W9-BTZ-408
D0123869

Fundamentals of Trusts and Estates

Fundamentals of Trusts and Estates

FIFTH EDITION

Roger W. Andersen

Professor of Law Emeritus
University of Toledo College of Law

Ira Mark Bloom

Justice David Josiah Brewer
Distinguished Professor of Law
Albany Law School

Carolina Academic Press
Durham, North Carolina

LCCN: 2017947248
ISBN: 978-1-5310-0121-6
eISBN: 978-1-53100-122-3

Carolina Academic Press, LLC
700 Kent Street
Durham, North Carolina 27701
Telephone (919) 489-7486
Fax (919) 493-5668
www.cap-press.com

Printed in the United States of America

Roger W. Andersen
In Memory of Howard & Ethel and Bobbie & Bill

Ira Mark Bloom
To my wife, Margaret Roberts, and our grandchildren,
Claudia Elena Bloom and Sofia Anna Bloom

Contents

Table of Cases

Y

Z

Table of Statutes

FEDERAL STATUTES, RULES AND REGULATIONS

Preface

This edition updates and selectively expands the prior edition to continue meeting the need for a lean set of materials, flexibly structured to accommodate 3-hour and 4-hour courses. The book seeks to present fundamental material clearly and concisely while providing creative vehicles for further inquiry. These materials, therefore, can also serve as the core for more extensive courses.

The trusts and estates course has always presented the range of human experience: caring and indifference, generosity and greed, comfort and pain, support and abandonment. In addition, current movements of the law provide a rich variety of debates, as new approaches challenge traditional doctrine. To help students develop skills and values to carry throughout their professional lives, this book's Questions and Problems illuminate both the human and the doctrinal dramas, often by placing students in various roles.

By focusing upon, expanding upon, or ignoring different Questions and Problems, teachers have the flexibility to structure their courses to meet their goals. The excerpted readings fulfill the same function—they can serve as background or as springboards for further inquiry. Policy debates, ethics issues, and practical considerations lace their way through the material.

Ira Bloom has taken primary responsibility for preparing this edition, which follows the largely traditional organization of earlier editions. The first chapter provides overviews of both the wealth transfer and the transfer tax systems, and introduces the topic of lawyer malpractice. Chapters on intestacy and wills develop the basic doctrines upon which the system depends. To facilitate an understanding of the law's movement toward integration, will substitutes are covered before discussing the problems caused by changed circumstances and the devices for protecting the family. The chapter on planning for incapacity serves as a bridge to a look at trusts, where we pay particular attention to the Uniform Trust Code and the Restatement (Third) of Trusts. A chapter covering future interests, including moves against the Rule Against Perpetuities, follows. The final chapter covers fiduciary administration. An Appendix contains forms that are useful at several stages in the course.

We also acknowledge with thanks the helpful and careful efforts of our editor, Elisabeth Ebben. Ira Bloom wishes to thank his research assistant, Bryan Bessette,

Albany Law School, Class of 2017, and his legal assistant, Theresa Colbert. Finally, and most importantly, we thank our families for their love and support.

Roger W. Andersen

Ira Mark Bloom

April 2017

Acknowledgments

The editors gratefully acknowledge permission to reprint photos, drawings, and other materials as noted below.

Photos

Dr. Barnes photo. Reprinted by permission of The Barnes Foundation.

Nancy Cruzan and Nancy Cruzan's Gravemarker photos. Courtesy of Chris Cruzan White.

Milton and Catherine Hershey photo appearing in Chapter 8. Courtesy of Hershey Community Archives, Hershey, PA.

Hershey School photo. Reproduced from the New York World-Telegram & Sun Collection of the Library of Congress.

The Mayo Brothers photo. Courtesy of the Mayo Foundation.

Memorial Stadium, Lincoln, Nebraska, photo. Courtesy of the University of Nebraska.

Cartoons and Drawings

Dilbert cartoon. Reprinted by permission of Universal/Uclick.

"I Love My Whole Family!" drawing by Brendan Blanchette. Reprinted by permission of Sharon Blanchette.

Trust Cartoon, reprinted by permission of R&R Newkirk Company.

Writings

Alexander, George J., *Premature Probate: A Different Perspective on Guardianship for the Elderly*, 31 Stan. L. Rev. 1003, 1018–19 (1979). Reprinted with the permission of Stanford Law Review and Fred B. Rothman & Co.

American Law Institute, Restatement (Second) of Property (Donative Transfers) §§ 2.1 (and part of the comment) & 2.2. Copyright © 1983. Restatement (Third) of Property (Donative Transfers) §§ 12.1, 21.2, 24.6, 25.3 & 25.4; Scope of Division VII and Introductory Note to chapter 27. Copyright © 1995 and 2012. Restatement (Third) of Trusts §§ 67, 81, 87 & 102. Copyrights © 1992, 2003. 2005 & 2012. Reprinted with the permission of the American Law Institute. All rights reserved.

Brashier, Ralph, *Disinheritance and the Modern Family*, 45 Case W. Res. L. Rev. 83, 164, 169–70, 173–74 (1994). Reprinted with the permission of Case Western Reserve Law Review.

Brown, Richard Lewis, *The Holograph Problem — The Case Against Holographic Wills*, 74 Tenn. L. Rev. 93, 95, 100, 110, 116–18, 120–22, 126–28 (2006). The full text of this article was published originally at 74 Tenn. L. Rev. 93 (2006) and the excerpts included here are reprinted by permission of the author and the Tennessee Law Review Association, Inc.

Colliton, James W., *Race and Sex Discrimination in Charitable Trusts*, 12 Cornell J.L. & Pub. Pol'y 275, 287 (2003). Reprinted with permission of the Cornell Journal of Law and Public Policy.

Cooper, Jeffrey A., *Shades of Gray: Applying the Benefit-the-Beneficiaries Rule to Trust Investment Directives*, 90 B.U. L. Rev. 2383, 2398 (2010). Reprinted with the permission of Jeffrey A. Cooper and Boston University Law Review.

Dukeminier, Jesse, *The Uniform Probate Code Upends the Law of Remainders*, 94 Mich. L. Rev. 148, 149–150, 166 (1995). Reprinted with the permission of Jesse Dukeminier and the University of Michigan Law Review Association.

Edward C. Halbach, Jr., *Trusts Investment Law in the Third Restatement*, 77 Iowa L. Rev. 1151, 1154–55, 1167–70 (1992) (reprinted with permission).

English, David, *A Checklist for Long-Term Care Coverage: Know the Policy and Know Your Client*, Prac. Law., June 1993, at 15–18. Reprinted with the permission of David English.

English, David & Meisel, Alan, *Uniform Health Care Decision Act Gives New Guidance*, Estate Planning at 355, 355, 356–57, 359–60, 362 (1994). Reprinted with the permission of Warren, Gorham & Lamont.

Fox, Lawrence J. and Martyn, Susan R., Red Flags: A Lawyer's Handbook on Legal Ethics, §§ 7.13(b), 7.32(b)-(d). (ALI-ABA 2d ed. 2010). Reprinted with the permission of ALI-ABA and the authors.

Gadsden, Christopher H., *Ethical Guidelines for the Fiduciary's Lawyer*, 134 Tr. & Est. 8, 13–16 (1995). Reprinted from Trusts & Estates, Mar. 1995. © 1996 Argus Inc., A Division of Intertec Publishing Corporation. Atlanta, GA. U.S.A.

Gary, Susan N., *Adapting Intestacy Laws to Changing Families*, 18 Law & Ineq. J. 1 (2000). Reprinted with permission.

Gordon, Deborah S., *Reflecting on the Language of Death*, 34 Seattle U. L. Rev. 379, 401, 407–09, 411 (2011). Reprinted with the permission of Deborah S. Gordon and Seattle University Law Review.

Gordon, Jeffrey, N., *The Puzzling Persistence of the Constrained Prudent Man Rule*, 62 N.Y.U. L. Rev. 52, 99–101 (1987). Reprinted with the permission of Jeffrey Gordon.

Halbach, Edward C. & Waggoner, Lawrence W., *The UPC's New Survivorship and Antilapse Provisions*, 55 Alb. L. Rev. 1091, 1131–33 (1992). Reprinted with the permission of the Albany Law Review.

Hirsch, Adam J., *Text and Time: A Theory of Testamentary Obsolescence*, 86 Wash. U. L. Rev. 609, 611–13, 615, 618, 620, 624–25, 630–33 (2009). Reprinted with the permission of Adam J. Hirsch and Washington University Law Review.

Hirsch, Adam J., *Spendthrift Trusts and Public Policy: Economic and Cognitive Perspectives*, 73 Wash. U. L.Q. 1, 2–3 (1995). Reprinted with the permission of Adam J. Hirsch and the Washington University Law Quarterly.

Johnson, Irene D., *Tortious Interference with Expectancy of Inheritance or Gift — Suggestions for Resort to the Tort*, 39 U. Tol. L. Rev. 769, 771, 774 (2008). Reprinted with the permission of Irene D. Johnson and Toledo Law Review.

Langbein, John H., *Reversing the Nondelegation Rule of Trust-Investment Law*, 59 Mo. L. Rev. 105, 105, 110 (1994). Reprinted with the permission of John H. Langbein and University of Missouri-Columbia Law Review.

Langbein, John H., *The Nonprobate Revolution and the Future of the Law of Succession*, 97 Harv. L. Rev. 1108, 1109, 1114, 1125–26, 1128–32, 1134–37 (1984). Copyright © 1984 by the Harvard Law Review Association. Reprinted with the permission of John H. Langbein and Harvard Law Review.

Langbein, John H., *Mandatory Rules in the Law of Trusts*, 98 Nw. U. L. Rev. 1105, 1112, 1115 (2004). Reprinted with the permission of John H. Langbein and the Northwestern University Law Review.

Langbein, John H. & Waggoner, Lawrence W., *Reformation of Wills on the Ground of Mistake: Change of Direction in American Law*, 130 U. Pa. L. Rev. 521, 524–28 (1982). Copyright © 1982 by and reprinted with the permission of John H. Langbein and Lawrence W. Waggoner and the University of Pennsylvania Law Review.

Lewis, Browne, *Children of Men: Balancing the Inheritance Rights of Marital and Non-marital Children*, 39 U. Tol. L. Rev. 1, 1–2, 6, 18 (2007). Reprinted with the permission of Browne Lewis and the Toledo Law Review.

Lindgren, James, *The Fall of Formalism*, 55 Alb. L. Rev. 1009 (1992). Reprinted with the permission of Albany Law Review.

Lynn, Robert J., *Perpetuities Literacy for the 21st Century*, 5 Ohio St. L.J. 219, 239–41 (1989). Reprinted with permission of Robert J. Lynn and the Ohio State Law Journal.

Mann, Bruce H., *Formalities and Formalism in the Uniform Probate Code*, 142 U. Pa. L. Rev. 1033, 1035–41 (1994). Copyright © 1994 by and reprinted with the permission of Bruce H. Mann and the University of Pennsylvania Law Review.

Roca, Robert P., *Determining Decisional Capacity: A Medical Perspective*, 62 Fordham L. Rev. 1177, 1195 (1994). Reprinted with the permission of Robert P. Roca and the Fordham Law Review.

Schenkel, Kent D., *Testamentary Fragmentation and the Diminishing Role of the Will: An Argument for Revival*, 41 Creighton L. Rev. 155–184 (2008). Reprinted with permission. Copyright © 1996 by Creighton University. Also with the permission of Kent D. Schenkel.

Shaffer, Thomas L., Death, Property and Lawyers at 72 (1970). Reprinted with the permission of Thomas L. Shaffer.

Sherman, Jeffrey G., *Posthumous Meddling: An Instrumentalist Theory of Testamentary Restraints on Conjugal and Religious Choices*, 1999 U. Ill. L. Rev. 1273, 1276–1281, 1301–04, 1329. Copyright © 1999 The Board of Trustees of the University of Illinois. Reprinted with the permission of the University of Illinois Law Review.

Simes, Lewis M. & Smith, Allan F., The Law of Future Interests, §§ 465, 468, 470 (John Boron 3d ed. 2002 West Group). Reprinted with the permission of Thomson Reuters.

Spivack, Carla, *Why the Testamentary Doctrine of Undue Influence Should Be Abolished?*, 58 U. Kan. L. Rev. 245, 250–51, 254, 258–60, 262, 267–68, 276, 281–83, 286–87, 290–91 (2010). Reprinted with the permission of Carla Spivack and the University of Kansas Law Review.

Sterk, Stewart E., *Rethinking Trust Law Reform: How Prudent Is Modern Prudent Investor Doctrine?*, 95 Cornell L. Rev. 851, 899–900, 903 (2010). Reprinted with the permission of Stewart E. Sterk and the Cornell Law Review.

Uniform Power of Attorney Act (© 2006), Uniform Probate Code (© 1990, with amendments through 2010), Uniform Trust Code (© 2000, with subsequent amendments), Uniform Principal and Income Act (© 1997, with subsequent amendments), and Uniform Prudent Investor Act (© 1994). Selected sections reprinted with the permission of the National Conference of Commissioners on Uniform State Laws.

Waggoner, Lawrence W., *The Multiple-Marriage Society and Spousal Rights Under the Uniform Probate Code*, 76 Iowa L. Rev. 223, 236–37, 239 (1991). Reprinted with the permission of Lawrence Waggoner.

Fundamentals of Trusts and Estates

Chapter 1

Lawyers, Estates, and Trusts

This chapter sets the context in which lawyers work with estates and trusts. It opens with a look at some of the career and personal-fulfillment opportunities this field offers. The chapter then presents an overview of the process for shifting wealth from one generation to the next. Next is an introduction to the federal wealth transfer tax system. The chapter closes with a discussion of duties lawyers owe clients.

§ 1.01 Opportunities

Welcome to one of the most enjoyable courses in law school. Rather than studying, as you might suppose, about dead people, you will be learning about ways to help living people solve real family problems. Such a task is both interesting and challenging: interesting because of the interplay between intellectual ideas and individual personalities; challenging because of the required attention to detail and the number of choices faced.

This class, of course, is just one step in what should become a career-long pursuit of learning and service, whatever direction you choose. Now is a good time to consider why you are taking *this* course and where it might lead.

Other students before you have found fulfillment in a wide variety of situations: bank trust departments, sections in large firms specializing in estate planning or combining that work with family law or business or retirement or disability planning; small and solo firms with similar combinations of specialties; legal services offices for low-income or elderly clients; litigation practices with particular expertise in this field; probate courts (as referees or judges); or charitable foundations. Whatever the individual experiences of their careers, these lawyers regularly experience both intellectual challenge and the satisfaction of working with people to face some of life's most fundamental questions.

For another take on the universality of these issues, consider some examples from legend, literature, history, and science: sibling rivalry (Cain & Abel), fraud (Jacob tricking Isaac), relations with stepparents (Hamlet), succession planning (King Lear), detailed preparation for the future (Egyptian tombs), and life after death (posthumous procreation). *See, e.g.*, G. Warren Whitaker, *Classic Issues in Family Succession Planning*, 6 Prob. & Prop. 32 (Mar./Apr. 2003).

This work can get very interesting indeed.

Question

As you contemplate your future as a lawyer, in what directions do you think learning this subject might take you?

§ 1.02 An Overview of Inter-Generational Wealth Transfer

This section introduces some terminology and basic concepts discussed in later chapters. Its major purpose is to provide a "big picture," so you will know the context in which particular doctrines operate. After a discussion of the probate system for transferring decedents' property, we will examine probate avoidance devices—lifetime transfers that can serve as substitutes for wills. Then we offer some basics about guardianships. The section closes with a word about the influence of various Restatements and Uniform Codes.

A. Probate

1. The Process

Probate systems developed to collect the assets of decedents, satisfy creditors, pay taxes, resolve conflicts among beneficiaries, and distribute what was left to the appropriate persons or institutions. Procedural details vary from place to place, but the basic concept of probate carries through differing approaches.

Only some property interests are "subject to probate." *See* Figure 1-1. Property the decedent held alone or as a tenant in common is subject to the system. It will pass according to the terms of a will or, if there is no will, according to an "intestate statute." On the other hand, a number of sources of wealth do not pass through probate. Joint tenancy (or tenancy by the entirety) property, life insurance proceeds on the decedent's life, property in lifetime trusts, pensions, and IRAs are all outside of probate. Notice how little wealth may actually be subject to probate. A typical married couple may hold virtually everything in joint tenancy—house, cars, bank accounts, investments. There may be no probate assets until the surviving spouse dies. If a family is wealthier, they may have most of their property in trust, again not subject to probate.

Despite the relatively narrow coverage, the probate system is fundamentally important to the entire inter-generational wealth transfer process. Much of the law governing wealth transfer developed in the context of probate. Moreover, it is the ultimate "fail-safe" system. If no other theory authorizes a shift of property from a decedent to another, the probate system comes into play.

Although the process of administration deals with the property of the dead, it is operated by, and affects, the living. For discussion purposes, it is therefore useful to assume a family situation. In our case, the principal living subjects are: Jeremy

Figure 1-1 Probate v. Non-Probate Property
A Decedent's Wealth

Probate Property

- In Decedent's Name
- ↓ Through Probate by Will or Intestacy
- ↓ Designated Surviors

Non-Probate Property

- Life Insurance
- Joint Property
- Retirement Benefits
- Property in Living Trusts
- P.O.D. Accounts
- → Designated Survivors

Newman, widower of Alice Newman, recently deceased; George Forbes, Alice's 53-year-old son by a prior marriage; and Alice's 51-year-old daughter, Ellen Forbes. Alice's will, of which Jeremy has a copy, names him executor of her estate.

Upon Alice's death, Jeremy may well suffer extreme psychic shock. It hardly needs saying that death can inflict massive trauma on a family. The last thing he may be thinking of is the process of wrapping up the financial pieces of Alice's life. The exigencies of life necessarily will intrude, however, and Jeremy will have tasks which he must perform. This effort may be painful, or it may be a comforting distraction from the grief and memory. First, he, perhaps in consultation with Ellen and George, must make the necessary funeral arrangements.[1] Second, he will look to the settling of Alice's affairs.

At some point after Alice's death, Jeremy will contact an attorney to assist him in that settlement process. The attorney undoubtedly will advise Jeremy that the first order of business is to locate Alice's signed will. Alice's attorney may have it, or it may be among Alice's effects. Second, the attorney will advise Jeremy to keep track of expenses, and to accumulate Alice's bills as they arrive at the house, because they will have to be paid once Jeremy is appointed executor. Finally, the attorney will tell Jeremy to determine what assets Alice owned when she died, and to protect those assets against theft and conversion by others.

The Will. When the will is located, the attorney will photocopy it and provide Jeremy, George, and Ellen with copies. In our case, Alice had the following, relatively simple, will:

1. Alice may have made pre-need funeral arrangements, including the appointment of an agent to make funeral arrangements.

Last Will of Alice Newman

I, Alice Newman, of 2912 Alhambra Circle, Coral Springs, Utopia, declare this to be my will. I revoke all prior wills and codicils.

ARTICLE I

I give all my tangible personal property to my husband Jeremy, if he survives me. If my husband does not survive me, I give all my tangible personal property to my son George and daughter Ellen, in equal shares.

ARTICLE II

I give one-half of the remainder of my estate to my husband Jeremy, if he survives me. The other half of the remainder, or all of the remainder, if Jeremy does not survive me, I give to my son George and my daughter Ellen, in equal shares.

ARTICLE III

I nominate my husband Jeremy to serve as executor of this will. If for any reason he fails to become or ceases to act as executor, I nominate the First Bank & Trust Company of Coral Springs, Utopia, or its successors in interest, to serve as executor of this will.

No executor shall be required to give bond, or surety, or security on a bond.

ARTICLE IV

My executor shall have all powers which I may lawfully give to an executor, including the power to sell and convey, lease or mortgage any real estate, all without leave of court.

I have signed this will on this 20th day of February, 2017.

[Signed Alice Newman]

We saw Alice Newman, in our presence, sign this instrument at its end. She then declared it to be her will and requested us to act as witnesses to it. We believe her to be of sound mind and memory and not under duress or constraint of any kind. We then, in her presence and in the presence of each other, signed our names as attesting witnesses. All of this was done on the date of this instrument.

____

____

Signature and Address of Witness #1

____

____

Signature and Address of Witness #2

Assets and Debts. The property Alice owned was also fairly typical. Most of "her" assets, including the family residence, checking and savings accounts, and stocks and bonds, were owned in joint tenancy with Jeremy. In her own name were her clothing, tools, and other personal possessions, an automobile licensed in Utopia, an old savings account, some valuable sculptures, and a summer cottage in the adjacent state of Vacationland. No one owed her any money at her death, and she had few debts.

Opening the Estate. Whether the decedent dies with or without a will, someone must oversee identifying the assets, paying the debts, and distributing the excess to the survivors. That person is now often called the "personal representative." In traditional usage, the person would be called an "executor" if named in the decedent's will. Otherwise, the traditional title of the personal representative is "administrator."[2] Statutes determine who is entitled to be appointed, normally a spouse, near relative, or person named by the decedent.

A court in the decedent's domicile will appoint the personal representative. Usually this court is called the probate court; in some jurisdictions, it is called the surrogate's court or orphan's court. The court may, however, be the court of general jurisdiction. Further, if the decedent owned property in another jurisdiction, an ancillary administration might be necessary there. Ancillary probate is designed to protect the local creditors and is particularly likely if the asset is real property, like Alice's cottage in Vacationland.

The process of administration begins with a petition to the probate court, usually on standard forms. In Alice's case, the petition is one to admit the will to probate. If Alice had died without a will, the petition would have been merely one for administration and appointment of a personal representative. If ancillary administration in Vacationland is necessary, the petition probably will request both administration and the appointment of an ancillary personal representative selected by the executor.

A will is proved by the testimony of its witnesses, either in person or by affidavit, and may be challenged by those who would take Alice's property if the will is invalid. Normally, the process begins with notice to interested persons, allowing a contested hearing of the witnesses. The court hears the testimony, and decides whether the will was valid. In some jurisdictions, however, the initial probate is informal, and ex parte, with notice given to interested persons after the will's admission to probate. In that case, interested parties may challenge the will by moving to set aside probate. In either event, however, the challenge is normally called a will contest. When a contest is not expected, executors usually prefer informal probate because its lack of formality tends to reduce costs.

Once the will has been proved valid, the court signs an order admitting the will to probate and issues letters testamentary to the executor, or letters of administration to other personal representatives. In our case, these "letters" give Jeremy authority to

2. Females holding these positions sometimes are called "executrix" and "administratrix," respectively. Because gender is irrelevant in this context, this book will follow the modern convention and avoid "trix" endings.

collect Alice's property and to convey it to those entitled to it. Alice's will waives a bond, so Jeremy need not file one with the court to guarantee his performance.

Administration. Once appointed personal representative, Jeremy begins the administration, which can be informal or formal. Formal administration is supervised by the court; informal administration requires only reporting of the completion of the administration.

The Uniform Probate Code allows a range of approaches. Although the traditional approach of full supervision is available, administration also may be largely unsupervised. The court can be called upon as needed. An interested party who feels that a low appraisal should be reviewed, for example, can obtain court supervision of that one controversy without at the same time invoking supervision of all other questions. In addition, the UPC offers the choice of universal succession, which skips administration entirely and gives title to the heirs[3] or residuary devisees,[4] subject to the claims of creditors and any other devisees.

The following discussion assumes a court's continuing supervision.

Formal administration begins with Jeremy collecting Alice's assets, including bringing any actions necessary to enforce claims Alice might have had against others. The assets are then listed on an inventory filed with the court. Appraisers may be needed if realty or valuable personal property is involved.

In Alice's case, the only assets to be collected are the car, personal possessions including clothes and tools, an old bank account, and a summer cottage. Jointly owned assets belong to Jeremy as a result of the survivorship provision in joint ownership, and the life insurance proceeds pass directly to the beneficiary under the provisions of the insurance contract. Jeremy will check Alice's casualty insurance to determine whether it insures her estate against loss. If it does not, he will want to purchase insurance, including liability insurance, if the car is to be driven.

Digital assets can pose challenges as the law inevitably lags behind both some technological and social changes. A wide variety of property once held in physical form—books, music, family photos, vacation videos, diaries—now appear in computerized storage, often in remote locations. Identifying a decedent's assets can be difficult; looking through a desk drawer for account statements no longer helps much. Moreover, questions arise as to whether the decedent or some other entity owns the content, where (for jurisdictional purposes) an asset is located, and whether an estate planning document like a will controls an asset's disposition. Fiduciary access to digital assets is discussed below.

---

3. The "heirs" are those who would take under the local intestate statute if there were no will.

4. Historically, the term "devisee" meant someone who took real property by will. The UPC defines "devisee" as anyone who takes real or personal property by will. UPC § 1-201(10), (11). The "residuary devisees" are those who would take under a will clause which follows any specific gifts and reads: "I give all the rest of my property to. . . ."

Next, Jeremy will open a bank account in his name as "executor of the estate of Alice Newman." He then requests the bank to transfer the funds in Alice's old savings account to the new account, giving the bank a copy of the Letters Testamentary to prove his authority. He will use the new bank account for paying Alice's debts, the attorney's fees, and other expenses.

Once the executor has assembled the assets and contacted the creditors,[5] estate administration enters a holding period. Since many problems regarding fiduciary administration are common to both personal representatives and trustees, we will discuss those issues in Chapter 10 after we have examined the law of trusts.

When the creditors file claims, Jeremy will decide whether the debt is valid, and if so, pay it. Otherwise, he will reject it, and leave the creditor to begin an action challenging his decision.

During the first few months of administration, Jeremy also will determine whether the estate needs to file and pay any estate, inheritance, or other death taxes. If it does, Jeremy will file the returns and pay any taxes. If necessary, he will sell assets to obtain the cash necessary to pay these and other debts. Even if no death tax returns are required to be filed, the estate will be required to file federal income tax returns, including the final income tax return for Alice and fiduciary income tax returns for the estate. State income tax returns may also need to be filed.

If he needs money to live on during administration, Jeremy can request that he be paid a family allowance from the assets of the estate. The amount will depend on local law, and, in some cases, on his need. Some states provide generous family allowances which, because they come before final distribution of the estate, can shift substantial amounts of assets to the spouse and dependent children.

Anna Nicole Smith and Federal Jurisdiction

Probate cases often involve greed, sometimes raise arcane points of law, and rarely reach the U.S. Supreme Court. Litigation involving Anna Nicole Smith did all of that in the context of celebrity and massive wealth. Smith (legal name, Vickie Lynn Marshall), an actress and *Playboy's* Playmate of the Year for 1993, married oil billionaire J. Howard Marshall the following year. She was 26; he was 89. After J. Howard died in 1995, the ultimate beneficiary of his estate plan was one of his sons, E. Pierce Marshall. Vickie claimed that J. Howard had promised her a share of his wealth. The dispute led to a series of lawsuits in several different courts.

Federal courts got involved because while J. Howard's estate was still open in a Texas probate court, Vickie declared bankruptcy in federal court in

5. Under *Tulsa Prof. Collection Serv., Inc. v. Pope*, 485 U.S. 478 (1988), unless personal representatives provide actual notice to known or reasonably ascertainable creditors, the probate process will not cut off the creditors' claims.

California. At that point, Pierce filed a claim in the bankruptcy proceeding that she had defamed him. Vickie counterclaimed that Pierce had tortiously interfered[6] with the lifetime gift she expected from J. Howard. The bankruptcy court rejected Pierce's defamation claim, and awarded Vickie compensatory damages of more than $449 million—less whatever she recovered in the ongoing probate action in Texas—as well as $25 million in punitive damages. Pierce ultimately sought to dismiss the bankruptcy award for lack of subject-matter jurisdiction, asserting that Vickie's tortious interference claim could be tried only in the Texas probate proceedings, rather than in federal court.

Pierce argued that the "probate exception" to what would otherwise be proper federal jurisdiction should apply in this case. In the words of Justice Ginsburg after the case reached her Court, "Among longstanding limitations on federal jurisdiction otherwise properly exercised are the so-called 'domestic relations' and 'probate' exceptions. Neither is compelled by the text of the Constitution or federal statute. Both are judicially created doctrines stemming in large measure from misty understandings of English legal history." *Marshall v. Marshall*, 547 U.S. 293, 299 (2006). "[T]he probate exception reserves to state probate courts the probate or annulment of a will and the administration of a decedent's estate; it also precludes federal courts from endeavoring to dispose of property that is in the custody of a state probate court. But it does not bar federal courts from adjudicating matters outside those confines and otherwise within federal jurisdiction." 547 U.S. at 311–12. The basic idea is that federal courts ought not to get too closely involved in matters traditionally reserved to the states, but at the same time should protect their jurisdiction in general. In *Marshall*, the Court held that federal jurisdiction was appropriate.

Pierce died June 20, 2006; Vickie died February 8, 2007, leaving an infant daughter. Pierce's widow, Vickie's executor, and the child's guardian continued the litigation. On remand, the Ninth Circuit ruled that the bankruptcy court had exceeded its statutory grant of power and should have afforded preclusive effect to the Texas Probate Court's findings (in favor of Pierce) on the intentional interference claim. *Marshall v. Stern*, 600 F.3d 1037 (9th Cir.), *cert. granted*, 131 S. Ct. 63 (2010).

Homestead and exempt property provisions also protect the family. Traditionally, homestead statutes protected real property while exempt property provisions applied to personalty, but modern statutes may ignore the distinction. Indeed, the UPC provides dollar amounts to provide homestead and exempt property protection. In whatever form, homestead and exempt property provisions typically assure spouses

6. For more on intentional interference with inheritance, see Chapter 3, § 3.02B5.

and children shares that come ahead of creditors' claims and distributions mandated by intestate succession or by will provisions. These statutes, which vary widely and may set different limits for different kinds of assets, are discussed in Chapter 2, § 2.01D.

After he has paid the creditors and taken into account the various allowances and exemptions, Jeremy will total the remaining assets, and divide them among himself and Alice's two children, as directed in the will. In other situations, distributions might be to individuals, to charities, to trustees of already existing trusts, or to trustees of trusts created by the decedent's will. When he delivers the assets, Jeremy will obtain a receipt, which he then will file with the court, along with an accounting of the transactions he engaged in during administration, and a petition that he be discharged from his duties as personal representative. Copies of the accounting will be given to the two children, who may object if they believe that he improperly managed the estate. If they make no objections, or if the court determines that he properly managed the estate, it will discharge him and administration comes to an end.

Question

A married man with children wants to appoint his long-time paramour to serve as his executor. Should a court refuse to appoint her because of her relationship with the testator? *See In re Estate of Nagle*, 317 N.E.2d 242 (Ohio Ct. App. 1974) (no).

Selected References

Jonathan J. Darrow & Gerald R. Ferrera, *Who Owns a Decedent's E-mails: Inheritable Probate Assets or Property of the Network?*, 10 N.Y.U. J. Legis. & Pub. Pol'y 281 (2006–2007).

Katarinna McBride, *The Anna Nicole Smith Case: An Opera in Five Acts*, 98 Ill. B.J. 266 (2010).

Gregory M. McCoskey, *Death and Debtors: What Every Probate Lawyer Should Know About Bankruptcy*, 34 Real Prop. Prob. & Tr. J. 669 (2000).

Paula A. Monopoli, American Probate (2003).

James E. Pfander and Michael J.T. Downey, *In Search of the Probate Exception*, 67 Vand. L. Rev. 1533 (2014).

2. Is Probate Necessary?

We sometimes assume that because the probate system is available it must be used. Instead, in each case, we ought to be recalling the functions of the system and asking whether this particular probate is necessary.

Consider Alice and Jeremy. If theirs had been a first marriage, with all of the assets held jointly except Alice's clothing, tools, and personal possessions, there would be little reason to bother probating Alice's estate. The only assets Alice owned alone—the tangible personal property—are already in the house, so there is no problem with assembling estate assets. Jeremy fully intends to pay off the pending bills, so creditors are not a worry. Since Jeremy's survivorship interest gives him the other property, there is no potential title problem.

Because Alice's situation is more complex, probate might be necessary. The bank might require letters of authority from a probate court before releasing the money in the savings account. On the other hand, perhaps something else could be worked out informally. Similarly, it might be possible to change title to the car by filing an affidavit in the motor vehicles office. If the children are questioning the will's validity, a hearing may be necessary, but a settlement may be possible. Because the vacation property was in Alice's name alone, probate probably would be necessary to clear the title. Some title insurance companies, however, might be willing to insure a title in Jeremy's or the children's names on the strength of affidavits, instead of requiring a probate court order. If Alice had owned a business, cutting off creditors' claims might be important. Though Jeremy must make reasonable efforts to find and notify creditors, going through probate would provide some security against creditors who appeared later. Before deciding, Jeremy would want to know how likely their appearance would be. For any number of reasons, you may want to advise Jeremy to use the probate process, but you ought to have reasons.

When someone has died, we need to collect the assets, take care of creditors, resolve any disputes among claimants, and get clear title into the hands of the right survivors. If we need the probate system to accomplish any of these goals, we should use it. If not, we shouldn't. Indeed, probate may be avoided in small estates under summary administration procedures. *See, e.g.* UPC §§ 3-1201-1204 (for estates of $25,000 or less) and N.Y. Surrogate's Court Procedure Act, art 13 (personal property of $30,000 or less).

Selected References

John H. Martin, *Reconfiguring Estate Settlement*, 94 Minn. L. Rev. 42 (2009).

John H. Martin, *Non-Judicial Estate Settlement*, 45 U. Mich. J.L. Reform 965 (2012).

Karen J. Sneddon, *Beyond the Personal Representative: The Potential of Succession Without Administration*, 50 S. Tex. L. Rev. 449 (2009).

B. Lifetime Transfers

We now turn to devices that effectively transfer wealth at someone's death, but that are not subject to the probate system. For this reason, they are often called "will substitutes" and "probate avoidance devices." Principal among them is the revocable living trust, which we will cover in detail in Chapter 4, § 4.05. This section introduces the trust concept and some terminology, and then describes other non-probate transfers.

1. Trusts

Because trusts are so flexible, they are the single most useful estate planning device. Professor Scott, the dominant figure of twentieth century trust law, reminds us "[t]he purposes for which trusts can be created are as unlimited as the imagination of lawyers." 1 Scott & Ascher on Trusts 4 (5th ed. 2006). Scott challenges us to use trusts creatively to meet the needs of our clients. Trusts are flexible because the essential elements are so few: (1) property (sometimes called the "res"), (2) held by someone (the trustee), (3) to benefit someone else (the beneficiary). The property serves as the principal (or corpus) of the trust, invested to generate income for the beneficiaries. Of course, there must be someone to create the trust. This person might be called the settlor, grantor, donor, trustor, or testator, depending upon the situation and local custom.

One person can assume any number of different roles, just so long as the trustee owes a duty to someone else. The settlor could be a trustee, by announcing that property she owned was now being held in trust for the benefit of others. One of those beneficiaries could even be the settlor/trustee herself. Of course, different people might assume each of those roles. It is quite common, for example, for a settlor to give money to a bank as trustee to invest for members of the settlor's family.

A settlor may create a trust either through a lifetime transfer or by will. A trust created during the settlor's life is called a lifetime (or inter vivos) trust. Questions involving lifetime trusts can be resolved in courts of general jurisdiction, but there is no ongoing judicial supervision. Lifetime trusts avoid the probate process. A trust created by will is called a testamentary trust. Testamentary trusts are typically subject to the continuing jurisdiction and supervision of the probate court.

2. Other Lifetime Transfers

While the lifetime trust is the most complex probate-avoidance device, others are more common. You will recall from your Property course how surviving joint tenants own the entire property when one joint tenant dies. This survivorship feature makes joint tenancy holdings extraordinarily popular, especially among persons of modest means. Real estate, bank accounts, stocks, and bonds can all be held in "joint with survivorship" form. Because the survivor no longer shares ownership with the one who has died, the decedent effectively has transferred wealth at death. Because of the legal theory that the survivor has owned the property all along, however, no probate process is required.

The law of contracts supplies another way around probate. Funds paid by a third party at the death of someone are often treated as contract rights of the beneficiary, rather than property of the one who died.

Life insurance is the most common example of this way of giving money at death. Though the industry has developed a wide array of products in recent years, they commonly fall into one of two basic categories. Term insurance covers the risk of someone dying during the term of the policy. Whole life insurance incorporates an investment feature as well. With either term or whole life, death benefits bypass the probate system because they are not viewed as property of the decedent. In recent years, the use of "payable-on-death" and "transfer-on-death" accounts has expanded significantly. Statutes have authorized bank accounts and, more recently, mutual funds and other securities, as well as real property, to be held in these forms. The explosion of retirement plans also has produced a new way of accumulating wealth and leaving it to survivors outside of probate.

These developments have profound implications for the law of wealth transfer. On the one hand, the law of wills is learning from the law that has developed around these other devices. On the other, wills' rules hold many lessons about how to interpret documents making non-probate transfers. As you consider the various doctrines discussed in this book, ask when it makes sense to borrow ideas from different areas of law and when it makes sense to maintain traditional distinctions.

C. Guardianships

People need guardians, who are also referred to as conservators in some states, when they cannot handle their own affairs. For example, if an accident kills both parents, their minor children, now orphans, will need someone to care for them and their property. The law's solution is for a court to appoint someone as *guardian of the person*, who has the responsibility and authority to care for the child. A court also may appoint the same person, or another (including a bank), as *guardian of the property*. A third type of guardian, a *guardian ad litem*, may be appointed to protect the children's interests in litigation. Guardianship also may be appropriate when adults, through accident or organic decline, lose their capacity to care for themselves or their property.

Comprehensive statutes commonly establish standards for creating guardianships and regulating guardians' behavior. The details differ from state to state.[7] Even the terminology varies. A "guardian" in one state may in another be called a "conservator," "curator," or a "committee," although the disabled person typically is referred to as the "ward."[8] Interested parties, often family members of the ward, ask courts to establish guardianships. The court, usually a probate court, will decide whether a guardianship is warranted, name a guardian and supervise the guardian's conduct.

7. The Uniform Adult Guardianship and Protective Proceedings Jurisdiction Act, which has been enacted in almost every state, provides for the transfer of a guardianship to another jurisdiction.

8. Indeed, even within a single state, the title given may depend on the nature of the ward. For example, a minor may have a "guardian" while an incompetent adult may have a "conservator."

The powers of the guardian vary among particular types of guardians. Guardians for incompetent adults, for example, may have more authority than guardians for competent minors.[9] Guardians ad litem have limited powers because their sole function is to protect the ward's interests in specific litigation. Guardians with similarly limited authority may be appointed for specific purposes, such as selling particular property for a minor.

Choosing guardians of the person of minor children is one of the most serious concerns of young parents, and one of the primary reasons they execute wills. Often, the parents do not agree with their state's statutory preferences for naming a guardian. For example, the children's grandparents may be too old, or the parents' siblings may hold values the parents do not share. Further, the statutes cannot specify which grandparents or siblings should be appointed. This circumstance poses the risk of acrimonious litigation if the families of the two parents disagree on who should take the children. If the parents are separated, the risk is even higher. Therefore, parents often use their wills to name guardians. Under the Uniform Probate Code, guardians so named can assume office upon probate of the will without court approval. UPC § 5-202. Even in jurisdictions in which courts must confirm appointments, the directions in the will normally control.

Guardians of the person are necessary for minors. Someone must be able to tell the children it is time for bed. On the other hand, guardians of property may not even be desirable, if other methods are available for handling the property. In particular, guardianships can be inefficient and expensive. Traditionally, the guardian of property has limited powers, usually exercisable only with court approval. Statutory limitations on permissible investments may effectively prevent the guardian from obtaining a reasonable rate of return on guardianship property. Additionally, required accountings and bonds increase attorney's fees and court costs, diminishing the assets available for the child. Recognizing these drawbacks, some jurisdictions have reformed guardianships of property. For example, the Uniform Probate Code grants the guardian (renamed "conservator") broad powers of management, exercisable without court approval, much as though the guardian were trustee of a privately established trust. UPC §§ 5-424, 425(a).

In those jurisdictions that have not liberalized property guardianships, wills of young parents often place assets in trust for the minors, should both parents die. Another solution is to make gifts to minors under uniform transfers to minors legislation. These statutes allow a "custodian" to take title of the property for the minor and to expend funds for the child's benefit, all without court supervision. Other alternatives to guardianship are covered in Chapter 7, Planning for Incapacity.

9. Subject to court approval, a guardian (conservator) may have access to a protected person's digital assets (electronic records) under Section 14 of the Revised Uniform Fiduciary Access to Digital Assets Act, discussed in Chapter 10, § 10.03A2(b)(ii).

Notes and Question

1. Deciding whether an adult needs a guardian can be a tricky business, fraught with conflicts. Sometimes younger relatives are trying to help; sometimes they are trying to take advantage of the adult. Children who seek guardianships for their parents face the risk that the parent (rightly or wrongly) will not appreciate their action. When some of Delphine C. Wagner's children sought to have a conservator appointed for her, she disinherited them. *See Estate of Wagner*, 522 N.W.2d 159 (Neb. 1994).

2. How far does the duty of the guardian's lawyer extend? *Fickett v. Superior Court*, 558 P.2d 988 (Ariz. Ct. App. 1976), involved a guardian who converted his ward's funds to his personal use. The court held that the guardian's lawyer owed a duty to the ward.

D. The Uniform Codes and the Restatements

Law reform engines have significantly affected the law of trusts and estates. The Uniform Probate Code (UPC) and the Uniform Trust Code (UTC) offer statutory language and commentary to state legislatures considering reform (and indirectly influence court decisions).[10] The Restatements of Property and of Trusts provide guidance to courts (and indirectly influence legislatures). Courts heavily rely on Restatements. *See, e.g., Noveletsky v. Metropolitan Life Insurance Company*, 49 F. Supp. 3d 123, 139 (D. Me. 2014) ("The common law applicable to Maine trusts can be found in the decisions of Maine's Law Court, which often rely on the Restatements pertaining to trusts").

In 1969, the Commissioners on Uniform State Laws promulgated the UPC as a comprehensive statute covering a broad range of issues related to family wealth transfers: jurisdiction, intestacy, wills, probate procedure, guardianship, and trust administration. Since then, a number of revisions have been made, most recently in 2008. As of 2017, 18 jurisdictions have adopted some version of the UPC.[11] The UTC was approved in 2000 and by 2017 had been adopted in more than 30 states.[12] Uniform acts in this area are monitored by the Joint Editorial Board for Uniform Trust and Estate Acts, a group of academic lawyers and practitioners.[13] Facilitated by overlap of interest and personnel, the Board has worked cooperatively with groups that revise the Restatements of Property and of Trusts.

---

10. Comments to uniform statutes provide a rich source of legislative history. Courts that have enacted a uniform statute may rely on a uniform law comment to resolve an issue. *See, e.g., In re Trust under Deed of Kulig*, 131 A.3d 494 (Pa. Super. Ct. 2015).

11. UPC jurisdictions include: Alaska, Arizona, Colorado, Hawaii, Idaho, Maine, Massachusetts, Michigan, Minnesota, Montana, Nebraska, New Jersey, New Mexico, North Dakota, South Carolina, South Dakota, U.S. Virgin Islands, and Utah.

12. Adopting UTC jurisdictions are listed in Footnote 3 on Page 393.

13. For current adoption information of uniform acts, *see* www.uniformlaws.org.

Those Restatements, like others you have learned about, are the product of the American Law Institute (ALI), an organization of judges, lawyers, and law professors founded in 1923 to clarify, simplify, and otherwise reform the law. Despite the name, a "Restatement" does not simply restate the law. Rather, it offers a recommended version of the common law.

As the continuing development of new Uniform Laws and new Restatements demonstrates, wills and trust law is not static. Indeed, the Revised Uniform Fiduciary Access to Digital Assets (RUFADAA), which was approved in 2015, is a very recent example.[14]

Some of the challenges—and joys—of working in this area are anticipating and creating new solutions to people's problems. Indeed, whatever direction your career takes, keep in mind the benefits—to you and to the larger community—of joining law reform efforts from the local to the international level.[15]

Selected References

Lawrence H. Averill, Jr. & Mary F. Radford, Uniform Probate Code and Uniform Trust Code in a Nutshell (6th ed. 2010).

David M. English, *The Uniform Trust Code (2000): Significant Provisions and Policy Issues*, 67 Mo. L. Rev. 143 (2002).

Organization Websites

BWRTX:ABA Real Property, Trust and Estate Section—http://www.americanbar.org/groups/real_property_trust_estate.html.

American College of Trust and Estate Counsel—http://www.actec.org/.

American Law Institute—http://www.ali.org/.

Uniform Law Commission—http://www.uniformlaws.org/.

§ 1.03 Federal Wealth Transfer Taxes

This section pursues a modest, but important, goal: to introduce you to the federal system for taxing transfers of wealth. With a basic understanding of what the system is about, you will be better able to follow cases involving estate plans constructed for tax reasons. Additionally, research and advanced course work should be easier. Most importantly, however, you should be able to identify situations which

14. RUFADAA is considered in detail in Chapter 10, § 10.02A2(b).

15. One career goal might be to join The American College of Trust and Estate Counsel, whose members are elected as the premier lawyers in this field. ACTEC provides in-depth analysis in a variety of forums.

call for more expertise than you have acquired. Then you will know it is time to learn more or to send your client elsewhere.

Not surprisingly, the current system developed over time. Although Congress had imposed various inheritance-related taxes for short periods in the 18th and 19th centuries, it turned to an estate tax in 1916, and we have had one since then. The gift tax followed, with some fits and starts, as a backup to the estate tax and the income tax. The estate and gift taxes operated separately from 1932 until 1976, when they were unified into one system which taxes cumulative lifetime transfers and an individual's estate at death. Major reforms in 1981 moved the tax burden off of the middle class, by raising effective exemption levels and allowing an unlimited marital deduction. Those reforms, however, left intact some loopholes benefiting the very rich who set up dynastic trusts. In 1986, Congress added a permanent separate generation-skipping transfer (GST) tax, which seeks to impose a wealth transfer tax once each generation, but with a generous exemption level so that practically the GST tax falls on only our wealthiest families.

Shifting directions in 2001, Congress started phasing out the system until there were no estate and GST taxes for decedents dying in 2010. The gift tax remained, but at lower rates. In an interesting political game, the 2001 legislation would have reinstituted much of the system in 2011, but at levels that would have applied before the 2001 Amendments. After much delay and haggling, Congress in late 2010 made some changes,[16] but basically kicked the can down the road for two years. For 2011 and 2012, the estate and GST taxes were reinstated, but with exemption levels increased to $5 million; the gift tax exemption was also increased to $5 million. Much like before, 2013 was scheduled to return to most of the pre-2001 rules unless Congress acted.

Congress did act to make the estate, gift and generation-skipping transfer (GST) tax systems "permanent," that is, there was no sunset provision as under the 2001 and 2010 Acts. Specifically, Congress enacted the American Taxpayer Relief Act of 2012, effective beginning in 2013. Pursuant to the Act, a new estate rate schedule, which was also applicable to gifts, established a top rate of 40 percent. IRC § 2001(c).[17] In addition, the estate, gift, and GST exemption level was set at $5 million as adjusted annually for inflation. IRC §§ 2010 and 2505.[18] For 2016, the exemption level was $5,450,000 and $5,490,000 in 2017.

With the election of Donald Trump, the fate of federal transfer taxes is uncertain. One option includes a temporary repeal of the federal transfer taxes. At the same

16. For 2010, the estate tax system was retroactively reimposed, but with a $5 million exemption and a top rate of 35% (down from 45% in 2009). GSTs in 2010 continued to be tax free, but under a slightly different formulation.

17. The maximum GST tax rate is also 40 percent. *See* IRC § 2641(a)(1).

18. Congress also continued the 2010 Act's introduction of an increased exemption for a surviving spouse, which is known as portability. *See* IRC §§ 2010(c)(2) and 2505(a)(1).

time, about 15 states, many of which rely on the federal estate tax structure, have some form of taxation at death that will likely continue.

The federal transfer taxes interface with the federal income tax at a number of points.[19] For our purpose here, the most important concept is "basis," which sets the starting value of capital assets to determine the extent of a gain or a loss on the sale of the assets. For example, if you buy 100 shares of stock for $1,000 and sell them for $1,500, your basis will be $1,000 and your gain will be the amount your sale price exceeds the basis (here, $500). *See* IRC § 1001(a).[20] Similarly, if you sell for less than your basis, your loss will be measured from the basis.

When gratuitous transfers—at death or during life—are involved, the basis of the property is determined by special rules.[21] The basis of property received on the death of someone is either the property's fair market value as of the date of death or the value six months later, depending upon which value the personal representative selects. *See* IRC § 1014.

Consider again the stock you purchased for $1,000. As we have seen, if you sell it for $1,500, your gain is $500. On the other hand, if you keep the stock and die when its value is $1,500, its basis will jump to $1,500. If the beneficiary of the stock sells it for $1,500, no taxable gain will occur since the sales price and the basis are the same amount. When there is a lifetime gift, the basis depends on whether the donee disposes of the property at a gain or a loss. If the donee transfers for a gain, the donee's basis for determining gain becomes whatever the donor's basis was. If the done transfers for a loss, the donee's basis is the lesser of the donor's basis or the fair market value at the time of the gift. *See* IRC § 1015. Estate planners need to keep in mind not only the estate and gift tax rules we discuss, but also the income tax consequences donees will face.[22]

A. A Unified System

Since 1977, the gift and estate tax system has worked rather like a large beaker, with a scale printed on the side. Each time we make a taxable transfer, we pour a little water into the beaker. Later additions are assessed at a higher rate, and we start

19. Although income tax rates will likely be reduced during the Trump administration, there is no talk of repealing the federal income tax systems.

20. Technically, gain and loss are determined by comparing the amount realized from the sale with the adjusted basis for the property. *See* IRC § 1011(a). Amount realized is generally the sales price less related selling expenses, such as commissions. *See* IRC § 1011(b). Adjusted basis is generally the cost of the property, although in some cases later events may cause the basis to be adjusted upward or downward. *See* IRC §§ 1011 and 1016.

21. It is possible that changes will be made to the basis rules under the Trump administration.

22. For decedents dying in 2010, the personal representative could elect out of the estate tax system, but the price to pay for the election is that the aggregate basis for property acquired from the decedent will be the decedent's adjusted basis, with a possible increase of $1.3 million and an additional $3 million increase for property passing to the surviving spouse in a qualifying way.

paying taxes once we fill past the threshold Congress has set. Until then we use bits and pieces of our "unified credit" to offset tax we would otherwise owe. *See* IRC §§ 2001(c), 2010, 2505. Our transfers are technically taxable transfers, but we use the credit instead of actually paying tax. The amount passing tax free is usually known as an "exemption," an "exemption equivalent," or "the applicable exclusion amount."

Beginning in 2013, the estate, gift, and GST exemption was set at $5 million, as adjusted for inflation since 2011, to the nearest multiple of $10,000. For 2016, the exemption level was $5,450,000. The exemption level is $5,490,000 in 2017.

To see how the unified credit worked, imagine Marc, who incurred no prior transfer tax liability. Because his son, Ben, needed a down payment for his first house, in 2015 Marc gave Ben $34,000, $14,000 of which was exempt from taxation under an annual exclusion designed to reduce the gift tax consequences of lifetime transfers. The other $20,000 was subject to gift tax. *See* IRC § 2501. Rather than actually paying any tax, however, Marc used up a small piece of his unified credit. Figure 1-2 below illustrates Marc's situation after making the gift.

Figure 1-2 Marc's First Gift

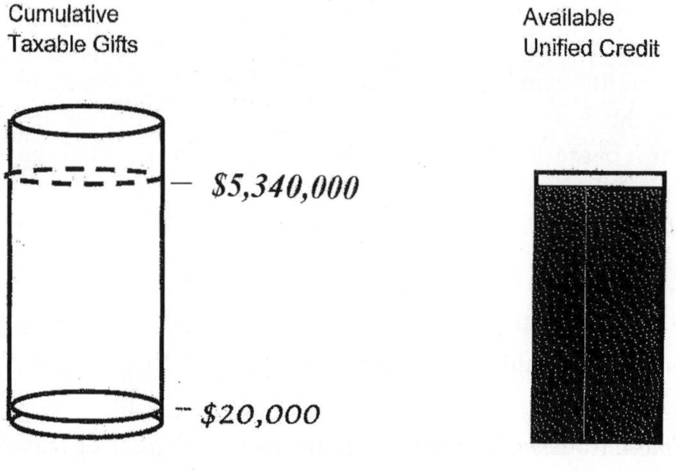

Cumulative Taxable Gifts

Available Unified Credit

$5,340,000

$20,000

Suppose further that in 2016, Ben's house was damaged in a storm, so Marc gave him another $34,000 for repairs. Because there was no inflation adjustment for gifts in 2016, the annual exclusion sheltered $14,000 and the other $20,000 was subject to tax. This second gift was taxed at a higher rate, however, because it came on top of Marc's earlier gift. To achieve that result as an accounting matter, we add in the prior gift for the purpose of figuring the tax on the new gift. Marc was not taxed twice on the first gift. The earlier gift only served to push the second gift into a higher bracket. Marc still used his unified credit and paid no tax. *See* Figure 1-3.

Figure 1-3 Marc's Second Gift

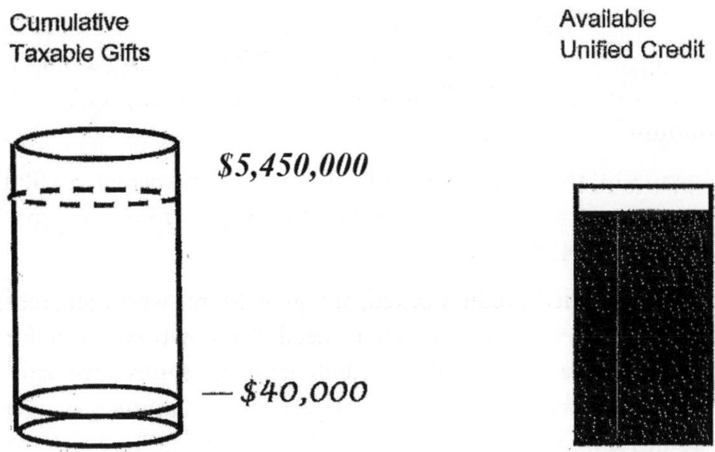

Other taxable gifts will be treated the same way. Suppose that Marc died at the end of 2016, having given away $100,000 in taxable gifts. Now the value of his taxable estate would be added in, just like the gifts. If the taxable estate was $5,350,000 or less, the rest of his unified credit would cover the tax.[23] If the taxable estate pushed his lifetime-plus-death total over $5,450,000, his estate would be able to use the rest of his available credit to offset some of the tax, but his estate would be liable for the excess over $5,450,000, all of which would be taxed at a 40 percent rate.

Rather than using up their unified credits in smaller bites throughout their lifetimes, some wealthy taxpayers elect to make lump sum gifts that would use the entire unified credit. By moving the assets out of their estates, they save both income tax on the income the property would generate and estate tax on any value the property would gain between the time of the gift and the donor's death.

With the basic framework in mind, we now turn to identifying taxable gifts and taxable estates.

B. The Gift Tax

The Internal Revenue Code imposes a tax on any "transfer of property by gift," while also excluding many gifts of up to $14,000, as that amount is indexed for

23. Although no federal estate tax will be payable if the combined lifetime transfers and the taxable estate was $5,450,000 or less, state death taxes may be payable in about 15 states which set the exemption or threshold level lower. For example, in Massachusetts **only** estates up to $1 million are exempt from estate taxation.

inflation. *See* IRC §§ 2502(a)(1), 2503(b). This section first addresses what constitutes a gift, and then turns to the annual exclusion.[24]

Deciding whether something is a "gift" for gift tax purposes often involves questions of valuation and of whether a transfer is complete. Some gifts are obvious. If Monica hands $50 to her son, Doug, and tells him "happy birthday," she has made a gift. Some are more subtle. Suppose Monica sells Doug her car for $2,000. If the car is worth $2,000, there is no gift, but if the car is worth $5,000, Monica has made a $3,000 gift. Valuation determines both whether there is a gift and how much the gift is.

Sometimes donors will give away property, but hold onto some strings. Then the question is whether the strings are strong enough to mean there was no completed gift. Only if the donor has parted with all "dominion and control" is there a gift. *See* Treas. Reg. § 25.2511-2. For example, if Monica creates a trust for Doug, but retains a power to revoke, she has not made a gift.

To avoid the record keeping that would follow if all gifts, including birthday presents, were taxable, Congress created the annual exclusion, indexed in $1,000 increments for inflation. In 2016 and 2017, the exclusion was $14,000. IRC § 2503(b). Because it allows each donor to make substantial annual gifts to each donee, however, the exclusion is large enough to encourage wealthy taxpayers to reduce their estates by making lifetime gifts. The annual exclusion applies only to unrestricted rights to the use, possession, or enjoyment of property or its income. Treas. Reg. § 25.2503-3(b). Thus, a donor cannot apply the exclusion to income interests given in trusts if the trustee has discretion to allocate income among various beneficiaries. Similarly, the exclusion does not cover future interests. But *see Crummey v. Commissioner*, 397 F.2d 82 (9th Cir. 1968) (allowing annual exclusions for future interest trust beneficiaries who are given the immediate right to demand the annual exclusion amount). Many taxpayers, however, want to use the annual exclusion, but restrict gifts to minors until they reach majority. In response, the Code allows the annual exclusion for future gifts to minors in some circumstances. *See* IRC § 2503(c). *See also Crummey v. Commissioner*, 397 F.2d 82 (9th Cir. 1968).

Question

Alicia, like most people, gives her family birthday presents. In June, Alicia gave her daughter, Elizabeth, a nice blouse. As part of year-end tax planning, Alicia wrote Elizabeth a check for $14,000. Should Alicia's lawyer ignore the incidental gifts and tell her she need not file a gift tax return because the annual exclusion covers her $14,000 check?

---

24. There are other minor gift tax exclusions, including tuition payments and payments for medical expenses. *See* IRC § 2503(e).

C. The Estate Tax

The federal estate tax resembles a fishing net. It snares a large number of different assets, but its holes allow some assets to escape in some situations. The basic approach is to include assets in a "gross estate," and allow some deductions to produce a "taxable estate." Much like the way later gifts are stacked on top of earlier gifts to assess gift tax, the taxable estate is added to lifetime gifts to determine estate tax liability. Again, the unified credit may cover all or part of that liability. This section first introduces the gross estate, then discusses the marital deduction, and closes with a look at how couples can use the marital deduction and unified credit together to shelter larger estates.

1. The Gross Estate

The gross estate is an accounting concept which attributes to a decedent property in the decedent's probate estate as well as non-probate property that benefits the decedent. When we say an asset is "in the gross estate," we do *not* mean that the asset itself becomes subject to the jurisdiction of a court. Rather, we are including its *value* in a computation to determine estate tax liability. *See* Figure 1-4.

Figure 1-4 The Gross Estate

A Decedent's Wealth

Probate Property	Non-Probate Property[25]
In Decedent's Name	Life Insurance
	Joint Survivorship Property
	Retirement Benefits
	Property in Lifetime Trusts
	P. O. D. Accounts

One of the most important points to get across to clients is that avoiding probate does not, of itself, mean avoiding federal estate taxes. A few basic provisions bring in most of the assets of typical families: separately-held property, joint property,[26] life insurance, and retirement benefits. IRC §§ 2033, 2039, 2040, 2042. Because of the political uncertainty about how Congress will set the exemption levels, many people—especially those with lots of life insurance or generous retirement benefits—may learn to their surprise that they could benefit from tax planning.

---

25. This list is illustrative, not complete.

26. When a married couple holds joint property, half its value is in the gross estate of the first to die. IRC § 2040(b). The value of an unmarried joint tenant's share will be based on the percentage the decedent contributed to the purchase. IRC § 2040(a). At the death of the last surviving joint tenant, all of the property will be included in that person's gross estate. IRC § 2033.

The estate tax, of course, also covers other forms of wealth. In particular, the Internal Revenue Code captures for the gross estate the value of lifetime transfers in which taxpayers retain beneficial interests. The gross estate will include the value of property in which the decedent kept: a life estate, a reversionary interest worth more than 5% of the value of the property which can only be enjoyed by surviving the decedent, or various powers to control the property. IRC §§ 2036, 2037, 2038. These provisions have generated a great deal of litigation, as taxpayers seek to retain benefits without suffering tax consequences. In general, the courts have looked at the substance, rather than the form, of the arrangements under question. Finally, the gross estate includes property subject to a general power of appointment. A power of appointment gives one person the authority to transfer someone else's property. A general power is one exercisable in favor of the person holding the power (the donee), the donee's creditors, the donee's estate, or creditors of the donee's estate. IRC § 2041(b)(2)(A).

In terms of taxing property a decedent has earned or received outright, the Internal Revenue Code casts a broad net. On the other hand, it is much more generous toward property received with strings attached. Gift recipients can receive a good deal of power over property, short of absolute ownership, without subjecting that property to tax in their own estates. For example, suppose Jennie creates a trust naming Sheila as trustee and giving her typical management powers. Jennie can also give Sheila, as beneficiary, a right to the trust's income, and a power to appoint the remainder to anyone except herself, her creditors, her estate or creditors of her estate. Sheila has something very close to complete ownership, yet the value of the trust will not be included in her gross estate.

2. The Marital Deduction

Once the value of the gross estate is established, various deductions apply, reducing the gross estate to the "taxable estate." For our purposes, the most important deduction is the one for transfers to surviving spouses.[27] Although the details can get quite complex, the basic principle of the marital deduction is straightforward: the law treats married couples as units, not individuals. It allows each spouse to give unlimited amounts of property to the other without incurring transfer taxes, so long as the property will be exposed to tax if and when it leaves the marital unit. A similar deduction is available for the gift tax, but this discussion will cover only the estate tax deduction. *Compare* IRC § 2523 (gift tax), *with* IRC § 2056 (estate tax).

---

27. In *United States v. Windsor*, 133 S. Ct. 2675 (2013), the Supreme Court effectively held that, for federal tax purposes, same-sex marriages must be constitutionally recognized. As a result, a marital deduction was allowed for transfers to the surviving spouse of a same-sex marriage. Deductions are also allowed, most noteworthy for qualifying contributions to charities, for administration and funeral expenses, and debts of the decedent.

Portability: A Portable Exemption

Until 2010, the unified credit (and its effective exemption amount) was personal to each taxpayer, so if a taxpayer died without using all of the credit, that benefit was simply lost. For example, one spouse might leave the entire estate to the other. On the death of the first, the marital deduction would cover everything, and there would be no need to use any of the credit. When the survivor died, only the survivor's own credit was available. Complicated estate plans were developed to subject to tax enough of the estate of the first-to-die spouse, so that spouse's credit was not wasted. (You may still see references to such "credit shelter" trusts.)

Now a decedent's personal representative can elect that the surviving spouse be allowed to "port" the deceased spouse's unused exclusion (DSUE) amount. IRC § 2010(c). This is known as portability. For example, if the deceased spouse died in 2016 with a taxable estate of $1 million and had made no taxable gifts, the DSUE amount would be $4,450,000. If the executor elected portability, the surviving spouse's exemption amount would be augmented by $4,450,000.

The combination of larger exemptions and their portability has led to rethinking many estate plans, which were structured around maximizing the unified credit and the marital deduction at the expense of others, e.g., children of a prior or current marriage.

The easiest way to be sure a transfer qualifies for the marital deduction is for the decedent spouse to give the property outright to the surviving spouse. In many situations, however, such an approach may be undesirable. The surviving spouse may need the management a trust provides, or the decedent spouse may want to be sure children from an earlier marriage get a share after the survivor's death. By carefully following the Internal Revenue Code's rules, drafters can create trusts to qualify for the marital deduction while not actually passing more than a life estate to the spouse. In each case, the tradeoff is that the property then will be in the survivor's gross estate.

Deciding how best to structure an estate plan utilizing the marital deduction requires lawyers and clients to consider a wide range of variables. In addition, marital deduction planning often places the lawyer in a difficult position, because the spouses' interests, or desires, may be different. In particular, spouses who expect to survive their mates may object to a plan that leaves them with less than complete ownership. In that connection, consider the following.

Lawrence J. Fox & Susan R. Martyn, Red Flags: A Lawyer's Handbook on Legal Ethics (ALI-ABA 2d ed. 2010)

§ 7.23(b) Handling Confidentiality in Joint Client Representations

Every joint representation requires attention to the issue of client confidentiality. Your written waiver should include the clients' choice of confidentiality provisions.

They can elect to have you disclose or not disclose to the other whatever either tells you in confidence. With respect to the attorney-client privilege, you must warn your clients that it attaches between commonly represented parties against opposing parties, but does not attach if litigation arises between these clients, including that initiated by a counterclaim.

If you do not include a confidentiality provision in your conflicts waiver, and one joint client tells you some material fact in confidence, your duty of confidentiality to that client will directly collide with your duty to keep the other client informed about material aspects of the matter. Your duties to one client now put you in a position of direct adversity to the other, and unless they have instructed you what to do in advance, you now must withdraw from the representation of both. Of course, withdrawal does not end the issue about disclosure. Here, absent a prior agreement between the parties, courts generally look to their own confidentiality exceptions to determine whether you may (or must) disclose.

Note

Careful preparation saved some headaches for the law firm in *A. v. B.*, 726 A.2d 924 (N.J. 1999). The firm had drafted wills for both a husband and a wife giving property to each other, with alternative gifts to the spouse's issue. Before the wills were executed, the firm—but not the wife—learned that the husband had a non- marital child who could qualify to take from the wife's estate. Because at the time of the representation the couple had agreed that information from one spouse could be shared with the other, the firm could disclose the existence of the non-marital child to the wife.

Problem

Jenny, age 50, and Richard, age 60, are a married couple in need of tax planning. How do you decide whether you can represent them both and what steps would you take if you did?

D. The Generation-Skipping Transfer Tax

To plug some holes which the gift and estate tax system had left open, Congress in 1986 enacted the generation-skipping transfer (GST) tax. IRC Ch. 13. The GST tax applies in addition to gift and estate taxes, but was designed with those taxes in mind. The rules surrounding the tax, and lawyer's strategies for coping with those rules, are very complex. The purpose of this section is not to summarize those rules but, rather, to help you understand why they developed.

The overall goal is to tax wealth once in each generation. To accomplish this, the GST tax system taxes transfers to a "skip person," someone two or more generations below the transferor's generation. IRC § 2613(a). To help visualize these transfers, consider gifts from Genevieve to her daughter Peggy, and to Peggy's son, Troy. From Genevieve's perspective, Troy is a skip person. Transfers to a skip person might happen any of three ways. There could be a "taxable termination," like a trust from Genevieve which ends at Peggy's death, with distribution to Troy. There could be a "taxable distribution," like Peggy's exercise as trustee of a power to invade for Troy's benefit the principal of a trust Genevieve established. Finally, to prevent direct avoidance of the rules aimed at trusts, there could be a "direct skip," like an outright gift from Genevieve to Troy. *See* IRC §§ 2611–2613.

The GST exemption is the same as the estate tax exemption, For example, if in 2016 Genevieve put $10,900,000 in trust for Peggy (her child) for life, remainder to Troy (grandchild), Genevieve could allocate all of her $5,450,000 exemption to the trust. When the GST became due at Peggy's death, half of the trust would be exempt. Notice that if the trust grew to $30 million before Peggy's death, $15 million would now be exempt. Taxable transfers exceeding the GST exemption limits generate tax liability at 40 percent, which is the federal estate tax's highest rate. IRC § 2602.

Problems

1. Harry and Wilma were married, and Harry died recently. At Harry's death, the following items of value were located:

Harry's separate property (probate estate):	$10,000,000
Life insurance on Harry's life payable to Wilma (Harry owned):	100,000
A power to appoint (only among his children) the principal of a trust created by his mother; value of trust:	200,000

(a) What is the size of Harry's gross estate?

(b) Assume Harry's will gave all of his probate estate to Wilma. Assuming no debts or administrative expenses, what is Harry's taxable estate?

2. Assume at Wilma's later death the value of the property which passed to her is the same as it was at Harry's death and that she died with no other property and no expenses. Upon what amount will Wilma have to pay estate taxes?

Selected References

Zoe Prebble & John Prebble, *The Morality of Tax Avoidance*, 43 Creighton L. Rev. 693 (2010).

John R. Price and Samuel A. Donaldson, Price On Contemporary Estate Planning (CCH 2016 ed.)

John R. Price, *In Honor of Professor John Gaubatz: The Fundamentals of Ethically Representing Multiple Clients in Estate Planning*, 62 U. Miami L. Rev. 735 (2008).

§ 1.04 Duties Lawyers Owe Clients (and Others)

A major goal of this book is to alert you to some underlying questions while helping you learn the basic doctrine and the skills necessary for applying that doctrine to the individual needs of your clients. If you serve those clients well, you will be upholding the highest standards of our profession.

On the other hand, if you pay insufficient attention to your clients' needs, you may find yourself liable for malpractice. That was not as true several decades ago, when a combination of traditional rules and the nature of estate planners' practices protected them from liability. First, because mistakes often only hurt non-clients—like intended will beneficiaries—lack of "privity" with the lawyer, whose only duty was to the client, barred will beneficiaries from recovering. Second, often no one noticed the mistake in a will until years later, when the testator died. A strict view of statutes of limitations protected lawyers by starting the running of the statute on the date of a document's execution, which may be many years before the mistake is found

These protections started to crumble, however, with *Lucas v. Hamm*, 364 P.2d 685 (Cal. 1961), *cert. denied*, 368 U.S. 987 (1962), which abolished the defense "there was no privity." Following that lead, and as illustrated by *Fabian v. Lindsay,* below, most recent cases have used either tort (negligence) or contract (third-party beneficiary) theory to allow will beneficiaries to recover against drafting lawyers. Recent cases have also interpreted statutes of limitation as running from the client's date of death, rather than the time of the will's execution. *See, e.g., Thorsen v. Richmond Society for the Prevention of Cruelty to Animals*, 292 Va. 257, 786 S.E.2d 453 (2016).

Fabian v. Lindsay

765 S.E.2d 132 (S.C. 2014)

Beatty, Justice.

Erika Fabian (Appellant) brought this action for legal malpractice and breach of contract by a third-party beneficiary, alleging attorney Ross M. Lindsay, III and his law firm Lindsay & Lindsay (collectively, Respondents) made a drafting error in preparing a trust instrument for her late uncle and, as a result, she was effectively disinherited. Appellant appeals from a circuit court order dismissing her action . . . for failure to state a claim and contends South Carolina should recognize a cause of action, in tort and in contract, by a third-party beneficiary of a will or estate planning document against a lawyer whose drafting error defeats or diminishes the client's intent. We agree, and we reverse and remand for further proceedings.

I. FACTS

[As written, a trust agreement unambiguously provided that the appellant would receive trust property only if another beneficiary predeceased the trust creator. The appellant contended that the trust creator intended that she receive trust property if the other beneficiary also failed to the trust creator's spouse, which was the case. . . .

The circuit court granted the [Respondents'] motion to dismiss, finding Appellant could not assert a claim for legal malpractice because South Carolina law recognizes no duty in the absence of an attorney-client relationship. In addition, the court stated no South Carolina court had ever recognized a breach of contract action by an intended beneficiary of estate planning documents. . . .]

. . . .

III. LAW/ANALYSIS

A. Privity Under Existing Law

In dismissing Appellant's claims, the circuit court essentially found Appellant was not in privity with Respondents and therefore failed to establish a viable cause of action. "'Privity' denotes [a] mutual or successive relationship to the same rights of property." *Thompson v. Hudgens*, 161 S.C. 450, 462, 159 S.E. 807, 812 (1931) (citation omitted); *see also Black's Law Dictionary* 1394 (10th ed. 2014) (defining "privity" as "[t]he connection or relationship between two parties, each having a legally recognized interest in the same subject matter (such as a transaction, proceeding, or piece of property); mutuality of interests"). South Carolina courts have equated privity with standing. [Citation omitted]. . . .

Privity for legal malpractice has traditionally been established by the existence of an attorney-client relationship. *See generally Rydde v. Morris*, 381 S.C. 643, 650, 675 S.E.2d 431, 435 (2009) (stating "existing law imposes a privity requirement as a condition to maintaining a legal malpractice claim in South Carolina"). "A plaintiff in a legal malpractice action must establish four elements: (1) the existence of an attorney-client relationship, (2) a breach of duty by the attorney, (3) damage to the client, and (4) proximate causation of the client's damages by the breach." *RFT Mgmt. Co. v. Tinsley & Adams L.L.P.*, 399 S.C. 322, 331, 732 S.E.2d 166, 170 (2012).

Appellant contends the current appeal presents an opportunity not available in prior cases for South Carolina to join the vast majority of states allowing intended third-party beneficiaries to bring claims against the lawyer who prepared the defective will or estate planning document. *See Chastain v. Hiltabidle*, 381 S.C. 508, 673 S.E.2d 826 (Ct. App. 2009) (stating whether a duty exists in regard to an alleged wrong is a question of law for the court). Appellant argues a lawyer's negligence in preparing an estate or testamentary document impacts three potential classes of plaintiffs: (1) the client, (2) the decedent's estate, and (3) the intended beneficiaries. As she aptly states:

> [O]f the three possible plaintiffs, only the beneficiaries have the motivation and sufficient damages to bring a malpractice claim. The client is deceased and the estate lacks a cause of action or damages or both. Indeed, because the beneficiaries were supposed to be the beneficial owners of estate assets, only the beneficiaries suffer directly due to the lawyer's negligence. If no cause of action is available to the beneficiaries, the negligent drafting lawyer is effectively immune from liability. Therefore, only the beneficiaries suffer the loss caused by the lawyer's negligence.

In the 1950s, after observing the problems created by the traditional privity requirement, jurisdictions in the United States began abandoning strict privity as an absolute bar to claims for legal malpractice. A majority of jurisdictions now recognize a cause of action by a third-party beneficiary of a will or estate planning document against the lawyer whose drafting error defeats or diminishes the client's intent, although they have done so using a variety of tests and formulations, whether in tort, contract, or both. [Citations omitted].

"The jurisdictions that have eased the strict privity requirement typically use one of the following three approaches to determine whether the intended beneficiary of a will has standing to bring an action for legal malpractice: (1) the balancing of factors test, which originated in California; (2) 'the Florida-Iowa rule[']; and (3) breach of contract based on a third-party beneficiary contract theory." [Citation omitted].

B. Theories for Imposing Liability in Tort or Contract

(1) Balancing of Factors Test

In an influential decision emanating from California in 1958, the rule on privity in legal malpractice actions began to evolve throughout the United States. In *Biakanja v. Irving*, 49 Cal. 2d 647, 320 P.2d 16 (Cal. 1958), the court held that where the defendant negligently prepared an invalid will, the beneficiary could recover for her loss in tort even though she was not in privity with the defendant. Although the defendant in that case was a notary public and not an attorney, the court also overruled prior cases involving attorneys.

The holding in *Biakanja* was formally extended to attorneys a few years later in *Lucas v. Hamm*, 56 Cal. 2d 583, 15 Cal. Rptr. 821, 364 P.2d 685 (Cal. 1961). In *Lucas*, the court allowed recovery both in tort and as a third-party beneficiary to a contract. In discussing whether to impose tort liability, the Lucas court reiterated all but one of the factors it originally delineated in *Biakanja* and stated, "[T]he determination whether in a specific case the defendant will be held liable to a third person not in privity is a matter of policy and involves the balancing of various factors, among which are the extent to which the transaction was intended to affect the plaintiff, the foreseeability of harm to him, the degree of certainty that the plaintiff suffered injury, the closeness of the connection between the defendant's conduct and the injury, and the policy of preventing future harm." *Id.* at 687 (citing *Biakanja*, 320 P.2d at 19).

Applying these factors, the court reasoned that "one of the main purposes which the transaction between defendant and the testator intended to accomplish was to provide for the transfer of property to plaintiffs; the damage to plaintiffs in the event of invalidity of the bequest was clearly foreseeable; it became certain, upon the death of the testator without change of the will, that plaintiffs would have received the intended benefits but for the asserted negligence of defendant; and if persons such as plaintiffs are not permitted to recover for the loss resulting from negligence of the draftsman, no one would be able to do so, and the policy of prevent[ing] future harm would be impaired." *Id.* at 688.

The court then noted since the defendant in this case was an attorney, it "must consider an additional factor not present in *Biakanja*, namely, whether the recognition of liability to beneficiaries of wills negligently drawn by attorneys would impose an undue burden on the profession." *Id.* The court found although in some situations liability could be large and unpredictable, this was also true for any attorney's liability to his client, and the extension of liability to beneficiaries injured by a negligently drawn will does not place an undue burden on the profession, particularly when taking into consideration that the opposite conclusion would cause the innocent beneficiary to bear the entire loss of the attorney's professional negligence. *Id.*

Other jurisdictions have engaged in a similar or modified "balancing of factors" analysis to generally determine whether an attorney should be liable to a third party in the absence of strict privity. [Citing cases from Arizona, Kansas and Florida].

(2) The Florida-Iowa Rule

In the event this Court joins the majority of jurisdictions allowing a third party beneficiary to seek recovery for the improper drafting of a will or estate planning document, Respondents and the amicus urge this Court to adopt an alternative theory of recovery known as the "Florida-Iowa Rule." It provides:

> An attorney preparing a will has a duty not only to the testator-client, but also to the testator's intended beneficiaries, who may maintain a legal malpractice action against the attorney on theories of either tort (negligence) or contract (third-party beneficiaries). However, liability to the testamentary beneficiary can arise only if, due to the attorney's professional negligence, the testamentary intent, *as expressed in the will*, is frustrated, and the beneficiary's legacy is lost or diminished as a direct result of that negligence.

DeMaris v. Asti, 426 So. 2d 1153, 1154 (Fla. Dist. Ct. App. 1983) (citations omitted)....

Respondents' desire, in the absence of this Court's retention of strict privity, is to promote the Florida-Iowa Rule because its essential feature, the imposition of a ban on all extrinsic evidence, obviously makes it more difficult for a plaintiff to establish a claim. [Citation omitted].

Appellant understandably opposes this theory [and the court agreed.]. As she correctly asserts: "The fundamental flaw in the Florida-Iowa [R]ule is that it focuses on the testamentary documents prepared by the lawyer rather than the source of the beneficiary's claim, which is not the allegedly defective will or trust document, but instead is the client-lawyer agreement that was intended to satisfy the client's testamentary intent. The proper approach in cases like this one where latent ambiguities exist in the will, trust agreement, or estate plan would be to allow the admission of extrinsic evidence to establish the client's intent as is generally allowed in a typical will contest."....

(3) Third-Party Beneficiary of Contract Theory

Another theory recognized for recovery is based on a third-party beneficiary approach. South Carolina law already generally recognizes a breach of contract claim for a third-party beneficiary of a contract and we find this principle is appropriate here.

"Generally, one not in privity of contract with another cannot maintain an action against him in breach of contract, and any damage resulting from the breach of a contract between the defendant and a third-party is not, as such, recoverable by the plaintiff." *Windsor Green Owners Ass'n v. Allied Signal, Inc.*, 362 S.C. 12, 17, 605 S.E.2d 750, 752 (Ct. App. 2004) (citation omitted). "However, if a contract is made for the benefit of a third person, that person may enforce the contract if the contracting parties intended to create a direct, rather than an incidental or consequential, benefit to such third person." *Id.* (citation omitted).

Courts in other jurisdictions have expressly extended this principle to frustrated third-party beneficiaries of estate instruments, although some have done so as a breach of contract action while others have used the "third-party beneficiary" principle as a basis to allow recovery in negligence. Some jurisdictions have recognized that a plaintiff may choose to proceed in contract, tort, or both. *See, e.g., Lucas*, 364 P.2d at 689 & n.2; *Stowe v. Smith*, 184 Conn. 194, 441 A.2d 81, 84 (Conn. 1981); *Blair v. Ing*, 95 Haw. 247, 21 P.3d 452, 464 (Haw. 2001).

In *Lucas*, in addition to allowing tort recovery, the California court found "that intended beneficiaries of a will who lose their testamentary rights because of failure of the attorney who drew the will to properly fulfill his obligations under his contract with the testator may recover as third-party beneficiaries." 364 P.2d at 689. The court stated, "Obviously the main purpose of a contract for the drafting of a will is to accomplish the future transfer of the estate of the testator to the beneficiaries named in the will, and therefore it seems improper to hold ... that the testator intended only 'remotely' to benefit those persons." *Id.* at 688. The court found this main purpose and "intent can be effectuated, in the event of a breach by the attorney, only by giving the beneficiaries a right of action, [so] we should recognize, as a matter of policy, that they are entitled to recover as third-party beneficiaries." *Id.* at 689. Moreover, the court noted the general rule is "where a case sounds in both tort and contract, the plaintiff will ordinarily have freedom of election between the two actions." *Id.* at 689 n.2.

We find this reasoning sound and adopt it here....

Recognizing a cause of action is not a radical departure from the existing law of legal malpractice that requires a lawyer-client relationship, which is equated with privity and standing. Where a client hires an attorney to carry out his intent for estate planning and to provide for his beneficiaries, there *is* an attorney-client relationship that forms the basis for the attorney's duty to carry out the client's intent. This intent in estate planning is directly and inescapably for the benefit of the third-party beneficiaries. Thus, imposing an avenue for recourse in the beneficiary, where the client is deceased, is effectively enforcing the *client's intent*, and the third party is in privity with the attorney. It is the breach of the attorney's duty to the client that is the actionable conduct in these cases....

In these circumstances, retaining strict privity in a legal malpractice action for negligence committed in preparing will or estate documents would serve to improperly immunize this particular subset of attorneys from liability for their professional negligence. Joining the majority of states that have recognized causes of action is the just result. This does not impose an undue burden on estate planning attorneys as it merely puts them in the same position as most other legal professionals by making them responsible for their professional negligence to the same extent as attorneys practicing in other areas.

In sum, today we affirmatively recognize causes of action both in tort and in contract by a third-party beneficiary of an existing will or estate planning document against a lawyer whose drafting error defeats or diminishes the client's intent. The focus of a will or estate document is, inherently, on third-party beneficiaries. That being the case, the action typically does not arise until the client is deceased....

IV. CONCLUSION

We recognize a cause of action, in both tort and contract, by a third-party beneficiary of an existing will or estate planning document against a lawyer whose drafting error defeats or diminishes the client's intent. Recovery under either cause of action is limited to persons who are named in the estate planning document or otherwise identified in the instrument by their status. Where the claim sounds in both tort and contract, the plaintiff may elect a recovery. We apply this holding in the instant appeal and to cases pending on appeal as of the date of this opinion. As a result, we reverse the order dismissing Appellant's complaint and remand the matter to the circuit court for further proceedings consistent with this opinion.

REVERSED AND REMANDED.[27]

Developments in the law of lawyer malpractice, however, have been uneven. Consider the next case.

Schneider v. Finmann

15 N.Y.3d 306 (2010)

Jones, J.

At issue in this appeal is whether an attorney may be held liable for damages resulting from negligent representation in estate tax planning that causes enhanced estate tax liability. We hold that a personal representative of an estate may maintain a legal malpractice claim for such pecuniary losses to the estate.

The complaint alleges the following facts. Defendants represented decedent Saul Schneider from at least April 2000 to his death in October 2006. In April 2000, decedent purchased a $1 million life insurance policy. Over several years, he transferred

27. Concurring and dissenting opinions omitted.

ownership of that property from himself to an entity of which he was principal owner, then to another entity of which he was principal owner and then, in 2005, back to himself. At his death in October 2006, the proceeds of the insurance policy were included as part of his gross taxable estate. Decedent's estate commenced this malpractice action in 2007, alleging that defendants negligently advised decedent to transfer, or failed to advise decedent not to transfer, the policy which resulted in an increased estate tax liability.

Supreme Court granted defendants' motion to dismiss the complaint for failure to state a cause of action. The Appellate Division affirmed (60 AD3d 892, 876 N.Y.S.2d 121), holding that, in the absence of privity, an estate may not maintain an action for legal malpractice. We now reverse and reinstate plaintiff's claim.

Strict privity, as applied in the context of estate planning malpractice actions, is a minority rule in the United States.[28] In New York, a third party, without privity, cannot maintain a claim against an attorney in professional negligence, "absent fraud, collusion, malicious acts or other special circumstances" (*Spivey v. Pulley*, 138 AD2d 563, 564, 526 N.Y.S.2d 145 [2d Dept 1988]). Some Appellate Division decisions, on which the Appellate Division here relied, have applied strict privity to estate planning malpractice lawsuits commenced by the estate's personal representative and beneficiaries alike.... This rule effectively protects attorneys from legal malpractice suits by indeterminate classes of plaintiffs whose interests may be at

28. Now only a handful of jurisdictions apply strict privity to malpractice actions commenced by beneficiaries against estate planning attorneys (*see Robinson v. Benton*, 842So2d 631, 637 [Ala 2002]; *Nevin v. Union Trust Co.*, 1999 ME 47, 726 A 2d 694, 701 [Me 1999]; *Noble v. Bruce*, 349 Md. 730, 709 A2d 1264, 1275 [Md 1998]; *Simon v. Zipperstein*, 32 Ohio St. 3d 74, 512 NE2d 636 [Ohio 1987]; *Lilyhorn v. Dier*, 214 Neb. 728, 335 NW2d 554 [Neb 1983]). Numerous jurisdictions have either relaxed the principle of privity or have granted standing to beneficiaries or estates (see *The Stanley L and Carolyn M. Watkins Trust*, 321 Mont 432, 438, 2004 MT 144, 92 P.3d 620 [2004] [an estate has standing to bring a legal malpractice action]; *Blair v. Ing*, 95 Haw. 247, 21 P3d 452, 464 [Hawai'I 2001] [non-client may bring a legal malpractice suit]; *Simpson v. Calivas*, 139 N.H. 1, 650 A2d 318, 321 [NH 1994] [named beneficiaries have standing to bring claims in negligence against an estate planning attorney]; *Espinosa v. Sparber, Shevin, Rosen and Heilbronner*, 612 So2d 1378, 1380 [Fla 1993][estate stands in the shoes of the testator and satisfies the privity requirement]; *Schreiner v. Scoville*, 410 NW2d 679, 681 [Iowa 1987][intended beneficiaries may maintain a malpractice action against the decedent's attorney despite the absence of privity]). The *Schreinder* court cited to numerous jurisdictions that had a similar rule in place (see *id. At 681-682*). Texas treats the malpractice claims brought by beneficiaries and personal representatives of decedent's estates differently (see *Barcelo v.* Elliott, 923 SW2d 575, 580 [Tex 1996] [non-client beneficiaries cannot maintain malpractice suits against estate planning attorneys because they lack privity]; *cf. Belt v. Oppenheimer, Blend, Harrison & Tate, Inc.*, 192 SW3d 780, 784–786 [Tex 2006] [departed from the *Barcelo* rule in suits brought by the personal representative of the decedent's estate and held that privity existed between the parties]). Texas treats the malpractice claims brought by beneficiaries and personal representatives of decedent's estates differently (*see Barcelo v. Elliott*, 923 SW2d 575, 580 [Tex 1996][non-client beneficiaries cannot maintain malpractice suits against estate planning attorneys because they lack privity]; *cf. Belt v. Oppenheimer, Blend, Harrison & Tate, Inc.*, 192 SW3d 780, 784–786 [Tex 2006] [departed from the *Barcelo* rule in suits brought by the personal representative of the decedent's estate and held that privity existed between the parties]).

odds with the interests of the client-decedent. However, it also leaves the estate with no recourse against an attorney who planned the estate negligently.

We now hold that privity, or a relationship sufficiently approaching privity, exists between the personal representative of an estate and the estate planning attorney. We agree with the Texas Supreme Court that the estate essentially "'stands in the shoes' of a decedent" and, therefore, "has the capacity to maintain the malpractice claim on the estate's behalf" (*Belt v. Oppenheimer, Blend, Harrison & Tate, Inc.*, 192 SW3d 780, 787 [Tex. 2006]). The personal representative of an estate should not be prevented from raising a negligent estate planning claim against the attorney who caused harm to the estate. The attorney estate planner surely knows that minimizing the tax burden of the estate is one of the central tasks entrusted to the professional. Moreover, such a result comports with EPTL § 11-3.2(b),[29] which generally permits the personal representative of a decedent to maintain an action for "injury to person or property" after that person's death.

Despite the holding in this case, strict privity remains a bar against beneficiaries' and other third-party individuals' estate planning malpractice claims absent fraud or other circumstances. Relaxing privity to permit third parties to commence professional negligence actions against estate planning attorneys would produce undesirable results—uncertainty and limitless liability. These concerns, however, are not present in the case of an estate planning malpractice action commenced by the estate's personal representative.

Accordingly, the order of the Appellate Division should be reversed, with costs, and defendants' motion to dismiss the complaint denied.

Order reversed, with costs, and defendants' motion to dismiss the complaint denied. Opinion by Judge Jones. Chief Judge Lippman, and Judges Ciparick, Graffeo, Read, Smith, and Pigott concur.

Questions and Notes

1. States that require privity are concerned that the threat of suit from third parties will compromise an attorney's representation of his or her client. *See, e.g., Baker v. Wood, Ris & Hames, PC*, 364 P.3d 872 (Colo. 2016). In what way might the threat of suit compromise the representation?

2. More broadly, courts see the privity requirement as a way to prevent attorneys from being subject to "almost unlimited liability." *See, e.g., Baker v. Wood, Ris & Hames, PC*, 364 P.3d 872 (Colo. 2016). Can a balance be achieved between policing lawyer behavior via the threat of malpractice liability while protecting against "almost unlimited liability"? *Cf. Estate of Agnew v. Ross*, 152 A.3d 247 (Pa. 2017) (plaintiff must be named in a document to sue on third-party beneficiary contract). *See*

29. No cause of action for injury to person or property is lost because of the death of the person in whose favor the cause of action existed. For any injury an action may be brought or continued by the personal representative of the decedent (EPTL § -11-3.2 [b]).

generally Gerry W. Beyer, *Avoid Being a Defendant: Estate Planning Malpractice and Ethical Concerns*, 5 St. Mary's J. Legal Mal. & Ethics 224 (2015).

3. Another potential source of liability comes while the client is still alive. "An attorney who regularly mails out newsletters or other communications to estate planning clients as part of a client-retention or marketing plan . . . may be fostering reasonable expectations in such clients that they will be advised about changes in the law that make their plan no longer appropriate or effective." 3d Rest. Prop. Ch. 5, Introductory Reporter's Note.

Problems

1. Oscar and Alma had their lawyer draft wills giving their property to each other. The lawyer mistakenly combined two different kinds of will clauses. First, each will made the gift to the other spouse contingent on survival by 30 days. Then each provided that if both spouses were killed in a "common disaster," their nephews would take. Oscar died of a stroke, and 15 days later Alma died of cancer. Neither spouse survived long enough to get the other's property, but the nephews did not qualify to take it because there was no common disaster. The nephews have consulted you to see if they might have a claim against Oscar and Alma's lawyer.

(a) What evidence would you develop to show the nephews were Oscar's and Alma's intended beneficiaries in this situation? Would it matter if the nephews' claim was in malpractice against the lawyer or if instead they sought an order interpreting the will to include them as beneficiaries?

(b) If the nephews brought an action to interpret the will, would the *estate* have any claim against the lawyer? What would be the measure of damages?

(c) How would you have drafted Oscar's and Alma's wills to avoid the problem? See the discussion on survivorship, supra.

2. Trent and Dawn became best friends as college roommates. Trent stayed on campus to attend law school and then joined a local practice. Dawn moved out of state and became an architect. Recently Dawn sent Trent an email asking Trent to draft him a will and email it. Should Trent be at risk for conducting unauthorized practice of law in the other state if he complied with Dawn's request?

Selected References

ACTEC Commentaries on the Model Rules of Professional Conduct (5th ed. 2016).

Martin D. Begleiter, *The Gambler Breaks Even: Legal Malpractice in Complicated Estate Planning Cases*, 20 Ga. St. U. L. Rev. 277 (2003).

Gerry W. Beyer, *Avoiding the Estate Planning "Blue Screen of Death"—Common Non-Tax Errors and How to Prevent Them*, 1 Est. Plan. & Comm. Prop. L.J. 61 (2008).

Bradley E.S. Fogel, *Attorney v. Client—Privity, Malpractice, and the Lack of Respect for the Primacy of the Attorney-Client Relationship in Estate Planning*, 68 Tenn. L. Rev. 261 (2001).

Martin L. Fried, *The Disappointed Heir: Going Beyond the Probate Process to Remedy Wrongdoing or Rectify Mistake*, 39 Real Prop. Prob. & Tr. J. 357 (2004).

Victoria J. Haneman, *Changing the Estate Planning Malpractice Landscape: Applying the Constructive Trust to Cure Testamentary Mistake*, 80 UMKC L. Rev. 91 (2011).

Catherine Houston Richardson, *A "Rest in Peace" Guide of Estate Planning Ethics*, 28 J. Legal Prof. 217 (2003–04).

Jacob L. Todres, *Tax Malpractice: Areas in Which It Occurs and the Measure of Damages: An Update*, 78 St. John's L. Rev. 1011 (2004).

Raymond J. Werner, *Licensed in One State, but Practicing in Another: Multijurisdictional Practice*, 17 Prob. & Prop. 6 (Mar./Apr. 2003).

Chapter 2

Intestacy

The law governing intestate distributions supports the entire field of family wealth transfers. You might compare these rules to the default provisions of a computer program. Unless the user (property owner) overrides the system with specific instructions, these rules apply to all probate property. For those who die without a will, and there are many,[1] an intestate statute provides an "estate plan" designed by the state legislature. This chapter first describes the structure of those plans. Then it addresses more detailed questions about which persons the plans benefit and what shares those persons take.

§ 2.01 Overview

Even if there is a will, it might not cover all of a decedent's probate property. For example, the will might only say "I give all of my real property to Helen." In the usual case, Helen would have no right to the decedent's personal property. The decedent would then die "partially intestate" as to the personalty, which would pass according to the intestate statute. Similarly, courts faced with incomplete disposition of trust interests may apply heirship principles to determine the ultimate takers of the trust property.

The influence of intestate statutes extends well beyond decedents without wills or those with gaps in their estate plans. Procedurally, intestate statutes help identify "interested persons" who may be able to challenge a will. These statutes also aid document interpretation. For example, a decedent may actually adopt the rules of intestacy by including will or trust language giving his property to his "heirs" or "next of kin." *See, e.g.*, Harris Trust & Sav. Bank v. Beach, 513 N.E.2d 833 (Ill. 1987), reproduced in Chapter 9. In addition, intestate statutes often serve as models for laws mandating shares for disinherited spouses or forgotten children. Many other concepts and definitions developed with reference to intestacy have carried over into will and trust law generally. Finally, intestate schemes provide document drafters with a variety of models to present to their clients who want wills or trusts.

---

1. A 2014 survey found that 64 percent of Americans do not have wills, including 90 percent between ages 18–34 and 80 percent from ages 35–54. Rocket Lawyer News at https://www.rocketlawyer.com/news/article-Make-a-Will-Month-2014.aspx.

A. Terminology

To understand much of the material in this course, you should master the technical meanings of common terms. "Heirs" are those people identified by statute to take the estate to the extent that the decedent dies intestate. "Ancestors" includes parents, grandparents, and the like, extending back into history. A phrase like "my [or Monica's] children" refers to a single generation. In most jurisdictions, both "descendants" and "issue" describe a multi-generational group including children, grandchildren, and the continuing line. As the inheritance rights of adopted children have grown, many states now use "descendants" instead of "issue," which contemplates a blood line. "Collaterals" means those people out of the lines of ascent and descent: aunts, uncles, brothers, sisters, cousins. These generalizations are subject to the refinements discussed below in the context of special situations such as adoption.

B. Survivorship

Intestate statutes give shares to the decedent's survivors. One question is what it means to be alive. Section 1 of the Uniform Determination of Death Act provides that someone is dead if there is irreversible cessation of all circulatory and respiratory functions or irreversible cessation of all functions of the entire brain, including the stem.

A more common question is who died first, especially in a "common disaster." Suppose Doris and Darlene were sisters who would have inherited from each other, but they both died in a plane crash. Who should inherit from whom? In response to this problem, an early version of the Uniform Simultaneous Death Act, adopted in many states, provided that where "there is no sufficient evidence that the persons have died otherwise than simultaneously, the property of each person shall be disposed of as if he had survived." Unif. Simultaneous Death Act § 1, 8A U.L.A. 561 (1940). The idea was to solve the dilemma of insufficient evidence and to distribute property to living people as much as possible. The statute was too narrow, however. Claimants were able to produce evidence of bare survival, thereby overcoming the statute and defeating its second purpose of not having property pass through a dead person's estate. For example, in one case about a couple who had died in a plane crash, carbon monoxide in the wife's blood indicated she had survived her husband whose blood had no carbon monoxide.[2]

To avoid that result, the UPC created a legal definition of survival, requiring one person to have survived another by 120 hours before being deemed to have survived that person. UPC § 2-104. A time requirement is better than a "simultaneous death" approach, because a time requirement covers deaths that occur together even if not at the same moment. A time requirement is also better than the "common disaster" approach, because the key is not whether people die of the same cause, but whether

2. *In re Bucci's Will*, 293 N.Y.S.2d 994 (Sur. Ct. 1968). New York has since adopted the UPC's approach discussed below. N.Y. Estates, Powers and Trusts Law § 2-1.6.

their deaths are too close temporally. For this reason, many wills and trusts override the default simultaneous death rules and instead require someone to survive by 30 days, or perhaps 60 days before qualifying as a beneficiary.[3]

Sometimes people simply disappear, like the pilot Amelia Earhart, the Teamster boss Jimmy Hoffa, and the hijacker D.B. Cooper. So the probate system can function in those circumstances, statutes create methods of establishing death in the absence of a body. For example, UPC § 1-107(4) provides that death can be established by clear and convincing circumstantial evidence. Someone who has not been heard from for a continuous period of five years "and whose absence is not satisfactorily explained after diligent search or inquiry" is generally presumed dead after five years. UPC § 1-107(5).

Uniform Probate Code

Section 2-104. Requirement of Survival by 120 Hours; Individual in Gestation.

(a) [**Requirement of Survival by 120 Hours; Individual in Gestation.**] For purposes of intestate succession, homestead allowance, and exempt property, and except as otherwise provided in subsection (b), the following rules apply:

> (1) An individual born before a decedent's death who fails to survive the decedent by 120 hours is deemed to have predeceased the decedent. If it is not established by clear and convincing evidence that an individual born before the decedent's death survived the decedent by 120 hours, it is deemed that the individual failed to survive for the required period.
>
> (2) An individual in gestation at a decedent's death[4] is deemed to be living at the decedent's death if the individual lives 120 hours after birth. If it is not established by clear and convincing evidence that an individual in gestation at the decedent's death lived 120 hours after birth, it is deemed that the individual failed to survive for the required period.

(b) [**Section Inapplicable If Estate Would Pass to State.**] This section does not apply if its application would cause the estate to pass to the state under Section 2-105.[5]

C. Choice of Law

When decedents have had ties to more than one state, choice-of-law questions may arise. Courts usually apply the law of the situs of the property to questions surrounding

3. Unfortunately, because language tends to remain in forms longer than it should, some documents make matters worse by replacing sensible statutory rules with the old "simultaneous death" approach.

4. A child conceived posthumously through assisted reproduction is treated as in gestation at a decedent's death if the child was in utero not later than 36 months after the individual's death or born not later than 45 months after the individual's death. UPC §§ 2-120(k), 2-121(h).

5. If there are no survivors who qualify under the intestate statute, the property is said to "escheat" to the state. *See, e.g.*, UPC § 2-105.

realty, and the law of the decedent's domicile to questions concerning personalty. *See* 2d Rest. Conflict of Laws §§ 236, 260 (1971). Some courts, however, apply the law of the situs to tangible personalty as well as to realty. *See, e.g., Riley v. New York Trust Co.*, 315 U.S. 343 (1942). Questions of relationship can also create conflict-of-laws problems. For example, a marriage valid where the marriage was contracted is likely to be recognized everywhere else, unless there are strong public policy reasons to the contrary. *See* 2d Rest. Conflict of Laws § 283 (1971).

Under normal choice-of-law principles, courts apply the whole law of a state whose law is deemed to control a transaction. Therefore, even though the law of the situs normally controls realty disposition, the conflict-of-laws rules of the situs state may require that the laws of another state, such as the state of domicile, control. A court in one state may therefore find that it must refer to the law of another state, only to be required by that law to consider the law of yet a third state.

Selected Reference

William M. Richman & William L. Reynolds, *Understanding Conflict of Laws*, Ch. 4 (4th ed. 2013).

D. Protective Provisions

The category "protective provisions" refers to another set of rules that, while not limited to intestacy, influences survivors' shares. Family members have a right to estate assets "off the top," before creditors' claims and before distribution according to the intestate statute (or the will, if there is one). The size and shape of these protections varies among states, but they fall into three main categories: (1) homestead property, (2) exempt property, and (3) support.

Traditionally, homestead and exempt property provisions protected, respectively, real estate (the actual homestead, especially for close family members) and personal property. Some jurisdictions now ignore the distinction and group both kinds of property under one of the labels. Rather than focusing on specific property, many statutes simply set monetary amounts. Sometimes state constitutions establish the protections, and sometimes they come through statutes.

Florida Constitution, Article X, Section 4
Homestead—exemptions

(a) There shall be exempt from forced sale under process of any court, and no judgment, decree or execution shall be a lien thereon, obligations contracted for the purpose, improvement or repair thereof, or obligations contracted for house, field or other labor performed on the realty, the following property owned by a natural person:

(1) homestead, if located outside a municipality, to the extent of one hundred sixty acres of contiguous land and improvements thereon, which shall

not be reduced without the owner's consent by reason of subsequent inclusion in a municipality; or if located within a municipality, to the extent of one-half acre of contiguous land, upon which the exemption shall be limited to the residence of the owner or his family;

(2) personal property to the value of one thousand dollars.

(b) These exemptions shall inure to the surviving spouse or heirs of the owner.

(c) The homestead shall not be subject to devise if the owner is survived by spouse or minor child, except the homestead may be devised to the owner's spouse if there be no minor child. The owner of home stead real estate, joined by the spouse if married, may alienate the homestead by mortgage, sale or gift and, if married, may by deed transfer the title to an estate by the entirety with the spouse. If the owner or spouse is incompetent, the method of alienation or encumbrance shall be as provided by law.

Although they arose primarily to protect farmers from creditors, homestead protections are not limited to farming property, but apply broadly to residential real property, including even condominiums used as the family home. The UPC provides the surviving spouse or children a monetary homestead allowance of $22,500. UPC § 2-402.

Although UPC § 2-403 provides an exempt property allowance of $15,000, some states provide that identified property, typically tangible personal property, will be exempt and set off in favor of the surviving spouse or minor children. For example, New York has a robust exempt property statute that can exceed $90,000. N.Y. Estates, Powers & Trusts Law § 5-3.1.

Florida's $1,000 limit on personal property illustrates how some states cap various protections (or the total available). When left unadjusted for inflation or deflation, such exemptions' value can change drastically. Both UPC amounts are subject to revision, based on changes in consumer prices. UPC § 1-109.

States also differ as to whether the protection applies to all children of the decedent or only to minor children. Some protect only against creditors of the decedent, but others also protect against disinheritance. Some provisions get very specific. For example, a Minnesota statute awards personal "property with sentimental value" to decedent's children of a "prior marriage" where there are current minor children entitled to a statutory allowance. Minn. Stat. § 525.152.

Another common, but not universal, protection comes in the form of support allowances to help the family live while the estate administration is open. Again, there are lots of variety. Some statutes fix the benefit; some allow the probate court to set an appropriate amount; some set maximums; some require adult children to be dependents in order to benefit. The UPC grants a "reasonable allowance" to the surviving spouse, minor children the decedent was obligated to support, and children the decedent was in fact supporting. UPC § 2-404.

E. The Structure of Intestate Schemes

Though the details of intestate statutes vary considerably from state to state, their basic structures are similar. Several key concepts work in various combinations, both to identify who qualifies to take the property and to determine their shares:

- *Blood relatives are favored.* When you think of the relatives who would inherit, think of those related by blood (and, in general, adoption). You may call the woman who married your mother's brother "Aunt Sophie," but she is not included. (She is related by "affinity.") In varying degrees, special provisions cover spouses, stepchildren, some adopted children, and children from reproductive technology.
- *Family lines matter.* As a starting place for identifying individuals, think first in terms of bloodlines. You will be well-served by applying a "look down, look up, look down, look up" technique. First look down for descendants. If there is more than one child, follow each child's line down, stopping when you find a survivor. If there are no descendants, look up to the parents. If none, look down again, to sisters and brothers and, if necessary, nieces and nephews. As we'll see, some states shift approaches at the point while others continue this process further (to grandparent lines and beyond) or use it in particular situations. Because it focuses on parentage, this approach is often called a "parentelic" system.[6]
- *Stop when you find survivors.* Living survivors cut off those further down the line.
- *Degree of relationship matters.* Here we count the steps ("degrees") between the decedent and various relatives. (See the Table of Consanguinity on Page 71) The level of "closeness" to the decedent can be relevant in two different situations. First, it can identify who inherits (fewest steps wins). Second, it can determine what shares people take (people of equal degree take equally). Be careful, however. Sometimes degree of relationship will trump other principles, sometimes other principles will prevail.
- *"Representation" can affect shares.* In some situations, intestate statutes will use a predeceased person as a placeholder to determine how shares are divided. Consider a decedent who left three surviving descendants: (1) a child and (2) two grandchildren who are daughters of a predeceased child. The intestate statue would use the predeceased child as a representative of the grandchildren and divide the estate with one-half to the surviving child and one-quarter each to the grandchildren. Caution: "representation" means different things in different jurisdictions.

---

6. Caution: Some discussions assume very specific meaning for "parentelic." We mean it in the general sense of following different lines through time. Note how you are in many parental lines: your parents', grandparents', great-grandparents' . . . .

Review the UPC provisions that follow, seeing how these concepts work in different situations. You may find it helpful to consult the statute's official comments, available in your library and online at http://www.uniformlaws.org/shared/docs/probate%20 code/UPC_Final_2016aug1.pdf.

Uniform Probate Code

Section 2-102. Share of Spouse.[7]

The intestate share of a decedent's surviving spouse is:

(1) the entire intestate estate if:

(i) no descendant or parent of the decedent survives the decedent; or

(ii) all of the decedent's surviving descendants are also descendants of the surviving spouse and there is no other descendant of the surviving spouse who survives the decedent;

(2) the first [$300,000], plus three-fourths of any balance of the intestate estate, if no descendant of the decedent survives the decedent, but a parent of the decedent survives the decedent;

(3) the first [$225,000], plus one-half of any balance of the intestate estate, if all of the decedent's surviving descendants are also descendants of the surviving spouse and the surviving spouse has one or more surviving descendants who are not descendants of the decedent;

(4) the first [$150,000], plus one-half of any balance of the intestate estate, if one or more of the decedent's surviving descendants are not descendants of the surviving spouse.

Section 2-103. Shares of Heirs other than Surviving Spouse

(a) Any part of the intestate estate not passing to a decedent's surviving spouse under Section 2-102, or the entire intestate estate if there is no surviving spouse, passes in the following order to the individuals who survive the decedent:

(1) to the decedent's descendants by representation;

(2) if there is no surviving descendant, to the decedent's parents equally if both survive, or to the surviving parent if only one survives;

(3) if there is no surviving descendant or parent, to the descendants of the decedent's parents or either of them by representation;

(4) if there is no surviving descendant, parent, or descendant of a parent, but the decedent is survived on both the paternal and maternal sides by one or more grandparents or descendants of grandparents:

---

7. This section is designed for states that have not adopted the community property system. An alternative provision (§ 2-102A) for community property states distributes separate property the same way, but gives all community property to the surviving spouse, even if children or parents survive the decedent. We consider community property in Chapter 6. [Eds.]

(A) half to the decedent's paternal grandparents equally if both survive, to the surviving paternal grandparent if only one survives, or to the descendants of the decedent's paternal grandparents or either of them if both are deceased, the descendants taking by representation; and

(B) half to the decedent's maternal grandparents equally if both survive, to the surviving maternal grandparent if only one survives, or to the descendants of the decedent's maternal grandparents or either of them if both are deceased, the descendants taking by representation;

(5) if there is no surviving descendant, parent, or descendant of a parent, but the decedent is survived by one or more grandparents or descendants of grandparents on the paternal but not the maternal side, or on the maternal but not the paternal side, to the decedent's relatives on the side with one or more surviving members in the manner described in paragraph (4).

(b) If there is no taker under subsection (a), but the decedent has:

(1) one deceased spouse who has one or more descendants who survive the decedent, the estate or part thereof passes to that spouse's descendants by representation; or

(2) more than one deceased spouse who has one or more descendants who survive the decedent, an equal share of the estate or part thereof passes to each set of descendants by representation.

Section 2-105. No Taker.

If there is no taker under the provisions of this Article, the intestate estate passes to the [state].

Section 2-106. Representation.

(a) [**Definitions.**] In this section:

(1) "Deceased descendant," "deceased parent," or "deceased grandparent" means a descendant, parent, or grandparent who either predeceased the decedent or is deemed to have predeceased the decedent under Section 2-104.

(2) "Surviving descendant" means a descendant who neither predeceased the decedent nor is deemed to have predeceased the decedent under Section 2-104.

(b) [**Decedent's Descendants.**] If, under Section 2-103(1), a decedent's intestate estate or a part thereof passes "by representation" to the decedent's descendants, the estate or part thereof is divided into as many equal shares as there are (i) surviving descendants in the generation nearest to the decedent which contains one or more surviving descendants and (ii) deceased descendants in the same generation who left surviving descendants, if any. Each surviving descendant in the nearest generation is allocated one share. The remaining shares, if any, are combined and then divided in the same manner among the surviving descendants of the deceased descendants as if the surviving descendants who were allocated a share and their surviving descendants had predeceased the decedent.

(c) [**Descendants of Parents or Grandparents.**] If, under Section 2-103(3) or (4), a decedent's intestate estate or a part thereof passes "by representation" to the descendants of the decedent's deceased parents or either of them or to the descendants of the decedent's deceased paternal or maternal grandparents or either of them, the estate or part thereof is divided into as many equal shares as there are (i) surviving descendants in the generation nearest the deceased parents or either of them, or the deceased grandparents or either of them, that contains one or more surviving descendants and (ii) deceased descendants in the same generation who left surviving descendants, if any. Each surviving descendant in the nearest generation is allocated one share. The remaining shares, if any, are combined and then divided in the same manner among the surviving descendants of the deceased descendants as if the surviving descendants who were allocated a share and their surviving descendants had predeceased the decedent.

Section 2-114. Parent Barred from Inheriting in Certain Circumstances.

(a) A parent is barred from inheriting from or through a child of the parent if:

(1) the parent's parental rights were terminated and the parent-child relationship was not judicially reestablished; or

(2) the child died before reaching [18] years of age and there is clear and convincing evidence that immediately before the child's death the parental rights of the parent could have been terminated under law of this state other than this [code] on the basis of nonsupport, abandonment, abuse, neglect, or other actions or inactions of the parent toward the child.

(b) For the purpose of intestate succession from or through the deceased child, a parent who is barred from inheriting under this section is treated as if the parent predeceased the child.

Because the details of intestate statutes vary widely among the states, you simply must consult the statutes in the jurisdictions in which you practice. In addition to knowing your own statutes, you need to be aware of movements around the country that may prompt your legislature to change your law.

Thoughtful intestate statutes pursue several goals. Perhaps the primary one is to reflect the presumed desires of decedents. Others include protecting dependent family members, keeping property in the nuclear family, and encouraging individuals to accumulate property. As you compare the law of your state to the UPC approaches discussed in this chapter, ask how well each furthers these policies, or other policies you identify.

Notes and Questions

1. Intestacy statutes divide property without reference to where the rest of a decedent's wealth goes. Suppose Louis died intestate, leaving only his children David and Edith. The children will share the probate estate equally even if Edith also now takes substantial property she had held with her father in joint tenancy. Similarly, David

would still get half, even if he were the beneficiary of a substantial living trust from his father.

(a) Should an intestate statute adjust heirs' shares to take into account other forms of wealth transfer?

(b) How would you design a statute to accomplish that result?

2. In some jurisdictions, if the decedent has a spouse but no children, the spouse will share the estate with the decedent's parents. What do you think of that approach?

3. If a decedent leaves children, they will cut off the decedent's parents. Does that approach make sense? Imagine a decedent in his 60's with elderly parents and grown children. Who has the greater need?

4. Intestate statutes ignore questions about the relative needs of survivors and the closeness or hostility between the decedent and the survivors. Should we give courts more discretion to fit the distribution to each family's circumstances?

5. In the context of parents and children, UPC § 2-114(a)(2) takes into account the quality of the relationship between the decedent and the intestate claimant. Should this principle apply to other situations, like abusive spouses or other relatives?

6. Many states limit the ability of aliens to inherit property, especially realty. *See, e.g.*, N.C. Gen. Stat. § 64-5 (alien cannot inherit real property unless alien's country reciprocates); Ill. Ann. Stat. ch. 6, § 2 (alien must dispose of inherited real property within six years).

Problems

1. John dies without a will, survived by his wife, Denise. John has neither issue nor surviving parents. At death, John separately owned stocks; real estate was held in joint tenancy with Denise; John was the owner of a life insurance policy on his life, with Denise as beneficiary; and John owned an Individual Retirement Account with Denise as beneficiary. What property will pass by intestacy?

2. If you were to die today, what property would pass under your state's intestate statute and who would take it? Under the UPC?

3. Albert is married to Shannon, and they have a daughter, Kate. Albert has two other surviving relatives: a brother, Bruce; and a cousin, Ellie, the daughter of his mother's sister. After applicable protective provisions, debts and expenses, Albert's probate estate is $90,000.

(a) If Albert died today, who would take what shares of his estate under your state's intestate statute? Under the UPC?

(b) Albert, Shannon, and Kate were involved in an auto accident. Kate was killed instantly; Albert died on the way to the hospital; Shannon died the following day. Who would take what shares of Albert's estate under your state's intestate statute? Under the UPC?

Selected References

Mary Louise Fellows, E. Gary Spitko & Charles Q. Strohm, *An Empirical Assessment of the Potential for Will Substitutes to Improve State Intestacy Statutes*, 85 Ind. L.J. 409 (2010).

Frances H. Foster, *Should Pets Inherit?*, 63 Fla. L. Rev. 801 (2011).

Rebecca Friedman, *Intestate Intent: Presumed Will Theory, Duty Theory, and the Flaw of Relying on Average Decedent Intent*, 49 Real Prop., Tr & Est. L.J. 565 (2015).

Ronald J. Scalise, Jr., *Honor Thy Father and Mother?: How Intestacy Law Goes Too Far in Protecting Parents*, 37 Seton Hall L. Rev. 171 (2006).

§ 2.02 Qualifying to Take

When statutes use terms such as "spouse," "children," "issue," and "descendants," questions arise as to who falls within the designated class. This section explores a number of problems surrounding definitions of those terms. First, consider how the changing structure of American families is altering traditional conceptions.

Susan N. Gary, *Adapting Intestacy Laws to Changing Families*

18 Law & Ineq. J. 1, 4, 27–28, 71 (2000)

The family structure in the United States has changed dramatically. Stepfamilies, blended families, unmarried heterosexual and gay and lesbian cohabitants with or without children—many persons now live in families that no longer fit the [married father and mother and their two children] norm....

Intestacy statutes attempt to distribute a decedent's property to the decedent's family, either because the intestacy statute strives to approximate the decedent's wishes or because society has decided that intestacy statutes should benefit and strengthen families if a decedent does not express a contrary wish in a will. If family is the focus of several goals behind intestacy statures, then understanding what "family" means is important....

Intestacy statutes almost uniformly use a formal definition of family: persons related by blood, marriage or adoption. Other areas of the law have begun to turn to a functional definition of family, although not in a consistent manner. In recent years, general discussions about families and the law have proposed either changing the formal definition of family to include more family relationships or relying more frequently on a functional definition of family in determining the rights and responsibilities of family members....

The objective approach that predominates in intestacy statutes carries with it the weight of history, the security of fixed rules and the benefit of efficiency for the probate court. Unfortunately, the objective "blood, marriage or adoption" approach means that increasingly property does not benefit the decedent's "family" nor follow the decedent's intent. The difficulty, of course, is that while ties through blood or adoption are relatively easy to establish, ties of affinity are not. Any determination of whether a decedent had a parent-child relationship with a survivor will require some degree of discretion. The uncertainty associated with the use of discretion likely will lead to increased litigation. Discretion carries with it risks, but given the state of today's families, some degree of discretion is necessary. . . .

Selected References

Frances H. Foster, *The Family Paradigm of Inheritance Law*, 80 N.C. L. Rev. 199 (2001).

Susan N. Gary, *The Probate Definition of Family: A Proposal for Guided Discretion in Intestacy*, 45 U. Mich. J.L. Reform 787 (2012).

Danaya C. Wright, Inheritance Equity: Reforming the Inheritance Penalties Facing Children in Nontraditional Families. 25 Cornell J.L. & Pub. Pol'y 1 (2015).

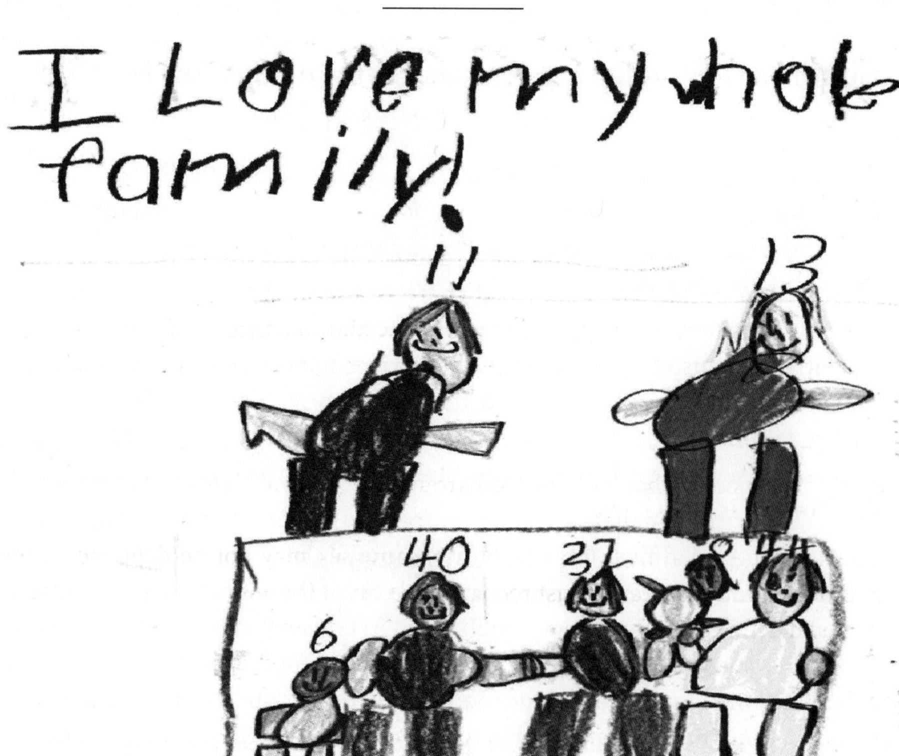

Brendan Blanchette's family included himself (then 6), his brother, sister, mother, father, father's second wife, and baby half-sister.

A. Spouses and Partners

Traditionally, a "spouse" means someone who is legally married. *But see, e.g.,* 15 Vt. Stat. Ann. § 1204(b) ("spouse" includes parties to a civil union). Because most Family Law courses examine in some detail questions about how a marital relationship is established, this discussion only highlights a few issues that impact inheritance. As with intestacy rights, statutes dominate this field. Except where the decedent dies while the parties are in the process of legalizing their relationship, courts generally require compliance with statutory formalities. *See, e.g., In re Estate of Biewald,* 468 N.E.2d 1321 (Ill. Ct. App. 1984) (Mary and Clarence were divorced in 1959, but continued to live together until Mary's death in 1982. Held: Clarence was not a "surviving spouse"). Some states recognize "common law marriages" based on the behavior of the couple, rather than a formal ceremony. Of course, a valid divorce or annulment precludes someone from claiming as a surviving spouse. *See* UPC § 2-802. Jurisdictions disagree on the question of how a separation decree affects the status of a surviving spouse. *Compare* N.Y. Estates, Powers & Trusts Law § 5-1.2 (not surviving spouse) *with* UPC § 2-802 (still surviving spouse).

Bigamous marriages pose special problems. Because a married person lacks the capacity to remarry without divorce, subsequent "spouses" have void relationships with the bigamist. Upon the bigamist's death, theoretically (and in most jurisdictions, practically) only the first spouse qualifies to inherit, even if long deserted by the decedent. Using the concept of "putative spouse," a few states recognize the intestate claims of innocent later consorts. Section 209 of the Uniform Marriage and Divorce Act provides: "Any person who has cohabited with another to whom he is not legally married in the good faith belief that he was married to that person is a putative spouse.... If there is a legal spouse or other putative spouses, ... the court shall apportion property, maintenance, and support rights among the claimants as appropriate in the circumstances and in the interests of justice."

In *Obergefell v. Hodges,* 135 S. Ct 2584 (2015), the U.S. Supreme Court resolved many of the questions that had revolved around the marital rights of persons of the same sex.[8] The court held that, under the due process and equal protection clauses of the Fourteenth Amendment, couples of the same sex may not be deprived of the right to marry and that states must recognize lawful same-sex marriages performed in other states.

---

8. Earlier, the Supreme Court effectively held that federal tax and other benefits could not be denied to same-sex married couples. *See United States v. Windsor,* 133 S. Ct. 2675 (2013).

Obergefell will also affect a broader range of marriage and inheritance issues. Because a person's gender no longer affects the right to marry, persons who have been identified as one sex at birth and later identified themselves as the other sex will no longer face challenges to the validity of their marriages (and accompanying inheritance rights).[9] Same-sex couples who have been living together may be surprised by "common law marriage" rules applying to them. It remains to be seen the extent to which states will modify various approaches to "domestic partnerships." Often domestic partnership rules arose as a way to grant some of the benefits of marriage to same-sex couples prohibited from marrying. Now that marriage is available, domestic partnerships may be redefined or disappear.

Selected References

David T. DuFault, *The Intricacies of Estate Planning for Same-Sex Couples*, 43 Est. Plan. 23 (2016).

Leslie J. Harris, *Same Sex Unions Around the World*, 19 Pro. & Prop. 31 (Sept./Oct. 2005).

Jeffrey S. Jacobi, *Two Spirits, Two Eras, Same Sex: For a Traditional Perspective on Native American Tribal Same-Sex Marriage Policy*, 39 U. Mich. J.L. Reform 823 (2006).

Paula A. Monopoli, *Inheritance Law and the Marital Presumption After* Obergefell, 8 Est. Plan. & Community Prop. L.J. 437 (2016).

Lawrence W. Waggoner, *With Marriage on the Decline and Cohabitation on the Rise, What about Marital Rights for Unmarried Partners?*, 41 ACTEC L.J. 49 (2015).

B. Descendants

1. Non-marital Children[10]

Children of unmarried women long suffered discrimination because of the decisions their parents made. Now their status alone does not prejudice their position in

9. In *Estate of Gardiner*, 42 (.3d 120 (Kan. 2002), a "marriage" between a man and a post-operative male-to-female was held void so that the survivor had no intestate rights as a surviving spouse.

10. Consider the following excerpt:

> At the outset the court wishes to express criticism of the use of the word "illegitimate" as applied to children. Not only is this term, when used in connection with children, repugnant to this court but its use in any local law, ordinance or resolution or in any public or judicial proceeding or in any process, notice, order, decree, judgment, record, public document or paper, is a violation of law (*see* General Construction Law, § 59). Despite this fact Judges, legal writers and others continuously use that term when writing about children born out of wedlock. In this decision wherever the words "non-marital child or

the intestate hierarchy, but a continuing challenge remains. Without unduly burdening claimants, we do need to be confident that there really is a paternal-child relationship between a particular man and his putative child.

Browne Lewis, *Children of Men: Balancing the Inheritance Rights of Marital and Non-marital Children*

39 U. Tol. L. Rev. 1, 1–2, 6, 18 (2007)

Children born out of wedlock were once the exception to the rule. They were called bastards and their rights were largely ignored. Today, however, having children out of wedlock has become commonplace in the United States.... In America, at least one out of every three babies born is a non-marital child....

...

Beginning in 1968, several cases involving the legal rights of non-marital children came before the U.S. Supreme Court ... involv[ing] a wide range of legal issues, including ... probate ....[11] The decisions ... broadly extended the legal relationship between parents and their non-marital children[,] ... changed the legal landscape for non-marital children[,] and influenced the enactment of state intestacy statutes....

... [I]n order for a state inheritance statute to survive a constitutional attack, it must provide non-marital children with the opportunity to inherit from their fathers. The Supreme Court has given states substantial leeway in probate matters; nevertheless, any statutory scheme that expressly or implicitly prevents non-marital children from establishing a father-child relationship for inheritance purposes would likely be invalidated. However, states are not required to permit non-marital children to have the exact same inheritance rights as marital children.... Therefore, the key is to provide equal opportunity, not strict equality.

...

... [S]tate legislatures must avoid extremes—total exclusion and total inclusion. Total exclusion is not fair to non-marital children because it punishes them for actions taken by their parents. On the other hand, total inclusion is not fair to the fathers or their marital children because it permits persons to file unchallenged claims against the estates of deceased men.... [S]tatutes in most states give non-marital

---

children" are used the references apply to the prohibited phrase "illegitimate child or children."

In re Estate of Leventritt, 400 N.Y.S.2d 298, 299 (Sup. Ct. 1977).

11. [*Trimbell v. Gordon*, 430 U.S. 762 (1977), which held that barring non-marital children from inheriting, violated the equal protection clause, was the most significant decision. Eds.]

children the opportunity to inherit from their fathers as long as they take the steps necessary to prove paternity.

. . . [T]he statutory requirements range from simple to complex. . . .

Aside from special situations, the UPC defers to the state's family law provisions for establishing paternity. In contrast, New York's intestacy provisions, like that of many states, address paternity generally.

Uniform Probate Code

Section 2-117. No Distinction Based on Marital Status.

Except as otherwise provided in Sections 2-114, 2-119, 2-120, or 2-121, a parent-child relationship exists between a child and the child's genetic parents, regardless of the parents' marital status.

Comment

Scope. This section, adopted in 2008, provides the general rule that a parent-child relationship exists between a child and the child's genetic parents, regardless of the parents' marital status. Exceptions to this general rule are contained in Sections 2-114 (Parent Barred from Inheriting in Certain Circumstances), 2-119 (Adoptee and Adoptee's Genetic Parents), 2-120 (Child Conceived by Assisted Reproduction Other than Child Born to Gestational Carrier), and 2-121(Child Born to Gestational Carrier).

N.Y. Estates, Powers & Trusts Law § 4-1.2
Inheritance by non-marital children

(a) For the purposes of this article:

(1) A non-marital child is the legitimate child of his mother so that he and his issue inherit from his mother and from his maternal kindred.

(2) non-marital child is the legitimate child of his father so that he and his issue inherit from his father and his paternal kindred if:

(A) a court of competent jurisdiction has, during the lifetime of the father, made an order of filiation declaring paternity or the mother and father of the child have executed an acknowledgment of paternity pursuant to section four thousand one hundred thirty-five-b of the public health law, which has been filed with the registrar of the district in which the birth certificate has been filed or;

(B) the father of the child has signed an instrument acknowledging paternity, provided that . . . [various requirements are met.]

(C) paternity has been established by clear and convincing evidence, which may include, but is not limited to: (i) evidence derived from a

> genetic marker test, or (ii) evidence that the father openly and notoriously acknowledged the child as his own; however nothing in this section regarding genetic marker tests shall be construed to expand or limit the current application of subdivision four of section forty-two hundred ten of the public health law.

New York's reference to DNA evidence is relatively unusual. However, as science becomes more sophisticated, proof-of-paternity problems get easier, and it becomes increasingly harder to justify disproportionate burdens placed on non-marital children. Meanwhile, the law has resisted change. *See, e.g, Phillips v. Ledford*, 590 S.E.2d 280 (N.C. 2004) (because statutory elements not met, daughter was unable to inherit despite DNA and other evidence of relationship); *Tuan Anh Nguyen v. INS*, 533 U.S. 53 (2001) (upholding extensive paternity proof requirements).

Selected References

Martha F. Davis, *Male Coverture: Law and the Illegitimate Family*, 56 Rutgers L. Rev. 73 (2003).

Kathleen R. Guzman, *What Price Paternity?*, 53 Okla. L. Rev. 77 (2000).

Paula A. Monopoli, *Toward Equality: Nonmarital Children and the Uniform Probate Code*, 45 U. Mich. J.L. Reform 995 (2012).

Kate Schuler, *The Liberalization of Posthumous Paternity Testing—Expanding the Rights of Illegitimate Children*, 17 Quinnipiac Prob. L.J. 150 (2003).

2. Adopted Persons

Because adoption creates new relationships with new families, it also creates a series of problems regarding inheritance rights.[12] The first step in examining adoption situations is to identify the various parties. The adoptee, of course, is the central character. On one side, we might have the adoptee's genetic parents[13] and their families. On the other side, we might find the adoptive parents and their families. Inheritance questions can flow in many directions: If the adoptee dies, can either side inherit? If parents on either side die, can the adoptee inherit? What about more distant relatives? Can the adoptee inherit from them or vice-versa? Should special

---

12. This section considers the impact of adoption in the context of intestate inheritance. A related problem arises in the context of interpreting documents, as when a will gives property to "children."

13. The term "natural parents" is commonly used to designate the biological parents of an adopted person. This book avoids the term because it carries the connotation that the adoptive parents are somehow "unnatural." "Birth," "genetic," or "biological" are terms carrying no such baggage.

rules apply when the adoptive parent is married to a genetic parent? What if they are unmarried partners?

Typically, adopted children can inherit from their adoptive parents, although the statutes vary in their specifics. More difficult is the question of whether adopted children can inherit from the genetic parents. Some statutes sever the adopted child's relationship with the genetic family in most situations. When statutes do not address the question, however, many courts allow such inheritance.

Another question is what happens if the child's adoptive or genetic grandparents (or other relatives) die. The answer is less certain. Some statutes allow the adopted child to inherit from the ancestors and collaterals of adoptive parents, but when statutes do not address the question, the courts are divided. On the other hand, courts tend to allow the adopted child to inherit from ancestors and collaterals of genetic parents to the same degree that they allow inheritance from the genetic parents themselves.

Similar problems occur when the adopted child dies. In the absence of express statutory language, often the genetic parents, but not the adoptive parents, can inherit from the child. The equitable doctrine of abandonment, however, may bar the genetic parents.

A number of states follow the UPC's solution to these problems and, in most situations, simply remove the child from the families of the genetic parents and drop it into the adoptive parents' families for all purposes. UPC §§ 2-118, 2-119(a). That approach has the advantages of clarity and of giving the child a "fresh start" in a new family.

On the other hand, many adoptions occur *within* a family. For example, when a remarriage follows a death or divorce the new spouse may adopt a child of remaining parent. The UPC's solution to stepparent adoptions is to place the child in the adoptive-stepparent's family, but then to distinguish between the genetic parents. The full parent-child relationship is maintained with the spouse of the adopting stepparent; each can inherit from the other. The relationship with the non-custodial genetic parent's family, however, runs only to the benefit of the child. The child can inherit from members of the non-custodial side of the birth family, but they cannot inherit from her. UPC § 2-119(b). If the adoption is by a relative of a genetic parent, or by the spouse or surviving spouse of a relative of a genetic parent, the UPC provides that the relationships to the genetic parents continue, but again only to the benefit of the child. UPC § 2-119(c).

Adoption also raises some unusual problems. For example, suppose Aunt Minnie has three nephews who would inherit equally. Because Jay lives nearby and has helped her, Minnie might try to adopt Jay so he could take everything as her child. Courts disagree about whether to recognize such adoptions.

Applying the theory of "equitable adoption," also known as "virtual adoption," courts sometimes treat a child as adopted, even in the absence of formal adoption proceedings. *Compare Matter of Heirs of Hodge*, 470 So. 2d 740 (Fla. Dist. Ct. App. 1985) (child treated as adopted when raised by others since age three and given their name), *with O'Neal v. Wilkes*, 439 S.E.2d 490 (Ga. 1994) (after shuffling among relatives, girl eventually raised by non-relatives, but not entitled to protection as "adopted" because aunt who last took care of her had no authority to enter into adoption contract). Equitable adoption may be recognized if a person had the authority to contract to adopt. *See Sanders v. Riley*, 770 S.E.2d 570 (Ga. 2015). *See also DeHart v. DeHart*, 986 N.E.2d 85 (Ill. 2013) (in addition to the contract-to-adopt theory, equitable adoption offers an independent way to prove parent-child relationship). *But see Estate of Scherer*, 336 P.3d 129 (Wyo. 2014) (Wyoming will not recognize doctrine of equitable adoption).

Courts have been wary of allowing the "adoptive parents" or their heirs to inherit from the unadopted child on such a theory.

Sometimes an adoption occurs in one state, and the intestate decedent lives in another. If the two states treat the rights of adopted children differently, a conflict of laws problem arises. The decedent's state may want to enforce its own law in the inheritance situation, even though the law of the place of adoption controls the child's status for most purposes. *See, e.g., Warren v. Foster*, 450 So. 2d 786 (Miss. 1984) (refusal by Mississippi court to follow Tennessee statute cutting off adoption from birth parent).

Uniform Probate Code

Section 2-115. Definitions. In this [subpart]:

(1) "Adoptee" means an individual who is adopted.

(2) "Assisted reproduction" means a method of causing pregnancy other than sexual intercourse.

(3) "Divorce" includes an annulment, dissolution, and declaration of invalidity of a marriage.

(4) "Functioned as a parent of the child" means behaving toward a child in a manner consistent with being the child's parent and performing functions that are customarily performed by a parent, including fulfilling parental responsibilities toward the child, recognizing or holding out the child as the individual's child, materially participating in the child's upbringing, and residing with the child in the same household as a regular member of that household.

(5) "Genetic father" means the man whose sperm fertilized the egg of a child's genetic mother. If the father-child relationship is established under the presumption of paternity under [insert applicable state law], the term means only the man for whom that relationship is established.

(6) "Genetic mother" means the woman whose egg was fertilized by the sperm of a child's genetic father.

(7) Genetic parent" means a child's genetic father or genetic mother.

(8) Incapacity" means the inability of an individual to function as a parent of a child because of the individual's physical or mental condition.

(9) Relative" means a grandparent or a descendant of a grandparent.

Section 2-118. Adoptee and Adoptee's Adoptive Parent or Parents.

(a) [**Parent-Child Relationship Between Adoptee and Adoptive Parent or Parents.**] A parent-child relationship exists between an adoptee and the adoptee's adoptive parent or parents.

Section 2-119. Adoptee and Adoptee's Genetic Parents.

(a) [**Parent-Child Relationship Between Adoptee and Genetic Parents.**]

Except as otherwise provided in subsections (b) through (e), a parent-child relationship does not exist between an adoptee and the adoptee's genetic parents.

(b) [**Stepchild Adopted by Stepparent.**] A parent-child relationship exists between an individual who is adopted by the spouse of either genetic parent and:

(1) the genetic parent whose spouse adopted the individual; and

(2) the other genetic parent, but only for the purpose of the right of the adoptee or a descendant of the adoptee to inherit from or through the other genetic parent.

(c) [**Individual Adopted by Relative of Genetic Parent.**] A parent-child relationship exists between both genetic parents and an individual who is adopted by a relative of a genetic parent, or by the spouse or surviving spouse of a relative of a genetic parent, but only for the purpose of the right of the adoptee or a descendant of the adoptee to inherit from or through either genetic parent.

(d) [**Individual Adopted after Death of Both Genetic Parents.**] A parent-child relationship exists between both genetic parents and an individual who is adopted after the death of both genetic parents, but only for the purpose of the right of the adoptee or a descendant of the adoptee to inherit through either genetic parent.

(e) [**Child of Assisted Reproduction or Gestational Child Who Is Subsequently Adopted.**] If, after a parent-child relationship is established between a child of assisted reproduction and a parent or parents under Section 2-120 or between a gestational child and a parent or parents under Section 2-121, the child is adopted by another or others, the child's parent or parents under Section 2-120 or 2-121 are treated as the child's genetic parent or parents for the purpose of this section.

Questions and Notes

1. Should it matter if the adopted "child" was an adult at the time of the adoption? *See generally* Richard C. Ausness, *Planned Parenthood: Adult Adoption and the Right of Adoptees to Inherit*, 41 ACTEC L. J. 241 (2015/2016).

2. Kate Hudson is the biological daughter of Goldie Hawn and Bill Hudson. Goldie and Bill divorced when Kate was young, and Kate was raised by Goldie and Kurt Russell,

Goldie's longtime partner. If Kurt, a step-partner, had adopted Kate, and thereafter Bill died intestate, would/should Kate still be entitled to inherit from and through Bill? See Peter Wendel, *Inheritance Rights and the Step-partner Adoption Paradigm: Shades of the Discrimination against Illegitimate Children*, 34 Hofstra L. Rev. 351 (2005).

3. Peggy's daughter, Roxanne, has battled drug addiction, joblessness, and jail time. As a consequence, Peggy had been raising Roxanne's son Jason for most of his life. Peggy died recently while caring for Jason because Roxanne is back in prison. Should Jason (now 10) be able to inherit from his grandmother?

4. Should a child who could not satisfy the rules governing inheritance by non-marital children, but lived with both parents, be able to inherit under an "equitable legitimization" theory, roughly similar to the "equitable adoption" theory?

5. In Chapter 9 we examine how courts interpret documents when beneficiaries have been adopted.

Problems

1. Bob was born to Doug and Wanda, who later divorced. Wanda then married Alphonse, who adopted Bob with Doug's consent.

(a) When Doug dies, does Bob inherit from him under the law of your state? Under the UPC?

(b) Would Doug inherit from Bob?

(c) Same results as in (a) and (b) if Doug and Wanda had adopted Bob?

(d) Same results as in (a) and (b) if Wanda and Alphonse cohabited without marriage and Alphonse adopted Bob?

(e) What results if, instead of marrying Alphonse, Wanda formed a domestic partnership (or civil union) with Marjorie, who adopted Bob?

2. Bob was born to Doug and Wanda. Then Doug died and Wanda married Alphonse, who adopted Bob. When Doug's father dies, would Bob inherit from him under the law of your state? Under the UPC?

3. After Sam's mother died, the widow of his mother's brother adopted him. Later, Sam's maternal grandfather died intestate. Would Sam inherit anything from his grandfather under the law of your state? Under the UPC?

Selected References

Richard C. Ausness, *Planned Parenthood: Adult Adoption and the Right of Adoptees to Inherit*, 41 ACTEC L. J. 241 (2015/2016).

Jason C. Beekman, *Same-sex Second-parent Adoption and Intestacy law: Applying the Sharon S. Model of "Simultaneous" Adoption to Parent-child Provisions of the Uniform Probate Code*, 96 Cornell L. Rev. 139 (2010).

Michael J. Higdon, *When Informal Adoption Meets Intestate Succession: The Cultural Myopia of the Equitable Adoption Doctrine*, 43 Wake Forest L. Rev. 223 (2008).

Neta Sazonov, *Expanding the Statutory Definition of "Child" in Intestacy Law: A Just Solution for the Inheritance Difficulties Grandparent Caregivers' Grandchildren Currently Face*, 17 Elder L.J. 401 (2010).

Peter T. Wendel, *Inheritance Rights and the Step-partner Adoption Paradigm: Shades of the Discrimination against Illegitimate Children*, 34 Hofstra L. Rev. 351 (2005).

Peter T. Wendel, *The Succession Rights of Adopted Adults: Trying to Fit a Square Peg into a Round Hole*, 43 Creighton L. Rev. 815 (2010).

3. Children of Assisted Reproduction

As often happens, the law lags behind science and technology. Consider the following case.

Finley v. Commissioner, Social Security Administration

270 S.W.3d 849 (Ark. 2008)

PAUL E. DANIELSON, ASSOCIATE JUSTICE.

This case involves a question of law certified to this court by the United States District Court for the Eastern District of Arkansas .... The question certified is the following:

> Does a child, who was created as an embryo through in vitro fertilization during his parents' marriage, but implanted into his mother's womb after the death of his father, inherit from the father under Arkansas intestacy law as a surviving child?

We conclude that the answer to this question is no.

According to the District Court's order, the certified question arises from an appeal by Amy Finley, from the final decision of the Commissioner of the Social Security Administration, Michael Astrue (the Commissioner), which denied her claim for "child's insurance benefits" under 42 U.S.C. § 402(d). The District Court's order reflects the following facts. On October 6, 1990, Ms. Finley and Wade W. Finley, Jr., were married. During the course of the marriage, the Finleys pursued fertility treatments at the University of Arkansas for Medical Sciences (UAMS), and, ultimately, participated in UAMS's In Vitro Fertilization and Embryo Transfer (IVF/ET) Program.[14] In June of 2001, doctors produced ten embryos using Ms. Finley's eggs and

---

14. In vitro fertilization is described as follows: After the woman has taken injectable ovulation-inducing medications ..., multiple oocytes are retrieved from the woman's ovaries by a minor

Mr. Finley's sperm. Two of the embryos were implanted into Ms. Finley's uterus and four embryos were frozen for preservation. Ms. Finely later suffered a miscarriage of both of the implanted embryos.

On July 19, 2001, Mr. Finley died intestate while domiciled here in Arkansas. A little less than one year later, on June 26, 2002, Ms. Finley had two of the previously frozen embryos thawed and transferred into her uterus, resulting in a single pregnancy. On February 14, 2003, prior to the child's birth, the Lonoke County Circuit Court entered an order providing that upon the baby's delivery ... [the child's birth certificate would show Wade Finley, Jr., as the father and that determination would be binding for all lawful purposes].

The child was born on March 4, 2003, and on April 11, 2003, Ms. Finley filed a claim for mother's insurance benefits and the child's claim for child's insurance benefits, based on the earnings record of Mr. Finley.... [Denied claims and various appeals led to the district court certifying the question to this court.] The claims were denied at the initial and reconsideration levels; however, an Administrative Law Judge (ALJ) issued a decision on June 16, 2006, awarding both mother's and child's insurance benefits.

... Ms. Finley argues that her child was "conceived" at the time her egg was fertilized by the father's sperm. She contends that there is no statutory prohibition in Arkansas preventing a natural child who was conceived by in vitro fertilization from inheriting from his father. She avers that the General Assembly was aware of in vitro fertilization procedures in light of the fact that it mandated all accident and health insurance companies include in vitro fertilization as a covered expense in Ark. Code Ann. § 23-85-137(a) (Repl. 2004) and was aware of assisted reproductive technologies by its reference to artificial insemination in Ark. Code Ann. § 28-9-209(c) (Repl. 2004). She urges that based upon the medical definitions of "conception," the child born of the Finleys' union was not posthumously conceived and that as a matter of public policy, all children's rights should be protected, including their rights to property and inheritance.

The Commissioner responds that Arkansas intestacy law does not provide inheritance rights from a biological father to a child who was created as an embryo through in vitro fertilization during his parents' marriage, but implanted into his mother's

---

surgical procedure. The oocytes are placed in a petri dish with her male partner's sperm (in vitro) and placed in an incubator for fertilization to occur. The embryos are allowed to grow for a period of three to five days before they are placed back into the woman's uterus.17-289 Attorneys' Textbook of Medicine P.289.65 (3d ed. 2007).It differs entirely from artificial insemination: Intrauterine insemination, also known as artificial insemination, refers to the placement of sperm into the uterine cavity. Intrauterine insemination may be performed at the time of ovulation in the woman's normal menstrual cycle, or with the use of medications that induce ovulation. In most cases, the female partner takes fertility medications in advance of the procedure. The man must produce sperm at the time the woman is ovulating; the sperm (after undergoing certain "washing" procedures) are then inserted into the woman's uterine cavity through a long, thin catheter.17-289 Attorney's Textbook of Medicine P.289.81 (3d ed. 2007).

womb after the death of the father. He argues that the Finleys' child was neither born nor conceived during the Finleys' marriage, which ended upon Mr. Finley's death. The Commissioner maintains that the logical interpretation of the term "conception" or "conceived," as used in Arkansas's intestacy provisions, is to mean the onset of pregnancy, or the successful implantation of an embryo in the womb. He asserts that the General Assembly has not amended the intestate succession statutes to expand the definition of conception to include the creation of embryos during the in vitro fertilization process.... He further points out that the General Assembly, and not the courts, determines public policy. Finally, the Commissioner submits, given the fact that inheritance laws require finality, it is unlikely that the legislature defined the term "conception" to include a medical procedure that could result in a biological birth many years after the father's death. Ms. Finley replies that the General Assembly has been well aware of assisted reproduction for a number of years and, had it chosen to do so, it could have enacted legislation to prevent such an inheritance.

... [T]he District Court's certification order ... provides that "[u]nder the Social Security Act, a child is entitled to child's insurance benefits if he is the child of an individual who dies while insured, if the child was dependent upon the insured at the time of the insured's death.... In determining whether a claimant is the "child" of a deceased insured, the Commissioner is instructed to "apply such law as would be applied in determining the devolution of intestate personal property ... by the courts of the State in which [the insured] was domiciled at the time of his death[.]" 42 U.S.C. § 416(h)(2)(A)...."

During the administrative proceedings in this case, Plaintiff claimed that there were no Arkansas statutes specifically addressing the inheritance rights of a child conceived through in vitro fertilization, but that, pursuant to Ark. Code Ann. § 28-9-209(c), W.F. was "conceived" as a "zygote" prior to his father's death, while his parents were married. Thus, she argued that W.F. had inheritance rights under that statute. The Commissioner acknowledged the lack of a "clear definition" of "conception" under Arkansas state law, but looked to "the generally accepted definition of the term in the medical community" and concluded that "conception" occurred when "the embryo was implanted in [Plaintiff's] uterus after the wage earner died." ...

...

... In order to inherit as a posthumous heir under Arkansas law, the child must not only have been born after the decedent's death, but must also have been conceived before the decedent's death:

> (a) Posthumous descendants of the intestate *conceived before his or her death* but born thereafter shall inherit in the same manner as if born in the lifetime of the intestate.

Ark. Code Ann. § 28-9-210(a) (Repl. 2004) (emphasis added). In order to answer the question certified to this court, we must, then, determine whether a child, created as an embryo through in vitro fertilization during the child's parents' marriage, but implanted into the child's mother's womb after the death of the child's father, was "conceived before" the decedent's death....

It is clear from the statute that in order to inherit through intestate succession as a posthumous descendant, the child must have been conceived before the decedent's death. However, the statutory scheme fails to define the term "conceived." While we could define that term, we find there is no need to do so, as we can definitively say that the General Assembly, in enacting Act 303 of 1969, § 12, now codified at Ark. Code Ann. § 28-9-210, did not intend for the statute to permit a child, created through in vitro fertilization and implanted after the father's death, to inherit under intestate succession. Not only does the instant statute fail to specifically address such a scenario, but it was enacted in 1969, which was well before the technology of in vitro fertilization was developed....

Both of the interested parties in this case cite to several decisions by both federal and state courts involving at least similar issues. *See Eng Khabbaz v. Comm'r, Soc. Sec. Admin.*, 155 N.H. 798, 930 A.2d 1180 (N.H. 2007) (holding that a child conceived after her father's death via artificial insemination was not a "surviving issue" under New Hampshire intestacy law and, thus, was not eligible to receive a portion of her father's estate); *Stephen v. Commissioner of Social Security*, 386 F. Supp. 2d 1257 (M.D. Fla. 2005) (holding that the Commissioner properly determined that the child was not entitled to child's survivor benefits, where under Florida law, a child conceived from the sperm of a person who died before the transfer of sperm to a woman's body was not eligible for a claim against the decedent's estate unless the child was provided for by the decedent's will); *Gillett-Netting v. Barnhart*, 371 F.3d 593 (9th Cir. 2004) (holding that because the children, both of whom were the result of in vitro fertilization of the mother's eggs by the decedent's sperm after his death, were the decedent's legitimate children under Arizona law, they were deemed dependent under 42 U.S.C. § 402(d) and did not need to demonstrate actual dependency nor deemed dependency under 42 U.S.C. § 416(h)); *Woodward v. Commissioner of Social Security*, 435 Mass. 536, 760 N.E.2d 257 (2002) (holding that where the surviving parent or the child's other legal representative demonstrates a genetic relationship between the posthumously reproduced child and the decedent, and where the survivor or representative establishes both that the decedent affirmatively consented to posthumous conception and to the support of any resulting child, the child may enjoy the inheritance rights of "issue" under Massachusetts's intestacy law, so long as time limitations do not preclude the commencement of succession rights on behalf of the child). While those opinions appear thoughtful and well-reasoned under each state's respective code provisions or lack thereof, they are of no assistance in interpreting our specific Arkansas statute....

While the parties would have us define the term "conceive," we decline to do so in the instant case. Our role is not to create the law, but to interpret the law and to give effect to the legislature's intent.... In vitro fertilization and other methods of assisted reproduction are new technologies that have created new legal issues not addressed by already-existing law.... Were we to define the term "conceive," we would be making a determination that would implicate many public policy concerns, including, but certainly not limited to, the finality of estates. That is not our role. The determination of public policy lies almost exclusively with the legislature, and we will not interfere with that determination in the absence of palpable errors.... With this is mind, we strongly encourage the General Assembly to revisit the intestacy succession statutes to address the issues involved in the instant case and those that have not but will likely evolve.

For the foregoing reasons, we answer the certified question in the negative.

Notes and Question

1. As of this writing, the Arkansas legislature has not embraced the court's suggestion. For commentary on this case. See *Note, Statutory Misconception: The Arkansas Supreme Court's Method in* Finley v. Astrue *Sets New Precedent for Uncertainty*, 63 Ark. L. Rev. 419 (2010).

2. In *Astrue v. Capato*, 132 S. Ct. 2021 (2012), the U.S. Supreme Court held that the provisions of the Social Security Act governing the status of posthumously conceived children are constitutional under rational-basis review. *See generally* Catherin Kim, *Posthumously Conceived Children and their Social Security Benefits Based on State Intestacy Law: How Astrue v. Capato Changes Future Social Security Benefits as Technology Advances*, 46 Loy. L.A. L. Rev. 1141 (2013).

3. Legislatures have taken different approaches to assisted reproduction. For example, on the question of whether to recognize posthumous conception, *compare* Ga. Code Ann. § 53-2-1(b)(1), Idaho Code Ann. § 15-2-108, and Tex. Prob. Code § 201.056 (not recognized), *with* Cal. Prob. Code § 249.5 and New York Estates, Powers and Trusts Law § 4-1.3 (recognized.)

4. How well do you think the UPC provisions below balance the competing interests of the child, each of the parents, donors, gestational carriers, the child's siblings, and the need to resolve inheritance questions in a timely fashion?

Uniform Probate Code

Section 2-115. Definitions.

In this [subpart]:

...

(2) "Assisted reproduction" means a method of causing pregnancy other than sexual intercourse.

...

(4) "Functioned as a parent of the child" means behaving toward a child in a manner consistent with being the child's parent and performing functions that are customarily performed by a parent, including fulfilling parental responsibilities toward the child, recognizing or holding out The child as the individual's child,

materially participating in the child's upbringing, and residing with the child in the same household as a regular member of that household.

(5) "Genetic father" means the man whose sperm fertilized the egg of a child's genetic mother. If the father-child relationship is established under the presumption of paternity under [insert applicable state law], the term means only the man for whom that relationship is established.

(6) "Genetic mother" means the woman whose egg was fertilized by the sperm of a child's genetic father.

(7) "Genetic parent" means a child's genetic father or genetic mother.

(8) "Incapacity" means the inability of an individual to function as a parent of a child because of the individual's physical or mental condition.

. . .

Section 2-120. Child Conceived by Assisted Reproduction Other Than Child Born to Gestational Carrier.

(a) [**Definitions.**] In this section:

(1) "Birth mother" means a woman, other than a gestational carrier under Section 2-121, who gives birth to a child of assisted reproduction. The term is not limited to a woman who is the child's genetic mother.

(2) "Child of assisted reproduction" means a child conceived by means of assisted reproduction by a woman other than a gestational carrier under Section 2-121.

(3) "Third-party donor" means an individual who produces eggs or sperm used for assisted reproduction, whether or not for consideration. The term does not include:

(A) a husband who provides sperm, or a wife who provides eggs, that are used for assisted reproduction by the wife;

(B) the birth mother of a child of assisted reproduction; or

(C) an individual who has been determined under subsection (e) or (f) to have a parent-child relationship with a child of assisted reproduction.

(b) [**Third-Party Donor.**] A parent-child relationship does not exist between a child of assisted reproduction and a third-party donor.

(c) [**Parent-Child Relationship with Birth Mother.**] A parent-child relationship exists between a child of assisted reproduction and the child's birth mother.

(d) [**Parent-Child Relationship with Husband Whose Sperm Were Used During His Lifetime by His Wife for Assisted Reproduction.**] Except as otherwise provided in subsections (i) and (j), a parent-child relationship exists between a child of assisted reproduction and the husband of the child's birth mother if the husband provided the sperm that the birth mother used during his lifetime for assisted reproduction.

(e) [**Birth Certificate: Presumptive Effect.**] A birth certificate identifying an individual other than the birth mother as the other parent of a child of assisted reproduction presumptively establishes a parent-child relationship between the child and that individual.

(f) [**Parent-Child Relationship with Another.**] Except as otherwise provided in subsections (g), (i), and (j), and unless a parent-child relationship is established under subsection (d) or (e), a parent-child relationship exists between a child of assisted reproduction and an individual other than the birth mother who consented to assisted reproduction by the birth mother with intent to be treated as the other parent of the child. Consent to assisted reproduction by the birth mother with intent to be treated as the other parent of the child is established if the individual:

(1) before or after the child's birth, signed a record that, considering all the facts and circumstances, evidences the individual's consent; or

(2) in the absence of a signed record under paragraph (1):

(A) functioned as a parent of the child no later than two years after the child's birth;

(B) intended to function as a parent of the child no later than two years after the child's birth but was prevented from carrying out that intent by death, incapacity, or other circumstances; or

(C) intended to be treated as a parent of a posthumously conceived child, if that intent is established by clear and convincing evidence.

(g) [**Record Signed More than Two Years after the Birth of the Child: Effect.**] For the purpose of subsection (f)(1), neither an individual who signed a record more than two years after the birth of the child, nor a relative of that individual who is not also a relative of the birth mother, inherits from or through the child unless the individual functioned as a parent of the child before the child reached [18] years of age.

(h) **Presumption: Birth Mother Is Married or Surviving Spouse.] For the purpose of subsection (f)(2), the following rules apply:**

(1) If the birth mother is married and no divorce proceeding is pending, in the absence of clear and convincing evidence to the contrary, her spouse satisfies subsection (f)(2)(A) or (B).

(2) If the birth mother is a surviving spouse and at her deceased spouse's death no divorce proceeding was pending, in the absence of clear and convincing evidence to the contrary, her deceased spouse satisfies subsection (f)(2)(B) or (C).

(i) [**Divorce Before Placement of Eggs, Sperm, or Embryos.**] If a married couple is divorced before placement of eggs, sperm, or embryos, a child resulting from the assisted reproduction is not a child of the birth mother's former spouse, unless the former spouse consented in a record that if assisted reproduction were to occur after divorce, the child would be treated as the former spouse's child.

(j) [**Withdrawal of Consent Before Placement of Eggs, Sperm, or Embryos.**] If, in a record, an individual withdraws consent to assisted reproduction before placement of eggs, sperm, or embryos, a child resulting from the assisted reproduction is not a child of that individual, unless the individual subsequently satisfies subsection (f).

(k) [**When Posthumously Conceived Child Treated as in Gestation.**] If, under this section, an individual is a parent of a child of assisted reproduction who is conceived after the individual's death, the child is treated as in gestation at the individual's death for purposes of Section 2-104(a)(2)[15] if the child is:

(1) in utero not later than 36 months after the individual's death; or

(2) born not later than 45 months after the individual's death.

Section 2-121. Child Born to Gestational Carrier.

(a) [**Definitions.**] In this section:

(1) Gestational agreement" means an enforceable or unenforceable agreement for assisted reproduction in which a woman agrees to carry a child to birth for an intended parent, intended parents, or an individual described in subsection (e).

(2) Gestational carrier" means a woman who is not an intended parent who gives birth to a child under a gestational agreement. The term is not limited to a woman who is the child's genetic mother.

(3) Gestational child" means a child born to a gestational carrier under a gestational agreement.

(4) Intended parent" means an individual who entered into a gestational agreement providing that the individual will be the parent of a child born to a gestational carrier by means of assisted reproduction. The term is not limited to an individual who has a genetic relationship with the child.

(b) [**Court Order Adjudicating Parentage: Effect.**] A parent-child relationship is conclusively established by a court order designating the parent or parents of a gestational child.

(c) [**Gestational Carrier.**] A parent-child relationship between a gestational child and the child's gestational carrier does not exist unless the gestational carrier is:

(1) designated as a parent of the child in a court order described in subsection (b); or

(2) the child's genetic mother and a parent-child relationship does not exist under this section with an individual other than the gestational carrier.

15. UPC § 2-104(a)(2) requires the child to survive birth by 120 hours.

(d) Parent-Child Relationship with Intended Parent or Parents.] In the absence of a court order under subsection (b), a parent-child relationship exists between a gestational child and an intended parent who:

(1) functioned as a parent of the child no later than two years after the child's birth; or

(2) died while the gestational carrier was pregnant if:

(A) there were two intended parents and the other intended parent functioned as a parent of the child no later than two years after the child's birth;

(B) there were two intended parents, the other intended parent also died while the gestational carrier was pregnant, and a relative of either deceased intended parent or the spouse or surviving spouse of a relative of either deceased intended parent functioned as a parent of the child no later than two years after the child's birth; or

(C) there was no other intended parent and a relative of or the spouse or surviving spouse of a relative of the deceased intended parent functioned as a parent of the child no later than two years after the child's birth.

. . .

(h) [When Posthumously Conceived Gestational Child Treated as in Gestation.] If, under this section, an individual is a parent of a gestational child who is conceived after the individual's death, the child is treated as in gestation at the individual's death for purposes of Section 2-104(a)(2) if the child is:

(1) in utero not later than 36 months after the individual's death; or

(2) born not later than 45 months after the individual's death.

(i) [No Effect on Other Law.] This section does not affect law of this state other than this [code] regarding the enforceability or validity of a gestational agreement.

Question

Would the result in *Finley* have been different if Arkansas had been using the UPC approach?

Problem

Paula was born to Mariel, who had been impregnated with the sperm of a third-party donor. Six months after Paula's birth, Mariel met Leslie and within a year they were sharing housing and child care for Paula. This arrangement continued until Leslie was killed in a car accident 10 years later. Last month, Leslie's father died intestate. In a UPC jurisdiction, what evidence would you gather to establish Paula right to inherit from Leslie's father?

Selected References

Amanda Horner, *I Consented to do What?: Posthumous Children and the Consent to Parent After-death*, 33 S. Ill. U. L.J. 157 (2008).

Charles P. Kindregan & Maureen McBrien, Assisted Reproductive Technology: A Lawyer's Guide to Emerging Law and Science (2010).

Kristine S. Knaplund, *Children of Assisted Reproduction*, 45 U. Mich. J.L. Reform 899 (2012).

Browne C. Lewis, *Dead Men Reproducing: Responding to the Existence of After-death Children*, 16 Geo. Mason L. Rev. 403 (2009).

Lee-ford Tritt, *Technical Correction or Tectonic Shift: Competing Default Rule Theories Under the New Uniform Probate Code*, 61 Ala. L. Rev. 273 (2010).

Lee-ford Tritt, *Sperms and Estates: An Unadulterated Functionally-Based Approach to Parent-Child Property Succession*, 62 SMU L. Rev. 367 (2009).

Morgan Kirkland Wood, *It Takes a Village: Considering the Other Interests at Stake When Extending Inheritance Rights to Posthumously Conceived Children*, 44 Ga. L. Rev. 873 (2010).

C. Half Bloods

Two people are in a half-blood relationship when they have one common ancestor. Consider the following family:

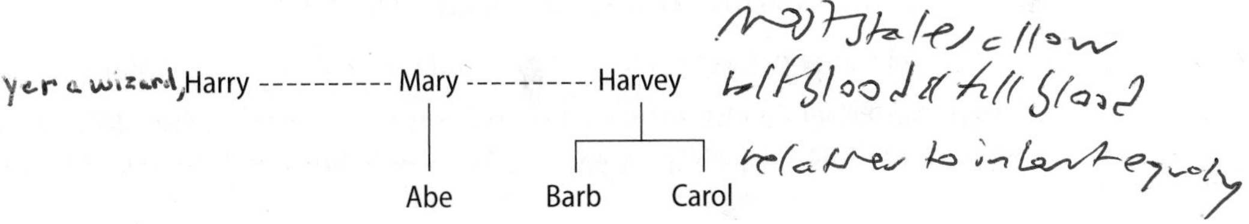

Mary and Harry had Abe. After a death or divorce, Mary and Harvey had Barb and Carol. As to Carol, Abe is a half-brother and Barb is a whole-blooded sister.

Most states allow half-blood and full-blood relatives to inherit equally. *See, e.g.*, UPC § 2-107. Some statutes, however, do not. E.g., Fla. Stat. § 732.105 (half bloods get half the share of whole bloods).

As the next section describes, traditionally there must be some blood relationship between the decedent and the heir (e.g., Abe would not inherit from Harvey).

Selected References

Ralph C. Brashier, *Half-bloods, Inheritance, and Family*, 37 U. Mem. L. Rev. 215 (2007).

Ralph C. Brashier, *Consanguinity, Sibling Relationships, and the Default Rules of Inheritance Law: Reshaping Half-blood Statutes to Reflect the Evolving Family*, 58 SMU L. Rev. 137, 137–94 (2005).

D. Stepchildren

One's stepchildren are the children of one's spouse. Until recently, stepchildren and other relatives by affinity have had no inheritance rights. The UPC and a few states allow stepchildren to take if there are no surviving blood relatives, as a last alternative to the property escheating to the state. *See* UPC § 2-103(b). In the right circumstances, a stepchild might be able to use the "equitable adoption" theory to qualify as an "adopted" child.

Question

Blended families may come from many sources: divorce and remarriage, death and remarriage (especially among older people), and shifting non-marital relationships. Should intestate statutes recognize any intergenerational, non-blood relationships? If so, which ones and how?

E. Ancestors and Collateral Relatives

Recall that as a starting place intestate statutes follow family lines when identifying which blood relations will inherit: first seek descendants, then move up one generation looking for parents, then down again seeking siblings and their offspring. After that, states disagree about when it is appropriate to modify the process or stop it entirely.

Many statutes, like the UPC, continue in the same vein for another generation: move up to the grandparents (half to the maternal and half to the paternal sides) and down their lines. If only one side of the family has survivors, they take everything. *See* UPC § 2-203(4). At that point the UPC stops the search for blood relatives (see below), but many states then begin looking for "next of kin." Other states omit the step of splitting between the grandparents' lines and instead start the "next of kin" search directly after not finding surviving descendants of parents. *See, e.g.*, Mass. Gen. Laws, ch. 190, § 3(6).

States identify next of kin various ways, often blending the familiar parentelic principle with a degree-of-relationship system that counts people connecting the decedent to the survivor. The numbers on the Table of Consanguinity indicate the number of steps ("degrees") from the decedent to various survivors. Under a strict degree-of-relationship system, the closest survivor wins. If counting yields a tie, some states return to the parentelic principle and thus favor those who claim through the decedent's nearest ancestor. If there is still a tie, the survivors take equally. *See* Mont. Code Ann. § 72-2-113(1)(e), (2). Because various states use different combinations, you must carefully check the details of local law.

Although giving the property to next of kin keeps it in the family, sometimes only very distant relatives survive a decedent. The cost of identifying them can be high, and their ties to the decedent may be minimal. Also, when the estate is large and the facts murky, many persons may be tempted to claim relationships they do not have. To avoid these problems, the UPC cuts off blood relatives more distant than descendants of the decedent's grandparents. *See* UPC §§ 2-103, 2-105.

As we have seen, the UPC and some states give to step-children before letting the property escheat to the state.

Table Of Consanguinity

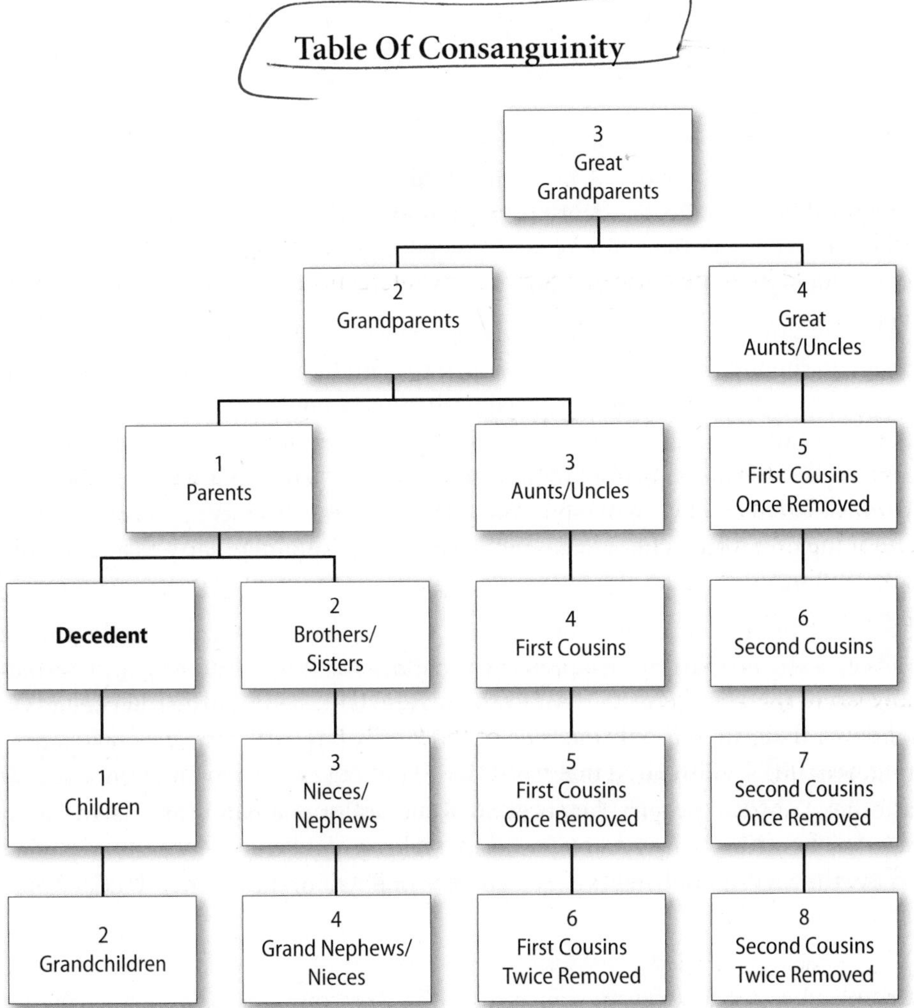

§ 2.03 Allocating Shares

Having examined the major questions surrounding who qualifies as an "heir," we now ask how the heirs should divide the property. As you review these questions, keep in mind the admonition to ask how well various approaches further the policies of reflecting the presumed desires of decedents, protecting dependent family members, keeping property in the nuclear family, and encouraging individuals to accumulate property. You may want to compare the UPC's approaches, reproduced above, with the laws of a non-UPC state.

A. Spouses

Like much of the law of spousal relations generally, the law governing spouses' intestate shares is changing. Traditionally, blood relationships were the key to inheritance rights, and spouses suffered by comparison. Slowly, focus shifted from bloodlines to the family unit. Spouses fared better. More recently, the law has started to respond to the reality that many persons have more than one spouse during a lifetime.

The size of a surviving spouse's share varies, depending upon both state law and who else survives. If the decedent left no children, the spouse might get everything or might share with the decedent's parents. If the decedent left children, the spouse will often share with them, for example, by taking half if there is one child, or one-third if there is more than one child.

Dividing an estate between the surviving spouse and the children might not leave enough to support the spouse. In addition, if the children are minors, they may need separate, costly guardianships. Especially when the amounts are small, splitting the estate may not be wise. As a rough way to avoid these problems, some states give the surviving spouse a lump-sum amount, sometimes called "front money," and then divide the balance between the spouse and the children. Another approach is to give everything to the surviving spouse and rely upon the spouse to serve as a "conduit" to the children.

Some states do not trust spouses to take care of the children, especially if there has been a second marriage. To protect the children in this situation, some jurisdictions lower the amount of the front money. The UPC distinguishes between two situations, based on the presumed trustworthiness of the surviving spouse as a conduit. First, if the surviving spouse is the parent of the decedent's children, but also has other children, the survivor takes $225,000,[16] plus one-half of the balance. On the other hand, if the *decedent* left children who are not children of the surviving spouse, the survivor only takes $150,000, plus one-half of the balance. UPC § 2-102.

16. Recall that the UPC adjusts dollar amounts to reflect changes in consumer prices. UPC § 1-109.

Problems

Shelley and Art had two children, Hope and Roy. When Art died, Shelley married John and they had a daughter, Beth.

(a) Shelley died leaving an estate of $400,000 in liquid assets. Who takes what shares of Shelley's estate under the law of your state? Under the UPC?

(b) Instead, John predeceased Shelley leaving an estate of $300,000 in liquid assets plus Greenacre (worth $100,000), a farm he inherited from his paternal uncle. Who takes what shares of John's estate under the law of your state? Under the UPC?

B. Descendants and Collaterals

Two basic notions work both independently and together in various schemes for allocating intestate shares. Familiarity with these concepts is important, both because you may encounter them when interpreting intestate statutes, and especially because they serve as alternative models you should present to your clients when they design their own estate plans. One, called a "*per capita*" approach, counts people. The other focuses on the generation that a survivor occupies and often treats people as if they were "standing in the shoes" of their parents or grandparents. The multi-generational approach comes in a variety of forms and carries different names, but generally fits the description of "representation." A *per capita* approach is common when all of the takers are in the same generation. When the survivors are among the descendants of the decedent's grandparents and are in different generations, virtually all states provide for some form of representation. Especially when the survivors are stretched out among three or more generations, states take different approaches in deciding just how to "represent."

Consider the following family, in which all of the intestate decedent's children have died, but two grandchildren (K & O) and six great-grandchildren (U, V, W, X, Y, Z) survive.[17]

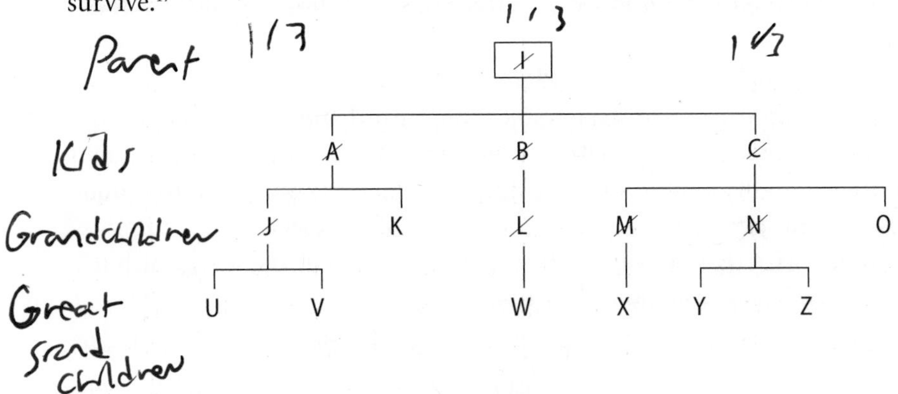

17. Using letters, rather than names, to represent people is a rather impersonal technique this text usually avoids. There is, however, some precedent for using numbers. An early settler in Ohio and Indiana, Benjamin Stickney, named his children "One" and "Two."

1. Per Capita

One possibility would be to divide the estate among the decedent's descendants *per capita*; K, O, U, V, W, X, Y, and Z would each take 1/8 shares. An intestate statute would be very unlikely to adopt such a scheme in this situation, with survivors in different generations. On the other hand, the concept of counting heads appears in other contexts. For example, if K and O had also died, so all the survivors were in the same generation, many states would give to the great-grandchildren equally.

2. Representation

Keeping straight the different ways in which representation can be structured is difficult because statutes, court decisions, and documents may use different terms to describe the same form of distribution. This section identifies the common patterns and the terms that tend to be associated with each.

a. Strict *Per Stirpes*

One possibility is to divide the estate into as many shares as there are surviving children or deceased children who left descendants surviving the decedent. Sometimes this approach is called "*per stirpes*," and sometimes, "by right of representation." To distinguish it from the division described next, many commentators call this one "strict *per stirpes*." In our example, the estate would be divided into three shares, one for each stock, and then subdivided from there. a's 1/3 would go to j and K (1/6 each), and j's share would go on to U and V (1/12 each). b's 1/3 would go to l and on to W. Similarly, c's 1/3 finds its way to O (1/9), X (1/9), and Y & Z (1/18 each).

Those who prefer this system view the family in vertical terms. In our example, they see a's family, b's family, and c's family. Those families share the property equally. As a result, however, people in the same generation may get widely-differing shares. W gets 1/3, but Y and Z only take 1/18 each. Their shares depend on how prolific their parents were. When survivors stretch among three generations, a more remote descendant can take more than a closer one. W gets 1/3, but K only takes 1/6, and O gets 1/9.

b. *Per Stirpes: Per Capita* with Representation

As a partial response to such uneven results, some jurisdictions use a compromise interpretation of "representation." These states skip older, "empty" generations and divide the estate into shares at the first generation leaving survivors. This technique sometimes is called "*per stirpes*," sometimes "by right of representation," and sometimes "*per capita* with representation." It is "*per capita*" at the first level which has survivors and "with representation" after that.

Until 1990, the UPC used this system. Examining the UPC's language both aids understanding and offers a model for drafting. The earlier UPC gave property to descendants "by representation" and then defined "representation" as follows in former § 2-106: ". . . the estate is divided into as many shares as there are surviving heirs in the nearest degree of kinship and deceased persons in the same degree who left issue who survive the decedent, each surviving heir in the nearest degree receiving one share and the share of each deceased person in the same degree being divided among his issue in the same manner."

Applying per capita with representation to our family would divide the estate into six shares. K and O get 1/6 each; j, l, m, and n's shares would descend as before. The differences among the great-grandchildren's shares have narrowed. W and X each get 1/6; and U, V, Y, and Z each get 1/12.

c. Representation: *Per Capita* at Each Generation

Borrowing an idea from North Carolina, N.C. Gen. Stat. § 29-16, the UPC now favors equal treatment of each generation. Called "*per capita* at each generation," this approach views the family horizontally. The language to accomplish this result is complicated. Study the following excerpt from § 2-106(b):

> (b) [**Decedent's Descendants.**] If, under Section 2-103(1), a decedent's intestate estate or a part thereof passes "by representation" to the decedent's descendants, the estate or part thereof is divided into as many equal shares as there are (i) surviving descendants in the generation nearest to the decedent which contains one or more surviving descendants and (ii) deceased descendants in the same generation who left surviving descendants, if any. Each surviving descendant in the nearest generation is allocated one share. The remaining shares, if any, are combined and then divided in the same manner among the surviving descendants of the deceased descendants as if the surviving descendants who were allocated a share and their surviving descendants had predeceased the decedent.

Consider again our hypothetical family. *A per-capita*-at-each-generation approach would ignore the children's generation because none survived. Start at the grandchildren's generation and add the number of survivors plus the number of those who died leaving descendants who survive. Here we divide it six ways and give K & O 1/6 each. Next, move down a generation and divide the remainder of the estate according to the same principle. Here all six of the great-grandchildren survived, so each gets 1/6 of the remaining 2/3. If some of those great-grandchildren had died leaving descendants, we would divide what was left in the pot the same way. This scheme has the advantage of treating equally those who are equally distant from the decedent.

Native American Inheritance

The uneven history of American Indian land ownership has created an inheritance system that combines federal, state, and tribal law, depending upon the circumstances. Individual allotments of land are held in "trust" or in "restricted" title for their owners by the United States. When such land is rented, the proceeds are held in individual Indian money (IIM) accounts by the federal government. Such land and the IIM accounts are subject to federal inheritance law. Other assets are usually subject to state law, though a few tribes have their own probate rules.

Because many Native Americans die intestate with large families, fractionalization of land ownership has become a significant problem over several generations. It is not unusual for 100 owners to share property. Congressional attempts to limit fractionalization, by declaring that small shares escheat to the tribe, failed on constitutional grounds. *See Hodel v. Irving*, 481 U.S. 704 (1987); *Babbitt v. Youpee*, 519 U.S. 234 (1997). The most recent effort—the American Indian Probate Reform Act, 118 Stat. 1773 (with different provisions effective on various dates in 2006 and 2007)—creates a uniform system for transferring trust or restricted land and IIM accounts at death. The Act also allows tribes to opt-out of the federal system by adopting their own probate codes. Recognizing the particular problems surrounding Indian ownership, the Act's intestacy provisions differ from more widely-applicable state law.

In particular, several devices seek to cut down on fractional ownership. Aside from a spouse, only "eligible heirs" can inherit. These are limited to Indians, a child or grandchild of an Indian, or another who is already a co-owner. Who is an "Indian" varies from tribe to tribe, but as intermarriage with non-Indians reduces the percentage of Indian blood required for qualification, fewer persons will meet the definition. Moreover, the only collateral relatives who can inherit are brothers and sisters (not, for example, nieces and nephews). In the absence of an eligible heir, the property goes to the tribe or the other co-owners. In a move that harkens back to the English rule of primogeniture, shares of less than five percent go to a single heir, instead of being divided further. In modern application, the rule does not favor males; the entire share goes to the eldest surviving child, grandchild, or great-grandchild, as the case may be. In the absence of one of those, the tribe or the co-owners take. Unless the decedent leaves a will, percentage ownership cannot drop below five percent.

3. *Drafting Lessons*

The various methods for dividing intestate estates can serve as models for drafting will and trust clauses which dispose of property. In particular, consider how the UPC's basic approach to dividing an estate can help you design an appropriate dispository clause for a will or trust. For example, § 2-106(b) starts by dividing property "into as many equal shares as there are (i) surviving descendants in the generation nearest to the decedent which contains one or more surviving descendants and (ii) deceased descendants in the same generation who left surviving descendants, if any." This approach gives property to living people. Note that good drafting does not rely upon one of the possibly ambiguous labels identified above; rather, it specifically describes how the property is to be divided.

Notice especially what the UPC does *not* do. It does not give property to all members of a class and then take it away if they have not survived (e.g., "to my children, but if any child predeceases me, then to that child's descendants"). By never giving the property to the predeceased child, the UPC approach avoids the extra language (and potential for mistake) needed to take the property away. Moreover, because this approach creates shares for groups of people, drafters can adapt the language easily to fit varying client intentions. For example, a client who wanted to include descendants' spouses could say "and (ii) deceased descendants in the same generation who left surviving spouses or surviving descendants, if any." *See generally* Edward C. Halbach, Jr., *Drafting and Overdrafting: A Voyeur's View of Recurring Problems*, Heckerling Inst. on Est. Plan. § 1303.7 (1985). Drafters can use the basic "divide into as many shares as there are . . ." approach to create any of the basic divisions of property described in this section.

If you are curious about how all this might fit into a larger context, check out the dispository clauses in the Appendix.

Problems

1. Assume the following family:

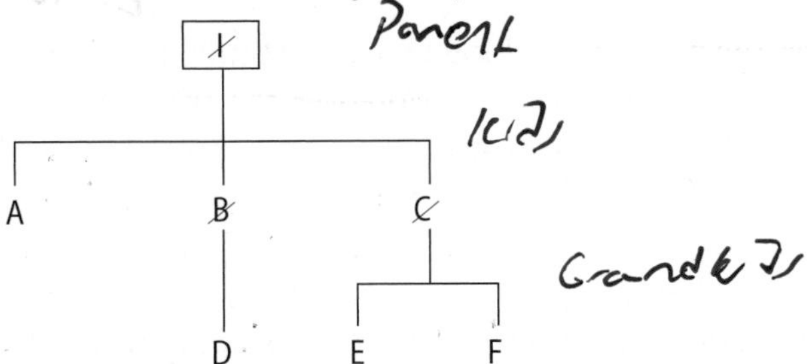

(a) How would the estate be distributed under a *per capita* with representation system?

(b) Under a *per capita* at each generation system?

2. Assume the following family:

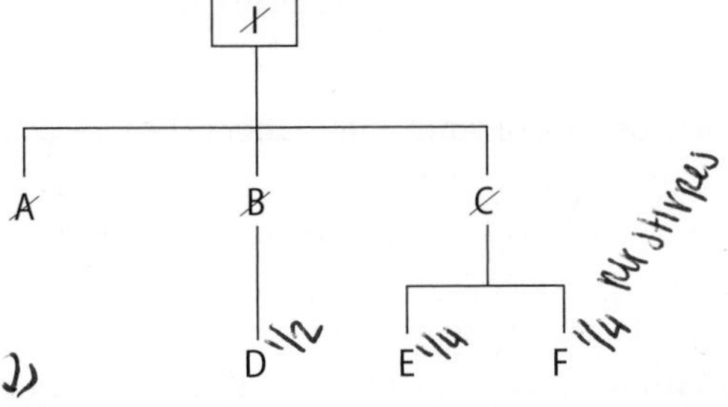

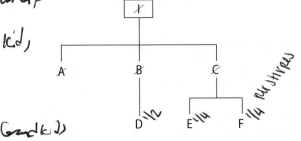

How would the estate be distributed under the law of your state? Under the UPC?

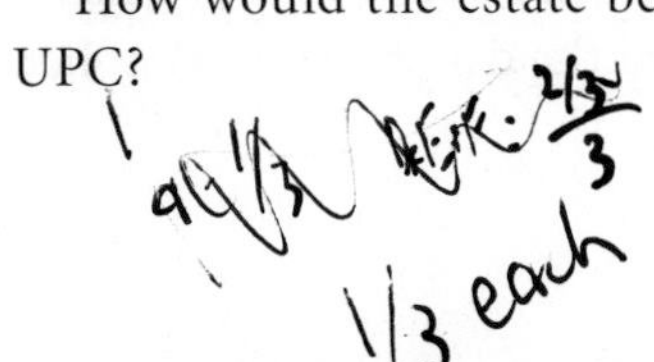

3. Assume the following family:

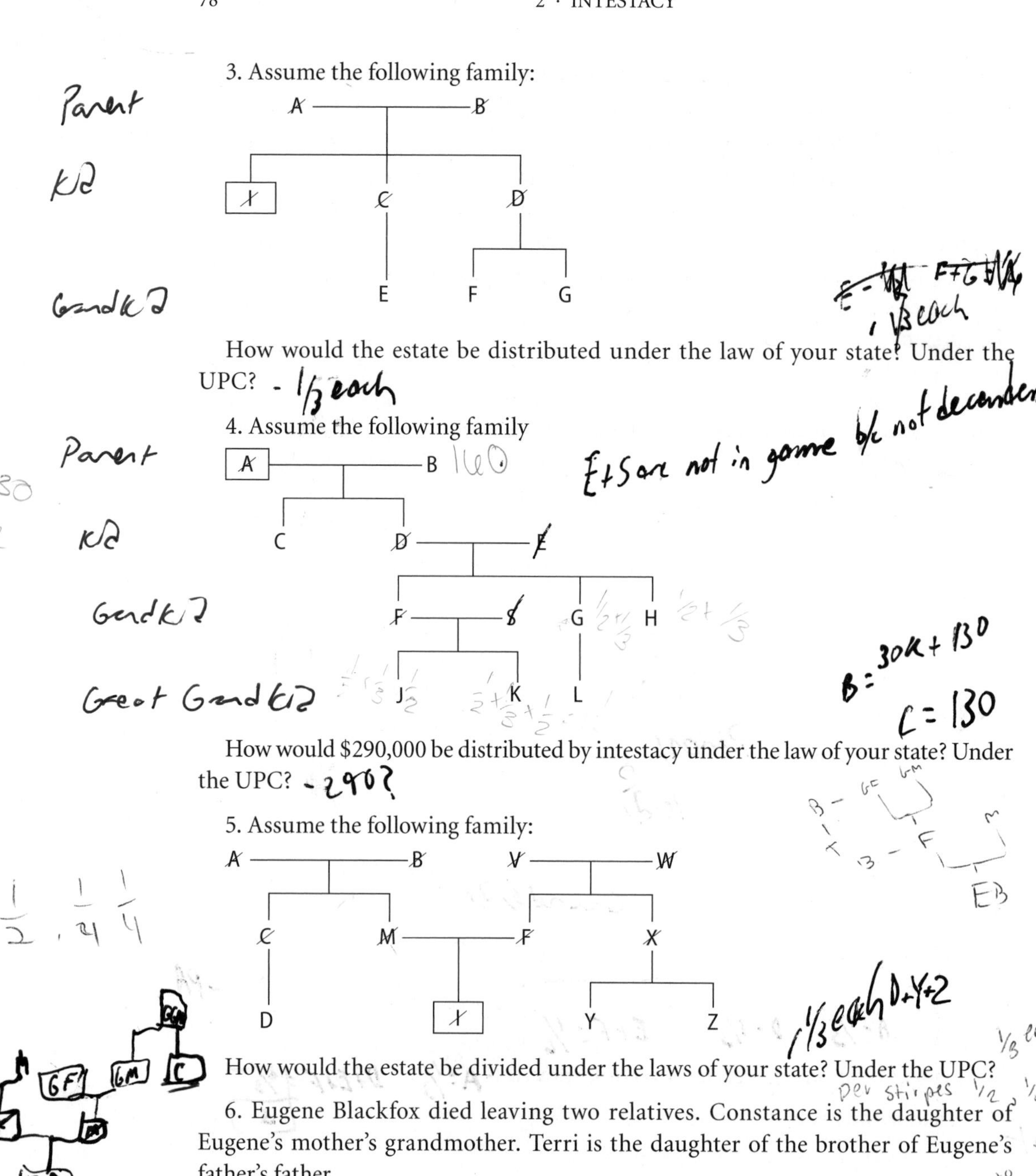

How would the estate be distributed under the law of your state? Under the UPC?

4. Assume the following family

How would $290,000 be distributed by intestacy under the law of your state? Under the UPC?

5. Assume the following family:

How would the estate be divided under the laws of your state? Under the UPC?

6. Eugene Blackfox died leaving two relatives. Constance is the daughter of Eugene's mother's grandmother. Terri is the daughter of the brother of Eugene's father's father.

(a) Who takes Eugene's estate under the law of your state? Under the UPC?

(b) Same result if Terri is the granddaughter of the brother of Eugene's father?

7. Rose McEwan died partially intestate because her will did not dispose of all of her property. Rose left no husband or children, and her parents (Kata and Frank) had predeceased her. On her mother's side, Rose was survived by her mother's half-brother and half-sisters (Karl, Joza, and Mary) and the daughter (Ana) of her

mother's whole-sister (Flora). On her father's side, Rose left the three children (Ann, Mary Ann, and Joseph) of her father's brother (Michael). Who are Rose's heirs under the law of your state? Under the UPC?

8. Some relatives of Betty Burk, who died last month, have asked you to handle her estate. She died intestate, an only child, unmarried with no children. Her parents predeceased her. Your investigations uncover the following facts.[18]

Betty's father, Bronce Burk, had one brother, Billy. Billy died leaving a daughter, Julie. Julie has two children, Ann and Tom.

Betty's mother, "Brownie," had one brother, Ed Smith, and two sisters, Lucy Smith Bacon and Ruby Smith Arnold.

Ed Smith is still living at age 91. He has a wife, Alice, and two children: Nan and Ed, Jr. Nan has one child, Joe; Ed. Jr. has 5 children: J1 through J5.

Lucy Bacon and her son, Bill Bacon, are dead. Bill Bacon has 4 children: BB1 through BB4. BB1 has two children and BB3 has 3 children. Lucy's daughter Bess has three children: MM1 children through MM3. Each of them has two children Ruby Smith Arnold died at age 101 (really!). Ruby had five children. Her sons Robert and Jim died childless and unmarried. Her daughter Dot died but is survived by her husband, George, and their four children: James, Cindy, Susan, and Cathy. James has two children; Cindy has three children and one grandchild; Susan has four children; and Cathy has three children.

Ruby's son Bill died but is survived by his wife, Della, and two sons from his first marriage: Hank and Eric. Hank has a child, Heidi.

Ruby's daughter Kay, a widow, has three children: Brian, Bob, and Becky. Brian has two children and Becky has two children.

Who should take what shares of Betty Burk's estate under your state's statute? Under the UPC?

9. Willfred Ranney, 28, is married to Charlotte, 29. They have three children: Robert (10), Cheryl (8), and Martha (5). Willfred wants a will naming Charlotte as his primary beneficiary, but if she predeceases him, he wants the property to go to his surviving descendants. Draft the dispository language necessary to divide the estate among Willfred's descendants according to each of the following schemes:

1. strict *per stirpes*
2. *per stirpes*: *per capita* with representation
3. representation: *per capita* at each generation.

Begin each clause with: "If my wife Charlotte does not survive me, ..." Do not use the labels for various schemes; rather, specifically identify how the estate is to be divided. For further discussion and sample language, see Roger W. Andersen & Karen Boxx, Skills & Values: Trusts and Estates, Ch. 2. (2009).

18. These facts are real. [Eds.]

Selected References

Roger W. Andersen & Douglas Oliver, *Communicating Clearly: Showing Dispository Preferences with Flowcharts*, 29 Okla. City U. L. Rev. 559 (2004).

David M. English, *A Uniform Probate Code for Indian Country at Last*, 20 Prob. & Prop. 20 (Mar./Apr. 2006).

Kristina L. McCulley, *The American Indian Probate Reform Act of 2004: The Death of Fractionation or Individual Native American Property Interests and Tribal Customs?*, 30 Am. Indian L. Rev. 401 (2005–2006).

Chapter 3

Wills

We now shift our attention from default doctrines that apply when a testamentary plan is lacking to a series of devices that people can use to construct estate plans. This chapter centers upon the will, the most basic of those devices. Properly drawn, a will covers property that would otherwise pass by intestacy.

As you work through this material, view it from different angles. Sometimes, assume the role of a litigator, examining documents after the fact, looking for arguments and anticipating counter-arguments about validity and meaning. Another approach, with which you may be less familiar, is to look forward, as a planner, paying particular attention to the details that make a plan able to withstand future challenges while retaining the flexibility to adapt to unforeseeable change. Finally, you should step back and ask what is going on here. What policies are being pursued, are they appropriate, and do the rules support or undermine those policies? That third question is not an empty academic exercise. Instead, it informs how you approach the first two as you seek to accomplish your clients' goals.

To set the tone for the way most lawyers spend their time working with wills, we begin with a look at the planning process. Then we turn to the requirements for creating wills and questions about just what language is included in a will. Because wills once put together also can be taken apart, doctrines surrounding will revocation come next. The chapter closes with a discussion of contracts to make wills.

§ 3.01 The Planning Process

The planning process places lawyers and their clients together, working to identify each client's goals and to develop a plan that meets, as nearly as possible, those goals. To accomplish that end, a lawyer must learn to listen to the client, to hear both what is said and what is not said. When a client's plans are unusual, the lawyer should learn what is behind the plan. When the client's situation is unusual, the lawyer should avoid the tendency to push the client into a "typical" plan. All of this service can be accomplished only if the lawyer treats the client as an individual, with very personal needs.

Because lawyers regularly work with wills and talk about death, they may, over time, start to undervalue both how important these questions are to their clients and how traumatic it may be to face them. As the following excerpt indicates, lawyers who are sensitive to their clients' situations have the opportunity to help them along some difficult steps in their lives.

Thomas Shaffer, Death, Property, and Lawyers

(1970)

Clients in "estate planning" are invited into a relation with property which is probably new to them and which may be unsettling. Death is a part of this confrontation, and death is an unpleasant fact to modern man.... Planning for death is encouraging because modern man is attracted to the idea of plans which will organize his future life for him, but traumatic because it involves planning for death and personal death is a thought modern man will do almost anything to avoid....

The testamentary experience is death-confronting, novel, and taboo-defying. For that reason it is probably much more vivid in the mind and heart of the client than lawyers who go through the experience every day suppose it to be. Taboo-defying experiences usually tend to be vivid. People going through them tend to be upset. People who are able to go through their upsetting experiences in the company of a competent, comfortable, accepting professional, however, come out more aware of their lives, more reconciled to what is real in their lives, and better able to make choices and to develop. The question here is not whether the lawyer is a counselor in this relationship, she cannot avoid being a counselor. The question is whether the lawyer realizes what she is doing, is able to accept what it involves for herself and for her client, and has the wisdom and courage to be a helpful companion.

Question

Do you have a will? If so, how did you feel at the time you decided what it should say? How do you feel about how your lawyer handled the process? If you do not have a will, have you been avoiding facing the need?

The planning process begins with gathering facts about the client, the client's assets, the beneficiaries and their assets, and the client's goals. It continues with considering the tools available to the planner—wills, trusts, gifts, and contracts—and reviewing the consequences of using those tools. The planning process ends temporarily after selecting the appropriate tools, honing them to the particular details of the plan, and drafting and executing the relevant documents. Planning begins again when the situation changes.

Gathering Information about Individuals. The planner needs information about the client, the beneficiaries, and the possible fiduciaries. What follows is a brief description of the types of information needed about each, and the reasons why the planner needs it. The lawyer can obtain most of this information at the time of the initial interview. When conducting that interview, planners should be especially careful not to cross-examine the client, but rather to use the conversation as a way to build rapport.

The client. Planners need both personal and financial information. Personal information includes such matters as age, domicile, marital status, children or other issue, and dependents. In the case of younger clients, age establishes legal capacity. For older clients, age may be needed to calculate future social security rights, or the value of life insurance policies. Domicile identifies the legal system within which the estate plan will operate. Marital or domestic partnership status clarifies the rights to an elective share, or other protected interest, and availability of the marital deduction for federal transfer tax purposes. As modern science has extended the time of procreation even beyond death, it is important to learn whether the client intends to use such technology. Knowing about issue also allows the planner to draft any language of disinheritance with them in mind. The presence of dependents suggests that the client's plan includes them.

Financial information about the client helps to clarify the client's present and future needs. The lawyer should know the client's financial lifestyle—specifically, consumption and investment habits—in order to determine (a) whether the client's assets and income exceed present or predictable future needs, and (b) whether the client emotionally could tolerate making lifetime gifts. Obtaining an inventory of digital property will be increasingly important.

The beneficiaries. Planners need several types of information concerning the client's intended beneficiaries. First, of course, we need the beneficiaries' names and enough of a description to distinguish them from others. Particularly delicate is the problem of learning whether any issues are non-marital. Special problems arise if there are beneficiaries unrelated to the client by blood. These beneficiaries increase the chances of a will contest, so the planner should know why the client is including them.

Second, the planner needs some personal information about the beneficiaries. Young beneficiaries may need a guardian or a trust. If beneficiaries are old, planning for their possible incompetence may be appropriate. The client's perception of the beneficiaries' personal habits is also important. Spendthrifts, professional students, or bad money managers may all need special treatment.

The planner also should identify contingent beneficiaries. The possibility of one or more beneficiaries predeceasing the client is real. Talking with clients about their children's possible early deaths requires tact, but is preferable to never learning what the clients would have wanted.

The fiduciaries. Planners also need to learn (a) who will be the executor of the client's estate, (b) who will be the trustee of any trust, and (c) who will be the guardian of any minor children. Clients often find those decisions difficult, so don't expect immediate answers. Indeed, the need to select a guardian is a common reason people with young children put off making a will at all. The ages and residences of some individuals may preclude them from serving as fiduciaries in the jurisdiction.

Similarly, the client should consider each individual's financial experience as relevant to qualifying and serving competently as a fiduciary. Knowing the proposed fiduciary's relationship to the client's family and to the principal beneficiaries helps avoid any antagonism in the estate administration.

Identifying the Property Involved. Information about the property of the client and of the beneficiaries is essential to the planning process.

The client's property. The planner needs to have accurate descriptions of the client's property, the manner in which title is held and the property's value. The property's value may affect tax liability or the impact of proposed gifts. The will is only one part of an overall plan, which must consider survivorship property, community property, insurance, and other forms of wealth. Knowing the forms that wealth takes, therefore, is a precondition to designing the plan. Special cautions arise when a client wants to give specific property to specific individuals ("my Rolex to Jane"). In the case of titled property and choses in action, the attorney should obtain a copy of the appropriate deed, note, or title document. In the case of important tangible personal property, the client should describe the property in writing. The planner also should develop a realistic picture of the client's future earnings and expenses, possible inheritances, and foreseeable growth or decline in asset value.

The beneficiaries' assets. The planner also needs some information about the beneficiaries' assets. For example, the relative wealth of different children may suggest different planning options for each.

Identifying the Client's Goals. Perhaps the most important information the planner must learn is what the client wants the plan to accomplish. Under pressures of time, lawyers can be tempted to assume a particular goal, rather than educating the client about options and letting the client decide. Often goals become clear only after a round-robin of lawyer suggestions, client reactions, and new proposals from all participants.

Choosing the Appropriate Tools. The next step in the planning process is to identify the tools appropriate to accomplishing the client's goals. The principal wealth transfer devices—wills, trusts, gifts, and contracts—were introduced in Chapter 1 and will receive detailed attention throughout this book. Virtually every estate plan will include a will, even if it only mirrors the intestate statute. In addition to naming personal representatives and guardians, wills can often simplify the probate process by specifying fiduciary powers or invoking simpler procedures. Lawyers also commonly advise their clients about the devices available when planning for possible disability—especially powers of attorney, both for financial management and for health care. We address disability planning in Chapter 7.

Question

What techniques might you use to help clients identify and develop their estate planning ideas?

Selected References

Georgia Akers, *On Death and Dying: Counseling the Terminally Ill Client and the Loved Ones Left Behind*, 1 Est. Plan. & Comm. Prop. L.J. 1 (2008).

Roger W. Andersen & Douglas Oliver, *Communicating Clearly: Showing Dispository Preferences with Flowcharts*, 29 Okla. City U. L. Rev. 559 (2004).

Mark Glover, *A Taxonomy of Testamentary Intent*. 23 Geo. Mason L. Rev. 569 (2016).

Deborah S. Gordon, *Reflecting on the Language of Death*, 34 Seattle Univ. L. Rev. 379 (2011).

David Horton, *Testation and Speech*, 101 Geo. L.J. 61 (2012).

Michael R. McCunney & Alyssa A. DiRusso, *Marketing Wills*, 16 Elder L.J. 33 (2008).

Marla Lyn Mitchell-Cichon, *What Mom Would Have Wanted: Lessons Learned from an Elder Law Clinic About Achieving Clients' Estate-Planning Goals*, 10 Elder L.J. 289 (2002).

Timothy P. O'Sullivan, *Family Harmony: An All Too Frequent Casualty of the Estate Planning Process*, 8 Marq. Elder's Advisor 253 (2007).

Ann Perry, The Wise Inheritor (2003).

Karen J. Sneddon, *Not Your Mother's Will: Gender, Language, and Wills*, 98 Marq. L. Rev. 1535 (2015).

Karen J. Sneddon, *In the Name of God, Amen: Language in Last Wills and Testaments*, 29 Quinnipiac L. Rev. 665 (2011).

§ 3.02 Creation of Wills

A will's validity depends both upon the testator's mental state and the formal steps taken at a "will execution" ceremony. We open with a look at what a will is and then turn to discussions of the mental element and the formalities required by a typical state statute. With that material in mind, this section closes by discussing ways to preserve a will in the face of potential challenges.

A. What's a Will?

The answer to this seemingly-simple question is familiar to law students: "it depends." For example, compare the definitions of New York and the UPC.

N.Y. Estates, Powers & Trusts Law

Section 1-2.19 Will

(a) A will is an oral declaration or written instrument [satisfying formal requirements] to take effect upon death, whereby a person disposes of property or directs how it shall not be disposed of, disposes of his body or any part thereof, exercises a power, appoints a fiduciary or makes any other provision for the administration of his estate, and which is revocable during his lifetime.

(b) Unless the context otherwise requires, the term "will" includes a "codicil".

Uniform Probate Code

Section 1-201. General Definitions.

(56)

"Will" includes codicil and any testamentary instrument that merely appoints an executor, revokes or revises another will, nominates a guardian, or expressly excludes or limits the right of an individual or class to succeed to property of the decedent passing by intestate succession.

Both statutes are broader than many definitions The recognition of "negative wills," documents that "merely" disinherit someone,[1] is unusual. Instead, most jurisdictions require a "will" to give away property. Such limitations on testamentary freedom are just a few of the many we will examine throughout this book. Protective provisions, discussed in Chapter 2, § 2.01D, also limit the ability of a decedent to dispose of certain property by will.

The UPC's failure to mention the disposition of the decedent's body or body parts is not surprising because Section 4 of the Uniform Anatomical Gift Act allows for such provision by will.[2] Although provision can be made in a will, it will make more sense to provide for anatomical dispositions by a lifetime document.

Although a will can also provide for the disposition of the decedent's remains, for example, by cremation, many states allow an individual to appoint an agent to make

---

1. Disinheritance is often prompted by feelings of ill-will. *See, e.g., In re* Estate of Beu, 333 N.Y.S.2d 858 (Sup. Ct. 1972), *aff'd*, 354 N.Y.S.2d 600 (App. Div. 1974) (disinherited daughter "has been disobedient and ungrateful and has failed to return the affection and trust that I have bestowed upon her"). Such strong language runs the risk that the testator's estate will be liable for testamentary libel. *See* Paul T. Whitcombe, *Defamation by Will: Theories and Liabilities*, 27 J. Marshall L. Rev. 749 (1994).

2. Virtually every state has enacted the Uniform Anatomical Gift Act or some equivalent. Anatomical gifts can only be made for "the purpose of transplantation, therapy, research, or education." Uniform Anatomical Gift Act § 2(3).

such decisions. *See, e.g.*, New York Health Law § 4201 (Disposition of Remains; Responsibility Therefor).

The UPC and New York refer to a "codicil," which simply means an amendment to a will. For a codicil to be effective, it must meet the same requirements as a will. Notice also the circularity in the UPC. A "will" includes a "testamentary instrument." But what's that? New York articulates the general understanding that we are talking about something taking effect upon death and revocable until then.

B. The Mental Element

The mental side of will making includes two principal requirements: testamentary intent and testamentary capacity.

1. Intention

Testamentary intent means the intent that the document or transaction control events (normally the disposition of property) at the maker's death, but create no rights or powers until that time. Normally, the testamentary nature of a decedent's intent is clear. Written documents say "Will" at the top; dying soldiers say "Give my watch to Anne." Occasionally, however, the intention behind a particular document may be unclear. In jurisdictions which recognize unwitnessed, handwritten wills, people named in letters may claim the letter was also intended to serve as a will. Ambiguous situations present difficult interpretation questions. Extrinsic evidence may help, but in some jurisdictions extrinsic evidence is not admissible to show the testamentary nature of a handwritten instrument. Consider the following case.

In re Estate of Kuralt

15 P.3d 931 (Mont. 2000)

Justice Terry N. Trieweiler delivered the Opinion of the Court.

Patricia Elizabeth Shannon, longtime personal companion of the deceased, Charles Kuralt, challenged the testamentary disposition of Kuralt's real and personal property. . . . [T]he District Court found that Kuralt executed a valid holographic codicil which expressed his testamentary intent to transfer the Madison County property to Shannon. The Estate now appeals from the order and judgment of the District Court. We affirm the District Court's order and judgment. . . .

. . . Charles Kuralt and Elizabeth Shannon maintained a longterm and intimate personal relationship. [They] desired to keep their relationship secret, and were so successful in doing so that even though Kuralt's wife, Petie, knew that Kuralt owned property in Montana, she was unaware, prior to Kuralt's untimely death, of his relationship with Shannon.

Over the nearly 30-year course of their relationship, Kuralt and Shannon saw each other regularly and maintained contact by phone and mail. Kuralt was the primary source of financial support for Shannon and established close, personal relationships with Shannon's three children. Kuralt provided financial support for a joint business venture managed by Shannon and transferred a home in Ireland to Shannon as a gift.

In 1985, Kuralt purchased a 20-acre parcel of property along the Big Hole River in Madison County, near Twin Bridges, Montana. Kuralt and Shannon constructed a cabin on this 20-acre parcel. In 1987, Kuralt purchased two additional parcels along the Big Hole which adjoined the original 20-acre parcel. These two additional parcels, one upstream and one downstream of the cabin, created a parcel of approximately 90 acres and are the primary subject of this appeal.

On May 3, 1989, Kuralt executed a holographic will[3] which stated as follows: May 3, 1989

> In the event of my death, I bequeath to Patricia Elizabeth Shannon all my interest in land, buildings, furnishings and personal belongings on Burma Road, Twin Bridges, Montana.
>
> Charles Kuralt 34 Bank St. New York, NY 10014

Although Kuralt mailed a copy of this holographic will to Shannon, he subsequently executed a formal will on May 4, 1994, in New York City. This Last Will and Testament, prepared with the assistance of counsel, does not specifically mention any of the real property owned by Kuralt. The beneficiaries of Kuralt's Last Will and Testament were his wife, Petie, and the Kuralts' two children. Neither Shannon nor her children are named as beneficiaries in Kuralt's formal will. Shannon had no knowledge of the formal will until the commencement of these proceedings.

On April 9, 1997, Kuralt deeded his interest in the original 20-acre parcel with the cabin to Shannon. The transaction was disguised as a sale. However, Kuralt supplied the "purchase" price for the 20-acre parcel to Shannon prior to the transfer. After the deed to the 20-acre parcel was filed, Shannon sent Kuralt, at his request, a blank buy-sell real estate form so that the remaining 90 acres along the Big Hole could be conveyed to Shannon in a similar manner. Apparently, it was again Kuralt's intention to provide the purchase price. The second transaction was to take place in September 1997 when Shannon, her son, and Kuralt agreed to meet at the Montana cabin.

Kuralt, however, became suddenly ill and entered a New York hospital on June 18, 1997. On that same date, Kuralt wrote the letter to Shannon which is now at the center of the current dispute:

> June 18, 1997 Dear Pat—
>
> Something is terribly wrong with me and they can't figure out what. After cat-scans and a variety of cardiograms, they agree it's not lung cancer or heart

3. Like Montana, many jurisdictions recognize wills made without witnesses, but in the testator's handwriting. *See* Page ____.

> trouble or blood clot. So they're putting me in the hospital today to concentrate on infectious diseases. I am getting worse, barely able to get out of bed, but still have high hopes for recovery . . . if only I can get a diagnosis! Curiouser and curiouser! I'll keep you informed. I'll have the lawyer visit the hospital to be sure you inherit the rest of the place in MT. if it comes to that.
>
> I send love to you & [your youngest daughter,] Shannon. Hope things are better there!
>
> Love, C.

Enclosed with this letter were two checks made payable to Shannon, one for $8000 and the other for $9000. Kuralt did not seek the assistance of an attorney to devise the remaining 90 acres of Big Hole land to Shannon. Therefore, when Kuralt died unexpectedly, Shannon sought to probate the letter of June 18, 1997, as a valid holographic codicil to Kuralt's formal 1994 will.

The Estate opposed Shannon's Petition for Ancillary Probate based on its contention that the June 18, 1997 letter expressed only a future intent to make a will. . . .

The record supports the District Court's finding that the June 18, 1997 letter expressed Kuralt's intent to effect a posthumous transfer of his Montana property to Shannon. Kuralt and Shannon enjoyed a long, close personal relationship which continued up to the last letter Kuralt wrote Shannon on June 18, 1997, in which he enclosed checks to her in the amounts of $8000 and $9000. Likewise, Kuralt and Shannon's children had a long, family-like relationship which included significant financial support.

The District Court focused on the last few months of Kuralt's life to find that the letter demonstrated his testamentary intent. The conveyance of the 20-acre parcel for no real consideration and extrinsic evidence that Kuralt intended to convey the remainder of the Montana property to Shannon in a similar fashion provides substantial factual support for the District Court's determination that Kuralt intended that Shannon have the rest of the Montana property.

The June 18, 1997 letter expressed Kuralt's desire that Shannon inherit the remainder of the Montana property. That Kuralt wrote the letter in extremis is supported by the fact that he died two weeks later. Although Kuralt intended to transfer the remaining land to Shannon, he was reluctant to consult a lawyer to formalize his intent because he wanted to keep their relationship secret. Finally, the use of the term "inherit" underlined by Kuralt reflected his intention to make a posthumous disposition of the property. . . .

. . . Accordingly, we affirm the judgment of the District Court.

Charles Kuralt's Codicil:

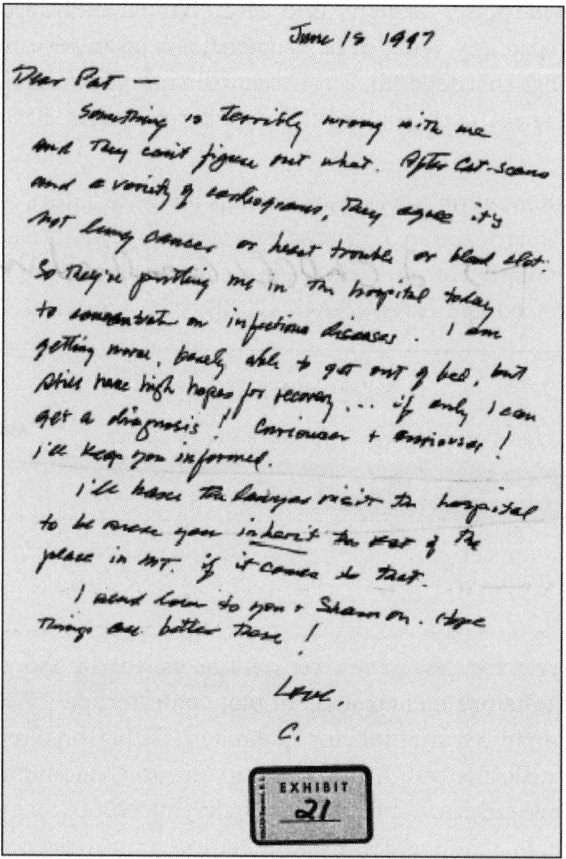

June 18 1997

Dear Pat —

Something is terribly wrong with me and they can't figure out what. After cat-scans and a variety of cardiograms, they agree it's not lung cancer or heart trouble or blood clot. So they're putting me in the hospital today to concentrate on infectious diseases. I am getting worse, barely able to get out of bed, but still have high hopes for recovery ... if only I can get a diagnosis!! Curiouser + curiouser! I'll keep you informed.

I'll have the lawyer visit the hospital to be sure you inherit the rest of the place in MT. if it comes to that.

I send love to you + Shannon. Hope things are better there!

Love,

C.

EXHIBIT 21

Notes and Questions

1. Charles Kuralt was a well-respected journalist perhaps best known, ironically enough, for his "On the Road" reports. For some video, see http://www.youtube.com/results?search_query=charles+kuralt+on+the+road&aq=0.

2. Oral W. Fountain left a handwritten document, titled "Last Will," listing her children's names and certain property under each name. The "will" was signed and witnessed, but failed because it lacked any dispositive language. *Edmundson v. Estate of Fountain*, 189 S.W.3d 427 (Ark. 2004).

3. A document that is by its terms contingent on the happening of future events may still exhibit testamentary intent. If the events occur, the will is entitled to probate; if they do not, probate will be denied. Conditional language is often ambiguous, however, and may indicate only the reason for making the will, not a condition upon its effectiveness. In the latter case, the will is valid even if the event does not occur. *Compare Mason v. Mason*, 268 S.E.2d 67 (W. Va. 1980) (Will read, "I am in the hospital for surgery, and in case I do not survive. . . ." Testator survived surgery and died later. Will valid.), *with Ellerbeck v. Haws*, 265 P.2d 404 (Utah 1953); *In re Estate of Perez*, 155 S.W.3d 599 (Tex. App. 2004) (wills invalid on very similar facts).

4. Sarah executed a handwritten document, internally described as a will, which purported to dispose of her property and which named executors. It contained a paragraph stating that "My Will not be Probated, it is just a personal conviction of my own. If any things are added Mr. T.T. Skeen will know about it." Should the document be probated as the decedent's will? *See Taylor v. Hodges*, 507 So. 2d 912 (Ala. 1987) (yes).

5. In a shift from focus on the *testator* to focus on the testator's *intention*, several states and the UPC have adopted an idea that started in South Dakota. They now recognize in some situations a will executed by a conservator. *See, e.g.*, Cal. Prob. Code § 2580(b)(13); S.D. Codified Laws § 29A-5-420(8); UPC § 5-411(a)(7), (b).

Selected Reference

Ralph C. Brashier, *Policy, Perspective, and the Proxy Will*, 61 S.C. L. Rev. 63 (2009).

2. Testamentary Capacity

A court requiring a testator to have "testamentary capacity" may be referring to the common rule that the testator be a certain age, usually 18. More commonly, the term refers to the testator's mental state. In that context, capacity might be lacking in either of two senses. First, the testator might be suffering from mental deficiency, the general lack of ability to put things together. Second, the testator may be operating under an "insane delusion" over something in particular.

Mental deficiency. Mental deficiency concerns the general capacity to make a will. Thus, a testator who has a guardian because he cannot handle his own affairs may still be able to make a will. *See Parish v. Parish*, 704 S.E.2d 99 (Va. 2011) (conservator appointed in 1983 after brain injury; will executed in 2002). The key question is whether the testator understands enough things relating to the will-making process. Though courts use a variety of formulations, they tend to require a testator to:

(1) know the nature and extent of his or her property;

(2) know "the natural objects of the testator's bounty," namely, those persons most of us would expect to take the property;

(3) understand the basics of the plan for disposing of the property; and

(4) understand how the above elements interrelate.

The testator's knowledge and understanding need not be perfect. Rather, they must be sufficient under the circumstances. The larger and more complex the estate, the greater the capacity required. If a testator suffers from mental deficiency at the time the will was executed, the whole will is invalid. On the other hand, if a testator fades in and out, but executes the will during a lucid interval, the will is valid.

Insane delusion. Insane delusion is different from mental deficiency. It relates to specific beliefs unsupported by any rational explanation. If particular provisions of the will are the result of the delusion, they are void. Frequently, the whole will fails when an individual is found to have an insane delusion.

In re Estate of Romero

126 P.3d 228 (Colo. App. 2005)

HAWTHORNE, JUDGE.

...

This case involves a contested probate of a formal will executed by decedent [Robert Ramon Romero].... Decedent devised a gift of $500 to each of his children and left the remainder of his estate to his mother and sister in equal shares, with a provision that if either his mother or sister predeceased him, the remaining beneficiary would take the entire remainder. Because decedent's mother predeceased him, his sister was left as the sole beneficiary of the residuary estate.

Contestants [his children] filed objections, claiming that decedent did not have the testamentary capacity to execute a will.... In support of their assertions, they relied primarily on the uncontested facts that decedent suffered from mental illness and that he had been a protected person under a Veterans Administration (VA) guardianship over his financial affairs.

A hearing was held on the petition for formal probate. Contestants presented, inter alia, expert witness testimony from the physician who treated decedent for schizophrenia. While this physician testified that decedent suffered from auditory hallucinations, the physician was unable to connect them with execution of decedent's will and, moreover, saw decedent for only a few minutes on three occasions during the eighteen months prior to the signing of the will. The probate court accordingly discounted his testimony.

Instead, the probate court credited the testimony of the attorney who prepared the will, because it found him to be the only individual with personal knowledge of decedent's testamentary capacity when the will was executed. The attorney testified that he met with decedent on four separate occasions, including one visit to decedent's home. He testified that although decedent's mother transported decedent to and from the attorney's office, she was present neither during his conversations with decedent nor during the actual execution of the will, but remained in the office waiting area. He further testified that decedent expressed his desire to leave his entire estate to his mother and his sister because of his minimal contact with his children and in return for all the love and support he had received from his mother and sister over the years. The attorney also testified that it was only upon his suggestion that decedent made a small bequest to his children to demonstrate that his exclusion of them as primary beneficiaries was intentional. He further testified that he had "no doubt in his mind" when the will was executed that decedent fully understood the consequences of his action.

After considering all the evidence, the probate court found that contestants did not prove by a preponderance of the evidence that decedent was not of sound mind when he executed his will. The court held that neither the evidence of mental illness nor the mere existence of a VA guardianship was sufficient, in and of itself, to prove lack of testamentary capacity. . . .

I.

Contestants first contend that the probate court erred in failing to conclude that the will was invalid because decedent lacked testamentary capacity. We disagree.

A person has testamentary capacity if he or she is an "individual eighteen or more years of age who is of sound mind." Section 15-11-501, C.R.S. 2004. A testator's soundness of mind may be evaluated under either the test set forth in *Cunningham v. Stender*, 127 Colo. 293, 255 P.2d 977 (1953), or the insane delusion test. *See Breeden v. Stone*, 992 P.2d 1167 (Colo. 2000).

Under the *Cunningham* test, a person has testamentary capacity when the person (1) understands the nature of the act, (2) knows the extent of his or her property, (3) understands the proposed testamentary disposition, and (4) knows the natural objects of his or her bounty, and (5) the will represents the person's wishes. . . . An individual lacks testamentary capacity under the insane delusion test when he or she suffers from an insane delusion that materially affects the disposition of the will.[4]

Once a proponent of a will has offered prima facie proof that the will was duly executed, any contestant has the burden of establishing lack of testamentary intent or capacity, undue influence, fraud, duress, mistake, or revocation by a preponderance of the evidence.

A.

Contestants maintain that the facts demonstrated that decedent did not know the extent of his property and therefore lacked testamentary capacity under that prong of the *Cunningham* test. We are not persuaded.

. . .

The appointment of a conservator or guardian is not a determination of testamentary incapacity of the protected person. Section 15-14-409(4), C.R.S. 2004.

There is scant Colorado case law detailing what specific knowledge is required for a testator to be deemed to know the extent of his or her property. However, the cases which touch upon this issue, including *Cunningham* itself, indicate that it is sufficient that a testator comprehend the "kind and character of his [or her] property" or understand, generally, the nature and extent of the property to be bequeathed. *Cunningham, supra*, 127 Colo. at 300, 255 P.2d at 981 . . . .

4. If the decedent suffered from an insane delusion that did not materially affect the will dispositions, then the will may be admitted to probate, but the specific disposition may be stricken. [Eds.]

In other words, "A perfect memory is not an element of testamentary capacity. A testator may forget the existence of part of his estate . . . and yet make a valid will." 1 *Page on Wills* § 12.22 (rev. 2003).

. . .

An ability to index the major categories of property constituting an individual's estate was found sufficient to establish testamentary capacity in *Breeden, supra*, 992 P.2d at 1173. This holding is consistent with the approach taken by courts in other jurisdictions with similar tests for testamentary capacity. . . .

Here, the probate court found that decedent understood that his assets comprised the accumulation of whatever amounts were left over from his VA and social security benefits after his living expenses had been deducted. The probate court concluded that decedent's failure to know the actual amount of money in his VA account was not surprising or fatal, given that the VA's routine practice was not to inform its wards how much money they had in their VA accounts, to protect the wards from exploitation. Further, the court found that the relative size of the estate was not a motivating factor in decedent's decision to leave his estate to his mother and sister, as decedent's attorney testified that decedent's original intent was to preclude his children from taking any of his estate at all.

Under these circumstances, we agree with the probate court that decedent's lack of knowledge of the actual value of his estate did not affect his testamentary capacity.

B.

Contestants next contend that the probate court erred in concluding that decedent did not have an insane delusion regarding the amount of his estate. Specifically, they argue that decedent had an insane delusion that his estate would be minimal or nominal and that if he had realized the actual value, he would have left a larger bequest to them. We conclude there was no error.

An insane delusion is a persistent belief in something that has no existence in fact, which belief is adhered to in spite of all evidence to the contrary. . . . The contestant bears the burden of proving that the testator suffered from an insane delusion, that he was under such a delusion at the time of making his will, that the insane delusion materially affected the disposition made in the will, and that the will was the product of the insane delusion. . . .

. . . [D]ecedent's estate was valued at approximately $90,000 when the will was executed and approximately $450,000 at decedent's death. His attorney testified that while decedent could not articulate the value of his assets, he expressed an understanding that his assets came from his VA benefits, that his VA guardian allocated him enough money to meet his personal needs and to pay for his living expenses, and that his estate would consist of the money left over in his accounts under VA supervision after his expenses were met. Moreover, his attorney testified that because he was familiar with the management of VA guardianship accounts, he did not press decedent about the value of the estate. While the attorney described decedent's account as nominal, this was his own assessment rather than a quote from decedent.

A field examiner for the VA testified that although a VA guardian is required to file an annual accounting with the court and with the VA, veterans would not usually be in a position to know the exact value of their estates because they were not furnished copies of their annual accounts. If veterans inquired, they were told they could get a copy of their accountings at the court where the documentation was filed.

The probate court concluded that it was not surprising that decedent did not know the value of his estate, given his apparent satisfaction with the money-handling arrangement and the lack of documentation as to the dollar amount of his VA account. Moreover, the probate court specifically credited the attorney's testimony that decedent was not motivated by the comparative size of the amounts passing to his children and to his mother and sister.

The probate court's findings are supported by the record, and under these circumstances, we conclude there was no error.

C.

Contestants maintain that the probate court erred in finding decedent had testamentary capacity in light of the VA guardianship.... We disagree.

... [C]ontestants point to a VA regulation that defines a mentally incompetent individual subject to guardianship as one who "lacks the mental capacity to contract or to manage his or her own affairs, including disbursement of funds without limitation." 38 C.F.R. § 3.353(a).

The VA regulations, however, specifically provide that "lack of testamentary capacity should not be confused with ... mental incompetence." 38 C.F.R. § 3.355(c). The regulations provide that there is a general but rebuttable presumption that every testator possessed testamentary capacity and reasonable doubts should be resolved in favor of testamentary capacity....

Here, a VA field administrator testified that the VA rating of incompetency meant that decedent was incompetent only as to the handling of his VA disability funds and did not mean he was incapacitated as to other matters. The field administrator further testified that a veteran, even if incompetent to handle VA funds, could still enter into contracts similar to wills by naming insurance beneficiaries and that, in fact, the VA had accepted such a designation from decedent. Accordingly, the VA had found decedent to have testamentary capacity, despite his VA guardianship, under a test similar to the testamentary capacity test established in Colorado....

Section 15-14-409(4), C.R.S. 2004, specifically provides that the appointment of a conservator or the entry of another protective order is not a determination of the testamentary incapacity of the protected person. Moreover, § 28-5-219, C.R.S. 2004, provides that neither the fact that a person has been rated incompetent by the VA nor the fact that a guardian has been appointed for the person shall be construed as a legal adjudication of insanity or mental incompetency....

Given the statutory framework and the record in this matter, we conclude that the probate court did not err in finding that decedent had testamentary capacity in spite of his VA guardianship.

... [The court also rejected the undue influence argument.]

The judgment is affirmed.

JUDGE MARQUEZ and JUDGE GRAHAM concur.

Robert P. Roca, *Determining Decisional Capacity: A Medical Perspective*

62 Fordham L. Rev. 1177, 1195 (1994)

The special role of physicians in determining decisional capacity lies in judging whether the symptoms of a mental disorder compromise the ability of a person to make a particular decision. Psychiatric diagnosis plays a major role in this judgment; it serves as an anchor and validator, helping protect persons against ageism and other inappropriate influences on capacity judgments. But psychiatric diagnosis is not sufficient. There must also be direct evidence that psychiatric symptoms are specifically interfering with decision-making. Thus the process of assessing decisional capacity has two principal components: (1) the psychiatric history and mental status examination—to determine whether a diagnosable psychiatric disorder is present—and (2) specific inquiry into the patient's understanding of and reasoning about the decision at hand—to determine whether psychiatric symptoms are disabling decision-making. When this process reveals that the symptoms of a psychiatric disorder are determining the patient's choice, a judgment of incapacity is clearly justified. But persons with psychiatric disorders, including dementia, may be quite capable of making particular decisions, and persons without psychiatric disorders may make unwise, unpopular or eccentric—but nonetheless competent—choices. Neither psychiatric disorders nor foolish choices by themselves signal incapacity.

Notes and Questions

1. Note how important the lawyer's testimony was in *Romero.* One lesson: keep good notes.

2. A lawyer preparing a will for someone who clearly lacks testamentary capacity would be committing fraud, an act prohibited by both tort law and ethical rules. *See* Paul G. Haskell, Preface to Wills, Trusts and Administration 324 (2d ed. 1994). Marginal cases pose a different problem. Consider Rule 1.14(9) of the Model Rules of Professional Conduct: "When a client's ability to make adequately considered decisions in connection with the representation is impaired, whether because of minority, mental disability or for some other reason, the lawyer shall, as far as reasonably

possible, maintain a normal client-lawyer relationship with the client." What steps might you take to maintain a "normal" relationship?

3. Although insane delusion and mental deficiency are separate doctrines, *Romero* illustrates how in a particular case arguments about one can dovetail with the other. In *Hargrove's Will*, 28 N.Y.S.2d 571 (App. Div. 1941), for example, a delusion as to family membership arguably negated the capacity to understand who were the natural objects of the testator's bounty. There the will was valid although testator mistakenly believed children of his ex-wife were not his.

4. Another complicating factor can be determining whether a belief comes from an insane delusion or a simple mistake.

5. Wills can be weird while being perfectly valid. For some interesting examples, see http://www.cnn.com/2009/LIVING/wayoflife/08/31/bizarre.will.stipulations/index.html. For a reality-TV approach, see http://investigation.discovery.com/videos/the-will/.

6. As a practical matter, the flexibility inherent in capacity doctrine allows for a balancing of testator autonomy on the one hand with protection of the family on the other. Such flexibility opens the door both for frivolous litigation from disappointed family members and for courts willing substitute their views for those of the testator. The undue influence doctrine we discuss next is subject to the same critique. A different question is how many actually pass through those doors.

Selected References

Bradley E.S. Fogel, *The Completely Insane Law of Partial Insanity: The Impact of Monomania on Testamentary Capacity*, 42 Real Prop. Prob. & Tr. J. 67 (2007).

Mark Glover, *Rethinking the Testamentary Capacity of Minors*, 79 Mo. L. Rev. 69 (2014).

Joseph Karl Grant, *Running Past Landmines—The Estate Attorney's Dilemma: Ethically Counseling the Client with Alzheimer's Disease*, 24 Elder L.J. 101 (2016).

Joyce Moore, *Will Contests: From Start to Finish*, 44 St. Mary's L.J. 97 (2013).

Thomas E. Simmons, *Testamentary Incapacity, Undue influence, and Insane Delusions*, 60 S.D. L. Rev. 175 (2015).

Fredrick E. Vars, *Toward a General Theory of Standards of Proof*, 60 Cath. U. L. Rev. 1 (2010).

3. *Undue Influence*

Contests based on lack of capacity often include the additional claim that the will was the product of undue influence. While distinct theories, the two often arise from the same sorts of fact patterns. If the person who benefited from the will also had a hand in its preparation, an undue influence claim is likely. Most courts focus on the notion that the influencer coerced the testator to create a will reflecting the influencer's intention, not the testator's. The Restatement (Third) of Property (Wills and Other Donative Transfers) offers the following in comment to § 8.3:

> [C]ircumstantial evidence is sufficient to raise an inference of undue influence if the contestant proves that (1) the donor was susceptible to undue influence, (2) the alleged wrongdoer had an opportunity to exert undue influence, (3) the alleged wrongdoer had a disposition to exert undue influence, and (4) there was a result appearing to be the effect of the undue influence.

A continuing question, however, is how to tell when influence is "undue." Courts tend to look at a variety of factors, in a variety of combinations, only some of which might be present in an individual case. In addition to the Restatement's list, among the most commonly-identified factors are:

- the existence of a confidential relationship;
- the influencing beneficiary's participation in some part of the will's preparation;
- the extent of secrecy and haste;
- the extent the new plan changes earlier plans;
- the extent the beneficiary's benefit is unwarranted or unfair in light of other possible claimants; and
- the existence of independent advice.

Establishing (or negating) the existence of a confidential relationship can be particularly important because the presence (or absence) of such a relationship can affect the burden of proof.

Restatement (Third) of Property (Wills and Other Donative Transfers)

§ 8.3, comments

f.

Presumption of undue influence. A presumption of undue influence arises if the alleged wrongdoer was in a confidential relationship with the donor and there were suspicious circumstances surrounding the preparation, formulation, or execution of the donative transfer. . . .

g.

Confidential relationship—fiduciary, reliant, or dominant-subservient. Traditionally, the single term "confidential relationship" has been used to describe a relationship that gives rise to a presumption of undue influence if coupled with suspicious circumstances. When examined more closely, the term "confidential relationship" embraces three sometimes distinct relationships—fiduciary, reliant, or dominant-subservient. . . .

A fiduciary relationship is one in which the confidential relationship arises from a settled category of fiduciary obligation. Some fiduciary relationships are between the donor and a hired professional. For example, an attorney is in a fiduciary relationship with his or her client. . . . Other fiduciary relationships are not necessarily between the donor and a hired professional. For example, an agent under a power of attorney is in a fiduciary relationship with his or her principal, but the donor's agent under a power of attorney frequently is a close family member or trusted friend who receives no fee for acting as agent. . . .

Whether a reliant relationship exists is a question of fact. The contestant must establish that there was a relationship based on special trust and confidence, for example, that the donor was accustomed to be guided by the judgment or advice of the alleged wrongdoer or was justified in placing confidence in the belief that the alleged wrongdoer would act in the interest of the donor. . . .

Whether a dominant-subservient relationship exists is a question of fact. The contestant must establish that the donor was subservient to the alleged wrongdoer's dominant influence. Such a relationship might exist between a hired caregiver and an ill or feeble donor or between an adult child and an ill or feeble parent.

In a particular case, these three relationships might overlap. . . .

h.

Suspicious circumstances. The existence of a confidential relationship is not sufficient to raise a presumption of undue influence. There must also be suspicious circumstances surrounding the preparation, execution, or formulation of the donative transfer. . . .

California recently tried to clarify the meaning of "undue influence" as follows:

California Probate Code

Section 86

"Undue influence" has the same meaning as defined in Section 15610.70 of the Welfare and Institutions Code. It is the intent of the Legislature that this section supplement the common law meaning of undue influence without superseding or interfering with the operation of that law.

California Welfare and Institutions Code

Section 15610.76

(a) "Undue influence" means excessive persuasion that causes another person to act or refrain from acting *by overcoming that person's free will* and results in inequity.

In determining whether a result was produced by undue influence, all of the following shall be considered:

(1) The vulnerability of the victim. Evidence of vulnerability may include, but is not limited to, incapacity, illness, disability, injury, age, education, impaired cognitive function, emotional distress, isolation, or dependency, and whether the influencer knew or should have known of the alleged victim's vulnerability.

(2) The influencer's apparent authority. Evidence of apparent authority may include, but is not limited to, status as a fiduciary, family member, care provider, health care professional, legal professional, spiritual adviser, expert, or other qualification.

(3) The actions or tactics used by the influencer. Evidence of actions or tactics used may include, but is not limited to, all of the following:

(A) Controlling necessaries of life, medication, the victim's interactions with others, access to information, or sleep.

(B) Use of affection, intimidation, or coercion.

(C) Initiation of changes in personal or property rights, use of haste or secrecy in effecting those changes, effecting changes at inappropriate times and places, and claims of expertise in effecting changes.

(4) The equity of the result. Evidence of the equity of the result may include, but is not limited to, the economic consequences to the victim, any divergence from the victim's prior intent or course of conduct or dealing, the relationship of the value conveyed to the value of any services or consideration received, or the appropriateness of the change in light of the length and nature of the relationship.

(b) Evidence of an inequitable result, without more, is not sufficient to prove undue influence.

In re Estate of Saucier

908 So. 2d 883 (2005)

Ishee, J., For the Court:

. . .

[Jerry Saucier died August 9, 2003, of congestive heart failure due to alcoholic cardiomyopathy.] During his life, Jerry executed two documents which were later produced and submitted to probate. The first will, later propounded by the Appellant [James Saucier, Jerry's father], was a holographic document[5] dated January 27, 2002. The second will was a typewritten will dated January 27, 2003, leaving all of Jerry's

5. Holographic wills are documents in the testator's handwriting. In some states, they are valid wills if they lack witnesses, but meet other requirements.

property, both real and personal, to [Susan] Tatum. There is no dispute as to the authenticity of the two wills presented for probate.

Under the holographic will the balance of Jerry's estate would have passed to his son, from whom Jerry was estranged at the time of his death. At trial, Saucier challenged the second will put forth by Tatum on the grounds that the will was the product of Tatum's undue influence over Jerry at the time it was executed. The facts presented at trial regarding the close relationship between Tatum and the decedent established that Tatum provided care and assistance to Jerry as his health declined by, for example, cleaning his house and by taking him to detoxification programs and psychiatric appointments. Tatum and Jerry also dated at least one year prior to his death. Testimony at trial illustrated that the pair saw each other every day of the year prior to his death, that they were physically intimate, and that at some point the pair had made plans to marry. Tatum was heavily involved in preparing his will. Tatum located and provided the form used for the second will, and accompanied Jerry to the bank where the instrument was executed. Upon learning that the will had not been properly executed, Tatum brought Jerry to the bank a second time in order to affect a valid execution.

... [T]he trial court found that Tatum "played an instrumental part in seeing that the will was created ...." While Jerry admitted to his father that he consumed approximately one-fifth of whisky a day, there was no testimony that Jerry was intoxicated at the time of the preparation and execution of his will. Witnesses from the bank where the instrument was executed provided that they thought Jerry was competent at the time of the execution, and that while present, Tatum did not appear to be an active or interfering force in the execution of the will. The judgment entered by the chancery court found that the will propounded by Tatum was not the result of undue influence, and allowed the document to be entered into probate. Aggrieved by this decision, Saucier asserts the following errors on appeal: (1) whether the chancery court erred in failing to find that the second will was the product of undue influence by Tatum; and (2) whether Tatum failed to rebut the presumption of undue influence by clear and convincing evidence.

ISSUES AND ANALYSIS

I. Whether the chancery court erred in failing to find that the second will was the product of undue influence by Tatum.

Saucier asserts that the trial court erred in failing to find that second will was the product of undue influence. Saucier asserts specifically that the relationship between Tatum and Jerry was confidential and that Tatum was instrumental in the formation of the second will, thereby creating a presumption of undue influence.

"In an action contesting a will, a presumption of undue influence arises where there is a confidential or fiduciary relationship." *In re Fankboner v. Pallatin*, 638 So. 2d 493, 495 (Miss. 1994) (citing *Mullins v. Ratcliff*, 515 So. 2d 1183, 1192 (Miss. 1987)). "Suspicious circumstances, along with the confidential relationship, also give rise to a presumption of undue influence." *Id.* (Citing *Estate of Lawler v. Weston*, 451 So. 2d

739, 741 (Miss. 1984)). In *Croft v. Alder*, 237 Miss. 713, 722-23, 115 So. 2d 683, 686 (1959), the Mississippi Supreme Court held:

> Where a confidential relation exists between a testator and a beneficiary under his will, and the beneficiary has been actively concerned in some way with the preparation or execution of it, the law raises a presumption that the beneficiary has exercised undue influence over the testator, and casts upon the beneficiary the burden of disproving undue influence by clear and convincing evidence.

Saucier argues on appeal that a confidential relationship, as well as suspicious circumstances, created such a presumption of undue influence in this case, and that as such, Tatum should have been forced to rebut that presumption by clear and convincing evidence.

The factors utilized by this court to determine whether a confidential relationship existed are as follows:

> (1) whether one person has been taken care of by others, (2) whether one person maintains a close relationship with another, (3) whether one person is provided transportation and has their medical care provided for by another, (4) whether one person maintains joint accounts with another, (5) whether one is physically or mentally weak, (6) whether one is of advanced age or poor health, and (7) whether there exists a power of attorney between one and another.

In re Estate of Dabney, 740 So. 2d 915, 919 (P12) (Miss. 1999). In examining factor one, Tatum's own testimony established that she provided assistance and care to Jerry. However, in many instances, despite his alcoholism, Jerry was capable of caring for himself in a manner common to functional alcoholics. Because the parties saw each other on a daily basis, were physically intimate, and had made some generalized plans to marry, these facts clearly indicate that a close relationship was maintained between Jerry and Tatum in regards to factor two. While Tatum did provide transportation for Jerry, most notably during the formation of the will, this was mostly due to the fact that Jerry's license had been suspended. There is some evidence to suggest that Tatum transported Jerry to a handful of psychiatric appointments, and provided other more generalized assistance as considered by factor three. As to factor four, there is no evidence to suggest that Jerry and Tatum held joint accounts, although we note that Jerry entrusted Tatum with the keys to his safety deposit box. As to factor five, Jerry was physically ravaged by his alcoholism. However, whether Jerry was mentally weak presents a closer question. Saucier asserts on appeal that Jerry's liquor consumption, and a past incident where police were called to his home after a bout of hallucinations evidences Jerry's weakened mental state. Saucier also claims that Jerry "badly mismanaged" some apartments owned by his father. Finally, Saucier cites the statement of Jerry's psychiatrist who observed that he was "shaky, tremulous," and that Jerry "just seemed uncomfortable."

Tatum has put forth ample evidence to indicate that Jerry was fully capable of conducting his own affairs, was able to manage his own business and employees, and for the most part was competent to handle his own affairs. In fact, his own psychiatrist, Shannon Johnson, stated that Jerry was "in his right mind." Although Jerry evidenced specific instances of mental weakness, the weight of the evidence mitigates against finding that he functioned within a continually weakened mental state. As to factors six and seven, we note that Jerry was in a weakened physical state, and that no power of attorney was granted to Tatum by Jerry.

Taking all of the *Dabney* factors as a whole, it is clear that the relationship between Jerry and Tatum was confidential in nature. Furthermore, the chancellor found that Tatum was "a moving force" in the creation of the second will. The confidential relationship of the parties and Tatum's role in the creation of the will suffice to create a presumption of undue influence. Furthermore, according to *Croft*, Tatum's status as a beneficiary under the will further bolsters this presumption. *Croft*, 115 So. 2d at 686....

II. Whether Tatum failed to rebut the presumption of undue influence by clear and convincing evidence.

Saucier asserts in his second assignment of error that Tatum failed to rebut the presumption of undue influence. In the case *sub judice*, due to the fact that the circumstances give rise to a presumption of undue influence, the burden off going forward with the proof shifted to Tatum to prove by clear and convincing evidence that (1) Tatum acted in good faith in the confidential relationship with Jerry; (2) Jerry acted with full knowledge and deliberation of his actions and their consequences when he executed the second will; and (3) that Jerry exhibited independent consent and action....

To determine whether Tatum acted in good faith, we must examine the facts surrounding the procurement of the second will. It is undisputed that Tatum was instrumental in the drafting of the will. However, she and Jerry worked together in this regard, and her role in drafting the will is not alone determinative of bad faith. Numerous disinterested persons witnessed the signing of the will. The first subscribing witness to the will, Teressa Rogers, an assistant manager at the bank, testified that she questioned Jerry regarding whether the will represented his wishes, and whether he wanted to sign the document. She further testified that Jerry answered both questions in the affirmative, and that Jerry appeared to be in his right mind and was not intoxicated. The testimony of the second subscribing witness, Jacque Forrester, was not heard as the parties stipulated that his testimony was merely corroborative of the testimony of Rogers. "Secondly, the place of the execution of the will and the persons in whose presence the will was executed are significant." *In re Will of Fankboner*, 638 So. 2d at 496. The second will of Jerry Saucier was executed in the open at a branch of the Union Planters Bank before two disinterested subscribing witnesses and a notary public. "The third and fourth factors are the consideration/fee that was paid and the identity of the person who paid the fee." *Id.* In this case, no consideration or fee was paid in the drafting of the will. The fifth and final factor that should be considered to determine the "good faith" of Tatum is the secrecy and openness given the execution of the will. *Id.* The evidence before us is clear that the execution of the will was open and well observed. We therefore find substantial evidence that supports a finding that Tatum acted in good faith.

We now turn to the question of whether Jerry acted with full knowledge and deliberation of his actions and their consequences when he signed the will. The testimony of the subscribing witnesses is again pertinent in this regard. All of the testimony provided regarding the signing of the will at the bank indicated that Jerry was acting in accordance with his own wishes and of his own volition. There is simply scant evidence to conclude that Tatum abused her relationship with Jerry either by asserting dominance over him or by substituting her intent for his. . . . As to the third factor . . . , we must determine whether Jerry exhibited independent consent and action. The evidence in this case is legion toward establishing that Jerry exhibited independent consent and action, and that the second will represents his final wishes independent and free from of any undue influence by Tatum. The evidence *sub judice* is clear and convincing in establishing that Tatum did not substitute her will for Jerry's, and any presumption to the contrary is clearly rebutted . . . .

THE JUDGMENT OF THE CHANCERY COURT OF FORREST COUNTY IS AFFIRMED. . . .

Notes

1. The burden of proving undue influence normally is upon the contestant. As *Saucier* illustrates, the burden may shift when the party charged with asserting influence was in a confidential relationship with the decedent, but courts disagree on the nature of any shift. As *Saucier* illustrates, the burden of proof typically shifts to the proponent when a contestant demonstrates the existence of a confidential relationship and suspicious circumstances. *But see Clinger v. Clinger*, 872 N.W.2d 37 (Neb. 2015) (rejecting will contestants' proposed jury instruction that the demonstration of a confidential relationship, coupled with other suspicious circumstances, gives rise to a presumption of undue influence, which shifts the burden of proof to the will's proponents, holding instead that such proof gives rise only to a "probable inference" and that the ultimate burden of proof remains on the contestants at all times).

Evidence that the testator received independent advice is often said to overcome the presumption. *See Heinrich v. Silvernail*, 500 N.E.2d 835 (Mass. App. Ct. 1986) (independent advice from lawyer). The adequacy of any independent review, however, can itself be challenged. *See In re Estate of Winans*, 183 Cal. App. 4th 102 (2010) (question of fact as to whether a certificate of independent review is valid).

2. Like an insane delusion, undue influence may affect either a bequest or the entire will. If the influence attacks the entire plan, then the will fails; if the influence affects only a single bequest, a court will invalidate that gift, leaving the remainder of the plan unaffected. *See, e.g., In re Estate of Kremer*, 845 N.W.2d 70 (Iowa Ct. App. 2014) (three of five beneficiaries exercised undue influence and lost their gifts, but gifts to

the other two could stand because they could remain without violating the testator's general intent.)

3. Undue influence can apply even when the benefit goes to someone other than the influencer. *See* Cal. Prob. Code § 21380 (among others: relatives, partners, and employees of the influencer); *Estate of Gerard*, 911 P.2d 266 (Okla. 1995) (Friend of the testator took increasing "interest" in him. Finding a confidential relationship between them, the court imputed the resulting undue influence to the friend's husband.); *Estate of Maheras*, 897 P.2d 268 (Okla. 1995) (influence by pastor, gift to church invalidated).

4. Evidence that the testator received independent advice is often said to overcome a presumption of undue influence. *See Heinrich v. Silvernail*, 500 N.E.2d 835 (Mass. App. Ct. 1986) (independent advice from lawyer). Advising a client to get independent advice as a way to "cleanse" a suspect gift may not only save the gift, but also save the lawyer from malpractice. *See Osornio v. Weingarten*, 21 Cal. Rptr. 3d 246 (Ct. App. 2004) (drafting lawyer owed duty of care to prospective beneficiary—who was also care custodian—to ensure that presumptive disqualification would be overcome).

5. Many jurisdictions apply special scrutiny to gifts to lawyers, for good reason. Florida actually invalidates gifts to lawyers or their relatives if the lawyer was involved in the will's drafting or execution, unless the lawyer or relative is also related to the testator. *See* Fla. Stat. 732.806. Most states raise a presumption of undue influence. *See, e.g., Matter of Putnam*, 257 N.Y. 140 (1931). Conflict of interest concerns can extend beyond a gift to oneself. In *Haynes v. First National State Bank of New Jersey*, 432 A.2d 890 (N.J. 1981), lawyer Grant drafted a will for Isabel, giving most of her estate to her daughter, another of Grant's clients. Isabel left only token gifts to the children of Isabel's predeceased other daughter. Because of the conflict of interest, the court raised a presumption of undue influence, which could be overcome only by clear and convincing evidence.

Whether or not a disposition to a lawyer is invalidated, a lawyer as a matter of ethics should not be the scrivener. Rule 1.8(c) of the Model Rules of Professional Conduct provides: "(c) A lawyer shall not solicit any substantial gift from a client, including a testamentary gift, or prepare on behalf of a client an instrument giving the lawyer or a person related to the lawyer any substantial gift unless the lawyer or other recipient of the gift is related to the client. For purposes of this paragraph, related persons include a spouse, child, grandchild, parent, grandparent or other relative or individual with whom the lawyer or the client maintains a close, familial relationship."

6. The not-uncommon practice of a drafting lawyer being named as executor raises solicitation and conflict of interest concerns. In New York, lawyers who are named in a will prepared by them (or anyone affiliated with them) must disclose the following to their clients before such a will is executed: (1) (almost) anyone can serve as an executor; (2) absent a contrary agreement, executors receive statutorily-set

commissions; (3) absent execution of a disclosure agreement, an attorney who serves as an executor is entitled to one-half of the commissions to which the attorney would otherwise be entitled; and (4) attorneys who serve as executors are entitled to both their executors' commissions and reasonable attorney's fees. A model disclosure form is available. *See* N.Y. Surr. Ct. Proc. Act § 2307-a.

7. The undue influence doctrine—and its testamentary capacity cousin—share a downside. In efforts to create vehicles for protecting testators' intentions, they also create room for disappointed family members to threaten or bring unfounded challenges and room for courts to substitute their own judgments about what the "appropriate" testamentary disposition should have been. Consider the following article:

Carla Spivack, *Why the Testamentary Doctrine of Undue Influence Should Be Abolished*

58 U. Kan. L. Rev. 245, 250–51, 254, 258–60, 262, 267–68, 276, 281–83, 286–87, 290–91 (2010)

Many scholars have criticized the doctrine of undue influence in wills, but none so far has called for its abolition. This call is long overdue. Three objections to the doctrine of undue influence—historical, doctrinal, and psychological—warrant its abandonment.

. . .

II. History

The history of undue influence sheds light on the question of how and why the doctrine has become distorted. In England, the policy of contesting wills deemed to be the result of unfair or unconscionable dealing began as an equitable action available in the courts of Chancery.... Over time, jurisdiction over these cases gradually shifted from Chancery to law courts for a number of reasons... and, law and equity were finally officially merged in the nineteenth century.

This shift in jurisdiction played a significant role in turning the doctrine into the vague and destructive one it is today. The differences between equity and law made the transportation of an equitable doctrine into law highly problematic. The equitable doctrine that shaped undue influence developed from "radically different" premises than those which underlay the growth of common law.

Equity's mandate was different from that of the law courts: Chancery's function was to supplement the common law and to alleviate some of the harsher results which rigid application of common law rules could produce.... The Chancellor's role was to see that justice was done when the mechanical application of legal rules failed to achieve it. Part of this project involved preventing the "weak and foolish" from being taken advantage of by technically legal but unfair contracts. A crucial aspect of this process was that each decision was based narrowly on the facts of the particular case and had no effect on general rules of law; each decision was binding only on the parties, not on any future litigants in either court....

The second notable feature of these decisions is that they clearly emanate from the perceived need to keep money in the family—and not just in the legal family. Their concern is the genetic family, referred to as the "Name and Blood" of the decedent. The essence of the injustice in these cases was a will that took the land away from the decedent's heirs . . . .

Equity courts enforce social norms of the time, which later ages may find anachronistic or disagreeable. . . . Equity is better positioned to perform this role for two reasons. Its decisions make explicit the social norms they are enforcing, and it, therefore, does not calcify these norms into mechanically applicable legal rules which then, abstracted from their context, carry them into future ages when the underlying biases no longer reflect social consensus. . . .

By 1868, the doctrine had shifted to a new and unfortunate track. . . . [T]he determination was no longer whether a person's will had been constrained more than a court's conscience considered fair. Now, the Court tries to answer the unanswerable question of whether the influenced person had exercised free will. This is a completely different inquiry and, as I will show, one impossible to conclude. . . .

III. The Doctrine Today and Why It Is Not Working

. . .

. . . [Scholars] argue that the doctrine is failing to achieve its purported goal of protecting testamentary freedom; rather, they conclude, behind its "mask" of realizing a testator's true intent, it is doing something else entirely. There are both psychological and doctrinal reasons that explain the "mask" and reveal what is going on behind it.

A. Psychology

The past hundred years of psychology, as well as recent clinical studies, indicate that the understanding of the "self" that courts use in deciding undue influence cases is deeply misguided. First, courts are ill-suited to analyze, and even understand, the shifting operations of power in intimate relationships. As most psychologists agree, and clinical studies show, power in relationships is nuanced, complex, and nearly impossible to understand from the outside. The insights of psychology, with its emphasis on ambiguity and ambivalence, are an ill fit in the law's evidentiary paradigms. Second, courts assume that there is such a thing as a "fully autonomous self," and that the line between that self and the influence of others can be clearly demarcated. In cases when courts (and juries) do recognize that the self exists in relation to others, and is a product of those relationships, they acknowledge this fact only with respect to family members, and are thus deeply suspicious of interdependent relationships among unrelated adults. . . .

B. Doctrinal Problems

. . .

The doctrine's vagueness leaves it at the mercy of the ideological forces in play in a culture at any given time. . . .

[While analyzing a series of examples, the article discusses *In re Estate of Reid*, 825 So. 2d 1 (Miss. 2002).]

Mary Lea Reid, a seventy-eight-year-old widow, had been befriended by—or had befriended—Michael B. Cupit. He was a twenty-four-year-old man, the court noted disapprovingly in the first sentence of the opinion, who had shown up to view Reid's antebellum home in Brookhaven, Mississippi. The two remained friends and saw each other frequently until Reid died; she adopted him and executed a deed and a will in his favor. A "potential heir" challenged these transfers as products of Cupit's fraud and undue influence. The court agreed, and went through numerous legal and verbal contortions to invalidate the adoption, the deed, and the will, ignoring the applicable statute of limitations to do so.

The opinion made clear that the court disapproved of Reid's relationship with Cupit, despite her apparent pleasure in it.... The court filings, however, tell a different story. Asked during deposition whether Cupit "unduly influenced or ... compelled" her to deed her land to him, Reid burst out "oh, that makes me fighting mad. The fellow that said that, I'd like to choke him, because that's a lie. He better go home and get down on his knees and ask God to forgive him .... That's just not right." Witnesses testified that Reid adopted Cupit due to her "strong desire to have a child which she had never had," that Reid "was proud to have Cupit as her adopted son and heir," and that she told everyone in the community that Cupit was "a good son to her." The court approvingly notes the trial court's disregard and discrediting of this evidence, however, saying "the chancellor [below] found that this testimony must be seen in the proper context. Those witnesses did not have the benefit of knowing the whole story"—a "whole story" apparently, the court knew better than those who knew Reid and had witnessed the relationship ....

There was no question that Reid had capacity and the evidence seemed to show, moreover, that she had had independent legal advice and consultation in executing the documents at issue.... [Regarding the role of independent advice, the] ... court acknowledged that in a ... meeting to draft her will, "[Cupit] did not participate in the discussion," and the attorney "took every precaution to ensure that she was competent and that no overreaching was involved." The court answers this objection, though, by smugly observing that "there was undue influence and overreaching arising from "antecedent circumstances' of which [the attorney] could not be aware." With the possibility of such "antecedent circumstances," of course, it would never be possible for independent legal advice to validate any transfer attacked on undue influence grounds....

In short, the court was hell bent on invalidating the will and deed and allowed neither facts nor law to get in its way.... My point, however, is not to show lacuna in the reasoning in these cases. That courts routinely ignore testamentary freedom to impose social norms and moral judgments on testators' decisions, that women in relationships with younger men are more likely to have their wishes ignored than men with younger women, that devises to others than relatives are likely to be deemed results of undue influence despite extensive evidence of capacity and independent decision-making, other scholars have proved before. Rather, that such violations of testamentary freedom continue to occur together with the other arguments made here supports my contention that the doctrine should be abolished. . . .

IV. The Costs of Continued Use

The continued use of this doctrine entails significant costs. The number of contested wills is increasing, and the most common method for contesting a will is an allegation of undue influence. On the one hand, the continued existence of the doctrine encourages numerous frivolous cases, often brought by one sibling against another who cared for an aging parent and then received a larger portion of the estate. In these cases, courts show awareness that the dependent testator is capable of having testamentary intent, ruling against the contestant on the grounds that the parent had wished to reward the caretaking sibling. Such cases waste the court's time. Second, the continued application of the doctrine creates wasteful litigation costs because heirs discontented with a will can use the threat of a will contest to force a settlement, which often distorts the decedent's intent and depletes the value of the estate.

V. Policy Concerns Are Amenable to Other Doctrines

So far I have argued that because the doctrine of undue influence fails to protect testamentary freedom and generates significant costs, we should abolish it. . . . [L]ess problematic doctrines more effectively address the concerns undue influence purports to address: coercion and overreaching, especially with respect to the elderly; protection of intended beneficiaries; and reassurance for a testator worried that future decline might leave her vulnerable to failing those she intended to benefit.

These are all parts of one dilemma—how best to protect and effectuate the testator's intent. . . . [O]ther doctrines and public policies can do so more effectively [than undue influence] . . . : capacity, duress, fraud, and tortious interference with expectations.

Question

Should the undue influence doctrine be abolished?

Problems

1. Harry, a widower aged 70, lived alone. A year before his death, Harry's favorite niece, Matilda, 30, came to live in the same city. Matilda made a point of visiting Harry once or twice a month—usually to join in Sunday dinner. Harry's two children, Rebecca and David, lived in other cities and he was able to see them only rarely. He was lonely and very much enjoyed the Sunday visits from Matilda. Six months before he died, Harry decided he needed a will. Harry and Matilda chatted several times about what might be an appropriate disposition of Harry's estate. Harry

mentioned that he intended to leave Matilda a bequest, in appreciation for her kindness. She replied that she appreciated the thought, but expected no particular benefit. Later, before executing the will, Harry also consulted his neighbor, George, a retired plumber, for his views on the estate plan. Though George knew none of the parties, and said he thought it was a good plan. Harry's estate was $50,000. His will gave $9,000 to Matilda, with the residue to be split between his children. David has asked your advice about whether he can defeat Matilda's gift. What will you tell him?

2. You have been in practice for several years. Your elderly grandmother wants you to prepare her will. In addition to providing for members of her family, your grandmother wishes to provide a substantial bequest for the charity upon whose Board you sit. What do you do?

3. Robin, a multimillionaire, artist and art patron who had little interest in financial matters, and Chris, a financial planner, lived together. Chris handled the couple's financial affairs. When Robin's will left everything to Chris, Robin's family challenged the will on undue influence grounds. What more would you want to know before deciding whether the undue influence claim might stick?

Selected References

Susanna L. Blumenthal, *The Deviance of the Will: Policing the Bounds of Testamentary Freedom in Nineteenth-Century America*, 119 Harv. L. Rev. 959 (2006).

Richard B. Keeton, *Balancing Testamentary Incapacity and Undue Influence: How to Handle Will Contests of Testators with Diminishing Capacity*, 57 S. Tex. L. Rev. 53 (2015).

Kevin Noble Millard, *The Color of Testamentary Freedom*, 62 SMU L. Rev. 1783 (2009).

Paula A. Monopoli, *Fiduciary Duty: New Ethical Paradigm for Lawyer/Fiduciaries*, 67 Mo. L. Rev. 309 (2002).

Paula A. Monopoli, *Drafting Attorneys as Fiduciaries: Fashioning an Optimal Ethical Rule of Conflicts of Interest*, 66 U. Pitt. L. Rev. 411 (2005).

Ashley E. Rathbun, *Marrying into Financial Abuse: A Solution to Protect the Elderly in California*, 47 San Diego L. Rev. 227 (2010).

Jeffrey G. Sherman, *Can Religious Influence Ever Be "Undue" Influence?*, 73 Brook. L. Rev. 579 (2008).

4. Fraud

Occasionally someone will contest a will on the basis of one of the two types of fraud—fraud in factum and fraud in the inducement. Fraud in factum means fooling the testator into signing a document purporting to be a will, or a document known to be a will, but including an undisclosed provision. Fraud in the inducement means getting the testator to execute a document by misrepresenting facts. In either situation, the will is denied probate.

The clearest case of fraud is the false will. Forged documents, of course, are not even the act of the decedent, and cannot be probated. Fraud also can exist when the decedent executes a document without knowing that it is a will, or that it contains a particular gift. Lacking testamentary intent, the document (or provision) would be denied probate.

For an example of fraud in the inducement, consider Max and his daughters, Lynn and Beth. To obtain a larger share, Lynn convinces Max that Beth is dead, and that Max should rewrite his will to exclude Beth. In this situation, Max actually intends to execute a new will, but that intent was the result of Lynn's fraud.

Problem

Martha was a divorcee with two children, James and Ethel. James lived with their father, and Ethel lived with Martha. The father died, and left his major assets and most of his estate to James. Ethel told Martha that the father had left his entire estate to James. Martha then executed a will leaving her entire estate to Ethel, disinheriting James. Should Martha's will be denied probate because of the misrepresentation?

5. *Tortious Interference with Expectancy*

Irene D. Johnson, *Tortious Interference with Expectancy of Inheritance or Gift—Suggestions for Resort to the Tort*

39 U. Tol. L. Rev. 769, 771, 774 (2008)

In 1979, the Restatement Second [of Torts § 774B] provided the following statement concerning the tort of intentional interference with expectancy: "one who by fraud, duress, or other tortious means intentionally prevents another from receiving from a third person an inheritance or gift that he would otherwise have received is subject to liability to the other for loss of the inheritance or gift." A common list of the elements plaintiff must prove in order to recover includes: "the existence of the expectancy; that the defendant intentionally interfered with the expectancy; that the interference involved tortious conduct such as fraud, duress, or undue influence; that there was a reasonable certainty that the plaintiff would have received the expectancy but for the defendant's interference; and damages." If the plaintiff cannot establish all of these elements, the cause of action for tortious interference with expectancy will fail. . . . [6]

---

6. *See, e.g.*, Cote v. Cote, 143 A.3d 117 (Me. 2016) (claim failed because of failure to prove "but for" undue influence expectancy would have been received). [Eds.]

[P]robate proceedings emphasize the effectuation of the testator's intent with respect to the disposition of the testator's probate estate (something difficult to establish with definiteness because the testator, at the point of probate, is necessarily dead). Conversely, tort actions aim to restore the plaintiff with the benefit arguably lost because of defendant's tortious conduct. A successful tort action results in a judgment against the defendant for money damages, not a determination of the validity of a particular will or other testamentary result.

While not all jurisdictions recognize a cause of action for tortious interference with expectancy of inheritance or gift, about half of all jurisdictions permit actions based on the tort. Some jurisdictions have not ruled on the availability of the tort, while other states appear to have rejected its use. Of the jurisdictions recognizing the tort, most take the position that a tort action will fail unless the party claiming injury can establish that probate is inadequate in some way.

In re Estate of Ellis

923 N.E.2d 237 (Ill. 2009)

BURKE, J.

Grace Ellis executed a will in 1964 naming Shriners Hospitals for Children (Shriners) as beneficiary of her estate if she died without direct descendants. In 1999, she executed a new will naming James G. Bauman as sole beneficiary. Bauman was the pastor of the church of which Ellis was a member. When Ellis died in 2003, the 1999 will was admitted to probate. It was not until 2006 that Shriners became aware of its interest in the 1964 will. Shriners filed the instant action to contest the 1999 will[7] based on theories of undue influence and fraud and included a tort count for intentional interference with an expectancy of inheritance. The circuit court of Cook County dismissed all counts as untimely pursuant to section 8-1 of the Probate Act of 1975 (755 ILCS 5/8-1 (West 2006)). On appeal, Shriners challenged only the dismissal of the tort claim. The appellate court affirmed the trial court's judgment. . . .

We . . . now hold that Shriners' tort claim for intentional interference with an expectancy of inheritance is not limited by the six-month limitation period in section 8-1. Accordingly, we reverse the appellate court's judgment and remand to the trial court for further proceedings.

BACKGROUND

. . .

Ellis died on October 8, 2003, at the age of 86, leaving no direct descendants. Her estate was worth more than $2 million dollars. The 1999 will was filed with the clerk of the circuit court of Cook County on October 9, 2003, and admitted to probate on October 29, 2003. Bauman was named independent executor of the estate.

---

7. Like Illinois, some jurisdictions admit the will to probate and then allow contests. Others hear challenges before admitting the will in the first place. *See* Chapter 1, § 1.02(A)(1). [Eds.]

Shriners first became aware of its interest in the 1964 will when Bauman filed the will with the circuit court in 2006 as part of a separate will contest brought by several of Ellis' heirs at law. . . . Shriners alleged that Ellis met Bauman in 1994 and became a member of St. John's Lutheran Church in Glenview, Illinois, where Bauman was a pastor. Ellis subsequently gave Bauman powers of attorney over her health care and property, changed title to more than $1 million of her assets to Bauman, and purchased gifts and an automobile for Bauman. Counts I and II of the petition contested the validity of the 1999 will based on theories of undue influence and mental incapacity. Both counts requested the vacation of the order admitting the 1999 will to probate, and the admission to probate of the 1964 will.

Count III, the count that is at issue in this appeal, set forth a tort claim for intentional interference with an expectancy of inheritance. It alleged that: (1) but for the 1999 will obtained by Bauman, Shriners would have received Ellis' entire estate; (2) with knowledge of the 1964 will, Bauman set forth on an intentional scheme to interfere with Shriners' expectancy for his personal benefit; (3) Bauman interfered with Shriners' expectancy by abusing his position of trust, unduly influencing Ellis 'to execute a new will and to buy him gifts, violating his fiduciary duty to Ellis, taking advantage of her age and diminished capacity, and failing to notify beneficiaries and interested parties after her death; and (4) but for Bauman's actions, the bequest to Shriners would have been received. Shriners asked that the circuit court enter judgment against Bauman. In its prayer for relief, it requested compensatory damages in excess of $2 million dollars, an accounting of all *inter vivos* transfers and gifts, and punitive damages.

Bauman filed a motion to dismiss the petition, asserting that it was filed more than six months after admission to probate of the 1999 will, in violation of section 8-1 of the Probate Act of 1975 (755 ILCS 5/8-1 (West 2006)).

Section 8-1 provides, in relevant part:

"Within 6 months after the admission to probate of a domestic will ***, any interested person may file a petition in the proceeding for the administration of the testator's estate or, if no proceeding is pending, in the court in which the will was admitted to probate, to contest the validity of the will." 755 ILCS 5/8-1 (West 2006).

The circuit court granted Bauman's motion, dismissed the entire petition with prejudice, and denied Shriners leave to amend.

. . . The appellate court affirmed [holding] . . . that the allegations in Shriners' tort claim were virtually identical to those in its will contest count based on undue influence. The court concluded that the legislature could not have intended "to bar a will contest as untimely after six months yet allow the same allegations to proceed in the tort arena." 381 Ill. App. 3d at 431. Therefore, the appellate court held, Shriners' tort claim amounted to an impermissible collateral attack on the order admitting the 1999 will to probate and was properly dismissed as time-barred under section 8-1 of the Probate Act of 1975. . . .

ANALYSIS

The sole issue in this appeal is the timeliness of Shriners' tort claim. As noted, the appellate court applied the six-month limitation period for filing a will contest set forth in section 8-1 of the Probate Act of 1975. This six-month limitation period is jurisdictional and not subject to tolling by fraudulent concealment or any other fact not expressly provided for by the Probate Act.... Whether the six-month limitation is applicable to a tort claim is a question of statutory construction subject to *de novo* review....

Shriners contends that the appellate court's application of section 8-1 of the Probate Act of 1975 to a tort claim for intentional interference with expectancy of inheritance contradicts the clear and unambiguous language of the statute and confuses the tort with a will contest. We agree. Under the plain language of section 8-1, the six-month statutory limitation period applies to a "petition *** to contest the validity of the will." 755 ILCS 5/8-1 (West 2006). A tort action for intentional interference with inheritance is distinct from a petition to contest the validity of a will, in several important respects. The single issue in a will contest is whether the writing produced is the will of the testator.... Any ground which, if proved, would invalidate the will, including undue influence, incapacity, fraud, or revocation, may state a cause of action.... The object of a will contest proceeding is not to secure a personal judgment against an individual defendant but is a *quasi in rem* proceeding to set aside a will....

By contrast, in a tort claim for intentional interference with inheritance, "[o]ne who by fraud, duress or other tortious means intentionally prevents another from receiving from a third person an inheritance or gift that he would otherwise have received is subject to liability to the other for loss of the inheritance or gift." Restatement (Second) of Torts § 774B (1979). The "widely recognized tort" does not contest the validity of the will; it is a personal action directed at an individual tortfeasor. See *Marshall v. Marshall*, 547 U.S. 293, 312 ... (2006) (the tort claim "seeks an *in personam* judgment against [the defendant], not the probate or annulment of a will"). Although some of the evidence may overlap with a will contest proceeding, a plaintiff filing a tort claim must establish the following distinct elements: (1) the existence of an expectancy; (2) defendant's intentional interference with the expectancy; (3) conduct that is tortious in itself, such as fraud, duress, or undue influence; (4) a reasonable certainty that the expectancy would have been realized but for the interference; and (5) damages.... The remedy for a tortious interference action is not the setting aside of the will, but a judgment against the individual defendant, and, where the defendant has himself received the benefit of the legacy, a constructive trust, an equitable lien, or "a simple monetary judgment to the extent of the benefits thus tortiously acquired." Restatement (Second) of Torts § 774B(e) (1979). Thus, a tort claim for intentional interference with an expectancy is not a "petition *** to contest the validity of the will" under the plain statutory language of section 8-1.

Although section 8-1 does not expressly limit a tort action, Illinois courts nevertheless have restricted the tort in certain circumstances where a plaintiff forgoes an opportunity to file a tort claim within the six-month period for a will contest. In *Robinson*, after the will and codicil were admitted to probate, plaintiffs entered into a settlement agreement with the estate, agreeing not to file a will contest in exchange for $125,000. More than six months later, plaintiffs filed a complaint for tortious interference with expectancy of inheritance. This court held that the tort action should have been dismissed where plaintiffs chose not to avail themselves of a will contest remedy. *Robinson [v. First State Bank of Monticello*, 97 Ill. 2d 174,] at 185. We stated:

"In this case, where a will has been admitted to probate and where the plaintiffs have engaged an attorney to determine whether they should file a will contest, have decided not to contest the will, have entered into a settlement agreement for $125,000 (agreeing to release the other parties to the agreement *** from any and all claims and causes of action arising from any will, codicil or other undertaking by the parties), and have allowed the statutorily prescribed period in which to contest the will to expire (thereby establishing the validity of the will), we will not recognize a tort action for intentional interference with inheritance.

...

Given the facts in this case, if we were to allow the plaintiffs to maintain their tort action, we would be giving them a second bite of the apple and defeating the purpose of the exclusivity of a will contest under section 8-1." *Robinson*, 97 Ill. 2d at 184-85.

...

This court noted in *Robinson* that the public policy underlying the enactment of section 8-1 is "an attempt to make the administration of an estate as orderly as possible because of the gravity of the interests at stake." *Robinson*, 97 Ill. 2d at 186. See also *Pedersen v. Dempsey*, 341 Ill. App. 141, 143, 93 N.E.2d 85 (1950) (reasons for restricting a will contest include "the pressing importance of securing an orderly settlement of estates, to prevent embarrassment to creditors and others, and to avoid as much confusion as possible in the vast amount of property rights and titles that pass through probate"). We said that to allow the plaintiffs to maintain a tort action "which in its practical effect would invalidate a will that has become valid under the Probate Act of 1975 *** would permit the issue of undue influence, which would have been grounds for a will contest, to be litigated years after the will was admitted to probate and immune from contest on this issue." *Robinson*, 97 Ill. 2d at 186.

The concern articulated in *Robinson* about the "practical effect" of allowing the plaintiffs to maintain the tort action must be read in the context of the facts of that case. Unlike Shriners, the plaintiffs in *Robinson* could have obtained complete relief had they filed a timely will contest. Instead, they settled with the estate and agreed not to file any further claims arising from the will and codicil. In the instant case, we cannot say that a will contest was "available" to Shriners, nor that a successful will contest would have furnished the relief sought by Shriners in its tort action. The parties agree that Shriners was unaware of its bequest in the 1964 will until more than two years after the 1999 will had been admitted to probate. Our holding in *Robinson* was limited to not recognizing the tort action where plaintiffs have an opportunity to contest a probated will but choose not to do so, and subsequently enter into an agreement to take no further court action. . . .

The facts in the case at bar are similar to *Schilling v. Herrera*, 952 So. 2d 1231 (Fla. App. 2007), where a Florida appellate court permitted the plaintiff's tortious interference with expectancy claim to go forward. The plaintiff was the decedent's only heir-at-law and was named the sole beneficiary in a 1996 will. In 2003, the defendant convinced the decedent to execute a new will naming the defendant as the sole beneficiary of her estate. The plaintiff did not learn of the decedent's death until after the defendant had petitioned the probate court for discharge of probate on the 2003 will. Shortly thereafter, the final order of discharge was entered by the probate court. *Schilling*, 952 So. 2d at 1233. The plaintiff subsequently filed his complaint for intentional interference with an expectancy of inheritance. . . . The [appellate] court acknowledged the rule in Florida that "'if adequate relief is available in a probate proceeding, then that remedy must be exhausted before a tortious interference claim may be pursued.'" *Schilling*, 952 So. 2d at 1236, quoting *De Witt v. Duce*, 408 So. 2d 216, 218 (Fla. 1981). The *Schilling* court held, however, that because the defendant's fraud was not discovered until after probate, the plaintiff was allowed to bring a later action for damages because relief in probate was impossible. *Schilling*, 952 So. 2d at 1236-37. Similarly, Shriners did not have a fair opportunity to pursue a remedy in probate because it was not aware of its expectancy under the earlier will, nor was it aware of Bauman's allegedly fraudulent conduct, until after the 1999 will was admitted to probate and the six-month deadline for a will contest had expired.

Furthermore, a will contest would not have provided sufficient relief to Shriners because it would not have extended to the alleged *inter vivos* transfers of property. Shriners alleged that Bauman depleted Ellis' estate by inducing her to transfer assets worth more than $1 million to him prior to her death. In a successful will contest, Shriners could have recovered only assets that were part of the estate upon Ellis' death but could not have reached the assets transferred during her lifetime.

. . .

Accordingly, we find that section 8-1 does not apply to the tort action filed by Shriners against Bauman. We emphasize that our holding applies to the particular parties under the circumstances of this case and does not extend to a plaintiff who fails to bring a tort claim within the period for filing a will contest, where the will contest remedy was available.

. . .

Reversed and remanded.

Notes and Questions

1. For more on the *Marshall* controversy that prompted the Supreme Court decision cited in *Ellis*, see Page 9.

2. If interference with an expectancy is a tort, not a will contest, why should claimants have to first use the probate process, if it is available?

3. In *Bjork v. O'Meara*, 986 N.E.2d 626 (Ill. 2013), the Supreme Court of Illinois held that the six-year statute of limitations for tortious interference applies if the tort claim does not seek or require an invalidation of the decedent's will.

4. Several states refuse to recognize the tort of intentional interference with inheritance. *See, e.g.*, *Vogt v. Witmeyer*, 87 N.Y.2d 998 (N.Y. 1996) (holding that New York does not recognize a right of action for tortious interference with prospective inheritance); and *Anderson v. Archer*, No. 03-13-00790-CV, 2016 Tex. App. LEXIS 2165 (Tex. Civ. App. Mar. 2, 2016) (expressly rejecting a cause of action for tortious interference with inheritance in Texas). In those states, aggrieved persons may obtain equitable relief in the form of the "constructive trust" remedy.

"The term 'constructive trust' is misleading. The theory does not impose management duties on the 'trustee.' Rather, constructive trust is [an equitable] remedy. The constructive trust theory is a device for preventing unjust enrichment by moving legal title from a person who has title but should not, to someone who should." Roger W. Andersen, Understanding Trusts and Estates 91 (5th ed. 2013).

Consider the famous case of *Latham v. Father Divine*, 299 N.Y. 22 (1949), where Father Divine, a cult figure, murdered the decedent to prevent her from revoking her will in favor of Father Divine and executing a new will in favor of others. The court imposed a "constructive trust" on Father Divine which required him to pay over the property he received as will beneficiary to the intended beneficiaries.

Problem

Mary had made a will giving much of her property to her minister. Near death but still mentally alert, Mary changed her mind and tried to execute a new will in favor of her friend, Jack. The minister intervened and prevented Mary from executing the new will. When Mary died with the old will intact, what arguments could you make for getting the property to Jack?

Selected References

Martin L. Fried, *The Disappointed Heir: Going Beyond the Probate Process to Remedy Wrongdoing or Rectify Mistake*, 39 Real Prop. Prob. & Tr. J. 357 (2004).

Diane J. Klein, *"Go West, Disappointed Heir": Tortious Interference with Expectation of Inheritance—A Survey with Analysis of State Approaches in the Pacific States*, 13 Lewis & Clark L. Rev. 209 (2009).

Diane J. Klein, *A Disappointed Yankee in Connecticut (or Nearby) Probate Court: Tortious Interference with Expectation of Inheritance—A Survey with Analysis of State of Approaches in the First, Second, and Third Circuits*, 66 U. Pitt. L. Rev. 235 (2004).

Diane J. Klein, *The Disappointed Heir's Revenge, Southern Style: Tortious Interference with Expectation of Inheritance—A Survey with Analysis of State Approaches in the Fifth and Eleventh Circuits*, 55 Baylor L. Rev. 79 (2003).

C. Will Execution

1. The Policies

The rules for executing a valid will are changing. Traditionally, the list of elements was long, and the judicial approach was strict. In some states, the list is shorter, and the courts are more forgiving. In order to understand these varying approaches, we must have in mind the policies underlying will execution rules.

Traditional analysis identifies four principal justifications for Statutes of Wills rules. Preservation of evidence is the most obvious one. We want to be confident that we have reliable information about what the testator wanted. Second, requiring a level of ceremony serves a cautionary function. It warns the testator, "This is something special." The very formality itself focuses the testator's mind, and gives survivors more confidence that a purported will is not just a set of tentative notes reflecting an unformed intention. Third, Statute of Wills elements may have a protective purpose, preventing others from overreaching. Finally, there is some value in "channeling" testators to use similar forms, features, and procedures. Such uniformity gives testators, lawyers, and courts a common language for approaching problems.

As you evaluate the appropriateness of pursuing those policies, consider the following:

James Lindgren, *The Fall of Formalism*

55 Alb. L. Rev. 1009 (1992)

People are not stupid. Yet for hundreds of years the law of wills has treated them as if they were. Sure, they don't know the law, but they usually know what they want. The fear that they might improvidently give away their property at death has left a legacy of formalism unmatched in American law.

In the law of wills, the story told about people is that their seriously intended statements about their property can't be trusted. They are so weak, old, feeble, and subject to pressure that they need extraordinary protection from themselves. Their spoken words are completely worthless. Their written statements are without meaning unless they're witnessed by two people. Even then, the witnesses must sign in the presence of the giver. And so on.

In the law of contracts, on the other hand, the story is completely different. People are intelligent and competent. They know their own mind. Other people can rely on their seriously made statements. They don't need protection from themselves. Their spoken words are enough to convey millions of dollars. And their written statements have meaning without witnesses.

Having formal rules may channel testators to visit lawyers, who then can offer helpful advice. The following article suggests, however, that we should not over-value uniformity of forms and formulae. Wills speak to a variety of audiences.

Deborah S. Gordon, *Reflecting on the Language of Death*

34 Seattle U. L. Rev. 379, 401, 407–09, 411 (2011)

Although formulaic language, like will-execution formalities, serves a "channeling" and ritual function, this language becomes problematic when it is adopted without mindful consideration of alternatives. . . . [B]y refusing to write robotically and instead choosing language that requires precision, variety, and thoughtfulness, by drafting with a "rich texture" that includes "emotion and particularity," a will can allow the testator to tell her story and thereby "help connect us to the person the testator was." Attention to a will's language is thus crucial to the formulation of testamentary intent in the first instance. . . .

A "technical terms" or "formula" approach to written language makes tremendous sense in the field of law. Drafting from forms is not only easier than creating documents from scratch, but it also allows lawyers to reduce the economic costs of planning. . . . The simpler and more formulaic a will is, one might argue, the cheaper and more accessible it will be both for lawyers and laymen to read and adapt.

. . . As costly as it may be for the testator to add more expressive language to a will, the costs of litigating a will contest, whether borne by the litigants or the estate, are likely to be far more onerous. . . . Faced with clients (testators and beneficiaries) who complain about fees and threaten malpractice suits, an approach that encourages lawyers to take the time to infuse a document with the client's deliberate preferences, and even her history or philosophy, has the potential to give the testator and the objects of her bounty—those remembered and those omitted—a sense of closure that counteracts other frustrations they might feel about costs, delays, or administrative burdens. In addition, if a will ends up in litigation, a jury may be more receptive to the intent of a testator when her goals are expressed clearly and in her individual voice. . . .

. . . [T]hose most likely to benefit from this suggested change are the different readers, including the beneficiaries, fiduciaries, and possibly the court. Along with facilitating the testator's ability to formulate her intent in the first instance and then fostering her ability to convey that intent on her own or with her lawyer's help, expressive writing also has the potential to bring the testator's loved ones together in a moment of loss. . . .

. . . [T]he audience most likely to welcome a more expressive approach to wills consists of the fiduciaries, such as executors and trustees, who essentially stand in the testator's shoes and act as the testator's surrogates with respect to distribution and ongoing administration of estate property. While a more expressive testamentary document may impose added restrictions on these fiduciaries, it can also provide them with crucial guidance in moments of uncertainty.

Selected Reference

Kent D. Schenkel, *Testamentary Fragmentation and the Diminishing Role of the Will: An Argument for Revival*, 41 Creighton L. Rev. 155 (2008).

2. A Typical "Statute of Wills"

The modern will has its roots in both Roman law and the English testament, the ecclesiastically-supervised death-bed directions for distributing personal property. The ability to transfer land at death, however, came in the Statute of Wills of 1540, 32 Hen. 8, c. 1, which required "some memorandum" of the decedent's will. To protect against perjury, in 1677 Parliament passed the Statute of Frauds, which included formal requirements, like a writing, signed by the testator before witnesses. 29 Car. 2, c. 3, § 5. The Wills Act of 1837 unified the rules for wills covering real or personal property. 7 Will. 4 & 1 Vict., c. 26, § 9.

Because many states still require a variety of elements derived from English law, we reproduce Ohio's traditional statute as an example. Compare it to the statute in your own state. As you will discover in the material below, almost every word is "loaded," filled with potential for litigation.

Ohio Rev. Code

§ 2107.03. Method of making will

Except oral wills, every will shall be in writing, but may be handwritten or typewritten. The will shall be signed at the end by the testator or by some other person in the testator's conscious presence and at the testator's express direction. The will shall be attested and subscribed in the conscious presence of the testator, by two or more competent witnesses, who saw the testator subscribe, or heard the testator acknowledge the testator's signature.

For purposes of this section, "conscious presence" means within the range of any of the testator's senses, excluding the sense of sight or sound that is sensed by telephonic, electronic, or other distant communication.

In part to cut down on litigation, the UPC has eliminated many of these technical requirements. Further, it has added notarization as alternative to the 2-witness requirement. *But see* Anne-Marie Rhodes, *Notarized Wills*, 27 Quinnipiac Prob. L. J. 419 (2014) (raising concerns about the notarized will option, which only Colorado and North Dakota have enacted).

Uniform Probate Code

Section 2-502. Execution; Witnessed Wills; Holographic Wills

(a) Except as provided in subsection (b) and in Sections 2-503, 2-506, and 2-513, a will must be:

(1) in writing;

(2) signed by the testator or in the testator's name by some other individual in the testator's conscious presence and by the testator's direction; and

(3) either:

(A) signed by at least two individuals, each of whom signed within a reasonable time after the individual witnessed either the signing of the will as described in paragraph (2) or the testator's acknowledgment of that signature or acknowledgment of the will; or

(B) acknowledged by the testator before a notary public or other individual authorized by law to take acknowledgements.

a. In an Original Writing (usually)

As a general rule, wills statutes contemplate the probate of an original writing and not a copy. However, under either a statute of wills or a lost or destroyed wills statute, a copy of a will may substitute for a lost or destroyed original will. *See, e.g., In re Estate of Winter*, 142 A.3d 796 (Pa. 2016) (admitting will copy under Pennsylvania's statute of wills).

While a written document is the general rule, some states allow oral wills in limited situations. Typical requirements for so-called "nuncupative wills" include: (1) the will must be made while the testator is in his or her last illness (some states are even more restrictive and require that the will be made while in extremis); (2) the will may pass only personalty under a specific (modest) dollar limit; (3) the witnesses must reduce the will to writing shortly after its making, usually within 10 days; (4) the testator must specifically ask the witnesses to witness the statement as a will; and (5) the will must be offered for probate within a limited period after the testator's death. An oral will may not be sufficient to revoke a prior written will.

A more common exception to the writing requirement is for "Soldiers' and Sailors' Wills." Some statutes are more precise than others in defining the scope and applicability of this doctrine. Typically, for soldiers to qualify they must be on active duty during a war. For sailors, they must be at sea. Most jurisdictions limit the doctrine to personal property.

As in so many areas, technology is prompting changes in traditional rules. So far, Nevada is the only state to have enacted legislation on electronic wills.

Nev. Rev. Stat.

Section 133.085. Electronic will.

1. An electronic will is a will of a testator that:

(a) Is written, created and stored in an electronic record;

(b) Contains the date and the electronic signature of the testator and which includes, without limitation, at least one authentication characteristic of the testator; and

(c) Is created and stored in such a manner that:

(1) Only one authoritative copy exists;

(2) The authoritative copy is maintained and controlled by the testator or a custodian designated by the testator in the electronic will;

(3) Any attempted alteration of the authoritative copy is readily identifiable; and

(4) Each copy of the authoritative copy is readily identifiable as a copy that is not the authoritative copy.

. . .

3. An electronic will that meets the requirements of this section is subject to no other form, and may be made in or out of this State. An electronic will is valid and has the same force and effect as if formally executed.

4. An electronic will shall be deemed to be executed in this State if the authoritative copy of the electronic will is:

(a) Transmitted to and maintained by a custodian designated in the electronic will at the custodian's place of business in this State or at the custodian's residence in this State; or

(b) Maintained by the testator at the testator's place of business in this State or at the testator's residence in this State.

. . .

6. As used in this section:

(a) "Authentication characteristic" means a characteristic of a certain person that is unique to that person and that is capable of measurement and recognition in an electronic record as a biological aspect of or physical act performed by that person. Such a characteristic may consist of a fingerprint, a retinal scan, voice recognition, facial recognition, a digitized signature or other authentication using a unique characteristic of the person.

(b) "Authoritative copy" means the original, unique, identifiable and unalterable electronic record of an electronic will.

(c) "Digitized signature" means a graphical image of a handwritten signature that is created, generated or stored by electronic means.

Question

Are a testator's recorded statements, posted to YouTube and linked to a document that includes other terms, effective parts of a will in Nevada?

Selected References

Gerry W. Beyer & Claire G. Hargrove, *Digital Wills: Has the Time Come for Wills to Join the Digital Revolution?*, 33 Ohio N.U. L. Rev. 865 (2007).

Scott S. Boddery, *Electronic Wills: Drawing a Line in the Sand against their Validity*, 47 Real Prop., Tr. & Est. L.J. 197 (2012).

Christopher J. Caldwell, *Should "E-Wills" Be Wills: Will Advances in Technology Be Recognized for Will Execution?*, 63 U. Pitt. L. Rev. 467 (2002).

Joseph Karl Grant, *Shattering and Moving Beyond the Gutenberg Paradigm: The Dawn of the Electronic Will*, 42 U. Mich. J.L. Reform 105 (2008).

b. Signed

All written wills must be signed by the testator. Witness's signatures may also be necessary. Thus, questions arise about what constitutes a "signature." Generally, any mark applied to the document with the intent that it operate as the decedent's signature will fulfill the "signature" requirement. While standard practice calls for a formal, complete signature, a variety of less formal approaches have worked. *See Kehr's Will*, 95 A.2d 647 (Pa. 1953) (initials); *Kimmel's Estate*, 123 A. 405 (Pa. 1924) ("Father"); *In re Estate of Deskovic*, 157 N.E.2d 769 (Ill. App. Ct. 1959) (fingerprints). Of course, the lack of formality might suggest a lack of intention that the mark serve to validate the document. Interpreting a statute defining "signature" to include "any other symbol or methodology executed or adopted by a party with intention to authenticate a writing," *Taylor v. Holt*, 134 S.W.3d 830 (Tenn. Ct. App. 2003), allowed a computer-generated signature.

Occasionally, someone present at the execution of the will attempts to assist the testator to sign. Courts typically allow an assistant to hold the testator's hand and even to hold the pen if the testator also touches it.

Most statutes allow assistants simply to sign on behalf of the testator, but that act must come at the testator's direction or sometimes "express" direction. Jurisdictions taking the latter approach are attempting to eliminate the argument that the testator impliedly asked for help. One case allowed a will "signed" by a rubber stamp. The testator directed someone to stamp her signature on the will, and then she placed her own X on each side of the stamp. *Phillips v. Najar*, 901 S.W.2d 561 (Tex. Ct. App. 1995). The safest approach for someone signing on behalf of another is to write out the full name of the testator and then add "signed by ____________________" and the signature of the subscriber. Some places allow this procedure only if the testator is unable to act alone.

Some statutes (like Ohio's) require the testator's signature to come "at the end." Because testators will forget to sign at the end, but leave signatures at various other places on the document, this simple-sounding requirement has generated considerable litigation. One way to interpret "at the end" is to require the signature to be at the physical end of the document, but the more common approach is to look for the will's "logical end." *See, e.g., Estate of Van Gilder*, 220 A.2d 21 (Pa. 1966) (folded notecard). Usually, if the signature is not at the end, the whole will fails. Some jurisdictions merely disregard the material appearing after the signature. *See* N.Y. Estates, Powers and Trusts Law § 3-2.1(a)(1).

> ***Selected Reference***
>
> Chad Michael Ross, *Probate: The Tennessee Court of Appeals Allows a Computer Generated Signature to Validate a Testamentary Will (*Taylor v. Holt, *134 S.W.3d 830, Tenn. Ct. App. 2003)*, 35 U. Mem. L. Rev. 603 (2005).

Question

Which is the best approach: invalidating wills not signed at the end, ignoring material which comes after the signature, or not imposing the "at the end" requirement at all?

c. Attested in the Testator's Presence

Unless the state allows so-called "holographic" wills,[8] wills must be signed by two witnesses.

Some states say the witnesses must themselves sign "in the presence of" the testator. Sometimes they must also sign in the presence of each other. If someone is signing the testator's signature on his behalf, the proxy must be in the testator's presence. In all of these contexts, courts have struggled with what "presence" means. Traditionally, they followed a "line-of-sight" test. As the Ohio and UPC statutes illustrate, the modern approach is to require persons to be in each other's "conscious presence."

In re Demaris' Estate

110 P.2d 571 (Or. 1941)

[The will in question was executed in a doctor's office. With the doctor and his wife in the room to serve as witnesses, the testator signed the will while he was on

8. These are unwitnessed wills in the testator's handwriting. *See* § 3.03C3.

the bed in the treatment room. (See the case for a diagram.) The witnesses then took the will to the desk in the consultation room to sign it themselves. The doors between the rooms remained open. The doctor's wife signed while standing on the south side of the desk, where the testator could have seen her. The doctor then sat at the chair, out of the testator's vision, and signed. Later, the doctor's signature was challenged as not having met the requirements of a statute which read "[e]very will shall be . . . attested by two or more competent witnesses, subscribing their names to the will, in the presence of the testator."]

ROSSMAN, J.

. . . The meaning of the phrase "in the presence of the testator" has been the subject of much controversy and of diversity of opinion. . . . Some of the decisions restrict a testator to his sense of sight in ascertaining whether his attesting witnesses are in his presence when they sign. They hold that if he and the attesters are in the same room all are prima facie in each other's presence, but if the attesting signatures are written in another room, then, prima facie, the statutory requirement was violated. If a counterpane stretched between the bedposts, to shield the testator from drafts, is between him and the attesters, the attestation is invalid: *Reed v. Roberts*, 26 Ga. 294, 71 Am. Dec. 210. These strict interpretation courts go further. For instance, in *In re Beggans' Will*, 68 N.J. Eq. 572, 59 Atl. 874, and *Graham v. Graham*, 32 N.C. 219, the courts held that before a finding could be authorized that the attesting witnesses signed in the testator's presence it must appear, not only that the testator could have seen them sign had he chosen to look, but that he did actually see the will and the writing of the signatures as the attestation took place. *Burney v. Allen*, 125 N.C. 314, 34 S.E. 500 . . . represents a slight restriction upon the interpretation just noticed. The court there merely demanded proof that the testator could have seen had he cared to look. It said: "He must have the opportunity, through the evidence of ocular observation, to see the attestation." . . .

The liberal interpretation courts apply to all attestations the test which is employed in strict interpretation jurisdictions to the wills of the blind only: the mental apprehension or conscious presence test. They seem to believe that if the lawmaker meant "within the sight of" or "in the same room with" he would have said so, and would not have employed the phrase "in the presence of." . . .

. . . We are convinced that any of the senses that a testator possesses, which enable him to know whether another is near at hand and what he is doing, may be employed by him in determining whether the attesters are in his presence as they sign his will. . . .

At least one of the objects of the statute was served in the present instance; that is, two disinterested persons were brought to the testator's bedside to be present while he executed his will. When two disinterested persons, who later tell the truth, are present, the testator has been afforded, in our opinion, the best protection against fraud that this statute is capable of yielding. . . .

In conclusion, we express the belief that if Dr. Gillis and his wife failed to comply with the strict letter of the statute when they attested the will, they, nevertheless, substantially complied with its requirements. To hold otherwise would be to observe the letter of the statute as interpreted strictly, and fail to give heed to the statute's obvious purpose. Thus, the statute would be turned against those for whose protection it had been written. The circuit court, in sustaining the will, committed no error....

Notes and Questions

1. Do the same policies support the rule that the witnesses must sign in the presence of the testator and the rule that the testator must sign (or acknowledge the signature) in the presence of the witnesses?

2. The UPC does not require witnesses to sign in either the testator's or each other's presence. They must, however, sign within a reasonable time. *See* UPC § 2-502(a)(3). Colorado's version makes clear that the signing can come after the testator's death. Colo. Rev. Stats. § 15-11-502. What policies should courts consider when identifying a "reasonable time"?

3. Although some courts require the testator to ask the witnesses to sign the will, others have found a request from more general words or conduct by the testator or the lawyer. *See, e.g., Hollingsworth v. Hollingsworth*, 401 S.W.2d 555 (Ark. 1966) (witnesses and testator signing in each other's presence left no doubt witnesses understood they were signing testator's will).

4. The requirement that witnesses "attest" (or "sign" or "subscribe") raises the same sorts of questions that apply to a testator's signature. *See, e.g., In re Estate of Leavey*, 202 P.3d 99 (Kan. Ct. App. 2009) (witness's initials on the corners of each page not enough where signature line at the end left blank). Some jurisdictions distinguish between "attest" and "subscribe." *See Estate of Griffith*, 30 So. 3d 1190 (Miss., 2010) (witnesses who did not know what they were signing were only subscribing witnesses, not attesting witnesses as required by the statute).

5. Suppose the will in *DeMaris* had been executed in a law office, with a lawyer and his secretary playing parallel roles to Dr. and Mrs. Gillis. Could the lawyer or another member of the firm represent the executor in the litigation that followed?

Subject to exceptions unlikely to apply in this situation, Rule 3.7 of the ABA Model Rules of Professional Conduct prohibits a lawyer from acting "as advocate at a trial in which the lawyer is likely to be a necessary witness."

d. By Competent Witnesses

Witnesses must not only be competent—in the mental capacity sense—at the time of the will's execution, but many states say part of being competent is being "disinterested," in the sense of not taking any gifts under the will. Strictly applied, the rule would invalidate most wills signed by interested witnesses. Rather than letting the will fail, however, states which follow this rule usually save the will through "purging statutes." One variety of these statutes invalidates the gift. Another approach, known as the "lesser of the two" rule, allows an interested witness to take the lesser of: (1) the gift, or (2) the amount the witness would have received had there been no new will.

UPC § 2-505(b) simply eliminates the interested-witness rule: "The signing of a will by an interested witness does not invalidate the will or any provision of it." Indeed, UPC § 2-502(a)(3)(B) allows a testator's notarized acknowledgement to validate a will without the need for any witnesses.

Estate of Parsons

163 Cal. Rptr. 70 (Ct. App. 1980)

Grodin, Associate Justice.

This case requires us to determine whether a subscribing witness to a will who is named in the will as a beneficiary becomes "disinterested" within the meaning of Probate Code section 51 by filing a disclaimer of her interest after the testatrix' death. While our own policy preferences tempt us to an affirmative answer, we feel constrained by existing law to hold that a disclaimer is ineffective for that purpose.

I

Geneve Parsons executed her will on May 3, 1976. Three persons signed the will as attesting witnesses: Evelyn Nielson, respondent Marie Gower, and Bob Warda, a notary public. Two of the witnesses, Nielson and Gower, were named in the will as beneficiaries. Nielson was given $100; Gower was given certain real property. Mrs. Parsons died on December 13, 1976, and her will was admitted to probate on the petition of her executors, respondents Gower and Lenice Haymond. On September 12, 1977, Nielson filed a disclaimer[9] of her $100 bequest. Appellants then claimed an interest in the estate on the ground that the devise to Gower was invalid.[10] The trial court rejected their argument, which is now the sole contention on appeal.

Appellants base their claim on Probate Code section 51, which provides that a gift to a subscribing witness is void "unless there are two other and disinterested subscribing witnesses to the will." Although Nielson disclaimed her bequest after subscribing the will, appellants submit that "a subsequent disclaimer is ineffective to transform an interested witness into a disinterested one." Appellants assert that because there was only one disinterested witness at the time of attestation, the devise to Gower is void by operation of law.

---

9. A disclaimer is the refusal to accept property, in this instance a bequest. *See* Pages ____

10. Appellants Phyllis Maschke and Roger, Donald, and Clifford Winelander are the assignees of their uncle Sydney Winelander, the decedent's first cousin once removed. Appellants Frances Areitio, Florence Rennaker, and Josephine, Henry, and Walter Marion are also the decedent's first cousins once removed. Mrs. Parsons' will contained no residuary clause. If the devise to Gower fails, appellants and other next of kin of equal degree will inherit the property.

Respondents contend that appellants' argument is "purely technical" and "completely disregards the obvious and ascertainable intent" of the testatrix. They urge that the property should go to the person named as devisee rather than to distant relatives who, as the testatrix stated in her will, "have not been overlooked but have been intentionally omitted." They stress that there has been no suggestion of any fraud or undue influence in this case, and they characterize Nielson's interest as a "token gift" which she relinquished pursuant to the disclaimer statute. (Prob. Code, § 190 et seq.) Finally, respondents point to the following language of Probate Code section 190.6: "In every case, the disclaimer shall relate back for all purposes to the date of the creation of the interest." On the basis of that language, respondents conclude that Nielson "effectively became disinterested" by reason of her timely disclaimer. According to respondents, the conditions of Probate Code section 51 have therefore been satisfied, and the devise to Gower should stand. . . .

In order to establish a will as genuine, it is not always necessary that each and every one of the subscribing witnesses testify in court. (Prob. Code, §§ 329, 372.) Moreover, Probate Code section 51 does not by its terms preclude any witness from testifying; nor does the section void the interest of a subscribing witness when "two other and disinterested" witnesses have also subscribed the will. It is therefore entirely conceivable and perfectly consistent with the statutory scheme that a will might be proved on the sole testimony of a subscribing witness who is named in the will as a beneficiary; and if the will had been attested by "two other and disinterested subscribing witnesses," the interested witness whose sole testimony established the will would also be permitted to take his gift, as provided in the instrument. (Prob. Code, §§ 51, 329, 372.) If Probate Code section 51 serves any purpose under such circumstances, its purpose must necessarily have been accomplished before the will was offered for probate. Otherwise, in its statutory context, the provision would have no effect at all.

The quintessential function of a subscribing witness is performed when the will is executed. . . . We believe that Probate Code section 51 looks in its operation solely to that time. . . . The section operates to ensure that at least two of the subscribing witnesses are disinterested. Although disinterest may be a token of credibility, as at common law, it also connotes an absence of selfish motives. We conclude that the purpose of the statute is to protect the testator from fraud and undue influence at the very moment when he executes his will, by ensuring that at least two persons are present "who would not be financially motivated to join in a scheme to procure the execution of a spurious will by dishonest methods, and who therefore presumably might be led by human impulses of fairness to resist the efforts of others in that direction." (Gulliver and Tilson, Classification of Gratuitous Transfers (1941) 51 Yale L.J. 1, 11. . . .)

No other possible construction which has been brought to our attention squares so closely with the statutory framework.

III

Because we hold that Probate Code section 51 looks solely to the time of execution and attestation of the will, it follows that a subsequent disclaimer will be ineffective to transform an interested witness into a "disinterested" one within the meaning of that section. If the execution of a release or the filing of a disclaimer after the will has been attested could effect such a transformation, the purpose of the statute as we have defined it would be undermined. . . .

Respondents' concern for the intentions of the testatrix is . . . misplaced. The construction of the will (Prob. Code, § 101) is not at issue here. We are faced instead with the operation of Probate Code section 51, which makes no reference to the intentions of the testatrix. Legislation voiding the interest of an attesting witness "often upsets genuine expressions of the testator's intent." (Chaffin, *Execution, Revocation, and Revalidation of Wills: A Critique of Existing Statutory Formalities* (1977) 11 Ga. L. Rev. 297, 317.) But that legislation controls the outcome of this case. . . .

Notes and Questions

1. California Probate Code § 6112 now allows "any person generally competent" to witness a will, but sets up a presumption that a witness who receives a devise "procured the devise by duress, menace or undue influence."

2. Notice that if Evelyn's disclaimer had been effective, Marie would not have lost her gift. Evelyn and Bob would have met the two-witness requirement. This result is an application of the general principle that extra ("supernumerary") interested witnesses are irrelevant.

3. If a lawyer had supervised the execution of Geneve Parsons' will, would it have been negligence to allow Marie and Evelyn to witness the will? To omit a residuary clause?

4. To save a will, a purging statute takes away a gift after the fact. How is that approach different from allowing a disclaimer to save a will after the fact?

5. For a poignant case, see *In re Moody's Will*, 154 A.2d 165 (Maine 1959). Elinor's will said "I also request my Executor to pay each of the signers, as witnesses, of this my last will, the sum of Five Dollars each, as a token of appreciation." In the absence of a purging statute, the will was denied probate because the will lacked disinterested witnesses.

6. Purging statutes can affect benefits beyond gifts under the will. The will in *Estate of Wu*, 877 N.Y.S.2d 886 (Sur. Ct. 2009), included a clause directing the executor to pay all "estate and inheritance taxes payable by reason of my death, whether passing under this will or otherwise." One of the witnesses was also the beneficiary of life insurance policies that triggered tax, and thus benefited from the clause. To eliminate him as an interested witness, the clause was not applied to him.

7. How "close" of a relationship does it take to be an interested witness? *See, e.g.*, *Pavletich v. Pavletich*, 428 P.2d 632 (N.M. 1967) (will valid although it directed executor to hire attorney who was also a witness); *In re Longworth*, 222 A.2d 561 (Me. 1966) (officials of bank/trustee could serve as witnesses); *Rosenbloom v. Kokofsky*, 369 N.E.2d 1142 (Mass. 1977) (spouse of beneficiary was interested witness); *In re Estate of Tkachuk*, 139 Cal. Rptr. 55 (Ct. App. 1977) (gift to church valid when minister witnessed will).

8. Should we go further than eliminating the interested-witness rule and simply abolish the witness requirement altogether?

Problem

Dorothy's will leaves $50,000 to her daughter Wanda and the residue ($30,000) to her son Robert. Wanda, who signed as one of the witnesses, would have received $40,000 had Dorothy died intestate. How much will Wanda receive in a Uniform Probate Code state? In a state which employs the "lesser of the two rule"?

e. Some Other Rules

Occasionally statutes or courts require or mention other elements:

Publication. A few statutes require that the testator "publish" the will by telling the witnesses that the document is his will.

Order of signing. Because witnesses formally are attesting to the testator's signature, the testator's signature should be there when the witnesses add theirs. Occasionally, however, witnesses will sign first. Courts generally validate such out-of-order signings if the signatures came as a part of "one transaction." *Waldrep v. Goodwin*, 195 S.E.2d 432 (Ga. 1973). Nonetheless, prudent attorneys ensure that testators sign first.

Wills having a relationship to other jurisdictions. Suppose a testator validly executes a will in State A but dies a domiciliary of State B, where the execution requirements were not met. Will the will be admitted to probate in State B? Clearly, the answer in this and other situations is yes in a UPC jurisdiction.

Uniform Probate Code

Section 2-502. Choice of Law as to Execution.

A written will is valid . . . if its execution complies with the law at the time of execution of the place where the will is executed, or of the law of the place where at the time of execution or at the time of death the testator is domiciled, has a place of abode, or is a national.

A similar result will likely obtain in non-UPC jurisdiction. *See, e.g.*, N.Y. Estates, Powers and Trusts Law § 3-5.1(c).

Selected Reference

Raymond J. Werner, *Licensed in One State, but Practicing in Another: Multi-jurisdictional Practice*, 17 Prob. & Prop. 6 (Mar./Apr. 2003).

f. Attestation Clauses and Self-Proving Affidavits

Neither attestation clauses nor self-proving affidavits are required as part of a valid will, but they are commonly included.

Attestation clauses typically appear after the testator's signature, but above the witnesses' signatures. They are phrased from the witnesses' point of view, attesting that the testator has met the elements of the local statute. They are important because in most states they set up a rebuttable presumption that the facts stated in the clause are correct. This feature can be particularly useful if, between the time of the ceremony and the time for admitting the will to probate, witnesses have died or forgotten the relevant events. In *Matter of Collins*, 458 N.E.2d 797 (N.Y. 1983), for example, the witnesses were bank employees who had, as a service to their customers, witnessed numerous wills. Though they could not recall the details of the particular will execution in question, the court upheld the will on the strength of the attestation clause. If someone challenges a will, the attestation clause can be used to refresh witnesses' recollections or to impeach their testimony. Here is a typical attestation clause:

> On this 16th day of September, 1996, Mary Smith declared to us, the undersigned witnesses, that the foregoing instrument was her last will, and she asked us to act as witnesses to her signature thereon. She then signed the will in our mutual presence. We now, at her request, in her presence, and in our mutual presence, subscribe our names as witnesses, each declaring that in his or her opinion the testator is of sound mind and not operating under undue influence.

The Uniform Probate Code has popularized self-proving affidavits. There are two big differences between self-proving affidavits and traditional attestation clauses: (1) the testator also signs the self-proving affidavit and (2) the affidavit is notarized. Under the UPC, self-proving affidavits raise a conclusive presumption that the testator and witnesses have satisfied the statute's signature requirements. The affidavits both avoid the need for calling witnesses and limit the grounds of challenge.

Uniform Probate Code

Section 2-504. Self-Proved Will.

(a) A will may be simultaneously executed, attested, and made self-proved, by acknowledgment thereof by the testator and affidavits of the witnesses, each made before an officer authorized to administer oaths under the laws of the state in which execution occurs and evidenced by the officer's certificate, under official seal, in substantially the following form:

I, ________________, the testator, sign my name to this instrument this day of ________________, and being first duly sworn, do hereby declare to the undersigned authority that I sign and execute this instrument as my will and that I sign it willingly (or willingly direct another to sign for me), that I execute it as my free and voluntary act for the purposes therein expressed, and that I am eighteen years of age or older, of sound mind, and under no constraint or undue influence.

________________ Testator

We, ________________, ________________, the witnesses, sign our names to this instrument, being first duly sworn, and do hereby declare to the undersigned authority that the testator signs and executes this instrument as [his] [her] will and that [he][she] signs it willingly (or willingly directs another to sign for [him][her]), and that each of us, in the presence and hearing of the testator, hereby signs this will as witness to the testator's signing, and that to the best of our knowledge the testator is eighteen years of age or older, of sound mind, and under no constraint or undue influence.

________________ Witness

________________ Witness

The State of ________________ County of ________________

Subscribed, sworn to and acknowledged before me by ________________, the testator, and subscribed and sworn to before me by ________________, and ________________, witness, this day of ________________.

________________ (Seal)/(Signed)

________________ (Official capacity of officer)

(b) An attested will may be made self-proved at any time after its execution by the acknowledgment thereof by the testator and the affidavits of the witnesses, each made before an officer authorized to administer oaths under the laws of the state in which the acknowledgment occurs and evidenced by the officer's certificate, under the official seal, attached or annexed to the will in substantially the following form:

The State of ________________

County of ________________

We, ________________, ________________, and ________________, the testator and the witnesses, respectively, whose names are signed to the attached or foregoing instrument, being first duly sworn, do hereby declare to the undersigned authority that the testator signed and executed the instrument as the testator's will and that [he][she] had signed willingly (or willingly directed another to sign for [him][her]), and that [he][she] executed it as [his][her] free and voluntary act for the purposes therein expressed, and that each of the witnesses, in the presence and hearing of the testator, signed the will as witness and that to the best of [his][her] knowledge the testator was at that time eighteen years of age or older, of sound mind, and under no constraint or undue influence.

________________ Testator

________________ Witness

________________ Witness

Subscribed, sworn to and acknowledged before me by ________________, the testator, and subscribed and sworn to before me by ________________, and ________________, witnesses, this of ________________.

(Seal)

(Signed)

(Official capacity of officer)

(c) A signature affixed to a self-proving affidavit attached to a will is considered a signature affixed to the will, if necessary to prove the will's due execution.

Like all parts of the will execution ceremony, self-proving affidavits should be handled with particular care. For example, several cases have held that signatures that appear in the affidavit, but not earlier, are insufficient to validate the will. *See, e.g., Orrell v. Cochran*, 695 S.W.2d 552 (Tex. 1985) (testator); *Estate of Ricketts*, 773 P.2d 93 (Wash. Ct. App. 1989) (witnesses); *but see Estate of Dellinger v. 1st Service Bank*, 793 N.E.2d 1041 (Ind. 2003) (will valid where witnesses only signed self-proved affidavit). UPC § 2-504(c) seeks to avoid that problem. Moreover, UPC § 2-502(a)(3)(B) allows a testator's notarized acknowledgement to validate a will without additional witnesses.

So long as the execution itself was good, a botched self-proving affidavit should not invalidate the will. *See Cutler v. Ament*, 726 S.W.2d 605 (Tex. Ct. App. 1987).

In the absence of attestation clauses or self-proving affidavits, witnesses may need to appear and testify concerning due execution of the will. If they are out of the jurisdiction, their testimony may have to be obtained through letters rogatory, administered outside of the jurisdiction. If the witnesses are unavailable, will proponents may need to prove the validity of the witnesses' and the testator's signatures. *See London v. Harris*, 507 So. 2d 468 (Ala. 1987) (unwillingness of witness to confirm signature constitutes "unavailability" of the witness, allowing her signature to be proved by other testimony).

Problems

1. The senior probate partner in your law firm has asked you to create a checklist or script, including the words which the attorney should use, to be followed by attorneys in the firm in supervising the execution of wills. Prepare the script.

2. Harry Johnson has come to you to draft his will. He has a wife (Wilma Johnson), a daughter (Dorothy), and a son (Samuel). Neither offspring is married. Assume for the purposes of this problem that after discussing various alternatives with you Harry has decided on a "simple will." Harry's chosen dispository scheme is as follows: All of his property to Wilma. If Wilma does not survive, the residue would go to the children equally. If either child does not survive, then to the child's (now unborn) descendants. If a predeceased child has no descendants, then to the other child (or descendants). If neither Wilma nor any descendants survive Harry, to the American Cancer Society.

Wilma is to be executor; alternative is Wilma's sister, Joan Veach. Draft a will for Harry. It should be typed, in a form (including appropriate affidavits) ready for execution. Pay particular attention to the dispository clauses. You may want to review the material in Chapter 2, § 2.03(B)(3) and in the Appendix.

3. An additional will drafting exercise with sample documents is available at Roger W. Andersen and Karen Boxx, Skills & Values: Trusts and Estates, ch. 5 (2009).

Selected Reference

Deborah S. Gordon, *Reflecting on the Language of Death*, 34 Seattle U. L. Rev. 379 (2011).

3. Holographic Wills

Recognizing that in some situations formality is not possible, and that some testators simply believe it is not necessary, about half of the states allow informal, handwritten wills in particular circumstances. Called "holographs," these wills qualify for recognition under an alternative set of rules. Most importantly, holographs need not be witnessed. In return for eliminating the need for witnesses, however, states require additional elements, primarily aimed at assuring the genuineness of the document.

The UPC sets bare-bones requirements: the signature and "material portions" must be in the testator's handwriting. UPC § 2-502(b). *Matter of Estate of Baker*, ___ P.3d ___, 2016 WL 7488253 (Ala. 2016), held that the signature requirement was satisfied by a signature in the exordium (initial) clause. Consistent with the UPC's general approach of allowing more extrinsic evidence, § 2-502(c) provides: "Intent that the document constitute the testator's will can be established by extrinsic evidence, including, for holographic wills, portions of the document that are not in the testator's handwriting."

Several states require the document to be "entirely" or "wholly" in the testator's handwriting. Because of their minimal requirements, holographic wills may appear in unlikely places. They may be written in letters[11] or on furniture, briefcases, walls,

11. *See, e.g., In Re Estate of Kuralt* on Page 87.

even car bumpers. Once a court validates such a writing, however, it carries the same weight as a beautifully drafted document executed with all the trimmings in a law office. Keep your eyes open for holographs.

Question

What reasons justify requiring a holographic will to be "wholly" in the handwriting of the testator?

Problems

1. Martina wrote her will using three copies of the same printed form. She started by filling in blanks in the opening clause on each page, identifying herself and her residency and declaring the document to be her will. Then she wrote "I wish to disburse certain moneys and properties to the following:" and proceeded to write out her wishes. She used the large blank areas on all three forms, crossing out printed material where it did not fit her needs. At the end, she again used some of the form's blanks to identify her executor, the date and place. Then she signed the last page. Is the will valid in a state requiring documents to be "entirely handwritten" by the testator?

2. Thomas filled in the blanks of a will form he purchased at a local stationery store. The form included printed language which read "I give devise and bequeath to" and left a space. Thomas listed eight people, showing 1/8 shares for each, and then he signed the form. Is the will valid in a state requiring a will's "material provisions" to be in the testator's handwriting?

3. Tai-Kin Wong, a biotech entrepreneur, left the following note written the day he died: "All Tai-Kin Wong's—>Xi Zhao, my best half TKW 12/31/92." He had been living with Xi Zhao for three years. Is the note a valid will? *See Estate of Wong*, 47 Cal. Rptr. 2d 707 (Ct. App. 1995) (no).

Not only do states disagree about whether holographs are a good idea, so do scholars. Your responses to the material below may also influence the ways you analyze the next section about how the law should handle mistakes.

Richard Lewis Brown, *The Holograph Problem—The Case Against Holographic Wills*

74 Tenn. L. Rev. 93, 95, 100, 110, 116–18, 120–22, 126–28 (2006).

Holographic wills are a problem on several different levels. They are a problem to the coherence of the law of wills, to the decedents who have relied on them to guide the distribution of their estates, and to the court systems that must grapple with their chronic issues of validity and interpretation.... [T]hey should be excised from the law of wills....

... The[ir] announced purpose is to allow for the creation of valid wills by those who are unable or unwilling to obtain the professional assistance of a lawyer. ... Because they are invariably homemade, holographic wills present a range of chronic and unnecessary problems. ...

III. What is Wrong with Holographic Wills?

A. Validity Issues

Holographic wills are notoriously prone to challenge. ...

1. The Wholly/Entirely/Materially in the Handwriting of the Testator Requirement

... The paradigmatic holographic will is a document that is entirely handwritten by the testator, with no words on the document that are printed, stamped, or written by the hand of another. Yet many documents offered for probate as holographic wills are not so unblemished. They may include very minor non-handwritten components, as seemingly insignificant as the printed heading on stationery or a printed date. At the other end of the spectrum, they may be pre-printed will forms in which the testator's handwriting only appears by filling in the blanks. ...

2. The Testamentary Intent Requirement

...

The testamentary intent requirement is usually not an issue with formal, attested wills. ... In contrast, holographic wills invite suspicion as to the existence of testamentary intent. Holographic wills are often informal documents, such as letters or memoranda, which lack any formal designation as a will or last testament. Even if the holograph is denominated a will, the absence of the ceremonial execution that accompanies attested wills, creates less certainty that the document was intended to be final. ...

3. Technical Execution Requirements

...

The signature requirement can lead to litigation and, in some instances, to the invalidation of holographic wills. ... Is the handwritten name a signature or is it simply a part of the text of the will? ...

B. Interpretation

... In some cases, the holographic will is so artlessly drafted, that the court simply cannot determine the testator's intended plan of disposition.

... [C]ases abound in which the testator's use of imprecise language potentially thwarts implementation of the testator's true intentions. Is a devise of the "farmhouse" intended to mean the "farmhouse" only, or the house and the entire farm? Does a devise of the testator's house "& its entire contents" include stocks, coins, and jewelry that were in the house? ...

The homemade nature of holographic wills inevitably leads to difficulties when the testator uses legal words of art. The term "heir," for instance, has a precise legal meaning . . . . But many lay will drafters . . . frequently use "heirs" when they mean something quite different, like devisees named elsewhere in the will. . . .

V. Conclusion — What to Do About Holographic Wills?

Simply stated, holographic wills are more trouble than they are worth. . . .

First, state legislatures should prospectively repeal statutes authorizing holographic wills. [Second, states should enact the dispensing power and, in the absence of legislation, courts should adopt the substantial compliance doctrine (both of which are discussed in the next section of this text).] . . .

. . . [Third, the] law of wills should provide effective mechanisms to allow testators to implement their testamentary intentions. . . . [T]hose mechanisms must be accessible not only to those currently served by well-trained professionals, but also to those who are unable to afford, or who are otherwise deterred from utilizing, lawyers.[12] How one accomplishes that goal is a serious question, but encouraging testators to create homemade handwritten wills is not the answer.

Holographs in Action

Professor Stephen Clowney sees holographic wills as devices that empower people to effectuate their testamentary wishes, even if unable (perhaps lacking time) or unwilling (perhaps lacking funds) to consult a lawyer. He analyzed all of the holographic testamentary documents submitted to the Allegheny County, Pennsylvania, Register of Wills, during a two year period. *See* Stephen Clowney, *In Their Own Hand: An Analysis of Holographic Wills and Homemade Willmaking*, 43 Real Prop. Tr. & Est. L.J. 27 (2008).

He was surprised by results that showed "the benefits of homemade wills far outweigh their potential for mischief" and cast doubt "upon any charge that holographic wills impose unreasonable or excessive probate costs on testators or their families." *Id.* at 31–32. Though holograph authors came from a variety of socio-economic backgrounds, they mostly used clear language, often had accumulated substantial property, and were not feeble. Their wills did not prompt a disproportionate share of litigation.

Clowney offers four reasons for legislatures to allow holographic wills:

1. They provide an inexpensive alternative to intestacy.
2. They allow an inexpensive way to amend complicated estate plans.

12. One approach, followed in some states, is to recognize approved fill-in-the-blank forms. *See* Me. Rev. Stat. Ann. tit. 18A, § 2-514; Wis. Stat. Ann. §§ 853.50–.62. *See generally* Gerry W. Beyer, *Statutory Fill-in Will Forms — The First Decade: Theoretical Constructs and Empirical Findings*, 72 Or. L. Rev. 769 (1993). [Eds.]

3. They serve people caught with little time to live.
4. "[I]n the overwhelming majority of cases, [they] distribute a decedent's property without fuss or objections." *Id.* at 54.

In addition to providing valuable empirical data and offering broader policy prescriptions, this article shares a wealth of stories giving valuable insights into how the law of wills affects people's lives.

4. *Mistake in Execution*

Some wills statutes include a long list of technical requirements. Others, like the UPC, have shortened the list, in part to lower the chances that innocent mistakes will thwart testators' intentions. However short the list, life being what it is, mistakes happen. The following excerpt explains the principal rationale for courts' traditionally strict approach to enforcing will execution requirements. Then we turn to the development of the UPC's reform.

George J. Alexander, *Premature Probate: A Different Perspective on Guardianship for the Elderly*

18 Stanford L. Rev. 1003, 1018–19 (1979)

Certainty of result is a significant, if not primary, feature of the law of inheritance. Consequently, fixed rules are commonplace and tend to apply even in the face of countervailing considerations of fairness. For example, in Estate of Moore [206 P.2d 413 (Cal. App. 3d Dist. 1949)], the California Court of Appeals invalidated a will which had been signed at the beginning rather than at the end, although the will complied with all other statutory requirements. There was no question that the document was the decedent's will, yet the court refused to allow it into probate. The court recognized the probable specific unfairness to the decedent's estate, but relied on a broad view of justice, noting that when they are strictly construed, "statutes in the long run promote justice—which is their sole object—by shutting out opportunities of fraud. When they defeat one honest purpose they prevent unnumbered frauds, which in their absence would be feasible and measurably safe." It is easy to find similar examples in the law of formalities which when disobeyed apparently thwart a drafter's intent in the interest of avoiding fraud.

Although insistence on correct form appears at first to thwart the accomplishment of property owners' wishes, the purpose of that insistence may actually be the opposite. By providing for a certain result, such rules enable those willing to take the trouble to adopt the proper form to be certain about the outcome of their actions. The formality prevents competing claims of unfairness from becoming issues. If form were not so important, courts would continuously be confronted with the invitation to balance countervailing interests against the precision of the property owner's statement of intent. But instead a court can reject a document when improperly expressed however "unfair" that rejection may be and accept a property owner's statement made in the proper form however "unfair" its disposition of property may be. In that light, one can understand the court's decision in Estate of Moore, even if the "unfairness" in that case is extreme. Ironically, individual fairness is better effected by rules leading to certain outcomes than by individual adjudication.

Bruce H. Mann, *Formalities and Formalism in the Uniform Probate Code*

142 U. Pa. L. Rev. 1033, 1035–41 (1994)

The centerpiece of the 1990 Uniform Probate Code is the most significant change in what constitutes a will since enactment of the Statute of Frauds in 1677. For over three hundred years, wills have been defined by their formal qualities. The details have varied, but the essential formal requirements—writing, signature, and attestation—have remained constant and inviolate. These three formal requirements remain in a modified § 2-502, but they are no longer essential. Indeed, one could say that they remain in form only. A new provision, § 2-503, permits a court to dispense with the formalities if it is satisfied "that the decedent intended the document . . . to constitute" his or her will.

The significance of this change cannot be overstated. Wills have always been creatures of form rather than substance. A document that meets the formal requirements of the applicable Wills Act is a will. Whether or not a decedent intended a formally executed document to be his or her will has always been secondary to whether or not the document complied with the statutory formalities. . . .

Section 2-503 is the most recent salvo in a long campaign against formalism in wills adjudication, the roots of which go back over fifty [now 70+] years. It is important to remember that the target of the campaign has always been formalism rather than the formalities themselves. . . .

The problem lies not with the formalities, but with judicial insistence on literal compliance with them. Was one of the attesting witnesses called from the room while the testator was in mid-signature? If so, the will is invalid because it was not signed in the presence of both witnesses. . . . This judicial rule of strict compliance with Wills Act formalities is what led [Professor John] Langbein to begin his call for reform with the charge that "[t]he law of wills is notorious for its harsh and relentless formalism" [citing John H. Langbein, *Substantial Compliance with the Wills Act*, 88 Harv. L. Rev. 489 (1975)].

Langbein rested his call on the proposition that "[t]he first principle of the law of wills is freedom of testation." . . . The practical consequence of this deference is that the many rules that govern what constitutes a will and how it should be construed all purport to promote discovery of what the dearly departed intended.

Rules, however, sometimes assume lives of their own, particularly in bureaucratic systems such as probate. When they do—when courts refuse to countenance even minor slips in compliance—the administrative convenience of the formalities becomes the slavish adherence to form of formalism. Langbein . . . [argued that courts should] accept substantial compliance with the formalities whenever they are satisfied that the document expresses the testator's intent and that its form, however imprecise, gives sufficient assurance that the purposes of the formalities have been served. Langbein's proposal . . . did not, however, sweep the courts. Court after court refused to apply substantial compliance to save defectively executed wills, sometimes saying that to do so "would lead to confusion and uncertainty" or "unsettle the probate process," but more often rejecting it with little or no comment. . . . Their refusal was so persistent that by the time a court bucked the trend and applied the doctrine [*see In re* Will of Ranney, 589 A.2d 1339 (N.J. 1991)], Langbein himself had switched his allegiance to the related solution that became § 2-503.

The "dispensing power" of § 2-503 did not originate with the Uniform Probate Code. While Langbein sought converts in the United States, two Australian states reformed their Wills Acts. One, Queensland, adopted Langbein's substantial compliance proposal. The other, South Australia, provided that documents that had not been executed with the requisite formalities could nonetheless be admitted to probate whenever the court was satisfied "that there can be no reasonable doubt that the deceased intended the document to constitute his will." The Queensland statute, in Langbein's words, "has been a flop," primarily because of judges who seem unable to relinquish the old certitude of literal compliance. The South Australia statute, on the other hand, has been a rousing success. Courts have applied it with impressive discrimination and liberality to admit formally noncomplying documents as wills. . . .

The dispensing power operates more directly than substantial compliance. It forgoes the functional analysis of the latter and instead allows the proponent of a purported will to prove what courts now infer from compliance with the formalities—that the decedent intended the document to be a will. It thus redresses the evidentiary imbalance of the traditional rule—that compliance with the formalities raises a rebuttable presumption that the document is a will, while failure to comply creates a conclusive presumption that it is not—by treating both presumptions as rebuttable. The degree of compliance with the formalities may still be relevant, but only insofar as it bears on the decedent's intent, not on how closely it approximates full compliance. By subordinating the formalities and their functions to the testator's intent, the dispensing power frees courts from the fiction that the formalities are of equal weight and importance. As a consequence, courts can treat minor defects in execution as just that—minor defects that need not invalidate a will. With the dispensing power, wills would not be admitted to probate any less routinely than they are now. The important difference is that they could not be rejected as routinely.

Notes

1. A follow-up study of Australia's experience reveals that over time Queensland judges have gotten a bit more forgiving in finding "substantial compliance." Even so, the author prefers the approach of UPC § 2-503. *See* Stephanie Lester, *Admitting Defective Wills to Probate, Twenty Years Later: New Evidence for the Adoption of the Harmless Error Rule*, 42 Real Prop. Prob. & Tr. J. 577 (2007).

2. The reform train eventually did leave its U.S. station after Professor Mann wrote the article above. Rather than using the term "dispensing power," however, statutes, courts, and commentators now commonly refer to "harmless error."

Uniform Probate Code

Section 2-503. Harmless Error

Although a document or writing added upon a document was not executed in compliance with Section 2-502, the document or writing is treated as if it had been executed in compliance with that section if the proponent of the document or writing establishes by clear and convincing evidence that the decedent intended the document or writing to constitute (i) the decedent's will, (ii) a partial or complete revocation of the will, (iii) an addition to or an alteration of the will, or (iv) a partial or complete revival of his [or her] formerly revoked will or of a formerly revoked portion of the will.

In re Estate of Wiltfong

148 P.3d 465 (Colo. App. 2006)

Opinion by Judge Bernard.

In this formal testacy probate proceeding, Randall Rex (proponent), the proponent of a document alleged to be a will, appeals the trial court's order finding decedent, Ronald Wiltfong, died intestate. We reverse and remand for further proceedings.

I. Background

... Proponent and decedent were domestic partners for twenty years until decedent's death. They lived together and intermingled most of their finances.

On proponent's birthday in 2003, proponent and decedent celebrated with two friends. In the presence of the friends, decedent gave proponent a birthday card containing a typed letter decedent had signed. The letter expressed decedent's wish that if anything should ever happen to him, everything he owned should go to proponent. The letter also stated that proponent, their pets, and an aunt were his only family, and "everyone else is dead to me." Decedent told proponent and the friends the letter represented his wishes.

Decedent died from a heart attack the following year.

Proponent filed a petition to have the letter admitted to probate as decedent's will. Margaret Tovrea (contestant), the mother of decedent's three nephews who would be decedent's heirs if he died intestate, objected to the petition.

The trial court ruled the letter was not a will because it did not meet the requirements of § 15-11-503(2), C.R.S. 2006, and therefore the nephews would take decedent's estate by intestate succession. This appeal followed.

Proponent contends the trial court erred in concluding decedent did not intend the letter to be his will. We conclude that further proceedings are necessary to resolve this question.

II. General Principles

. . .

B. Execution of Wills

The underlying purposes of the Colorado Probate Code (Code) are to simplify and clarify the law concerning the affairs of decedents; to discover and make effective the intent of decedents in distributing their property; and to promote a speedy and efficient system for settling estates of decedents and distributing their property to their successors. The Code is to be liberally construed and applied to promote these purposes. Section 15-10-102, C.R.S. 2006.

As relevant here, § 15-11-502(1), C.R.S. 2006, establishes three requirements for a will: (1) it must be in writing; (2) it must bear the testator's signature or be signed in the testator's name; and (3) it must also bear the signatures of at least two persons who witnessed either the testator's signature or the testator's acknowledgment of the signature. There is no need to publish the document as the testator's will or to have witnesses sign the document in the presence of the testator or the other witnesses. *In re Estate of Royal*, 826 P.2d, 1236 (Colo.1992).

Although these three formalities represent a reduction over time in the number of formalities surrounding the execution of wills, *compare* § 15-3-502, C.R.S.1963, *with* § 15-11-502(1), they "require strict adherence in order to prevent fraud because statutes governing execution are designed to safeguard and protect the decedent's estate." *In re Estate of Royal, supra*, 826 P.2d at 1238 (citation omitted).

C. Holographic Wills

Section 15-11-502(2), C.R.S. 2006, provides that handwritten wills may also be valid: "A will that does not comply with subsection (1) of this section is valid as a holographic will, whether or not witnessed, if the signature and material portions of the document are in the testator's handwriting."

Proof of a decedent's intent that a document serve as a holographic will can be established by extrinsic evidence, including parts of the document that are not in the decedent's handwriting. Section 15-11-502(3), C.R.S. 2006. Holographic wills are viewed as valid even if "immaterial parts such as date or introductory wording are printed, typed, or stamped" or if printed will forms are used and the "material portions of the document are handwritten." Uniform Probate Code § 2-502 cmt. subsec. (b).

Here, the trial court found the letter was not a holographic will. Neither party disputes this finding on appeal.

D. Harmless Error

While scrupulous adherence to the formalities associated with executing wills serves the important purpose of preventing fraud, it can also "defeat intention . . . [or] work unjust enrichment." Restatement (Third) of Property: Wills & Other Donative Transfers § 3.3 cmt. b (1999). To address this concern, among others, the Code was amended in 1994 to align Colorado's law with extensive changes suggested by the Uniform Probate Code. *In re Estate of Sky Dancer*, 13 P.3d 1231 (Colo. App.2000).

One of these changes was effected by § 15-11-503(1), C.R.S.2006. This statute governs how potential donative documents are treated when they have not been executed pursuant to the three requirements established by § 15-11-502(1). Sections 15-11-503(1) states:

Although a document, or writing added upon a document, was not executed in compliance with section 15-11-502, the document or writing is treated as if it had been executed in compliance with that section if the proponent of the document or writing establishes by clear and convincing evidence that the decedent intended the document or writing to constitute: (a) The decedent's will. . . .

The purpose of adding § 15-11-503(1) was to provide a mechanism for the application of harmless error analysis when a probate court considers whether the formal requirements of executing a will have been met. Applying a harmless error standard in these circumstances supports the purposes of the Code and follows the general trend of the Uniform Probate Code extending the principle of harmless error to probate transfers. . . .

Thus, the question is whether a defect is harmless in light of the statutory purposes, not in light of the satisfaction of each statutory formality, viewed in isolation. To achieve those purposes, the issue is whether the evidence of the conduct proves the decedent intended the document to be a will. Restatement, *supra* , § 3.3 cmt. b.

Certain errors cannot be excused as harmless, like the failure of a proponent to produce a document. Other errors are difficult, although not impossible, to excuse as harmless, like the absence of a signature on a document. Restatement, *supra* , § 3.3 cmt. b. In this regard, § 15-11-503(2) reads: "Subsection (1) of this section shall apply only if the document is signed or acknowledged by the decedent as his or her will . . . ."

Adopted in 2001, Colo. Sess. Laws 2001, ch. 249 at 887, § 15-11-503(2) was designed to limit the harmless error concept to minor flaws in the execution of wills. *In re Estate of Sky Dancer, supra* ; H. Tucker, D. Swank & T. Hill, *Holographic and Nonconforming Wills: Dispensing with Formalities-Part II*, 32 Colo. Law. 53 (Jan.2003). Thus, § 15-11-503(2) establishes the condition precedent that a document be "signed or acknowledged by the decedent as his or her will" before a court may move to the next step and decide whether there is clear and convincing evidence the decedent intended the document to be a will.

The kinds of errors viewed as harmless in Colorado are technical drafting mistakes that frustrate the testator's intent. . . .

E. Burden of Proof Under § 15-11-503

Under § 15-11-503, a proponent of a document must show, by clear and convincing evidence, the decedent intended the document to be a will. This enhanced burden is "appropriate to the seriousness of the issue." Uniform Probate Code § 2-503 cmt. Clear and convincing evidence is stronger than a mere preponderance; it is highly probable evidence free from serious or substantial doubt. . . .

The greater the deviation from the requirements of due execution established by § 15-11-502, the heavier the burden on the document's proponent to prove, by clear and convincing evidence, that the instrument establishes the decedent's intent. *In re Estate of Sky Dancer, supra.*

. . .

IV. Conclusion

In this case, the court found decedent's letter did not satisfy the formal requirements of a will pursuant to § 15-11-502(1) and that it was not a holographic will pursuant to § 15-11-502(2). We agree.

Two of the formal requirements of § 15-11-502 were met in this case because the letter was in writing and signed by decedent. However, the letter was not signed by at least two witnesses who had witnessed either decedent's signing of the letter or decedent's acknowledgment of the signature or of the document as a will. Thus, the letter was not a formal will.

The letter was also not a holographic will. Although it was signed by decedent, the material portions of the letter were typed, and, therefore, they were not in decedent's handwriting.

Thus, it was appropriate to determine whether the letter was a writing intended as a will under § 15-11-503. However, [the trial court read the statute's requirement that the testator "sign or acknowledge" the document to mean "sign *and* acknowledge." The court thus required a person to announce, "This is my will."[13] On appeal, this court reversed and remanded, because the statute does not include that additional requirement.] . . .

On remand, the court should determine whether the defects in decedent's letter were technical drafting mistakes that should not be allowed to frustrate decedent's testamentary intent and, thus, harmless error under § 15-11-503(1) and (2). . . . Under a proper formulation of the harmless error analysis, once a court determines a decedent has signed or acknowledged a document as a will, as the trial court did here, the issue becomes whether the proponent can establish by clear and convincing evidence the decedent intended the document to be a will.

---

13. This requirement is often called "publication." *See* § 3.03C2(e). [Eds.]

This proof may take the form of extrinsic evidence, such as decedent's statements to others about the letter. Section 15-11-502(3) ("Intent that the document constitutes the testator's will can be established by extrinsic evidence. . . ."); Tucker, *supra*, 32 Colo. Law. at 55 ("A critical adjunct to . . . § 15-11-503 is . . . § 15-11-502(3), which gives teeth to that statute.").

The language of the letter is also relevant evidence, including, for example, whether the letter disposes of all decedent's property and whether the letter identifies a beneficiary. *See In re Estate of Lewis*, 93 P.3d 605 (Colo.App.2004) (courts ascertain intent of the decedent from will's language) . . . .

Here, the letter and the circumstances surrounding it are manifestly distinguishable from the document the division invalidated in *In re Estate of Sky Dancer, supra.* The purported will discussed in that opinion was flawed by more than technical drafting mistakes. For example, information produced in a police investigation suggested the proponent of the document may have been involved in causing the decedent's death. The dispositive portion of the document was neither signed by the decedent nor written in her hand. There was no evidence the decedent told anyone the document was to serve as her will. Last, the division indicated there was a possibility another person had created the dispositive portions of the document. Those concerns do not apply in this case.

Therefore, the trial court's order is reversed, and the case is remanded for further proceedings consistent with the views expressed in this opinion.

JUDGE MARQUEZ and JUDGE GRAHAM concur.

Notes

1. Note the order in which the *Wiltfong* court addressed questions surrounding the will's validity.

2. Despite their policy similarities, these reform doctrines differ. "Substantial compliance" focuses on being "close." Even if it can justify eschewing the traditional strict-compliance approach, a court using substantial compliance must eventually apply the statutory elements themselves. *See, e.g., Pomar v. Hash*, 2017 WL 639416 (Va. 2017) (no substantial compliance if witness fails to sign). In contrast, the UPC's "harmless error" approach allows courts to focus directly on whether the testator intended the document to be effective. *But cf. Pomar v. Hash*, 2017 WL 639416 (Va. 2017) (Virginia's harmless error statute will not be considered if will not probated within one year of death).

A third approach, reforming the document, is a possibility in some situations. *In re Snide*, 418 N.E.2d 656 (N.Y. 1981), involved Harvey and Rose, who had signed each other's wills. When the mistake was discovered after Harvey died, the court admitted the will Harvey had signed, even though it clearly referred to Rose as the testator and Harvey as beneficiary. To make sense of "Harvey's" will, the court reformed that will by substituting "Harvey" wherever "Rose" appeared, and vice versa. More recently, courts and commentators have concentrated on substantial compliance or harmless error when addressing mistakes in *execution*. We consider the reformation doctrine in § 3.04(b).

3. Compare the UPC's broader language with Colorado's insistence that the testator either sign or acknowledge the document as a will. In New Jersey, which tracks the UPC language, an *unexecuted* copy of a will could be admitted to probate where there was clear and convincing evidence that the document reflected the testator's intent. *In re Estate of Ehrlich*, 427 N.J. Super. 64 (App. Div. 2012), appeal dismissed by the parties, 64 A.3d (N.J. 2013). *Accord Estate of Attia*, ___ N.W.2d ___, 2016 WL 6652492 (Mich. Ct. App. 2016).

Signatures also may be especially important if a court is applying the substantial compliance doctrine. The testator in *Estate of Kuhn*, 612 N.W.2d 385 (Wis. App. 2000), failed to follow the requirements of a statutory form will when he only placed his signature after the name of three (of four) beneficiaries. The gift to the fourth beneficiary failed. *See also Brown v. Fluharty*, 748 S.E.2d 809 (W.Va. 2013) (substantial compliance doctrine does not validate will that physically disabled testator did not sign.)

4. Restatement (Third) of Property § 3.3 encourages legislatures to adopt a harmless error rule paralleling the UPC, but also endorses a substantial compliance approach in the absence of legislation.

Questions

1. You are a member of a State Bar committee considering whether to recommend that the legislature adopt UPC § 2-503. Most of the discussion has centered around the question of whether the flexibility gained by adopting a harmless error rule would carry too high a price by encouraging a flood of litigation. One participant just suggested that the "clear and convincing" standard is sufficient protection against the floodgates risk. When they turn to you, what do you say?

2. Since Nevada is the only state so far to recognize electronic wills by statute, *see* Page 122, should an electronic will be admitted to probate under a state's harmless error statute? *See Estate of Castro*, No. 2013ES00140 (Lorain County Ohio Ct. Com. Pl. June 19, 2013)) (yes). *See generally Gökalp* Y. Gürer, *No Paper? No Problem: Ushering In Electronic Wills through California's "Harmless Error" Provision*, 49 U.C. Davis L. Rev. 1955 (2016) (arguing that the harmless error rule should apply to admit electronic wills).

Problems

1. At the end of a long handwritten letter, the writer says "Finally, I just want you to know, you'll get everything when I'm gone." Should a court recognize that language as a will under UPC § 2-503?

2. Mi-Ling Wong, a resident of a nursing home, sat in her room with two friends, Jennifer and Julie. After a conversation about the need for making a will, she wrote the following in her handwriting: "I give all of my property at my death to my good friend Robert. Mi-Ling Wong." She then said to her friends, "Now I want both of you to sign this." Before they could do so, however, the fire alarm rang, and everyone fled the room. Mi-Ling Wong died in the fire. Jennifer and Julie survived, found the paper, and signed it. Is the paper a valid will?

Selected References

Jane B. Baron, *Irresolute Testators, Clear and Convincing Wills Law*, 73 Wash. & Lee L. Rev. 3 (2016).

Mark Glover, *Decoupling the Law of Will-Execution*, 88 St. John's L. Rev. 597 (2014).

John H. Langbein, *Excusing Harmless Errors in the Execution of Wills: A Report on Australia's Tranquil Revolution in Probate Law*, 87 Colum. L. Rev. 1 (1987).

John H. Langbein, *Substantial Compliance with the Wills Act*, 88 Harv. L. Rev. 489 (1975).

John V. Orth, *Wills Act Formalities: How Much Compliance Is Enough?*, 43 Real Prop. Tr. & Est. L.J. 73 (2008).

Emily Sherwin, *Clear and Convincing Evidence of Testamentary Intent: The Search for a Compromise Between Formality and Adjudicative Justice*, 34 Conn. L. Rev. 453 (2002).

Leigh A. Shipp, *Equitable Remedies for Nonconforming Wills: New Choices for Probate Courts in the United States*, 79 Tul. L. Rev. 723 (2005).

D. Protective Planning

After wearing the hats of litigators and policy wonks, we now return to the role of estate planner. In particular, our concern is how to protect estate plans from attack. Protection starts with heightened awareness. Which situations are likely to invite challenges? Who is likely to bring one? Some situations are obvious: the client may show signs of lack of capacity or over-dependence upon one person. Others may take some digging. The testator may want to make a substantial gift outside the biological family. The testator may have children from each of two marriages. Second-marriage situations are particularly tricky, because all may seem well when both spouses agree on a plan, only to degenerate following one spouse's death. After a look at the question of who has standing to challenge a will, this section examines two categories of strategies for protecting clients' intention: structural elements in the plan and conduct when carrying out the plan.

1. Who Might Challenge

Only those who would benefit from a finding of invalidity have standing to contest a will. Perhaps the clearest example is an heir whose share under the will is smaller than the intestate share would be. When there is more than one will, the analysis gets more complicated. For example, because an unchallenged earlier will left out the decedent's son, the son could not challenge a later will in its entirety. He did have standing, however, to challenge just the residuary clause of the later will. That way the "all prior wills revoked" clause of the later will would still apply to revoke the earlier will that had left him out. Then, invalidating the later will's residuary clause would cause a partial intestacy. *See Estate of Luongo*, 823 A.2d 942 (Pa. Super. Ct. 2003); *but see Estate of Burger*, 898 A.2d 547 (Pa. 2006) (heir lacked standing because a valid substitute gift to other residuary beneficiaries prevented partial intestacy). *See also Gordon v. Kleinman*, 120 So. 3d 120 (Fla. App. 2013) (beneficiary of 1983 will had standing by challenging validity of all four later wills from 1992–2009). Similarly, someone who took a larger share under an earlier will could challenge a later will that reduces (or eliminates) the first gift. Courts disagree on whether creditors of an heir (or creditors of a beneficiary of an earlier will) can contest a later will, but secured creditors are more likely to have standing than general creditors. Finally, fiduciaries usually have standing to contest later wills on behalf of the people who would be hurt.

Melvin Higginbotham was a wealthy industrialist who loved sea otters and founded the Higginbotham Otter Aquarium. By far the greatest source of his wealth was his stock in Higgs, Inc., in which he held a controlling interest. After making substantial gifts to his family, Melvin's will left the majority of his estate to the Aquarium, which would be run by three directors. Later, he changed his mind and executed a new will giving most of his Higgs, Inc., stock to his son, Bill, as trustee to manage the property and pay the income to the Aquarium. Bill's daughter, Marcia, was named as contingent trustee in case Bill died. Later still, Melvin executed a third will giving the stock directly to the Aquarium.

Marcia alleges that the third will was the result of the undue influence of Melvin's lawyer, Gordon. Gordon, the dominant person among the Aquarium's directors, owned a substantial block of Higgs, Inc., stock in his own name and stood to gain effective control of Higgs, Inc., once the Aquarium acquired the stock. Bill, also an Aquarium director, is still alive. Does Marcia have standing to challenge the last will? If she does not, who can raise the undue influence claim? *See In re Estate of Getty*, 85 Cal. App. 3d 755 (1978) (no standing).

2. Structural Elements

An estate plan might include any combination of several features designed to discourage bringing, or limit the chances of winning, a will contest. This subsection identifies the principal techniques.

No-contest clauses. One possibility is to include a no-contest clause, which denies gifts to any beneficiary who challenges the will. These clauses sometimes go under the label "*in terrorem*" because they are designed to terrorize beneficiaries tempted to bring a contest. The clause can only work, however, if it is accompanied by a gift to the potential contestants. (See box.) Note that in many will contests involving issues of capacity, undue influence, or improper execution, if the contest is successful, the no-contest clause will have no effect. It will fall with the will or the other challenged clauses.

If the contest fails, however, the question becomes whether to enforce the clause against the contestant. Courts are divided on whether no-contest clauses are a good idea. To the extent they actually discourage litigation, they reduce the incidence of strike suits filed to get the estate beneficiaries to settle with the contestants so the estate can be closed. Discouraging such suits may preserve some measure of family harmony. Since on their face the clauses apply to all contests, however, they may also stifle valid claims. To balance these competing consequences, many jurisdictions refuse to apply no-contest clauses if there was "probable cause" to bring the contest. *See* Restatement (Second) of Property § 9.1; UPC § 3-905. Under that approach, even if you lose the contest, if you had probable cause for bringing it, there will be no penalty. *See, e.g., Hamel v. Hamel*, 299 P.3d 278 (Kan. 2013). A no-contest provision in a will that voided a disposition even if based on probable cause was unenforceable as violative of Mississippi public policy. *Parker v. Benoist*, 160 So. 3d 198 (Miss. 2015).

Make Them Think

For an example of a useless no-contest clause, consider *Lipper v. Weslow*, 369 S.W.2d 698 (Tex. Civ. App. 1963). The testator had two sons, only one of whom survived her. Because she was favoring her surviving son over the family of her predeceased son, and she wanted to discourage a contest by the losers, she provided that any legatee who contested the will would lose his or her share. The will, however, entirely disinherited her predeceased son's family; they had nothing to lose by bringing the contest. She should have included a gift to the potential contestants large enough to make them think about whether the amount they would gain through a successful contest was enough to justify the risk of losing everything if they lost the contest and the court enforced the no-contest clause.

One common source of litigation is deciding whether a particular action is a contest at all. New York statutes provide a so-called "safe harbor" identifying specific acts that are not contests. *See* Surrogate's Court Procedure Act § 1404; Estates, Powers and Trusts Law § 3-3.5. *See also In re Estate of Singer*, 920 N.E.2d 943 (N.Y. 2009) (statutory list not exclusive). Courts often, but not always, construe such clauses narrowly.[14]

14. *Compare Estate of Davies*, 26 Cal. Rptr. 3d 239 (Ct. App. 2005) (action seeking clarification of whether beneficiary met survival requirement is not a contest), and *Harrison v. Morrow*, 977 So. 2d 457 (Ala. 2007) (clause prohibiting challenges to procedures for distribution of bequests or their

Despite these limits, no-contest clauses can be powerful devices. Consider Dawn Roddenberry's decision to challenge the will of her father and "Star Trek" creator, Gene. Despite a no-contest clause, Dawn filed a contest based on fraud, undue influence, and lack of testamentary capacity. She pursued the litigation for nearly two years, before voluntarily dismissing the action the day it was set to go to trial. The court found that she had brought a contest and thereby forfeited her $500,000 cash legacy plus her share of a trust that could be worth hundreds of millions of dollars, depending upon the continued success of "Star Trek" films and merchandise. *See* Los Angeles Times, June 28, 1996, at B4.

Mediation or Arbitration Clauses. Some jurisdictions authorize documents to mandate alternative dispute resolution (ADR).[15] *See* Ariz. Rev. Stat. § 14-10205 (applies to trusts). However, if these clauses are analyzed under contract principles, they are not likely to be enforceable against a beneficiary, who is not a party to any contract. *See, e.g., Rachal v. Reitz*, 347 S.W.3d 305 (Tex. App. 2011); *Diaz v. Bukey*, 195 Cal. App. 4th 315 (2011). Even if the local jurisdiction does not enforce directions to mediate or arbitrate, the mere presence of a clause directing or encouraging disputants to engage in ADR may be enough. Also, a testator may tie such a clause to a no-contest clause; for example, one might provide that a contestant who has first engaged in good-faith mediation will still receive some percentage of the gift that would otherwise be lost after an unsuccessful contest.

Explanations. When a testator wants to leave out some family members, or reduce their shares, one option is for the testator to explain in the will the reasons for doing so. If the testator is equalizing treatment among various takers, as when one child's gift is reduced to take into account a lifetime gift, this technique may work well. What otherwise would have looked like unjustified favoritism (and might have prompted a bitter response) becomes more understandable. Easing family tensions at an emotional time can be an especially valuable final gift from the testator.

When favoritism of one side of the family is prompted by ill-will toward the other side, however, displaying the family laundry in public can be risky. In *Lipper v. Weslow*, the no-contest clause case discussed infra, the testator complained in a long paragraph about how the wife and children of her predeceased son had ignored her. Airing such complaints is unlikely to discourage a contest from the disinherited relatives. Moreover, such an approach may fuel a contest. Failure to get the facts right could strengthen a challenge based on lack of capacity. Unfounded accusations could produce a claim of testamentary libel.

Living Probate. A few jurisdictions allow wills to be admitted to probate before the testator's death. Though the details vary, the basic idea is to allow a testator to

---

percentages did not apply to contest of the whole will), *with Cook v. Cook*, 99 Cal. Rptr. 3d 913 (Ct. App. 2009) (clause applied to beneficiary who argued that settlors' debts to him should not be offset against his share), and *McKenzie v. Vanderpoel*, 61 Cal. Rptr. 3d 129 (Ct. App. 2007) (petition seeking reallocation of trust income and principal was a contest).

15. We also discuss ADR in Chapter 10, § 10.04.

give interested parties notice of an intent to probate the will. If anyone objects, a hearing is held to determine whether the will should be admitted. If there are no objections, or if the objections are overcome, the will is admitted to probate and controls distribution of the estate unless the testator later revokes it.

Lifetime trusts and other gifts. Another way to get property to a favored beneficiary without risking a will contest is to make lifetime gifts. Family members could challenge gifts while the client is alive, but as a practical matter, challenges are unlikely. Because the property would not be in the estate, a will contest would be irrelevant. If the client made a gift by creating a living trust with an independent trustee, the continuing nature of the trust during the lifetime of the client/donor may negate challenges of incapacity or undue influence. Other options include: outright gifts, the creation of joint and survivor or payable-on-death accounts, and life insurance. Of course, the client should have the financial means to make gifts like these and still maintain an appropriate standard of living.

Family Law Options. In some situations, testators may be able to protect their estate plans by using devices from family law. Couples who are not married may decide that the protections they gain through marriage outweigh the disadvantages. Adoption may be a good choice if the client has no children and wants to give the estate to a non-family member. By adopting the beneficiary, the client may be able to prevent other relatives from challenging the will. Adoption may be an option for homosexual couples. *But see In re Robert Paul P.*, 471 N.E.2d 424 (N.Y. 1984) (a 57-year-old male was not allowed to adopt a 50-year-old male with whom he had shared a homosexual relationship for more than 25 years). Another possibility would be for a couple to agree to a cohabitation contract, setting out their rights and obligations. *See Marvin v. Marvin*, 557 P.2d 106 (Cal. 1976) (court enforced oral contract between cohabitating couple thereby giving non-working partner, who provided domestic services, legal rights in working partner's property).

3. Conduct

By acting defensively, lawyers can build a record to discourage contests. Working with one eye viewing the elements of mental capacity and undue influence, lawyers can preserve evidence establishing that their clients were acting competently and on their own at the time they executed the wills. If the testator is disinheriting someone for private reasons, the lawyer could ask the testator to write out an explanation or prepare an audio or video recording to keep on file. Using the testator's own handwriting supports both the authenticity of the document and its weight as actually reflecting the testator's intention. A recording of the testator explaining the will could be powerful evidence of competency and actual intention. Even if the recording is not admissible in court, it may well convince the family that the testator really wanted the result shown in the will. On the other hand, what may only be innocent disinterest—once recorded—can help challengers. (See box below.)

Caution: Recordings Can Be Dangerous

Looking ahead to preparing Kay's will, Bruce tape recorded a conversation with her. Affirming a decision to deny probate of the resulting will, the Montana Supreme Court relied in part on the tape:

> . . . [T]he tape-recorded conversation between Bruce and Kay in which they discussed the proposed changes to Kay's will reveals that Kay was unaware that she owned stock until reminded by Bruce.
>
> BRUCE [the son]: You own stock in Ford Motor Company and stock in Australia New Zealand Bank.
>
> KAY [the mother]: I do? (laughs)
>
> BRUCE: Yes, which has your's, mine, and Jean's [the daughter] names on them as tenants in common. Okay. How do you want to handle those stocks? That's also the Montana Power Stock that Dad bought prior.
>
> KAY: I am no good at that kind of thing. I have no idea.
>
> The foregoing evidence indicates that Kay did not have the "clearness of mind and memory to know, in general, without prompting, the nature and extent of [her] property." *See Bodin's Estate*, 398 P.2d at 619. Without such clearness of mind, and absent the mental capacity to recollect the nature and situation of her property, Kay was not competent to execute a will.
>
> Dr. Paul Bach . . . , a clinical psychologist, . . . also was concerned about Kay's mental competence based on his review of the tape-recorded conversation between Bruce and Kay. [Bach testified:]
>
> Most remarkable was the number of times [Kay] responded to questions put to her by saying something on the order [of] . . . "I'm not good at that kind of thing . . . , decisions to make . . . , I wish . . . , I want someone else to do it . . . , I don't know . . . , I don't remember, I can't remember." Particularly her mention was made of stocks and bonds, and she responded, "I do have some?", as if uncertain that she did. But basically, her verbal responses indicated a woman who was uncertain at the time of the tape recording, and just would continuously give inaccurate responses to a question at different points throughout the tape.

Estate of Brooks, 927 P.2d 1024, 1028–29 (Mont. 1996).

Because witnesses in these situations are more likely to be called to appear in court, clients should choose them with care. Are they young enough to be likely survivors of the testator? Will they come across as strong, independent people? Right after the will execution ceremony, lawyers could ask the witnesses to dictate their recollections of the event. These statements could then be used in later litigation to refresh recollections. Using a psychiatrist as a witness is probably a bad idea, because it would alert challengers to the competency issue. It might be prudent, however, to include a psychiatrist's statement in the file for later use.

An often-overlooked technique is to disclose the plan, especially to those who might be disappointed. Like the ante-mortem probate available in a few places, this approach gets things out in the open. It can foster family discussions, explain reasoning, and even prompt reconciliations. Perhaps most importantly, by avoiding surprises, disclosure gives beneficiaries time to let disappointment or anger dissipate.

Problems

1. Violet Quirin's first two wills had divided her property equally between her two daughters. However, her final will, in 2010, acknowledged her "love and respect" for her daughters, but explicitly made "no provision for them in this will." Instead, it gave her estate to friends and charities. The unhappy daughters challenged the will. In affirming a decision finding testamentary capacity, the court in *Estate of Quirin*, 2015 WL 2405484 (Mont. 2015), described the setting:

> The 2010 will was the product of Quirin's interactions with attorney Nancy Moe. Quirin contacted Moe on June 2, 2010, and asked her to draft a new will for Quirin. Moe met with Quirin for around an hour and a half on June 4, 2010. Quirin told Moe that her daughters were the current beneficiaries of her will and that she no longer wished for them to benefit from her estate. She told Moe that she would like to change her will to benefit organizations and individuals with whom she had long, trusting relationships. Moe advised Quirin that a will contest might result from such a change, but Quirin persisted, stating that she and her daughters were "not close." . . .
>
> Moe concluded that Quirin intended to make a new will, understood that she was making a new will, understood her assets, and otherwise understood the consequences of what she was doing. Moe, therefore, drafted a will based on her June 4 discussion with Quirin. . . . Moe, accompanied by two paralegals from her office, visited Quirin's home. Moe and the paralegals observed that Quirin was dressed and articulate and that there was nothing to suggest that Quirin did not have testamentary capacity. Quirin and Moe spoke about the will and their June 4 conversation. Quirin signed the will prepared by Moe during this visit. The paralegals signed the will as witnesses.

What additional techniques might have saved Quirin's estate the costs of a trial and an appeal?

2. For a problem that requires a client letter discussing the issue of a potential challenge to her will on grounds she lacked testamentary capacity, and suggesting protective strategies, *see* Roger W. Andersen and Karen E. Boxx, Skills and Values: Trusts and Estates, Ch. 6 (2009).

Selected References

Katherine M. Arango, *Trial and Heirs: Antemortem Probate for the Changing American Family*, 81 Brook. L. Rev. 779 (2016).

Dennis W. Collins, *Avoiding a Will Contest—The Impossible Dream?*, 34 Creighton L. Rev. 7 (2000).

Dara Greene, *Antemortem Probate: A Mediation Model*, 14 Ohio St. J. on Disp. Resol. 663 (1999).

Erin Katzen, *Arbitration Clauses in Wills and Trusts: Defining the Parameters for Mandatory Arbitration of Wills and Trusts*, 24 Quinnipiac Prob. L.J. 118 (2011).

Lela P. Love & Stewart E. Sterk, *Leaving More Than Money: Mediation Clauses in Estate Planning Documents*, 65 Wash. & Lee L. Rev. 539 (2008).

Calvin Massey, *Designation of Heirs: A Modest Proposal to Diminish Will Contests*, 37 Real Prop. Prob. & Tr. J. 577 (2003).

Susan G. Thatch, Ante-*Mortem Probate in New Jersey—An Idea Resurrected?*, 39 **Seton Hall Legis.** J. 331 (2015).

Paul T. Whitcombe, *Defamation by Will: Theories and Liabilities*, 27 J. Marshall L. Rev. 749 (1994).

§ 3.03 Components of the Will

A separate set of issues centers around the question: What items constitute the will? The doctrine of "integration" addresses the question in the physical sense: Which pieces of paper were meant to be in the will? The doctrine of "incorporation by reference" allows a testator to give testamentary effect to words not physically present at the execution ceremony. The doctrine of "acts of independent significance" allows reference to facts outside of the will.

A. Integration

Usually it is easy to determine which papers make up a will: all of the pages are found stapled together in numbered order, with the signatures at the end. Presumably, that is the way they were when the will was executed. Integration problems arise when pages are loose or scattered or piled together with some stapled and others not. Then the question becomes: what papers were present and intended to be part of the will at the time of the execution ceremony? Planners use a variety of techniques to avoid such controversy: the attestation clause may specify the number of pages, the words may carry over from one page to the next to show that no new pages were inserted later, or the testator and witnesses may have initialed each page.

The practice of initialing pages is risky, however, because it is so easy to miss a page and thereby raise a suspicion that something is wrong.

B. Incorporation by Reference

Incorporation by reference is a way to give testamentary effect to a document not present at the execution ceremony.

Simon v. Grayson

102 P.2d 1081 (Cal. 1940)

WASTE, C.J.

The question presented for determination upon this appeal involves the construction and effect to be given a provision in a will purporting to incorporate a letter by reference. Respondent's claim to certain of the estate's funds is based upon the terms of the letter. The appellants, who are residuary legatees under the will, contend that the attempted incorporation by reference was ineffectual. The facts, which were presented to the trial court upon an agreed statement, are as follows:

S.M. Seeligsohn died in 1935. His safe deposit box was found to contain, among other things, a will and codicil and a letter addressed to his executors. The will, which was dated March 25, 1932, contained a provision in paragraph four, leaving $6,000 to his executors "to be paid by them in certain amounts to certain persons as shall be directed by me in a letter that will be found in my effects and which said letter will be addressed to Martin E. Simon and Arthur W. Green [the executors] and will be dated March 25, 1932." ...

The letter found in the testator's safe deposit box was dated July 3, 1933, and stated: "In paragraph VIII of my will I have left you $6,000 to be paid to the persons named in a letter and this letter is also mentioned in said paragraph. I direct that after my death you shall pay said $6,000 as follows: To Mrs. Esther Cohn, 1755 Van Ness Ave. San Francisco, Calif. the sum of $4,000. . . ." This letter was written, dated and signed entirely in the handwriting of the testator. No letter dated March 25, 1932, was found among his effects.

The codicil to the will was executed November 25, 1933. It made no changes in paragraph IV of the will and contained no reference to the letter, but recited, "Except as expressly modified by this Codicil, my Will of March 25th 1932 shall remain in full force and effect."

Esther Cohn's whereabouts was known to the testator's executors immediately following his death, but she herself died a week later. Respondent, as her executrix, claimed the $4,000 mentioned in the letter....

It is settled law in this state that a testator may incorporate an extrinsic document into his will, provided the document is in existence at the time and provided, further, that the reference to it in the will clearly identifies it, or renders it capable of identification by extrinsic proof. . . . An attempt to incorporate a future document is ineffectual, because a testator cannot be permitted to create for himself the power to dispose of his property without complying with the formalities required in making a will. . . .

In the case at bar the letter presumably was not in existence when the will was executed, for the letter bore a date subsequent to the date of the will. . . . However, the letter was in existence at the time the codicil to the will was executed. The respondent points out that under the law the execution of a codicil has the effect of republishing the will which it modifies (Prob. Code, sec. 25), and argues from this that Seeligsohn's letter was an "existing document" within the incorporation rule. The only authorities cited by the parties on this point are several English decisions. These cases hold that although an informal document is not in existence when the will referring to it is executed, a later republication of the will by codicil will satisfy the "existing document" rule and will incorporate it by reference provided the testamentary instruments sufficiently identify it. *In re Goods of Lady Truro*, [1886] L. R. 1 P. & D. 201; *compare In re Goods of Smart*, [1902], L. R. Prob. Div. 238; 4 Cal. L. Rev. 356. The principle of republication thus applied is unquestionably sound. In revising his scheme of testamentary disposition by codicil a testator presumably reviews and reaffirms those portions of his will which remain unaffected. In substance, the will is reexecuted as of that time. Therefore, the testator's execution of the codicil in the present case must be taken as confirming the incorporation of the letter then in existence, provided the letter can be satisfactorily identified as the one referred to in the will. And this is true, notwithstanding the codicil made no reference to the letter and recited that the will should remain in full force "except as expressly modified by this codicil," for the letter, if properly incorporated, would be an integral part of the republished will.

We are also of the opinion that the trial court did not err in concluding that the letter found with the will was the letter referred to in the will. Conceding the contrary force of the discrepancy in dates, the evidence of identity was, nevertheless, sufficient to overcome the effect of that factor. The controlling authorities in this state do not require that the informal document be identified with exact precision; it is enough that the descriptive words and extrinsic circumstances combine to produce a reasonable certainty that the document in question is the one referred to by the testator in his will. . . . Here the letter was found in the safe deposit box with the will. It was addressed to the executors, as the will stated it would be. No other letter was found. Moreover, the letter is conceded to have been written by the testator, and its terms conform unmistakably to the letter described in the will. It identifies itself as the letter mentioned in the will and deals with the identical subject matter referred to in that portion of the will. All these circumstances leave no doubt that the letter of July 3, 1933, is the one that the testator intended to incorporate in paragraph four of his will. . . .

Notes and Questions

1. What other arguments could you make for saving the letter's gift in *Simon v. Grayson*?

2. Typically-stated requirements for a document to be incorporated by reference include:

- The writing must be in existence at the time the will is executed.
- The will must describe the writing as in existence at the time the will is executed.
- The will must describe the writing with sufficient detail to identify it.
- The writing must fit the description.
- The will must show an intent to incorporate the writing into the will.

The UPC eliminates the second element, which in particular has troubled courts. UPC § 2-510.

3. As we will see in Chapter 6, statutes often give part of a parent's estate to children born after the parent's will was executed. Patricia was born after her father executed his will, but before the date of a codicil. The court in *Azcunce v. Estate of Azcunce*, 586 So. 2d 1216 (Fla. Dist. Ct. App. 1991), held that the codicil republished the will, so Patricia was not an afterborn child protected by the statute. *Compare* Restatement (Third) of Property (Wills and Other Donative Transfers) § 3.4, Reporter's Note ("The mere fact that the codicil expressly republished the prior will should not require that the doctrine of republication by codicil always be applied.").

4. Testators often have specific desires about who should get various pieces of personal property: "I want the silver platter from Aunt Martha to go to her son George and the green wing-back chair to go to Marjorie, because she's always liked it." Lists like this can be long and are especially subject to change. Incorporation by reference cannot cope with such changes because the doctrine requires the document to exist when the will is executed. To address these problems, the UPC allows wills to refer to a separate, signed writing which identifies who should get particular items of tangible personal property, and allows the testator to change the writing after the will has been executed. UPC § 2-513. Does the interest of validating peoples' intentions override the risk of fraud in these situations?

Problems

1. You practice in a jurisdiction which has not adopted UPC § 2-513 (*see* note 4, *above*). Your client has acquired a number of pieces of jewelry she wants to leave to different relatives. She may, of course, acquire new items or change her mind about who should get them. How would you handle her problem?

2. Dexter Johnson's will is reproduced below from *Johnson v. Johnson*, 279 P.2d 928, 933 (Okla. 1954). The handwritten portion is in Dexter's handwriting and reads: "To my brother James I give ten dollars only. This will shall be complete unless hereafter altered, changed or rewritten. Witness my hand this April 6, 1947. Easter Sunday, 2:30 p.m. D.G. Johnson Dexter G. Johnson." In a jurisdiction recognizing holographs, should the will be probated?

JOHNSON v. JOHNSON Okl. 933
Cite as, Okl., 279 P.2d 928

31691

FILED IN COUNTY COURT
OKLAHOMA COUNTY, OKLA.
JUL 2 1952
CLIFF MYERS, COURT CLERK
By .... DEPUTY

129067

I, D. G. Johnson also known as Dexter G. Johnson, of Oklahoma City, Oklahoma County, State of Oklahoma do hereby make, publish and declare this to be my last Will and Testamnt and revoke all former wills and codocils by me made.

FIRST: I direct my Executor to pay my just debts,last illness and burial expense.

SECOND: I give, devise and bequeath to my sister Beulah Johnson also known as Beulah J. Johnson and my brother V. C. Johnson also known as Victor C. Johnson all of the rest, residue and rrmainder of my estate, real, personal and mixed propertt, wherever situated and whatsoever kind and/or character, subject only to the following requests of my said brother and sister,namely and specifically that at a time when in the jydgment of my said sister and brother they shall deem the cpndition of the estate in a proper and suitable condition so to do without material ~~injuryxxxx~~ damage to or otherwise detremental to said estate and the properties reasonably disposed of to pay intc a trust fund to be governed by my said sister and brother the sum of Fifty thousand dollars to be used for the erection of a new church in Montrose,Effingham County, State of Illinois on the site where the present church now stands being the church formerly attended by our family regularily and to build a parsonage of not less than six rooms,nor more than eight rooms on the lots owned by me across the street from said church site and said lots to be deeded to said church organization for the use of the minister to preside over the church aforesaid; also to use any sum remaining for a mauseloeum or suitable arrangement as my said sister and brother may determine proper and fitting for the graves of our family now buried there and any sum then remaining to generally improve said cemetery a ll as my said sister and brother may determine; if there be difference of opinions or desires in any matter, then the will and desire of my sister shall prevail. and further that a fund of Ten thousand dollars to be set up and invested in SAFE SECURITIES with reasonable rate of interest for the use and benefit of my great neice Joanna Johnson and a similiar sum for Joanna's sister with same conditions and to be paid to each of them in monthly payments of Seventy-five dollars each month beginning on their seventeenth birthday and thereafter until exhausted ans each shall have received the full sum together with it's accruals of ten thousand dollars or a total of twenty thousand dollars; I also request that a fund of ten thousand dollars be set up for the purpose of paying to my brother Joseph Evera d Johnson a monthoy stipend of fifty dollars each and every month during his life to begin ninety days after my death and to end with the death of my said brother or the exhaustinn of the funds if they shall exhaust prior to his death with any sum remaining to remune to the use and benefit of my brother Victor C. Johnson and sister Beulah J. Johnson, and yhe further sum of Five yhousand dollars to be paid within reasonable time to Alma L. Kloss friend of my sister Beulah J.Johnson in appreciation for her kindness and sincere friendship to and for my sister Beulah J. Johnson with the request that said Alma L. Kloss invest same in some good securities, government bonds or annuity, ~~xxxxxxx~~. I further suggest that my said sister and brother employ Claude Monnett, attorney and friend of mine be employed for a reasonable fee, to be agreed upon by ~~xxxxxxxxxx~~ my sister, brother and Mr. Monnett for complete service but should they not agree then my said brother and sister shall employ whomsoever they may desire, being contious that nothing to be done without their consent and knowledge

To my brother James I give ten dollars only
This will shall be complete unless hereafter altered changed or rewritten
Witness my hand this April 6, 1947
Easter Sunday 2:30 P.m.
D G Johnson
Dexter G Johnson

C. Independent Significance

Courts regularly give testamentary effect to information outside of a will. Most frequently, they identify people ("my children") and property ("my house on Maple Street") by looking at other evidence. Some situations require more obvious references to additional information. Suppose Mikiso's will reads "all the books in my library to Rodney" or "$500 to each of the members of the Galesburg Debate Club." In order to interpret these gifts, a court might rely upon a library catalog or an after-death inventory, a club mailing list, or a dues record. Courts routinely consider such evidence under the doctrine of independent significance. The key to the doctrine is the notion of significance independent of the will. Presumably, Mikiso would not move books in or out of a library in order to change the gift to Rodney. Mikiso would not invite people to join a debate club in order to qualify under the will. These facts have a separate, non-testamentary significance. Reference to them does no violence to the policies behind the Statute of Wills.

Problem

Are the following bequests valid?

(a) "The automobile I own at my death."

(b) "The contents of my safe deposit box at the Last National Bank." Found in the box were the testator's jewelry, cash, stock certificates, and a savings bank passbook.

(c) "The contents of my safe deposit box at the Last National Bank, to the individuals indicated on the envelopes contained therein." Found in the box were seven envelopes, each containing cash or stocks, and each addressed by the testator to a different individual.

§ 3.04 Interpreting Wills: Extrinsic Evidence

Courts, traditionally, have been reluctant to look beyond the language of a document when they try to determine its meaning. They may give effect to the "plain meaning" of particular technical words or stretch a bit further and consider the whole document. Of course, what is plain to a particular judge may not be so plain to other people. Increasingly, courts are recognizing that giving meaning to words in the abstract, rather than in the context of a particular family's situation, often can be arbitrary. Understanding the circumstances, however, requires a court to consider extrinsic evidence. The principal traditional reason to allow extrinsic evidence is to resolve ambiguity.

Extrinsic evidence helps resolve ambiguity

A. Patent and Latent Ambiguities

A patent ambiguity is one apparent from the face of a document, while a latent ambiguity is one only discoverable by considering evidence extrinsic to the document. For example, "I give Arnie one of my two houses in Toledo" creates a patent ambiguity. The document itself reveals that we cannot tell which house to give Arnie. In contrast, "I give $5,000 to my cousin in Urbana" looks fine until we learn that the donor had one cousin in Urbana, Ohio, and one in Urbana, Illinois. Then we have a latent ambiguity.

Under the traditional rule, extrinsic evidence is not admissible to resolve patent ambiguities but can be used to resolve latent ambiguities. *See, e.g., Bagley v. Mousel*, 715 N.W.2d 490 (Neb. 2006). Many courts now reject the distinction and allow extrinsic evidence in either situation. *See, e.g., University of S. Ind. Found. v. Baker*, 843 N.E.2d 528 (Ind. 2006). Section 11.1 of the Restatement (Third) of Property (Wills and Other Donative Transfers) states: "An ambiguity in a donative document is an uncertainty in meaning that is revealed by the text or by extrinsic evidence other than direct evidence of intention contradicting the plain meaning of the text."

In re Estate of Gibbs

111 N.W.2d 413 (Wis. 1961)

[George and Lena Gibbs had substantially similar wills giving one percent of their estates "to Robert J. Krause, now of 4708 North 46th Street, Milwaukee, Wisconsin." He lived at that address, but did not know the Gibbses. Arguing there must have been a mistake, Robert W. Krause, a longtime employee of George, claimed the gift.]

Fairchild, J. . . . 1. The evidence leads irresistibly to the conclusion that Mr. and Mrs. Gibbs intended legacies to respondent [Robert W.], and that the use of the middle initial "J." and the address of North 46th Street resulted from some sort of mistake. . . .

The attorney who drew several wills for Mr. and Mrs. Gibbs produced copies of most of them. They were similar in outline to the wills admitted to probate except that Mr. Gibbs' wills executed before Mrs. Gibb's death bequeathed his property to her, if she survived. The first ones were drawn in 1953 and each contained a bequest to "Robert Krause, of Milwaukee, Wisconsin, if he survives me, one per cent (1%)." There was testimony that Mrs. Gibbs' will, executed in August, 1955, contained the same language. In the 1957 wills the same bequest was made to "Robert Krause, now of 4708 North 46th Street, Milwaukee, Wisconsin."

In several other instances street addresses of legatees were given for the first time in 1957. In the 1958 wills the same bequest was made to "Robert J. Krause, now of 4708 North 46th Street, Milwaukee, Wisconsin." The scrivener also produced a handwritten memorandum given to him by Mr. Gibbs for the purpose of preparing Mr. Gibbs' 1958 will, and the reference on that memorandum corresponding to the Krause bequest is "Bob, 1%." Four bequests (to Gruener, Krause, Preuschl and Owen) appear in the same order in each of the wills and are reflected in the memorandum referred to as "Fred Gruener, Bob, Mike, and Ed." Gruener, Preuschl and Owen were former employees of Gibbs Steel Company, as was respondent. Owen's residence is given as Jefferson, Wisconsin, in all the wills. In the 1953 wills, the residence of Gruener, Krause and Preuschl was given only as Milwaukee, Wisconsin. A street address was inserted for the first time in each case in the 1957 wills, and repeated in the later ones. . . .

The only evidence which suggests even a possibility that Mr. or Mrs. Gibbs may have known of appellant [Robert J.] may be summarized as follows:

For a time, appellant had a second job as a part time taxi driver, and he recalled an elderly lady who was his passenger on a lengthy taxi trip in June, 1955. He did not recall where he picked her up. He had driven her across the city, waiting for her while she visited in a hospital, and then driven her back across the city. The place where he let her out, however, was not her home. He did not recall that she had given him her name, but she had inquired as to his. They had conversed about the illness of appellant's wife and his working at an extra job in order to make ends meet. She had expressed sympathy and approval of his efforts. Presumably when he was notified that his name appeared in the Gibbs' wills as legatee, he endeavored to find an explanation of his good fortune and concluded that the lady in question must have been Mrs. Gibbs. The 1955 taxi ride, however, could not explain the gift to Robert Krause in the 1953 wills, and it is clear that the same legatee was intended in the Krause bequests in all the wills. Moreover, appellant's description of his taxi passenger differed in several particulars from the description of Mrs. Gibbs given by other witnesses.

. . . [T]he county court could reach no other conclusion upon consideration of the extrinsic evidence than that Mr. and Mrs. Gibbs intended to designate respondent as their legatee. The difficult question is whether the court could properly consider such evidence in determining testamentary intent.

Under rules as to construction of a will, unless there is ambiguity in the text of the will read in the light of surrounding circumstances, extrinsic evidence is inadmissible for the purpose of determining intent.

A latent ambiguity exists where the language of the will, though clear on its face, is susceptible of more than one meaning, when applied to the extrinsic facts to which it refers.

There are two classes of latent ambiguity. One, where there are two or more persons or things exactly measuring up to the description in the will; the other where no person or thing exactly answers the declarations and descriptions of the will, but two or more persons or things answer the description imperfectly. Extrinsic evidence must be resorted to under these circumstances to identify which of the parties, unspecified with particularity in the will, was intended by the testator.

Had the probated wills used the language of the 1953 wills "To Robert Krause of Milwaukee," such terms would have described both appellant and respondent, as well as a number of other people. Upon such ambiguity of the first type above mentioned becoming apparent, extrinsic evidence would be admissible in order to determine which Robert Krause Mr. and Mrs. Gibbs had in mind as their legatee.

Had the will said "To my former employee, Robert J. Krause of 4708 North 46th Street," neither appellant nor respondent would have exactly fulfilled the terms. Latent ambiguity of the second type would thus have appeared, and again extrinsic evidence would be admissible to determine what individual testators had in mind.

The wills containing, as they do, similar bequests to a long list of individuals, each bearing some relationship of blood, friendship, or former employment to Mr. or Mrs. Gibbs, come close to implying that every legatee named has some such relationship. Nevertheless the wills do not refer to Krause as standing in any particular relationship.

The terms of the bequest exactly fit appellant and no one else. There is no ambiguity.

"An ambiguity is not that which may be made doubtful by extrinsic proof tending to show an intention different from that manifested in the will, but it must grow out of the difficulty of identifying the person whose name and description correspond with the terms of the will." [*Ward v. Espy*, 1846, 6 Humph. 447, 25 Tenn. 447.]

Under the circumstances before us, can a court properly consider evidence showing that some of the words were used by mistake and should be stricken or disregarded? It is traditional doctrine that wills must not be reformed even in the case of demonstrable mistake. This doctrine doubtless rests upon policy reasons. The courts deem it wise to avoid entertaining claims of disappointed persons who may be able to make very plausible claims of mistake after the testator is no longer able to refute them.

Although the courts subscribe to an inflexible rule against reformation of a will, it seems that they have often strained a point in matters of identification of property or beneficiaries in order to reach a desired result by way of construction. In *Will of Stack*, [251 N.W. 470 (Wis. 1934)] where the will devised "Block 64," the court included part of block 175 in the provision to conform to the unexpressed intent of the testator. In *Will of Boeck*, [152 N.W. 155 (Wis. 1915)] where the will devised the "northeast quarter of the northwest quarter" of a section, which was not owned by the testator, the court held such provision passed the southeast quarter of the northwest quarter, to conform to the misexpressed intent of the testator. In *Moseley v. Goodman*, [195 S.W. 590 (Tenn. 1917)] where testator bequeathed property to "Mrs. Moseley," the court denied the claim of Mrs. Lenoir Moseley to the gift and held that Mrs. Trimble had been intended by the testator. Mrs. Trimble was known to the testator by the nickname "Mrs. Moseley." . . .

We are also aware of the rule which allows a court in probating a will to deny probate to a provision in the document which was included by mistake. British courts will deny probate to a single word, or part of a sentence, thereby completely altering the provided dispositions. [1 Bowe-Parker: Page on Wills (1961 ed.), p. 675, sec. 13.7.]

We conclude that details of identification, particularly such matters as middle initials, street addresses, and the like, which are highly susceptible to mistake, particularly in metropolitan areas, should not be accorded such sanctity as to frustrate an otherwise clearly demonstrable intent. Where such details of identification are involved, courts should receive evidence tending to show that a mistake has been made and should disregard the details when the proof establishes to the highest degree of certainty that a mistake was, in fact, made.

We therefore consider that the county court properly disregarded the middle initial and street address, and determined that respondent was the Robert Krause whom testators had in mind.

Orders affirmed.

Notes and Questions

1. *Gibbs* supports the comment that "[a]lthough the question posed is usually whether extrinsic evidence is 'admissible,' the trial court in fact usually hears it, and the strength of the evidence may determine the outcome." William M. McGovern Jr. & Sheldon F. Kurtz, Wills, Trusts & Estates 264 (3d ed. 2004).

2. Would there have been a latent ambiguity in Gibbs if the will had read simply "to Robert Krause"? What if it had said "to my longtime employee Robert J. Krause"?

3. Under the traditional rule, if construction of the will is possible, extrinsic evidence is inadmissible. The rule preserves formality in will execution and may avoid litigation. Professor Corbin—of contracts fame—notes, however, that "when a judge refuses to consider relevant extrinsic evidence on the ground that the meaning of written words is to him plain and clear, his decision is formed by and wholly based upon the completely extrinsic evidence of his own personal education and experience." Arthur L. Corbin, The Interpretation of Words and the Parole Evidence Rule, 50 Cornell L.Q. 161, 164 (1965).

Compare the views of Humpty Dumpty:

> "When I use a word," Humpty Dumpty said in rather a scornful tone, "it means just what I choose it to mean—neither more nor less."
>
> "The question is," said Alice, "whether you can make words mean so many different things."
>
> "The question is," said Humpty Dumpty, "which is to be master—that's all."

Lewis Carroll, Through the Looking-Glass and What Alice Found There (1871).

Some courts, therefore, allow extrinsic evidence to determine whether there is an ambiguity. *See, e.g.*, *Estate of Russell*, 444 P.2d 353 (Cal. 1968). If the evidence is inadmissible or unhelpful, the gift fails.

4. UPC § 2-601 reads: "In the absence of a finding of contrary intention, the rules of construction in this Part control the construction of a will." The earlier version had included the words "contrary intention indicated by the will." The comment explains that this change allows extrinsic evidence for the purpose of rebutting the rules of construction.

5. A reluctant court would find more support in Restatement (Third) of Property (Wills and Other Donative Transfers) § 10.2: "In seeking to determine a donor's intention, all relevant evidence, whether direct or circumstantial, may be considered. Thus, the text of the donative document and relevant extrinsic evidence may both be considered."

6. To what extent and to whom is the attorney who drafts an ambiguous gift liable? Should it matter whether extrinsic evidence is admissible to resolve the ambiguity?

Problems

1. Identify the actual or potential ambiguities in the following:
   (a) "I give my money and coin collection."
   (b) "I give my farm."
   (c) "To the Heart Association."
   (d) "Equally between my brothers, David and Richard, and their children."
2. Making reasonable assumptions, redraft the language in problem 1.

B. Interpretation or Reformation?

Courts faced with mistakes in drafting often purport to "interpret" or "construe" a document in order to correct the mistake. One reason they resort to this approach is that, as the court in *Gibbs* noted, traditional rules preclude reforming wills. To do so would give testamentary effect to language not put through the Statute of Wills wringer. The excerpt below from a comprehensive and influential article has prompted change in some places, including California and Texas. *See Estate of Duke v. Jewish National Fund*, 352 P.3d 863 (Cal. 2015); Tex. Prob. Code § 201.056 (2015).

In re O'Donnell, 815 N.W.2d 640 (Neb. App. 2012), involved a testator who wrote her own will, but failed to specify what was to happen to money left in testamentary trusts if the beneficiaries died before exhausting the trust funds. Based upon a draft will, and other provisions of the executed will, the court reformed the will to give the property to a cousin, rather than the will's residuary beneficiary.

John H. Langbein & Lawrence W. Waggoner *Reformation of Wills on the Ground of Mistake: Change of Direction in American Law?*

130 U. Pa. L. Rev. 521, 524–28 (1982)

The no-reformation rule is peculiar to the law of wills. It does not apply to other modes of gratuitous transfer—the so-called nonprobate transfers—even though many are virtually indistinguishable from the will in function. Reformation lies routinely to correct mistakes, both of expression and of omission, in deeds of gift, inter vivos trusts, life insurance contracts, and other instruments that serve to transfer wealth to donees upon the transferor's death. Alternatively, courts sometimes find it necessary to remedy mistakes in these nonprobate transfers by imposing a constructive trust on the mistakenly named beneficiary in favor of the intended beneficiary.

Courts have been willing to use their equity powers in these nonprobate situations, because a case of well-proven mistake necessarily invokes the fundamental principle of the law of restitution: preventing unjust enrichment. If the mistake is not corrected, the mistaken beneficiary is unjustly enriched at the expense of the intended beneficiary. Moreover, when the mistake results from the wrong of a third party, the courts sometimes speak of a second policy: protecting an innocent party (here, the intended beneficiary) from suffering the consequences of another's wrongdoing.

Judicial intervention to prevent unjust enrichment or to protect the victim of wrongdoing has such a manifestly compelling doctrinal basis that the puzzle is to explain why the courts have not been willing to act similarly when the document affected by the mistake is a will. Unjust enrichment (or third-party negligence) is equally wrong whether the resulting error occurs in an inter vivos transfer or in a will. Both transfers are gratuitous, both unilateral. Accordingly, we emphasize as a starting point that the no-reformation rule for wills cannot rest on the notion that there is no wrong to remedy. Why, then, does equity refuse to remedy unjust enrichment in the case of a mistake in a will?

The customary justification has to do with the nature of the evidence in cases of testation. A will is by definition "ambulatory," meaning ineffective to pass property until the death of the testator. Evidence suggesting that the document is affected by mistake—that the will is at variance with the testator's actual intent—must necessarily be presented when death has placed the testator beyond reply. The testimony will typically involve statements allegedly made by the testator, so-called direct declarations of intent, which he can now neither corroborate nor deny. The testator's main protection against fabricated or mistaken evidence is the will itself. Therefore, it is argued, evidence extrinsic to the will should be excluded. And if extrinsic evidence is excluded, the court can have no grounds to reform.

There are, we think, two persuasive answers. First, although the living donor under an inter vivos instrument can take the stand and testify about his true intent, this testimony does not have automatic reliability. . . .

Second, and still more telling, reformation of documents effecting gratuitous inter vivos transfers is routinely granted even after the death of the donor. . . . The essential safeguard in these cases has been the clear-and-convincing-evidence standard, which appellate courts have policed rigorously.

Accordingly, we think that there is no principled way to reconcile the exclusion of extrinsic evidence in the law of wills with the rule of admissibility in the law of nonprobate transfers. . . .

Restatement (Third) of Property (Donative Transfers)

§ 12.1 Reforming Donative Documents to Correct Mistakes

A donative document, though unambiguous, may be reformed to conform the text to the donor's intention if the following are established by clear and convincing evidence:

(1) that a mistake of fact or law, whether in expression or inducement, affected specific terms of the document; and

(2) what the donor's intention was.

Direct evidence of intention contradicting the plain meaning of the text as well as other evidence of intention may be considered in determining whether elements (1) and (2) have been established by clear and convincing evidence.

§ 12.2 Modifying Donative Documents to Achieve Donor's Tax Objectives

A donative document may be modified, in a manner that does not violate the donor's probable intention, to achieve the donor's tax objectives.

Note

Because Rest. 3d Prop. § 12.1 refers to "a donative document," it covers more than wills and trusts. *See, e.g., Estate of Irvine v. Oaas*, 309 P.3d 986 (Mont. 2013) (beneficiary designations in investment contracts); *Pullum v. Pullum*, 58 So. 3d 752 (Ala. 2010) (land description in deed).

The notion of reforming wills has met resistance in the courts. Consider the following case.

Flannery v. McNamara

738 N.E.2d 739 (Mass. 2000)

IRELAND, J.

The plaintiffs, Helen M. Flannery and Margaret M. Moran (Flannerys), filed a complaint against the defendants, Paul J. McNamara, administrator of the estate of

William H. White, Jr. (decedent), and the decedent's heirs, the Daleys and the Whites (heirs), seeking declaratory relief and reformation of the decedent's will. The Flannerys alleged that they, and not the decedent's heirs, are the rightful beneficiaries under the will. . . .

The judge granted the heirs' motions for summary judgment, ruling that, because the will was unambiguous on its face, extrinsic evidence of the decedent's alleged intent was inadmissible. Moreover, she held that, because the will did not provide for disposition of the decedent's property in the event his wife predeceased him, his property passed to the heirs by way of intestacy.

. . . The Flannerys argue that the Probate Court judge erred by holding inadmissible extrinsic evidence that might persuade the court to (1) construe; or (2) reform a poorly drawn will, albeit unambiguous on its face, to reflect the decedent's intent, thereby avoiding unjust enrichment.

This appeal presents the question whether we should overrule (1) the so-called "plain meaning" rule, that prohibits the admission of extrinsic evidence to construe unambiguous wills; and (2) the rule prohibiting the reformation of wills. We decline to do so, and thus, affirm the Probate Court's decision.

1. Statement of Facts.

On September 30, 1995, the decedent died in Arlington. The decedent's will, dated January 20, 1973, left his entire estate to his wife, Katherine M. White (Katherine). The relevant part of the will provides that:

"I give, devise, and bequeath all of the property of which I die possessed real, personal, and mixed of whatsoever nature and wheresoever located to my beloved wife, Katherine M. White."

The decedent's will failed to name a contingent beneficiary and it did not contain a residuary clause.

Katherine died October 14, 1993, survived by the decedent and her two sisters, the Flannerys. The couple had no children. McNamara, the decedent's attorney, repeatedly advised the decedent to let him review the will, but the decedent never showed the will to McNamara. The decedent died survived by his intestate heirs who were discovered through a genealogical search. The heirs are the decedent's first cousins, once removed.

The Flannerys make the following allegations. For almost five decades, they had a close relationship with the decedent. Moreover, after Katherine's death, the decedent relied heavily on the Flannerys for advice and assistance with daily matters. After the decedent died, he was buried in the Flannerys' family plot. On several occasions, the decedent told members of the Flannerys' family that his Arlington residence and its contents "will be [theirs] some day." Additionally, the decedent informed McNamara that he understood that, if Katherine were to predecease him, his will provided for his property to go to the Flannerys. In contrast, the decedent did not have a close relationship with the heirs.

After the decedent died in 1995, McNamara was appointed administrator of the decedent's estate. He received the decedent's will for probate and was preparing to distribute the estate to the heirs by way of intestate succession, when the Flannerys filed for declaratory relief and reformation of the will on November 25, 1997.

2. Discussion.

The Flannerys claim that, although the decedent's will made no mention of them, he intended to pass his estate to them in the event that Katherine predeceased him. Specifically, the Flannerys contend that the portion of the will that reads, "all . . . to my beloved wife, Katherine M. White," should be either construed or reformed to read, "all . . . to my beloved wife, Katherine M. White, if she survives me, but if not, then to her sisters who survive me," namely, the Flannerys. We disagree.

a. Construction. "The fundamental object in the construction of a will is to ascertain the testator's intention from the whole instrument, attributing due weight to all its language, considered in light of the circumstances known to the testator at the time of its execution, and to give effect to that intent unless some positive rule of law forbids." *Putnam v. Putnam*, 366 Mass. 261, 266, 316 N.E.2d 729 (1974). . . .

Here, the Flannerys assert that the decedent intended to name them as the beneficiaries of his estate in the event that his wife predeceased him. To prove this, the Flannerys seek to introduce extrinsic evidence of their relationship with the decedent and the decedent's statements concerning his intent.

Under current Massachusetts law, however, "if a will is not ambiguous, extrinsic evidence to explain its terms is inadmissible . . . even where the language involved has a legal consequence either not likely to have been understood by the testator . . . or contrary to his intention expressed orally" (citations omitted). *Putnam v. Putnam, . . . supra*. . . . The will before us is not ambiguous. . . .

b. Reformation. Reformation of wills is presently prohibited in Massachusetts. . . . Moreover, "the fact that [the will] was not in conformity to the instructions given to the draftsman who prepared it or that he made a mistake does not authorize a court to reform or alter it or remould it by amendments." *Mahoney v. Grainger*, 283 Mass. 189, 191, 186 N.E. 86 (1933).

Nevertheless, the Flannerys urge us to reject this basic tenet. Specifically, they point to *Putnam v. Putnam*, 425 Mass. 770, 772 n.3, 682 N.E.2d 1351 (1997), where in the dictum of a footnote we noted that "the case may be hard to make . . . for denying reformation of a will where in substantively similar circumstances, we would allow reformation of a trust instrument. . . . Evidence of intention may be relevant and admissible on the issue of mistake, that is, to support the reformation of the instrument." The Flannerys use this statement to argue that we should join, what the Restatement terms, "the minority but growing view," under which mistaken wills can be reformed. Restatement, supra at § 12.1 Reporter's Note at 134.

Section 12.1 of the Restatement provides for the reformation of an unambiguous donative document in order to conform the text to the donor's intention. Such reformation is permitted where the party seeking reformation can establish (1) a mistake of fact or law in the document; and (2) the donor's intention by clear and convincing evidence. . . .

However, the reformation of a will, which would dispose of estate property based on unattested testamentary language, would violate the Statute of Wills. . . . Strong policy reasons also militate against the requested reformation. To allow for reformation in this case would open the floodgates of litigation and lead to untold confusion in the probate of wills. It would essentially invite disgruntled individuals excluded from a will to demonstrate extrinsic evidence of the decedent's "intent" to include them. The number of groundless will contests could soar. We disagree that employing "full, clear and decisive proof" as the standard for reformation of wills would suffice to remedy such problems. . . . Judicial resources are simply too scarce to squander on such consequences. . . .

Additionally, the Flannerys urge us to apply the holdings of *Putnam v. Putnam*, . . . and *Shawmut Bank, N.A. v. Buckley*, 422 Mass. 706, 665 N.E.2d 29 (1996), that allowed for the reformation of wills to achieve the testators' intent with respect to tax objectives.[16] In *Putnam v. Putnam* . . . we construed a will to resolve a conflict, as we would an ambiguity, to conform to the decedent's intentions to take advantage of the maximum marital deduction permitted under the Federal estate tax law. The Flannerys interpret this case to mean that we implicitly ordered reformation. In *Shawmut Bank, N.A. v. Buckley* . . . we eliminated a clause from a will to effectuate the testator's intention to minimize the Federal estate taxation of her testamentary trust.

Both cases are distinguishable from the present claim for reformation. First, the decisions permitted reformation in very limited circumstances: namely, achieving favorable Federal estate tax treatment with respect to testamentary trusts. . . . However, given the absence of any tax issues here, it certainly does not fall within the ambit of that very narrow exception.

Second, neither the *Putnam* nor the *Buckley* case admitted extrinsic evidence to ascertain the testators' intent, as the Flannerys urge us to do. . . .

Third, in both cases, none of the parties to the proceedings objected to the construction or reformation of the wills. . . .

The order of the Probate Court granting the defendants' motions for summary judgment is affirmed, and a declaratory judgment shall issue.

Greaney, J. (concurring in the result, with whom Abrams, J., joins)

. . . I write separately because I disagree with the court's reasoning on the reformation issue.

16. The Flannerys note that this court has allowed for the reformation of inter vivos trusts where the results of the trust were clearly inconsistent with the settlors' tax objectives. . . . However, inter vivos trusts are not testamentary documents, and therefore need not meet the formalities required for the execution of a will. . . .

. . . [T]he court concludes that our rule prohibiting the reformation of a will applies and precludes consideration of the remedy. In reaching this conclusion, the court effectively shuts the door on consideration, in an appropriate case, of reformation of a will to correct a mistake which negates the testator's intent.

In writing for the court in *Putnam v. Putnam*, 425 Mass. 770, 772 n.3, 682 N.E.2d 1351 (1997), Chief Justice Wilkins stated: "For reasons that may no longer be meaningful, we have been less willing to recognize the possibility of proof of mistake in the drafting of a will (as opposed to an inter vivos trust) that is unambiguous on its face. The case may be hard to make, however, for denying reformation of a will where, in substantively similar circumstances, we would allow reformation of a trust instrument. [. . .]" . . . As the Restatement points out, and cases demonstrate, there are instances where mistakes in a will . . . caused by scrivener's error, incorrect legal advice, misrepresentations, and the like, may call for reformation of an unambiguous text. . . .

I suspect that, in an appropriate case, the court will conclude that an unambiguous will should be reformed because of a proven mistake in expression or inducement. When that case arrives, the court will either have to reject or revise what is said about reformation in this opinion or struggle to create an ambiguity, where none exists, in order to permit reformation. . . .

Notes and Questions

1. In unusual cases, a court in a plain-meaning jurisdiction may imply a gift by implication, especially to avoid intestacy. *See, e.g., Matter of Warren*, 39 N.Y.S.3d 282 (N.Y. App. 2016). 21.

2. The Restatement distinguishes between "reformation" and "modification" to achieve tax objectives. Modification is possible without the clear and convincing evidence required for reformation. Florida also follows that approach. Fla. Stat. §§ 732.615–.616. Similarly, Massachusetts allows reformation to testamentary trust beneficiaries seeking tax savings, but not will beneficiaries seeking changes for non-tax reasons. *See also Sowder v. United States*, 407 F. Supp. 2d 1230 (E.D. Wash. 2005) (ignoring will language that would have precluded claiming the marital deduction). Does the different treatment for tax and non-tax issues make sense?

3. The extent to which the Internal Revenue Service will accept retroactive corrections is not clear. *See* Rev. Rul. 93-79, 1993-2 C.B. 269 (no retroactive effect recognized for state court order reforming trust).

4. In footnote 10, the *Flannery* court distinguished cases reforming revocable trusts because such trusts are not testamentary documents. Compare the cases in § 4.04[B] which in some situations treat trusts more like wills. *See* § 8.04[A] (general reformation of lifetime trusts).

5. If courts correct documents, will lawyers become less careful?

Selected References

Jane B. Baron, *Irresolute Testators, Clear and Convincing Wills Law*, 73 Wash. & Lee L. Rev. 3 (2016).

Andrea W. Cornelison, *Dead Man Talking: Are Courts Ready to Listen? The Erosion of the Plain Meaning Rule*, 35 Real Prop. Prob. & Tr. J. 811 (2001).

Wayne M. Gazur, *Coming to Terms With the Uniform Probate Code's Reformation of Wills*, 64 S.C. L. Rev. 403 (2012).

Mark Glover, *Minimizing Probate-Error Risk*, 49 U. Mich. J.L. Reform 335 (2016).

Victoria J. Haneman, *Changing the Estate Planning Malpractice Landscape: Applying the Constructive Trust to Cure Testamentary Mistake*, 80 UMKC L. Rev. 91 (2011).

David Hasan, *Unwinding*, 57 Emory L. Rev. 871 (2008).

Richard F. Storrow, *Judicial Discretion and the Disappearing Distinction Between Will Interpretation and Construction*, 56 Case W. Res. L. Rev. 65 (2005).

§ 3.05 Revocation

As times change, estate plans may also need to change. A testator's estate may grow or shrink, leaving specific bequests too small or too large. A particular item may be lost or sold, so that a replacement gift would be appropriate. A beneficiary might die; a beneficiary or the testator might divorce; the relationship between the testator and various beneficiaries might improve or worsen. Each of these events suggests the need to rethink will provisions. The law has established specific methods for revoking or amending wills. Moreover, if the testator does not act, the law may revoke a will in situations in which the legislature thinks the typical testator would have wanted that result.

A. By a Writing or Physical Act

Statutes allow testators to modify or revoke their wills by either of two basic methods. First, a later writing meeting the statutory requirements can expressly or impliedly supersede the earlier will. Second, testators can revoke wills by specific acts that do physical damage to the document. Either method might cause a total, or a partial, revocation, but in any case, the act must be accompanied by an intention to revoke. Courts traditionally have taken the same strict approach toward revocation requirements as they have toward will executions, sometimes with familiar intention-defeating results.

A Writing. The surest way to revoke a will is by validly executing a later document expressly revoking the will. Usually, this later document is a new will that simply replaces the old one. To avoid confusion, most well-drafted wills begin with a statement like "I revoke all of my prior wills." Writings can also revoke part of a will. These amendments, called "codicils," usually make specific changes and expressly reaffirm the will in all other respect.

Note carefully that the revoking document itself must satisfy the will-execution rules. In a jurisdiction allowing holographs, a short handwritten note might revoke a long, formal, printed will. Similarly, a court might use the substantial compliance or harmless error doctrines to save a document that itself revokes an earlier will.

Problems arise if a later will is inconsistent with a prior will, but lacks a clause expressly revoking all or part of the prior one. Suppose Sandi executed a will giving $3,000 to Lee and the rest of her estate to Randy. Later Sandi executed a second document which reads "At my death, I give Debbie $3,000." The question is whether Sandi intended the second writing to be a codicil supplementing the first or a new will replacing it. Courts have struggled with where to draw the line. *See, e.g., In re Last Will and Testament of Carney*, 758 So. 2d 1017 (Miss. 2000) (court read five holographs together, harmonizing the conflicting provisions). To avoid litigation in these situations, the UPC offers some presumptions. *See* UPC § 2-507(c) & (d); *see also* Restatement (Second) of Property § 34.2, cmt. b.

Physical Act. Testators can also revoke wills by physically altering the document with the intent to revoke it. Standards for what constitutes a sufficient act of revocation often hinge upon the particular phrasing of the local statute. Notice that some of the permissible methods focus on interfering with the will's words themselves ("canceling"), while others refer to the paper ("burning"). *See, e.g., Estate of Eglee*, 383 A.2d 586 (R.I. 1978) (red pencil interlineations through every word and signature, and diagonally across each clause not "otherwise destroying"); *Estate of Funk*, 654 N.E.2d 1174 (Ind. Ct. App. 1995) (handwritten notes, changes in beneficiaries and bequests, missing page, and page cut out but reattached not enough to "destroy or mutilate"); *Kronauge v. Stoecklein*, 293 N.E.2d 320 (Ohio Ct. App. 1972) (writing in margin not "canceling").

Uniform Probate Code

Section 2-507. Revocation by Writing or by Act.

(a) A will or any part thereof is revoked:

(1) by executing a subsequent will that revokes the previous will or part expressly or by inconsistency, or

(2) by performing a revocatory act on the will, if the testator performed the act with the intent and for the purpose of revoking the will or part or if another individual performed the act in the testator's conscious presence and by the testator's direction. For purposes of this paragraph, "revocatory

act on the will" includes burning, tearing, canceling, obliterating, or destroying the will or any part of it. A burning, tearing, or canceling is a "revocatory act on the will," whether or not the burn, tear, or cancellation touched any of the words on the will.

(b) If a subsequent will does not expressly revoke a previous will, the execution of the subsequent will wholly revokes the previous will by inconsistency if the testator intended the subsequent will to replace rather than supplement the previous will.

(c) The testator is presumed to have intended a subsequent will to replace rather than supplement a previous will if the subsequent will makes a complete disposition of the testator's estate. If this presumption arises and is not rebutted by clear and convincing evidence, the previous will is revoked; only the subsequent will is operative on the testator's death.

(d) The testator is presumed to have intended a subsequent will to supplement rather than replace a previous will if the subsequent will does not make a complete disposition of the testator's estate. If this presumption arises and is not rebutted by clear and convincing evidence, the subsequent will revokes the previous will only to the extent the subsequent will is inconsistent with the previous will; each will is fully operative on the testator's death to the extent they are not inconsistent.

Estate of Gushwa

197 P.3d 1 (N. Mex. 2008)

Bosson, Justice.

The New Mexico Probate Code specifies the means by which a testator may revoke a prior will. See NMSA 1978, §45-2-507(A) (1993) (stating that a will may be revoked by either executing a subsequent will or by performing a revocatory act on the will). The district court, concluding that the purported revocation in this case was legally ineffective, granted summary judgment, and the Court of Appeals affirmed in a well-reasoned opinion. On certiorari, we affirm most of that opinion, reversing only a small part and remanding for the district court to adjudicate a remaining allegation of fraud and to consider the propriety of a constructive trust in this case.

BACKGROUND

In June 2000, with the help of his niece, Betty Dale, and her husband (Ted), George Gushwa prepared and executed his will, putting property in trust to support his wife, Zane (called "Wife" in this opinion), for life, with the remainder to his nieces and nephews, not including the Dales. Ted, who was named trustee, was given the original for safekeeping. Evidently George soon thereafter decided to revoke some or all of the will. There was conflicting testimony about how much of the will George wanted Zane to see. Ultimately, Ted sent George photocopies of three pages from the will.

In February 2001, a new lawyer drafted a document entitled "Revocation of Missing Will(s)," signed by George and two witnesses and notarized. George also wrote

"Revoked" on the copy of three pages of the will, presumably the same three pages that he received from Ted, and attached those pages to the Revocation of Missing Will(s) document. In April 2001, George obtained a photocopy of the entire will from his previous attorney and wrote "Revoked" on each page of that copy of the will.

After George's death in 2005, Zane applied to serve as personal representative and asserted that George had died intestate. One of George's nieces objected, arguing that the June 2000 will was in force. Zane argued the will had been revoked by the Revocation document and also by writing on the photocopied pages. Zane further contended that Ted's behavior had prevented George from obtaining possession of the original will so that he could write "Revoked" on the original instead of just a copy. She asked the court to impose a constructive trust in her favor if the court found the will had not been revoked.]

. . .

DISCUSSION

This appeal raises two questions under the Probate Code and one question of equity. First, we consider whether Decedent's execution of the Revocation of Missing Will(s) document satisfies the requirements of Section 45-2-507(A)(1), dealing with revocation by writing. Second, we determine whether Decedent's act of writing "Revoked" on a photocopy is a revocatory act within the meaning of Section 45-2-507(A)(2). Finally, we examine whether the allegations of fraud against Ted create a genuine issue of material fact that, if proven, might justify relief and preclude summary judgment.

. . .

Our Probate Code provides that a will or any part thereof may be revoked in one of two ways. See § 45-2-507. A testator may revoke a previous will "by executing a subsequent will that revokes the previous will or part expressly or by inconsistency." Section 45-2-507(A)(1). A testator may also revoke a previous will "by performing a revocatory act on the will if the testator performed the act with the intent and for the purpose of revoking the will or part." Section 45-2-507(A)(2). A "revocatory act on the will" includes "burning, tearing, canceling, obliterating or destroying the will or any part of it." Id. For purposes of this appeal, we concentrate on the word "canceling," but we turn first to the requirement in Section 45-2-507(A)(1) for revocation by a "subsequent will."

Revocation by Writing

. . . [W]e note that our Probate Code, unlike that of other states, does not allow for revocation of a will by any "other writing." Compare § 45-2-507(A)(1)[17] ("A will or any part thereof is revoked . . . by executing a subsequent will that revokes the previous will or part expressly or by inconsistency . . . .") with Fla. Stat. § 732.505(2) (2002) ("A will or codicil, or any part of either, is revoked . . . [b]y a subsequent will,

17. Based on UPC § 2-507. [Eds.]

codicil, *or other writing* executed with the same formalities required for the execution of wills declaring the revocation." (Emphasis added.)). . . . Wife argues that the Revocation of Missing Will(s) document should be given the effect of a subsequent will because of its language expressly revoking Decedent's prior will. Wife relies on the definition of "will" contained in the definitions section of the Probate Code. See NMSA 1978, § 45-1-201(A)(53) (1995) (defining a will as "any testamentary instrument that . . . revokes or revises another will").[18]

Wife's position, however, is at odds with the Code's specific language describing the only legally effective methods of revocation. If a will could be revoked by any writing that simply revoked another will, without the necessary testamentary language—or that it be in fact a "subsequent will"—then a will could be revoked by "any other writing," contrary to the Code's specific language and the legislative intent to limit the available means of revocation. Because our Probate Code requires revocation by a subsequent will, we are guided by this more specific statement rather than a generic definition. Accordingly, we reject Wife's argument . . . Our Probate Code requires an exacting attention to form as well as intent to validate a revocation. . . .

Similarly, Wife's argument that other language in the Revocation of Missing Will(s) document gives it the effect of a subsequent will does not persuade us. Instead, the language chosen by Decedent clearly shows that he knew he was not drafting a subsequent will. . . .

. . . [T]he Revocation of Missing Will(s) document was never intended to be a subsequent will and should not be given the effect of a subsequent will by this Court. Therefore, as a matter of law consistent with the clear language of the Probate Code, this document did not revoke Decedent's prior will.

The Effect of a Revocatory Act on a Photocopy of the Will

In addition to revoking a will by executing a subsequent will, the Probate Code provides that a will may be revoked by performing a revocatory act on the will. Section 45-2-507(A)(2). ("A will . . . is revoked . . . by performing a revocatory act on the will if the testator performed the act with the intent and for the purpose of revoking the will . . . ."). The district court concluded that Decedent's act of writing "Revoked" on a photocopy was insufficient to revoke the Will because a photocopy of a will does not have the same legal status as an executed copy of a will. The Court of Appeals agreed. . . .

. . . [O]ur Probate Code mandates that a revocatory act be performed "on the will." Section 45-2-507(A)(2). While the Code does not explicitly require that the act be performed on the original or on an executed original, such a requirement is implicit in the statutory term "will." . . .

Further, we agree with our Court of Appeals that treating photocopies differently from originals is important as a matter of policy. As that Court explained, the

18. *See also* § 3.02A of this text (What's a Will?). [Eds.]

requirement of an original can protect against fraudulent reproduction of unauthorized wills. . . . Photocopies can be readily produced and the existence of multiple copies of a will can engender confusion, especially when the issue is whether the will has been validly revoked. . . .

Imposition of a Constructive Trust

Because we conclude that Decedent's attempt to revoke the Will was legally ineffective, we decline to remand for a trial on that issue. We are, however, mindful of the inequity that this holding may work under the circumstances of this particular case if, as alleged, Decedent was fraudulently prevented from regaining possession of his original Will.[19]

. . . Specifically, Wife argued that Ted's refusal to return the original created a disputed issue of fact that should have been resolved at trial. To this Court, Wife again asks that we remand for a trial to remedy what she perceives as an unjust result arising from a formalistic interpretation of the Probate Code.

. . .

A court will impose a constructive trust "to prevent the unjust enrichment that would result if the person having the property were permitted to retain it." *In re Estate of Duran*, 133 N.M. 553, 66 P.3d 326, 2003 NMSC 8, P 34. Courts have held that certain conduct, "such as fraud, constructive fraud, duress, undue influence, breach of a fiduciary duty, or similar wrongful conduct[,]" may warrant the imposition of a constructive trust. *Id.* (quoted authority omitted). "If a court imposes a constructive trust, the person holding legal title is subjected to an equitable duty to convey the property to a person to whom the court has determined that duty is owed." *Id.*

Wife maintains that Ted wrongfully prevented Decedent from regaining possession of his original Will. Decedent's niece, Wanda, disputes these allegations with an affidavit from Ted. In response to Wife's allegation that he refused to send Decedent the original Will, Ted denies ever receiving a call from Decedent requesting the original Will. Instead, he explains that it was Wife, not Decedent, who called him asking for the original Will. Ted also states that Decedent instructed him not to send Wife the original and to send Decedent a copy of only certain pages of the Will.

Viewing this evidence in the light most favorable to Wife, as the party opposing summary judgment, and drawing all inferences in favor of a trial on the merits, we conclude that summary judgment was not appropriate with respect to this issue. . . . A disputed issue of material fact remains unresolved, namely whether Ted wrongfully prevented Decedent from obtaining the original Will, thereby making it virtually impossible for Decedent to comply with the statutory requirements for revocation. Thus, we remand to the district court to adjudicate that issue and decide whether, as a consequence, a constructive trust should be imposed under the facts of this case.

19. Compare § 3.02B5 regarding tortious interference with an inheritance. [Eds.]

CONCLUSION

We affirm in part and reverse in part and remand to the district court for further proceedings consistent with this Opinion.

[Justices Serna, Maes, and Daniels concurred.]

Chavez, Chief Justice (dissenting).

... I recognize that the Revocation of Missing Will(s) document is not an ideal will, and indeed that Decedent apparently believed that it did not constitute a will under New Mexico law. Decedent used language suggesting that he did not consider the document a will and that he intended to revoke his prior will by the ineffective means of performing a revocatory act on a partial photocopy of his prior will. Because of this confusion, the majority concludes as a matter of law that Decedent's document was not a will, and as such failed to satisfy New Mexico's statutory requirements for the revocation of a prior will. I respectfully disagree. The document met all of the formalities necessary to create a will, and the district court's responsibility was simply to determine the testator's intent.... Given the document's ambiguity, we should remand to the district court to determine, on the basis of extrinsic evidence of the testator's intent, whether the Revocation of Missing Will(s) document should be considered a will.... Only if the document is found not to be a will would I raise the issue of constructive trust. Accordingly, I respectfully dissent....

Notes and Questions

1. Even though UPC § 2-507 only allows a will to revoke a prior will, would the "Revocation of Missing Will(s)" document have been effective to revoke the will in a jurisdiction following UPC § 2-503's harmless error rule?

2. Considering the traditional emphasis on meeting a long list of formal requirements for executing wills, why does the law so casually allow revocation by physical act?

3. Usually, revocatory acts must be done by the testator or in the testator's presence at his direction. Resolving the "presence" question in this context involves the same issues as whether witnesses are in the testator's "presence" at a will's execution. See § 3.02(C)(2)(c).

4. Sometimes a previously-executed will cannot be found after the testator's death. If such a will has not been revoked, proponents can prove its validity and terms by other evidence. The best evidence is probably an unexecuted copy from the lawyer's office. The language in some "lost wills" statutes complicates the analysis by, for example, requiring the will to have been "in existence" at the testator's death. Under a literal reading, a will accidently thrown away could not be probated even if there were no intention to revoke it. Courts have usually allowed such a will under the ruse that it was still in "legal existence"—although not in physical existence—or that it had been "fraudulently destroyed." *See, e.g., In re Estate of Wheadon*, 579 P. 2d 930 (Utah 1978) (legal existence). In other states, an original will that was validly

executed can be probated if it was not "revoked." *See, e.g.*, N.Y. Sur. Ct. Proc. Act § 1407. Thus, if a will was accidentally thrown away, it would not have been revoked and if due execution and the will contents can be proved, probate will be allowed.

If the lost will was last in the testator's hands, courts will presume the testator revoked the will. Suspicious circumstances, however, may help a proponent overcome the presumption. *Compare Estate of Markofske*, 178 N.W.2d 9 (Wis. 1970) (Testator's sister, who was an intestate heir but was not named in the will, cleaned out testator's house but found no will. Copy admitted to probate.), *with In re Estate of Bakhaus*, 102 N.E.2d 818 (Ill. 1951) (Will with signature cut off found in shop others had access to. Held: revoked.).

5. Some states allow partial revocations by physical act, as where a testator crosses out or cuts out one provision but leaves the rest of the will alone. Sometimes it is hard to tell whether the testator intended to revoke the whole document, several provisions, or only a particular provision. Also, if a will contains a residuary clause, the effect of allowing revocation of a specific gift is to increase the residuary gift. For these reasons, other states do not recognize partial revocation by physical act. *See, e.g.*, N.Y. Estates, Powers and Trusts Law § 3-4-1(a)(2). For them, it is all or nothing.

Problems

1. Margaret had made a will giving her residuary estate to Thomas Hart, but then she changed her mind. At her request, a friend wrote a note to the executor, who had the will, saying "Please destroy the will I made in favor of Thomas Hart." Margaret then signed the letter, and two friends who were present witnessed it.

(a) If the executor did not destroy the will, is Margaret's attempted revocation effective?

(b) What if the executor did as requested and destroyed the will?

2. Larry executed Will I giving his car to Gary, $3,000 to Maria, and the rest of his property to Frank. Later, he executed a document he also called a "will," which made no mention of Will I and gave his car to Monica and $4,000 to Maria. How would you divide Larry's estate?

3. Harvey, old and blind, had a will leaving a substantial gift to Sidney, his valet. One night, Harvey asked for his will. When Sidney brought it, Harvey felt it, recognized it, and asked Sidney to throw it into the nearby blazing fireplace. Sidney instead put a different paper into the fire. Harvey smiled, thinking his will had burned; then he died. Should the will be probated?

4. Martina wanted to revoke her will and let the intestate statute control. Her lawyer convinced her to keep her old will as a memorandum to be used if she changed her mind. On the cover of the will, the lawyer wrote "This will is null and void." Martina signed the statement.

(a) Is the will revoked by physical act?

(b) If not, is the lawyer liable to Martina's heirs in malpractice?

Selected Reference

Mark Glover, *Formal Execution and Informal Revocation: Manifestations of Probate's Family Protection Policy*, 34 Okla. City U. L. Rev. 411 (2009).

B. By Operation of Law

Sometimes people divorce, but do not amend their wills to take into account the change in their lives. Many states have statutes that invalidate some of the will's provisions that relate to the former spouse. Some refer to this process as revocation "by operation of law." Because the logic of this approach could also apply to non-probate transfers, we cover the topic in Chapter 5, § 5.01C.

Closely related to statutes that revoke will provisions are statutes that give new spouses or children rights to claim intestate shares if a will omits them. Chapter 6 covers these rules in connection with other devices to protect family members from disinheritance.

§ 3.06 Revival

Suppose Wayne executes Will I, and then sometime later executes Will II, which revokes Will I. Changing his mind again, Wayne revokes Will II. Various jurisdictions take different approaches regarding whether Will I is good again. Though strictly speaking only one approach amounts to "revival," that term is generally used to identify the issues surrounding this circumstance.

Some places follow the English common law rule which said that because wills speak only at the testator's death, Will I was never really revoked by Will II, so Will I still stands as the testator's "last will." Under this view, Will I is not revived so much as it is "uncovered."

Other jurisdictions say that because Will I was revoked by Will II, the only way to get back Will I is to re-execute it. Under this approach, Will I is not revived so much as it is "reborn." Rather than re-executing the same document, the safest approach is to reproduce the old will and execute the new, clean copy. An alternative is to execute a codicil to Will I, thereby republishing it on the date of the codicil.

The most common approach really is "revival." If the testator intends to revive Will I at the time of revoking Will II, that intention will prevail. Otherwise, Will I stays revoked. Even here, however, there is a split of opinion. Some jurisdictions allow revival only if the "terms of the revocation" of Will II indicate an intention to revive. The UPC reflects a more liberal view.

Uniform Probate Code

Section 2-509. Revival of Revoked Will.

(a) If a subsequent will that wholly revoked a previous will is thereafter revoked by a revocatory act under Section 2-507(a)(2) [identifying physical acts], the previous will remains revoked unless it is revived. The previous will is revived if it is evident from the circumstances of the revocation of the subsequent will or from the testator's contemporary or subsequent declarations that the testator intended the previous will to take effect as executed.

(b) If a subsequent will that partly revoked a previous will is thereafter revoked by a revocatory act under Section 2-507(a)(2), a revoked part of the previous will is revived unless it is evident from the circumstances of the revocation of the subsequent will or from the testator's contemporary or subsequent declarations that the testator did not intend the revoked part to take effect as executed.

(c) If a subsequent will that revoked a previous will in whole or in part is thereafter revoked by another, later, will, the previous will remains revoked in whole or in part, unless it or its revoked part is revived. The previous will or its revoked part is revived to the extent it appears from the terms of the later will that the testator intended the previous will to take effect.

Section 1-201. General Definitions.

. . . .

(56) "Will" includes codicil and any testamentary instrument that merely appoints an executor, revokes or revises another will, nominates a guardian, or expressly excludes or limits the right of an individual or class to succeed to property of the decedent passing by intestate succession.

Problems

1. Assume that Marcus validly executed Will I and that the Uniform Probate Code applies.

a. Marcus validly executed Will II, which revoked Will I. A day before he died, Marcus tore up Will II. What more would you want to know before deciding whether Will I was revived?

b. Marcus validly executed a codicil to Will I. A day before he died, Marcus tore up the codicil. What more would you want to know before deciding whether part of Will I was revived?

c. Marcus validly executed a codicil to Will I. A day before he died, Marcus validly executed a paper that read "I hereby revoke my codicil to Will I." What more would you want to know before deciding whether part of Will I was revived?

2. Clarence left several sheets of paper attempting to dispose of his property:

(1) Dated 10/1/91, numbered #0, appointed executors and included administrative directions, signed.

(2) Dated 10/12/91, numbered #1, captioned "Embody in Will," included 13 pecuniary bequests, unsigned.

(3) Dated 10/12/91, numbered #2, captioned "Embody in Will"; included six pecuniary bequests, a gift of clothes, directions for the funeral, and a residuary clause; unsigned.

(4) Dated 5/12/92, numbered #3, includes "The following I consider as some of friends—and I will to them as follows," lists seven pecuniary bequests, unsigned.

(5) Dated 9/19/94, unnumbered, disposes of several items of personal property, signed.

(a) If the last page (including the signature) had been crossed out, which pages, if any, would be entitled to probate?

(b) What if, instead, the first page (numbered #0) had been crossed out?

3. Ralph executed a properly witnessed document which only says "Should I die with this document still in force, I revoke my will of March 15, 1995." Later, he tears up the revoking document. Under UPC § 2-509, is the will of March 15, 1995 revalidated?

§ 3.07 Dependent Relative Revocation[20]

The most intriguing of the doctrines relating to will revocation is the one carrying the name "dependent relative revocation," known to generations of law students as "DRR." DRR works rather like the "undo" command for a word processor. Fundamentally a doctrine for correcting what turn out to have been mistakes, it carries an odd title because courts—traditionally reluctant to correct mistakes involving wills—engage in a fiction. When they decide to ignore a mistaken revocation, they pretend that the revocation itself was really dependent on some condition. When (because of the mistake) the condition is not met, the courts may then treat the mistaken revocation as though it never really happened. Because there has been no revocation, the will in question stands.

A classic DRR scenario involves a testator who has revised her will. Something goes wrong at the execution ceremony, however, and the new will is not valid. Without realizing that the new will is invalid, she tears up the old will. A court applying DRR would save the old will on the theory that her destruction of that will was

20. Section 4.3 of the Restatement (Third) of Property (Wills and Other Donative Transfers) renames the doctrine "Ineffective Revocation." We retain the traditional, if convoluted, name because courts have so far kept it.

conditional on the new will being valid. Because the new will fails, the tearing did not revoke the old one.

Notice that the doctrine does not give the testator what she really wanted, and thought she had, the new will. Rather, when the choice is intestacy or the old will, she gets the old will she thought she had revoked. One continuing problem in many DRR cases is trying to choose among unfavored alternatives. The UPC thus refers to the doctrine as "the law of second best." UPC § 2-507, comment. Most courts look at the circumstances, compare the various wills and the intestate statute, and then choose what they believe the testator would have done had the testator known what hindsight has revealed.

The following case shows a lawyer's creative attempt to save a lost will which the court presumed was revoked. Rather than recognizing DRR as a fiction, the court searches for the testator's intention to make a conditional revocation.

In re Estate of Patten

587 P.2d 1307 (Mont. 1978)

Haswell, C.J.

This is an appeal from the granting of summary judgment by the District Court, Pondera County, denying admission to probate of a copy of the purported Last Will and Testament of Ella D. Patten, deceased.

[Ella had executed two wills. The first was validly executed in 1968; the second was invalidly executed in 1970. She died in 1973, survived by two sons, Donald and Robert. At her death, only the 1970 will was found. Shortly after her death, the court denied probate of the 1970 will, because there was no evidence she signed in the presence of witnesses or declared the document to be her will. Donald then tried to probate the 1968 will as a lost will.]

Both wills left the bulk of decedent's estate, approximately $200,000, to Donald Patten. There are some differences between the wills. In the 1968 will, Robert Patten was named executor of the estate. In the 1970 will, this appointment was deleted. The 1970 will omits some specific bequests which were in the 1968 will. The remaining paragraphs in the wills are almost identical in language and in form. . . .

The principal issue in this appeal is the District Court's refusal to apply the doctrine of dependent relative revocation and admit the copy of the 1968 will to probate. This is a case of first impression in Montana. We have not previously determined if the doctrine of dependent relative revocation is a part of Montana law. . . .

The doctrine of dependent relative revocation comes from the common law. The doctrine has been outlined in this manner:

> "Under what has been termed the doctrine of 'dependent relative revocation,' if a testator, having made a will and desiring to make a new one, cancels the first will preparatory to making the second and thereafter fails lawfully to execute the same or make[s] therein an invalid disposition of his property,

> it will be presumed that he preferred the old will to an intestacy, and the old will is not revoked. The doctrine is said to be one of presumed intention, it being presumed that cancellation or destruction of the old will was intended to be dependent upon making of a new one as a substitute for the old one. If the cancellation of the old will and the making of the new one were parts of one scheme, and the revocation of the old will was so related to the making of the new as to be dependent upon it, then if the new will be not made, or if made is invalid for any reason, the old will, though canceled, should be given effect, if its contents can be ascertained in any legal manner." Thompson on Wills § 168, p. 262.

The doctrine is applied with caution. The mere fact that a testator made a new will, which failed of effect, will not of itself prevent the destruction of an earlier will from operating as a revocation. The doctrine can only apply where there is a clear intent of the testator that the revocation of the old is conditional upon the validity of the new will.... For the doctrine to apply, the new will must also not have changed the testamentary purpose of the old will and essentially repeated the same dispositive plans such that it is clear that the first will is revoked only because the second duplicated its purpose.... Thus, while the doctrine may be widely recognized, it is narrowly applied.

In deciding whether to apply the doctrine in a given case, the testator's "intent" is the controlling factor. The testator must intend that the destruction of the old will is dependent upon the validity of the new will.... Evidence of this intent cannot be left to speculation, supposition, conjecture or possibility. The condition that revocation of a will is based upon the validity of the new will must be proved by substantial evidence of probative value.... A showing of immediate intent to make a new will and of conditional destruction are required to reestablish a destroyed will under the theory of dependent relative revocation. *In re Estate of Hall* (1972), 7 Wash. App. 341, 499 P.2d 912. In Hall, the court stated that to prove this intent the proponents of the revoked will must show that the new will was executed concurrently with or shortly after the destruction of the old will and both wills must be similar in content. In the present case, Donald Patten, the proponent of the copy of the 1968 will, has not proven that decedent intended the destruction of the 1968 will to depend upon the validity of the 1970 will.

The original of the 1968 will was given to Ella D. Patten after it was executed. At her death, it could not be found. Under Montana law, a will, last seen in the possession of a testator, which cannot be found after a careful and exhaustive search following death is presumed to have been destroyed by the testator with the intent of revoking it.... This presumption that decedent destroyed the 1968 will with the intent to revoke it must apply in this case. No one knows when the decedent destroyed her will or how she did it. The record does not show that the 1970 will was executed concurrently or shortly after the destruction of the 1968 will.

While the content of both wills is similar in some respects, the dissimilarities are such that they reveal decedent's revocation of the 1968 will was not conditioned on the validity of the 1970 will. In the 1968 will, decedent bequeathed $5,000 and $2,500 to her grandchildren, the son and daughter of Robert Patten. In the 1970 will, Donald Patten's name was written in by pen and ink as the executor. In the 1968 will, Robert Patten was the named executor. These differences in the wills show that decedent may not have intended the same dispositive plan.

Here, the evidence that decedent intended the revocation of the 1968 will to depend upon the validity of the 1970 will is merely conjecture and speculation. As that is the case, the District Court was correct in granting summary judgment to Robert L. Patten. The doctrine of dependent relative revocation can only be applied where the evidence of the testator's intent is clear and convincing. Such is not the case here.

In a similar factual situation, the Illinois Supreme Court refused to apply the doctrine. *In re Moos' Estate* (1953), 414 Ill. 54, 110 N.E.2d 194. In *Moos' Estate*, the original will of the decedent could not be found after his death and the presumption of revocation arose. There, like here, a copy of the will alleged to have been lost was presented to the court for probate. Admission of the copy of the will to probate was denied. The court holding that, where the evidence was insufficient to overcome the presumption of revocation, the doctrine of dependent relative revocation had no application in absence of evidence that the revocation of the old will depended upon the efficacy of the new will. Here, we have no evidence that the revocation of the 1968 will depended upon the validity of the 1970 will. The doctrine of dependent relative revocation has no application under these circumstances. . . .

Notes and Questions

1. Why didn't the court ask whether Ella would have preferred the 1968 will to intestacy?

Compare Estate of Bowers, 131 P.3d 916 (Wash. Ct. App. 2006). Alice Bowers' 1991 will made a large charitable gift and left her residuary estate to her daughter. In 2004, Alice revised the will to reduce her daughter's gift to $500, but Alice never executed the revised will. When she died, the 1991 will could not be found, which would have left the daughter with an intestate share. Invoking DRR principles, the court noted the 2004 "will" showed that Alice did not intend to die intestate. Although the 1991 will was presumed revoked, it could be proved under the local statute because it was "lost or destroyed under circumstances such that the loss or destruction does not have the effect of revoking the will."

2. Would the result in *Patten* have been different if the case had arisen after Montana adopted UPC § 2-503 (harmless error)?

3. Section 4.3 of the Restatement (Third) of Property (Wills and Other Donative Transfers) attempts to clarify the doctrine, in part by renaming it "Ineffective Revocation." A revocation is presumed to be ineffective if it was made "because of a false assumption of law, or because of a false belief about an objective fact, that is either recited in the revoking instrument or established by clear and convincing evidence."

However, "the presumption is rebutted if allowing the revocation to remain in effect would be more consistent with the testator's probable intention."

4. Other courts have followed *Patten's* insistence that the testator must have intended to revoke a prior will on the condition that a later will was effective. *See, e.g., Estate of Sharp*, 889 N.Y.S.2d 323 (N.Y. App. Div. 2009). Comment c to § 4.3 of the Restatement (Third) of Property views this requirement as "misguided":

> *Revocation intending to make a replacement will.* A revocation is presumptively ineffective if a testator, failing in an attempt to replace one will (the first will) with another will (the replacement will), revokes the first will by revocatory act. In such a case, the failed dispositive objective that the testator intended to achieve in connection with revoking the first will is the pattern of distribution contained in the replacement will. If the testator initiated steps toward executing a replacement will that are sufficient to make the dispositive plan that he or she wanted to achieve provable, it is presumed that the testator's revocation of the first will was made in connection with an intent to replace it with the replacement will. After death, the only evidence available may be the ineffectively executed replacement will, and sometimes but not necessarily the revoked first will. Consequently, the doctrine of ineffective revocation would be too restricted if it required evidence of the time of revocation and of a contemporaneous intent to make a replacement will. There need not be affirmative proof of the time of revocation or that, at the time of revocation, the testator intended to replace the first will with a replacement will.

5. Courts have disagreed about whether to apply DRR to revocations by writing. In the face of absolute language like "I revoke all my prior wills," a court may have trouble saying the revocation was nonetheless conditional. The question can arise when a testator executes a new will which both expressly revokes the old one and creates a new gift which itself is invalid. To enforce the revocation clause of the new will, but not allow the new disposition, strikes some courts (and the Restatement) as being unfair to the testator. They correct the mistake by viewing the new will's revocation clauses as having been dependent on the effectiveness of the new gift. Other courts enforce the revocation clause, however, because its language is clearly not conditional. *Compare Linkins v. Protestant Episcopal Cathedral Found.*, 187 F.2d 357 (D.C. Cir. 1950) (DRR applied), *with Crosby v. Alton Ochsner Medical Found.*, 276 So. 2d 661 (Miss. 1973) (not applied).

6. It is possible, if very rare, for DRR to realize the testator's first choice. In *In re Estate of Boysen*, 309 N.W.2d 45 (Minn. 1981), the testator, apparently believing both of his wills provided the same distribution when they in fact did not, revoked Will II. Lack of intention to revive Will I left the decedent intestate. Had DRR been applied to ignore Will II's revocation, the testator's intention would have been honored. *See* John H. Langbein & Lawrence W. Waggoner, *Reforming the Law of Gratuitous Transfers: The New Uniform Probate Code*, 55 Alb. L. Rev. 871, 887 n.34 (1992).

Problems

1. Olivia executed a will cutting out some relatives. Later, she revised the will, but kept the same basic scheme. Later still, she tore up Will II and told a friend she wanted Will I to stand. Under local law, however, she could only get the first will back by re-executing it. Should her property pass by intestacy or under Will II?

2. Steve's first will left everything to Janet. His second will revoked the first and divided his property equally between Janet and Claire. The second will was typed, but not witnessed. Can DRR apply to save the first will?

3. Marge's first will gave her estate to Peter, and named a bank as executor. A later will repeated the gift to Peter, but also named him as executor. Peter was one of two witnesses to the second will, but not to the first. What does Peter take?

4. Howard's printed will includes a gift of "$5,000 to my friend Michael Andrews." The "$5,000" is crossed out and "$7,500" is written above in Howard's handwriting, along with his initials.

   (a) How much does Michael take when Howard dies?

   (b) What if the change were to $2,500?

Selected Reference

Frank L Schiavo, *Dependent Relative Revocation Has Gone Astray: It Should Return to Its Roots*, 13 Widener L. Rev. 73 (2006).

Richard F. Storrow, *Dependent Relative Revocation: Presumption or Probability?*, 48 Real Prop. Tr. & Est. L.J. 497 (2014).

§ 3.08 Options for Safeguarding Wills

As much of the material in this chapter indicates, wills can be dangerous instruments in the hands of some clients. They can lose them, mangle them, "correct" them, use them for scratch paper. For good reason, lawyers have long wanted to keep wills out of temptation's reach. One solution is for the lawyer to keep the will for the client. That way it will be protected from harm and easily available when needed. Not so coincidentally, later updating and, most lucratively, the ultimate probating are likely to be handled by the law office where the will has been stored. Many law firms view a safe full of wills as a capital investment in the future. The practice has its practical drawbacks, however, especially for solo practitioners. If the lawyer dies while still keeping a practice, those handling the lawyer's estate can spend considerable time and money trying to track down the clients and former clients whose wills have been in safekeeping.

Concerned about lawyer overreaching, Wisconsin appears to be unique among the states in prohibiting the practice unless the will is kept by the attorney "upon specific unsolicited request of the client." *State v. Gulbankian*, 196 N.W.2d 733, 736 (Wis. 1972). One commentator believes that approach does not go far enough. "[T]he best and most effective ethical rule is one based on an outright prohibition of such attorney practices. The other logical choice, attempting to determine whether the drafting attorney or the testator requested the safekeeping, is simply too elusive to be meaningful or effective." Gerald P. Johnston, *An Ethical Analysis of Common Estate Planning Practices—Is Good Business Bad Ethics?*, 45 Ohio St. L.J. 57, 133 (1984).

Notes and Questions

1. Compare how presumptions of undue influence can arise when lawyers appear as beneficiaries of the wills they draft.

2. See the copy below of Mary Horst's will for an example of a client who decided to revise her own will. *See Horst v. Horst*, 184 Ohio App. 3d 281 (2009). Which is the greater risk: that lawyers will overreach to obtain business or that clients will handle their wills incorrectly?

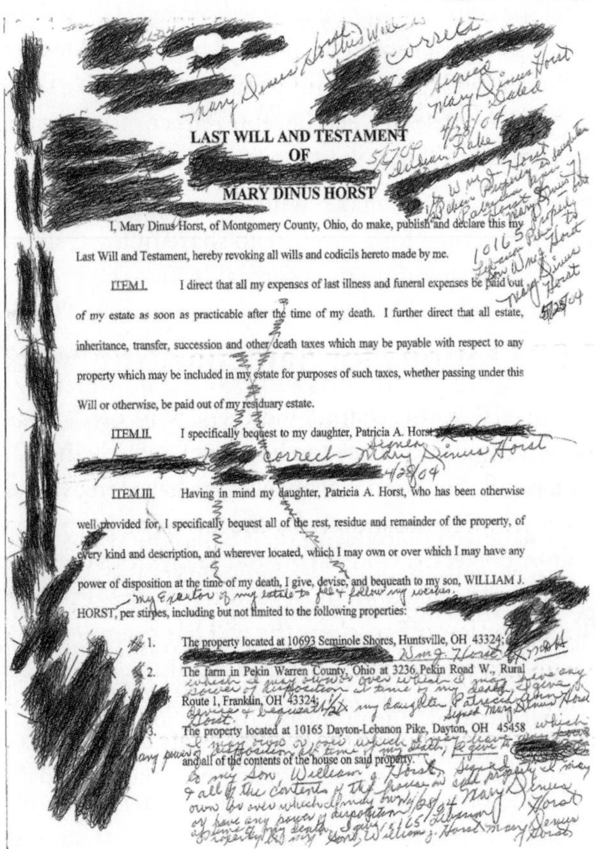

LAST WILL AND TESTAMENT
OF
MARY DINUS HORST

I, Mary Dinus Horst, of Montgomery County, Ohio, do make, publish and declare this my Last Will and Testament, hereby revoking all wills and codicils hereto made by me.

ITEM I. I direct that all my expenses of last illness and funeral expenses be paid out of my estate as soon as practicable after the time of my death. I further direct that all estate, inheritance, transfer, succession and other death taxes which may be payable with respect to any property which may be included in my estate for purposes of such taxes, whether passing under this Will or otherwise, be paid out of my residuary estate.

ITEM II. I specifically bequest to my daughter, Patricia A. Horst

ITEM III. Having in mind my daughter, Patricia A. Horst, who has been otherwise well provided for, I specifically bequest all of the rest, residue and remainder of the property, of every kind and description, and wherever located, which I may own or over which I may have any power of disposition at the time of my death, I give, devise, and bequeath to my son, WILLIAM J. HORST, per stirpes, including but not limited to the following properties:

1. The property located at 10693 Seminole Shores, Huntsville, OH 43324;
2. The farm in Pekin Warren County, Ohio at 3236 Pekin Road W., Rural Route 1, Franklin, OH 43324;
3. The property located at 10165 Dayton-Lebanon Pike, Dayton, OH 45458 and all of the contents of the house on said property.

3. Walter Deardoff's will directed his executrix to hire either of two identified lawyers and provided that if she failed to do so, she "shall be replaced." The named executrix declined to serve, and her replacement wanted to choose her own lawyer. The court in *Estate of Deardoff*, 461 N.E.2d 1292 (Ohio 1984), ruled that the direction was not binding. If the two lawyers were also involved in the drafting of the will, should they be subject to professional discipline? To malpractice liability?

§ 3.09 Contracts Regarding Wills

In addition to being able to create and revoke wills, people can also execute contracts to make, or not make, or revoke, or not revoke, wills. These contracts do not change wills law—wills can still be made or revoked despite the promises—but they do affect how property is ultimately distributed. The two most common areas of dispute involve contracts to make wills and contracts not to revoke them. If a promise to make or not to revoke a will is enforceable under contract law, it may be enforced against the estate of the breaching promisor.

A common remedy will be to create a constructive trust in favor of the promisee and then enforce it against the assets of those who otherwise would be unjustly enriched. Recall that the court in *Estate of Gushwa*, *see Page 173*, remanded for findings of whether a constructive trust should be imposed because the testator had been prevented from revoking his will. Note carefully that a constructive trust is not a trust in the ongoing management sense of that concept. Rather, it is a remedy ordering the person who is not entitled to the property to turn it over to the person who is.

Litigation over contracts to make wills frequently involves someone who worked for a testator in return for a promise to share in the testator's estate. Often the promise was oral and therefore unenforceable, but the promisee may bring a quantum meruit action for the value of services rendered. The amount recoverable, however, may be a far cry from the promised share of the estate. *See, e.g.*, *Green v. Richmond*, 337 N.E.2d 691 (Mass. 1975) (estate worth $7,000,000). Contracts to make a will may arise in other contexts. *See, e.g.*, *Leonardi v. Leonardi*, 950 N.Y.S.2d 723 (N.Y. Sup. Ct., 2012) (contract to leave property by will based on separation agreement).

Individuals can also agree not to revoke their wills. Questions about whether there has been such an agreement generally arise between spouses who execute wills with reciprocal terms. Such wills are called "mutual" or "reciprocal" wills. Sometimes these wills are also "joint," one will serving two persons. Using a joint and reciprocal will may make it more likely for a court to find that the survivor promised not to revoke the will. In part to avoid the problems these contracts pose, the UPC specifically negates any such presumption. UPC § 2-514.

Wills can also be reciprocal without being joint. Married couples typically execute wills with reciprocal terms. Sometimes, as in the next case, the wills include express agreements, usually promises that the survivor will not revoke all or part of the plan. Almost always, a trust is a better solution. *See* note 4, below.

Ernest v. Chumley

936 N.E.2d 602 (Ill. App. Ct. 2010)

JUSTICE STEIGMANN delivered the opinion of the court:

. . .

[Robert and Dorothy Sonneborn executed mutual wills with reciprocal terms. If the other survived, each gave the other their entire estate to the exclusion of their children. The wills also included language paralleling the following, taken from Dorothy's version:

Since my husband and I each have children from a prior marriage, it is our intent that upon the death of the survivor of us, that my estate or his estate, as the case may be, be divided one-half to my children and one-half to his children designated as beneficiaries in Article III. Accordingly, it is further our intent that upon the death of the first of us, the terms of the will of the surviving spouse shall become irrevocable.]

In April 2003, Robert died, owning assets in joint tenancy with Dorothy . . . , which included their home and several bank accounts. Two months after Robert's death, Dorothy executed a new will that bequeathed her entire estate to her biological children.

In December 2004, Dorothy married Thomas Chumley. The following month, Dorothy executed another will, in which she bequeathed her entire estate to (1) Thomas and, should he predecease her, then to (2) her biological children and Thomas's two children in equal shares. In February 2006, Dorothy sold the home she had shared with Robert . . . [and ultimately deposited the proceeds in three certificates of deposit held jointly with Thomas].

. . .

In October 2004—two months before Dorothy married Thomas—[Robert's children] Deborah and John filed a complaint to construe the will, requesting that the trial court (1) find Dorothy's August 2000 mutual will irrevocable, (2) order Dorothy to itemize the assets she owned with Robert immediately before his death, and (3) impose a constructive trust, prohibiting (a) Dorothy from making gratuitous transfers of those assets and (b) Thomas's or Dorothy's future spouses from making any statutory claims on the itemized assets. . . . [The court denied complete relief, and Deborah and John appealed.]

. . .

II. THE APPLICABILITY OF DOROTHY'S MUTUAL WILL DURING HER LIFETIME

A. The Legal Implications of Mutual Wills

Mutual wills are the separate instruments of two or more testators that contain reciprocal terms such that each testator disposes of his or her respective property to the other. . . . In contrast, a joint will is a single instrument that contains the wills of two or more persons, and may be considered mutual if it contains reciprocal provisions. . . . In the case of mutual and reciprocal wills, "'a judicial presumption arises in favor of the existence of the contract from the existence of the mutual wills themselves.'" *In re Estate of Aimone*, 590 N.E.2d 94, 98 ([Ill. App.] 1992), quoting *In re Estate of Kritsch*, 382 N.E.2d 50, 53 ([Ill. App.]1978). A contract embodied in a mutual will becomes irrevocable as to the survivor upon the death of the first testator.

B. Deborah and John's Claim That Dorothy's Mutual Will Implicitly Restricted Her Use of Certain Assets During Her Lifetime

We first note that Deborah and John do not contest the trial court's findings that (1) in April 2003, Dorothy's mutual will became irrevocable because of Robert's death; (2) the expressed terms of Robert's and Dorothy's mutual wills (a) did not restrict Dorothy's use of the assets during her lifetime and (b) show that Robert and Dorothy entered into a contractual agreement; and (3) regardless of how Dorothy obtained the assets at issue, they were subject to the testamentary scheme of their respective mutual wills.

Instead, Deborah and John argue only that the trial court erred by denying, in part, their complaint to construe the will because they are entitled to (1) an accounting and (2) the imposition of a constructive trust upon the assets owned by Robert at his death. Specifically, Deborah and John contend that although the contract embodied by Robert's and Dorothy's mutual wills did not explicitly restrict Dorothy's use of the assets at issue during her lifetime, it implicitly restricted Dorothy from (1) executing new wills, (2) selling the home she shared with Robert, and (3) transferring money into a joint account with Thomas. Thus, the narrow question before this court is whether Robert's and Dorothy's mutual wills implied restrictions upon Dorothy's *use* of the aforementioned assets during her lifetime. With one exception, we conclude that they did not. That exception is that we conclude that Dorothy's transfer of funds from the sale of her home into three certificates of deposit that she held in joint tenancy with Thomas violated the terms of the irrevocable contract created by the execution of her joint and mutual will.

. . .

[The court distinguished cases that had arisen after the death of the surviving spouse.]

3. *Restrictions Placed on a Surviving Spouse's Use of Bequeathed Assets During Her Lifetime*

Over three decades ago in *First United Presbyterian Church v. Christenson*, . . . 356 N.E.2d 532 ([Ill.] 1976), the supreme court considered the effect of explicit restrictions on the use of bequeathed assets during a surviving spouse's lifetime. In *Christenson*, ... Margaret and her then-husband, Lewis, executed a joint and mutual will that (1) gave the surviving spouse possession of the entirety of the other spouse's estate upon either spouse's death; (2) explicitly prohibited Margaret, as the surviving spouse, from selling two parcels of land devised to the First United Presbyterian Church; and (3) upon the surviving spouse's death, bequeathed the remaining estate to their nieces and nephews to "share and share alike."

Approximately three years after Lewis's death, Margaret executed two warranty deeds conveying the two parcels of land devised to the church to her nieces and nephews.... The church brought suit, requesting, in part, that the trial court set aside the warranty deed....

... [T]he supreme court held that the plain language of Margaret's and Lewis's will did not prohibit Margaret from conveying the parcels to her nieces and nephews during Margaret's lifetime.... In so holding, the supreme court directed the trial court to enter an order (1) finding Margaret's nieces and nephews owners of the parcels until Margaret's death and (2) enjoining them from executing any instrument that would convey the parcels in a manner inconsistent with the church's ownership interest after Margaret's death.[21] ...

4. *The Plain Language of Robert's and Dorothy's Respective Mutual Wills*

...

In this case, the plain, unambiguous language of Robert's and Dorothy's respective August 2000 mutual wills shows, in pertinent part, that (1) upon Robert's April 2003 death, (a) Dorothy was immediately entitled to the entirety of Robert's assets without restriction, (b) Deborah and John were not entitled to any of Robert's assets, and (c) Dorothy's mutual will became irrevocable, and (2) upon Dorothy's death, Deborah and John would each be entitled to a one-quarter interest in Dorothy's estate. If Robert and Dorothy intended to place restrictions on Dorothy's use of the bequeathed assets during her lifetime, they could have easily expressed their intent to do so in their mutual wills as the parties did in *Christenson.* They did not, and we decline to infer otherwise. Thus, we reject Deborah and John's contention that Robert's and Dorothy's mutual wills implicitly created a life estate that restricted Dorothy's use of the assets at issue during her lifetime. However, our analysis does not end here.

5. *Dorothy's Ownership of Assets in Joint Tenancy*[22] *With Robert*

... Dorothy was still bound by the expressed intent of the underlying irrevocable contract created by her mutual will. Specifically, that upon Dorothy's death, Deborah and John would each inherit one-quarter of her remaining estate. See *Rauch v. Rauch*, 445 N.E.2d 77, 79 ([Ill. App.]1983) ("A joint and mutual will must be

21. The court gave the nieces and nephews life estates for the life of another, in this case Margaret.

22. We discuss joint tenancy in Chapter 4, §4.02A. [Eds.]

executed pursuant to a contract between the testators, requiring the survivor of them to dispose of the property as the will's provisions instruct").

Although assets held in joint tenancy do not pass under a joint and mutual will, they can be the subject of a contractual agreement contained within a joint and mutual will and a court, under the appropriate circumstances, can enforce the agreement by limiting the surviving spouse's disposition of property.... Although not immediately entitled to possession until the death of the surviving spouse, third-party beneficiaries of a joint and mutual will are entitled to enforcement of the underlying contract....

In this case, the record shows that Robert and Dorothy expressly bequeathed the entirety of their respective estates to the surviving spouse—in this case Dorothy—intending to leave the residue of that estate, however much that estate might be at the time of her death, to Robert's and Dorothy's biological children in equal shares. The record also shows that after Robert's death, Dorothy deposited a substantial portion of the funds she received from the sale of the home she previously owned with Robert into three separate certificates of deposit, which she held in joint tenancy with Thomas. However, in so doing, Dorothy effectively breached the expressed intent of her irrevocable contract by removing those funds from her estate by operation of law....

Accordingly, we remand to the trial court with directions that it enter an order mandating that Dorothy (1) terminate Thomas's interest in the aforementioned certificates of deposit and (2) refrain from taking any future action that is inconsistent with Deborah and John's future interest in her estate except expenditures made for her own support....

Notes

1. Professor Alice Noble-Allgire of Southern Illinois University has noted that *Ernest v. Chumley* may have muddied the waters inadvertently about whether Illinois law implies a contract from the use of mutual and reciprocal wills (as opposed to a joint will). The case illustrates the importance of precision when quoting other material.

The problem arises in the court's background information in section II A of the *Ernest* opinion. See Page 190. Quoting *Aimone*, which in turn quoted *Kritsch*, the *Ernest* court says: "In the case of mutual and reciprocal wills, 'a judicial presumption arises in favor of the existence of the contract....'" However, the quoted language actually reads: "... in the case of *such* mutual and reciprocal wills..." (emphasis added). The "mutual and reciprocal" wills in *Kritsch*, like those in *Ernest*, actually included specific language making each survivor's will irrevocable. In Illinois, "such" wills—not just *any* mutual and reciprocal wills—appear to be the ones that give rise to the presumption of a contract.

On the revocability question, many states treat joint wills differently from mutual/reciprocal wills. *Compare Curry v. Cotton,* 191 N.E. 307 (Ill. 1934) (a joint will becomes irrevocable after the death of one of the makers if the survivor accepts any of the benefits made for him by such will) with *Oursler v. Armstrong,* 179 N.E.2d 489 (N.Y. 1961) (mutually reciprocal wills may have created a moral obligation for the survivor not to revoke the will, but not a contractual one.)

Cases like *Ernest* illustrate that whatever the case law says, even reciprocal wills pose a litigation risk if the survivor changes his or her will. Unless the local law is very specific, see Note 3, *below*, couples signing mirror-image wills while also wanting to preserve flexibility for their survivor should consider including specific language saying no contract is intended.

Joint wills—a single will for two people—breed litigation on a wide range of issues. Avoid them. For two cases—nine years apart—interpreting the same joint will, see *Shimp v. Shimp*, 412 A.2d 1228 (Md. 1980) (finding a contract not to revoke), and *Shimp v. Huff*, 556 A.2d 252 (Md. Ct. App. 1989) (establishing spousal election rights).

3. Many jurisdictions require that a contract to make or not revoke a will must be in writing. The UPC requires that the contract be: (1) expressed in the will, (2) expressly referred to in the will and provable by extrinsic evidence, or (3) in writing. UPC § 2-514. Based on this provision, reciprocal will provisions did not result in a contract not to revoke the survivor's will. *See Taylor v. Robertson*, 485 S.W.3d 393 (Ct. App. Mo. 2016). Some statutes go further, and require also that the contract be witnessed by two persons. *See, e.g.*, Fla. Stat. § 732.701(1).

For an interesting twist on the oral contract question, see *Ryan v. Ryan*, 642 N.E.2d 1028 (Mass. 1994). In the course of seeking the cooperation of his former wife, Marion, in obtaining a church annulment of their marriage, Paul Ryan, a lawyer, allegedly orally promised that their children would inherit two-thirds of his estate. He also allegedly advised Marion that the oral contract was enforceable. Paul remarried and executed a new will which did not leave two-thirds to his children. When Marion and the children lost the contract claim because the promise was oral, they brought a legal malpractice claim against Paul's estate because Paul had advised Marion incorrectly. The malpractice claim failed for lack of sufficient evidence that Paul ever told Marion that his oral promise was enforceable. The uncorroborated testimony of one of the children was not enough to warrant submitting the claim to the jury. Concerned that malpractice claims like this might provide an end run around the Statute of Frauds and Statute of Wills, the court required the plaintiffs to prove by clear and convincing evidence both the existence of an attorney-client relationship and the legal advice given.

4. Contracts not to revoke wills are almost always a bad idea. They lock survivors into an estate plan which may not become effective until a time when its terms have become inappropriate. In the meantime, the contract clouds the rights of the

survivors, often prompting litigation. The particular contract language will affect the result, but most provisions leave ambiguities. Some examples:

(a) Can a survivor who promised not to revoke the will effectively avoid the contract by transferring assets during their lifetime? *Compare Self v. Slaughter*, 16 So. 3d 781 (Ala. 2008) (no) with *In re Leix Estate*, 797 N.W.2d 673 (Ct. App. Mich. 2010 (yes).

(b) Are gifts allowed if the assets are "the sole property of the one who survives. To be used at their own discretion." *Klooz v. Cox*, 496 P.2d 1350 (Kan. 1972) (no). Or to "use the proceeds of such property as he or she sees fit"? *Swearingin v. Estate of Swearingin*, 2006 Tex. App. LEXIS 5187 (June 15, 2006) (yes).

(c) If the survivor remarries and the new spouse gives investment advice which greatly increases the value of the property, does the new spouse have any claim to the increased value? *Robison v. Graham*, 799 P.2d 610 (Okla. 1990) (no).

(d) Does the contract apply to life insurance proceeds the survivor receives? *Bergheger v. Boyle*, 629 N.E.2d 1168 (Ill. App. Ct. 1994) (no).

(e) Does the contract apply to the wrongful death award the survivor receives for the death of the spouse? *In re Estate of Jud*, 710 P.2d 1241 (Kan. 1985) (yes).

(f) Is a contract to keep the property "on the Brubaker side of the family" met by a will provision "to my blood nephews," excluding nieces? *Kretzer v. Brubaker*, 660 N.E.2d 446 (Ohio 1996) (yes).

(g) May the lawyer who drafted a joint and mutual will, and later drafted an instrument for the surviving spouse which may have violated the will, represent devisees under the will in a challenge to the later instrument? ABA Formal Opinion 64 (1932) (no).

Clients, especially those involved in second marriages, need to protect the interests of all of the family members. Usually a trust will be the best way to accomplish that goal.

Problems

1. Jennie and Martin are planning to marry. They each have children from prior marriages and want you to work out a plan which is fair to everyone. What ethical problems will you face if you represent them both? How will you structure the lawyer-client relationship?

2. Martha Jones died recently and her daughter, Abby, has come to you for advice. Martha divorced her husband when her children were young. With the help of her unmarried sister, Susan, Martha managed a farm while raising two children, now both in their 40's: Abby, who now lives in another city; and Bob, who lived with Martha and Susan and eventually took over management of the farm.

Martha left a will dated May 16, 1970. It revoked all prior wills, left the farm to Susan, and split the remainder of the estate equally between Abby and Bob. The will contained a "no-contest" clause under which anyone who challenged the will would lose their share. The will was signed by Martha and witnessed by Barbara Smith (the drafting attorney) and Matilda Morin (a secretary in Smith's office).

Also among Martha's documents was a note written entirely in Martha's hand and dated December 28, 2005. It reads: "I don't want Susan to get the farm when I die." It is signed "Martha." The note was torn in half and found in a blank envelope. Abby relates that when she was home for the holidays in 1995, Martha and Susan had a confrontation over what was to be served at Christmas dinner. Martha accused Susan of always being too "bossy." Abby overheard Bob suggest to Martha that perhaps Susan didn't deserve to get the farm after all. Abby's next visit home was in the summer of 1996; at that time Martha and Susan were getting along very well. As far as Abby knows, the good relations continued until Martha's sudden death last month. About 80 percent of the net value of Martha's estate is tied up in the farm. Abby has no interest in running the farm, but would like to maximize her own share of her mother's estate. However, she is reluctant to pursue all possible arguments, because she doesn't want to end up with the worst of both worlds: no larger share and an alienated family. Advise Abby.

Chapter 4

Lifetime Alternatives to Wills

In Chapter 1 we noted that large amounts of property pass outside the probate system through a series of devices commonly known as "will substitutes." We now turn to a more detailed look at the ways a property owner can avoid the probate process by making gifts, by establishing living trusts, or by creating contract rights in third parties.

Individuals choose these devices for a variety of reasons: to benefit the donee, to retain a modicum of secrecy regarding family assets and plans, to defeat the claims of creditors or the donor's spouse, to minimize or eliminate taxes, or simply to avoid the necessity of dealing with lawyers. Perhaps the most common reason is to avoid the delays and expenses of probate administration.

In the past, the law treated probate and non-probate transfers separately, each in its own box with its own set of rules. Slowly and unevenly, doctrinal barriers have been coming down. On one hand, the relaxation of standards for executing non-probate documents has helped liberalize standards for will execution. On the other, doctrines developed in the context of wills are being applied to will substitutes. Over time, the law of probate and of non-probate transfers is becoming increasingly integrated. While that change is happening, lawyers must understand both the traditional rules and the likely directions in which the law may move. The now-classic article excerpted below describes the theoretical framework within which these changes continue.

John H. Langbein, *The Nonprobate Revolution and the Future of the Law of Succession*

97 Harv. L. Rev. 1108, 1109, 1114, 1125–26, 1128–32 (1984)

Over the course of the twentieth century, persistent tides of change have been lapping at the once-quiet shores of the law of succession. Probate, our court-operated system for transferring wealth at death, is declining in importance. Institutions that administer noncourt modes of transfer are displacing the probate system. Life insurance companies, pension plan operators, commercial banks, savings banks, investment companies, brokerage houses, stock transfer agents, and a variety of other financial intermediaries are functioning as free-market competitors of the probate system and enabling property to pass on death without probate and without will. The law of wills and the rules of descent no longer govern succession to most of the property of most decedents. Increasingly, probate bears to the actual practice of succession about the relation that bankruptcy bears to enterprise: it is an indispensable institution, but hardly one that everybody need use.

I. THE WILL SUBSTITUTES

Four main will substitutes constitute the core of the nonprobate system: life insurance, pension accounts, joint accounts, and revocable trusts. When properly created, each is functionally indistinguishable from a will—each reserves to the owner complete lifetime dominion, including the power to name and to change beneficiaries until death. These devices I shall call "pure" will substitutes, in contradistinction to "imperfect" will substitutes (primarily joint tenancies), which more closely resemble completed lifetime transfers. The four pure will substitutes may also be described as mass will substitutes: they are marketed by financial intermediaries using standard form instruments with fill-in-the-blank beneficiary designations. . . .

The "pure" will substitutes are not the only instruments of the nonprobate revolution; "imperfect" will substitutes—most prominent among them the common-law joint tenancy—also serve to transfer property at death without probate. Joint tenancies in real estate and in securities are quite common; joint tenancies in automobiles and other vehicles are also fairly widespread. Because they ordinarily effect lifetime transfers, joint tenancies are "imperfect" rather than "pure" will substitutes. When the owner of a house, a car, a boat, or a block of IBM common stock arranges to take title jointly, his cotenant acquires an interest that is no longer revocable and ambulatory. Under the governing recording act or stock transfer act, both cotenants must ordinarily join in any subsequent transfer. Yet like the pure will substitutes, joint tenancy arrangements allow the survivor to obtain marketable title without probate: under joint tenancy, a death certificate rather than a probate decree suffices to transfer title.

People seeking to transfer property at death without using the probate system have thus been tempted to use the common-law joint tenancy as a will substitute notwithstanding its lifetime consequences. . . .

III. THE JURIDICAL BASIS OF THE NONPROBATE SYSTEM

The nonprobate revolution has posed a conceptual problem for the law of wills that is still not cleanly answered in the case law or in the literature: How is it that will-like transfers escape being treated like wills? In the law of wills, the least departure from Wills Act formality routinely voids the transfer. Yet the will substitutes almost never comply with the attestation requirements for attested wills, nor do they satisfy the handwriting requirement for holographic wills. What, then, sustains the will substitutes against the Wills Act?

Our law has dealt with this question by indulging in a pretense—by denying that the will substitutes are will-like and by validating them as gifts. I shall urge a more candid answer, for which I think there is much support in existing practice and doctrine.

A. The Present-Interest Test

The essential difference between a gift and a will can be simply stated: a gift is a lifetime transfer, ordinarily effected by present delivery of the property, whereas a will transfers property only on the transferor's death .... [P]ure will substitutes fall ... clearly on the will side of the gift/will line. Each maintains the transferor's complete lifetime dominion and creates no interest in the transferee until the transferor's death. Nevertheless, the case law that has legitimated the pure will substitutes treats them as lifetime transfers. The main stratagem has been to identify some so-called "present interest" in the transferee, acquired during the lifetime of the transferor, which makes the transferee a donee and distinguishes the will substitute from a will....

The odor of legal fiction hangs heavily over the present-interest test. We see courts straining to reach right results for wrong reasons and insisting that will-like transfers possess gift-like incidents. Courts have used such doctrinal ruses to validate not only the revocable inter-vivos trust, but the other will substitutes as well. Why is a transfer by life insurance policy or by pension plan not void for violation of the Wills Act? Because the beneficiary's interest is "vested" during the transferor's lifetime. But how can it be vested when the transferor may freely revoke the beneficiary's interest? Well, the power to revoke simply makes the interest "vested subject to defeasance." What is the difference between the revocable and ambulatory interest created by a will, and a vested but defeasible interest in life insurance or pension proceeds? None at all, except for the form of words. Similarly, the joint bank account created merely as a probate avoidance device has been treated as a true joint tenancy, despite the depositor's power to exercise total lifetime dominion over the account. Of the pure will substitutes, only the transparently labeled P.O.D. [Payable On Death] account has persistently failed the present-interest test and has had to depend for the most part upon statutory validation.

B. Probate Monopoly or Transferor's Intent?

The courts have been uncomfortable with the present-interest test, and they have attempted to provide a further justification for exempting the will substitutes from the Wills Act—the concept of "alternative formality." ...

The notion of alternative formality offers an important insight. The will substitutes do exhibit formalities—written terms and signature—that parallel the requirements of the Wills Act. And in some cases, the involvement of third parties such as bank officers and insurance agents may serve some of the purposes of attestation. Motivated by considerations of efficiency and accuracy, the financial intermediaries who operate the nonprobate system have developed simplified formalities that largely serve the purposes of the Wills Act. Indeed, the needs of business practice incline the nonprobate system to a level of formality for the will substitutes that is well above the minimum permitted in jurisdictions that allow holographic wills....

Alternative formality is not a test for compliance with the Wills Act; it is a test for not having to comply with the Wills Act .... Alternative formality is a test that tells us when a mode of transfer should be fairly regarded as an effective will substitute operating outside the probate system. Alternative formality thus defines the bounds of the nonprobate system.

Modern practice supplies only one theory that can reconcile wills and will substitutes in a workable and honest manner: the rule of transferor's intent. The real state of the law is that the transferor may choose to pass his property on death in either the probate or the nonprobate system or in both. The transferor who takes no steps to form or disclose his intent will be remitted to probate, the state system. The transferor who elects to use any of the devices of the non-probate system will be protected in his decision, provided that the mode of non-probate transfer is sufficiently formal to meet the burden of proof on the question of intent to transfer. The alternative formalities of the standard form instruments that serve as mass will substitutes satisfy this requirement so easily that the issue of intent almost never needs to be litigated. The transferor's-intent theory thus replaces the probate monopoly theory. Transferors are free to opt out of probate by selecting any of the well-demarcated non-probate modes of transfer. . . .

Kent D. Schenkel, *Testamentary Fragmentation and the Diminishing Role of the Will: An Argument for Revival*

41 Creighton L. Rev. 155, 157–58 (2008).

Professor John Langbein identified four major types of "will substitutes" . . . [:] life insurance, pension accounts, the revocable inter vivos trust and the so-called "imperfect will substitutes" such as common-law joint tenancy. Since that time, new techniques have been popularized. The devices are best divided into three major legal categories: those based on a third-party beneficiary contract; those based on the revocable living trust; and those based on titling of property. Those based on contract include the pay-on-death or "POD" designations, which generally are enabled by legislation . . . . The UPC permits the contracting parties (the depositor institution and the account owner/depositor) to enter into a contract that allows the depositor to benefit a third party by making the account payable on the death of the depositor to one or more designated beneficiaries. Similar in concept are the "transfer-on-death" ("TOD") provisions of the Uniform TOD Security Registration Act . . . allowing for the transfer-on-death of security accounts by a comparable third party beneficiary arrangement. Also based on contract . . . are provisions for multiple party accounts. Another major category of assets are those assets transferred by designated beneficiary form. Specifically, these assets include insurance policies, annuities, and a wide variety of retirement plans and pension accounts.

Uniform Probate Code

Section 6-101. Nonprobate Transfers On Death.

A provision for a nonprobate transfer on death in an insurance policy, contract of employment, bond, mortgage, promissory note, certificated or uncertificated security, account agreement, custodial agreement, deposit agreement, compensation plan, pension plan, individual retirement plan, employee benefit plan, trust, conveyance, deed of gift, marital property agreement, or other written instrument of a similar nature is nontestamentary. This subsection includes a written provision that:

(1) money or other benefits due to, controlled by, or owned by a decedent before death must be paid after the decedent's death to a person whom the decedent designates either in the instrument or in a separate writing, including a will, executed either before or at the same time as the instrument, or later;

(2) money due or to become due under the instrument ceases to be payable in the event of death of the promisee or the promisor before payment or demand; or

(3) any property controlled by or owned by the decedent before death which is the subject of the instrument passes to a person the decedent designates either in the instrument or in a separate writing, including a will, executed either before or at the same time as the instrument, or later.

Comment

. . .

Because the modes of transfer authorized by an instrument under this section are declared to be nontestamentary, the instrument does not have to be executed in compliance with the formalities for wills prescribed under Section 2-502; nor does the instrument have to be probated, nor does the personal representative have any power or duty with respect to the assets. . . .

Question

If a provision in a Limited Liability Corporation's agreement disposes of a decedent's LLC interest, should the agreement control or should the interest pass by probate? *See Blechman v. Estate of Blechman*, 160 So. 3d 152 (Fla. Dist. Ct. App. 2015) (LLC interest passes pursuant to LLC agreement).

Selected References

Mary Louise Fellows, E. Gary Spitko & Charles Q. Strohm, *An Empirical Assessment of the Potential for Will Substitutes to Improve State Intestacy Statutes*, 85 Ind. L.J. 409 (2010).

David Horton, *In Partial Defense of Probate: Evidence from Alameda County, California*, 103 Geo. L.J. 605 (2015).

Melanie B. Leslie and Stewart E. Sterk, *Revisiting the Revolution: Reintegrating the Wealth Transmission System*, 56 B.C. L. Rev. 61 (2015).

§ 4.01 Lifetime Gifts

Traditionally, to make an effective gift, the donor must deliver the property with the intention to make a gift, and the donee must accept it. In a major doctrinal shift, Restatement (Third) of Property § 6.2 adds an option to the delivery requirement: using an inter vivos donative document.

Proving intent can be difficult, especially if the donor has died. Often "deadman" statutes prohibit testimony from persons who conversed with the decedent, leaving no proof of the decedent's intent one way or the other. *See* McCormick on Evidence, 4th ed., Vol. 1, pp. 250–53 (1992).

Because some tangible items (like a piano) are too big for easy manual delivery, constructive delivery may suffice. Among the more common controversies is whether handing over the key to a locked receptacle is sufficient symbolic delivery to allow the recipient to take the contents.[1] The cases usually turn on whether it was practical for the donor to transfer the stored items manually, instead of merely giving the key. If courts adopt the view of Restatement (Third) of Property § 6.2, comment c, that physical delivery, even if feasible, is not required, these disputes will no longer arise; constructive or symbolic delivery will work as well as physical delivery. Because intangible property, like stocks or bank accounts, is not subject to manual transfer, even traditional rules allow manually delivering the stock certificate or bank book evidencing the property. Sometimes, special rules apply. *See* United States v. Chandler, 410 U.S. 257 (1973) (physical transfer of U.S. Savings Bonds ineffective because government regulations required more). Transfer of realty requires a deed, but the deed itself need not be handed over to the donee. *See* Ferrell v. Stinson, 11 N.W.2d 701 (Iowa 1943) (deed of Iowa land to Iowa donees placed in box in Arizona).

Donors often deliver property by turning it over to an "escrow agent," someone the donor designated to hold the property as agent for the donee. For example, a donor might deliver stock to the corporation for reissuance in the name of a donee. *See, e.g.*, Panzirer v. Deco Purchasing & Distrib. Co., 448 So. 2d 1197 (Fla. Dist. Ct. App. 1984) (gift of stock by delivery of notarized letter of authorization to broker). Such transfers can allow delivery to be complete without notice to the donee. The danger is that if the donee is not to receive the property until the donor's death, the transaction appears to be testamentary, violating the Wills Act. As the Langbein article notes,

1. Sometimes "constructive" delivery and "symbolic" delivery are used interchangeably. The classic work on personal property draws a distinction between the two concepts: -

> A delivery is symbolic, when instead of the thing itself, some other object is handed over in its name and stead. A delivery is constructive, when in place of actual manual transfer the donor delivers . . . the means of obtaining possession and control . . . or in some other manner relinquishes to the donee power and dominion . . . .

Ray A. Brown, The Law of Personal Property 92 (3d ed. by Walter B. Rausenbush, 1975). Under traditional rules, symbolic delivery alone, without giving up power and dominion, is said to be insufficient to make a gift.

however, courts often validate these transfers by finding the donee got something before the donor died.

The requirement that a gift be accepted is there to protect donees. Courts will presume acceptance, even if the donee lacks notice of the gift, unless the gift does not benefit the donee, as when it is subject to unfavorable restrictions or conditions.

Gifts can be effective probate-avoidance devices, but they should be used with care. Lay people usually are unaware of the law's distinction between lifetime and testamentary gifts. From the law's perspective, many donors seem to want it both ways. For example, a donor may intend for a transfer to look like a lifetime gift, thereby avoiding probate, but may also intend that it not be effective until the donor's death. Courts are often liberal about allowing as "gifts" transfers with a distinctly testamentary look, but they are reluctant to allow a donor to undo a gift, which in form was a lifetime transfer.

Henkle v. Henkle

600 N.E.2d 791 (Ohio Ct. App. 1991)

Koehler, J. On September 8, 1988, plaintiff-appellant, Clarriette C. Henkle, filed a complaint against defendants-appellees, Annette J. Henkle, both individually and as administrator for the estate of John R. Henkle, deceased, and Jacob R. Henkle, the sole surviving son of John R. Henkle. The complaint alleged that a real estate transfer from appellant to her grandson John R. Henkle was void and should be set aside....

The record reveals that appellant had owned a two-hundred-twenty-acre farm, popularly known as the "Henkle Farm," since the 1950s. Starting in the early 1980s, appellant permitted her grandson John Henkle to operate and manage her farm. John Henkle demonstrated considerable skill and knowledge in managing the farm and appellant entrusted many of her farm-related and business affairs to him.

On February 4, 1988, appellant executed a warranty deed conveying most of the Henkle Farm to John Henkle, while reserving a life estate for herself. At the same time, she also executed another warranty deed conveying 1.7 acres of the farm to her son, Robert Henkle....

John Henkle died intestate on April 21, 1988. He was survived by his wife, Annette J. Henkle, and his son, Jacob R. Henkle, both of whom stand to inherit the Henkle Farm as the statutory beneficiaries of his estate. It was after John Henkle's death that appellant decided to file a lawsuit to set aside the deed....

In [her] deposition, appellant indicated that it was always her desire that the Henkle Farm should remain in the Henkle family. It was her understanding that John Henkle would operate the farm and that some time in the future he would convey home sites on the property to three of his brothers. She stated that she was aware in the two and one-half months following the execution of the deed but before John's death that she had signed the deed that conveyed the property to John and that he had not conveyed the home sites to his brothers as he promised. She indicated that she did not object because at that time his brothers did not want the property.

. . . Appellant's first claim for relief was undue influence. She alleged that she and John Henkle maintained a confidential relationship and that because of this relationship John Henkle was able to exert undue influence over her, thereby coercing her to convey to him the Henkle farm.

A deed executed in the correct form is presumed to be valid and will not be set aside except upon clear and convincing evidence. Therefore, a party seeking rescission and cancellation of a deed because of undue influence bears the burden of proof by clear and convincing evidence. . . .

In an affidavit filed in support of her memorandum contra to defendant's motion to summary judgment, appellant stated that "[w]hen I did sign the deeds, which ultimately transferred my real estate, I did so at the direction, insistence, influence and guidance of my grandson, John R. Henkle." . . . Nothing in the record supports the inference that John Henkle exerted such influence over appellant that her will was overborne. To the contrary, in her deposition, when asked if she relied upon the advice of her attorney in making the conveyance to her grandson, she replied, "I don't think so. I decided on my own. I have had a mind of my own a long time. . . ."

[The court rejected arguments based on mistake and turned to arguments that unjust enrichment justified imposition of a constructive trust.]

The Ohio Supreme Court discussed constructive trusts in *Ferguson v. Owens* (1984), 9 Ohio St. 3d 223, 459 N.E.2d 1293, 9 OBR 565, in which it stated: . . . "In *Beatty v. Guggenheim Exploration Co.* (1919), 225 N.Y. 380, 122 N.E. 378, we find the following pertinent commentary by Justice Cardozo, at pages 386 and 389 [122 N.E. at 380, 381]: . . . 'A constructive trust is the formula through which the conscience of equity finds expression. When property has been acquired in such circumstances that the holder of the legal title may not in good conscience retain the beneficial interest, equity converts him into a trustee . . . .' A court of equity in decreeing a constructive trust is bound by no unyielding formula . . . ." *Ferguson, supra*, 9 Ohio St. 3d at 225-226, 9 OBR at 567, 459 N.E.2d at 1295.

Although a constructive trust is usually invoked when property has been acquired by fraud, it may also be imposed where it is inequitable that a person retain the property even if it was acquired without fraud. . . .

Construing the material supporting and opposing summary judgment in appellant's favor, the record shows only that appellant conveyed the property to John Henkle with the understanding that at some unspecified time in the future he would give his three brothers home sites on the farm. Appellant indicated that she believed that John would convey these tracts of unspecified description to his brothers and that John was to have the rest of the farm. She did not object when John did not make the conveyances to appellant's other grandchildren prior to his death because "they didn't want it." The record does not support the assertion that John Henkle made any sort of misrepresentation, but rather that he died before he could fulfill his promises because the intended beneficiaries did not want the land. Appellant has shown no basis in equity for which she was entitled for relief. Instead, it is clear that appellant made a gift to John Henkle, and that neither he nor his beneficiaries were unjustly enriched at her expense. Consequently, there are no grounds for the operation of a constructive trust. . . .

Question and Notes

1. If Clarriette had asked you for advice before she executed the deed to John, what would you have said?

One temptation—which you should resist—would be to suggest a revocable deed. Revocable deeds and deeds subject to various conditions are infamous litigation-breeders. *See* Olin L. Browder, Jr., *Giving or Leaving—What Is a Will?*, 75 Mich. L. Rev. 845 (1977).

Several states now allow an attractive alternative: a transfer-on-death (TOD) deed. *See* § 4.04.

2. Usually gifts are irrevocable. Sometimes a person in fear of imminent death will give personal property to another, but then recover and want the property back. Such transfers, called "gifts causa mortis" are presumed revocable if the donor either survives the imminent peril or survives the donee. *See* Restatement (Second) of Property § 31.3; Restatement (Third) of Property § 6.2.

3. Should the presumption that a transfer to a close family member was a gift also apply to a transfer to an in-law of the donor? *See Cohen v. Raymond*, 128 A.3d 1072 (N.H. 2015) (no).

4. Questions can arise about whether a transfer is a gift or a bailment. *See Westleigh v. Conger*, 755 A.2d 518 (Me. 2000) (cash held in decedent's niece's safety deposit box was a bailment).

Problems

1. J.O. and Nannie executed a deed containing the grant "[W]e, the undersigned J.O. HEGWOOD and wife, NANNIE MAY HEGWOOD, do hereby sell, convey and warrant to our son, CARROLL DENNIS HEGWOOD, and HIS OWN BLOOD HEIRS, at OUR DEATH, the following described land . . . ," and delivered the deed to Carroll, who did not record the deed until after his father's death. Was the deed valid without complying with the Statute of Wills? *See Ford v. Hegwood*, 485 So. 2d 1044 (Miss. 1986) (yes).

2. Donna signed a check, making it payable to Anne, and left it on a table in the apartment they shared. Donna then left the apartment and committed suicide. Is

Anne entitled to the check? If Donna had survived the suicide attempt, could she have gotten back the check?

Note: Gifts to Minors

Gifts made directly to minors pose a problem: a court-supervised guardianship may be necessary. In response, almost every state has a gifts to minors act, based on the more flexible and inclusive Uniform Transfers to Minors Act (UTMA); South Carolina and Vermont still have its predecessor, the Uniform Gift to Minors Act (UGMA). These acts allow a donor to give property to a "custodian" who manages the property on behalf of the minor and may use it to benefit the minor. A custodian is a fiduciary who owes loyalty to the minor. *See* Uniform Transfer to Minors Act § 11. We examine fiduciary duty in Chapter 10.

Because states used different versions of the act, their statutes vary. Unsurprisingly, more recent versions have expanded to cover more kinds of property acquired in various different ways. Some versions allow a will or trust to authorize the appropriate fiduciary to give property to custodians, rather than directly to minors. Even if the governing document has not allowed such a gift, some states allow a personal representative, trustee, or guardian to effectively end a guardianship by giving a minor's property to a new custodian (or adding property to an existing custodial arrangement). *See* Uniform Transfer to Minors Act § 6.

A few shortcomings remain. In particular, the Act allows only a single minor to be the subject of a single custodianship. This restriction prevents a donor from pooling funds to allow discretionary distributions to several minors according to their needs. Second, the minor's attaining majority terminates the custodianship. A donor who wants to pool funds or delay distribution must use a trust.

Selected References

Ray A. Brown, The Law of Personal Property, Chs. 7–8 (3d ed. 1975).

Richard Hyland, Gifts: A Study in Comparative Law (2009).

§ 4.02 Joint Interests

Creating joint interests in real or personal property is perhaps the most common probate-avoidance device. The right of the survivor to own the whole is the distinguishing feature of these interests. When one owner dies, her interest simply disappears, leaving the survivor(s) owning the whole.

As a doctrinal matter, most estate planning problems involving joint interests center around whether and when grantors intended a completed gift. Courts usually, but not always, take people at their word when they say they are creating joint interests.

A. Joint Tenancy

Joint tenancy can be an effective probate avoidance device. Notice, however, that a joint tenancy between two people only avoids probate once. The survivor becomes sole owner. Clients also need to understand that a deed creating a joint tenancy, unlike a will naming a beneficiary, is irrevocable. All of the grantees become owners, with the consequences of that status.

Note and Questions

1. To discourage the fractionalization of Native American land titles, the American Indian Probate Reform Act reverses the modern general rule and presumes that a devise to two or more persons creates a joint tenancy with right of survivorship, rather than a tenancy in common. 25 U.S.C. § 2206(c).

2. Suppose Frances and Jack held real property as joint tenants with right of survivorship. Jack, without telling Frances, executed a deed of his half interest to his daughter, Julie. Traditional doctrine would leave Frances and Julie as tenants in common, effectively cutting off Frances' survivorship interest. *See Carmack v. Place*, 535 P.2d 197 (Colo. 1975).

(a) Is there any way for the law to protect Frances from that sort of surprise?

(b) If Jack had asked you to prepare the deed to Julie, would you have asked him why? What if you did not like his reasons? Consider the following excerpt.

3. As part of probate avoidance, creditors of the deceased tenant in a joint tenancy will not be allowed to recover from the joint property. It becomes the sole property of the surviving tenant. *See Ex parte Arvest Bank*, ___ So. 3d ___, 2016 WL 4943250 (Ala. 2016).

Problems

1. Seeking to avoid probate, Frank, a widower in his 80s who had had a stroke, transferred property to himself and his son, Sam, as joint tenants. Later, Frank remarried and asked Sam to reconvey the property. Sam refused and Frank sued, asking that the deeds be declared void, claiming he had not intended to convey a present interest in the property. Frank lost, having failed to overcome the presumption of delivery that arose from having recorded the deed. If Frank had asked you to help him avoid probate by preparing some joint tenancy deeds with his son, would you have thought to have warned him that if he married again, he might not want such an arrangement?

2. Manuel and Sharon, who each have children from prior marriages, recently took title to property as joint tenants with right of survivorship. If their survivor dies intestate, who will take the property?

Selected Reference

John V. Orth, *The Perils of Joint Tenancies*, 44 Real Prop. Prob. & Tr. J. 427 (2009).

B. Multiple Party Accounts

Jointly-held stocks, bonds, mutual funds and bank accounts are common. Perhaps the principal reason courts have struggled with these forms of ownership is that they do not fit into traditional boxes. A joint account is "neither a common law joint tenancy, an ordinary inter-vivos gift, a trust nor a will, yet it partakes of the features of all of these." N. William Hines, *Personal Property Joint Tenancies: More Law, Fact and Fancy*, 54 Minn. L. Rev. 509, 531 (1970). Bank accounts, perhaps because they are so widespread, have caused the most trouble. Slowly, the law is coming to recognize that people may use the joint form for a variety of reasons. Rather than burdening these devices with the baggage of other doctrines, legislation has emerged to validate various approaches in their own right. *See* UPC Article VI.

Convenience Accounts. Questions arise regularly about whether a particular jointly-held account was opened only for the "convenience" of one depositor. In *Franklin v. Anna National Bank of Anna*, 488 N.E.2d 1117 (Ill. App. Ct. 1986), Frank was a widower with failing eyesight, whose sister-in-law, Cora, moved in to care for him. To make it easier for Cora to get funds, Frank had Cora's name placed on the savings account he had had with his wife. After Frank's death, Cora (as surviving joint tenant) and Frank's executor (as successor to Frank) both claimed the money. The court found clear and convincing evidence that Frank had not intended to make a gift to Cora, but rather had added her as a signatory for his own convenience. This evidence was enough to overcome the usual presumption of joint ownership established by the bank's signature card.[2] The UPC seeks to avoid litigation by providing a "check off what you want" form, which includes a "multiple-party account without right of survivorship." *See* UPC § 6-204 (emphasis added).

Totten Trusts, POD, and TOD Accounts. A form of ownership peculiar to savings accounts is the so-called "Totten Trust," sometimes also known simply as a "savings account trust." The former term comes from the name of a New York case validating the device. *In re Totten*, 71 N.E. 748 (N.Y. 1904). In form, the depositor opens an account "as trustee" for someone else. In fact, there is really no trust relationship established. Rather, the account functions like an account in which the depositor can withdraw the funds at any time and the "beneficiary" gets what is left when the depositor/trustee dies. Often such accounts are labeled "Payable on Death" (POD). In the past, courts have been hostile to straightforward POD accounts (as too blatantly testamentary), but legislatures have authorized them in virtually all states.

Almost every state has extended the concept of POD accounts beyond bank accounts by enacting some form of the Uniform Transfer on Death [TOD] Security Registration Act, adopted in 1989 and incorporated in 1990 into the UPC under §§ 6-301 to 6-311. Provided the person who originates or transfers a security title by registration (the registering entity) agrees, the act allows the owner of a security to

---

2. A statute creating a strong presumption that both signatories own the property in the account can also lead to abuse, as one co-owner drains the account. See *Russ ex rel. Schwartz v. Russ*, 734 N.W.2d 874 (Wis. 2007) on Page 358.

designate a beneficiary or beneficiaries who will become the owner(s) of the security on the death of the owner. The transfer is accomplished by registering a security in beneficiary form, indicating the owner's name and her intention to have a beneficiary become the owner on the owner's death. For example, if a beneficiary form provides "Jane Doe TOD John Doe," the registering entity will transfer the security directly to John Doe on the death of Jane Doe.

Securities registered in TOD form pass to the beneficiary without probate. In contrast to securities held in joint ownership with right of survivorship, TOD security registration allows probate avoidance without the need to share ownership during one's lifetime. The owner of the security can retain all control until death.[3]

§ 4.03 Property in Marriage

In addition to offering the option of holding property jointly, some states allow married couples to create survivorship interests by holding as tenants by the entireties or by holding a survivorship form of community property.

Tenancy by the entireties is quite similar to joint tenancy, except that the tenants must be married and neither can transfer his or her interest alone. In addition to preventing unilateral severance, this latter feature protects entireties property from the creditors of just one spouse. *See Sharp v. Hamilton*, 495 So. 2d 235 (Fla. Dist. Ct. App. 1986) (dissolution decree awarding all of tenancy-by-entireties property to wife cut off husband's mortgage and judgment creditors' claims).

A number of states allow spouses to hold property as community property. Usually, when one spouse dies, the decedent's share of the community property passes through probate. In what is becoming a trend, however, several community property states recognize an estate in community property with right of survivorship. We will discuss community property in more detail in Chapter 6, § 6.01A.

§ 4.04 Transfer on Death Deeds

In response to some of the disadvantages of other probate-avoidance tools, over the last several years states have adapted for real property the idea of using TOD designations that have been popular for investment accounts. [4] The device goes by different names, but has grown in popularity and prompted the creation in 2009 of the Uniform Real Property Transfer on Death Act. [5] Like its personal property counterparts, a TOD deed allows the property owner to name a beneficiary who

3. In contrast, a joint tenancy may be severed during lifetime.

4. *See* § 4.02(B).

5. As of late 2016, Alaska, District of Columbia, Hawaii, Illinois, Nebraska, Nevada, New Mexico, North Dakota, Oregon, South Dakota, Texas, Virginia, Washington, and West Virginia have adopted the Act. Other enactments are likely. More than 10 other states have enacted non-uniform

will succeed to ownership at the owner's death. Because an effective TOD deed does not create a current interest in the grantee, there is no completed gift for either ownership or tax purposes. Moreover, the deed is revocable.

The most important advantage of this device is that the owner retains control. There is no completed gift,[6] no tax consequence,[7] and the owner can change or revoke deed. These features make a TOD deed a good way to avoid probate without adding the complications of giving away a remainder interest[8] or creating a joint tenancy.[9] Moreover, the cost is minimal.

Like all easy-to-use devices, this one runs the risk that individuals will make mistakes if acting without competent legal advice. The owner might fail to meet writing and signature requirements, or might lack sufficient mental capacity. Perhaps the greatest risk—shared by all of the devices noted in this chapter—is that the deed might not fit with the rest of the owner's estate plan. Unlike some of the other alternatives to probate, a TOD deed may delay the ability to sell the property quickly, because the authorizing statute may give persons with a claim against the property time to file their claims.

Question and Note

1. If real property is transferred by a transfer on death deed, might the decedent's estate be liable for the mortgage on the real property? *See In re Estate of Carlson*, 367 P.3d 486 (Okla. 2016) (yes).

2. Some states have enacted transfer on death legislation for certain personal property. *See e.g.,* Colo. Rev. Stat. §42-6-110.5 (2016) (vehicles); Minn. Rev. Stat. §86B.841 (Transfer-on-Death Title to Watercraft) and §168A.125 (Transfer-on-Death Title to Motor Vehicle).

Selected References

Susan N. Gary, *Transfer-On-Death Deeds: The Nonprobate Revolution Continues*, 41 Real Prop. Prob. & Tr. J. 529 (2006).

Dennis M. Horn & Susan N. Gary, *Death Without Probate: TOD Deeds—The Latest Tool in the Toolbox*, Prob. & Prop., Mar./Apr. 2010 at 13.

David Major, *Revocable Transfer on Death Deeds: Cheap, Simple, and Has California's Trusts & Estates Attorneys Heading for the Hills*, 49 Santa Clara L. Rev. 285 (2009).

---

transfer on death deed legislation. *See* Cal. Prob. Code §§5620–5628 (2016); Okla. Stat. tit. 58, §1252 (2015).

6. *See* §4.01.

7. *See* Chapter 1, §1.03(B).

8. *See Henkle v. Henkle* on Page 203.

9. *See* §4.02(A).

§ 4.05 Lifetime Trusts

You will recall from Chapter 1 that trusts are among the most popular and most flexible of estate planning devices. You may want to review that discussion before reading the following material. Trusts involve at least one person (the trustee) holding property for the benefit of one or more persons (the beneficiary or beneficiaries). People who create trusts can declare that they themselves serve as trustee or they can give property to someone else to fill that role. Testators can create trusts by including trust provisions as part of a will, in which case the trust property will be subject to the probate system. Another option—the subject of this section—is to avoid probate by creating a trust before death.[10] To preserve flexibility, settlors who establish lifetime trusts usually retain the power to revoke their trusts.[11]

DILBERT © Scott Adams/Dist. by United Feature Syndicate, Inc.

In addition to providing probate-avoidance, revocable and irrevocable trusts (as well as testamentary trusts) have other uses. For example, trusts allow one person to manage property for another. If the settlor becomes disabled, for example, the trustee can provide for the settlor's care and support, thereby avoiding the need for guardianship. In a similar way, trusts for minors can avoid guardianships. Trusts also allow someone to give property successively to two or more beneficiaries. Rather than giving everything to a surviving spouse, a client might prefer to support the spouse during the survivor's life, but then transfer assets to the client's children. In Chapters 8, 9, and 10, we will comprehensively explore the subject of trusts, including other uses for trusts. *See* § 8.01[E], *infra*. For now, however, we consider below some of the problems associated with using a revocable trust as a way to avoid probate. This section first establishes that a revocable trust can be valid to transfer property even though the trust may function much like a will. Then we turn to the developing principle that a trust may be valid to transfer property while the trust form is ignored in other contexts.

---

10. It is also possible to make TOD designations effective on the death of the surviving joint owner or on the death of the surviving multiple owner of the security. *See* UPC § 6-307.

11. For tax or personal reasons, some clients may want to establish irrevocable trusts. The flexibility inherent in retaining a power to revoke, however, makes revocable trusts the dominant choice. For a sample of a revocable trust, see Page 714 of the Appendix.

A. Validity of Revocable Trusts

The key problem is that when a settlor retains the power to revoke, the trust arrangement is one in which the settlor, for practical purposes, still "owns" the property. A settlor who experiences a change of heart can simply end the trust and take the property back. Imagine Jessica, who places property in trust while retaining both the power to revoke and the right to income from the property during her life. At her death, the trust is to terminate, with Michael getting the trust property. Especially if Jessica names herself as trustee, such an arrangement looks very much like a will. Should such trusts be valid if not executed with the formalities of wills?

Farkas v. Williams

125 N.E.2d 600 (Ill. 1955)

MR. JUSTICE HERSHEY delivered the opinion of the court:

This is an appeal from a decision of the Appellate Court, First District, which affirmed a decree of the circuit court of Cook County finding that certain declarations of trust executed by Albert B. Farkas and naming Richard J. Williams as beneficiary were invalid....

Albert B. Farkas died intestate at the age of sixty-seven years, a resident of Chicago, leaving as his only heirs-at-law brothers, sisters, a nephew and a niece. Although retired at the time of his death, he had for many years practiced veterinary medicine and operated a veterinarian establishment in Chicago. During a considerable portion of that time, he employed the defendant Williams, who was not related to him.

On four occasions (December 8, 1948; February 7, 1949; February 14, 1950; and March 1, 1950) Farkas purchased stock of Investors Mutual, Inc. At the time of each purchase he executed a written application to Investors Mutual, Inc., instructing them to issue the stock in his name "as trustee for Richard J. Williams." Investors Mutual, Inc., by its agent, accepted each of these applications in writing by signature on the face of the application. Coincident with the execution of these applications, Farkas signed separate declarations of trust, all of which were identical except as to dates. The terms of said trust instruments are as follows:

> DECLARATION OF TRUST—REVOCABLE. I, the undersigned, having purchased or declared my intention to purchase certain shares of capital stock of Investors Mutual, Inc. (the Company), and having directed that the certificate for said stock be issued in my name as trustee for Richard J. Williams as beneficiary, whose address is 1704 W. North Ave. Chicago, Ill., under this Declaration of Trust do Hereby Declare that the terms and conditions upon which I shall hold said stock in trust and any additional stock resulting from reinvestments of cash dividends upon such original or additional shares are as follows:

(1) During my lifetime all cash dividends are to be paid to me individually for my own personal account and use. . . .

(2) Upon my death the title to any stock subject hereto and the right to any subsequent payments or distributions shall be vested absolutely in the beneficiary. . . .

(3) During my lifetime I reserve the right, as trustee, to vote, sell, redeem, exchange or otherwise deal in or with the stock subject hereto, but upon any sale or redemption of said stock or any part thereof, the trust hereby declared shall terminate as to the stock sold or redeemed, and I shall be entitled to retain the proceeds of sale or redemption for my own personal account and use.

(4) I reserve the right at any time to change the beneficiary or revoke this trust, but it is understood that no change of beneficiary and no revocation of this trust except by death of the beneficiary, shall be effective as to the Company for any purpose unless and until written notice thereof in such form as the Company shall prescribe is delivered to the Company at Minneapolis, Minnesota. The decease of the beneficiary before my death shall operate as a revocation of this trust.

(5) In the event this trust shall be revoked or otherwise terminated, said stock and all rights and privileges thereunder shall belong to and be exercised by me in my individual capacity. . . .

The applications and declarations of trust were delivered to Investors Mutual, Inc., and held by the company until Farkas' death. The stock certificates were issued in the name of Farkas as "trustee for Richard J. Williams" and were discovered in a safety-deposit box of Farkas after his death, along with other securities, some of which were in the name of Williams alone. . . .

If no interest passed to Williams before the death of Farkas, the intended trusts are testamentary and hence invalid for failure to comply with the statute on wills. . . .

But considering the terms of these instruments we believe Farkas did intend to presently give Williams an interest in the property referred to. For it may be said, at the very least, that upon his executing one of these instruments, he showed an intention to presently part with some of the incidents of ownership in the stock. Immediately after the execution of each of these instruments, he could not deal with the stock therein referred to the same as if he owned the property absolutely, but only in accordance with the terms of the instrument. He purported to set himself up as trustee of the stock for the benefit of Williams, and the stock was registered in his name as trustee for Williams. Thus assuming to act as trustee, he is held to have intended to take on those obligations, which are expressly set out in the instrument, as well as those fiduciary obligations implied by law. In addition, he manifested an intention to bind himself to having this property pass upon his death to Williams, unless he changed the beneficiary or revoked the trust, and then such change of beneficiary or revocation was not to be effective as to Investors Mutual, Inc., unless and until written notice thereof in such form as the company prescribed was delivered to them at Minneapolis, Minnesota. An absolute owner can dispose of his property, either in his lifetime or by will, in any way he sees fit without notifying or securing approval from anyone and without being held to the duties of a fiduciary in so doing. . . .

An additional problem is presented here, however, for it is to be noted that the trust instruments provide: "The decease of the beneficiary before my death shall operate as a revocation of this trust." The plaintiffs argue that the presence of this provision removes the only possible distinction, which might have been drawn between these instruments and a will. Being thus conditioned on his surviving, it is argued that the "interest" of Williams until the death of Farkas was a mere expectancy. Conversely, they assert, the interest of Farkas in the securities until his death was precisely the same as that of a testator who bequeaths securities by his will, since he had all the rights accruing to an absolute owner.

Admittedly, had this provision been absent the interest of Williams would have been greater, since he would then have had an inheritable interest in the lifetime of Farkas. But to say his interest would have been greater is not to say that he here did not have a beneficial interest, properly so-called, during the lifetime of Farkas. The provision purports to set up but another "contingency" which would serve to terminate the trust. The disposition is not testamentary and the intended trust is valid, even though the interest of the beneficiary is contingent upon the existence of a certain state of facts at the time of the settlor's death. (Restatement of the Law of Trusts, section 56, comment f.) . . . .

[D]id Farkas retain such control over the subject matter of the trust as to render said trust instruments attempted testamentary dispositions?

In each of these trust instruments, Farkas reserved to himself as settlor the following powers: (1) the right to receive during his lifetime all cash dividends; (2) the right at any time to change the beneficiary or revoke the trust; and (3) upon sale or redemption of any portion of the trust property, the right to retain the proceeds therefrom for his own use.

Additionally, Farkas reserved the right to act as sole trustee, and in such capacity, he was accorded the right to vote, sell, redeem, exchange or otherwise deal in the stock which formed the subject matter of the trust. . . .

It is well established that the retention by the settlor of the power to revoke, even when coupled with the reservation of a life interest in the trust property, does not render the trust inoperative for want of execution as a will. . . .

A more difficult problem is posed, however, by the fact that Farkas is also trustee, and as such, is empowered to vote, sell, redeem, exchange and otherwise deal in and with the subject matter of the trusts.

That a settlor may create a trust of personal property whereby he names himself as trustee and acts as such for the beneficiary is clear. Restatement of the Law of Trusts, section 17.

Moreover, the later cases indicate that the mere fact that the settlor in addition to making himself sole trustee also reserves a life interest and a power of revocation does not render the trust invalid as testamentary in character. (32 A.L.R.2d 1286.) . . . .

In the instant case the plaintiffs contend that Farkas, as settlor-trustee, retained complete control and dominion over the securities for his own benefit during his lifetime. . . .

It is obvious that a settlor with the power to revoke and to amend the trust at any time is, for all practical purpose, in a position to exert considerable control over the trustee regarding the administration of the trust. For anything believed to be inimicable to his best interests can be thwarted or prevented by simply revoking the trust or amending it in such a way as to conform to his wishes. Indeed, it seems that many of those powers which from time to time have been viewed as "additional powers" are already, in a sense, virtually contained within the overriding power of revocation or the power to amend the trust. . . .

In the case at bar, the power of Farkas to vote, sell, redeem, exchange or otherwise deal in the stock was reserved to him as trustee, and it was only upon sale or redemption that he was entitled to keep the proceeds for his own use. Thus, the control reserved is not as great as in those cases where said power is reserved to the owner as settlor. For as trustee he must so conduct himself in accordance with standards applicable to trustees generally. It is not a valid objection to this to say that Williams would never question Farkas' conduct, inasmuch as Farkas could then revoke the trust and destroy what interest Williams has. Such a possibility exists in any case where the settlor has the power of revocation. Still, Williams has rights the same as any beneficiary, although it may not be feasible for him to exercise them. Moreover, it is entirely possible that he might in certain situations have a right to hold Farkas' estate liable for breaches of trust committed by Farkas during his lifetime. In this regard, consider what would happen if, without having revoked the trust, Farkas as trustee had given the stock away without receiving any consideration therefor, had pledged the stock improperly for his own personal debt and allowed it to be lost by foreclosure or had exchanged the stock for another security or other worthless property in such manner as to constitute gross impropriety and gross negligence. In such instances, it would seem in accordance with the terms of these instruments that Williams would have had an enforceable claim against Farkas' estate for whatever damage had been suffered. Contrast this with the rights of a legatee or devisee under a will. The testator could waste the property or do anything with it he wished during his lifetime without incurring any liability to those designated by the will to inherit the property. . . .

Another factor often considered in determining whether an inter vivos trust is an attempted testamentary disposition is the formality of the transaction. (Restatement of the Law of Trusts, section 57, comment g.) . . . Historically, the purpose behind the enactment of the statute on wills was the prevention of fraud. The requirement as to witnesses was deemed necessary because a will is ordinarily an expression of the secret wish of the testator, signed out of the presence of all concerned. The possibility of forgery and fraud are ever present in such situations. Here, Farkas executed four separate applications for stock of Investors Mutual, Inc., in which he directed that the stock be issued in his name as trustee for Williams, and he executed four separate declarations of trust in which he declared he was holding said stock in trust for Williams. The stock certificates in question were issued in his name as trustee for Williams. He thus manifested his intention in a solemn and formal manner. . . .

Reversed and remanded, with directions.

Notes

1. Compare the first part of the Farkas opinion, in which the court searches for something Farkas intended presently to give to Williams, with Professor Langbein's discussion of the "present-interest test" in the law review excerpt that opens this chapter.

Modern doctrine dispenses with the fiction, and recognizes the trust despite the settlor's control. Original Uniform Trust Code (UTC) § 603(a) provided that "rights of the beneficiaries are subject to the control of, and the duties of the trustee are owed exclusively to, the settlor" if the settlor had the capacity to revoke the revocable trust. *Accord* Restatement (Third) of Trusts § 74. In part to harmonize the treatment of revocable trusts with the law of wills, a 2004 amendment to UTC § 603(a) made optional the requirement that the settlor have the capacity to revoke the trust. In effect, even if the settlor lacks the capacity to revoke, the revised section recognizes that enacting states may still deny trust beneficiaries rights until the settlor dies. As we saw in Chapter 3, will beneficiaries have no rights before the testator dies.

During the settlor's lifetime, remainder beneficiaries of a revocable trust are neither entitled to an accounting, *see e.g. State v. Thompson* 836 N.W.2d 470, 474 (Iowa. 2013), nor able to sue a trustee who commits a breach of a revocable trust during the settlor's lifetime. *See, e.g., In re Estate of Giraldin,* 290 P.3d 199 (Cal. 2012). In effect, and as provided by UTC 603(a), the trustee of a revocable trust owes no fiduciary duty to remainder beneficiaries since their rights are subject to the settlor's right to revoke. *See Fulp v. Gilliland*, 998 N.E.2d 204 (Ind. 2013). However, trust beneficiaries who were adversely affected by the breach of duty owed *to the settlor* may be able to sue the trustee for such breach after the settlor dies. *See In re Estate of Giraldin,* 290 P.3d 199 (Cal. 2012). *Contra In re Trust of Trimble,* 826 N.W.2d 474 (Iowa 2013).

2. Because property in a revocable trust avoids probate, the revocable trust device has overtaken the will as the primary means to have property pass at death where a state's probate process is considered onerous, For example, the use of revocable trusts predominates in such states as California, Florida, Massachusetts, and Ohio. Even where probate avoidance is not of particular concern, revocable trusts are useful, especially to keep matters private because revocable trusts (unlike wills) do not typically become public documents. In addition, revocable trusts are very useful to

provide for the settlor's possible disability, including the avoidance of guardianship in case the settlor becomes incapacitated. There is also virtual agreement that a revocable trust should be created for real property located outside the settlor's domicile to avoid the necessity for *ancillary* probate of the real property. *See Mason v. Torrellas*, 792 S.E.2d 12 (W.Va. 2016) (ancillary probate may be denied even though will admitted to probate in domiciliary state of testator if fraud can be proved in procuring original probate).

3. Of course, a settlor must have the capacity to form an intention to create a revocable trust. Courts disagree whether a person who creates a revocable trust needs a level of capacity greater than the capacity required to execute a will. *Compare Kibbee v. First Interstate Bank*, 242 P3d 973 (Wyo. 2010) (higher standard required), *with In re Tisdale*, 655 N.Y.S.2d 809 (Sur. Ct. 1997) (same standard). Restatement (Third) of Trusts § 11(2) and UTC § 601 impose the lower wills standard for revocable lifetime trusts. UTC § 604 also provides time limits to contest the validity of revocable trusts: the earlier of 120 days after receiving notice of the existence of the revocable trust or, if notice is not given, the same time period that the state allows to contest a will when notice of the will was not given.

4. The trust document should say whether, and how, the trust is revocable. In the face of silence, most courts and state statutes presume that the trust is irrevocable. Statutes in a few states establish a presumption of revocability. UTC § 602(a) adopts the minority position, but only for trusts created after the code is adopted in the state. In comparison, the Restatement (Third) of Trusts takes the position that the trust will be revocable only if the settlor retains some interest in the trust; otherwise the trust will be presumed to be irrevocable. *See* Restatement (Third) of Trusts § 63, cmt. c.

5. When a trust instrument specifies a method to modify or revoke the trust, the settlor must generally follow that method. *See, e.g., In re DelFosse*, 442 B.R. 481 (2010) (settlor required by revocable trust to deliver notice of revocation or amendment to trustee but failed to do so); *Austin v. City of Alexandria*, 574 S.E.2d 289 (Va. 2003) (because revocable trust required a deed by settlor-trustee to himself, real property in the trust was not validly withdrawn when no deed was executed). *See also McCarthy v. Taylor*, 17 N.E.3d 807 (Ill. App. Ct. 2014) (settlor's handwritten modifications to revocable trust instrument were valid and complied with the trust agreement's requirement that all amendments be "in writing," which, as a matter of law, does not require that the writing be a formal legal document).

The UTC liberalizes the traditional rules on revocation and modification. *Compare* UTC § 602(c)(2)(A) (trust revocation by will possible even if not allowed by trust), *with Will of Tamplin*, 48 P.3d 471 (Alaska 2002) (trust revocation by will not allowed if not authorized by trust).

California allows a jointly-created trust to include a provision that the surviving spouse (or any other person) can revoke the portion contributed by the deceased settlor. *See* Cal. Prob. Code §§ 15401 and 15410.

Uniform Trust Code

Section 602. Revocation or Amendment of Revocable Trust.

(c) The settlor may revoke or amend a revocable trust:

(1) by substantial compliance with a method provided in the terms of the trust; or

(2) if the terms of the trust do not provide a method or the method provided in the terms is not expressly made exclusive, by:

(A) a later will or codicil that expressly refers to the trust or specifically devises property that would otherwise have passed according to the terms of the trust; or

(B) any other method manifesting clear and convincing evidence of the settlor's intent.

Notes and Questions

1. If a trust instrument is ambiguous as to whether the settlor intended that the trust be revocable, should evidence besides the settlor's testimony be allowed to resolve the ambiguity? *See In re Durosko Marital Trust*, 862 A.2d 914 (D.C. 2004) (allowing lawyer's testimony that contradicted settlor's).

2. Should a revocable trust be revocable by physical act with intent to revoke, as in the law of wills?

3. Settlor's revocable trust provided that she needed the consent of her lawyer-draftsperson to revoke or amend the trust. Do you see any ethical issues raised by the lawyer's action? *See Dunn v. Patterson* I, 919 N.E.2d 404 (Ill. App. Ct. 2009).

4. The settlor of a revocable trust amends the trust to exclude a beneficiary and add a new beneficiary instead. While the settlor is alive, can a trust beneficiary contest the amendment based on claim that new beneficiary exerted undue influence over the settlor? *See Linthicum v. Rudi*, 148 P.3d 746 (Nev. 2006). Would your answer change if the settlor was dead? *See MacIntyre v. Wedell*, 12 So. 3d 273 (Fla. Dist. Ct. App. 2009).

5. A trust may be created by more than one person and, depending on the trust terms, revocable by one or more during the settlors' lifetimes. Absent a contrary provision, one settlor generally can revoke only the property he or she contributed. In recognition of the unique nature of community property, either spouse in a community property jurisdiction can revoke a joint revocable trust to the extent of the community property held in the trust. *See* Restatement (Third) of Trusts § 63, cmt. k; UTC § 602(b)(1). We will discuss community property in Chapter 6. Issues also may arise regarding a surviving settlor's power to amend or revoke. *See, e.g.*, *Scalfaro v. Rudloff*, 934 A.2d 1254 (Pa. 2007), *rev'g and remanding*, 884 A.2d 904 (Pa. Super. Ct.

2005) (survivor had no power to revoke because trust specifically required joint action which was impossible since other settlor was dead); *Mangels v. Cornell*, 189 P.3d 573 (Kan. Ct. App. 2008) (joint revocable trust was contractual so survivor could not amend trust).

Note: Pour-Over Wills

Closely-tied to revocable trusts, pour-over wills designate the trustee of a revocable trust as a will beneficiary.[12] Often pour-over wills include a number of dispositive provisions (cash to individuals, real estate or specifically-identified items of personal property to particular family members) and then give the rest of the testator's probate property to the trustee of a pre-existing revocable trust.

A common estate plan using the pour-over device includes two basic elements. First, the client creates a revocable trust, but intends it as a shell to be activated later, rather than as a current management device. Second, the client creates a will naming the trustee of the revocable trust as a will beneficiary. After the client's death, the will pours the decedent's residuary probate property, into the revocable trust, which then serves as a management (and, sometimes, tax-savings) device to care for the survivors.[13]

When pour-overs first appeared, courts struggled with how, and under what circumstances, to allow trust provisions to control the distribution of what had been probate property. Because the terms of a revocable trust usually would not have met the Statute of Wills' requirements, courts were reluctant to let those terms control the probate property. To the extent that courts allowed such plans, they relied either on incorporation by reference or on the doctrine of independent significance. Because each of these doctrines posed other problems, legislatures acted to allow testamentary gifts to pre-existing trusts. The Uniform Testamentary Additions to Trusts Act appeared in 1960 and later became part of the UPC. UPC § 2-511 applies not only to revocable trusts but to irrevocable and testamentary trusts as well. The few states which have not adopted a version of the Uniform Act have statutes which reach substantially the same results.

Uniform Probate Code

Section 2-511. Testamentary Additions to Trusts.

(a) A will may validly devise property to the trustee of a trust established or to be established (i) during the testator's lifetime by the testator, by the testator and some

---

12. For sample language, see Page 713 of the Appendix.

13. Life insurance proceeds and retirement benefits may also be funneled into a revocable trust by naming the trustee as beneficiary of the policy and retirement benefits.

other person, or by some other person, including a funded or unfunded life insurance trust, although the settlor has reserved any or all rights of ownership of the insurance contracts, or (ii) at the testator's death by the testator's devise to the trustee, if the trust is identified in the testator's will and its terms are set forth in a written instrument, other than a will, executed before, concurrently with, or after the execution of the testator's will or in another individual's will if that other individual has predeceased the testator, regardless of the existence, size or character of the corpus of the trust. The devise is not invalid because the trust is amendable or revocable, or because the trust was amended after the execution of the will or the testator's death.

(b) Unless the testator's will provides otherwise, property devised to a trust described in subsection (a) is not held under a testamentary trust of the testator, but it becomes a part of the trust to which it is devised, and must be administered and disposed of in accordance with the provisions of the governing instrument setting forth the terms of the trust, including any amendments thereto made before or after the testator's death.

(c) Unless the testator's will provides otherwise, a revocation or termination of the trust before the testator's death causes the devise to lapse.

Question

A will provided for the pour-over of assets into a pre-existing trust, but the trust was later revoked. Anticipating that possibility, the will also provided that if the trust were revoked, the assets should be disposed of according to the terms of the trust. What result? *See Estate of Coleman*, 129 Cal. App. 4th 380 (Ct. App. 2005) (trust terms incorporated by reference into will, so assets pass under a testamentary trust).

Selected References

Frances H. Foster, *Privacy and the Elusive Quest for Uniformity in the Law of Trusts*, 38 Ariz. St. L.J. 713 (2006).

Frances H. Foster, *Trust Privacy*, 93 Cornell L. Rev. 555 (2008).

Richard Gould, *The Living Trust: Fact v. Fiction*, 15 Quinnipiac Prob. L.J. 133 (2000).

Dennis M. Patrick, *Living Trusts: Snake Oil or Better than Sliced Bread?*, 27 Wm. Mitchell L. Rev. 1083 (2000).

Robert H. Sitkoff, *Revocable Trusts and Incapacity Planning: More than Just a Will Substitute*, 24 Elder L.J. 1 (2016).

B. Ignoring Trust Form: Creditors' Rights in Revocable Trusts

Because revocable trusts are widely accepted as a way to transfer property without probate, courts may treat such trusts as separate entities for all purposes. Courts should exercise caution before saying, "A trust is a trust is a trust."[14]

State St. Bank & Trust Co. v. Reiser

389 N.E.2d 768 (Mass. App. Ct. 1979)

[Wilfred Dunnebier was a home-builder who set up a lifetime trust to hold the capital stock of five closely-held corporations. He retained both the power to revoke and the power to direct the disposition of income and principal during his lifetime. When he died, a bank tried to collect its substantial working-capital loan, only to find that the probate estate was not large enough to cover the debt. The bank then sought trust assets.]

KASS, J.

During the lifetime of the settlor, to be sure, the bank would have had access to the assets of the trust. When a person creates for his own benefit a trust for support or a discretionary trust, his creditors can reach the maximum amount which the trustee, under the terms of the trust, could pay to him or apply for his benefit. . . .

We then face the question whether Dunnebier's death broke the vital chain. . . .

As an estate planning vehicle, the inter vivos trust has become common currency. See Second Bank-State-St. Trust Co. v. Pinion, 341 Mass. 366, 371, 170 N.E.2d 350 (1960). Frequently, as Dunnebier did in the instant case, the settlor retains all the substantial incidents of ownership because access to the trust property is necessary or desirable as a matter of sound financial planning. Psychologically, the settlor thinks of the trust property as "his," as Dunnebier did when he took the bank's officer to visit the real estate owned by the corporation whose stock he had put in trust. See Fiduciary Trust Co. v. First Natl. Bank, 344 Mass. 1, 9, 181 N.E.2d 6 (1962). In other circumstances, persons place property in trust in order to obtain expert management of their assets, while retaining the power to invade principal and to amend and revoke the trust. It is excessive obeisance to the form in which property is held to prevent creditors from reaching property placed in trust under such terms. See Restatement of Property § 328, Comment a (1940). . . .

We hold, therefore, that where a person places property in trust and reserves the right to amend and revoke, or to direct disposition of principal and income, the settlor's creditors may, following the death of the settlor, reach in satisfaction of the settlor's debts to them, to the extent not satisfied by the settlor's estate, those assets owned by the trust over which the settlor had such control at the time of his death as would have enabled the settlor to use the trust assets for his own benefit. . . .

---

14. In Chapters 5 and 6 we explore, in part, the extent to which rules applicable to wills should also apply to revocable trusts.

Note and Problems

1. In effect, with respect to creditors' claims the settlor of a revocable trust is treated as the owner of the trust property even though title is technically in the trustee. *See* 3d Rest. Trusts § 25(2). "This result . . . is based on the sound public policy of basing the rights of creditors on the substance rather than the form of the debtor's property rights." *Id.* Comment e.

2. The UTC addresses the rights of creditors with respect to revocable trusts. First, during the settlor's lifetime, trust property is subject to the claims of creditors. UTC § 505(a)(1). Second, after the settlor dies, and subject to the settlor providing a different order of liability, creditors can reach property that was held in the revocable trust but only after exhausting the deceased settlor's probate assets. UTC § 505(a)(3). Not surprisingly, revocable trusts are considered assets of a bankrupt estate under federal law. *See, e.g., In re Dennis Ekstrom*, 2010 Bankr. LEXIS 982 (debtor concedes that assets in revocable trust were part of bankruptcy estate); *In re Tougas*, 338 B.R. 164 (Bankr. D. Mass. 2006) (holding assets in revocable trusts were part of bankruptcy estate).

3. One of your clients is the State Banking Association, which would like to propose a statute establishing rules regarding creditor's rights in revocable trusts. Banks might be creditors making claims or trustees resisting them. What topics should such a statute cover?

§ 4.06 Life Insurance and Other Contracts

In terms of estate planning, life insurance may be the most important asset of middle-class Americans. Typically, an insurance company (the insurer), in return for the payment of a premium or premiums by the owner (the policy-holder), agrees to pay an identified person or entity (the beneficiary) specified death benefits upon the death of the person whose life is insured. Despite its functional similarity to wills, life insurance has escaped the "testamentary transfer" label. Traditionally, contract law, not the law of wills, governs the enforceability of life insurance policies. *See* Thomas E. Atkinson, Law of Wills § 39 (2d ed. 1953).

The most common purpose of life insurance is to provide support for dependents whose breadwinner died prematurely. Life insurance also supplies ready cash to pay estate taxes or buy out shares of a business. Other uses include saving for retirement and making charitable gifts.

There are two basic features of life insurance policies. One, present in all policies, covers the risk of death. The other, present in some policies and in a variety of forms, provides a savings option.

Term life insurance covers only the risk of death and runs for a specific period of time, often renewable. If the insured dies during the term, the beneficiaries collect a predetermined amount, the face amount of the policy. If the insured does not die during the term, the premium is gone. In this way, term life insurance is similar to auto or homeowner's insurance.

The amount of coverage during the term usually remains level. Sometimes, however, the coverage may increase or decrease. For example, if an insured bought a $150,000 decreasing term policy to cover a mortgage loan, the coverage would decline as the outstanding amount of the mortgage declined. Unless the coverage declines, annual premiums usually go up to reflect the insured's greater likelihood of dying during the new term of the policy.

Policies including a savings feature come in a variety of forms. Traditional whole life insurance differs from term life insurance in several ways. Rather than lasting for a term of years, it lasts the insured's whole lifetime, provided that premiums are paid. Also, the premiums usually remain constant. Most importantly, premiums not only pay for life insurance, but also the company invests some of the premium. The policy sets a schedule for the increase in its cash value over time. The cash value serves two main purposes. First, the insured is developing a low-risk investment, which can provide cash for college expenses, retirement, or other needs if the insurance coverage is no longer necessary. Second, the insured may borrow against the cash value of the policy at a pre-determined rate of interest.

In response to market pressures, insurance companies have developed a range of products that combine risk-of-loss coverage and investment opportunities. Current assumption whole life is similar to traditional whole life, except that the premium and cash value accumulations are not fixed. If investment performance is better than the "current assumption" when the policy was issued, the policyholder can reduce the premium from a pre-set maximum or accumulate more cash value than the preset minimum schedule. Universal life insurance is more flexible than whole life. Once the policy is in force, the insured can make premium payments at any time and in any amount, subject to built-in limits. The insured may increase the death benefit or the cash value by applying more of the premium to the insurance part or the investment part of the policy. With variable life insurance, the insurance company lets the insured choose how to allocate the cash value portion of the account among stocks, bonds, mutual funds, or other investments. Such policies offer greater owner control, with the possibility of higher investment returns at the cost of increased risk of loss.

Problems

1. Roley's life insurance policy named his wife, Sarah, as his beneficiary. They were involved in a plane crash. Roley was killed instantly and Sarah died the next day. Who should get the insurance proceeds?

2. Phillip and Roberta have two young children. Like many young families, they have a heavily-mortgaged house and minimal savings. Their principal "assets" are term life insurance policies through their respective employers. What elements would you recommend they include in their estate plan?

3. Thomas Kickingbird's will provided as follows: "I name Gina as beneficiary of my MONY life insurance policy." Thomas had earlier designated Margaret as beneficiary on the life insurance application. Who is entitled to the life insurance proceeds? *See McCarthy v. Aetna Life Ins. Co.*, 704 N.E.2d 557 (N.Y. 1998).

Notes

1. Creditors are typically barred from reaching the proceeds of life insurance. *See, e.g.*, N.Y. Ins. Law § 3212(b). If, however, insurance proceeds are payable to the owner's estate, the proceeds may be reachable by creditors of the deceased owner. *See generally* George J. Couch, Cyclopedia of Insurance § 28.12 (Rev. 2d ed. 1984). One clear lesson is to provide for contingent beneficiaries to avoid payment of life insurance proceeds to the policy owner's estate.

2. Section 529 of the Internal Revenue Code provides tax benefits for college savings plans authorized under applicable state law. An individual (the account owner) creates an account for a named beneficiary (the future student) by transferring cash to a fund manager the state designates. Most states allow the account owner to designate a new owner on the account owner's death, so the account transfers free from probate. In effect, college savings plan accounts are another type of non-probate transfer. Although the creation of a 529 plan constitutes a completed gift for gift tax purposes, creditors of the account owner can reach the account. *See In re Addison,* 540 F.3d 805, 819–20 (8th Cir. 2008).

Selected Reference

Jon J. Gallo, *The Use of Life Insurance in Estate Planning: A Guide to Planning and Drafting—Part I*, 33 Real Prop. Prob. & Tr. J. 685 (1999), and *Part II*, 34 Real Prop. Prob. & Tr. J. 55 (2000).

§ 4.07 Retirement Funds

Retirement planning—as opposed to estate planning—has become an increasingly larger part of many law practices. Individuals may establish a variety of tax-advantaged accounts to save for their retirement. These accounts supplement the retirement income that individuals receive from social security and other governmental plans. Additionally, employers often include pension benefits, usually in the form of an annuity, as a part of their employees' fringe benefit package.

A. Annuities

Annuities are of two basic types, straight and refund, although other distinctions exist within each category. All provide periodic payments over time; many also allow for a payment to the annuitant's estate or other survivor. A straight annuity pays out funds until the death of one or more of the annuitants. There is no death benefit. A refund annuity guarantees payment of a stated amount. If the annuitant dies before all the money is paid, the balance is payable to the annuitants' estate or a designated beneficiary. Annuities may be for a term of years, for the life or lives of one or more individuals, or for some other term. If the annuitant can terminate payments voluntarily, the annuity is a term annuity. If both annuitants are to receive payments until the death of the first annuitant, with payments to continue in the survivor, the contract is a joint and survivor annuity.

B. Pensions

1. Private Sector Benefit Plans

Many employers maintain retirement and death benefit plans for their employees as fringe benefits. Additionally, many employees and self-employed individuals buy their own plans. As a practical matter, the Employee Retirement Income Security Act (ERISA), 88 Stat. 829 (1974), and the Internal Revenue Code (IRC) govern most plans. The two statutes work together toward the goals of encouraging retirement investments, assuring that the funds really are available at retirement, and that employees get fair treatment. From the individual's perspective, private pension plans offer two principal tax benefits. First, employees can exclude contributions to the plan from their income; thus they invest "pre-tax" dollars. Second, employees can defer taxation until distribution at retirement age. This feature means re-invested income is also pre-tax, and that when taxation does come, the taxpayer may well be in a lower (retirement-level) tax bracket.

Employer plans fall into two broad categories. "Defined benefit" plans establish each employee's benefit according to a formula. For example, someone's retirement pay might be 60 percent of the average of their highest three years of salary. Years of service might also be part of the formula. Those with 20 years service might get 40 percent, while those with 40 years get 60 percent. The employer then funds the plan according to actuarial calculations regarding age, life expectancy, current salary, and the like. Except for the risk that the employer may become insolvent, the employee has no risk of a low return on the investments made during the employee's working years. The benefit is already defined. On the other hand, the employee does not benefit from any return which turns out to be higher than that anticipated.

The second principal category of employer-funded plans is "defined contribution" plans. These come in a variety of forms. Rather than starting at the benefit end and working backwards to determine an employer's obligation, these plans either require or allow employer contributions at various levels. Accounts are kept for each employee, and whatever has been accumulated before retirement becomes available to that person. The employee bears the risk of poor returns and benefits from high returns. Within the context of extraordinarily complex Treasury and Labor Department regulations, a wide variety of employee benefit plans have developed. Employee stock ownership plans (ESOPs) require investments in the stock of the employer corporation, while stock bonus plans merely provide for distribution of such stock in the future. Other plans bear such exotic descriptions as profit-sharing plans, money purchase pension plans, bond purchase pension plans, target benefit plans, and thrift or savings plans. A cash or deferred plan (commonly called a 401(k) plan from the authorizing section of the Internal Revenue Code) is part of a profit-sharing or stock bonus plan; an employee may elect to have the employer reduce her salary and instead contribute (within limits) to her retirement account.

ERISA controls the design of the vast majority of all pension plans. It imposes minimum standards on participation, vesting, and funding, and it requires annual reporting of plan performance to the Labor Department, and annual disclosure to plan participants. It also creates a government corporation, the Pension Benefit Guaranty Corporation, to insure plan benefits against underfunded termination. ERISA further requires that employers operate pension plans as trusts or insured plans, and imposes fiduciary responsibilities on plan trustees and other fiduciaries. The Act mandates civil and criminal sanctions for violation of those responsibilities. Finally, the Act provides that benefits under the plans are not assignable to others.

The Retirement Equity Act, 98 Stat. 1426 (1984), amended ERISA to mandate that, if a plan beneficiary dies before the benefits start, his or her spouse must get some or all of the employee's benefit. Perhaps more importantly, when an employee retires, the plan usually must pay out in the form of a joint and survivor annuity. The employee's spouse can consent to another arrangement. A divorced spouse can share in retirement rights if the divorce court so provides in a properly-structured order.

As part of the effort to provide basic, nationwide protection to employees, ERISA preempts "any and all State laws insofar as they may now or hereafter relate to any employee benefit plan" covered by the Act. 29 U.S.C. § 1144(a). The "relate to" language is very broad and, consequently, has generated both a lot of commentary and a continuing stream of litigation. ERISA may apply to a number of problems traditionally viewed as part of wills and trusts law. For example, in *Egelhoff v. Egelhoff*, 121 S. Ct. 1322 (2001), the Supreme Court held that ERISA preempted a Washington State statute that would have revoked the designation of a divorced spouse as beneficiary of an employer-provided group life insurance policy. Moreover, ERISA sets its own standard of duty for trustees administering pension plans, and that body of law promises to influence the law of private trusts. Lawyers working on private estate plans need to be aware that ERISA is lurking in the background.

The income tax Code provides the second major control on the structure of employer-provided retirement and death benefit plans. *See* I.R.C. § 401 *et seq.* In order to be deemed "qualified" under the Code, plans must meet stringent requirements. Qualified plans must be non-discriminatory in the sense that they cannot favor management or highly compensated employees. Such plans also must satisfy minimum participation, vesting, and funding standards. The Code also limits the amount of tax-advantaged contributions to qualified plans.

Many individuals set up their own retirement plans. These arrangements, known as individual retirement accounts (IRAs) and Keogh (or H.R. 10) plans, allow self-employed individuals, and certain employees, some of the tax-deferral advantages otherwise available under employer-financed qualified plans. If the employee is covered by an employer-provided retirement plan, however, the tax benefit of IRAs may be severely restricted.

2. Public Retirement Plans

Public funds contribute to retirement through the federal Social Security system and in retirement plans for federal, state, and local employees. Financed by employment taxes from approximately 95 percent of the country's work force and their employers, the Social Security system is the nation's primary public retirement, death benefit and disability insurance system. The Old Age, Survivors and Disability Insurance System (OASDI), as Social Security is properly called, provides retirement income, death and disability benefits, and a health insurance component under Medicare. Social Security benefits are paid monthly, in an amount determined by applying a benefit formula to the worker's average monthly earnings for an index period. The payment is subject to a cost of living adjustment and may be reduced by employment earnings. Spouses of participants are also entitled to benefits. Workers at the lower end of the earnings spectrum may also be protected by other assistance programs. Finally, lump sum death benefits are payable to the participant's surviving spouse or child.

The federal and state governments also maintain retirement plans for their employees, many of whom are not covered by the Social Security system. A separate retirement system applies to railroad employees under the Railway Retirement Act.

Selected References

Thomas P. Gallanis, *ERISA and the Law of Succession*, 65 Ohio St. L.J. 185 (2004).

Louis A. Mezzullo, An Estate Planner's Guide to Qualified Retirement Plan Benefits (5th ed. 2016).

Stewart E. Sterk & Melanie B. Leslie, *Accidental Inheritance: Retirement Accounts and the Hidden Law of Succession*, 89 N.Y.U. L. Rev. 165 (2014).

Concluding Note on Non-Probate Transfers

This chapter has brought together a series of doctrines related by the fact that they all involve at-death events, which are not part of the probate process. For example, recall the joint tenancy with right of survivorship and various transfer-on-death arrangements. Despite their commonalities, they tend to be governed by different sets of rules. For example, although a will can change a revocable trust disposition and a beneficiary designation in a TOD security, a will cannot change beneficiary designations in life insurance policies and in retirement plans. Nor can joint tenancy arrangements be changed by will. When acting as a planner, be sure to respect their differences.

Problems

1. Thomas Kickingbird's will made a variety of gifts, including Thomas's car to Margaret and to Gina: (1) a TOD Security that itself had named Margaret as beneficiary and (2) "my MONY life insurance policy," which also had named Margaret as beneficiary. What should Gina and Margaret take?

2. Dominic Pruselli, 76, has come to you for legal advice. His wife died about a year ago. He has three middle-aged children and several grandchildren. He owns his house, a Winnebago, a car, some mutual fund shares, some bank CDs, and some bank accounts. His net worth is about $120,000, half in the house. All assets were joint with his wife, so he avoided probate costs at her death. Dominic now wants to avoid probate when he dies. You have talked with him about creating a living trust, but he does not trust anyone else to manage his property and does not feel comfortable being a trustee himself. Advise Dominic.

Selected References

Kent D. Schenkel, *The Trust-As-Will Portmanteau: Trill or Spork?*, 27 Quinnipiac Prob. L.J. 40 (2013).

Judith T. Younger, *Falling in Love,* 58 St. Louis U. L.J. 767 (2014).

Chapter 5

Changed Circumstances

One of life's constants is change. This chapter examines how the law copes with changes that affect property distributions at death. One set of questions is whether and in what circumstances courts or legislatures should intervene to change a previously-prepared plan. As the following article suggests, the questions do not admit to easy answers.

Adam J. Hirsch, *Text and Time: A Theory of Testamentary Obsolescence*

86 Wash. U. L. Rev. 609, 611–613, 615, 618, 620, 624–25, 630–33 (2009)

... If a hiatus separates the time when a will is executed from the time when it matures, intervening occurrences—changes in the testator's life—may render it less well adapted to his or her subsequent circumstances.

This is the problem of *testamentary obsolescence*....

... When, if ever, should courts step in to update a text on its maker's behalf?

I. Intervention in the Presence of Friction

... "A will may be so easily revoked by the testator in his lifetime," one judge opined, "that the courts have been slow in permitting changes in circumstances to do by implication what the testator may so readily do for himself."

That said, we can nonetheless identify settings in which this assumption breaks down, settings in which testators pursuing a path to will revision are bound to encounter "friction" of various kinds and degrees....

One circumstance that could stymie self-revision of a will is incapacity. Lawmakers deny incapacitated testators the right to alter their wills, lest they cease to display the detailed thoughtfulness that comprises one of the social benefits of granting freedom of testation in the first place. Still, an unalterable estate plan may grow thoughtless anyway, given its unresponsiveness to the drift of events....

Once we acknowledge that inability to update a will could provide grounds for legal intervention, we have to consider the range of situations where such a handicap could arise. Executing a will requires more than just mental capacity. It also requires time—always a scarce resource and sometimes very scarce....

Consider the case where a testator and a beneficiary named under the will suffer a common calamity—for instance, an automobile accident in which one is the driver and the other a passenger—that mortally wounds both of them. Even if the beneficiary survives the testator by a short while, we can predict that the testator would prefer to substitute a different taker. Now on death's door, the beneficiary will have no occasion to enjoy the bequest, and it will pass in short order to others selected to inherit under the beneficiary's, instead of the testator's, estate plan. Yet, the testator has no chance to revise the will to take account of this change of circumstance. . . .

. . . Consider a beneficiary who slays the testator. Pointing a sharp metal object at the testator's throat and thrusting it forward is the sort of act likely to snap the sociological bonds that previously tied the testator to his or her assailant. But the testator lacks time to communicate the change of intent following from that act: in this instance, the sword is mightier than the pen. . . .

II. Intervention in the Absence of Friction

. . .

When we turn to changes of circumstance that testators remain at liberty to answer by revising their wills, the case for legal activism to update text becomes uneasy. Yet, where the change is of a nature as to make the original estate plan impossible to implement, some sort of intervention has to occur. . . .

Impossibility in the context of wills arises chiefly in two situations: (1) where property testators bequeathed no longer remains within their inventory of possessions and hence is no longer theirs to give away; and (2) where named beneficiaries (by analogy) are no longer alive and hence are unavailable to accept bequests. By striving to effectuate probable intent in these situations, lawmakers can . . . destratify the inheritance process and reduce transaction costs. . . .

We are left, finally, with changed circumstances that neither disable the testator from revising the will nor render the estate plan impossible by its terms to carry out. Whether lawmakers should update an estate plan by implication of such circumstances when the testator has not lifted a finger to amend the will is ultimately the most interesting—and most neglected—question we have before us. And, theoretically, we can imagine a range of responses.

The *formalistic* move is to give effect to the literal terms of the will. Circumstances change every day of our lives. Lawmakers may reasonably require testators to execute a codicil to reflect a change of mind, at least when nothing stands in the way of their doing so. Insistence on formal execution of revisions eases the task of verifying the substance and finality of testamentary intent. At any rate, if testators have gone to the trouble of executing an initial will, lawmakers have some cause to assume that testators will update the will if and when it suits them to do so.

The alternative *antiformalistic* move would allow courts to weigh the effects that changed circumstances have on a testator's intent and to implement that reading even in want of a codicil. The virtue of this approach is its flexibility "amidst the endless variety of human affairs," recognizing that, for whatever reason, testators may lose sight of their estate plans. Its vice, though, is the danger that courts will fail accurately to reconstruct intent due to error or fraud, coupled with the potential administrative cost when every will is subject to such reconstruction.

As a matter of law, nearly all jurisdictions reject the antiformalistic move. . . .

Still and all, no jurisdiction follows the formalistic move scrupulously either. At least after erecting fences, lawmakers have ventured out into the field of speculation, amending an estate plan in discrete situations that vary from state to state. Three triggering events predominate: where the execution of a will is followed by divorce, by marriage, or by childbirth.[1] In most jurisdictions, if a testator makes a will and subsequently marries, the new spouse receives an intestate share under the premarital will; likewise, if a testator makes a will and subsequently gets divorced, the former spouse loses his or her bequest under the predissolution will; finally, if a testator makes a will and subsequently becomes a parent, the new child receives an intestate share under the prenatal will.

These rules effect what is known, rather deceptively, as implied revocation (or alternatively, revocation by operation of law). In truth, the testator performs no action that is intended, implicitly or explicitly, to revoke the estate plan in these situations; lawmakers simply reckon that these dramatic changes of circumstance will likely precipitate a shift of testamentary intent. . . .

Implied revocation nevertheless has an underside. Even if we can establish the empirical likelihood that testators would respond to a particular change of circumstance with a particular revision of the estate plan, we cannot surmise that amending a will on its author's behalf effectuates intent with the same likelihood. The issue is not whether someone would probably want to revise a will following a consequential event, but whether someone *who has not done so* would probably want to do so. . . .

Another set of questions continues those raised in the last chapter: to what extent should the rules developed for wills apply to various alternatives to wills? Consider the following excerpt from an influential article:

John H. Langbein, *The Nonprobate Revolution and the Future of the Law of Succession*

97 Harv. L. Rev. 1108, 1134–37 (1984)

In most fields of law, rules can be divided into two sorts—mandatory and subsidiary, jus strictum and jus dispositivum—according to whether they override or yield to the contrary intentions of the parties. In the law of wills, the formal

1. In Chapter 6, we discuss the rights of "after-acquired" spouses and children. [Eds.].

requirements of the Wills Act exemplify mandatory law: the testator is not free to invent his own formalities. But most rules of the law of wills are rules of subsidiary law that apply only when a will is silent or unclear. Because of the long delay that often intervenes between the writing and implementing of a will, the process of testation invites the creation of subsidiary law. Circumstances often change across the decades in ways that testators do not address.

A simple example of such a "stale will" situation is that of the testator who gets divorced after writing a will in favor of his spouse. Good divorce lawyers take it as part of their job to see to it that clients revise their wills, but not every client is represented by counsel, much less good counsel, nor do clients inevitably act promptly in accordance with counsel's advice. Suppose, therefore, that John and Mary become divorced and that—months or years later—John dies without having revised a will naming Mary as the primary beneficiary. It can be argued that the will should be enforced as written—indeed, that a testator's will should be enforced unless and until he revokes it. We are not accustomed to inquiring into the motivations for devises; and in any case, not all divorces are bitter. John may have wished Mary to take under the will notwithstanding the divorce. If John had wanted to condition Mary's devise on the persistence of their marriage, he could have said so in the will.

This position has, however, been decisively rejected in American law. Either by statute or by case law, most of our jurisdictions have reached the result that is codified in the Uniform Probate Code: the divorce extinguishes Mary's interest. If John wants Mary to take, he must write a new will or revise the existing will by codicil after the divorce. The premise of the rule is that, because most testators do not want to benefit ex-spouses, such a will no longer reflects the intentions of the testator. Justice will more often be served if divorce is treated as a species of partial revocation and litigation on the question is foreclosed.

What of the will substitutes? Suppose that John had been equally careless in leaving the beneficiary designation in his life insurance policy unaltered. Chances are excellent that Mary would take, unless the language of any marital property settlement between them could be construed to reach the case. An Illinois court handled one of these cases in the 1970's as follows:

> Illinois followed the majority rule that a decree of divorce in no way affects the rights of the divorced wife as a beneficiary in a husband's life insurance policy.... Surely, if the insured had wished to substitute another person or his estate as beneficiary following the divorce, he would have at least attempted to effect a change with the insurer or included a provision in the property settlement agreement indicating such intention. [*O'Toole v. Central Laborers' Pension & Welfare Funds*, 299 N.E.2d 392, 394 (Ill. App. 1973).]

The Illinois case is typical in that the court felt itself under no obligation to mention, much less to reconcile, the contrary rule and rationale of the law of wills.... The doctrinal ruse that courts use to escape the probate monopoly theory thus comes back to haunt the law of will substitutes. Because the will substitutes are improperly deemed lifetime transfers, principles of construction and presumptions of transferors' intent that have been developed in the law of wills do not apply....

These cases would often solve themselves if the courts admitted the will-like character of the will substitutes. Transferors use will substitutes to avoid probate, not to avoid the subsidiary law of wills. The subsidiary rules are the product of centuries of legal experience in attempting to discern transferors' wishes and suppress litigation. These rules should be treated as presumptively correct for will substitutes as well as for wills. Once we understand that will substitutes are nothing more than "nonprobate wills" and that no harm results from admitting that truth, we have no basis for interpreting will substitutes differently from wills. Both as a matter of legislative policy and as a principle of judicial construction, we should aspire to uniformity in the subsidiary rules for probate and non-probate transfers. Even when the subsidiary law of wills has been reduced to statute, it represents a determination about what testators ordinarily intend or would have intended.

Uniform Trust Code

[SECTION 112. RULES OF CONSTRUCTION.[2] The rules of construction that apply in this State to the interpretation of and disposition of property by will also apply as appropriate to the interpretation of the terms of a trust and the disposition of the trust property.]

Comment

This section is patterned after Restatement (Third) of Trusts § 25(2) and comment e (Tentative Draft No. 1, approved 1996), although this section, unlike the Restatement, also applies to irrevocable trusts. The revocable trust is used primarily as a will substitute, with its key provision being the determination of the persons to receive the trust property upon the settlor's death. Given this functional equivalence between the revocable trust and a will, the rules for interpreting the disposition of property at death should be the same whether the individual has chosen a will or revocable trust as the individual's primary estate planning instrument....

Because of the wide variation among the States on the rules of construction applicable to wills, this Code does not attempt to prescribe the exact rules to be applied to trusts but instead adopts the philosophy of the Restatement that the rules applicable to trusts ought to be the same, whatever those rules might be....

Rules of construction attribute intention to individual donors based on assumptions of common intention.... Rules of construction also address situations the donor failed to anticipate. These include the failure to anticipate the predecease of a beneficiary or to specify the source from which expenses are to be paid. Rules of construction can also concern assumptions as to how a donor would have revised donative documents in light of certain events occurring after execution. These include rules

2. About half the states that have adopted the UTC included this section in their versions. [Eds.]

dealing with the effect of a divorce and whether a specific devisee will receive a substitute gift if the subject matter of the devise is disposed of during the testator's lifetime....

In contrast to the UTC, the UPC provides different rules of construction for wills and for trusts and other instruments. *See* UPC art. 2, pts. 6 & 7. Professor Newman argues that in a variety of circumstances (including rules of construction) different rules should apply. Alan Newman, *Revocable Trusts and the Law of Wills: An Imperfect Fit*, 43 Real Prop. Tr. & Est. L.J. 523 (2008).

Selected Reference

Shelley Kreiczer-Levy, *Deliberative Accountability Rules in Inheritance Law: Promoting Accountable Estate Planning*, 45 U. Mich. J.L. Reform 937(2012).

§ 5.01 Acts of the Property Holder

Actions property holders take before death can affect how their property will be divided after death. They can, for example, give property to people who will be their intestate heirs or will beneficiaries. The Langbein excerpt above suggests another way property holders can change what beneficiaries get: they can divorce the beneficiaries. This section addresses the doctrines that cope with those actions.

Advancements

A. Advancements

Advancements are gifts that the donor intends to be charged against the recipient's share of the donor's intestate estate. Two problems arise. First, how do we tell whether a donor intended a gift to be an advancement? Second, how does an advancement affect the shares of other heirs?

Evidence of a donor's intention is often circumstantial. To help solve the proof problem, the common law presumed a parent's gift of a substantial sum to a child to be an advancement. Some jurisdictions extended the presumption to cover gifts to other relatives as well. This approach invites people to make long lists of whatever gifts the donor made throughout a lifetime and then to fight about whether those gifts were advancements. In response, many states have reversed the presumption and recognized gifts as advancements only if the donee acknowledges them as such or if the donor indicates in a contemporaneous writing that the gift is meant as an advancement. *See* UPC § 2-109. Professor Fried comments that the UPC's approach "virtually removes the doctrine of advancements from the law of intestate succession." Martin L. Fried, *The Uniform Probate Code: Intestate Succession and Related Matters*, 55 Alb. L. Rev. 927, 937 (1992).

If the donor has made an advancement, courts conduct what is called a "hotch-potch" calculation. The court adds the value of each advancement to the total amount available for distribution from the estate. It then divides the total "hotchpot" (on paper) among the heirs according to the intestate statute. The court credits each donee with the gifts already received, and distributes the rest of the property. The advancements themselves are not returned to the estate. Rather the court adds in their value only for the purpose of calculating shares.

For example, consider Casey's estate, worth $20,000 with three children entitled to inherit. Suppose Casey had given her daughter, Lucy, an advancement of $1,000. To determine everyone's shares, add the $1,000 advancement to the $20,000 estate to create a hotchpot of $21,000. Then divide by three to get a $7,000 share of the hotchpot for each child. The estate, of course, does not have that much, so when you distribute the estate, you credit Lucy with the value of her advancement. Lucy takes only $6,000, and the other children take $7,000 each. If Lucy's advancement had been larger than her share of the hotchpot, she simply would not share in the estate, which would go to the other two children.

Notes and Questions

1. Recall various gifts you have made and received. Were they intended as advancements? Even if not, could someone else argue that they were? What evidence would you develop to overcome a presumption that they were advancements?

2. In the example in the text, Casey gave Lucy an advancement of $1,000. Suppose Lucy died before Casey and left a son, Ethan. When Casey dies, should Ethan be charged with the $1,000 advancement to his mother? *Compare Mow v. Baker*, 24 S.W.2d 1 (Tex. 1930) (yes), *with* UPC § 2-109(c) (no).

3. Disputes sometimes arise regarding valuation. The UPC values an advancement "as of the time the heir came into possession or enjoyment of the property or as of the time of the decedent's death, whichever first occurs." UPC § 2-109(b).

Problem

Ada died a widow, leaving daughters Lucille, Florence, and Naomi. During her lifetime, Ada gave Lucille advancements totaling $20,000 and Naomi advancements totaling $30,000. Ada left a net distributable estate of $100,000. How should the estate be divided under the UPC? Under the law of your state?

B. Satisfaction

What the advancements doctrine is to intestate succession, the satisfaction doctrine is to wills law.[3] Some of the details differ, but the basic idea is the same. Suppose

3. Because satisfaction is similar to ademption (the doctrine surrounding gifts of property no longer in an estate), satisfaction sometimes carries the label "ademption by satisfaction."

Hugh wrote a will giving Melanie half of his estate and later gave Melanie $5,000 intended to come out of her ultimate share. If a court recognized the $5,000 as being "in partial satisfaction" of the gift under the will, other will beneficiaries could force a hotchpot calculation to credit Melanie with the money she already received.

As with advancements, disputes arise about the intention behind lifetime gifts, and courts have relied upon presumptions. Traditionally, courts have presumed that gifts of money from parents to children after a will's execution are in satisfaction of any legacies under the will. Courts have disagreed about whether testamentary gifts of real estate or specific personal property could ever be satisfied by a lifetime gift of different property. The modern view would allow lifetime gifts to replace testamentary gifts of different character, where that is the intention. *See* Thomas E. Atkinson, Law of Wills 737–41 (2d ed. 1953).

Because will beneficiaries need not be heirs, satisfaction potentially covers a wider range of lifetime gifts than does the advancements doctrine. Consider the following case.

Yivo Institute for Jewish Research v. Zaleski

874 A.2d 411 (Md. 2005)

Greene, J.

In this case we are asked to revise the Maryland law of ademption by satisfaction and require that a testator's intention to adeem a legacy can be proven only by a writing made contemporaneous with an inter vivos gift. Petitioner, in its attempt to persuade us to change the law, relies in part on the assertion that the doctrine of ademption is in conflict with Md. Code (2001), § 3-106 of the Estates & Trusts Article, the Restatement (Third) of the Law of Property (Wills and Other Donative Transfers) § 5.4 (1999), and the Uniform Probate Code § 2-609 (amended 1990).... For reasons to follow in this opinion, we decline the invitation to rewrite the law of ademption and affirm the judgment of the intermediate appellate court.

On September 25, 2002, the Orphans' Court for Montgomery County denied petitioner's, the YIVO Institute for Jewish Research ("YIVO"), request to receive distribution of a bequest in the Will of Jan Karski ("Dr. Karski"). The Orphans' Court concluded that Dr. Karski's inter vivos gifts to YIVO were intended by Dr. Karski as a fulfillment of the legacy under his will. The petition was opposed by respondents, the personal representative of Dr. Karski's estate and two residuary legatees under Dr. Karski's Will—the American Center of Polish Culture and the Kosciusko Foundation. YIVO appealed to the Court of Special Appeals seeking reversal of the decision of the Orphans' Court.

YIVO argued in the Court of Special Appeals, as they do here, that the specific bequest to YIVO in the will was not adeemed by the lifetime gifts. YIVO also contends that the Orphans' Court erred in admitting the testimony of Dr. Hanna Kaya Ploss ("Dr. Ploss") as to oral statements made by Dr. Karski after satisfaction of

Dr. Karski's pledge to YIVO. The intermediate appellate court affirmed the decision of the Orphans' Court....

Background

Dr. Karski was a hero of the Polish underground during World War II. He reported to Allied powers on the events transpiring in Poland until he was captured by the Nazis. During his confinement he was tortured and suffered greatly. After attempting suicide to avoid disclosures that could have endangered the underground movement, Dr. Karski was taken to a Nazi-controlled hospital in critical condition. He was rescued from the hospital by members of the underground movement. Several lives were lost during the rescue effort and one rescuer, Zofia Hanuszkiewicz ("Zofia"), spent several years in a German prison camp for her involvement.

Jan Karski standing before a wall map of the Warsaw Ghetto at the United States Holocaust Memorial Museum in 1994. Photo by E. Thomas Wood.

After the war, Dr. Karski emigrated to the United States and settled in Chevy Chase, Maryland. Dr. Karski remained committed to Polish culture until his death, developing ties with several Polish organizations, including The Kosciusko Foundation ("Foundation") and The American Center of Polish Culture ("Center"). He spent much of his life attempting to mend the relationship between Jewish and non-Jewish Poles which had been fractured by events occurring in Poland during WW II. Following the death of his wife, Pola Nirenska, Dr. Karski developed a plan to memorialize both of them by creating an award to acknowledge Jewish authors of Polish origin. In 1992, Dr. Karski entered into an agreement with YIVO to establish an endowment fund to provide an annual award of $5,000 to authors whose works focused on or otherwise described contributions to Polish culture and Polish science by Poles of Jewish origin. Dr. Karski formalized his pledge in a letter dated November 25, 1992 ("Letter Agreement"). The Letter Agreement provided, in pertinent part:

> The endowment will consist of a gift of $100,000.00 in cash to be made by me to YIVO in my will, or in cash and/or marketable securities of the same total market value during my lifetime.

A second letter, identical to the November 25, 1992, letter, was signed February 25, 1993. It is unclear from the record, however, why the second letter was executed.

On October 25, 1993, eight months after writing the second Letter Agreement, Dr. Karski executed his will. Article SECOND of the will provides:

> I hereby give and bequeath to YIVO—Institute for Jewish Research (tax exempt organization Dr. Lucjan Dobroszycki and Dr. Ludwik Seidenman)—all my shares of Northern States Power (N.St.Pw.) of which 400 share certificates are located in Riggs National Bank, Friendship Branch (4249 block of Wisconsin Avenue), Safe Deposit Box 240, and the rest approximately 1,780 shares, is held by Northern States Power as automatic reinvestment. All these shares (approximately 2,180) should be transferred (not sold) to YIVO.

At the time the will was executed, Northern States Power Company shares had a value of about $100,000. At the time of Dr. Karski's death the shares were worth $113,527.64.

In addition, pursuant to the Third Clause of the will, stock in two other utilities, New York State Gas & Electric and Ohio Edison, was left to the Washington Performing Arts Society ("WPAS"). Most of the remaining estate was bequeathed in equal shares to the Foundation, the Center, three of Dr. Karski's elderly relatives in Poland, and Zofia, the woman who had helped rescue him from the hands of the Nazis.

During the period November 28, 1995, to January 22, 1996, Dr. Karski made a series of lifetime gifts of utility stocks to YIVO consisting of 1,809 shares of New York State Electric & Gas Corporation, 2,300 shares of Ohio Edison Company, and cash. Because the New York State Gas & Electric and Ohio Edison shares that were given to YIVO during Dr. Karski's lifetime were the same stock as bequeathed to WPAS in the will, the bequest to WPAS was treated by the Personal Representative as adeemed by extinguishment.[4] The value of these stock gifts totaled $99,997.69. On February 7, 1996, Dr. Karski made a further gift of $2.31, bringing the total value of the gifts to YIVO to exactly $100,000. Dr. Karski did not amend his will to reflect the inter vivos transfer of utility stock and cash to YIVO.

Dr. Karski died on July 12, 2000. At that time, the shares of Northern States Power Company remained an asset of his estate. Paul Zaleski, who qualified as personal representative, denied YIVO's request for payment of the bequest on the basis that Dr. Karski's earlier gift satisfied the legacy. As a result, YIVO filed a Petition for Order Directing Distribution of Specific Bequest.

The Orphans' Court conducted an evidentiary hearing and rendered an oral opinion finding that Dr. Karski intended for his lifetime gifts to YIVO to satisfy the legacy under the will. Following the entry of final judgment, YIVO appealed to the Court of Special Appeals which affirmed the judgment of the Orphans' Court. We granted YIVO's petition for a writ of certiorari.

. . .

Discussion

. . . "[W]hen a testator in his lifetime pays to a legatee the amount of money given by the will, and such payment is intended to be in satisfaction of the legacy, the legacy is thereby adeemed." *Rhein v. Wheltle*, 206 Md. 1, 6, 109 A.2d 923, 925 (1954). . . . Therefore, if a testator intended that an inter vivos gift should abrogate the legacy, the legacy is adeemed either in whole or in part; but if a testator intended that the

4. Ademption by extinguishment generally applies to specific legacies and occurs because the unique property that is the subject of a specific bequest has been sold, given away, or destroyed, or is not otherwise in existence at the time of the testator's death. Black's Law Dictionary 42 (8th ed., 2004). In this case, the shares bequeathed to WPAS were given away and, thus, not in existence at the time of Dr. Karski's death.

legatee should receive both the testamentary gift and the inter vivos benefit, the legacy is not adeemed. *Id.*

It is a general rule that "where a testator is the parent of the legatee or in loco parentis, and after executing his will makes a gift to the same child, it will be presumed that the gift was intended to be in satisfaction of the legacy." *Rhein*, 206 Md. at 6, 109 A.2d at 926. The legacy will be considered adeemed unless the presumption is rebutted. Id. This principle was founded upon the equitable presumption that a parent, who has the natural obligation to provide for his children, after executing a will establishing the portion of his estate that each child should receive, would not give one of his children a double portion of his estate to the detriment of the others. Id.... On the other hand, it is accepted as a general rule that where a testator is not the parent of the legatee or does not stand in loco parentis, it will be presumed that the subsequent gift did not adeem the legacy by satisfaction....

Petitioner argues that a subsequent writing is necessary to show a clear intention of satisfaction. YIVO relies upon revisions to Maryland's law in 1968 concerning advancements and intestate estates which resulted from the Governor's Commission to Review the Testamentary Law of Maryland ("The Henderson Commission"). The Henderson Commission recommended, and the Maryland Code now reflects, that for an inter vivos gift to be treated as an advancement, there must be written evidence of such an intent. Petitioner posits that there is no reason to "maintain standards for ademption of a legacy by satisfaction that differ from those applicable to advancement of an intestate share."

In our view, principles governing advancement and intestate shares do not help resolve the issues in this case. In the present case, the decedent did not die intestate, he died with a will. The laws of intestate succession concern disposition of property by operation of law under circumstances where the decedent failed to declare his or her intention with regard to the disposition of his or her property at the time of death. The law of ademption by satisfaction, however, is concerned with the intention of the testator at the time the inter vivos gift was made.... Second, petitioner's reliance upon the Henderson Commission Report is of no avail because that Commission did not recommend any changes to the common law of ademption by satisfaction. In fact, there is no mention of any discussion in the Report with regard to the general law of ademption....

In addition, petitioner contends we should adopt the view of 1 Restatement (Third) of the Law of Property (Wills and Other Donative Transfers) § 5.4 (1999) (hereinafter, "Restatement") and the Uniform Probate Code § 2-609 (amended 1990), 8 U.L.A. 179 (1998) (hereinafter, "UPC"). Section 5.4 of the Restatement: Ademption by Satisfaction provides:

> An inter vivos gift made by a testator to a devisee or to a member of the devisee's family adeems the devise by satisfaction, in whole or in part, if the testator indicated in a contemporaneous writing, or if the devisee acknowledged in writing, that the gift was so to operate.

Under the Revised UPC, § 2-609 Ademption by Satisfaction, the required evidence of intent can take one of three forms: (I) a statement in the will itself providing for deduction of the gift or any future gifts, (ii) a written statement of the testator in a contemporaneous writing indicating that the gift is in full or partial satisfaction of the devise, or (iii) a written statement of the devisee acknowledging that the gift is in full, partial satisfaction of the devise.[5] Maryland, however, has neither expressly adopted the Restatement § 5.4 nor the UPC. Both provisions require a writing to prove that an inter vivos gift operates as an ademption by satisfaction. We are not persuaded, however, to adopt either view. We are guided by the long-standing rule that the intention of the testator at the time of the inter vivos gift is the heart of ademption by satisfaction. . . .

The doctrine of ademption by satisfaction is an intent-effecting doctrine. The doctrine operates to prevent the legatee from receiving a double gift against the testator's wishes.[6] The question is one wholly of intention, and the burden is upon those who assert that the inter vivos gift was intended to satisfy the legacy. . . . [T]here are, however, certain circumstances where the intent to adeem will be presumed. For example, "in the case of a legacy to one towards whom the testator does not stand in loco parentis, the rule is that if the bequests are for a particular purpose, a subsequent gift to the legatee by the testator in his lifetime for the same purpose operates as a satisfaction of the legacy to the amount of the gift." *Loyola College*, 137 Md. at 550, 113 A. at 83. The rule, however, is subject to the qualification that the inter vivos gift must not be substantially different in kind from the legacy. Id. Additionally, it is well established that "if a testator has given a legacy in order to accomplish a certain purpose, and he subsequently accomplishes that purpose himself, the legacy is presumed to be adeemed." *Rhein*, 206 Md. at 7, 109 A.2d at 926.

In reaching its conclusion that Dr. Karski's lifetime gifts of $100,000 to YIVO were given to adeem the legacy of approximately $100,000, the Orphans' Court first needed to determine the purpose of the legacy in the will. The Court deemed it reasonable

5. Eleven states have enacted the Revised UPC § 2-609 or some variation of it: Alaska, Arizona, Colorado, Hawaii, Michigan, Minnesota, Montana, New Mexico, North Dakota, South Dakota, and Utah. Twelve states enacted the original UPC ademption by satisfaction section (Original UPC § 2-612) or a close variation of it: Alabama, California, Florida, Idaho, Maine, Missouri, Nebraska, New Jersey, Oregon, South Carolina, Virginia, and Wisconsin. A few other states have enacted nonuniform legislation on ademption by satisfaction, but the majority of states have not developed specific statues addressing ademption by satisfaction. Maryland is one such state.

6. Comment (a) of the Restatement suggests that "ideally, the testator would effect that intent by making the gift and revoking the devise. . . ." "The doctrine of ademption by satisfaction operates when the testator neglected to revoke or partly revoke the devise." Unlike the Restatement and the UPC, we think the better policy is to not limit proof of the testator's intent only to written documentation. In our view, it is conceivable that a testator could effectuate his or her intent to adeem by satisfaction by making an inter vivos gift and neglect to either revoke the devise or to declare his or her intent to revoke in writing. Thus, the testator's intent to adeem could be drawn, not only from what he or she wrote but also from what he or she said or did.

in assessing the purpose of the legacy to look to the facts surrounding it, the commitment Dr. Karski made to YIVO, and the Letter Agreement. In this context, the Court found, as a matter of fact, that the purpose of the legacy was to fulfill or otherwise provide security for the commitment that Dr. Karski made to YIVO. . . .

Once it was determined that the purpose of the legacy was security, the Orphans' Court could properly find, based upon the evidence in the record, that the lifetime gifts had a purpose identical to that of the legacy. Dr. Karski gave the lifetime gifts to secure his promise in the Letter Agreement to provide a bequest of $100,000 to YIVO. This finding of a same purpose operates as a satisfaction of the legacy, unless the lifetime gift was substantially different in kind. . . .

Dr. Karski bequeathed shares of Northern States Power to YIVO. At the time Dr. Karski drafted his will these shares were worth approximately $100,000. Dr. Karski's lifetime gift to YIVO consisted of shares of New York State Gas & Electric, shares of Ohio Edison, and cash in the amount of $2.31, thus bringing the total value of the gifts to $100,000. While the stock given to YIVO during Dr. Karski's life were shares from a different company than that named in the will, we agree with the Orphans' Court and the intermediate appellate court that there was no evidence that the stock in the legacy had any particular significance. Dr. Karski's own Letter Agreement referred to "cash and/or marketable securities," evidencing that Dr. Karski treated the shares as equivalent to cash. The Orphans' Court correctly found that Dr. Karski intended that the different company shares and the cash were identical to one another. Thus, the shares were not substantially different in kind. . . .

Having established that the inter vivos gifts to YIVO were the same in purpose and in kind as the bequest to YIVO in Dr. Karski's Will, the Orphans' Court found a presumption of ademption. . . .

Parol Evidence

We next turn to petitioner's last claim of error with respect to the Orphans' Court's ruling on the admission of the testimony of Dr. Hanna-Kaya Ploss, Executive Director of the American Center of Polish Culture and a friend of Dr. Karski's, regarding statements made by Dr. Karski in 1998 and the years preceding his death. Specifically, Dr. Ploss testified that,

> I don't know what was in that will, but Dr. Karski was not a compulsive man who would pound on something over and over, but from time to time he said, "You know, maybe I should change my will just in case the YIVO Institute will come and ask once more for the money when I already have given it to them," and then he always answered his own question, "No. They are much too decent to do such [a] thing. No." . . .
>
> He was absolutely sure they will not come a second time and ask for the money when I have already given it to them, that is something that sticks in my mind, "I have already given them the money."

We find that the court did not err in allowing the testimony. . . .

JUDGMENT OF THE COURT OF SPECIAL APPEALS AFFIRMED. PETITIONER TO PAY COSTS.

Notes and Questions

1. Should Dr. Karski have updated his will? How else might he have avoided what appears to be YIVO's attempt at double-dipping?

2. The UPC's stricter approach to advancements and gifts in satisfaction should limit the number of disputes about a donor's intention. Compare the Code's willingness to dispense with formalities in § 2-503 (harmless error).

3. The UPC allows a lifetime gift to one person to satisfy a testamentary gift made to another. For example, a wealthy person might want to give money to a grandchild in satisfaction of a will provision in favor of the grandchild's parent. *See* UPC § 2-609.

4. Suppose James makes two lifetime gifts. First, he gives Blanche $15,000 and attaches a note saying "This gift is in satisfaction of all provisions for you in my Living Trust Agreement dated March 15, 1995." Then he gives Peter $5,000 and a note saying "This gift is in satisfaction of my having named you as beneficiary of my Prudential Life Insurance Policy # 87493." When James dies leaving both the trust and the life insurance policy unchanged, should the doctrine of satisfaction apply? If so, how?

C. Divorce

Donors can also change gifts by divorcing the donee. Suppose Rae's will leaves everything to her husband, Ollie. Later, they divorce and then Rae dies without changing her will. Virtually all states have statutes which would prevent Ollie from taking under Rae's will. The statutes, however, differ widely in their details.

When approaching a problem like this one, it is helpful to have a series of questions in mind.

(1) What acts trigger the statute? Divorce alone? Divorce plus a property settlement? Separation? Divorce and later remarriage?

(2) What documents does the statute cover? Only the will? A trust? Life insurance? A joint tenancy deed?

(3) Who loses out? Only the former spouse? The former spouse's relatives?

(4) What happens to the property? Is it distributed as if the former spouse had predeceased the decedent?

The following material explores these questions.

Friedman v. Hannan

987 A.2d 60 (Md. Ct. App. 2010)

Opinion by ADKINS, J.

In this case we interpret Section 4-105(4) of Md. Code Estates & Trusts Article ("ET"), which directs that provisions in a will "relating to the spouse" be revoked upon divorce from that person. We hold that the automatic revocation provision of ET Section 4-105(4) is not limited to bequests to a former spouse, and may include bequests to a former spouse's family members. A court should utilize the terms of the will and circumstances surrounding its execution to determine whether a bequest "relat[es] to the spouse" within the meaning of Section 4-105(4). . . .

. . . [James Hannan married Anna Zelinski. He executed the will in question here before they separated and finally divorced.] As part of the separation, both parties entered into a property settlement agreement. Zelinski testified that Decedent met all of his obligations under that agreement. Decedent subsequently died on September 10, 2006. He had never remarried.

This action involves a will that Decedent executed during his marriage to Zelinski ("the Will"), the relevant provisions of which state:

> . . .
>
> ITEM THREE: I give and bequeath to my Wife, ANNA MARIE COVERT HANNAN, provided she survives me, all of my possessions . . . .
>
> ITEM FOUR: Should my Wife, ANNA MARIE COVERT HANNAN, and myself die together by accident or otherwise, the estate is to be handled by LYDIA ELIZABETH COVERT FRIEDMAN and KEVIN HANNAN. All real and personal property, except jewelry belonging to my Wife and myself, be liquidated and proceeds there of [sic] be divided equally between my surviving immediate family members and those surving [sic] immediate family members of my Wife: JEROME B. HANNAN, KEVIN HANNAN, MICHAEL HANNAN, KATHLEEN HANNAN and DANIEL HANNAN, LYDIA ELIZABETH COVERT FRIEDMAN, PATRICIA JO COVERT TOLLEY, BARBARA JANE COVERT, GENIA LOUISE COVERT, and KELLEY ANN FRIEDMAN (said KELLEY is to share her part with her sister KIMBERLY BETH FRIEDMAN). . . .

. . . [T]he Orphans' Court for Baltimore City concluded that "[t]he remaining clause [in Item Four] pertaining to distribution provides that certain family members, including [Friedman], are entitled to distribution only if the Decedent died in a common disaster with his wife[.]"[7] Accordingly, the Orphans' Court ordered that the Will not be admitted to probate, effectively leaving Decedent intestate. [His

7. This case provides another example of why you should avoid a "common disaster" clause. The parties and the court all assumed this was a homemade will, but we suspect it drew language from a form originally drafted by a lawyer. [Eds.]

brother, Jerome Hannan, served as personal representative of the estate. In the discussion below, "Hannan" refers to Jerome.]

... [On appeal to the circuit court,] Zelinski testified that her named family members were her sisters and two of her nieces. She admitted that Decedent did not know her named family members prior to their marriage, and that those family members did not live with them during the marriage. Decedent's divorce attorney, Susan Huesman-Mitchell, testified that Decedent was a merchant marine, an avocation that required him to live away from his wife on a boat for several weeks at a time.

The Circuit Court agreed with the parties' interpretation of Item Four as a residuary clause, and therefore found that Decedent died testate. The court then considered the Will as a whole and determined that its provisions relating to the immediate family of Decedent's wife could not be fulfilled because of the divorce....

Friedman contends that in Item Four Decedent crafted individual bequests with the intent that those gifts survive any divorce between Decedent and Zelinski. Hannan responds that the bequest to Friedman was contingent upon Decedent being married to Zelinski at the time of his death. Hannan views the bequest as one intended to be a gift to a class, which fails because of the divorce. They also differ on the meaning of ET Section 4-105, with Friedman arguing for a narrow interpretation, and Hannon urging the opposite.

The starting point of our analysis will be ET Section 4-105, which sets forth the methods or circumstances under which a will may be revoked. Subsection (4) thereof includes divorce as a cause of dissolution to this extent:

Divorce or annulment.—By an absolute divorce of a testator and his spouse or the annulment of the marriage, either of which occurs subsequent to the execution of the testator's will; *and all provisions in the will relating to the spouse, and only those provisions*, shall be revoked unless otherwise provided in the will or decree.

(Emphasis added). Both parties agree that the statute applies, and that the case turns on the meaning of "relating to the spouse[.]" Although neither party contends that this provision is ambiguous, they divide on its meaning. Hannan argues that the phrase "provisions in the will relating to the spouse" mandates revocation when, in the mind of the testator, the connection between the legatees and the ex-spouse is "substantial and logical" and that there is "no other basis for a connection[.]" Friedman, on the other hand, advances a narrow interpretation, which would apply only to bequests to or for the direct benefit of the spouse....

... [W]e start by considering the plain meaning of "relate," which is "[t]o stand in some relation; to have bearing or concern; to pertain; refer; to bring into association with or connection with; with 'to.'" BLACK'S LAW DICTIONARY 1288 (6th ed. 1990) .... Thus, the ordinary meaning of "relate" is the existence of a connection between two subjects, not that the two subjects need be the same....

. . . [W]e read "relating to" as a broad term, and hold that the trier of fact, when applying the statutory language of section 4-105(4) to decide whether a particular bequest is one "relating to the spouse," is not limited to bequests to or for the benefit of the spouse. In other words, the trier of fact may determine that bequests to other persons nonetheless "relate to" the spouse. . . . If the General Assembly had intended Section 4-105(4) to apply more narrowly, it had no reason to use the term "relating to." It could have simply said that upon divorce, "all provisions in the will for the former spouse are revoked." Its choice not to do this, but instead to use the broader "relating to" language, must be respected and enforced by this Court.

We are not persuaded by Friedman's argument that "[t]he deliberate inclusion of 'and only those provisions' is clear evidence that the legislature intended to limit the scope of [ET Section 4-105(4)] to revoke only those provisions relating to the former spouse." This language simply clarifies that the balance of the will remains intact. It adds nothing that would further define or limit the meaning of the phrase "relating to the spouse."

With such a broadly worded statute, the task of determining, on a case by case basis, whether a particular bequest in a will was "related to" the decedent's former spouse, falls to the courts. . . .

The Circuit Court's decision and Friedman's criticism of it can best be understood if we set forth the key portions in the language of the Court:

> Looking at the will itself, taking the decedent's wife out of the will, it is clear that the testator intended to create two classes of persons to share equally in the proceeds of the estate.
>
> The first class of individuals was the decedent's immediate family members, comprising of five persons. The second class, or group, consisted of six persons, namely his wife's immediate family members. . . .
>
> At the time of his death, the decedent was unmarried. He did not have a wife. Since he did not have a wife, there were no immediate family members of a wife at the time of his death.
>
> Absent any evidence to the contrary, this was a condition that the decedent—that decedent did not contemplate at the time that he signed the will.
>
> The condition, namely passing of proceeds to his wife and/or her immediate family members, cannot be fulfilled.
>
> I find that the case of *Herman v. Ortego*, 39 California App. 4th, 1529 to be particularly instructive in this case. In that case, which is extremely similar to the case at hand, the court indicated the decisive inquiry is whether or not the testator in making the particular gift in question did so with group mindiness.
>
> Whether, in other words, he was looking at the body of persons in question as a whole or a unit, rather than individual members of the group as individuals, if the former they take as a class.

> According to the holding in that case, the court found that we think it more logical construction to hold that when a testator provides for his spouses' children, he normally intends to exclude children of an ex-spouse after dissolution unless a contrary intention is indicated elsewhere in the will. We clearly do not have a contrary indication indicated elsewhere in the will.
>
> And I also find that—that consistent with the out of state opinion, this testator clearly made a gift in terms of group mindiness. And I find that as evidence of six individuals on the immediate—six immediate family members on the wife's side have to share in half the estate, but only five members of the decedent's immediate family have to share in this—the estate.

Friedman argues that the Circuit Court made an error of law in classifying the Item Four bequest as conditioned on Decedent remaining married to Zelinski at his death....

[The Circuit Court had discussed whether the will created a "class gift" to his wife's relatives, as opposed to individual gifts to each of them. This court concluded that it was proper to use class gift analysis to determine how the Maryland statute applied to this will.]

... We conclude that in creating the automatic revocation of will provisions "relating to" a former spouse, the General Assembly recognized two pertinent features of divorce. First, divorce usually results in a separation of assets that were jointly owned, thus reducing each spouse's assets available to bequeath to his or her own family. Second, divorce is often acrimonious, with the acrimony spilling over to the former spouse's family. Also, it is common in writing wills during a marriage that two spouses divide their assets between their respective family members because they have agreed that is fair. Even without acrimony, this viewpoint is likely to change upon divorce. In enacting Section 4-105(4), the Legislature created a remedy to avoid unintended consequences for people who neglect to change their wills upon divorce.

For these reasons it is permissible for an Orphans' Court or circuit court to find that a will provision is "relating to" the former spouse within the meaning of Section 4-105(4) if it considers that the provision was primarily motivated by the marriage or given at the request of the spouse. As we mentioned above, a testator may provide for the children of a spouse simply because each spouse agrees to benefit the other's family, without any independent desire to devise property to those children.[8] On the other hand, a court could find that a bequest did not "relate to" the spouse when the evidence shows that the testator formed a close personal relationship with the legatee and likely desired to provide for him or her regardless of whether the marriage continued.

8. This principle might apply as well when a court is considering a bequest to non-relatives, such as a "spouse's caretaker" or "spouse's church."

Decedent's naming of the individuals included in the bequest to his wife's relatives, in addition to referring to them by a group name, does not foreclose a finding that Decedent viewed them as a group of persons who would only inherit if he remained married. . . . Although Decedent individually named each family member who would take pursuant to Item Four, he *first* identified those people according to their respective groups before listing their names. Additionally, Decedent placed the conjunction "and" before the last person comprising *each* group, thus suggesting an intent to create two lists, rather than one. Finally, instead of specifically referring to Zelinski when classifying the Friedman group, Decedent described them as the "immediate family members of *my Wife* [.]" (emphasis added).

Petitioner advances an argument based on a comparison of the Uniform Probate Code ("UPC") and ET Section 4-105(4) and purported legislative history. UPC Section 2-508, in effect in 1969, called for revocation of will provisions "to the spouse." At the same time, the precursor to Maryland's ET Section 4-105 contained largely the same language as the statute does today, in that it called for revocation of provisions "relating to the spouse." *See* Md. Code (1957), Article 93, § 351. In 1990, the UPC was amended to add a provision that the automatic revocation upon divorce also applied to any bequests "to a relative of the divorced individual's former spouse[.]" UPC § 2-804(b)(1) (1990) Petitioner posits that the UPC did in its revision exactly what [Hannan] asks this Court to do—expand the concept of revocation beyond the former spouse to also include the former spouse's relatives. But Maryland has not adopted this portion of the UPC nor in any way indicated that it wished to expand this statute in such a manner. . . .

. . .

CONCLUSION

In sum, we hold that ET Section 4-105(4) is not limited in its effect to provisions for the direct benefit of the spouse. The decision as to whether a particular provision is one "relating to" a former spouse is a factual one to be made by the trial court. In doing so, a court should decide whether the testator in creating the provision was primarily motivated by the marriage or whether the testator had independent reasons for the bequest. In making that decision, the court may infer that bequests made to a former spouse's family were made primarily because of the marriage unless there is evidence of some independent reason in the will itself or the circumstances existing at the time of execution. For the reasons set forth above, we conclude that the Circuit Court did not err in finding that Decedent was "group-minded" in the Item Four residuary bequest, and that the bequest to Friedman failed as a result of the divorce.

JUDGMENT OF THE COURT OF SPECIAL APPEALS AFFIRMED. COSTS TO BE PAID BY PETITIONERS.

Uniform Probate Code

Section 2-804. Revocation of Probate and Nonprobate Transfers by Divorce; No Revocation by other Changes of Circumstances.

(a) [Definitions.] In this section:

(1) "Disposition or appointment of property" includes a transfer of an item of property or any other benefit to a beneficiary designated in a governing instrument.

(2) "Divorce or annulment" means any divorce or annulment, or any dissolution or declaration of invalidity of a marriage that would exclude the spouse as a surviving spouse within the meaning of Section 2-802. A decree of separation that does not terminate the status of husband and wife is not a divorce for purposes of this section.

(3) "Divorced individual" includes an individual whose marriage has been annulled.

(4) "Governing instrument" means a governing instrument executed by the divorced individual before the divorce or annulment of his [or her] marriage to his [or her] former spouse.

(5) "Relative of the divorced individual's former spouse" means an individual who is related to the divorced individual's former spouse by blood, adoption, or affinity and who, after the divorce or annulment, is not related to the divorced individual by blood, adoption, or affinity.

(6) "Revocable," with respect to a disposition, appointment, provision, or nomination, means one under which the divorced individual, at the time of the divorce or annulment, was alone empowered, by law or under the governing instrument, to cancel the designation in favor of his [or her] former spouse or former spouse's relative, whether or not the divorced individual was then empowered to designate himself [or herself] in place of his [or her] former spouse or in place of his [or her] former spouse's relative and whether or not the divorced individual then had the capacity to exercise the power.

(b) [Revocation Upon Divorce.] Except as provided by the express terms of a governing instrument, a court order, or a contract relating to the division of the marital estate made between the divorced individuals before or after the marriage, divorce, or annulment, the divorce or annulment of a marriage:

(1) revokes any revocable (i) disposition or appointment of property made by a divorced individual to his [or her] former spouse in a governing instrument and any disposition or appointment created by law or in a governing instrument to a relative of the divorced individual's former spouse, (ii) provision in a governing instrument covering a general or nongeneral power of appointment on the divorced individual's former spouse or on a relative of the divorced individual's former spouse, and (iii) nomination in

a governing instrument, nominating a divorced individual's former spouse or a relative of the divorced individual's former spouse to serve in any fiduciary or representative capacity, including a personal representative, executor, trustee, conservator, agent, or guardian; and

(2) severs the interests of the former spouses in property held by them at the time of the divorce or annulment as joint tenants with the right of survivorship [or as community property with the right of survivorship], transforming the interests of the former spouses into tenancies in common.

(c) [Effect of Severance.] A severance under subsection (b)(2) does not affect any third-party interest in property acquired for value and in good faith reliance on an apparent title by survivorship in the survivor of the former spouses unless a writing declaring the severance has been noted, registered, filed, or recorded in records appropriate to the kind and location of the property which are relied upon, in the ordinary course of transactions involving such property, as evidence of ownership.

(d) [Effect of Revocation.] Provisions of a governing instrument are given effect as if the former spouse and relatives of the former spouse disclaimed all provisions revoked by this section or, in the case of a revoked nomination in a fiduciary or representative capacity, as if the former spouse and relatives of the former spouse died immediately before the divorce or annulment.

(e) [Revival if Divorce Nullified.] Provisions revoked solely by this section are revived by the divorced individual's remarriage to the former spouse or by a nullification of the divorce or annulment.

(f) [No Revocation for Other Change of Circumstances.] No change of circumstances other than as described in this section and in Section 2-803 effects a revocation.

(g) [Protection of Payors and Other Third Parties.]

(1) A payor or other third party is not liable for having made a payment or transferred an item of property or any other benefit to a beneficiary designated in a governing instrument affected by a divorce, annulment, or remarriage, or for having taken any other action in good faith reliance on the validity of the governing instrument, before the payor or other third party received written notice of the divorce, annulment, or remarriage. . . .

(h) [Protection of Bona Fide Purchasers; Personal Liability of Recipient.]

(1) A person who purchases property from a former spouse, relative of a former spouse, or any other person for value and without notice, or who receives from a former spouse, relative of a former spouse, or any other person a payment or other item of property in partial or full satisfaction of a legally enforceable obligation, is neither obligated under this section to return the payment, item of property, or benefit nor is liable under this section for the amount of the payment or the value of the item of property or benefit. . . .

Notes and Questions

1. Compare the Maryland statute's "relating to the former spouse" language with the more specific provisions in the UPC, covering a variety of issues. Note also that the UPC's result can only be overcome by the "express terms" of the relevant document. Is it better to create specific standards that require special effort to overcome, or to give courts some "wiggle room" to interpret particular documents as Maryland does, *see Nichols v. Suiter,* 78 A.3d 344 (Md. 2013)? Should courts (or legislators) be more reluctant to "correct" language that has been left unchanged for some period of time after the new circumstance (like a divorce) took place? How long?

2. By extending its reach to non-probate assets, § 2-804 is part of the UPC's effort to integrate the law. *See also* 3d Rest. Prop. (Wills and Other Donative Transfers) § 4.1, cmt. p (apply to will substitutes the presumption that a marriage dissolution revokes any provision in favor of the former spouse). Should integration apply in this context? In particular, does the statute sufficiently recognize the former spouse's contributions to acquiring the assets in question?

3. The revocation-by-divorce doctrine typically does not apply to beneficiaries who divorce someone other than the donor. *See, e.g., Matter of Breder*, 432 N.Y.S.2d 441 (Sur. Ct. 1980) (a gift to the testator's nephew and the nephew's wife went to both, even though they divorced before testator's death). *But see Grady v. Grady*, 395 So. 2d 643 (Fla. Dist. Ct. App. 1981) (a gift of trust income to the testator's daughter and her husband for their support went solely to the daughter after the parties dissolved their marriage).

4. In *Egelhoff v. Egelhoff*, 532 U.S. 141 (2001), the Supreme Court held that ERISA preempted a Washington State statute that would have revoked the designation of a divorced spouse as beneficiary of an employer-provided group life insurance policy.

In *Hillman v. Maretta*, 133 S. Ct. 1943 (2013), the Supreme Court forbade a Virginia court from ordering a former spouse, whose rights would have ended under Virginia law, to restore life insurance benefits subject to ERISA.

Problem

Jeffery's only will included a gift of all his estate "To my wife, Elaine, if she survives me by 30 days, and if she does not, to her daughter, Gloria." Later, Jeffery and Elaine divorced, and Jeffery died without revising his will. Elaine and Gloria both survived Jeffery. Jeffery's closest surviving relative is a cousin, a descendant of one of his great-grandparents. Who should take Jeffery's estate under:

(a) the UPC?

(b) a statute that reads "If a testator has divorced, the will must be read as if the testator's former spouse had failed to survive the testator"?

(c) a statute that reads "If a testator has divorced, all provisions in the will in favor of the testator's former spouse must be read as if the former spouse failed to survive the testator"?

Selected References

Susan N. Gary, *Applying Revocation-on-Divorce Statutes to Will Substitutes*, 18 Quinnipiac Prob. L.J. 83 (2004).

John H. Langbein, *Destructive Federal Preemption of State Wealth Transfer Law in Beneficiary Designation Cases:* Hillman *Doubles Down on* Egelhoff, 67 Vand. L. Rev. 1665 (2014).

Lawrence W. Waggoner, *The Creeping Federalization of Wealth-Transfer Law*, 64 Vand. L. Rev. 1635 (2014).

§ 5.02 Acts of Beneficiaries

Another way shares can change is by acts of the beneficiaries themselves. Courts often deny beneficiaries their shares because of the beneficiary's misconduct. In addition, a beneficiary may turn down an inheritance or attempt to give away one not yet received.

A. Disclaimers[9]

Beneficiaries use disclaimers to change the distribution of an estate or trust by refusing to accept its benefits. They are the principal tool for "post-mortem"—after death—estate planning. Probably the most common reason for disclaiming property is to save taxes, although the device often can be used to avoid creditors or simply allow others, more needy, to take the property. Before executing disclaimers, potential recipients should be fully aware of the consequences.

In re Estate of Holden

539 S.E.2d 703 (S.C. 2000)

Justice Burnett:

This is a probate matter involving the validity of two disclaimers of interest in an estate and the validity of two documents revoking the disclaimers. The decision of the Court of Appeals is affirmed as modified.

FACTS

William Holden, Sr. (Father) died intestate on January 3, 1992. He was survived by his wife Julia S. Holden (Mother), two sons Petitioner William Holden, Jr., and

9. In the past, statutes and case opinions tended to use the term "renunciation," especially when referring to heirs. "Disclaimer" is probably now more common. Both the Internal Revenue Code and the UPC now use "disclaimer." IRC § 2518; UPC Article II, Part 11.

Robert Holden (Sons), and one grandchild. A second grandchild was born within ten months of Father's death.

After Father's death, Sons filed disclaimers of their interests in Father's estate. In relevant part, the disclaimers state: "I hereby disclaim and renounce any interest in the estate and relinquish any claim I may have to it." Their attorney's letter accompanying the filing describes the disclaimers as "Disclaimers of the decedent's children in favor of the decedent's spouse." The personal representative subsequently distributed the proceeds of the estate to Mother.

After reviewing the estate's closing documents, the probate court informed the personal representative that, as a result of Sons' disclaimers, Respondents Zachary David Holden and Julia Lynn Holden (Grandchildren), as Father's lineal descendants, may inherit a portion of the estate.[10] To avoid this unintended result, each Son executed a document entitled "Revocation and Withdrawal of Disclaimer" which provides, in part: ". . . it was my intent in entering into this said Disclaimer and Renunciation of Interest to disclaim and renounce my intestate interest in favor of [Mother] . . . the spouse of [Father], so that she would become the sole heir of the Estate. . . ."

The probate court appointed a guardian ad litem for Grandchildren and conducted a hearing to determine the validity of the disclaimers and revocations. The probate court held Sons' disclaimers were valid for federal tax law purposes and the revocations were ineffective. The court ordered 50% of the estate's assets distributed to Grandchildren.

The circuit court held the attorney's filing letter accompanying the disclaimers expressly provided Sons intended to direct their interest in the estate to their Mother. Concluding this intention was contrary to applicable provisions of the Internal Revenue Code, the circuit court held the disclaimers ineffective. In a two to one decision, the Court of Appeals held the disclaimers were valid and reversed the circuit court. . . .

DISCUSSION

. . .

[S.C. Code Ann.] Section 12-16-1910 addresses the effect of a disclaimer of property interests for purposes of estate taxes. It provides "if a person as defined in Section 62-2-801 makes a disclaimer as provided in Internal Revenue Code Section 2518 with respect to any interest in property, this chapter applies as if the interest had never been transferred to the person." § 12-16-1910 (Supp. 1999).

---

10. S.C. Code Ann. § 62-2-801(d) (1987) provides ". . . the disclaimed interest shall be transferred (or fail to be transferred, as the case may be) as if the disclaimant had predeceased the date of the effectiveness of the transfer of the interest; the disclaimer shall relate back to the date of effectiveness for all purposes. . . ." Where the transferor died intestate, the date of effectiveness of the transfer of the disclaimed interest is the date of the transferor's death. § 62-2-801(e)(1). Under the intestacy statutes, one-half of the decedent's estate passes to the surviving spouse and one-half passes to the decedent's issue. § 62-2-102(2). "Issue" is defined as all lineal descendants. § 62-1-201(21).

In relevant part, Internal Revenue Code § 2518 defines a "qualified disclaimer" for purposes of federal estate and gift tax laws as follows:

> (a) General rule.—For purposes of this subtitle, if a person makes a qualified disclaimer with respect to any interest in property, this subtitle shall apply with respect to such interest as if the interest had never been transferred to such person.
>
> (b) Qualified disclaimer defined.—For purposes of subsection (a), the term "qualified disclaimer" means an irrevocable and unqualified refusal by a person to accept an interest in property but only if—
>
> (1) such refusal is in writing,
>
> [(2) such writing is received by the transferor of the interest, his legal representative, or the holder of the legal title to the property to which the interest relates not later than the date which is 9 months after the later of—
>
> (A) the day on which the transfer creating the interest in such person is made, or
>
> (B) the day on which such person attains age 21]
>
> (3) [the disclaimant] has not accepted the interest or any of its benefits, and
>
> (4) as a result of such refusal, the interest passes without any direction on the part of the person making the disclaimer and passes either—
>
> (A) to the spouse of the decedent, or
>
> (B) to a person other than the person making the disclaimer.

26 U.S.C.A. § 2518 (1989).

A United States Treasury Department regulation interprets Internal Revenue Code § 2518(b)(4) as follows:

Passage without direction by the disclaimant of beneficial enjoyment of disclaimed interest—

> (1) In general. A disclaimer is not a qualified disclaimer unless the disclaimed interest passes without any direction on the part of the disclaimant to a person other than the disclaimant. . . . If there is an express or implied agreement that the disclaimed interest in property is to be given or bequeathed to a person specified by the disclaimant, the disclaimant shall be treated as directing the transfer of the property interest.

26 C.F.R. § 25.2518-2(e)(1) (1998).[11]

11. But see Treas. Reg. 25.2518-2(e)(4) (the "without direction" requirement is not violated by precatory language in the disclaimer naming the takers of disclaimed property if the language has no effect under local law).

"The requirement that the disclaimed property pass 'without any direction' from the person making the disclaimer means that the disclaimer must result in a valid passing of the disclaimed interest . . . by operation of state law." The "without any direction" requirement is satisfied "only if the interest passes to the ultimate recipient by virtue of the instrument of transfer or by operation of law; it prevents the disclaimant from designating a beneficiary." 5 Boris I. Bittker and Lawrence Lokken, Federal Taxation of Income, Estates & Gifts § 121.7.6 (2d ed. 1993). . . .

In addition, a qualified disclaimer must also meet any state law requirements. *Delaune v. U.S.*, 143 F.3d 995, 1001 (5th Cir. 1998) ("The clear terms of § 2518(b)(4) necessarily require the disclaimer itself be valid under state law, because only in such a situation can it be said that the interest passes 'as a result of the refusal' and 'without any direction on the part of the person making the disclaimer.' "); Estate of Bennett, 100 T.C. 42, 67 (1993) ("There must be a valid passing of an interest under State law requirements before a valid passing of an interest can be considered to have occurred for Federal estate tax law purposes."). . . .

I.

Sons argue the Court of Appeals erred by holding their disclaimers met the requirements of qualified disclaimers under I.R.C. § 2518(b)(4). Specifically, Sons argue their intention to direct their interests is apparent from 1) their attorney's filing letter accompanying the disclaimers, 2) the fact that two of the three heirs disclaimed their interest, indicating an intent to direct the disclaimed interest in favor of the third heir, and 3) their revocations once they realized the disclaimers might not transfer their interests to Mother. They assert each of these factors suggest an implied agreement to disclaim their interests in favor of Mother, that parol evidence of these factors was properly admitted without objection before the probate court, and that their disclaimers are ineffective. We disagree.

A.

"The parol evidence rule prevents the introduction of extrinsic evidence of agreements or understandings contemporaneous with or prior to execution of a written instrument when the extrinsic evidence is to be used to contradict, vary or explain the written instrument." *Gilliland v. Elmwood Properties*, 301 S.C. 295, 302, 391 S.E.2d 577, 581 (1990). . . .

The express language of Sons' written disclaimers is unambiguous. The disclaimers do not direct the transfer of Sons' interests in Father's estate. It is undisputed that, based on the written disclaimers alone, Sons' interests pass by operation of state law (the descent and distribution statutes) to Grandchildren as lineal descendants of Father. . . .

Neither Sons' attorney's letter filed with the disclaimers nor the fact that two of the three intestate heirs filed a disclaimer (suggesting a desire to direct their interests to the third heir) were admissible to explain or contradict the written disclaimers.

Both factors are extrinsic evidence created contemporaneously with or prior to the written disclaimers. . . . Even though Grandchildren failed to object to this parol evidence, the evidence is nonetheless incompetent. It would have been improper for the probate court to consider the evidence to contradict or explain the disclaimers. . . .

Finally, Sons' revocations thirteen months after the filing of their disclaimers are not parol evidence. Nonetheless, the revocations were not proper evidence of Sons' intent in filing the disclaimers. The revocations were filed to correct Sons' mistake of law. Since equity will not correct a mistake of law, see Discussion III, it would have been improper to consider the revocations as evidence of Sons' intent in filing the disclaimers in the first instance. Since Sons offered no competent evidence that they directed their interests in favor of Mother, the disclaimers met the requirements of I.R.C. § 2518(b)(4), and their interests passed to Grandchildren by operation of state law.

. . .

III.

Sons argue the Court of Appeals should have applied equity principles to set aside their disclaimers. We disagree.

. . .

"Equitable relief is available where the parties acted under a mistake of fact going to the essence of the particular transaction, but not if the mistake was one of law." 27A Am. Jur. 2d Equity § 7 (1996); *Smothers v. U.S. Fidelity and Guar. Co.*, 322 S.C. 207, 470 S.E.2d 858 (Ct. App. 1996) (a court of equity will not, in the absence of fraud or undue influence, grant relief from the consequence of a mistake of law). "Relief will not be granted where the complaining party took measures to secure knowledge as to the state of the law and, being misinformed, placed himself in the prejudicial situation of which he later complains. Everyone is presumed to have knowledge of the law and must exercise reasonable care to protect his interests." Id. S.C. at 210-211, S.E.2d at 860.

. . .

Sons' execution of the disclaimers was not the result of a mistake of fact. Sons were fully aware of all facts (they were aware of the existence of at least one of the Grandchildren at the time they filed the disclaimers), but they did not realize the legal consequences of their disclaimers. Sons' error was a mistake of law and is not subject to equitable relief. *Webb v. Webb*, 171 W. Va. 614, 301 S.E.2d 570 (W. Va. 1983) (son's error in executing disclaimer of interest by intestate succession in an attempt to vest title to his share of the estate in decedent's widow was mistake of law and could not be set aside on grounds of mistake).

The decision of the Court of Appeals is AFFIRMED.

Notes

1. As *Holden* illustrates, two sets of rules govern disclaimer questions. State statutes and decisions control how a disclaimer affects ownership. The Internal Revenue Code controls federal tax consequences. Some states (like South Carolina) effectively incorporate some of the federal rules into state law. Others create their own distinct disclaimer systems. In either case, a lawyer might be liable for malpractice for failing to advise about the tax savings available by a disclaimer. *See Sims v. Hall*, 592 S.E.2d 315 (S.C. Ct. App. 2003).

Did Holden's lawyer commit malpractice for failing to advise correctly that the decedent's grandchildren, instead of his wife, would take the disclaimed property? What would be the damages?

2. Theodore Kolb's father had established a trust giving a life estate to Theodore's mother and a contingent remainder (contingent on survival) to Theodore. When applying for some loans, Theodore listed his trust interest among his assets. Facing an impending bankruptcy, Theodore attempted to disclaim his trust interest while his mother was still alive. Held: Theodore's listing of the interest on his loan application constituted acceptance of the interest, precluding his later disclaimer. *In re Kolb*, 326 F.3d 1030 (9th Cir. 2003).

3. Survivors may want to disclaim their gifts to keep the property out of the hands of creditors or to keep government benefits. Courts often recognize disclaimers for these purposes, but the law is not uniform. *See, e.g., Citizens State Bank v. Kaiser*, 750 P.2d 422 (Kan. Ct. App. 1988) (disclaimer of interest in joint tenancy accounts does not relate back to the date of co-tenant's death, and thus does not defeat judgment creditor's interest acquired through garnishment); *Stein v. Brown*, 480 N.E.2d 1121 (Ohio 1985) (where a will beneficiary seeks to disclaim an inheritance with the actual intent to defraud a present or future creditor, the disclaimer is a fraudulent conveyance and has no legal effect); *Compare Nielsen v. Cass County Social Serv. Bd.*, 395 N.W.2d 157 (N.D. 1986) (disclaimer effective to maintain Medicaid benefits) *with Schell v. Pa. Dep't of Pub. Welfare*, 80 A.3d 844 (Pa. Comm. 2013) and *Molloy v. Bane*, 631 N.Y.S.2d 910 (N.Y. App. Div. 1995) (disclaimer not effective for Medicaid purposes).

4. For an example of a creative, if unsuccessful, use of a disclaimer, see *Estate of Parsons*, Page 127. There, a witness/beneficiary disclaimed her gift in an effort to become disinterested.

5. Somewhat related to disclaimers are settlement agreements under which various beneficiaries agree to share the decedent's assets differently from what the intestate statute, will, or trust provides. Courts generally favor these agreements as useful for avoiding will contests or preserving family harmony. *See* Paul G. Haskell, Preface to Wills, Trusts and Administration 220–23 (2d ed. 1994).

The Uniform Disclaimer of Property Interests Act, now incorporated into the UPC, covers a wide range of interests and situations.

Uniform Probate Code

Section 2-1105. Power to Disclaim; General Requirements; When Irrevocable.

(a) A person may disclaim, in whole or part, any interest in or power over property, including a power of appointment. A person may disclaim the interest or power even if its creator imposed a spendthrift provision or similar restriction on transfer or a restriction or limitation on the right to disclaim.

(b) Except to the extent a fiduciary's right to disclaim is expressly restricted or limited by another statute of this State or by the instrument creating the fiduciary relationship, a fiduciary may disclaim, in whole or part, any interest in or power over property, including a power of appointment, whether acting in a personal or representative capacity. A fiduciary may disclaim the interest or power even if its creator imposed a spendthrift provision or similar restriction on transfer or a restriction or limitation on the right to disclaim, or an instrument other than the instrument that created the fiduciary relationship imposed a restriction or limitation on the right to disclaim.

(c) To be effective, a disclaimer must be in a writing or other record, declare the disclaimer, describe the interest or power disclaimed, be signed by the person making the disclaimer, and be delivered or filed in the manner provided in Section 2-1112. In this subsection:

(1) "record" means information that is inscribed on a tangible medium or that is stored in an electronic or other medium and is retrievable in perceivable form;

(2) "signed" means, with present intent to authenticate or adopt a record, to;

(A) execute or adopt a tangible symbol; or

(B) attach to or logically associate with the record an electronic sound, symbol, or process.

(d) A partial disclaimer may be expressed as a fraction, percentage, monetary amount, term of years, limitation of a power, or any other interest or estate in the property.

(e) A disclaimer becomes irrevocable when it is delivered or filed pursuant to Section 2-1112 or when it becomes effective as provided in Sections 2-1106 through 2-1111, whichever occurs later.

(f) A disclaimer made under this Part is not a transfer, assignment, or release.

Section 2-1106. Disclaimer of Interest in Property.

(a) In this section:

(1) "Future interest" means an interest that takes effect in possession or enjoyment, if at all, later than the time of its creation.

(2) "Time of distribution" means the time when a disclaimed interest would have taken effect in possession or enjoyment.

(b) Except for a disclaimer governed by Section 2-1107 [Jointly Held Property] or 2-1108 [Disclaimer by Trustee], the following rules apply to a disclaimer of an interest in property:

(1) The disclaimer takes effect as of the time the instrument creating the interest becomes irrevocable, or, if the interest arose under the law of intestate succession, as of the time of the intestate's death.

(2) The disclaimed interest passes according to any provision in the instrument creating the interest providing for the disposition of the interest, should it be disclaimed, or of disclaimed interests in general.

(3) If the instrument does not contain a provision described in paragraph (2), the following rules apply:

(A) If the disclaimant is not an individual, the disclaimed interest passes as if the disclaimant did not exist.

(B) If the disclaimant is an individual, except as otherwise provided in subparagraphs (C) and (D), the disclaimed interest passes as if the disclaimant had died immediately before the time of distribution.

(C) If by law or under the instrument, the descendants of the disclaimant would share in the disclaimed interest by any method of representation had the disclaimant died before the time of distribution, the disclaimed interest passes only to the descendants of the disclaimant who survive the time of distribution.

(D) If the disclaimed interest would pass to the disclaimant's estate had the disclaimant died before the time of distribution, the disclaimed interest instead passes by representation to the descendants of the disclaimant who survive the time of distribution. If no descendant of the disclaimant survives the time of distribution, the disclaimed interest passes to those persons, including the state but excluding the disclaimant, and in such shares as would succeed to the transferor's intestate estate under the intestate succession law of the transferor's domicile had the transferor died at the time of distribution. However, if the transferor's surviving spouse is living but is remarried at the time of distribution, the transferor is deemed to have died unmarried at the time of distribution.

(4) Upon the disclaimer of a preceding interest, a future interest held by a person than the disclaimant takes effect as if the disclaimant had died or ceased to exist immediately before the time of distribution, but a future interest held by the disclaimant is not accelerated in possession or enjoyment.

Don has died intestate, leaving his son Art, Art's three children, and Bill, the child of Don's predeceased daughter, Betty. If Art disclaims, how will Don's estate be divided under the intestate law of your state if the disclaimer statute says to treat the disclaimant as having predeceased the decedent? Under the UPC?

Selected References

Adam J. Hirsch, *Disclaimer Law and UDPIA's Unintended Consequences*, Est. Plan., Apr. 2009, at 34.

William P. LaPiana, *Some Property Law Issues in the Law of Disclaimers*, 38 Real Prop. Prob. & Tr. J. 207 (2003).

B. Assignments of Expectancies

An expectancy is a hoped-for inheritance. Sometimes people want to transfer their expectancies to others. Perhaps they want to make a gift; perhaps they want to cash in early. From the recipient's perspective, the risk is that the expectancy will never amount to anything. The potential donor could always make (or revise) a will or the expectant heir could die too soon. The tenuous nature of expectancies has led courts to restrict severely the situations in which any transfer would be effective. According to orthodox doctrine, outright transfers of expectancies are invalid. *See* Rest. Prop. § 313, cmt. a. Despite this rule, some people still try them. *See Harper v. Harper*, 243 S.E.2d 74 (Ga. 1978) (a deed transferring grantor's interest from his future inheritance void). One way which courts have softened the doctrine is to enforce in equity contracts to transfer expectancies, if the agreement is supported by fair consideration. *See Rector v. Tatham*, 196 P.3d 364 (Kan. 2008) (agreement among siblings that after mother's death, one sibling would receive the remaining balance from sale of mother's house).

A parallel doctrine recognizes transfers of a child's expectancy back to the parent, again if supported by fair consideration. These transfers are called "releases" and are treated like advancements. *See* Thomas E. Atkinson, Law of Wills 725 (2d ed. 1953). The parent's payment for the release is really just an early transfer of an expected share.

In Chapter 8, we discuss the ability of a trust beneficiary to transfer his or her trust interest.

Selected Reference

Katheleen R. Guzman, *Releasing the Expectancy*, 34 Ariz. St. L.J. 775 (2002).

C. Misconduct

A beneficiary's misconduct can change the beneficiary's expected share. Suppose, for example, Arnie kills his father, Peter. Can Arnie then inherit from Peter? In response to the unfairness of allowing Arnie to benefit from his wrong, let alone the risk of encouraging such conduct, courts and legislatures would often deny Arnie his share. Depending on the facts, however, that response may not seem fair. What if the killing was the result of reckless driving? Or mental illness? Or a response to abuse? Or helping with a suicide? Sometimes statutes answer those questions, sometimes not.

In the absence of applicable legislation, courts, based on the principle established in *Riggs v. Palmer*, 115 N.Y. 506 (1889) that a murderer should not profit from his or her wrongdoing, may impose a constructive trust against the property Arnie would otherwise get from Peter. *See, e.g., In re Estate of Safran*, 306 N.W.2d 27 (Wis. 1981). You will recall that a constructive trust is a remedy courts use to prevent unjust enrichment.[12]

A large number of states have statutes denying wrongdoers property in certain circumstances. Unfortunately, legislatures often have merely responded to notorious cases and therefore have missed the opportunity to work out a comprehensive solution. As a consequence, the statutes vary widely in their details. The list of acts of misconduct can extend beyond killings, and the restrictions can apply to non-probate property.[13]

In the face of this confusion, it can be helpful to have a series of questions you can ask about whatever statute you face:

- What bad actions disqualify the wrongdoer?
- What property interests are affected?
- What is the effect of applying the statute?
- Is a bona-fide purchaser who takes property from a wrongdoer protected?

Consider how well the UPC answers these questions.

---

12. See Chapter 3, §§ 3.02B5, 3.05A, 3.09.

13. *See, e.g.*, Cal. Prob. Code § 259(a) (takers under will, trust, or intestacy, found to have engaged in physical abuse, neglect, or fiduciary abuse of elder or dependent adult); Va. Code Ann. § 64.1-16.3 (persons who willfully desert or abandon a child or spouse and such situation continues until the death of the child or spouse are barred from intestate succession, elective share, exempt property, family allowance, and homestead allowance); N.Y. Estates, Powers and Trusts Law §§ 4-1.4 (intestate takers who refuse to provide for, or who abandon, a child under 21 years of age) and 4-1.6 (joint bank account property of convicted murderer).

Uniform Probate Code

Section 2-803. Effect of Homicide on Intestate Succession, Wills, Trusts, Joint Assets, Life Insurance, and Beneficiary Designations.

(a) [Definitions.] In this section:

(1) "Disposition or appointment of property" includes a transfer of an item of property or any other benefit to a beneficiary designated in a governing instrument.

(2) "Governing instrument" means a governing instrument executed by the decedent.

(3) "Revocable," with respect to a disposition, appointment, provision, or nomination, means one under which the decedent, at the time of or immediately before death, was alone empowered, by law or under the governing instrument, to cancel the designation in favor of the killer, whether or not the decedent was then empowered to designate himself [or herself] in place of his [or her] killer and whether or not the decedent then had capacity to exercise the power.

(b) [Forfeiture of Statutory Benefits.] An individual who feloniously and intentionally kills the decedent forfeits all benefits under this Article with respect to the decedent's estate, including an intestate share, an elective, an omitted spouse's or child's share, a homestead allowance, exempt property, and a family allowance. If the decedent died intestate, the decedent's intestate estate passes as if the killer disclaimed his [or her] intestate share.

(c) [Revocation of Benefits Under Governing Instruments.] The felonious and intentional killing of the decedent:

(1) revokes any revocable (i) disposition or appointment of property made by the decedent to the killer in a governing instrument, (ii) provision in a governing instrument conferring a general or nongeneral power of appointment on the killer, and (iii) nomination of the killer in a governing instrument, nominating or appointing the killer to serve in any fiduciary or representative capacity, including a personal representative, executor, trustee, or agent; and

(2) severs the interests of the decedent and killer in property held by them at the time of the killing as joint tenants with the right of survivorship [or as community property with the right of survivorship], transforming the interests of the decedent and killer into tenancies in common.

(d) [Effect of Severance.] A severance under subsection (c)(2) does not affect any third-party interest in property acquired for value and in good faith reliance on an apparent title by survivorship in the killer unless a writing declaring the severance has been noted, registered, filed, or recorded in records appropriate to the kind and location of the property which are relied upon, in the ordinary course of transactions involving such property, as evidence of ownership.

(e) [Effect of Revocation.] Provisions of a governing instrument are given effect as if the killer disclaimed all provisions revoked by this section or, in the case of a revoked nomination in a fiduciary or representative capacity, as if the killer predeceased the decedent.

(f) [Wrongful Acquisition of Property.] A wrongful acquisition of property or interest by a killer not covered by this section must be treated in accordance with the principle that a killer cannot profit from his [or her] wrong.

(g) [Felonious and Intentional Killing; How Determined.] After all right to appeal has been exhausted, a judgment of conviction establishing criminal accountability for the felonious and intentional killing of the decedent conclusively establishes the convicted individual as the decedent's killer for purposes of this section. In the absence of a conviction, the court, upon the petition of an interested person, must determine whether, under the preponderance of evidence standard, the individual would be found criminally accountable for the felonious and intentional killing of the decedent. If the court determines that, under that standard, the individual would be found criminally accountable for the felonious and intentional killing of the decedent, the determination conclusively establishes that individual as the decedent's killer for purposes of this section.

(h) [Protection of Payors and Other Third Parties.]

(1) A payor or other third party is not liable for having made a payment or transferred an item of property or any other benefit to a beneficiary designated in a governing instrument affected by an intentional and felonious killing....

(i) [Protection of Bona Fide Purchasers; Personal Liability of Recipient.]

(1) A person who purchases property for value and without notice, or who receives a payment or other item of property in partial or full satisfaction of a legally enforceable obligation, is neither obligated under this section to return the payment, item of property, or benefit nor is liable under this section for the amount of the payment or the value of the item of property or benefit....

In the Matter of the Swansons' Estates

187 P.3d 631 (Mont. 2008)

Justice W. William Leaphart delivered the Opinion of the Court.

Gene Swanson, the personal representative of the estates of Louisa Ann Swanson and Swen Paul Swanson, moved the District Court to forfeit Jeanette Swanson's interest in the estates. The District Court granted the motion. Jeanette Swanson appeals. We reverse and remand....

Jeanette Swanson ("Jeanette") shot and killed two of her children, Louisa Ann and Swen Paul. Immediately afterwards, Jeanette called 911 to report that she shot the children. Jeanette was charged with two counts of deliberate homicide [and pled guilty to both] . . . .

[Prior to sentencing, Jeanette underwent a series of psychological examinations. All of the doctors agreed that she had been suffering from a severe mental disorder.] . . . Jeanette suffered from the delusion that someone in the Augusta area wanted to harm her children. In the days before the shootings, her hallucinations and delusions intensified. Jeanette believed she had to shoot the children in order to protect them from this impending and imminent harm. She believed that by shooting them, she was sending them to heaven where they would be safe. Since the time of the shooting, Jeanette has consistently maintained that she killed the children to protect them. . . .

The District Court . . . for each count of deliberate homicide, committed Jeanette to the custody of the director of the department of public health and human services for placement and treatment at the state hospital for the term of her natural life.

Gene Swanson ("Gene"), the children's father, served as the personal representative for Louisa Ann's and Swen Paul's estates. Gene petitioned the District Court to forfeit Jeanette's interest in the children's estates [under Montana's "slayer statute"] . . . . The District Court granted the petition and found that as a matter of law Jeanette had forfeited her rights of inheritance to the children's estates. Jeanette appeals this order. . . .

DISCUSSION

Did the District Court err in concluding, as a matter of law, that Jeanette forfeited her right to inherit from the children's estates under § 72-2-813, MCA?

Gene invokes § 72-2-813, MCA, Montana's "slayer statute," to prevent Jeanette from inheriting or otherwise benefiting from her deceased children's estates. Section 72-2-813(2), MCA, provides in relevant part:

> An individual who feloniously and intentionally kills the decedent forfeits all benefits under this chapter with respect to the decedent's estate, including an intestate share, an elective share, and omitted spouse's or child's share, a homestead allowance, exempt property, and a family allowance. If the decedent died intestate, the decedent's intestate estate passes as if the killer disclaimed the killer's intestate share.

. . . This statute codifies the long-standing common law principle that a killer should not profit from his own wrongdoing. . . . [T]he plain language of the statute excludes slayers who lack the requisite intent and homicides that are not "felonious."

On appeal, Jeanette argues that the District Court erred as a matter of law by giving conclusive effect to her guilty plea in the previous criminal case and by extending the presumption found in § 72-2-813(7), MCA, beyond the plain language of the statute.

1. Does the fact that Jeanette pled guilty to the charges of deliberate homicide in a previous criminal case conclusively establish that she killed the children "feloniously and intentionally" for purposes of § 72-2-813, MCA?

The District Court's order summarily denied Jeanette the right to inherit by treating her guilty plea as conclusive evidence that she "feloniously and intention ally" killed her children . . . .The District Court's conclusion effectively precluded Jeanette from litigating two issues in this civil case: whether she acted with the requisite intent, and whether the killings were felonious. However, the District Court neglected to analyze whether it was appropriate to apply the doctrine of collateral estoppel to either issue in this case. . . .

. . . When a criminal defendant enters a plea of guilty to the charge of deliberate homicide, the issues of whether a killer acted with intent and whether the killing was felonious are not "established" through litigation. By contrast, when a defendant undergoes a bench or jury trial, these elements are proven beyond a reasonable doubt. A guilty verdict establishes these elements, but a guilty plea does not. Thus, a guilty verdict has a conclusive effect for the purposes of the slayer statute that a guilty plea does not.

This distinction between a guilty verdict and a guilty plea is recognized by the Legislature in § 72-2-813(7), MCA, which provides:

> After all right to appeal has been exhausted, a judgment of conviction *establishing criminal accountability* for the felonious and intentional killing of the decedent conclusively establishes the convicted individual as the decedent's killer for purposes of this section.

Section 72-2-813(7), MCA (emphasis added). . . . [A] guilty plea does not establish, in an evidentiary sense, criminal accountability for a felonious and intentional killing. As a result, under the plain language of § 72-2-813(7), MCA, a guilty plea does not conclusively establish that a killer acted feloniously and intentionally for the purposes of the slayer statute.

The case at bar illustrates the purpose of distinguishing a guilty plea from a guilty verdict. . . . [I]t is difficult to discern a defendant's motive for pleading guilty. Jeanette pled guilty to the shootings, but all the while maintained that she intended to protect the children, not to hurt them. Jeanette's guilty plea may have been a strategic decision, or perhaps even a choice to spare her family the added trauma of a public trial. Due to the fact that she entered a guilty plea, the issues of whether she intended to kill the children and whether the killings were felonious were never fully examined at trial.

In sum, we conclude that there has not been a trial resulting in a final judgment on the merits of whether Jeanette acted "feloniously and intentionally" when she shot her children. Thus, her guilty plea in the previous criminal action does not preclude her from raising these issues in the instant civil case.

2. Do § 72-2-813(7) and § 72-2-813(10), MCA, read together, create a statutory presumption that conclusively establishes that Jeanette acted "feloniously and intentionally"?

Gene next argues that the statutory presumption found in § 72-2-813(7), MCA, conclusively establishes that Jeanette acted feloniously and intentionally:

After all right to appeal has been exhausted, a judgment of conviction establishing criminal accountability for the felonious and intentional killing of the decedent conclusively establishes the convicted individual as the decedent's killer for purposes of this section.

Section 72-2-813(7), MCA. He reaches this interpretation of the statute by reading § 72-2-813(7), MCA, together with § 72-2-813(10), MCA. Section 72-2-813(10), MCA, provides that "[f]or the purposes of this section, a felonious and intentional killing includes a deliberate homicide as defined in 45-5-102 and a mitigated deliberate homicide as defined in 45-5-103." Gene argues that, read together, these subsections establish a conclusive presumption that one who has been convicted of deliberate homicide is presumed to have acted feloniously and intentionally for the purposes of this section.

We disagree. The Official Comment to § 72-2-813(7), MCA, clearly expresses the purpose of the section's presumption:

> Subsection (g) [72-2-813(7)] leaves no doubt that, for purposes of this section, a killing can be "felonious and intentional," whether or not the killer has actually been convicted in a criminal prosecution. Under subsection (g) [72-2-813(7)], after all right to appeal has been exhausted, *a judgment of conviction establishing criminal accountability for the felonious and intentional killing of the decedent conclusively establishes the convicted individual as the decedent's killer for purposes of this section.* Acquittal, however, does not preclude the acquitted individual from being regarded as the decedent's killer for purposes of this section.

Section 72-2-813(7), MCA cmt. (emphasis added). The section's purpose is to establish that a killer may be barred civilly from inheriting under this statute even if he or she was acquitted in a criminal proceeding. In doing so, the Legislature has expressly rejected the logic of some of our sister states, who have held that the acquittal of a killer bars the application of the slayer statute. *See e.g. Turner v. Estate of Turner*, 454 N.E.2d 1247 (Ind. App. 1 Dist. 1983)....

... [T]he purpose of the statutory caveat found in § 72-2-813(10), MCA, is to distinguish Montana's slayer statute from those in other states, where courts have narrowly interpreted slayer statutes to apply only where the homicide is deliberate and unmitigated. *See e.g. Quick v. United Benefit Life Ins. Co.*, 287 N.C. 47, 213 S.E.2d 563, 568 (N.C. 1975) (noting that the slayer statute does not apply to justifiable or excusable homicide). The plain language of our statute provides that a "felonious and intentional killing" may include both a deliberate homicide and a mitigated deliberate homicide. Section 72-2-813(10), MCA. Gene, however, apparently interprets the statute to mean that all deliberate homicides are "felonious and intentional killings" for the purposes of the slayer statute. Nothing in the plain language of the statute supports this reading, and Gene has not advanced any other authority in support of his interpretation. . . .

On remand, Gene has the burden of proving that Jeanette acted "intentionally" and "feloniously" for the purposes of § 72-2-813, MCA. We take this opportunity to note the difference between the term "feloniously" as it is used in § 72-2-813, MCA, and the statutory definition of a felony . . . . Section 45-2-101(23), MCA, defines a "felony" as "an offense in which the sentence imposed upon conviction is death or imprisonment in a state prison for a term exceeding 1 year." . . . . Technically, Jeanette was not sentenced to any prison time. If courts were to measure whether a killer acted "feloniously" for purposes of § 72-2-813, MCA, by whether or not the killer's sentence comported with the definition of "felony" found in § 45-2-101(23), MCA, then the slayer statute could not be applied to any killer who was not sentenced to death or imprisoned for more than a year.

Other states to grapple with this question have noted that, in the specific context of the slayer statutes, the term "feloniously" has been historically construed as a synonym for "unlawful" or "wrongful." . . . Several of our sister states have refused to presume that a killer acted "feloniously" simply because the homicide was statutorily classified as a felony. . . .

Like Montana, North Dakota's slayer statute is derived from § 2-803 of the Uniform Probate Code. N.D. Cent. Code § 30.1-10-03 (2007); Unif. Probate Code § 2-803, 8 U.L.A. 211 (1998). In a recent decision interpreting § 2-803(b), the North Dakota Supreme Court explicitly rejected the notion that the term "feloniously" encompassed only those intentional acts statutorily designated as felonies. *Matter of Estates of Josephson*, 297 N.W.2d at 448. Instead the court defined the term more broadly, and held that in the specific context of the slayer statute, the term "feloniously" "refers to a killing that is wrongful, that is without legal excuse or justification." *Matter of Estates of Josephson*, 297 N.W.2d at 448. This definition of "feloniously" comports with the construction we have given to the term in prior cases. . . .

. . . Finally, on remand, Gene also has the burden of proving that Jeanette acted with the requisite intent under § 72-2-813, MCA. Evidence of Jeanette's guilty plea is admissible on the independent ground that it is an admission, but it may not be given conclusive effect. . . . In considering whether Jeanette was capable of forming the requisite intent, the District Court must take into account the evidence concerning Jeanette's mental condition, as required by § 46-14-101(1), MCA. . . .

In sum, we hold that the District Court erred by concluding, as a matter of law, that Jeanette was precluded from inheriting from her children's estates. . . . Thus, we reverse and remand for further proceedings consistent with this opinion.

Notes and Questions

1. On remand, the lower court found that Gene did not meet the burden of proving that Jeanette acted with the requisite intent, because of her mental disease or defect. Ultimately the parties agreed to a global settlement that also included the terms of a divorce. Among the twists of this tragic situation was that most of the available funds came from a settlement under a homeowner's insurance umbrella policy that allowed recovery (by the children) for wrongful death and negligent infliction of emotional distress (by the mother).[14]

2. For more on this case, see Peter Arant, *Note: In re Estates of Swansons: The Slayer Statute and the Impact of a Guilty Plea on Collateral Estoppel in Montana*, 71 Mont. L. Rev. 217 (2010). Other states have taken similar approaches despite the somewhat different phrasing of their statutes. *See Dougherty v. Cole*, 934 N.E.2d 16 (Ill. App. Ct. 2010) (slayer barred despite being found not guilty by reason of insanity because facts showed slayer "intentionally and unjustifiably" killed his mother); *In re Estate of Kissinger*, 206 P.3d 665 (Wash. 2009) (slayer barred despite being found not guilty by reason of insanity because facts showed a "willful and unlawful" killing). *But see Estate of Armstrong v. Armstrong*, 170 So. 3d 510 (Miss. 2015) (slayer who was insane at time of killing did not "willfully" cause death under Mississippi statute). In contrast, New York, which does not have a slayer statute, would not bar a slayer from taking if the slayer was insane at the time of the act. *See In re Bobula*, 19 N.Y.2d 818 (1967).

3. Note one of the advantages of uniform statutes: one court (Montana) uses another jurisdiction's (North Dakota's) decision to help interpret the first jurisdiction's statute.

4. What if two people own property as joint tenants with right of survivorship and one kills the other? The UPC's equal division is a common approach. *Accord* In re Covert, 97 N.Y.2d 68 (2001). It denies the wrongdoer a gain while it recognizes that the wrongdoer already owned an interest in the property since the slayer could have converted the joint tenancy into a tenancy in common at any time. Of course, the wrongdoer does lose something—the right of survivorship.

Courts often reach the same result with respect to tenancy by the entireties property. *See Preston v. Chabot*, 412 A.2d 930 (Vt. 1980) (Edward killed Norma and later married Shirley. The court imposed a constructive trust in favor of Norma's children on one-half of entireties property Edward had held with Norma and later held with Shirley). According to the comments to UPC § 2-803, this is the proper result, since the slayer could have obtained a no-fault divorce and wound up with one-half of the property.

According to the Restatement of Restitution, the survivor should receive only a life interest in one-half of the property. By killing the co-tenant, the wrongdoer

14. Conversation between Michael G. Moses, who represented the father, and Roger W. Andersen, Apr. 27, 2011.

forfeited the right to sever and receive one-half of the whole. Restatement of Restitution § 188, cmt. b. Several states follow this rule. *See, e.g., Estate of Mathew,* 706 N.Y.S.2d 432 (N.Y. App. Div. 2000).

The Restatement (Third) of Property (Wills and Other Donative Transfers) adopts a compromise position between the divergent positions under the UPC and the Restatement of Restitution. Unless a statute provides otherwise, the slayer will receive one-half of the joint tenancy or tenancy by the entirety property only if the court finds that there is an equitable justification to treat the homicide as effecting a severance. Otherwise, the slayer will be limited to a life estate in one half of the property. *See* 3d Rest. Prop. § 8.4, cmts. l and m.

5. Brandon pleaded guilty to first degree manslaughter for killing his mother-in-law, Dianne, who died leaving Brandon's wife, Deanna, as the sole beneficiary of her will. Before Dianne's estate was distributed, Deanna died intestate, with Brandon as her sole heir and owning only the property acquired from her mother. To prevent Brandon from benefiting from the wrong, the court barred Brandon from collecting from his wife's estate. *See Matter of Edwards,* 991 N.Y.S.2d 431 (N.Y. App. Div. 2014).

6. Should any of the following persons be barred from inheriting from the decedent:

(a) Someone who facilitates suicide—for example, by providing a gun or putting sleeping pills within reach?

(b) A supposed caregiver who largely ignored a needy individual?

(c) Someone whose parental rights had been terminated?

(d) Someone who kept the secret of another relative's planned crime and who would inherit if the criminal were barred?

Problems

1. Mary had made a will giving much of her property to her minister. Near death, but still mentally alert, Mary changed her mind and tried to execute a new will in favor of her friend, Jack. The minister intervened and prevented Mary from executing the new will. When Mary died, with the old will intact, what arguments could you make for getting the property to Jack?

2. Shannon shot her husband, Michael, wounding him, and thereby prevented him from continuing chemotherapy. When a resurgence of existing cancer killed Michael, would Shannon take his estate under UPC § 2-803?

3. Don, a widower, had two children, Alice and Barb. Alice had three children, and Barb had one child. A week after Barb died, Alice killed Don. If Don died intestate, how should his estate be distributed under the UPC?

4. Byron shot Martha and then himself, but there was insufficient evidence of who died first. Should Martha's estate share in Byron's estate?

5. You are a legislative assistant to a State Representative who was outraged to read that a murderer was able to inherit from his victim. Your Representative is preparing reform legislation and wants your ideas about two topics. What acts should trigger the statute? What forms of property should it cover and how should it treat them?

Selected References

Allison Bridges, *Marital Fault as a Basis for Terminating Inheritance Rights: Protecting the Institution of Marriage and Those Who Abide by Their Vows—'Til Death Do Them Part*, 45 Real Prop. Prob. & Tr. J. 559 (2010).

Richard Lewis Brown, *Undeserving Heirs?—The Case of the "Terminated" Parent*, 40 U. Rich. L. Rev. 547 (2006).

Lisa C. Dumond, *The Undeserving Heir: Domestic Elder Abuser's Right to Inherit*, 23 Quinnipiac Prob. L.J. 214 (2010).

Callie Kramer, *Guilty by Association: Inadequacies in the Uniform Probate Code Slayer Statute*, 19 N.Y.L. Sch. J. Hum. Rts. 697 (2003).

Matthew Barry Reisig, *O to A, for Helping Kill O: Wisconsin's Decision Not to Bar Inheritance to Individuals Who Assist a Decedent in Suicide*, 17 Am. U. J. Gender Soc. Pol'y & L. 785 (2009).

Anne-Marie Rhodes, *Consequences of Heirs' Misconduct: Moving from Rules to Discretion*, 33 Ohio N.U. L. Rev. 975 (2007).

Thomas H. Shepherd, *Comment: It's the 21st Century . . . Time for Probate Codes to Address Family Violence: A Proposal That Deals with the Realities of the Problem*, 20 St. Louis U. Pub. L. Rev. 449 (2001).

Karen J. Sneddon, *Should Cain's Children Inherit Abel's Property?: Wading into the Extended Slayer Rule Quagmire*, 76 UMKC L. Rev. 101 (2007).

Carla Spivack, *Killers Shouldn't Inherit From Their Victims—Or Should They?*, 48 Ga. L. Rev. 145 (2013).

§ 5.03 Changes in Property

Much can happen to property between the time when a document is drafted and the time it becomes effective. These changes can affect both what property passes and who gets it. Suppose Mary Jane's will gives 50 shares of Glasstech stock to Walter. Before Mary Jane's death, the stock might split, with additional shares issued for each share owned. Another possibility is that Supertech might buy out Glasstech. Different risks are that Mary Jane might simply sell the stock and replace it with a new investment, or her guardian may sell it to raise money for her care.

This section addresses the doctrines that affect what Walter would receive in those various circumstances. First, it identifies the various classifications the law has created for gifts. Often the way a court classifies a gift will determine how well the donee fares. Second, we will view the special problem of stock dividends and splits. Third comes the doctrine of ademption, which asks what to do when the subject of the gift is no longer there.

A. Classification of Gifts

Courts and legislatures have identified four classes of gifts: specific, general, demonstrative, and residuary. *See generally* 3d Rest. Prop. § 5.1. Although courts often get formalistic when assigning such labels, the idea of the different categories is to recognize that transferors may have different ideas about various gifts. The familiar goal is to identify the testator's intention.

Often classification is easy. *Specific gifts* are just that: gifts specifically identified. "My oak desk," "my 100 shares of General Motors Preferred Stock," and "my house and lot on Derby Street in Pullman" are all specific gifts. *General gifts* are often legacies, but they need not be. "$3,000 to Marsha" is a general gift. *Demonstrative gifts* are rare. They are a cross between specific and general gifts. Demonstrative gifts are ones which a testator intends to come from a specific source, but which can also come out of general estate assets. "$6,000 to come first from my credit union account, but if the account is too small, from my other funds" is a demonstrative gift. Finally, *residuary gifts* are the catch-alls giving "everything else I own."

The biggest problem is trying to distinguish—on the margin—between specific and general gifts. One reason for the trouble is that the characterization has different consequences in different circumstances. As we shall see, from the perspective of a will beneficiary, a "specific" label is a good thing if there is some accrued, but unpaid, income. The beneficiary usually gets the income. On the other hand, a "specific" label is bad if the question involves a gift of property which is not an estate asset at the testator's death. In this situation, specific gifts usually fail, but general gifts do not. Predictably, courts sometimes read similar language in different ways as they strain to push a gift into a particular category to produce the result they believe makes the most sense in the case before them.

Problem

Classify each of the following dispositions:

(a) "I leave Jess 100 shares of Dana Corporation common stock."

(b) "I leave Jess my 100 shares of Dana Corporation common stock."

(c) "I leave Jess all my shares of Dana Corporation common stock."

(d) "I leave Jess one-half of my personal property."

(e) "I leave Jess an annuity of $300.00 per month, to be paid out of my Chase bank account"

(f) "I leave Jess one-third of my net estate."

B. Dividends and Stock Splits

Testators often gain wealth between the time of a will's execution and the date of death. This happy event poses construction problems, however, when the growth (sometimes called "accretion") stems from securities specifically devised in the will. The basic question is: does the specific gift include the gain?

For example, assume that 100 shares of specifically devised stock were worth $10,000 when the will was executed, but $15,000 at the testator's death, and produced $1,000 per year in cash dividends. At the testator's death, the entire $15,000 value would pass to the beneficiary, but any dividends declared (but not paid) before the testator's death would be part of the residuary estate.

This distinction between capital growth and current income creates problems when a corporation restructures by means of stock splits or stock dividends. A testator would hold both the shares owned at the time of the will execution and the additional shares gained from the split or dividend. The question then becomes whether these new shares follow the original shares or belong to the residuary estate as would cash dividends. Because stock splits merely reallocate capital among a greater number of shares, most modern courts give the new shares to the beneficiary of the old. *See Bostwick v. Hurstel*, 304 N.E.2d 186 (Mass. 1973) (gift of 25 shares of AT&T stock grew to 150 shares after two stock splits before the testator's death). Some courts take this approach only if the gift is specific. *See Boerstler v. Andrews*, 506 N.E.2d 279 (Ohio Ct. App. 1986).

Stock dividends, however, resemble both cash dividends and stock splits. Because a stock dividend normally converts accrued corporate earnings into stated capital, it substitutes for a cash dividend. On the other hand, from the investor's point of view, the "dividend" serves only to spread the market value of the corporation among a greater number of shares, so the post-dividend stock carries a lower market value. The stock dividend thus looks like a restructuring of the investor's market investment, much like a stock split. Courts, therefore, disagree about whether stock dividends should go with a specific gift of the underlying stock.

Under the UPC, a devise of securities usually will include additional securities acquired "as a result of the testator's ownership." UPC § 2-605(a). *Accord* 3d Rest. Prop. § 5.3. Thus, both stock dividends and stock splits would go with the original shares, regardless of the gift's classification as general or specific.

C. Ademption

The doctrine of ademption seeks to answer questions about what to do if a document gives away property which is not available when the document becomes effective.[15] The dominant approach relies upon classifying the gift as general or specific. If the gift is general, the fiduciary uses general estate assets to buy property for the beneficiary. If the gift is specific, the beneficiary loses out under the "identity" theory which says that a specific gift fails if the subject matter is not an estate asset at death.[16]

The identity theory is easy to understand and, superficially at least, easy to apply. In many situations, however, it defeats testators' probable intentions, so courts have developed various devices for avoiding the strict doctrine. The UPC goes further and abolishes the identity theory in favor of one which seeks out the testator's intention. UPC § 2-606. *Accord* 3d Rest. Prop. § 5.3, cmt. b.

The next case retains the traditional rule, but applies it in a new context.

Wasserman v. Cohen

606 N.E.2d 901 (Mass. 1993)

LYNCH, J.

This appeal raises the question whether the doctrine of ademption by extinction applies to a specific gift of real estate contained in a revocable inter vivos trust. . . .

1.

We summarize the relevant facts. Frieda Drapkin created the Joseph and Frieda Drapkin Memorial Trust (trust) in December, 1982, naming herself both settlor and trustee. She funded the trust with "certain property" delivered on the date of execution, and retained the right to add property by inter vivos transfer and by will. Drapkin also reserved the right to receive and to direct the payment of income or principal during her lifetime, to amend or to revoke the trust, and to withdraw property from the trust. On her death, the trustee was directed to distribute the property as set out in the trust. The trustee was ordered to convey to the plaintiff "12-14 Newton Street, Waltham, Massachusetts, Apartment Building, (consisting of approximately 11,296 square feet)."

When she executed the trust, Drapkin held record title to the property at 12-14 Newton Street in Waltham, as trustee of Z.P.Q. Realty Trust. However, she sold the

---

15. Some jurisdictions use the term "ademption by extinction" to distinguish the theory from what they label "ademption by satisfaction." We discuss "satisfaction" on § 5.01[B].

16. The identity theory seems to have gotten its start in decisions penned by Lord Thurlow in the 1780s. For this reason, the doctrine is sometimes called "Lord Thurlow's rule." *See* John C. Paulus, *Ademption by Extinction: Smiting Lord Thurlow's Ghost*, 2 Tex. Tech. L. Rev. 195 (1971). The rule was a response to dissatisfaction with attempted searches for testators' intentions.

property on September 29, 1988, for $575,000, and had never conveyed her interest in the property to the trust.

Drapkin died on March 28, 1989. Her will, dated December 26, 1982, devised all property in her residuary estate to the trust to be disposed of in accordance with the trust's provisions.

2.

The plaintiff first contends that the probate judge erred in failing to consider Drapkin's intent in regard to the gift when she sold the property. We disagree.

We have long adhered to the rule that, when a testator disposes, during his lifetime, of the subject of a specific legacy or devise in his will, that legacy or devise is held to be adeemed, "whatever may have been the intent or motive of the testator in doing so." *Walsh v. Gillespie*, 338 Mass. 278, 280, 154 N.E.2d 906 (1959), quoting *Richards v. Humphreys*, 15 Pick. 133, 135 (1833).... The focus is on the actual existence or nonexistence of the bequeathed property, and not on the intent of the testator with respect to it. *Bostwick v. Hurstel*, 364 Mass. 282, 295, 304 N.E.2d 186 (1973). To be effective, a specific legacy or devise must be in existence and owned by the testator at the time of his death....

The plaintiff asks us to abandon the doctrine of ademption. She contends that, because the doctrine ignores the testator's intent, it produces harsh and inequitable results and thus fosters litigation that the rule was intended to preclude. See Note, Ademption and the Testator's Intent, 74 Harv. L. Rev. 741 (1961). This rule has been followed in this Commonwealth for nearly 160 years. See *Richards v. Humphreys, supra*. Whatever else may be said about it, it is easily understood and applied by draftsmen, testators, and fiduciaries. The doctrine seeks to give effect to a testator's probable intent by presuming he intended to extinguish a specific gift of property when he disposed of that property prior to his death. As with any rule, exceptions have emerged.[17] These limited exceptions do not lead us to the abandonment of the rule. Its so-called harsh results can be easily avoided by careful draftsmanship and its existence must be recognized by any competent practitioner. When we consider the myriad of instruments drafted in reliance on its application, we conclude that stability in the field of trusts and estates requires that we continue the doctrine.

---

17. This court has created two exceptions to the "identity" theory. In *Walsh v. Gillespie*, 338 Mass. 278 (1959), a conservator appointed for the testatrix five years after her will was executed sold shares of stock that were the subject of a specific legacy. The court held that the sale did not operate as an ademption as to the unexpended balance remaining in the hands of the conservator at the death of the testatrix. *Id.* at 284. In *Bostwick v. Hurstel*, 364 Mass. 282 (1973), a conservator had sold, then repurchased, stock that was the subject of a specific legacy and that had been split twice, before the death of the testatrix. The court held that the bequest of stock was not adeemed but emphasized, "we do not violate our rule that 'identity' and not 'intent' governs ademption cases." *Id.* at 296.

3.

The plaintiff also argues that deciding ademption questions based on a determination that a devise is general or specific is overly formalistic and fails to serve the testator's likely intent. She maintains that the court in *Bostwick v. Hurstel*, supra, moved away from making such classifications. In Bostwick, the court held that a gift of stock was not adeemed where the stock had been sold and repurchased prior to the death of the testatrix, and where it had been subject to two stock splits. However, the court confined the holding specifically to its facts. See *Bostwick v. Hurstel*, supra at 294-295, 304 N.E.2d 186. In addition, the court stated: "Our holding does not indicate that we have abandoned the classification of bequests as general or specific for all purposes. We have no occasion at this time to express any opinion on the continuing validity of such distinctions in those cases where abatement or ademption of the legacy is at issue. . . ." *Id.* at 292, 304 N.E.2d 186. We now have such an occasion, and we hold that, at least in regard to the conveyance of real estate at issue here, the practice of determining whether a devise is general or specific is the proper first step in deciding questions of ademption.

4.

We have held that a trust, particularly when executed as part of a comprehensive estate plan, should be construed according to the same rules traditionally applied to wills. . . . . We agree with this reasoning. As discussed above, the doctrine of ademption has a "long established recognition" in Massachusetts. . . . Furthermore, Drapkin created the trust along with her will as part of a comprehensive estate plan. Under the residuary clause of her will, Drapkin gave the majority of her estate to the trustee, who was then to dispose of the property on her death according to the terms of the trust. We see no reason to apply a different rule because she conveyed the property under the terms of the trust, rather than her will. Thus, we conclude that the doctrine of ademption, as traditionally applied to wills, should also apply to the trust in the instant case.

5.

Conclusion

Since the plaintiff does not contest that the devise of 12-14 Newton Street was a specific devise,[18] it follows that the devise was adeemed by the act of Drapkin.

---

18. "A specific legacy is one which separates and distinguishes the property bequeathed from the other property of the testator, so that it can be identified. It can only be satisfied by the thing bequeathed; if that has no existence, when the bequest would otherwise become operative, the legacy has no effect." -*Moffatt v. Heon*, 242 Mass. 201, 203 (1922), quoting *Tomlinson v. Bury*, 145 Mass. 346, 347 (1887).

Notes and Question

1. A different sort of ademption can occur if a donor anticipates an at-death gift by transferring equivalent property to a beneficiary during the donor's life. Called "ademption by satisfaction," or simply "satisfaction," this doctrine is very similar to the advancements theory of intestate succession. See §§ 5.01 (A) & (B).

2. Like most clear rules, the identity theory can yield some harsh results. Consider *In re Estate of Nakoneczny*, 319 A.2d 893 (Pa. 1974). Michael's will left real estate to his son, Paul. The Urban Redevelopment Authority later acquired the land and Michael put most of the proceeds into bonds. When Paul claimed the bonds after his father's death, the court applied the identity theory and declined to trace the gift. *See also Matter of Braunstein*, 4 N.Y.S.3d 63 (N.Y. App Div. 2015) (real estate adeemed by its transfer to limited partnership as decedent because partner had no interest in specific partnership assets); *In re Estate of Bauer*, 700 N.W.2d 572 (Neb. 2005) (son sold real estate under a durable power of attorney; gift to son adeemed); *In re Hilpert's Estate*, 300 N.Y.S. 886 (Sur. Ct. 1937) (library burned; beneficiary denied insurance proceeds); *Price v. Johnson*, 563 S.W.2d 188 (Tenn. Ct. App. 1977) (testator exchanged stock for cash and installment note from the corporation; gift of stock adeemed).

3. In response to the identity rule's harshness, courts and legislatures have developed several avoidance devices. As the *Wasserman* opinion notes, if the testator becomes incompetent, courts often trace assets when someone acting on behalf of the incompetent has transferred property subject to a specific devise. *See Morse v. Converse*, 113 A. 214 (N.H. 1921) (where guardian took money from a savings account to buy a Liberty Bond, devisee of the savings account got the bond); *Brown v. Labow*, 69 Cal. Rptr. 3d 417 (Ct. App. 2007) (stock gift traced to proceeds from dissolution of close corporation after trust settlor's incapacity). Where a guardian has sold specifically devised property to pay the ward's expenses, but some of the proceeds of the sale are left over, courts have allowed tracing to the extent of the remaining funds. *See, e.g., Rodgers v. Rodgers*, 406 S.W.3d 422 (Ark. 2012) (timber rights); *In re Estate of Honse*, 392 S.W.3d 511 (Mo. Ct. App. 2013) (farm and associated property).

If the gift is clearly "specific," the "change in form" exception may come into play. Thus, if a will devised ABC stock, before a buyout by Disney, the devisee would take the new Disney stock. *See In re Estate of Watkins*, 284 So. 2d 679 (Fla. 1973) (no ademption where testator's gift of 400 shares of Amerada Petroleum Corporation was converted into shares issued by the Amerada Hess corporation after the two corporations merged); *Johnston v. Estate of Wheeler*, 745 A.2d 345 (D.C. 2000) (no ademption where will referred to testator's "pension" and testator rolled her benefits into an IRA). Courts sometimes take the change in form exception for granted. *See Nobbe v. Nobbe*, 831 N.E.2d 835 (Ind. Ct. App. 2005) (increased value of new corporation's stock goes with the original gift; ademption not discussed).

Also, courts can usually construe a will as speaking at the time of the testator's death. Thus, a gift of "my car" would almost certainly apply to the car owned at death.

4. The technique of tracing assets, of following proceeds through different forms, emphasizes the beneficiary's importance to the donor. The theory is that the donor wanted the beneficiary to get something. Sometimes, however, perhaps the focus should be more on the gift itself—like a keepsake tied to particular memories. If so, perhaps ademption should apply. Should courts seek to identify the testator's intention?

The UPC reverses the identity theory and creates a rule based on intention. *Accord* 3d Rest. Prop. § 5.3, cmt. b.

Uniform Probate Code

Section 2-606. Nonademption of Specific Devises; Unpaid Proceeds of Sale, Condemnation, or Insurance; Sale by Conservator or Agent.

(a) A specific devisee has a right to the specifically devised property in the testator's estate at death and:

> (1) any balance of the purchase price, together with any security agreement, owing from a purchaser to the testator at death by reason of sale of the property;
>
> (2) any amount of a condemnation award for the taking of the property unpaid at death;
>
> (3) any proceeds unpaid at death on fire or casualty insurance on or other recovery for injury to the property;
>
> (4) property owned by the testator at death and acquired as a result of foreclosure, or obtained in lieu of foreclosure, of the security interest for a specifically devised obligation;
>
> (5) real or tangible personal property owned by the testator at death which the testator acquired as a replacement for specifically devised real or tangible personal property; and
>
> (6) unless the facts and circumstances indicate that ademption of the devise was intended by the testator or ademption of the devise is consistent with the testator's manifested plan of distribution, the value of the specifically devised property to the extent the specifically devised property is not in the testator's estate at death and its value or its replacement is not covered by paragraphs (1) through (5).

(b) If specifically devised property is sold or mortgaged by a conservator or by an agent acting within the authority of a durable power of attorney for an incapacitated principal, or if a condemnation award, insurance proceeds, or recovery for injury to the property are paid to a conservator or to an agent acting within the authority of a durable power of attorney for an incapacitated principal, the specific devisee has the right to a general pecuniary devise equal to the net sale price, the amount of the unpaid loan, the condemnation award, the insurance proceeds, or the recovery.

(c) The right of a specific devisee under subsection (b) is reduced by any right the devisee has under subsection (a).

(d) For the purposes of the references in subsection (b) to a conservator, subsection (b) does not apply if after the sale, mortgage, condemnation, casualty, or recovery, it was adjudicated that the testator's incapacity ceased and the testator survived the adjudication by one year.

(e) For the purposes of the references in subsection (b) to an agent acting within the authority of a durable power of attorney for an incapacitated principal,

(i) "incapacitated principal" means a principal who is an incapacitated person,

(ii) no adjudication of incapacity before death is necessary, and

(iii) the acts of an agent within the authority of a durable power of attorney are presumed to be for an incapacitated principal.

Questions

1. *Wasserman* applies the ademption doctrine to revocable trusts. The UPC does not. (The 2-600 series of sections apply only to wills.) Is this an instance where rules developed for wills should also apply to trusts?

2. *Wasserman* sticks to the identity rule. The UPC looks to intention. In this context are simple, clear rules better, even if they are arbitrary?

Problems

1. Suppose Bill's will says "to my son, Dick, my Sporterized 30-06 Springfield rifle, with a hand-made Herter stock and a Weaver 2.5 scope, in memory of our good times together in the Blue Mountains." If the rifle is insured and stolen the week before Bill's death, what would Dick receive under UPC § 2-606?

2. Terrell's will gave her 4-wheel drive Jeep Wrangler SUV to Martha. Terrell then sold the Jeep and bought a Mini sportscar. Under UPC § 2-606, would Martha take the Mini?

Selected References

Gregory S. Alexander, *Ademption and the Domain of Formality in Wills Law*, 55 Alb. L. Rev. 1067 (1992).

Mark L. Ascher, *The 1990 Uniform Probate Code: Older and Better, or More Like the Internal Revenue Code?*, 77 Minn. L. Rev. 639 (1993).

Mary Louise Fellows, *Traveling the Road of Probate Reform: Finding the Way to Your Will (A Response to Professor Ascher)*, 77 Minn. L. Rev. 659 (1993).

Mary K. Lundwall, *The Case Against the Ademption by Extinction Rule: A Proposal for Reform*, 29 Gonz. L. Rev. 105 (1994).

D. Abatement and Exoneration

Two other doctrines relate not so much to changes in property as to creditors' claims, but they traditionally depend so heavily upon the classification of gifts that it makes sense to consider them here. Abatement addresses what to do when there is not enough money to go around. Exoneration considers the impact of liens on specifically-devised property.

Suppose Ralph's will creates the following gifts: "(1) my woodworking tools to my daughter Victoria, (2) $8,000 to my son Michael, (3) $4,000 to my daughter Marie, and (4) the rest of my estate to my brother Bob." Suppose further that the tools are worth $6,000 and other estate assets total $24,000, for a total of $30,000. Debts total $15,000. Which beneficiaries' shares go to pay the creditors? Typically, gifts to will beneficiaries "abate," or fail in the face of inadequate funds, in the following order: (1) residuary, (2) general, and (3) demonstrative and specific as a single class. Multiple gifts in the same class abate proportionately. This hierarchy would mean that Bob would get nothing because the residuary is worth $12,000 and the debts total $15,000. The remaining $3,000 comes from the general gifts to Michael and Marie. Reduced proportionately, Michael's gift is $6,000, Marie's is $3,000. Victoria takes the tools. A rule making the residuary bear the creditors' claims presents a warning to drafters. If the residuary beneficiary is primary, the will should not be too generous with specific and general gifts.

Boilerplate clauses can cause trouble when lawyers insert them without thinking about their possible applications. One common clause—a general direction to pay one's debts—is not only unnecessary, but often unwise. As you learned in Chapter 1, debts will be paid. Such a clause can also prompt litigation about whether the exoneration doctrine should apply. For example, in *Estate of Fussell v. Fortney*, 730 S.E.2d 405 (W.Va. 2012), a general direction to pay "just debts" meant that two specific devises of land subject to mortgages should pass free of the mortgages. Most likely, neither the lawyer nor the testator thought about whether the residuary beneficiary or the specific devisees should bear the burden of any mortgages.

Exoneration is the common law doctrine that a specific devise transfers free from any outstanding mortgage, which has to be paid by the residuary estate. For example, suppose you owned a house (subject to a mortgage) and a car (subject to a lien) and suppose your will gave the house to your sister, the car to your brother, and all the rest of your property to your mother. If your jurisdiction followed the exoneration doctrine, your mother's gift would be reduced by the amount necessary to pay off the mortgage and the car loan. Some jurisdictions recognize the doctrine, while others do not. *Compare In re Estate of Payne*, 895 A.2d 428 (N.J. 2006) (letter to attorney evidenced probable intention that realty pass without debt), *with* UPC § 2-607 (no right of exoneration). The important point for document drafters is that if they include a specific gift, they should say whether it passes free from creditors' encumbrances, or subject to them.

Problems

1. Bill wants to make several pecuniary and specific bequests to friends and family and leave the bulk of his estate to his wife, Bobby. How would you draft the will to protect Bobby's position as primary beneficiary?

2. Karen wants you to draft a will provision giving her car, titled in her name but encumbered by a security interest of $6,000, to her husband, Tokutaro. What other information would you need and what factors would you consider before drafting the provision?

§ 5.04 Lapse

Suppose James leaves a will giving his car to Kerry, but that she predeceases him. At common law, Kerry's gift would "lapse," or fail. The car would pass under the residuary clause, or, if the will lacked one, by intestacy. Because legislators thought that in some cases such a result would be contrary to a common testator's intention, they passed "antilapse" statutes. Rather than letting gifts fail, these statutes give the property to specified alternative takers. The statutes vary in detail, in terms of whose gifts they save and what alternative takers they designate. Questions also arise about the extent to which antilapse statutes, originally applied only to wills, cover will substitutes. This section first addresses traditional antilapse statutes and then turns to the changes proposed by the UPC.

A. Traditional Antilapse Statutes

Because antilapse statutes vary in detail, it can be helpful to have a series of questions you can ask about each situation you face:

- Is the predeceased beneficiary in a class protected by the statute?
- Did the beneficiary die before the document was executed?
- Did the beneficiary leave survivors who qualify under the statute to take the gift?
- How does the document's language affect the statute?

Start by identifying the relationship between the testator and the predeceased beneficiary. Some statutes protect gifts to all beneficiaries. Some apply only to gifts to relatives; for this purpose, spouses usually do not qualify as "relatives," because applying the statute could shift property to the spouse's family. For example, suppose Anna dies leaving a will giving everything to her husband Joe, who has predeceased. If the antilapse statute applies to Joe, his successors, rather than Anna's, would take the property. Some statutes only cover gifts to "descendants" or "issue"; here, familiar problems arise as to whether adopted or non-marital children fit the statute's definitions.

Under the common law, a gift to someone dead when the will was executed did not lapse; rather, it was "void." Most statutes expressly cover both lapsed and void gifts, but some do not.

Antilapse statutes prevent lapse only in the sense that they identify alternative takers. The key question is the relationship between the predeceased beneficiary and that person's survivors. If appropriate survivors exist, they will take the gift. By far the most common substitute takers are issue of the beneficiary.

Because they are remedial statutes, designed to effectuate presumed intention, antilapse statutes will yield to contrary expressions of intent. The problem is deciding what expressions will remove the document from the statute's grasp. Because extrinsic evidence traditionally is not admissible, we are left with the document's words.

Estate of Kehler

411 A.2d 748 (Pa. 1980)

Roberts, Justice.

Testator, Emerson Kehler, died in April of 1975. By paragraph THIRD of his will, he disposed of the residue of his estate:

> "All the rest, residue and remainder of my estate, real, personal and mixed, of whatsoever nature and wheresoever situated, I give, devise and bequeath unto my brother, RALPH KEHLER, of Reading, Pennsylvania, and my sisters, VIOLA WELKER, of Lavelle, Pennsylvania,
>
> ADA SHARTEL, of Reading, Pennsylvania, and GERTRUDE KRAPF, of Stroudsburg, Pennsylvania, and to the survivor or survivors of them, equally, share and share alike, to have and to hold unto themselves, their heirs and assigns forever."

Ralph Kehler predeceased testator, but Ralph Kehler's daughter, appellant Ethel Chupp, survived testator.

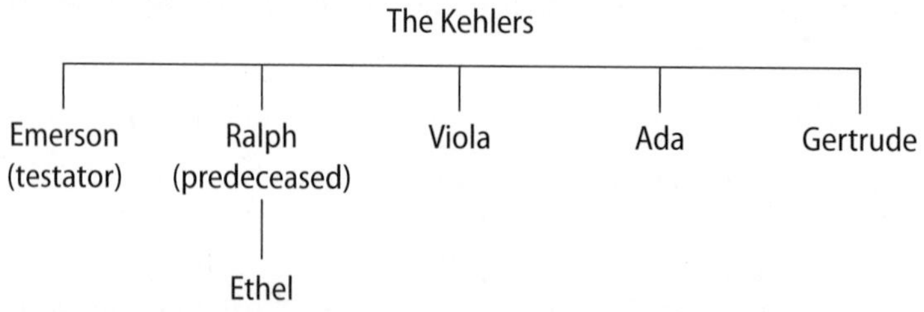

At issue on this appeal is whether appellant may take the share of the residue her father Ralph Kehler would have received had he survived testator. Appellant takes the position that testator's intent concerning the disposition of the bequest to a predeceased sibling is ambiguous. She maintains, therefore, that the relevant "antilapse" statute, 20 Pa. C.S. § 2514(9), applies. Section 2514(9) provides:

Rules of interpretation

> In the absence of a contrary intent appearing therein, wills shall be construed as to real and personal estate in accordance with the following rules: . . .
>
> (9) Lapsed and void devises and legacies; substitution of issue. A devise or bequest to a child or other issue of the testator or to his brother or sister or to a child of his brother or sister whether designated by name or as one of a class shall not lapse if the beneficiary shall fail to survive the testator and shall leave issue surviving the testator but shall pass to such surviving issue who shall take per stirpes the share which their deceased ancestor would have taken had he survived the testator. . . .

The Orphans' Court Division of the Court of Common Pleas of Northumberland County disagreed. It concluded that the language of testator's will, particularly "and to the survivor or survivors of them," manifests testator's "contrary intent" within the meaning of section 2514 to limit takers to those named siblings who are living at testator's death, thus precluding operation of subsection (9). We agree with appellant that the orphans' court misinterpreted testator's will.

This Court has not yet held that a testator must expressly provide for a possible lapse to manifest "contrary intent" overcoming operation of the anti-lapse statute. *See Corbett Estate*, 430 Pa. 54, 61 n.7, 241 A.2d 524, 527 n.7 (1968). Surely, however, a "contrary intent" must appear with reasonable certainty. See *id.*, at 62-63, 241 A.2d at 527-28. . . .

Testator's will here permits no such certainty. In paragraph THIRD of his will, Testator fails to make an express statement concerning his intended disposition of residue in the event a named beneficiary predeceases him. Instead, he merely states his desire to leave the residue to his named siblings "and to the survivor or survivors of them." By contrast, in other paragraphs of his will, testator expressly provides for the possibility of lapse. In paragraph FIRST, in which testator gives his nephew Emerson Asher Shoemaker a monetary gift, testator provides:

> "I give and bequeath the sum of One Thousand ($1,000.00) Dollars, unto my nephew, EMERSON ASHER SHOEMAKER, of Reading, Pennsylvania, should he survive me, but if he predeceases me, then this paragraph of my Will shall be null and void and of no effect." . . .

Testator's careful use of express language directing a lapse of these bequests in his will raises considerable doubt that he intended a lapse in paragraph THIRD, where no such language is used. It cannot now be said with the requisite reasonable certainty that testator intended a lapse of residuary bequests under paragraph THIRD. In accordance with the Legislature's directive contained in 20 Pa.C.S. § 2514(9), it must be presumed that testator did not intend his bequest to Ralph Kehler to lapse. By way of the same statute, appellant may share in the residuary estate.

Decree vacated and case remanded for proceedings consistent with this opinion. Each party pays own costs.

LARSEN, JUSTICE, dissenting.

I dissent. I believe the testator clearly expressed his intention in Paragraph Third to distribute the residue of his estate to the survivor or survivors of the four named siblings. It is not surprising that testator used different language in the first and second paragraphs as those paragraphs mentioned only one individual each—each paragraph was a specific monetary legacy to a specific individual.

The majority observes the testator "merely states his desire to leave the residue to his named siblings and to the survivor or survivors of them." I agree with this observation, but contrary to the majority, I would affirm the Orphans' Court because of this "merely stated" expression of intent, and would affirm the distribution of the estate in accordance with his intent.

Notes

1. *Kehler* interpreted a residuary clause. Under traditional rules, a lapsed gift to a residuary beneficiary goes to intestate takers, unless saved by an antilapse statute. The theory is that there can be "no residue of a residue"; there is nothing to catch the failed gift. Both UPC § 2-604(b) and Restatement (Third) of Property § 5.5, comment o, reject the rule, and would let the other residuary beneficiaries take. *See also In re Estate of Zilles*, 200 P.3d 1024 (Ariz. Ct. App. 2008) (allowing other residuary beneficiaries of a revocable trust to take). Despite a dissent noting that 37 states have abolished the "no residue of a residue" rule, *In re Estate of McFarland*, 167 S.W.3d 299 (Tenn. 2005), reaffirmed an 1852 case taking the traditional approach.

A court might avoid the "no residue of a residue" rule if the residuary clause also created a class gift, like one to "children" or "brothers and sisters." If the antilapse statute does not apply to class gifts, the surviving class members take larger shares. Many antilapse statutes expressly apply to class gifts. When the statute is not clear, most, but not all, courts apply their statutes to class gifts.

Disputes may arise about whether a gift even is a class gift. We address that question in Chapter 9.

2. Because antilapse statutes yield to a showing of contrary intent, courts regularly struggle with whether language in a particular document is sufficient to avoid a statute. *See, e.g., Estate of Kuruzovich*, 78 S.W.3d 226 (Mo. Ct. App. 2002) (residuary gift to three people "share and share alike" insufficient to override antilapse statute). One might expect that "to Mary, if she survives me," would be enough. The gift looks contingent: no survival, no gift. The vast majority of cases hold that an express survivorship requirement shows an intention that the antilapse statute not apply, but that rule is under attack.

The latest Restatement argues that such language does not conclusively evidence the testator's intention that the antilapse statute not apply. *See* 3d Rest. Prop. § 5.5, cmt. h (". . . [T]he trier of fact should be especially reluctant to find that survival language manifests a contrary intent [to the antilapse statute applying] in cases in which the deceased devisee is one of the testator's children, or other direct descendant, and the effect of refusing to apply the antilapse statute would be to disinherit one or more grandchildren or great-grandchildren."). The comment to UPC § 2-603 warns: "Lawyers who believe that the attachment of words of survivorship to a devise is a foolproof method of defeating an antilapse statute are mistaken." *See, e.g., Ruotolo v. Tietjen*, 890 A.2d 166 (Conn. App.), *appeal granted*, 896 A.2d 101 (Conn. 2006) (residuary gift to Hazel "if she survives me" insufficient to prevent antilapse statute from saving gift for Hazel's daughter).

Courts also may require a "gift over" to someone else. *Detzel v. Nieberding*, 219 N.E.2d 327 (Ohio Prob. Ct. 1966) (gift over required); *but see Shalkhauser v. Beach*, 233 N.E.2d 527 (Ohio Prob. Ct. 1968) (words of survivorship alone usually enough). Kehler illustrates, moreover, that even language giving property to survivors may not be enough to avoid the statute. On the other hand, it might be. Compare the will's language in *Kehler* to: "should any of my said children die before my decease I hereby give, will, devise and bequeath the share of said deceased child to the survivor or survivors of my said children, share and share alike." That language was enough to avoid the statute's application when the testator's daughter predeceased her. *See In re Estate of Evans*, 227 N.W.2d 603 (Neb. 1975).

The search for an alternative gift can take courts to strange places. One common rule of construction is that a gift to one person "or" someone else places a condition of survivorship on the first named, with the second person as the alternative beneficiary. In turn, because a survivorship condition followed by an alternative beneficiary often avoids the antilapse statute, courts sometimes stretch language to find an "or." *See Estate of Mangel v. Strong*, 186 N.W.2d 276 (1971) ("to my beloved wife Irene E. Mangel and to her heirs and assigns . . ." interpreted as "or her heirs and assigns").

Another problem appears if both the primary and secondary beneficiaries predecease the testator, with one or more of them leaving issue. Courts disagree about who should take. For this reason, drafters often provide a series of alternative beneficiaries. Although it is possible to get carried away with too many options, providing alternative takers in different generations offers some protection against a gap appearing. Naming a charity as the last alternative beneficiary usually preserves the gift.

3. In more than half the states, antilapse statutes—previously limited to wills—now apply to lifetime trusts. The Restatement advocates this approach. *See* 3d Rest. Prop. § 5.5, cmt. p. *See also* UTC § 112 (will construction rules also apply to trusts). *But see Baldwin v. Branch*, 888 So. 2d 482 (Ala. 2004) (leaving the question to the legislature). Some statutes apply to other documents as well. *See* Cal. Prob. Code §§ 21101 & 21110 (wills, trusts, deeds, and other instruments).

4. Because antilapse statutes have no applicability unless the beneficiary failed to survive, questions arise about whether the beneficiary survived. Well drafted documents will define "survives" to mean survival by a defined time period. Recall our discussion of this issue earlier in the book.

5. Questions sometimes arise about the relationship of antilapse statutes to other doctrines. Consider the following examples:

- *Misconduct.* Margaret's will gave her property equally to her three children. When son Steven killed her, he forfeited his share because of Florida's slayer's statute. The antilapse statute, however, gave Steven's share to his children. *In re Estate of Benson*, 548 So. 2d 775 (Fla. Dist. Ct. App. 1989).
- *Disclaimer.* Lillian was a residuary beneficiary who disclaimed her share. In the absence of a contingent beneficiary, the court applied the antilapse statute to give the property to Lillian's children. *Estate of Cooper*, 342 N.Y.S.2d 995 (Sur. Ct. 1973).
- *Adoption.* When Julie was two years old, her mother married Neil. Neil agreed to adopt Julie, but never got around to it, though Julie took his surname as a youth. Julie predeceased Neil, leaving two children. The "equitable adoption" theory did not apply to treat Julie as someone covered by the antilapse statute. *In re Estate of Seader*, 76 P.3d 1236 (Wyo. 2003).
- *Conflict of Laws.* Ella died in Ohio leaving a will giving her husband a life estate in land in Indiana, with a remainder to her brother and sister, who had predeceased her. Under Indiana law the remainder lapsed; Ohio's antilapse statute would save it. To save the gift while applying traditional choice of law principles, the court applied the equitable conversion doctrine, which said that the will "converted" the realty to personalty. Because the property was personalty, the law of Ella's domicile, Ohio, could apply. *Duckwall v. Lease*, 20 N.E.2d 204 (Ind. Ct. App. 1939).
- *No-contest Clause.* Violet's will gave Howard a legacy if he survived her. When Howard challenged part of his mother's will, he lost his share under a no-contest clause that treated him as predeceased. However, because the legacy gift included survivorship language, the anti-lapse statute did not apply to save the gift for his children. *In re Camac*, 772 N.Y.S.2d 792 (Sur. Ct. 2004).

Problems

1. Terry's will includes a clause giving property "to my sisters, Mary, if she survives me, and Jane."

(a) If Mary predeceases Terry, leaving a daughter, Meghan, does Meghan take a share?

(b) If Jane predeceases Terry, leaving a daughter, Janice, does Janice take a share?

2. Harry and Nancy executed a joint and mutual will under which their survivor received "all the estate of every description which either or both of us may own, to be used and occupied during the survivor's life, and upon the survivor's death, all of

such property shall belong to Gordon." Harry died, then Gordon died, then Nancy died. Should Gordon's children take under an antilapse statute?

3. Daryl and Gary were sole and equal residuary beneficiaries under their mother's will. Because Gary was disabled and needed a place to live, Daryl disclaimed his share. Should Gary or Daryl's minor children get Daryl's interest if the local disclaimer statute says "disclaimed property passes as if the disclaimant had predeceased the testator"?

4. Draft clauses to effectuate the following gifts. You may need to make some additional assumptions.

(a) Don wants to leave to his daughter, Rebecca, the painting he received when he moved from Ohio.

(b) Myrna wants to leave her stock portfolio to her sister Agnes. Myrna currently owns 30 shares of GM common stock and 5 shares of Westinghouse preferred.

B. The Uniform Probate Code

In an effort to solve many of the problems that have plagued antilapse statutes, the UPC offered a comprehensive, complicated proposal in 1990. The current version appears below. You may also want to consult the extensive comments to this section.

Uniform Probate Code

Section 2-603. Antilapse; Deceased Devisee; Class Gifts.

(a) [Definitions.] In this section:

(1) "Alternative devise" means a devise that is expressly created by the will and, under the terms of the will, can take effect instead of another devise on the happening of one or more events, including survival of the testator or failure to survive the testator, whether an event is expressed in condition-precedent, condition-subsequent, or any other form. A residuary clause constitutes an alternative devise with respect to a nonresiduary devise only if the will specifically provides that, upon lapse or failure, the nonresiduary devise, or non-residuary devises in general, pass under the residuary clause.

(2) "Class member" includes an individual who fails to survive the testator but who would have taken under a devise in the form of a class gift had he [or she] survived the testator.

(3) "Devise" includes an alternative devise, a devise in the form of a class gift, and an exercise of a power of appointment.

(4) "Devisee" includes (i) a class member if the devise is in the form of a class gift, (ii) an individual or class member who was deceased at the time the testator executed his [or her] will as well as an individual or class member who was then living but who failed to survive the testator, and (iii) an appointee under a power of appointment exercised by the testator's will.

(5) "Stepchild" means a child of the surviving, deceased, or former spouse of the testator or of the donor of a power of appointment, and not of the testator or donor.

(6) "Surviving devisee" or "surviving descendant" means a devisee or a descendant who neither predeceased the testator nor is deemed to have predeceased the testator under Section 2-702.

(7) "Testator" includes the donee of a power of appointment if the power is exercised in the testator's will.

(b) [Substitute Gift.] If a devisee fails to survive the testator and is a grandparent, a descendant of a grandparent, or a stepchild of either the testator or the donor of a power of appointment exercised by the testator's will, the following apply:

(1) Except as provided in paragraph (4), if the devise is not in the form of a class gift and the deceased devisee leaves surviving descendants, a substitute gift is created in the devisee's surviving descendants. They take by representation the property to which the devisee would have been entitled had the devisee survived the testator.

(2) Except as provided in paragraph (4), if the devise is in the form of a class gift, other than a devise to "issue," "descendants," "heirs of the body," "heirs," "next of kin," "relatives," or "family," or a class described by language of similar import, a substitute gift is created in the surviving descendants of any deceased devisee. The property to which the devisees would have been entitled had all of them survived the testator passes to the surviving devisees and the surviving descendants of the deceased devisees. Each surviving devisee takes the share to which he [or she] would have been entitled had the deceased devisees survived the testator. Each deceased devisee's surviving descendants who are substituted for the deceased devisee take by representation the share to which the deceased devisee would have been entitled had the deceased devisee survived the testator. For the purposes of this paragraph, "deceased devisee" means a class member who failed to survive the testator and left one or more surviving descendants.

(3) For the purposes of Section 2-601 [stating that UPC rules of construction control in the absence of a contrary intention], words of survivorship, such as in a devise to an individual "if he survives me," or in a devise to "my surviving children," are not, in the absence of additional evidence, a sufficient indication of an intent contrary to the application of this section.

(4) If the will creates an alternative devise with respect to a devise for which a substitute gift is created by paragraph (1) or (2), the substitute gift is superseded by the alternative devise only if an expressly designated devisee of the alternative devise is entitled to take under the will.

(5) Unless the language creating a power of appointment expressly excludes the substitution of the descendants of an appointee for the appointee, a surviving descendant of a deceased appointee of a power of appointment can be substituted for the appointee under this section, whether or not the descendant is an object of the power.

(c) [More Than One Substitute Gift; Which One Takes.] If, under sub-section (b), substitute gifts are created and not superseded with respect to more than one devise and the devises are alternative devises, one to the other, the determination of which of the substitute gifts takes effect is resolved as follows:

(1) Except as provided in paragraph (2), the devised property passes under the primary substitute gift.

(2) If there is a younger-generation devise, the devised property passes under the younger-generation substitute gift and not under the primary substitute gift.

(3) In this subsection:

(i) "Primary devise" means the devise that would have taken effect had all the deceased devisees of the alternative devises who left surviving descendants survived the testator.

(ii) "Primary substitute gift" means the substitute gift created with respect to the primary devise.

(iii) "Younger-generation devise" means a devise that (A) is to a descendant of a devisee of the primary devise, (B) is an alternative devise with respect to the primary devise, (C) is a devise for which a substitute gift is created, and (D) would have taken effect had all the deceased devisees who left surviving descendants survived the testator except the deceased devisee or devisees of the primary devise.

(iv) "Younger-generation substitute gift" means the substitute gift created with respect to the younger-generation devise.

Notes and Question

1. A parallel provision extends antilapse provisions to a variety of will substitutes, including life insurance, retirement plans, and POD accounts. UPC § 2-706.

2. Recall that "survival" under the UPC requires survival by 120 hours. UPC § 2-702.

3. The UPC antilapse statute has been controversial. Two criticisms predominate. First, subsection (b)(3) reverses the usual rule that words of survivorship are enough to remove a gift from the statute's application. Critics variously see the change as unnecessary, as likely to defeat testators' intentions and to pose malpractice risks for practitioners who follow their well-established habits. Defenders respond that the traditional rule is too shaky to be reliable as a drafting guide and that many testators had never formed any intention about lapse issues. Defenders also suggest that survivorship language, rather than reflecting testators' informed decisions about lapse, often merely appears from forms. The second main critique is more general: the UPC is simply too complex. Untangling it is not worth the effort. Defenders respond that the statute can save time and reduce litigation because the UPC provides answers other statutes and most case law leave unresolved.

4. Imagine that you are a member of the National Conference of Commissioners on Uniform State Laws. They have been debating the tension between achieving uniformity and encouraging law reform, using UPC § 2-603 as an example. If a proposal is too controversial, many states may reject it. On the other hand, playing to the lowest common denominator sacrifices opportunities for clarifying or otherwise improving the law. In this context, which do you value more, uniformity or reform?

Problems

1. Tanya left her stamp collection "to my son Ben, if he survives me, and if he does not, to my daughter Nancy." Assume Ben predeceased Tanya, but left descendants.

(a) Under UPC § 2-603, who takes the stamps if Nancy survives Tanya?

(b) What if Nancy also predeceases Tanya, leaving descendants?

2. Joseph had three children: Ralph, Richard, and Robert. Joseph's will left a gift "to my surviving children." Ralph predeceased Joseph, leaving four children. Richard survived. Robert predeceased Joseph, leaving three children. Under UPC § 2-603, who takes what shares of the gift?

Selected Reference

Adam J. Hirsch, *Default Rules in Inheritance Law: A Problem in Search of Its Context*, 73 Fordham L. Rev. 1031 (2004).

Eloisa C. Rodriguez-Dod, *"I'm Not Quite Dead Yet!": Rethinking the Anti-Lapse Redistribution of a Dead Beneficiary's Gift*, 61 Clev. St. L. Rev. 1017 (2013).

Richard F. Storrow, *Wills and Survival*, 34 Quinnipiac L. Rev. 447 (2016).

Chapter 6

Protecting the Family

Courts have long honored the principle of free testation, the notion that testators can leave their property however and to whomever they wish. Free testation is an extension of a free-market economy; testators choose how they want to "spend" their money. Because this approach gives people the ability to affect events after their own deaths, commentators commonly refer to the power of the "dead hand." One can imagine a large hand rising—in horror movie style—out of a grave and pointing the direction survivors should take or hold them back from where they want to go. At some point the principle of free testation collides with other principles. One such principle is that property owners owe a duty to provide for their families. Another is that living people should control their own destinies, unshackled by restrictions from the past.

This chapter explores ways the law protects family members from a decedent's caprice.[1] We start with a look at spouses' claims on the family wealth. Here, the law is moving from "protecting" or "supporting" the survivor toward recognizing each spouse's ownership interest in the couple's assets. We then turn to the claims of spouses and children who have been left out of a will, usually because they came along after the will was executed. The chapter closes with discussions of limitations on gifts to charity and the more general limits "public policy" places on testamentary gifts.

For a thoughtful discussion of several topics in this chapter, see Adam J. Hirsch, *Freedom of Testation/Freedom of Contract,* 95 Minn. L. Rev. 2180 (2011).

§ 6.01 Disinherited Spouses

We are in the midst of a movement to reform spousal inheritance rights in response to the changing structure of families, as the traditional prototype (propertied husband, with dependent wife and children) becomes increasingly less representative. This section examines the shape and direction of that reform movement.

For two reasons, we start with the law of community property. First, community property rules apply directly to more than one-fourth of all Americans.[2] Second,

1. Protective provisions, introduced in Chapter 2, § 2.01D, also prevent a decedent by will from disinheriting a surviving spouse and in certain instances minor children.

2. Community property is the law in Arizona, California, Idaho, Louisiana, Nevada, New Mexico, Texas, and Washington. Wisconsin has adopted the Uniform Marital Property Act (which uses

community property principles are influencing "common law" jurisdictions (i.e., those that have not adopted community property). Then we turn back in time to the common law doctrine of dower, which still applies in a few states. The discussion next shifts to this sections' principal topic, the evolving right of a surviving spouse to claim a share of a decedent spouse's wealth in a common law state. The section then views the problems posed for couples who move between common law and community property jurisdictions. The section closes with a look at contracts spouses can use to adjust (or waive) their rights.

A. Community Property

Community property states have created a form of property ownership that recognizes the mutuality of marital relationships. Basically, community property includes (1) property acquired through the efforts of either spouse during the marriage and while domiciled in a community property jurisdiction and (2) income or proceeds from the sale of community property. For example, rather than treating spouses' earnings as the separate property of each, this doctrine lumps together both spouses' earnings and calls them "community property." In contrast, property each spouse brings into the marriage (or acquires by gift or inheritance intended for themselves individually) is called "separate property."

Each spouse owns one-half of the community property and all of his or her separate property. In general, each spouse can manage the community property, but transfers of real estate or substantial gifts to third parties usually require the consent of both spouses. At death, both spouses usually have the power to dispose of their own separate property and half of the community property. Sometimes one spouse's will tries to dispose of both spouses' shares, for example, by putting all the community property in a trust for the survivor, with a remainder to the children. In that circumstance, the survivor faces a choice (traditionally called a "widow's election") between claiming either the trust benefits or the survivor's share of the community property.

Because the next case comes from Wisconsin, it uses the term "marital property" where other jurisdictions would use "community property." The problems it covers, however, transcend the different terminology.

---

different terminology, but basically adopts the same system) and should also be counted as a community property state. In these states, couples have various ways to "opt out" of the system that otherwise applies. In contrast, Alaska allows its couples to choose to hold assets as community property; Arkansas, South Dakota, and Tennessee allow couples to create community property trusts. The purpose for these statutes is to facilitate favorable income tax treatment for the surviving spouse by obtaining a step-up in basis under IRC § 1014(b)(6). The Service has not ruled on whether this tax advantage will be allowed.

In re Kobylski

503 N.W.2d 369 (Wis. Ct. App. 1993)

Nettesheim[, P.J.]

. . . The principal issues on this appeal concern the "mixed property" provisions of sec. 766.63, Stats., of Wisconsin's Marital Property Act (MPA). Genevieve Hellstern's estate appeals from a judgment in favor of Genevieve's surviving husband, Geza Hellstern. The estate challenges the probate court's determination that a residence, titled in Genevieve's name and brought to the marriage by her, was reclassified to marital property. . . .

We reverse the probate court's ruling that the residence was reclassified to marital property and we remand for further proceedings on this issue. . . .

I. FACTS

Genevieve, age 58, and Geza, age 71, married on February 20, 1982. At that time, both were widowed and had children from their prior marriages. Their marriage produced no children.

At the time of the marriage, Genevieve owned a residence where she and her first husband had lived and raised their children. Genevieve and Geza lived in this residence for the duration of their marriage. Genevieve retained title to the property in her own name. During the marriage, Genevieve and Geza made several improvements to the residence that were paid for by funds from their joint checking and savings accounts. They also used these accounts to pay for property taxes, utilities, insurance and other household expenses. Additionally, Geza painted the interior and exterior of the residence, assisted Genevieve's son in enlarging the one-car garage, and did the yard work. . . .

In June 1979, three years before Genevieve and Geza married, Genevieve executed her will which distributed her entire estate to her four children from her prior marriage. Following Genevieve's death in June 1990, Geza filed notice to take under the widower's election of deferred and augmented marital property. . . . Geza sought either: (1) reimbursement for the funds expended on the residence for improvements if the probate court ruled that the residence was Genevieve's nonmarital property, or (2) the value of his one-half marital interest in the residence if the court ruled that the residence was reclassified to marital property because he and Genevieve had contributed marital funds for improvements and because he also had applied uncompensated labor to improve the residence. The estate objected to Geza's claims. . . .

The probate court ruled in Geza's favor on all issues. The court held that the residence was mixed property under sec. 766.63, Stats., of the MPA because "substantive labor, efforts and marital cash were applied" during the marriage. The court further ruled that the residence was reclassified to marital property because "tracing is [not] possible." The court therefore awarded Geza the value of a one-half interest in the residence. . . .

II. MARITAL PROPERTY LAW

. . . .

B. Marital Property Principles Generally

All property of married persons either is, or is presumed to be, marital property unless it is proven to be otherwise. . . . Likewise, any property determined not to be marital property is presumed to be deferred marital property and may be subject to a surviving spouse's elective rights. . . . At death, the deceased spouse may freely dispose of only the one-half interest the decedent owns in each item of marital property. The decedent may also dispose of the whole of each item of his or her nonmarital property. . . .

Despite the MPA's presumption that all spousal property is marital, spouses are permitted to own individual and predetermination date property [owned before Wisconsin switched from a common law to a community property system]. . . . [D]uring marriage, predetermination date property is treated as if it were individual property, and at death it may be subject to a deferred marital property analysis if the marital property presumption is overcome.

The party challenging the marital property (or deferred marital property) presumption has the burden to establish that the property at issue is not marital. . . . Demonstrating that the time, method or source of the property's acquisition establishes the property as nonmarital rebuts the presumption as to that item of property. . . .

III. THE RESIDENCE

The probate court concluded that Genevieve's nonmarital residence was reclassified to marital property under sec. 766.63(1) and (2), Stats., because "substantive labor, efforts and marital cash were applied" during the marriage and "tracing is [not] possible . . . as unreimbursed labor is involved." We construe the court's ruling as resting upon two independent determinations under sec. 766.63: (1) Genevieve and Geza's use of their marital funds for improvements to the residence constituted a mixing of marital and nonmarital property which reclassified the residence to marital property pursuant to sec. 766.63(1) because its nonmarital component could not be traced, and (2) the application of Geza's substantial uncompensated labor to the residence served to reclassify the residence under sec. 766.63(2) because the value of the labor could not be traced. We address each of these determinations in turn.

A. Mixing Marital Property With Nonmarital Property Pursuant to Sec. 766.63(1), Stats.

1. Trial Court Ruling

The probate court made the following factual findings, none of which is disputed on appeal. Genevieve owned the residence when she and Geza married, and she retained title in her sole name during her life. During the marriage, Geza received a pension and social security, while Genevieve received social security and the interest from her CD's. Generally, all of Genevieve's and Geza's funds were deposited into and transferred between their joint savings and checking accounts to pay for property taxes, utilities, insurance and other related residence expenses. After their determination date [Jan. 1, 1986, when the statute went into effect], the spouses paid $ 3970.08 from their joint checking account for improvements to the residence. . . .

2. Statutory Presumption

Ordinarily, we would begin any classification discussion under the MPA with the statutory presumption that all spousal property is marital property. . . . However, Geza's argument is premised upon a reclassification claim—a contention which necessarily concedes on a threshold basis that the residence is Genevieve's nonmarital property.[3] Thus, we begin our discussion in this case with the premise that the residence is Genevieve's nonmarital property and remained so unless reclassified.

3. Reclassification of Property Under the MPA

The MPA recognizes a variety of ways that reclassification may occur. Pursuant to sec. 766.31(10), Stats., a spouse may voluntarily reclassify his or her nonmarital property to marital property by, inter alia, gift, conveyance or marital property agreement. Geza's claim, however, does not rest on this statute. Instead, he claims that the property was reclassified pursuant to the mixed property provisions of sec. 766.63, Stats., which recognizes another method by which reclassification can occur. Under this statute, nonmarital property is reclassified to marital property if the two are mixed to the point where the nonmarital component of the property cannot be traced. However, if the "component of the mixed property which is not marital property can be traced," reclassification does not result. See sec. 766.63(1).

4. Burden of Proof in a Mixed Property Proceeding

Geza's reclassification claim is based on "mixing." As with any claimant, we conclude that the burden to establish mixing is properly assigned to Geza. If this burden is satisfied, the marital asset is reclassified "unless the component of the mixed property which is not marital property can be traced." Section 766.63(1), Stats. (emphasis added). We think it logical that the party seeking to avoid reclassification by establishing tracing should carry the burden to do so. . . . In this case, that party is the estate.

5. Tracing

In [*In re*] *Lloyd*, we addressed the tracing rules applicable to a reclassification claim under sec. 766.63, Stats. *Lloyd*, 170 Wis. 2d at 257–60, 487 N.W.2d at 653–54

Borrowing from divorce property division law, we performed an identity analysis. . . .

3. Even if we were to indulge in the statutory presumption, it is readily rebutted in this case because Genevieve owned the residence before the spouses' January 1, 1986 determination date. . . .

Identity addresses whether the nonmarital component has been preserved in some present identifiable form so that it can be meaningfully valued and assigned—in other words, "traced." . . . Thus, where individual or predetermination date property is mixed with marital property, the critical inquiry is whether, despite mixing, the nonmarital component of the property can be identified and valued. . . . At the same time, this inquiry is also used to determine the proportionate marital and nonmarital ownership.

6. Analysis

We now turn to the application of the statute to the facts of this case. As we have previously noted, Geza had the burden of establishing mixing. At trial, the documentary evidence established the following payments, totaling $ 3970.08, by Genevieve and Geza from their joint checking account for the following "improvements" to the residence:

New siding and gutters	$1016.00
New siding and gutters	500.00
Wind damage	150.00
Carpet purchase	490.28
Carpet installation	250.50
Garage door purchase	440.00
Labor paid to Peter Kobylski (new 2-car garage)	300.00
Sewer till replacement	219.00
Concrete for new garage	122.06
Building material for new garage	482.24

By this undisputed documentary evidence, Geza established that his and Genevieve's marital property was mixed with Genevieve's nonmarital property. Thus, Geza met his burden to establish mixing under the statute. The question then becomes whether "the component of the mixed property which is not marital property can be traced." Section 766.63(1), Stats. As we have already held, this burden to establish tracing was on the estate.

Here, the same evidence which shows mixing also demonstrates that tracing can be easily accomplished. The "paper trail" of Geza and Genevieve's contribution of their marital funds to Genevieve's nonmarital residence provides a ready basis for segregating the nonmarital component of the marital property. Therefore, the estate met its burden of tracing the residence's nonmarital component. We conclude that the probate court erred when it concluded that tracing was not possible.

7. The Remedy When Tracing Can Be Performed

This does not end our inquiry, however. As we have noted, sec. 766.63(1), Stats., precludes reclassification when tracing can be performed. However, the question remains as to what remedy other than reclassification the marital estate is entitled in such a setting. . . .

The majority of community property states hold that when marital funds are used to improve the separate property of one of the spouses and tracing is established, the improvements acquire the classification of the underlying property. . . . However, the marital estate has a right of reimbursement for the funds expended by the community for the improvements. . . . [4]

Many of the community property decisions which allow reimbursement, however, differ on whether the amount of reimbursement should be the actual amount expended by the community, the enhanced value attributable to the improvements, or whichever is less. . . .

In *Anderson* [*v. Gilliland*, 684 S.W.2d 673 (Tex. 1985)], the Texas Supreme Court had occasion to examine the measure of reimbursement for funds expended by the community to improve separate property of one of the spouses. There, the spouses spent $20,238 to build a home on a lot owned by the wife prior to the marriage. At the time of the husband's death, this improvement had increased the value of the wife's separate property by $54,000. The husband's estate sought to include in the estate one-half the reimbursement due the community for the improvements to the wife's separate property. . . .

[T]he Texas Supreme Court ultimately ruled that a claim for reimbursement is measured by the enhancement in value to the benefited estate, stating:

> The "cost only" rule, if followed, would provide an easy-to-apply measure since it would not require proof of enhancement. However, such a rule would, in many instances, permit the owner of the benefited estate to be enriched at the expense of the contributing estate. This is true because the estate which contributes the capital necessary to construct the improvements would not share in the increase in value resulting from the investment. The "enhancement or cost, whichever is less" rule, however, would permit the benefited estate the maximum recovery at the expense of the contributing estate in all situations. This does not comport with equity.

---

4. There are two theories for dealing with the issue of mixing marital and nonmarital property:(1) the spouses' contribution of marital to nonmarital property creates an ownership interest in the asset based on the classification of funds contributed, and (2) one spouse will own the asset as nonmarital property and the other spouse will be entitled to a right of reimbursement for the marital property funds expended. . . . The community property states have adopted variations of either "reimbursement" or "community ownership" theories. Common to both theories is the general concept that the community should receive whatever remuneration is paid to a spouse for his or her time and effort because the time and effort of each spouse belongs to the community. Though sharing a common conceptual basis, the two theories diverge when it comes to valuation of the community's claim against separately owned stock that has appreciated by virtue of a spouse's time and effort. The "reimbursement" theory provides that the stock, as it appreciates, remains the separate property of the owner spouse. Under this theory, the community is entitled to reimbursement for the reasonable value of the time and effort of both or either of the spouses which contributed to the increase in value of the stock. The "community ownership" theory, on the other hand, holds that any increase in the value of the stock as a result of the time and effort of the owner spouse becomes community property. . . .

Anderson, 684 S.W.2d at 675. *See also Portillo* [*v. Shappie*, 636 P.2d 878] at 883 [(N.M. 1981)] (tying the community's recovery to the amount of money spent may produce results which, depending on the circumstances, would be unfair to either the separate estate or the community. By treating such expenditures as an equity investment of community funds, rather than a loan, the community shares in the fluctuations of the market, taking both the gains and the losses).

We are persuaded by the *Anderson/Portillo* rationale that measuring reimbursement by the enhancement in value to the property is more likely to ensure the equitable treatment of both the contributing estate and the benefited estate in most situations. The rule is sensible and consistent with the equitable principles of our MPA, and we expressly adopt it here. *See* sec. 766.95, Stats. Where marital funds are used to improve the separate property of one of the spouses, a claim for reimbursement exists in favor of the marital estate measured by the property's enhanced value attributable to the improvements, not the amount of marital funds actually expended.[5] Thus, expenditures that relate merely to the maintenance of the property or which do not enhance the property's value are not to be considered. The party seeking such reimbursement has the burden of demonstrating that the improvement funds expended have enhanced the value of the spouse's separate property and the amount of enhancement. . . .

. . . [S]ince this is the first Wisconsin appellate case to speak to this issue, we conclude that the fairer approach is to remand for further proceedings to allow the parties to present additional evidence on this question. Following such proceedings, the court shall determine which of the expenditures relate to mere maintenance of the property and which constitute improvements to the property. As to the latter, the court shall also determine the amount, if any, by which Genevieve and Geza's contributions of their marital property enhanced the value of the residence. The court shall then fix Geza's recovery accordingly.

B. Mixing Industry With Nonmarital Property Pursuant to Sec. 766.63(2), Stats.

. . . .

Geza's claim also was made pursuant to sec. 766.63(2), Stats., which recognizes a second type of mixing: a spouse's contribution of uncompensated industry to the other spouse's nonmarital property. The statute provides:

> (2) Application by one spouse of substantial labor, effort, inventiveness, physical or intellectual skill, creativity or managerial activity to either spouse's property other than marital property creates marital property attributable to that application if both of the following apply:

5. Of course, because a spouse may freely dispose of the one-half interest he or she has in each item of marital property, . . . a surviving spouse would only be entitled to one-half the reimbursement amount to which the marital estate is entitled.

(a) Reasonable compensation is not received for the application.

(b) Substantial appreciation of the property results from the application.

It is important to note that, unlike subsec. (1) of the statute, this subsection does not contemplate any reclassification of existing nonmarital property to marital property. Rather, it contemplates creation of a marital property interest attributable to the application of the industry. In this case, therefore, Geza's industry created a marital property component in Genevieve's nonmarital residence if:

(1) Geza applied substantial labor or skill to the residence, (2) Geza received no reasonable compensation for his efforts, and (3) the efforts produced a substantial appreciation of the residence.

Geza testified that during the marriage he painted the interior and exterior of the residence, assisted Genevieve's son in enlarging the one-car garage, and did the yard work around the residence. Further, he testified that he received no compensation from Genevieve for these efforts....

Before applying the statute to the facts, we first address burden of proof considerations in an "industry mixing" claim under sec. 766.63(2), Stats. Just as with a "property mixing" claim under subsec. (1), we conclude that an "industry mixing" claim under subsec. (2) requires the claimant to establish the contribution of the industry. This burden lies with Geza in this case.

However, unlike a subsec. (1) "property mixing" case in which the mixing produces reclassification of the property unless tracing can be performed, a subsec. (2) "industry mixing" case does not produce any reclassification. Instead, if mixing is established, the statute provides that marital property is created to the extent of the additional value of the property attributable to the industry. Thus, unlike a "property mixing" case, the statute does not require proof of tracing; rather, it presumes such as a matter of law if substantial appreciation can be established. Therefore, the burden does not shift to the other spouse to establish tracing....

We now apply the statute to the facts of this case. For two reasons, we conclude that certain of the probate court's findings do not satisfy the legal standard set out under sec. 766.63(2), Stats., and thus do not support its ultimate conclusion awarding Geza a marital property interest in the residence.

First, under the very words of the statute, the application of substantial uncompensated labor to a spouse's nonmarital property followed by substantial appreciation thereof does not serve to reclassify the whole or any portion of the property to marital property. Rather, it creates marital property, and then only to the extent of the additional value of the property that is attributable to the substantial uncompensated labor.... Thus, the probate court's conclusion that the property was totally reclassified was error.

Second, we conclude that certain of Geza's labors and efforts do not constitute the "substantial" contribution required by the statute. Although the statute offers no insight as to what constitutes "substantial" effort, § 14 of the Uniform Marital

Property Act is identical to sec. 766.63, Stats. The comment to § 14 related to physical labor explains substantial effort as follows:

> The rule of the section is strict. It articulates a bias against creation of marital property from such an act unless the effort has been substantial and has been responsible for substantial appreciation. Routine, normal, and usual effort is not substantial. [. . .]

Unif. Marital Property Act § 14 comment, 9A U.L.A. 131–32 (1987). . . .

Under the facts of this case, we conclude that Geza's painting and yard work, without more, qualify only as routine, normal and usual maintenance of the property and did not operate to create a marital property component in Genevieve's nonmarital residence. . . . Therefore, we additionally reverse this portion of the probate court's ruling.

We do agree, however, with the probate court's conclusion that Geza's efforts and labors in enlarging the garage qualified as a "substantial" contribution of industry. But this satisfies only half the statute since the industry must also produce a "substantial appreciation" of the nonmarital asset. Here, the probate court concluded that there was no evidence of an increase in market value. Nonetheless, the court reasoned that Geza had established substantial appreciation because his efforts had contributed to the "utility and comfort of the home." While the court's ruling was an attempt to do fairness, it does not comport with the statutory requirement of substantial appreciation. Fair or not, the legislature has decreed that the contributing party cannot recover for uncompensated substantial industry if there is no resulting substantial appreciation.

As with the preceding issue, . . . we choose to remand for reconsideration and further evidence, if the parties wish, on the question of substantial appreciation.

Question and Notes

1. In light of the movement toward equal treatment of women, why haven't other common law states followed Wisconsin and turned to a community property system?

2. *Kobylski* illustrates that record keeping is important if a couple wants to maintain both separate and community property. For example, property purchased with community funds is itself community property, as is property purchased with a combination of separate and community funds that have been commingled. Compensation for personal injuries suffered during marriage generally is separate property. On the other hand, jurisdictions differ about whether to treat income from separate property as separate or community property. When someone uses both separate and community funds to acquire an asset over time, the asset may be part "separate" and part "community."

3. ERISA, the federal statute regulating retirement plans and employee benefits, preempts local laws that otherwise would apply to accounts covered by the statute. *See Boggs v. Boggs*, 520 U.S. 833 (1997) (Louisiana community-property law preempted).

4. After we have examined other systems for protecting spousal interests, we will return to community property in the context of addressing problems that arise when couples change their domicile.

Problems

1. Sue owned a consulting firm when she married Warren. Her continued efforts after her marriage greatly increased the firm's value. How and to what extent, if any, should Warren share the benefits of Sue's labor after Sue's death?

2. Lew and Grace are married and live in a community property state. Lew had paid $20,000 toward his home before he married Grace. Over the first several years of the marriage, Lew finished the purchase by paying another $20,000 out of his earnings. Lew's will left all of his separate and community property to his daughter, Annique. The house is now worth $90,000. What is Annique's share of the house?

Washington appears to be the only state that applies community property principles to non-marital couples in the absence of something more, like registration. *See Oliver v. Fowler*, 168 P.3d 448 (Wash. 2007). *Compare* Cal. Fam. Code § 297.5(a) (registered domestic partners treated as spouses).

Selected References

Jonathan G. Blattmachr, Howard M. Zaritsky & Mark L. Ascher, *Tax Planning with Consensual Community Property: Alaska's New Community Property Law*, 33 Real Prop. Prob. & Tr. J. 615 (1999).

Kathy T. Graham, *The Uniform Marital Property Act: A Solution for Common Law Property Systems?*, 48 S.D. L. Rev. 455 (2003).

David R. Knauss, *What Part of Yours Is Mine?: The Creation of a Marital Property Ownership Interest by Improving Nonmarital Property Under Wisconsin's Marital Property Law*, 2005 Wis. L. Rev. 855.

B. Dower

In creating protections for surviving spouses, the common law distinguished between widowers and widows. A widower received a life estate in all of the lands his wife owned during the marriage, if issue who could inherit the land were born of that marriage. The widower's right, granted "by the curtesy of England," came to be called "curtesy." A widow, on the other hand, received a life estate in one-third of the lands her husband owned during the marriage; issue were not required, but the estate to which the right attached had to be one that issue could inherit if they were born. The widow's right was called "dower." Most states have abolished both doctrines. Because of equal protection concerns, most of those that have retained dower and curtesy have collapsed them into a single right, available to both men and women.

Dower and curtesy had some utility in a society in which most of the wealth was held as land, but do not work very well to protect surviving spouses today. In particular, most of our wealth is now personal property, to which the doctrines do not apply. There is also a downside to the doctrines: they tend to clog land titles. As a practical matter, the right of modern spouses to elect against a will has replaced dower and curtesy.

Note

As a practical matter, a homestead allowance assures surviving spouses some protection against being left with nothing. The extent of the allowance, however, varies widely among the states. *See* Chapter 1.

Problem

Blake owned a house when he married Ellen. Later, Blake put the house into a joint tenancy between himself and his daughter, Erika.

(a) In a state recognizing dower, does Ellen have any dower interest in the house?

(b) What if Blake had created the joint tenancy before his marriage to Ellen?

Selected References

Areila R. Dubler, *In the Shadow of Marriage: Single Women and the Legal Construction of the Family and the State*, 112 Yale L.J. 1641 (2003).

Joslyn R. Muller, *Haven't Women Obtained Equality? An Analysis of the Constitutionality of Dower in Michigan*, 87 U. Det. Mercy L. Rev. 533 (2010).

C. The Right to Elect

Except in community property states and Georgia, surviving spouses have the right to claim a share of their predeceased spouse's estate.[6] The size of the share varies among different jurisdictions, as does the size of the "estate" to which the right attaches. First, we will discuss the traditional approach to structuring an elective

6. Georgia offers a surviving spouse only a "year's support." Ga. Code Ann. § 53-5-1.

share. Then we will examine some exceptions to the traditional rules. Finally, we will close with a look at the two waves of reform the UPC has generated.

1. *The Basics*

Elective share statutes developed as an alternative to dower. In states where dower has not been abolished, spouses are often given the choice of whether to claim dower or an elective share (which may also be called "dower"). Regardless of a will's provisions, under traditional elective share statutes a surviving spouse can claim a share of the decedent's probate estate.

While shares of one-third or one-half are common, states take a variety of approaches to determining just what the elective share should be. The share may parallel the spouse's share under the local intestate succession statute. Sometimes other schemes appear, basing shares upon various factors, such as the number of children. Some statutes reflect their origins in dower.

One problem, which will become increasingly common as our population ages, is how to handle elections on behalf of incompetent surviving spouses. Often statutes allow such elections when they would be in the "best interests" of the surviving spouse. Some courts say "best interests" includes all of the facts and circumstances surrounding a particular case, while others focus more narrowly on the monetary value of the election. *Compare Kinnett v. Hood*, 185 N.E.2d 888 (Ill. 1962) (court denied a petition to renounce a will which created a trust for the decedent's incompetent wife because the will "was designed to protect her best interests"), with *In re Estate of Clarkson*, 226 N.W.2d 334 (Neb. 1975) (Court allowed election to take money out of trust, because ownership unencumbered by a trust is more valuable. Because the spouse was incompetent, however, a guardianship would be required), and *In re Estate of Cross*, 664 N.E.2d 905 (Ohio 1996) (election required because non-election would leave spouse both without Medicaid eligibility and without funds). *See also In re Estate of Shipman,* 832 N.W.2d 335 (S.D. 2013) (invalidating purported "disclaimer" of right to elect by incompetent spouse's son acting under power of attorney).

The UPC places elective property in trust for an incompetent survivor. UPC § 2-212(b). At the survivor's death, anything left passes under the predeceased spouse's will or to the predeceased spouse's intestate heirs. UPC § 2-212(c)(3).

Exercising an elective share necessarily disrupts any estate plan. The property to satisfy the share must come from somewhere. Some states place the burden on the residuary takers of the decedent's will. Others share the burden among all of the beneficiaries. If the electing spouse were giving up a life estate, a court might "sequester" the life estate and use the income to reimburse beneficiaries particularly disadvantaged by the election. For example, *Sellick v. Sellick*, 173 N.W. 609 (Mich. 1919), involved an election against William Sellick's will, which included gifts to several people and gave his wife, Caroline, a life estate in $25,000, with the remainder to William's niece and nephew. Under the local rule, Caroline's elective share came at the expense of the residuary beneficiary. Instead of treating Caroline as predeceased and accelerating the remainder following her life estate, the court "sequestered" the $25,000 during Caroline's life. The income from this $25,000 was paid to the residuary beneficiary to diminish the amount of his disappointment. Upon Caroline's death, the remainder would pass to the niece and nephew.

Notes and Questions

1. After Thomas left Joyce, she filed for divorce. Before the divorce was final, Thomas died, so Joyce lost her claim to equitable distribution of their property. Because she and Thomas were living apart at his death, Joyce had no right to an elective share under New Jersey's statute. Rather than leave her with nothing, the court held she could assert a constructive trust against the marital property in Thomas' estate. *Carr v. Carr*, 576 A.2d 872 (N.J. 1990).

2. Irving Berk, 99, married his caretaker, Hua Wang, 47, two months after he had been diagnosed with dementia. After Irving died, Hua's election against his will presented a question of fact regarding whether she forfeited her right to election by marrying for the purpose of obtaining pecuniary benefits that become available by virtue of being the decedent's spouse. *In re Berk*, 897 N.Y.S.2d 475 (App. Div. 2010).

3. In addition to the elective share, states offer a variety of protections or preferences for surviving spouses. The details vary widely, but topics include homestead provisions (protecting against the decedent's creditors), rights to claim various pieces of personal property, first options on the family home, and support allowances. *See, e.g.*, UPC §§ 2-401 to 2-405. *See also* § 2.01(D) of this text.

4. Should a domestic partner have a right to elect against the decedent's will? *See, e.g.*, 15 Vt. Stat. Ann. § 1204(b) ("spouse" includes parties to a civil union, so same-sex civil union partners have the right to elect). How about committed couples? *See generally* Lawrence W. Waggoner, *With Marriage on the Decline and Cohabitation on the Rise, What About Marital Rights for Unmarried Partners?*, 41 ACTEC L.J. 49 (2015).

5. Under the UPC, the trust established for an incompetent surviving spouse eventually passes back through the estate of the spouse against whom the election was made. Should that property pass instead according to the surviving spouse's will?

6. In England, a court can order that an appropriate amount of a decedent's property be placed in trust, to be used for the surviving spouse and children, as "would be reasonable in all circumstances." Inheritance Act 1975, § 2(b). Is such a system preferable to our fixed-share election system?

7. Suppose a couple agrees not to revoke their wills, one spouse dies, and the survivor leaves the will intact. If the survivor remarries and the new spouse exercises a right of election, should the contract be honored before the elective share is calculated?

Selected References

Julia Belian, *Medicaid, Elective Shares, and the Ghosts of Tenures Past*, 38 Creighton L. Rev. 1111 (2005).

Paul J. Buser, *Domestic Partner and Non-Marital Claims Against Probate Estates: Marvin Theories Put to a Different Use*, 38 Fam. L.Q. 315 (2004).

2. Exceptions

Because traditional elective share statutes apply only to the probate estate, people who want to defeat their spouse's claims often shift their wealth into forms which will not pass through probate and, therefore, will not be subject to election.

Some courts and legislatures have found troubling the specter of someone "emptying" the probate estate to defeat a surviving spouse's claim. Various theories protect a disinherited spouse by extending the right of election to non-probate assets. It may be helpful to group most of the cases along two general—but not clearly delineated—lines. One approach focuses on intent (sometimes "fraudulent" intent), and tends to consider a variety of factors, giving different weight to each in particular instances.[7] Courts sometimes consider motive, timing, the amount of support otherwise available to the spouse, or the relationship of the spouses.

Rather than using the language of fraud, most jurisdictions ask (in one way or another) whether there has been an illusory transfer, an approach popularized by *Newman v. Dore*, 9 N.E.2d 966 (N.Y. 1937). There the court allowed an election against a trust the testator had established three days before he died, retaining income to himself for life and powers to control the trust administration. The court asked whether the testator "in good faith divested himself of ownership of his property or has made an illusory transfer." 9 N.E.2d at 969. The required good faith referred not to the purpose of disinheriting his wife, but rather whether he intended to give up his ownership in the property. In most states taking this approach, the question is not whether the spouse is being disinherited, but rather whether the transfer was effective in property law terms. If so, the surviving spouse has no claim.

Sometimes courts confuse the issue by speaking of "fraud" when they are really talking about something else. Sometimes "intent" doesn't refer to fraudulent intent, but intent to make an incomplete (aka "illusory") transfer. In a long opinion, the Supreme Court of Maryland sought to explain and clarify its approach in *Karsenty v. Schoukroun*, 959 A.2d 1147 (Md. 2008). In the process, it refers to several terms used in other cases.

---

7. Although Kentucky employs the fraudulent transfer approach with respect to property transferred by a deceased spouse, life insurance is not considered such an asset. *See Bays v. Kiphart*, 486 S.W.3d 283 (Ky. 2016).

> ... [T]he body of precedents forming the doctrine that, until now, has been referred to as 'fraud on marital rights' has really little to do with common law fraud as typically understood....
>
> ... [W]hen a surviving spouse seeks to invalidate the non-probate disposition of an asset, a scrutinizing court must focus on the nature of the underlying *inter vivos* transfer. If it was "complete and bona fide" or done in "good faith" (both phrases meaning the same thing in this context), the court must respect the estate planning arrangements of the decedent and may not invalidate the transaction; however if it was "a mere device or contrivance," "a mere fiction," "a sham," or "colorable" (each also sharing the same meaning in this context), the court shall invalidate the underlying transaction as to the surviving spouse.... In order to answer this question, a court must consider whether the decedent truly intended that the *inter vivos* transfer divest her or him of ownership in form, but not in substance.

Id. at 1151, 1172–73. Under Maryland's approach, factors relevant to that determination include: the extent the decedent retained an interest in, actual enjoyment of, or control over the transferred property; whether the transfer was part of a reasonable and legitimate estate planning arrangement; the decedent's motives (e.g., to keep a business in the family); the survivor's motives (e.g., acting under an implicit understanding that the transfer was not real); and the degree to which the survivor would be deprived of assets they would otherwise expect to inherit; the familial relationship between the decedent and those who would benefit from the transfer. *See also In re Estate of Thompson,* 434 S.W.3d 877 (Ark. 2014) (following *Karsenty*).

In response to the uncertainty of those approaches, some courts have adopted an objective test based on the power the decedent—as a practical matter—had over property. The following case debates which property should be subject to spousal election, and along the way asks who—courts or legislatures—should be deciding that question.

Bongaards v. Millen

793 N.E.2d 335 (Mass. 2003)

SOSMAN, J.

The plaintiff filed a complaint in the Probate and Family Court, seeking a declaration that certain property held in trust by his deceased wife, Jean Bongaards (Jean), should be considered part of her estate for purposes of determining his elective share under G.L. c. 191, § 15, the statute permitting a surviving spouse to waive will provisions and elect instead to receive a statutory portion of the estate of the deceased spouse. The plaintiff's first amended complaint also asserted that assets in a bank savings account maintained by Jean should be subject to his elective share.... [T]he judge rejected both claims . . . and the Appeals Court affirmed in part and reversed in part. . . . The Appeals Court concluded that the prospective rule announced by this court in *Sullivan v. Burkin*, 390 Mass. 864, 867, 460 N.E.2d 572 (1984) (*Sullivan*), which treats assets of certain types of trusts as part of a decedent's estate for purposes of G.L. c. 191, § 15, did not apply to Jean's trust, but that the bank savings account should have been included in the elective share estate. . . . We now conclude that the result reached by the Appeals Court was correct. . . .

1. Facts.

In 1978, Josephine D'Amore, who was Jean's mother, created the 291 Commonwealth Avenue Trust (trust) and conveyed to the trust real estate consisting of an apartment building located at that address in Boston. D'Amore declared herself the sole trustee and sole beneficiary of the trust during her lifetime. The terms of the trust provided that, on D'Amore's death, her daughter Jean would, if she accepted, become the sole trustee and sole lifetime beneficiary.

D'Amore intended the trust property to pass solely to her children and then to her grandchildren. The trust incorporated by reference a schedule of beneficiaries, which provided D'Amore a life estate and, following the termination of D'Amore's life estate, a life estate to Jean, and then to D'Amore's living grand-children [or others as Jean might appoint]. . . . After D'Amore's death and until Jean appointed one or more successor beneficiaries, the terms of the trust permitted Jean . . . to amend the terms of the trust or to terminate the trust and vest title to the trust property in herself individually.

In 1979, D'Amore executed a deed, signed by her as an individual, which purported to convey the real estate to Jean [but] . . . made no reference to the trust. D'Amore died later that year. Jean and the plaintiff, who had lived in one of the apartments at 291 Commonwealth Avenue since their marriage in 1965, continued to live there, and Jean managed the property until her death.

In 1988, Jean executed a certificate of acceptance of her appointment as trustee. This document apparently was never recorded. On July 19, 1996, Jean executed the following documents: a second acceptance of her appointment as trustee (which subsequently was recorded); . . . and an amendment inserting a so-called spendthrift clause into the trust document. At the same time, Jean executed a confirmatory deed . . . to herself as trustee. That document's stated purpose was "to clarify any such potential uncertainty or conflict" stemming from the 1979 deed and "to the extent that clear title [to the property] is not already held by said Trust or the Trustee thereof, then it shall be so transferred to the said Trustee by virtue of this deed." Jean died ten days later on July 28, 1996.

During her lifetime, Jean maintained a bank savings account in the name of "Jean A. Bongaards ATF [as trustee for] Nina Millen." Jean retained the power to withdraw funds from the account at any time. . . . Her will stated that she intentionally had not provided for her husband, the plaintiff.

2. Discussion.

. . . .

The question before us is whether Jean's estate, for purposes of determining the plaintiff's statutory share, includes the property located at 291 Commonwealth Avenue and the funds in the bank savings account.

a. The trust property.

[The court rejected claims that the trust was not valid and that estoppel should apply to ignore the trust.] . . .

(iii) Inclusion of trust property in the elective share estate pursuant to Sullivan.

We now turn to the plaintiff's argument that the property, regardless that it was held by Jean at all times in a valid inter vivos trust created by her mother in 1978, should nevertheless be part of Jean's estate subject to his elective share, pursuant to principles expressed in *Sullivan*. . . .

Until 1984, the rule of this Commonwealth was that spouses had an absolute right to dispose of any or all of their personal property in their lifetime, with the result that it would not form part of their "estate" subject to their spouse's elective share at their death. See *Kerwin v. Donaghy*, 317 Mass. 559, 571, 59 N.E.2d 299 (1945). It was thus possible for a husband effectively to disinherit his wife, without her knowledge or consent, by transferring his property into a trust created for his own benefit during his lifetime, with the sole purpose of removing the property from his estate at death and thereby preventing his wife from asserting her rights under G.L. c. 191, § 15. See id. This court's decision in Sullivan eliminated this option.

In *Sullivan*, the husband had conveyed real estate to an inter vivos trust, with himself as trustee. He retained the right to the income, as well as the right to revoke the trust at any time, and directed that, on his death, the principal and any undistributed income were to be paid to two other persons, neither of whom was his wife. The husband intentionally left no provision in his will for his wife. *See id.* at 865. Considering the wife's claim to an elective share of the trust, the court concluded that, because *Kerwin v. Donaghy, supra*, had been the law for almost forty years, and because counsel and clients were entitled to rely on that precedent, the wife was not entitled to a statutory share of the trust assets. *Sullivan, supra* at 870-871. The court went on to state:

> For the future, however, as to any inter vivos trust created or amended after the date of this opinion, we announce that the estate of a decedent, for the purposes of G.L. c. 191, § 15, shall include the value of assets held in an inter vivos trust *created by the deceased spouse* as to which the deceased spouse alone retained the power during his or her life to direct the disposition of those trust assets for his or her benefit, as, for example, by the exercise of a power of appointment or by revocation of the trust. (emphasis added).

Id. at 867. Rather than engage in the difficult analyses other jurisdictions had employed to prevent a spouse's evasion of the elective share statute by way of an inter vivos trust (e.g., analysis of the deceased spouse's "motive" or "intention," or the "illusory" or "fraudulent" nature of the spouse's creation of the trust), the court prospectively adopted a bright-line rule that a spouse's creation of a trust over which the spouse alone retained control would not suffice to defeat the surviving spouse's interest in the property placed in that trust....

Under that rule ... the trust property at issue here is ... not subject to the plaintiff's elective share for the simple reason that the trust was created by a third party, D'Amore, and not by Jean. The rule announced in Sullivan applies only to assets of a trust "created during the marriage by the deceased spouse." *Id.* at 872. This limitation on the rule announced in *Sullivan* was based, in part, on principles set forth in the then current publication of the American Law Institute on the issue of a surviving spouse's rights to assets of an inter vivos trust held by the deceased spouse, the Restatement (Second) of Property: Donative Transfers, Supplement to Tent. Draft No. 5 (1984), now embodied in the Restatement (Second) Property: Donative Transfers § 13.7 (1986). *See Sullivan, supra* at 869. Section 13.7 treated trust assets as assets of a deceased spouse for purposes of determining a surviving spouse's elective share "if the deceased spouse was both the donor and donee of a general power of appointment that was exercisable by the donee alone, unless the controlling statute provides otherwise." Assets in a trust created by a third person were specifically excluded, even though the deceased spouse may have held a general power of appointment. *See* Restatement (Second) of Property: Donative Transfers, *supra* at § 13.7 comment a (section applies "if, and only if, the donor and donee were the same person," and assets are not part of elective share estate "when the donor and donee were different persons"). Accordingly, the rule of Sullivan does not apply to the trust established by D'Amore.

The plaintiff contends that, even though the property was placed in the trust by D'Amore and not by Jean, Jean's control over the property under the terms of the trust was so great that the property should be included in Jean's estate for purposes of G.L. c. 191, § 15. This contention is not a valid basis for ignoring the restrictions of the Sullivan rule, which is already premised on the spouse having effective control over the trust and its assets....

(iv) Proposed modification of the Sullivan rule to include all "marital property" in the elective share estate.

A more expansive rationale for reaching the result urged by the plaintiff has been advanced by the amicus, the Women's Bar Association of Massachusetts. That rationale, although echoing some of the *Sullivan* court's reasons for over-ruling *Kerwin v. Donaghy, supra*, should not be extended in the far-reaching and literal manner now suggested. Sullivan noted that, since the court's decision in Kerwin, "the interests of one spouse in the property of the other have been substantially increased upon the dissolution of a marriage by divorce." *Sullivan, supra* at 872. In the wake of those changes in the divorce laws, the court observed that "it is neither equitable nor logical to extend to a divorced spouse greater rights in the assets of an inter vivos trust created and controlled by the other spouse than are extended to a spouse who remains married until the death of his or her spouse" (emphasis added). *Id.* The amicus suggests—and one of today's dissenting opinions essentially agrees—that we should now ignore the limiting language in that observation from *Sullivan* and simply include in the elective share estate any property, including any trust assets, that would have been treated as marital property to be divided on divorce.

Before turning to the specific defects in that proposed equation of property rights on divorce with property rights upon a spouse's death, we note a fundamental flaw in the entire analysis, namely, that it completely ignores basic principles of statutory construction. At issue here is the definition of the term "estate of the deceased" in G.L. c. 191, § 15. Under the statute, a surviving spouse may waive the provisions of the decedent spouse's will and "claim such portion of the estate of the deceased as he or she is given the right to claim under this section" (emphasis added). *Id.* . . . The question before us is what "estate" the Legislature intended as the "estate" to be divided under that formula. . . .

. . . [T]here does not appear to be any ambiguity in the Legislature's use of the term "estate of the deceased" in G.L. c. 191, § 15. In context, "estate of the deceased" refers to the decedent's probate estate. . . .

Regardless whether changing times and the modern array of possible will substitutes may make it advisable to expand the term beyond the mere probate estate, we are not at liberty to update statutes merely because, in our view, they no longer suffice to serve their intended purpose. This is particularly true when the Legislature itself has recently considered numerous proposals to modernize the elective share statute, with differing approaches regarding how the elective share should be harmonized with contemporary concepts of marriage and property, and has yet to adopt any of them. . . . That the current version of the statute is woefully inadequate to satisfy modern notions of a decedent spouse's obligation to support the surviving spouse or modern notions of marital property does not authorize us to tinker with the statute's provisions in order to remedy those inadequacies. It is up to the Legislature to choose between the complex—and apparently controversial—options for modernizing this outdated scheme, not up to us to modernize it piecemeal according to our views of what remedies should be made available to a disinherited spouse.

It could be argued that *Sullivan* already represents such a tinkering with the definition of "estate" for purposes of G.L. c. 191, § 15, and that ordinary principles of statutory construction should therefore not prevent us from continuing the process begun in *Sullivan*. However, that justification for a significant expansion of the term "estate" in G.L. c. 191, § 15, ignores the fact that Sullivan merely closed a loophole through which spouses had been able to evade § 15. As articulated in *Sullivan*, what was to remain part of the "estate" subject to the elective share was property that previously belonged to the deceased spouse. But for the spouse's artificially distancing the property from that "estate" by the creation of a trust while still, for all practical purposes, retaining absolute control over and use of the property, the property would have been part of the deceased spouse's probate, and hence the elective share, "estate." In other words, *Sullivan* kept in the elective share "estate" property that would ordinarily have been in that "estate," refusing to give effect to a spouse's attempt to remove that property from the elective share "estate" but still retain access to it by means of a "trust."

It is one thing for this court to plug loopholes to prevent a spouse's evasion of the elective share statute. It is quite another to expand the reach of the elective share statute itself and, by so doing, frustrate the intent of a third party who is a stranger to the marriage. The recognition in *Sullivan* that property in a trust created by a third party presents "a different situation" from property in a trust "created during the marriage by the deceased spouse," *id.* at 872, 873, was not some hypertechnical distinction. A third party has no obligation to support someone else's spouse, and property owned by a third party has never been part of someone else's spouse's elective share "estate." Thus, when a third party places that property in a trust, the property is not being removed—artificially or otherwise—from that elective share "estate." The property was never in that "estate" in the first place, and the only question before us is whether the settlor's giving of certain powers to a trustee who is (or later becomes) married will now, for the first time, place additional property into that elective share "estate" in contravention of the third-party settlor's plans with respect to the disposition of that property.[8] The proposed revision of the definition of "estate" to include trust property that was never, prior to the trust's creation, the property of either spouse is not designed merely to prevent evasion of the elective share statute. Rather, it would represent a judicially created expansion of the reach of the statute. It goes far beyond the modest prophylactic measure announced in *Sullivan* and cannot be justified as a mere "extension" of *Sullivan*.

Nor do we see substantive merit to the proposed equation of the "estate" for purposes of the elective share with the marital property of the decedent that would have been divisible if the couple had divorced. Whatever the superficial appeal of equating the two, it is an equation that does not withstand scrutiny....

On divorce, marital property is divided based on a judge's assessment of multiple factors—length of the marriage, conduct of the parties, age, health, occupation, amount and sources of income, vocational skills, employability, liabilities, needs of the children, needs of the spouses, "and the opportunity of each for future acquisition of capital assets and income." G.L. c. 208, § 34. The division of marital property also takes into account "the contribution of each of the parties in the acquisition, preservation or appreciation in value of their respective estates and the contribution of each of the parties as a homemaker to the family unit." Id. An expansive approach

8. *Sullivan* did not explicitly address how the elective share is to be satisfied if the decedent's probate estate is insufficient to pay the elective share that has been calculated including trust assets. However, as the Appeals Court noted, the *Sullivan* rule would have little practical effect unless the trust assets themselves could be reached to satisfy the spouse's claim.... While we have not addressed the issue directly, the logic of that analysis is compelling.

to what constitutes marital property is appropriate and fair, where that marital property will then be divided equitably based on the contributions, needs, and circumstances of the two divorcing spouses. Under that approach, trust assets available to a spouse are included in the marital property subject to equitable division in the judge's discretion based on the § 34 factors. . . .

By comparison, the elective share statute grants the surviving spouse a fixed percentage of the elective share "estate," based solely on the surviving spouse's unilateral decision to reject the decedent's will. . . . There is no assessment of the surviving spouse's needs, or the equities of that elective share percentage, or the equities of applying that percentage to a particular trust that was created and funded by some third party. Thus, if assets in a trust created by a third party are to be included in the elective share estate, there is no way of accounting equitably for the fact that the surviving spouse made no contribution toward the acquisition of that asset, and no way of accounting for the fact that the beneficiaries identified by the original settlor may have far greater need for the trust assets than does the surviving spouse. The expansive definition of marital property used in divorce cases causes no injustice, and indeed promotes justice, because of the fine-tuned and case-specific approach to the equitable distribution of that marital property. There is no such fine-tuned or case-specific approach in the elective share statute. . . .

It is also apparent that, on divorce, the fact that one spouse has considerable power over or access to trust assets is an important consideration in any equitable division of the marital estate, regardless of the source of those trust assets. While the spouse with such power over the trust may not have exercised that power yet, the spouse will continue to have that power after the divorce. . . .

The same is not true when a spouse dies without having exercised powers given to that spouse under a trust established by a third party. There is no prospect of the deceased spouse exercising any of those powers after death. . . . The fact that the spouse could have exercised such powers during his or her lifetime does not change the fact that, on death, the opportunity to acquire property from the trust has passed. The power over a trust formerly held by a now-deceased spouse is not the equivalent of a power over trust assets held by a divorcing spouse who is still very much alive and remains empowered to use and dispose of the trust assets.

Moreover, while the amicus proposes that modern notions of marital property should be used to identify property of the decedent spouse that will be subject to the elective share, the elective share statute takes no heed of the surviving spouse's property that would also be marital property. If the idea is to provide the surviving spouse roughly what he or she would have obtained in the event of a divorce, that goal is defeated by not only the elective share statute's fixed percentage formula but also by the fact that divorce divides the entirety of the couple's marital property, while the elective share divides only the property previously owned by the decedent spouse. Thus, for example, if the bulk of the marital property is owned by one spouse, divorce would ordinarily have required that spouse to transfer some of that marital property to the other spouse. Under the elective share statute, however, the surviving spouse may claim a portion of the decedent's property for himself or herself, without regard to how much of the couple's marital property is already held by the surviving spouse.[9] The elective share statute cannot operate in a manner comparable to property division on divorce unless the elective share "estate" includes all of the property—including that of the surviving spouse—that the court would divide in the event of divorce.

(v) Restatement (Third) of Property.

Justice Greaney's dissent proposes yet another approach to the calculation of the elective share estate, namely, that we adopt prospectively the definition recently approved by the American Law Institute in the Restatement (Third) of Property: Wills and Other Donative Transfers § 9.1(c) (2003), which includes in the elective share estate "the value of property owned or owned in substance by the decedent immediately before death that passed outside of probate at the decedent's death to donees other than the surviving spouse." . . . Comment j to § 9.1(c) explains that property may be "owned in substance by the decedent through various powers or rights, such as the power to revoke, withdraw, invade, or sever, or to appoint the decedent or the decedent's estate as beneficiary. . . . It is irrelevant whether the decedent acquired substantive ownership of the property before or after the marriage by gift or otherwise from someone else." Restatement (Third) of Property, supra at 212. . . . [W]e think it is inappropriate to adopt § 9.1(c) of the Restatement (Third) of Property at this time.

None of the materials presently before us—the parties' briefs, the amicus brief, the decision of the judge below, or the decision of the Appeals Court—contains any reference to § 9.1(c) or any other section of the Restatement (Third) of Property. As a fundamental principle, appellate courts should not reach out to decide issues that have not been briefed by any party (or even any amicus).

However well intentioned, appellate courts create much mischief when they ignore that principle. . . . Before adopting § 9.1(c), *sua sponte*, we should await an appropriate case where the parties have presented us with the relative merits of the current as opposed to the former Restatement position on this complex issue. . . .

. . . To the extent that the Legislature wishes to amend the elective share statute to insert more modern concepts from the current Restatement, that is the legislature's prerogative. We, however, should not insert such concepts into the statutory scheme absent some basis for believing that those concepts comport with the Legislature's intent. We see no basis for such a belief at this time, although appropriate briefing—or legislative action—might convince us otherwise in the future.

9. By comparison, the Uniform Probate Code, which includes the surviving spouse's assets in the "estate" to be divided by the elective share, effectively applies the elective share to the entirety of the couple's marital property. See Uniform Probate Code §§ 2-203, 2-205, 8 U.L.A. 103-107 (Master ed.1998).

We are also troubled by the uncertain scope of the new Restatement position. Section 9.1(c) provides no definition of the rather murky phrase "owned in substance," but comment j to that section explains that property is "owned in substance" if the decedent had "various powers or rights, such as the power to revoke, withdraw, invade, or sever, or to appoint the decedent or the decedent's estate as beneficiary," and that "the decedent's motive in creating, exercising, or not exercising any of these powers is irrelevant." Comment j thus indicates that the existence of "various powers or rights" held by the decedent spouse will render the trust property "owned in substance" by the decedent and thus subject to the elective share, but fails to specify precisely what "powers" or "rights" suffice or, conversely, what "powers" or "rights" will not be great enough to make the decedent the owner "in substance" of the property. Some settlors have sound reasons for giving a trustee considerable powers over a trust, but they would have to be warned that the mere existence of such powers may give the trustee's spouse rights to a portion of the trust property in the event that the trustee predeceases his or her spouse. The ambiguities inherent in the concept of "owned in substance" would be the source of much drafting uncertainty and, ultimately, litigation to determine what trust provisions will or will not provide a safe harbor for such trusts.

We thus think that it is inadvisable to announce any prospective rule on this complex subject at this time. We do, however, agree with the observation that our elective share statute may fail to provide sufficient support for disinherited spouses and that it has failed to keep pace with the changing principles on which the property rights of married couples are now based. Indeed, there appears to be no dispute that our elective share statute is outdated and inadequate. The dispute centers solely on which of the various models for a modern elective share statute would best achieve the desired goals. . . .

b. The bank account.

. . . .

We . . . agree with the Appeals Court that the bank savings account was a valid inter vivos trust to which the *Sullivan* rule unquestionably applies. The bank savings account, while a valid trust, could be revoked by Jean, its settlor, at any time, by merely withdrawing its funds, and Jean retained unlimited power to use assets in the bank account trust during her lifetime.

3. Conclusion.

We vacate the judgment dismissing the complaint. A declaration is to enter that the real estate at issue is not to be considered part of the estate of Jean Bongaards, but that the assets in the bank savings account are to be considered part of her estate, for purposes of calculating the plaintiff's elective share. . . .

MARSHALL, C.J. (concurring in part and dissenting in part).

. . . .

This is a simple case, controlled by *Sullivan*. As the court correctly notes, *Sullivan* applies only to inter vivos trusts created by a deceased spouse. . . . The trust at issue here was not created by the deceased spouse, and under *Sullivan*, is not part of the decedent's estate for purposes of G.L. c. 191, § 15. *See Sullivan, supra* at 872. As the plaintiff makes no other claim, that should end the court's inquiry. . . .

GREANEY, J. (concurring in part and dissenting in part, with whom SPINA, J., joins).

I agree with the court's conclusion that the plaintiff cannot recover in this case on the theories argued. I favor adopting, however, the principles expressed in § 9.1(c) of the Restatement (Third) of Property: Wills and Other Donative Transfers (2003), to govern assets held by a decedent in a trust with terms like this trust, which permit the decedent to control the trust assets entirely for his or her sole benefit, whether those assets were placed in the trust by the deceased spouse or by a third person. . . . If the protection contemplated by the statutory elective share is to have any practical significance in an age where conventional estate planning offers scores of will substitutes, a deceased's "estate" cannot be limited solely to the probate estate.[10] The possible disruption of one's estate plan does not diminish the importance of a statutory approach that provides a minimum measure of economic security to surviving spouses, usually women, who would otherwise be disinherited. Indeed, at its most elemental level, the elective share was designed to frustrate the intent of a settlor or testator whose estate plan otherwise would operate totally (or substantially) to disinherit his or her spouse.

It is not quite right to say, as the court does, that this issue has not been briefed. Although the plaintiff has not specifically cited the Restatement, his arguments are entirely congruent with that authority. More directly, the plaintiff relies (as does the amicus, the Women's Bar Association of Massachusetts), as might be expected, on the decision of *Sullivan v. Burkin, supra*, which has Restatement (Second) principles and thinking at its core. The Restatement (Second) is also referenced specifically in the decision of the Appeals Court. . . .

As noted by the court, the Restatement (Third) now expressly includes, as part of the deceased spouse's estate for purposes of a surviving spouse's elective share, "the value of property owned or owned in substance by the decedent immediately before death that passed outside of probate at the decedent's death to donees other than the surviving spouse." Restatement (Third) of Property: Wills and Other Donative Transfers § 9.1(c) (2003). The court's criticism of the ALI and its Restatement (Third) of Property: Wills and Other Donative Transfers is quite remarkable. The court suggests in various ways that the approach adopted by the ALI is vague, unsupported, contradictory, and poorly reasoned. I disagree.

10. The purpose of G.L. c. 191, § 15, is twofold. The obvious purpose is to provide support to the surviving spouse, thus underscoring the proposition that the obligation to support one's spouse continues after death. In addition, the statute attempts to return to the surviving spouse his or her economic contribution to the marriage, thus recognizing the contemporary philosophy that marriage is an economic partnership. Neither purpose is served when a spouse has the practical advantage of entire ownership in trust property as long as he or she lives, yet is permitted to deprive his or her spouse of an elective share in the property on death.

The text of the Restatement makes reasonably plain that the ALI is adopting, and building on, the acknowledged and well-reasoned change made by this court in *Sullivan v. Burkin, supra*, to extend spousal elective share rights to property owned outright or virtually outright by the deceased spouse. The definition of "owned in substance" in the Restatement is not, as characterized by the court, "murky." ... Comment j to § 9.1(c) explains that property may be "owned in substance by the decedent through various powers or rights, such as the power to revoke, withdraw, invade, or sever, or to appoint the decedent or the decedent's estate as beneficiary.... It is irrelevant whether the decedent acquired substantive ownership of the property before or after the marriage by gift or otherwise from someone else. The objective is to equate property owned in substance with probate property, which includes property that the decedent acquired before or after the marriage by gift or otherwise from someone else." The term is further illustrated in a definitional section of Restatement text as "property that the decedent did not own but over which the decedent had sufficient control, such as through a power to become the owner, to be treated as the owner for some purposes, such as the federal estate tax or the spouse's elective share. Thus, property subject to a revocable trust is part of the decedent's gross estate for purposes of the federal estate tax and is subject to the spouse's elective share, but is not part of the decedent's probate estate. The same applies to property in a trust over which the decedent had a general power of appointment....." Restatement (Third) of Property: Wills and Other Donative Transfers § 1.1 comment b (1999). This definition clearly identifies that it pertains to transfers made (as here) by a third party; that it "refers to property ... over which the decedent had sufficient control, such as through a power to become the owner" (which is the case here); and that it includes property held by the decedent which is subject to the "federal estate tax" (which is also the case here). *Id.* In other words, the Restatement (Third) makes clear what common sense suggests: if the deceased spouse has complete control over assets in a trust, the deceased spouse should be treated as the trust's owner for purposes of the surviving spouse's elective share rights.[11]

....

The court suggests that my dissent rests on principles of equitable property division under G.L. c. 208, § 34. This is not so.[12] I simply recognize, as the *Sullivan* court did, that the area of marital property division bears some intrinsic relevance to the

11. The court bolsters its conclusion today with the observation that a person who could have, but did not, exercise powers over trust property during his or her lifetime should not fairly be treated as the property's owner.... This somewhat myopic view of ownership was implicitly rejected by the Sullivan court when it concluded that it is the extent of control over the disposition of trust assets (rather than the actual disposition of those assets), that is determinative of the trust property's inclusion in a surviving spouse's elective share....

12. Indeed, the court's opinion appears to respond primarily to the expansive position on this issue advanced in the amicus brief, rather than the more limited view set forth in my dissent. It should be obvious that I favor prospective expansion of the "estate of the deceased" no further than to include assets held in an inter vivos trust when the terms of the trust (as they did here) permit the decedent alone to alter, amend, or revoke the trust to devote the assets entirely to his or her sole

operation of G.L. c. 191, § 15. . . . Doubtless there may be instances in which the statute's mechanical formula for determining the elective share amount, regardless of what property is included in the "estate of the deceased," might overcompensate a surviving spouse of independent means or one who has been otherwise provided for by life insurance, pension death benefits, or other will substitutes. It could also provide a windfall to one who, due to the short duration of the marriage, should not be entitled to a full statutory share of the deceased spouse's estate. Such occurrences, undoubtedly infrequent, are part and parcel of any elective share statute. In the vast majority of cases, however, the statute, interpreted to include assets in trusts with terms such as the trust before us, would not operate to create unjust results but rather would provide a measure of equity and justice to an effectively disinherited spouse, typically a wife. There thus is imbedded in the entire scheme a gender issue of societal importance that can be appropriately addressed and solved straightforwardly by a common-law court, without hand-wringing over statutory construction.[13]

My position is supported by the observations that: (1) in almost every situation, the elective share does not come into play because the deceased spouse did not directly or indirectly seek to disinherit the surviving spouse; and (2) settlors such as D'Amore could, by appropriate wording, achieve the ends apparently sought here by not giving the sole trustee and primary beneficiary a power akin to a general power.

I recognize that a sweeping judicial change in this area could have unintended far reaching consequences and adhere to the view expressed by the *Sullivan* court, that "the question of the rights of a surviving spouse in the estate of a deceased spouse, using the word 'estate' in its broad sense, is one that can best be handled by legislation." *Sullivan v. Burkin, supra* at 873. . . . Based on the lack of legislative action to date, it cannot be expected that the Legislature will promptly act in the wake of the court's decision today. . . .

---

benefit, regardless whether those assets were placed in the trust by the deceased spouse or by a third person.

13. I specifically disagree with the court's notion that I am ignoring basic principles of statutory construction because we are construing a legislative term, namely, the "estate of the deceased," that, in the court's view, is unambiguously confined to the deceased's probate estate. The entire elective share statute is underpinned with common-law concepts drawn from trust law and from the law of donative transfers, and its terms, thus, must be construed in light of common-law notions of pro-bate and nonprobate assets and concepts of equity. The *Sullivan* court had no hesitation in taking a trust that was nontestamentary in nature and making it a part of the "estate of the deceased" for purposes of the elective share statute. To distinguish the *Sullivan* decision by pointing out that it dealt with a trust created by the decedent and not by a third party is to beg the precise question we have undertaken to address—whether the "estate of the deceased" should include trust property over which the decedent (like Ernest G. Sullivan or Jean A. Bongaards) enjoyed absolute control and use so as to be treated, for all practical purposes, as the property's owner during his or her lifetime, regardless of the property's original ownership?

Notes and Questions

1. As you review *Bongaards*, note that both the majority and the dissent express frustration with the legislature. Consider the following call to action from *Sullivan* back in 1984: "What we have announced as a rule for the future hardly resolves all the problems that may arise. [giving examples] . . . The question of the rights of a surviving spouse in the estate of a deceased spouse, using the word "estate" in its broad sense, is one that can best be handled by legislation. . . . But, until it is, the answers to these problems will 'be determined in the usual way through the decisional process.'" *Sullivan v. Burkin*, 460 N.E.2d 572, 577–78 (Mass. 1984). Does the legislature's failure to act influence your view of the appropriate role for the court?

2. As the *Bongaards* court noted, *Sullivan v. Burkin* applied its new rule prospectively. Is that a good way to change in estate planning rules? One observer suggests a more nuanced approach: the party successfully challenging the old rule should receive compensation, perhaps from a discretionary judicial fund, to the extent of what that party would have received under the new rule. Such compensation would encourage law reform without penalizing those who relied on existing rules. In *Sullivan*, for example, "everyone wins. Mr. Sullivan successfully cut his wife out of his will because that's what the old rule allowed him to do. Mrs. Sullivan would collect what she is entitled to collect under the new rule. And lastly, the state wins because it has an interest in seeing the common law evolve to fit the public policies of the time." Gil J. Ghatan, *The Incentive Problem with Prospective Overruling: A Critique of the Practice*, 45 Real Prop. Prob. & Tr. J. 179, 205 (2010).

3. In the context of defining "separate property" for spousal election purposes, the Virginia Supreme Court looked more favorably on analogies to family law than did the Massachusetts court in *Bongaards.* "Since the primary purpose of the equitable distribution statute is to provide a fair manner for classifying assets accumulated during a marriage, we find that this body of law is sufficiently analogous to the issue at hand to inform our decision." *Dowling v. Rowan*, 621 S.E.2d 397, 401 (Va. 2005). *But see Pestrikoff v. Hoff*, 278 P.3d 281 (Alaska 2012) (principles of equitable distribution of marital property in divorce do not apply in probate of intestate's estate.)

How much should be borrowed? In particular, family law's "equitable distribution" approach requires case-by-case determinations foreign to the various formulas applied in the spousal election situation. Should we shift to a system under which probate courts make individualized distributions in response to a spousal election?

4. The "Is the trust valid?" focus of the illusory transfer test poses problems for a court trying to protect the spouse. For a case invalidating, as opposed to allowing a claim against, a revocable lifetime trust, see *Seifert v. Southern National Bank of South Carolina*, 409 S.E.2d 337 (S.C. 1991). The South Carolina legislature later remedied the court's having thrown the trust baby out with the bath water. S.C. Code Ann. § 62-7-112 (finding that trust is "illusory" does not invalidate trust, but merely makes trust assets subject to spousal election claim). Compare the discussion in Chapter 4 on Pages 221–222 about whether a trust might be valid for one purpose, but ignored for another.

5. Lack of uniformity on the law of spousal election encourages forum shopping. Suppose Stewart and Marjorie live in a state allowing election against a revocable trust and that Stewart wants to disinherit Marjorie. Trying to avoid Marjorie's claim, Stewart may create a trust in a different, more traditional state, naming someone there as trustee. Another technique would be for Stewart's trust to select a traditional state's law as the law governing the trust. *See, e.g., National Shawmut Bank v. Cumming*, 91 N.E.2d 337 (Mass. 1950) (law of trustee's domicile determines spousal election rights); *In re Estate of Renard*, 453 N.Y.S.2d 625 (1982) (law of personalty's situs controls); UPC §§ 2-202(d) (law of decedent's domicile), 2-703 (law selected by governing instrument controls unless contrary to elective share provisions, exempt property and allowances provisions, or other public policy).

6. Emory Law School Research Assistants studied probate records in nine counties in Georgia, the only state that has neither community property nor spousal election statutes. They found that 75 percent of the cases in which a decedent disinherited or minimized the share of a surviving spouse involved either trusts or legal life estates benefiting the survivor. Diminished shares appeared where part of a tax-saving plan, or where the survivor was the beneficiary of insurance or employee benefits, or had sufficient wealth in their own name, or had agreed to the plan. *See* Jeffrey N. Pennell, *Minimizing the Surviving Spouse's Elective Share*, 32 Heckerling Inst. on Est. Plan., Ch. 9 (2002). Can spousal disinheritance be appropriate?

Problems

1. You are the law clerk for a Justice of the highest court in your state. The case on appeal involves a surviving spouse's attempt to claim an elective share against property held in a revocable lifetime trust the decedent established. Local (but dated) precedent would deny the claim. Your Justice would like to see the law change, but wants your view on the best way to accomplish that result. What do you recommend?

2. Yesterday you supervised the execution of a series of documents for Sam and Anna, a couple in their 50s who have been married 20 years and always kept assets in their own names. Neither has children. Sam has few assets; Anna is "comfortable." They executed wills giving property to each other, with alternative gifts to charity if the spouse did not survive. Anna put her substantial investment portfolio in a revocable trust which will pay income to her for life, then income to Sam for his life, and then distribute the principal to charity.

This morning, Anna called to say she wants to amend the trust to eliminate Sam's life estate and pay the principal to charity at her death.

What ethical problems do you face? See the Fox & Martyn excerpt on Page 25.

Selected References

Martin D. Begleiter, *Grim Fairy Tails: Studies of Wicked Stepmothers, Poisoned Apples, and the Elective Share*, 78 Alb. L. Rev. 521 (2015).

Angela M. Vallario, *Spousal Election: Suggested Equitable Reform for the Division of Property at Death*, 52 Cath. U. L. Rev. 519 (2003).

3. *The Uniform Probate Code*

Much of the weakness of the traditional elective share system grows out of its title-based approach. If the decedent spouse held property in her or his own name, so that the property becomes an asset of the probate estate, the survivor has a claim. If property is held in trust (or in some other will substitute), survivors normally cannot reach it. Form prevails over substance. The title-based approach is arbitrary in another sense as well. Whether the marriage lasted a day or a half-century, the elective share is the same. These results do not fit with the idea that a marriage is a cooperative venture to which both parties contribute over time.

The UPC's effort to reform the law of spousal election has come in stages.

a. The Original Augmented Estate

In 1969, the UPC drew upon the experiences of New York and Pennsylvania to develop an "augmented estate" designed to prevent people from taking advantage of the title-based system. We have seen how, by not including the decedent's non-probate assets within its reach, the traditional system can leave a survivor under-protected. For the same reason, the traditional approach can over-protect a survivor. Suppose Cindy puts most of her wealth in a trust for John, but leaves a will giving most of the probate property to charity. John could "double-dip" by enjoying the trust and also electing against the will.

To remedy these under and over protection problems, the UPC adopted an expanded, "augmented," estate against which surviving spouses could elect. UPC § 2-202 (pre-1990). In some ways, it is a system made not to be used. The drafters hoped that by making it virtually impossible for one spouse to defeat the other's share, or for a survivor who was well-cared-for to "double dip" by electing and taking more, people would not bother on either score.

This version of the augmented estate has three basic parts. The first can be called the "net probate estate." This is the property in the decedent spouse's probate estate, less debts, expenses, and allowances. UPC § 2-202 (pre-1990). Though the details differ among jurisdictions, this is the estate against which spouses elect under traditional statutes.

To the net probate estate the original UPC adds the value of will substitutes benefiting persons other than the surviving spouse. UPC § 2-202(1) (pre-1990). In concept, but not detail, this part of the augmented estate draws upon the definition of the gross estate for purposes of the Federal Estate Tax. *See* § 1.03(C)(1). It reaches property which continued to benefit the decedent, but which was held in a form that avoided probate. In particular, it includes a revocable inter vivos trust with a non-spouse as beneficiary. In an exception to the general thrust of this approach and in response to industry lobbying, life insurance benefiting a non-spouse is not included. Also, because the goal is to avoid "fraud" on the elective share, only transfers during the marriage are subject to this sort of recapture.

The third part of the original augmented estate includes property which the decedent gave the surviving spouse before death. UPC § 2-202(2) (pre-1990). This device is meant to preclude elections by spouses who have already gotten a fair share of the decedent's wealth. For this reason, life insurance which benefits the surviving spouse is included. This part of the augmented estate covers both (a) gifts which the survivor still owns, and (b) property that the survivor received as gifts from the decedent and in turn gave away to others in ways that would include them in the *survivor's* augmented estate. The second element prevents a survivor from manipulating the statute by setting up his or her own avoidance devices.

Selected Reference

Sheldon F. Kurtz, *The Augmented Estate Concept Under the Uniform Probate Code: In Search of an Equitable Elective Share*, 62 Iowa L. Rev. 981 (1977).

b. A Partnership Approach

The next step of the UPC's reform effort came in 1990, in an effort to apply the "partnership theory of marriage" to spousal election. The code still used the "augmented estate" term, but thoroughly revised the approach. Tweaks were made in 1993 and 2008. Less than 10 states have enacted the latest UPC version. Professor Lawrence W. Waggoner served as the project's Director of Research and Chief Reporter.

Lawrence W. Waggoner, *The Multiple-Marriage Society and Spousal Rights Under the Uniform Probate Code*

76 Iowa L. Rev. 223, 236–37, 239 (1991)

1. THE PARTNERSHIP THEORY OF MARRIAGE

Disinheritance of a surviving spouse brings into question the fundamental nature of the economic rights of each spouse in a marital relationship and the manner in which society views the institution of marriage. The contemporary view of marriage is that it is an economic partnership. The partnership theory of marriage, sometimes called the marital-sharing theory, is stated in various ways. Sometimes it is portrayed "as an expression of the presumed intent of husbands and wives to pool their fortunes on an equal basis, share and share alike." Under this approach, the economic rights of each spouse are seen as deriving from an unspoken marital bargain under which the partners agree that each is to enjoy a half interest in the fruits of the marriage, that is, in the property nominally acquired by and titled in the sole name of either partner during the marriage other than property acquired by gift or inheritance. A decedent who disinherits her surviving spouse is seen as having reneged on the bargain. Sometimes the theory is couched in restitutionary terms, a return-of-contribution notion. Under this approach, the law grants each spouse an entitlement to compensation for nonmonetary contributions to the marital enterprise, as "a recognition of the activity of one spouse in the home and to compensate not only for this activity but for opportunities lost." Sometimes the theory is stated in aspirational and behavior-shaping terms: ["T]he ideal to which marriage aspires [is] that of equal partnerships between spouses who share resources, responsibilities, and risks . . . [."]

No matter how the rationale is expressed, the community-property system recognizes the partnership theory. . . .

The common-law states, however, also give effect or purport to give effect to the partnership theory when it perhaps counts most—at dissolution of a marriage upon divorce. If the marriage ends in divorce, a spouse who sacrificed her financial-earning opportunities to contribute so-called domestic services to the marital enterprise, such as childrearing and homemaking, or a spouse who pursued a lower-paying career or who engaged in volunteer work, stands to be recompensed. . . .

Elective-share law in the common-law states has not caught up to the partnership theory of marriage. Under typical American elective-share law, including the elective share provided by the pre-1990 UPC, a surviving spouse is granted a right to claim a one-third share of the decedent's estate, not a right to claim the fifty percent share of the couple's combined assets that the partnership theory would imply. The redesigned elective share promulgated in the 1990 UPC is intended to bring elective-share law into line with the partnership theory of marriage.

The 1990 UPC's basic device was to create a sliding scale that gave a surviving spouse an increasing percentage of the augmented estate as the marriage continued. After 15 years, the survivor could claim half of the augmented estate. Critics noted that such a system could unduly benefit the surviving spouse of a later-in-life marriage and that it served only as an approximation of what the marital assets would be in a particular marriage. The next excerpt opens by explaining the logic behind the 2008 version, designed in response to experience under the statute.

Uniform Probate Code Article II, Part 2 Elective Share of Surviving Spouse General Comment

In [a] long-term marriage . . . , the effect of implementing a partnership theory is to increase the entitlement of the surviving spouse when the marital assets were disproportionately titled in the decedent's name; and to decrease or even eliminate the entitlement of the surviving spouse when the marital assets were more or less equally titled or disproportionately titled in the surviving spouse's name. Put differently, the effect is both to reward the surviving spouse who sacrificed his or her financial-earning opportunities in order to contribute so-called domestic services to the marital enterprise and to deny an additional windfall to the surviving spouse in whose name the fruits of a long-term marriage were mostly titled.

In [a] short-term, later-in-life marriage . . . , the effect of implementing a partnership theory is to decrease or even eliminate the entitlement of the surviving spouse because in such a marriage neither spouse is likely to have contributed much, if anything, to the acquisition of the other's wealth. Put differently, the effect is to deny a windfall to the survivor who contributed little to the decedent's wealth, and ultimately to deny a windfall to the survivor's children by a prior marriage at the expense of the decedent's children by a prior marriage. Bear in mind that in such a marriage, which produces no children, a decedent who disinherits or largely disinherits the surviving spouse may not be acting so much from malice or spite toward the surviving spouse, but from a natural instinct to want to leave most or all of his or her property to the children of his or her former, long-term marriage. In hardship cases, however, as explained later, a special supplemental elective-share amount is provided when the surviving spouse would otherwise be left without sufficient funds for support.

2008 Revisions. When first promulgated in the early 1990s, the statute provided that the "elective-share percentage" increased annually according to a graduated schedule. . . . The "elective-share percentage" did double duty. The system equated the "elective-share percentage" of the couple's combined assets with 50 percent of the marital-property portion of the couple's assets—the assets that are subject to equalization under the partnership theory of marriage. Consequently, the elective share effected the partnership theory rather indirectly. Although the schedule was designed to represent by approximation a constant fifty percent of the marital-property portion of the couple's assets (the augmented estate), it did not say so explicitly.

The 2008 revisions are designed to present the system in a more direct form, one that makes the system more transparent and therefore more understandable. The 2008 revisions disentangle the elective-share percentage from the system that approximates the marital-property portion of the augmented estate. As revised, the statute provides that the "elective-share percentage" is always 50 percent, but it is not 50 percent of the augmented estate but 50 percent of the "marital-property portion" of the augmented estate. The marital-property portion of the augmented estate is computed by approximation—by applying the percentages set forth in a graduated schedule that increases annually with the length of the marriage (each "marital-portion percentage" being double the percentage previously set forth in the "elective-share percentage" schedule)....

... An important byproduct of the revision is that it facilitates the inclusion of an alternative provision for enacting states that want to implement the partnership theory of marriage but prefer not to define the marital-property portion by approximation but by classification.... [See alternative § 2-203(b) in brackets below.]

Section 2-202. Elective Share

(a) [Elective-Share Amount.] The surviving spouse of a decedent who dies domiciled in this State has a right of election, under the limitations and conditions stated in this Part, to take an elective-share amount equal to 50 percent of the value of the marital-property portion of the augmented estate.

(b) [Supplemental Elective-Share Amount.] If the sum of the amounts described in Sections 2-207, 2-209(a)(1), and that part of the elective-share amount payable from the decedent's probate estate and nonprobate transfers to others under Section 2-209(b) and (c) is less than [$75,000], the surviving spouse is entitled to a supplemental elective-share amount equal to [$75,000], minus the sum of the amounts described in those sections. The supplemental elective-share amount is payable from the decedent's probate estate and from recipients of the decedent's nonprobate transfers to others in the order of priority set forth in Section 2-209 (b) and (c).

(c) [Effect of Election on Statutory Benefits.] If the right of election is exercised by or on behalf of the surviving spouse, the surviving spouse's homestead allowance, exempt property, and family allowance, if any, are not charged against but are in addition to the elective-share and supplemental elective-share amounts.

(d) [Non-Domiciliary.] The right, if any, of the surviving spouse of a decedent who dies domiciled outside this State to take an elective share in property in this State is governed by the law of the decedent's domicile at death.

Section 2-203. Composition of the Augmented Estate

(a) Subject to Section 2-208, the value of the augmented estate, to the extent provided in Sections 2-204, 2-205, 2-206, and 2-207, consists of the sum of the values of all property, whether real or personal, movable or immovable, tangible or intangible, wherever situated, that constitute:

(1) the decedent's net probate estate;

(2) the decedent's nonprobate transfers to others;

(3) the decedent's nonprobate transfers to the surviving spouse; and

(4) the surviving spouse's property and nonprobate transfers to others.

(b) The value of the marital-property portion of the augmented estate consists of the sum of the values of the four components of the augmented estate as determined under subsection (a) multiplied by the following percentage:

If the decedent and the spouse were married to each other:	The percentage is:
Less than 1 year	3%
1 year but less than 2 years	6%
2 years but less than 3 years	12%
3 years but less than 4 years	18%
4 years but less than 5 years	24%
5 years but less than 6 years	30%
6 years but less than 7 years	36%
7 years but less than 8 years	42%
8 years but less than 9 years	48%
9 years but less than 10 years	54%
10 years but less than 11 years	60%
11 years but less than 12 years	68%
12 years but less than 13 years	76%
13 years but less than 14 years	84%
14 years but less than 15 years	92%
15 years or more[14]	100%

[Alternative Subsection (b) for States Preferring a Deferred-Marital-Property System]

[(b) The value of the marital-property portion of the augmented estate equals the value of that portion of the augmented estate that would be marital property at the decedent's death under [the Model Marital Property Act] [copy in definition from Model Marital Property Act, including the presumption that all property is marital property] [copy in other definition chosen by the enacting state].]

Section 2-204. Decedent's Net Probate Estate

The value of the augmented estate includes the value of the decedent's probate estate, reduced by funeral and administration expenses, homestead allowance, family allowances, exempt property, and enforceable claims.

---

14. The comment to this section includes the following: "The schedule deems by approximation that 100 percent of the components of the augmented estate is marital property after 15 years of marriage. Government data indicate that the median length of a first marriage that does not end in divorce is 46.3 years, the median length of a post-divorce remarriage that does not end in divorce is 35.1 years, and the median length of a post-widowhood remarriage that does not end in divorce is 14.4 years. Enacting states may determine that this data supports lengthening the schedule in subsection (b) to 20 or even 25 years." [Eds.]

Section 2-205. Decedent's Nonprobate Transfers to Others

The value of the augmented estate includes the value of the decedent's nonprobate transfers to others, not included under Section 2-204, of any of the following types, in the amount provided respectively for each type of transfer:

(1) Property owned or owned in substance by the decedent immediately before death that passed outside probate at the decedent's death. Property included under this category consists of:

(A) Property over which the decedent alone, immediately before death, held a presently exercisable general power of appointment. The amount included is the value of the property subject to the power, to the extent the property passed at the decedent's death, by exercise, release, lapse, in default, or otherwise, to or for the benefit of any person other than the decedent's estate or surviving spouse.

(B) The decedent's fractional interest in property held by the decedent in joint tenancy with the right of survivorship. The amount included is the value of the decedent's fractional interest, to the extent the fractional interest passed by right of survivorship at the decedent's death to a surviving joint tenant other than the decedent's surviving spouse.

(C) The decedent's ownership interest in property or accounts held in POD, TOD, or co-ownership registration with the right of survivorship. The amount included is the value of the decedent's ownership interest, to the extent the decedent's ownership interest passed at the decedent's death to or for the benefit of any person other than the decedent's estate or surviving spouse.

(D) Proceeds of insurance, including accidental death benefits, on the life of the decedent, if the decedent owned the insurance policy immediately before death or if and to the extent the decedent alone and immediately before death held a presently exercisable general power of appointment over the policy or its proceeds. The amount included is the value of the proceeds, to the extent they were payable at the decedent's death to or for the benefit of any person other than the decedent's estate or surviving spouse.

(2) Property transferred in any of the following forms by the decedent during marriage:

(A) Any irrevocable transfer in which the decedent retained the right to the possession or enjoyment of, or to the income from, the property if and to the extent the decedent's right terminated at or continued beyond the decedent's death. The amount included is the value of the fraction of the property to which the decedent's right related, to the extent the fraction of the property passed outside probate to or for the benefit of any person other than the decedent's estate or surviving spouse.

(B) Any transfer in which the decedent created a power over income or property, exercisable by the decedent alone or in conjunction with any other person, or exercisable by a nonadverse party, to or for the benefit of the decedent, creditors of the decedent, the decedent's estate, or creditors of the decedent's estate. The amount included with respect to a power over property is the value of the property subject to the power, and the amount included with respect to a power over income is the value of the property that produces or produced the income, to the extent the power in either case was exercisable at the decedent's death to or for the benefit of any person other than the decedent's surviving spouse or to the extent the property passed at the decedent's death, by exercise, release, lapse, in default, or otherwise, to or for the benefit of any person other than the decedent's estate or surviving spouse. If the power is a power over both income and property and the preceding sentence produces different amounts, the amount included is the greater amount.

(3) Property that passed during marriage and during the two-year period next preceding the decedent's death as a result of a transfer by the decedent if the transfer was of any of the following types:

(A) Any property that passed as a result of the termination of a right or interest in, or power over, property that would have been included in the augmented estate under paragraph (1)(A), (B), or (C), or under paragraph (2), if the right, interest, or power had not terminated until the decedent's death. The amount included is the value of the property that would have been included under those paragraphs if the property were valued at the time the right, interest, or power terminated, and is included only to the extent the property passed upon termination to or for the benefit of any person other than the decedent or the decedent's estate, spouse, or surviving spouse. As used in this subparagraph, "termination," with respect to a right or interest in property, occurs when the right or interest terminated by the terms of the governing instrument or the decedent transferred or relinquished the right or interest, and, with respect to a power over property, occurs when the power terminated by exercise, release, lapse, default, or otherwise, but, with respect to a power described in paragraph (1)(A), "termination" occurs when the power terminated by exercise or release, but not otherwise.

(B) Any transfer of or relating to an insurance policy on the life of the decedent if the proceeds would have been included in the augmented estate under paragraph (1)(iv) had the transfer not occurred. The amount included is the value of the insurance proceeds to the extent the proceeds were payable at the decedent's death to or for the benefit of any person other than the decedent's estate or surviving spouse.

(C) Any transfer of property, to the extent not otherwise included in the augmented estate, made to or for the benefit of a person other than the decedent's surviving spouse. The amount included is the value of the transferred property to the extent the aggregate transfers to any one donee in either of the two years exceeded [$12,000] [the amount excludable from taxable gifts under 26 U.S.C. Section 2503(b) [or its successor] on the date next preceding the date of the decedent's death].

Section 2-206. Decedent's Nonprobate Transfers to the Surviving Spouse

Excluding property passing to the surviving spouse under the federal Social Security system, the value of the augmented estate includes the value of the decedent's nonprobate transfers to the decedent's surviving spouse, which consist of all property that passed outside probate at the decedent's death from the decedent to the surviving spouse by reason of the decedent's death, including:

(1) the decedent's fractional interest in property held as a joint tenant with the right of survivorship, to the extent that the decedent's fractional interest passed to the surviving spouse as surviving joint tenant,

(2) the decedent's ownership interest in property or accounts held in co-ownership registration with the right of survivorship, to the extent the decedent's ownership interest passed to the surviving spouse as surviving co-owner, and

(3) all other property that would have been included in the augmented estate under Section 2-205(1) or (2) had it passed to or for the benefit of a person other than the decedent's spouse, surviving spouse, the decedent, or the decedent's creditors, estate, or estate creditors.

Section 2-207. Surviving Spouse's Property and Non-Probate Transfers to Others

(a) [Included Property.] Except to the extent included in the augmented estate under Section 2-204 or 2-206, the value of the augmented estate includes the value of:

(1) property that was owned by the decedent's surviving spouse at the decedent's death, including:

(i) the surviving spouse's fractional interest in property held in joint tenancy with the right of survivorship,

(ii) the surviving spouse's ownership interest in property or accounts held in co-ownership registration with the right of survivorship, and

(iii) property that passed to the surviving spouse by reason of the decedent's death, but not including the spouse's right to homestead allowance, family allowance, exempt property, or payments under the federal Social Security system; and

(2) property that would have been included in the surviving spouse's nonprobate transfers to others, other than the spouse's fractional and ownership interests included under subsection (a)(1)(i) or (ii), had the spouse been the decedent.

(b) [Time of Valuation.] Property included under this section is valued at the decedent's death, taking the fact that the decedent predeceased the spouse into account, but, for purposes of subsection (a)(1)(i) and (ii), the values of the spouse's fractional and ownership interests are determined immediately before the decedent's death if the decedent was then a joint tenant or a co-owner of the property or accounts. For purposes of subsection (a)(2), proceeds of insurance that would have been included in the spouse's nonprobate transfers to others under Section 2-205(1)(iv) are not valued as if he [or she] were deceased.

(c) [Reduction for Enforceable Claims.] The value of property included under this section is reduced by enforceable claims against the surviving spouse.

Section 2-208. Exclusions, Valuation, and Overlapping Application.

(a) [**Exclusions.**] The value of any property is excluded from the decedent's nonprobate transfers to others (i) to the extent the decedent received adequate and full consideration in money or money's worth for a transfer of the property or (ii) if the property was transferred with the written joinder of, or if the transfer was consented to in writing before or after the transfer by, the surviving spouse. . . .

Section 2-209. Sources from Which Elective Share Payable.

(a) [**Elective-Share Amount Only.**] In a proceeding for an elective share, the following are applied first to satisfy the elective-share amount and to reduce or eliminate any contributions due from the decedent's probate estate and recipients of the decedent's nonprobate transfers to others:

(1) amounts included in the augmented estate under Section 2-204 which pass or have passed to the surviving spouse by testate or intestate succession and amounts included in the augmented estate under Section 2-206; and

(2) the marital-property portion of amounts included in the augmented estate under Section 2-207.

(b) [**Marital Property Portion.**] The marital-property portion under subsection (a)(2) is computed by multiplying the value of the amounts included in the augmented estate under Section 2-207 by the percentage of the augmented estate set forth in the schedule in Section 2-203(b) appropriate to the length of time the spouse and the decedent were married to each other.

(c) [**Unsatisfied Balance of Elective-Share Amount; Supplemental Elective-Share Amount.**] If, after the application of subsection (a), the elective-share amount is not fully satisfied, or the surviving spouse is entitled to a supplemental elective-share amount, amounts included in the decedent's net probate estate, other than assets passing to the surviving spouse by testate or intestate succession, and in the decedent's nonprobate transfers to others under Section 2-205(1), (2), and (3)(B) are applied first to satisfy the unsatisfied balance of the elective-share amount or the supplemental elective-share amount. The decedent's net probate estate and that portion of the decedent's nonprobate transfers to others are so applied that liability for the unsatisfied balance of the elective-share amount or for the supplemental elective-share amount is apportioned among the recipients of the decedent's net probate estate and of that portion of the decedent's nonprobate transfers to others in proportion to the value of their interests therein.

(d) [Unsatisfied Balance of Elective-Share and Supplemental Elective-Share Amount.] If, after the application of subsections (a) and (c), the elective-share or supplemental elective-share amount is not fully satisfied, the remaining portion of the decedent's nonprobate transfers to others is so applied that liability for the unsatisfied balance of the elective-share or supplemental elective-share amount is apportioned among the recipients of the remaining portion of the decedent's nonprobate transfers to others in proportion to the value of their interests therein....

Section 2-210. Personal Liability of Recipients

(a) Only original recipients of the decedent's nonprobate transfers to others, and the donees of the recipients of the decedent's nonprobate transfers to others, to the extent the donees have the property or its proceeds, are liable to make a proportional contribution toward satisfaction of the surviving spouse's elective-share or supplemental elective-share amount. A person liable to make contribution may choose to give up the proportional part of the decedent's nonprobate transfers to him [or her] or to pay the value of the amount for which he [or she] is liable.

Note: Determining the Elective Share

Determining the elective share under the UPC requires four basic steps:

First, calculate the augmented estate. *See* UPC § 2-203(a). The basic idea is to include all assets of both spouses, regardless of how title is held. The process includes four steps:

(a) Start with the decedent's net probate estate. UPC § 2-204.

(b) Add the value of nonprobate transfers the decedent made to others than the surviving spouse, except to the extent the recipients gave value or the surviving spouse joined in the transfer. UPC §§ 2-205, 2-208.

(c) Add the value of nonprobate property going from the decedent to the surviving spouse. UPC § 2-206.

(d) Add the value of the spouse's property (including what would have been included among the surviving spouse's nonprobate transfers to others if the spouse had been the decedent). UPC § 2-207.

Second, determine the marital-property portion by multiplying the appropriate percentage based on the length of the marriage. UPC § 2-203(b).

Third, multiply the marital portion by 50 percent to determine the elective share. If the amount is less than $75,000, add "supplemental elective-share amount" to bring the total up to $75,000. UPC § 2-202(b).[15]

---

15. The spouse's homestead allowance, exempt property, and family allowance are in addition to the elective share and supplemental share amounts. UPC § 2-202(c).

Fourth, identify the property used to satisfy the elective share. *See* UPC § 2-209. First use property the spouse already has:

(a) Property received by will or intestate succession,

(b) Will substitutes benefiting the survivor, and

(c) The marital-property portion of property the survivor already owned (broadly defined to include the spouse's non-probate transfers).[16]

If that property satisfies the share, of course, there will be no election because the spouse will gain nothing. If the spouse's property is not enough or the spouse qualifies for a supplemental elective-share amount, then turn to the non-spousal survivors, in the following order:

(d) Persons who at the decedent's death received property from the will or will substitutes, and persons who received life insurance within two years of the decedent's death. They contribute to the spouse pro rata.

(e) Other persons who received irrevocable gifts from the decedent within two years of death.

Question

Why does the UPC allow election against an intestate estate?

Problems

1. Barb Bogert died last week leaving a will giving all of her property to her husband of 12 years. Barb's husband, Bill, and her daughter, Debbie, are her only survivors. Barb's only probate asset is a summer house worth $100,000. She also was a joint tenant (with Debbie) of a farm worth $200,000. Bill is beneficiary of a life insurance policy he bought on Barb, with a face value of $100,000 and a current value of $50,000. Bill and Barb held joint bank accounts worth $10,000 and a house (in joint tenancy) worth $190,000. Bill owns in his own name a stock portfolio worth $50,000.

(a) Under a traditional elective-share statute, what would Bill's elective share be?

(b) Under the UPC, what would Bill's elective share be? What property would satisfy his share?

(c) If Bill had died instead, leaving everything to Barb, what would Barb's elective share be under the UPC? What property would satisfy her share?

16. Determine the marital-property portion by multiplying the appropriate percentage, based on the length of the marriage.

2. Helen Bryant, 72, is president of Sell, Inc., an advertising firm which she formed 40 years ago and which has been highly successful. She has two sons from her first marriage, Ben and Lyle Bradford. Their father died when the boys were young, and Helen raised them as a single parent. Four years ago, Helen married Bill Bryant, a wealthy stockbroker. Bill has a 20-year-old daughter, Nora; Helen did not adopt her. There was no premarital agreement.

Helen's wealth consists of the following: controlling interest in Sell, Inc.; life insurance under a policy Sell, Inc., has been paying premiums on for 40 years; a substantial blue-chip stock portfolio; a lake cabin; a Mercedes sedan. She sold her home and moved into Bill's home at the time of their marriage. Helen has never lived in a community property state.

Helen has come to you for advice on how best to achieve the following split of her estate at her death: token gifts to Bill and to Nora, one-half of the rest to Mark Morris (a business associate), one-quarter each to sons Ben and Lyle Bradford. She explains that Bill and Nora should "do just fine" on Bill's money.

When pressed about Mark Morris, she calls him an "old friend" who has worked closely with her while handling the financial side of the advertising business from the beginning. You learn that Mark Morris lived with the Bradford family for a five-year period when the boys were teenagers; Mark served as a "father" to the boys. You also learn that in the last two years Helen has increasingly relied on Mark's advice in all aspects of her financial planning. Her once-fierce independence has mellowed to an acceptance of virtually any advice he offers.

How would you design a plan to meet Helen's goals and what steps would you take to protect the plan from attack?

(a) First, assume you are in a common law (i.e., non-community property) jurisdiction that has not passed the Uniform Probate Code.

(b) Next, assume that you are in a common law jurisdiction which has adopted the Uniform Probate Code. In what ways would you plan differently?

Questions

1. If the justices of the Massachusetts Supreme Judicial Court who decided the *Bongaard* were instead members of the legislature, how many of them do you think would vote for the UPC proposal?

2. You are a state legislator. In response to a call for reform from your state's highest court, the state bar association is recommending the UPC's spousal election scheme. Do you support the proposal? What changes, if any, would you make?

Selected References

Alan Newman, *Incorporating the Partnership Theory of Marriage into Elective-Share Law: The Approximation System of the Uniform Probate Code and the Deferred-Community-Property Alternative*, 49 Emory L.J. 487 (2000).

Raymond C. O'Brien, *Integrating Marital Property into a Spouse's Elective Share*, 59 Cath. U. L. Rev. 617 (2010).

Lawrence W. Waggoner, *The Uniform Probate Code's Elective Share: Time for a Reassessment*, 37 U. Mich. J.L. Reform 1 (2003).

D. Changes in Domicile

Couples who move face a variety of problems regarding their rights to property. They may move between a community property and a common law state. Even if they move within either of those systems, different spousal election rules may apply. Under traditional conflict of laws rules, different laws can apply to different aspects of marital property. Typically, but not universally, the law of the situs of real property controls that property; the law of the marital domicile at the time personal property is acquired determines its character (community or separate); and the law of the marital domicile at death determines the surviving spouse's rights.

Estate of Hanau v. Hanau

730 S.W.2d 663 (Tex. 1987)

Robertson, Justice. . . .

Robert and Dorris Hanau were married in Illinois in 1974 and five years later moved to Texas. After moving here, Robert prepared a will leaving his separate property to his children by a prior marriage, and his community property to Dorris. Robert and Dorris each had substantial amounts of separate property before the marriage, and at all times kept such property under their own names. While married and in Illinois, Robert accumulated numerous shares of stock through the use of his separate property. Under Illinois common law, this would have remained his separate property. Robert died in Texas in 1982 and Dorris was granted letters testamentary on May 10, 1982. . . . The only question presented to the trial court was the status of those stocks bought during the marriage in Illinois using Robert's separate property. . . .

The long-standing general rule is that property which is separate property in the state of the matrimonial domicile at the time of its acquisition will not be treated for probate purposes as though acquired in Texas. . . . In *Cameron* [*v. Cameron*, 641 S.W.2d 210 (Tex. 1982)], we held, however, that separate property acquired in common law jurisdictions merits different treatment in the limited context of divorce or annulment. While there were solid reasons for creating the Cameron rule in those situations, the same rationales are not applicable to probate procedures. . . .

Without [the power to effect an equitable distribution of property in the context of divorce], unfair results could occur because one spouse's equitable share of the other spouse's separate property under common law might not be considered under our community property definition of separate property. . . . The key is that there is no similar right in a probate proceeding, nor is there any need for any. If there is a valid will, the will should usually be enforced regardless of the equity of the devises or bequests within. . . . Similarly, if the property is to pass through intestacy, a specified statutory formula is invoked which operates without the need to make equitable determinations. *See* Tex. Prob. Code Ann. § 38 (Vernon 1980).

In sum, to extend *Cameron* would make a shambles of 150 years of Texas probate law, thus, without a clear showing of supporting case law, statutory authority or a clear need for such broad power in the trial court, we refuse to do so.

Notes and Questions

1. If Robert and Dorris had gotten a divorce in Texas, the stock would have been subject to the court's jurisdiction for the purpose of achieving an equitable distribution of the property. Why should Dorris fair less well when she remained married?

2. Because community property states rely on their basic system to allocate wealth between spouses, these states generally do not provide survivors a right of election against their predeceased spouse's property. The survivor merely keeps his or her half of the community property. A propertyless migrant spouse from a common law jurisdiction may be left with no community property and no right of election. A few states recognize "quasi-community property," which is personal property acquired elsewhere that would have been community property if acquired in the new home state. If the acquiring spouse dies first, the survivor gets half of the quasi-community property. *See, e.g.*, Cal. Prob. Code §§ 66, 101.

3. Couples moving the other direction—from a community property state to a common law state—face different problems. Their community property should continue to retain that characterization, but lawyers, judges, and transfer agents unaccustomed to community property may try to force the couple to change the ownership to something more familiar, like a joint tenancy. If the couple does manage to preserve the community status of its property, they may also be creating a situation in which a surviving spouse can double dip. Unless courts or legislatures adapt elective share laws to reflect the presence of community property, the survivor could retain his or her half of the community and still elect to take part of the decedent's half. The Uniform Disposition of Community Property Rights at Death Act, adopted in several common law states, gives each spouse the right to dispose of half of the community property at death and removes the right of election as to that property.

4. Lydia lived in Indiana but owned real estate in Illinois. Her will was probated in both states. Should her widower be able to elect against the will in one state, but take under it in the other? *See In re Estate of Conrad*, 422 N.E.2d 884 (Ill. App. Ct. 1981) (no).

Selected Reference

Katherine D. Black, Mary K. Black & Julie M. Black, *Community Property for Non-Community Property States*, 24 Quinnipiac Prob. L.J. 260 (2011).

Karen E. Boxx, *Community Property Across State Lines: Square Pegs and Round Holes*, 19 Prob. & Prop. 9 (Jan./Feb. 2005).

E. Agreements Waiving Marital Rights

Sometimes potential (or current) spouses are not comfortable with their counterparts having available a right to elect, or some other marital claim. In particular, people with children from an earlier marriage may want to prevent a new spouse from electing against a will benefiting those children. One solution is for one or both parties to waive their spousal rights. People usually make these agreements before marriage. In a few cases contracts come after the marriage, but while it is still happy, and sometimes they arise with separation or divorce on the horizon.

When reviewing these agreements, courts sometimes struggle with the extent to which the rules for commercial contracts should apply.

In re Estate of Greiff

703 N.E.2d 752 (N.Y. 1998)

Bellacosa, J.

. . . .

Appellant Helen Greiff married Herman Greiff in 1988 when they were 65 and 77 years of age, respectively. They had entered into reciprocal prenuptial agreements in which each expressed the usual waiver of the statutory right of election as against the estate of the other. The husband died three months after the marriage, leaving a will that made no provision for his surviving spouse. The will left the entire estate to Mr. Greiff's children from a prior marriage. When Mrs. Greiff filed a petition seeking a statutory elective share of the estate, Mr. Greiff 's children countered with the two prenuptial agreements which they claimed precluded Mrs. Greiff from exercising a right of election against her husband's estate (see, EPTL 5-1.1[f]).

A trial was held in Surrogate's Court, Kings County, on the issue of the validity and enforceability of the prenuptial agreements. The Surrogate explicitly found that the husband "was in a position of great influence and advantage" in his relationship with his wife-to-be, and that he was able to subordinate her interests, to her prejudice and detriment. The court further determined that the husband "exercised bad faith, unfair and inequitable dealings, undue influence and overreaching when he induced the petitioner to sign the proffered antenuptial agreements," particularly noting that the husband "selected and paid for" the wife's attorney. Predicated on this proof, the credibility of witnesses and the inferences it drew from all the evidence, Surrogate's Court invalidated the prenuptial agree ments and granted a statutory elective share of decedent's estate to the surviving spouse.

The Appellate Division reversed, on the law, simply declaring that Mrs. Greiff had failed to establish that her execution of the prenuptial agreements was procured through her then-fiancée's fraud or overreaching. This Court granted the widow leave to appeal. We now reverse.

A party seeking to vitiate a contract on the ground of fraud bears the burden of proving the impediment attributable to the proponent seeking enforcement (*see*, *Matter of Gordon v. Bialystoker Ctr. & Bikur Cholim*, 45 NY2d 692, 698, *supra*). This rubric also applies generally to controversies involving prenuptial agreements (*see*, *Matter of Phillips*, 293 NY 483, 488). Indeed, as an incentive toward the strong public policy favoring individuals ordering and deciding their own interests through contractual arrangements, including prenuptial agreements . . . , this Court has eschewed subjecting proponents of these agreements to special evidentiary or freighted burdens (*see*, *Matter of Sunshine*, 40 NY2d 875, 876).

Importantly, however, neither *Sunshine* in 1976 *(supra)* nor *Phillips* in 1944 *(supra)* entirely insulates prenuptial agreements from typical contract avoidances. That proposition includes the kind of counterpoint advanced by the surviving spouse in this case to offset her stepchildren's use of the prenuptial agreements against her claim for her statutory elective share. . . .

This Court has held, in analogous contractual contexts, that where parties to an agreement find or place themselves in a relationship of trust and confidence at the time of execution, a special burden may be shifted to the party in whom the trust is reposed (or to the proponent of the party's interest, as in this case) to disprove fraud or overreaching. . . .

As an illustration, in *Gordon (supra)*, the administrator of the decedent's estate challenged the transfer of funds by the decedent, one month before her death, to the nursing home in which she was a patient. The Court restated its applied guidance, as part of the invalidation of the transfer, as follows:

> "Whenever . . . the relations between the contracting parties appear to be of such a character as to render it certain that . . . either on the one side from superior knowledge of the matter derived from a fiduciary relation, or from an overmastering influence, or on the other from weakness, dependence, or trust justifiably reposed, unfair advantage in a transaction is rendered probable, . . . *it is incumbent upon the stronger party to show affirmatively that no deception was practiced, no undue influence was used, and that all was fair, open,*

voluntary and well understood" (Gordon v. Bialystoker Ctr. & Bikur Cholim, at 698-699 [emphasis added], *quoting Cowee v. Cornell, 75 NY 91, 99-100).*

This enduring, nuanced balance of fair assessment can be applicable in the context of prenuptial agreements (*see*, ... *Graham v. Graham*, 143 NY 573, 579-580). We emphasize, however, that the burden shift is neither presumptively applicable nor precluded. We eschew absolutist rubrics that might ill serve the interests of fair conflict resolution as between proponents or opponents of these kinds of ordinarily useful agreements.

This Court's role here is to clarify, harmonize and find a happy medium of views reflected in the cases. For example, *Graham* has been read as holding that prenuptial agreements were presumptively fraudulent due to the nature of the relationship between prospective spouses. *Phillips*, on the other hand, has been urged to suggest that prenuptial agreements may never be subject to burden-shifting regardless of the relationship of the parties at the time of execution and the evidence of their respective conduct.

Graham was decided in 1894 and indicated that prospective spouses stand in a relationship of confidence which necessarily casts doubt on or requires strict scrutiny concerning the validity of an antenuptial agreement. Its outdated premise, however, was that the man "naturally" had disproportionate influence over the woman he was to marry....

A century later society and law reflect a more progressive view and they now reject the inherent inequality assumption as between men and women, in favor of a fairer, realistic appreciation of cultural and economic realities.... Indeed, the law starts marital partners off on an equal plane. Thus, whichever spouse contests a prenuptial agreement bears the burden to establish a fact-based, particularized inequality before a proponent of a prenuptial agreement suffers the shift in burden to disprove fraud or overreaching. This rule is less rigid than *Graham*'s presumptive equation.

Phillips tugs in the opposite direction from *Graham*. On close and careful analysis, however, *Phillips* does not upset the balanced set of operating principles we pull together by today's decision. While holding that antenuptial agreements are not enveloped by a presumption of fraud, the Court in *Phillips* indicated that some extra leverage could arise from the "circumstances in which the agreement was proposed" (*Matter of Phillips, supra*, at 491). This language does not turn its back entirely on *Graham*. Rather, it is generous enough to encompass the unique character of the inchoate bond between prospective spouses—a relationship by its nature permeated with trust, confidence, honesty and reliance. It allows further for a reasonable expectation that these relationships are almost universally beyond the pale of ordinary commercial transactions. Yet, the dispositive tests of legitimacy and enforceability of their prenuptial agreements need not pivot on the legalism or concept of presumptiveness. Instead, a particularized and exceptional scrutiny obtains.

The Appellate Division's approach here did not allow for the calibration and application of these legal principles.... A specific frame of reference for that court should be whether, based on all of the relevant evidence and standards, the nature of the relationship between the couple at the time they executed their prenuptial agreements rose to the level to shift the burden to the proponents of the agreements to prove freedom from fraud, deception or undue influence. . . .

Order reversed.

Uniform Probate Code

Section 2-213. Waiver of Right to Elect and of Other Rights.

(a) The right of election of a surviving spouse and the rights of the surviving spouse to homestead allowance, exempt property, and family allowance, or any of them, may be waived, wholly or partially, before or after marriage, by a written contract, agreement, or waiver signed by the surviving spouse.

(b) A surviving spouse's waiver is not enforceable if the surviving spouse proves that:

(1) he [or she] did not execute the waiver voluntarily; or

(2) the waiver was unconscionable when it was executed and, before execution of the waiver, he [or she]:

(i) was not provided a fair and reasonable disclosure of the property or financial obligations of the decedent;

(ii) did not voluntarily and expressly waive, in writing, any right to disclosure of the property or financial obligations of the decedent beyond the disclosure provided; and

(iii) did not have, or reasonably could not have had, an adequate knowledge of the property or financial obligations of the decedent.

(c) An issue of unconscionability of a waiver is for decision by the court as a matter of law.

(d) Unless it provides to the contrary, a waiver of "all rights," or equivalent language, in the property or estate of a present or prospective spouse or a complete property settlement entered into after or in anticipation of separation or divorce is a waiver of all rights of elective share, homestead allowance, exempt property, and family allowance by each spouse in the property of the other and a renunciation by each of all benefits that would otherwise pass to him [or her] from the other by intestate succession or by virtue of any will executed before the waiver or property settlement.

Notes and Questions

1. In judging whether parties have made fair disclosure, courts may consider a number of factors. *See, e.g., In re Marriage of Norris*, 624 P.2d 636 (Or. Ct. App. 1981) (no fair disclosure when agreement was presented on morning of wedding); *In re Marriage of Matson*, 705 P.2d 817 (Wash. Ct. App. 1985) (no fair disclosure when one

party was much less sophisticated than the other); *Hawkins v. Hawkins*, 185 N.E.2d 89 (Ohio Prob. Ct. 1962) (fair disclosure when both parties were competent professionals); *In re Marriage of Foran*, 834 P.2d 1081 (Wash. Ct. App. 1992) (no fair disclosure when one spouse's net worth was $8200 compared to the other spouse's net worth of $198,500); *Geddings v. Geddings*, 460 S.E.2d 376 (S.C. 1995) (no fair disclosure despite language in the agreement that there had been disclosure, when wife had no knowledge of the value of husband's estate). Courts disagree about how to handle the question of legal representation. *See In re Marriage of Bonds*, 5 P.3d 815 (Cal. 2000) (Barry Bonds' premarital agreement enforceable even though wife was not represented by independent counsel).

2. How much are pre-marital agreements like other contracts? Should a court shift the burden of proof? If so, in what circumstances? Should a court review these agreements on substantive grounds? If so, should it consider substantive fairness on the date of the contract, or in light of later events? What factors should it consider when judging substantive fairness on the date of the contract, or in light of later events? What factors should it consider when judging substantive fairness? Should a court ask whether parties have made fair disclosure? If so, what factors should it consider? Should it matter whether the agreement is being interpreted in the context of a divorce or a death?

3. Chapter 7 of the American Law Institute's Principles of the Law of Family Dissolution covers agreements between spouses, those planning to marry, and those who are or plan to become domestic partners.

Problem

Chris and Pat have been living together, unmarried, for three years. They want to formalize their sharing arrangements. Can you represent them both? How would you avoid the ethical problems that might arise?

Selected References

Dennis I. Belcher & Laura O. Pomeroy, *A Practitioner's Guide for Negotiating, Drafting and Enforcing Premarital Agreements*, 37 Real Prop. Prob. & Tr. J. 1 (2002).

Erika L. Haupt, *For Better, for Worse, for Richer, for Poorer: Premarital Agreement Case Studies*, 37 Real Prop. Prob. & Tr. J. 29 (2002).

Jennifer Tulin McGrath, *The Ethical Responsibilities of Estate Planning Attorneys in the Representation of Non-traditional Couples*, 27 Seattle U. L. Rev. 75 (2003).

Jeffrey G. Sherman, *Prenuptial Agreements: A New Reason to Revive an Old Rule*, 53 Clev. St. L. Rev. 359 (2005/2006).

§ 6.02 Forgotten Spouses and Children

Another way the law protects families is to guarantee a minimum share to family members omitted from a will. The typical scenario involves someone who makes a will and sometime later marries or has a child (or additional children), but neglects to amend the will. A person not covered is often called "pretermitted," or overlooked. Many states provide protection to spouses who were not included in premarital wills. *See, e.g.,* UPC § 2-301. Virtually all states have statutes that provide some protection to children who have been omitted from wills. *See* 2d Rest. Prop. § 34.2, Statutory Note. Because the statutes vary in detail, but pose similar issues, it can be helpful to have a series of questions you can ask about whatever statute you face.

Which categories of relatives are protected? Many jurisdictions view the problem as one of following a testator's presumed intention in light of changed circumstances; they effectively partially revoke the will to include "after-acquired" relatives.[17] Several protect spouses in this situation, most protect children, and some protect descendants of omitted children. Some states take a different approach and protect all children, whether born before or after the will's execution. Rather than relying upon a "changed circumstances" rationale, these jurisdictions are simply forcing testators to disinherit expressly, if that is their desire.

Does other evidence preclude application of the statute? In contrast to spousal election statutes, pretermitted heir statutes are subject to testators' expressions of contrary intent.[18] Thus, an omitted person could be in a class protected by the statute, but still not get a share, if evidence indicated the testator's intention to disinherit that person. Numerous questions surround evidence of testators' intentions to disinherit. First, states differ on what sort of evidence is admissible. Some places allow extrinsic evidence (sometimes called "Missouri type" statutes), but others restrict the evidence to language in the will ("Massachusetts type"). Second, the effect of particular statements has been the subject of much litigation. See the note on Intentional Disinheritance.

What share does the relative take? An omitted relative normally takes an intestate share. Some statutes, however, adjust the share in different situations. For example, under the UPC, if a testator gives something to children living when the will was executed, afterborns get only a share of what was given to their older siblings. UPC § 2-302(a)(2).

---

17. Indeed, marriage revokes the whole will in some states. *See, e.g.,* Ga. Code Ann. § 53-2-76. Some states require marriage and birth of a child. *See, e.g.,* Kan. Stat. Ann. § 59-610. Some treat the will as revoked only if the new spouse survives the testator. *See, e.g.,* Or. Rev. Stat. § 112.305. In other places, marriage has no effect on a pre-existing will. *See, e.g.,* Ohio Rev. Code Ann. § 2107.37.

18. The one exception is Louisiana, which recognizes the legitime, a device of the civil law to guarantee a share for protected relatives. *See* La. Civ. Code Ann. art. 1493–1501; *Succession of Lauga*, 624 So. 2d 1156 (La. 1993) (extensive discussion).

Where does the money come from? In many states, the taker under the residuary clause will bear the primary burden of satisfying a pretermitted claim. This approach is consistent with the way most claims are handled. See the discussion of abatement. In particular circumstances, however, others may pay for the claim. In Ohio, for example, the pretermitted child takes property from all will beneficiaries except the surviving spouse. Ohio Rev. Code Ann. § 2107.34. Under the UPC, a pretermitted spouse cannot take property from the testator's children born before the marriage (unless they are also the spouse's children). UPC § 2-301(b).

Uniform Probate Code

Section 2-302. Omitted Children

(a) Except as provided in subsection (b), if a testator fails to provide in his [or her] will for any of his [or her] children born or adopted after the execution of the will, the omitted after-born or after-adopted child receives a share in the estate as follows:

(1) If the testator had no child living when he [or she] executed the will, an omitted after-born or after-adopted child receives a share in the estate equal in value to that which the child would have received had the testator died intestate, unless the will devised all or substantially all the estate to the other parent of the omitted child and that other parent survives the testator and is entitled to take under the will.

(2) If the testator had one or more children living when he [or she] executed the will, and the will devised property or an interest in property to one or more of the then-living children, an omitted after-born or after-adopted child is entitled to share in the testator 's estate as follows:

(i) The portion of the testator's estate in which the omitted after-born or after-adopted child is entitled to share is limited to devises made to the testator's then-living children under the will.

(ii) The omitted after-born or after-adopted child is entitled to receive the share of the testator's estate, as limited in subparagraph (i), that the child would have received had the testator included all omitted after-born and after-adopted children with the children to whom devises were made under the will and had given an equal share of the estate to each child.

(iii) To the extent feasible, the interest granted an omitted after-born or after-adopted child under this section must be of the same character, whether equitable or legal, present or future, as that devised to the testator's then-living children under the will.

(iv) In satisfying a share provided by this paragraph, devises to the testator's children who were living when the will was executed abate ratably, in abating the devises of the then-living children, the court shall preserve to the maximum extent possible the character of the testamentary plan adopted by the testator.

(b) Neither subsection (a)(1) nor subsection (a)(2) applies if:

(1) it appears from the will that the omission was intentional; or

(2) the testator provided for the omitted after-born or after-adopted child by transfer outside the will and the intent that the transfer be in lieu of a testamentary provision is shown by the testator's statements or is reasonably inferred from the amount of the transfer or other evidence.

(c) If at the time of execution of the will the testator fails to provide in his [or her] will for a living child solely because he [or she] believes the child to be dead, the child is entitled to share in the estate as if the child were an omitted afterborn or after-adopted child.

(d) In satisfying a share provided by subsection (a)(1), devises made by the will abate under Section 3-902.

Notes and Questions

1. UPC § 2-302(c) is unusual because it treats as a pretermission problem a testator's mistaken belief in the prior death of a child. Traditionally, courts treated that problem as a mistake in inducement to make the will and allowed relief only if the mistake appeared on the face of the will and the will disclosed what the bequest would be but for the mistake. *See Gifford v. Dyer*, 2 R.I. 99 (1852).

2. Spousal pretermitted statutes differ from spousal election statutes. First, pretermitted protection is automatic. In contrast, a surviving spouse exercising an election right often must comply with a cumbersome election procedure. If the spouse dies before the election or before a given time period, the rights will not survive. Second, each statute may mandate different shares. Third, the pretermitted share is unlikely to extend beyond probate property, but a spousal election right might.[19] Fourth, language in a will can defeat a pretermitted share but not an elective share.

3. Are pretermitted heir statutes designed to protect people who are unintentionally omitted from a will, or are they designed to protect relatives from disinheritance? Consider Elizabeth, who while domiciled in New York, executed a will omitting her son, Rudolph. Elizabeth later became mentally incapacitated and moved to New Hampshire, where she died. Does your view of the purpose of pretermitted heir statutes help you decide whether New York's or New Hampshire's statute should apply?

---

19. *But see In re Trust Under Deed of Kulig*, 131 A.3d 494 (Pa. Super. Ct. 2015) (applying Pennsylvania's version of UTC § 112, reproduced on Page 233, to allow a surviving spouse rights when decedent's revocable trust omitted spouse.)

4. Should pretermitted heir statutes apply to revocable lifetime trusts? *Compare Kidwell v. Rhew,* 268 S.W.3d 309 (Ark. 2007) (no), *with* Restatement (Second) of Property: Donative Transfers § 34.2 (yes).

5. Pretermitted heir statutes often protect children "born or adopted" after the will's execution. What about unknown children "discovered" later? *Compare In re Gilmore,* 925 N.Y.S.2d 567 (N.Y. App. 2011) (in the absence of specific statutory language "after-known" children not covered), *with* Cal. Prob. Code, § 21622 (child covered if decedent was "unaware" of the child).

6. Pretermitted heir statutes typically apply to children who are adopted after will execution. Should these statutes apply to children who were not actually adopted but would take under intestate statutes based on equitable adoption or virtual adoption? *See Johnson v. Rogers,* 774 S.E.2d 647 (Ga. 2015) (no).

7. UPC § 2-302(b)(2) allows transfers *outside* the will to trump the protections of § 2-302(a) if the intention that the transfers were intended to be in lieu of a testamentary provision "is reasonably inferred from the amount of the transfer or other evidence." What sort of evidence would you need? *Cf. Ferguson v. Critopoulos,* 2014 WL 4666935 (Ala. 2014) (providing guidelines to cover similar language in a pretermitted spouse case).

Problems

1. Bill and Mary had no children. Their wills gave everything to each other, with alternative gifts (half and half) to their parents. Then their daughter, Myrna, was born.

(a) If Bill died without revoking his will, what share of his estate would Myrna take in your state? Under the UPC?

(b) If Bill revised his will to give his fishing pole to Myrna and $1,000 to United Way, what share would Myrna take in your state? Under the UPC?

(c) Assume Bill revised his will as noted in (b), but that a son, Martin, was born thereafter. If Bill then died, what share would Martin take in your state? Under the UPC?

(d) Would your answers to (c) be the same if right after Myrna and Martin's respective births, Bill had purchased $500 U.S. Savings bonds in his name and "Payable on Death" to each respective child?

(e) What if Bill bought a bond for Myrna, but did not buy one for Martin. Would Martin have a share of Myrna's bond in your state? Under the UPC?

2. Philip and Donna currently have two children, Michael and Jennifer. Philip wants to leave his estate to Donna, or, if she predeceases him, in equal shares to his children who may survive. Draft the appropriate language.

Note: Intentional Disinheritance

Sometimes clients will want to disinherit their children because the parents and children are estranged. Except in Louisiana, testators have that power. Using it, however, may not be wise. For one thing, that approach may well prompt a will contest, based on lack of capacity or undue influence. Recall the planning options available to reduce the likelihood of a successful contest. *See* 3.02[D]. Secondly, disinheriting one child may put enormous strains on the favored children, precluding reconciliation for another generation. Clients should appreciate that disinheritance is a drastic step, not to be taken lightly.

Similarly, lawyers should be careful in drafting the necessary language of disinheritance. Questions about whether particular language is sufficient to overcome the protections of a pretermitted heir statute have prompted considerable litigation. In general, the more specific the language, the more likely it will defeat a relative's claim. Courts traditionally have not allowed "negative wills," which only disinherit, but do not give property to anyone. However, the UPC allows them. UPC § 2-101(b). *See also* § 3.02A of this text.

Another question is whether the disinherited child should be told about the decision. Some experienced estate planners give three reasons for informing the child. First, notice gives the child time to adjust financial plans. Second, knowing ahead of time avoids the confusion a surprise disinheritance creates. Finally, "telling your child he has been cut out may motivate him to shape up and change his ways. It can even lead to reconciliation." *See* Gerald M. Condon & Jeffrey L. Condon, Beyond the Grave 92 (1995).

Problems

1. Valerie has two children, Dionne and Larry. Draft language to preclude Larry from claiming a pretermitted share in Valerie's estate.

2. Suppose Valerie's will read, "To my descendants (except my son Larry), or their survivors by right of representation." If Larry predeceases Valerie, should his son Athan take under Valerie's will?

3. Suppose Valerie's will read, "I give my son Larry twenty dollars." If Larry predeceases Valerie, should his son Athan be able to take a pretermitted share?

For many years, commentators have been urging that states adopt some form of protection against disinheritance. Consider the following.

Ralph C. Brashier, *Disinheritance and the Modern Family*

45 Case W. Res. L. Rev. 84, 164, 169–70, 173–74 (1994)

The law of decedents' estates has failed to account for . . . modern changes in family structures, and consequently the interests of millions of American children have been marginalized. . . .

The intentional disinheritance of a child by a competent testator is both permissible and unchallengeable. Even if disinheritance of minor children were proven to be less frequent than disinheritance of spouses, there remains a crucial distinction between the positions of the disinherited spouse and the disinherited minor child: because of her minority, the minor child with few exceptions has no ability or opportunity to protect herself from disinheritance. The child has no choice concerning her existence and has no choice concerning the parent/child relationship that follows. Unable to provide for herself or terminate the relationship, she is bound to a family which she neither created nor can change. Moreover, the ability to disinherit is not mutual: because in most states a child under eighteen cannot make a will, the child cannot disinherit her parent. Ironically, the effect is that the parent receives the benefit of forced heirship which is denied to his child. . . .

In a society where noncustodial parents frequently shirk their inter vivos child support obligations and are perhaps even more likely to exclude the children from their wills, jurisdictions could protect the disinherited child by recognizing the parent's posthumous duty to support the child during minority. Statutory recognition of the parent's posthumous duty to support the child would make explicit the obligation implicit in the conduit theory under dower and the forced share. Moreover, the loopholes currently permitting children in nontraditional families to be disinherited would be closed. A well-planned scheme of this sort could be easily and efficiently administered and would infringe upon testamentary freedom only to the extent necessary to support the child until she attains the age of majority.

Note

For a brief commentary on how Europeans resolve the conflict between testamentary freedom and mandating shares for family members, see http://www.economist.com/research/articlesBySubject/displaystory.cfm?subjectid=3856661&story_id=14644403.

Question

Should we establish a minimum share for children? If so, how should it be defined?

Selected References

Brian C. Brennan, *Disinheritance of Dependent Children: Why Isn't America Fulfilling Its Moral Obligation?*, 14 Quinnipiac Prob. L.J. 125 (1999).

Adam J. Hirsch, *Airbrushed Heirs: The Problem of Children Omitted from Wills*, 50 Reap Prop. Tr. & Est. L. J. 175 (2015).

Max Nathan, Jr., *Forced Heirship: The Unheralded "New" Disinherison Rules*, 74 Tul. L. Rev. 1027 (2000).

J. Thomas Oldham, *What Does the U.S. System Regarding Inheritance Rights of Children Reveal About American Families?*, 33 Fam. L.Q. 265 (1999).

§ 6.03 Charitable Gifts

At one time a number of states had so-called "mortmain statutes"[20] limiting gifts to charity. Such statutes had two overlapping aims: to protect family members against disinheritance and to protect the testator (and the family) from the temptation of buying one's way into heaven by making a deathbed transfer.

Mortmain statutes took either or both of two approaches. They limited the percentage of property which testators could give to charity, or they prohibited (or limited) charitable gifts made in a set period before death. Mortmain statutes have been abolished but, in many places, only recently. Untangling some not-so-old cases may require understanding what these statutes were trying to accomplish.

§ 6.04 Public Policy Limits

Even without specific legislative authorization, courts sometimes, if rarely, act on their own to invalidate various will provisions as violative of public policy. The public policy doctrine nicely illustrates a question important in this chapter and much of wills and trusts law: how much control should we allow people to exercise after their deaths? The following commentary focuses upon a relatively narrow question, but one with broad implications.

---

20. The name comes from the English Statute of Mortmain. 7 Edw. 1, stat. 2, ch. 13 (1279).

Jeffrey G. Sherman, *Posthumous Meddling: An Instrumentalist Theory of Testamentary Restraints on Conjugal and Religious Choices*

1999 U. Ill. L. Rev. 1273, 1276–81, 1301–04, 1329

Courts traditionally have upheld . . . testamentary conditions calculated to restrain legatees' personal conduct, unless the conditions violate public policy. As one might imagine, however, the courts' application of this public policy standard has led to a "welter of conflict and confusion" from which it is difficult to distill any consistent principles. . . .

This confusion as to result bespeaks confusion as to underlying theory. An individual who wishes her nephew to remain unmarried can, upon his marriage, revoke a will she had previously made in his favor, and the nephew will have no legal right to reinstate the bequest. One may disinherit family members for any reason at all, however arbitrary or even hateful the reason may be; unconditional testamentary dispositions are not subjected to any "reasonableness" standard. And a testator is permitted to stipulate in her will that a particular bequest is to be paid to her nephew only if he is unmarried at the date of her death. But if the testator 's will conditions her bounty to the nephew on the nephew's remaining unmarried—even after her death—such a provision probably will be declared invalid on public policy grounds. Why are conditional bequests subjected to a reasonableness test while unconditional bequests are not? And why is the former condition (nephew must be unmarried at testator's death) permissible, while the latter (nephew must remain unmarried even after testator's death) is not?

The traditional explanation for striking down only the latter condition is that the restraint it imposes continues beyond the testator's death and therefore exerts its influence when it is no longer amendable by appeal to the transferor's reason and reflection upon changed circumstances. I shall call this explanation the "continuing influence" rationale. . . .

Under this traditional analysis, a condition that purports to influence the legatee's conjugal or religious choices after the testator's death is subject to challenge on public policy grounds, but a similar condition that exerts no posthumous influence is perfectly acceptable. For example, a testamentary condition requiring that the legatee eventually divorce his spouse might be invalidated on public policy grounds, but a testamentary condition requiring that the legatee divorce his spouse before the testator's death would be regarded universally as valid.

The problem with the "continuing influence" rationale for striking down certain testamentary conditions is that it proves too much, for every testamentary disposition restrains people's use of property after the testator's death has put him beyond the reach of argument and reflection. If a testator devises successive interests in Blackacre to A and B, the arrangement is put equally beyond the reach of subsequent persuasion whether B's interest is to take effect upon the expiration of a ten-year term in A (valid) or upon A's marriage (probably invalid). The objection that the "continuing influence" rationale makes to these testamentary restraints is no different from the broader objections to "dead-hand" control. If all that concerns us are the inequities of dead-hand control, there is no reason why the condition relating to marriage should be more objectionable than the ten-year term provision.

At the same time as the "continuing influence" rationale proves too much, it also proves too little. Suppose a testator's will provides: "I devise Blackacre to A, if A has killed B before my death; but if A has not killed B before my death, then I devise Blackacre to C." The condition attached to A's devise offers no continuing inducement to commit homicide; after the testator's death, it is too late for A to satisfy the condition if she has not already satisfied it. Yet most assuredly the condition would be struck down on public policy grounds. . . .

The purpose of this article is to offer a new theory for responding to these testamentary restraints: a theory that, it is hoped, will not only yield more consistent and explainable results than the free-floating "public policy" analysis but also restrict the enforceability of these intrusive, divisive conditions even more than current law. . . .

Testation is an anomaly. We don't let the dead vote; why do we let them tell us what to do with material resources? . . .

If we did not allow property owners to bequeath, they would employ other devices to achieve the same result: joint tenancies, life insurance, inter vivos trusts. Unless we were willing to abolish inter vivos transfers as well, legal prohibitions against testation would prove to be a paper tiger, as property owners would simply learn to mold their intended transactions into allowable forms. And if we succeeded in abolishing inter vivos gratuitous transfers of property as a backstop to our abolition of testation, we might, in fairness, have to prohibit implicit inter vivos transfers, such as a parent's providing her children with better-than-average nutrition and education. . . .

Prohibiting testation would cause efficiency losses as well. . . .

If one knew that one's resources were, upon one's death, to revert to the state or be redistributed by lottery, one's incentive to invest in the preservation of those resources would diminish as death approached. . . . But to minimize the incentive problem, all the law need do is allow the property owner to designate his successors; it is not necessary to grant the property owner the right to condition his bounty on such things as religious and conjugal choices. . . .

One might argue that if allowing a property owner to designate a posthumous successor promotes efficiency, allowing a property owner also to impose testamentary conditions on the successor would promote efficiency still more. The argument would run as follows: it is good for efficiency if the property owner knows she can regulate the property to the same extent after death as she can while still alive; inasmuch as a living property owner can withhold bounty from her child because she does not like the child's conjugal choices, she ought to be able likewise to condition her posthumous bounty on the child's conforming to her wishes.

There are two responses to this argument. First, if we define efficiency in terms of aggregate personal satisfaction, posthumous conditions may decrease efficiency inasmuch as the successor's enjoyment of an asset is less untrammeled than his predecessor's. Second, and more important, is the question of society's proper role. If a living person wishes to deny bounty to an adult child because she disapproves of the child's conjugal choices, she need not enlist society's aid in denying wealth to the child (beyond society's general recognition of private property rights). But if a person wishes to extend her influence over her child from beyond the grave by imposing testamentary conditions, society's aid must be enlisted; and . . . it should be considered offensive and unsuitable for society to bring its power to bear when the objective is control by the dead over the personal conduct of the living. . . .

Testamentary conditions calculated to restrain legatees' personal conduct should not be enforced. We allow testation only to the extent necessary to avoid the harms that the abolition of testation would produce. To avoid those harms it is crucial to allow property owners to designate their successors, but it is not necessary to allow them also to superintend their successors' behavior. Consequently, although a property owner may enlist society's aid to the extent necessary to convey her property to her successors, she may not properly enlist society's aid in governing their conduct.

Although this argument has been advanced only in the context of testamentary conditions affecting conjugal or religious choices, it must be admitted that no limiting principle has been offered by means of which this argument can be so confined. The minimalist testation theory would invalidate all testamentary conditions calculated to restrain or induce particular personal conduct on the part of the legatees, even if the conduct in question has nothing to do with marriage or religion and even if the conduct sought to be induced is "good" or the conduct sought to be restrained is "bad." . . .

Notes and Questions

1. Despite courts' deference to testamentary freedom, they regularly invalidate on public policy grounds instructions to destroy property. For example, in *Eyerman v. Mercantile Trust Co.*, 524 S.W.2d 210 (Mo. Ct. App. 1975), the court enjoined Louise Johnston's executor from razing her house according to directions in her will. Other directions to destroy property may not present such clear cases. Should a court invalidate a movie star's order to burn love letters which have value in the tabloid marketplace, but whose exposure would offend notions of privacy?

2. In an effort to influence their children's behavior, testators may make gifts conditional on meeting various requirements. As Professor Sherman notes, usually courts uphold such restrictions, but not always. *See also* Restatement (Second) of Property §§ 6 & 7. Consider some examples regarding marriage:

(a) Isaac Liberman created a trust giving his son Harry a lifetime income. If Harry married someone approved by his mother and the executors and trustees named in the will (his brother and sister), the principal of the trust would go to Harry's issue. If not, the principal would go to Harry's brother and sister. The brother and sister refused consent. Although seemingly convinced that the brother and sister were not acting out of greed, the court invalidated the restriction because of its "natural tendency . . . to restrain all marriage." *Liberman v. Liberman*, 18 N.E.2d 658, 662 (N.Y. 1939).

(b) Linn Eaton gave his married daughter, Cynthia, a remainder interest in some real estate, subject to the provision that if she were married at the time she came into possession, the property would go into trust. Commenting that "[n]ot every encouragement of divorce is objectionable," the court upheld the restriction. *Hall v. Eaton*, 631 N.E.2d 805, 808 (Ill. App. Ct. 1994).

(c) Adolph Donner created a trust for his daughters, but denied one of them any income or right to the principal until she reached 65, or until her husband Martin died or the couple divorced. Evidently Adolph believed Martin had tricked him into investing in a worthless venture. Given what the court called "a reasonable economic basis" for the condition, the court upheld the restriction. *Estate of Donner*, 623 A.2d 307, 309 (N.J. Super. App. Div. 1993).

(d) Joseph Gordon left his property to his children, with a provision revoking the gift of any child who married a person "not born in the Hebrew faith." In May, 1949, son Harold married Veronica, who had been raised a Roman Catholic. In December, 1949, culminating training that had begun before the marriage, Veronica converted to Judaism, an act which some, but not all, Jews view as having a retroactive effect back to birth. The court cut off Harold's interest as of the date of his marriage. *Gordon v. Gordon*, 124 N.E.2d 228 (Mass. 1954).

(e) Erla Feinberg exercised a power of appointment she'd been given over a trust established by her husband. Following the basic policy he had established, but changing the method, she conditioned remainder interests to his grandchildren on their not being married to someone outside their Jewish faith. The court upheld the restriction. *In re Estate of Feinberg*, 919 N.E.2d 888 (Ill. 2009).

3. Conditional gifts based on lifestyle may well fail in their purpose. "When-ever a client confides that he must impose restrictions on a gift to an heir, the attorney should remind himself that if the client has been unable to control his child's or grandchild's behavior while he's alive, there is little likelihood that the conditional gift will curb the heir's rebelliousness once the testator is gone." John A. Warnick, *The Ungrateful Living: An Estate Planner's Nightmare—The Trial Attorney's Dream*, 24 Land & Water L. Rev. 401, 413 (1989).

4. For a will with very specific directions for how to dispose of the testator's body to make a series of political points, see http://www.peta.org/feat/newkirk/will.html.

5. Biotechnology raises more troubling public policy questions. Do you agree with the following opinion?

Hecht v. Superior Court

20 Cal. Rptr. 2d 275 (Ct. App. 1993)[21]

LILLIE, P.J.

Petitioner, the girlfriend of decedent William E. Kane, seeks a peremptory writ of mandate/prohibition to vacate a January 4, 1993, order directing the personal representative of decedent's estate to destroy all of the decedent's sperm in the custody and control of California Cryobank, Inc. The real parties in interest are the administrator of the decedent's estate (Robert L. Greene) and the decedent's adult son (William E. Kane, Jr.) and adult daughter (Katherine E. Kane). We issued an order to show cause and order staying execution of the January 4, 1993, order.

This proceeding presents several matters of first impression involving the disposition of cryogenically preserved sperm of a deceased. We conclude that the trial court's order constituted an abuse of discretion in the procedural posture of this case which compels us to set aside such order....

[Kane committed suicide on October 30, 1991, leaving his live-in friend of five years, Deborah E. Hecht, and two college-age children from a marriage which ended in 1976. During the month before his death, Kane deposited 15 vials of his sperm with California Cryobank, a Los Angeles sperm bank. His "Specimen Storage Agreement" instructed Cryobank to either hold or release the specimens, according to his executor's request.]

On September 27, 1991, decedent executed a will which was filed with the Los Angeles County Superior Court and admitted to probate. The will named Hecht as executor of the estate, and provides, "I bequeath all right, title, and interest that I may have in any specimens of my sperm stored with any sperm bank or similar facility for storage to Deborah Ellen Hecht." A portion of the will entitled "Statement of Wishes" provided, "It being my intention that samples of my sperm will be stored at a sperm bank for the use of Deborah Ellen Hecht, should she so desire, it is my wish that, should [Hecht] become impregnated with my sperm, before or after my death, she disregard the wishes expressed in Paragraph 3 above [pertaining to disposition of decedent's "diplomas and framed mementoes,"] to the extent that she wishes to preserve any or all of my mementoes and diplomas and the like for our future child or children."...

[After efforts at compromise failed, the estate's administrator asked for court instructions on how to respond to requests from Kane's children that the sperm either be destroyed or that they be given all (or most) of it. The children argued that the sperm's destruction would guard their family unit by preventing the birth of children who would never know their father and by preventing the disruption of their existing family by such an afterborn.]

21. This opinion was modified by *59 Cal. Rptr. 2d 222 (1996)*, and the California Supreme Court directed that the movified version neither be published in the official reports nor cited, *1997 Cal. LEXIS 131*. We include it to prompt discussion of the issues involved. [Eds.]

Hecht filed a Brief in response to the administrator's petition. She argued that neither the estate nor the children currently hold any property interest in, or right to distribution of, the sperm; it was gifted to her at the time of its deposit into the sperm bank and is either an inter vivos gift or a gift causa mortis. Hecht also maintained that even if the semen is an asset of the estate, the estate should be directed to distribute it to her because (1) the parties entered into a settlement agreement providing she is entitled to sole possession and control of the semen; (2) the will specifically directs that she is to be the sole beneficiary of the sperm; (3) destruction of the semen against her wishes would violate her rights to privacy and procreation under the federal and California Constitutions; and (4) she faces irreparable harm if the semen is not quickly distributed to her because her "advanced maternal age" will adversely affect her ability to conceive using the semen.

At the December 9, 1992, hearing on the petition, the court ordered that the sperm be destroyed....

I. PROBATE PRINCIPLES

... As we hereinafter explain, the decedent's interest in his frozen sperm vials, even if not governed by the general law of personal property, occupies "an interim category that entitles them to special respect because of their potential for human life" (*see Davis v. Davis* (Tenn. 1992) 842 S.W.2d 588, 597), and at the time of his death, decedent had an interest, in the nature of ownership, to the extent that he had decisionmaking authority as to the sperm within the scope of policy set by law. (*Ibid.*) Thus, decedent had an interest in his sperm which falls within the broad definition of property in Probate Code section 62, as "anything that may be the subject of ownership and includes both real and personal property and any interest therein."

II. NATURE OF RIGHTS IN SEMEN

"The present legal position toward property rights in the human body is unsettled and reflects no consistent philosophy or approach. Until recently, the common law either refused to recognize a property right in human bodies or recognized only a quasi-property right.... [The court in *Moore v. Regents of University of California*, 793 P.2d 479 (Cal. 1990),] did not resolve the debate over the existence or extent of a property interest in one's body. Nor does the existing statutory scheme quiet the debate. The statutes that address individuals' control over their bodies delineate the extent of that control in specific situations, but do not establish a general principle." (Note, *Personalizing Personalty: Toward a Property Right in Human Bodies* (1990) 69 Tex. L. Rev. 209, 220, fns. omitted.) ...

... Although it has not yet been joined with an egg to form a preembryo, as in *Davis*, the value of sperm lies in its potential to create a child after fertilization, growth, and birth. We conclude that at the time of his death, decedent had an interest, in the nature of ownership, to the extent that he had decisionmaking authority as to the use of his sperm for reproduction. Such interest is sufficient to constitute "property" within the meaning of Probate Code section 62. Accordingly, the probate court had jurisdiction with respect to the vials of sperm.

In concluding that the sperm is properly part of decedent's estate, we do not address the issue of the validity or enforceability of any contract or will purporting to express decedent's intent with respect to the stored sperm. In view of the nature of sperm as reproductive material which is a unique type of "property," we also decline petitioner's invitation to apply to this case the general law relating to gifts of personal property or the statutory provisions for gifts in view of impending death. (*See* Prob. Code, § 5700 et seq.)

We now address the propriety of the trial court's order that the sperm be destroyed....

Real parties attempt to justify the order as premised upon the theory that even if decedent had sufficient right of possession or ownership of the sperm so as to bring it within the jurisdiction of the probate court, his assumed intended use or disposition of the sperm—artificial insemination of Hecht—is invalid on two purported public policy grounds: (1) public policy forbids the artificial insemination of an unmarried woman, and (2) public policy forbids artificial insemination of Hecht with the stored sperm of a deceased man....

III. ARTIFICIAL INSEMINATION AND UNMARRIED WOMEN

... Real parties fail to cite any pertinent authority which indicates that the state has a policy of preventing the formation of single-parent families. We also point out that, at this time, the issue is speculative, as it assumes that Hecht will bear a child into a single-parent family....

Given the foregoing we also find without merit the argument of real parties that "The state's interest in protecting the institutions of family and marriage dictates petitioner should be denied access to the sperm." Clearly the institution of marriage is not implicated in this case, especially where there was no existing marriage relationship involving decedent at the time of his death and obviously there can be none after his death. (*See Jhordan C. v. Mary K., supra*, 179 Cal. App. 3d 386, 395, 224 Cal. Rptr. 530.) It is also premature for us to address the issue of family integrity and, in any case, there is no factual basis in this record to support any contention that the artificial insemination of Hecht would have an impact on any other family, including any family involving decedent's surviving adult children.

We thus conclude that real parties fail to establish with any pertinent authority that the public policy of California prohibits the artificial insemination of Hecht because of her status as an unmarried women.

IV. POSTMORTEM ARTIFICIAL INSEMINATION

We are aware of only one other court which has addressed the issue of the right of a woman to the sperm of a decedent. In 1984, in Parpalaix v. CECOS, the French tribunaux de grande instance ordered CECOS, a government run sperm bank in a Paris suburb, to return stored sperm of a decedent to a doctor chosen by his surviving wife. In light of the discussion in the preceding section pertaining to unmarried women, we find the Parpalaix case instructive and pertinent to the issue before us although it dealt with a married couple. We glean the following facts and decision in the Parpalaix case from a discussion of it in Shapiro and Sonnenblick, *supra*, 1 Journal of Law and Health at pages 229–233.

In 1981, Alain Parpalaix, suffering from testicular cancer, made one deposit of sperm at CECOS but left no instructions as to the future use of the sperm. At the time of the deposit, he was living with Corinne, whom he later married on December 23, 1983; as his condition was rapidly deteriorating, Alain died on December 25, 1983 at the age of 26. Corinne requested Alain's sperm deposit from CECOS, which denied the request as other centers had denied the requests of other widows. Corinne, joined by her in-laws, pursued the matter in court, where they contended that as Alain's natural heirs (spouse and parents), they had become the owners of the sperm and CECOS had broken the contract, which was in the nature of a bailment; they also argued they had a moral right to the sperm. . . .

According to Shapiro and Sonnenblick, the French court offered no solutions to the obstacles created by the [French] laws, but implied that, given the various new methods of procreation, the laws were outdated. . . . The court framed the issues it had to decide as only whether Alain Parpalaix intended his widow to be artificially inseminated with his sperm and whether that intent was "unequivocable." The court found that the testimony of the widow and Alain's parents established his "deep desire" to make his wife "the mother of a common child." (*Ibid.*) CECOS did not appeal the decision of the court and Corinne was artificially inseminated in November 1984; due to the small quantity and poor quality, she did not become pregnant. (*Ibid.*)

"Although the Parpalaix decision has been generally acclaimed as eminently humane, it has been criticized by doctors and lawyers alike. The court's order is a victory for the widow and even for the father who can sire a child from the grave, but it may be detrimental to the child. Though the court permitted Corinne Parpalaix to continue expressing her love for Alain by bearing his child, nowhere in the Parpalaix decision did it address and consider the best interests of the child. Commentators have suggested that the child could suffer psychologically from being conceived by a dead man. How such psychological effects would differ from those experienced by a child born to an unmarried woman by AID [artificial insemination by donor] or a child who, at a very young age, loses his father, remains to be explained." (Shapiro & Sonnenblick, *supra*, 1 J. Law & Health at pp. 246-247; fns. omitted.)

Echoing some of the concerns expressed by Shapiro and Sonnenblick, real parties argue that "this court should adopt a state policy against posthumous conception," because it is "in truth, the creation of orphaned children by artificial means with state authorization," a result which they characterize as "tragic." However, real parties do not cite any authority establishing the propriety of this court, or any court, to make the value judgment as to whether it is better for such a potential child not to be born, assuming that both gamete providers wish to conceive the child. In other words, assuming that both Hecht and decedent desired to conceive a child using decedent's sperm, real parties fail to establish a state interest sufficient to justify interference with that decision. As in Tennessee, we are aware of no statutes in California which contain a "statement of public policy which reveals an interest that could justify infringing on gamete-providers' decisional authority. . . ." (*Davis v. Davis, supra*, 842 S.W.2d 588, 602.) . . .

Real parties also intimate that the birth of a child by Hecht using decedent's sperm will create psychological burdens on them, decedent's surviving adult children, as well as financial burdens on society and on the estate.

In light of the UPA and Probate Code sections 6407 and 6408,[22] it is unlikely that the estate would be subject to claims with respect to any such children. If the Second Settlement Agreement is enforceable against Hecht, the estate may also be protected from any claims with respect to such children. . . .

Decedent's adult children also fail to provide any legal or factual basis to support their contention that the birth of a child through the artificial insemination of Hecht with decedent's sperm implicates their "fundamental right to protection of their family integrity," and thus their psychological well-being.

At this point, it is also entirely speculative as to whether any child born to Hecht using decedent's sperm will be a burden on society. . . .

For the foregoing reasons we conclude that the trial court abused its discretion in ordering decedent's sperm destroyed. . . .

Notes

1. After several more trips to court, Hecht was finally able to obtain all of the vials, but she was unable to get pregnant from Kane's sperm. She later married, and the new couple adopted a child. *The Easy Reader*, Hermosa Beach, Cal., Mar. 29, 2001.

2. Compare the questions that arise if post-mortem conceptions are successful. See Chapter 2, § 2.03B(3).

Problems

1. Stephen Merrill has come to you for advice about his will. Stephen is a devout Mormon with four children. His major concern is his 25-year-old son, Joseph, a "free spirit" who has lost interest in religion. As a way of encouraging Joseph to settle down and return to the church, Stephen wants to include the following language in his will: "One-fourth to my son Joseph, provided that within five years of my death Joseph marry a member of the Church of Jesus Christ of Latter-Day Saints." What is your

---

22. In California, Probate Code section 6407 provides that "Relatives of the decedent conceived before the decedent's death, but born thereafter inherit as if they had been born in the lifetime of the decedent."

advice? Does it matter whether Joseph lives in Salt Lake City, Utah, or West Ossipee, New Hampshire? What if the gift were to Joseph "so long as he does not enter into a civil union or domestic partnership"?

2. Richie Alford, a wealthy widower and a devout member of the First Episcopal Church, had his minister, Reverend John Rector, over for dinner to celebrate his 84th birthday. After dinner, he asked Rector to join him in the library to discuss his will. Alford noted that his adopted son, Ethan, who had run away from home at 15, had been an ungrateful bum. Rector advised that Alford bequeath $3,000 to Clara Witness (a good friend) and the residue of his estate to charities.

The next day, May 23, Alford typed a document he labeled "My Will." It reads as follows:

"I, Richie Alford, being of sound mind, do hereby declare this to be my last will, revoking all prior wills.

"I give my son Edward $10,000.

"I give $5,000 to my dear friend Clara Witness. "I give my Pontiac Firebird to Lucy Lincoln. "I give $10,000 to the First Episcopal Church.

"I give the rest, residue and remainder of my estate to the National Rifle Association."

The will contained a typed signature and had space for three witnesses to sign.

The next day, May 24, Alford invited the Witness sisters (Anna, Bessie, and Clara) over for coffee. As they were about to leave, he asked them to witness his will. They agreed, so he got out the will and placed it face up on the table. He requested that they not read the document, which he said was his will. Anna left the room to get her coat. While she was gone, Alford initialed his typed name in the presence of the other two witnesses. He then sat down in an armchair across the room. Bessie and Clara each signed the document, but because of the places they were standing, blocked Alford's view of the table. Anna then returned with her coat. Alford told her he had signed the will already; she observed his initials and added her signature. The sisters then departed.

On June 1, Alford gave Edward $5,000.

On June 15, Alford went to a meeting of the American Cancer Society and became inspired. In his own hand he wrote, "On June 15, I decided to rewrite my will. It is my desire that the American Cancer Society get my property. Richie Alford."

On June 30, Lucy Lincoln died.

At a July 4 picnic, Alford was told by a trusted friend that the American Cancer Society had disbanded. (In fact, it had not.) When he got home, he tore up the paper he had written on June 15, but left it in his file.

July 15, Alford died leaving an estate of $600,000. A paper in Alford's handwriting was found with Alford's papers. It read: "July 7. The birds in the park are making a mess of everything. My estate should still go to the NRA. Richie Alford."

The typed will and the handwritten "wills" were offered for probate. Ethan has appeared to claim a share of the estate.

Ethan and Edward (the only heirs or potential heirs at law) have consulted your senior partner. What arguments would you make and what problems would you face if you represent Ethan and Edward?

Selected References

R. Alta Charo, *Skin and Bones: Post-Mortem Markets in Human Tissue*, 26 Nova L. Rev. 421 (2002).

Ilene S. Cooper & Robert M. Harper, *Life After Death: The Authority of Estate Fiduciaries to Dispose of Decedents' Reproductive Matter*, 26 Touro L. Rev. 649 (2010).

William A. Drennan, *Wills, Trusts, Schadenfreude, and the Wild, Wacky Right of Publicity: Exploring the Enforceability of Dead-Hand Restrictions*, 58 Ark. L. Rev. 43 (2005).

Bridget M. Fuselier, *Pre-embryos in Probate: Property, Person, or Something Else?*, 24 Prob. & Prop. 31 (Sept./Oct. 2010).

Meeland Hanna, *Discriminatory Strings Attached: Reining in the Testator's Intent in Conditioning Will and Trust Bequests*, 25 U. Fla. J. L. & Pub. Pol'y 331 (2014).

Charles M. Jordan, Jr. & Casey J. Price, *First Moore, Then Hecht: Isn't It Time We Recognize a Property Interest in Tissues, Cells, and Gametes?*, 37 Real Prop. Prob. & Tr. J. 151, 152 (2002).

Aaron H. Kaplan, *The "Jewish Clause" and Public Policy: Preserving the Testamentary Right to Oppose Religious Intermarriage*, 8 Geo. J.L. & Pub. Pol'y 295 (2010).

Tracie M. Kester, Uniform Acts—*Can the Dead Hand Control the Dead Body? The Case for a Uniform Bodily Remains Law*, 29 W. New Eng. L. Rev. 571 (2007).

Emalee G. Popoff, *Testamentary Conditions in Restraint of the Marriage of Homosexual Donees*, 7 Drexel L. Rev. 163 (2014).

Ronald J. Scalise, Jr., *Public Policy and Antisocial Testators*, 32 Cardozo L. Rev. 1315 (2011).

Abigail J. Sykas, *Waste Not, Want Not: Can the Public Policy Doctrine Prohibit the Destruction of Property by Testamentary Direction?*, 25 Vt. L. Rev. 911 (2001).

Chapter 7

Planning for Incapacity

Because people live longer than ever before, and because medical technology often can keep even severely incapacitated people alive, clients often want to plan for their own possible incapacity. Consequently, lawyers who in the past merely drafted "simple" wills for clients of modest means are now developing plans both for property management and preservation and for control of health care decisions during incapacity. *See generally* Katherine C. Pearson, *Capacity, Conflict, and Change: Elder Law and Estate Planning Themes in an Aging World*, 117 Penn St. L. Rev. 979 (2013).

Both lawyers and their clients need to fight the temptation to think that only elderly people need to plan for the possibility of incapacity. Incapacity can strike any person at any time.

§ 7.01 Property Management and Preservation

For property management the trust, especially the revocable trust discussed in Chapter 4, § 4.05, provides great flexibility—making it preferable to guardianship, discussed in Chapter 1, § 1.02C. *See* Robert H. Sitkoff, *Revocable Trusts and Incapacity Planning: More than Just a Will Substitute*, 24 Elder L.J. 1 (2016). Here we discuss the lower-cost—and thus more widely used—durable power of attorney for property management Then we turn briefly to the oft-ignored "elephant in the room" of an aging population: long-term health insurance.

A. Durable Powers of Attorney

A power of attorney is an arrangement under which one person (the principal) gives another person (the agent) the power to act on behalf of the person executing the power. Powers of attorney might be executed for a specific purpose, like allowing someone else to participate in the closing of a house sale when either the buyer or the seller cannot be present. Powers of attorney can also be quite broad, authorizing the agent to act in all sorts of ways for the principal. They can be particularly useful in allowing a helper to handle the affairs of someone who is home-bound or in a nursing home.

Under traditional agency law, the power of the agent ends if the principal becomes incompetent. *See* Restatement (Second) of Agency §§ 120 and 122. To overcome that restriction, all states authorize some form of a "durable" power of attorney, under which the agent retains authority despite the principal's incapacity. As durable powers became more widespread, states developed a variety of responses to detailed questions like execution requirements and default rules regarding the scope of an agent's authority. To offer greater uniformity and a comprehensive approach, a new Uniform Power of Attorney Act was promulgated in 2006.[1] One important change eliminated the common requirement that the power of attorney form expressly state that it was creating a durable power; under the new act, a power is durable unless it expressly indicates otherwise. A new statutory form can serve as a drafting guide even in jurisdictions that have not adopted the new act. Compare the form in the Appendix, *infra*.

One overriding concern is to protect the principal from abuse. As the next case illustrates, informal family solutions can raise difficult questions.

Russ ex rel. Schwartz v. Russ

734 N.W.2d 874 (Wis. 2007)

N. Patrick Crooks, J.

... Johnnie Russ (Johnnie) appeals from an order ... dismissing Johnnie's complaint against her son, Elliott Russ (Elliott), with prejudice. The complaint, which was filed on Johnnie's behalf by her guardian, Marion Schwartz (Schwartz), alleged that Elliott breached his fiduciary duty as Johnnie's agent under a power of attorney (POA), and that he engaged in conversion of funds from a joint checking account[2] that he and Johnnie opened prior to the execution of the POA document.

...

Johnnie was born in 1926. In 1985, she suffered a stroke and had health problems thereafter. In 1992, Johnnie moved in with her son, Elliott, and his wife, Doris Russ (Doris), where she remained for the next nine years. That same year, Johnnie and Elliott opened a joint bank account into which they agreed to deposit all of Johnnie's income .... There is no evidence that Elliott or Doris deposited any of their income into the account.

On February 26, 1999, without the assistance of an attorney, Johnnie executed a durable Wisconsin Basic Power of Attorney for Finances and Property, pursuant to Wis. Stat. §§ 243.10 and 243.07, designating Elliott as her agent. It is undisputed that the entire document was read aloud at the time of execution. Johnnie granted Elliott all the powers on the first page of the form, authorizing him to, among other things,

---

1. The Uniform Power of Attorney Act has been enacted in more than 20 states. Several other states have their own comprehensive power of attorney statutes, which typically authorize durable powers of attorney. *See, e.g.*, Del. Code Ann. Ch 49-A (durable powers of attorney act) and N.Y. Gen. Oblig. Law §§ 5-1501 to 5-1514.

2. For more on multi-party accounts, *see* Chapter 4 § 4.02B. [Eds.]

pay her bills and manage her bank accounts. However, she left the second page blank, choosing not to authorize Elliott to be compensated for his services or to have general authority, which would allow him to make gifts. She also did not obligate Elliott to provide her with a periodic accounting.

After executing the POA, the parties continued living together as they had before, maintaining their previous financial arrangement.... On October 10, 2002, the circuit court declared Johnnie incompetent, appointed Schwartz as Johnnie's guardian, and terminated the durable POA.[3]

On March 10, 2003, Schwartz filed this suit on Johnnie's behalf. Johnnie sought recovery of funds that Elliott withdrew from the joint account between March 1999 and April 2002, while he was her POA agent, for expenses related to himself, his business, and his wife. Johnnie alleged that by using the joint account, which contained her funds, for his own expenses, Elliott breached his fiduciary duty as her POA agent. During the contested period, $45,172.44 of Johnnie's funds were deposited into the joint account. The parties stipulated that, between February 1999 and October 2002, the total amount of checks written from the joint account for the benefit of Elliott was $34,379.91.

In the circuit court, Johnnie argued that Elliott's use of her funds from the joint account constituted self-dealing. She maintained that ... because the POA did not authorize Elliott to make gifts or be compensated, it did not permit him to self-deal. Elliott argued that because the funds in a joint account belong to all account holders under Wis. Stat. § 705.03, he was entitled to spend the money, regardless of his role as Johnnie's POA agent. He also argued that any money he used for his own benefit was offset by the value of the care he had provided Johnnie.

[The circuit court ultimately ruled that Elliott has assumed a fiduciary duty to "take care of" Johnnie and that he had not breached the duty. Based on mutual mistake, the court reformed the POA to authorize Elliott's free use of the money in the joint account. Johnnie appealed dismissal of her claim.]

...

... [A] POA agent has a fiduciary duty to the principal, and ... the agent is usually prohibited from self-dealing unless the power to self-deal is written in the POA document.... However, in this case, the prohibition against self-dealing is complicated by the fact that Elliott and Johnnie opened a joint checking account in 1992, shared the joint account for more than six years before they executed the POA document in 1999, and continued to use the joint account after the execution of the POA document.

---

3. Appointment of a guardian does not necessarily end the agent's authority under a POA, but a court might order such a result to protect the ward. *See, e.g., Russell v. Chase Investment Services Corp.*, 212 P.3d 1178 (Okla. 2009). However, that result was common practice in Wisconsin at the time of this litigation. Telephone conversation between Roger W. Andersen and Jeffrey Myer, who represented Johnnie, July 15, 2011. [Eds.]

Under Wis. Stat. § 705.03, "unless there is clear and convincing evidence of a different intent," the parties to a joint account may withdraw and use the funds in the account without being required to account to any other party to the joint account. In this case, the POA document itself is not clear as to the parties' intent.... Johnnie did not check the box on the second page of the POA document that would have required Elliott to provide an accounting, nor did she write instructions for how the joint account should be handled.

...

We hold that, when a POA agent and a principal share a preexisting joint checking account, the execution of a POA document, in and of itself, is not "clear and convincing evidence of a different intent" under Wis. Stat. § 705.03. We are satisfied that § 705.03, under which Elliott owed no duty to Johnnie as a joint account holder, appears to conflict with Elliott's fiduciary duty as a POA agent pursuant to Wis. Stat. § 243.10. This case involves conflicting and inconsistent presumptions. When funds are deposited into a joint bank account, donative intent is presumed.... [4]

On the other hand, a fiduciary, such as a POA agent, has an obligation not to engage in self-dealing.... When a POA agent, for the agent's own use, transfers funds deposited by the principal, without written authority in the POA document to do so, a presumption of fraud is created, regardless of whether the funds were deposited before or after the execution of the POA.

... In *Estate of Rybolt*, 258 Ill.App.3d 886, 197 Ill.Dec. 570, 631 N.E.2d 792, 795 (1994), the Illinois court of appeals stated that "where such conflicting presumptions exist they cancel each other out, leaving the trial court free to make a determination based upon facts and credibility of the witnesses." The court cited *In re Estate of Harms*, 236 Ill.App.3d 630, 177 Ill.Dec. 256, 603 N.E.2d 37, 44 (Ill.App.1992), another Illinois court of appeals case, in which there were joint accounts that existed prior to the fiduciary relationship created by a POA. Income was deposited into the joint account while the fiduciary relationship existed. The court held for the POA agent, reasoning that the deposits made to the accounts followed a procedure that was used prior to the existence of the fiduciary relationship. *Id.* at 45.

Then, in *In re Estate of Teall*, 329 Ill.App.3d 83, 263 Ill.Dec. 364, 768 N.E.2d 124 (2002), the Illinois court of appeals limited the holding in *Harms* to apply only when a joint account was created before the fiduciary relationship began, and where deposits made during the fiduciary relationship followed a procedure that was established before that relationship. The court stated, "'[W]here the attorney-in-fact actively uses his position to create the joint tenancies the presumptions do not cancel; instead,

4. "Unless there is clear and convincing evidence of a different intent" the presumption is conclusive, because the statue continues: "The application of any withdrawn from a joint account by a party thereto shall not be subject to inquiry by any person, including any other party to the account and not withstanding such other party's minority or other disability." Wis. Stat. § 705.03(1). [Eds.]

the controlling presumption is the presumption of fraud, which requires strong evidence to overcome.'" *Id.* at 130 (citations omitted).

... We hold that a joint checking account established under Wis. Stat. § 705.03 prior to the execution of a POA creates a presumption of donative intent. We further hold that when an agent acting under a POA transfers funds deposited by the principal from such joint account, but for the agent's own use, a presumption of fraud is created. When these two conflicting and inconsistent presumptions coexist, the circuit court is then free to make a determination based upon the facts and the credibility of the witnesses....

In arriving at its conclusion that Elliott did not breach his fiduciary duty nor engage in conversion, the circuit court reformed the POA document on grounds of mutual mistake and applied the doctrine of equitable estoppel to bar Johnnie's claim.... [W]e decline to take that approach here because such approach, if followed by other circuit courts, would likely be very time consuming. Those doctrines are often difficult to apply, especially in cases such as the one presented here.... We are satisfied that the conflicting presumptions approach taken by Illinois courts, and adopted here, will be more efficient and less time consuming....

The order of the circuit court is affirmed.

Shirley S. Abrahamson, Chief Justice, (concurrence).

I join the majority opinion but write to put this case in the larger societal and legal context of elder abuse generally and durable powers of attorney and joint accounts more specifically....

The durable power of attorney has been appropriately characterized as "a simple yet powerful tool." But it is at the same time a troublesome document, creating the potential for abuse. By merely signing a durable power of attorney, a principal may give an agent tremendous power, including the power to sell the principal's home and any other assets, to make investments, to cancel insurance policies or name new beneficiaries, and even to empty the bank accounts.

... Most of the litigation involving durable powers of attorney seems to arise when an agent allegedly makes improper gifts or engages in more broadly-stated "self-dealing."

Yet the problems involving durable powers of attorney do not arise just from the acts of selfish and conniving agents. Commentators have also expressed concern about the difficulties created by the confusing nature of the fiduciary duty imposed by a durable power. As one commentator aptly summarized, "[t]he most serious problem with durable powers is the uncertainty as to the agent's powers." Little guidance is given to agents in the statutes or case law, and few guidelines have been clearly established as to the standard agents are to use in making decisions for the principal under the durable power and the extent of their duty to communicate with the principal.

So how is a well-intentioned agent supposed to behave? Assumptions have been made that an agent under a durable power is governed by traditional agency rules, or by rules analogous to those governing guardians and trustees, or by general fiduciary principles. Merely to say that the principal is a fiduciary, however, is not sufficient. Many different types of fiduciary relationships exist, and the obligations of the agent vary depending on the specific context of the fiduciary relationship.

The Restatement (Third) of Agency explains that

> The relationship created by a durable power resembles agency because it is a mechanism to enable the legal consequences of one person's acts to be attributed to another person. In other respects, the relationship at this point resembles a trust in which the power holder is similar to a trustee because the person acting is not under the control of the person for whom the actor's conduct has consequences and on whose behalf the actor has a duty to act.
>
> 1 Restatement (Third) Agency, Introduction, at 10 (2006).

Problems are also specifically posed by the "durable" nature of the durable power of attorney. Perhaps when a principal is competent and is aware of the agent's actions one set of fiduciary duties comes into play under a durable power, but a different set of fiduciary duties may govern after the principal becomes incompetent. Having different standards, however, may prove not only difficult but may also be contrary to the goals of the durable power of attorney. The determination of incompetency is complicated and the durable power of attorney is designed to avoid a judicial declaration of incompetency.

. . .

The majority opinion adopts the "intention of the principal" as the standard for testing the agent's decision-making in the present case. An agent is to act according to the principal's wishes. Such a standard may be fine when the principal can supervise the agent. This standard, however, may be subject to abuse when the principal can no longer supervise the agent and cannot testify because he or she is incompetent or deceased.

Moreover, this standard may become problematic when the principal's wishes are at odds with the principal's best interests. The principal, for instance, may not want to move into an assisted living facility even though he or she can no longer live alone, or may not want to sell certain assets even though he or she is financially strapped. What is the well-intentioned agent to do, when what is clearly in the principal's best interests is against the principal's intentions?

. . .

This case illustrates the complexity of the problem and how simple reforms may not work. In the instant case, the principal was an elderly woman who, without benefit of counsel, appointed her adult son as the agent under a standard durable power of attorney form and who later became incompetent. In completing the durable power form, the mother did not explicitly allow her son to make gifts or engage in self-dealing. Nevertheless, because of the circumstances and relationship, the circuit court (and this court) treat the power of attorney as if it had these provisions.

Further complicating the agency relationship in the present case is that the mother and son had a joint account that predated the execution of the durable power. . . .

. . . This case illustrates that the durable power of attorney implicates other areas of the law, and any reform must be mindful of these other legal issues.

. . .

There are significant issues bubbling and brewing just below the surface of today's decision that need to be addressed. Courts have not had the opportunity to define the role of an agent under a durable power of attorney sufficiently because litigation is too infrequent and too fact-specific. Legislative study of the use and abuse of durable powers of attorney may be called for. . . .

I am authorized to state that Justice Ann Walsh Bradley joins this opinion.

Wisconsin adopted the Uniform Power of Attorney Act in 2009,[5] including the form that appears below. *See* Wis. Stat. ch. 244.

WISCONSIN STATUTORY FORM POWER OF ATTORNEY FOR FINANCES AND PROPERTY

IMPORTANT INFORMATION

THIS POWER OF ATTORNEY AUTHORIZES ANOTHER PERSON (YOUR AGENT) TO MAKE DECISIONS CONCERNING YOUR PROPERTY FOR YOU (THE PRINCIPAL). YOUR AGENT WILL BE ABLE TO MAKE DECISIONS AND ACT WITH RESPECT TO YOUR PROPERTY (INCLUDING YOUR MONEY) WHETHER OR NOT YOU ARE ABLE TO ACT FOR YOURSELF. THE MEANING OF AUTHORITY OVER SUBJECTS LISTED ON THIS FORM IS EXPLAINED IN THE UNIFORM POWER OF ATTORNEY FOR FINANCES AND PROPERTY ACT IN CHAPTER 244 OF THE WISCONSIN STATUTES.

THIS POWER OF ATTORNEY DOES NOT AUTHORIZE THE AGENT TO MAKE HEALTH-CARE DECISIONS FOR YOU.

YOU SHOULD SELECT SOMEONE YOU TRUST TO SERVE AS YOUR AGENT. UNLESS YOU SPECIFY OTHERWISE, GENERALLY THE AGENT'S AUTHORITY WILL CONTINUE UNTIL YOU DIE OR REVOKE THE POWER OF ATTORNEY OR THE AGENT RESIGNS OR IS UNABLE TO ACT FOR YOU.

5. The Act has been adopted in more than 20 states. Current status is available at http://uniformlaws.org/LegislativeFactSheet.aspx?title=Power%20of%20Attorney.

YOUR AGENT IS ENTITLED TO REASONABLE COMPENSATION UNLESS YOU STATE OTHERWISE IN THE SPECIAL INSTRUCTIONS.

THIS FORM PROVIDES FOR DESIGNATION OF ONE AGENT. IF YOU WISH TO NAME MORE THAN ONE AGENT YOU MAY NAME A COAGENT IN THE SPECIAL INSTRUCTIONS. COAGENTS ARE NOT REQUIRED TO ACT TOGETHER UNLESS YOU INCLUDE THAT REQUIREMENT IN THE SPECIAL INSTRUCTIONS.

IF YOUR AGENT IS UNABLE OR UNWILLING TO ACT FOR YOU, YOUR POWER OF ATTORNEY WILL END UNLESS YOU HAVE NAMED A SUCCESSOR AGENT. YOU MAY ALSO NAME A 2ND SUCCESSOR AGENT.

THIS POWER OF ATTORNEY BECOMES EFFECTIVE IMMEDIATELY UNLESS YOU STATE OTHERWISE IN THE SPECIAL INSTRUCTIONS. THIS POWER OF ATTORNEY DOES NOT REVOKE ANY POWER OF ATTORNEY EXECUTED PREVIOUSLY UNLESS YOU SO PROVIDE IN THE SPECIAL INSTRUCTIONS.

IF YOU REVOKE THIS POWER OF ATTORNEY, YOU SHOULD NOTIFY YOUR AGENT AND ANY OTHER PERSON TO WHOM YOU HAVE GIVEN A COPY. IF YOUR AGENT IS YOUR SPOUSE OR DOMESTIC PARTNER AND YOUR MARRIAGE IS ANNULLED OR YOU ARE DIVORCED OR LEGALLY SEPARATED OR THE DOMES TIC PARTNERSHIP IS TERMINATED AFTER SIGNING THIS DOCUMENT, THE DOCUMENT IS INVALID.

IF YOU HAVE QUESTIONS ABOUT THE POWER OF ATTORNEY OR THE AUTHORITY YOU ARE GRANTING TO YOUR AGENT, YOU SHOULD SEEK LEGAL ADVICE BEFORE SIGNING THIS FORM.

DESIGNATION OF AGENT

I .... (name of principal) name the following person as my agent:

Name of agent: ....

Agent's address: ....

Agent's telephone number: ....

DESIGNATION OF SUCCESSOR AGENT(S) (OPTIONAL)

If my agent is unable or unwilling to act for me, I name as my successor agent:

Name of successor agent: ....

Successor agent's address: ....

Successor agent's telephone number: ....

If my successor agent is unable or unwilling to act for me, I name as my 2nd successor agent:

Name of 2nd successor agent: ....

Second successor agent's address: ....

Second successor agent's telephone number: ....

GRANT OF GENERAL AUTHORITY

I grant my agent and any successor agent general authority to act for me with respect to the following subjects as defined in the Uniform Power of Attorney for Finances and Property Act in chapter 244 of the Wisconsin statutes:

INITIAL each subject you want to include in the agent's general authority.

Real property

Tangible personal property

Stocks and bonds

Commodities and options

Banks and other financial institutions

Operation of entity or business

Insurance and annuities

Estates, trusts, and other beneficial interests

Claims and litigation

Personal and family maintenance

Benefits from governmental programs or civil or military service

Retirement plans

Taxes

LIMITATION ON AGENT'S AUTHORITY

An agent who is not my spouse or domestic partner MAY NOT use my property to benefit the agent or a person to whom the agent owes an obligation of support unless I have included that authority in the special instructions.

SPECIAL INSTRUCTIONS (OPTIONAL)

You may give special instructions in the following space ....

EFFECTIVE DATE

This power of attorney is effective immediately unless I have stated otherwise in the special instructions.

NOMINATION OF GUARDIAN (OPTIONAL)

If it becomes necessary for a court to appoint a guardian of my estate or guardian of my person, I nominate the following person(s) for appointment:

Name of nominee for guardian of my estate: ....

Nominee's address: ....

Nominee's telephone number: ....

Name of nominee for guardian of my person: ....

Nominee's address: ....

Nominee's telephone number: ....

RELIANCE ON THIS POWER OF ATTORNEY FOR FINANCES AND PROPERTY

Any person, including my agent, may rely upon the validity of this power of attorney or a copy of it unless that person knows that the power of attorney has been terminated or is invalid.

SIGNATURE AND ACKNOWLEDGMENT

Your signature .... Date ....

Your name printed ....

Your address ....

Your telephone number ....

State of ....

County of ....

This document was acknowledged before me on .... (date), by .... (name of principal).

(Seal, if any)

Signature of notary ....

My commission expires: ....

This document prepared by: ....

IMPORTANT INFORMATION FOR AGENT

AGENT'S DUTIES

WHEN YOU ACCEPT THE AUTHORITY GRANTED UNDER THIS POWER OF ATTORNEY, A SPECIAL LEGAL RELATIONSHIP IS CREATED BETWEEN YOU AND THE PRINCIPAL. THIS RELATIONSHIP IMPOSES UPON YOU LEGAL DUTIES THAT CONTINUE UNTIL YOU RESIGN OR THE POWER OF ATTORNEY IS TERMINATED OR REVOKED. YOU MUST DO ALL OF THE FOLLOWING:

(1) DO WHAT YOU KNOW THE PRINCIPAL REASONABLY EXPECTS YOU TO DO WITH THE PRINCIPAL'S PROPERTY OR, IF YOU DO NOT KNOW THE PRINCIPAL'S EXPECTATIONS, ACT IN THE PRINCIPAL'S BEST INTEREST.

(2) ACT IN GOOD FAITH.

(3) DO NOTHING BEYOND THE AUTHORITY GRANTED IN THIS POWER OF ATTORNEY.

(4) DISCLOSE YOUR IDENTITY AS AN AGENT WHENEVER YOU ACT FOR THE PRINCIPAL BY WRITING OR PRINTING THE NAME OF THE PRINCIPAL AND SIGNING YOUR OWN NAME AS "AGENT" IN THE FOLLOWING MANNER:

(principal's name) by .... (your signature) as agent

UNLESS THE SPECIAL INSTRUCTIONS IN THIS POWER OF ATTORNEY STATE OTHERWISE, YOU MUST ALSO DO ALL OF THE FOLLOWING:

(1) ACT LOYALLY FOR THE PRINCIPAL'S BENEFIT.

(2) AVOID CONFLICTS THAT WOULD IMPAIR YOUR ABILITY TO ACT IN THE PRINCIPAL'S BEST INTEREST.

(3) ACT WITH CARE, COMPETENCE, AND DILIGENCE.

(4) KEEP A RECORD OF ALL RECEIPTS, DISBURSEMENTS, AND TRANSACTIONS MADE ON BEHALF OF THE PRINCIPAL.

(5) COOPERATE WITH ANY PERSON THAT HAS AUTHORITY TO MAKE HEALTH-CARE DECISIONS FOR THE PRINCIPAL TO DO WHAT YOU KNOW THE PRINCIPAL REASONABLY EXPECTS OR, IF YOU DO NOT KNOW THE PRINCIPAL'S EXPECTATIONS, TO ACT IN THE PRINCIPAL'S BEST INTEREST.

(6) ATTEMPT TO PRESERVE THE PRINCIPAL'S ESTATE PLAN IF YOU KNOW THE PLAN AND PRESERVING THE PLAN IS CONSISTENT WITH THE PRINCIPAL'S BEST INTEREST.

TERMINATION OF AGENT'S AUTHORITY

YOU MUST STOP ACTING ON BEHALF OF THE PRINCIPAL IF YOU LEARN OF ANY EVENT THAT TERMINATES THIS POWER OF ATTORNEY OR YOUR AUTHORITY UNDER THIS POWER OF ATTORNEY. EVENTS THAT TERMINATE A POWER OF ATTORNEY OR YOUR AUTHORITY TO ACT UNDER A POWER OF ATTORNEY INCLUDE ALL OF THE FOLLOWING:

(1) DEATH OF THE PRINCIPAL.

(2) THE PRINCIPAL'S REVOCATION OF THE POWER OF ATTORNEY OR YOUR AUTHORITY.

(3) THE OCCURRENCE OF A TERMINATION EVENT STATED IN THE POWER OF ATTORNEY.

(4) THE PURPOSE OF THE POWER OF ATTORNEY IS FULLY ACCOMPLISHED.

(5) IF YOU ARE MARRIED TO THE PRINCIPAL, A LEGAL ACTION IS FILED WITH A COURT TO END YOUR MARRIAGE, OR FOR YOUR LEGAL SEPARATION, UNLESS THE SPECIAL INSTRUCTIONS IN THIS POWER OF ATTORNEY STATE THAT SUCH AN ACTION WILL NOT TERMINATE YOUR AUTHORITY.

(6) IF YOU ARE THE PRINCIPAL'S DOMESTIC PARTNER AND YOUR DOMESTIC PARTNERSHIP IS TERMINATED, UNLESS THE SPECIAL INSTRUCTIONS IN THIS POWER OF ATTORNEY STATE THAT SUCH AN ACTION WILL NOT TERMINATE YOUR AUTHORITY.

LIABILITY OF AGENT

THE MEANING OF THE AUTHORITY GRANTED TO YOU IS DEFINED IN THE UNIFORM POWER OF ATTORNEY FOR FINANCES AND PROPERTY ACT IN CHAPTER 244 OF THE WISCONSIN STATUTES. IF YOU VIOLATE THE UNIFORM POWER OF ATTORNEY FOR FINANCES AND PROPERTY ACT IN CHAPTER 244 OF THE WISCONSIN STATUTES OR ACT OUTSIDE THE AUTHORITY GRANTED, YOU MAY BE LIABLE FOR ANY DAMAGES CAUSED BY YOUR VIOLATION.

IF THERE IS ANYTHING ABOUT THIS DOCUMENT OR YOUR DUTIES THAT YOU DO NOT UNDERSTAND, YOU SHOULD SEEK LEGAL ADVICE.

OPTIONAL SIGNATURE OF AGENT

I HAVE READ AND ACCEPT THE DUTIES AND LIABILITIES OF THE AGENT AS SPECIFIED IN THIS POWER OF ATTORNEY.

Agent's signature _____ Date _____

Uniform Power of Attorney Act

Section 201. Authority That Requires Specific Grant; Grant Of General Authority.

(a) An agent under a power of attorney may do the following on behalf of the principal or with the principal's property only if the power of attorney expressly grants the agent the authority and exercise of the authority is not otherwise prohibited by another agreement or instrument to which the authority or property is subject:

(1) create, amend, revoke, or terminate an inter vivos trust;

(2) make a gift;

(3) create or change rights of survivorship;

(4) create or change a beneficiary designation;

(5) delegate authority granted under the power of attorney;

(6) waive the principal's right to be a beneficiary of a joint and survivor annuity, including a survivor benefit under a retirement plan; [or]

(7) exercise fiduciary powers that the principal has authority to delegate [; or

(8) disclaim property, including a power of appointment].

(b) Notwithstanding a grant of authority to do an act described in subsection (a), unless the power of attorney otherwise provides, an agent that is not an ancestor, spouse, or descendant of the principal, may not exercise authority under a power of attorney to create in the agent, or in an individual to whom the agent owes a legal obligation of support, an interest in the principal's property, whether by gift, right of survivorship, beneficiary designation, disclaimer, or otherwise.

(c) Subject to subsections (a), (b), (d), and (e), if a power of attorney grants to an agent authority to do all acts that a principal could do, the agent has the general authority described in Sections 204 through 216.

(d) Unless the power of attorney otherwise provides, a grant of authority to make a gift is subject to Section 217.

(e) Subject to subsections (a), (b), and (d), if the subjects over which authority is granted in a power of attorney are similar or overlap, the broadest authority controls.

(f) Authority granted in a power of attorney is exercisable with respect to property that the principal has when the power of attorney is executed or acquires later, whether or not the property is located in this state and whether or not the authority is exercised or the power of attorney is executed in this state.

(g) An act performed by an agent pursuant to a power of attorney has the same effect and inures to the benefit of and binds the principal and the principal's successors in interest as if the principal had performed the act.

Section 217. Gifts.

(a) In this section, a gift "for the benefit of" a person includes a gift to a trust, an account under the Uniform Transfers to Minors Act, and a tuition savings account or prepaid tuition plan as defined under Internal Revenue Code Section 529, 26 U.S.C. Section 529 [, as amended].

(b) Unless the power of attorney otherwise provides, language in a power of attorney granting general authority with respect to gifts authorizes the agent only to:

(1) make outright to, or for the benefit of, a person, a gift of any of the principal's property, including by the exercise of a presently exercisable general power of appointment held by the principal, in an amount per donee not to exceed the annual dollar limits of the federal gift tax exclusion under Internal Revenue Code Section 2503(b), 26 U.S.C. Section 2503(b), [as amended,] without regard to whether the federal gift tax exclusion applies to the gift, or if the principal's spouse agrees to consent to a split gift pursuant to Internal Revenue Code Section 56 2513, 26 U.S.C. 2513, [as amended,]

in an amount per donee not to exceed twice the annual federal gift tax exclusion limit; and

(2) consent, pursuant to Internal Revenue Code Section 2513, 26 U.S.C. Section 2513, [as amended,] to the splitting of a gift made by the principal's spouse in an amount per donee not to exceed the aggregate annual gift tax exclusions for both spouses.

(c) An agent may make a gift of the principal's property only as the agent determines is consistent with the principal's objectives if actually known by the agent and, if unknown, as the agent determines is consistent with the principal's best interest based on all relevant factors, including:

(1) the value and nature of the principal's property;

(2) the principal's foreseeable obligations and need for maintenance;

(3) minimization of taxes, including income, estate, inheritance, generation skipping transfer, and gift taxes;

(4) eligibility for a benefit, a program, or assistance under a statute or regulation; and

(5) the principal's personal history of making or joining in making gifts.

Notes and Questions

1. Do you think the *Russ* litigation would have been avoided if the form above had been available when Johnnie executed her Power of Attorney? What if the provisions of the Uniform Power of Attorney Act excerpted above had been in force at the time?

2. Sections 9 and 10 of the Revised Uniform Fiduciary Access to Digital Assets Act, discussed in Chapter 10, § 10.03A(2)(b)(ii), provide rules for an agent acting under a power of attorney to access digital assets (electronic records) of the principal.[6] Generally, access by the agent will need to have been authorized by the principal.

3. Powers of attorney can either be immediately effective or can be written to "spring" into action upon the happening of a future event, usually the disability of the principal. Powers invite litigation if they merely provide that they are effective upon the principal's "incapacity." The power should define "incapacity," and probably should designate a committee (with flexible membership) to certify that incapacity exists. In Section 109(d), the Uniform Power of Attorney Act authorizes a person designated to determine the principal's incapacity to be able to access health care information and communicate with the health care provider under the Health Insurance Portability and Accountability Act [HIPAA], 42 U.S.C. § 1320d. Well-drafted springing powers will include HIPAA authorization.

---

6. Section 14 of RUFADAA, discussed in Chapter 10, § 10.03A(2)(b)(ii), provides rules for conservators (guardians) to access digital assets of a protected person. Generally, court authorization will be necessary for the conservator (guardian) to obtain access to the digital assets of a ward.

4. Some clients do not want to trouble themselves with a lifetime trust while they are competent, but do want its protection should they become incompetent. One solution is to establish a nominally-funded trust and create a durable power of attorney that authorizes the agent to add funds to the trust. The power of attorney functions much like a pour-over will,[7] but the assets can be transferred to the trust while the principal is still alive.

5. Some power of attorney forms authorize the agent to create a new trust on behalf of the principal. *See, e.g., Reineck v. Lemen*, 792 S.E.2d 269 (Va. 2016) (upholding agent's creation of trust in agent's favor because within best interests of principal).

Both the agent and the new trustee are subject to fiduciary duties. *See In re Estate of Kurrelmeyer*, 895 A.2d 207 (Vt. 2006) (upholding such a power, but reserving the question of whether the agent breached her fiduciary duty under the power by creating a trust favorable to herself); *In re Dentler Family Trust*, 873 A.2d 738 (Pa. Super. Ct. 2005) (when the agent created a trust naming himself and his lawyer as co-trustees, the court ignored an exculpatory clause setting a lower standard of care for the trustees). We discuss fiduciary duties in Chapter 10.

6. Should an agent acting under a durable power of attorney be able to revoke a trust? With or without specific authorization? *See Perosi v. LiGreci*, 948 N.Y.S.2d 629 (N.Y. App. Div. 2012) (attorney-in-fact can amend trust without specific authorization to do so in trust instrument or in power of attorney).

7. Should a power of attorney that was executed in one state be recognized in another state? Although the Uniform Recognition of Substitute Decision-Making Documents Act so provides, it has only be enacted in Idaho. *See* Idaho. Code Ann. § 15-15-101.

8. It is not unusual for a younger-generation person to help an older friend or relative by arranging to meet with a lawyer or accompanying the older person to the lawyer's office. Sometimes the helper offers to pay for the work. This situation poses a series of ethical problems for the lawyer. If the older person is not mobile, things get even more complicated. Consider the following:

Lawrence J. Fox & Susan R. Martyn, Red Flags: A Lawyer's Handbook on Legal Ethics

(ALI-ABA 2d ed. 2010).

§ 7.32(b) Relative Matters?

This kid shows up the other day. Tells us his dad needs a new will. Seems dad is quite infirm. So son comes down to tell me what dad wants. Nice fellow. Dad wants to set up an education fund for the grandkids. I prepare the will; son will get dad to sign it.

7. *See* Chapter 4, § 4.05.

We think it's time to start making house calls. Remember dad is your client. . . . You've got to make sure of two things. What are dad's wishes? And is dad fully capable of making decisions? When clients suffer from a disability, we are supposed to treat them as competent to the greatest extent possible. But if we conclude the client cannot order his affairs, we have to make sure we are taking directions from someone who has dad's best interest at heart. That may be true here. But you just don't know enough right now. Go visit dad or decline the engagement.

§ 7.32(c) Third-Party Payment

Someone other than your client can pay for the representation, as long as the 5 C's[8] you owe your client remains uncompromised. Three specific requirements are designed to make this happen:

1. The client must know about the payment and who makes it, and give informed consent . . . ;

2. You must make sure that there is no interference with your independent professional judgment, or the client-lawyer relationship; and

3. Confidences of your client remain sacrosanct, protected by your fiduciary duty to the client, not the third party. In other words, the payor has no right to call the tune, whether it's an employer paying for the representation of an employee . . . , one codefendant paying for the representation of all . . . , parents paying for the representation of a child . . . , nondebtor third parties paying for the representation of debtor's counsel in bankruptcy, or a nonprofit organization that pays for the legal representation of its clients.

§ 7.32(d) Third-Party Influence

Even when third parties do not pay for the representation of another, they nevertheless may seek to influence a client-lawyer relationship.

Red Flag Do not assume that the person you talk to or the person who pays you is a client. Although this will often be the case, you have the obligation to clarify whom you represent and to make clear to third parties that they have no right to learn anything about the representation nor to influence it unless your client wants them to do so.

If you have been recommended, employed, or paid to provide legal services to another, you have the obligation to remember that your client is not the person who regularly or occasionally recommends you, or the person who perhaps speaks to you on behalf of another, say a family member . . . . You must not allow that other person to direct or regulate your professional judgment on behalf of your client.

---

8. [Client] Control, Competence, Communication, Confidentiality, and [resolving] Conflicts of Interest. [Eds.]

Problem

One of the biggest problems with durable powers is that third parties might not honor them. How would you solve the following potential questions: Did the principal have the mental capacity to create the power? Is the principal "incapacitated" enough to trigger a springing power? Does the power authorize the particular activity for which it is being relied upon? Has the principal revoked the power?

Selected References

Roger W. Andersen, Plan While You Can: Legal Solutions for Facing Disability, Ch. 3 (2003).

Jane A. Black, *The Not-So-Golden Years: Power of Attorney, Elder Abuse, and Why Our Laws Are Failing a Vulnerable Population*, 82 St. John's L. Rev. 289 (2008).

Karen E. Boxx, *The Durable Power of Attorney's Place in the Family of Fiduciary Relationships*, 36 Ga. L. Rev. 1 (2001).

Ralph C. Brashier, *The Ghostwritten Will*, 93 B.U. L. Rev. 1803 (2013).

Jacqueline Myles Crain, *HIPAA—A Shield for Health Information and a Snag for Estate Planning and Corporate Documents*, 40 Real Prop. Prob. & Tr. J. 357 (2005).

Marshall B. Kapp, *Older Clients with Questionable Legal Competence: Elder Law Practitioners and Treating Physicians*, 37 Wm. Mitchell L. Rev. 99 (2010).

Nancy J. Knauer, *Gay and Lesbian Elders: Estate Planning and End-of-Life Decision Making*, 12 Fl. Coastal L. Rev. 164 (2010).

Nina A. Kohn, *Elder Empowerment as a Strategy for Curbing the Hidden Abuses of Durable Powers of Attorney*, 59 Rutgers L. Rev. 1 (2006).

Catherine Seal, *Power of Attorney: Convenient Contract or Dangerous Document?*, 11 Marq. Elder's Advisor 307 (2010).

Linda S. Whitton, *The Uniform Power of Attorney Act: Striking a Balance Between Autonomy and Protection*, 1 Phoenix L. Rev. 343 (2008).

B. Long-Term Care Insurance

Another property-related concern of persons anticipating disability is whether they can afford the health care they may need and at the same time preserve their estates for their families. Some clients will need Medicaid planning, a topic we will discuss in connection with trust creditors' claims. *See* § 8.03(C)(4). Another solution will be to invest in long-term health insurance.

David M. English, *A Checklist for Long-Term Coverage: Know the Policy and Know Your Client*

Prac. Law., June 1993, at 15–18

Insurance coverage for long-term care will play an increasingly important role in a society where people are living longer and longer. Long-term care insurance is widely available and fairly easy to obtain. But the types of coverages vary widely. Although nearly all states have regulations governing minimum policy terms, the policies on the market offer very different services, levels of coverage, and conditions which must be met before benefits will be paid. The following checklist will help you to decide whether long-term care insurance makes sense for your client and to choose the right kind of policy.

Checklist for Choosing a Long-Term Care Policy Full Information

1. Before recommending that a client purchase a particular policy, be certain that both you and the client have complete information:

- The insurance agent may have little knowledge of the product which he or she is selling. Consequently, except for agents in whom you have full confidence, never rely on the oral statements of the agent alone, or even worse, the client's translation of the agent's statements.
- Sales literature distributed by the company may or may not be complete concerning some of the more critical policy terms. The best advice is to insist on a copy of a prototype policy.

Assessing the Client

1. Long-term care insurance isn't for everyone. Before recommending a long-term care policy, determine whether other planning devices can meet the client's long-term care needs:

- As a general rule, it is probably a mistake to recommend long-term care insurance to a client who can easily qualify for Medicaid.
- Furthermore, there is a high lapse rate on long-term care insurance policies. The client may otherwise be an excellent candidate for a long-term care policy, but not if the client lacks the commitment to continue premium payments.

2. Assess the downside risk of not purchasing a policy:

- What is the probability that the client will need nursing home care? There is a 43 per cent probability that a 65-year-old will at some time need nursing home care. But the rate is considerably higher for women than men, and the rate will be higher in some families than it will be in others.
- What is the probable stay in the nursing home? Over half of all stays are for four months or less but 10 per cent are for five years or longer.
- What level of financial resources must the client dissipate before qualifying for Medicaid? If relatively small, it may be cheaper to simply spend down these assets instead of paying premiums, possibly over many years.

3. Weigh the client's reasons for considering a long-term care policy:

- To protect an inheritance;
- To avoid a possible burden on the family;
- To enable the client to stay out of a nursing home. Some policies provide extensive home care benefits;
- To permit the client to enter a nursing home of choice. Medicaid beds are limited and nursing homes are generally more receptive to patients who can pay their own way;
- To provide peace of mind that the client's long-term care needs will be met.

Assessing the Policy

1. Long-term care policies vary widely in their provisions, and, of course, the better the coverage, the higher the premium. The following are some of the more important questions to ask:

- How are covered benefits defined? Levels of care covered by the policy may include some or all of homemaker services, home care, custodial care, intermediate care, and skilled care, each of which may have its own detailed definition. As a general rule, avoid policies which cover only skilled care.
- Is prior medical treatment required for coverage? Some policies require a period of hospitalization before nursing home admission or require nursing home care before qualification for home care benefits. Neither type of provision is desirable.
- What is the waiting period for benefits? Waiting periods may vary from zero to 365 days. A longer waiting period will result in a significant reduction of premiums. In assessing a waiting period, the client must determine her goals.
- What is the benefit level? The policy may pay either a fixed amount per day or may pay a percentage of the costs of care.
- Does the policy include an inflation adjustment? This provision is important, particularly for clients who may not need long-term care for many years. Also, does the provision adjust for inflation at a simple rate or does it more desirably adjust at a compound rate?
- Does the policy contain an exclusion for preexisting conditions? Obviously, if the client has the preexisting condition described, the policy should not be purchased.
- Does the policy waive premiums while being paid? Following admission to a nursing home, resources for the payment of premiums may quickly become exhausted, particularly if the policy doesn't cover the full costs of care.
- What is the duration of benefits—one year, two years, five years, or life-time? As a general rule, it is probably better to opt for a longer period of benefits with a less favorable waiting period instead of electing a short waiting period and having benefits run out too soon.

- What is the benefit trigger? Does the policy require a cognitive impairment, or is the trigger instead phrased in terms of an inability to engage in one or more activities of daily living? Does the policy cover Alzheimer's?

Selected References

Roger W. Andersen, Plan While You Can: Legal Solutions for Facing Disability, Ch. 6 (2003).

William S. Friedlander, *Step by Step: Help Your Clients Pick a Nursing Home*, Trial, July 2010, at 16.

Robert D. Hayes, Nancy G. Boyd & Kenneth W. Hollman, *What Attorneys Should Know About Long-Term Care Insurance*, 7 Elder L.J. 1 (1999).

Christopher C. Jennings & Christopher J. Dawe, *Long-Term Care: The Forgotten Health Care Challenge*, 17 Stan. L. & Pol'y Rev. 57, 57–66 (2006).

§ 7.02 Health Care Decisionmaking

Prompted by changes in medical technology, courts and legislatures have grappled with the question of when and how to allow people to die, even though they might be kept alive. Clients seeking wills now regularly ask their lawyers to prepare appropriate documents to allow the client some control over end-of-life decisions.[9] These variously-named documents go under the general title "advance directives." For sample documents, see the Appendix.

The oldest, and perhaps best-known, form of advance directive is the "living will." Created by analogy to wills disposing of property and operating against a backdrop of case law, living wills speak directly for the patient to various potential care-givers. These documents got a boost from the publicity surrounding Karen Ann Quinlan, whose father ultimately obtained court permission to disconnect her respirator. *See In re Quinlan*, 355 A.2d 647 (N.J. 1976). Living wills try to anticipate various medical situations which could arise and identify the type of care the patient would want. Many states impose various execution requirements similar to those which apply to wills of property. For example, most living wills require a writing signed before witnesses.

The term "living will" can confuse the lay public. Sometimes people think it is a different form of the familiar will for property, rather like a will version of the "living trusts" they hear about. Sometimes they apply the "living will" label to all forms of advance directives regarding health care. In an effort to stem the confusion, the

9. Preparation requires facing questions most of us do not like to consider. Helpful sources for starting the conversation include http://med.stanford.edu/letter.html and Paula Span, *When the Time Comes* (2009).

Uniform Health-Care Decisions Act uses the term "individual instruction." Unif. Health-Care Decisions Act § 1(1).

A New Tattoo

St. Petersburg Times, Feb. 5, 1995, at 3F

Maria Rodriguez was so fearful of one day being put on life support, she had a living will tattooed on her stomach. The 40-year-old Gary, Indiana nurse said she has seen enough patients and their families suffer when lives are prolonged.

The red and black tattoo features a red heart slashed with the universal "no" sign and the words "No Code." The will reads: "Pain and comfort only. Organ donor." It ends with her initials, "M.R."

Rodriguez said the "No Code" instructs medical workers not to resuscitate her or keep her alive by artificial means.

"When my name gets called, I don't want anything holding me up," she said.

Note and Question

Mary Wohlford, a retired nurse in Dyersville, Iowa, had the words "DO NOT RESUSCITATE" tattooed on her chest. *See* Ken Fuson, *80-year-old's tattoo spells out last wishes*, The Seattle Times, May 17, 2006, at A2. Is it just a coincidence that these tattoo stories involve nurses?

One weakness of living wills (or "individual instructions") is that anticipating all possible situations is virtually impossible. Further, it is one thing to decide in the abstract how we would like to be treated; it is another to stare an end-of-life decision in the face. To create some flexibility, lawyers have drawn an analogy to durable powers of attorney granting authority to make property-related decisions on behalf of an incompetent. Now many clients will give to a trusted friend or relative the power to make end-of-life health-care decisions on behalf of the principal. The following case is responsible for some of the increased use of such durable powers, commonly referred to as health care proxies.

Cruzan v. Director, Missouri Department of Health

497 U.S. 261 (1990)

Chief Justice Rehnquist delivered the opinion of the Court.

Petitioner Nancy Beth Cruzan was rendered incompetent as a result of severe injuries sustained during an automobile accident. Copetitioners Lester and Joyce Cruzan, Nancy's parents and coguardians, sought a court order directing the withdrawal of their daughter's artificial feeding and hydration equipment after it became apparent that she had virtually no chance of recovering her cognitive faculties. The Supreme Court of Missouri held that because there was no clear and convincing evidence of Nancy's desire to have lifesustaining treatment withdrawn under such circumstances, her parents lacked authority to effectuate such a request. We granted certiorari, 492 U.S. 917 (1989), and now affirm.

Nancy Cruzan December 25, 1982

On the night of January 11, 1983, Nancy Cruzan lost control of her car as she traveled down Elm Road in Jasper County, Missouri. The vehicle overturned, and Cruzan was discovered lying face down in a ditch without detectable respiratory or cardiac function. Paramedics were able to restore her breathing and heartbeat at the accident site, and she was transported to a hospital in an unconscious state. An attending neurosurgeon diagnosed her as having sustained probable cerebral contusions compounded by significant anoxia (lack of oxygen). The Missouri trial court in this case found that permanent brain damage generally results after 6 minutes in an anoxic state; it was estimated that Cruzan was deprived of oxygen from 12 to 14 minutes. She remained in a coma for approximately three weeks and then progressed to an unconscious state in which she was able to orally ingest some nutrition. In order to ease feeding and further the recovery, surgeons implanted a gastrostomy feeding and hydration tube in Cruzan with the consent of her then husband. Subsequent rehabilitative efforts proved unavailing. She now lies in a Missouri state hospital in what is commonly referred to as a persistent vegetative state: generally, a condition in which a person exhibits motor reflexes but evinces no indications of significant cognitive function.[10] The State of Missouri is bearing the cost of her care.

10. The State Supreme Court, adopting much of the trial court's findings, described Nancy Cruzan's medical condition as follows:

After it had become apparent that Nancy Cruzan had virtually no chance of regaining her mental faculties, her parents asked hospital employees to terminate the artificial nutrition and hydration procedures. All agree that such a removal would cause her death. The employees refused to honor the request without court approval. The parents then sought and received authorization from the state trial court for termination.

The Supreme Court of Missouri reversed by a divided vote....

We granted certiorari to consider the question whether Cruzan has a right under the United States Constitution which would require the hospital to withdraw life-sustaining treatment from her under these circumstances....

The logical corollary of the doctrine of informed consent is that the patient generally possesses the right not to consent, that is, to refuse treatment. Until about 15 years ago and the seminal decision in *In re Quinlan*, 70 N.J. 10, 355 A.2d 647, *cert. denied sub nom. Garger v. New Jersey*, 429 U.S. 922 (1976), the number of right-to-refuse-treatment decisions was relatively few .... [After a review of *Quinlan* and the cases that followed, the court concluded:]

As these cases demonstrate, the common-law doctrine of informed consent is viewed as generally encompassing the right of a competent individual to refuse medical treatment. Beyond that, these cases demonstrate both similarity and diversity in their approaches to decision of what all agree is a perplexing question with unusually strong moral and ethical overtones. State courts have available to them for decision a number of sources—state constitutions, statutes, and common law—which are not available to us. In this Court, the question is simply and starkly whether the United States Constitution prohibits Missouri from choosing the rule of decision which it did. This is the first case in which we have been squarely presented with the issue whether the United States Constitution grants what is in common parlance referred to as a "right to die." We follow the judicious counsel of our decision in *Twin City Bank v. Nebeker*, 167 U.S. 196, 202 (1897), where we said that in deciding "a

---

> (1) [H]er respiration and circulation are not artificially maintained and are within the normal limits of a thirty-year-old female; (2) she is oblivious to her environment except for reflexive responses to sound and perhaps painful stimuli; (3) she suffered anoxia of the brain resulting in a massive enlargement of the ventricles filling with cerebrospinal fluid in the area where the brain has degenerated and [her] cerebral cortical atrophy is irreversible, permanent, progressive and ongoing; (4) her highest cognitive brain function is exhibited by her grimacing perhaps in recognition of ordinarily painful stimuli, indicating the experience of pain and apparent response to sound; (5) she is a spastic quadriplegic; (6) her four extremities are contracted with irreversible muscular and tendon damage to all extremities; (7) she has no cognitive or reflexive ability to swallow food or water to maintain her daily essential needs and ... she will never recover her ability to swallow sufficient [sic] to satisfy her needs. In sum, Nancy is diagnosed as in a persistent vegetative state. She is not dead. She is not terminally ill. Medical experts testified that she could live another thirty years.

Cruzan v. Harmon, 760 S.W.2d 408, 411 (Mo. 1988) (en banc) (quotations omitted; footnote omitted).

question of such magnitude and importance . . . it is the [better] part of wisdom not to attempt, by any general statement, to cover every possible phase of the subject."

The Fourteenth Amendment provides that no State shall "deprive any person of life, liberty, or property, without due process of law." The principle that a competent person has a constitutionally protected liberty interest in refusing unwanted medical treatment may be inferred from our prior decisions. . . .

But determining that a person has a "liberty interest" under the Due Process Clause does not end the inquiry;[11] "whether respondent's constitutional rights have been violated must be determined by balancing his liberty interests against the relevant state interests." *Youngberg v. Romeo*, 457 U.S. 307, 321 (1982). . . .

Petitioners . . . assert that an incompetent person should possess the same right [to refuse lifesaving hydration and nutrition] . . . as is possessed by a competent person. . . .

The difficulty with petitioners' claim is that in a sense it begs the question: An incompetent person is not able to make an informed and voluntary choice to exercise a hypothetical right to refuse treatment or any other right. Such a "right" must be exercised for her, if at all, by some sort of surrogate. Here, Missouri has in effect recognized that under certain circumstances a surrogate may act for the patient in electing to have hydration and nutrition withdrawn in such a way as to cause death, but it has established a procedural safeguard to assure that the action of the surrogate conforms as best it may to the wishes expressed by the patient while competent. Missouri requires that evidence of the incompetent's wishes as to the withdrawal of treatment be proved by clear and convincing evidence. The question, then, is whether the United States Constitution forbids the establishment of this procedural requirement by the State. We hold that it does not.

Whether or not Missouri's clear and convincing evidence requirement comports with the United States Constitution depends in part on what interests the State may properly seek to protect in this situation. Missouri relies on its interest in the protection and preservation of human life, and there can be no gainsaying this interest . . . . We do not think a State is required to remain neutral in the face of an informed and voluntary decision by a physically able adult to starve to death.

But in the context presented here, a State has more particular interests at stake. The choice between life and death is a deeply personal decision of obvious and overwhelming finality. We believe Missouri may legitimately seek to safeguard the personal element of this choice through the imposition of heightened evidentiary requirements. . . .

---

11. Although many state courts have held that a right to refuse treatment is encompassed by a generalized constitutional right of privacy, we have never so held. We believe this issue is more properly analyzed in terms of a Fourteenth Amendment liberty interest. *See Bowers v. Hardwick*, 478 U.S. 186, 194–95 (1986).

We think it self-evident that the interests at stake in the instant proceedings are more substantial, both on an individual and societal level, than those involved in a run-of-the-mine civil dispute. But not only does the standard of proof reflect the importance of a particular adjudication, it also serves as "a societal judgment about how the risk of error should be distributed between the litigants." *Santosky* [*v. Kramer*, 455 U.S. 745,] 755 [1982]; *Addington* [*v. Texas*, 441 U.S. 418,] 423 [1979]. The more stringent the burden of proof a party must bear, the more that party bears the risk of an erroneous decision. We believe that Missouri may permissibly place an increased risk of an erroneous decision on those seeking to terminate an incompetent individual's life-sustaining treatment. An erroneous decision not to terminate results in a maintenance of the status quo; the possibility of subsequent developments such as advancements in medical science, the discovery of new evidence regarding the patient's intent, changes in the law, or simply the unexpected death of the patient despite the administration of life-sustaining treatment at least create the potential that a wrong decision will eventually be corrected or its impact mitigated. An erroneous decision to withdraw life-sustaining treatment, however, is not susceptible of correction....

Petitioners alternatively contend that Missouri must accept the "substituted judgment" of close family members even in the absence of substantial proof that their views reflect the views of the patient....

No doubt is engendered by anything in this record but that Nancy Cruzan's mother and father are loving and caring parents. If the State were required by the United States Constitution to repose a right of "substituted judgment" with anyone, the Cruzans would surely qualify. But we do not think the Due Process Clause requires the State to repose judgment on these matters with anyone but the patient herself. Close family members may have a strong feeling—a feeling not at all ignoble or unworthy, but not entirely disinterested, either—that they do not wish to witness the continuation of the life of a loved one which they regard as hopeless, meaningless, and even degrading. But there is no automatic assurance that the view of close family members will necessarily be the same as the patient's would have been had she been confronted with the prospect of her situation while competent. All of the reasons previously discussed for allowing Missouri to require clear and convincing evidence of the patient's wishes lead us to conclude that the State may choose to defer only to those wishes, rather than confide the decision to close family members.[12]

The judgment of the Supreme Court of Missouri is Affirmed. Justice O'Connor, concurring.

12. We are not faced in this case with the question whether a State might be required to defer to the decision of a surrogate if competent and probative evidence established that the patient herself had expressed a desire that the decision to terminate life-sustaining treatment be made for her by that individual.

I agree that a protected liberty interest in refusing unwanted medical treatment may be inferred from our prior decisions, . . . and that the refusal of artificially delivered food and water is encompassed within that liberty interest. . . .

I also write separately to emphasize that the Court does not today decide the issue whether a State must also give effect to the decisions of a surrogate decisionmaker . . . . In my view, such a duty may well be constitutionally required to protect the patient's liberty interest in refusing medical treatment. Few individuals provide explicit oral or written instructions regarding their intent to refuse medical treatment should they become incompetent.[13] States which decline to consider any evidence other than such instructions may frequently fail to honor a patient's intent. Such failures might be avoided if the State considered an equally probative source of evidence: the patient's appointment of a proxy to make health care decisions on her behalf. Delegating the authority to make medical decisions to a family member or friend is becoming a common method of planning for the future. *See, e.g.*, Areen, *The Legal Status of Consent Obtained from Families of Adult Patients to Withhold or Withdraw Treatment*, 258 JAMA 229, 230 (1987). Several States have recognized the practical wisdom of such a procedure by enacting durable power of attorney statutes that specifically authorize an individual to appoint a surrogate to make medical treatment decisions. Some state courts have suggested that an agent appointed pursuant to a general durable power of attorney statute would also be empowered to make health care decisions on behalf of the patient . . . . Other States allow an individual to designate a proxy to carry out the intent of a living will. These procedures for surrogate decisionmaking, which appear to be rapidly gaining in acceptance, may be a valuable additional safeguard of the patient's interest in directing his medical care. . . .

. . . Today we decide only that one State's practice does not violate the Constitution; the more challenging task of crafting appropriate procedures for safeguarding incompetents' liberty interests is entrusted to the "laboratory" of the States, *New State Ice Co. v. Liebmann*, 285 U.S. 262, 311 (1932) (Brandeis, J., dissenting), in the first instance.

13. *See* 2 President's Commission for the Study of Ethical Problems in Medicine and Biomedical and Behavioral Research, Making Health Care Decisions 241–42 (1982) (thirty-six percent of those surveyed gave instructions regarding how they would like to be treated if they ever became too sick to make decisions; 23% put those instructions in writing) (Lou Harris Poll, September 1982); American Medical Association Surveys of Physician and Public Opinion on Health Care Issues 29–30 (1988) (fifty-six percent of those surveyed had told family members their wishes concerning the use of life-sustaining treatment if they entered an irreversible coma; 15% had filled out a living will specifying those wishes).

Nancy Cruzan's Grave Marker

Notes

1. On remand, the state trial court heard additional evidence and found clear and convincing evidence that Nancy Cruzan would not want the feeding tube. She died 12 days after it was removed.

2. Advance directives proliferated in response to Justice O'Connor's opinion in *Cruzan*, the Patient Self-Determination Act (42 U.S.C. § 1395) (requiring hospitals receiving federal funds to advise patients of their right to sign such documents), and a variety of public-education efforts. Given our mobile society, it may make sense to adopt a uniform approach.

David M. English & Alan Meisel, *Uniform Health-Care Decisions Act Gives New Guidance*

21 Est. Plan. 355, 356–57, 359–60, 362 (1994)

Every state now has legislation authorizing the use of some form of advance health-care directive—power of attorney, a living will, or, in most cases, both. In addition, more than 30 states have "surrogate decision-making" statutes, allowing family members and, in some instances, others to make health-care decisions for individuals who lack decision-making capacity and who have not executed an advance directive.

The premise of both the case law and these statutes is that competent persons have a common-law and possibly constitutional right of self-determination and the right to be free from unwanted interferences with their bodily integrity. In the health-care setting, this translates into a right to make decisions about their care, including the right to decline treatment even when that decision would probably or even certainly lead to death. This right ordinarily is implemented through informed consent or refusal. Although decision making for competent patients presents few legal difficulties, the same cannot be said for patients who have lost capacity since they no longer can make a decision, informed or otherwise.

This existing legislation, however, has developed in fits and starts, resulting in an often fragmented, incomplete, and sometimes inconsistent set of rules. Statutes enacted within a single state sometimes conflict with each other, and conflicts between statutes of different states are common. In an increasingly mobile society where an advance health-care directive made in one state must frequently be implemented in another, there is a need for greater consistency.

Much of the present state legislation also inappropriately inhibits, rather than facilitates, the use of advance health-care directives. The execution requirements, for example, often go well beyond what is required even for the execution of a will. Furthermore, many of the statutes unnecessarily limit the circumstances when life-sustaining treatment may be withheld or withdrawn to situations in which a person is either "terminally ill" or "permanently unconscious." There is a need for simplicity and greater flexibility.

The Uniform Health-Care Decisions Act (the Act), which was approved by the Uniform Law Commissioners in August 1993, was drafted with these problems very much in mind. Unlike most current state statutes dealing with medical decision making for patients who no longer possess the capacity to do so personally, the Act is comprehensive and will enable an enacting jurisdiction to replace its existing legislation on the subject with a single statute. Moreover, the overriding objective of the new Act is to facilitate the use of advance health-care directives. . . .

. . . The heart of the Act is found in Sections 1 to 14. Following a series of definitions (§ 1), the Act contains provisions on making and revoking advance health-care directives (§§ 2 and 3). An optional statutory form for making a directive is provided as well (§ 4).

The Act encourages and facilitates the use of advance health-care directives, but it also recognizes that many individuals fail to plan. Consequently, two back-up provisions are included. One is Section 5, which specifies when individuals other than a patient's agent or guardian may act as "surrogate" and make health-care decisions for the patient. The other is Section 6, addressing health-care decision making by guardians. . . .

The optional form

In drafting the Act, the optional form (§ 4) received more attention than any other section. The drafters unanimously concluded that (1) the Act should include a form, (2) its use should be optional, and (3) it should be written in a style accessible to the lay public.

The drafting committee opted for a single form that combines both the designation of an agent and the opportunity to give individual instructions, should the individual be so inclined. The committee favored comprehensiveness over brevity and included many provisions typical of forms drafted by attorneys. Even though a brief form would be easier to read and execute, it runs the risk of failing to deal with the many issues that an individual might wish to address.

Practical advice. Although an individual ideally should consult with his attorney or other qualified professional before making an advance health-care directive, the drafting committee recognized that such consultation will frequently not occur. For this reason, the form includes an extended introductory explanation describing the contents of the form, various options, and procedures for completion. Also included in the explanation is practical advice on steps to take after the form's completion. The signer is advised to give a copy of the completed form to his physician, other health-care providers, and to any health-care agents he may have named. In addition, the signer is advised to talk to the designated agent to make sure that the agent understands the signer's wishes and is willing to take the responsibility.

Preference for power of attorney. The power of attorney appears first on the form so as to assure, to the extent possible, that it will come to the attention of a casual reader. This reflects the reality that the appointment of an agent is increasingly viewed, especially by physicians, as more helpful to the making of health-care decisions for incompetent patients than is the provision of specific instructions. . . .

Organ and tissue donation. Included in the form is space for an individual to express an intent to make an organ or tissue donation. It is included on the assumption that an advance health-care directive is more likely to come to light than a donor card. . . .

Designation of primary physician. Finally, the form provides space for an individual to designate a primary physician. The vast majority of existing state statutes contain no such provision. In contrast, these statutes refer to, and impose obligations on, the "attending physician," a term that the Act specifically avoids and that is usually understood to mean the physician currently responsible for providing treatment and not the physician whom the patient would select if able to do so.

Surrogates

The reality is that a substantial majority of Americans fail to execute directives (as they fail to execute wills or purchase life insurance) because of their general unwillingness to plan for death. Furthermore, there is no reason to believe that this situation will change significantly even if the Act is widely enacted. Health-care decision making for individuals who fail to plan is therefore an important concern, and the Act (§ 5) provides for the designation of a decision maker in the absence of the written appointment of an agent or judicial appointment of a guardian, or if an agent or guardian has been appointed but is not "reasonably available." Following the common-law terminology, the Act refers to this decision maker as a "surrogate." The term "surrogate" applies as well to an agent who is orally appointed by the patient. . . .

Conclusion

The Act represents a major advance over existing law. It is comprehensive, facilitates making advance health-care directives, addresses decision making for those who have failed to plan, and eliminates many of the current restrictions. The Act also provides physicians, health care administrators, and their legal counsel with increased assurance that they are on firm legal footing when implementing decisions to terminate life-sustaining medical treatment.

Notes

1. Should a health care proxy that was executed in one state be recognized in another state?

Although the Uniform Recognition of Substitute Decision-Making Documents Act so provides, it has only been enacted in Idaho. *See* Idaho. Code Ann. § 15–15–101.

2. Related questions about physician-assisted suicide promise to influence the law surrounding advance directives. *See Washington v. Glucksberg*, 521 U.S. 702 (1997), and *Vacco v. Quill*, 521 U.S. 793 (1997) (companion cases upholding prohibitions of physician-assisted suicide in the face of due process and equal protection challenges). Five states allow physician-assisted suicide by statute. *See* Cal. Health & Safety Code § 443.2 (2016); Co. Rev.Stat. ____; Or. Rev. Stat. § 127.805 (1999); Vt. Stat. Ann. tit. 18, § 5283 (2013); Wash. Rev. Code § 70.245.020 (2009). Montana allows physician-assisted suicide based on the Montana Supreme Court decision in *Baxter v. State*, 224 P.3d 1211 (Mont. 2009).

3. Persons suffering from Alzheimer's Disease and other forms of dementia fall between those being kept alive on ventilators, on one hand, and competent people who can consent to assisted suicide, on the other. There is no "plug" to pull, and incompetence precludes legal assisted suicide. Nonetheless, many do not want to continue to live if they are no longer functioning at a certain level.

Key questions include both how to end life and how to decide on the timing. Some commentators advocate directives to voluntarily stop eating and drinking (VSED), phased-in over a few weeks to avoid a traumatic instead of peaceful end. For guidance in developing a standard for when life is worth living, consider the following:

When Is It Time to Go?

Jerome Medalie, a retired lawyer who has long been involved with end-of-life issues, developed the following list of factors for his own advanced directive. [To see the full document, go to https://sites.google.com/site/jeromemedalie/jm-files.]

More specifically, with respect to the deterioration or erosion of my cognitive capacity, I do not want it to progress to the point when, as examples:

(1) I cannot recognize my loved ones;

(2) I cannot remember the names of my wife/husband or one or more of my children;

(3) I cannot articulate coherent thoughts and sentences;

(4) I cannot read books with understanding and enjoyment;

(5) I cannot watch or listen to television or other media with understanding and enjoyment;

(6) I cannot intelligently discuss an issue with intellectual proportions;

(7) I have forgotten when or how to eat or drink without assistance;

(8) I have forgotten when or how to perform personal hygiene on a regular basis without assistance;

(9) I remain uncommunicative for long periods of time;

(10) I babble incoherently or curse erratically or without apparent provocation exhibit anger, antisocial or other bizarre behavior.

I want "out" long before any modest combination of these instances or events occurs repeatedly or continuously. As a guide, I suggest that whenever any three of these events have occurred and have been repeated or persist over the course of several weeks the time for the withdrawal of life support has arrived.

4. As medical technology has improved, so has the demand for organ transplants. Many lawyers now ask their clients whether they want to execute organ donor designations in addition to the wills, durable powers of attorney, and health-care directives that have become routine. *See* Unif. Anatomical Gift Act, 8A U. L. A. 19. For examples of these forms, see the Appendix, *infra*.

Questions

1. What directions would you give in an "individual instruction" regarding your health care? Who would you appoint to make health-care decisions on your behalf, and in what ways would you limit your agent's authority?

2. Who should a statute designate as surrogate decision makers to act in the absence of an advance directive?

3. Why do you suppose that the end-of-life cases generating the most publicity have centered on young women—Karen Ann Quinlan, Nancy Cruzan, and Terry Schiavo?

Problem

Bobby and Bill are in their mid-70s and have been married for 50 years. Their total assets, all joint, are worth about $500,000, and they have a steady retirement income. They divide their time between their long-term home in the north and a mobile home in the south. Avid golfers, they are in good health. Although Bobby had bypass surgery a few years ago, she exercises regularly. They have two adult children. Because they have not revised their wills since the children were little, Bobby and Bill have scheduled an appointment with you to discuss making new wills. What topics will you plan to discuss with them?

Selected References

Georgia Akers, *On Death and Dying: Counseling the Terminally Ill Client and the Loved Ones Left Behind*, 1 Est. Plan. & Comm. Prop. L.J. 1 (2008).

Roger W. Andersen, Plan While You Can: Legal Solutions for Facing Disability, Chs. 7 and 8 (2003).

Lisa Brodoff, *Planning for Alzheimer's Disease with Mental Health Advance Directives*, 17 Elder L.J. 239 (2010).

Norman L. Cantor, *Twenty-Five Years After Quinlan: A Review of the Jurisprudence of Death and Dying*, 29 J.L. Med. & Ethics 182 (2001).

Vanessa Cavallaro, *Advance Directive Accessibility: Unlocking the Toolbox Containing Our End-of Life Decisions*, 31 Touro L. Rev. 555 (2015).

T.P. Gallanis, *Aging and the Nontraditional Family*, 32 U. Mem. L. Rev. 607 (2002).

Rebecca K. Glatzer, *Equality at the End: Amending State Surrogacy Statutes to Honor Same-Sex Couples' End-of-Life Decisions*, 13 Elder L.J. 255 (2005).

Daniel P. Hickey, *The Disutility of Advance Directives: We Know the Problems, But Are There Solutions?*, 36 J. Health L. 455 (2003).

A. Frank Johns, *Older Clients with Diminishing Capacity and Their Advance Directives*, 39 Real Prop. Prob. & Tr. J. 107 (2004).

Shari A. Levitan & Helen Adrian, *Brave New World: Ethical Issues Involving Surrogate Health Care Decisions*, 20 Prob. & Prop. 30 (Jan./Feb. 2006).

Alan Meisel, & Kathy L. Cerminara, *The Right To Die: The Law of End-of-Life Decisionmaking* (3d ed., with supplements).

Sam J. Saad III, *Living Wills: Validity and Morality*, 30 Vt. L. Rev. 71 (2005).

Samuel W. Wardle, *The Advance Directive Statute Revisited*, 67 U. Miami L. Rev. 861 (2013).

Linda S. Whitton, *Planning for End-of-Life Health Care Decisions: What National Survey Results Reveal*, 20 Prob. & Prop. 38 (Jan./Feb. 2006).

Robert B. Wolf et al., *The Physician Orders for Life-Sustaining Treatment (POLST) Coming Soon to a Health Care Community Near You*, 40 ACTEC L.J. 57 (2014).

Chapter 8

Trusts

Trusts provide lawyers with a continuing series of interesting opportunities.[1] Because trusts are so flexible, they allow us to help clients in an enormous range of circumstances. We have already seen how revocable trusts can serve as will substitutes. Now we turn to those doctrines that apply to trusts generally. This chapter opens with an overview designed to complement our earlier coverage. Then come discussions of what is needed to create a trust, the nature of a beneficiary's interest, and how a trust can be changed or terminated. The chapter closes with a look at the special problems surrounding charitable trusts.

§ 8.01 An Overview

The contemporary trust can only be understood in the context of its unique history. As will be seen, the overriding feature of the trust device is the fiduciary relationship between the trustee and trust beneficiary as a result of the separation of legal and equitable title to property held in trust.

A. History

The modern trust is an outgrowth of the use device that was employed during medieval times. After the law courts ruled in the thirteenth century that real property was not capable of being devised, lawyers of that time tried to avoid operation of this rule by having the property owner (feoffor) transfer the property to a third party (feoffee to uses), under the proviso that the transferee hold the property for the use of the transferor for his life, and upon his death for someone else whom the transferor had designated. In the normal case, such person was selected by the transferor at his death in a testament (as opposed to a will).

If the transferee refused to recognize the rights of the transferor or his successor, the Chancellor, acting as a court of equity, would compel compliance with the duty

1. The trusts that we consider in this book are trusts for gratuitous purposes: the donative transfer of property during lifetime or at death. Trusts, however, are important vehicles in the commercial and business world. Indeed a substantial amount of commercial and business property is held in some type of trust, including business trusts, pension trusts, mutual fund investment trusts, land trusts, and real estate investment trusts. *See generally* John H. Langbein, *The Secret Life of the Trust: The Trust as an Instrument of Commerce*, 107 Yale L.J. 165 (1997). Their study is more appropriate in other courses.

expressed in the transfer. The law courts would do nothing because the rights alleged were not legal rights. The Chancellor, however, enforced the duties, and as a result the "use" became a recognized form of conveyance. Later, when the transferor died, the rules of intestacy would not apply because he no longer owned the property; rather, the transferor owned only the right to enforce the duties against the transferee. Further, because the Chancellor also was willing to enforce those duties in favor of the person the transferor appointed in his testament, a substitute for the devise by will had been created.

The Statute of Uses, passed in 1536, put a stop to the loss of revenue to the Crown from the use device. The effect of the Statute of Uses was to execute the use, that is, to bypass the feoffee to uses by giving legal title to the real property to the individual for whom the use of the property was intended, referred to as cestui que use. In the normal case, in which the transferor was the cestui que use, the result was to leave the transferor with legal title, and subject to the burdens of the incidents of medieval tenure. In 1540, the Statute of Wills was enacted to mollify the wishes of the landowners; it sanctioned the right to devise real property by will.

Inventive lawyers soon found ways (created loopholes) to avoid the Statute of Uses. The principal gambit was for the owner of real property (feoffor) to convey legal title in real property to the feoffee to uses whereby the feoffee had active duties to perform for the cestui que use. The Chancellor promptly ruled that the Statute of Uses was intended only to execute "passive" uses (the mere holding of title) and not to negate actual duties imposed on the feoffee to uses.

The recognition that active duties avoided the operation of the Statute of Uses marked the beginning of the modern trust. Simply substitute trust language for that employed under the use device, that is, the feoffor is the settlor; the feofee to uses is the trustee and the cestui que use is the beneficiary who even today is sometimes referred to as the cestui que trust.

The Statute of Uses still exists in many states (and has even been extended to personal property in some jurisdictions) so that a trust will not be created if a trustee has no active duties to perform. *See generally* 3d Rest. Trusts § 6. Since courts almost invariably find that the transferor intended to impose active duties on the trustee, the Statute will only apply if a court concludes that the intended trustee was a mere title holder. In such case, however, the trust will be a dry or passive trust and the intended trust beneficiary will have legal title. *See Provident Life and Accident Ins. Co. v. Little*, 88 F. Supp. 2d 604 (S.D. W. Va. 2000) (applying West Virginia law).

B. Modern Trust Law

The hallmark of the modern trust device is the fiduciary relationship between the trustee and trust beneficiary that results from the separation of the legal and equitable interests in the property. Legal title to the property, which may include personal as well as real property, is held by the trustee subject to enforceable rights in the trust beneficiary. In operation, the trustee has active duties to perform for the trust beneficiary, even though the trustee holds legal title to the trust property as far as the outside world is concerned. Even today, these fiduciary duties and the trust beneficiary's correlative rights are enforceable based on equitable principles, just as the original use was enforced in the Chancery Court.

Trusts are recognized in every state in the United States. Generally, trust law is based on common-law principles that are compiled in the Restatement (Second) of Trusts and in the recently-completed Restatement (Third) of Trusts.[2] The Restatement (Third) of Trusts is destined to have a significant impact on American trust law, as has had the Restatement (Second) of Trusts, because courts tend to rely on the Restatements when there is no authority in their jurisdiction. *See, e.g., Estate of Somers*, 89 P.3d 898, 904 (Kan. 2004) ("When there is no law directly on point, Kansas courts turn to the Restatement of Trusts."). *But cf. In re Estate of Stephano*, 981 A.2d 138 (Pa. 2009) (lower courts must follow existing precedent until Supreme Court adopts new Restatement position). In addition to judicial pronouncements and the Restatements of Trusts, certain aspects of trust law may have been codified by a particular jurisdiction, including California, New York, and Texas. The Uniform Trust Code (UTC), approved in 2000, is the latest national effort to codify most, but not all, aspects of trust law. Significantly, most of the provisions in the UTC are intended to have retroactive effect. As of this writing over 30 states and the District of Columbia have enacted the UTC and more enactments are likely to follow.[3] This chapter will make frequent references to the UTC and to the Restatement (Third) of Trusts.

C. Express, Resulting and Constructive Trusts

The principal type of trust studied in this book is the private express trust, that is, a transfer of legal title to property to a person (a trustee) whereby the transferor (settlor) expressly intends to impose active duties on the trustee for the benefit of one or more private persons (beneficiaries). Although a charitable trust is also an express trust, in that a trustee will have active duties to perform, the settlor expressly

---

2. Despite its name, the Restatement of Trusts (or any Restatement) does not simply restate the common-law. As explained by Professor Edward C. Halbach, Jr., Reporter for the Restatement of Trusts: "[Restatements] purport to state an authoritative or recommended view of the current American common law." *See* Edward C. Halbach, Jr., *Symposium on Law in the Twentieth Century: Uniform Acts, Restatements, and Trends in American Trust Law at Century's End*, 88 Cal. L. Rev. 1877, 1881 (2000).

3. The states include: Alabama, Arizona, Arkansas, Florida, Kansas, Kentucky, Maine, Maryland, Massachusetts, Michigan, Minnesota, Mississippi, Missouri, Nebraska, New Hampshire, New Mexico, New Jersey, North Carolina, North Dakota, Ohio Oregon, Pennsylvania, South Carolina, Tennessee, Utah, Vermont, Virginia, West Virginia, Wisconsin, and Wyoming.

intends that the trust property be devoted by the trustee exclusively for charitable purposes. A mixed express trust has both private beneficiaries and charitable purposes and is usually created for tax purposes.

Express trusts must be distinguished from two other types of trusts that arise by operation of law: resulting trusts and constructive trusts. A resulting trust typically arises when a person: (1) intends to create an express trust; (2) validly transfers property to a person as trustee; but (3) for some reason the trust fails in whole or in part. *See* 3d Rest. Trusts § 8. Because the transferor did not intend that the trustee have the beneficial enjoyment of the property, the law infers that the transferor would want the property returned.

To carry out this legally inferred intent, a resulting trust is imposed, whereby the transferee becomes a trustee with the duty to return the property to the transferor or the transferor's successors in interest. For example, if the transferor conveyed property to a trustee but failed to identify the beneficiaries, an express trust would not be created. Instead, the transferee would hold the trust property and would have the duty to give the property back to the transferor. In this chapter we will encounter many instances when a resulting trust arises.

A less common type of resulting trust is called a purchase money resulting trust. *See* 3d Rest. Trusts § 9. For example, if Judy pays Donna to transfer property to Judy's friend, Leo, a court may infer that Leo was to hold the property under a "purchase money resulting trust" for Judy's benefit. If Judy wanted the property, she could get an order directing Leo to transfer it to her. *See, e.g., State v. Sanders*, 8 P.3d 124 (Mont. 2000). If Leo were a relative, however, a court will presume Judy intended to make a gift. *See, e.g., In re Marriage of Kendra*, 815 N.E.2d 22 (Ill. App. Ct. 2004). *Cf. Gregoire v. Gregoire*, 987 A.2d 909 (Vt. 2009) (presumption of gift rebutted and resulting trust arose in favor of parent). In many states, the purchase money resulting trust has been abolished by statute.

A constructive trust is a trust only in the sense that a person upon whom a constructive trust is imposed is obligated to surrender property to another. In essence, a constructive trust is a remedial device that is designed to avoid unjust enrichment of the legal title holder, be it in the donative transfer area or any other area. Indeed, the constructive trust device is covered in Restatement of Restitution § 160, rather than in the Restatement of Trusts.

We have already encountered the constructive trust device in the context of wills. *See, e.g., Ernest v. Chumley*, reproduced in this book, (court discusses the imposition of a constructive trust on a person who breaches a contract not to revoke a will). *See also* In re Estate of Horrigan v. Ladner, 757 So. 2d 165 (Miss. 1999) (constructive trust imposed over money invested with decedent where decedent breached promise to leave property by will). In this chapter, we'll encounter constructive trusts in the context of a breach of promise to create or hold property in trust.

D. Terminology

Common labels are normally applied to the three actors involved in the creation and operation of an express trust: the settlor (sometimes referred to as the "donor," "grantor," or "trustor," or "trust creator"), the trustee (the person who receives legal title from the settlor and holds the property during the term of the trust), and the beneficiary (sometimes referred to as the cestui que trust). The sum of the rights of the beneficiaries constitute the "equitable title" to the property.

settlor, Trustee, & Beneficiary

Uniform Trust Code

Section 103. Definitions.

"Settlor" means a person, including a testator, who creates, or contributes property to, a trust. If more than one person creates or contributes property to a trust, each person is a settlor of the portion of the trust property attributable to that person's contribution except to the extent another person has the power to revoke or withdraw that portion.

"Trustee" includes an original, additional, and successor trustee, and a cotrustee.

"Beneficiary" means a person that: (A) has a present or future beneficial interest in a trust, vested or contingent; or (B) in a capacity other than that of trustee, holds a power of appointment over trust property.[4]

Trusts are distinguished by reference to the time of their creation. A lifetime (also referred to by the Latin "inter vivos") trust is one that is created by a transfer during the life of the settlor. Lifetime trusts are also commonly called "living" trusts, a term describing the trust that is used as a substitute for a will—one in which the grantor reserves the income from the trust for his life, the power to revoke the trust, and other accouterments of continued ownership.

In contrast to lifetime trusts, testamentary trusts are created by the settlor's will. Note that the two terms refer to the manner of creating the trust, not to their operation after they are created. Many lifetime trusts survive the death of the settlor, but this fact does not turn them into testamentary trusts. Only those created by will are categorized using the latter term.

Trusts also are categorized by the identity of the trustee. Declared trusts are trusts in which the settlor is the sole trustee. They are formed by a "declaration of trust." Declared trusts are thus distinguished from trusts that have a third party as trustee, and arise from a "trust agreement," "deed of trust," or "trust indenture."

Trusts in which the beneficial interests are vested beyond recall by the settlor are irrevocable, while those in which the settlor retains the power to reclaim the beneficial interest are revocable. As we saw in earlier chapters, the power of revocation has significant impact on the rights of creditors and the settlor's spouse.

Finally, trusts are distinguished by reference to the setting in which they arise. Those discussed in these materials are gratuitous trusts—trusts used for the purposes of making gifts either during lifetime or at death. Surprisingly, almost 90 percent of the wealth held in trust form is for non-gratuitous reasons; these trusts include federally regulated mutual fund trusts, business operating trusts, and retirement (pension) trusts.

---

4. The power of appointment prong will be discussed in Chapter 9, §9.03. [Eds.]

E. Contemporary Reasons for Trusts

People create gratuitous trusts for many different non-tax reasons. As discussed previously, lifetime trusts may be used for probate avoidance and to allow for the successive enjoyment of trust property. Another major reason to create a trust is to provide asset management. Whether the beneficiaries are young children or disabled adults, the trust device can take the burdens of management out of the settlors' hands.

You will recall that trusts can also save estate taxes by splitting family assets among various family members to maximize the use of the applicable exclusion amount (exemption) available under federal gift and estate tax law. Trusts may also be used to minimize income taxes by shifting the incidents of income tax to persons in low income tax brackets and to minimize generation-skipping transfer taxes.

Clients must first decide whether they want to use a lifetime trust, a testamentary trust, or both. Of course, if a client is seeking current asset management, or probate avoidance, then a lifetime trust is appropriate. If these are not current needs, however, the client could create a testamentary trust or open a lifetime trust, but keep it as an empty shell until death or disability.

In general, lifetime trusts are more complicated to set up, but are more flexible once they are in operation. Testamentary trusts are easier to establish, but generally subject to more restrictions when funded. If someone other than the settlor is to serve as trustee of a lifetime trust, that person (or institution) must be involved in creating, as well as amending the trust if the lifetime trust so allows. On the other hand, a settlor can establish or change a testamentary trust unilaterally. Once the testator dies, however, a testamentary trust becomes subject to the jurisdiction and, usually the supervision of the probate court. For example, courts may require reports or restrict investments, and they may retain control of the trust even if the family moves out of the jurisdiction. Additionally, the document will be part of the public record.

F. Choice of Law

Because the location of the settlor, the trustee, the beneficiaries, and the trust property could all be different, choice-of-law questions may arise over trust validity, interpretation, and effect.[5] Regarding validity, UPC § 2-506 and UTC § 403 encourage trust creation by allowing the law of one of several jurisdictions to govern. For example, UTC § 403 (applicable to the validity of lifetime trusts) would allow the law of the jurisdiction of any of the following to validate the trust: the settlor's domicile, the trustee's domicile, or the trust property's location.

Regarding issues involving interpretation and effect, default rules apply unless the settlor validly designates a different jurisdiction. The law of the situs governs real property (immovables). *See* 2d Rest. Conflict of Laws § 277. With respect to personal

5. Choice of law rules for trust administration are discussed in Chapter 10, § 10.01.

property (movables), the choice of law will depend on whether the trust was created during lifetime or by will. If the trust was created during lifetime, the law of the jurisdiction having the most significant relationship to the trust will govern; if personal property is the subject matter of a testamentary trust, then the testator's domicile will usually control since that jurisdiction will likely have the most significant contacts. *See* 2d Rest. Conflict of Laws §§ 268 and 269.

Uniform Trust Code

Section 107. Governing Law.

The meaning and effect of the terms of a trust are determined by: (1) the law of the jurisdiction designated in the terms unless the designation of that jurisdiction's law is contrary to a strong public policy of the jurisdiction having the most significant relationship to the matter at issue; or (2) in the absence of a controlling designation in the terms of the trust, the law of the jurisdiction having the most significant relationship to the matter at issue.

Notes and Question

1. Georgia has no elective share system. Should a settlor be able to avoid his state's elective share protection for trust property by designating Georgia law as the controlling law in the trust?

2. Challenging choice of law questions arise when more than one country has some relationship to a trust, especially since many countries do not specifically recognize a trust per se. *See generally* Jeffrey A. Schoenblum, *The Rise of the International Trust*, 32 Vand. J. Transnat'l L. 3 (1999); Jonathan Harris, The Hague Trusts Convention: Scope, Application and Preliminary Issues (2002).

Selected References

George G. Bogert & George T. Bogert, The Law of Trusts (Rev. 2d ed. 1983) (Multi-volume treatise).

David M. English, *The Uniform Trust Code (2000): Significant Provisions and Policy Issues*, 67 Mo. L. Rev. 143 (2002).

Deborah S. Gordon, *Trusting Trust*, 63 U. Kan. L. Rev. 497 (2015).

Edward C. Halbach, *Uniform Acts, Restatements, and Trends in American Trust Law at Century's End*, **88 Cal. L. Rev. 1881 (Dec. 2000).**

Henry Hansmann & Ugo Mattei, *The Functions of Trust Law: A Comparative Legal and Economic Analysis*, 73 N.Y.U. L. Rev. 434 (1998).

Joseph Kartiganer & Raymond H. Young, *The UTC: Help for Beneficiaries and Their Attorneys*, 17 Prob. & Prop. 18 (2003).

John H. Langbein, *The Secret Life of the Trust: The Trust as an Instrument of Commerce*, 107 Yale L.J. 165 (1997).

John H. Langbein, *Rise of the Management Trust*, 143 Tr. & Est. 52 (Oct. 2004).

Judith W. McCue, *How To Greet New Uniform Trust and Estates Act?: With Rational Exuberance*, 36 U. Miami Inst. on Est. Plan. ch. 11 (2001).

Charles E. Rounds Jr. and Charles E. Rounds III, Loring and Rounds: A Trustee's Handbook (2017 edition).

Eugene F. Scoles, *Choice of Law in Trusts: Uniform Trust Code, Sections 107 and 403*, 67 Mo. L. Rev. 213 (2002)

Scott and Ascher on Trusts (5th ed. 2006)

Robert H. Sitkoff, *An Agency Costs Theory of Trust Law*, 89 Cornell L. Rev. 621 (2004).

Lee-ford Tritt, *The Limitations of an Economic Agency Cost Theory of Trust Law*, 32 Cardozo L. Rev. 2579 (2011).

§ 8.02 Creation

A valid trust requires: (1) an intention to create a fiduciary relationship, (2) property (and delivery), (3) a beneficiary, (4) a trustee, (5) a valid trust purpose, and (6) compliance with formalities. The key concept is creation of a fiduciary relationship by separating ownership into two parts: "legal title" in a trustee with management duties and "equitable title" in a beneficiary who can enforce those duties. Because a trust is an alternative to the gratuitous transfer of outright ownership by gift or will, consideration is not necessary to create a present trust; a promise to create a trust in the future, however, must be supported by consideration. *See* 3d Rest. Trusts § 15.

A. Intent

Usually the intention to create a trust is quite clear: a multi-page document carries the label "Trust Agreement," or a will section reads "Family Trust." Some situations, however, are ambiguous.

Burton v. Irwin

181 S.E.2d 624 (Va. 1971)

Cochran, J., delivered the opinion of the court. On this appeal we are concerned with the construction of the holographic will of the late Blanche Burton Mallory.

Mrs. Mallory, a widow 86 years old, died without issue on November 10, 1967, leaving as her heirs at law and distributees two sisters, a brother, various nieces and nephews and great-nieces and great-nephews. Her will, admitted to probate in the clerk's office of the Chancery Court of the City of Richmond, reads as follows:

> "Richmond Virginia
>
> June 26 1962
>
> This is my last will & testament [sic].
>
> I appoint my Brother William L Burton as executor and Trustee of my estate. To my Brother William L Burton I present herewith & without recourse the accompaning [sic] Bonds, Stocks, Mortage [sic] Notes, real estate, and Bank Accounts and valuables of all descriptions in my safty [sic] box, at First & Merchants Bank Richmond Va. or at home or any other place in Richmond Va. My Brother knows my wishes and will carry them out, to the best of his ability.
>
> Blanche Burton Mallory"

[When William claimed that he was entitled to keep the entire estate himself, the testator's heirs countered that William held the estate on resulting trust for their benefit on the theory that the testator had intended to a testamentary trust but had failed to name the trust beneficiaries. The lower court agreed with the heirs. The court herein reversed and remanded.]

The evidence . . . shows a relationship approaching that of motherson between the testatrix and her brother, financial dependence of William upon his sister and a motive for her to leave her estate to him. In light of these circumstances we consider the language of the Mallory will.

Her brother is the only person mentioned by the testatrix, and he is referred to three times in the brief writing. The word "trustee" is found only once and then in conjunction with "executor." No trust beneficiaries are named nor are any trust purposes specified. The conclusion is inescapable that in naming her brother "executor and Trustee" Mrs. Mallory, acting without knowledge of the legal terminology employed, merely intended that her brother administer her estate. . . .

Precatory words are prima facie construed to create a trust when they are directed to an executor. . . . But here, while the brother is personal representative as well as sole devisee and legatee, the precatory words are addressed to him as "Brother" and not as fiduciary. . . . [I]n Boutelle v. Boutelle, 231 Md. 69, 188 A.2d 559 (1963), an absolute devise and bequest to the testator 's wife, also named as his executrix, followed by the words "to be held for the benefit of herself and our children", was held to be no trust but an outright gift.

Under the modern view, approved by us and by a majority of other courts, no trust is created by precatory language directed to a legatee unless there is testamentary intent to impose a legal obligation upon him to make a particular disposition of property. . . .

In following the majority rule we have stated that more than mere precatory words are required to create a trust. . . . The precatory language will not be made imperative if it comprises merely words of suggestion and advice. . . .

We conclude that the language found in Mrs. Mallory's will falls short of establishing an intent to create a trust and that it constitutes a devise and bequest of her property in fee simple and absolute estate to her brother William L. Burton . . .

Notes and Questions

1. Although a court may be able to determine whether language is precatory based on the instrument alone, *see In re Estate of Lattig*, 2001 Wash. App. LEXIS 1644 (July 27, 2001). Most cases like *Burton* are decided on the basis of surrounding circumstances, rather than just the language used. *Compare Clalit Health Servs. v. Isr. Humanitarian Found.*, 385 F. Supp. 2d 392 (S.D.N.Y. 2005) ("request" was mandatory) *with Archer v. Archer*, 2014 WL 2802735 (Tex. App., 2014) ("request" was precatory) and *In re Palma*, 52 Misc. 3d 1216(A) (N.Y. Sur. Ct. 2016) ("wishes" were precatory). *Compare also In re Estate of Hogan*, 146 N.W.2d 257 (Iowa 1966) ("recommendation" was not a mandatory direction) with *Farmer v. Broadhead*, 230 So. 2d 779 (Miss. 1970) ("recommended" use of a trust form was mandatory). *See also In re Estate of Sanger*, 673 N.W.2d 411 (Wis. Ct. App. 2003). What factors should courts consider when deciding between whether to treat language as mandatory or precatory? *See, e.g., In re Estate of Curry*, 988 P.2d 505 (Wash. Ct. App. 1999) (I "trust" executrix to divide proceeds equally was mandatory).

2. Precatory trust disputes can result in a finding of an intention to create a trust because a fiduciary relationship was intended. But a person may intend to create a fiduciary relationship without intending to create a trust. *See, e.g., Eychaner v. Gross*, 779 N.E.2d 1115 (Ill. 2002) (agency relationship created, not a trust). Moreover, even if a document describes that property is being held in trust, an express trust will not be created unless the putative settlor manifested an intention to create a trust. *See, e.g., Palozie v. Palozie*, 927 A.2d 903 (Conn.. 2007) (no trust created because unclear whether purported settlor intended to create trust); *Meima v. Broemmel*, 117 P.3d 429 (Wyo. 2005) (evidence established that a house was held for lease and purchase, not in trust); *In re Mannara*, 785 N.Y.S.2d 274 (Sur. Ct. 2004) (no trust intended despite will which left property to nephews in trust for their education).

3. If one person gives property to another, subject to a requirement that the donee pay a third person some amount of money, courts will say that the donee takes free from any trust, but subject to an "equitable charge" in favor of the third person. The third person would have a security interest in the property given to the donee. *See, e.g., Estate of Stephano*, 981 A.2d 138 (Pa. 2009) (bequest of stock on condition that beneficiary pay stock dividends to another resulted in debtor-creditor relationship, not a trust). *See generally* 3d Rest. Trusts § 5, cmt. h.

In re Estate of Zukerman

578 N.E.2d 248 (Ill. App. Ct. 1991)

[Before dying together in an auto accident in December, 1988, Louis Rotfeld and Audrey Zukerman had been living together for 12 years. Rotfeld's will gave Zukerman specific items of personal property and 45% of his residuary estate if she survived him by 30 days.

In June, 1987, Rotfeld had opened a customer safekeeping account at Oak Trust and Savings Bank, where Robert Sullivan served as a vice-president. At Rotfeld's request, Sullivan had Rotfeld's $125,000 Commonwealth Edison bond reissued in the name of "Louis Rotfeld, as Trustee for Audrey Zukerman." Rotfeld never executed a formal trust agreement.

In August, 1987, Rotfeld asked Sullivan to make the same arrangements for a $75,000 Ford Motor Credit Corporation bond. The bank issued a safekeeping receipt to "Louis Rotfeld, as Trustee for Audrey Zukerman," but because of some mistakes, the bond's registration did not get changed before the fatal accident.]

Justice Laposta delivered the opinion of the court. On March 22, 1990, the administrator of the estate of Zukerman instituted citation proceedings in the Probate Division of the circuit court of Cook County, seeking to recover the Commonwealth Edison bond and the proceeds of the Ford bond. After an evidentiary hearing, the trial court found that Zukerman was the beneficiary of an express inter vivos trust created by Rotfeld and that her estate was entitled to possession of both bonds.

The executor of the estate of Rotfeld appeals, asserting that there was insufficient evidence that Rotfeld intended to establish a trust for the benefit of Zukerman and insufficient evidence of the trust purpose or the manner in which that purpose was to be accomplished.

The trial court in the case at bar specifically found that Rotfeld established a valid inter vivos trust for the benefit of Zukerman, and we hold that this finding was not against the manifest weight of the evidence.

The requirements of a valid express trust include (1) intent of the parties to create a trust, which may be shown by a declaration of trust by the settlor or by circumstances which show that the settlor intended to create a trust; (2) a definite subject matter or trust property; (3) ascertainable beneficiaries; (4) a trustee; (5) specifications of a trust purpose and how the trust is to be performed; and (6) delivery of the trust property to the trustee....

An oral express trust is valid and may be established by parol evidence, but must be proven by clear and convincing evidence.... The acts or words relied upon must be so unequivocal as to lead to but one conclusion, and if the evidence is doubtful or capable of reasonable explanation upon any other theory, it is not sufficient to establish an oral express trust....

Yet, no particular form of words is necessary to create a trust, when the writing makes clear the existence of a trust. . . . Wherever an intention to create a trust can be fairly collected from the language of the instrument and the terms employed, such intention will be supported by the courts. . . .

In the instant case, the evidence established that all of the requirements of a valid inter vivos trust were satisfied. Rotfeld deliberately and voluntarily acted to have both bonds retitled in his name "as trustee for" Zukerman. Rotfeld repeatedly told Sullivan that he wanted the bonds to be turned over to Zukerman upon his death or "if anything happened to him." This conduct clearly indicates that he intended to create a trust for the benefit of Zukerman. The trust property, beneficiary, and trustee were specifically identified.

Although the trust purpose and manner in which it was to be performed were not spelled out in detail, it is not necessary to the validity of a trust that every required element be so clearly expressed in detail that nothing can be left to inference or implication. . . . It can fairly be inferred that Rotfeld created the trust in order to provide additional financial security to his long-time companion after his death. The manner in which this purpose was to be effectuated was clear from Rotfeld's instructions to Sullivan that he was to receive the interest income as trustee for Zukerman and control of the two bonds was to be turned over to Zukerman upon Rotfeld's demise. . . .

Although the bonds were registered under Rotfeld's social security number and the interest income was declared on his individual income tax return, we do not believe that these circumstances alone are sufficient to indicate that Rotfeld did not intend to create a trust for the benefit of Zukerman. It was necessary that the bonds be registered and that the interest payments be declared as income in filings with the Internal Revenue Service. We hold that the manifest weight of the evidence supports the finding of the trial court that Rotfeld intended and created a trust for the benefit of Zukerman.

Zukerman was the sole beneficiary, and there was no evidence that Rotfeld reserved the power to revoke the trust. Thus, when Rotfeld declared the trust, Zukerman acquired a vested equitable interest in the entire trust property and, at her death, it passed to her estate.

Respondent, the executor of the estate of Rotfeld, contends that the trust was invalid as an attempted testamentary disposition or the creation of a "Totten" trust. The trial court rejected this contention, and we hold that this determination was not against the manifest weight of the evidence.

Rotfeld's conduct indicates an intent to create an immediate trust in his life-time and to have the bonds turned over to Zukerman at his death. This conclusion is confirmed by the fact that Rotfeld left other property to Zukerman in his will and could have done the same with the bonds at issue. Yet, he did not. Rather, Rotfeld deliberately had the bonds retitled in his name as trustee for Zukerman and told Sullivan that he was to receive the interest income as trustee for her.

A settlor may create a trust of personal property whereby he names himself trustee for the beneficiary, and the reservation of a life interest in the property will not defeat the trust. (*Farkas v. Williams* (1955), 5 Ill. 2d 417, 425-26, 125 N.E.2d 600, 605 . . . .) A settlor may reserve the power to consume the interest income or the principal of the trust property without destroying the vested equitable interest of the beneficiary. *Farkas*, 5 Ill. 2d at 429-30, 125 N.E.2d at 607. . . .

The declaration of trust immediately creates an equitable interest in the beneficiary although the enjoyment of that interest is postponed until the death of the settlor. The fact that the beneficiary's actual enjoyment of the trust is contingent upon the settlor's death does not negate the existence of a present interest in the beneficiary during the settlor 's lifetime. *Farkas*, 5 Ill. 2d at 425-26, 125 N.E.2d at 605. . . .

Notes and Question

1. As we shall see in Chapter 10, trustees owe their beneficiaries a duty to invest trust assets prudently. Part of prudence is avoiding foreseeable losses. Another part is spreading risk through diversification. Suppose that an accident at a Commonwealth Edison nuclear power plant threatened the company's solvency and greatly reduced the bond's market value, but that Rotfeld held onto the bond. Could Zukerman recover damages for Rotfeld's breach of fiduciary duty?

2. Compare the trust in *Zukerman* with the TOD account discussed in Chapter 4.

3. The capacity to form an intention is indispensable for trust creation. Standard rules regarding testamentary capacity apply to testamentary trusts, while a heightened gift standard applies to create an irrevocable lifetime trust. *See* 3d Rest. Trusts § 11(3). As discussed earlier, there is disagreement over the level of capacity necessary to execute a revocable lifetime trust. Both the Restatement (Third) of Trusts § 11 (2) and UTC § 601 impose the lower wills standard for revocable lifetime trusts.

As in the case of wills, a lifetime trust may be invalid to the extent trust creation "was induced by fraud, duress or undue influence." UTC § 406.

4. As in the case of wills, lifetime trusts may contain a "no-contest" provision that attempts to dissuade challenges to trust validity on the grounds of lack of capacity or due execution. In addition, lifetime trusts (as well as, testamentary trusts) may contain no-contest provisions for other reasons, e.g., attempting to have a specific dispositive provision voided on the ground of undue influence.

Cook v. Cook, 99 Cal. Rptr. 3d 913, 916 (Ct. App. 2009), illustrates a no-contest provision in a trust:

"If any beneficiary under this instrument . . . directly or indirectly contests this instrument, any amendment to this instrument, . . . or opposes, objects to, or seeks to invalidate any of the provisions of this instrument . . . or seeks to succeed to any part of the estate of the settlors other than in the manner specified in this instrument . . . , then the right of that person to take any interest given to him or her by this instrument or any amendment to this instrument shall be void, and any gift or other interest in the trust property to which the beneficiary would otherwise have been entitled shall pass as if he or she had predeceased the settlors without issue."

No-contest provisions in trusts tend to be strictly construed. *See, e.g.*, *Rafalko v. Georgiadis*, 777 S.E.2d 870 (Va. 2015) (no forfeiture under unique facts) and *Johnson v. Greenelsh*, 217 P.3d 1194 (Cal. 2009) (contesting a settlor's mental competence to exercise rights under a trust did not violate no-contest clause). *See also In re Estate of Stan*, 839 N.W.2d 498 (Mich. Ct. App. 2013) (although challenging the appointment of a personal representative violated a no-contest clause in a revocable trust, forfeiture would not result because probable cause existed for the challenge). In any event, a no-contest clause will not be enforced if it "would interfere with the enforcement or proper administration of the trust." 3d Rest. Trusts § 96(2).

5. Trusts that have third-party trustees typically are captioned as trust agreements and recite that the trust is an agreement between the settlor and trustee. If the settlor reserves the right to amend the trust, is the amendment invalid if the trustee does not agree to the change on the theory that the trust is in the nature of a bilateral contract? *See Moore v. Valley View State Bk.*, 89 P.3d 595 (Kan. 2004) (no).

Problems

1. Mary Jones offered to give a collection of rare law books to the Blackstone University Law School, and its dean gratefully assented to the proposed gift. Thereafter, the law school held a luncheon in Mary's honor. At the luncheon, Mary described the collection to the many notables who attended, and announced its gift. The next day Mary initialed a newspaper release, prepared by the University, which announced that she was giving the collection to the law school. Later, Mary gave the University a memorandum listing most of the collection, particularly the most important books. She then commenced the task of arranging and cataloging the collection for crating and shipping to the University, and corresponded with the law school about delivering it. Mary died six months after the luncheon, before shipping the collection. Mary's will gave her entire estate to her children. Who is entitled to the collection?

2. You represent Lincoln Insurance and Fidelity Endowment Company (LIFE). LIFE insurance policies allow the insured to choose the manner of payment, or settlement, of the proceeds. The most popular "settlement option" is payment in a lump sum to the beneficiary. Some insureds, however, choose to have the company retain the policy proceeds, and pay the beneficiary interest on the sum for a period, with the principal amount payable in the future. Under one LIFE policy, Ralph Whipple elected to have interest paid to his surviving daughter, Shirley, until age 21, at which time she would take the principal amount.

Ralph died and LIFE has been handling the proceeds as directed. Ralph's exwife is Shirley's guardian, and has sued LIFE, alleging that the company holds the principal sum in trust, and requesting approval to invade the trust to satisfy Shirley's current needs. If the funds are in fact a trust, the court is likely to order the invasion. LIFE wants your advice on whether to defend against the suit. What considerations are relevant to your client's decision?

Selected References

David Horton, *Unconscionability in the Law of Trusts*, 84 Notre Dame L. Rev. 1675 (2009).

John H. Langbein, *The Contractarian Basis of the Law of Trusts*, 105 Yale L.J. 625 (1995).

Alan Newman, *The Intention of the Settlor Under the Uniform Trust Code: Whose Property Is It Anyway?*, 38 Akron L. Rev. 649 (2005).

Frank L. Schiavo, *Does the Use of "Request," "Wish," or "Desire" Create a Precatory Trust or Not?*, 40 Real Prop. Prob. & Tr. J. 647 (2006).

B. Trust Property

In most cases, there is no question about trust property. Assets from an estate fill a testamentary trust, or stocks, bonds, and cash fund a lifetime trust. In some situations, however, a purported trust's subject matter can be less substantial. Then the question becomes whether the item counts as "property" (or "res") for the purposes of sustaining a trust, or whether it is a mere expectancy that cannot be the subject of a trust. *See* 3d Rest. Trusts § 41.

Kully v. Goldman

305 N.W.2d 800 (Neb. 1981)

CLINTON, J.

This action was brought in the District Court for Douglas County by the plaintiff, Robert I. Kully, against the defendant, William A. Goldman, asking the court to temporarily and permanently enjoin Goldman from withholding "the transfer to plaintiff" annually of season tickets to four specific seats to the University of Nebraska varsity football games and from doing anything to prejudice Goldman's "future ability to receive such tickets from the University." The prayer further asked that Goldman be declared trustee of said tickets for Kully's use. . . .

[W]e accept the factual findings of the trial court that in about 1961 the parties made an agreement that Goldman would obtain from the University of Nebraska Athletic Department four season tickets for his own use and four for the use of Kully; that ticket reservations were made in Goldman's name; and that from the time the agreement was made in about 1961 until 1979, with the exception of the year 1972, Goldman purchased the four tickets and was paid annually by Kully either before or after the tickets were obtained. . . .

It is fundamental that in order for a present trust, . . . to be created, there must be a defined interest or ascertainable object of ownership. Bogert, Trusts and Trustees §§ 111, 113 (2d ed. 1965), and § 451 (Rev. 2d ed. 1977). An agreement to create a trust in the future in order to be specifically enforceable must be supported by a consideration. Op. cit. § 113 at 578-79; Restatement (Second) of Trusts § 26, Comment m (1959). . . .

In this case the evidence shows that Goldman had no contractual right with the university which bound it to annually, for any period of time, sell him tickets upon tender by him of the purchase price. Because Goldman was on the list of annual purchasers, his prospect of obtaining the same seats and the same number of seats each year was good. It was not, however, a property right which he could enforce. The university could, at any time if it chose, refuse to sell tickets to Goldman. Although it is undoubtedly true that the university, barring some change in circumstances, was most likely to continue to sell Goldman tickets, it was not required to do so. . . .

Memorial Stadium, Lincoln, Nebraska

It appears to be the universal rule that mere expectancies cannot be held in trust. Restatement (Second) of Trusts § 86 (1959); Bogert, Trusts and Trustees § 113 (2d ed. 1965). The courts have uniformly held that no trust can be created unless there exists some property interest which may be held by the trustee for the claimant. American Sodium Co. v. Shelley, 51 Nev. 344, 276 P. 11 (1929) (a revocable permit). . . .

In order for equity to recognize a promise to create a trust in the future when a property or property interest comes into existence, the promise must be supported by a consideration. Restatement (Second) of Trusts § 75, Comment b, § 86, Comments b and c (1959). If no consideration exists the promise is not specifically enforceable. Restatement of Contracts § 366 (1932). . . .

In the case before us, the court's decree directing specific performance was improper because there was no existing res which could be the subject of a present trust and because, insofar as a promise related to acquisition of tickets for "all" future seasons, it was unsupported by a consideration. . . .

Notes and Question

1. Suppose Oscar placed $50,000 in a trust giving income to his son Andy during his life and at Andy's death giving the principal to whomever Andy appointed by his will. If Andy did not appoint anyone, the property would go to Oscar's other son, Matthew, if he survived Andy. If Matthew did not survive, the property would go to Oscar's sister, Dawn, if she survived Andy. Dawn's interest is a contingent remainder. A contingent remainder is a property interest which Dawn could place in a new trust. *See* 3d Rest. Trusts § 40.

Suppose further that Andy is a healthy 40-year-old father of three. His brother Matthew is 30, and Aunt Dawn is 62. Would you rather have Dawn's contingent remainder or William Goldman's chance of getting Nebraska football tickets?

2. The rights to acquire Nebraska football tickets are a sufficient property interest to make them subject to court division in a marriage dissolution action. *See Kullbom v. Kullbom*, 306 N.W.2d 844 (Neb. 1981) (awarding "all rights, if any" to the husband).

3. *Brainard v. Comm'r*, 91 F.2d 880 (7th Cir. 1937), *cert. dismissed*, 303 U.S. 665 (1938), involved a taxpayer who was trying to reduce his income taxes by spreading his gains among a variety of family members. In December 1927, he orally declared to his wife and mother that he was holding in trust for various family members the profits he would make from trading stocks in 1928. The IRS argued that he had not created a trust, so all trading profits earned in 1928 were attributable to him. The court agreed with the IRS reasoning that there were no 1928 profits in existence at the time of the declaration of trust.

One of the most useful estate planning devices is to create a revocable trust that can serve as a shell to catch estate assets and life insurance proceeds which appear at the settlor's death. From the perspective of trust doctrine, a key question is whether a trustee's beneficial interest in life insurance is a "property interest" sufficient to sustain the trust.

4. Gun trusts created during lifetime are becoming popular vehicles to allow the continuation of gun ownership, especially for firearms that are subject to federal regulation. *See generally* Lee-ford Tritt, *Dispatches from the Trenches of America's Great Gun Trust Wars*, 108 Nw. U.L. Rev. 743 (2014).

Gordon v. Portland Trust Bank

271 P.2d 653 (Or. 1954)

[Albert Gordon delivered a series of life insurance policies to the Portland Trust Bank under an agreement naming the bank as trustee. Albert designated the bank as beneficiary of the policies, but the bank was not responsible for paying the premiums. Albert retained a series of rights under the policies, such as obtaining loans or cashing them in. After Albert's death the bank purported to hold the insurance proceeds in trust under the terms of the agreement. Albert's wife, Leotta, as executrix of Albert's will, claimed that the trust agreement did not create a trust, but was actually a testamentary disposition which was revoked by a later will.]

Lusk, Justice. . . . In modern times, the real incidents of ownership are indisputably vested in the insured and it was only logical that many courts should take the position that the beneficiary, where he is subject to divestment at the mere whim of the insured, takes only a contingent interest or an expectancy. Thus, today there is considerable authority for the view that the beneficiary gets a vested right only as his expectancy or contingent interest matures on the death of the insured. . . . But the courts are by no means in accord on the issue. Many hold that the beneficiary takes a vested interest subject to divestment upon change of beneficiary in accordance with the provisions of the policy. . . .

Under the general view that the beneficiary has no more than an expectancy, it is more difficult to find the necessary res for a present trust. Rather, the transaction appears to be a contract with the trust-beneficiary to create a trust at the insured's death. The courts, however, have not felt constrained to arrive at this conclusion, and the cases are legion which have upheld the usual form of unfunded insurance trust even where the court had previously announced that the beneficiary has no more than a mere expectancy. . . . A right of revocation of the trust deed in the case of any trust cannot really be distinguished from the power reserved by the insured to change the beneficiary. The extent of control reserved to the donor and the insured is the same in both cases, and the vested interest of the beneficiary of the ordinary trust is not open to question, despite the fact that the donor might revoke the trust at his pleasure. *See, Allen v. Hendrick*, 104 Or. 202, 224, 206 P. 733. A close analogy is found in the so-called "Totten" or tentative savings bank trust, under which complete control is likewise reserved by the donor during his lifetime, but the beneficiary is permitted to take the money on his death. See, *Matter of Totten*, 179 N.Y. 112, 71 N.E. 748, 70 L.R.A. 711.

. . . Our own view is that the ownership of the modern policy is actually divided between the beneficiary and the insured. The various marketing or sales features, such as the loan and cash surrender values, are clearly the property of the insured. On the other hand, the beneficiary is the owner of a promise to pay the proceeds at the death of insured, subject to insured's right of revocation. It seems to us that the right of the beneficiary is actually the primary right under the policy, whereas the insured's rights are secondary and have nothing to do with the basic purpose of life insurance....

It follows from the foregoing analysis of the nature and incidents of an insurance trust that Mr. Gordon intended to, and did, transfer to the bank a present interest in the insurance policies, *Allen v. Hendrick*, 104 Or. 202, 225, 206 P. 733, and that the plaintiff's contention that the instrument is testamentary in character, rather than a trust, must fail....

Notes and Questions

1. The current version of the Uniform Testamentary Additions to Trusts Act allows testamentary gifts to lifetime trusts "regardless of the existence, size, or character of the corpus of the trust." UPC § 2-511(a).

2. Recall that in *Farkas v. Williams* on Page 212, the court struggled with whether the beneficiary (Williams) had received anything during Farkas' lifetime. Was Williams' interest in the trust Farkas created a property interest that Williams could in turn place in his own trust?

3. An attempted trust may fail because a court cannot tell what property the settlor intended to put in trust. *See Wilkerson v. McClary*, 647 S.W.2d 79 (Tex. App. 1983) (unclear which of four bank accounts should be held in trust); *Matter of Estate of Chong*, 906 P.2d 710 (Nev. 1995) (remand to determine whether checking account had been retitled from settlor to trustee).

4. Can property acquired after a trust has been created be treated as trust property by a recitation that after-acquired property be part of the trust? *Rose v. Waldrip*, 730 S.E.2d 529 (Ga. App. 2012), following 2d Rest. Trusts 86 and 3d Rest, Trusts 41, decided that an interest that is not in existence on trust creation cannot be held in trust. Of course, once the property comes into existence, it may become part of the trust by transfer or even by declaration in almost all states. See Note on Page 412.

Selected Reference

Jane B. Baron, *The Trust Res and Donative Intent*, 61 Tul. L. Rev. 45 (1986).v

C. Trustee

From a doctrinal perspective, the requirement that a trust have a trustee is the least onerous of the basic elements. Rather than letting a trust fail, a court will almost invariably appoint a trustee if a testator intended to create a trust, but did not name a trustee, or if a sitting trustee dies or resigns. Hence the maxim "A trust will not fail for want of a trustee." However, a trust will fail if the settlor intended that the trust operate only while a specific person was trustee and that specific person failed to serve as trustee.

In the context of an intended lifetime trust where the settlor will not be the sole trustee, the trust will fail if the intended trust property is not validly delivered to the intended trustee. In such case, carefully distinguish between two required trust elements. In that situation, the trust will fail for want of delivery, rather than for want of a trustee. In contrast, there is no delivery problem, with respect to a testamentary trust; probate of the will substitutes for delivery.

The real challenges for a settlor lie in the selection of the trustee (and successor trustee) and the powers the settlor wishes to give to the trustee. As we shall see in Chapter 10, trustees' powers and duties are many and varied. They must handle both the financial and the personal sides of administration.

Identifying a trustee who can monitor investments, file tax forms, and make sensitive decisions about how much to spend for a beneficiary's "comfortable support" can be difficult. In an effort to combine professional competence and a personal touch, settlors sometimes appoint two co-trustees, one a corporation and the other an individual. The corporate trustee, usually a bank, provides continuity and expertise, and the individual provides the personal touch. A co-trustee arrangement can be unwieldy, however, because both trustees usually must join in acting on the trust's behalf. *See* 3d Rest. Trusts § 81. To avoid that problem, some settlors try to divide the authority and responsibility of each trustee with varying degrees of success. Another approach is for an individual trustee to delegate investment and other responsibilities to experts. As we will see in Chaper 10, delegation of certain duties is generally allowed.

Yet another solution to the complexity of managing trusts is for the settlor to require that a trustee follow the directions of a "trust advisor" or "trust director." Known as directed trusts, the most common directions by trust advisors are with respect to trust investments but may also involve other administrative powers and discretionary distributions.

More recently, settlors have also begun to appoint "trust protectors," who may be given even greater powers to direct trustees, including the power to terminate or modify a trust. Both directed trusts and trust protectors are considered further in Chapter 10 § 10.03B3(b).

For the very wealthy, a new paradigm has emerged for trusteeship: the family trust company. A corporation is formed with family members with the expectation that the resulting family trust company will serve as the trustee for generations over the family's fortune. As a result, the limitations inherent with individual and corporate trustees can be avoided. *See generally* Iris J. Goodwin, *How the Rich Stay Rich: Using a Family Trust Company to Secure a Family Fortune*, 40 Seton Hall L. Rev. 467 (2010). Several states have enacted legislation that allows family trust companies to be either lightly regulated or even unregulated.[6]

---

6. *See* Iris J. Goodwin, *How the Rich Stay Rich: Using a Family Trust Company to Secure a Family Fortune*, 40 Seton Hall L. Rev. 467, 473–75 (2010).

Should a Family Member Be a Trustee?

Both to save money and because they know the people involved, clients are often tempted to name a family member to serve as a trustee. Noting that "[a]lthough some individuals may feel honored when selected as a trustee, the office of trustee is not an honorary position," two observers stress that a variety of factors should influence the choice of a trustee. *See* Kathryn A. Johnson & Adam J. Wiensch, *Trustee Selection for Successful Trust Administration*, 8 Prob. & Prop., May/June 1994, at 38, 40.

Here are some issues to consider:

- Whether it is appropriate to assume (as is often the case) that the trustee will (or should) serve without compensation.[7]
- Whether by naming a family member one might actually increase costs because that person may need to hire more professionals (accountants, lawyers, investment advisors) than would a corporate trustee with greater expertise.
- Whether the trust is too large for an individual to be able to manage (or too small for a corporate trustee to want to take on).
- Whether the nature of the trust assets requires special expertise.
- Whether the trust will likely outlive the named trustee and successors.
- Whether the family member trustee will have conflicts of interest or personality conflicts with trust beneficiaries.
- Whether tax issues can be appropriately handled.

Note

In situations involving third-party trustees, legal title of the trust property cannot vest in the trustee unless there has been "delivery." *See, e.g., Trott v. Jones*, 157 S.W.3d 592 (Ark. Ct. App. 2004). Recall our discussion of delivery as an element in the law of gifts. Depending on the nature of the asset, delivery alone may not be sufficient. *See, e.g., Estate of Washburn*, 581 S.E.2d 148 (N.C. Ct. App. 2003) (no trust created over security absent indorsement and delivery of certificate as required under Article 8 of UCC).

If the settlor has declared that she holds property in trust, delivery from settlor to trustee is not necessary to satisfy the "property" element of trust creation. *See, e.g., Rose v. Waldrip*, 730 S.E.2d 529 (Ga. App. 2012). *But see* N.Y. Estates, Powers and

7. In the absence of a compensation provision in the trust instrument, the trustee may be entitled to statutory commissions. *See, e.g.*, N.Y. Sur. Ct. Proc. Act § 2309.

Trusts Law § 7-1.18 (requiring written documentation even if settlor is sole trustee). The settlor already has the trust principal. On the other hand, delivery of something to someone may help meet the "intent" element. Often the settlor's delivery of a written instrument of trust to the principal beneficiary provides the evidence. If the settlor orally declares a trust, evidence of the settlor's intent may appear in statements to third parties, letters, bookkeeping entries, and the like.

D. Beneficiaries[8]

Just as virtually all trusts clearly have property, so do they have identifiable beneficiaries separate from the trustee. Doctrinally, beneficiaries are required in order to achieve the separation of legal and equitable title that characterizes the trust relationship. A trustee must owe duties to someone else. Otherwise, there never would be anyone to enforce the trustee's duties.

Selected References

Steve R. Akers, *Twenty-five Things You Have to Know about Appointing Trustees*, 17 Prob. & Prop. 36 (July/Aug. 2003).

Richard C. Ausness, *The Role of Trust Protectors in American Trust Law*, 45 Real Prop. Tr. & Est. L.J. 319 (2011).

Iris J. Goodwin, *How the Rich Stay Rich: Using a Family Trust Company to Secure a Family Fortune*, 40 Seton Hall L. Rev. 467 (2010).

Barbara Hauser, *How to Interview a Corporate Trustee*, 146 Tr. & Est. 60 (Mar. 2007).

I.M. Cohen, *Appreciating Individual Trustees*, 145 Tr. & Est. 32 (Dec. 2006).

Deborah S. Gordon, *Trusting Trust*, 63 Kan. L. Rev. 497 (2015).

K. Street, *Growls or Gratitude? Practical Guidelines for Selection of Individual Trustees and Design of Trustee Succession Plans*, 40 Heckerling Inst. on Est. Plan. ¶ 3.1 (2006).

Hannah Shaw Grove & Russ Alan Prince, *Choosing a Trustee*, 143 Tr. & Est. 52 (Feb. 2004).

Barbara Hauser, *Appreciating Corporate Trustees*, 144 Tr. & Est. 52 (Aug. 2005).

James P. Weller & Alan V. Ytterberg, *Managing Family Wealth Through a Private Trust Company*, 36 ACTEC L.J. 623 (2010).

---

8. A beneficiary may be called a cestui que trust.

Morsman v. Commissioner

90 F.2d 18 (8th Cir. 1937)

[Robert Morsman on January 28, 1929, executed a "Trust Agreement" making himself trustee of shares of stock he owned individually. The United States Trust Company was to be successor trustee, to whom Morsman had to turn over the property on or before January 1, 1939. The income earned prior to 1934 was to be accumulated and added to principal. Thereafter, income was to be paid to Morsman for his life. The trust was to terminate upon his death if he were childless. If he died leaving issue surviving, the income was to be paid to his surviving issue for twenty years, at which time the trust would terminate. Upon termination, the principal was to be distributed (a) per stirpes to his then surviving issue; (b) to his widow; or (c) to his heirs. At the time he executed the trust, Morsman was unmarried and childless, although he had a living brother.

In February, 1929, Morsman sold some of the stock at a profit. In May, 1929, he turned over all funds in the trust to the United States Trust Company as successor trustee. The trustee reported the gain as trust income. Morsman did not report it as individual income. The Commissioner ruled that he should have reported the income as his, and the Board of Tax Appeals concurred.]

THOMAS, CIRCUIT JUDGE. . . . The petitioner contends that a private express trust did exist during the period in question and that the profits realized from the sale of the securities should be taxed as income to the trust and not as income to himself individually. . . .

First. With respect to the position of Morsman, it is settled that a trust cannot exist where the same person possesses both the legal and equitable titles to the trust fund at the same time. In such a case the two titles are said to merge. . . . This principle is not denied. The result, of course, is different where one person conveys property to another who agrees to hold in trust for the grantor. . . . In such a case there is an immediate severance of the legal and equitable titles, and a trust arises at once. In the instant case that provision of the agreement by which the petitioner undertook to hold for himself, standing alone, therefore, contributes nothing toward the creation of a trust. . . .

Second. With respect to the possibility of issue, it will be observed that in designating beneficiaries and providing for the enjoyment of the property the petitioner has looked to the future. . . . The distinction thus noted between the case where A declares himself trustee for his unborn issue and where he conveys to B to hold in trust for such issue is vital; and this is the point at which Morsman failed in his attempt to create a present trust. Where the beneficiary is in being, the beneficial interest may be vested in him though its enjoyment be postponed. But by "no distortion of language or legal principles" . . . can a present severance of legal and equitable titles, an essential element of any completed trust . . . , be spelled out where one makes a purported declaration of trust naming himself as trustee for unborn issue or other nonexistent persons. . . .

It has been said that "If a beneficiary of a trust has not been born or conceived, a suit can be maintained on his behalf by a next friend or guardian to enforce the duties of the trustee." Trusts, Restatement, § 214, Comment a. . . . It is true that a guardian may be appointed for an unborn child which is in esse . . . but it is difficult to understand how such an appointment can be made for a child not yet conceived where there is no other basis of jurisdiction. . . . To say that because a guardian may be appointed for an unborn child and that for that reason a present trust exists although the legal and equitable titles be merged in the same person is a plain case of putting the cart before the horse. It is only where there is a present severance of legal and equitable titles, which effect a trust, and which gives equity jurisdiction to act, that a court of equity can appoint a guardian to act in behalf of unborn issue. . . .

Third. With respect to the "heirs" as present beneficiaries and to the possible suggestion that petitioner 's brother now living may take a present equitable interest under paragraph (8) of the trust agreement, it is observed that one of the elementary rules of law is that "A living person has no heirs." . . . Only on death do heirs come into existence. . . . What has been said with reference to the rights of unborn children applies with equal force to the rights of heirs, two classes equally nonexistent. "Heirs," therefore, have no present beneficial interest, and cannot be considered beneficiaries. . . .

Finally, with respect to the status of a widow as a beneficiary, what has been said in reference to the nonexistence of issue and heirs is applicable here. The record . . . does not show the existence of a wife. A widow is, therefore, a mere potentiality without existence and with no one to represent her. . . .

The trust agreement, therefore, failed to effect the creation of a trust on January 28, 1929. This results from the fact that no existing beneficiaries were named therein and, consequently, there was no present severance of the legal and equitable titles to the property. . . .

Notes and Question

1. How might you meet the *Morsman* court's requirement of achieving separation of title, other than by using a third-party trustee?

2. Tax cases are suspect authority for statements regarding other areas of law. In particular, courts handling tax questions may be tempted to interpret state law with an eye to what they view as the best tax result. A court seeking to sustain the trust in *Morsman* might have recognized Morsman's brother as someone with an interest in enforcing trustee duties, or the court might have named a guardian to represent as-yet-unidentified beneficiaries if the need arose.

3. Early in his career, the late Professor William F. Fratcher, who became one of the country's noted authorities on trust law, commented, "[I]nsofar as the majority opinion in Morsman . . . purports to declare the law of trusts, it is unsound and ought

not to be followed. The settlor of a private trust can be the sole trustee and the only presently ascertainable beneficiary so long as the other beneficiaries will be ascertainable within the period of the rule against perpetuities." William F. Fratcher, *Trustor as Sole Trustee and Only Ascertainable Beneficiary*, 47 Mich. L. Rev. 907, 934 (1949).

4. *Senfour Investment Co. v. King County*, 401 P.2d 319 (Wash. 1965), is a sales tax case in which the court ruled in favor of the taxpayer. Fred Streib offered to purchase a hotel on behalf of an as yet non-existent corporation. Since the corporation was not yet formed on the closing date, Streib and two others purchased the hotel in place of the corporation. They were taxed on this transaction. After the corporation was formed, Streib and the others quitclaimed the hotel to the new corporation. The county treasurer assessed a second tax. Streib argued that he at all times acted as trustee of the property, and the court agreed, saying "It is not necessary that the cestui que trust be in existence at the time of the creation of the trust."

5. The merger doctrine would apply if the trustee was the only beneficiary. For example, if Morsman was the sole trustee, had the right to income for life, and the remainder was payable to his estate, no trust would have been created. *Cf. In re Wells*, 259 B.R. 776 (Bankr. M.D. Fla. 2001) (merger when income beneficiary died and sole trustee was sole remainder beneficiary). *See generally* 3d Rest. Trusts § 69.

Note: Unidentifiable Beneficiaries and Resulting Trusts

Beneficiaries of a private trust must be definite. The trustee must be able to identify who should get the property, and a court should have a standard by which to judge whether the trustee has distributed trust benefits to the right persons. The question in any particular case is whether the description is sufficient to meet those goals. Some are easy: "children," "husband," "wife," "nieces," "nephews." On the other hand, "relatives" has caused some trouble. If construed to mean any relation, the description is probably too broad to be enforceable. *Binns v. Vick*, 538 S.W.2d 283 (Ark. 1976). If construed to mean those relatives who would take under the intestate statute, the term has enough specificity. *Reagh v. Kelley*, 89 Cal. Rptr. 425 (Ct. App. 1970).

What about an indefinite term like "friends"? Clearly, if the trust required the trustee to distribute equal amounts to each friend, the trust would fail since it would be impossible to determine the total number of friends who constitute the class. *See* 3d Rest. Trusts § 46(1). But suppose the trustee was directed to distribute the trust property to one or more of the settlor's friends? *Clark v. Campbell*, 133 A. 166 (N.H. 1926), involved such a case since the testator wanted tangible personal property—books, photos, artwork—to go to his friends as mementos of the friendship. Rather than listing which individual items should go to which person, he gave them all to his trustees with directions to distribute them "to such of my friends as they, my trustees, shall select." Because it found no criterion by which to judge the trustees' choices, the court invalidated the attempted trust. Although the trust failed, the testator clearly did not intend to leave the property to the trustees personally. Therefore, a "resulting trust" arose in favor of the estate; the personal items became estate assets, free from trust.

The result in *Clark* frustrated the intent of the settlor, especially since the settlor could have validly given the trustee a permissive, rather than a mandatory power to make distributions to friends. Such a permissive power is called a power of appointment—a power created by the owner of property giving someone else (the donee) the power to transfer the property. The permissible transferees (objects) might, or might not, be limited to a particular class. If the power identifies a class, the typical plan is to allow the donee to choose among possible objects. The description of the class need not be particularly precise. The question for a court is not whether all possible members of the class of objects are identifiable, but whether a particular appointee is a member of the class. Powers of appointment are considered in detail in Chapter 9, § 9.03.

The court in *Clark* rejected the trustees' argument that they had a valid power of appointment. Because the power was held in trust, the court required the level of specificity appropriate for determining trust beneficiaries, rather than the lower level required to sustain a power of appointment exercisable by non-trustees.

Restatement (Third) of Trusts § 46(2) takes the position that a trustee should be allowed to make distributions to identifiable individuals within an indefinite class. *See also* 2d Rest. Prop. (Donative Transfers) § 12.1. In his article, *Uniform Acts, Restatements, and Trends in American Trust Law at Century's End*, 88 Cal. L. Rev. 1877, 1891 (2000), Professor Edward Halbach, Jr., Reporter for the Restatement (Third) of Trusts, explained Section 46(2) as follows:

> [I]ntended mandatory provisions of otherwise valid trusts that cannot be enforced as such may be allowed as "adapted trusts." That is, the intended purpose may be carried out, within reasonable time limits (normally limited to a twenty-one-year period derived, by analogy, from the rule against perpetuities' twenty-one-year period in gross), if the devisee or legatee will do so by exercising a nonmandatory, generally personal "power" to appoint or expend (to or for the members of an indefinite class . . .) funds that are otherwise held in trust for distribution in default of appointment to beneficiaries implied by law—that is, for the testator's successors in interest, or for the other beneficiaries of an otherwise enforceable trust. Thus, the adapted trust is a true trust that is enforceable by the reversionary beneficiaries, subject to the trustee's power of distribution (not mandatory as intended, but analogous to a power of appointment). As adapted in this fashion, the trust avoids the complete failure of the decedent's purpose that would occur under traditional doctrine, which has simply required the devisee to hold immediately on resulting trust.

Uniform Trust Code

Section 402. Requirements for Creation.

(c) A power in a trustee to select a beneficiary from an indefinite class is valid. If the power is not exercised within a reasonable time, the power fails and the property subject to the power passes to the persons who would have taken the property had the power not been conferred.

Note: Purpose Trusts (Trusts without Beneficiaries)

A trust that has no beneficiaries and is created exclusively for charitable purposes will be recognized as an express charitable trust, as distinct from a private express trust. Charitable trusts are enforceable by the applicable state's attorney general. Absent unusual situations, resulting trusts will not come into play with charitable trusts.

The common law has recognized arrangements whereby a settlor intends to create a private express trust for certain non-charitable, non-capricious purposes, such as trusts to care for pets and trusts to erect and maintain tomb-stones. Because there is no person to enforce the trust, a true express trust cannot be created. Rather an honorary trust is created, so-called because the trustee is honor-bound to carry out the settlor's intended but unenforceable terms. Pursuant to the honorary trust doctrine, the settlor or the settlor's successors in interest may force the honorary trustee to convey the property to them if the trustee fails to honor the wishes of the settlor after a reasonable period. If the purpose is capricious, however, the trust will fail from the inception.

The UTC goes beyond the honorary trust doctrine by allowing the settlor to appoint a person who can enforce the trust, or if none has been validly appointed by the settlor, a court can appoint an enforcer. *See* UTC §§ 408(b) and 409. Except for trusts to care for animals alive during the settlor's lifetime, UTC § 409 permits enforcement of noncharitable purpose trusts for no more than 21 years. On the other hand, trusts for the care of animals who were alive during the settlor's lifetime will last until the animal or last of the animals die. *See* UTC § 408(a). *Cf.* UPC § 2-907 (recognizing trusts for pets but limiting trust duration to a 21-year period). Unless the trust provides otherwise, the trustee must distribute to the settlor (or the settlor's successors) any property not required for the intended use. *See* UTC §§ 408(c) and 409.

In an open attempt to attract trust business, several states, including Delaware, Idaho, Maine, New Hampshire, Wisconsin, and Wyoming, have recently enacted legislation that is intended to allow trusts for noncharitable purposes to last indefinitely. *See generally* Richard Nenno, *Perpetual Dynasty Trusts: Tax Planning* and *Jurisdiction Selection Appendix L in ALI-ABA Planning Techniques for Large Estates* (May 2011) (listing states, including a few that allow noncharitable purpose trusts to last for 90 years). For example, a trust to maintain a building for 200, or even two million, years is clearly permissible in Delaware and, despite Professor Hirsch's reservations, see Adam J. Hirsch, *Delaware Unifies the Law of Charitable and Noncharitable Purpose Trusts*, 36 Est. Plan. 13 (2009), most likely in all of the other enacting states. Otherwise, their legislation would make no sense. Also, trust purpose statutes typically provide that a person be designated to ensure that the intended use of the trust property be carried out; such person is referred as a trust enforcer.

Settlors may also attempt to create trusts for indefinite purposes. An example would be a trust for benevolent purposes. If the purposes are deemed exclusively charitable, then the trust will be recognized as a charitable trust. Assuming the purposes were not exclusively charitable purposes, no express trust will be created for want of a definite beneficiary. Similar to the position taken on trusts for indefinite persons under Restatement (Third) of Trusts § 46(2), Restatement § 47(1) provides that a trust for a noncharitable purpose may be created if the trustee is willing to carry out the purposes. *Accord* UTC § 409.

Note: Other Situations Involving Resulting Trusts

A resulting trust can arise when a trust fails because of illegality, impossibility, or a violation of the Rule Against Perpetuities. If the trust principal generates more income than the trust purposes require (for example, to supply a set monthly stipend), a resulting trust may arise with respect to the surplus income.

A resulting trust will also arise from an incomplete disposition. Suppose Sarah's will gives property to Bruce in trust with income to Beth for life, and principal to Ira if he survives Beth. If Ira does not survive Beth, Bruce does not get to keep the money. Rather, a resulting trust arises in favor of Sarah's estate. In this context, the resulting trust is serving as an "equitable reversion," a name courts sometimes apply.

To avoid a resulting trust when there has been an incomplete disposition, courts may imply gifts to fill the gap. Imagine a trust giving "income to Don and Stewart, and on the death of the survivor, principal to Ron." What happens to the income when either Don or Stewart dies? Consider Professor Scott's comments:

> Four possible dispositions might be made of the share of the income of the deceased beneficiary: (1) it might be paid to the surviving life beneficiar[y]; (2) it might be paid to the estate of the deceased beneficiary; (3) it might be paid to the estate of the settlor as property not disposed of by his will; (4) it might be accumulated and on the termination of the trust paid to the persons entitled to the principal of the trust estate.

William F. Fratcher, Scott on Trusts § 143 (4th ed. 1989).

The most common approach is to imply a gift of income to the surviving life tenant. *See, e.g., Heisinger v. Dillon*, 147 A.3d 123 (2016). *Accord* 3d Rest. Prop. § 26.9, cmt. e(1). However, if the remainder interest is in favor of the issue of the income beneficiaries upon the survivor's death, the Restatement position is that a gift should first be implied to the predeceasing beneficiary's issue for the life of the surviving life tenant. *See* 3d Rest. Trusts § 49, cmt. c and 3d Rest. Prop. § 26.9, cmt. e(1).

Problems

1. Frank's will gave his estate to a trustee to be distributed "among my employees." Is the trust valid?

2. Marilyn Monroe gave the residue of her estate to her friend Lee Strasberg, with instructions to distribute it among Marilyn's "friends, colleagues and those to whom I am devoted." Robert S. Menchin, Where There's a Will 138 (1979). If the gift were in trust, would it be valid?

3. What do you think would be a capricious purpose so that the attempt to create a private express trust would fail?

4. Helen Cummings is a healthy 85-year-old. Anticipating eventualities, she wants to create a trust for the person who provides her the best care at home during her declining years. Helen views the trust as both an incentive for good home care and a thank you. What language would you use to identify her intended beneficiary?

5. Do you think a trust beneficiary can disclaim an interest in trust?

Selected References

Richard C. Ausness, *Non-Charitable Purpose Trusts: Past, Present, and* Future, 51 Real Prop, Trust and Estate L. J. 321 (2016).

Gerry W. Beyer, *Pet Animals: What Happens When Their Humans Die?*, 40 Santa Clara L. Rev. 617 (2000).

Alexander A. Bove, Jr., *The Purpose of Purpose Trusts*, 18 Prob. & Prop. 34 (May/June 2004).

Estate Planning for Pets website, www.estateplanningforpets.org (listing pet trust statutes).

Adam J. Hirsch, *Trusts for Purposes: Policy, Ambiguity, and Anomaly in the Uniform Laws*, 26 Fla. St. U. L. Rev. 913 (1999) and *Bequests for Purposes: A Unified Theory*, 56 Wash. & Lee L. Rev. 33 (1999).

Rachel Hirschfeld, *The Perfect Pet Trust: Saving Your Dog from the Unexpected*, 9 Alb. Gov't L. Rev. 107 (2016).

Igor Levenberg, *Personal Revival Trusts: If You Can't Take It With You, Can You Come Back to Get It?*, 83 St. John's L. Rev. 1469 (2009).

Breahn Vokolek, *America Gets What It Wants: Pet Trusts and a Future for Its Companion Animals*, 76 UMKC L. Rev. 1109 (2008).

E. Trust Purposes

Uniform Trust Code

Section 404. Trust Purposes.

A trust may be created only to the extent its purposes are lawful, not contrary to public policy, and possible to achieve. A trust and its terms must be for the benefit of its beneficiaries.

Comment

Generally, a trust has a purpose which is illegal if: (1) its performance involves the commission of a criminal or tortious act by the trustee; (2) the settlor's purpose in creating the trust was to defraud creditors or others; or (3) the consideration for the creation of the trust was illegal. See Restatement (Third) of Trusts § 28 cmt. a (Tentative Draft No. 2, approved 1999). . . .

The general purpose of trusts having identifiable beneficiaries is to benefit those beneficiaries in accordance with their interests as defined in the trust's terms. The requirement of this section that a trust and its terms be for the benefit of its beneficiaries, which is derived from Restatement (Third) of Trusts § 27(2), implements this general purpose. While a settlor has considerable latitude in specifying how a particular trust purpose is to be pursued, the administrative and other nondispositive trust terms must reasonably relate to this purpose and not divert the trust property to achieve a trust purpose that is invalid, such as one which is frivolous or capricious. *See* Restatement (Third) of Trusts § 27 cmt. b.

Even though a trust is created for a lawful purpose, it may be invalidated in whole or in part if there is a perpetuities violation. As discussed later in the chapter, there is a well-established policy that bars a settlor from making a trust nonterminable beyond the applicable perpetuities period. *See* 3d Rest. Trusts § 29, cmt. c. The effect of a beneficiary's interest vesting remotely as a perpetuities violation will be examined in Chapter 9.

We have already encountered how public policy may be used to strike down a will provision. As explained in the Comment to UTC § 404, the same public policy considerations apply in the context of trusts:

> Purposes violative of public policy include those that tend to encourage criminal or tortious conduct, that interfere with freedom to marry or encourage divorce, that limit religious freedom, or which are frivolous or capricious. See Restatement (Third) of Trusts § 29 cmt. d–h (Tentative Draft No. 2, 1999).

According to Professor Langbein, the benefit-the-beneficiaries standard that is articulated in UTC § 404 provides the rationale for the rule that bars carrying out a settlor's capricious purposes.[9] *See* John H. Langbein, *Burn the Rembrandt? Trust Law's Limits on the Settlor's Power to Direct Investments*, 90 B.U. L. Rev. 375, 376 (2010). Yet, as the title of Professor Langbein's article suggests, the most pressing question is whether settlor investment directions may violate the benefit-the-beneficiaries standard and therefore be disregarded because capricious. We will return to this question in chapter 10.

Questions

1. Would a trust violate public policy if it provided for a child if she graduates from college with an overall B average, receives a law degree, has a child, marries before age 30, and is free from illicit drugs based on monthly testing arranged by the trustee?

2. What would be the consequences for a trust if a trust provision were struck down because it conflicts with public policy?

Selected References

Howard M. McCue, III, *Planning and Drafting to Influence Behavior*, 34 Heckerling Inst. on Est. Plan. ch. 6 (2000).

Marjorie J. Stephens, *Incentive Trusts: Considerations, Uses, and Alternatives*, 29 ACTEC J. 5 (2003).

Joshua C. Tate, *Conditional Love: Incentive Trusts and the Inflexibility Problem*, 41 Real Prop. Prob. & Tr. J. 445 (2006).

F. Formalities for Trust Creation

The formalities for trust creation depend on the type of trust that is sought to be created. The applicable jurisdiction's Statute of Wills must be complied with to create a testamentary trust. As we saw in Chapter 4, *Farkas v. Williams* is the seminal case for the proposition that a revocable lifetime trust need not comply with the Statute of Wills, but only with any formalities for lifetime trusts. *See* 3d Rest. Trusts § 25(1).

The formalities to create a lifetime trust are quite state-specific. *See* George G. Bogert & George T. Bogert, The Law of Trusts §§ 62–65 (Rev. 2d ed. 1984) (providing state-specific rules). With respect to real property, most states have an applicable Statute of Frauds that must be satisfied to create a lifetime trust. In at least one state, Massachusetts, the trust also must be recorded in its entirety. On the other hand,

---

9. We earlier encountered the public policy doctrine as a means to strike down certain will provisions.

in some states no writing is required to create a trust over real property. *See Cody v. United States*, 348 F. Supp. 2d 682 (E.D. Va. 2004).

In all states other than Georgia, Indiana, Louisiana, New York, and West Virginia (which did not adopt UTC § 407), no writing is required to create a lifetime trust over personal property. Adopting the overwhelming majority position as illustrated by *In re Zukerman*, 578 N.E.2d 248 (Ill. App. Ct. 1991), reproduced on Page 402, UTC § 407 dispenses with the need for any writing provided an oral trust is established by clear and convincing evidence. *See In re Estate of Fournier*, 902 A.2d 852 (Me. 2006) (oral trust created based on clear and convincing evidence).

New York not only requires that trusts over personal property be in writing but also imposes strict formalities requirements for trusts over both personal property and real property. N.Y. Estates, Powers and Trusts Law § 7.1.17. Florida now imposes wills formalities for all revocable trusts having testamentary aspects. Fla. Stat. § 736.0403(2)(b). Should the law provide a remedy if the settlor's failure to comply with Statute of Frauds will have the effect of unjustly enriching the transferee? Suppose Javier delivers a deed for Blackacre, absolute on its face, to Maria, but Maria orally promises to hold the land in trust for Javier for life and then transfer it to Frank. If Maria refuses to turn over the land to Frank, we have a conflict between the policy of limiting oral evidence (and thereby the danger of false claims) and the policy of preventing people from unjustly enriching themselves. To avoid unfair results, courts may impose a constructive trust upon a donee like Maria to prevent her from holding in her own behalf. Relief will be appropriate when at the time of the conveyance the transferee acted fraudulently, exerted undue influence, was guilty of duress, or was in a confidential relationship to the transferor. *See* 3d Rest. Trusts § 24[2].

A trust is also "secret" if a gift under a will is absolute on its face, but there is an oral agreement on the side. To prevent unjust enrichment in this situation, a court must admit testimony of the oral agreement. Once the court has the details, it is likely to impose a constructive trust in favor of the intended beneficiaries. *See* 3d Rest. Trusts § 18[1].

Unjust enrichment can also arise when there is a lifetime or testamentary gift made subject to a promise to give the property to someone else. *Olliffe v. Wells*, 130 Mass. 221 (1881), is a classic old case which involved a residuary gift to the Reverend Eleazer M. P. Wells. Ellen Donovan's will required Wells to distribute the property in his discretion "to carry out wishes which I have expressed to him or may express to him." Wells made no personal claim to the funds, but said that Donovan had told him to use the money for charity. Donovan's heirs claimed the property under a resulting trust theory. They argued that the trust failed because its terms were not shown in the will. The court agreed.

A trust like the one in *Olliffe* is sometimes called "semi-secret." The document shows a trust intention on its face, but the details are oral. A court can exclude the oral evidence and still prevent unjust enrichment by imposing a resulting trust to deny the beneficiary the right to keep the property. Because the imposition of a resulting trust may unjustly enrich the testator's innocent successors in interest, the Restatement (Third) of Trusts § 18[1] supports the minority position among the states that would impose a constructive trust on the will beneficiary for the intended trust beneficiaries. *Pickelner v. Adler*, 229 S.W.3d 516 (Tex. App. 2007), reflects the majority position by rejecting the imposition of a constructive trust in semi-secret trust situations as contrary to established Texas law.

Problems

1. If the intended trustee was not in a confidential relationship to the transferor at the time real property was deeded, should the trustee be allowed to keep the property if she intended to act as trustee at the time of conveyance but subsequently fails to carry out her oral promise?

2. Suppose the settlor otherwise complied with the requirements of Statute of Frauds but the writing failed to name a trust beneficiary. Should the trustee get to keep the property?

3. Hans, a trustee under an oral trust, offers to sell your client some of the trust's personal property. What inquiries will you want to make?

Selected Reference:

Frank S. Berall, *Oral Trusts and Wills: Are They Valid?*, 33 Est. Plan. 17 (Nov. 2006).

§ 8.03 The Nature of a Beneficiary's Interest

A major reason for the popularity of trusts is their ability to provide financial resources for those in need. Trust doctrine gives settlors broad freedom to design beneficiaries' interests in whatever way the settlor deems appropriate. The trust creator will need to decide the rights he or she wishes to confer on the designated beneficiaries with respect to trust income and principal. The choices range from mandatory rights to permissive rights or to some combination thereof.

This section first addresses the rights of trust beneficiaries vis-a-vis the trustee in mandatory, discretionary, and support trusts. Thereafter, we explore the beneficiary's right to assign trust interests and creditors' rights to a trust beneficiary's interest, including the effect of spendthrift provisions. The rights of creditors to trust property in which the settlor is a beneficiary—so-called asset protection trusts—are also explored. Finally, we address the important area of how trusts impact beneficiaries' entitlement to government benefits in the Medicaid context.

A. Mandatory Trusts

1. Right to Income Trusts

A trust to "Amos for life, remainder to Beth" illustrates the nature of mandatory rights for trust beneficiaries. As income beneficiary, Amos is mandatorily entitled to receive from the trustee the income derived from the trust. The default rule is that income must be distributed at least annually, although more frequent distributions are often directed. As principal beneficiary, Beth is mandatorily entitled to the trust principal on the death of Amos. As we will see in Chapter 10, there are numerous issues regarding whether a particular receipt constitutes trust income or principal, as well as how a particular disbursement should be charged against trust income and trust principal.

A less common example of mandatory income rights involve mandatory accumulation trusts. Consider a trust that provides for the accumulation of trust income for 10 years, with trust principal (and accumulations) payable to Alice after 10 years. Alice has no present right to trust income, but is entitled to the accumulated income and principal after 10 years.

2. Annuity Trusts

A settlor may also provide a beneficiary with mandatory trust rights by creating an annuity trust. The typical annuity trust gives a beneficiary the right to a fixed dollar amount annually, that is, an annuity. For example, a settlor might provide that Arthur is entitled to $5,000 annually for life, with remainder to Bonnie. Unlike the traditional mandatory income trust where distinctions between trust income and principal are critical, it generally will make no difference whether Arthur is paid $5,000 out of income or principal. The annuity trust suffers from inflexibility since Arthur will be entitled to the same $5,000 in year 1 and in year 20, so that Arthur will not really be receiving the equivalent of $5,000 in later years.

3. Unitrusts

A unitrust is a variant of the annuity trust. Under the unitrust model, the settlor decides on what percentage of the trust principal the intended "income" beneficiary will receive; the trustee is then mandated to pay out to the intended "income" beneficiary the amount determined by applying that percentage to the value of the trust principal. Consider the operation of a four percent unitrust for the life of Angela, with remainder to Barbara. The trust provides that after the first year Angela will receive four percent of the principal valued at the end of the preceding year. If at the end of year one, the trust principal is worth $500,000, Angela will be entitled to $20,000 in year two.

In contrast to the mandatory income trust, the unitrust is attractive because the trustee does not have to make investments that produce income, since income is not the benchmark for distributions. The trustee of a mandatory income trust will find it difficult to generate a reasonable amount of income other than by fixed investments (such as bonds and certificates of deposit) since the return on stocks is abysmally low, about one percent annually). At the same time, by foregoing stock investments, the principal beneficiary may be disadvantaged in that the principal will have no opportunity for growth, nor will inflation be taken into account. Unitrusts avoid these problems.

In Chapter 10, we will see how unitrusts allow trustees to invest for total return without worrying about whether a receipt is income or principal and how existing trusts may be converted to unitrusts in some states. We will also see how the latest Uniform Principal and Income Act provides that trustees of mandatory income trusts can make compensating adjustments in order to invest for total return.

B. Discretionary and Support Trusts

Trusts can last a long time. Circumstances will change as beneficiaries are born or go to college or get sick or die. Families may get richer or poorer; rates of return may fall; inflation may erode purchasing power. Mandatory trusts, like that directing a trustee to pay "all of the net income" to a beneficiary, annuity trusts and even unitrusts, can hinder a trustee's ability to respond to change.

Fortunately, trusts can allow trustees to adjust to different circumstances. Some trusts authorize the trustee to pay the beneficiaries "such amount of income or principal as the trustee in its absolute discretion shall deem advisable." These are commonly called "discretionary trusts." Some trusts will attempt to control the trustee's discretion by limiting distributions to those "necessary for the comfortable support of the beneficiary." These are commonly called "support trusts." Sometimes a settlor will create a hybrid, a "discretionary support trust," by giving the trustee "uncontrolled discretion" to pay funds "for support." Both Restatement (Third) of Trusts § 50 and UTC § 504 attempt to simplify the area by treating support trusts as merely a type of discretionary trust; in effect, only the category of discretionary trusts survives under the Restatement (Third) of Trusts and the UTC.

In choosing between discretionary trusts with or without standards, a client must balance between providing flexibility and controlling abuse of discretion. In Chapter 9, we will see how additional trust flexibility can be achieved by using powers of appointment in lieu of fixed remainder interests.

Emmert v. Old National Bank of Martinsburg

246 S.E.2d 236 (W. Va. 1978)

[Allen Emmert's will established a trust for his two sons and included the following clause:

> Earnings accumulated from the operation of said trust estate, or principal if said accumulations are insufficient, may be used by said Trustee for the

> purpose of adequately providing for the comfort and support of either or both of my said sons, if necessary at any time. Advances or expenditures for either son in excess of advances or expenditures for the other son shall be charged against the share of the one for whom the advances or expenditures are made.

Emmert's son, Frank, asked the trustee to distribute to him $100,000 from the $230,000 trust. The bank trustee refused. At trial, Frank showed that he was $48,000 in debt and owned virtually no assets other than household furnishings. He was unemployed, and suffered from a disease which caused weight loss, frequent nausea and general lassitude. His only income came from the trust in question and one-half of the income from another, $60,000 trust. The trustee introduced evidence showing that Frank had squandered large sums of money from his father's estate, and argued that the trust income was sufficient to keep Frank in comfort.

The bank also cited a trust provision that "I [testator] desire that each of my sons be treated equally in the payments, advances, and the distribution of income and the corpus of said trust." The bank argued that to comply with Frank's request would virtually bankrupt the trust, and prevent meeting future obligations to make $250 per month payments to the sons, and contingent payments to other beneficiaries upon the death of the sons. The trial court upheld the bank's position.]

NEELY, JUSTICE. . . .

We need not resort to interpretation or construction to say that [this] provision plainly authorizes the use of trust principal for the comfort and support of the trust beneficiaries, including the appellant, Frank S. Emmert. The ambiguity with respect to principal distributions is not whether they are permitted, but rather, under what circumstances they are required. It appears there is a two-pronged standard. First, there must be some necessity for making a distribution, i.e., "if necessary at any time." Second, the distribution is limited to an amount which provides an adequate level of "comfort and support" to the beneficiary receiving the distribution. To be useful as a guideline for the trustee, this vague, two-pronged standard requires judicial construction. . . .

What then was intended by the testator to be an adequate level of comfort and support? We believe the testator had reference to the standard of living to which each of his sons was accustomed when he died and which his upbringing of them led them to expect. Our interpretation is reinforced and supported by an interpretation of a similar support-maintenance provision in the case of Smith v. Smith, 134 W. Va. 842, 62 S.E.2d 347 (1950). The adequate standard of living the testator had in mind for his beneficiaries would not permit them to enjoy new extravagances or to suffer unexpected deprivations.

A reading of the whole will and examination of the surrounding circumstances makes clear the testator's intention with respect to the second part of his standard, the requirement that there be some necessity for the principal distributions. The testamentary trust was established out of the residue of the testator's estate and the bulk of his assets went into it. Its design and operating principles quite naturally evidence a concern for the testator's primary beneficiaries, his two sons. Nonetheless, as so often is the case with large residuary bequests, the testator wanted later generations of his lineal descendants or collateral relatives to enjoy such of the fruits of his estate as were not consumed by the primary beneficiaries. Thus the testator created a trust which benefitted his two sons and yet had the potential to spread his generosity out over several generations. It should be pointed out here that the testator, who died in 1961, was very likely mindful of the tax advantages to be gained from generation-skipping gifts. To accommodate his primary interest in his sons' welfare with his secondary interest in extending the scope of his generosity to include others, the testator imposed the "necessity" requirement which had to be satisfied before his sons could encroach on the trust corpus for their comfort and support. This requirement made the trust corpus available to the sons as a last resort to sustain them only after their other financial resources were exhausted. This interpretation is in accord with Re Martin's Will, 269 N.Y. 305, 199 N.E. 491 (1936), which, on the question of whether other financial resources of the beneficiary ought to be taken into account, draws the following distinctions:

> The primary question in this class of cases always is, Does the will constitute an absolute gift of support or maintenance which makes it a charge upon the income from the estate and upon principal? If so, then the private income of the beneficiary cannot be considered. If, however, the gift is of income coupled with a provision that the principal may be invaded in case of need, the private income of the beneficiary must be considered in determining whether such need exists.
>
> Of course the testator must have hoped such manifest necessity would not arise, so that his residuary estate could pass intact to the testator's other lineal descendants or collateral relatives. . . .

At this point the question arises whether a principal distribution from the testamentary trust to provide adequate support and comfort for Frank S. Emmert is necessary. A fair reading of all the evidence in the case indicates that such a distribution is necessary. The appellant has exhausted all financial resources available to him and is seeking a level of comfort and support to which he was accustomed at the time of his father's death and which is in accord with the station in life his upbringing prepared him to assume. Much of his present financial misfortune, with respect both to his accumulated debt and to his reduced earning capacity, stems from his poor health, which, of course, neither he nor his father could have anticipated. Catastrophic illness is one of the exceptional circumstances the testator very likely had in mind when he made provision for principal distributions from the testamentary trust in time of necessity.

While the trust used words of discretion such as "may", the discretion of the trustee is not without limits. When the trustee acts outside the bounds of reasonable judgment the court will intervene.... Since it was the testator's intent that distributions from corpus for the beneficiary's comfort and support were to be made when necessary and such distributions are necessary, the appellee ... abused its discretion in refusing to pay any portion of the corpus to Frank S. Emmert.

It is obvious that any principal distributions made to Frank S. Emmert will reduce the trust remainder available to the contingent beneficiaries. Also, if the distributions are large enough, the trust may be unable to meet certain specified contingent obligations such as the payment of $25,000 to Frank S. Emmert's wife, assuming, as seems likely, he dies without issue. Any time a corpus invasion privilege is granted there exists the possibility, as here, that remainder interests will be reduced or eliminated. Such a possibility is inherent in the nature of corpus invasion privileges and cannot be used to defeat a lawful and proper invasion of corpus. The trustee's arguments in this respect are not well taken. Furthermore, it is evident that the testator's primary concern was the welfare of his closest blood kin, his sons, and for that welfare all else could be sacrificed, if necessary. Accordingly we hold that provisions such as the one under consideration should be given a liberal interpretation by trustees, who are frequently overly concerned about potential liability.[10] ...

Finally, we come to the question of appellant's needs. Having determined that The Old National Bank of Martinsburg, as trustee, has abused its discretion in refusing to make distributions to Frank S. Emmert, we are remanding this case to the Circuit Court of Berkeley County for a hearing to determine the frequency and amount of principal distributions. The circuit court should consider all the evidence concerning the appellant's assets, liabilities, and available financial resources. It is the present needs of the appellant and not his past extravagances that should control the court's determination.... At the same time, blind approval of appellant's demand for $100,000 should not be given because it is the amount necessary for comfort and support and not what the beneficiary desires that is controlling.... The court can easily determine support but meaning must also be given to "comfort."

10. A rule which in many circumstances implies a liberal construction of invasion provisions comes from a recognition that only discretionary invasion is consistent with substantial tax savings ..., a fact of which settlors' attorneys (as a class) have usually been aware, while settlors (as a class) have usually been unmindful of the inherent rigidities in dealing with professional trustees who are given discretionary powers. Settlors have usually followed advice of counsel, who may them-selves have working relationships with professional trustees, and notwithstanding the particular settlor's intention that such provisions be construed as liberally as possible, broad discretion to with-hold assets must necessarily be given to the trustee for tax reasons. For example, ... a settlor will provide that a trustee "may" invade for the benefit of the life income beneficiary to gain favorable tax treatment when he intends the trustee "shall" invade as a practical matter. However, a professional trustee has a vested interest in retention in the form of charges and fees proportionate to the value of property administered. Furthermore, professional trustees are reluctant to make discretionary decisions because of potential liability and usually prefer to follow, in normal bureaucratic style, the safest of all paths....

The circuit court should keep in mind that comfort is not a "mere quantum sufficient to eat, to drink and to wear. . . ." but that it denotes whatever is necessary to give security from want, including reasonable physical, mental and spiritual fulfillment. *Forman v. Whitney*, 2 Keyes (N.Y.) 165, 2 Abb. Pr. 163 (1865). A meager distribution might not fulfill the testator's intentions, but at the same time one too large could cause detriment to the beneficiary himself. The court should weigh the possibility that too rapid a reduction of principal could leave the beneficiary in want later in life (contrary to the testator 's intention that he be provided for) and at the same time consider the beneficiary's needs and his station in life. . . . Furthermore the bank should consider the probable life expectancy of Frank Emmert and the maximum benefit which combined interest and principal can provide him during his remaining life in the event he is totally destitute of other sources of income.

We hope the hearing fairly accommodates all the competing interests of existing and contingent beneficiaries, is faithful to the testator's intent, and is just under all the circumstances. We hope that it marks the end of protracted and expensive litigation in this case, but we cannot say that in the event of some extraordinary and unanticipated circumstances the appellant's needs may not change. In such event we hope the trustee will voluntarily exercise its creation to increase the distributions if the appellant's needs are greater, and we hope the appellant will voluntarily accept a reduction in the principal if the circumstances warrant.

Reversed and remanded.

Restatement (Third) of Trusts

§ 87. Judicial Control of Discretionary Powers

When a trustee has discretion with respect to the exercise of a power, its exercise is subject to supervision by a court only to prevent abuse of discretion.

Uniform Trust Code

Section 814. Discretionary Powers . . . .

(a) Notwithstanding the breadth of discretion granted to a trustee in the terms of the trust, including the use of such terms as "absolute," "sole," or "uncontrolled," the trustee shall exercise a discretionary power in good faith and in accordance with the terms and purposes of the trust and the interests of the beneficiaries.

Notes and Questions

1. Abuse of discretion giving rise to court control of a trustee may arise from acts of bad faith, from improper motive (including the exercise of judgment that is contrary to the terms and purposes of the trust), from the exercise of judgment that is contrary to a trustee's fiduciary duties, and from failing to exercise discretion. *See, e.g., Rafalko v. Georgiadis*, 777 S.E.2d 870 (Va. 2015) and *In re G.B. Van Dusen Marital Trust,* 834 N.W.2d 514 (Minn. 2013). *See generally* 3d Rest. Trusts § 87 and comments thereto.

Although abuse of discretion may also be found if the trustee acts beyond the bounds of reasonable judgment, the grant of absolute discretion or words to that effect relieve the trustee from liability for acting unreasonably. *See generally* 3d Rest. Trusts § 87 and comments thereto.

2. When determining a trustee's discretion, courts often emphasize the notion that terms like "comfort" and "support" are relative, and should be judged in the context of the level to which the beneficiary "has become accustomed" or what is appropriate for the beneficiary's "station in life." To what extent does this approach reflect or reinforce class biases?

3. Trustees, especially corporate trustees, have a reputation for being less than generous when exercising their discretion to distribute funds to beneficiaries. Why are trustees so conservative?

4. General authorizations in a document often leave questions unanswered, at least from the trustee's perspective. Consider the following:

(a) A trust that authorizes trustee to use trust funds for an individual's "support" includes amounts for the private school education of that individual's children. *See Estate of Stevens, 617 S.E.2d 736* (S.C. Ct. App. 2005).

(b) A trust that authorizes trustee to invade trust principal for "any need or condition which may arise or develop" includes power to distribute trust principal for estate planning needs of income beneficiaries. *See Smith v. First Cmty. Bancshares*, 575 S.E.2d 419 (W. Va. 2002); *see also Finch v. Wachovia Bank & Trust Co., N.A.*, 577 S.E.2d 306 (N.C. Ct. App. 2003).

(c) A trust authorizing expenditures for the "college or post high school education" of the testator's issue only included education up to the level of a bachelor's degree. *See Austin v. Nelson*, 1998 Conn. Super. LEXIS 1997 (July 15th, 1998). *Accord Southern Bank & Trust Co. v. Brown*, 246 S.E.2d 598 (S.C. 1978).

(d) A trustee's power to invade corpus "as may be necessary to keep Ruth Ann Welch in health," included expenses for "food, clothing, medicine, doctor's services, and hospital care," but only after a showing that she has exhausted other resources. *See Loar v. Massey*, 261 S.E.2d 83 (W. Va. 1979).

(e) A trustee's power to invade corpus for "any expense of sickness," covered the beneficiary's nursing home care. *See Thiele v. Whittenbaugh*, 291 N.W.2d 324 (Iowa 1980).

The drafting lesson: be specific.

5. Among the most often litigated questions is the extent to which a trustee should consider other resources available to the beneficiary. Emmert suggests a black and white constructional approach to whether a beneficiary's resources are to be taken into account, that is, either the trustee is prohibited from taking into account the beneficiary's other resources or the trustee is required to take other resources into account. *Compare Lanagan v. Rorke*, 182 S.W.3d 596 (Mo. Ct. App. 2005) (other resources irrelevant), *with Hertel v. Nationsbank N.A.*, 37 S.W.3d 408 (Mo. Ct. App. 2001) (other resources should be taken into account). Restatement (Third) of Trusts § 50, comment e, advances a middle ground where the settlor has not made clear his or her intentions: the trustee should consider the beneficiary's resources but has some discretion to make distributions even if the beneficiary has other available resources. *See In re Druck*, 790 N.Y.S.2d 837 (Sur. Ct. 2005) (applying Restatement position).

6. Should the lawyers who drafted the documents that prompted the litigation cited in this set of notes be liable for the cost of that litigation?

7. Should the grant of absolute discretion to a trustee make the trustee's decisions final and unreviewable by a court?

8. How can annuity trusts and a unitrusts be made more flexible?

Problem

Ellen has come to you to draft a will establishing a trust for her daughter, Beth.

(a) What techniques can you propose to encourage the trustee to be generous, but not be so directive as to defeat the trust's adaptability?

(b) Draft the specific language necessary to allow the trustee to invade the principal to pay for Beth's education.

Selected References

Evelyn G. Abravanel, *Discretionary Support Trusts*, 68 Iowa L. Rev. 273 (1983).

Edward C. Halbach, Jr., *Problems of Discretion in Discretionary Trusts*, 61 Colum. L. Rev. 1425 (1961).

Ivan Taback, *When the Rubber Meets the Road: A Discussion Regarding a Trustee's Exercise of Discretion*, 49 Real Prop. Tr. & Est. L.J. 491 (2015).

C. Transfers of Beneficial Interests in Trust

1. General Principles

Uniform Trust Code

Section 501. Rights of Beneficiary's Creditor or Assignee.

To the extent a beneficiary's interest is not protected by a spendthrift provision, the court may authorize a creditor or assignee of the beneficiary to reach the beneficiary's interest by attachment of present or future distributions to or for the benefit of the beneficiary or other means. The court may limit the award to such relief as is appropriate under the circumstances.

UTC § 501 codifies the two principles that underlie much of the law surrounding the transfer of a trust beneficiary's interest. First, unless a statute or the trust document provides otherwise, a trust beneficiary generally can transfer his or her interest to another person. Secondly, creditors' rights typically follow alienability: the creditor usually can get what the beneficiary can transfer. More specifically, creditors can satisfy their claims by reaching a trust beneficiary's interest. The procedure varies among the states, but familiar creditors' devices like attachment, garnishment, and execution tend to be available. Creditors usually have a choice between waiting for the beneficiary's payment to come due, and then collecting it, or attempting to sell the beneficiary's interest and taking what the market will bring at that time. A beneficiary's interest will pass to his trustee in bankruptcy. 11 U.S.C. § 541.

Problems

Sandy creates a trust by transferring $100,000 to Thelma, as trustee. The terms of the trust provide that Amy receives income for life, with trust corpus payable to Bob at Amy's death.

(a) Can Amy assign her trust interest?

(b) Can Amy devise her trust interest?

(c) Can Bob assign his trust interest?

(d) If Bob dies before Amy, and Bob dies without a will, who will receive the trust property on Amy's death?

(e) Could a creditor of Amy reach her trust interest?

(f) Could a creditor of Bob reach his trust interest?

2. *Spendthrift Provisions and Other Restraints on Alienation*

Most settlors attempt to restrict the alienability of their beneficiaries' interests as a way of protecting the beneficiaries both from themselves and from creditors. The classic device for achieving this result is a "spendthrift clause" phrased something like this: "No interest of my wife or of any lineal descendant of mine in income or principal shall be anticipated, encumbered or assigned. No such interest shall be subject to the claims of such person's creditors, spouse or divorced spouse or others." *Domo v. McCarthy*, 612 N.E.2d 706, 709 (Ohio 1993). UTC § 502(b) provides that a trust interest will be spendthrifted merely by providing in the trust that it is subject to a "spendthrift trust" or like wording.

Adam J. Hirsch, *Spendthrift Trusts and Public Policy: Economic and Cognitive Perspectives*

73 Wash. U. L.Q. 1, 2–3 (1995)

The spendthrift trust is a device whereby benefactors shield gratuitous transfers from immediate consumption by their beneficiaries. Adorned with a spendthrift clause (or a "disabling restraint," as it is technically known), a trust provides benefits that are legally inalienable. Though the trust generates a steady income stream with an ascertainable present value, the beneficiary is powerless to accelerate her interest by selling it for a lump sum; the trustee will ignore the sale and continue paying over the income to the beneficiary. Likewise, creditors cannot satisfy their claims by levying execution against the corpus; courts will enforce no lien against the trust. Spendthrift trusts thus differ from ordinary income-producing trusts, whose beneficial interests can be sold at will and used for any purpose at all. A disabling restraint does not dictate the substantive use of trust income (that is, it does not require one sort of spending or another), but it does limit the temporal use of income to the singular purpose of periodic consumption. Once a trust distribution is in her hands, the beneficiary is free to consume it as prudently or as frivolously as she pleases. And once a trust distribution is in her hands, the beneficiary's creditors are also empowered to reach it—assuming they can find it, for in practice what may follow is a game of hide-and-seek, the trustee (at the beneficiary's direction) depositing the income each month into a different bank. In short, a spendthrift trust provides a stable source of passive income, conducing to the beneficiary's long-term support. If the income suffices, it can enable her to live in high style, even as her creditors go empty-handed.

Other ways for settlors to restrict beneficiaries and their creditors are to establish discretionary or support trusts that allow access to trust income or principal only under defined conditions. Even greater restrictions may be realized by imposing spendthrift restraints on discretionary and support trusts.

a. Restraints on Voluntary Transfers

Just as you can give an old armchair to a friend, so can a trust beneficiary give away or sell a life estate or a remainder interest in a trust. Purchasers of present or future interests are placing bets about how long others will live. For example, in 1965, Andre-Francois Raffray, then 47, agreed to pay 90-year-old Jeanne Calment the equivalent of $500 per month until she died and then move into her apartment in Arles, France. He died in 1995, still making payments. Calment (age 120) was quoted saying, "In life, one sometimes makes bad deals." Toledo Blade, Dec. 29, 1995, at p. 1, col. 6.

The possibility of bad deals is one reason settlors limit or eliminate their beneficiaries' power to make such transfers: settlors want to protect the beneficiaries from the temptation to sell their trust interests for immediate cash and then blow the money. Sometimes settlors are so enamored of the notion of protecting against creditors' claims that the settlors restrict voluntary transfers without even thinking about the issue. Sometimes spendthrift clauses simply appear because they were part of a trust form's "boilerplate."

Although a trust beneficiary can assign his or her rights to receive discretionary trust distributions absent a spendthrift provision, the assignee basically has no recourse against the trustee absent an abuse of discretion. On the other hand, a beneficiary's interest in a support trust has been considered as inalienable since such transfer would defeat the purposes of the trust. Restatement (Third) of Trusts § 60 and UTC § 504 take a new position that support trusts are merely a type of discretionary trust with the effect that assignment may be permitted absent a spendthrift provision, but with the likely result that the assignee will have no recourse against the trustee.

Discretionary, support, and spendthrift trusts can affect the ability of both trustees and beneficiaries to adjust to changing situations. The discretionary power that can shield a beneficiary from temptation may also leave the beneficiary with little recourse against a stingy trustee. The spendthrift clause which might prevent a beneficiary from selling a trust share for party money might also prohibit the beneficiary from giving it away to save taxes. Protective settlors should consider what they hope to protect against.

Question and Problem

1. Assume a settlor has provided that all trust interests are spendthrifted. Dying before the income beneficiary, a remainder beneficiary devises his remainder interest. Does the will provision violate the spendthrift restriction? *See In re Townley Bypass Unified Credit Trust*, 252 S.W.3d 715 (Tex. App. 2008) (no, following 3d Rest. Trusts § 58, cmt. g).

2. Rebecca and David, in their 50s, have consulted you for advice about their son, Carl, age 26. Carl, an only child, has a steady job as a traffic engineer for the city, but from his parent's perspective, he is not a good money manager. Unmarried, he lives

in a nice apartment complex and drives a two-year-old Ford. He's paying off college and car loans, but otherwise has no substantial debts. The problem is that Carl is not saving anything, and his parents are savers. Rebecca and David have about $200,000 in mutual funds, and their deaths would generate another $200,000 in life insurance proceeds. Their modest house is worth about $65,000. They fear that Carl's habit of "spending whatever's available" will mean he would dissipate their estate in short order. How would you approach their problem?

b. Restraints on Involuntary Transfers

For as long as there have been creditors, there have been people trying to avoid them. In the late nineteenth century, the case that follows gave the spendthrift trust device a significant boost.

Broadway National Bank v. Adams

133 Mass. 170 (1882)

Morton, C.J.

The object of this bill in equity is to reach and apply in payment of the plaintiff's debt due from the defendant Adams the income of a trust fund created for his benefit by the will of his brother. The eleventh article of the will is as follows: "I give the sum of seventy-five thousand dollars to my said executors and the survivors or survivor of them, in trust to invest the same in such manner as to them may seem prudent, and to pay the net income thereof, semi-annually, to my said brother Charles W. Adams, during his natural life, such payments to be made to him personally when convenient, otherwise, upon his order or receipt in writing; in either case free from the interference or control of his creditors, my intention being that the use of said income shall not be anticipated by assignment." . . .

There is no room for doubt as to the intention of the testator. It is clear that, if the trustee was to pay the income to the plaintiff under an order of the court, it would be in direct violation of the intention of the testator and of the provisions of his will. The court will not compel the trustee thus to do what the will forbids him to do, unless the provisions and intention of the testator are unlawful.

The question whether the founder of a trust can secure the income of it to the object of his bounty, by providing that it shall not be alienable by him or be subject to be taken by his creditors, has not been directly adjudicated in this Commonwealth. The tendency of our decisions, however, has been in favor of such a power in the founder. . . .

It is true that the rule of the common law is, that a man cannot attach to a grant or transfer of property, otherwise absolute, the condition that it shall not be alienated; such condition being repugnant to the nature of the estate granted. Co. Lit. 223 a. Blackstone Bank v. Davis, 21 Pick. 42.

Lord Coke gives as the reason of the rule, that "it is absurd and repugnant to reason that he, that hath no possibility to have the land revert to him, should restrain his feoffee in fee simple of all his power to alien," and that this is "against the height and puritie of a fee simple." By such a condition, the grantor undertakes to deprive the property in the hands of the grantee of one of its legal incidents and attributes, namely, its alienability, which is deemed to be against public policy. But the reasons of the rule do not apply in the case of a transfer of property in trust. By the creation of a trust like the one before us, the trust property passes to the trustee with all its incidents and attributes unimpaired. He takes the whole legal title to the property, with the power of alienation; the cestui que trust takes the whole legal title to the accrued income at the moment it is paid over to him. Neither the principal nor the income is at any time inalienable.

The question whether the rule of the common law should be applied to equitable life estates created by will or deed, has been the subject of conflicting adjudications by different courts. . . .

We are not able to see that it would violate any principles of sound public policy to permit a testator to give to the object of his bounty such a qualified interest in the income of a trust fund, and thus provide against the improvidence or misfortune of the beneficiary. The only ground upon which it can be held to be against public policy is, that it defrauds the creditors of the beneficiary.

It is argued that investing a man with apparent wealth tends to mislead creditors, and to induce them to give him credit. The answer is, that creditors have no right to rely upon the property thus held, and to give him credit upon the basis of an estate which, by the instrument creating it, is declared to be inalienable by him, and not liable for his debts. By the exercise of proper diligence they can ascertain the nature and extent of his estate, especially in this Commonwealth, where all wills and most deeds are spread upon the public records. There is the same danger of their being misled by false appearances, and induced to give credit to the equitable life tenant when the will or deed of trust provides for a cesser or limitation over, in case of an attempted alienation, or of bankruptcy or attachment, and the argument would lead to the conclusion that the English rule is equally in violation of public policy. We do not see why the founder of a trust may not directly provide that his property shall go to his beneficiary with the restriction that it shall not be alienable by anticipation, and that his creditors shall not have the right to attach it in advance, instead of indirectly reaching the same result by a provision for a cesser or a limitation over, or by giving his trustees a discretion as to paying it. He has the entire jus disponendi, which imports that he may give it absolutely, or may impose any restrictions or fetters not repugnant to the nature of the estate which he gives. Under our system, creditors may reach all the property of the debtor not exempted by law, but they cannot enlarge the gift of the founder of a trust, and take more than he has given. . . .

Whether a man can settle his own property in trust for his own benefit, so as to exempt the income from alienation by him or attachment in advance by his creditors, is a different question, which we are not called upon to consider in this case. But we are of opinion that any other person, having the entire right to dispose of his property, may settle it in trust in favor of a beneficiary, and may provide that it shall not be alienated by him by anticipation, and shall not be subject to be seized by his creditors in advance of its payment to him.

It follows that, under the provisions of the will which we are considering, the income of the trust fund created for the benefit of the defendant Adams cannot be reached by attachment, either at law or in equity, before it is paid to him. Bill dismissed. . . .

Notes and Questions

1. Spendthrift clauses do not cut off creditors, but they do put creditors at a distinct disadvantage. As a general rule, creditors cannot obtain their debtor's beneficial interest in the trust if the interest is spendthrifted. *See, e.g.*, UTC § 502(c). And in most states, general creditors cannot force the trustee to pay them directly. *See, e.g.*, UTC § 502(c). Instead, they must wait until the trustee pays the beneficiary and then try to catch the money there. *See, e.g. Fannie Mae v. Heather Apartments Ltd. Partnership*, 811 N.W.2d 596 (Minn. 2012).

As Professor Hirsch notes, this approach can prompt a game of hide-and-seek.

In a few states, general creditors are given some rights even under spendthrift trusts. For example, in California, general creditors can obtain a court order that requires a trustee to distribute up to 25 percent of trust income to a judgment creditor and any principal required to be distributed to a beneficiary. *See* Cal. Prob. Code §§ 15306.5, 15301(b). New York allows a general creditor to reach up to 10 percent of trust income and principal and even greater amounts if not necessary for the reasonable needs of the beneficiary. *See* N.Y. Civil Practice Law and Rules §5205(d); *see also* N.Y. Estates, Powers and Trusts Law § 7-3.4.

2. Spendthrift clauses under applicable state law will also be effective in bankruptcy. *See* 11 U.S.C. § 541(c)(2). *See, e.g., In re Wachter*, 314 B.R. 365 (Bankr. E.D. Tenn. 2004) (debtor's remainder interest in spendthrift trust, valid under Tennessee law, was not part of the bankruptcy estate).

3. Do you agree with the position under the Restatement (Third) of Trusts § 58(1) and UTC § 502(a) that a spendthrift provision will not be effective unless both voluntary and involuntary alienation are barred?

4. Legendary Harvard Professor John Chipman Gray attacked spendthrift trusts in a book laced with comments like "it is not the function of the law to join in the futile effort to save the foolish and the vicious from the consequences of their own vice and folly." John Chipman Gray, Restraints on the Alienation of Property 243 (2d ed. 1895).

One argument in favor of recognizing spendthrift clauses is that "the law should allow the property owner, within reason, to dispose of her property as she chooses." *Scott v. Bank One Trust Co.*, N.A., 577 N.E.2d 1077, 1084 (Ohio 1991). Notice, however, how the argument cuts both ways. To the extent the law recognizes the freedom of donors to shape their gifts by attaching strings, the law also undercuts the freedom of donees to dispose of their property as they choose.

What other arguments can you make for (and against) recognizing spendthrift trusts? Although now virtually all jurisdictions recognize spendthrift clauses, the question is not irrelevant. As the next case illustrates, courts continue to struggle with the extent to which they should recognize exceptions to this general rule, particularly in the form of preferred classes of creditors. *See generally* 3d Rest. Trusts § 59.

Shelley v. Shelley

354 P.2d 282 (Or. 1960)

O'Connell, Justice.

This is an appeal from a decree of the circuit court for Multnomah county establishing the rights of the parties to the income and corpus of a trust of which the defendant, the United States National Bank of Portland (Oregon) is trustee. The assignments of error are directed at the trial court's interpretation of the trust. The trust involved in this suit was created by Hugh T. Shelley. The pertinent parts of the trust are as follows:

"Ninth: All of the rest, residue, and remainder of my said estate, . . . I give, devise, and bequeath to the United States National Bank of Portland (Oregon), in trust, . . . upon the following trusts: . . .

"(2) I direct that, all income derived from my trust estate be paid to my wife, Gertrude R. Shelley, as long as she lives, said income to be paid to her at intervals of not less than three (3) months apart; . . .

"(4) If my said wife, Gertrude R. Shelley, shall predecease me, and my said son is then alive, or upon my wife's death after my death and my son being alive, it is my desire, and I direct, that, the United States National Bank of Portland (Oregon), as trustee, shall continue this estate in trust and pay all income derived therefrom to my son, Grant R. Shelley, as long as he lives, said income to be paid to him at intervals not less than three (3) months apart; Provided, Further, That when my son, Grant R. Shelley, arrives at the age of thirty (30) years, my trustee may then, or at any time thereafter, and from time to time, distribute to said son absolutely and as his own all or any part of the principal of said trust fund that it may then or from time to time thereafter deem him capable of successfully investing without the restraints of this trust; Provided, However, That such disbursements of principal of said trust so made to my son after he attains the age of thirty (30) years shall be first approved in writing by either one of my brothers-in-law, that is: Dr. Frank L. Ralston, now of Walla Walla, Washington, or Russell C. Ralston, now of Palo Alto, California, if either of them is then living, but if neither of them is then living, then my trustee is authorized to make said disbursements of principal to my son in the exercise of its sole and absolute judgment and discretion; Provided, Further, That, said trust shall continue as to all or any part of the undistributed portion of the principal thereof to and until the death of my said son.

"(5) I further direct and authorize my trustee, from time to time (but only upon the written approval of my said wife if she be then living, otherwise in the exercise of my trustee's sole discretion) to make disbursements for the use and benefit of my son, Grant R. Shelley, or his children, in case of any emergency arising whereby unusual and extraordinary expenses are necessary for the proper support and care of my said son, or said children. . . .

"(8) Each beneficiary hereunder is hereby restrained from alienating, anticipating, encumbering, or in any manner assigning his or her interest or estate, either in principal or income, and is without power so to do, nor shall such interest or estate be subject to his or her liabilities or obligations nor to judgment or other legal process, bankruptcy proceedings or claims of creditors or others."

The principal question on appeal is whether the income and corpus of the Shelley trust can be reached by Grant Shelley's former wives and his children.

Grant Shelley was first married to defendant, Patricia C. Shelley. Two children were born of this marriage. Patricia divorced Grant in 1951. The decree required Grant to pay support money for the children; the decree did not call for the payment of alimony. Thereafter, Grant married the plaintiff, Betty Shelley. Two children were born of this marriage. The plaintiff obtained a divorce from Grant in August, 1958. The decree in this latter suit required the payment of both alimony and a designated monthly amount for the support of the children of that marriage.

Sometime after his marriage to the plaintiff, Grant disappeared and his whereabouts was not known at the time of this suit. The defendant bank, as trustee, invested the trust assets in securities which are now held by it, together with undisbursed income from the trust estate. The plaintiff obtained an injunction restraining the defendant trustee from disbursing any of the trust assets. Patricia Shelley brought a garnishment proceeding against the trustee, by which she sought to subject the trust to the claim for support money provided for in the 1951 decree of divorce. . . .

The defendant bank finally brought a bill of interpleader tendering to the court for disbursement all of the funds held in trust, praying for an order establishing the respective rights of the interpleaded parties to the trust assets. . . .

We shall first consider that part of the decree which subjects the income of the trust to the claims of plaintiff and of defendant, Patricia Shelley. The trust places no conditions upon the right of Grant Shelley to receive the trust income during his lifetime. Therefore, plaintiff and Patricia Shelley may reach such income unless the spendthrift provision of the trust precludes them from doing so.

The validity of spendthrift trusts has been established by our former cases.... The question on this appeal is whether the spendthrift provision will be given effect to bar the claims of the beneficiary's children for support and the plaintiff's claim for alimony.

In *Cogswell v. Cogswell* et al., 1946, 178 Or. 417, 167 P.2d 324, 335, we held that the spendthrift provision of a trust is not effective against the claims of the beneficiary's former wife for alimony and for support of the beneficiary's child. In that case the court adopted the rule stated in 1 Restatement, Trusts, § 157, which reads in part as follows:

> "§ 157. Particular Classes of Claimants.
>
> "Although a trust is a spendthrift trust or trust for support, the interest of the beneficiary can be reached in satisfaction of an enforceable claim against the beneficiary,
>
> "(a) by the wife or child of the beneficiary for support, or by the wife for alimony;"

The defendant bank concedes that the Cogswell case is controlling in the case at bar, but asks us to overrule it on the ground that it is inconsistent with our own cases recognizing the testator's privilege to dispose of his property as he pleases and, further, that it is inconsistent with various Oregon statutes expressing the same policy of free alienation. If we should accept the premise urged by the defendant bank, that a testator has an inviolable right to dispose of his property as he pleases subject only to legislative restriction, the conclusion is inevitable that the testator may create in a beneficiary an interest free from all claims, including those for support and alimony.

But the premise is not sound. The privilege of disposing of property is not absolute; it is hedged with various restrictions where there are policy considerations warranting the limitation.... Not all of these restrictions are imposed by statute. The rule against perpetuities, the rule against restraints on alienation, the refusal to recognize trusts for capricious purposes or for illegal purposes, or for any purpose contrary to public policy, are all instances of judge-made rules limiting the privilege of alienation. Many others could be recited. Griswold, Spendthrift Trusts (2d Ed.) § 553.... It is within the court's power to impose upon the privilege of disposing of property such restrictions as are consistent with its view of sound public policy, unless, of course, the legislature has expressed a contrary view. Our own statutes do not purport to deal with the specific question before us, which is as to whether there should be limitations on the owner's privilege to create a spendthrift trust....

In holding that a spendthrift trust is subject to claims for alimony and support the court, in *Cogswell v. Cogswell et al., supra*, did not disclose the reasoning by which it reached its conclusion. This failure to examine the question of public policy in the area of spendthrift trusts is not unusual, for as Griswold, Spendthrift Trusts (2d Ed.), p. 634 points out in discussing the validity of spendthrift trusts, "examination [of public policy] has rarely, if ever, been attempted by the courts," and he admits that "it is obviously a matter difficult to approach and one about which dogmatic conclusions cannot be reached." But once having recognized the validity of spendthrift trusts, which we have and which conclusion defendant bank endorses, the more specific question of the validity of the restraint of such a trust as against the claims of children for support and of the beneficiary's former wife for alimony presents a narrower question of policy which, we believe, is easier to answer. The question is whether a person should be entitled to enjoy the benefits of a trust and at the same time refuse to pay the obligations arising out of his marriage.

We have no hesitation in declaring that public policy requires that the interest of the beneficiary of a trust should be subject to the claims for support of his children. . . . Certainly the defendant will accept the societal postulate that parents have the obligation to support their children. If we give effect to the spendthrift provision to bar the claims for support, we have the spectacle of a man enjoying the benefits of a trust immune from claims which are justly due, while the community pays for the support of his children. *Wetmore v. Wetmore*, 1896, 149 N.Y. 520, 44 N.E. 169, 33 L.R.A. 708. We do not believe that it is sound policy to use the welfare funds of this state in support of the beneficiary's children, while he stands behind the shield of immunity created by a spendthrift trust provision. To endorse such a policy and to permit the spectacle which we have described above would be to invite disrespect for the administration of justice. *Seidenberg v. Seidenberg*, D.C. Cir., 1954, 126 F. Supp. 19, 21, *affirmed*, 225 F.2d 545, 96 U.S. App. D.C. 245. One who wishes to dispose of his property through the device of a trust must do so subject to these considerations of policy and he cannot force the courts to sanction his scheme of disposition if it is inimical to the interests of the state. . . .

The justification for permitting a claim for alimony is, perhaps, not as clear. The adjustment of the economic interests of the parties to a divorce may depend upon a variety of factors, including the respective fault of the parties, the ability of the wife to support herself, the duration of the marriage, and other considerations. Whether alimony is to be granted and its amount are questions which are determined in light of these various interests. It is probably fair to say that the duties created by the marriage relation, at least as they are evaluated upon the termination of the marriage, are conceived of as more qualified than those arising out of the paternal relationship. On the theory that divorce terminates the husband's duty to support his former wife and that she stands in no better position than other creditors, some courts have held that the spendthrift provision insulates the beneficiary's interest in the trust from her claim. *Lippincott v. Lippincott*, 1944, 349 Pa. 501, 37 A.2d 741. Recognizing the difference in marital and parental duties suggested above, it has been held that a spendthrift trust is subject to the claims for the support of children but free from the claims of the former wife. *Eaton v. Eaton*, 1926, 82 N.H. 216, 132 A. 10, commented upon in 35 Yale L.J. 1025 (1926). . . . A majority of the cases, however, hold that a spendthrift provision will not bar a claim for alimony....

As we have already mentioned, the case of *Cogswell v. Cogswell, supra*, is in accord with this latter view. We are of the opinion that the conclusion there reached should be reaffirmed. The duty of the husband to support his former wife should override the restriction called for by the spendthrift provision. The same reason advanced above for requiring the support of the beneficiary's children will, in many cases, be applicable to the claim of a divorced wife; if the beneficiary's interest cannot be reached, the state may be called upon to support her.... The case of *Seidenberg v. Seidenberg*, D.C. 1954, 126 F. Supp. 19, 23, *affirmed*, 225 F.2d 545, 96 U.S. App. D.C. 245, contains an excellent review of the problem. In summary the court said:

> "The family is the foundation of society. The duty of a married man to support and protect his wife and children is inherent in human nature. It is a part of natural law, as well as a requirement of the law of every civilized country. It is not an ordinary indebtedness, such as a contractual obligation or a judgment for damages arising out of a tort. It is a responsibility far superior to that of paying one's debts, important as the latter obligation is. No part of a man's property or income should be exempt from meeting this liability, for he is under at least as great a duty to provide shelter, clothing, and food for his immediate family as he is to furnish them for his own person. The law should not regard with complacency any man who repudiates or ignores this obligation, which is instinctive in mankind, and should not permit him to flout it with impunity."

The text writers take the same view and in justifying the rule overriding the spendthrift restraint, generally no distinction is made between the claims of dependent children and the claims of the wife for support or alimony. Thus, 2 Scott on Trusts, § 157.1, states:

> "... The claim of a wife and dependent children to support is based upon the clearest grounds of public policy. They are in quite a different position from ordinary creditors who have voluntarily extended credit. It would be shocking indeed to permit a husband to receive and enjoy the whole of the income from a large trust fund and make no provision for his needy dependents."

Accord: 6 American Law of Property, § 29.130; 1A Bogert, Trusts and Trustees, § 223; Griswold, Spendthrift Trusts (2d Ed.), § 339....

We hold that the beneficiary's interest in the income of the Shelley Trust is subject to the claims of the plaintiff for alimony and to the claims for the support of Grant Shelley's children as provided for under both decrees for divorce....

The question of the claimants' rights to reach the corpus of the trust involves other consideration. For the reasons heretofore stated, the beneficiary's interest in the corpus is not made immune from these claims. But, by the terms of the trust, the disbursement of the corpus is within the discretion of the trustee (or, in some instances subject to the approval of others), and, therefore, Grant Shelley's right to receive any part of the corpus does not arise until the trustee has exercised his discretion and has decided to invade the corpus. Until that time, the plaintiff and Patricia Shelley cannot reach the corpus of the trust because the beneficiary has no realizable interest in it. . . . In some jurisdictions a creditor of the beneficiary of a discretionary trust may attach the potential interest of the beneficiary. . . . There is no such procedure in Oregon available to the creditor. And at least with respect to the corpus, ORS 29.175(2) makes the interest constituting the subject matter of the trust free from attachment. It follows that the decree of the lower court in making the corpus of the Shelley Trust subject to the plaintiff's claim for alimony was erroneous.

The claims for the support of Grant Shelley's children, provided for in the two divorce decrees, involve a different problem. The trust directed and authorized the trustee, in the exercise of its sole discretion upon the death of settlor's wife, to make disbursements for the use and benefit not only of Grant Shelley, but also for his children. The disbursements were to be made "in case of any emergency arising whereby unusual and extraordinary expenses are necessary for the proper support and care of my said son, or said children." Here the children are named as beneficiaries of the trust and need not claim derivatively through their father. However, they are entitled to a share of the corpus only if, in the trustee's discretion, it is determined that an emergency exists. The defendant bank contends that the expenses of supporting Grant Shelley's children claimed in this case were for the usual and ordinary costs of support and do not, therefore, constitute "unusual and extraordinary expenses" within the meaning of the trust provision. It is contended that there was no "emergency" calling for "unusual and extraordinary expenses" because there was no proof of an unexpected occurrence or of an unexpected situation requiring immediate action. We disagree with defendant's interpretation. We construe the clause to include the circumstances involved here, i.e., where the children are deserted by their father and are in need of support. We think that the testator intended to provide that in the event that the income from the trust was not sufficient to cover disbursements for the support and case of either the son or his children an "emergency" had arisen and the corpus could then be invaded. . . .

It is to be noted that the children of Grant Shelley are not beneficiaries of the income of the trust; they may reach it only as persons having claims against the beneficiary, Grant Shelley. If, for example, Grant Shelley should decide to support his children out of assets other than income of the trust, the children would have no claim whatsoever against his interest in the trust. The decree, therefore, should have permitted an invasion of the corpus only if it was necessary to first reach the income under the circumstances just mentioned and such income was insufficient. And further, the decree should have made such corpus available only in the event of the trustee's exercise of discretion authorizing the disbursement for the support of the children under the emergency circumstances provided for in the trust. . . .

Notes and Questions

1. Did Hugh Shelley create a spendthrift trust, a support trust, or a discretionary trust for his son? Both Restatement (Third) of Trusts § 60 and UTC § 504 take the position that a support trust is merely a type of discretionary trust. Apart from a narrow group of favored creditors and even without a spendthrift provision, UTC § 504(b) would bar all other creditors (but not the beneficiary) from compelling a trust distribution under any discretionary trusts even if a trustee has abused its discretion. *See also Pfannenstiehl v. Pfannenstiehl*, 55 N.E.3d 933 (Mass. 2016); *Paulson v. Paulson*, 783 N.W.2d 262 (N.D. 2010) (spouse's interest in discretionary trust not an asset for equitable distribution purposes).

2. A well-accepted exception involves claims by the United States or a State against a trust beneficiary to the extent a statute bars recognition of a spendthrift provision. *See* 3d Rest. Trusts § 59 and UTC § 503(b)(3). Thus, the federal government is permitted to reach a spendthrifted trust interest of beneficiary for unpaid taxes. *See, e.g., United States v. Greer*, 360 F. Supp. 2d 760 (W.D.N.C. 2005).

3. What other classes of creditors are candidates for favored treatment? Suppliers of "necessary" services? Creditors, like appliance repairers, for whom checking credit histories does not make sense? *Compare* 3d Rest. of Trusts § 59(b) (excepting spendthrift protection from claimants who furnished necessary supplies and services to the beneficiary), *with* UTC § 503 (no exception for claimants furnishing necessaries). On the other hand, both Restatement (Third) of Trusts § 59(b) and UTC § 503(b) would permit claimants who furnished services to protect the beneficiary's interest, such as a lawyer engaged to resist an attack on the validity of the trust, to reach a spendthrifted interest.

4. Arguably tort victims, essentially "involuntary creditors," should have the benefit of exemptions from the spendthrift trusts but this is not the usual result. In *Sligh v. First Nat'l Bank*, 704 So. 2d 1020 (Miss. 1997), the Mississippi Supreme Court, based on public policy considerations, allowed a tort victim to recover from the tortfeasor's spendthrifted trust. In response, the Mississippi legislature promptly barred such recoveries. *See* Miss. Code Ann. § 91-9-503 (1999). *See also Duvall v. McGee*, 826 A.2d 416 (Md. 2003) (trust beneficiary's spendthrifted interest not reachable to satisfy judgment for battery that resulted in victim's death); *Scheffel v. Krueger*, 782 A.2d 410 (N.H. 2001) (trust beneficiary's spendthrifted interest not reachable to satisfy tort judgment for sexual assault of minor child).

Recognizing the unfairness of the spendthrift exemption, Cal. Prob. Code § 15305.5 authorizes a court to order restitution judgment from a spendthrifted interest if the trust beneficiary committed a felony.

5. Settlors may authorize a trustee to make distributions of trust income or principal to himself or herself. Should creditors have any rights in such trusts? Should it depend on whether the trustee discretion is not limited, albeit subject to judicial supervision, or is it limited by an ascertainable standard, such as for support? UTC § 505(e) bars creditor relief if the trustee-beneficiary's power is limited by an ascertainable standard. *Contra* 3d Rest. Trusts § 60, cmt. g.

Selected References

Robert T. Danforth, *Article Five of the UTC and the Future of Creditors' Rights in Trusts*, 27 Cardozo L. Rev. 2551 (2006), and *Rethinking the Law of Creditors' Rights in Trusts*, 53 Hastings L.J. 287 (2002).

Kevin D. Millard, *Rights of a Trust Beneficiary's Creditors Under the Uniform Trust Code*, 34 ACTEC L.J. 58 (2008).

Victoria Hasseler, *Trustee-Beneficiaries, Creditors, and New York's EPTL: The Surprises that Result and How the UTC Solves Them*, 69 Alb. L. Rev. 1169 (2006).

Alan Newman, *Spendthrift and Discretionary Trusts: Alive and Well Under the Uniform Trust Code*, 40 Real Prop. Prob. & Tr. J. 567 (2005).

Jeffrey A. Schoenblum, *In Search of a Unifying Principle for Article V of the Uniform Trust Code: A Response to Professor Danforth*, 27 Cardozo L. Rev. 2609 (2006).

Timothy J. Vitollo, *Uniform Trust Code Section 503: Applying Hamilton Orders to Spendthrift Trusts*, 43 Real Prop. Tr. & Est. L.J. 169 (2008).

3. Asset Protection Trusts

In recent years, lawyers have given increasing attention to protecting the assets of wealthy clients, especially those who are engaged in relatively risky situations: doctors who fear a catastrophic malpractice claim, business owners who fear a market shift which would destroy what they have built. Many asset protection devices are available, including the creation of family limited partnerships, devotion of assets to retirement plans that are protected from creditors, and use of tenancies by the entireties in certain jurisdictions.

An Asset Protection Trust (APT) is another potential way to prevent creditors from reaching assets. An APT relies on favorable legislation in offshore jurisdictions, and most recently, favorable legislation in several states. The basic paradigm of the APT is as follows: a settlor creates a trust over his or her assets, naming a third party, but friendly, trustee. The trust terms empower the trustee to make discretionary distributions of trust income or principal to the settlor. Under applicable legislation, creditors cannot reach the trust property while in trust.

APTs have been used effectively for many years in off-shore trust havens. Notable jurisdictions include Bermuda, the Cayman Islands, and the Cook Islands. However, offshore APTs have not been effective in some egregious situations. *See, e.g., FTC v. Affordable Media*, LLC, 179 F.3d 1228 (9th Cir. 1999) (settlor held in civil contempt for failing to comply with injunction that ordered repatriation of trust assets); *In re Coker*, 251 B.R. 902 (Bankr. M.D. Fla. 2000) (bankrupt settlor debtor held in civil contempt by bankruptcy court for failure to repatriate trust assets).

The reason settlors used offshore trust havens to create APTs was the long-standing position under American common law, codified in many states, that public policy would be offended if a settlor's creditors were not permitted to reach assets in a self-settled trust. *See* 2d Rest. Trusts § 156; Indeed, the latest Restatement maintains the position that APTs are not effective against a settlor's creditors. 3d Rest. Trusts § 58(2). *See also* N.Y. Estates, Powers and Trusts Law § 7-3.1(a); *Rush University Medical Center v. Sessions,* 980 N.E.2d 45 (Ill. 2012). Significantly, UTC § 505(a)(1) codifies the rule: a settlor's creditors "may reach the maximum amount that can be distributed to or for the settlor's benefit." Like the Restatement (Third) of Trusts § 58(2), UTC § 505(a)(1) allows a settlor's creditors to reach trust property where discretionary or mandatory distributions are authorized.

In the late 1990s, Alaska and Delaware decided to compete for APT business that was flowing to off-shore trust havens. The gambit? Enact domestic APT legislation making it available to residents and non-residents alike. Quite understandably, other states decided that they should compete with Alaska and Delaware, in part to garner business from out-of-staters but also to encourage their wealthy citizens to create in-state APTs. To date, over 10 other states have become APT jurisdictions: Hawaii, Mississippi, Missouri, Nevada, New Hampshire, Ohio, Oklahoma, Rhode Island, South Dakota, Tennessee, Utah, West Virginia, and Wyoming.

Domestic APT legislation flies in the face of the traditional American doctrine that prevents the insulation of a settlor's trust assets from creditors. The Comments to UTC § 505(a)(1) make clear that the drafters believed that the doctrine represented "sound policy."

Whether one favors or disfavors APT legislation, the effectiveness of domestic APTs is far from clear. APTs created by nonresident settlors, e.g., New Yorkers creating APTs in Delaware, appear most vulnerable in the bankruptcy arena since bankruptcy courts have jurisdiction over assets located nationally. *See In re Huber,* 493 B.R. 798 (W.D. Wash. 2013) (Washington resident created a trust for which Alaska's asset protection laws were to apply. Because Alaska had no substantial relation to the trust property, the bankruptcy court held that Washington law applied.).

Even in APT jurisdictions, creditors will have recourse if a settlor makes a fraudulent transfer under state law. *See generally* Uniform Voidable Transactions Act (Formerly Uniform Fraudulent Transfer Act) (as amended in 2014.) Transfers may also be fraudulent under bankruptcy law. *See In re Huber,* 493 B.R. 798 (W.D. Wash. 2013) (trust transfers were fraudulent under Bankruptcy Law § 548(e) and thus void). *Accord In re Mortensen,* 2011 Bank Lexis 5004 (D. Alaska 2011).

Question

Your client, a domiciliary of a state that does not permit a settlor to avoid creditors by creating a self-settled trust, would like to have that benefit. Is it wrong to assist such person? How would you decide whether to recommend a self-settled trust in a domestic asset protection state or one in an offshore haven?

Selected References

Richard C. Ausness, *The Offshore Asset Protection Trust: A Prudent Financial Planning Device or the Last Refuge of a Scoundrel?*, 45 Duq. L. Rev. 147 (2007).

John K. Eason, *Policy, Logic, and Persuasion in the Evolving Realm of Trust Asset Protection*, 27 Cardozo L. Rev. 2621 (2006).

Adam J. Hirsch, *Fear Not the Asset Protection Trust*, 27 Cardozo L. Rev. 2685 (2006).

Henry J. Lischer, Jr., *Professional Responsibility Issues Associated with Asset Protection Trusts*, 39 Real Prop. Prob. & Tr. J. 561 (2004).

Ronald J. Mann, *A Fresh Look at State Asset Protection Trust Statutes*, 67 Vand. L. Rev. 1741 (2014).

Richard W. Nenno, *Planning with Domestic Asset-Protection Trusts: Parts I and II*, 40 Real Prop. Prob. & Tr. J. 263 and 477 (2005).

Gideon S. Rothschild, *The United States of Asset Protection*, 147 Tr. & Est. 38 (2008).

Jay Soled and Mitchell M. Gans, *Asset Preservation and the Evolving Role of Trusts in the Twenty-First Century*, 72 Wash. & Lee L. Rev. 257 (2015).

Stewart E. Sterk, *Asset Protection Trusts: Trust Law's Race to the Bottom?*, 85 Cornell L. Rev. 1035 (2000).

4. Medicaid Eligibility

Pohlmann v. Nebraska Department of Health and Human Services

710 N.W.2d 639 (Neb. 2006)

Stephan, J.

This is an appeal from an order of the district court for Lancaster County affirming an order of the Nebraska Department of Health and Human Services (DHHS) which denied Ruth Pohlmann's application for Medicaid benefits. The denial was based upon Ruth's status as a beneficiary of a testamentary trust established by her late husband, Herman Pohlmann. We reverse, based upon our conclusion that DHHS and the district court erred in determining that the trust corpus was a disqualifying asset.

FACTS

On August 10, 1982, Herman executed his last will and testament, which [created a Family Trust with income payable to his wife, Ruth, for life] "and such portion of the principal as [the trustee] may, from time to time, deem appropriate for her health, education, support or maintenance." . . . Herman and Ruth's children and grandchildren were beneficiaries of the remainder of the Family Trust. Herman's will appointed Ruth as personal representative of his estate or, alternatively, their two children Merlyn Pohlmann and Verona Lee Gumaer as copersonal representatives.

Following Herman's death, his will was admitted to probate, and on January 24, 2000, the copersonal representatives executed two deeds of distribution conveying four parcels of real property to the trustee of the Family Trust.

On June 6, 2003, Merlyn, as attorney in fact for Ruth, applied to DHHS for Medicaid benefits on her behalf. At that time and during the pendency of this case, Ruth was a resident of a nursing home in Deshler, Nebraska. On June 30, DHHS denied Ruth's request for Medicaid benefits after determining that she was ineligible for assistance because she had available resources exceeding the program standard of $ 4,000. The decision was based in part upon the balance in her bank accounts and in part upon resources which DHHS believed were available to Ruth under the testamentary trust established by Herman's will. Merlyn appealed the decision on Ruth's behalf, contending that while the income from the Family Trust was an available resource, the corpus of the trust was not. . . . At the time of the hearing, the balance in Ruth's bank accounts was less than the $ 4,000 disqualification limit. The hearing officer affirmed the DHHS decision, [as did a district court, by] . . . application of 42 U.S.C. § 1396p(d)(3)(B)(i) (2000), which deems that resources of an irrevocable trust are available to an applicant if there are "any circumstances" under which payment could be made for the benefit of the applicant. . . .

ASSIGNMENT OF ERROR

Ruth assigns, restated, that the district court erred in determining that the corpus of the Family Trust was an available resource for purposes of determining her eligibility for Medicaid benefits. . . .

ANALYSIS. . . . We are presented with the question of whether the corpus of an irrevocable, discretionary testamentary trust is a resource available to the beneficiary spouse of the grantor for purposes of determining the spouse's eligibility for Medicaid benefits. Medicaid is a cooperative federal program supervised by the U.S. Department of Health and Human Services through the Health Care Financing Administration. See, 42 U.S.C. § 1396 et seq. (2000). . . . Medicaid funds are used to provide medical assistance to persons whose resources are insufficient to meet the cost of necessary medical care. A state is not obligated to participate in the Medicaid program; however, once it has voluntarily elected to participate, it must comply with standards and requirements imposed by federal statutes and regulations. Nebraska has elected to participate in the Medicaid program . . . and DHHS is responsible for the administration of the Medicaid program in this state.

Under federal law, a state participating in the Medicaid program must establish resource standards for the determination of eligibility. § 1396a(a)(17)(B). These standards must take into account "only such income and resources as are, as determined in accordance with standards prescribed by the Secretary [of the U.S. Department of Health and Human Services], available to the applicant or recipient." § 1396a(a)(17)(B).

Both DHHS and the district court utilized § 1396p(d) in determining whether the Family Trust corpus was a resource available to Ruth. For purposes of that subsection,

> an individual shall be considered to have established a trust if assets of the individual were used to form all or part of the corpus of the trust and if any of the following individuals established such trust other *than by will*:
>
> (i) The individual.
>
> (ii) The individual's spouse.
>
> (iii) A person, including a court or administrative body, with legal authority to act in place of or on behalf of the individual or the individual's spouse.
>
> (iv) A person, including any court or administrative body, acting at the direction or upon the request of the individual or the individual's spouse.

(Emphasis supplied.) § 1396p(d)(2)(A). With respect to irrevocable trusts, the federal statute further provides that

> there are any circumstances under which payment from the trust could be made to or for the benefit of the individual, the portion of the corpus from which, or the income on the corpus from which, payment to the individual could be made shall be considered resources available to the individual.

§ 1396p(d)(3)(B)(i).

In this case, DHHS and the district court applied the "any circumstances" test of § 1396p(d)(3)(B)(i) and the corresponding provision in 469 Neb. Admin. Code, ch. 2, § 009.07A5b(2), and concluded that because the trustee in the exercise of his discretion could make payments from the Family Trust to Ruth, the corpus was an available resource which disqualified her from receiving Medicaid benefits. This reasoning mirrors that of the *Nebraska Court of Appeals in Boruch v. Nebraska Dept. of Health & Human Servs.*, 11 Neb. App. 713, 718, 659 N.W.2d 848, 853 (2003), in which the Court of Appeals wrote that under the plain language of § 1396p(d), if a person establishes an irrevocable trust with his or her assets and the individual is able, under any circumstances, to benefit from the corpus of the trust or the income derived from the trust, the individual is considered to have formed a trust which is counted in the determination of Medicaid eligibility.

However, Boruch involved a self-settled inter vivos trust in which the Medicaid applicant was both the grantor and the beneficiary. Here, it is undisputed that the Family Trust was established through the will of Herman. Ruth argues that this fact precludes application of the "any circumstances" test because the "other than by will" language in § 1396p(d)(2)(A) specifically exempts testamentary trusts from the scope of § 1396p. . . .

We find merit in this argument. As the Court of Appeals noted in Boruch, § 1396p was enacted in 1993 to restrict a loophole in the Medicaid act through which self-settled trusts were used to exclude assets from consideration for Medicaid eligibility purposes. *See, also, Skindzier v. Comm'r of Soc. Servs.*, 258 Conn. 642, 784 A.2d 323 (2001). For Medicaid eligibility purposes, the corpus of a self-settled trust is an available resource under § 1396p(d)(3)(B)(i) if the "any circumstances" test is met. If the test is not met, the corpus is considered an asset disposed of by the individual for purposes of § 1 3 9 6 p (c). See § 1396p(d)(3)(B)(ii). However, the plain meaning of the phrase "other than by will" in § 1396p(d)(2)(A) and the corresponding Nebraska regulation make it clear that a Medicaid applicant cannot be considered to have established a trust for purposes of the restrictions imposed by § 1396p(d) if the trust was established by will. See *Skindzier v. Comm'r of Social Services, supra*. The State Medicaid Manual, promulgated by the Health Care Financing Administration as a means of issuing policies and procedures to state agencies administrating Medicaid, specifically provides that for purposes of determining eligibility under § 1396p, the term trust "does not cover trusts established by will." Health Care Fin. Admin., U.S. Dept. of Health and Human Servs., Pub. No. 45, State Medicaid Manual § 3259.1(A)(1) at 3-3-109.24 (rev. 64, Nov. 1994). Because the trust at issue here was not self-settled, but, rather, was testamentary, it was not within the purview of § 1396p(d)(3)(B)(i) and 469 Neb. Admin. Code, ch. 2, § 009.07A5b(2). DHHS and the district court thus erred in applying the "any circumstances" test to determine the availability of the trust corpus for purposes of Ruth's Medicaid eligibility.

We acknowledge the argument made by DHHS that the statutory exemption of testamentary trusts from § 1396p seems inconsistent with the underlying purpose of Medicaid, which is to provide medical assistance to those who have no other financial means. However, we must also agree with the statement by the Supreme Court of Connecticut in Skindzier that "we have no authority to impose a different rule simply because, in our opinion, it would better implement the legislative policy of minimizing the fiscal risk to [Medicaid]." *Id.* at 661, 784 A.2d at 335. Instead, like the Connecticut court, we are "'precluded from substituting [our] own ideas of what might be a wise provision in place of a clear expression of legislative will.'" *See id.* at 661, 784 A.2d at 336.

DHHS alternatively argues that by not exercising her right of election as a surviving spouse, Ruth allowed her assets to fund the Family Trust created by Herman's will, thus bringing the trust within the scope of § 1396p(d). DHHS relies upon *Miller v. SRS*, 275 Kan. 349, 64 P.3d 395 (2003), in which the Kansas Supreme Court upheld an administrative determination that a widow's decision not to claim her spousal elective share resulted in a trust established by the widow with her own funds for her own benefit, and not a trust created by will, thereby bringing the trust corpus within the scope of § 1396p(d). We do not reach this issue because neither DHHS nor the district court was asked to make a determination that Ruth created a self-settled trust by not electing her spousal share, and the record is silent on the issue. An appellate court will not consider an issue on appeal that was not presented to or passed upon by the trial court. . . .

Our determination that the "any circumstances" test was erroneously applied in this case does not conclusively resolve the question of whether the Family Trust corpus was an available resource for Medicaid eligibility purposes. Nebraska regulations provide that "testamentary trusts may be excluded as resources, depending on the terms of the trust." . . . Under the Nebraska Uniform Trust Code, "'terms of a trust' means the manifestation of the settlor's intent regarding a trust's provisions as expressed in the trust instrument or as may be established by other evidence that would be admissible in a judicial proceeding." Neb. Rev. Stat. § 30-3803(19) (Supp. 2005). . . . In analyzing the terms of a testamentary trust to determine if the corpus is "available" to a beneficiary for purposes of Medicaid eligibility, courts have looked to whether the trust is a support trust or a discretionary trust. *See, Miller v. SRS, supra*; *Eckes v. Richland Cty. Soc. Serv.*, 2001 ND 16, 621 N.W.2d 851 (N.D. 2001). We find the following formulation by the Supreme Court of North Dakota helpful where, as here, the beneficiary is not a cotrustee:

> The settlor's intent determines whether a trust is classified as a support or a discretionary trust, which in turn determines what portion of the trust is available to an applicant for the purpose of qualifying for Medicaid benefits. . . . A support trust essentially provides the trustee "shall pay or apply only so much of the income and principal or either as is necessary for the education or support of a beneficiary." . . . A support trust allows a beneficiary to compel distributions of income, principal, or both, for expenses necessary for the beneficiary's support, and an agency may consider the support trust as an available asset when evaluating eligibility for assistance. . . . Conversely, a discretionary trust grants the trustee "uncontrolled discretion over payment to the beneficiary" and may reference the "general welfare" of the beneficiary. . . . Because the beneficiary of a discretionary trust does not have the ability to compel distributions from the trust, only those distributions of income, principal, or both, actually made by the trustee may be considered by the agency as available assets when evaluating eligibility for assistance.

(Citations omitted.) *Eckes v. Richland Cty. Soc. Serv.*, 621 N.W.2d at 855-56. See, also, Restatement (Third) of Trusts § 60 (2003).

The key provision of the Family Trust stated that the trustee was to pay Ruth "all of the accumulative income from the individual funds and such portion of the principal as it may, from time to time, deem appropriate for her health, education, support or maintenance." (Emphasis supplied.) Although not in the context of a Medicaid eligibility determination, we have held that similar discretionary powers granted to a trustee do not create a right of the beneficiary to compel payments from the trust. *See, Doksansky v. Norwest Bank Neb.*, 260 Neb. 100, 615 N.W.2d 104 (2000); *Smith v. Smith*, 246 Neb. 193, 517 N.W.2d 394 (1994). In this case, DHHS concedes that the Family Trust is discretionary with respect to distributions of corpus, and we likewise conclude. Because Ruth cannot compel a distribution from the Family Trust corpus, it is not an available asset for purposes of determining her eligibility for Medicaid benefits.

CONCLUSION

The judgment of the district court affirming the order of DHHS does not conform to the law because it is based upon the "any circumstances" test of § 1396p(d)(3)(B)(i) and 469 Neb. Admin. Code, ch. 2, § 009.07A5b(2), both of which are inapplicable to the testamentary trust at issue in this case. We conclude as a matter of law that the Family Trust created by Herman's will is discretionary in nature, such that the beneficiary, Ruth, may not compel a distribution from its corpus and that therefore, such corpus is not an available asset for purposes of determining Ruth's eligibility for Medicaid benefits but must be excluded for this purpose under 469 Neb. Admin. Code, ch. 2, § 009.07A5g. Accordingly, we reverse the judgment of the district court and remand the cause with directions to vacate the DHHS order and remand to that agency for further proceedings consistent with this opinion.

Reversed and remanded with directions.

Notes and Questions

1. As *Pohlmann* suggests, Medicaid is a highly complex area involving both federal and state laws. No attempt is made in this book to comprehensively treat Medicaid, which is the proper subject for an Elder Law course; rather, we focus, as does *Pohlmann*, on the intersection between Medicaid eligibility for a trust beneficiary. The key issue is whether trust property is an available resource to the beneficiary; if so, the trust beneficiary may be ineligible for Medicaid, since a person must generally be "poor" to receive such welfare benefits.

2. Trust property may be treated as an available resource, thereby preventing a trust beneficiary's Medicaid eligibility in self-settled trusts, see Notes 5 and 6, as well as trusts created by a third party. Although a trust beneficiary's right to income will not be counted as an available resource to qualify for Medicaid eligibility and the furnishing of nursing home care, the income received by the beneficiary must be used to pay for the beneficiary's nursing home care with Medicaid picking up any balance.

What about trusts for a beneficiary's support or where the trustee has discretion over trust distributions? The cases addressing the problem have generally focused on whether the trust was a support trust or a discretionary trust. If the trust was a discretionary trust, without any support standard, the trust property will not be treated as an available resource. On the other hand, if the trustee was mandated to use the trust property for the beneficiary's support, without taking into account any of the beneficiary's resources, then the trust property would be an available resource.

As *Pohlmann* illustrates, the current problem area involves the so-called discretionary support trust, where the trustee has some discretion in making distributions for support. Although *Pohlmann* treated the discretionary support trust as discretionary, *accord In re Horton Irrevocable Trust*, 668 N.W.2d 208 (Minn. Ct. App. 2003), other courts have held that the trust property is an available resource. *In re Flygare*, 725 N.W.2d 114 (Miss. Ct. App. 2006); *Corcoran v. Dep't of Soc. Servs.*, 859 A.2d 533 (Conn. 2004); *Kryzsko v. Ramsey County Soc. Servs.*, 607 N.W.2d 237 (N.D. 2000); *Shaak v. Pa. Dep't of Pub. Welfare*, 747 A.2d 883 (Pa. 2000).

Recall that the Restatement (Third) of Trusts § 50, as followed by UTC § 504, eliminates the distinction between support and discretionary trusts. Indeed, the Restatement takes the sensible position that a settlor would not have intended a trustee to make distributions under a support trust if Medicaid disqualification would result. *See* 3d Rest. Trusts § 50, cmt. e; *accord* UTC § 814.

3. If a governmental body provides support to a trust beneficiary could it prevail in a suit against the trustees of a discretionary support trust to recover expenditures on behalf of the beneficiary? If viewed as a creditors' rights issue, UTC § 504(c) resoundingly answers the question in the negative. On the other hand, the Restatement position would allow recovery under certain circumstances. *See* 3d Rest. Trusts § 60, cmt. (e)(1) (trustee's refusal may constitute abuse of discretion).

If a creditor could not reach trust property in a discretionary trust for support, does it necessarily follow that the trust property is not an available resource to the beneficiary for Medicaid qualification purposes?

If recovery is based on a state's statutory right to recover from a decedent's estate assets, where the decedent had received Medicaid benefits, a court may permit recovery by a state even under a discretionary support trust. *See In re Trust of Barkema*, 690 N.W.2d 50 (Iowa 2004); *but cf. Emmet County Bd. of Supervisors v. Ridout*, 692 N.W.2d 821 (Iowa 2005) (no recovery in capacity as special creditor furnishing support).

4. Clients with disabled relatives often want to establish trusts to help care for those relatives. Such a client will want to avoid subjecting the trust to state claims for the cost of the relative's care, and to avoid disqualifying the relative for state aid. The most widely-accepted approach is to create a "supplemental needs trust" (SNT) which limits the trustee's authority to providing only those benefits the state will not provide and limits spending so as not to disqualify the beneficiary from state assistance. (Under certain circumstances a SNT may be self-settled by a disabled person provided that governmental bodies can recover for expenditures on the death of the settlor.)

Several states have statutes defining the limits of such trusts. Caution: this is an area calling for special care. The rules are often very detailed and subject to sudden change.

Why would legislatures endorse trusts like these?

5. Trusts may involve the self-settled type, comparable to the asset protection trust paradigm, where a third-party trustee has the discretion to make trust distributions to the settlor. Federal legislation contained in the Omnibus Budget Reconciliation Act (OBRA) of 1993 provides that assets in such a self-settled trust, referred to as a Medicaid Qualifying (Disqualifying might be the better word) Trust, will generally count against the settlor. In effect, the Medicaid rules reject self-settled trusts as asset protection devices. *See Strand v. Rasmussen*, 648 N.W.2d 95 (Iowa 2002) (trust created by conservator treated as self-settled).

As set forth in *Pohlmann*, federal law also treats lifetime trusts created by a spouse for the other spouse as an available resource. Query: why did Congress exclude comparable testamentary trusts?

6. In response to the Medicaid Qualifying Trust rules, elder law practitioners began to rely on self-settled irrevocable trusts where the settlor would only have the mandatory right to income for a term of years or life so that only the income would be treated as an available resource for Medicaid qualification. The remainder would be payable to a third party or parties, typically a family member. Because the remainder could not return to the settlor, the remainder would not be treated as an available resource under the Medicaid Qualifying Trust rules. The net result was that members of a settlor's family could receive the trust principal on the settlor's death (or at the end of the term) free from Medicaid.

The Medicaid Look-Back Period

Not unmindful of the Medicaid Trust and other devices, Congress created a five year look-back period for all trusts created, to the effect that trusts created within five years of applying for Medicaid would be taken into account under a penalty period provision. (In 2005, Congress extended the look-back period to five years for non-trust transfers made after February 8, 2006.) In other words, Congress believed that a claimant should not able to qualify for benefits by becoming "suddenly poor," that is, by giving away enough property to meet the qualifying standards.

The 2005 federal legislation significantly changed the penalty period rules for trust and other transfers made before a person is entitled to nursing home benefits under Medicaid. Prior to the legislation, uncompensated transfers during the look-back period were deemed made in the month following the transfer and a person would not be eligible for nursing home care under Medicaid for a number of months.

Consider the following example: On March 1, 2005, Settlor created an irrevocable trust over $90,000 with income payable to Able for life, remainder to Beth. On April 1, 2005, the average monthly cost of nursing home care in the settlor's region was $10,000. Pursuant to the penalty period rules,[11] Settlor would be eligible for nursing home care on January 1, 2006, assuming he or she otherwise would qualify on January 1, 2006.

Under the 2005 federal legislation, effective for transfers made after February 8, 2006, the penalty period generally begins on the date a person would otherwise be eligible for nursing home treatment but for a transfer made within the look-back period. *See* 42 U.S.C. § 1396p(c)(1)(D).

The operation of this harsh penalty rule can be illustrated by modifying the above example: Settlor created the same trust over $90,000 one on March 1, 2011, and on January 1, 2012, would otherwise be eligible for nursing home care under Medicaid. For comparative purposes, assume the nursing home monthly rate remained at $10,000.

Based on the new penalty period rules, Settlor would not be eligible for nursing home care until October 1, 2012, even though he needed to enter a nursing home on January 1, 2012!

In effect, under the new penalty period rules, the $90,000 will be deemed transferred on the date the nursing home care is needed, rather than one month after the transfer. The nine months of ineligibility ($90,000/$10,000) begins on the date that the nursing home care becomes necessary.

7. Is it wrong to help a person with assets become "legally poor" and qualify for Medicaid? Do you agree that: "There is no greater issue in establishing a lawful Medicaid eligibility trust than there is in taking a lawful deduction on an income tax return"? Dwight E. Bickel, Medicaid Eligibility Planning After the 1993 Omnibus Budget Reconciliation Act Amendments, Prac. Law., Jan. 1994, at 21, 23.

8. You are on the staff of a legislative committee working on Medicaid reform.

Your project is to develop a memorandum addressing the concerns of citizens who have worked hard to accumulate assets they would like to pass on to their children, but who fear watching it all drain away to cover nursing home expenses. At the same time, you have been told that the government simply cannot afford to pay the health care costs of those who are not "truly needy." What factors will you consider as you balance these competing policies? What solutions will you propose?

11. Number of months ineligible equals amount transferred divided by the monthly nursing home amount. In example, $90,000/$10,000=9 months of ineligibility starting April 1, 2005.

Selected References

Thomas Begley, Jr., *Serving Special Needs,* 143 Tr. & Est. 29 (May 2004).

Joel C. Dobris, *Medicaid Asset Planning by the Elderly: A Policy View of Expectations, Entitlement, and Inheritance,* 24 Real Prop. Prob. & Tr. J. 1 (1989).

David M. English et al., Elder Law and the Deficit Reduction Act of 2005 (LexisNexis 2006).

Joseph A. Rosenberg, *Supplemental Needs Trusts for People with Disabilities: The Development of a Private Trust in the Public Interest,* 10 B.U. Pub. Int. L.J. 91 (2000).

Jack Sullivan, *Pooled Special-Needs Trusts: An Exception That Should Be the Rule to Protect Adults with Developmental Disabilities,* 27 Law & Ineq. 441 (2009).

§ 8.04 Reformation, Modification, and Termination

A. Reformation and Modification Based on Ambiguity and Mistake

Ambiguities and mistakes in trust instruments raise the same problems as those discussed in connection with will interpretation and reformation. *See* § 3.04[B], *supra.* Consistently, UTC § 415 and Restatement (Third) of Trusts § 62 take the position that trust instruments can be reformed to correct mistakes even if the trust language is unambiguous, provided the mistake was proved by clear and convincing evidence. *See, e.g., Megiel-Rollo v. Megiel,* 162 So. 3d 1088 (Fla. Dist. Ct. App. 2015) and *In re Matthew Larson Trust Agreement,* 831 N.W.2d 388 (ND. 2013) (applying UTC § 415 to allow reformation). *See also In re Irrevocable Trust Agreement of 1979,* 331 P.3d 881 (Nev. 2014) (rescission also possible).

The more traditional jurisprudence would allow for the correction of mistakes, *see, e.g., In re Irrevocable Trust Agreement of 1979,* 331 P.3d 881 (Nev. 2014) (irrevocable lifetime trust can be reformed or rescinded if the settlor can prove unilateral mistake by clear and convincing evidence), even though the correction was made after the settlor died.) *Popp v. Rex,* 916 So. 2d 954 (Fla. Dist. Ct. App. 2005) (pre-UTC § 415 case).

Reformation for mistakes in testamentary trusts, however, is traditionally not allowed. Following the wills rule, UTC § 416 follows the judicial trend, *see, e.g., Martin v. Martin,* 685 S.E.2d 288 (Ga. 2009) and *Booth v. Kornegay,* 892 N.E.2d 332 (2008), and allows trust modification to achieve the settlor's tax objectives. *See In re Paul F. Suhr Trust,* 222 P.3d 506 (Kan. 2010) (UTC § 416 applied).

Question

If the settlor is still alive and language is ambiguous, should settlor's post-execution testimony be conclusive on intention? *See In re Durosko Marital Trust*, 862 A.2d 914 (D.C. 2004) (allowing testimony of lawyer who drafted trust).

Selected Reference

Fred Franke and Anna Katherine Moody, *The Terms of the Trust: Extrinsic Evidence of Settlor Intent*, 40 ACTEC L.J. 1 (2014).

B. Termination and Modification Prescribed by Settlor

A trust will normally terminate on the death of the last income beneficiary, at the end of a prescribed number of years, or when the purposes for the trust have been accomplished. *See* 3d Rest. Trusts § 61 and UTC § 410(a). As we saw in Chapter 4, a trust may be prematurely terminated or modified if the settlor has retained such power. *See generally* 3d Rest. Trusts § 63. Typically, the trust will provide for methods of amending and revoking, and the settlor must follow those methods as discussed, supra. A settlor who has not reserved a power to revoke, however, will need the beneficiaries' consent before making any changes. *See* UTC § 411(a). In *Matter of Frei Irrevocable Trust Dated Oct. 29, 1996*, 133 Nev. 8, ___ P.3d ___ (2017), the court allowed the survivor settlor and affected beneficiaries to modify a trust to remove a spendthrift provision.

In addition, a trust may be prematurely terminated or modified if the settlor has given someone else (invested another) with the power of termination. The power to terminate may be granted to the trustee or a beneficiary. *See* 3d Rest. Trusts § 64(1). Even a third person, usually referred to as a trust protector, may be granted termination or modification powers; however, the trust protector will be presumed to hold these powers in a fiduciary capacity. *See* 3d Rest. Trusts § 64(2) and UTC § 808(d).

Note on Decanting

Irrevocable trusts that provide trustees with discretionary dispositive powers may also allow a trustee to terminate an existing irrevocable trust by pouring over the trust assets into a new irrevocable trust with different terms. The trustee's action of creating a new trust is known as "decanting." Although decanting was earlier recognized by a few state courts, *see, e.g., Phipps v. Palm Beach Trust Co.*, 196 So. 299 (Fla. 1940), and most recently in *Morse v. Kraft*, 992 N.E.2d 1021 (Mass. 2013), in recent years, several states have enacted "decanting" statutes to provide authority and guidance to trustees.[12] *See generally* Alan S. Halperin & Lindsay O'Donnell, *Modifying Irrevocable Trusts: State Law and Tax Considerations in Trust Decanting*, 42 Heckerling Inst. on Est. Plan. Ch. 13 (2008).

In summer 2015, the Uniform Law Commission approved a comprehensive Uniform Trust Decanting Act. The Act has been enacted by Colorado, New Mexico, Virginia, and Washington; additional enactments are expected. *See generally* Kristin T. Abati & Renat V. Lumpac, *The Uniform Trust Decanting Act*, Trusts & Estates at 15 (Feb. 2016).

Decanting can be illustrated by the following example: S creates an irrevocable trust with income to Alice until age 25, with principal payable to Alice at age 25. The trustee has the power to distribute trust principal to Alice as the trustee decides. By decanting, the trustee, who is concerned that Alice may not be able to handle the principal at age 25, could create a new trust with income payable to Alice until age 40, with remainder to Alice at age 40.

Decanting can be used to change both dispositive and administrative provisions by decanting trust assets into a new trust with different terms. Both nontax and tax benefits may be achieved by decanting. For example, a trustee may wish to decant so that the new trust becomes subject to new and more favorable state laws. Or, the trustee may wish to utilize decanting to prolong the imposition of generation-skipping transfer taxes.

C. Termination and Modification by the Trust Beneficiaries

Sometimes those involved with a trust want to change it, or end it before its time. Often the motivating factor is an unanticipated financial need that arises after the settlor has established the trust. What happens if the settlor creates an irrevocable lifetime trust or a testamentary trust, but has not provided a means for premature termination (or modification)? Can such a trust be terminated if all of the beneficiaries consent? After the settlor has died, or even while the settlor is alive, the beneficiaries may seek changes, either to adjust to emergencies or simply to get access to the fund.

The next case established the principle that courts will protect the trust's purpose on the settlor's behalf.

12. New York recently amended its earlier decanting statute to allow greater flexibility, which includes allowing a trustee to decant not only from purely discretionary trusts (as in the past) but also trusts with powers subject to an ascertainable standard. *See* N.Y. Estates, Powers and Trusts Law § 10-6.6.

1. The Claflin *Doctrine*

Claflin v. Claflin

20 N.E. 454 (Mass. 1889)

Field, J.

By the eleventh article of his will as modified by a codicil, Wilbur F. Claflin gave all the residue of his personal estate to trustees, "to sell and dispose of the same, and to pay to my wife, Mary A. Claflin, one-third part of the proceeds thereof, and to pay to my son Clarence A. Claflin one-third part of the proceeds thereof, and to pay the remaining one-third part thereof to my son Adelbert E. Claflin, in the manner following, viz. ten thousand dollars when he is of the age of twenty-one years, ten thousand dollars when he is of the age of twenty-five years, and the balance when he is of the age of thirty years."

Apparently, Adelbert E. Claflin was not quite twenty-one years old when his father died, but he some time ago reached that age and received ten thousand dollars from the trust. He has not yet reached the age of twenty-five years, and he brings this bill to compel the trustees to pay to him the remainder of the trust fund. His contention is, in effect, that the provisions of the will postponing the payment of the money beyond the time when he is twenty-one years old are void. There is no doubt that his interest in the trust fund is vested and absolute, and that no other person has any interest in it, and the authority is undisputed that the provisions postponing payment to him until sometime after he reaches the age of twenty-one years would be treated as void by those courts which hold that restrictions against the alienation of absolute interests in the income of trust property are void.... These decisions do not proceed on the ground that it was the intention of the testator that the property should be conveyed to the beneficiary on his reaching the age of twenty-one years, because in each case it was clear that such was not his intention, but on the ground that the direction to withhold the possession of the property from the beneficiary after he reached his majority was inconsistent with the absolute rights of property given him by the will.

This court has ordered trust property to be conveyed by the trustee to the beneficiary when there was a dry trust, or when the purposes of the trust had been accomplished, or when no good reason was shown why the trust should continue, and all the persons interested in it were sui juris and desired that it be terminated; but we have found no expression of any opinion in our reports that provisions requiring a trustee to hold and manage the trust property until the beneficiary reached an age beyond that of twenty-one years are necessarily void if the interest of the beneficiary is vested and absolute. See ... *Sears v. Choate*, 146 Mass. 395, 15 N.E. Rep. 786. This is not a dry trust, and the purposes of the trust have not been accomplished if the intention of the testator is to be carried out.

In *Sears v. Choate* it is said, "Where property is given to certain persons for their benefit, and in such a manner that no other person has or can have any interest in it, they are in effect the absolute owners of it, and it is reasonable and just that they should have the control and disposal of it unless some good cause appears to the contrary." In that case the plaintiff was the absolute owner of the whole property, subject to an annuity of ten thousand dollars payable to himself. The whole of the principal of the trust fund, and all of the income not expressly made payable to the plaintiff, had become vested in him when he reached the age of twenty-one years, by way of resulting trust, as property undisposed of by the will. Apparently the testator had not contemplated such a result, and had made no provision for it, and the court saw no reason why the trust should not be terminated, and the property conveyed to the plaintiff. . . . In the case at bar nothing has happened which the testator did not anticipate, and for which he has not made provision. It is plainly his will that neither the income nor any part of the principal should now be paid to the plaintiff. It is true that the plaintiff's interest is alienable by him, and can be taken by his creditors to pay his debts, but it does not follow that, because the testator has not imposed all possible restrictions, the restrictions which he has imposed should not be carried into effect. The decision in *[Broadway National] Bank v. Adams*, 133 Mass. 170, rests upon the doctrine that a testator has a right to dispose of his own property with such restrictions and limitations, not repugnant to law, as he sees fit, and that his intentions ought to be carried out unless they contravene some positive rule of law, or are against public policy. The rule contended for by the plaintiff in that case was founded upon the same considerations as that contended for by the plaintiff in this, and the grounds on which this court decline to follow the English rule in that case are applicable to this; and for the reasons there given we are unable to see that the directions of the testator to the trustees, to pay the money to the plaintiff when he reaches the age of twenty-five and thirty years, and not before, are against public policy, or are so far inconsistent with the rights of property given to the plaintiff that they should not be carried into effect. It cannot be said that these restrictions upon the plaintiff's possession and control of the property are altogether useless, for there is not the same danger that he will spend the property while it is in the hands of the trustees as there would be if it were in his own. . . .

Notes and Questions

1. *Claflin* is the leading case applying the "material purpose doctrine," sometimes known as the "Claflin Doctrine," that beneficiaries may not force the termination of trusts whose "material purpose" has yet to be accomplished. This is the prevailing judicial view. *See* William F. Fratcher, Scott on Trusts § 337 (4th ed. 1987); *but see Fisher v. Ladd*, 268 S.E.2d 20 (N.C. Ct. App. 1980) (allowing termination by agreement of all living beneficiaries). On the other hand, a trust may be prematurely terminated (or modified) with the consent of all the beneficiaries if no material purpose of the settlor exists for trust continuation. *See* UTC § 411(b).

What evidence indicates a "material purpose" that prevents early termination? Consider the following candidates:

(a) Terms describing the trust as one for education and maintenance. *In re Estate of Brown*, 528 A.2d 752 (Vt. 1987) (no early termination).

(b) Income payable to one beneficiary for life, with a remainder over to another with principal payable to income beneficiary but not for primary support. *See Estate of Bonardi*, 871 A.2d 103 (N.J. App. Div. 2005) (material purpose barred termination in favor of income beneficiary).

(c) Income or principal payable "in the Trustee's discretion." *Compare* 3d Rest. Trusts § 65, cmt. e (early termination may still be possible), *with* 2d Rest. Trusts § 337, cmts. l, m, n (no early termination).

The typical judicial approach has been that, because a material purpose exists as a result of a trust being spendthrifted, such an irrevocable trust cannot be terminated even with the consent of all trust beneficiaries. *See, e.g., White v. Fleet Bank of Maine*, 875 A.2d 680 (Me. 2005) (decided under pre-UTC law). *But see In re Pike Family Trusts*, 38 A.3d 329 (Me. 2012) (applying UTC § 411(c) that spendthrift provision is not presumed to be a material purpose). Because spendthrift provisions tend to be boilerplate and thereby inserted in trusts without much thought, UTC § 411(c) takes the position that a spendthrift provision "is not presumed to constitute a material purpose of the trust." *Accord* 3d Rest. Trusts § 65, cmt. e. Based on Kansas law, which modified UTC § 401(c) to presume that a material purpose exists if any trust interest is spendthrifted, a material purpose was found because it was not rebutted. *See Trust D Created Under the Last Will and Testament of Harry Darby*, 234 P.3d 793 (Kan. 2010).

2. If a material purpose exists for trust continuation so that trust termination will not be allowed under the *Claflin* doctrine, a trust modification that is not inconsistent with the trust's material purpose may be permitted. *See* 3d Rest. Trusts § 65, cmt. f.

3. A beneficiary desiring to change an irrevocable trust while the settlor is alive has the option of trying to convince the settlor to endorse the change, that is, the settlor would state that no material purpose remains for trust continuation. Even if a material purpose exists for trust continuation, a settlor may also be able to revoke an irrevocable trust if all trust beneficiaries agree. *See* UTC § 411(a).

Once the settlor has died, however, negotiations to modify or terminate a trust are no longer possible. Should courts be reluctant to fix a settlor's plans in stone? Compare note 1, describing courts' general willingness to enforce continuing restrictions on beneficiaries' behavior. *See also In re Trust under Will of Flint,* 118 A.3d 182 (Del. Ch. Ct. 2015). Restatement (Third) of Trusts § 65 (2) takes the position that, after the settlor's death, an irrevocable trust may be terminated or modified even if a material purpose exists, provided the consent of all trust beneficiaries is obtained and the court finds "that the reason for termination or modification outweighs the material purpose."

4. Do you think a court should allow a partial modification or termination if all of the trust beneficiaries do not give their consent? *See* UTC § 411.

5. Assuming a bona fide dispute exists, *see Fleisch v. First Am. Bank*, 710 N.E.2d 1281 (Ill. App. Ct. 1999) (no bona fide dispute), a court should approve the settlement of a will contest even though it will defeat the testator's purpose to establish a trust. *See* 3d Rest. Trusts § 65, cmt. h. *Contra Adams v. Link*, 145 A.2d 753 (Conn. 1958) (court refused to approve a will-contest settlement agreement because the compromise would have defeated the testator's purpose to establish a trust called for in the will).

6. In contrast to the traditional approach in this country, courts in England have broad power to modify or terminate trusts for the benefit of the beneficiaries. English Variation of Trusts Act, 1958, 6 & Eliz. 2, ch 53. Do you favor allowing courts to eliminate the power of the dead hand in this context? What standards would you apply?

Problems

1. In the following situations, can the beneficiary (or beneficiaries) compel the trustee to terminate the trust if the settlor is dead?

(a) Megan created a living trust to pay the income to Megan's daughter, Jennie, until Jennie reaches age 35, and then to pay Jennie the principal, but if Jennie should die before attaining 35, the trustee is to pay the principal to Jennie's estate. Jennie seeks to terminate the trust when she is 30.

(b) Ray created a trust to pay income to his wife Dorothy for life and on her death to pay the principal to their son Robert. Dorothy and Robert wish to terminate the trust.

(c) Wilbur set up a testamentary trust to pay income to his friend Ed as necessary for Ed's support, and on Ed's death to pay the accumulated income, if any, and the principal to their friend Larry. Ed seeks termination, with Larry's consent.

2. You are a bank trust officer with responsibility for the Partridge Testamentary Trust, which has assets of $100,000. George Partridge died a widower. The residuary clause of his will created the trust to provide income to his only child, Macy, for her life, with the principal to go to her surviving children. The trust has neither a spendthrift clause nor any powers to invade the principal. Macy, now 42 and divorced, has a 22-year-old son, Jonathan. Macy and Jonathan have asked that you terminate the trust and distribute the principal to them. What is your response?

Selected Referencse:

Richard C. Ausness, *Sherlock Holmes and the Problem of the Dead Hand: The Modification and Termination of "Irrevocable" Trusts*, 28 Quinnipiac Prob. L.J. 237 (2015).

Bradley E.S. Fogel, *Terminating or Modifying Irrevocable Trusts by Consent of the Beneficiaries—A Proposal to Respect the Primacy of the Settlor's Intent*, 50 Real Prop. Tr. & Est. L.J. 337 (2016).

2. Indestructible Trusts

Suppose the settlor had as an irrefutable material purpose that the trust last for a long time, for example, 200 years, 500 years, or even in perpetuity. Should the beneficiaries be able to compel trust termination at some point or can a settlor, long dead, continue to impose her will so that the trust will be indestructible? Restatement (Second) of Property § 2.1 (Donative Transfers) sets forth the well-established common law rule that a trust may be prematurely terminated with the consent of all beneficiaries after the expiration of the applicable rule against perpetuities:

Restatement (Second) of Property (Donative Transfers)

§ 2.1 Duration of Trust

A trust created in a donative transfer, which has not terminated within the period of the rule against perpetuities as applied to such trust, shall continue until the trust terminates in accordance with its terms, except that a trust, other than a charitable trust, may be terminated at any time after the period of the rule against perpetuities expires by a written agreement of all of the beneficiaries of the trust delivered to the trustee, which agreement informs the trustee that the trust is terminated and gives the trustee directions as to the distribution of the trust property.

Comment

When all the beneficiaries of a trust are ascertained and sui juris, they, acting together, can force a termination of the trust, unless thereby a material purpose of the trust will be defeated. . . . The rule of this section places a limit on the period of time that the creator of a trust is allowed to force the effectuation of the material purpose of the trust, when the continued accomplishment of such purpose is against the wishes and desires of the current beneficial owners of the trust property. Some limit is desirable in order to prevent the possible undesirable social consequences of the views of persons long removed from the current scene influencing unduly the wishes and desires of those living in the present.

Without an effective rule against perpetuities, it would seem that a trust may be made indestructible even though all trust beneficiaries would desire the trust to be terminated. Although Restatement (Third) of Trusts § 65(2) allows a court to compel termination even though a material purpose remains for trust continuation, it is highly unlikely that a court would intervene if a state had repealed its rule against perpetuities for the express purpose to permit perpetual trusts. Unfortunately, that is precisely what has been happening in recent years. Almost 20 states have repealed their rule against perpetuities for the express purpose of encouraging wealthy non-residents and residents to create dynasty (perpetual) trusts to exploit the federal generation-skipping transfer tax system. *See generally* Ira Mark Bloom, *The GST Tax Is Killing the Rule Against Perpetuities*, 87 Tax Notes 569 (2000). We further consider the perpetuities repeal movement at the end of the next chapter.

Note: Representing Unidentified and Incapacitated Beneficiaries

Even if there is no material purpose for trust continuation, or the perpetuities period has run, a trust may not be terminated by the beneficiaries unless all trust beneficiaries consent to termination. This can be a very serious problem since many trusts have beneficiaries who are unascertained or unborn. One possible solution is for a court to appoint a guardian ad litem to represent such unidentified persons, as well as to represent incapacitated persons, especially minors.

Hatch v. Riggs National Bank, 361 F.2d 559 (D.C. Cir. 1966), illustrates how courts might use a guardian ad litem. Anna Hatch created an irrevocable trust reserving a lifetime income and a testamentary power of appointment to herself. Her next of kin were to take the property if she did not exercise the power. When she had trouble living on the trust income, Anna sought to revoke the trust, but she needed consent from her next of kin, who would not be identified until her death. To solve the problem, the court suggested that a guardian ad litem be appointed to negotiate on their behalf.

UTC § 305(c) would permit a guardian ad litem acting on behalf of unidentified persons to "consider general benefits accruing to the living members of the individual's family." In fact, UTC § 305 broadens representation to allow court appointment of a representative to act on non-judicial matters for represented persons, as well as the traditional representative role in judicial proceedings.

The doctrine of "virtual representation" might also be effective to modify an irrevocable trust when the consent of all beneficiaries cannot be obtained. The "virtual representation" doctrine relies upon the logic that one person can speak for an unknown person who, if identified, would be in the same situation as the speaker. For example, suppose Tracy has a remainder interest following her mother's life estate, but if Tracy does not survive her mother, Tracy's (yet unborn) children would take her interest. Tracy's consent to modify an administrative provision probably would bind her children because when protecting her own interests, she will protect the unborn beneficiaries. Virtual representation is attractive because it allows currently living persons to make some decisions even though other beneficiaries may appear later.

Uniform Trust Code

Section 304. Representation by Person Having Substantially Identical Interests.

Unless otherwise represented, a minor, incapacitated, or unborn individual, or a person whose identity or location is unknown and not reasonably ascertainable, may be represented by and bound by another having a substantially identical interest with respect to the particular question or dispute, but only to the extent there is no conflict of interest between the representative and the person represented.

Questions

1. In a state without an effective rule against trust duration, why would application of the *Claflin* doctrine mean that an irrevocable trust could be indestructible in perpetuity? Might such a perpetual trust be prematurely terminated if all of the living beneficiaries desire to terminate the trust? What might be some of the adverse societal consequences if the trust is not terminated?

2. Why will virtual representation of unborn, unascertained, and incapacitated beneficiaries ordinarily be ineffective for trust termination?

Selected References

Martin D. Begleiter, *The Guardian Ad Litem in Estate Proceedings*, 20 Willamette L. Rev. 643 (1984).

William R. Culp, Jr., and Briani Bennett Mellen, *Trust Decanting: An Overview and Introduction to Creative Planning Opportunities*, 45 Real Prop. Tr. & Est. L.J. 1 (2010).

Gail B. Bird, *Trust Termination: Unborn, Living, and Dead Hands—Too Many Fingers in the Trust Pie*, 36 Hastings L.J. 563 (1985).

Thomas E. Simmons, *Decanting and Its Alternatives: Remodeling and Revamping Irrevocable Trusts*, 55 S.D. L. Rev. 253 (2010).

D. Judicial Modification or Termination

The following case raises the issue of whether and when a court may modify the trust terms.

In re Trusteeship of Mayo

105 N.W.2d 900 (Minn. 1960)

Dell, Chief Justice.

Appeals from orders of the district court denying the petitions of Esther Mayo Hartzell, as beneficiary, for orders authorizing the trustees of two separate trusts created by the late Dr. Charles H. Mayo on August 17, 1917, and March 28, 1919, to deviate from identical investment restrictions in the trust instruments or to construe the term "other forms of income bearing property" as used therein as authorizing investment of trust funds in corporate stock. The donor died May 26, 1939. . . .

Charles and William Mayo

With reference to investments the provisions of both trusts are in substance as follows:

> ". . . The TRUSTEES shall hold said property as a trust fund and collect the interest, income and profits therefrom as the same accrue; manage, care for and protect said fund all in accordance with their best judgment and discretion, invest and re-invest the same in real estate mortgages, municipal bonds or any other form of income bearing property (but not real estate nor corporate stock), ..." (Italics supplied.)

At the time of the hearing the value of the assets of the first trust was approximately $1,000,000, invested mostly in municipal bonds and in 1,944 shares of common stock of the Kahler Corporation, the latter coming into the trust at the time of its creation from the donor. The value of the assets of the second trust at the time of the hearing was approximately $186,000 invested mostly in municipal bonds. . . .

Petitioner urges that the donor's ultimate and dominant intention was to pre-serve the value of the trust corpus and that this will be circumvented unless the court authorizes the trustees to deviate from the investment provisions of the trusts and invest part of the funds in corporate stocks; that it is common practice of trustees of large trusts which have no restrictive investment provisions (including the First National Bank of Minneapolis, one of the trustees in both trusts here) to invest substantial proportions of trust assets in corporate stocks to protect such trusts against inflation, and she asserts that if no deviation is permitted and the next 20 years parallel the last 20 years the ultimate beneficiaries of these trusts will be presented with assets having less than one-fourth of the value which they had at the time of the donor 's death.

In opposition to the petition, the trustees refer to the donor's clear intention, as expressed in the trust instruments, that no part of the trust funds should be invested in real estate or corporate stocks, and urge that, since no emergency or change of circumstances which could not have been foreseen or experienced by the donor during his lifetime has been shown, no deviation from the donor's clearly expressed intention would be justified. They urge that the rule is well established that where prospective changes of conditions are substantially known to or anticipated by the settlor of a trust the courts will not grant a deviation from its provisions. They point out that the donor here had survived some 20 years after the creation of the trusts during a period in which there had been both a great inflation and a severe depression; that after creating such trusts he had observed the inflation of the post-World-War-I period, the stock market fever of the pre-1929 era, the market crash of 1929, and the subsequent depression and lowering of bond interest rates during the late 1930's; that despite these economic changes he had never altered the investment restrictions in these trusts. . . .

The general principles governing deviation to which this court has adhered whenever the question has been presented are set forth in Restatement, Trusts (2d ed) § 167, comment c:

> "Where by the terms of the trust the scope of investment which would otherwise be proper is restricted, the court will permit the trustee to deviate from the restriction, if, but only if, the accomplishment of the purposes of the trust would otherwise be defeated or substantially impaired. Thus the court will permit the investment if owing to changes since the creation of the trust, such as the fall in interest rates, the danger of inflation, and other circumstances, the accomplishment of the purposes of the trust would otherwise be defeated or substantially impaired. Where by the terms of the trust the trustee is not permitted to invest in shares of stock, the court will not permit such an investment merely because it would be advantageous to the beneficiaries to make it."

In applying the foregoing rule the courts have adopted certain rules for guidance. It is only in exceptional circumstances described as cases of emergency, urgency, or necessity that deviation from the intention of the donor, as evidenced by the trust instrument, has been authorized. In most of the cases where deviation was authorized, the fact that the donor could not have foreseen the changed circumstances played an important part. Even under such circumstances deviation will not be authorized unless it is reasonably certain that the purposes of the trust would otherwise be defeated or impaired in carrying out the donor's dominant intention.

In our opinion the evidence here, together with economic and financial conditions which may properly be judicially noticed, compels us to hold that unless deviation is ordered the dominant intention of the donor to prevent a loss of the principal of the two trusts will be frustrated....

It appears without substantial dispute that if deviation is not permitted the accomplishment of the purposes of the trusts will be substantially impaired because of changed conditions due to inflation since the trusts were created; that unless deviation is allowed the assets of the trusts, within the next 20 years, will, in all likelihood, be worth less than one-fourth of the value they had at the time of the donor's death. To avoid this we conclude that in equity the trustees should have the right and be authorized to deviate from the restrictive provisions of the trusts by permitting them, when and as they deem it advisable, to invest a reasonable amount of the trust assets in corporate stocks of good, sound investment issues....

Uniform Trust Code

Section 412. Modification or Termination Because of Unanticipated Circumstances or Inability to Administer Trust Effectively.

(a) The court may modify the administrative or dispositive terms of a trust or terminate the trust if, because of circumstances not anticipated by the settlor, modification or termination will further the purposes of the trust. To the extent practicable, the modification must be made in accordance with the settlor's probable intention.

Notes

1. *Mayo* illustrates the application, albeit a very liberal one, of the longstanding doctrine of administrative deviation, often called equitable deviation. *See, e.g., In re Cove Irrevocable Trust*, 893 A.2d 344 (Vt. 2006) (sale of trust property settlor provided should not be sold).

UTC § 412, following the Restatement (Third) of Trusts § 66(1), liberalizes the equitable deviation doctrine by authorizing a change if trust purposes will be furthered, and not only where the purposes of the trust would be defeated or substantially impaired. *See Niemann v. Vaughn Cmty. Church*, 113 P.3d 463 (Wash. 2005) (applying equitable deviation doctrine where change would further trust purposes in a charitable trust) and *In re Estate of Wilson*, on Page 496.

Pursuant to the equitable deviation doctrine, a court may change trust provisions that affect trust administration based on changed circumstances not anticipated by the settlor. *Carnahan v. Johnson*, 711 N.E.2d 1093 (Ohio Ct. App. 1998) (trustee authorized to sell property that settlor had barred trustee from selling). UTC § 412(b) broadens the doctrine to allow for modification of an administrative provision "if continuation of the trust on its existing terms would be impracticable or wasteful or impair the trust's administration." Not all courts, however, have been willing to apply equitable deviation. *See, e.g., Toledo Trust Co. v. Toledo Hospital*, 187 N.E.2d 36 (Ohio 1962) (enforcing a direction to invest only in federal, state, or municipal bonds despite possible ravages of inflation); *In re Trust Under Will of Flint*, 118 A.3d 182 (Del. Ch. 2015) (refusing to allow a directed trust even though all trust beneficiaries requested); *In re Mary R. Latimer Trust*, 78 A.3d 875 (Del. Ch. 2013) (refusing to deviate from terms of a private trust to maintain specific burial plots by allowing for general cemetery maintenance despite anticipated financial deterioration of the cemetery).

2. Until recently, the generally accepted doctrine was that a court should not change dispositive dispositions. *But cf. Univ. of Me. Found. v. Fleet Bank of Me.*, 817 A.2d 871 (Me. 2003) (court allowed partial termination in favor of remainder beneficiary even though income interest spendthrifted). UTC § 412(a), following the lead of Restatement (Third) of Trusts § 66(1), represents a major development by allowing for judicial dispositive deviation, as well as administrative deviation, to carry out the settlor's probable intent. *Compare In re Somers*, 89 P.3d 898 (Kan. 2004) (the court exercised its power under Kansas' version of UTC § 412(a) to partially terminate a trust because of changed circumstances by distributing $3 million to a remainder beneficiary), *with Trust D Created Under the Last Will and Testament of Harry Darby*, 234 P.3d 793 (Kan. 2010) (no reformation because no unanticipated circumstance involved). *See also Kristoff v. Centier Bank*, 985 N.E.2d 20 (Ind. 2013) (modification denied because there were no unanticipated circumstances).

3. Both Restatement (Third) of Trusts § 66, comment d, and UTC § 414(b) authorize a court to terminate a trust that has become uneconomical. UTC § 414(a) would also allow a trustee without judicial approval to terminate trusts of less than $50,000 if "the trustee concludes that the value of the trust property is insufficient to justify the cost of administration." UTC § 417 would also allow a trustee to combine or divide trusts provided "the result does not impair rights of any beneficiary or adversely affect achievement of the purposes of the trust." Trust combination may result in more efficient trust administration, while trust division is frequently useful to better accomplish tax objectives.

Problem

In 1980, Sally created a testamentary trust to accumulate income until Sally's infant child, Carla, began attending college at which time the trustee would pay $10,000 a year for Carla's college tuition. When Carla finished her education, the trust would terminate in favor of Carla's children, but if she had none, then the trust principal would be payable to Carla's brother, Barry. At the time of trust creation, $10,000 reflected the average annual tuition at a private university. By the time Carla began attending a private college, the average annual tuition at a private university far exceeded $10,000. Should a court allow the trustee to invade principal to make up the shortfall in tuition?

Selected Reference

Ronald Chester, *Modification and Termination of Trusts in the 21st Century: The Uniform Trust Code Leads a Quiet Revolution*, 35 Real Prop. Prob. & Tr. J. 697 (2001).

§ 8.05 Charitable Trusts[13]

Because of the broad public policy favoring charitable work, charitable trusts operate under some different rules. First, a charitable trust need not have definite beneficiaries.[14] In most situations, the job of enforcing the trust falls to the state's Attorney General. In addition, a charitable trust is not subject to the Rule Against Perpetuities. *See, e.g.*, *United Bank, Inc. v. Blosser*, 624 S.E.2d 815 (W. Va. 2005).

Finally, there is a long tradition allowing courts to modify charitable trusts to further trust purposes in the face of changed circumstances. In order to qualify for this special treatment, however, a trust must have a "charitable purpose."

Because charitable trusts are also favored under the tax laws, charitable trusts invariably involve compliance with tax rules. Indeed, as Professor Ascher recently opined in his extensive article, "Congress and the federal courts [have] federalized the law of charity." Mark L. Ascher, *Federalization of the Law of Charity*, 67 Vand. L. Rev. 1581 (2014).

A. Creation and Enforcement of Charitable Trusts

St. Mary's Medical Center, Inc. v. McCarthy

829 N.E.2d 1068 (Ind. Ct. App. 2005)

Barnes, J.

St. Mary's Medical Center, Inc. ("St. Mary's") appeals the trial court's entry of declaratory judgment and a permanent injunction in favor of Vincent McCarthy. We reverse.

---

13. Charitable activities my also be carried out in other forms, most significantly, the charitable corporation. In fact, the charitable corporation is the preferred form of organization for charitable activities in the United States. *See* Principles of the Law of Nonprofit Organizations, § 200, Reporter's Note on Statistical Information (Prelim. Draft No. 3, 2005) (IRS statistics reveal there are over 500,000 charitable corporations, about 12,000 charitable trusts, and 122,000 charitable associations that conduct non-religious and private foundation activities).

14. Although there are differences between charitable trusts and charitable corporations, most of the trust law principles apply equally to charitable corporations.

ISSUE

The sole restated issue we consider is whether the trial court properly concluded that St. Mary's cannot demolish a chapel on its campus constructed in the 1950's with funds provided by the estate of one of McCarthy's relatives.

FACTS

In 1950, Cornelia G. Haney executed her last will and testament. . . . The will provided in part as follows, after listing several other dispositions:

> E. Thirty-two (32) per cent thereof to THE CITIZENS NATIONAL BANK OF EVANSVILLE, of Evansville, Indiana, in trust, never- theless, for the use and benefit of ST. MARY'S HOSPITAL, of Evansville, Indiana, upon and subject to the following uses and trusts, to-wit:
>
> * * *
>
> 3. The corpus and income of said trust estate shall be used by said trustee for the purpose of creating at or in connection with said ST. MARY'S HOSPITAL, of Evansville, Indiana, a HANEY MEMORIAL, the exact nature and form of which shall be determined by [a] committee . . . or the successor member or members of said committee, and in furtherance of such purpose said trustee shall expend the corpus and income of the trust estate for the use and benefit of said hospital or transfer the same or any part thereof to said hospital, at any time or from time to time, upon such terms and conditions as the members or a majority of the members of said committee in their sole discretion shall determine and direct the trustee.

Haney died on July 21, 1951. On March 30, 1954, the trust committee decided to use the trust funds to build a chapel at St. Mary's. Construction of the chapel, financed by over $ 250,000 from Haney's estate, was completed in early 1956. On February 29, 1956, the chapel was consecrated in Catholic fashion and dedicated as the Chapel of Mary, Queen, with a plaque noting it was a memorial to Haney. . . .

In 2003, St. Mary's determined that it would be necessary to expand its facilities, and that such expansion would require demolition of the chapel funded by Haney's estate. In 2004, St. Mary's took steps to deconsecrate and dismantle the chapel, including moving the Eucharist to another chapel at the hospital and removing the stained glass windows. As evidenced by local newspaper coverage . . . , the decision to demolish the Chapel of Mary, Queen, was unacceptable to many persons in the Evansville community.

On July 30, 2004, McCarthy filed his complaint for declaratory judgment and a permanent injunction to prevent St. Mary's from demolishing the chapel. McCarthy is the grandson of Daniel McCarthy, one of the trust committee members who voted to use the funds from Haney's estate to build the chapel. He is also a distant relative of Haney; he is her first cousin, three times removed, and was born in 1965, or fourteen years after her death. On September 28, 2004, the trial court entered its judgment, with accompanying findings and conclusions, providing that St. Mary's "is permanently enjoined from destroying the Chapel of Mary, Queen" and requiring St. Mary's to restore the chapel to its original condition. . . . St. Mary's now appeals.

ANALYSIS

McCarthy argued before the trial court and argues on appeal that Haney's bequest to St. Mary's for the creation of a Haney Memorial essentially was intended to create a charitable trust, with St. Mary's now trustee for the donated assets that were converted into the Chapel of Mary, Queen. He essentially contends that the first trust created by Haney's will for the benefit of St. Mary's morphed into a second trust with St. Mary's as trustee when it received the funds for construction of the chapel. St. Mary's counters first that McCarthy, who is separated from Haney by seven degrees of consanguinity, lacked standing to initiate this action, and second that there is no current charitable trust in this case. . . .

Turning first to McCarthy's standing, the general rule is that only those persons who have a personal stake in the outcome of the litigation and who show that they have suffered or were in immediate danger of suffering a direct injury as a result of the complained-of conduct will be found to have standing. *State ex rel. Cittadine v. Indiana Dep't of Transp.*, 790 N.E.2d 978, 979 (Ind. 2003). "Absent this showing, complainants may not invoke the jurisdiction of the court." Id. A plaintiff must have more than a general interest common to all members of the public. Id.

This court held in *Boice v. Mallers*, 121 Ind. App. 210, 216-17, 96 N.E.2d 342, 344-45 (1950), trans. denied.

> The law is well settled that inasmuch as the enforcement of public charities are matters of public interest the attorney general appearing as a public officer is the proper party to maintain litigation involving questions of public charitable trusts. And an individual member of the public has no right as such to maintain a suit of such character.

In the present case, the Attorney General was notified of McCarthy's lawsuit but declined to intervene. McCarthy also concedes that he is not an heir-at-law of Haney. Nevertheless, in order to address the merits of this case we will assume without deciding that McCarthy, a person with ties to the Haney family whose grandfather voted to use the funds from Haney's estate to build the chapel, had standing to bring this action.

> Resolution of this case turns on construction of Haney's will. . . . "The 'four-corners' rule has long been the law in Indiana and requires that, as to any matter expressly covered by a written instrument, the provisions therein, if unambiguous, determine the terms of the instrument." [*East v. Estate of East*, 785 N.E.2d 597, 601 (Ind. Ct. App. 2003).]

McCarthy insists that St. Mary's holds the Chapel of Mary, Queen, as trustee for the benefit of those whose use it, such as medical personnel and visitors at the hospital. We note the difference between an absolute devise or gift and one in trust to a charitable institution.[15] "In the former, the property becomes an asset of the corporation to be used in such manner as the corporation deemed best, while in the latter, the property is held by the corporation, not as its own, but in the capacity as a trustee, or as an instrumentality of the settlor in carrying out the directions." *Stockton v. Northwestern Branch of Women's Foreign Missionary Soc'y of Methodist Episcopal Church*, 127 Ind. App. 193, 201, 133 N.E.2d 875, 878-79 (1956). Whether the language of a will or other document was intended to create a charitable trust, binding on the recipient, has been litigated in a number of cases, here and in other jurisdictions, over the course of many years. One commentator has stated generally:

> The court will examine carefully all the clauses of the instrument and the situation of the parties in order to decide whether the phrases used were intended to be binding upon the donee and to make him trustee for charity, or whether he was to be an absolute owner with only moral obligations by reason of the suggestions or requests from the donor as to the use of the property given.

George Gleason Bogert & George Taylor Bogert, The Law of Trusts and Trustees § 324, pp. 376–77 (1992). "In determining the question of the testator's intention, the generally accepted rules of construction must apply and it will be presumed that he used precatory words in their ordinary and usual sense unless there is something to show that he intended that they be given a different meaning." *Lewis v. Atkins*, 122 Ind. App. 618, 623, 105 N.E.2d 183, 185 (1952). "The mere statement in a will of the purpose for which the subject property is to be used does not create a trust." *Ebenezer 's Old People's Home of Evangelical Ass'n of Ebenezer, N. Y. v. South Bend Old People's Home*, 113 Ind. App. 382, 391, 48 N.E.2d 851, 854 (1943) (holding that language in will devising property to "an institution in the City of South Bend . . . which has for its purpose of its existence the maintenance of a home for old people irrespective of their religious beliefs upon at least a partial charitable basis" did not create a charitable trust, and devisee was entitled to retain property even though it was unable to operate said institution).

It has also been noted as a general proposition that charitable trusts are favored by the law, "and the most liberal rules of construction will be employed to sustain and uphold every attempt of a person to donate his property to a charitable use. . . . The charitable character of the trust being made apparent, all doubts are to be resolved in its favor." *Hays v. Harmon*, 809 N.E.2d 460, 467 (Ind. Ct. App. 2004), trans. denied.

---

15. We reject St. Mary's assertion that Haney's devise to St. Mary's, whether construed as a gift or a trust, was not a charitable one because it was intended to create a memorial in her family's name. It is well-settled that a gift does not lose its charitable character simply because the donor also wants the gift to be recognized as a personal or family memorial. See *Scobey v. Beckman*, 111 Ind. App. 574, 580-81, 41 N.E.2d 847, 850 (1942) ("It is our opinion, therefore, that a bequest for the support of a minister, or for the payment of a minister's salary, or the furnishing of a house in which a minister may live, should all be recognized as gifts for charitable uses. The fact that the testatrix also desired to perpetuate by this gift the memory of her deceased son, does not render this devise less charitable."). Here, Haney clearly intended to make a charitable gift to St. Mary's, which could be considered either a medical or religious institution, and the chapel clearly is a religious building.

In Hays, however, there was no question of whether the decedent intended to create a charitable trust by his will. The will expressly referenced the creation of a trust. The issue in Hays was whether, given the clear intention to create a trust, the terms of the trust were sufficiently definite to make it valid. *Id.* at 469. Here, we must address the initial question: whether Haney intended to create a perpetual charitable trust after her assets were transferred to St. Mary's. There is also no question here that Haney intended to make a charitable gift of some kind to St. Mary's; the question is what form the gift took. That we should be liberal in construing testamentary charitable gifts does not mean that we may create a charitable trust out of whole cloth.

Both McCarthy and the trial court, in concluding that Haney devised her property to St. Mary's in the form of a charitable trust, have relied upon *Bible Institute Colportage Ass'n v. St. Joseph Bank & Trust Co.*, 118 Ind. App. 592, 75 N.E.2d 666 (1947). There, two judges of this court concluded that a devise to the Bible Institute Colportage Association of Chicago "to be used in the publication and dissemination of evangelical Christian literature in harmony with its Articles of Incorporation" created a charitable trust that was for the benefit of those who might receive the literature and was binding on the Association's successor as trustee of the bequeathed assets. *Id.* at 606-07, 75 N.E.2d at 672. Judge Royse wrote an opinion concurring in result only, pointing out that the majority's conclusion seemed to conflict with the established rule that a mere statement in a will of an intended purpose for a devise to a charity does not convert the gift into a charitable trust. *Id.* at 608-10, 75 N.E.2d at 673 (Royse, J., concurring in result) (citing *Ebenezer*, 113 Ind. App. at 391, 48 N.E.2d at 854).

Another case in Indiana, besides Ebenezer, that reached the conclusion that a devise in a will was an outright gift, and not a charitable trust, was Stockton. There, a will devised assets to the Methodist Church "to the Northwestern Branch of the Women's Foreign Missionary Society to be used for China, India and Africa ...." *Stockton*, 127 Ind. App. at 198, 133 N.E.2d at 877. This court held this devise was "a gift absolute without restrictions as to use" and did not create a charitable trust. *Id.* at 201, 133 N.E.2d at 879. In another case from Ohio, a will devised a house to a church "to be used as a parsonage." *First Presbyterian Church of Salem v. Tarr*, 63 Ohio App. 286, 26 N.E.2d 597, 597 (Ohio Ct. App. 1939). The Ohio Court of Appeals held that this language did not devise the home in trust to the church for charitable purposes, and the church received a fee simple title to the house and could sell it rather than using it as a parsonage. *Id.* at 599.

We conclude the Colportage case, even if we were to assume it was correctly decided, does not control the outcome here. In the Colportage case, evidently the bequeathed funds had not been used for their stated purpose and funds remained for that use, and could continue being used in that way indefinitely or until the funds ran out. Here, to the extent there was a stated purpose for the funds in this case—i.e. for the creation of a Haney Memorial—that purpose was met when the chapel was constructed and a plaque memorializing Haney was placed there. Additionally, the general rule is that the mere statement of the purpose for a charitable devise does not transform it into a charitable trust. See, e.g., 14 C.J.S. Charities § 31 (1991). Beyond that, Haney's will says nothing as to how long the memorial had to exist in order for the devise to be valid, or what would happen should St. Mary's no longer want the chapel before the end of its useful life. . . .

Haney's will also expressly states that the corpus and income of the trust created for the benefit of St. Mary's should be used for creation of the Haney Memorial. It is axiomatic that transferring title and the entire equitable interest in property to one person as sole beneficiary and sole trustee destroys the existing trust. See, e.g., Ind. Code § 30-4-2-8; Restatement (Third) of Trusts, § 69 (2003). Thus, the trust created by Haney's will clearly was terminated when St. Mary's, that trust's sole named beneficiary, also received the entire corpus of the trust for the creation of the Chapel of Mary, Queen. . . .

Even if Haney's will did not create a charitable trust with St. Mary's as trustee of the funds she bequeathed to it, McCarthy's argument also essentially amounts, in the alternative, to a claim that the bequest/gift was subject to a condition subsequent. That is, he seems to contend that the devise is revocable should St. Mary's want to destroy the chapel at any time before it collapses of its own accord after an indeterminate period of use. "Although no definite or particular form of expression is absolutely essential to the creation of a condition subsequent, it must be manifest from the terms of the will that the devise or bequest was made on condition and the absence of the words usually used for such purpose is significant." *Ebenezer*, 113 Ind. App. at 390, 48 N.E.2d at 854. Conditions subsequent are not favored in law and always receive a strict construction. Id. A condition subsequent will not be implied from a mere declaration in the deed that the grant or devise is made for a special purpose. Id.

The clear majority rule is "that nothing short of express provisions for forfeiture and either a reverter, a gift over or a right to retake the property in the donor or his heirs would enable a donor to effectively impose a condition subsequent." Bogert, § 324 p. 392. An application of this rule is apparent in *Herron v. Stanton*, 79 Ind. App. 683, 147 N.E. 305 (1920). There, a decedent's will devised assets for the creation of an art gallery and school in Indianapolis, upon condition that the gallery and/or school be perpetually named for the decedent, John Herron. In the event the gallery and/or school no longer wanted to use Herron's name, the will provided that it would be divested of the assets and such would be distributed to other charitable institutions in Indianapolis. This court held that the devise was a valid charitable gift with a valid condition subsequent or conditional limitation upon the gift. 79 Ind. App. at 695-96, 147 N.E. at 308.

Here, Haney's will contains nothing to indicate the required duration of the Haney Memorial, in contrast to John Herron's will expressly stating that the art school created by his assets should be named for him in perpetuity. Haney's will also contains no reverter language to indicate what should happen to the chapel, or the funds used to build it, if St. Mary's no longer wanted the chapel on its premises, again in contrast to Herron's will. . . .

Here, given the disfavor of conditions subsequent and the absence of clear reverter language or the required length of any Haney Memorial created by Haney's estate, the most that can be said of her devise to St. Mary's through her trust committee was that she and the committee expressed confidence in St. Mary's that it would "use the property so far as may be reasonable and practicable to effect the purpose of the grant." *Gray*, 64 A.2d at 110. Indeed, the Chapel of Mary, Queen apparently was an integral part of St. Mary's for nearly fifty years, until such time as the hospital's governance decided that it was no longer practicable for the chapel to remain and, in fact, was an impediment to expansion of the hospital. We will not second-guess the reasonableness of St. Mary's determination on this point. We also note that although charitable gifts should be encouraged so far as possible, charities themselves should not be bound to one particular use of bequeathed property for multiple generations unless they are on clear notice that such is a requirement of the bequest.[16]

In any event, there are Indiana cases suggesting that St. Mary's use of the chapel for nearly fifty years constituted substantial compliance with any charitable trust or condition subsequent imposed by Haney's will. For example, in *Higbee v. Rodeman*, 129 Ind. 244, 28 N.E. 442 (1891), the court considered the effect of a donation of real estate to a township with the condition that it be used for school purposes. The opinion holds that even if this represented a valid condition subsequent, which the court doubted, the township substantially complied with the condition by using the property for school purposes for thirty years and that it could then sell the property. *Id.* at 247, 28 N.E. at 443. A similar case is *General Convention of New Church in U.S. v. Smith*, 52 Ind. App. 136, 100 N.E. 384 (1913). There, the decedent bequeathed $2,000 and real estate to his brother, which pursuant to the will the brother promised to use to build a library and hall for the benefit of a church organization. Apparently, the brother died twenty years after the library and hall were built and his heirs sought to recover the property over the objections of the church organization. This court first expressed skepticism that the brother was intended to hold the property in trust for the church organization. We went on to hold that even if there had been a trust, "the purposes of the bequest were fully carried out by the erection of this building of which plaintiffs had the use and benefit for nearly 20 years, and it does not appear that they are still entitled to its use and benefit. In other words, it does not appear that the trust, if any was created, has not been fully terminated." *Id.* at 138, 100 N.E. at 385.

In sum, in looking at the four corners of Haney's will there is nothing expressing an intent that St. Mary's was to hold any assets bequeathed to it as a charitable trust. There also is nothing in the will indicating the existence of a valid condition subsequent upon the bequest. There is no indication the trust committee created by Haney's will imposed any such condition or created a second trust with St. Mary's as trustee.

16. There was evidence presented here that the Chapel of Mary, Queen could stand for another fifty to seventy-five years, if not longer. McCarthy essentially asserts that St. Mary's must allow the chapel to stand for at least that long; the wording of the trial court's order also would seem to require St. Mary's to do nothing that might hasten the chapel's demise and that it would have to wait until the chapel crumbled of its own accord before it could put the property on which it stands to another use. We decline to so hold in the absence of clear evidence that St. Mary's knew it was irrevocably tying up a substantial piece of its grounds for at least 100 to 125 years when it agreed to use the funds from Haney's estate to build the chapel.

Finally, even if there was a charitable trust or valid condition subsequent, St. Mary's use of the chapel for nearly fifty years represents substantial compliance with any such trust or condition.

CONCLUSION

The trial court erred as a matter of law in concluding that St. Mary's cannot dismantle the Chapel of Mary, Queen. Haney's will neither created a charitable trust with St. Mary's as trustee of the devised assets, nor gave property to St. Mary's as a gift with a condition subsequent. The trust committee also imposed no restrictions on St. Mary's use of the chapel built with funds from Haney's estate, except for having to indicate that it was a memorial to Haney in accordance with her will. We reverse the declaratory judgment and permanent injunction against St. Mary's and direct that judgment be entered in favor of St. Mary's.

Reversed.

Notes

1. As in the case of private express trusts, *McCarthy* illustrates that a charitable trust will only arise if intended by a charitably-minded transferor. That a transferor had charitable purpose in mind for contributed funds does not mean that a trust was intended; rather the words may be considered precatory in nature.

2. If the requisite trust intent is lacking, the likely option is that the transferor intended an absolute gift to a charitable organization, as was found in *McCarthy. Accord Isanogel Ctr., Inc. v. Father Flanagan's Boy's Home, Inc.*, 839 N.E.2d 237 (Ind. Ct. App. 2005). If an absolute gift was not intended, then a charitable gift subject to a condition subsequent may have been intended with a forfeiture in favor of the transferor or the transferor's successors, effectively a reversion. *See, e.g., Tenn. Div. of the United Daughters of the Confederacy v. Vanderbilt Univ.*, 174 S.W.3d 98 (Tenn. Ct. App. 2005) (transferor corporation would be entitled to return of gifted funds, based on present value of contribution, if it ceased to use the name "Confederate Memorial" on a dormitory). Alternatively, the charitable donee may forfeit the gift on the happening of the condition either in favor of another charity or in favor of a non-charitable beneficiary. In the latter case, the gift over would be subject to any applicable rule against perpetuities.

3. *McCarthy* also involved the issue of standing: Who is entitled to ensure that the terms of a charitable gift are carried out? Clearly, the state attorney general has standing to enforce charitable trusts (as well as charitable corporations). As explained by Professor Brody (who was the Reporter for ALI project on Principles of the Law of Nonprofit Organizations) in her article entitled *Charity Governance: What's Trust Law Got to Do with It?*, 80 Chi.-Kent. L. Rev. 641, 672 (2005):

> Every state attorney general enjoys the role known as 'parens patriae'—inherited from the English view of the sovereign as father of the country—to oversee the performance of charitable trusts and their fiduciaries. Attorney

general oversight extends, generally, to those nonprofit corporations that are charities.

4. Relators, persons hired by the attorney general to act on the state's behalf, will also have standing, as will persons with a special interest in the enforcement of the charitable trust. *See* 2d Rest. Trusts § 391. For example, if a charitable trust is created to benefit a law school, the school would have a special interest in having the trust enforced. *But see Lucker v. Bayside Cemetery*, 979 N.Y.S.2d 8 (N.Y. App. Div. 2013) (denying "special interest" status to family members of deceased individuals who purchased perpetual care contracts because as a group they were neither "sharply defined" or "limited in number.").

5. A current and controversial issue is whether the settlor has standing to enforce a trust or other charitable gift that contains restrictions if the settlor has not reserved the enforcement right in the trust instrument or in the deed of gift. The issue is important because the state attorney general may decide not to get involved in a case, as in *McCarthy*, or the attorney general may have a conflict of interest. Denial of standing is the usual result. *See, e.g., Russell v. Yale Univ.*, 737 A.2d 941 (Conn. App. Ct. 1999) (denying standing to settlor's heirs because settlor would not have standing). *See also Courtenay C. & Lucy Patten Davis Found. v. Colo. State Univ. Research Found.*, 320 P.3d 1115 (Wyo. 2014) (denying standing to donor to enforce the terms of the gift not in trust). In *Carl J. Herzog Found. v. Univ. of Bridgeport*, 699 A.2d 995 (Conn. 1997), the Supreme Court of Connecticut denied standing to the donor in a suit against a university under the Uniform Management of Institutional Funds Act based on the common law principle denying a settlor standing to sue under a charitable trust absent the reservation of that right. *But see Smithers v. St. Luke's-Roosevelt Hosp. Ctr.*, 281 A.D.2d 127 (N.Y. 2001) (donor's estate had standing to enforce $10 million gift to hospital).

UTC § 405(c) makes a dramatic change in the standing area by granting standing to the settlor as the default rule. *Contra* 2d Rest. Trusts § 391.

The newly-adopted Uniform Prudent Management of Institutional Funds Act, which applies to charitable trusts that have a charitable institution as trustee, has no provision on donor standing. On the other hand, a preliminary ALI draft on Principles of the Law of Nonprofit Organizations (Section 405) would give a donor standing but only if the instrument so provided, a sufficient amount was involved, and suit was brought within a reasonable time.

Question

Donor contributed $1 million to the UCLA Foundation to establish an endowed chair with the proviso that the funds would be transferred to another school within the University of California system under certain circumstances. Donor claimed that UCLA failed to properly use the funds and sued for specific performance claiming a breach of contract. UCLA claimed a charitable trust was created and only the Attorney General could sue. What should be the result? *See L.B. Research & Educ. Found. v. UCLA Found.*, 130 Cal. App. 4th 171 (2005).

The Hershey (Chocolate) Trust Story: The Attorney General's Right to Protect Broader Public Interests at the Expense of the Settlor's Intended Charitable Beneficiaries

For over 100 years, the sweet smell of chocolate has wafted over Hershey, Pennsylvania. The struggle to keep things that way evolved into a dispute about the appropriate role of attorneys general in supervising charitable trusts and other charities.

Hershey started as a classic company "model town," created when Milton Hershey moved his confectionary business from Philadelphia at the beginning of the last century. Among much else, Milton Hershey and his wife Catherine founded the Milton Hershey School for underprivileged children, supported by a charitable trust funded with Hershey company stock. As a result, the trust also became the controlling shareholder of the corporation. The resulting concentrations—company stock in the trust and trustee power in the company—set the stage for conflict.

In 2002, the trustees, acting pursuant to Milton Hershey's express grant of the power to sell any trust securities, announced plans to take bids for all of the trust's remaining shares of Hershey stock. The trustees' laudable goal was to diversify their investments and maximize the value of trust assets for the School, thereby fulfilling Milton Hershey's specific charitable wishes for the School as charitable beneficiary. Fearing the plant closures that could follow from loss of local control, government officials, workers, managers, union leaders, and local businesspeople objected. The Pennsylvania Attorney General—in the role of supervising charities—claimed the authority to prevent the trustees from selling the stock (despite their authority under the trust document) if the sale would be inimical to the public interest. Traditionally, an attorney general's supervision has been limited to preventing fraud and insuring that the terms of the trust are followed.

Milton S. and Catherine Hershey, Hershey Archives, Library of Congress

Over a dissent raising concerns that under a broad grant of authority the attorney general could become too involved in decision-making of every charity in Pennsylvania, an injunction was upheld against any sale that would lose controlling interest in the company. *In re Milton Hershey School Trust*, 807 A.2d 324 (Pa. Commw. Ct. 2002).

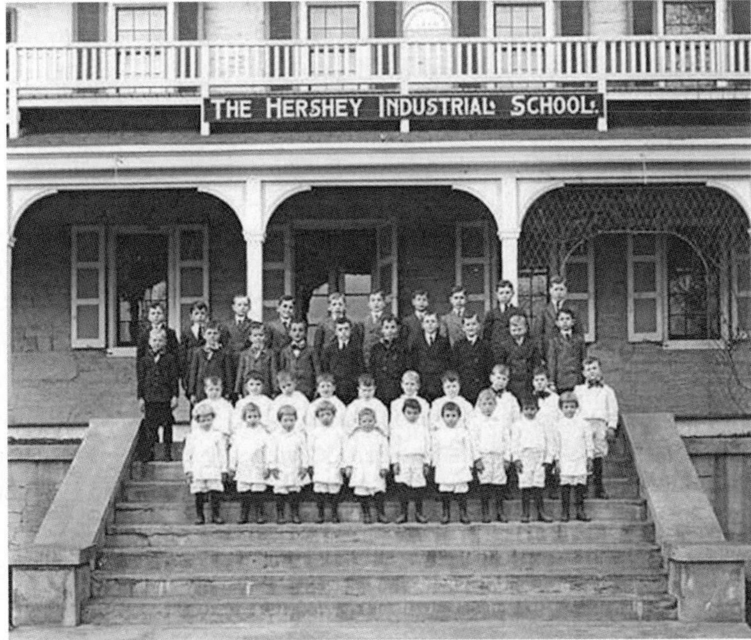

The Hershey Industrial School, Hershey Archives, Library of Congress

Perhaps in response to the dissent, the Pennsylvania legislature quickly enacted legislation authorizing the attorney general to obtain judicial review of charitable trust fiduciaries' decisions to sell controlling interests in a publicly-traded corporation. The standard for approval: clear and convincing evidence that the change in control is necessary for the corporation's economic viability. 20 Pa. Cons. Stat. Ann. § 7203(d). The trustees ultimately reached an agreement with the attorney general not to sell their controlling interest. [17]

Questions about the scope of an attorney general's supervisory role are just part of a larger, continuing debate about the appropriate role of charities in our society.

17. The agreement didn't please everyone. Although the alumni association of the Milton Hershey School was initially granted standing to contest the arrangement, the Supreme Court of Pennsylvania held otherwise. *In re Milton Hershey School*, 867 A.2d 674 (Pa. Commw. Ct. 2005), *rev'd*, 911 A.2d 1258 (2006).

Selected References

Evelyn Brody, *From the Dead Hand to the Living Dead: The Conundrum of Charitable Donor Standing*, 41 Ga. L. Rev. 1183 (2007), and *Charity Governance: What's Trust Law Got to Do with It?*, 80 Chi.-Kent. L. Rev. 641 (2005).

Ronald Chester, *Grantor Standing to Enforce Charitable Transfers Under Section 405(c) of the Uniform Trust Code and Related Law: How Important Is It and How Extensive Should It Be?*, 37 Real Prop. Prob. & Tr. J. 611 (2003).

Alan L. Feld, *Who Are the Beneficiaries of Fisk University's Stieglitz Collection?*, 91 B.U. L. Rev. 873 (2011).

Susan N. Gary, *The Problems with Donor Intent: Interpretation, Enforcement, and Doing the Right Thing*, 85 Chi.-Kent L. Rev. 977 (2010).

Iris J. Goodwin, *Donor Standing to Enforce Charitable Gifts: Civil Society vs. Donor Empowerment*, 58 Vand. L. Rev. 1093 (2005).

Jonathon Klick & Robert H. Sitkoff, *Agency Costs, Charitable Trusts, and Corporate Control: Evidence from Hershey's Kiss-Off*, 108 Colum. L. Rev. 749 (2008).

Jennifer L. Komoroski, *The Hershey Trust's Quest to Diversify: Redefining the State Attorney General's Role When Charitable Trusts Wish to Diversify*, 45 Wm. &. Mary L. Rev. 1769 (2004).

Mark Sidel, *The Struggle for Hershey: Community Accountability and the Law in Modern American Philanthropy*, 65 U. Pitt. L. Rev. 1 (2003).

Joshua C. Tate, *Should Charitable Trust Enforcement Rights Be Assignable?*, 85 Chi.-Kent L. Rev. 1045 (2010).

B. Charitable Purposes

Definitions of "charitable" are necessarily open-ended and, perhaps more than most definitions, a function of the time and place in which they are made. The basic concept of a charitable purpose, however, is something that benefits the community in general. According to Restatement (Third) of Trusts § 28, "Charitable purposes include: (a) the relief of poverty; (b) the advancement of education; (c) the advancement of religion; (d) the promotion of health; (e) governmental or municipal purposes; (f) other purposes that are beneficial to the community." *Accord* UTC § 405(a).

In some ways, it is easier to identify what is not a charitable purpose:

A Trust for Too Narrow a Benefited Class. For example, a trust to provide for the health and education of the grantor's family would not be charitable, even though trusts for health and education are traditional charitable trust categories. *Hardage v. Hardage*, 84 S.E.2d 54 (Ga. 1954) (income to be used for "blood relatives . . . who because of poverty, hardships or old age are unable to properly provide such care out of their own resources" and for "educational loans" to "dependent[s] of any of my blood relatives"). Similarly, a trust to pay for medical insurance for employees of a particular company might be too narrow to be deemed charitable, particularly if the company were small. *See* George T. Bogert, Trusts § 365 (6th ed. 1987). *But cf. United Bank, Inc. v. Blosser*, 624 S.E.2d 815, 823 (W. Va. 2005) ("a trust that is created to provide educational scholarships to an indefinite class of beneficiaries but which also contains a preference for certain family members of the grantor, is a valid charitable trust educational trust . . . ."

The mere fact that only a few individuals will benefit from the trust, however, does not prevent the trust from being charitable. Thus, a trust to provide medical care for victims of a particular disease should be valid even if the disease were rare, because the number of persons who could possibly contract the illness is large.

Benefits Not Tied to the Charitable Purpose. Occasionally, a trust instrument is phrased in terms of a recognized charitable purpose, but the effect of the trust is not charitable. Moreover, generosity is not "charity" in the sense used here. *See Shenandoah Valley National Bank v. Taylor*, 63 S.E.2d 786 (Va. 1951). Charles Henry left his estate to be invested and the income divided among the local primary school children on the last day of school before Easter and before Christmas "in furtherance of his or her obtainment of an education." The court saw the plan for what it was: a generous gift to schoolchildren, not a charitable gift to advance the social interests of the community. In contrast, *Bakos v. Kryder*, 543 S.W.2d 216 (Ark. 1976), regarded as charitable a direction to pay $100 or $200 to each child leaving a specified children's home at about age 18, where most of the children in the home were impoverished and all were in the home because of unfortunate circumstances.

Trusts for Political Purposes. On the theory that society benefits from law reform, courts over time have become more sympathetic to trusts pursuing that purpose. *Compare Jackson v. Phillips*, 96 Mass. (14 Allen) 539 (1867) (trust assisting women to obtain equal rights was not charitable), *with Register of Wills v. Cook*, 216 A.2d 542 (Md. 1966) (trust to further passage of equal rights amendment was charitable). Further, many valid charitable trusts may produce incidental political activity because of the breadth of powers given to the trustees to accomplish the goals of the trust. On the other hand, a trust endowing a political party would be invalid as noncharitable. *See* Scott and Ascher on Trusts § 34.1 (5th ed. 2006).

Notes and Question

1. Would an accumulation trust to eventually provide $1 million for every American be a charitable trust and therefore be exempt from the rule against perpetuities? *See Marsh v. Frost Nat'l Bank*, 129 S.W.3d 174 (Tex. App. 2004).

2. A trust can be "charitable" for the private-law purposes of avoiding the requirement of definite beneficiaries and the Rule Against Perpetuities, even though some of its activities would preclude it from qualifying as a charity for federal tax purposes.

See, e.g., Crisp Area YMCA v. NationsBank, N.A., 526 S.E.2d 63 (Ga. 2000) (tax benefits would not be allowed because YMCA was inactive). In contrast, the State of Pennsylvania sought to deny sales tax exemption to the American Law Institute, a Section 501(c)(3) organization, on the grounds that its educational programs benefitted only lawyers and did not benefit a substantial and indefinite class of persons; disagreeing, the court upheld the exemption because ALI's continuing legal education activities benefitted the public generally by ensuring that lawyers properly discharge their duties to the public. *See Am. Law Inst. v. Commonwealth*, 882 A.2d 1088 (Pa. Commw. Ct. 2005), *aff'd*, 901 A.2d 1030 (Pa. 2006).

3. A drafting hint: when referring to the trust's purpose, include the appropriate terms from the Restatement (Third) of Trusts § 28, quoted *supr* a. In particular, use the word "charitable" and avoid the word "benevolent."

4. Gifts in trust may be unrestricted or restricted. For example, if a settlor creates a trust to benefit a school, the trustees could use the trust funds for any school purpose without restriction. On the other hand, if a gift was made to the trust with the proviso that the trust funds were to be applied for scholarships, then the gift would be restricted to scholarships. Section 410 of the Principles of the Law of Nonprofit Organizations (Prelim. Draft No. 3, 2005), illustrates the types of restrictions that might be applied:

§ 410 Permitted Restrictions

> A donor may restrict the charitable gift, as provided in § 405, with one or more requirements, including but not limited to a requirement that the gift must be
>
> 1. Used for a specified charitable purpose or activity.
>
> 2. Maintained for a particular length of time or in perpetuity, or until the occurrence of a specified event.
>
> 3. Used to provide benefits within a specific geographic area.
>
> 4. Administered in a particular manner.
>
> 5. Accepted with a specified form of acknowledgment or recognition of the donor.

5. One type of restriction—acceptance by a charitable trust or corporation with a specified form of acknowledgment or donor recognition—can generate interesting problems. For example, should Seton Hall University be able to remove the name Kozlowski from its business school facility center now that Dennis Kozlowski, former CEO of Tyco, has been convicted of stealing $600 million from the company and was sentenced up to 25 years?

6. Private trusts often favor beneficiaries of particular social groups, religions, or political persuasions. Unless a trust offends the state's public policy, courts will allow its particular agenda. *See* 3d Rest. Trusts § 28, cmt. f. The test is whether the limitation is "inconsistent with the nature of charitable purposes. Provisions of these types in charitable trusts are not valid if they involve invidious discrimination." *See* id.

Do you think that a trust to provide a scholarship that excludes Roman Catholics as applicants constitutes invidious discrimination? What about a trust to establish a scholarship for rabbis to study in a university's philosophy department?

7. The validity of racially discriminatory trusts at one point depended on whether or not state action was involved. If state action was involved, for example, where a city was the trustee of a trust for a park that only benefited white persons, the trust was struck down as violative of the Equal Protection Clause. *See Evans v. Abney*, 396 U.S 435 (1970). On the other hand, if no state action was involved, the racially discriminatory trust was upheld. *See First Nat'l Bank v. Danforth*, 523 S.W.2d 808 (Mo. 1975), *cert. denied sub nom. Lakeside Hosp. Ass'n v. First Nat'l Bank*, 421 U.S. 1016 (1975).

Since the *Danforth* case in 1975, no court has upheld any racially discriminatory trust. As explained by James W. Colliton, *Race and Sex Discrimination in Charitable Trusts*, 12 Cornell J.L. & Pub. Pol'y 275, 287 (2003):

> [T]he cases seem to reflect a general, unstated, and possibly unrecognized feeling on the part of judges that charitable trusts are not really private and that it is not appropriate in our society to allow them to be racially discriminatory. They seem to show a general, but inadequately articulated, shift in our law away from enforcing these trusts. This general shift may be reflected in the fact that no party in a number of recent cases has been willing to argue for the validity of the discriminatory provisions. Trustees, heirs, attorneys general, and judges often agree that the discriminatory provision is invalid and move to the question of whether to reform the trust or terminate it.

In contrast, trusts that discriminate on the basis of sex are generally upheld. The issue of state action involving sexual discriminatory trusts is considered in *In re Estate of Wilson*.

Problem

You represent Winston Snodgrass, an affluent widower in his early 60's, whose parents are deceased and who has no children. He indicates that his only living "close" relatives are wealthy, greedy nephews. After his death, he wishes his substantial fortune to be used, for as long as the law permits, to provide Winston Snodgrass Memorial Scholarships to needy, meritorious law students who are white, male, and Protestant. You are an atheist and a strong believer in affirmative action.

(a) How would you feel working with this client?

(b) What are your ethical and professional responsibilities in this matter?

Selected References

Elizabeth R. Carter, *Tipping the Scales in Favor of Charitable Bequests: A Critique*, 34 Pace L. Rev. 983 (2014).

James W. Colliton, *Race and Sex Discrimination in Charitable Trusts*, 12 Cornell J.L. & Pub. Pol'y 275, 287 (2003).

William A. Drennan, *Surnamed Charitable Trusts: Immortality at Taxpayer Expense*, 61 Ala. L. Rev. 225 (2010).

John K. Eason, *Motive, Duty, and the Management of Restricted Charitable Gifts*, 45 Wake Forest L. Rev. 123 (2010).

John K. Eason, *Private Motive and Perpetual Conditions in Charitable Naming Gifts: When Good Names Go Bad*, 38 U.C. Davis L. Rev. 375 (2005).

Kristine S. Knaplund, *Becoming Charitable: Predicting and Encouraging Charitable Bequests in Wills*, 77 U. Pitt. L. Rev. 1 (2015).

C. Modification (Cy Pres and Equitable Deviation)

1. Cy Pres

Sometimes settlors give property for charitable purposes that later become impossible or impractical to pursue. If the settlor also had a general intention to support charitable purposes, a court can apply the trust proceeds to another charitable purpose consistent with the settlor's general intention. *See* 3d Rest. Trusts § 67. The authority to substitute a charitable purpose in a charitable trust is called the power of cy pres. Literally defined "as near as possible," cy pres power enables a court to substitute a charitable purpose which as nearly as possible carries out the settlor's intent. For example, a court might exercise its cy pres power to substitute computer technicians under a trust created to educate typewriter repairmen.

Obermeyer v. Bank of Am., N.A.

140 S.W.3d 18 (Mo. 2004)

WOLFF, J.

INTRODUCTION

When the late Dr. Joseph Kimbrough established his estate plan in 1955, Washington University had a dental school and a Dental Alumni Development Fund that existed to benefit the school. His 1955 estate plan included a trust to provide benefits for his niece and nephews during their lifetimes after Dr. Kimbrough's death.

The trust provided that, upon the death of the survivor of the niece and nephews, the trust estate would be "paid over and distributed free of trust unto Washington University . . . for the exclusive use and benefit of its Dental Alumni Development Fund." [The trust did not contain a reversionary provision providing for an alternate disposition of the trust estate.]

Dr. Kimbrough died in 1963. Washington University discontinued the Dental Alumni Development Fund in 1965, and the university closed its dental school in 1991. The fund no longer exists. The trust paid benefits to the niece and nephews until 2000, when the last of the three died. The death of the last survivor in 2000 was the event that triggered the clause that the trust estate be paid to Washington University for the exclusive use and benefit of the Dental Alumni Development Fund.

Louise Obermeyer and Elizabeth Salmon, the great, great-nieces of Dr. Kimbrough, brought this action for declaratory judgment and construction of Dr. Kimbrough's inter vivos trust, which was valued at approximately $ 2.8 million in 2000. The circuit court held that Dr. Kimbrough established the trust with a general charitable intent and applied the cy pres doctrine, ruling in favor of Washington University, and directing that the university use the funds to support two dental-related professorships in the name of Dr. Kimbrough.

The gift "free from trust" was an absolute gift to Washington University. The circuit court appropriately provided for the disposition of the trust estate. The judgment of the circuit court is affirmed.

DR. KIMBROUGH GAVE A GIFT "FREE FROM TRUST" TO WASHINGTON UNIVERSITY

The parties maintain that a charitable trust is at issue. Dr. Kimbrough, instead, created a trust for life beneficiaries with the remainder as a gift "free from trust" to Washington University "for the exclusive use and benefit of its Dental Alumni Development Fund." The property was in trust during the relevant life estates, but the amendment specifically provides that the distribution to the university shall be "free from trust." Once Dr. Kimbrough's named heirs died, there was no longer a trust and the distribution was to occur in accordance with the trust instrument.

APPLICATION OF THE CY PRES DOCTRINE

The cy pres doctrine is based on the concern of equity to protect and preserve charitable bequests. *Levings v. Danforth*, 512 S.W.2d 207, 209 (Mo. App. 1974). The original French phrase was "cy pres comme possible," meaning "as near as possible." George T. Bogert, Trusts 520 (6th ed. 1987). The doctrine of cy pres exists "to permit the main purpose of the donor of a charitable trust to be carried out as nearly as possible where it cannot be done to the letter." *Thatcher v. Lewis*, 335 Mo. 1130, 76 S.W.2d 677, 682 (Mo. 1934).

It was the policy of courts of equity "to declare valid, if possible, gifts to charity." *Burrier v. Jones*, 338 Mo. 679, 92 S.W.2d 885, 889 (Mo. banc 1936). Charitable trusts are favorites of equity, and they are "given effect wherever possible, by applying the most liberal rules of which the nature of the case will permit." *First Nat'l Bank of Kansas City v. Stevenson*, 293 S.W.2d at 367. Courts have the power and duty to apply the cy pres doctrine to seek to determine "as nearly as may be" the general purpose and intent of the settlor and adopt a plan or carry the general intent into fruition, thus preventing a failure of the charitable trust. Restatement (Second) of Trusts, sec. 399, p. 298 (1959).

The cy pres power is generally confined to charitable trusts. Bogert, Trusts at 520. Missouri courts have previously applied the cy pres doctrine only to charitable trusts; this Court has held that "absent the creation of a trust, there is no room for the application of the doctrine of cy pres." *Burrier*, 92 S.W.2d at 889.

While acknowledging the historical limitation of the cy pres doctrine to trusts, the doctrine is appropriate in certain cases involving gifts to charitable corporations. At issue here is a gift with direction from the grantor indicating the intended use of the trust assets. While the cy pres power is applied to gifts in trust, other jurisdictions have applied cy pres "to absolute gifts to charitable corporations or other organizations." George T. Bogert, Trusts and Trustees, sec. 431, p. 105 (2d ed. 1991).

Although the trust itself has ceased to exist, the gift comes from a trust. Moreover, most cy pres cases involve situations where many years have passed since the creation of a trust or other origination of the gift and the time the gift is to be given effect. Cy pres exists to conform the terms of the gift to current conditions. The money in the trust was to be "distributed free from trust unto Washington University, St. Louis, Missouri, for the exclusive use and benefit of its Dental Alumni Development Fund." Were Dr. Kimbrough's gift a charitable trust, the Court would readily apply the cy pres doctrine as the parties suggest. Dr. Kimbrough's gift from the trust is an absolute gift to Washington University with an instruction that can no longer be observed because the fund ceased to exist in 1965. Although courts typically reserve application of the cy pres doctrine for charitable trusts, and the absolute gift to the university may not fall under the categories listed above, the cy pres analysis is adopted to carry out Dr. Kimbrough's intent.

CY PRES ANALYSIS

Missouri courts hold that to apply the doctrine of cy pres, three requirements must be met. First, the trust in question must be a valid charitable trust. Second, it is or becomes impossible, impracticable, or illegal to carry out the specific terms of the trust. Finally, the settlor must have established the trust with a general charitable intent. *Comfort*, 576 S.W.2d at 336, holds that "unless and until it is determined that a trust has failed, the question of general or specific charitable intent is irrelevant." If the settlor's intent was specific, the cy pres doctrine cannot be applied. The result would be a reversion for the settlor or the settlor's heirs. Id.

The parties agree that a trust was created with a charitable intent and that the trust has failed because the dental school was closed and the Dental Alumni Development Fund no longer exists. The parties maintain that the issue is whether the trust was created with general or specific charitable intent.

A general charitable intent exists where there is an intent to assist a certain general type or kind of charity. *Ramsey v. City of Brookfield*, 361 Mo. 857, 237 S.W.2d 143, 145 (Mo. 1951). General charitable intent "is an intent that a gift be continued within the limits of its general purpose and that shall not cease when a particular thing is accomplished. Unquestionably, when the intent is to apply the gift to a continuing problem, there is a general charitable intent." *Thatcher*, 76 S.W.2d at 683. Gifts made to aid "education, science, literature, the poor, the sick, and so on" demonstrate general charitable intent. *Comfort*, 576 S.W.2d at 338. Because most charitable gifts are made to ameliorate a continuing problem, it must be determined whether the donor "intended to benefit all those affected by the continuing problem, or only certain of those persons." Id. The grantor's intent is specific when the grantor intended to "aid that kind of charity only in a particular way or by a particular method or means" and further intended that, "if the particular means failed, the gift failed." Id.

Dr. Kimbrough's gift to Washington University for the Dental Alumni Development Fund was not for a particular task to be accomplished, but to support dental medicine at Washington University, a profession of which he was deeply proud. The trust document contained no suggestion that the gift should fail if the particular fund ceased to exist.

In determining whether the charitable intent of the grantor is specific or general, the Court in Comfort v. Higgins set forth additional factors courts should consider.

First, Comfort distinguished between gifts of money and land, finding that courts have viewed gifts of land as "strong evidence of an absence of general charitable intent," while monetary gifts suggest general intent. *Id.* at 338. Dr. Kimbrough gave a gift of money, not real property, thus indicating general charitable intent.

The second factor is the existence of a reverter clause associated with the gift. Use of a direction for a reversion to the settlor in the case of failure indicates specific charitable intent, while the absence of a reverter clause supports general charitable intent. Id. Dr. Kimbrough's estate plan included reverter clauses as to the bequests for all of the individuals, which instructed the gifts to go to Washington University; however, it did not include a reverter clause as to the gift to Washington University in the will or trust.

The conclusion that a general charitable intent exists is typically reached where the heirs were either specifically excluded or had received other gifts in the will, indicating that no further gifts were included. Id. In his last will and testament, Dr. Kimbrough granted to Washington University the rest and remainder of his estate. In his will, Dr. Kimbrough left Louise Obermeyer $ 5,000 and did not provide for Elizabeth Salmon in his estate plan. The lack of a reverter clause for the charitable gift and the provision for one of his great, great-nieces are indicative of Dr. Kimbrough's general charitable intent.

The third relevant factor is whether the charitable gift was made in trust or outright. A gift in trust is indicative of specific charitable intent, while a gift made outright indicates general intent. *Id.* at 339. The trust provides that at the death of the survivor of the life beneficiaries, the trust is to be paid to Washington University "free from trust." Dr. Kimbrough's gift "free from trust" suggests general charitable intent.

The heirs argue that the use of the language, "for the exclusive use and benefit," requires a finding of specific charitable intent. Where the terms of a charitable trust direct a means of execution or dedicate the fund to a type of charity "forever" or "for no other purpose," or upon condition that it be applied "to no other purpose," these provisions do not necessarily demonstrate absence of a general charitable intent. *Ramsey*, 237 S.W.2d at 146. In Ramsey, a grant for the "sole purpose of building and equipping and maintaining a City hospital" and "no other" did "not necessarily show absence of a general charitable intent." Id. "Such provisions do not, ipso facto, show an intent that the trust should cease in the event of impossibility or impracticability of using the specified means." Id.

DR. KIMBROUGH'S CHARITABLE INTENT

The question remains what Dr. Kimbrough would desire if he knew that his gift could not be used by the Dental Alumni Development Fund for the continued operation and prestige of the dental school.

"The accomplishment of the ultimate purpose of the testator is the matter of paramount importance and its achievement must be the object of any judicial permission to alter or deviate from the trust terms." *Reed v. Eagleton*, 384 S.W.2d 578, 586 (Mo. 1964). The Court considers whether unforeseen circumstances have arisen that threaten the fulfillment of the charity and whether or not such circumstances warrant a court's exercise of its jurisdiction to enforce and protect charitable trusts. *Id.* at 585-86. In discerning the intent of the grantor, the basic equitable issue is what the settlor would desire if he or she knew that the trust could not be carried out. *Levings*, 512 S.W.2d at 211. A court is required to consider all the surrounding circumstances evidencing the grantor's intent. See *First Nat'l Bank of Kansas City v. Jacques*, 470 S.W.2d at 560. To adhere too strictly to the words of the testator may result in the defeat of the testator's ultimate purpose. IVA Scott on Trusts, sec. 399.4, p. 535 (4th ed. 1989). If the testator intended to make the property useful for charitable purposes, to render it useless for such purposes defeats the testator's intention. Id. "Under the guise of fulfilling a bequest, this is making a dead man's intentions for a single day a rule for subsequent centuries, when we know not whether he himself would have made it a rule even for the morrow." John Stuart Mill, quoted in IVA Scott on Trusts, sec. 399 at 535.

The record repeatedly shows that Dr. Kimbrough loved dentistry and was very proud of his profession. Dr. Kimbrough graduated from the Washington University Dental School, taught at the Washington University Dental School, gave unrestricted gifts to Washington University, and left the remainder of his trust to Washington University, not to the dental school.

This Court agrees with the circuit court's conclusion that Dr. Kimbrough's charitable intent was to further education and dental medicine at Washington University. There is no evidence that Dr. Kimbrough wanted his gift so narrowly drawn and so inflexible that if it could not be used in a specifically named fund, it should lapse. The circuit court's decision to establish one or two chairs in Dr. Kimbrough's name for research and practice in dental fields is consistent with Dr. Kimbrough's charitable intent.

From 1954 to 1963, Dr. Kimbrough made 11 gifts to Washington University, including gifts to the Dental Alumni Development Fund, the Washington University School of Medicine, the Second Century Development Program, the Alumni Fund, and the Century Club. The gift in question was made to Washington University, not to the dental school. The only limitation on the gift was that it be used in the fund. The fact that Dr. Kimbrough made multiple other inter vivos gifts to Washington University that were unrelated to the dental school suggests that he had a general charitable intent to support dental education at Washington University, not only through the Dental Alumni Development Fund.

This Court also recognizes that under the tax law in effect before 1969, virtually all charitable remainder trusts provided substantial tax savings to the grantor 's estate. See *Ellis First Nat'l Bank v. United States*, 550 F.2d 9, 11-12, 213 Ct. Cl. 44 (Ct. Claims 1977). Dr. Kimbrough's 1955 amendment to the trust, giving the remainder interest to Washington University as opposed to his heirs, was essential to the tax savings and may be evidence of his general charitable intent.

DENTAL MEDICINE CONTINUES AT WASHINGTON UNIVERSITY

The basic aspects of dental education at Washington University Dental School were the treatment of patients, education of dental students, and research of the faculty. Applying the funds to Washington University for dental-related endeavors most nearly carries out Dr. Kimbrough's intent because treatment of patients, post- graduate dental education, and research are ongoing at Washington University.

Although the dental school has been closed and the university no longer grants the basic degree in dental medicine, some dentistry continues through the medical school. Dr. Donald E. Huebener and Dr. W. Donald Gay were both faculty members of the dental school. Dr. Huebener is a member of a team of physicians, dentists, and orthodontists at the Cleft Palate Cranial Facial Deformity Institute, of which he is a founding member. He is a pediatric dentist in the City of St. Louis and provides routine dental care to 20 to 22 children daily at the dental clinic and provides dental care to children with special health care needs and serves on the cleft palate team. Dr. Gay, a maxillofacial prosthodontist, serves as the Director of the Division of Maxillofacial Prosthetics of the Otolaryngology Department at the School of Medicine. He does primarily the same work at the School of Medicine as he did at the dental school. He fits dental prostheses for people with birth defects or who have suffered trauma or cancer. The circuit court's judgment directing one or two chairs in Dr. Kimbrough's name would support one or two such professorships.

Richard Smith, the last dean of the dental school and chairman of its orthodontics department, became a professor of anthropology at the university, where he and others educate students in dental-related topics and do research in the area of dental genetics and biomechanics of the face. The medical library at Washington University has two dental book collections. The circuit court found that "dental medicine is still a necessary component of Washington University Medical School," and remarked on the "borderline miraculous healing work" the university's professors continue to perform.

Neither the closing of the dental school nor the change in the Dental Alumni Development Fund make Dr. Kimbrough's gift useless. The trust estate can be used to continue treatment of dental patients, research, and post-graduate education in dental medicine.

CONCLUSION

Cy pres literally means "as near as." Dr. Kimbrough's objective was to further dental education at Washington University. The circuit court's disposition of the gift attempts to fulfill Dr. Kimbrough's intent as near as possible because it requires Washington University to use the money for dental-related education. The fact that the Dental Alumni Development Fund and the dental school no longer exist does not frustrate that objective, as the medical school at Washington University continues to teach and practice dental medicine.

There is no evidence that Dr. Kimbrough ever contemplated that the money would go to his great, great-nieces, and he did not include a provision for the reversion of the property to his heirs in the event that the fund or dental school would cease to exist.

The general purpose of Dr. Kimbrough's gift to support educational programs and projects in dental fields at Washington University can be accomplished. While the specific fund designated by the grantor to carry out this purpose no longer exists, the circuit court's disposition of the trust assets carries out Dr. Kimbrough's intent.

The judgment of the circuit court is affirmed.

Restatement (Third) of Trusts

§ 67. Failure of Designated Charitable Purpose: The Doctrine of Cy Pres

Unless the terms of the trust provide otherwise, where property is placed in trust to be applied to a designated charitable purpose and it is or becomes unlawful, impossible, or impracticable to carry out that purpose, or to the extent it is or becomes wasteful to apply all of the property to the designated purpose, the charitable trust will not fail but the court will direct application of the property or appropriate portion thereof to a charitable purpose that reasonably approximates the designated purpose.

Uniform Trust Code

Section 413. Cy Pres.

(a) Except as otherwise provided in subsection (b), if a particular charitable purpose becomes unlawful, impracticable, impossible to achieve, or wasteful:

(1) the trust does not fail, in whole or in part;

(2) the trust property does not revert to the settlor or the settlor's successors in interest; and

(3) the court may apply cy pres to modify or terminate the trust by directing that the trust property be applied or distributed, in whole or in part, in a manner consistent with the settlor's charitable purposes.

(b) A provision in the terms of a charitable trust that would result in distribution of the trust property to a noncharitable beneficiary prevails over the power of the court under subsection (a) to apply cy pres to modify or terminate the trust only if, when the provision takes effect:

(1) the trust property is to revert to the settlor and the settlor is still living; or

(2) fewer than 21 years have elapsed since the date of the trust's creation.

Notes and Questions

1. Section 67 of the Restatement (Third) of Trusts and UTC § 413(a) liberalize the cy pres rules in three ways: (1) a settlor is presumed to have a general charitable intent unless the trust terms provide otherwise; (2) cy pres is allowed when it would be wasteful not to do so; and (3) only a reasonable approximation of the settlor's intent, rather than the closest possible approximation, need be made when a court substitutes a new charitable purpose. UTC § 413(b) also elevates the role of cy pres over reversions in favor of a deceased settlor's successors and gift over provisions that have not occurred within 21 years.

Section 6 of Uniform Prudent Management of Institutional Funds (UPMIFA), approved in the summer of 2006, applies the equitable deviation and cy pres doctrines to funds held by charities either in trustee or corporate capacity. Unlike UTC § 410(b), which permits the settlor of a trust to initiate a cy pres proceeding, donors of charitable corporation are not granted standing under UPMIFA. UPMIFA Section 6(d) would allow for the exercise of cy pres power in small trusts (under $25,000) that had been in existence for over 20 years without judicial approval.

2. Unlike *Obermeyer*, the disputed issue may involve not only whether cy pres should be applied but how the court should exercise its cy pres power. For example, in *Estate of Elkins*, 888 A.2d 815 (Pa. Super. Ct. 2005), the testator created charitable trusts for two hospitals in different locations. When one of the hospitals ceased to be a not-for-profit corporation, the court had little difficulty in finding that the cy

pres doctrine should be applied. The issue was which charity should be substituted, which according to the court was "a charity that most closely resembles the one that was to be the recipient of the trust." Reversing the lower court, which exercised its cy pres power in favor of the other hospital, the appellate court remanded the case to determine if a closer hospital should be the recipient.

The UTC is now the law of Pennsylvania. Do you think the result in *Elkins* would be different? Under the Restatement (Third) of Trusts § 67 standard?

3. By finding that the settlor lacked a general charitable intent, courts can avoid exercising their cy pres power. *See, e.g., Vollmann v. Rosenburg*, 972 S.W.2d 490 (Mo. Ct. App. 1998). Do you think a donor evidences a specific charitable intent if his or her name is required to be associated with a charitable endeavor?

4. There appears to be a judicial tendency to find that it was not impracticable nor impossible to carry out the trust's charitable purpose and thus cy pres was not needed. *See, e.g., In re R.B. Plummer Mem. Loan Fund Trust*, 661 N.W.2d 307 (Neb. 2003) (no cy pres to allow trust funds to be used for university scholarships because making of student loans, as required by trust, was neither impossible nor impracticable); *In re Ruth Easton Fund*, 680 N.W.2d 541 (Minn. Ct. App. 2004) (no cy pres because literal compliance was not impracticable, impossible, or inexpedient); *Crisp Area YMCA v. NationsBank, N.A.*, 526 S.E.2d 63 (Ga. 2000) (no cy pres even though charity was inactive). *See also Wilson. But see Kolb v. City of Storm Lake*, 736 N.W.2d 546 (Iowa 2007) (impossibility found even though created by city while acting as trustee).

Consider the judicial unwillingness to apply the cy pres doctrine in another case: In 1975, Beryl Buck left the residue of her estate (mostly about $9 million worth of Beldridge Oil stock) to the San Francisco Foundation, to be spent in prosperous Marin County. After a takeover by Shell and changes in the market, the value ballooned to over $300 million by 1984. Based on the "changed circumstances" of the increase in value, the foundation sought approval to spend some of the money outside of Marin County. Finding charitable needs in the county, the court denied the request. The story appears with commentary in a series of articles starting at 21 U.S.F. L. Rev. 585 (1987).

5. If the original purpose becomes impossible or illegal and a court cannot apply cy pres because it cannot identify a general charitable purpose, the trust fails and a resulting trust will arise. For example, in 1931, George Hoffman created a trust for a hospital, but by 1972 the hospital had to close. George's will provided an alternative gift to a non-charity, but that gift violated the Rule Against Perpetuities. The alternative gift, however, negated the possibility of applying cy pres because the gift showed George had a specific, as opposed to general, charitable intent. *See Nelson v. Kring*, 592 P.2d 438 (Kan. 1979).

How would *Kring* be decided under the Restatement (Third) of Trusts § 67? Under UTC § 413(b)?

6. Even if a state has not enacted UTC § 413(b), a gift over provision will not always bar the application of the cy pres doctrine, especially when an illegal racial restriction is involved as was the case of *Home for Incurables of Baltimore City v. Univ. of Md. Med. Sys. Corp.*, 797 A.2d 746 (Md. 2002). Testator left property to a private hospital to construct a facility for the physical rehabilitation of white patients only, but if the bequest was not acceptable to the hospital the bequest would go to a university hospital for physical rehabilitation without regard to race. Pursuant to applicable state law, a hospital cannot discriminate on the basis of race, so the hospital could not use the funds as intended. The court excised the racial restriction and, by applying the *cy pres* doctrine, allowed the private hospital to keep the $28 Million bequest.

7. Gifts to a second charity after the failure of the first charitable gift do not violate the Rule Against Perpetuities. *See, e.g., Wilbur v. Univ. of Vt.*, 270 A.2d 889 (Vt. 1970) (gift to University of Vermont on certain conditions, followed by gift to Library of Congress Trust Fund Board).

Problem

Marie wants to establish a trust to provide college scholarships for students from Ainsworth, a small ranching town in Nebraska. What issues would you want to raise with her before drafting the appropriate language?

2. Equitable Deviation

Closely related to the cy pres power is a court's equitable deviation power. In addition to applying to private trusts, see *Mayo*, equitable deviation allows a court to deviate from administrative terms in a charitable trust. In *Daloia v. Franciscan Health Sys.*, 679 N.E.2d 1084, 1092 (Ohio 1997), the Supreme Court of Ohio quoted with approval from an earlier lower court's explanation of the differences between the two doctrines:

> The cy pres doctrine is a rule of judicial construction under which the court is required to first find a general charitable intent in the instrument creating the trust; the general charitable purpose of the settlor moves the court to substitute a different charitable purpose for the one which has failed. Cy pres is applied only in the field of charitable trusts, whereas, a court of equity may order a deviation in private as well as charitable trusts. * * * In ordering a deviation a court of equity is merely exercising its general power over the administration of trusts; it is an essential element of equity jurisdiction. In ordering a deviation the court does not touch the question of the purpose or object of the trust, nor vary the class of beneficiaries, nor divert the fund from the charitable purpose designated. * * * The cy pres doctrine requires the exercise of a more extensive power than the ordinary power of a court of equity in ordering deviation. The jurisdiction merely to vary the details of the administration of a trust is more liberally exercised, more firmly

established and more widely recognized than the cy pres power of the court. (Emphasis added and citations omitted.)

In short, "courts apply equitable deviation to make changes in the manner in which a charitable trust is carried out while courts apply cy pres in situations where trustees seek to modify or redefine the settlor's specific charitable purpose." *Niemann v. Vaughn Cmty. Church*, 113 P.3d 463, 469 (Wash. 2005) (holding that equitable deviation applied to permit trustees to remove restriction preventing sale of church property that was not large enough for increased congregation).

RULE:

In re Estate of Wilson

452 N.E.2d 1228 (N.Y. 1983)

Appeal

[This decision involves combined appeals in two proceedings to determine the validity of charitable trusts. In "Wilson Trust," the trust was to pay college expenses of top male graduates of a high school, as certified by the then Superintendent. In "Johnson Trust," the trust with a Board of Education as trustee was to pay scholarships to male graduates of a high school "who shall be selected by the Board of Education . . . with the assistance of the principal of such High School." In Wilson Trust, the Appellate Division exercised its cy pres power over the trust to allow male students to apply directly to the trustee. In Johnson Trust, the Appellate Division exercised its cy pres power over the trust to eliminate the gender restriction.]

COOKE, CH. J.

On these appeals, this court is called upon to consider the testator's intent in establishing these trusts, evaluate the public policy implications of gender restrictive trusts generally, and determine whether the judicial reformation of these trusts violates the equal protection clause of the Fourteenth Amendment.

There can be no question that these trusts, established for the promotion of education, are for a charitable purpose within the meaning of the law. . . . Charitable trusts are encouraged and favored by the law . . . and may serve any of a variety of benevolent purposes. . . . Among the advantages the law extends to charitable trusts are their exemption from the rules against perpetuities . . . and accumulations . . . and their favorable tax treatment. . . . Moreover, unlike other trusts, a charitable trust will not necessarily fail when the settlor's specific charitable purpose or direction can no longer be accomplished.

When a court determines that changed circumstances have rendered the administration of a charitable trust according to its literal terms either "impracticable or impossible," the court may exercise its cy pres power to reform the trust in a matter that "will most effectively accomplish its general purposes" (EPTL 8-1.1, subd. [c]). In reforming trusts pursuant to this power, care must be taken to evaluate the precise purpose or direction of the testator, so that when the court directs the trust towards another charitable end, it will "give effect insofar as practicable to the full design of the testator as manifested by his will and codicil" (*Matter of Scott*, 8 N.Y.2d 419, 427, 208 N.Y.S.2d 984, 171 N.E.2d 326; . . .).

The court . . . cannot invoke its cy pres power without first determining that the testator's specific charitable purpose is no longer capable of being performed by the trust. . . . In establishing these trusts, the testators expressly and unequivocally intended that they provide for the educational expenses of male students. It cannot be said that the accomplishment of the testators' specific expression of charitable intent is "impossible or impracticable." So long as the subject high schools graduate boys with the requisite qualifications, the testators' specific charitable intent can be fulfilled.

Nor are the trusts' particular limitation of beneficiaries by gender invalid and incapable of being accomplished as violative of public policy. It is true that the eradication in this State of gender-based discrimination is an important public policy. Indeed, the Legislature has barred gender-based discrimination in education, . . . employment, . . . housing, . . . credit, . . . and many other areas. As a result, women, once viewed as able to assume only restricted roles in our society . . . now project significant numbers "in business, in the professions, in government and, indeed, in all walks of life where education is a desirable, if not always a necessary antecedent" (*Stanton v. Stanton*, 421 US 7, 15 . . .). The restrictions in these trusts run contrary to this policy favoring equal opportunity and treatment of men and women. A provision in a charitable trust, however, that is central to the testator 's or settlor's charitable purpose, and is not illegal, should not be invalidated on public policy grounds unless that provision, if given effect, would substantially mitigate the general charitable effect of the gift (see IV Scott on Trusts, [3d ed.] § 399.4).

Proscribing the enforcement of gender restrictions in private charitable trusts would operate with equal force towards trusts whose benefits are bestowed exclusively on women. "Reduction of disparity in economic condition between men and women caused by the long history of discrimination against women has been recognized as . . . an important governmental objective" (*Califano v. Webster*, 430 US 313, 317 . . .). There can be little doubt that important efforts in effecting this type of social change can be and are performed through private philanthropy. . . . And, the private funding of programs for the advancement of women is substantial and growing. . . . Indeed, one compilation of financial assistance offered primarily or exclusively to women lists 854 sources of funding (see Schlacter, Directory of Financial Aids for Women [2d Ed. 1981]; see, also, Note, Sex Restricted Scholarships and the Charitable Trust, 59 Iowa L. Rev. 1000, 1000-1001 & nn. 10, 11). Current thinking in private philanthropic institutions advocates that funding offered by such institutions and the opportunities within institutions themselves be directly responsive to the needs of particular groups. . . . It is evident, therefore, that the focusing of private philanthropy on certain classes within society may be consistent with public policy. Consequently, that the restrictions in the trusts before this court may run contrary to public efforts promoting equality of opportunity for women does not justify imposing a per se rule that gender restrictions in private charitable trusts violate public policy.

Finally, this is not an instance in which the restriction of the trusts serves to frustrate a paramount charitable purpose. In *Howard Sav. Inst. v. Peep*, 34 N.J. 494, 170 A.2d 39, for example, the testator made a charitable bequest to Amherst College to be placed in trust and to provide scholarships for "deserving American born, Protestant, Gentile boys of good moral repute, not given to gambling, smoking, drinking or similar acts." Due to the religious restrictions, the college declined to accept the bequest as contrary to its charter. The court found that the college was the principal beneficiary of the trust, so that removing the religious restriction and thereby allowing the college to accept the gift would permit administration of the trust in a manner most closely effectuating the testator 's intent. . . .

. . . [T]he trusts subject to these appeals were not intended to directly benefit the school districts. Although the testators sought the school districts' participation, this was incidental to their primary intent of financing part of the college education of boys who attended the schools. Consequently, severance of the school districts' role in the trusts' administration will not frustrate any part of the testators' charitable purposes. Inasmuch as the specific charitable intent of the testators is not inherently "impossible or impracticable" of being achieved by the trusts, there is no occasion to exercise cy pres power.

Although not inherently so, these trusts are currently incapable of being administered as originally intended because of the school districts' unwillingness to cooperate. These impediments, however, may be remedied by an exercise of a court's general equitable power over all trusts to permit a deviation from the administrative terms of a trust and to appoint a successor trustee.

A testamentary trust will not fail for want of a trustee . . . and, in the event a trustee is unwilling or unable to act, a court may replace the trustee with another. . . . Accordingly, the proper means of continuing the Johnson Trust would be to replace the School District with someone able and willing to administer the trust according to its terms.

When an impasse is reached in the administration of a trust due to an incidental requirement of its terms, a court may effect, or permit the trustee to effect, a deviation from the trust's literal terms. . . . This power differs from a court's cy pres power in that "[t]hrough exercise of its deviation power the court alters or amends administrative provisions in the trust instrument but does not alter the purpose of the charitable trust or change its dispositive provisions" (Bogert, Trusts and Trustees, [Rev 2d. ed] § 394, p. 249 . . .). The Wilson Trust provision that the School District certify a list of students is an incidental part of the trust's administrative requirements, which no longer can be satisfied in light of the District's refusal to cooperate. The same result intended by the testator may be accomplished by permitting the students to apply directly to the trustee. Therefore, a deviation from the Wilson Trust's administrative terms by eliminating the certification requirement would be the appropriate method of continuing that trust's administration. . . .

It is argued before this court that the judicial facilitation of the continued administration of gender-restrictive charitable trusts violates the equal protection clause of the Fourteenth Amendment (see US Const., 14th Amdt., § 1). The strictures of the equal protection clause are invoked when the State engages in invidious discrimination. . . . Indeed, the State itself cannot, consistent with the Fourteenth Amendment, award scholarships that are gender restrictive (see *Mississippi Univ. for Women v. Hogan*, 458 US 718, . . .).

The Fourteenth Amendment, however, "erects no shield against merely private conduct, however discriminatory or wrongful." (*Shelley v. Kraemer*, 334 US 1, 13 . . .). . . .

In the present appeals, the coercive power of the State has never been enlisted to enforce private discrimination. Upon finding that requisite formalities of creating a trust had been met, the courts below determined the testator's intent, and applied the relevant law permitting those intentions to be privately carried out. The court's power compelled no discrimination. That discrimination had been sealed in the private execution of the wills. Recourse to the courts was had here only for the purpose of facilitating the administration of the trusts, not for enforcement of their discriminatory dispositive provisions. . . . [18]

[The court affirmed the Appellate Division's order in *Wilson* and reversed the order in *Johnson*.]

Note

As *Wilson* illustrates, the line between a court's exercise of its cy pres power and its equitable deviation power is sometimes difficult to draw. Indeed, it has been argued that the distinction between the two doctrines is "specious and without merit." *See* Alex M. Johnson, Jr., *Limiting Dead Hand Control of Charitable Trusts: Expanding the Use of the Cy Pres Doctrine*, 21 U. Haw. L. Rev. 353, 380 (1999).

The Barnes Foundation Controversy: Equitable Deviation Applied to Move the Location of a Museum

The Barnes Foundation litigation illustrates the tenuous distinction between an administrative change sanctioned by equitable deviation and a substantive change sanctioned by cy pres. *See* Barnes Foundation, a Corporation, 25 Fiduc. Rep. 2d 39 (Dec. 2004) and 24 Fiduc. Rep. 2d 94 (Jan. 2004). In 1922, Dr. Albert Barnes created the Barnes Foundation, a charitable corporation to which he transferred his art collection, property, and funds. Pursuant to a trust indenture, Dr. Barnes specified a code of procedure for the maintenance and operation of the Barnes Foundation; the trust terms were incorporated in their entirety into the Foundation's bylaws.

18. [Editor 's Note: In *In re Certain Scholarship Funds*, 575 A.2d 1325 (N.H. 1990), the court refused to substitute a private trustee for the publicly named trustee on the ground that such reformation would involve state action in violate of New Hampshire's equal protection clause; instead the court removed the discriminatory provision.]

Central to the litigation is the following trust (and by-law) provision which sets forth Dr. Barnes's wishes:

> to promote the advancement of education and the appreciation of the fine arts; and for this purpose to erect, found and maintain, in the Township of Lower Merion, County of Montgomery and State of Pennsylvania, an art gallery and other necessary buildings for the exhibition of works of ancient and modern art, and the maintenance in connection therewith of an arboretum, wherein shall be cultivated and maintained trees and shrubs for the study and for the encouragement of arboriculture and forestry. . . .

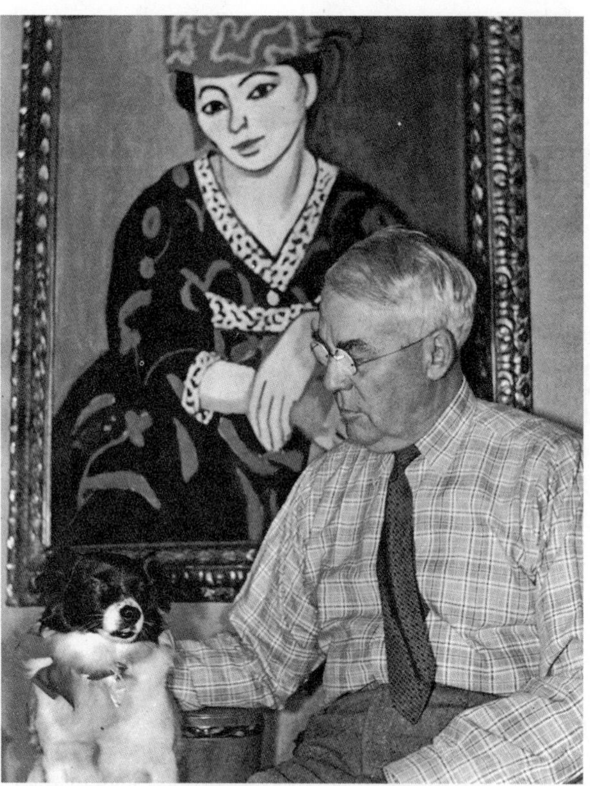

Albert C. Barnes and Fidèle with Matisse's "Red Madras Headdress (Le Madras rouge)" (BF448), 1942. Photograph by Pinto Studios. Credit line: Photograph Collection, Barnes Foundation Archives.

The art collection held by the Barnes Foundation is one of the most important collections in the world, comprising vast holdings of Renoir, Cezanne, Matisse, and Picasso, important works of many other impressionist painters, and other ancient and modern art. The Barnes collection is estimated to be worth $25 billion.

Despite its vast net worth, the Barnes Foundation is cash poor, due in part to restrictions placed by Dr. Barnes. These include prohibitions on selling or loaning any art works.[19] Indeed, the latest litigation was triggered by the trustees' announcement that it was insolvent, which triggered its petition to allow the art collection to be moved from Merion, a small town outside of Philadelphia, to a major museum to be constructed in the city of Philadelphia, with funding by several charitable organizations and the State of Pennsylvania. The court effectively couched the issue in terms of whether moving the art collection to Philadelphia would constitute an administrative deviation as distinct from a substantive change under the cy pres doctrine. The court pointed to Comment j of Section 381 of the Restatement (Second) of Trusts, which in general allows a court to order deviation by relocating an institution to other land subject to the following:

If, however, the testator provided that if the institution should not be maintained upon the land devised the charitable trust should cease, the trustee will not be directed or permitted to maintain the institution on other land.

So also, if the maintenance of the institution on the land devised was an essential part of the testator's purpose, the court will not direct or permit the trustee to maintain the institution on other land.

Dr. Barnes did not expressly provide that the collection had to be maintained in the Merion location. Yet, it is clear that the location in Merion was extremely important. Indeed, the trust even prohibits rearrangement of the paintings after Dr. Barnes' death. But was the maintenance of the collection in Merion an essential part of Dr. Barnes's purpose so that administrative deviation—relocating the collection—could not be authorized?

The court resolved "this very close question" in the negative: the maintenance of the collection in Merion was not an essential part of his purpose. But this decision did not mean that relocation would be automatically authorized. Instead, the court demanded that the trustees prove that relocation was the least drastic alternative. Another round of hearings convinced the judge that relocation was the least drastic action, despite considerable evidence that the collection could be maintained in Merion by less drastic means.

Although relocation could also have been allowed under the cy pres doctrine if the court found that maintenance of the collection in Merion was an essential part of Dr. Barnes's purpose, the court would likely have found that the loan of some of the collection would have been less drastic than relocation.

In any event, as a result of the 2004 ruling, the Barnes collection has been moved to a newly-constructed museum in Philadelphia. *See* http://www.barnesfoundation.org/.

---

19. In 1992, the Court of Common Pleas exercised administrative deviation by granting a petition to send some of the collection on a worldwide tour. *See Barnes Foundation, a Corporation*, 12 Fiduc. Rep. 349 (1992).

Selected References

Donald Argott, The Art of the Steal (documentary film 2010).

Rob Atkinson, *The Low Road to Cy Pres Reform: Principled Practice to Remove Dead Hand Control of Charitable Assets*, 58 Case W. Res. L. Rev. 97 (2007).

John K. Eason, *Private Motive and Perpetual Conditions in Charitable Naming Gifts: When Good Names Go Bad*, 38 U.C. Davis L. Rev. 375 (2005).

Jonathan Scott Goldman, *Just What the Doctor Ordered? The Doctrine of Deviation, the Case of Doctor Barnes's Trust and the Future Location of the Barnes Foundation*, 39 Real Prop. Prob. & Tr. J. 711 (2005).

Iris J. Goodwin, *Ask Not What Your Charity Can Do for You:* Robertson v. Princeton *Provides Liberal-Democratic Insights into the Dilemma of Cy Pres Reform*, 51 Ariz. L. Rev. 75 (2009).

Alex M. Johnson, Jr., *Limiting Dead Hand Control of Charitable Trusts: Expanding the Use of the Cy Pres Doctrine*, 21 U. Haw. L. Rev. 353 (1999).

Terrance A. Kline, *Comment on the Barnes Foundation Case*, 31 ACTEC J. 245 (2005).

Alberto B. Lopez, *A Revaluation of Cy Pres Redux*, 78 U. Cin. L. Rev. 1307 (2010).

Katie Magallanes, *Beyond Donor Intent: Leveraging Cy Pres to Remedy Unintended Burdens Caused by Charitable Gifts*, 40 ACTEC L.J. 407 (2014).

John Nivala, *Droit Patrimoine: The Barnes Collection, the Public Interest, and Protecting Our Cultural Inheritance*, 55 Rutgers L. Rev. 477 (2003).

Eric G. Pearson, *Reforming the Reform of the Cy Pres Doctrine: A Proposal to Protect Testator Intent*, 90 Marq. L. Rev. 127 (2006).

Frances Howell Rudko, *The Cy Pres Doctrine in the United States: From Extreme Reluctance to Affirmative Action*, 46 Clev. St. L. Rev. 471 (1998).

Heinrich Schweizer, *Settlor's Intent vs. Trustee's Will: The Barnes Foundation Case*, 29 Colum. J.L. & Arts 63 (2005).

Allison Anna Tait, *The Secret Economy of Charitable Giving*, 95 B.U. L.Rev. 1663 (2015).

Reid Kress Weisbord, *Reservations About Donor Standing: Should the Law Allow Charitable Donors to Reserve the Right to Enforce a Gift Restriction?*, 42 Real Prop. Prob. & Tr. J. 245 (2007).

Chapter 9

Planning for The Future: Successive Trust Interests

Clients creating trusts usually will want those trusts to stretch over parts of one or more generations. For example, the settlor of a lifetime trust may want to retain the income for life and then use the fund to pay children's or grandchildren's education expenses. Similarly, a common plan for a testamentary trust is to give the surviving spouse income for life, then give income to the testator's children during their lives, and finally distribute the principal to the grandchildren. To fulfill such goals, lawyers help their clients create both present and future interests.

This chapter emphasizes how lawyers can use present and future interests in the modern-day trust world.[1] Mastering this material may take some time, but success is neither impossible nor irrelevant. Indeed, the concepts discussed here are the basic building blocks of trusts since the creation of a trust will invariably involve at least one future interest. Even if the names fade from your memory, the ideas they represent will be crucial to your ability both to present estate planning choices to your clients and to draft documents that fulfill clients' wishes. The power you have over their plans carries a special responsibility to do the job well. This chapter begins with some basics to refresh your recollection of material you probably covered in a Property course. Then we turn to a series of interpretation questions as we seek to identify language to avoid and techniques for creating effective gifts. Next we examine the device most responsible for preserving flexibility over time: powers of appointment. The chapter closes with the Rule Against Perpetuities and related rules on dead hand control.

§ 9.01 Fundamentals

This section discusses some fundamental concepts that cut across the entire topic and then introduces the interests found in most modern estate plans.

1. Future interests may also be created in non-trust dispositions; the devise of a life estate in a farm to one person with remainder to another is an example. Indeed, the law of future interests developed during a period in English history when trusts were not commonly used. Today, however, dispositions in trust are usually preferable to non-trust dispositions because the trustee can transfer the underlying trust property without obtaining the consent of the trust beneficiaries.

A. Dividing by Time

This area of law developed over a period of hundreds of years to meet landowners' needs. Although these concepts now apply most often to personal property held in trust, viewing the question initially in terms of land can help with the fundamentals. First, the law separates the notion of ownership from the thing owned. We own "interests" in land, rather than the dirt itself. Second, we can divide our interests among different people according to when they have the right to use the land. Third, we treat these individual interests as if they were things in themselves. We give them unique characteristics and speak as if they behave in various ways.

The biggest, most complete interest is the fee simple absolute. If Howard owns a fee simple absolute interest in a lot, he owns an interest which extends forward in time for infinity. Suppose Howard died owning the property. His fee simple absolute would not end just because he died. Rather, it would go to someone else, by intestacy or by will. If it went intact, the recipient would get exactly what Howard had, an interest extending ahead in time for infinity.

Suppose, however, Howard left a will dividing the ownership: he gave Ethel the right to use the lot during her lifetime and said that after her death Andrew can use it. Howard's will created both a present interest and a future interest. Because Ethel can now use the lot, she has what we call a present interest, in this case a life estate. Because it ends at her death, however, her interest is not as large as Howard's. Because we know now that Andrew's interest will entitle him (or his successor) to use the lot after Ethel's death, we say Andrew now has a future interest, in this case a remainder. Future interests are not things people get in the future. Rather, they are things people own in the present, but which carry a right of possession in the future, rather like a ticket to next week's concert.

Future interests are really just present interests pushed out ahead of us. When Ethel dies, whoever holds Andrew's interest will be able to use the land. That person then will have a present interest, in this case, a fee simple absolute. When considering a future interest, you might imagine it as a box. On the outside is a label identifying the type of future interest; inside, however, is a present interest currently hidden from view.

The notion of dividing ownership according to time has allowed the development of modern trust law. In place of Ethel's right to use the lot, we give her the right to receive income from a trust. In place of Andrew's right to use the lot next, we give him a right to distribution of the trust principal after Ethel's death. Because the trustee holds legal title, Ethel and Andrew have equitable interests, but they behave in much the same way as the legal interests invented centuries ago.

B. Defeasibility

Some present and future interests can be lost if, from the perspective of the interest holder, the wrong things happen. An interest under this cloud is subject to "defeasance." Interests can end one of two ways, according to the language that created them in the first place: they can expire or they can be divested. "Limitational" language—like "until" and "so long as"—creates interests which may expire. If a grantor uses "conditional" language—like "but if"; "provided, however"; and "on the condition that"—the resulting interest will be an estate subject to divestment.

To see the differences between expiration and divestment, consider two of the "defeasible fee" estates. These estates are present interests that conceivably could go on forever, but that may also end. Although lawyers seldom use defeasible fee estates anymore, *cf. Cooley v. Williams*, 31 S.W.3d 810 (Tex. App. 2000) (layperson's holographic will construed to create fee simple determinable), the concepts they embody remain important in modern trusts. A grant from Stacey "to Brian so long as the church stands, then to Cheryl if she is then living" gives Brian a fee simple determinable and Cheryl an executory interest. [2] In contrast, a grant "to Brian, but if the church falls, then to Cheryl if she is then living" gives Brian a fee simple subject to an executory limitation and Cheryl an executory interest. The fee simple determinable is limited by time. The fee simple subject to an executory limitation is subject to a condition. The difference in language explains the difference in the way these estates end.

Figure 9-1 illustrates a fee simple determinable (the circle) followed by an executory interest (the dashed arrow). (The solid dot inside the executory interest represents the potential fee simple absolute hidden inside.) The dashed arrow points away from the circle to illustrate that when the church no longer stands, the present interest will expire on its own, leaving the future interest to take its place.

Figure 9-1 Fee Simple Determinable and Executory Interest

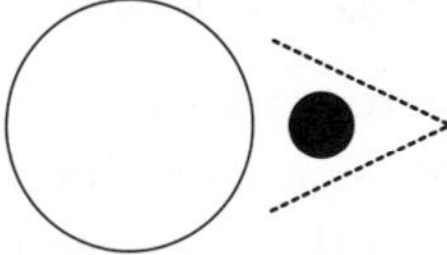

Figure 9-2 illustrates a fee simple subject to an executory limitation (the cross-hatched circle), and an executory interest (the arrow). This time, the arrow points toward the circle to indicate that if the condition is broken the executory interest will move in and end ("divest") the present interest.

Figure 9-2 Fee Simple Subject to an Executory Limitation and Executory Interest

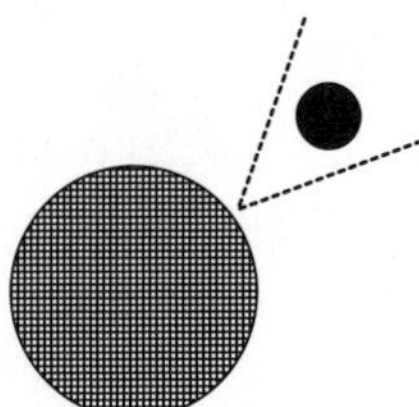

2. "Executory interest" is the label the law gives to a particular category of future interests.

What difference does it make whether we say an interest expires or is divested? Suppose Cheryl dies while the church is still standing, but it later collapses. Because Cheryl is not living when the church falls, she cannot take the property. If Stacey had created a fee simple determinable, Brian's interest would still expire on its own accord, and Stacey would retake the property as grantor. On the other hand, if Stacey had created a fee simple subject to an executory limitation, Brian would keep the property although the church no longer stood. His interest could be lost only by divestment, and with Cheryl gone, there is no one to divest Brian. Because he holds an estate subject to divestment by nobody, we recognize that he has a fee simple absolute.

This difference between expiration and divestment can apply to either present or future interests and allows lawyers to design estate plans with very specific circumstances in mind. Consider Andrea, who wants to leave a trust fund for her husband, Quinn, but also wants his income to stop if he remarries. At Quinn's remarriage or death, the trust will end and the property will go to Andrea's daughter, Kristin. If Andrea's main objective is to end Quinn's interest, no matter what, she can use language which follows the form "to Quinn for life so long as he remains unmarried, then to Kristin if she is then living." Even if Kristin does not survive, Quinn's interest will expire upon his remarriage. On the other hand, if Andrea wants to end Quinn's interest only if Kristin is around to benefit, Andrea can use language following the pattern of "to Quinn for life, but if he remarries, to Kristin if she is then living, and if he does not remarry, to Kristin if she is living at his death." Quinn's remarriage will end his interest only if Kristin is then alive.

C. Life Estates, Term of Years and Reversions

Modern estate plans regularly create life estates[3] or estates for a term of years[4] and therefore often include reversions. A grantor who creates only a life estate, or creates a life estate plus a remainder other than a vested remainder in a fee simple estate, necessarily retains a reversion. In the simplest example, if Geoffrey gives property "to Helen for life," Helen has a legal life estate and Geoffrey has a legal reversion. Assume Geoffrey also used a trust, giving property to Second Bank, to hold as trustee for Helen for 20 years. After 20 years, the bank will hold the property subject to a "resulting trust" in favor of Geoffrey. Such a resulting trust is also known as an "equitable reversion."

---

3. There may be a question whether a disposition creates a fee simple or a life estate. *See, e.g., Anderson v. Anderson*, 791 S.E.2d 40 (Ga. 2016) (only life estate created in individual).

4. Section 24.6 of the Restatement (Third) of Property defines a term of years as follows:

> The term of years is a present interest that terminates on the expiration of a term that is measured in one or more years, in units of a year, or in multiples or divisions thereof. A term of years can be qualified by language that specifies one or more events that can terminate the estate before or extend the estate beyond the expiration of the term.

Because reversions are retained interests that need not be expressed, they are easy to miss. Watch for them in the discussion that follows.

D. Remainders and Executory Interests

Remainders and executory interests are future interests held by third parties, people who are neither the grantor nor the present interest holder. One way to help distinguish between remainders and executory interests is by assigning each a personality characteristic. Remainders are patient; they snuggle up against a present interest and wait for its natural expiration; they have pillows. In contrast, executory interests are aggressive; they go around cutting short other interests; they have hatchets.[5] Remainders come in two types, vested and contingent, to which we now turn.

1. Vested Remainders

A remainder is "vested" if it satisfies three tests. First, the holder of the remainder must be someone who has been born. Second, that person must be identified. Third, there can be no express or implied condition precedent to that person taking. If a remainder is vested, it might be any of three types:

Indefeasibly Vested. Just as a fee simple is the largest interest, an indefeasibly vested remainder is the largest remainder. It is just a fee simple absolute, pushed out into the future. Suppose Joseph's will gives property "to Rose for life, remainder to Barbara." Rose has a life estate, and Barbara has an indefeasibly vested remainder.

Subject to Complete Defeasance. Just as a fee simple can be defeasible, so can a vested remainder. Many vested remainders subject to complete defeasance are just defeasible fees, pushed out into the future. Others are life estates in future garb. The key characteristic of these remainders is that they can be completely lost. Consider a trust disposition "to Alice for 20 years, remainder to Bob, but if Bob drinks liquor, to Peggy." Bob has a vested remainder subject to complete defeasance.

Subject to Open. Sometimes settlors will give property to a group of people whose membership is not fixed at the time of drafting. The usual idea of using such a class gift is to allow people born after the drafting, but before the time for distribution, to share in the gift. For example, Stan may create a trust for "my wife Mia for life, and then to her children." We call the remainder to the children a class gift, a concept we will examine more completely below. Because children born later could qualify as class members, we say the class is "open" during Mia's life. Suppose Stan and Mia have one child, Frieda. Frieda's remainder is vested because we can identify who is

---

5. The one exception, illustrated in Figure 9-1, is that an executory interest following a fee simple determinable does not cut short the fee simple, because the fee simple determinable expires automatically. In this situation, the executory interest is acting more like a remainder, but for historical reasons usually still carries the "executory interest" label.

getting it and because it is not subject to a condition precedent. However, Frieda may have to share her remainder with a later-born sibling. To account for that possibility, we say her remainder is vested, subject to partial divestment. Because this situation arises only when we have an open class, most lawyers use the shorter term "vested, subject to open."

2. Contingent Remainders

If remainders are not vested, they are contingent. The way to identify contingent remainders, therefore, is to work through the definition of vested remainders to see if the interest in question fails one of those tests. Ask: (1) Is the holder of the remainder someone who has not yet been born? (2) Is the holder of the remainder unidentified? (3) Is there any express or implied condition precedent to that person taking? If the answer to any question is "yes," the remainder is contingent.

A remainder "to Scott's children" is contingent if Scott has no children. A remainder "to the first child of my departed brother Taylor who graduates from college," is contingent if none of Taylor's children has graduated from college. We do not yet know who will qualify. A remainder "to Taylor's first child if that child graduates from college" is contingent if the eldest child has not graduated. Notice that this time we can identify the remainderman, but that person faces the condition precedent of graduating. Although it is correct to say each of these grants creates a contingent remainder, we also need to understand why each remainder is contingent. Without that information, we cannot determine the preconditions for the interest holder benefiting, and we cannot judge the interest's validity under the Rule Against Perpetuities. *See infra* § 9.04.

As a practical matter, a person must survive the termination of the present interest in order to enjoy a remainder personally, but that fact does not make all remainders contingent. For an interest to be contingent, the right to enjoy the property must be contingent. Suppose Bill gives property "to Susan for life, remainder to Peter." Under traditional analysis, Peter has an indefeasibly vested remainder. If Peter dies before Susan, his successors (through intestacy, will, or deed) would take his vested remainder, and get the property at Susan's death.

Settlors often create alternative gifts, in case the favored person does not qualify to take. These gifts may take the form of alternative contingent remainders. Suppose Joanne grants property "to Scott for life, then to Taylor if he survives Scott, and if he does not, to Todd." Taylor has a contingent remainder, contingent on survival.[6] Todd

---

6. An old case haunts this analysis if the contingency involves reaching a certain age. *Edwards v. Hammond*, 83 Eng. Rep. 614 (K.B. 1683), says, in effect, if you repeat an age contingency, a court will ignore your first reference as surplusage, leaving a vested, subject construction. Thus, if you grant "to Michael for life, then if Polly reaches 21 to Polly, but if Polly does not reach 21, to Chris," a court may read it like this: "to Michael for life, then to Polly, but if Polly does not reach 21, to Chris." Polly gets a vested remainder, subject to complete defeasance. Modern courts less

also has a contingent remainder, this one contingent upon Taylor's nonsurvival of Scott (although Joanne has not imposed the additional contingency that Todd survive Scott). Joanne has a reversion.

Why does Joanne have a reversion? Surely Taylor will either survive Scott and take the remainder, or not survive, so Todd will take. The answer lies in history and the ancient concept of seisin.[7] In particular, in medieval times a life estate might end by forfeiture (say, for treason) before the life tenant's death. Because neither remainderman would yet have qualified to take, the property would go to the grantor. Today, interests may be forfeited for certain crimes. Saying the grantor retains a reversion recognizes the very remote possibility that the life estate will end before the life tenant actually dies. *See* Lewis M. Simes & Allan F. Smith, The Law of Future Interests §85 (3d ed. 2002). For modern use, simply remember: if there is a contingent remainder, there must be a reversion.

When drafters create alternative future interests following a life estate (as in the example above), classifying those interests may be particularly difficult. Usually two possible constructions appear: (1) two alternative contingent remainders followed by a reversion, or (2) a vested remainder followed by an executory interest. The key to classification in this context usually is the first future interest.

When distinguishing between a remainder that is contingent and one that is vested but subject to defeasance, a mental image of the difference between the two interests may be helpful. Someone holding a contingent remainder is rather like an applicant in a job interview, hoping to be hired. Someone with a vested remainder, subject to defeasance, is more like a new employee, still in a "probationary" period, worried about being fired.

In order to determine whether a remainder is contingent, or vested subject to complete defeasance, we must look carefully at the words of the grant. If the language of condition is part of the description of the taker ("my children who survive me") or comes before words like "but" and "however" ("to Lori if she attends law school; but if she does not, to Ellen"), the condition is precedent and the remainder, contingent. If the modifying language comes after a conjunction ("to Lori, but if Lori does not attend law school, to Ellen") courts will usually find a vested remainder, subject to complete defeasance. Sometimes it helps to assume the life tenant has died before the contingency has been resolved. Under such circumstances, if you would say the remainderman has not yet qualified to take

---

committed to the tradition of favoring vested constructions might not follow the rule, especially in a trust context. In any case, the rule does not apply to age contingencies tied to the description of a class. *See Festing v. Allen*, 152 Eng. Rep. 1204 (Ex. 1843) (gift "to Martha's children who reach 21" was contingent).

7. "[W]e can 'get by' if we treat [seisin] as possession plus a mystical something which described a man's claim to an estate of freehold in land." John E. Cribbet & Corwin W. Johnson, Principles of the Law of Property 15 (3d ed. 1989).

the property, the remainder is contingent. On the other hand, if the remainderman takes, the remainder is vested.

We can use the various concepts described above to create an endless variety of combinations: vested remainders for life, subject to open . . . contingent remainders subject to open . . . contingent remainders which, if they ever vest, will nonetheless be subject to complete defeasance . . . executory interests subject to open . . . . If choices like those sound discouraging, cheer up! The very flexibility of the system of estates is what has kept it alive after so many centuries. Lawyers use these different combinations to effectuate their clients' estate plans.

E. Trusts and Future Interests

The use of trusts to create future interests introduces an added dimension to any discussion of future interests because trusts involve both legal and equitable interests. Thus, if Sue transfers property to Ted in trust to pay the income to Bill for Bill's life, and the principal to Carl upon the death of Bill, we must determine ownership of both the legal and equitable fees. Normally the legal interest is owned by Ted in fee simple subject to the rights of the trust beneficiaries. As for the equitable title, Bill has an equitable life estate, and Carl an equitable remainder. Second, analysis differs slightly between recognized equitable future interests and legal future interests. The major difference is that equitable interests not successfully given away by the settlor are sometimes called resulting trust interests, although equitable reversionary interest is technically correct. *See* 3d Rest. Prop. § 7. Finally, the necessity under the Statute of Uses for active duties running from the legal title holder to the equitable title holder suggests that if identical legal and equitable interests vest in the same person, no trust can exist because one cannot owe a duty to oneself. This is the trust merger doctrine and necessitates comparing the legal and equitable interests in trusts to determine the validity of the trust.

F. Problems in Classification

Although it is possible to define future interests in terms of reversionary, remainder, and executory interests, classification of a particular interest is not a simple task. For example, suppose Alice transfers property to Beth for the life of Beth, then to Cindy's children in remainder. It is impossible to know merely from the terms of the grant the nature of the future interest. If, at the time of the transfer, Cindy is dead and no children of Cindy survive, Alice has an indefeasible reversion. If Cindy is dead but children of Cindy survive, those children take vested remainders. If Cindy is alive and at least one child of Cindy is alive, that child takes a vested remainder subject to open. If Cindy is alive but has no children alive, the remainder in "Cindy's children" is a contingent remainder, and Alice has a reversion. Obviously, classification depends not only upon the instrument, but also upon the surrounding facts. Classification in the abstract is impossible!

Problems

1. Assume that the first person mentioned was the settlor of a lifetime trust, that the trustee held the legal title, and that all of the named parties are alive. Classify the equitable interests created by the following dispositions in trust:

(a) Olive to Agnes for life, then to Boyd for life, then to Charlotte.

(b) Tammy to Alvin for life, then to Alvin's widow for her life, then to Jay, if he survives Alvin's widow.

(c) Olive to Harriet for life, then to Herb if he survives Harriet, and if not to Hazel.

(d) Mark to Gilbert for life, then to James, but if James dies before Gilbert, to Vivien.

(e) Rebecca to Margaret for life, remainder to Viola's heirs. [Viola is alive at the time of the grant.]

(f) Paul to Carl for life so long as Carl remains unmarried; at the earlier of Carl's death and/or his remarriage, to Fred.

2. Tanya's will gave property "to Eric for life, then to Eric's children, but if none of Eric's children survive Eric, then to Violet, if she survives Eric." Consider how the classifications change over time.

(a) At Tanya's death, Eric had two children, Jay and Katina. Who owns what interests?

(b) Jay died, leaving all of his property to Lisa. Who owns what interests?

(c) Violet died, leaving all of her property to Katherine. Who owns what interests?

(d) Eric died. Who owns what interests?

3. Tanya's will gave property "to Eric for life, then to those of Eric's children who survive him, but if none of Eric's children survive him, then to Violet, if she survives Eric." Who owns what interests in each of the fact situations noted in problem 2?

4. Dale left property "to Colleen for life, then if Rita reaches age 21 to Rita, but if Rita dies before age 21, then to Audrey." Colleen, Rita, and Audrey all survive Dale. Rita is 16. Who owns what interests?

5. Draft the dispository clause of your own will giving a life estate to one person and remainders to others.

6. Nina Santora, 56, is married to Henry Santora and has two children from a prior marriage (Conrad and Joseph Lahann). She is creating a trust for Henry, Conrad, and Joseph. She wants to give Henry the trust income during his lifetime, with the principal going equally to the sons, or all to the surviving son. If neither son survives, the property should go to the National Multiple Sclerosis Society. If Henry remarries, however, Nina wants Henry's interest to end and the sons to take at that time. Draft the dispository language necessary to achieve Nina's goals.

G. The Restatement (Third) of Property's Simplified Classification System

Division VII of the Restatement (Third) of Property simplifies the classification of both present and future interests. As explained in the Scope of Division VII:

> Today, present and future interests are predominantly created as equitable interests in trust, not as legal interests in land. For modern purposes, the system of classification based on English land law is unnecessarily complex. As noted in a prominent treatise on the English law of real property: "English real property law has tended to have an unenviable reputation for its complexity." Much of the complexity serves no purpose in modern circumstances. England simplified its land law by legislation in 1925. This Restatement simplifies classification for American law. The principal function of classification today is descriptive—a shorthand way of labeling an interest that has specific characteristics.[8]

Regarding present interests, simplification comes about by conflating the three types of fee simple defeasible estates into simply the fee simple defeasible. *See* 3d Rest. Prop. § 24.3. Simplification in the future interests arena is more complex. First, future interests can only be classified as reversions or remainders. *See* 3d Rest. Prop. § 25.2. In the process, the following future interests are discontinued: the executory interest, the possibility of reverter, and the right of entry. *See* 3d Rest. Prop. § 25.2, cmts. c and d. Further, a future interest must be classified as vested or contingent pursuant to Section 25.3 of the Restatement (Third) of Property:

> A future interest is either contingent or vested. A future interest is contingent if it might not take effect in possession or enjoyment. A future interest is vested if it is certain to take effect in possession or enjoyment. A contingent or a vested future interest may additionally be classified according to the present interest into which the future interest will ripen once and if it takes effect in possession or enjoyment—as a fee simple absolute (or absolute ownership), a fee simple defeasible, a life estate, or a term of years.

As a result of this new definition, the traditional classifications of indefeasibly vested remainders and vested remainders subject to complete divestment are eliminated. Both are simply classified as vested remainders. Reversions, which traditionally are always classified as vested, will either be classified as vested or contingent depending on the disposition. *Compare* 3d Rest. Prop. § 25.3, Illustration 5 (vested reversion), *with* Illustration 5 (contingent reversion).

Section 25.4 of the Restatement (Third) of Property treats postponed class gifts:

> In the case of a postponed class gift that is open to new entrants, the future interest of each class member existing from time to time is classified as subject to open. Under the rule of § 25.3, the future interest can be either vested

8. Footnotes have been omitted.

or contingent. The future interest of a potential class member is always classified as contingent.

This new definition continues the traditional classification of vested remainder subject to open. *See* 3d Rest. Prop. § 25.4, Illustration 1. However, the historical classification of contingent is replaced by contingent remainder subject to open. *See* 3d Rest. Prop. § 25.4, Illustrations 2–5.

It will be interesting to see whether courts and legislatures embrace the welcome changes in classification that are made by the Restatement (Third) of Property.

Selected References

Roger W. Andersen, *Present and Future Interests: A Graphic Explanation*, 19 Seattle U. L. Rev. 101 (1995).

D. Benjamin Barros, *Toward a Model Law of Estates and Future Interests*, 66 Wash & Lee L. Rev. 3 (2009).

Jesse J. Dukeminier, Jr., *Contingent Remainders and Executory Interests: A Requiem for the Distinction*, 43 Minn. L. Rev. 13 (1958).

T.P. Gallanis, *The Future of Future Interests*, 60 Wash. & Lee L. Rev. 513 (2003).

Lewis M. Simes & Allan F. Smith, The Law of Future Interests (3d ed. 2002).

§ 9.02 Interpretation Questions

As we saw in Chapter 3, wills, including testamentary trusts, can give rise to issues of interpretation (construction) in determining the intention of the testator. Such issues also may be encountered with lifetime trusts and deeds. Whatever type of donative document, the ultimate goal of the constructional process is to determine the transferor's intention.

In this section, we consider recurrent problems in the law of future interests where a trust instrument contains an ambiguity that cannot be resolved by resorting to evidence of the settlor's actual intention, including the trust language, the dispositive scheme and extrinsic evidence. Specifically, we address three areas that haunt modern drafters. First, we examine conditions of survival. Traditionally a source of trouble, this area faces new controversy in the form of a radical UPC position. Then we turn to a series of topics involving gifts to classes. The section closes with rules for interpreting words like "dies without issue." Simple-sounding, the term is loaded.

Rules of construction, including constructional preferences, have developed a way to attribute intention when actual intent cannot be discovered. Although these rules are treated as presumptions[9] (or perhaps even "special-purpose presumptions"), in

9. *See* 3d Rest. Prop. § 11.3, cmt. a.

most cases the presumption cannot be overcome due to a lack of evidence. The settlor did not think about the problem that raises the ambiguity.

Although it is said that rules of construction are designed to carry out subjective intent, they actually may exist to further societal objectives. Consider the following from Lewis M. Simes & Allan F. Smith, The Law of Future Interests §465 (3d ed. 2002):

> Do these rules of construction aid in determining testator's subjective intention, or do they serve other ends? No one will deny that some of the rules of construction are based upon probabilities in the light of human experience so that their application tends in a majority of cases to effectuate the actual subjective intention of the testator. Thus, some of the general rules of construction, such as the preference for keeping property in the line of blood relatives of the testator, seem to express a viewpoint prevalent among a majority of humans. It may be urged, therefore, that a choice of assumptions which gives language meaning by which property is given to blood relatives rather than collateral relatives is a choice aimed at discovering the subjective intention of the testator. It may be equally urged, however, that the choice is made simply because of a social judgment that blood relatives ought to be preferred over collaterals, and that this rule of construction is aimed at achieving that result. It is submitted that many rules of construction necessarily contain something more than guides for finding subjective intent.

Accepting the notion that rules of construction in future interests also may be designed to carry out societal goals, what goals are involved and are there competing goals? Consider the views of Lewis M. Simes & Allan F. Smith, The Law of Future Interests §§468, 470 (3d ed. 2002):

> First, rules may exist to further the alienability of property; such appear to be the rules favoring vesting and early vesting, and favoring a substitutional construction. Second, the purpose may be to keep the property in the family. Third, the purpose may be to favor the natural objects of the testator's bounty—near relatives or dependents, such as a wife and children, or other dependent members of his household. Fourth, rules may exist for the purpose of avoiding intestacy, a mere arbitrary method of deciding the case, of somewhat more dignified and judicial character than tossing a coin or rolling dice. After all, the lay public is inclined to criticize a judge who holds a will invalid; for a will is like a constitution, in that one can get rid of it much more easily by construing it than by holding it void. Fifth, the rule may have nothing to do with objectives; it may be employed as a part of a postrationalizing process to justify a decision in a case where the judge is unable or unwilling to state his actual objectives. Rules of this sort not uncommonly exist in pairs. If one result is desired, one rule is used; if the opposite result, we use the other. Thus we have the rule that, if two parts of a will are contradictory, the latter prevails. We also have the rule that if a fee simple or

> absolute interest is given, it requires very plain language to cut it down by a later clause. Obviously, if the judge wishes one result, he explains it by the first rule; if the opposite result, he uses the second rule.
>
> [B]ecause the general rules of construction are so widely applicable, it is not uncommon to discover that two general rules are applicable to the same transaction, but that they produce opposite results. Thus, application of the rule of construction favoring vested interests rather than contingent interests may result in property leaving the blood line of the testator, even though there is a general preference for a construction which will give property to the blood relatives of the testator.

A. Survival

Document drafters regularly include survival language when they create future interests. Slight differences in the way drafters shape that language, however, can have significant consequences for the families involved. This section first examines traditional approaches and then discusses the substantial changes the UPC proposes.

1. *Traditional Approaches*

Traditional doctrine tells us that if Herb's will gave property in trust "to Barry for life, remainder to Leslie," Leslie's equitable remainder is indefeasibly vested. *See, e.g., In re Hobert*, 794 N.Y.S.2d 783 (Surr. Ct. 2004). *Accord* 3d Rest. Prop. § 26.3 (no implied condition of survivorship). If Leslie predeceases Barry and has not transferred her remainder during her lifetime, the remainder will pass to her successors, by intestacy or by will. Because her remainder interest was not subject to a condition of survivorship, it is not lost at her death.

In many situations, clients probably want future interest holders to survive until the time the beneficiary would take either income or principal. Drafting alternative gifts if a beneficiary predeceases requires special care. Consider whether the testator in the following case intended the result that occurred.

Swanson v. Swanson

514 S.E.2d 822 (Ga. 1999)

Fletcher, Presiding Justice.

The issue in this appeal is whether Laura C. "Peggy" Swanson inherits from her deceased husband Bennie Swanson the remainder interests he had in trusts created by his father. Because Bennie Swanson's remainder interests vested before his death and conditions subsequent contained in the trust provisions did not occur before the life beneficiary of the trusts died, Bennie's vested remainder was not defeased and instead passed according to the terms of his will. Therefore, we reverse.

When George Swanson died testate in 1970 he was survived by his wife Gertrude Swanson and his nine children. George's will created two trusts in which Gertrude had a life estate with the remainder left to the nine children, who were all named in the will. Bennie Swanson was one of these children. Bennie died testate prior to Gertrude. He had no children, but was survived by his wife Peggy Swanson, who is the sole beneficiary under his will. After Gertrude's death, Peggy Swanson and other relatives of George and Gertrude brought this action seeking a declaration of their rights under the trusts. The trial court granted summary judgment against Peggy on her claim that she was entitled to Bennie's remainder interests in the trusts. Peggy appeals and six of George and Gertrude's children are appellees.

1. To distinguish between vested remainders and contingent remainders, a court must determine whether at the time the instrument takes effect there is "a person who in his own right, or as a part of his estate, would take all of this property if [the life estate] ended now." [Richard R. Powell, Powell on Real Property, § 20.04 [2] (1998); Restatement of the Law of Property (1936) § 157, comment on clause (c).] If there is such a person, then the remainder is vested subject to partial or complete defeasance. If no such person is identifiable, then the remainder is subject to a condition precedent and is a contingent remainder. In determining the type of remainder created, Georgia has consistently followed two common-law principles: (a) the law favors construing "conditions to be subsequent" and (b) the law favors the "vesting of remainders in all cases of doubt," which is also called the "early vesting" of remainders.[10]

THE ITEM IV TRUST

2. The Item IV trust provided that, the corpus of this trust shall be disposed of according to the directions of my wife, Gertrude Swanson, either given by her appointment during her lifetime or by will upon her death. If she fails to make such disposition, then and in that event, the corpus of this trust, upon her death, shall pass to my nine children, herein above named, to be divided among them in equal shares, share and share alike. If any of my children should not be in life at the time of death of my said wife, the share of such deceased child shall go to his or her surviving children, per stirpes.

Following George's death, there were immediately identifiable persons who would take if the life estate ended: George's nine children. Therefore, each child had a vested remainder interest. Additionally, there were two conditions subsequent attached to the vested remainder. These conditions, which could bring about total defeasance of the vested remainder, were: (1) Gertrude's exercise of her power of appointment;[11] and (2) a child predeceasing Gertrude, but leaving children who survived Gertrude. Neither of these conditions occurred prior to the termination of Gertrude's life estate. She did not exercise her power of appointment and although Bennie died before

10. Georgia statute on early vesting, Ga. Code Ann. § 44-6-66, provides as follows: The law favors the vesting of remainders in all cases of doubt. In construing wills, words of survivorship shall refer to those survivors living at the time of the death of the testator in order to vest remainders unless a manifest intention to the contrary shall appear.

11. Exercise of a power of appointment is viewed as operating as a condition subsequent on the remainder in default of appointment. *See* Powell on Real Property, at § 20.04[5].

Gertrude, he left no children who survived Gertrude. Furthermore, the Swanson trusts contain no "very clear conditions of survivorship," and, therefore, Bennie's interest remained fully vested and passed under his will.

Holding these remainders to be vested and not defeased by the occurrence of a condition subsequent is consistent with our prior decisions. In *Witcher v. Witcher*, [231 Ga. 49, 200 S.E.2d 110 (1973)] the testator devised a life estate to his wife with "remainder over to my children, share and share alike" and "in the event either of my children should predecease me or my wife, then it is my will . . . the child or children of such deceased child take the share that would have gone to his or her parent, per stirpes." The testator was survived by his wife and four sons. One of the sons predeceased his mother and left no children, but his wife survived him. Finding that the condition subsequent did not occur, this Court held that the son's vested remainder passed by inheritance to his widow.

Similarly, in *Fields v. Lewis*, [118 Ga. 573, 45 S.437 (1903)] the grantor conveyed a life estate to his wife with remainder over "to such child or children or representatives of child or children as above mentioned or that she may bring forth by the said [grantor] and leaves in life." One child, who was living when the deed was executed, died intestate without children prior to the termination of the life estate. Thus, the sole condition that could cause a defeasance, dying before the life tenant and leaving a child who survived the life tenant, did not occur. Therefore, we held that the vested remainder was not divested and passed to the child's surviving spouse and sole heir.

The plain language of the Item IV trust, which follows the language of Witcher and Fields, evidences the testator's intent that the remainder be shared by nine families.

THE ITEM V TRUST

3. The Item V trust provided that "the remaining assets of this trust shall be divided into nine equal shares, one share for each of my surviving children or for the then surviving issue of each deceased child of ours." As with the Item IV trust, there were immediately identifiable persons who would take if the life estate ended: the surviving children. [Georgia Code Ann § 44-6-66, set forth in footnote 10] directs that we construe words of survivorship to refer to the death of the testator in order to vest remainders. There was one condition subsequent attached that could have caused a total defeasement of the vested remainder in each of George's children: the child predeceasing Gertrude, but leaving children who survived Gertrude. Although Bennie died prior to Gertrude, he had no children and, therefore, just as with the Item IV Trust, Bennie's vested remainder was not defeased and his one-ninth interest flowed into his estate.

In conclusion, we hold that Bennie Swanson's one-ninth interest in the trusts passes to his wife, his sole heir and beneficiary under his will because (1) his remainder was vested; (2) no condition subsequent occurred prior to the termination of the life estate; (3) there is no language in the will that plainly manifests a contrary intent; and (4) this construction is supported by case law and the applicable common-law principles.

Judgment reversed. All the Justices CONCUR, EXCEPT BENHAM, C. J., SEARS AND HINES, JJ., who dissent.

[Dissenting opinion omitted.]

Notes and Questions

1. Do you agree with the Swanson majority that George intended Bennie to lose his remainder only if he predeceased his father and left surviving descendants? The dissent argued that this result contravened the testator's intent based on reading the disposition in the context of the entire will. In *Martino v. Martino*, 35 S.W.3d 252 (Tex. App. 2000), the court construed a trust devise to the testator's spouse for life, with remainder to the testator's brothers and sisters with a substitutionary gift in favor of each siblings' surviving issue who predeceased the life tenant. In holding that the siblings who survived the life tenant succeeded to the predeceasing child's share, the court construed the substitutionary gift to surviving issue to mean that the testator could not have intended that the property should pass through the sibling's estate even though there were no surviving issue.

2. Notice the similarity between Bennie's remainder in Swanson and Brian's fee simple subject to an executory limitation illustrated in Figure 9-2.

3. Should survivorship be implied until the settlor of a revocable trust dies? For example, if a revocable trust provides income to settlor for life, remainder to B, will B's interest lapse if she predeceases the settlor or will B's interest be vested subject to divestment on the exercise of the power of revocation? *Compare Tait v. Community First Trust Co.*, 425 S.W.3d 684 (Ark. 2012) and *Baldwin v. Branch*, 888 So. 2d 482 (Ala. 2004) (vested so that B's successors in interest take on death of settlor where B predeceased settlor), *with* Cal. Prob. Code § 21109 (transferee does not take if fails to survive transferor). The Restatement (Third) of Property follows the California approach, which treats a revocable trust as a will for survival purposes. *See* 3d Rest. Prop. §§ 5.5, cmt. p and 15.2, cmt. d.

4. Sometimes survivorship language leaves open the question of how long the beneficiary must survive. Suppose that George's will had read, "To Eliese for life, then to Florence, but if Florence dies before Eliese, then to Florence's surviving children," and that Florence had a child, Rose. Would Rose have to survive George, Florence, or Elise? *Compare In re Nass's Estate*, 182 A. 401 (Pa. 1936) (survive the testator), *with In re Colman's Will*, 33 N.W.2d 237 (Wis. 1948) (survive immediate ancestor), *and In re Gustafson*, 547 N.E.2d 1152 (N.Y. 1989), *and* 3d Rest. Prop. § 26.4 (survive until the time for distribution). The lesson for drafters, of course, is to be clear.

5. Consider the following testamentary trust of the testator's residuary estate: Income to Al for life, 1/2 of the remainder to Boyce and Carol or the survivor; 1/2 to Charity. Boyce and Carol survive the testator but predecease Al. Does 1/2 pass to the heirs of Boyce and 1/2 to heirs of Carol? *See Estate of Zucker*, 761 A.2d 148 (Pa. Super. Ct. 2000) (yes).

6. Sam created a trust for his spouse Ann for life, remainder to his son, Charles, but if Charles fails to survive Ann, to Charles's child, Debbie. What interest was created in Charles? If Charles survives Ann but dies before the trust principal is distributed to him will Debbie be entitled to receive the distribution of trust principal? *See Wilson v. Rhodes*, 258 S.W.3d 873 (Mo. Ct. App. 2008) (no).

7. Even if a remainder beneficiary is required to survive until distribution by the trustee, the interest may become vested if the beneficiary dies before distribution and the distribution was unreasonably delayed by the trustee. *See In re Cornell*, 367 P.3d 173 (Idaho 2016).

Note: Implied Survival Requirements

In general, courts do not imply survivorship requirements in gifts of future interests, including single-generation class gifts, such as a gift to children or a gift to grandchildren. *See* 3d Rest. Prop. § 15.4. There are exceptions, however.

Multi-generational classes. Courts will imply conditions of survivorship when donors give to multi-generational classes, like "issue," "heirs," and "descendants." *See generally* 3d Rest. Prop. § 15.3. Courts generally define these terms as having a built-in survivorship requirement and alternative gift to those who survive.

Alternative gifts. If a gift is phrased in alternative terms—to Bea for life, then to Don or Nancy—courts usually will read it to mean that the gift to the first person is contingent upon survival. *See* 3d Rest. Prop. § 26.5. If Don predeceases Bea, Nancy will take. If both Don and Nancy predecease Bea, the general rule would not imply a condition with respect to Nancy's gift, so Nancy's successors will take.

Clobberie's Case. Under the rule of *Clobberie's Case*, 86 Eng. Rep. 476 (K.B. 1677), a gift to someone "at" a particular age will require the donee to survive until that age. On the other hand, other rules from that case direct courts to read "to Stanley, payable at 21," "to Stanley, to be paid at 21," and "to Stanley at 21 with interest" as creating vested interests, with no survival requirement. Under these latter interpretations, if Stanley dies, his successors can demand payment when Stanley would have reached 21. Section 26.6 of the Restatement (Third) of Property rejects the distinctions made in *Clobberie's Case* and would treat all of the above dispositions as requiring survival until the given age.

Another contingency. In a distinctly minority approach, some courts imply a condition of survival from another condition making a remainder contingent. *See, e.g.*, Lawson v. Lawson, 148 S.E.2d 546 (N.C. 1966) (remainder to life tenant's siblings expressly contingent upon life tenant having no children or leaving no surviving children was also impliedly contingent on surviving life tenant).

Divide and Pay Over. Some courts have held that if language requires property to be "divided and paid over" to a group of beneficiaries, they must survive until the time for distribution. See, e.g., *Harris Trust & Sav. Bank v. Beach*, *infra*. Most courts have repudiated or ignored the rule, and the Restatement rejects it. *See* 3d Rest. Prop. § 26.3, cmt. i. *But cf. Chavin v. PNC Bank*, 816 A.2d 781 (Del. 2003) (payment from revocable trust on death of settlor if beneficiary "then" be living construed as requiring beneficiary to survive until trust distribution).

Problems

1. Tim and Kathy had no children, but each had several siblings. Tim's will created a trust "for Kathy for life, remainder equally to my surviving nieces and nephews." What problems do you identify with this language?

2. Charley's will creates a trust "income to Andrea for life, remainder to Gary in fee simple, but if Gary dies before Andrea, remainder to Gary's first born child." Gary has one child, Tracy. Gary dies before Tracy, who dies before Andrea. Does Tracy's interest terminate on her death before Andrea?

3. Beth's will left property to "Ira for life, remainder to Maia, to be paid to her at age 21." Maia survived Beth, but died before reaching age 21. Ira died the next day. What happens to the property?

4. Hugh's will gave Sue a legal life estate in his home, with the remainder "to Jared or Melanie." If both Jared and Melanie survive Hugh, but predecease Sue, who gets the property when Sue dies?

5. Nathan created a testamentary trust with "income to my wife, Rose, remainder to our descendants." Nathan and Rose had three children, Jacob, Pauline, and Sylvia, none of whom survived Rose. Jacob had two children, Sara and Bill. Sara did not survive Rose, but Sara's children, Nancy and Eve, did. Bill survived. Pauline's daughter, Wendy, did not survive, but Wendy's son, Eric, did. None of Sylvia's descendants survived. How should the remainder be divided?

Selected References

Edward C. Halbach, Jr., *Future Interests: Express and Implied Conditions of Survival, Parts I & II*, 49 Cal. L. Rev. 297 & 431 (1961).

Edward C. Halbach, Jr., *Issues About Issue: Some Recurrent Class Gift Problems*, 48 Mo. L. Rev. 333 (1983).

Edward H. Rabin, *The Law Favors the Vesting of Estates. Why?*, 65 Colum. L. Rev. 467 (1965).

2. The UPC

In light of the confusion surrounding survivorship requirements for future interests, the UPC proposes significant reform. Taking an approach that parallels the antilapse statutes discussed supra, UPC § 2-707 applies to future interests under the terms of trusts. It requires beneficiaries to survive[12] until the time of distribution, and it provides an alternative distribution for a predeceased beneficiary's interest. In addition to the statute reproduced below, you may want to consult the UPC's extensive comments.

Uniform Probate Code

Section 2-707. Survivorship with Respect to Future Interests under Terms of Trust; Substitute Takers.

(a) [**Definitions.**] **In this section:**

(1) "Alternative future interest" means an expressly created future interest that can take effect in possession or enjoyment instead of another future interest on the happening of one or more events, including survival of an event or failure to survive an event, whether an event is expressed in condition-precedent, condition subsequent, or any other form. A residuary clause in a will does not create an alternative future interest with respect to a future interest created in a nonresiduary devise in the will, whether or not the will specifically provides that lapsed or failed devises are to pass under the residuary clause.

(2) "Beneficiary" means the beneficiary of a future interest and includes a class member if the future interest is in the form of a class gift.

(3) "Class member" includes an individual who fails to survive the distribution date but who would have taken under a future interest in the form of a class gift had he [or she] survived the distribution date.

(4) "Distribution date," with respect to a future interest, means the time when the future interest is to take effect in possession or enjoyment. The distribution date need not occur at the beginning or end of a calendar day, but can occur at a time during the course of a day.

(5) "Future interest" includes an alternative future interest and a future interest in the form of a class gift.

(6) "Future interest under the terms of a trust" means a future interest that was created by a transfer creating a trust or to an existing trust or by an exercise of a power of appointment to an existing trust, directing the continuance of an existing trust, designating a beneficiary of an existing trust, or creating a trust.

(7) "Surviving beneficiary" or "surviving descendant" means a beneficiary or a descendant who neither predeceased the distribution date nor is deemed to have predeceased the distribution date under Section 2-702 [generally requiring survivorship by 120 hours].

12. Recall that under the UPC "survival" means survival by 120 hours. UPC § 2-702.

(b) [**Survivorship required; Substitute Gift.**] A future interest under the terms of a trust is contingent on the beneficiary's surviving the distribution date. If a beneficiary of a future interest under the terms of a trust fails to survive the distribution date, the following apply:

(1) Except as provided in paragraph (4), if the future interest is not in the form of a class gift and the deceased beneficiary leaves surviving descendants, a substitute gift is created in the beneficiary's surviving descendants. They take by representation the property to which the beneficiary would have been entitled had the beneficiary survived the distribution date.

(2) Except as provided in paragraph (4), if the future interest is in the form of a class gift, other than a future interest to "issue," "descendants," "heirs of the body," "heirs," "next of kin," "relatives," or "family," or a class described by language of similar import, a substitute gift is created in the surviving descendants of any deceased beneficiary. The property to which the beneficiaries would have been entitled had all of them survived the distribution date passes to the surviving beneficiaries and the surviving descendants of the deceased beneficiaries. Each surviving beneficiary takes the share to which he [or she] would have been entitled had the deceased beneficiaries survived the distribution date. Each deceased beneficiary's surviving descendants who are substituted for the deceased beneficiary take by representation the share to which the deceased beneficiary would have been entitled had the deceased beneficiary survived the distribution date. For the purposes of this paragraph, "deceased beneficiary" means a class member who failed to survive the distribution date and left one or more surviving descendants.

(3) For the purposes of Section 2-701 [which says statutory rules control in the absence of a finding of contrary intention], words of survivorship attached to a future interest are not, in the absence of additional evidence, a sufficient indication of an intent contrary to the application of this section. Words of survivorship include words of survivorship that relate to the distribution date or to an earlier or an unspecified time, whether those words of survivorship are expressed in condition-precedent, condition-subsequent, or any other form.

(4) If a governing instrument creates an alternative future interest with respect to a future interest for which a substitute gift is created by paragraph (1) or (2), the substitute gift is superseded by the alternative future interest only if an expressly designated beneficiary of the alternative future interest is entitled to take in possession or enjoyment.

(c) [**More Than One Substitute Gift; Which One Takes.**] If, under subsection (b), substitute gifts are created and not superseded with respect to more than one future interest and the future interests are alternative future interests, one to the other, the determination of which the substitute gifts takes effect is resolved as follows:

(1) Except as provided in paragraph (2), the property passes under the primary substitute gift.

(2) If there is a younger-generation future interest, the property passes under the younger-generation substitute gift and not under the primary substitute gift.

(3) In this subsection:

(i) "Primary future interest" means the future interest that would have taken effect had all the deceased beneficiaries of the alternative future interests who left surviving descendants survived the distribution date.

(ii) "Primary substitute gift" means the substitute gift created with respect to the primary future interest.

(iii) "Younger-generation future interest" means a future interest that (A) is to a descendant of a beneficiary of the primary future interest, (B) is an alternative future interest with respect to the primary future interest, (C) is a future interest for which a substitute gift is created, and (D) would have taken effect had all the deceased beneficiaries who left surviving descendants survived the distribution date except the deceased beneficiary or beneficiaries of the primary future interest.

(iv) "Younger-generation substitute gift" means the substitute gift created with respect to the younger-generation future interest.

(d) [**If No Other Takers, Property Passes Under Residuary Clause or to Transferor's Heirs.**] Except as provided in subsection (e), if after the application of subsections (b) and (c), there is no surviving taker, the property passes in the following order:

(1) if the trust was created in a nonresiduary devise in the transferor's will or in a codicil to the transferor's will, the property passes under the residuary clause in the transferor's will; for purposes of this section, the residuary clause is treated as creating a future interest under the terms of a trust.

(2) if no taker is produced by the application of paragraph (a), the property passes to the transferor's heirs under Section 2-711.

(e) [**If No Other Takers and If Future Interest Created by Exercise of Power of Appointment.**] If, after the application of subsections (b) and (c), there is no surviving taker and if the future interest was created by the exercise of a power of appointment:

(1) the property passes under the donor's gift-in-default clause, if any, which clause is treated as creating a future interest under the terms of a trust; and

(2) if no taker is produced by the application of paragraph (1), the property passes as provided in subsection (d). For purposes of subsection (d), "transferor" means the donor if the power was a nongeneral power and means the donee if the power was a general power.

Edward C. Halbach, Jr. & Lawrence W. Waggoner, *The UPC's New Survivorship and Antilapse Provisions*

55 Alb. L. Rev. 1091, 1131–33 (1992)

In structure and theory, section 2-707 of the UPC parallels the antilapse provisions of sections 2-603 and 2-706. Unlike traditional antilapse statutes, section 2-707 expressly applies to future interests under the terms of a trust. Section 2-707 must be understood against the background of the common-law rules it replaces and the practices estate planners have adopted in drafting trusts in the light of those common-law rules. One of the recurring problems in future interests law concerns survivorship: Is a future interest extinguished (terminated) if its holder dies after the creation of the interest but before the time of possession or enjoyment?

Future interests are normally given to persons in one or more generations younger than that of the income beneficiary. If the income interest is granted to the grantor's surviving spouse, the remainder interest is likely to be granted to the couple's children or descendants; if the income interest is granted to a child of the grantor, the remainder interest is likely to be granted to the child's children or descendants. It is unusual, in other words, to grant an income interest to the grantor's grandchild and follow it with a remainder interest to the grantor's parents.

Consequently, when the beneficiary of a future interest predeceases the time of possession or enjoyment, the event is unexpected, typically caused by the remainder beneficiary's premature death or the life beneficiary's unusually long life span. When the unusual or unexpected happens, however, and a beneficiary dies before the time of possession or enjoyment, the first place to look to see if that event was anticipated and provided for is the governing instrument. If the governing instrument expressly imposes a condition of survival—as, for example, in the disposition "to A for life, remainder to B if B survives A"—then survival is required, of course. Conversely, if the governing instrument expressly states that no condition of survival is imposed—as, for example, in the disposition "to A for life, remainder to B whether or not B survives A"—then, of course, B need not survive A. What happens if the governing instrument expresses neither intention—as, for example, in the disposition "to A for life, remainder to B"? The basic rule of construction at common law is that a condition of survival is not implied, except in the case of flexible, multiple-generation classes such as "issue" or "descendants." Several rationales are offered in support of this rule. The rule, it is said, (i) furthers the constructional preference for complete dispositions of property; (ii) furthers the constructional preference for equality of distribution among the different lines of descent; (iii) is supported by the constructional preferences for vested over contingent interests, for vesting at the earliest possible time, and for indefeasible vesting at the earliest possible time; and (iv) furthers the alienability of property.

Of these four, the first, second, and fourth rationales are the most convincing, and the second probably the most forceful. The constructional preference for vested interests is an inconsistently respected relic of the past, having to do with avoidance of once important but now widely abolished rules, such as the doctrine of destructibility of contingent remainders, and the once overly harsh but now widely liberalized Rule Against Perpetuities.

The framers of the 1990 UPC concluded that the first and second rationales can be about as well or better served by a statute such as section 2-707 and that the fourth rationale can be served by limiting the statute to future interests created under the terms of a trust, where the trustee usually has the power to convey and mortgage the trust property.

How can the first and second rationales be similarly or better served by a statute such as section 2-707? The first rationale, the constructional preference for complete dispositions, is about equally served by traditional doctrine or by the substitutionary gifts created by the statute, so that the imposition of a condition of survival ordinarily does not cause the disposition to become incomplete. The second rationale, however, the strong constructional preference against inadvertently cutting off a branch of the family as a result of the early death of its ancestor, is much better served by the substitutionary gifts created by the statute than it is by the rule of construction against implied conditions of survival. The reason is that the rule of construction applies whether or not the predeceased beneficiary leaves any descendants who survive the time of possession and enjoyment. Thus, in either event it produces a future interest that is transmissible at death and thereby permits the deceased beneficiary to divert the property to others (such as a spouse or charity) rather than having the property pass, as it appears most transferors would prefer, to the beneficiary's descendants or other descendants of the transferor, as the case may be. Section 2-707, on the other hand, provides for a substitutionary gift to descendants when there are descendants who survive the time of possession and enjoyment (by 120 hours), but allows the particular future interest to fail if the predeceased beneficiary leaves no surviving descendants. Finally, section 2-707 avoids another set of disadvantages of the common-law rule, which is the need for reopening or tracing through the estates of predeceased beneficiaries when it is later discovered that the decedent had a transmissible future interest, with the accompanying risk of unnecessary, fortuitous taxation. In short, the results better correspond to the beneficiary preferences, administrative efficiencies, and tax objectives that could be expected to follow from careful state planning and drafting.

Jesse Dukeminier, *The Uniform Probate Code Upends the Law of Remainders*

94 Mich. L. Rev. 148, 149–50, 166 (1995)

Nothing is more settled in the law of remainders than that an indefeasibly vested remainder is transmissible to the remainderman's heirs or devisees upon the remainderman's death. Thus, where a grantor conveys property "to A for life, then to B and her heirs," B's remainder passes to B's heirs or devisees if B dies during the life of A.

Inheritability of vested remainders was recognized in the time of Edward I, and divisibility was recognized with the Statute of Wills in 1540.

Section 2-707 of the Uniform Probate Code (UPC), adopted in 1990, upends this law. In a comprehensive remake of the law of remainders, section 2-707 provides that, unless the trust instrument provides otherwise, all future interests in trust are contingent on the beneficiary's surviving the distribution date. Additionally, if a remainderman does not survive to the distribution date, the UPC creates a substitute gift in the remainderman's then-surviving descendants. If the remainderman has no surviving descendants, the remainder fails, and on the life tenant's death the property passes to the testator's residuary devisees or to the settlor's heirs.

This sea change in the law of remainders was set in motion by the Code's revisers when they expanded the antilapse idea of the law of wills to include trust remainders . . .

The proposal to supplant the existing law of remainders with an antilapse-like statute may have merit, not by analogy to will substitutes but as an independent claim that the antilapse idea better carries out the settlor's intent and better serves subsidiary public policies. There are two crucial questions. First, does the antilapse idea carry out the settlor's intent better than the traditional law of remainders? Second, does an antilapse law or the common law of remainders better serve public policy concerns, including reducing litigation and complexity? As for the first question, neither the Official Comment nor the drafters' law review commentary presents empirical evidence indicating that most trust settlors want a remainderman to lose the remainder if he does not survive the life tenant, substituting his descendants for him if he leaves descendants. The drafters appear to be proceeding purely on their own speculation. In fact, it seems just as likely that trust settlors intend to cede control of the remainder to the remainderman to permit the remainderman to deal with changes in his family circumstances during the life tenant's life. Before a fundamental change in the law of remainders is made, some empirical evidence should show that the common law has read people wrong for centuries . . .

It is not possible to say whether the common law or section 2-707 of the UPC most likely carries out the intent of the average trust settlor. There is no empirical evidence one way or the other. Judged by other criteria, the common law looks much more attractive than section 2-707. It gives flexibility to family members to deal with changes occurring during the life tenant's life, flexibility that section 2-707 eliminates. Section 2-707 will make more difficult modification or termination of trusts that, with the passage of time, become disadvantageous to the family. Section 2-707 will likely increase litigation, complexity in the law, and malpractice exposure. The only advantage of section 2-707 is that it eliminates remainders from remaindermen's probate estates, possibly saving probate costs. If there are probate administration costs associated with remainders, which have never been documented, they are a small price to pay for the flexibility of the common law . . . .

Notes and Questions

1. UPC § 2-707 applies only to future interests in trust. Sometimes planners will create legal life estates and vested remainders in land, especially farmland. The traditional rules would apply in that setting.

As Professor Dukeminier notes, however, in the trust context the UPC stands the traditional rule on its head. At the cost of potentially higher taxes and administration expenses, the traditional rule gives remaindermen control of their vested remainders, in particular, the power to transfer them by will. Compared to the common-law rule, the UPC shifts power away from beneficiaries and back to donors.

Actually, the claim by UPC § 2-707 proponents that the traditional rule will cause unnecessary estate taxes may only be true for the very wealthy, who will likely have legal advice. Because of the high federal exemption levels, no federal estate taxes will be payable by the vast majority even though the value of the remainder interest will be included in a remainder-person's gross estate. Indeed, from a tax perspective inclusion of the remainder interest in the gross estate may actually be advantageous since the trust property will get a higher basis for income tax purposes.

2. Beware of over-reading the UPC proposal. It only establishes rules of construction, which yield to a finding of contrary intention. UPC § 2-701. On the other hand, § 2-707(b)(3) says, "words of survivorship ... are not, in the absence of additional evidence, a sufficient indication of an intent" to override § 2-707's scheme of creating substitute gifts. Moreover, even words of survivorship which relate to a different distribution date or which use condition-subsequent form do not change the result. The UPC allows drafters to create indefeasibly vested remainders, but makes the task difficult.

3. The UPC's rules parallel the statute's complicated antilapse provisions. *See* UPC §§ 2-603, 2-706. Many arguments about those sections apply to § 2-707 as well.

4. Under the traditional rule, if Bob holds an indefeasibly vested remainder but dies before the life tenant, Bob's remainder passes through his estate. The UPC would give the remainder directly to Bob's descendants. As analyzed in the article cited below, Professor Susan French would give the remainder to those persons Bob identified by exercising a power of appointment. A power of appointment is a power one person has to transfer another person's property. *See infra* § 9.03. So long as the power could not be exercised in favor of the holder of the power, his estate, his creditors or the creditors of his estate, the property would not be subject to federal estate tax in the beneficiary's estate. This technique would avoid the tax and administration problems of the traditional vested interest approach, but (unlike the UPC) would preserve beneficiaries' power to make different dispositions. For example, such control might allow a beneficiary to adjust trust shares to help a needy sibling.

5. You are on the Probate Revision Committee of your state bar association. In light of decisions which have interpreted very similar language, but reached different conclusions about whether a remainder was vested or contingent upon survivorship, some committee members have called for reform. Do you favor the UPC approach, Professor French's proposal, or no reform?

6. Disclaimers of vested remainders in trust—either based on the traditional rule that survivorship will not be implied or in a UPC § 2-707 state where the constructional preference for survivorship is overridden—raise an interesting problem. Consider a testamentary trust with income to Amy for life, with an indefeasible remainder to Bob. What happens if after the testator dies Bob disclaims his remainder interest? Since Bob is still alive, the remainder cannot pass through his estate. Should it pass to the persons who would have been the intestate takers if Bob died intestate immediately before the testator died? What if Bob had a will? There are no cases on point. Following the UPC § 2-707 approach, Uniform Disclaimer of Property Interests Act § 6(b)(3)(D) (UPC § 2-1106 (b)(3)(D)) would pass the property to Bob's issue, but if he had none, then the remainder would pass to the applicable intestate takers of the testator.

Problems

1. Zena created a trust "to Richard for life, remainder to Stephanie, but if Stephanie dies before Richard, to Lisa." Under UPC § 2-707, who owns what interests?

2. Rose created a trust "for Tanya for life, then to Ben, if he survives Tanya, and if he does not, to Nancy." Assume Ben predeceased Tanya, but left descendants.

(a) If Nancy survives Tanya, who takes the remainder under UPC § 2-707?

(b) If Nancy also predeceases Tanya, leaving descendants, who takes the remainder under UPC § 2-707?

3. Viola's will created a trust "to Joseph for life, then to my surviving children." Viola had three children: Ralph, Richard, and Robert. At Joseph's death, only Richard survived. Ralph's four children and Robert's three children also survived Joseph. Under UPC § 2-707, who takes what shares of the trust principal

4. Sam's will creates a trust "to Pearl for life, and if Richard survives me, then to Richard as an indefeasibly vested remainder in fee." Richard survives Sam but dies before Pearl. Would Richard's devisee, his second wife, prevail over his surviving children under UPC § 2-207? *Cf.* In re Trust Fund A, 693 N.W.2d 790 (Iowa 2005) (holding that language overrode Iowa's constructional preference for survival until time of distribution).

Selected References

David M. Becker, *Uniform Probate Code Section 2-707 and the Experienced Estate Planner: Unexpected Disasters and How to Avoid Them*, 47 UCLA L. Rev. 339 (1999).

Laura E. Cunningham, *The Hazards of Tinkering with the Common Law of Future Interests: The California Experience*, 48 Hastings L.J. 667 (1997).

Susan F. French, *Imposing a General Survival Requirement on Beneficiaries of Future Interests: Solving the Problems Caused by the Death of a Beneficiary Before the Time Set for Distribution*, 27 Ariz. L. Rev. 801 (1985).

Lawrence W. Waggoner, *The Uniform Probate Code Extends Antilapse-Type Protection to Poorly Drafted Trusts*, 94 Mich. L. Rev. 2309 (1996).

B. Class Gifts[13]

In everyday speech, we use the language of class gifts: "children," "nieces and nephews," "grandparents." Lawyers add others: "heirs," "descendants," "issue." From a planning perspective, creating gifts to classes offers flexibility because, over time, classes typically can grow or shrink.[14] Without knowing who actually will get the property, we can create a trust with "income to Gary for life, principal to his children who survive him." If Gary later has more children, they will take. If some die before he does, they will drop out.

Although most classes are easy to identify, some are not. For example, language combining a class label with a list of members can cause problems. *See, e.g.*, Luke v. Stevenson, 696 N.W.2d 553 (S.D. 2005) (gift to "my minor great grandchildren, Jennifer Sampson, Jason Sampson, and Andrea Brown," was gift to individuals so that after-born was not a trust beneficiary). The Restatement (Third) of Property presumes that a class gift was not intended, subject to rebuttal "if the language or circumstances indicate that the transferor intended the beneficiaries to take as a group." *See* 3d Rest. Prop § 13.2(c).

This section considers a number of subsidiary problems class gifts present in addition to survivorship interests which were raised in § 9.02[A]. We first examine the rules of construction for deciding whether a person is treated as a "child" under various circumstances, e.g., adoption and birth outside of marriage. In effect, these are status questions which pervade the class gift area (as well as the law of intestacy as you saw in Chapter 2). Thereafter, we consider other important issues, including class closing issues and multigenerational class gifts to descendants, heirs, and the like. We conclude by looking at rules for construing "dies with" and "dies without" issue.

1. Status Questions

Individuals who are non-marital children or who claim class membership by way of adoption face familiar discriminatory barriers. In the absence of an identifiable intent to include non-marital children in class gifts, traditional rules excluded them. Adopted children fared a bit better. They were presumed included in an appropriate class gift created by their adopting parents, but courts refused to include them in class gifts created by others who did not know of the adoption. The idea was that "strangers to the adoption" should not have adopted family members foisted upon them. Although the law is uneven, both adopted and non-marital children are more likely than they were in the past to be included in class gifts. Some of the change has come through case law and some through legislation.

---

13. The Restatement (Third) of Property contains an entire division on class gifts. *See* 3d Rest. Prop. Division V (Class Gifts), chs. 13–16.

14. In an unusual case, a class gift may be static, *i.e.*, fluctuation is not possible. Consider a deed that leaves property "to my sister's children" where the sister has predeceased. *See* 3d Rest. Prop. § 13.1, cmt. h.

First National Bank of Chicago v. King

651 N.E.2d 127 (Ill. 1995)

JUSTICE HARRISON delivered the opinion of the court.

The issue in this case is whether section 2-4(f) of the Probate Act of 1975 (Ill. Rev. Stat. 1989, ch. 110 ½, par. 2-4(f)) should be construed to permit the adopted child of a testator's grandson to receive proceeds from a trust created by a will executed in 1936 under which the class of beneficiaries was limited to the "lawful descendants" of the testator's son and daughter-in-law.

The circuit court answered this question in the negative, holding that the presumption created by the statute in favor of adopted children cannot be applied here because "[t]he intent to exclude such child is demonstrated by the terms of the instrument by clear and convincing evidence." (Ill. Rev. Stat. 1989, ch. 110 ___, par. 2-4(f)(1).) .... [T]he appellate court subsequently reversed and remanded for further proceedings ... [a]nd the matter is now before us for review.

At the center of this dispute is the will left by Louis F. Swift, Sr., who died in 1937. Dated December 11, 1936, the will created three separate trust funds .... The Lydia Niblack Swift Fund (LNS Fund) is the one that concerns us on this appeal.

In section 10 of his will, Swift provided:

> "After the creation of the [LNS Fund], I direct that my trustee shall pay in quarter-yearly installments the net income from said Fund to my said daughter-in-law, Lydia Niblack Swift, during her natural life, if she shall be then surviving; provided, however, that if my said daughter-in-law, Lydia Niblack Swift, shall die after the creation, but before the termination, of said [LNS Fund], or if my said daughter-in-law, Lydia Niblack Swift, shall not survive me, the net income of said [LNS Fund] shall be paid in quarter-yearly installments to the lawful descendants, then surviving, in equal shares per stirpes, of my deceased son, Alden B. Swift, and said Lydia Niblack Swift." ...

Alden B. Swift and Lydia Niblack Swift had three children, Lydia, Nathan, and Narcissa. Lydia and Narcissa survived their mother. Although Nathan predeceased her, he left behind a son, Nathan Jr. and a daughter, Martha. Nathan Jr. was his biological child. Martha was not. She was the biological child of Nathan Jr.'s mother, who was Nathan Sr.'s second wife.

Nathan, Sr., adopted Martha after he married her mother. Both Nathan, Jr., and Martha survived Lydia Niblack Swift, and both are alive today.

The LNS Fund has not been terminated and is still in existence. Lydia Niblack Swift received all of the income from the Fund until her death in 1968. After that, her two surviving children, Lydia and Narcissa, each became entitled to one third of the Fund's income. The remaining third, which would have been payable to Nathan, Sr., had he survived his mother, was paid instead to Nathan's son, Nathan, Jr. Because Martha was adopted, the trustee took the position that she was not a "descendant" of Alden B. and Lydia Niblack Swift within the meaning of the testamentary trust.

The trustee therefore paid her nothing, and she claimed no share of the Fund's income.

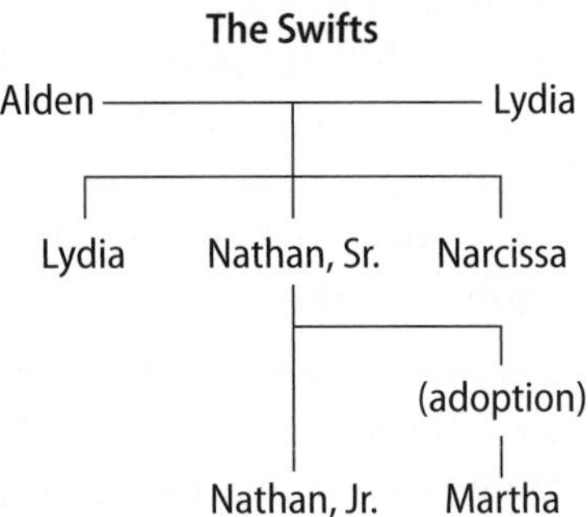

The situation changed with enactment of the 1989 revisions to section 2-4 of the Probate Act (Ill. Rev. Stat. 1989, ch. 110 ½>, par. 2-4). Those revisions added a new subsection (f), which provides:

> "After September 30, 1989, a child adopted at any time before or after that date is deemed a child born to the adopting parent for the purpose of determining the property rights of any person under any instrument executed before September 1, 1955, unless one or more of the following conditions applies:
>
> (1) The intent to exclude such child is demonstrated by the terms of the instrument by clear and convincing evidence.
>
> (2) An adopting parent of an adopted child, in the belief that the adopted child would not take property under an instrument executed before September 1, 1955, acted to substantially benefit such adopted child when compared to the benefits conferred by such parent on the child or children born to the adopting parent." (Ill. Rev. Stat. 1989, ch. 110 ½, par. 2-4(f).)

Identical provisions were also codified under section 1(b) of the Instruments Regarding Adopted Children Act (Ill. Rev. Stat. 1989, ch. 40, par. 1652(b)).

Following enactment of section 2-4(f), Martha requested that the First National Bank of Chicago, trustee of the LNS Fund, begin treating her as a beneficiary of the Fund. The trust responded by filing an action for declaratory judgment (Ill. Rev. Stat. 1989, ch. 110, par. 2-701) in the circuit court of Cook County to construe the terms of the LNS Fund in light of section 2-4(f) and to determine whether Martha should, in fact, be treated as a beneficiary. Martha counterclaimed, contending that the statute is constitutional and that it entitles her to share in the income of the Fund as a beneficiary . . . .

Nathan, Jr., and his son, Nathan Swift IV, . . . asserted that the statute is unconstitutional. In the alternative, they contended that even if the statute is valid, the statutory presumption cannot be extended to Martha because the testator's intent to exclude her "is demonstrated by the terms of the instrument by clear and convincing evidence" as set forth in section 2-4(f)(1) . . . .

The parties agree that section 2-4(f) expands a statutory presumption, applicable to the determination of property rights under written instruments, which no distinction is to be drawn between adopted children and natural offspring .... Under the statute, a testator is presumed to have intended for children adopted by their parents to be treated just as if they had been born to them. Previously, that presumption applied only to the construction of instruments executed on or after September 1, 1955. (See Ill. Rev. Stat. 1987, ch. 110 ½, par. 2-4(e).) Section 2-4(f) now extends it to also embrace instruments, such as Louis Swift's will, executed before September 1, 1955.

If section 2-4(f)'s presumption applies, Martha is unquestionably entitled to be treated as a beneficiary of the LNS Fund, just as her half-brother, Nathan, Jr., is. The dispute here has arisen because that presumption is not conclusive. As suggested earlier in this opinion, it can be rebutted where "the intent to exclude [the adopted] child is demonstrated by the terms of the instrument by clear and convincing evidence." Ill. Rev. Stat. 1989, ch. 110 ½, par. 2-4(f)(1).

The two Nathans assert that this standard has been satisfied here because sections 10 and 11 of the will specify that money from the LNS Fund is to be paid to the "lawful descendants" of Alden B. Swift and Lydia Niblack Swift, in equal shares "per stirpes." The ultimate question for us to resolve then is whether the terms "lawful descendants" and "per stirpes" in a document executed prior to 1955 are sufficient, by themselves, to demonstrate by clear and convincing evidence an intent to exclude adopteds.

This issue was addressed by the appellate court in *Continental Bank, N.A. v. Herguth* (1993), 248 Ill. App. 3d 292, 187 Ill. Dec. 395, 617 N.E.2d 852. There, the court reviewed the law in effect in 1926, when the settlor created the trust involved in that case, and concluded that the term "descendants" had a definite and certain meaning that encompassed only blood offspring. The court further held that the method of distribution provided by the settlor—per stirpes—automatically disqualified adopted persons under the then-existing law. Because the settlor is presumed to have known these legal principles when he executed the trust, the court reasoned that his use of the terms "descendant" and "per stirpes" "unmistakably evidenced his [actual] intent to limit the class of beneficiaries to his natural born progeny" and to exclude adopteds. (*Continental Bank*, 248 Ill. App. 3d at 296 ....) Because the settlor's actual intent was clear, the court concluded that the presumption created by section 2-4(f) was inapplicable, and that adopted heirs could not take under the trust.

Justice Inglis dissented ....

In Inglis' view, the settlor's use of the terms "descendants" and "per stirpes" in the trust do not demonstrate that [the testator] even considered the question of adopted heirs, much less that he intended to exclude them. Accordingly, Inglis would have applied the statutory presumption created by section 2-4(f) and held that the adopted heirs were entitled to share in the trust. Continental Bank, 248 Ill. App. 3d at 300-01 ... (Inglis, P.J., dissenting).

In the case before us, the appellate court agreed with Justice Inglis' analysis and declined to adopt the holding of the Continental Bank majority ....

We believe that the approach taken by the appellate court in this case is the better-reasoned one and should prevail over the analysis adopted by the majority in Continental Bank, 248 Ill. App. 3d 292, 187 Ill. Dec. 395, 617 N.E.2d 852. As a result, we agree with the appellate court's conclusion that the testator's use of the terms "lawful descendants" and "per stirpes" are not sufficient to demonstrate by clear and convincing evidence that he intended to exclude adopted children such as Martha.

The two Nathans argue that application of section 2-4(f)'s presumption under the facts present here violates the doctrine of separation of powers and infringes Nathan Jr.'s due process rights. We disagree.... Section 2-4(f) did not effect a change in substantive law. It merely expanded the evidentiary presumption that an adopted child is a natural child, so that the presumption now applies to all documents, regardless of whether they were drafted before or after September 1, 1955.

The legislature has the power to prescribe new Rules of Evidence and alter existing ones, and to prescribe methods of proof. Such action does not offend the separation-of-powers clause of our constitution.... With respect to the question of due process, Nathan, Jr., asserts that the statute is invalid because it defeats his settled expectations and those of his great-grandfather. We note, however, that Rules of Evidence such as this are procedural in nature..., and no one has a vested right in any particular mode of procedure.... The Nathans' constitutional challenge must therefore be rejected.

For the foregoing reasons, the judgment of the appellate court is affirmed.

Uniform Probate Code

Section 2-705. Class Gifts Construed to Accord With Intestate Succession; Exceptions.

(a) [**Definitions.**][15] In this section:

(1) "Adoptee" has the meaning set forth in Section 2-115.

(2) "Child of assisted reproduction" has the meaning set forth in Section 2-120.

(3) "Distribution date" means the date when an immediate or postponed class gift takes effect in possession or enjoyment.

(4) "Functioned as a parent of the adoptee" has the meaning set forth in Section 2-115, substituting "adoptee" for "child" in that definition.

(5) "Functioned as a parent of the child" has the meaning set forth in Section 2-115.

(6) "Genetic parent" has the meaning set forth in Section 2-115.

(7) "Gestational child" has the meaning set forth in Section 2-121.

(8) "Relative" has the meaning set forth in Section 2-115.

---

15. Certain definitions are set forth in the relevant UPC sections which are reproduced in Chapter 2.

(b) [**Terms of Relationship.**] A class gift that uses a term of relationship to identify the class members includes a child of assisted reproduction, a gestational child, and, except as otherwise provided in subsections (e) and (f), an adoptee and a child born to parents who are not married to each other, and their respective descendants if appropriate to the class, in accordance with the rules for intestate succession regarding parent-child relationships.

(c) [**Relatives by Marriage.**] Terms of relationship in a governing instrument that do not differentiate relationships by blood from those by marriage, such as uncles, aunts, nieces, or nephews, are construed to exclude relatives by marriage, unless:

(1) when the governing instrument was executed, the class was then and foreseeably would be empty; or

(2) the language or circumstances otherwise establish that relatives by marriage were intended to be included.

(d) [**Half-Blood Relatives.**] Terms of relationship in a governing instrument that do not differentiate relationships by the half blood from those by the whole blood, such as brothers, sisters, nieces, or nephews, are construed to include both types of relationships.

(e) [**Transferor Not Genetic Parent.**] In construing a dispositive provision of a transferor who is not the genetic parent, a child of a genetic parent is not considered the child of the genetic parent unless the genetic parent, a relative of the genetic parent, or the spouse or surviving spouse of the genetic parent or of a relative of the genetic parent functioned as a parent of the child before the child reached [18] years of age.

(f) [**Transferor Not Adoptive Parent.**] In construing a dispositive provision of a transferor who is not the adoptive parent, an adoptee is not considered the child of the adoptive parent unless:

(1) the adoption took place before the adoptee reached [18] years of age;

(2) the adoptive parent was the adoptee's stepparent or foster parent; or

(3) the adoptive parent functioned as a parent of the adoptee before the adoptee reached [18] years of age . . . .

Notes and Questions on Changing the Rules

1. When new rules of construction come along, the question arises whether those rules should apply only prospectively to new documents or whether they should govern existing documents. Applying rules prospectively gives the old rules a long shelf-life and complicates analysis by requiring research into what the law was at any particular time, sometimes long in the past. *See, e.g.*, *Watson v. Baker*, 829 N.E.2d 648 (Mass. 2005) (applying constructional rule applicable in 1936 to exclude adopted person from class); *In re Medeiros Testamentary Trust*, 96 P.3d 1098 (Haw. 2004) (applying constructional rules applicable during 1940s to exclude adopted persons); *Commerce Bank, N.A. v. Blasdel*, 141 S.W.3d 434 (Mo. Ct. App. 2004) (applying constructional rules applicable in 1949 to include adopted persons).

Courts that issue prospective rulings effectively protect the donor's reliance on what the law was at the time the document was executed. Should the law at time of will execution or at the testator's death control? Should there be a different result for revocable trusts? *See In re Medeiros Testamentary Trust*, 96 P.3d 1098 (Haw. 2004) (applying law at time irrevocable lifetime trust executed but law at time testator died, not law at time of will execution for testamentary trust).

2. As explained in *King*, the Illinois legislature decided to apply its new rule to existing documents. UPC § 8-101(b)(5) takes the same constructional approach except that the decedent must have died after a state enacted the UPC. *See Scribner v. Berry*, 489 A.2d 8 (Me. 1985).[16] Indiana generally applies its 2003 statutory abrogation of the stranger to the adoption rule retroactively. *See Paloutzian v. Taggart*, 931 N.E.2d 921 (Ind. Ct. App. 2010).

3. Retroactive application of a statute may raise constitutional questions. *See, e.g., Lake of the Woods Ass'n v. McHugh*, 380 S.E.2d 872 (Va. 1989) (wait-and-see perpetuities reform unconstitutional as applied retroactively to vested interests). *See generally* John M. Gradwohl & William H. Lyons, *Constitutional and Other Issues in the Application of the Nebraska Uniform Trust Code to Preexisting Trusts*, 82 Neb. L. Rev. 312 (2003).

For the most part, *King* reflects the tendency of courts to treat constructional rules as not substantive in nature, thereby avoiding the constitutional concern that substantive rights are violated. *But see Bird Anderson v. BNY Mellon, N.A.*, 974 N.E.2d 21 (Mass. 2012) (retroactive application of adoption statute by 2009 amendment to 1942 trust was unreasonable and violated substantive due process rights) and *Whirlpool Corp. v. Ritter*, 929 F.2d 1318 (8th Cir. 1991) (violation of Contracts Clause by applying new constructional rule). In response to *Ritter*, the Joint Editorial Board issued a statement explaining why it believes no constitutional violation existed. *See* Comment to UPC Article 2, Part 7.

Notes and Questions on Adoption Issues

1. As a general rule, an adopted child is no longer considered to be a child of his genetic parents. For example, a testator creates a testamentary trust for his child for life, remainder to his grandchildren. After testator dies, a grandchild is adopted by a new family. Because of the adoption out of the family, the adopted child will not share in the trust principal on the death of the life tenant. *See, e.g., Miller v. Walker*, 514 S.E.2d 22 (Ga. 1999).

Should there be an exception to the adopted-out rule if the adopted child was adopted by a step-parent? How about if a close relative adopted the child? *See* UPC § 2-705(b) (applying intestate rules that include these exceptions).

2. Adult adoptions are recognized in many states, subject to fraudulent adoption claims and possibly other requirements where the transferor is not the adopting

16. The UTC generally applies its constructional rules and presumptions to trusts created before state adoption of the UTC. *See* UTC § 1106(a)(4).

parent. *Compare Otto v. Gore*, 45 A.3d 120 (De. 2012) (adoption by former spouse of 65-year-old ex-husband was not intended by settlor to be a grandchild of trust) with *In re Estate of Weidner v. Peifer*, ___ N.E.3d ___, 2016 WL 7373924 (Ill.App. 2016) (child adopted at age 22 allowed to take as a "descendant" under trust as adoption was not an act of subterfuge).

The Restatement (Third) of Property § 14.5 also attempts to limit the effectiveness of adult adoptions, that is, an adoption after the individual attains age 18, not involving transferors. However, an adult adopted by a step-parent or foster parent as a child would be effective. Other adopted adults would only be treated as a child if the adoptive parent functioned as a parent during minority. *Accord* UPC § 2-705.

3. State law may also vary on the effect of an adult adoption. For example, in Colorado an adult adoption does not make an adopted person the child of the adopting party but does make the person an heir. On the other hand, valid adult adoptions in California are recognized to determine whether a person is a child under a will, trust, or other document. The disparity in state law treatment can lead to interesting results. For example, in *Ehrenclou v. MacDonald*, 117 Cal. App. 4th 364 (Ct. App. 2004), the question was whether an adult adopted in Colorado would be considered an issue of the adopting party where the trust provided that California law applied. The court held that the person was not issue since California would look to the state where the adoption occurred and by so doing, Colorado would not treat the person as a child although it would treat the person as an heir. *Cf. Sanders v. Yanez,* 190 Cal. Rptr. 3d 495 (Cal. Ct. App. 2015) (adult adoption in Texas recognized in California trust employing term "issue" because parent-child relationship created under Texas law).

Notes and Questions on Other Status Issues

1. The inclusion of nonmarital children within a class gift raises difficult problems. Traditionally, nonmarital children were excluded from the class absent a contrary intent. *See, e.g., Estate of Boynton v. Clark*, 584 S.E.2d 154 (S.C. Ct. App. 2003) (applying law in 1954). However, in some states, including New York and Pennsylvania, nonmarital children are included absent a contrary intent. Before amendment in 2008, UPC § 2-705(b), adopted in about 10 states, would treat a nonmarital child of the transferor as part of the class, but if the transferor was not the parent then the nonmarital child would be included only if the child was a regular member of the parent's or close relative's household. *Cf.* Current UPC § 2-705(b) and (e), set forth above.

The Restatement (Third) of Property § 14.7(2) would also treat a nonmarital child as a child of the transferor but is more nuanced; if the transferor is not the parent, such child will be included if the parent of the nonmarital child functioned as the parent of the child or was prevented from doing so by incapacity or death.

When designing a clause to cover the question, note that a client may well want to define the terms separately for different situations. For example, a blanket "lawful children" could disinherit children or grandchildren the client would really want to include. *See, e.g., Hood v. Todd*, 695 S.E.2d 31 (Ga. 2010) ("lawful" blood descendants did not include settlor's nonmarital child).

2. Regarding a child of assisted reproduction, Section 14.8 of the Restatement (Third) of Property treats such child "for class-gift purposes as a child of a person who consented to function as a parent to the child and who functioned in that capacity or was prevented from doing so by an event such as death or incapacity." *Cf.* UPC § 2-705(b) (applying intestacy rules regarding parent-child relationships).

3. Do you think a posthumously-born child should be included in a class gift?

4. Do you think stepchildren should be presumptively included within a class gift? How about other relatives by marriage? For example, should a gift to "brothers" include a brother-in-law? *See* UPC § 2-705(c).

Problems

1. Wilbert created a testamentary trust "to Faye for life, remainder to Stanley's children who reach age 21." Faye, Stanley, and Stanley's 23-year-old son, Lloyd, survived Wilbert. Then Faye died. A year later, Stanley adopted Jake, age 3. Will Jake share in the trust?

2. Harmon Harris wants you to draft a trust agreement in a state that does not bar gay men and lesbians from adopting. *See Rickard v. McKesson*, 774 So. 2d 838 (Fla. Dist. Ct. App. 2000) (adoption of 78-year-old man by an 88–year-old man was fraud on court obviating need to decide if Florida's statutory prohibition on adoptions by a homosexual person was unconstitutional). Several years ago Harmon's cousin adopted an adult lover so the lover could share in a trust Harmon's aunt had established. Harmon believes adopted children should receive full shares, but does not want anyone to "mess with my estate plan like my cousin did." Draft a definition of "descendant" which meets Harmon's needs.

3. Settlor created a trust that provided a disposition to issue who were "related by blood." Amy was born to settlor's child, Chester, while he was married and Amy's birth certificate listed Chester as her father. Several years later DNA testing conclusively proved that Chester was not Amy's father. Should Amy be treated as "issue" of the settlor who created the trust at a time when limiting dispositions to blood relatives was intended to exclude adopted children?

4. Suppose a will specifically excludes nonmarital children from a class gift. Should a posthumously-conceived child be excluded from the gift because the widow, who used the sperm of her deceased husband, was technically not married when the child was born? *See* UPC § 2-705(b) (last sentence added in 2010) and comment thereunder which would allow posthumous child to be included in class.

2. Class Closing

Class closing rules set the maximum size of a class. Because members still can drop out, the class closing rules do not establish a class' exact size, but only its ceiling. The rules are important for two reasons. First, they help courts decide which people have a claim to property. Second, Rule Against Perpetuities analysis often depends upon class closure.

Classes can close two ways, physiologically or according to the "rule of convenience." *See generally* 3d Rest. Prop. § 15.1.

Physiological Closing. Classes close physiologically when all the persons who can feed the class are dead. In general, the law conclusively presumes that living people can procreate. Often, one class will have many feeders, which can only be identified by extrinsic evidence. For example, a gift "to my nieces and nephews" would close physiologically only after the deaths of the donor's parents and all of the donor's siblings.

The Rule of Convenience. A class will close according to the rule of convenience when any class member has a right to demand possession. This rebuttable rule of construction strikes a balance between a donor's presumed desire to include all possible members of the class and the desire to allow distribution to those who have qualified to take. The rule also avoids the administrative problems that would develop if living beneficiaries took property, subject to giving some back as new class members appeared. The following examples illustrate the rule of convenience.

Example 9-1. Philip's will gives $10,000 "to Linda's children."

If Linda has a child, the class closes at Philip's death because that child can then demand possession.

Example 9-2. Noel established a trust to pay "income to Jay for life, remainder to Leyla's children." At Noel's death, Leyla has one child, David. Before Jay dies, Leyla has Ricky.

The class closes at Jay's death, when David and Ricky (or their successors) can demand distribution. Any of Leyla's children born after Jay's death are cut out.

Example 9-3. Matilda's will gave $10,000 "to Robert's children who reach 21." Robert has one child, Maggie, age 3. One year later he has Peter.

The class remains open until the first child reaches 21, with Maggie and Peter as class members. If before the class closes Robert has another child, that child would join the class. Any child who did not reach 21 would drop out of the class.

Example 9-4. Samuel's will created a trust to pay "income to Ida for life, remainder to Frank's children who reach 21." At Ida's death, Frank has one child, Ethan, age 10. A year later, Casey is born.

If Ethan reaches 21, the class closes so he does not have to wait to get his half of the fund. If Casey reaches 21, she will get the other half. If not, it will go to Ethan.

There are four general exceptions to the rule of convenience. *See generally* Lewis M. Simes & Allan F. Smith, The Law of Future Interest §§ 648–50 (3d ed. 2002). First, if no class member is alive when the time for distribution arrives, the class usually will stay open for all members whenever born. Thus, in Example 9-1, if Linda has no children at the time of Philip's death, the class remains open until Linda's death, even if she later has a child who otherwise would have closed the class. This exception to the general principle is based on the theory that Philip knew Linda had no children, so he must have intended to benefit all of her children, whenever born. *See* 3d Rest. Prop. § 15.1, cmt. k (but suggesting circumstances might justify failure of gift in its entirety).

Second, when a testator has made a gift of a specific sum to each member of a class, the class generally will close at the testator's death. If Helen's will gives $3,000 "to each of my grandchildren," the total amount of the gift would vary with the number of grandchildren. To avoid keeping the estate open until there can be no more grandchildren, the class closes at Helen's death. This result would follow even if Helen had no grandchildren.

Third, following the general rule that conception, not birth, is the key time, a child in gestation at the time the class closes is a class member. *See* UPC § 2-705(g)(1).

Finally, the rule of convenience normally does not apply to income interests. Because trustees can reallocate income as new class members arrive, there is no inconvenience in keeping the class open.

Problems

1. Michelle's will gave "$30,000 to Ashley's children to be paid at age 21." Ashley and her only child, Lisa (age 16), survived Michelle. A year later, Lisa died in a car accident. When does the class close?

2. Steven's will placed property in trust, with directions to terminate the trust and distribute the principal among Edna's children "when Edna's youngest child reaches age 21." Edna and her sons, James (22) and John (20), survive Steven. When does the trust terminate?

3. Kate's will left property in trust "to Molly for life, remainder to Joelle's children who reach age 21." Molly survived Kate, as did Joelle and her two children, Mary (age 8) and Phil (age 6). After Kate's death, events occurred in the following order: Joelle had a daughter, Addy. Mary reached 21. Molly died. Joelle had a son, Jay. Who, if anyone, is entitled to the trust principal, and what shares should they take in the following situations:

(a) At Molly's death.

(b) At Phil's death at age 20.

(c) When Addy reaches age 21.

(d) When Jay reaches age 21.

4. Marshall's will left property in trust "to Richard for life, remainder to his children." Richard and his two children survived Marshall. If Richard disclaims his interest, when will the class close? *See* UPC § 2-1106.

5. Settlor provides income to A for life, remainder to A's children. A is actually survived by child B. Child C is born to A's widow, who used A's frozen sperm, three

years after A dies. Does C share in the trust principal? *See* 3d Rest. Prop. § 15.1, cmt. j and UPC § 2-705(g)(2) (yes). *See also Matter of Martin B.*, 17 Misc. 3d 198 (Surr. Ct. N.Y. 2007).

3. *Class Gifts Involving Multiple Generations*

a. Gifts to Descendants

Gifts to descendants are the heart of many dispository schemes. Apart from the all-important status questions, the drafter should ascertain the client's wishes regarding how qualifying descendants will divide the property. In other words, how should shares be allocated among the descendants? You have seen this topic in the context of construing intestate statutes. *See* Ch. 2. To the public policy questions relevant to intestacy, we now add the complicating factor of honoring (at some level) the donor's intention. Consider the rules of construction noted below not as guides to rely upon, but as warnings of the need to provide careful, express directions regarding the issues they cover.

The problem of allocating shares can be illustrated by the following disposition: Hope created a trust "to Gordon for life, remainder to his surviving descendants."

After Gordon's death, should the trust be divided per capita, strict per stirpes, per stirpes (per capita with representation), representation (per capita at each generation), or according to some other scheme? The most common approach is to interpret documents according to the way the local intestate statute would handle the problem. *See* UPC § 2-708; 3d Rest. Prop. § 14.4.

The best solution, of course, is to draft documents that do not raise the question. Otherwise, protracted litigation may be necessary to resolve the issue. *See, e.g.*, *In re Annie Quon Ann Lock Trust*, 123 P.3d 1241 (Haw. 2005) ("per stirpes, to my then living brothers and sisters in equal shares" entitled surviving siblings to share to exclusion of children of predeceasing sibling); *In re Goodwin*, 739 N.Y.S.2d 239 (N.Y. Sur. Ct. 2002) ("to descendants of John H. Goodwin, share and share alike" held to require per capita distribution). In *In re Damon*, 128 P.3d 815 (Haw. 2006), testator, who died in 1924, left trust property "to all of my issue who shall then be living per stirpes and not per capita." The court held that the initial division should be based on the number of testator's children even though no child was then alive; this result accords with UPC § 2-709 (c), effectively strict per stirpes.

Uniform Probate Code

Section 2-709. Representation; Per Capita at Each Generation; Per Stirpes.

(a) **[Definitions.] In this section:**

(1) "Deceased child" or "deceased descendant" means a child or a descendant who either predeceased the distribution date or is deemed to have predeceased the distribution date under Section 2- 702.

(2) "Distribution date," with respect to an interest, means the time when the interest is to take effect in possession or enjoyment. The distribution date need not occur at the beginning or end of a calendar day, but can occur at a time during the course of a date.

(3) "Surviving ancestor," "surviving child," or "surviving descendant" means an ancestor, a child, or a descendant who neither predeceased the distribution date nor is deemed to have predeceased the distribution date under Section 2-702.

(b) [**Representation; Per Capita at Each Generation.**] If an applicable statute or a governing instrument calls for property to be distributed "by representation" or "per capita at each generation," the property is divided into as many equal shares as there are (i) surviving descendants in the generation nearest to the designated ancestor which contains one or more surviving descendants (ii) and deceased descendants in the same generation who left surviving descendants, if any. Each surviving descendant in the nearest generation is allocated one share. The remaining shares, if any, are combined and then divided in the same manner among the surviving descendants of the deceased descendants as if the surviving descendants who were allocated a share and their surviving descendants had predeceased the distribution date.

(c) [**Per Stirpes.**] If a governing instrument calls for property to be distributed "per stripes," the property is divided into as many equal shares as there are (i) surviving children of the designated ancestor and (ii) deceased children who left surviving descendants. Each surviving child, if any, is allocated one share. The share of each deceased child with surviving descendants is divided in the same manner, with subdivision repeating at each succeeding generation until the property is fully allocated among surviving descendants.

(d) [**Deceased Descendant With No Surviving Descendant Disregarded.**] For the purposes of subsections (b) and (c), an individual who is deceased and left no surviving descendant is disregarded, and an individual who leaves a surviving ancestor who is a descendant of the designated ancestor is not entitled to a share.

Problems

Before pursuing the projects below, you might want to review Chapter 2.

1. Willfred Ranney, 28, is married to Charlotte, 29. They have three children: Robert (10), Cheryl (8), and Martha (5). Willfred wants a will naming Charlotte as his primary beneficiary, but if she predeceases him, he wants the property to go to his surviving descendants. Draft the dispository language necessary to divide the estate among Willfred's descendants according to each of the following schemes:

(a) strict per stirpes

(b) per stirpes (per capita with representation)

(c) representation (per capita at each generation).

Begin each clause with: "If my wife Charlotte does not survive me."

2. Your senior partner has left you the following note:

John and Elizabeth Schaech are in their mid-30s. They have three young daughters: Helen, Kelly, and Shannon. They want to establish a trust to give themselves income and to take care of the girls (and any later children), in case John and Elizabeth die before the children reach age 25.

After their parents' deaths, children 25 or over will get their share of the principal. The children under 25 will get income interests in the trust, with principal distributed at age 25. If a child dies before getting the principal, distribute that child's share first to the child's descendants, or if there are none, on a per capita, with representation basis among John and Elizabeth's descendants.

Draft only the dispository language necessary to create the various future interests necessary. Begin your draft with "After the death of the survivor of John and Elizabeth."

Selected References

William F. Fratcher, *Class Gifts to "Heirs," "Issue," and Like Groups*, 55 Alb. L. Rev. 1205 (1992).

Edward C. Halbach, Jr., *Issues About Issue: Some Recurrent Class Gift Problems*, 48 Mo. L. Rev. 333, 334–55 (1983).

Kristine S. Knaplund, *Children of Assisted Reproduction*, 45 U. Mich. J. of Law Reform 899 (2012).

Paula A. Monopoli, *Toward Equality: Nonmarital Children and the Uniform Probate Code*, 45 U. Mich. J. of Law Reform 995 (2012).

Frederic S. Schwartz, *The New Restatement of Property and Class Gifts: Losing Sight of the Testator's Intention*, 22 Quinnipiac Prob. L.J. 221 (2009).

Lawrence W. Waggoner, *Class Gifts Under the Restatement (Third) of Property*, 33 Ohio N.U.L. Rev. 993 (2007).

b. Gifts to Heirs

Gifts to heirs present some of the most notorious construction problems in the law. The goal of this section is to help you identify those problems so you can recognize them when you review documents and so you can draft error-free documents. We begin with the question of how to identify "heirs," and then turn to two old troublemakers, the Rule in Shelley's Case and the Doctrine of Worthier Title.

i. Identifying Heirs

A court deciding who fits the description of "heirs" starts by looking at an intestate statute. Two principal problems emerge. First, what statute should apply? Second, when?

Suppose Edwin died an Illinois resident in 1970, leaving personal property in trust "to Lois for life, remainder to Joyce's heirs." Joyce, who lived in Indiana, died in 1996. Should the law of Illinois (the testator's domicile) or Indiana (the designated person's domicile) identify Joyce's heirs? There is authority for each position. If the gift were of a vacation cabin in Wisconsin, that law would probably apply. Suppose Illinois law applies, but the statute was revised in 1975. Should the new or the old version control? Again, the authorities are split.

Timing can also be a problem in another sense. As a starting place, we expect to determine someone's heirs at the time of the ancestor's death. Because in some situations such a reading would not match a donor's likely intention, courts struggle with when to make exceptions.

Suppose Edwin gave property "to Lois for life, remainder to the heirs of her sister, Joyce." Suppose that before Edwin's death, Joyce had died leaving only her sister, Lois, and Lois's son, Peter. (*See* Figure 9-3.) Normally, we would expect a court to determine Joyce's heirs at her death, naming Lois. In this situation, that interpretation would give Lois both the life estate and the remainder, which would merge into a fee simple.

Figure 9-3 Facts at Edwin's Death

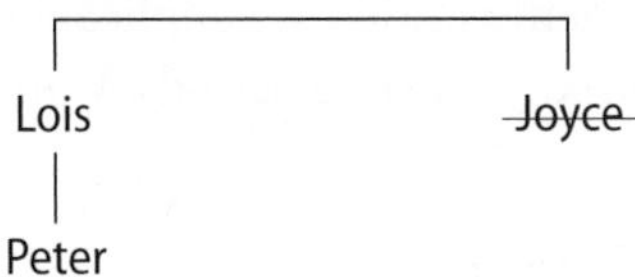

On the other hand, to preserve Edwin's intention to restrict Lois to a life estate, a court might postpone determination of Joyce's heirs until Lois's death. On these facts, that approach would exclude Lois, but keep the property in the family. The key, of course, is for the document to identify the time for determining heirship.

Uniform Probate Code

Section 2-711. Interests in "Heirs" and Like.

If an applicable statute or a governing instrument calls for a present or future distribution to or creates a present or future interest in a designated individual's "heirs," "heirs at law," "next of kin," "relatives," or "family," or language of similar import, the property passes to those persons, including the state, and in such shares as would succeed to the designated individual's intestate estate under the intestate succession law of the designated individual's domicile if the designated individual died when the disposition is to take effect in possession or enjoyment. If the designated individual's surviving spouse is living but is remarried at the time the disposition is to take effect in possession or enjoyment, the surviving spouse is not an heir of the designated individual.

Note and Problems

1. The Restatement (Third) of Property § 16.1 follows the UPC § 2-711 approach: heirs are determined at time of distribution. However, many jurisdictions adhere to the rule that heirs are determined when the ancestor dies, based on a preference for early vesting. For example, in *Schmidt v. Wachovia Bank, N.A.*, 624 S.E.2d 34 (Va. 2006), the testator effectively created a trust for a child for life, with remainder to testator's heirs at law. The Supreme Court of Virginia held that the testator's heirs were to be determined when the testator died, not when the child died. As it turned out in *Schmidt*, the child was the testator's sole heir when he died, so when she died the property passed to beneficiaries under her will.

2. Ralph's will gave his daughter, Lois, a life estate, with a remainder to Ralph's heirs. If all of Ralph's heirs determined as of his death assign their interests to Lois, can she convey a fee simple interest in the property?

3. In 1967, testator created a testamentary trust with income to A for life, remainder to B, but if B failed to survive the life tenant, then to the deceased child's "heirs at law." Testator died in 1968. The distribution scheme under the applicable intestate statute in 1968 was different from the distribution scheme when testator executed her will in 1967. B died in 1984. A died in 2006. The distribution scheme under the applicable intestate statute in 1984 was different from the 1967 and 1968 schemes. In turn, the distribution scheme under the applicable intestate statute in 2006 was different from that in the three prior time periods. Which distribution scheme should control?

ii. The Rule in Shelley's Case

Perhaps the most infamous of the old medieval rules is the Rule in Shelley's Case. In classic operation, the Rule applies to gifts of land to a life tenant, with an attempted remainder to the heirs of the life tenant.[17] Regardless of the intention of the donor, the rule invalidates the attempted remainder to the heirs and substitutes in its place a remainder to the life tenant. Thus, if Edwin gave realty "to Joyce for life, remainder to her heirs," the rule would change that grant to read "to Joyce for life, remainder to Joyce." At that point, the doctrine of merger would apply to create a fee simple absolute in Joyce. Although the Rule did not apply to personal property, it could affect trusts that included land.

The Restatement (Third) of Property § 16.2 repudiates the Rule since it has no place in modern-day society. Unfortunately, even if long ago abolished, the Rule may require litigation over preexisting instruments. As explained in *In re Estate of Hendrickson*, 736 A.2d 540, 541 (N.J. Sup. Ct. 1999) (considering, but rejecting, application of Rule in Shelley's case under a 1928 will that was unaffected by New Jersey's repeal of Rule in 1934):

---

17. Although the Rule did not apply to personal property, it could affect trusts that included land.

> It seems unimaginable that a court, near the end of this millennium, would be asked to consider the application of the long-abolished "Rule in Shelley's Case." Yet, this anachronistic doctrine, like Banquo's Ghost, has raised its hoary head and must be addressed not as an academic puzzle but as the key to a very real and substantial property dispute.

Problems

1. Horace gave his farm "to Gertrude for life, then to Lois for life, then to Gertrude's heirs." In a state recognizing the Rule in Shelley's Case, can Gertrude sell a fee simple interest in the farm?

2. You practice in a jurisdiction which recognizes the Rule in Shelley's Case. Draft language which gives Diane the right to use property for her lifetime and also transfers the property to her heirs after her death.

iii. The Doctrine of Worthier Title

Where recognized, the Doctrine of Worthier Title usually establishes a presumption that a grantor's[18] gift of a remainder to the grantor's own heirs was not intended as a remainder at all, but rather as a way of retaining a reversion. Unlike Shelley, in modern form the Doctrine of Worthier Title applies to both real and personal property, so it is more likely to affect modern trusts. Additionally, rather than being an unmodifiable rule of property, it usually is a rule of construction. The Restatement (Third) of Property § 16.3 repudiates the Doctrine of Worthier Title both as a rule of law and as a rule of construction.

An easy way to remember the doctrine's impact is to say it simply invalidates remainders to heirs of the grantor. Thus, if Edwin created a trust giving "income to Michael for life, remainder to my heirs," the doctrine would strike the remainder, leaving only "income to Michael for life." Without more granted, Edwin has a resulting trust (an equitable reversion).

The doctrine is not in good health, but it is still a force to consider. Many jurisdictions have abolished it, but some have done so only recently and prospectively. *See* UPC § 2-710; 3d Rest. Prop. § 16.3 (Reporter's Notes). In at least one jurisdiction that has abolished the Rule, a lifetime trust may be terminated with the consent of the settlor and living beneficiaries even though the settlor's heirs are the remainder beneficiaries of the trust. *See* N.Y. EPTL § 7-1.9(b).

---

18. There is also a "testamentary branch" to the doctrine, to the effect that gifts to heirs of the testator passed by descent instead of by will. Because in modern law it very seldom makes any difference whether someone takes by will or by descent, this branch of the doctrine is believed dead. *See* 3d Rest. Prop. § 16.3, cmt. c. It may not be, however. *See In re Estate of Kern*, 274 N.W.2d 325 (Iowa 1979) (prospectively abolishing the testamentary branch). In any event, the Restatement (Third) of Property § 16.3, comment c, repudiates the testamentary branch of the worthier title doctrine.

Selected Reference

Stanley M. Johanson, *Reversions, Remainders, and the Doctrine of Worthier Title*, 45 Tex. L. Rev. 1 (1966).

iv. Drafting Gifts to Heirs

Gifts to heirs can often be useful. They serve as the ultimate catch-all if known beneficiaries do not survive until the date for distribution and the client does not want to make charitable gifts. On the other hand, creating gifts to heirs requires careful drafting to identify which statute applies (and when) and to avoid the ghosts of Shelley and Worthier Title. Consider the following case.

Harris Trust and Savings Bank v. Beach

513 N.E.2d 833 (Ill. 1987)

[Pursuant to a 1921 antenuptial agreement between Frank Hixon and his eventual wife, Alice, Frank created a trust with income for Alice for life, a reversion to Frank if he survived Alice, but if Alice survived Frank, a remainder to be divided among Frank's heirs "share and share alike." In return, Alice relinquished all interest in Frank's estate.

Bold indicates heir at Frank's death; Italics indicates heir at Alice's death

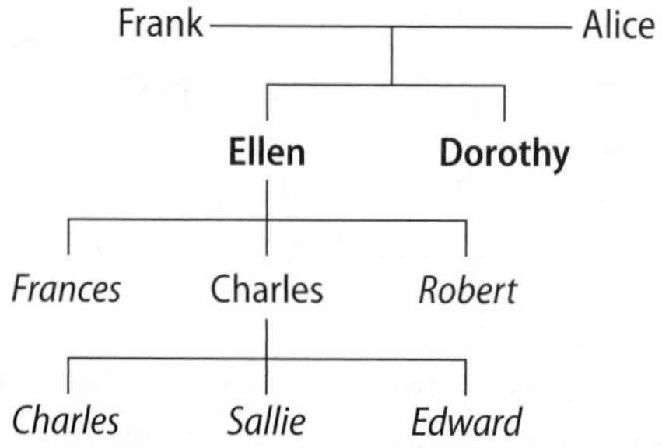

In 1931, Frank died, survived by Alice; his children, Dorothy and Ellen; and Ellen's three children. Both Dorothy and Ellen died in 1973. Dorothy had no issue and left the bulk of her estate to named charities. Ellen left two children and three grandchildren. Alice died in 1982, survived by the two grandchildren and three great-grandchildren.

The trial court held that trust property passed under the wills of Dorothy and Ellen. In effect, each had a vested remainder by virtue of being Frank's sole heirs as determined in 1931. (Alice was excluded as an heir under the antenuptial agreement.) The appellate court held that trust property passed under the residue of Frank's will because the doctrine of worthier title applied.]

Justice Simon delivered the opinion of the court . . . .

Three issues are presented on review: (1) whether the heirs are those surviving [Frank] Hixon's death or Alice's death; (2) whether the doctrine [of worthier title] is applicable, and if so, whether it applies as a rule of construction or a rule of law; and (3) whether, if the heirs are determined at Alice's death, the shares should be distributed per stirpes or per capita. Since the meaning of the word "heirs" as used in the trust is a necessary predicate to the applicability of the doctrine to this case, we begin by deciding at what point the heirs are to be determined.

I

The word "heirs" refers to "those persons appointed by the law to inherit an estate in case of intestacy." . . . When used in its technical sense, the testator's or settlor's heirs are, of course, determined at the time of his or her death . . . . This court, however, has never adopted the technical meaning of the word "heirs" as a rule of law. We have observed that " 'heirs' when used in a will does not necessarily have a fixed meaning. It may mean children or, where there are no children, it may mean some other class of heirs . . . if the context of the entire will plainly shows such to have been the intention of the testator." (Emphasis added.) (*Stites v. Gray* (1955), 4 Ill.2d 510, 513, 123 N.E.2d 483.) A determination of the class of heirs, therefore, is governed by the settlor's or testator's intention rather than by a fixed rule of law. The rule in Illinois, however, has been that, unless the settlor's intention to the contrary is "plainly shown" in the trust document, courts will rely upon the technical meaning of the term "heirs" by applying it as a rule of construction . . . . The charities are, therefore, correct in their observation that presently our rule of construction requires us to determine heirs at the settlor's death unless the trust or will provides clear evidence to the contrary . . . . The initial question we must address is whether we should continue to adhere to this standard of proof.

The charities contend that this high degree of proof is necessary to rebut the rule of construction because of the policy favoring early vesting of remainders . . . . However, they overlook that two eminent scholars in the field of Illinois future interest law revised their views regarding the policy in favor of early vesting. In the supplement to their treatise entitled the Illinois Law of Future Interests, Carey and Schuyler observe that "it was the rule regarding the destructibility of contingent remainders that caused courts to favor the early vesting of estates . . . . But now, in this state and in many others, there is no rule of destructibility.[19] If the original reason for favoring early vesting is gone, why continue to favor it?" H. Carey and D. Schuyler, Illinois Law of Future Interests 190 (Cum. Pocket Part 1954); Ill. Rev. Stat.1985, ch. 30, par. 40 . . . .

Early vesting frequently frustrates intentions by casting property to strangers . . . .

19. [Editor's Note: Section 25.5 of the Restatement (Third) of Property provides in part as follows: The Rule of Destructibility of Contingent Remainders is not recognized as part of American law.]

> . . . In the instant case, we have an interest following a life estate. If we follow both the circuit and appellate court's decision and vest the heirs' interest as quickly as possible, a large portion of the estate will fall into the hands of strangers. If we reduce the burden of proving that a grantor intended to use "heirs" in a nontechnical sense and if that vests the gift at the termination of the life estate, obviously only those heirs surviving the life tenant will share in the remainder . . . .

We agree with Professors Carey and Schuyler that early vesting of remainders should no longer be followed in this State without question. Early vesting is an axiom which must not get in the way when a contrary intent is demonstrated by a preponderance of the evidence. Requiring clear and convincing evidence or a plain showing to rebut the presumption in favor of the technical meaning of the term "heirs" . . . has its roots in the maxim favoring early vesting of remainders. Frequently this policy, as is the case here, frustrates what the ordinary settlor would have intended. We hold that because the primary reason for early vesting is no longer as important as it formerly was, proof by the preponderance of the evidence that the settlor, testator, or donor intended to use the term "heirs" in its nontechnical sense is sufficient to delay the vesting of a gift to a time other than at the grantor's death.

The result of delaying a gift to the heirs is not dramatic. The fear that a contingent remainder could be prematurely destroyed no longer exists. Further, should a predeceased member of the class be excluded from the gift, the result is not drastic. If the predeceased "heir" leaves issue, as is the case here, the settlor's own blood still enjoys the gift. If, on the other hand, a predeceased member fails to leave issue, as also occurred here, the gift is prevented from falling into the hands of strangers. In sum, by altering the degree of proof necessary to delay the vesting of a gift to the heirs, we do no harm. Instead, we further the ordinary grantor's intent, which is exactly what a proper rule of construction ought to do. Consequently, in this case we must determine which parties have offered the preponderant proof as to Hixon's intent—the charities or the grand-children and great-grandchildren.

Hixon's trusts, as the charities stress, do not explicitly state the point at which his heirs should be determined . . . . When the trusts are considered as a whole, however, it becomes apparent that the documents revolve totally around Alice's life and death; Hixon's life and death play only secondary roles . . .

The circumstances under which Hixon created the trust provide additional evidence of his intent to vest the gift at Alice's death. Hixon was 20 years older than Alice and he would consequently have expected her trusts to last for a considerable time after his own death. During this time, changes in the family through births and deaths would certainly occur. Rather than leave the remainder of the principal to his daughters, as he left the residue of his estate in his will, his use of an indefinite term such as "heirs" covered the inevitable changes in family circumstances that might occur . . . .

The grandchildren and great-grandchildren also claim that the language in the trusts instructing the trustees to "divide or distribute" the principal "equally among the heirs" invokes the "divide and pay over rule," which would operate to vest the gift at Alice's death. This rule is one of construction to aid courts in determining whether a gift to a class is a vested or contingent remainder ....

Under the "divide and pay over rule," when a trustee is directed to divide or distribute a gift to a class at a time after the settlor's death, the gift is contingent and possession and enjoyment of that gift are delayed until the time of distribution. The gift is contingent under the rule not only because it is dependent upon the happening of an event—the trustee dividing and distributing the assets—but also because the members of the class who would be alive and able to enjoy the gift would not be ascertained until the trustees performed their duty of distributing the assets ....

In the present case, Hixon left the trust gift to a class—the heirs—and he employed the key phrase to "divide and/or distribute the trust principal"; it therefore appears that this rule is applicable ....

... [I]n view of the ambiguity confronting us, [the divide and pay over rule] gives us an additional clue as to Hixon's intent.

The provision in the 1921 trust creating a reversion in Hixon should Alice predecease him also advances the grandchildren's and great-grandchildren's argument that Hixon's intention was that the heirs be determined at Alice's death. The reversionary clause conditioned the duration of the trust on Alice's survival. If Alice failed to survive Hixon, the trust would terminate and Hixon's reversion would operate. On the other hand, if Alice survived Hixon, the reversion would not take effect and the principal would be distributed to the heirs. The grand-children and great-grandchildren persuasively stress that considering the heirs at Hixon's death would lead to nearly the same result as if the reversion had occurred. In both instances the bulk of the principal would pass through the estates of Hixon's two daughters. Hixon's intention that the result was to be different should Alice survive and the reversion fail is an indication that Hixon must have intended that his heirs be determined at Alice's death. Viewing all of these indications with respect to Hixon's intent together, we conclude that the preponderant proof favors the position of the grandchildren and great-grandchildren and Hixon's heirs should therefore be determined at Alice's death.

II

Because we have concluded that it was Hixon's intention that the heirs were to be ascertained at Alice's death, the doctrine of worthier title is not applicable ....

III

The final question is whether the gift to the grandchildren and great-grandchildren should be distributed per stirpes or per capita. The great-grandchildren contend that because Hixon used the words "share and share alike" and instructed the trustees to distribute the gift "equally," the gift must be divided on a per capita basis .... When a testator leaves his estate to his or her heirs, courts generally conclude that the testator intended the gift to be distributed in accordance with laws of descent and distribution which provide for a per stirpes distribution. Under these circumstances we have stated that "a gift to issue 'equally' and 'share and share alike' does not require that each of such issue shall have an equal share with the other; that the mandate is satisfied if the issue of equal degree taking per stirpes share equally." *Condee v. Trout* (1942), 379 Ill. 89, 93, 39 N.E.2d 350.

In the present case, Hixon left the remainder in the trust principal to his heirs. That he provided for his heirs to share equally in that gift fails to rebut the presumption in favor of a per stirpes distribution; the gift to the class of heirs is a sufficient indication that Hixon intended the remainder to be divided in accordance with the laws of descent and distribution . . . .

We conclude that the remainder in the heirs should be distributed per stirpes with the three great-grandchildren each taking one-ninth of the estate and the two grandchildren each taking one-third. The judgments of both the circuit and appellate courts are reversed and the case is remanded for a distribution of the trust principal in a manner consistent with this opinion.

Notes

1. Compare this court's concern about property going to "strangers" with *Estate of Kehler*, and with the debate over the UPC's proposal regarding survivorship of holders of future interests in trust.

2. Terms like "relatives" and "family" present a myriad of problems and should be avoided unless carefully defined. The UPC treats many of these terms the same. *See* UPC § 2-711.

3. You should ask four questions if you see a remainder to the "heirs" of some person.

(a) Is the person alive, so the remainder is contingent?

(b) Is the person a life tenant, so Shelley might apply?

(c) Is the person the grantor, so Worthier Title might apply?

(d) When should "heirs" be determined?

Problems

1. Your senior partner has asked you to prepare a list of drafting phrases either to avoid or to use only with the greatest caution. Prepare the list with a brief note identifying the danger(s) involved.

2. Christopher wants you to draft a trust agreement which gives property to various descendants and creates an ultimate remainder in Christopher's heirs. You practice in a jurisdiction which recognizes the Doctrine of Worthier Title. Assume you have already created a series of life estates and contingent remainders for the descendants. Now draft only the dispository language necessary to create a contingent remainder in Christopher's heirs. Begin your draft with "If none of my descendants are then living, the trustee shall distribute the principal and accumulated income."

Selected References

William F. Fratcher, *Class Gifts to "Heirs," "Issue," and Like Groups*, 55 Alb. L. Rev. 1205 (1992).

John L. Garvey, *Drafting Wills and Trusts: Anticipating the Birth and Death of Possible Beneficiaries*, 71 Or. L. Rev. 47 (1992).

4. *The Rule in* Wild's Case

Suppose Evelyn gave her farm to "my son Delison and his children." (This language derives from *Wild's Case*, 77 Eng. Rep. 277 (K.B. 1599).) Delison and his two daughters, Susan and Angela, survived Evelyn. A year later, Delison's third child, Sarah, was born. Consider some possible interpretations. Maybe Delison, Susan, and Angela own the farm as joint tenants, or as tenants in common. Maybe Delison has a life estate, and the daughters have vested remainders, subject to open.

The rule in *Wild's Case* would create a joint tenancy among Delison, Susan, and Angela. Restatement (Third) of Property § 14.2, comment f, repudiates the rule in *Wild's Case.* In its place, the disposition would give successive ownership—a life estate in the parent, Delison, with a vested remainder, subject to open in his children.

The Restatement's successive, rather than current, construction would not apply to income interests in trust. For example, a trust in favor of Delison and his children would entitle each to share the income. On the other hand, absent a contrary expression of intention, the remainder would be given a successive construction. *See* 3d Rest. Prop. § 14.2, cmt. h. For example, a trust in favor of Alan for life, remainder to Delison and his children, would be construed to give Delison a secondary life estate, with remainder to his children.

As in all class gift dispositions, the drafting lesson is clear: be specific about your clients' intentions!

C. Death without (or with) Issue

Drafters of trust agreements must constantly be on the lookout for familiar, lawyer-like sounding phrases which are loaded with trouble. "Dies without issue" is one of the most deadly. The phrase haunts in many ways. *See* Lewis M. Simes & Allan F. Smith, The Law of Future Interests §§ 521–51 (3d ed. 2002).

First, a bit of history. When the fee tail[20] was still used, English courts read "if Dorthea dies without issue" to mean "if her line runs out." This approach is called

20. "After [the statute] DeDonis [Conditionalibus in 1285], a gift of land to 'B and the heirs of his body' created an estate in fee tail in B. This estate would last so long as there were any lineal descendants of B living and upon the failure of such issue the land would revert to the donor or his heirs." Sheldon F. Kurtz, Moynihan's Introduction to the Law of Real Property 50–51 (4th ed. 2005).

an indefinite failure of issue construction. Suppose Dorthea died leaving a son, who died leaving his daughter, who died leaving her son, who died leaving no issue. Under an "indefinite failure" approach, a court would say Dorthea died without issue when her great-grandson died.

Most states now adopt a definite failure of issue construction, which means that we look to a definite time—the time the person dies—to determine whether or not the person actually dies with or without issue. *See* 3d Rest. Prop. § 26.8. In our example, because Dorthea left a son, she would not have died without issue.

Another question is whether gifts should be treated as "substitutional" or "successive." Suppose George created a trust "to Marilyn for life, remainder to Dorthea, but if she dies without issue, to William." The question is one of timing. Some courts adopt a substitutional construction which says the key time is Marilyn's death. If Dorthea survives Marilyn, Dorthea gets a fee simple absolute. William was a substitute taker, in case Dorthea died without issue before Marilyn. *Accord* 3d Rest. Prop. § 26.8, Illust. 2. Other courts treat the gift as successive. Under such an interpretation, the critical moment is Dorthea's death. If Dorthea survives Marilyn, Dorthea gets a fee simple subject to an executory limitation, and William has an executory interest.

"To Marilyn for life, remainder to Dorthea, but if she dies without issue, to William" raises another problem if Dorthea dies with issue. By its terms, the grant does not cover the question. Despite their reluctance to fill gaps in dispositions, in this situation a remainder to those issue should be implied. *See* 3d Rest. Prop. § 26.9, cmt. b.

Similar construction problems arise if a grantor uses a phrase like "dies with issue." Suppose Peter created a trust "to Henry for life, then to Bob, but if Bob dies with issue, then to those issue." Does the phrase mean, "dies with issue before Henry dies" or "dies with issue when Bob dies"? The preferred, but not universal, construction is the first: Bob gets an indefeasible interest if he survives Henry. *See* 3d Rest. Prop. § 26.8, Illust. 5. Under the minority view, after Henry's death Bob gets a fee simple subject to an executory limitation and his issue would have an executory interest. Suppose Bob predeceases Henry and leaves a daughter, Marcia, who also predeceases Henry. Does Marcia have to survive only Bob or also Henry? Again, the cases conflict, but the general trend toward requiring survivorship until the time for distribution supports the conclusion that Marcia should survive the life tenant, Henry. *See* 3d Rest. Prop. § 26.8, Illust. 5.

Using the phrase "dies without issue" is asking for trouble. If you do use it, elaborate its meaning with the greatest care.

Problems

1. Elias created a testamentary trust with income "to Maya for life, remainder to Robert, but if Robert dies without issue, to Aisha." Maya survived Elias. Who should take the property after Maya's death under the following circumstances?

(a) Robert predeceases Elias, survived by issue who survive Elias.

(b) Robert predeceases Elias without issue.

(c) Robert predeceases Elias without issue, and Aisha predeceases Maya.

(d) Robert survives Elias, but predeceases Maya with issue who also predecease Maya.

(e) Robert survives Elias, but dies before Maya without issue.

(f) Robert survives Maya, but then dies without issue.

2. Redraft the language in problem 1 to avoid the construction problems you encountered.

3. May's will left her entire estate to her husband, Joseph, and said that if both of them died in a common disaster her estate should go to her nieces Evelyn and Megan. Joseph died of a heart attack and six years later May died of cancer. Who should take May's estate?

Selected Reference

John L. Garvey, *Drafting Wills and Trusts: Anticipating the Birth and Death of Possible Beneficiaries*, 71 Or. L. Rev. 47, 66–72 (1992).

§ 9.03 Powers of Appointment[21]

"The power of appointment is the most efficient dispositive device that the ingenuity of Anglo-American lawyers has ever worked out." In its broadest sense,[22] a power of appointment is a power one person has to designate who will take property subject to the power, or what shares the takers will receive. We have seen such powers already when we examined discretionary and support trusts. *See* Chapter 8. For the purposes of this discussion, however, a general reference to a "power" refers to a power of appointment an individual can hold outside of a fiduciary relationship.[23]

In 2013, the Uniform Law Commission approved the Uniform Powers of Appointment Act (UPOAA), which generally translates the Restatement (Third) of Property's Division on Powers of Appointment into legislation.[24] Colorado, Missouri, Montana, New Mexico, North Carolina, Utah and Virginia have enacted a version of the UPOAA, with other enactments likely.

21. The Restatement (Third) of Property contains an entire division on powers of appointment. *See* 3d Rest. Prop. Division VI (Powers of Appointment), chapters 17–23.

22. W. Barton Leach, *Powers of Appointment*, 24 A.B.A. J. 807 (1938).

23. Restatement (Third) of Property § 17.1 continues the position under the Restatement (Second) of Property § 11.1 that a fiduciary power is a power of appointment.

24. There are some exceptions. For example, contrary to the Restatement position, *see* Note 23, UPOAA § 103(13) excludes fiduciary powers as powers of appointment.

This section concerns powers to allocate the shares of a trust after its creation. First we introduce powers' terminology and concepts. Then we consider questions surrounding the creation and exercise of powers, with particular emphasis on structuring powers in ways which avoid problems.

A. The Basics

Powers of appointment are useful because they can buy time and save taxes. For example, powers allow members of one generation to give property to their grandchildren's generation, but postpone decisions about exactly how to divide that property. At the same time, powers allow tax savings in their children's generation.

Consider Edna, a widow with one son, James, a young adult without children. Suppose that Edna wants to set up a trust for James. She might give James the trust income for his life, with the principal distributed equally among his (yet unborn) children at James' death. The problem is that Edna cannot know if James will have children, or how many, or what their needs will be by the time James dies. Rather than arbitrarily fixing the shares ahead of time, Edna instead could give James (or someone else) a power of appointment to identify who should take the trust principal and in what shares. By creating a power of appointment, Edna can keep her trust adaptable to changed circumstances. For a generation, she can postpone decisions about how that money will be spent. At the same time, if Edna properly limits the scope of James' power, the property subject to the power will not be included in James' taxable estate.

1. The Players

The law of powers has its own terminology. *See* 3d Rest. Prop. § 17.2. The "**donor**" is the person who creates the power. The person who gets the power is called the "**donee**," who may include the donor. The donee can give the property only to people the donor identifies as "**objects**" of the power, which may or may not include the donee. If the donee exercises the power, the recipient is called an "**appointee.**" An appointee must come from the class of "**objects**" (sometimes called "**permissible appointees**"). If the donee does not exercise the power, the property may go to a "**taker in default of appointment**" who the donor specifically or impliedly identified. The taker in default usually has a remainder, subject to divestment by the power's exercise. Depending upon the estate plan, the same person may assume several roles. Thus, someone reserving a power to appoint to himself and then exercising that power would be donor, donee, object, and appointee.

2. Classification of Powers

Two different ways of classifying powers are critically important. One is based on who can get the property subject to the power, the other on the mechanics of how the power can be exercised.

a. Objects (Permissible Appointees)

The breadth of the class of objects is one criterion for dividing powers. Until recent times, a **general** power was one in which a donee could give the property to anyone, including himself or his estate. *See* Rest. Prop. § 320 (1940). A **special** power was one in which a donee was limited to a particular class of objects. These definitions left a gap: a power that could be exercised to benefit anyone except the donee. Earlier, the gap caused little trouble because people saw little utility in creating such "**hybrid**" powers. The increased importance of tax planning, however, has prompted drafters to create such powers because they avoid the tax consequences of a general power, but they also give the donee enormous discretion.

In response to this change, the Restatement (Third) of Property identifies two categories of powers: general and nongeneral. According to the Restatement, but subject to a few limited exceptions, a general power is one "exercisable in favor of any one or more of the following: the donee, the donee's estate, or the creditors of either . . . " 3d Rest. Prop. § 17.3. *Accord* UPOAA § 102(6).[25] The "**nongeneral**" category includes both special and hybrid powers. This grouping has the advantage of bringing tax and property terminology closer together, but it can be awkward because not all nongeneral powers raise the same questions.

Lawyers and courts still refer to "general" and "special" powers, and readers understand those terms according to their context. In most situations, "general" probably means a power exercisable in favor of the donee, his estate, his creditors or the creditors of his estate. If the question involves tax, "special" probably means "not general." If the question does not involve tax, "special" means "for a limited class of objects" (excluding the donee, the donee's creditors, the donee's estate, or creditors of the donee's estate as class members). This discussion will follow that approach.

b. Method of Exercise

The other way of classifying powers centers upon how and when powers can be exercised. **Inter vivos powers** are exercisable by a deed during the donee's lifetime (or some shorter time). **Testamentary powers** are exercisable by will. The same power can be both inter vivos and testamentary, exercisable either way at the donee's option.

These two basic lines of division—permissible appointees and method of exercise—overlap. We can have general inter vivos powers and special inter vivos powers. We can also have general testamentary powers and special testamentary powers. These options give planners enormous flexibility to design plans that can meet the needs of their clients.

---

25. Federal transfer tax laws provide the same general definition for a general power of appointment, albeit with more exceptions. *See, e.g.*, I.R.C. § 2041(b).

3. Estate Tax Treatment

The details of taxing property subject to powers can get very complex, but the general principles are straightforward. It may help to review the discussion in § 1.03, *supra.* If a donee dies holding a general power of appointment, the property subject to that power will be included in the donee's gross estate for estate tax purposes.[26] IRC § 2041(a). Property subject to a special power, however, is generally not included.[27] Because of this distinction, donors may create different sorts of powers in different situations.

4. Who Owns the Property

Like much of the law of property, the law surrounding powers of appointment is moving from strict reliance upon the logic of traditional doctrine to a more flexible examination of the realities involved. For example, UTC § 103(2)(B) takes the novel position that the holder of a power of appointment created under a trust is a trust beneficiary. As explained in the Comment:

> While the holder of a power of appointment is not considered a trust beneficiary under the common law of trusts, holders of powers are classified as beneficiaries under the Uniform Trust Code. Holders of powers are included on the assumption that their interests are significant enough that they should be afforded the rights of beneficiaries.

Another illustration of this development is the conflict surrounding how much of an interest a donee of a power has in the property subject to the power. The question is important largely because persons who have claims on the donee often want to treat the property subject to the power as the donee's property, so they can use the property to satisfy the donee's obligations.

Traditionally, the law viewed a donee of a power almost as an agent of the donor, who retained ownership of the property until the donee exercised the power. Under this view, the exercise of the power then relates back to the power's creation, so the exercise fills in blanks that had been left in the document creating the power. The appointee thus gets the property from the donor, not the donee (*see* Figure 9-4). Because the property subject to the power was not the donee's, claimants against the donee came away empty-handed even if the donee exercised a general testamentary power of appointment. *See, e.g., Johnson v. Shriver*, 216 P.2d 653 (Colo. 1950).

---

26. For tax purposes, a power is not general if it is properly limited by an ascertainable standard. IRC § 2041(b)(1)(A). For example, a donee may not have a general power even though she has access to trust principal for her own use if she can only invade to pay the "reasonable expenses of her higher education."

27. Comparable tax treatment applies to powers exercised during the donee's lifetime. If a donee exercises a general power, gift taxation results; exercise of a special power generally has no gift tax consequences. *See* IRC § 2514, applicable IRC §§ 2041(a)(3) and 2514(d) provide exceptions where a special power may be exercisable beyond the applicable perpetuities period.

Figure 9-4 Relation Back

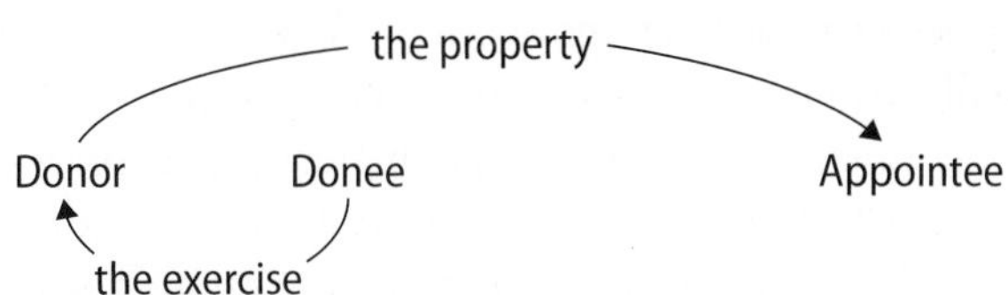

The relation-back theory makes sense in the context of a special power. Because the donee cannot appoint the property to herself, the property is not in any practical sense hers and should not be subject to claims against her.

On the other hand, the donee of a presently-exercisable general power is only a paper-thin line away from absolute ownership since the donee can get the property simply by signing some forms. In this context, treating the property as the donor's, and thus not subject to claims against the donee, is hard to justify. As a result, the law is changing. Indeed the Restatement (Third) of Property specifically rejects use of the relation-back theory to resolve most issues. *See* 3d Rest. Prop. § 17.4, cmt. f.

The Restatement (Third) of Property and UPOAA provide rules that treat the donee (powerholder) of a presently exercisable general power as if the powerholder owned the property that was the subject of the general power, albeit creditors must first access the powerholder's other owned assets. *See* 3d Rest Prop. § 22.3 and UPOAA § 502.[28] Also, under bankruptcy law, a presently exercisable general power of appointment is included in the estate of a bankrupt donee. *See* 11 U.S.C. § 541(b).

The Restatement (Third) of Property and UPOAA also treat the donee (powerholder) of a testamentary general power as if the powerholder owned the property that was the subject of the general power, albeit creditors must first access the powerholder's other owned assets. *See* 3d Rest Prop. § 22.3 and UPOAA § 502. For example, on the death of the donee of testamentary general power of appointment, the property subject to the power is reachable by creditors and available to pay expenses to the extent probate assets are insufficient whether or not the power is exercised. *See* 3d Rest. Property § 22.3(b) and UPOAA § 502(a)(1).

The law regarding the rights of a surviving spouse to reach property subject to a presently exercisable general power of appointment is in a state of flux. The traditional rule has been that the surviving spouse could not reach such property. *See Bongaards v. Millen*, 793 N.E.2d 335 (Mass. 2003) (where power created by third party). The latest UPC elective share version treats, as a testamentary substitute, property over which the deceased spouse was the donee of a presently exercisable general power of appointment but not a testamentary general power of appointment. *See* UPC § 2-205(1). *Accord* 3d Rest. Prop. § 23.1.

28. UTC § 505(b) treats the donee of a presently exercisable general power of appointment as if the donee were the settlor of a revocable trust; but, unlike the Restatement (Third) and UPOAA, creditors need not first access other owned assets.

Note and Problems

1. The interplay between the law of powers and federal taxation is extremely important. If the donee of a lifetime power is allowed to exercise it in his favor or in favor of his creditors, the power will be general. This classification may cause adverse income, gift, and estate tax consequences. If the donee of a testamentary power may exercise it in favor of her estate or the creditors of her estate, the power will be general and may cause adverse estate tax consequences. Recognizing the potential tax problems, courts may narrowly construe powers to avoid adverse tax results. For example, *In re Hillman*, 744 N.E.2d 1078 (Mass. 2001), involved a trust that gave the settlor's child a power exercisable during lifetime in favor of the settlor's "issue." Because the donee was also one of the settlor's issue, traditional doctrine would allow the child to appoint to himself, so the power would be general. To avoid the adverse tax consequences of classifying the power as general, the court interpreted the trust as creating a power to appoint to any of the settlor's other issue. *See also In re Pierce*, 816 N.E.2d 1212 (Mass. 2004) (will reformed to convert general power into special power to avoid estate taxation).

2. Libbey's will gave property in trust to First Bank, with income to George for life and the remainder "to those persons among my descendants to whom George appoints by will, and to the extent that George does not so appoint, then to Lori." Identify the players and characterize the nature of the power of appointment.

3. Think of your family. Are there any situations in which a power of appointment could be useful?

Selected References

Ira Mark Bloom, *Power of Appointment Legislation in New York: It's Time for Modernization*, 76 Alb. L. Rev. 9 (2012/2013).

Ira Mark Bloom, *Powers of Appointment under the Restatement (Third) of Property*, 33 Ohio N.U.L. Rev. 755 (2007).

B. Creation and Exercise

The fundamental question about powers is familiar: what did the donor intend to create? On the margin, disputes arise about whether a donor intended to create a power of appointment at all. *See, e.g., In re Estate of Stewart*, 473 A.2d 572 (Pa. Super. Ct. 1984) (a close family friend authorized to "handle" the decedent's estate "as she sees fit" had a general power). Closer to the center are arguments about the nature of the power. What steps must the donee follow to exercise it? Who are the permissible appointees? What interests can the donee create? A lawyer creating a power must look ahead and anticipate problems that could arise at the time the power will be exercised. For that reason, we start with some problems surrounding effective exercise of a power, and then circle back to examine how careful planning when creating a power can avoid trouble later.

Beals v. State St. Bank and Trust Co.

326 N.E.2d 896 (Mass. 1975)

Wilkins, J.

. . . Arthur Hunnewell died, a resident of Wellesley, in 1904, leaving his wife and four daughters. His will placed the residue of his property in a trust, the income of which was to be paid to his wife during her life. At the death of his wife the trust was to be divided in portions, one for each then surviving daughter and one for the then surviving issue of any deceased daughter. Mrs. Hunnewell died in 1930. One of the four daughters predeceased her mother, leaving no issue. The trust was divided, therefore, in three portions at the death of Mrs. Hunnewell. The will directed that the income of each portion held for a surviving daughter should be paid to her during her life and on her death the principal of such portion should "be paid and disposed of as she may direct and appoint by her last Will and Testament duly probated." In default of appointment, the will directed that a daughter's share should be distributed to "the persons who would be entitled to such estate under the laws then governing the distribution of intestate estates."

This petition concerns the distribution of the trust portion held for the testator's daughter Isabella H. Hunnewell, later Isabella H. Dexter (Isabella). Following the death of her mother, Isabella requested the trustees to exercise their discretionary power to make principal payments by transferring substantially all of her trust share "to the Dexter family office in Boston, there to be managed in the first instance by her husband, Mr. Gordon Dexter." This request was granted, and cash and securities were transferred to her account at the Dexter office. The Hunnewell trustees, however, retained in Isabella's share a relatively small cash balance, an undivided one-third interest in a mortgage and undivided one-third interests in various parcels of real estate in the Commonwealth, which Isabella did not want in kind and which the trustees could not sell at a reasonable price at the time. . . .

In February, 1944, Isabella, . . . partially released her general power of appointment . . . "to the extent that such power empowers me to appoint to anyone other than one or more of the . . . descendants me surviving of Arthur Hunnewell." [This release converted the power to a special power in response to changes in the estate tax law.]

On December 14, 1968, Isabella, who survived her husband, died without issue, . . . a resident of New York, leaving a will dated May 21, 1965 . . . . Isabella did not expressly exercise her power of appointment under her father's will. The residuary clause of her will provided in effect for the distribution of all "the rest, residue and remainder of my property" to the issue per stirpes of her sister Margaret Blake, who had predeceased Isabella.[29] The Blake issue would take one-half of Isabella's trust share, as takers in default of appointment, in all events. If, however, Isabella's will should be treated as effectively exercising her power of appointment under her father's will, the Blake issue would take the entire trust share, and the executors of the will of Isabella's sister Jane (who survived Isabella and has since died) would not receive that one-half of the trust share which would go to Jane in default of appointment.

In support of their argument that Isabella's will did not exercise the power of appointment under her father's will, the executors of Jane's estate contend that (1) Massachusetts substantive law governs all questions relating to the power of appointment, including the interpretation of Isabella's will; (2) the power should be treated as a special power of appointment because of its partial release by Isabella; and (3) because Isabella's will neither expresses nor implies any intention to exercise the power, the applicable rule of construction in this Commonwealth is that a general residuary clause does not exercise a special power of appointment. The Blake issue, in support of their argument that the power was exercised, contends that (1) Isabella's will manifests an intention to exercise the power and that no rule of construction need be applied; (2) the law of New York should govern the question whether Isabella's will exercised the power and, if it does, by statute New York has adopted a rule that a special power of appointment is exercised by a testamentary disposition of all of the donee's property; and (3) if Massachusetts law does apply, and the will is silent on the subject of the exercise of the power, the principles underlying our rule of construction that a residuary clause exercises a general power of appointment are applicable in these circumstances.

1. We turn first to a consideration of the question whether Isabella's will should be construed according to the law of this Commonwealth or the law of New York.[30]

---

29. The significant portion of the residuary clause reads as follows:

> All the rest, residue and remainder of my property of whatever kind and wherever situated (including any property not effectively disposed of by the preceding provisions of this my will and all property over which I have or may have the power of appointment under or by virtue of the last will and testament dated November 27, 1933 and codicils thereto dated January 7, 1935 and January 8, 1935 of my husband, the late Gordon Dexter) . . . I give, devise, bequeath and appoint in equal shares to such of my said nephew GEORGE BATY BLAKE and my said nieces MARGARET CABOT and JULIA O. BEALS as shall survive me and the issue who shall survive me of any of my said nephew or nieces who may predecease me, such issue to take per stirpes.

30. The applicable rules of construction where a donee's intention is not clear from his will differ between the two States. In the absence of a requirement by the donor that the donee refer to the power in order to exercise it, New York provides by statute that a residuary clause in a will exercises not only a general power of appointment but also a special power of appointment, unless the will expressly or by necessary implication shows the contrary . . . . In Massachusetts, unless the donor has provided that the donee of the power can exercise it only by explicit reference to the power, a general residuary clause in a will exercises a general power of appointment unless there is a clear indication of a contrary intent . . . . However, in *Fiduciary Trust Co. v. First Natl. Bank*, 344 Mass. 1, 6–10, 181 N.E.2d 226 (1962), we held that a general residuary clause did not exercise a special testamentary power of appointment in the circumstances of that case.

There are strong, logical reasons for turning to the law of the donee's domicil at the time of death to determine whether a donee's will has exercised a testamentary power of appointment over movables. See Restatement (Second) Conflict of Laws, § 275, comment c (1971); . . . Most courts in this country which have considered the question, however, interpret the donee's will under the law governing the administration of the trust, which is usually the law of the donor's domicil . . . . This has long been the rule in Massachusetts. *Sewall v. Wilmer*, 132 Mass. 131, 136–137 (1882) . . . .

If the question were before us now for the first time, we might well adopt a choice of law rule which would turn to the substantive law of the donee's domicil, for the purpose of determining whether the donee's will exercised a power of appointment. However, in a field where much depends on certainty and consistency as to the applicable rules of law, we think that we should adhere to our well established rule. Thus, in interpreting the will of a donee to determine whether a power of appointment was exercised, we apply the substantive law of the jurisdiction whose law governs the administration of the trust.

2. Considering the arguments of the parties, we conclude that there is no indication in Isabella's will of an intention to exercise or not to exercise the power of appointment given to her under her father's will . . . . In the absence of an intention disclosed by her will, construed in light of circumstances known to her when she executed it, we must adopt some Massachusetts rule of construction to resolve the issue before us. The question is what rule of construction. We are unaware of any decided case which, in this context, has dealt with a testamentary general power, reduced to a special power by action of the donee.

3. We conclude that the residuary clause of Isabella's will should be presumed to have exercised the power of appointment. We reach this result by a consideration of the reasons underlying the canons of construction applicable to general and special testamentary powers of appointment. Considered in this way, we believe that a presumption of exercise is more appropriate in the circumstances of this case than a presumption of nonexercise.

When this court first decided not to extend to a special power of appointment the rule of construction that a general residuary clause executes a general testamentary power (unless a contrary intent is shown by the will), we noted significant distinctions between a general power and a special power . . . . A general power was said to be a close approximation to a property interest, a "virtually unlimited power of disposition," . . . while a special power of appointment lacked this quality. We observed that a layman having a general testamentary power over property might not be expected to distinguish between the appointive property and that which he owns outright, and thus "he can reasonably be presumed to regard this appointive property as his own" . . . . On the other hand, the donee of a special power would not reasonably regard such appointive property as his own: "[h]e would more likely consider himself to be, as the donor of the power intended, merely the person chosen by the donor to decide who of the possible appointees should share in the property (if the power is exclusive), and the respective shares of the appointees" . . .

Considering the power of appointment given to Isabella and her treatment of that power during her life, the rationale for the canon of construction applicable to general powers of appointment should be applied in this case. This power was a general testamentary power at its inception. During her life, as a result of her request, Isabella had the use and enjoyment of the major portion of the property initially placed in her trust share. Prior use and enjoyment of the appointive property is a factor properly considered as weighing in favor of the exercise of a power of appointment by a will.... Isabella voluntarily limited the power by selecting the possible appointees. In thus relinquishing the right to add the trust assets to her estate, she was treating the property as her own. Moreover, the gift under her residuary clause was consistent with the terms of the reduced power which she retained. In these circumstances, the partial release of a general power does not obviate the application of that rule of construction which presumes that a general residuary clause exercises a general power of appointment.

4. A decree shall be entered determining that Isabella H. Dexter did exercise the power of appointment....

Notes and Questions

1. What are the "strong, logical reasons" for applying the law of the donee's domicil to determine whether a donee's will has exercised a power?

2. The *Beals* court applied a rule of construction that a general residuary clause exercises a general testamentary power, in part because Isabella treated the appointive property as her own. After she converted her power to a special power, when did she treat the property as her own?

Massachusetts now presumes non-exercise. Mass. Gen. L. ch. 191, § 1A(4), but New York still presumes exercise of a power by a general residuary clause subject to certain exceptions. *See* N.Y. EPTL § 10.6–1(a)(4). North Carolina statutorily presumes exercise but only for general powers of appointment. *See First Nat'l Bk v. Ingold*, 523 S.E.2d 725 (1999) (construing power as general so that N.C. Gen. Stat. § 31-43 applied).

3. Review Isabella's residuary clause. How might you argue it reflects an intention not to exercise the power she held from her father?

4. Under the UPC, a general residuary clause in a will, without more, will not exercise a power. UPC § 2-608. However, a general residuary clause in a will is deemed to exercise a power if the donor has not required specific reference to the power, and if "the power is general and there is no gift in default." UPC § 2-608(i). *Cf.* 3d Rest. Prop. § 19.4 and UPOAA § 302 (general power exercised under similar circumstances by residuary clause in a will or revocable trust).

5. Lawyers drafting documents that exercise previously created powers of appointment should examine carefully the document that created the power. For example, is the exercise in favor of a permissible appointee? *See, e.g.*, *Timmons v. Ingrahm*, 36 So. 3d 861 (Fla. Dist. Ct. App. 2010) (exercise in favor of step-children invalid when class limited to lineal descendants). In addition to defining the class of permissible

appointees, the donor may have given specific directions for exercising the power. *See, e.g., Cessac v. Stevens*, 127 So. 3d 675 (Fla. Dist. Ct. App. 2013) (power not validly exercised when instrument creating power required specific reference to power on exercise and donee only evidenced a general intent to exercise the power in his will); *Catch v. Phillips*, 86 Cal. Rptr. 2d 584 (Ct. App. 1999) (power not validly exercised by lifetime document when instrument creating power required exercise by will or codicil) If a power is required to be exercisable by will, the Restatement (Third) of Property § 19.9, comment b, takes the position that validity of exercise should not depend on whether the will is actually probated unless the donor required probate. *But see Estate of Scott*, 77 P.3d 906 (Colo. Ct. App. 2003).

Should a revocable trust be treated as a will for exercise purposes? *See* 3d Rest. Prop. § 19.9, cmt. b (yes). Can a lifetime power be validly exercised by a revocable trust in lieu of an actual deed? *See In re Edwards*, 99 P.3d 256 (Okla. Civ. App. 2004) (yes). *Accord* 3d Rest. Prop. § 19.9, cmt. d.

Donees who exercise powers to create new trusts or new powers need to be especially wary of the Rule Against Perpetuities. *See* Pages 578–580.

6. Under traditional doctrine, an unexercised general power simply left the property where it was, in the hands of the donor, unless the donor identified takers-in-default. The Restatement (Third) of Property § 19.22 wisely departs from tradition by allowing the unappointed property under a general power to pass to the donee or the donee's estate. *Accord* UPOAA § 310.

Under traditional doctrine, an ineffectively exercised general power raised the question whether the donee intended to assume control over the property for more than the limited purpose of exercising the power. If so, the donee may have "captured" the property for his own estate. *See Hochberg v. Proctor*, 805 N.E.2d 979 (Mass. 2004). The most common indicator of an intention to capture property is a general blending clause, one which mixes the donee's own property and the property subject to the power.

The Restatement (Third) of Property § 19.21 wisely departs from the capture doctrine if the donee ineffectively exercises a general power of appointment, for example, because the exercise violates the Rule Against Perpetuities. If the donor provided for takers by a takers-in-default-clause, the property will pass to the takers. If there are no takers in default, the property ineffectively appointed passes to the donee or the donee's estate without having to determine if the donee intended to capture the property. In effect, the Restatement (Third) of Property § 19.21 repudiates the capture doctrine in favor of a modern approach to the problem of ineffectively exercised powers. *Accord* UPOAA § 309.

7. When special powers are exercisable in favor of a definite class but remain unexercised, or an attempted exercise fails, and there are no takers in default, the property usually will go equally to the class members. Some courts imply a gift in default to the objects. *Accord* 3d Rest. Prop. § 19.23 and UPOAA § 311. Other courts say the donee has a "power in trust," sometimes called "an imperative power," with a duty

to exercise the power. *But cf.* 3d Rest. Prop. § 17.1, cmt. k and § 19.23 (rejecting imperative power in favor of implied gift). Because the donee has violated that obligation, a court will impose a constructive trust on those who would otherwise take, in favor of the objects of the power.

8. Although a spendthrift trust usually bars voluntary alienation by a trust beneficiary, if such beneficiary also has a general power of appointment exercisable during lifetime, the beneficiary effectively will have the power of alienation. *See Dickinson v. Wilmington Trust Co.*, 734 A.2d 605 (Del. Ch. Ct. 1999) (construing power to appoint to "such person or persons as the donee may designate" as a general power); *In re Gilroy*, 235 B.R. 512 (D. Mass. 1999) (bankrupt's estate includes spendthrifted trust interest where bankrupt had lifetime general power of appointment). Nor will the imposition of a spendthrift provision over principal be effective if the settlor has a testamentary general power of appointment. *See Phillips v. Moore*, 690 S.E.2d 620 (Ga. 2010).

9. As *Beals* illustrates, conflict of laws problems can arise in the powers arena. *See* 3d Rest. Prop. § 19.1, cmt. e (applying law of donee's domicil to determine effectiveness of donee's exercise). Consider another situation involving the cy pres doctrine, that of *Toledo Trust Co. v. Santa Barbara Foundation*, 512 N.E.2d 664 (Ohio 1987), *cert. denied*, 485 U.S. 916 (1988), recognized a California court's use of cy pres to modify an Ohio trust. Marcia Rivas' mother had created a trust in Toledo giving Marcia a power of appointment to designate in her will which charitable beneficiaries should take the trust principal. Marcia died in Santa Barbara, leaving a will naming Alcoholics Anonymous, but AA declined part of the gift. The California court then applied cy pres to substitute the Santa Barbara Foundation (SBF). The Toledo bank refused SBF's request for funds and brought a declaratory judgment action in Ohio. The Ohio court said that California law, the law of the domicile of the power's donee, controlled.

Note: The Scope of Special Powers

By definition, donees of special powers lack the authority to appoint property to persons or entities who are not objects of the power. In one case, a lawyer failed to advise the client that her exercise to a non-object would fail. The mistake cost the lawyer $300,000. *See Merrick v. Mercantile-Safe Deposit & Trust Co.*, 855 F.2d 1095, 1099 (4th Cir. 1988).

Because special powers limit donees' choices of appointees, some courts have viewed special powers as smaller than general powers in other respects as well. For example, some courts have denied donees of special powers the ability to create new powers of appointment or new trusts. This limited view of the authority granted by special powers is losing favor. *See, e.g., Estate of Reisman*, 702 N.W.2d 658 (Mich. Ct. App. 2005); *see generally* 3d Rest. Prop. § 19.4. To be safe, however, good drafters will identify the sorts of interests they want their donees to be able to create.

Special powers also present the question of how much power the donee has to choose among the class of objects. A special power can be either **exclusive** or **non-exclusive**. In this context, "exclusive" means having the power to exclude some of the objects of the power in favor of others. If a special power is non-exclusive, the donee must give each object something. *See, e.g., Hargrove v. Rich*, 604 S.E.2d 475 (Ga. 2004) (power to appoint to nieces and nephews was non-exclusive so exercise in favor of one niece was invalid). The question becomes: how much? Some jurisdictions require each object to get a substantial part of the assets subject to the power. Others say that nominal gifts to some objects still satisfy the restriction that a donee cannot exclude anyone. *See* 3d Rest. Prop. § 17.5.

Problem

Examine the form reproduced below. Explain the function and consider the wisdom of the phrases and sentences that appear in italics.

Michael's Special Power of Appointment

Upon Michael's death, the trustee shall pay all remaining principal and undistributed income, or hold it, according to the directions Michael makes under the special power of appointment created by this section. Michael may make such appointment by a written instrument he has signed and delivered to the trustee during Michael's lifetime but after my death or by a provision in a will executed after my death and specifically referring to the power created by this trust agreement. Michael may appoint to, or for the benefit of, any one or more of his lineal descendants, in whatever shares he deems appropriate. He may not appoint to himself, his estate, his creditors or the creditors of his estate.

He may appoint the property outright or in trust according to whatever terms he chooses as if the property were his own, subject to the limitations imposed by this section with regard to the persons who may benefit from this trust. In particular, but not by way of further limiting his discretion, he may: create new powers of appointment and new present or future interests in any appointee; create new powers of appointment in any other person living at my death (including a trustee), except that such new power may not be exercised in favor of persons other than the objects of this power; and impose spendthrift or other lawful restrictions.

To the extent that Michael does not expressly exercise this power of appointment effectively, the trustee shall distribute the property subject to this power according to the terms of section 3(B)(2) of this trust agreement.

Selected Reference

Susan F. French, *Exercise of Powers of Appointment: Should Intent to Exercise Be Inferred from a General Disposition of Property?*, 1979 Duke L.J. 747.

§ 9.04 The Rule Against Perpetuities

The Rule Against Perpetuities is among those rules of law that limit the power of one generation to restrict the uses future generations put to property. In contrast to other "dead hand" doctrines that focus on the substance of various restrictions, the Rule[31] is concerned with time. Roughly speaking, the Rule allows people to tie up property for 100 years. Although our focus is on estate planning, you should appreciate that some, but not all, courts will apply the Rule in a variety of commercial contexts: options to purchase property, rights of first refusal, easements, covenants, leases. *See, e.g.*, *Barnes v. Oceanus Nav. Corp.*, 21 A.D.3d 975 (N.Y. Ct. App. 2005) (right of first refusal violated common-law Rule). *See generally* William M. McGovern, Jr., Sheldon F. Kurtz & David M. English, Wills, Trusts, and Estates § 11.7 (3d ed. 2004).

In the context of modern estate planning, the Rule's original purpose of furthering land's alienability is no longer relevant. The Rule now serves as an arbiter between generations:

> With the emergence of trusts and corporations—entities which can alienate specific property—the rule has been justified as striking a fair balance between the desires of the living and the rights of the deceased to control enjoyment of property, with the consequent advantages of having property more freely available for the needs of current generations.

Ira Mark Bloom, *Transfer Tax Avoidance: The Impact of Perpetuities Restrictions Before and After Generation-Skipping Taxation*, 45 Alb. L. Rev. 261, 265 (1981).

This section aims to help you to identify perpetuities problems and to avoid those problems through careful drafting. We start with a framework for approaching perpetuities questions and then examine how the Rule applies in various situations. Next we view saving clauses, powerful tools which, if handled properly, can protect against many of the Rule's infamous traps. We then discuss the reforms that continue to command legislative attention and the recent perpetuities repeal movement. Finally, we consider important dead hand control rules other than the Rule Against Perpetuities.

A. Framework for Analysis

In the late nineteenth century, John Chipman Gray articulated the Rule as follows: "No interest is good unless it must vest, if at all, not later than twenty-one years after some life in being at the creation of the interest." John C. Gray, The Rule Against Perpetuities 191 (4th ed. 1942). Gray's formulation still dominates the way courts and commentators think about the Rule.

Three ideas permeate the analysis. First, the Rule is concerned about questions that stay unresolved too long, as measured by people's lives.

31. In this section the capitalized word "Rule" refers to the common-law Rule Against Perpetuities.

Second, the Rule judges each interest based on facts we know at the beginning of the perpetuities period. If a deed creates the interest, the relevant time is that of the deed's delivery. If a will creates the interest, the time is the testator's date of death. If a revocable trust creates the interest, the time is the expiration of the power to revoke (usually the settlor's death). For property subject to a general, presently-exercisable power of appointment, the perpetuities period should not start to run until the expiration of the power. *See* 2d Rest. Prop. § 1.2. Gray's shorthand way of referring to these various times was "at the creation of the interest."

Third, the Rule applies a possibilities test, so that if anything could go wrong, you must assume it will.

When judging the validity of any future interest, you may find it useful to work through the following steps:

(1) **Ask whether the interest is contingent.** In general, the Rule applies to all contingent remainders and executory interests, and it does not apply to vested interests. (For a review of these interests, *see supra* § 9.01.) Courts have, however, refined this general rule. For example, vested remainders subject to open, despite their "vested" label, are subject to the Rule. The openness of the class is a contingency that must be resolved within the perpetuities period. Also, a contingent gift to a second charity, following a gift to a first charity, is not subject to the Rule.

(2) **Identify exactly what we will need to know in order to say whether the interest has vested.**

(3) **Seek a "validating life."**[32] *See* Figure 9-5. Start with "relevant lives," those persons who have something to do with the contingency. In this connection, recall those problems that make interests contingent. Relevant lives might be among: (1) the beneficiaries themselves, (2) people who can affect the identity of the beneficiaries, and (3) people who can affect any condition precedent.

Figure 9-5 Identifying Validating Lives

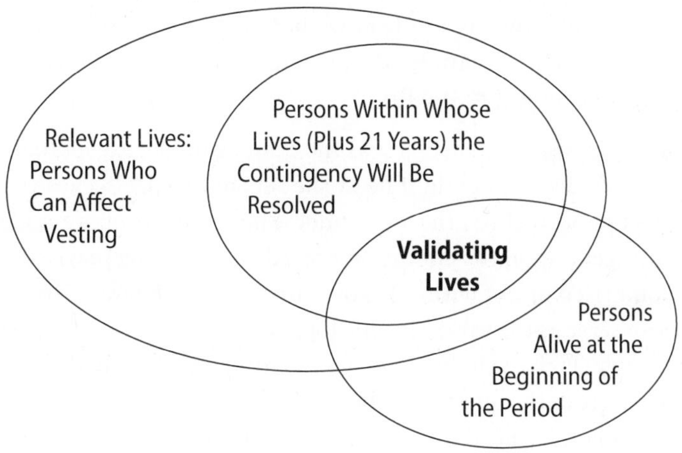

32. Some writers use the term "measuring life."

As to each person, ask whether we can be sure we will have resolved the problem by the time of that person's death (plus 21 years). If the answer is "yes," verify that the person is certain to have been alive at the beginning of the perpetuities period. (Caution: pay close attention if the potential validating life is someone identified by label, e.g., one of "Martina's children.") If so, that life can be a "validating life," establishing that the interest satisfies the Rule. If the answer is "no," try another life.

When you run out of relevant lives, and none works, the interest is void under the Rule unless it must either vest or fail within 21 years. The examples below illustrate these three steps.

Example 9-5. Suppose a grant from Matt "to Jennifer for life, remainder to Carla if she survives Jennifer." Jennifer's life estate is a present interest—presently vested, not subject to the Rule. Carla's remainder is contingent upon surviving Jennifer. Here we have two relevant lives, Jennifer and Carla. We also have two validating lives, because we now know that at the death of either one we will be able to tell whether Carla survives Jennifer, and both of them were alive at the time of the grant. The contingent remainder is valid. By definition, reversions are vested; hence, Matt's reversion is not subject to the Rule.

Example 9-6. Suppose David grants property "to Virginia for life, remainder to her first child to get married." At the time, Virginia has one child, Joe, who is not married. Virginia's life estate is presently vested and not subject to the Rule. The remainder is contingent upon identification as being Virginia's first child to get married. Virginia is a relevant life, because she supplies the children. She is not a validating life, however, because we cannot be sure that within 21 years after her death one of her children will get married. Joe is also a relevant life, but he, too, fails as a validating life. He may or may not get married, and thus meet the condition, within his lifetime. Furthermore, Joe might die tomorrow, and Virginia might have another child who would get married more than 21 years after Joe's death. The later child cannot be a validating life because he or she was not alive at the time of the grant. Having run out of relevant lives to test, we have established that the remainder is void under the Rule. The remainder drops out, leaving David's reversion, which is presently vested, not subject to the Rule.

Example 9-7. Suppose the same facts as the prior example, except that the remainder is "to Virginia's firstborn child if he or she gets married." Because we know that Joe is Virginia's firstborn child, the remainder is not contingent upon identification, but rather contingent upon the condition precedent of getting married. Because Joe will either get married or not within his own lifetime and he was alive at the time of the grant, he can serve as the validating life for his own remainder. Notice three things about this example. First, a slight change in wording made a big difference because it changed the nature of the question to be resolved. Second, in order to be valid under the Rule, Joe's remainder need not ever vest. The Rule's concern is not whether the remainder vests, but how long we must wait to find out. Third, the holder of the interest in question (Joe) can be his own validating life.

Example 9-8. If an interest is subject to more than one contingency, then we must analyze each contingency. What looks at first to be a void gift may in fact be valid. Suppose a gift "to the city so long as used as a park, then to Joyce if she is then living." Joyce's executory interest is subject to two contingencies: the land not being used as a park and Joyce being alive at that time. If the park-use contingency were the only one, Joyce's gift would fail for lack of a validating life. Joyce's interest is good, however, because Joyce cannot take unless she survives. Because Joyce's interest will either vest or not within her lifetime, she is her own validating life.

With this background in mind, look back to Gray's classic statement and note its assumptions:

- "Interest" includes either legal or equitable property interests in persons other than the grantor.
- "Must" means absolute certainty.
- "Vest" means vesting in interest and does not require a present possessory interest.
- "If at all" means that the interest need not vest, but we must know that the question (about whether the interest will vest) will be resolved within the period.
- "No later than" allows the possibility of early vesting.
- "Twenty-one years after" includes both that period in gross and actual periods of gestation.
- "Some life in being" means any one of a not unreasonably large number of human lives, and includes the period of gestation of that life.

This introduction prompts some generalizations. Like all generalizations, these must be used with care, because they will not always apply. They can, however, help identify probable trouble spots. Imagine a typical estate plan, with a life estate, a remainder for life, and an ultimate remainder.

Consider each of the interests:

(1) The life estate is presently vested, not subject to the rule.

(2) The remainder for life is likely to be valid, because often the contingencies surrounding it will be resolved at the end of the first life estate. If that is the case, the first life tenant will be someone alive when the interests were created and can serve as a validating life.

(3) The ultimate remainder, however, is more likely to be in trouble. The problem will arise because the lives relevant to that interest often will be those who hold the intermediate remainder for life. Those people may not qualify as validating lives because they might not have been alive at the beginning of the perpetuities period. While their own interest may be good, they may not be able to validate the ultimate remainder.

Problems

Which of the interests in the following fact patterns violate the Rule?

1. Judith's will includes a gift to "my youngest child who shall be living 35 years after the death of my friend Chris." Judith's two children, Anthony (age 3) and Beth (age 15), and Chris survived Judith.

2. Albert left his real estate to a named hospital but if the property is ever sold then the property goes to X. *See Kennewick Pub. Hosp. Dist. v. Hawe,* 214 P.3d 163 (Wash. Ct. App. 2009) (X has executory interest that violates the Rule resulting in fee simple absolute estate in the hospital). Why is X's interest void?

3. Carrie's will gave property "to City Hospital for its general purposes, but if the hospital ever ceases to operate, to Mark if he is then alive." Mark survived Carrie.

4. Thomas left property "to Michele for life, remainder to Michele's children, but if Michele dies without issue, remainder to Erich." At Thomas' death, Michele survived, unmarried and childless.

5. Jason left property in trust to Amanda for life, remainder to "Amanda's first child who reaches age 30." Jason is survived by Amanda and her two children:

(a) Ben, age 5, and Jeff, age 7.

(b) Ben, age 25, and Jeff, age 27.

(c) Ben, age 29, and Jeff, age 31.

Selected References

David M. Becker, *A Methodology for Solving Perpetuities Problems Under the Common Law Rule: A Step-by-Step Process That Carefully Identifies All Testing Lives in Being*, 67 Wash. U. L.Q. 949 (1989).

Jesse Dukeminier, *A Modern Guide to Perpetuities*, 74 Cal. L. Rev. 1867 (1986).

W. Barton Leach, *Perpetuities in a Nutshell*, 51 Harv. L. Rev. 638 (1938).

Mark Reutlinger, *When Words Fail Me: Diagramming The Rule Against Perpetuities*, 59 Mo. L. Rev. 157 (1994).

B. A Possibilities Test

One troublesome aspect of the Rule is its requirement that the mere chance, however unlikely, of something going wrong is enough to invalidate an interest. The Rule will snare a drafter who makes reasonable assumptions about the way life works, but does not consider remote possibilities.

Perkins v. Iglehart

39 A.2d 672 (Md. Ct. App. 1944)

Marbury, C.J.

This case arose through a trustee's petition filed in the Circuit Court for Baltimore County, asking for a construction of the will of Lucy James Dun. She died in 1921, a widow with one child, a son, William James Rucker. . . .

Mrs. Dun, in her will, gave various specific and pecuniary bequests, and then by the fourteenth clause provided as follows:

[To my son for life and] from and after the death of my said son to set apart one-third of said trust estate and pay the net income thereof to his widow during her life or widowhood, . . . and from and after the death or remarriage of the widow of my said son, to hold the one-third part of the trust estate, so as above set apart for her, for the benefit of the child or children of my said son then living and the descendants then living of his deceased children . . . but if there shall be no such children or descendants then surviving, or if all of them shall die before attaining the age of twenty-one years, to divide, pay over and transfer the same, free of any trust, to and among the persons who would be the next of kin of my said son according to the laws of Maryland if he were living at the time of the death or remarriage of his widow . . . .

The son, William J. Rucker, was twice married; both wives predeceased him . . . .

All of the questions here involved concern that part of the residuary clause of Mrs. Dun's will which disposes of one-third of the residuary estate, after the death of the testatrix's son. . . .

It is contended by the Rucker executors that the two gifts over, each to take effect from and after the death or remarriage of the son's widow, violate the rule against perpetuities . . . . "In determining [the] question of remoteness, there is an invariable principle that regard is to be had to possible, and not merely actual events. It is not determined by looking back on events which have occurred and seeing whether the estate has extended beyond the prescribed limit, but by looking forward from the time the limitation was made and seeing whether, according to its terms, there was then a possibility that it might so extend . . . . The event upon the happening of which the remainder is to vest must be one that is certain to happen within the prescribed period, or the limitation will be bad." [*Gambrill v. Gambrill*, 122 Md. 563, 569, 89 A. 1094, 1095] . . .

The contention of the Rucker executors is that the widow of the son of the testatrix might have been born after the death of the testatrix, and might have lived longer than twenty-one years and the period allowed for gestation after the death of the son. Therefore, the gift over to the children and descendants, and the gift over to the next of kin in the absence of children and descendants are both void, because both might fail to vest within the required period. This view, which was adopted by the chancellor, seems to be correct, if we read the residuary clause as it is written . . .

. The whole intention of the testatrix is to be ascertained from the entire will, as well as any specific intention shown in the particular clause under discussion. This intention is to be gathered not only from the will, but from pertinent circumstances surrounding the testatrix at the time of making the will. In cases where it is claimed that the rule against perpetuities is violated, the Court first decides what the will means, and then determines whether the will so interpreted violates the rule. There is a presumption against intestacy, especially where there is a residuary clause, indicating that the testatrix intended to dispose of her entire estate. If there are two constructions, either of which can be adopted without straining the words of the will, the Court will adopt that one which disposes of the entire estate, rather than one which results in a total or partial intestacy. But the Court will not write a new will, nor attempt to surmise what the testatrix would have done had she thought of the contingency which has arisen. Nor will the Court substitute its own judgment for hers, as to what she should have done. It will interpret what she has said, in the light of the circumstances which have arisen, and determine, from the will itself, what she meant.

The general intention of the residuary clause before us seems to be to provide for the son of the testatrix, his widow, his descendants and his next of kin. The entire clause revolves around the son. No question arises, or could arise, as to the estate given to the son's widow during her unmarried life. It vests within the required period. The question arises as to the two subsequent bequests of the one-third taking effect "from and after the death or remarriage of the widow." . . .

[The appellants contend] that neither the bequest to the children and descendants, nor that to the next of kin are void because the word "widow" in the will does not mean widow in the usually accepted sense of a surviving wife, but means Sally Woods who was engaged to the son at the time the will was made on April 7, 1910, and who married him twenty-one days later. She was in being at the death of the testatrix, dying on December 20, 1932. The surrounding circumstances which we are asked to consider in connection with this contention are that the will was made at the time when Mrs. Dun had come to Baltimore to take part in the festivities in connection with her son's approaching marriage to Sally Woods; that she undoubtedly had no other thought except that Sally Woods would ultimately become her son's wife, and might become his widow; that she did not name Sally Woods because of a natural delicacy under the circumstances, but that she meant Sally Woods when she used the word "widow."

[The court discussed cases interpreting "widow" to mean the person to whom the beneficiary was married when the beneficiary was married when the will was made.] In the case before us we are asked to go much further. We are asked to hold that a person who is not married to the testatrix's son is the person she means by her son's widow. It so happened that this person did marry the son, that she died before he did, and that he then married another wife who also predeceased him, and that he died leaving no widow at all. If we should say that Mrs. Dun meant Sally Woods by the word "widow" she used, and if it should have happened that Sally Woods had not married the son at all, but that he had married someone else who survived him, it would necessarily follow that Sally Woods would get the bequest although she had never actually become connected with the testatrix by marriage to her son. The real widow would not take at all. This possible contingency illustrates the instability of the contention. What Mrs. Dun was interested in doing was to take care of her son and his relations. He was taken care of for his life, his widow was taken care of for her unmarried life, his children and descendants and finally his next of kin were attempted to be taken care of. All the residuary clause related to the son, and all the beneficiaries were to take by virtue of their relationship to the son. It was the relationship to the son, and not any particular friendship for Sally Woods which motivated the bequest. Mrs. Dun said she was providing for her son's widow. We must assume that was what she was doing, and not that she was trying to take care of a particular person, even though she thought that person might someday be the widow of her son. . . .

We therefore hold that the bequests of the one-third of the residue of the estate, after the death or remarriage of the widow, are too remote and are void for that reason, and that there is a partial intestacy as to this one-third. . . .

Notes

1. Perkins illustrates the traditional approach of first construing a document and then applying the Rule, rather than seeking a construction that would validate the gift. Some more recent cases reflect the view that a testator would not have intended to create an invalid gift, so courts should seek a valid construction. *See, e.g., White v. Fleet Bk*, 739 A.2d 373 (Me. 1999) (language construed to limit duration of trust). *Cf. Coulter & Smith, Ltd. v. Russell*, 966 P.2d 852 (Utah 1998) (contract construed so that exercise of option must occur within reasonable time no later than 21 years from creation of option).

2. Another potential trap is the law's assumption that people, no matter what age, can always have children. *See, e.g., Jee v. Audley*, 1 Cox 324, 29 Eng. Rep. 1186 (Ch. Ct. 1787) (invalidating future interests because a couple in their 70s could have more children). This assumption poses problems because it limits the number of people who can qualify as validating lives. Validating lives identified by label (e.g. "children") cannot come from a class that could possibly include afterborns.

The presumption of fertility makes some sense in a modern context. Someone might use modern technology to have a child late in life or even after death. Also, an older adult might still adopt a child. The common law's conclusive presumption, however, is hard to justify. By statute or judicial decisions, a few states allow courts to consider evidence of inability to have children, apply the presumption of validity only to persons of specified ages, or treat the possibility of adoption as irrelevant to perpetuities analysis. Anticipating frozen sperm and other new biological advances, the UPC disregards "the possibility that a child will be born to an individual after the individual's death." UPC § 2-901(d).

3. Another category of problems created by the Rule's willingness to consider all possibilities involves references to events that people expect will be completed within perpetuities period, but which might not be. *See, e.g., In re Campbell's Estate*, 82 P.2d 22 (Cal. Ct. App. 1938) (gift to persons "in office at the time of distribution of my estate" invalid because the estate might not be distributed within 21 years after the lives of people alive at the testator's death); *In re Wood*, [1894] 3 Ch. 381 ("when the mortgage is paid").

Problem

Assume that the *Perkins* court is correct that Lucy Dun wanted to benefit William's widow, rather than the woman he was then planning to marry. How would you draft Lucy's will so both William's widow and his descendants who survive her could take the property?

C. Class Gifts

Class gifts pose special problems under the Rule because for any class member's gift to be valid, the uncertainties surrounding all class members must be resolved in time. If a condition precedent for one class member might not be resolved in time, the whole class loses out. Moreover, for purposes of the Rule, one of the "uncertainties" that must be resolved is whether the class will remain open. Thus, vested remainders subject to open are, despite their "vested" label, subject to the Rule. *Leake v. Robinson*, 2 Mer. 363, 35 Eng. Rep. 979 (Ch. 1817), popularized this "all or nothing" rule and it remains a fixture of perpetuities analysis.

The rule that all uncertainties, including class closing, be resolved for all class members means that class gift problems require a multiple-step analysis.

First, ask whether the class will close in time. Search for someone alive when the interest was created and within whose lifetime (plus 21 years) the class will close. Because classes may close either physiologically or under the rule of convenience, you have two opportunities in your search for a validating life. To check physiological closing, ask whether there is some validating life (or set of lives) you can look to and be sure that after that life (or set) there will be no more "feeders" for the class. To check closing by convenience, ask whether anyone's right to distribution will be certain to close the class. If neither search uncovers a validating life, the gift is void.

Second, ask whether all conditions precedent for every class member will be resolved in time. This inquiry may yield different validating lives than the ones used to close the class. If you can find validating lives both to close the class and to resolve all of the conditions precedent, then the interests of all class members will be valid. If not, they will all be void.

Some examples illustrate how these rules operate. First, consider a family headed by John, a widower. John has a married son, Peter. Peter and his wife, Karen, have two children, Tracy and Lucinda. Tracy has a child, Jamie.

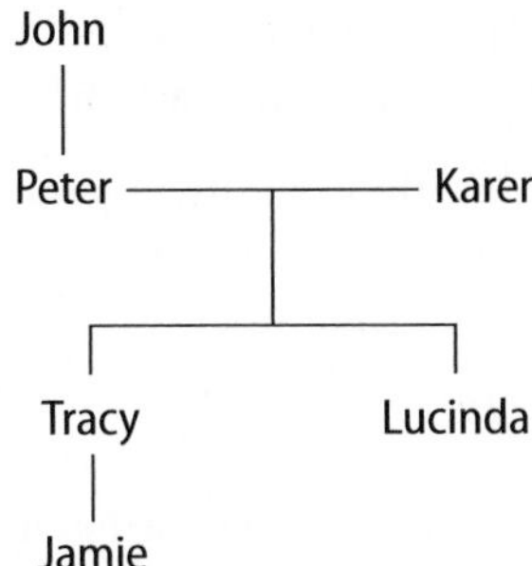

Example 9-9. Suppose John's will gives property "to Peter for life, then to his children for their joint lives, remainder to Peter's grandchildren." Assume all five family members survive John. Peter's life estate is presently vested, not subject to the rule. The children have vested remainders for their joint lives, subject to open. Their remainder is good because the uncertainty about their class closing will be resolved physiologically at Peter's death. Peter is the validating life. Jamie has a vested remainder subject to open. Her interest is void because the class of grandchildren cannot close until the death of the last survivor among Peter's children. Because Peter is alive, his children cannot be validating lives. Peter could have another child, Sue. Sue could have a child who could take more than 21 years after the deaths of all people now alive. Therefore, the entire gift to the grandchildren fails. John's estate is left with a reversion that follows the children's remainders.

Example 9-10(a). John's will gives property "to Lucinda for life, remainder to her nieces and nephews." Lucinda's life estate is presently vested, not subject to the rule. Whether the remainder is valid will depend upon who survives John. First suppose that all five family members survive John. Jamie has a vested remainder, subject to open. It is valid, because the class of nieces and nephews will close under the rule of convenience at Lucinda's death. At that time, Jamie will be able to demand distribution. Lucinda is the validating life.

Example 9-10(b). Suppose instead that Peter and Karen have died, and Tracy has no children. Tracy's unborn children have contingent remainders (on being born), subject to open. Their interests are good because Tracy's death will resolve both contingencies (whether anyone is born and when the class closes). Although not named in the gift, Tracy can serve as a validating life. John's estate has a reversion, not subject to the Rule.

Example 9-10(c). Now suppose that Tracy has no children, but that Peter and Karen are still alive. Under these facts, the remainder is void. Tracy cannot be a validating life because she cannot close the class of nieces and nephews physiologically. Because her parents are still alive, Tracy is not the class' only possible "feeder." Moreover, Lucinda (the life tenant) cannot be a validating life, because no one now living will be certain to close the class under the rule of convenience. In the absence of a validating life to close the class, the remainder fails.

Recall that in order for a class gift to be valid, not only must the class close in time, but also all conditions precedent regarding all class members must be resolved in time. The next series of examples considers the same family, but John's will reads: "to Lucinda for life, remainder to her nieces and nephews who reach age 21."

Example 9-11(a). Suppose that all five family members survive John and that Jamie is 22. Lucinda's life estate is presently vested, not subject to the Rule. Jamie has a vested remainder subject to open that is valid under the Rule. Because she has met the condition precedent of reaching 21, Jamie will be able to demand distribution at Lucinda's death. That event will close the class. Lucinda serves as the validating life, because the class will close at her death and the age contingency for all class members will be resolved within 21 years of her death.

Example 9-11(b). Suppose instead that Peter and Karen have died, and that Jamie is 15. Jamie's remainder is now contingent, subject to open. Tracy can serve as the validating life. Her death will close the class physiologically, and the age contingency will be resolved within 21 years thereafter. John's estate has a reversion, not subject to the Rule.

Example 9-11(c). Now suppose that Peter and Karen are alive, and that Jamie is 15. The remainder is void. Lucinda cannot serve as the validating life. Because Jamie is not yet 21, we cannot count on her to close the class under the rule of convenience at Lucinda's death. Tracy cannot be a validating life because the class that feeds nieces and nephews is still open. Peter and Karen could have another child, Sue. Everyone now living could die. More than 21 years later, Sue's child could reach 21 and take the remainder.

Example 9-12. Suppose John's will gives property "to Lucinda for life, remainder to Tracy's children who reach age 30." Peter and Karen have both died, but Lucinda, Tracy, and Jamie (age 32) survive John. Lucinda's life estate is presently vested, not subject to the Rule. Jamie has a vested remainder, subject to open. The remainder is void. The class will close physiologically at Tracy's death and, because Jamie is 32 we know that she will close the class under the rule of convenience at Lucinda's death. Either way, we have a validating life on the question of class closing. Even though the class will close in time, however, we cannot be sure that all class members will reach 30 in time. Neither Tracy nor Lucinda qualify as validating lives on this question because Tracy could have another child who is younger than nine when Tracy and Lucinda die. Although a member of the class, that child could still reach 30 more than 21 years later. John's estate has a reversion, not subject to the Rule, which follows Lucinda's life estate.

Although the "all or nothing" rule usually applies to class gifts, courts recognize two exceptions:

Gifts of a specific sum to each member of a class. Suppose Danya's will gave "$5,000 to each of my grandchildren, whether born before or after my death, who reach age 30." The "each" language means that rather than being grouped together, every grandchild is treated separately. Those grandchildren alive at Danya's death take valid gifts. Because we will know within their lifetimes whether they reach age 30, they can be their own validating lives. Those grandchildren born later lose out, but their loss does not taint the other gifts.

Gifts to subclasses. Donors create subclasses when they divide a class gift among groups of class members. For example, the following language would create subclasses: "the trustee shall pay income to my children for each of their respective lives, and upon the death of each, distribute the share from which that child has been receiving income to his or her children then surviving." For perpetuities purposes, the gifts to each different group of grandchildren would stand or fall separately. In most situations, the key will be whether their parents can serve as validating lives. *See generally* Lewis M. Simes & Allan F. Smith, The Law of Future Interests § 1267 (2d ed. 1956). This rule may also protect some contingent interests to heirs "by representation," since the notion of stocks, inherent in the representation concept, automatically produces sub-classes.

Problems

Which of the interests in the following fact patterns violate the Rule Against Perpetuities?

1. Doug's will created a trust, "income payable to my wife Kaye for her life, principal to my children who attain the age of 25 years." Doug is survived by Kaye and one child, Monica (age 3).

2. Ruben executes an irrevocable trust, "income payable to my wife Amy for her life, principal to my children who attain the age of 25 years." At the time of the transfer, Amy is alive and Ruben has two children, Melissa (age 35), and Brett (age 36).

3. Michelle's will left property in trust, "income payable to Paul for life, principal to Paul's grandchildren, to be paid to each as he or she reaches the age of twenty-five years."

(a) At Michelle's death, Paul survives, childless.

(b) At Michelle's death, Paul is dead, leaving two children, but no grandchildren, surviving Michelle.

(c) At Michelle's death, Paul, two of Paul's children, and one grandchild of Paul, age five, survive.

4. Shawn executes an irrevocable living trust, "income to my son Jon for life, and then principal to my grandchildren who reach age 21."

(a) Jon has two children, ages 12 and 14.

(b) Jon has one child, age 22.

5. Teresa's will included a bequest "to Mac's children who attain the age of twenty-five."

(a) At Teresa's death, Mac survives, childless.

(b) At Teresa's death, Mac survives, as do two of his children, two and five years of age, respectively.

(c) At Teresa's death, Mac survives, as do two of his children, twenty-four and thirty years of age, respectively.

6. Shirley's will left property in trust, income to her husband Brandon for his life. After Brandon's death, income to Shirley's children for their lives, then income to Shirley's grandchildren for their lives, and principal to those who would be Shirley's heirs if she had died at the time her last grandchild died. Brandon, two children and twelve grandchildren survive Shirley.

7. Kareem's will left $1,000 "to each of Rasha's children who reach age thirty." At Kareem's death, Rasha survives, as do two of her children, two and five years of age, respectively.

8. Terri devises property "to Stephanie if living when my estate is distributed, and if not to my children then living." Terri's two children and Stephanie survive Terri.

9. Abe's will created a trust with income for life to Hanasah. At her death one share of trust income would be allocated for life to each of Hanasah's surviving children and one share (collectively) for the surviving descendants of each of her children who predeceased Hanasah, but who left descendants who survived Hanasah. Upon the death of each of the income beneficiaries (or the last survivor of a group), the trustee would distribute the trust principal to that person's heirs. At Abe's death, Hanasah had a son, Yousef. Two years later, Hanasah had a daughter, Mona. Hanasah died leaving both children surviving her.

D. Powers of Appointment

Applying the Rule to powers of appointment requires two steps. First, we judge the validity of the power itself. Next, we judge the validity of the interests created by the power's exercise. *See generally* Lewis M. Simes & Allan F. Smith, The Law of Future Interests §§ 1272–73 (3d ed. 2002).

For these purposes, the Rule distinguishes between two groups: (1) general presently exercisable powers and (2) the group of general testamentary powers and special powers.[33] The reason for the distinction is that the donee of a general presently-exercisable power has something very close to absolute ownership because the donee can appoint to herself. The Rule judges these powers just like other contingent interests. In contrast, donees holding general testamentary or special powers cannot benefit themselves directly. Because these powers begin limiting the donee's freedom at the time the donor creates the power, courts have applied special rules to them.

1. Validity of the Power

A power that allows the donee to benefit himself or his creditors is substantially the same as complete ownership. Consequently, a general presently-exercisable power

33. Recall that this book frequently uses the term "special powers" to include what are coming to be called "nongeneral" powers. Because they do not give the donee the right to benefit from the property, nongeneral powers are subject to the same perpetuities rules as powers available to a limited class. *See* 3d Rest. Prop. § 19.19 cmt. g.

is valid if the donee can exercise it within the period. To judge its validity, apply standard perpetuities analysis, asking whether we know now that the power either will or will not become exercisable within the period.

In contrast, a general testamentary or special power is void if the donee can exercise it beyond the period. Now the question is not just getting the power into the hands of the donee in time, but assuring that the donee must exercise the power (or not) within the period. The lesson: unless you take special precautions, do not create a general testamentary or a special power for someone not yet alive, because the donee might be able to exercise it more than 21 years after the death of everyone now alive. You might give a power to an as-yet-unborn person (say, a grandchild), if you limited the time for the power's exercise to within lives in being (plus 21 years) at the time the donor's document became irrevocable.

2. *Validity of the Appointed Interests*

Because a general presently-exercisable power is akin to ownership, each interest created by the power's exercise is valid if contingencies surrounding it will be resolved within lives in being (plus 21 years) at the power's exercise. Exercising the power is just like creating other interests.

If a donee exercises a general testamentary or a special power, the Rule judges the validity of the appointed interests from the power's creation. Here the Rule is following the notion that the donee of a special power is the donor's agent, filling in words in the donor's document to identify who takes the property. Although we read the words as if the donor had written them, we consider facts we know at the time the donee actually exercises the power. The ability to consider facts at the time of exercise is called the "second look" doctrine. Perhaps a more accurate label would be the "later look" doctrine. Sometimes the later look saves the gift, sometimes not. Thus, the validity of interests appointed by the exercise of a special power or a general testamentary power are measured from the time of the power's creation, but taking into account facts known at the time of the power's exercise.

3. *Takers in Default*

Well-drafted documents creating powers of appointment will also identify people to take if the donee fails to exercise the power completely, or if the power fails for some other reason. These gifts in default may raise perpetuities issues. Conceptually, gifts in default are remainders subject to divestment by the exercise of the power. There is no perpetuities problem unless the default gift is to an open class or subject to a condition precedent. Many gifts in default, however, add these uncertainties. The question then becomes whether the second look doctrine applies to gifts in default. Case law is slim, and the commentators disagree. *Compare* American Law of Property § 24.36 (A. James Casner ed. 1952) (advocating taking a second look), *with* Lewis M. Simes & Allan F. Smith, The Law of Future Interests § 1276 (3d ed. 2002) (opposing that view).

Problems

1. Lisa's will gave property in trust—"income to Barry for life, then income to his children jointly for their lives, and after the death of Barry's last surviving child, principal to Planned Parenthood." Lisa also gave the trustee the power to allocate trust income among Barry's children. If Barry survives Lisa, what perpetuities problems, if any, does the trust present?

2. Kristen's will created a trust with "income to Tara for life, then to Tara's children for their lives, principal to whomever among Tara's issue, Tara's youngest child who survives Tara appoints." When Kristen died, Tara survived with her two children, Greg (age 12) and Carla (age 8). Later, Tara died leaving only Greg and Carla. Carla died leaving two children and a will that appointed the trust property "to my grandchildren." Which of the interests, if any, violate the Rule?

3. Toni's will created a trust with "income to my husband Andre for life, principal to whomever he appoints by will." Andre and his two children, Bill and Sam, survived Toni. Andre then died, leaving a will appointing the trust property in further trust with "income to my children jointly for their lives, and on the death of my last surviving child, to my issue then living." Which of the interests, if any, violate the Rule if:

(a) Bill and Sam were Andre's only surviving children.

(b) Bill, Sam, and Marc (born after Toni's death) were Andre's only surviving children.

E. Saving Clauses

Because the Rule is so technical and so easily violated, drafters have developed fail-safe devices called "saving clauses." Properly drafted, these clauses protect the plan from the possibility that the Rule will strike some gifts, sending property back through the grantor's estate. It is, of course, possible to draft a faulty saving clause.

In re Estate of Lee

299 P.2d 1066 (Wash. 1956)

Rosellini, J.

> This appeal from a decree of distribution involves the construction of the trust provisions of a will. The pertinent provisions are as follows:
>
> "Fifth: Upon the death of my said son, Fairman Burbidge Lee, my trustee, Seattle-First National Bank, is authorized to pay to each of my said grandchildren so much from the income and/or principal of my said estate as my said trustee shall deem necessary and proper for the maintenance, health and education of such grandchild until he shall have completed his education, but not after he shall have attained the age of twenty-five (25) years.

> Thereafter, my said trustee shall pay to each of my said grandchildren after he has completed his education, as aforesaid, the sum of Twenty-five and No/100 Dollars ($ 25.00) per month from the income and/or principal of my said estate, until the youngest of my said grandchildren shall have attained the age of forty (40) years, at which time my said estate shall be distributed to my grandchildren then living at said time, share and share alike; provided further that in the event none of my said grandchildren shall live to attain the age of forty (40) years, then upon the death of my last grandchild prior to attaining the age of forty (40) years, the trustee shall then distribute my estate to my great-grandchildren.
>
> "Sixth: If all of my grandchildren shall die prior to attaining the age of forty (40) years, without issue, then all of the remainder of the estate in the hands of my trustee shall be used by my trustee to endow beds in the Children's Orthopedic Hospital of Seattle, Washington, in the names of Anna Williams Lee, Chester Fairman Lee and Fairman Burbidge Lee.
>
> "Eighth: If any provisions of this Will should be void on account of the rule of perpetuities or any other rule of law pertaining to such trusts, then the trusts herein provided shall continue in force for the full period permitted by law and on the day prior to the expiration of such full period, trustee shall make distribution of any remainder of the trust estate to the persons herein named who would be entitled to take distribution thereon upon termination of the trust.
>
> "Tenth: I direct that if any part or provision of this, my Will, shall be declared illegal or void by any court, such illegality or invalidity shall not affect any other portion of this instrument. . . . "

In the fourth paragraph of her will, the testatrix provided a life estate for her son, which is concededly valid. It was also conceded in the trial court that the remainders provided in the fifth and sixth paragraphs violate the rule against perpetuities; and the only question which the trial court was asked to decide was whether the trust was saved by the eighth and tenth paragraphs.

The trial court concluded that the provision for distributing the estate to the "persons herein named who would be entitled to take distribution thereon at the termination of the trust" was sufficiently definite to enable the court to ascertain to whom distribution was to be made upon termination of the trust one day before the expiration of the full period permitted by law. It is the contention of the appellants that the provision is too indefinite to be enforced, that if this paragraph is ineffective, the dispositive scheme is destroyed and the entire trust has failed. Consequently, they say, Mrs. Lee died intestate and the estate should be distributed immediately to her only heir at law, her son, Fairman Burbidge Lee . . . .

[I]t is clear that the gifts of the remainders to the grandchildren are void, for they will vest only if one or more grandchildren survive until the youngest reaches age forty; and since grandchildren may be born after the death of the testatrix, and within the gestation period after the death of her son (the measuring life in being at the time of the testatrix' death), the youngest may reach age forty more than twenty-one years after the death of the son. By the same token, the gifts over to the great-grandchildren and to the hospital are void, for they are contingent upon events which may occur more than twenty-one years after the death of the son.

Since the remainders are void, by the expressed intent of the testatrix, the eighth paragraph of the will applies, and the trust is to terminate one day before the expiration of the full period allowed by law, that is, twenty-one years after the death of the son. The question to be decided is, Whom did the testatrix intend to receive distribution at that time.

The words of the testatrix are ambiguous and subject to two interpretations. It is the position of the appellant that the phrase "persons herein named who would be entitled to take distribution thereon at the termination of the trust" means those persons who would be entitled to take distribution of the corpus if the trust were terminated under the provisions of the fifth and sixth paragraphs of the will. Consequently, they say, it will be impossible to determine the beneficiaries at the termination of the trust; and for this reason, the provision is too indefinite to enforce.

The respondents, on the other hand, argue that the obvious intent was to provide for distribution of the corpus to those persons named in the preceding paragraphs who would be entitled to take distribution thereof if those paragraphs provided for the termination of the trust at the end of the lawful period rather than at the time designated in the invalid provisions of the will.

If the interpretation placed upon the phrase by the appellants is adopted, the clause is unenforceable, for the persons entitled to take distribution under the fifth and sixth paragraphs cannot be determined until the youngest grandchild has reached age forty, or all of the grandchildren have died before reaching age forty. It is exactly these contingencies which violate the rule against perpetuities, and it was just such a violation which paragraph eight was designed to guard against. Although she expressed herself ineptly, it is plain that the testatrix, in paragraph eight, intended to substitute a valid disposition for any invalid disposition which she may have made in the earlier paragraphs.

The eighth paragraph can be given effect only if the persons entitled to receive the corpus can be ascertained at the time of the termination of the trust—one day before the expiration of the period allowed by law. The law presumes that a valid disposition is intended. Atkinson, Wills, 815, § 146 .... [T]he testatrix did not intend to substitute an invalid disposition for a prior invalid disposition....

We conclude that the testatrix intended by the language used in paragraph eight to provide for the acceleration of the date on which distribution was to be made if the prior dispositive clauses should prove invalid; and for the distribution of the corpus on that date to her grandchildren if any were then living, otherwise to her great-grandchildren; and if all of her grandchildren had died without issue, to the Children's Orthopedic Hospital ....

The trial court, in its decree of distribution, provided that the trust should continue until the youngest grandchild reached age forty, or until the death of the last surviving grandchild prior to reaching age forty, or until twenty-one years, less one day, after the death of the son, whichever event should occur first. Such a disposition goes beyond any expressed intent of the testatrix. The will provides that in the event any provision of the will should be void, the trust should terminate one day before the end of the full period allowed by law, not that the trust should terminate in accordance with the provisions contained in paragraphs five and six or one day before the end of the full period allowed by law, whichever date was earlier.

The cause is remanded, with direction to modify the decree accordingly. In all other respects, the judgment is affirmed.

Notes and Questions

1. Most saving clauses have two basic components: one establishes an event that terminates the trust, and the other identifies an alternative disposition to replace the gift that the Rule prohibits. Identify the two parts of the saving clause in Lee's estate and describe why they were inadequate.

2. Is Mrs. Lee's lawyer liable for the cost of this litigation?

3. The tenth clause in Lee's will is designed to avoid the doctrine of infectious invalidity that would invalidate all of the gifts. *See* Lewis M. Simes & Allan F. Smith, The Law of Future Interests § 1262 (3d ed. 2002).

4. The following is a typical type of saving clause: "Notwithstanding other terms of this document, this trust shall end no later than 21 years after the death of the last surviving trust beneficiary living when this trust becomes irrevocable. If the trust terminates as a result of this clause, the trustee shall distribute the principal and accumulated income to the income beneficiaries at that time, in the same shares as they were then entitled to the trust income."

(a) Would this clause have been effective in Lee's estate?

(b) Assume a testamentary trust included this clause and a gift of "income to my wife for life, principal to my grandchildren who reach age 21." What is the longest time the trust would continue if the testator had no grandchildren living at his death?

(c) Assume a testamentary trust included this clause and a gift of "income to Elias for life, then income to Elias' children for their lives, then principal to the American Heart Association." What is the longest time the trust would continue if the Elias survived the testator and then had a daughter, Peggy?

(d) In light of problems like those in (b) and (c), Professor Becker comments: "One saving clause simply cannot meet the needs of every estate plan. The thoughtless use of one 'boilerplate' clause in every will and trust can wreak havoc on estate owners' dispositive plans and on an estate planner's reputation." David M. Becker, *Tailoring Perpetuities Provisions to Avoid Problems*, 9 Prob. & Prop. 10, 13 (Mar./Apr. 1995). He encourages lawyers to draft "tailormade" clauses to achieve perpetuities compliance.

Selected References

David M. Becker, *Estate Planning and the Reality of Perpetuities Problems Today: Reliance Upon Statutory Reform and Savings Clauses Is Not Enough*, 64 Wash. U. L.Q. 287 (1986).

William M. McGovern, Jr., *Perpetuities Pitfalls and How Best to Avoid Them*, 6 Real Prop. Prob. & Tr. J. 155 (1971).

F. Reform

Courts and legislatures have reacted to the Rule's arbitrariness in various ways. A few states aim at particular perpetuities problems. New York, for example, has a set of provisions aimed at administrative contingencies, unborn widows, age contingencies over 21, precocious toddlers (girls under 12 and boys under 14), and fertile octogenarians (women over 55). N.Y. Estates, Powers and Trusts Law §§ 9-1.2 and 9-1.3. More popular are broadly applicable reforms of two types. One, called wait-and-see, judges the validity of interests based on actual, rather than hypothetically possible, events. Although a few states rely on actual wait-and-see events, including Iowa, Mississippi and Vermont, the vast majority of states in the wait-and-see camp have enacted the 90-year wait and see period as provided in the Uniform Statutory Rule Against Perpetuities (USRAP). The other technique, sometimes called "cy pres," reforms documents to make them conform to the rule. Texas allows for immediate reformation, while USRAP provides for deferred reformation. In fact, USRAP—which combines both techniques—has gained numerous adherents around the country.[34] USRAP appears in the UPC in §§ 2-901 to 2-906.

1. Wait-and-See

The basic idea of this approach is to wait until after a testator's death to see if the horribles the Rule imagines actually take place. The basic problem is: how can we tell how long to wait?

---

34. USRAP has been enacted in the following jurisdictions: Alabama, Arizona, Arkansas, California, Colorado, Connecticut, District of Columbia, Florida, Georgia, Hawaii, Indiana, Kansas, Massachusetts, Minnesota, Montana, Nebraska, Nevada, New Mexico, North Carolina, North Dakota, Oregon, South Carolina, Tennessee, Utah, Virginia, Washington, West Virginia.

In some USRAP states, the original 90-year USRAP period has been extended. For example, Florida uses a 360-year period; Utah uses a 1000-year period. In other USRAP states, USRAP has been effectively repealed for most trusts. *See* § 9.04G (discussing perpetuities repeal movement).

In re Estate of Anderson

541 So. 2d 423 (Miss. 1989)

I.

Robertson, Justice.

Today's testator, a bachelor during his lifetime, by will made substantial bequests to his favorite nephew. The rest of his estate he placed in trust to provide for the education of his nephews and nieces for the next twenty-five years, at the end of which the trust corpus and any undistributed income will also go to the favorite nephew.

We are told that the bequest in trust violates the Rule against Perpetuities, and by this we are told that testator has misjudged the nephew much more than the measure of the Rule. The Chancery Court rejected the attack and upheld the trust. With but slight modification, we affirm.

II.

[The will of Charles Maurice Anderson, who died on December 12, 1984, left specific bequests to his nephew, Howard W. Davis, the son of Charles' sister. Charles also created a trust and directed the trustee to use all of the income "for the education of the descendants of F. A. Anderson, Sr. [Charles' father] for a period of twenty-five (25) years from the date of the admission of this last will and testament for probate." After 25 years, the trust would terminate and the principal pass to Howard but if Howard died before then, to the heirs of his body. Howard challenged the trust's validity.] ...

The descendants of the testator's late father, Fred Alvin Anderson, Sr., a/k/a F. A. Anderson, Sr., living on December 12, 1984, included five grandchildren and ten great-grandchildren. Two more great-grandchildren have been born since that date ...

IV.

Does the Twenty-Five Year Private Educational Testamentary Trust Violate the Rule Against Perpetuities, and Thus Fail?

A. The Rule Declared

... Public convenience today demands a rule of law (1) that will limit "dead hand" control over property which prevents the present generation from using the property as it sees fit, (2) that will keep property marketable and available for productive development in accordance with market demands, and (3) that will curb trusts which can protect wealthy beneficiaries from creditors, decrease the amount of risk capital available for economic development and, after a period of time and change in circumstances, tie up the family in disadvantageous and undesirable arrangements.

One response our law has made to these concerns has been the promulgation and enforcement of the Rule against Perpetuities....

The very able brief of Appellant Davis concentrates upon Gray's traditional statement of the Rule and then struggles mightily to avoid the import of this state's three major modifications of the Rule:

(1) Our shifting of emphasis from what-might-happen to wait-and-see, *C&D Investment Co. v. Gulf Transport Co.*, 526 So. 2d 526, 530 (Miss. 1988)....

(2) the abolition of the all-or-nothing rule for class gifts, *Carter v. Berry*, 243 Miss. 321, 140 So. 2d 843 (1962)... and

(3) the empowerment of our courts to imply a savings clause into any devise which would otherwise violate the Rule, to become operative only when it becomes apparent that remote vesting will otherwise occur.

Indeed, reflection upon the argument advanced by Appellant Davis makes clear that at least for today far greater inconvenience may result from the dead hand of John Chipman Gray than from the dead hand of Charles Maurice Anderson.

B. The Rule Applied

Will the interest vest within twenty-one years after the death of all descendants of F. A. Anderson who were in being on December 12, 1984?

... [T]he trust is to terminate "twenty-five years from the date of the admission of this last will and testament for probate," the termination date thus being December 21, 2009. As of December 12, 1984, the date of the death of Charles Maurice Anderson, it was theoretically possible that all of the descendants of F. A. Anderson, Sr. would die more than twenty-one years before the scheduled termination of the trust. It was also possible that no descendant of F. A. Anderson, Sr. would qualify for benefits within the term of the trust. If we turn back the clock to December 12, 1984, and look at the facts as they then existed, the conclusion was then inescapable the interest created by Item IX of the will might not vest within twenty-one years after the death of all persons in being on December 12, 1984, who could affect the vesting of the interest. From this conclusion, invoking the dead hand of John Chipman Gray, Appellant Davis argues that the Rule must be "remorselessly applied." Our law demurs, and with authority.

One evil experience has revealed is that treating the Rule as a rule of logical proof and mechanical application produces distributions of property neither intended nor desired by the testator.... Established within our law is the principle that a person's will should be enforced so as to avoid clearly unintended consequences.... Any reader of the will at issue may say with confidence that Charles Maurice Anderson did not intend that Howard W. Davis take Anderson's entire estate to the exclusion of the educational needs of Anderson's nieces and nephews and their children. It is this conclusion that triggers the Court's responsibility to apply one or more of our ameliorative doctrines and save this testamentary trust.

... [O]ur wait-and-see doctrine ... ought here be employed as it may save all, not just most, of Charles Maurice Anderson's private educational testamentary trust. Under wait-and-see, the validity of an interest is not judged by what might happen, but rather by what does happen, by whether the interest in fact vests or fails within the perpetuities period ....

For one thing, the record reflects that by the time of trial (August, 1986), several beneficiaries had already qualified for and received substantial educational benefits. Some income and, of course, the entire principal remained untouched, in 1986 and, we presume, today as well. It is true that what remains may never vest in any member of the beneficiary class, as it is possible that no further descendants of F. A. Anderson, Sr., may qualify for educational benefits. That the interests thus remain contingent is no longer of concern, as the period of the Anderson testamentary trust will end on December 21, 2009, which is less than twenty-one years from this day. As there are now in being a host of measuring lives, ... we may say with certainty that all interests created under the testamentary trust will either vest or fail within twenty-one years after the end of all measuring lives.[35] "There is no precedent in this state which compels us to close our eyes to the facts occurring after the death of the testat[or]." *Phelps v. Shropshire*, 254 Miss. at 785, 183 So. 2d at 162; quoted in *C&D Investment Co.*, 526 So. 2d at 529.

Davis' able counsel notes that the result we decree: that the trust be upheld, would allow this private educational testamentary trust to "go on for twenty-five years." Counsel tells us that this "not only violates the Rule against Perpetuities, it makes a shambles of it." The point revealed is that the Rule itself, at least without the Mississippi modifiers, is a shambles. But a moment's reflection reveals that an adept lawyer can tie up property "for an unconscionable period—viz., twenty-one years after the deaths of a dozen or so babies chosen from families noted for longevity, a term which, in the ordinary course of events, will add up to about a century."[36] If this be so, what sense does it make that the mere twenty-five years the Anderson trust will last are too much? Moreover, the twenty-five years these trust assets will be dominated by Charles Maurice Anderson's dead hand pale into insignificance when compared with the ninety year wait-and-see period which is the centerpiece of the new Uniform Statutory Rule Against Perpetuities

35. Our cases have not yet fleshed out the meaning of our wait-and-see doctrine. One objection to wait-and-see is the practical problems that may result from not knowing whether an interest is valid or void, perhaps for several decades. *See* R. Powell, The Law of Real Property §§ 827[A]—827[H] (P. Rohan rev. ed. 1986); *see also* Simes and Smith, The Law of Future Interests § 1230 (2d ed. 1956). Here we only had to wait and see for four years and nine days from December 12, 1984, a period which, alas, because of the slow pace of litigation, has come and gone. We have not concerned our-selves with the outer limits of wait-and-see and nothing said here should be taken as expressing a view on the point

36. 6 American Law of Property § 24.16, at 52 (A. James Casner ed. 1952).

promulgated in 1986 by the National Conference of Commissioners on Uniform State Laws. 8A U.L.A. 80 (Supp. 1987).

Notions of wait-and-see and an implied savings clause may be found in our cases dating back at least two decades, and in that sense our decision this day is nothing new. On the other hand, we have never recognized the two so forcefully as today. We need not sacrifice civil justice on the altar of legal formalism or the purist's nostalgia, as it is beyond comprehension that Howard W. Davis, or any other citizen of this state, has in fact placed legally cognizable reliance—to his detriment—upon the dead hand Rule of John Chipman Gray . . . .

[The executory interests in the heirs of Howard's body were valid because they would be determined at Howard's death or at the trust's later termination, which would be within 21 years of the court's decision.]

Uniform Probate Code

Section 2-901(a). Statutory Rule Against Perpetuities.

(a) [Validity of Nonvested Property Interest.] A nonvested property interest is invalid unless:

(1) when the interest is created, it is certain to vest or terminate no later than 21 years after the death of an individual then alive; or

(2) the interest either vests or terminates within 90 years after its creation.

Notes and Question

1. How long would the court in *Anderson* wait in the following situation: Bill's will created a trust "income to Ruth for life, then principal to her children who reach age 30"? The court would likely choose among three major alternatives:

The **causal-lives method** involves three steps. First, identify those individuals in being who can affect vesting. Second, test for certainty of vesting within the lifetimes, plus 21 years, of the identified persons. Third, if the event will not, with absolute certainty, occur within 21 years after the death of any identified person, wait-and-see whether the event actually occurs within 21 years after the deaths of those identified persons—the measuring lives.

The **formula method** comes from the Restatement and identifies the measuring lives by prescribing specific categories of candidates against which to measure the validity of interests. 2d Rest. Prop. § 1.4.

The **period-in-gross method** is a creature of USRAP, which waits 90 years.

2. In USRAP states certain exercises of a special power of appointment may adversely impact both the exemption from the federal generation-skipping transfer tax and, where a special power of appointment is exercised, the grand-fathering protections the GST offers certain trusts. *See* Jesse Dukeminier, *The Uniform Statutory Rule Against Perpetuities and the GST Tax: New Perils for Practitioners and New Opportunities*, 30 Real Prop. Prob. & Tr. J. 185 (1995).

Selected References

Ira Mark Bloom, *Perpetuities Refinement: There Is an Alternative*, 62 Wash. L. Rev. 23 (1987).

Jesse Dukeminier, *Perpetuities: The Measuring Lives*, 85 Colum. L. Rev. 1648 (1985), and *The Uniform Statutory Rule Against Perpetuities: Ninety Years in Limbo*, 34 UCLA L. Rev. 1023 (1987).

Mary Louise Fellows, *Testing Perpetuity Reforms: A Study of Perpetuity Cases 1984-89*, 25 Real Prop. Prob. & Tr. J. 597 (1991).

Lawrence W. Waggoner, *Perpetuities: A Perspective on Wait-and-See*, 85 Colum. L. Rev. 1714 (1985), *Perpetuities Reform*, 81 Mich. L. Rev. 1718 (1983), and *The Uniform Statutory Rule Against Perpetuities: The Rationale of the 90-Year Waiting Period*, 73 Cornell L. Rev. 157 (1988).

2. *Reformation*

Another method for easing the Rule's harshness is for courts to reform offending documents to bring them into compliance with the Rule. Courts either might reform the document immediately upon discovering the perpetuities violation. *See, e.g., Meduna v. Holder*, 2003 Tex. App. LEXIS 10568 (Dec. 18, 2003) (applying Texas' immediate reformation statute). Or they might first wait to see how things turn out, and then reform if they must, which will be the usual approach under USRAP § 903. In either case, the basic problem is: how do we reform?

Berry v. Union National Bank

262 S.E.2d 766 (W. Va. 1980)

Harshbarger, Justice.

This case presents the issue whether a private testamentary trust which violates the rule against perpetuities should be modified to effectuate a testatrix' intent or should fail.

Clara Clayton Post died on June 20, 1975, in Harrison County. Her will and codicil were admitted to probate on June 23, 1975 .... After a series of specific bequests ... Ms. Post created a private educational trust for the descendants of her late husband's brothers and sisters, giving her trustee absolute discretion to provide educational expenses for class members meeting certain criteria. The trust was to endure for twenty-five years after testatrix' death or until the principal was reduced to less than $5,000.00, whichever should first occur. At the termination of the trust the principal and interest were to be distributed per stirpes to the then living descendants of her husband's brothers and sisters. The Union National Bank of Clarksburg, appellee, was named trustee ....

The analysis of any problem concerning a will must begin with the fundamental principle that a testator's intent shall be ascertained and followed to the extent possible . . . .

The rule against perpetuities is a common-law rule which reflects the public policy that a testator or trustor cannot control the devolution of his property for an inordinate period of time . . . .

It is here that principles of law collide: a testator may not indefinitely control the devolution of his property; but a testator's intent should be honored and intestacy avoided whenever feasible. To remedy this apparent conflict, we adopt a doctrine of equitable modification which courts should apply to certain devises that on their face appear to violate the rule against perpetuities but meet the conditions enumerated below. Our action accords with a developing trend to ameliorate the harsh consequences of "remorseless application" of the rule. The theory which we endorse today is akin to the doctrine of cy pres which was initially developed in the area of charitable trusts and was legislatively enacted in West Virginia in 1931 for that purpose. W. Va. Code, 35-2-2.

The purpose of equitable modification is to revise an instrument in a fashion that effectuates a testator's general intent within the limitations established by the rule.

We support the underlying policies of the rule against perpetuities and will deny validity to an interest which vests beyond the time limitations provided in the rule. However, before a testamentary scheme is totally obliterated by application of the rule, we will determine whether the testamentary disposition can be equitably modified to comport with the rule's underlying policy.

A non-charitable devise or bequest which violates the rule will be modified if the following conditions are met:

(1) The testator's intent is expressed in the instrument or can be readily determined by a court;

(2) The testator's general intent does not violate the rule against perpetuities;

(3) The testator's particular intent, which does violate the rule, is not a critical aspect of the testamentary scheme; and

(4) The proposed modification will effectuate the testator's general intent, will avoid the consequences of intestacy, and will conform to the policy considerations underlying the rule.

The testamentary trust here meets all these criteria for application of the equitable modification doctrine.

Testatrix clearly expressed her general intent in Section IX of her will when she stated:

> I believe it was the desire of my husband that such funds as I might have at my death should be used to help such persons [who are later defined in this

> section] obtain educations. This is the only expression I ever heard him make relative to the disposition of such funds.

Her general intention to provide funds for education of her husband's nieces, nephews and their families does not contravene the rule. Her particular intention—to have the trust continue for twenty-five years after her death or until the principal was less than $5,000.00—violates the rule .... There is no indication that the twenty-five year period is a critical aspect of her testamentary scheme. If the trust is modified to reduce that twenty-five year period to twenty-one years before distribution of the remaining principal to the then living descendants of her husband's siblings, the general intent to provide for their education will be effectuated, intestacy for that portion of her estate will be avoided, and property will not be controlled by her beyond the perpetuities' limitation ....

Uniform Probate Code

Section 2-903. Reformation.

Upon the petition of an interested person, a court shall reform a disposition in the manner that most closely approximates the transferor's manifested plan of distribution and is within the 90 years allowed by Section 2-901(a)(2), 2-901(b)(2), or 2-901(c)(2) if:

> (1) a nonvested property interest or a power of appointment becomes invalid under Section 2-901 (statutory rule against perpetuities);
>
> (2) a class gift is not but might become invalid under Section 2-901 (statutory rule against perpetuities) and the time has arrived when the share of any class member is to take effect in possession or enjoyment; or
>
> (3) a nonvested property interest that is not validated by Section 2-901(a)(1) can vest but not within 90 years after its creation.

Notes and Questions

1. What should the *Berry* court have done if evidence had showed that Clara Post wanted the trust to extend 25 years so that its beneficiaries could use the funds to attend graduate school?

2. West Virginia has now enacted USRAP, including cy pres reformation. W. Va. Code Ann. §§ 36-1A-1 to 36-1A-8.

3. In general, USRAP applies prospectively. *See* UPC § 2-905(b). However, § 2-903's authority to allow reformation appears to permit a back-door method of applying wait-and-see. The comments encourage courts to reform existing documents by inserting saving clauses, which themselves often take a wait-and-see approach. UPC § 2-905, cmt.

4. Although nondonative transfers are not subject to the statutory rule against perpetuities, see UPC § 2-904, it is unclear whether nondonative transfers are still subject to the common-law Rule. *Compare Juliano & Sons Enters. v. Chevron, Inc.*, 593

A.2d 814 (N.J. Super. Ct. App. Div. 1991) (not subject to common-law Rule), *with Buck v. Banks*, 668 N.E.2d 1259 (Ind. Ct. App. 1996) (subject to common-law Rule). A Nebraska court declined to rule on the issue since it found that a right of first refusal would not have violated the common-law Rule. *See Greenhall Invs., L.L.C. v. Wiese Dev. Corp.*, 706 N.W.2d 552 (Neb. Ct. App. 2005).

5. You are the member of a State Bar committee considering whether to recommend USRAP to your legislature. What is your position?

Problem

You are a judge in a jurisdiction that applies cy pres immediately, rather than waiting until the end of a wait-and-see period. You are faced with the following situation. Warren's will created a trust giving "income for life to Jim and principal to his children who reach 30." Jim survived Warren with three children: Jack (age 12), Connie (8), and Kathy (5). How should you reform the will?

Robert J. Lynn, *Perpetuities Literacy for the 21st Century*

5 Ohio St. L.J. 219, 239–41 (1989)

What and how should we think about the Rule as we leave the twentieth century and move into the twenty-first?

First, as drafters of deeds, wills, and trusts, we should advise clients not to create future interests unless both the nature of the subject matter and the objectives sought to be achieved justify doing so. Persons with little property usually should make outright gifts, uncomplicated by future interests, and lawyers are obligated to point that out.

Second, although reform versions of the Rule facilitate saving gifts that violate the Rule in orthodox form, as drafters of legal documents, we should make certain that the documents we draft conform to the requirements of the Rule in orthodox form. If those requirements are met, there is no need to resort to either wait-and-see or cy pres, and if a dispute arises and litigation ensues, a declaration of validity is appropriate. The existence of a reform version of the Rule in a jurisdiction might tempt the drafter to be less cautious than he or she otherwise would be. That temptation should be resisted. Persons owning property and executing documents change domiciles with great regularity. They own property in states other than that where they are domiciled. A document drafted in one jurisdiction might be construed and applied years later in another jurisdiction. Drafting should conform to the requirements of the Rule in its most stringent form, and careful drafting should be complemented by inclusion of a perpetuities savings clause in the document.

Third, ... [I]f the Rule did not exist, some kind of device to curb the whims of the egotist would have to be invented .... [W]e should not assume that the Rule has outlived its usefulness and can be forgotten. The Rule exists, and it will persist in some form.

Fourth, there are a number of versions of the Rule, and we must identify the version of the Rule that will be controlling in a particular case. Doing so requires us not only to identify the appropriate jurisdiction, but also to fix the time frame within which relevant events occurred. Changes in property law are rarely retroactive. Perpetuities questions sometimes arise years after relevant events have occurred. A version of the Rule that exists in a jurisdiction today might not be the version of the Rule that is decisive in the case we are considering.

Fifth, although the Rule was created by judges to police the transmission of wealth from generation to generation among families, it has been applied to commercial transactions, and, indeed, a significant share of the relatively few recently reported perpetuities problems arose in a commercial rather than a family setting. Therefore, we should not assume that if a law practice does not include family law, estate planning, or administration of estates, the strictures of the Rule can be ignored. It is just as embarrassing for the real estate development lawyer to learn that he or she has violated the Rule as it is for the estate planner to learn that a dispositive scheme has been skewed by a violation of the Rule.

Sixth, when we examine a document that might pose a perpetuities problem, we should remind ourselves that our ability to identify a violation of the Rule turns on our knowledge of all the relevant facts. The Rule applies to a limited number of future interests, and our ability to identify a future interest subject to the Rule requires us to classify interests in accordance with the rules of construction ....

Finally, we should not assume that modifications of the Rule recommended or made from time to time indicate any significant shift in American attitudes on control of wealth by the dead .... Although the listing of measuring lives in the Restatement (Second) and the recommendation of a ninety-year period in gross by the Commissioners on Uniform State Laws in this last decade are departures in the United States from simplicity in reform, neither of these events shows a remarkable change in contemporary views on the use of trusts and wills to provide for families over several generations.

... [A]s we move into the twenty-first century ... any version of the Rule that we encounter presupposes mastery of the Rule in orthodox form, and ... no version of the Rule that we encounter frees us from our obligation to draft documents that conform to the Rule in orthodox form. Documents that clearly conform to the Rule in orthodox form reduce the likelihood of the dispute and litigation that disrupt families and reduce the donor's gifts by costs and fees. Promoting family harmony and keeping the donor's gifts intact are clearly in the public interest.

Selected Reference

Sharona Hoffman & Andrew P. Morris, *Birth After Death: Perpetuities and the New Reproductive Technologies*, 38 Ga. L. Rev. 575 (2004).

Les A. McCrimmon, *Gametes, Embryos and the Life in Being: The Impact of Reproductive Technology on the Rule Against Perpetuities*, 34 Real Prop. Prob. & Tr. J. 697 (2000).

3. The Restatement of Property's New Formulation of the Rule Against Perpetuities

In 1978, the Restatement (Second) of Property reformulated the common-law Rule, which uses a "what might have been" approach to invalidate remote nonvested interests at their inception. The reformulation was to create a "wait-and-see" rule: remote nonvested interests would not fail at the inception but only after waiting to see if the interest failed to vest by the end of the perpetuities period.[37] In turn, the Restatement (Second) of Property provided that any failed interest could then be judicially modified to comply with the Rule.[38]

In 2010, the American Law Institute approved the latest reformulation of the Rule under the Restatement (Third) of Property.[39] In a nutshell, the new Rule does four major things. First, the new formulation eliminates lives in being and 21 years as the benchmark for the perpetuity period. Second, it substitutes prescribed measuring lives, whether or not alive at trust (or nontrust) creation, as the benchmark for the perpetuity period; the measuring lives generally include "the transferor, the beneficiaries of the disposition who are related to the beneficiary and no more than two generations younger than the transferor and the beneficiaries of the disposition who are unrelated to the transferor, and no more than the equivalent of two generations younger than the transferor."[40] Third, the new Rule does not void a remote nonvested interest but generally makes a trust (or nontrust disposition) that has not terminated by the end of the perpetuity period (the death of the last surviving measuring life) subject to judicial modification.[41] Fourth, pursuant to the judicial modification section, a court shall modify the disposition to make it fall within the perpetuity period consistent with the transferor's approximate plan of distribution.[42]

What was the rationale for reformulating the Rule? Consider the following ALI statement:

> The shift from lives in being to a generations-based limit on dead-hand control. This Restatement continues to recognize the desirability of a rule of public policy that curbs excessive dead-hand control, but implements that rule in a more tailored manner than the limit based on lives in being plus 21 years. An unexamined assumption of the common-law Rule and the wait-and-see movement is that the perpetuity period—the maximum limit—must be measured by lives in being at the creation of the interest. Requiring the lives to be in being at the creation of the interest prevents the perpetuity

37. *See* 2d Rest. Prop. (Donative Transfers) § 1.4.

38. *Id.* at § 1.5.

39. The reformulation was contained in 3d Rest. Prop. § 27.1 (Tent. Dft. No. 6), which was approved in May 2010. *See* http://www.ali.org/index.cfm?fuseaction=projects.proj_ip&projectid=13.

40. 3d Rest. Prop. § 27.1(b)(1).

41. *See* 3d Rest Prop § 27.1(a).

42. *See* 3d Rest Prop § 27.2.

period from adjusting to the trust and family circumstances, because that requirement often divides members of the same generation into measuring and non-measuring lives. Although trusts commonly confer lifetime benefits on members of one generation before passing benefits to the next generation, the life-in-being requirement means that only those members of a generation who are in being at the creation of the interest can be used to measure the perpetuity period. Members of the same generation who come into being later cannot be used. This Restatement replaces the "in being" requirement with a rule that measures the perpetuity period by generations. Basically, with certain qualifications and exceptions, the Rule—as promulgated in this Restatement—limits dead-hand control to granting benefits through, but not beyond, two generations younger than the transferor. The result is that the perpetuity period becomes more consistent with the know-and-see theory[43] than the lives-in-being approach and is tailored to the individual trust and family circumstances.[44]

G. Perpetuities Repeal Movement[45]

The Rule Against Perpetuities (Rule) is under siege in the United States. As of this writing, the following states have effectively repealed the Rule, especially for trusts in which the trustee has the power to transfer the trust property, so-called "qualified trusts": Alaska, Delaware, District of Columbia, Idaho, Illinois, Kentucky, Maine, Maryland, Michigan, Missouri, New Hampshire, New Jersey, North Carolina, Ohio, Oklahoma, Pennsylvania, Rhode Island, South Dakota, Virginia, and Wisconsin.[46] Several states have extended the period for lengthy trust periods, including: Alabama (360 years), Arizona (500 years), Colorado (1,000 years), Florida (360 years) and Washington (now 150 years), Nevada (now 365 years) and Tennessee (360 years),

43. As Professor Waggoner, the Reporter for the Restatement (Third), earlier explained: "[T]he [know-and-see] standard [arguably means] that donors should be allowed to exert control through the youngest generation of descendants they knew and saw, or at least one or more but not necessarily all of whom they knew and saw." Lawrence W. Waggoner, *The Uniform Statutory Rule Against Perpetuities*, 21 Real Prop. Prob. & Tr. J. 569, 587 (1986).

44. 3d Rest. Prop. Intro. to ch. 27.

45. Adapted from Ira Mark Bloom, *How Federal Transfer Taxes Affect the Development of Property Law*, 48 Clev. St. L. Rev. 661 (2000) and Ira Mark Bloom, *The GST Tax Tail Is Killing the Rule Against Perpetuities*, 87 Tax Notes 569 (2000).

46. Repeal methods vary considerably. For example, in Illinois the Rule applies to qualified trusts unless the settlor opts out of the Rule, while in North Carolina the Rule simply does not apply to qualified trusts. *See generally* Note, *Dynasty Trusts and the Rule Against Perpetuities*, 116 Harv. L. Rev. 2588, 2590–95 (2003). Hawaii now allows perpetual trusts that are governed by the permitted transfers in trust act. *See* Haw. Rev. Stat § 525-4(6) (involving cash, marketable securities, life insurance contracts, and non-private annuities). Apart from Rhode Island, the common-law Rule, USRAP or the rule against unduly suspending the power of alienation, *see* § 9.05[A], may still apply to non-vested interests in non-qualified trusts and those outside of trust.

Utah (1,000 years), Washington ("only" 150 years) and Wyoming (1,000 years). Other states are seriously considering repeal.

What has sparked the perpetuities repeal movement? Is it the recognition that this ancient property rule no longer serves any social policy? No! Since 1997, the Rule has been repealed so that wealthy individuals will be able to create perpetual dynasty trusts to exploit the generation-skipping transfer (GST) tax system.[47]

By repealing the Rule, the GST exemption amount can be enjoyed in perpetuity under a properly crafted GST exempt-trust, also referred to as dynasty trusts. Recognizing the interrelationship between perpetuities and the GST exemption, Alaska repealed the Rule in 1997 to encourage non-residents to create Alaska trusts. Soon other states joined in the quest for more trust business and to ensure that their wealthy residents did not need to leave their home to create a trust that would be perpetually exempt for GST tax purposes.

North Carolina, which has repealed the Rule, and four states (Arizona, Nevada, Utah, and Wyoming), which allow trusts to last for multiple centuries, have constitutional prohibitions on perpetuities. The question is whether the constitutional prohibition effectively prevents such states from allowing perpetual or near-perpetual trusts. *See generally*, Robert H. Sitkoff and Steven J. Horowitz, *Unconstitutional Perpetual Trusts*, 67 Vand. L. Rev. 1769 (2014). *Cf. Bullion Monarch Mining, Inc., v. Barrick Gold Strike Mines, Inc.*, 345 P.3d 1040 (Nev. 2015) (suggesting that Nevada's original constitutional provision is not "static").

The perpetuities repeal movement—a race to the bottom—is quite understandable. Unless a state repeals its Rule, its wealthy residents will create GST exempt trusts in those states that have repealed the Rule. Indeed, an empirical study shows that $100 billion has moved into perpetual trust states through 2003, particularly into those states that also do not impose state fiduciary income taxation. *See* Robert H. Sitkoff & Max M. Schanzenbach, *Jurisdictional Competition for Trust Funds: An Empirical Analysis of Perpetuities and Taxes*, 115 Yale L.J. 356 (2005).[48]

In their haste to jump on the repeal bandwagon, no repealing state appears to have seriously considered the negative consequences of sanctioning GST exempt perpetual trusts. Unfortunately, there will be serious negative consequences under the settlor's infinite dead hand control.

Consider some of the problems with long-lasting, perhaps even perpetual trusts. The wealth that can be amassed from a one million dollar trust after relatively short periods of time, based on an after-tax return of five percent is startling.[49] Imagine the wealth and power the lucky dynastic family members might enjoy from

47. Three states, Idaho, South Dakota, and Wisconsin, had effectively repealed the Rule before 1984.

48. Although several of these states also have self-settled asset protection laws, the study was not able to evaluate the impact of APT laws.

49. The value after 100 years would be $140 million; after 200 years it would be almost $20 billion; after 300 years, the value would be $2.7 trillion. *See* Ira Mark Bloom, *Transfer Tax Avoidance:*

GST-exempt trusts. Such trusts will likely name as fiduciaries already powerful corporate trustees whose wealth and power will grow as trustees over dynasty trusts.

In a dynasty trust, the trustees will likely be given discretionary powers over trust property for the trust creator's lineal descendants. Consider why Professor Lawrence W. Waggoner, Director of Research of the Joint Editorial Board for the Uniform Probate Code, predicts that such discretionary trusts will become an administrative nightmare:

> Overtime, the administration of such trusts is likely to become unwieldy and very costly.
>
> Government statistics indicate that the average married couple has 2.1 children. Under this assumption, the average settlor will have more than 100 descendants (who are beneficiaries of the trust) 150 years after the trust is created, around 2,500 beneficiaries 250 years after the trust is created, and 45,000 beneficiaries 350 years after the trust is created. Five hundred years after the trust is created, the number of living beneficiaries could rise to an astounding 3.4 million.[50]

The American Law Institute Rejects Perpetual and Multiple Centuries Trusts

In 2010, the American Law Institute approved the following position,[51] which in part provides:[52]

> It is the considered judgment of The American Law Institute that the recent statutory movement allowing the creation of perpetual or multiple-centuries trusts is ill advised. The movement to abrogate the Rule Against Perpetuities has not been based on the merits of removing its curb on excessive dead-hand control. The policy issues associated with allowing perpetual or multiple-centuries trusts have not been seriously discussed in the legislatures. The driving force has been the effort to take some trust-industry (financial-services) jobs from other states.
>
> A rule that curbs excessive dead-hand control is deeply rooted in this nation's history and tradition, and for good reason. A 360-year trust created in the year 2010 could endure until the year 2370 and have over 100,000 beneficiaries. A 1000-year trust created in 2010 could terminate

---

The Impact of Perpetuities Restrictions Before and After Generation-Skipping Taxation, 45 Alb. L. Rev. 260, 301 n.219 (1981).

50. Letter from Lawrence W. Waggoner, Lewis M. Simes Professor of Law, to Ira Mark Bloom (Oct. 26, 2001).

51. The position was contained in 3d Rest. Prop, Tent. Draft No. 6, which was approved in May 2010. *See* http://www.ali.org/index.cfm?fuseaction=projects.proj_ip&projectid=13.

52. *See* 3d Rest. Prop., Introductory Note to Chapter 27.

> in the year 3010 and have millions of beneficiaries. No transferor has enough wisdom to make sound dispositions of property across such vast intervals and for beneficiaries so remote and so numerous. A 1000-year or 360-year trust created in 2010 might incorporate what are currently considered to be flexible provisions for a trust that could last that far into the future. To put that claim into perspective, consider the devices for controlling family wealth through subsequent generations that were available 360 or more years ago, in the year 1650 or earlier. Such devices, drafted before the invention of the typewriter,[53] first took the form of the unbarrable entail and, after the entail became barrable, the strict settlement. These devices became archaic long ago. If that which was considered sophisticated 360 or more years ago is considered primitive today, there is reason to suspect that that which is considered sophisticated today will be considered primitive 360 or more years from now.
>
> The traditional limit on dead-hand control of a life in being plus 21 years allows trusts or other property arrangements to continue for about a century, which is an extraordinarily long period of time.[54] The length of the traditional limit can perhaps be justified on the ground that it allows a transferor to benefit remote but known or partially known generations. But the traditional limit does not allow a transferor to benefit hundreds, thousands, or millions of remote descendants born or adopted centuries or millennia after the transferor's death.[55]
>
> An important reason for maintaining a reasonable limit on dead-hand control is that the limit forces full control of encumbered property to be shifted periodically to the living, free of restrictions imposed by the original transferor. The living can then use the property as they wish, including retransferring it into new trusts with up-to-date provisions.[56]

53. The first commercially successful typewriter was invented in 1867. *See* 1001 Inventions That Changed the World 327 (Jack Challoner ed. 2009).

54. It is now understood that Lord Nottingham's decision in the Duke of Norfolk's Case announced a rule *of* perpetuities, not a rule *against* perpetuities.

55. If Samuel Hinckley, who died in Massachusetts in 1662, had created a perpetual or a multiple-centuries trust for his descendants, the more-than-100,000 beneficiaries living in 2010 would include President Barack Obama and his descendants and former President George H.W. Bush and his descendants (including former President George W. Bush). If Mareen Duvall, who died in Maryland in 1694, had created a perpetual or a multiple-centuries trust for her descendants, the more-than-100,000 beneficiaries living in 2010 would include President Obama and his descendants and former Vice President Richard Cheney and his descendants.

56. *See* Ruth L. Deech, *Lives in Being Revived*, 97 L.Q. Rev. 593, 594 (1981) ("If a settlor or testator had total liberty to dispose of his property among future beneficiaries, the recipients, being fettered by his wishes, would never enjoy that same freedom in their turn. The liberty to make fresh rearrangements of assets is necessary not only in order to be rid of irksome conditions attached by earlier donors to the enjoyment of income but also in order to be able to maneuver in the light of

Selected References

Mark L. Ascher, *But I Thought the Earth Belonged to the Living*, 89 Tex. L. Rev. 1149 (2011)

Ronald Chester, *The Psychology of Dead Hand Control*, 43 Real Prop. Tr. and Est. L.J. 504 (Fall 2008).

Wendy Davis, *Remember the Rule Against Perpetuities? Well, Forget it! New Jersey Undoes Centuries of Jurisprudence with a Pen Stroke*, 157 N.J.L.J. 217 (1999).

Joel C. Dobris, *Undoing Repeal of the Rule Against Perpetuities: Federal and State Tools for Breaking Dynasty Trusts*, 27 Cardozo L. Rev. 2537 (2006).

Jesse Dukeminier & James E. Krier, *The Rise of the Perpetual Trust*, 50 UCLA L. Rev. 1303 (2003).

Mary Louise Fellows, *Why the Generation-Skipping Transfer Tax Sparked Perpetual Trusts*, 27 Cardozo L. Rev. 2511 (2006).

Tye J. Klooster, *Are the Justifications for the Rule Against Perpetuities Still Persuasive?*, 30 ACTEC J. 95 (2004).

Max M. Schanzenbach & Robert H. Sitkoff, *Perpetuities or Taxes? Explaining the Rise of the Perpetual Trust*, 27 Cardozo L. Rev. 2465 (2006).

Robert H. Sitkoff & Max M. Schanzenbach, *Jurisdictional Competition for Trust Funds: An Empirical Analysis of Perpetuities and Taxes*, 115 Yale L.J. 356 (2005).

Stewart E. Sterk, *Jurisdictional Competition to Abolish the Rule Against Perpetuities: R.I.P. for the R.A.P.*, 24 Cardozo L. Rev. 2097 (2003).

Joshua C. Tate, *Perpetual Trusts and the Settlor's Intent*, 53 Kan. L. Rev. 595 (2005).

William J Turnier & Jeffrey L. Harrison, *A Malthusian Analysis of the So-Called Dynasty Trust*, 28 Va. Tax Rev. 779 (2009).

Reid Kress Weisbord, *Trust Term Extension*, 67 Fla. L. Rev. 73 (2015).

§ 9.05 Other Rules on Dead Hand Control Over Trusts

The perpetuities reform and repeal movements do not mean that there will be no restrictions on dead hand controls over trusts created in the future. Two other rules may be applicable in a particular state: the rule against the undue suspension of the

new tax laws, changes in the nature of the property and in the personal circumstances of the beneficiaries, unforeseeable by the best-intentioned and most perspicacious of donors.").

power of alienation and the rule against the unreasonable accumulation of trust income. The rule that restricts the duration of trusts was discussed in Chapter 8.

A. The Rule Against the Undue Suspension of the Power of Alienation

Enacted in 1969, the following Wisconsin statute, Wis. Stat. Ann. § 700.16, has been the model for other states (Alaska, Kentucky, New Jersey, North Carolina, and South Dakota) that have repealed their rule against perpetuities in its entirety:

> (1) (a) A future interest or trust is void if it suspends the power of alienation for longer than the permissible period. The permissible period is a life or lives in being plus a period of 30 years . . . .
>
> (2) The power of alienation is suspended when there are no persons in being who, alone or in combination with others, can convey an absolute fee in possession of land, or full ownership of personalty.
>
> (3) There is no suspension of the power of alienation by a trust or by equitable interests under a trust if the trustee has power to sell, either expressed or implied, or if there is an unlimited power to terminate in one or more persons in being . . . .
>
> (5) The common-law rule against perpetuities is not in force in this state.

Although some states use 21 years instead of Wisconsin's 30-year add-on period, statutes based on this model still allow dead hand control over trusts (and non-trust interests). In the context of trusts, the key is whether the trustee has the power to sell the trust property or a person has the power to terminate the trust. If either of these powers is granted under a trust, there can be no violation of the undue suspension rule; as a result, the trust can last in perpetuity. On the other hand, if neither power exists under a trust, then trust validity will be measured by the common-law lives in being approach, with a number of years added on.

For example, suppose Steven creates an irrevocable trust to last for 100 years, but bars Thomas, as trustee, from selling the property. Moreover, the trust does not give the unlimited power to terminate the trust. According to the statute, the power of alienation of the trust property is "suspended" because the trustee cannot sell the property and no person can terminate the trust. The suspension extends too long because every life in being at the creation of the trust may die immediately after trust creation and yet the suspension may continue for more than another 30 years. As a result, the trust is void.

The important point to note under these statutes is that there will be no suspension of the power of alienation during the period that the trustee can sell the trust property or a person can terminate the trust. In contrast, New York has an undue suspension statute, N.Y. EPTL § 9-1.1(a), that applies to trusts even if the trustee has the power to sell the trust property. In effect, an undue suspension can occur in New York if alienation of the equitable interests in the trust are unduly suspended.

B. The Rule Against the Unreasonable Accumulation of Trust Income

Restatement (Second) of Property (Donative Transfers)

§ 2.2. Accumulation of Trust Income

(1) An accumulation of trust income under a non-charitable trust created in a donative transfer is valid until the period of the rule against perpetuities expires with respect to such trust and any accumulation thereafter is invalid.

(2) An accumulation of trust income under a charitable trust created in a donative transfer is valid to the extent the accumulation is reasonable in the light of the purposes, facts and circumstances of the particular trust.

(3) The trust income released by an invalid accumulation shall be paid to such recipients and in such shares and in such manner as most closely effectuates the transferor's manifested plan of distribution.

(4) An accumulation of trust income occurs when part or all of the current income of the trust can be and is retained in the trust, or can be and is so applied by the trustee as to increase the fund subject to the trust, and such retention or application is not found to be merely in the course of judicious management of the trust.

Although relying on the perpetuities period, the rule against unreasonable accumulations does not deal with remote vesting. Rather it addresses the societal problem of trust principal becoming unreasonably large due to extended periods when the trust income is added to the trust principal, rather than distributed out of the trust.

Several states have specific statutes against unreasonable accumulations of trust income, including California, and New York. Other states have applied the rule by case law, including Connecticut, Kansas and Maine. Whether statutorily or judicially imposed, the common-law period is used as the measuring rod, as contrasted by the Restatement's use of a wait-and-see perpetuities period. *See* White v. Fleet Bank, 739 A.2d 373 (Me. 1999) (applying common-law rule against unreasonable accumulations despite enactment of USRAP 90 year wait-and-see period).

There may also be a question whether the rule against unreasonable accumulations applies in states that have effectively repealed the rule against perpetuities for qualified trusts but have not specifically enacted legislation repealing the rule against unreasonable accumulations. Presumably a court would find that the rule against unreasonable accumulations did not apply, as using the repealed time marker would make little sense. A few states, including Delaware, Illinois, South Dakota and Wisconsin, have legislatively abrogated the rule against unreasonable accumulations.

Question

In a state that has effectively repealed the Rule Against Perpetuities for trusts, does it necessarily follow that the state's rule against the unreasonable accumulation of trust income has also been repealed? *See generally* Karen J. Sneddon, *The Sleeper Has Awakened: The Rule Against Accumulations and Perpetual Trusts*, 76 Tul. L. Rev. 189 (2001).

Selected Reference

Robert H. Sitkoff, *The Lurking Rule Against Accumulations of Income*, 100 Nw. U.L. Rev. 501 (2006).

Chapter 10

Problems in Administration

§ 10.01 An Overview

This chapter considers problems fiduciaries face when administering estates or trusts, and thereby complements the discussion in Chapter 1 on probate administration. Many of the same problems may also face other fiduciaries in donative transfers—custodians serving under the Uniform Transfer to Minors Acts, guardians, conservators, and agents acting under powers of attorney.[1]

The major focus of this chapter is on the fiduciary duties and powers of personal representatives (executors and administrators) and trustees. We start with the fundamental duty of loyalty and then focus on fiduciary powers and duties in the managerial area. Included within this discussion are the evolving areas of fiduciary investment conduct and of principal and income allocation. We also highlight other important areas of fiduciary responsibility, such as the fiduciary duty to inform and report, as well as fiduciary liability to third persons. We close the chapter with the remedies that beneficiaries have when fiduciaries breach their fiduciary obligations.

As you will see, fiduciary administration cases typically raise three questions: (1) Did the fiduciary have a particular duty? (2) Did the fiduciary breach that duty? and (3) What are the remedies of the beneficiaries if a breach has occurred? As a result, although most of the cases in the early part of the chapter inevitably involve aspects of remedies, we have saved a discussion of the major issues in the remedies area for the end of the chapter.

The chapter will frequently reference UTC provisions on trustee administration since the area is comprehensively treated therein, as well as the Restatement (Third) of Trusts, which is now complete.

As you study this chapter, you should understand that, with few exceptions, the examined duties and powers are default rules. As a result, absent public policy constraints, the decedent or settlor can impose (or waive) whatever fiduciary duties and sanction whatever fiduciary powers that the decedent or settlor desires. UTC § 105

1. Trustees of trusts governed by ERISA are subject to a standard of prudence (*see* 29 U.S.C. § 1104(a)(1)(B)) and to other rules that are similar to those that govern other trustees. *See, e.g.*, *California Ironworkers Field Pension Trust v. Loomis Sayles & Co.*, 259 F.3d 1036 (9th Cir. 2001) (involving prudence rule, duty to disclose and duty of loyalty).

refers to default and mandatory rules. As an overarching principle, the fiduciary has the fundamental obligation to act in good faith, follow the terms and purposes of the will or trust, and serve the interests of the beneficiaries. See UTC § 801). *See also* 3d Rest. Trusts § 76.

One final introductory point: as with other trusts and estates matters, choice of law issues may arise in the fiduciary administration area. Generally, the law where estate or trust administration occurs will govern, particularly with respect to real estate. *See* 2d Rest. Conflicts §§ 271(b), 272(b), 279, 316, 334. However, the decedent or settlor may be able to designate a state in which the principal place of administration is deemed to take place and that designation will be respected if possible. *See* 2d Rest. Conflicts §§ 271(a), 272(a); UTC § 108 (settlor's designation of principal place of administration will be recognized if trustee is resident of or has office in jurisdiction or if all or part of administration occurs in the jurisdiction). *See In re Peierls Family Inter Vivos Trusts,* 77 A.3d 249 (Del. 2013) (illustrating complexities involved in changing the law governing trust administration).

Conflict of laws issues also may involve jurisdictional matters. For example, in *Rose v. Firstar Bank*, 819 A.2d 1247 (R.I. 2003), an Ohio corporate trustee had insufficient minimum contacts with Rhode Island to allow Rhode Island beneficiaries to obtain personal jurisdiction over the trustee. A further issue involves the transfer of trust administration to another jurisdiction; UTC § 108(c) specifically authorizes a trustee to transfer trust administration if appropriate under the circumstances, however, court order, disapproval or approval is also possible; in addition, transfer without court approval is not permitted if a qualified beneficiary objects. *See* UTC § 108(e).

The Bishop Estate: "A World Record for Breaches of Trust"

Enormous wealth, greed, mismanagement, and political manipulation combined to set a shameful world record. It all started with good intentions in 1884. Princess Pauahi Bishop—a member of the royal family that had ruled Hawaii before it was annexed and became a U.S. Territory—died leaving a testamentary trust to support two schools. Known as the Bishop Estate, the trust became by the 1990's the wealthiest charitable trust in the country, surpassing the combined endowments of Harvard and Yale. Among much else, the Bishop Estate owned over 10 percent of the land in Hawaii.

On its face, the trust management plan looked sound: successors to the five initial trustees would be appointed by the justices of Princess Pauahi Bishop the Hawaii Supreme Court as vacancies occurred. What more distinguished group to choose persons of skill and integrity for such an important task? Unfortunately, politics and cronyism held sway, and many trustees appeared more interested in benefitting personally than in discharging fiduciary duties. Here are just a few examples:

Source: Hawaii State Archives.

One trustee took junkets that were paid out of trust funds.

Another trustee invested personal funds in the same deals the trust invested.

All trustees were paid unreasonable compensation.

University of Hawaii Trusts & Estates Professor Randall Roth, federal district court Judge Samuel King, and others broke the story in the mid-1990's in a Honolulu newspaper essay. King and Roth's 2006 book, Broken Trust, tells the riveting tale that led to the removal of one trustee and the forced resignations of the four others. In achieving what Professor Roth called "a world record for breaches of trust," the trustees appear to have broken virtually every fiduciary duty including: loyalty, prudence, care and diligence, furnishing information, and following the terms of the trust. Because a charity was involved, the Hawaii Attorney General and the federal Internal Revenue Service also had roles. One of the main lessons is an old one: it's important to have someone other than the fox watching the henhouse.

Selected References

Karen E. Boxx, *Distinguishing Trustees and Protecting Beneficiaries: A Response to Professor Leslie*, 27 Cardozo L. Rev. 2753 (2006).

Frederick R. Franke, Jr., *Resisting the Contractarian Insurgency: The Uniform Trust Code, Fiduciary Duty, and Good Faith in Contract*, 36 ACTEC L.J. 517 (2010).

John H. Langbein, *The Contractarian Basis of the Law of Trusts*, 105 Yale L.J. 625 (1995).

Melanie Leslie, *Common Law, Common Sense: Fiduciary Standards and Trustee Identity*, 27 Cardozo L. Rev. 2713 (2006).

Robert J. Rosepink, *Punctilio of an Honor—A Trustee's Duties*, 28 ACTEC J. 101 (2001).

Charles E. Rounds, Jr., *The Case for a Return to Mandatory Instruction in the Fiduciary Aspects of Agency and Trusts in the American Law School, Together with a Model Fiduciary Relations Course Syllabus*, 18 Regent U. L. Rev. 251 (2005/2006).

Robert Sitkoff, *An Agency Costs Theory of Trust Law*, 89 Cornell L. Rev. 621 (2004), and *The Economic Structure of Fiduciary Law*, 91 B.U. L. Rev. 1039 (2011).

Symposium, *The Bishop Estate Controversy*, 21 U. Haw. L. Rev. 353-714 (1999).

---

§ 10.02 Duty of Loyalty

Loyalty: honor, dedication, trustworthiness. Personal representatives and trustees owe it to beneficiaries. Lawyers owe it to clients. Only at their peril do fiduciaries allow the interests of others, or their own self-interest, to compromise the duty of loyalty.

In re Estate of Hines

715 A.2d 116 (D.C. 1998)

TERRY, ASSOCIATE JUDGE:

This case arises out of the administration of a decedent's estate. Appellant, the court-appointed personal representative, sold the real property of the estate to herself and her brother without court permission and without the knowledge or written consent of the other heirs of the decedent. Two of those heirs, claiming that appellant had acted improperly, brought suit seeking her removal as personal representative, appointment of a successor personal representative, and nullification of the sale of the property. Ruling that appellant had breached her fiduciary duty to the estate and had acted in contravention of statute and court order, the trial court granted appellees' motion for summary judgment. We affirm.

I

Charles H. Hines died on February 25, 1981. He devised a life estate in the family home on Florida Avenue, N.W., to his wife Ruth, with the remainder to their three children, William Hines, Marjorie Burke, and Sallie Archie, in equal shares, as tenants in common. Mr. Hines' will designated William Hines as the personal representative of the estate, but William never submitted the will to probate. William predeceased his mother and left his one-third interest in the property to his children, Caryn and Gary Hines, in equal shares. Some time thereafter Marjorie assigned one-tenth of her interest to her daughter, Tanya Hall.

On December 30, 1992, following the death of Ruth Hines, Caryn petitioned the court to appoint her as the personal representative of the estate of Charles Hines. The court issued an Abbreviated Probate Order appointing her as personal representative and requiring her to post a general bond in the amount of $1,000. The order also stated that she must file an additional bond, in an amount to be fixed by the court, before accepting assets in excess of that amount. Caryn posted a general bond in the amount of $1,000, which was never increased.

....

In May 1993 Marjorie told Caryn that she wanted to purchase the house for herself. Accordingly, on May 8 Marjorie and Caryn executed a sales contract which provided, among other things, that the sales price would be $70,000, that the property would be sold "as is," that the seller (the estate) would pay $ 3,000 toward the closing costs, that the seller could declare the contract null and void if the purchaser (Marjorie) failed to obtain financing within fifteen days, and that settlement was to occur within sixty days after the date of the contract.

By June 1994, Marjorie had not settled on the property, and Caryn had received only one other offer to purchase the property. On June 14 Caryn and her brother Gary executed a contract to purchase the property for themselves. The contract provided, among other things, that the sale price would be $70,000 and the seller (the estate) would pay $3,000 towards closing costs. Caryn signed the contract both as seller (on behalf of the estate) and as purchaser. The contract was silent as to who would pay for repairs to the house, nor did it expressly disclaim any warranties. Caryn admittedly concealed the transaction from Marjorie, failed to obtain court approval for the purchase, and did not obtain consent for the transaction from either Marjorie or Sallie, the other two principal heirs.

... On September 7 Caryn and Gary closed on the purchase of the property. Sometime later, in her Second and Final Account as personal representative, Caryn reported to the court that the estate had received $60,481.15 from the sale of the property to herself and her brother Gary.

Marjorie thereupon filed a complaint seeking Caryn's removal as personal representative and asking the court to set aside the sale of the property; her daughter Tanya later joined as a co-plaintiff. In her answer to the complaint, Caryn admitted that she had sold the house to herself and her brother without the knowledge and consent of either Marjorie or Sallie, each of whom held a one-third interest. She also admitted that she had paid only $70,000, which was $14,000 less than the appraised value of the property at the time of the sale. Along with her answer, Caryn filed a motion seeking nunc pro tunc authorization of the sale. The parties then filed cross-motions for summary judgment, and the court granted Marjorie and Tanya's motion in a fourteen-page order reciting the facts as we have summarized them here. Caryn noted this appeal, con-tending that the trial court erred in setting aside the sale of the property.

II

. . . .

The general rule applicable to this case was stated by the Supreme Court more than 150 years ago:

> The law . . . prohibits a party from purchasing on his own account that which his duty or trust requires him to sell on account of another, and from purchasing on account of another that which he sells on his own account. In effect, he is not allowed to unite the two opposite characters of buyer and seller, because his interests, when he is the seller or buyer on his own account, are directly conflicting with those of the person on whose account he buys or sells.

Michoud v. Girod, 45 U.S. (4 How.) 503, 555, 11 L. Ed. 1076 (1846). "Confidence in the loyalty and impartiality of a fiduciary is not maintained by one who is at once the seller and the buyer of the subject of sale." *Harlan v. Lee*, 174 Md. 579, 592, 199 A. 862, 869 (1938). Thus it has long been settled in the District of Columbia that a fiduciary may not purchase property which he holds in a fiduciary capacity "for his own benefit or on his own behalf, directly or indirectly," and that the person or persons to whom the fiduciary duty is owed—in this case, the other heirs—may seek to have any such sale voided or nullified. *Holman v. Ryon*, 56 F.2d 307, 310, 61 App. D.C. 10, 13 (1932) (citations omitted); see *Goldman v. Rubin*, 292 Md. 693, 441 A.2d 713, 720 (1982); Uniform Probate Code (U.L.A.) § 3-713 (1983). A personal representative owes a fiduciary duty to the estate and its beneficiaries. D.C. Code § 20-701 (a) (1989). This duty is breached when the personal representative's exercise of power over the estate is contrary to law or in violation of a court order. See D.C. Code § 20-743 (1989). Moreover, a fiduciary breaches her duty when she fails to disclose material information to the beneficiaries. See *Vicki Bagley Realty, Inc. v. Laufer*, 482 A.2d 359, 365 (D.C. 1984) (fiduciary duty "encompasses an obligation to inform the principal of every development affecting his interest" (citing cases)); Eddy v. Colonial Life Insurance Co., 919 F.2d 747, 750, 287 U.S. App. D.C. 76, 79 (1990).

. . . .

Appellant argues nevertheless that summary judgment was improper because there is a genuine issue as to whether she and her brother purchased the property for less than its fair market value. We disagree. Although this may be a disputed issue of fact, it is not material because it does not affect the outcome of the case. See *Anderson v. Liberty Lobby*, 477 U.S. at 248. The law does not differentiate between an unauthorized sale at fair market value and an unauthorized sale below fair market value; both are prohibited. Moreover:

> It is a wholesome doctrine, based upon reasons of public policy, that a [fiduciary] may not purchase or deal in [the] property [of the estate] for his own benefit or on his own behalf... "So jealous is the law of dealings of this character by persons holding confidential relations to each other that the [beneficiary] may avoid the transaction, even though the sale was without fraud, the property sold for its full value, and no actual injury to his interests be proven...."

Holman v. Ryon, supra, 61 App. D.C. at 13, 56 F.2d at 310 (citations omitted); cf. *Mosser v. Darrow*, 341 U.S. 267, 272-273, 71 S. Ct. 680, 95 L. Ed. 927 (1951). Therefore, "it is wholly immaterial whether the property brings its full value." *Bassett v. Shoemaker*, 46 N.J. Eq. 538, 20 A. 52, 53 (1890); *accord Potter v. Smith*, 36 Ind. 231, 239 (1871) ("however innocent the purchase may be in a given case, it is poisonous in its consequences"), quoted in *In re Estate of Garwood*, 272 Ind. 519, 400 N.E.2d 758, 763 (1980). Thus any factual dispute as to the fair market value of the property does not preclude the entry of summary judgment.

....

In summary, when a personal representative directly or indirectly purchases on her own account an asset of the estate at a sale which was not authorized by the court or the beneficiaries, the sale is voidable at the behest of any beneficiary.... In this case it is undisputed that appellant purchased real property belonging to the estate without the necessary authorization. Her conflict of interest was obvious and flagrant. We therefore hold that the trial court, after appellees raised an objection to the sale, acted properly in declaring the transaction void. That judgment is accordingly

Affirmed.

Notes and Questions

1. As *Hines* illustrates, the law follows a "no further inquiry" approach when an executor or administrator engages in a transaction that is not solely in the interests of the estate beneficiaries. In *Estate of Rothko*, conflicts of interest existed because fiduciaries could indirectly benefit from the sale of estate property to an art gallery. *See also Martin v. Dieringer*, 108 P.3d 234 (Alaska 2005) (loans by executor to corporation in which executor was stockholder). Do you think an executor breaches her duty of loyalty by claiming that property was held by the decedent and herself as joint tenants? *See In re Estate of Rosso*, 701 N.W.2d 355 (Neb. 2005) (no).

By application of the "no further inquiry" rule, the estate fiduciary may be accountable, regardless of the deal's underlying fairness.

2. Judge Cardozo famously described the trustee's fiduciary duty of loyalty in *Meinhard v. Salmon*, 164 N.E. 545, 546 (N.Y. 1928):

> Many forms of conduct permissible in a workaday world for those acting at arm's length, are forbidden to those bound by fiduciary ties. A trustee is held to something stricter than the morals of the market place. Not honesty alone, but the punctilio of an honor the most sensitive, is then the standard of behavior. As to this there has developed a tradition that is unbending and inveterate. Uncompromising rigidity has been the attitude of courts of equity when petitioned to undermine the rule of undivided loyalty by the 'disintegrating erosion' of particular exceptions. Only thus has the level of conduct for fiduciaries been kept at a level higher than that trodden by the crowd.

3. The rule of undivided loyalty clearly applies in the trust context. In effect, the trustee must act solely in the beneficiaries' interests or in furtherance of a charitable trust's charitable purposes; failing to do so invokes the "no further inquiry rule." As Restatement (Third) Trusts § 78 explains:

> The fiduciary duty of undivided loyalty in the trust context . . . is particularly intense so that, in most circumstances, its prohibitions are absolute for prophylactic reasons. The rationale begins with a recognition that it may be difficult for a trustee to resist temptation when personal interests conflict with fiduciary duty. In such situations, for reasons peculiar to typical trust relationships, the policy of the trust law is to prefer (as a matter of default law) to remove altogether the occasions of temptation rather than to monitor fiduciary behavior and attempt to uncover and punish abuses when a trustee has actually succumbed to temptation. This policy of strict prohibition also provides a reasonable circumstantial assurance (except as waived by the settlor or an affected beneficiary) that beneficiaries will not be deprived of a trustee's disinterested and objective judgment.

4. Transactions by trustees that implicate the duty of loyalty may be broken down into two general categories: (1) self-dealing by the trustee and (2) dealings that "otherwise involve or create a conflict between the trustee's fiduciary duties and personal interests." 3d Rest. Trusts § 78(2). Self-dealing includes transactions between the trustee and himself or herself. Buying or selling trust property are classic examples of self-dealing. *See, e.g., In re Trust Created by Inman*, 693 N.W.2d 514 (Neb. 2005) (trustee not allowed to purchase trust asset for himself). Mortgaging trust property to obtain a personal loan is another. *See In re Paxson Trust I*, 893 A.2d 99 (Pa. Super. Ct. 2006). If a trustee also has a special power of appointment might the exercise constitute a breach of the duty of loyalty? *See Herring v. Herring*, 891 So. 2d 143 (Miss. 2004).

Other conflicting interests or loyalties involve dealings with third persons. For example, the sale of trust property to a family member would constitute a breach of the duty of loyalty even if the sale was fair and was made in the best interests of the trust beneficiaries. *See* 3d Rest. Trusts § 78, cmt. e.

5. The prohibition on conflicted transactions is not absolute; there are justifiable qualifications. Thus, if the trustee fully discloses the proposed transaction to the beneficiary, the transaction is fair and reasonable, and the beneficiary gives informed consent, then the beneficiary cannot hold the fiduciary liable for breaching the duty of loyalty. *See* 3d Rest. Trusts § 78, cmt. c(3); UTC § 1009. Approval or permission for self-dealing in the will or trust may also vitiate liability for self-dealing. *See* 3d Rest. Trusts § 78, cmt. c(1)–(2); UTC § 802.

The duty of loyalty is a default duty, rather than a mandatory duty. *See* UTC § 105. *See generally* Mark L. Ascher, 3 Scott & Ascher on Trusts § 16.1 (5th ed. 2007). As a result, a settlor may relieve a trustee from the duty of loyalty. *See, e.g., Noveletsky v. Metropolitan Life Insurance Company*, 49 F. Supp. 3d 123 (D. Me. 2014).

The litigated cases seek to determine whether the settlor authorized self-dealing. *See, e.g., In re Estate of Stevenson*, 605 N.W.2d 818 (S.D. 2000) (trust did not provide authorization for trustee to lease trust property to relatives). *See also Wood v. U.S. Bank*, 828 N.E.2d 1072 (Ohio Ct. App. 2005) (trustee did not breach duty of loyalty by continuing to hold its own stock in trust where settlor provided that trustee was authorized to retain securities).

6. Despite Justice Cardozo's admonitions, see Note 1, exceptions, some controversial have crept into the duty of loyalty area. Seemingly uncontroversial is the exception for the trustee to be reasonably compensated, including compensation for special services. *See* 3d Rest. Trusts § 78, cmt. c(4)–(5). More controversial, but growing in acceptance, is the statutory license for a corporate trustee to invest in its proprietary mutual funds and to receive in effect dual compensation-trustee commissions on top of brokerage commissions. The Restatement (Third) of Trusts, comment c(8) and UTC § 802(f) codify the proprietary mutual fund exception on the grounds that the arrangement is advantageous for trust beneficiaries. *But see* Melanie B. Leslie, *In Defense of the No Further Inquiry Rule: A Response to Professor John Langbein*, 47 Wm. & Mary L. Rev. 541, 571–579 (2005) (criticizing UTC § 802(f)).

7. UTC § 802(c) departs from the common law by excepting from the no further inquiry rule certain transactions that do not involve self-dealing. Thus, transactions with a spouse, other close relatives, a trustee's agent or attorney as well as transactions with corporations and other businesses in which the trustee's judgment might be affected are not prohibited as a breach of the duty of loyalty. Instead, the transaction is presumptively a conflict but may be rebutted by a showing that the "transaction was not affected by a conflict between personal and fiduciary interests." *See* UTC § 802(c) and cmts. Professor Leslie seriously objects to the UTC's relaxation of the rule. *See* Melanie B. Leslie, *In Defense of the No Further Inquiry Rule: A Response to Professor John Langbein*, 47 Wm. & Mary L. Rev. 541, 571–579 (2005).

8. Professor Langbein advocates eliminating the no further inquiry rule even when a trustee self-deals. *See* John H. Langbein, *Questioning the Trust Law Duty of*

Loyalty: Sole Interest or Best Interest?, 114 Yale L.J. 929 (2005), criticized in Melanie B. Leslie, *In Defense of the No Further Inquiry Rule: A Response to Professor John Langbein*, 47 Wm. & Mary L. Rev. 541 (2005). For example, Professor Langbein sees no reason why a trustee should not be able to buy trust property at an auction for the trustee's personal benefit if the trustee can later show, if challenged, that the purchase was in the best interests of the trust beneficiaries even though not in the sole interest of the beneficiaries since the trustee also benefitted. Although corporate law employs a business judgment rule rather than trust law's sole interest rule, the corporate approach was rejected in *Stegemeier v. Magness*, 728 A.2d 557 (Del. 1999) (refusing to apply the lower corporate business judgment standard to determine whether the trustee breached its duty of loyalty).

What problems do you foresee with eliminating the no further inquiry rule for self-dealing? Is there a way that the trustee can purchase trust property at auction even under the traditional no further inquiry rule?

9. Absent express authority to self-deal, an agent under a power of attorney will be liable for breaching the duty of loyalty by transferring the principal's property to herself and her family. *See, e.g.*, *Crosby v. Luehrs*, 669 N.W.2d 635 (Neb. 2003); *accord* Uniform Power of Attorney Act §§ 114, 117.

A fiduciary's duty of impartiality to estate or trust beneficiaries is another facet of the duty of loyalty. *Compare Estate of Greenblatt*, 86 A.3d 1215 (Me. 2013) (personal representative did not violate the duty of impartiality) with *Zim Israel Navigation Co. v. 3-D Imports, Inc.*, 29 F. Supp. 2d 186 (S.D.N.Y. 1998) (trustee breached duty of impartiality by not treating all beneficiaries equally when distributing a fund to compensate for cargo losses).

Uniform Trust Code

Section 803. Impartiality.

If a trust has two or more beneficiaries, the trustee shall act impartially in investing, managing, and distributing the trust property, giving due regard to the beneficiaries' respective interests.

Comment

The duty of impartiality is an important aspect of the duty of loyalty. . . .

The duty to act impartially does not mean that the trustee must treat the beneficiaries equally. Rather, the trustee must treat the beneficiaries equitably in light of the purposes and terms of the trust. A settlor who prefers that the trustee, when making decisions, generally favor the interests of one beneficiary over those of others should provide appropriate guidance in the terms of the trust. See Restatement (Second) of Trusts, cmt. a (1959).

The duty of impartiality cuts across every facet of fiduciary administration. *See, e.g., McNeil v. McNeil*, 798 A.2d 503 (Del. 2002) (duty breached by not sharing information with one of the beneficiaries). *See generally* 3d Rest. Trusts § 79. However, the duty of impartiality will most often arise in connection with trust investments, see, e.g., *SunTrust Bank v. Merritt*, 612 S.E.2d 818 (Ga. Ct. App. 2005) (investment in tax exempt bonds did not unduly favor income beneficiary) and with principal and income allocations. See UPIA § 103(b). One persistent problem is how to allocate tax benefits and burdens fairly. For example, the Internal Revenue Code gives the executor the choice of claiming the expenses of estate administration against the income taxes due from the estate or against estate taxes. IRC § 642(g). An executor who saves income taxes at the cost of higher estate taxes (or vice-versa) should allocate some of the savings to those who suffered the higher bill. *See Estate of Bixby*, 295 P.2d 68 (Cal. Ct. App. 1956) (executor saved over $100,000 in income taxes, but increased estate taxes by almost $60,000). Section 506 of the 1997 Uniform Principal & Income Act authorizes a fiduciary to make adjustments between beneficiaries to take into account tax elections and decisions.

Problems

1. You work in the trust department of a regional bank which has branches in a number of small communities, including your hometown, where the bank is currently serving as executor of the estate of a prominent citizen. You are assigned to supervise an "estate sale" of the decedent's tangible personal property. Can you sell to any of the following: your spouse, your mother, your best friend?

2. Over the last 10 years, you have developed a thriving law practice and a number of helpful contacts. You have especially good relationships with three insurance agents, an accountant, an estate sales agent who appraises personal property, and a real estate appraiser. Some have become personal friends. You often hire them or refer clients to them. They do the same for you. Are you violating your duty of loyalty to your clients?

3. If a trustee holds a minority interest in a corporation and the trustee is also a director of the corporation, should the trustee vis-à-vis his corporate duties be held to the higher trustee-level standard rather than the lower corporate-level standard? *Rollins v. Rollins*, 780 S.E.2d 328, 344 (Ga. 2015) and *Rollins v. Rollins*, 755 S.E.2d 727 (Ga. 2014) (no; lower corporate-level standard applies).

Christopher H. Gadsden, *Ethical Guidelines for the Fiduciary's Lawyer*[2]

134 Tr. & Est. 8, 13–16 (Mar. 1995).

The counseling of executors, administrators, special administrators and other personal representatives in estate administration (collectively described in this article as "executors") and trustees, is an integral part of the practice of virtually all trust and estate lawyers. In some cases, the lawyer is representing only the fiduciary but must consider what duties, if any, he or she may owe to beneficiaries and others. In other situations, the engagement to represent the fiduciary is the outgrowth of previous estate planning work for several family members and the lawyer finds that he or she now is representing multiple clients, both the fiduciary and some or all of the beneficiaries....

As the Comment to Model Rule 1.7 aptly notes, "[i]n estate administration the identity of the client may be unclear under the law of a particular jurisdiction. Under one view, the client is the fiduciary; under another view the client is the estate or trust, including its beneficiaries."

... [T]he great majority of court decisions have concluded that the client is the fiduciary.... However, some courts and commentators have suggested that the lawyer for a fiduciary may owe some derivative duties to the beneficiaries served by that fiduciary....

Any lawyer who represents a fiduciary with respect to estate or trust administration would be well served by an express statement that sets forth the duties of the lawyer and clarifies the relationships of the fiduciary, the beneficiaries and the lawyer....

In a substantial number of estates or trusts the lawyer who is asked to represent the fiduciary already represents one or more of the beneficiaries. The lawyer may have been the grantor's attorney for estate planning purposes and may have been serving the same role for the grantor's spouse and other family members....

The lawyer should identify those beneficiaries who may reasonably believe that the lawyer represents them with respect to estate or trust administration.... Any uncertainty on the lawyer's part about the beneficiary's current status as a client suggests that a potential misunderstanding between lawyer and beneficiary on this issue might exist. It is good practice to contact the beneficiary and clarify the relationship....

As a general rule, a lawyer may represent both the fiduciary and one or more beneficiaries. Conflicts of interest will not necessarily be present in estate administration; in many cases that may constitute only a theoretical possibility. On the other hand, if the lawyer knows of antipathy between the fiduciary and the beneficiary, the

2. Reprinted from Trusts & Estates, March 1995. © 1996 Argus, Inc., A Division of Intertec Publishing Corporation. Atlanta, GA, U.S.A.

lawyer should consider whether it is wise to represent either or both. The lawyer also should consider whether the particular circumstances of the estate or trust are likely to make a later withdrawal by the lawyer so harmful to one or both of the clients that representation of both clients is advisable. . . .

In some situations, the lawyer may recognize at the outset that substantial potential for conflict exists. Sometimes this potential may result not so much from the relationship between the fiduciary and the beneficiary itself but from other conflicting interests of the parties. In other words, the personal interests of the fiduciary conflict with the interests of one or more beneficiaries. . . .

Potential for conflict also may develop when the duties of the fiduciary are in conflict with the interests of a beneficiary. . . . For example, the beneficiary may ask the lawyer to review the fiduciary's accounting and to analyze critically the performance of the fiduciary. Because such an analysis may result in the identification of potential claims against the fiduciary, it would not be in the best interest of the fiduciary for its lawyer to evaluate such claims. As another example, the beneficiary may ask the lawyer to influence discretionary actions by the fiduciary in favor of that beneficiary. Tax elections, choices of investment and principal/income allocations all fall into this category. To advocate on behalf of one beneficiary would run counter to the duty not to advise or assist partiality among beneficiaries, one of the negative duties that the lawyer derived from his or her fiduciary/client.

Potential for conflict also may stem from positions taken by the fiduciary. For example, the fiduciary might demand additional compensation. . . .

If the lawyer discerns that substantial potential for conflict exists, Model Rule 1.7 requires the lawyer to discuss with each client the advantages and disadvantages of dual representation and obtain each client's consent. If the lawyer is not able to obtain the consent of both clients to the dual representation, the lawyer must withdraw from the representation of one or both clients. . . . Model Rule 1.9 . . . requires consent of the former client if the interests of the two parties are materially adverse and it is a substantially similar matter. In some circumstances, the lawyer may withdraw only with respect to the dispute or other source of conflict. In other cases, the potential for conflict may pervade the entire estate or trust administration and require a total withdrawal. . . .

More often, actual adversity will develop during administration of the estate or trust. The beneficiary may want to negotiate for the purchase of a trust asset, such as the stock of a family business. . . .

Actual adversity also will develop if the beneficiary requests that lawyer to assert claims against the fiduciary. The beneficiary may want to challenge the fiduciary's proposed compensation. The beneficiary may wish to seek removal of the fiduciary from office. The beneficiary may want the fiduciary to be surcharged. When actual adversity develops, the lawyer should not continue to represent both parties.

Notes and Question

1. The Gadsden article notes that a lawyer who represents a fiduciary may be liable to the estate's or trust's beneficiaries. *But see Audette v. Poulin*, 127 A.3d 908 (R.I. 2015) (no duty of care owed to trust beneficiaries by attorney for trust; hence malpractice claim failed); *Trask v. Butler*, 844, 872 P.2d 1080, 1085 (1994) (holding that estate attorney is not liable to beneficiaries for legal malpractice, and explaining that beneficiaries have adequate alternative remedies against the personal representative). In *Trask v. Butler*, the court gave three reasons for holding that the lawyer hired by the personal representative should not be liable to the estate or the estate's beneficiaries: (1) the estate beneficiaries were incidental, rather than intended, beneficiaries of the lawyer-client relationship; (2) the estate beneficiaries could sue the personal representative directly for breach of fiduciary duty; and (3) the legal profession would be unduly burdened by the unresolvable conflict of interest a lawyer would face in deciding whether to represent the personal representative, the estate, or the beneficiaries. What do you think of the court's reasons?

2. A lawyer who represents a fiduciary may still owe limited duties to beneficiaries. As explained in the ACTEC Commentaries on the Model Rules of Professional Conduct, MRPC 1.2 (Scope of Representation):

> The lawyer for the fiduciary owes some duties to the beneficiaries of the fiduciary estate although he or she does not represent them. The duties, which are largely restrictive in nature, prohibit the lawyer from taking advantage of his or her position to the disadvantage of the fiduciary estate or the beneficiaries. In addition, in some circumstances the lawyer may be obligated to take affirmative action to protect the interests of the beneficiaries.

3. The UTC decided against resolving an important issue: Can a beneficiary obtain information from the trustee's attorney or does the attorney-client privilege apply? *Compare Riggs Nat'l Bank v. Zimmer*, 355 A.2d 709 (Del. Ch. 1976) (beneficiary is really the client and can therefore obtain information from trustee's attorney), *with Wells Fargo Bank v. Superior Court*, 990 P.2d 591 (Cal. 2000) (attorney-client privilege between trustee and trustee's lawyer bars trust beneficiary from obtaining information).

Restatement (Third) of Trusts § 82, cmt f, approves the fiduciary exception:

> [L]egal consultations and advice obtained in the trustee's fiduciary capacity concerning decisions or actions to be taken in the course of administering the trust . . . are subject to the general principle entitling a beneficiary to information that is reasonably necessary to the prevention or redress of a breach of trust or otherwise to the enforcement of the beneficiary's rights under the trust.

The fiduciary exception to the attorney-client privilege may also allow for a successor trustee to receive otherwise privileged information from a predecessor trustee on matters relevant to trust administration. *See Hammerman v. Northern Trust Co.*,

329 P.3d 1055 (Ariz. Ct. App. 2014) (reasoning that allowing predecessor trustee to assert attorney-client privilege against successor trustee would impede successor trustee's duty to keep beneficiaries reasonably informed).

What about estate beneficiaries obtaining information from the attorney for the executor or administrator?

New York recently amended its statute, Civil Practice Law and Rules §4503(a)(2), on attorney-client privilege, to make clear that a fiduciary exception does not apply for estate beneficiaries:

> **(a)(2) Personal representatives.**
>
> (A) For purposes of the attorney-client privilege, if the client is a personal representative and the attorney represents the personal representative in that capacity, in the absence of an agreement between the attorney and the personal representative to the contrary:
>
> (i) No beneficiary of the estate is, or shall be treated as, the client of the attorney solely by reason of his or her status as beneficiary; and
>
> (ii) The existence of a fiduciary relationship between the personal representative and a beneficiary of the estate does not by itself constitute or give rise to any waiver of the privilege for confidential communications made in the course of professional employment between the attorney or his or her employee and the personal representative who is the client.

Notwithstanding New York's rejection of the fiduciary exception, NY Civil Practice Law and Rules §4503(b), requires an attorney to disclose certain information:

> **(b) Wills and revocable trusts.** In any action involving the probate, validity or construction of a will or, after the grantor's death, a revocable trust, an attorney or his employee shall be required to disclose information as to the preparation, execution or revocation of any will, revocable trust, or other relevant instrument, but he shall not be allowed to disclose any communication privileged ... which would tend to disgrace the memory of the decedent.

On the issue of whether the decedent's personal representative may waive the attorney-client privilege between the attorney and the decedent, the courts unanimously hold that waiver of the privilege is permitted. *See, e.g., In re Bassin*, 813 N.Y.S.2d 200 (N.Y. App. Div. 2006).

Problem

Your longtime client, Marvin, was killed in a car accident, and you are serving as his executor. Can you hire yourself as lawyer for Marvin's estate? Can you represent Marvin's daughter in a wrongful death action against the driver of the other car?

Selected References

Charles M. Bennett, *Frontiers in Ethics: The Estate Lawyer's Duty of Loyalty and Confidentiality to the Fiduciary Client: Examining the Past to Make Wise Choices Now and in the Future*, 33 Ohio N.U. L. Rev. 807 (2007).

Virginia L. Blackwell, *Conflicts of Interest When an Attorney Represents an Estate*, 27 J. Legal. Prof. 141 (2002).

Dominic J. Campisi, *Competence and the Duty of Impartiality*, 139 Tr. & Est. 45 (Nov. 2000).

Robert S. Held, *A Trust Counsel's Duty to Beneficiaries*, 92 Ill. B.J. 636 (2004).

Ronald C. Link, *Developments Regarding the Professional Responsibility of the Estate Administration Lawyer: The Effect of the Model Rules of Professional Conduct*, 26 Real Prop. Prob. & Tr. J. 1 (1991).

Jeffrey N. Pennell, *Representations Involving Fiduciary Entities: Who is the Client?*, 62 Fordham L. Rev. 1319 (1994).

Report of the Special Study Committee on Professional Responsibility: Counseling the Fiduciary, 28 Real Prop. Prob. & Tr. J. 825 (1994).

§ 10.03 Managerial Issues

A. Duties and Powers

1. In General

Questions of fiduciary duty and fiduciary power tend to fold back upon each other. With their beneficiaries' interests firmly in mind, fiduciaries must exercise their powers prudently. Indeed, Restatement (Third) Trusts § 86 provides that the exercise of powers by a trustee are subject to all of the fiduciary duties that are imposed on the trustee.[3] Duties and powers can come from several sources.[4]

---

3. Besides the duties referred to in UTC §§ 801, 804, and 806, which are set out in the text, a trustee has many other duties under either the UTC or under common law. For example, a trustee has the duty to act as prudent investor. *See* § 10.03[4]. *See also* § 10.02, (duty of loyalty) and § 10.03[D] (other duties).

4. Under UPC § 3-703(a), personal representatives are subject to the standard of care comparable to that described in UTC §§ 804 and 806. *See* UPC § 7-302. UPC § 3-715 gives personal representatives powers similar to those prescribed for trustees by the UTC.

Uniform Trust Code

Section 801. Duty to Administer Trust.

Upon acceptance of a trusteeship, the trustee shall administer the trust in good faith, in accordance with its terms and purposes and the interests of the beneficiaries, and in accordance with this [Code].

Section 804. Prudent Administration.

A trustee shall administer the trust as a prudent person would, by considering the purposes, terms, distributional requirements, and other circumstances of the trust. In satisfying this standard, the trustee shall exercise reasonable care, skill, and caution.

Comment

The duty to administer a trust with prudence is a fundamental duty of the trustee. This duty does not depend on whether the trustee receives compensation. The duty may be altered by the terms of the trust. . . .

A settlor who wishes to modify the standard of care specified in this section is free to do so, but there is a limit. Section 1008 prohibits a settlor from exculpating a trustee from liability for breach of trust committed in bad faith or with reckless indifference to the purposes of the trust or to the interests of the beneficiaries.

Section 806. Trustee's Skills.

A trustee who has special skills or expertise, or is named trustee in reliance upon the trustee's representation that the trustee has special skills or expertise, shall use those special skills or expertise.

Section 815. General Powers of Trustee.

(a) A trustee, without authorization by the court, may exercise:

(1) powers conferred by the terms of the trust; or

(2) except as limited by the terms of the trust:

(A) all powers over the trust property which an unmarried competent owner has over individually owned property;

(B) any other powers appropriate to achieve the proper investment, management, and distribution of the trust property; and

(C) any other powers conferred by this [Code].

(b) The exercise of a power is subject to the fiduciary duties prescribed by this [article].

Comment

This section is intended to grant trustees the broadest possible powers, but to be exercised always in accordance with the duties of the trustee and any limitations stated in the terms of the trust. This broad authority is denoted by granting the trustee the powers of an unmarried competent owner of individually owned property, unlimited by restrictions that might be placed on it by marriage, disability, or cotenancy. . . .

A power differs from a duty. A duty imposes an obligation or a mandatory prohibition. A power, on the other hand, is a discretion, the exercise of which is not obligatory. The existence of a power, however created or granted, does not speak to the question of whether it is prudent under the circumstances to exercise the power.

Section 816. Specific Powers of Trustee.

Without limiting the authority conferred by Section 815, a trustee may:

(1) collect trust property and accept or reject additions to the trust property from a settlor or any other person;

(2) acquire or sell property, for cash or on credit, at public or private sale;

(3) exchange, partition, or otherwise change the character of trust property;

(4) deposit trust money in an account in a regulated financial-service institution;

(5) borrow money, with or without security, and mortgage or pledge trust property for a period within or extending beyond the duration of the trust;

(6) with respect to an interest in a proprietorship, partnership, limited liability company, business trust, corporation, or other form of business or enterprise, continue the business or other enterprise and take any action that may be taken by shareholders, members, or property owners, including merging, dissolving, or otherwise changing the form of business organization or contributing additional capital;

(7) with respect to stocks or other securities, exercise the rights of an absolute owner, including the right to:

(A) vote, or give proxies to vote, with or without power of substitution, or enter into or continue a voting trust agreement;

(B) hold a security in the name of a nominee or in other form without disclosure of the trust so that title may pass by delivery;

(C) pay calls, assessments, and other sums chargeable or accruing against the securities, and sell or exercise stock subscription or conversion rights; and

(D) deposit the securities with a depositary or other regulated financial-service institution;

(8) with respect to an interest in real property, construct, or make ordinary or extraordinary repairs to, alterations to, or improvements in, buildings or other structures, demolish improvements, raze existing or erect new party walls or buildings, subdivide or develop land, dedicate land to public use or grant public or private easements, and make or vacate plats and adjust boundaries;

(9) enter into a lease for any purpose as lessor or lessee, including a lease or other arrangement for exploration and removal of natural resources, with

or without the option to purchase or renew, for a period within or extending beyond the duration of the trust;

(10) grant an option involving a sale, lease, or other disposition of trust property or acquire an option for the acquisition of property, including an option exercisable beyond the duration of the trust, and exercise an option so acquired;

(11) insure the property of the trust against damage or loss and insure the trustee, the trustee's agents, and beneficiaries against liability arising from the administration of the trust;

(12) abandon or decline to administer property of no value or of insufficient value to justify its collection or continued administration;

(13) with respect to possible liability for violation of environmental law:

(A) inspect or investigate property the trustee holds or has been asked to hold, or property owned or operated by an organization in which the trustee holds or has been asked to hold an interest, for the purpose of determining the application of environmental law with respect to the property;

(B) take action to prevent, abate, or otherwise remedy any actual or potential violation of any environmental law affecting property held directly or indirectly by the trustee, whether taken before or after the assertion of a claim or the initiation of governmental enforcement;

(C) decline to accept property into trust or disclaim any power with respect to property that is or may be burdened with liability for violation of environmental law;

(D) compromise claims against the trust which may be asserted for an alleged violation of environmental law; and

(F) pay the expense of any inspection, review, abatement, or remedial action to comply with environmental law;

(14) pay or contest any claim, settle a claim by or against the trust, and release, in whole or in part, a claim belonging to the trust;

(15) pay taxes, assessments, compensation of the trustee and of employees and agents of the trust, and other expenses incurred in the administration of the trust;

(16) exercise elections with respect to federal, state, and local taxes;

(17) select a mode of payment under any employee benefit or retirement plan, annuity, or life insurance payable to the trustee, exercise rights thereunder, including exercise of the right to indemnification for expenses and against liabilities, and take appropriate action to collect the proceeds;

(18) make loans out of trust property, including loans to a beneficiary on terms and conditions the trustee considers to be fair and reasonable under

the circumstances, and the trustee has a lien on future distributions for repayment of those loans;

(19) pledge trust property to guarantee loans made by others to the beneficiary;

(20) appoint a trustee to act in another jurisdiction with respect to trust property located in the other jurisdiction, confer upon the appointed trustee all of the powers and duties of the appointing trustee, require that the appointed trustee furnish security, and remove any trustee so appointed;

(21) pay an amount distributable to a beneficiary who is under a legal disability or who the trustee reasonably believes is incapacitated, by paying it directly to the beneficiary or applying it for the beneficiary's benefit, or by:

(A) paying it to the beneficiary's [conservator] or, if the beneficiary does not have a [conservator], the beneficiary's [guardian];

(B) paying it to the beneficiary's custodian under [the Uniform Transfers to Minors Act] or custodial trustee under [the Uniform Custodial Trust Act], and, for that purpose, creating a custodianship or custodial trust;

(C) if the trustee does not know of a [conservator], [guardian], custodian, or custodial trustee, paying it to an adult relative or other person having legal or physical care or custody of the beneficiary, to be expended on the beneficiary's behalf; or

(D) managing it as a separate fund on the beneficiary's behalf, subject to the beneficiary's continuing right to withdraw the distribution;

(22) on distribution of trust property or the division or termination of a trust, make distributions in divided or undivided interests, allocate particular assets in proportionate or disproportionate shares, value the trust property for those purposes, and adjust for resulting differences in valuation;

(23) resolve a dispute concerning the interpretation of the trust or its administration by mediation, arbitration, or other procedure for alternative dispute resolution;

(24) prosecute or defend an action, claim, or judicial proceeding in any jurisdiction to protect trust property and the trustee in the performance of the trustee's duties;

(25) sign and deliver contracts and other instruments that are useful to achieve or facilitate the exercise of the trustee's powers; and

(26) on termination of the trust, exercise the powers appropriate to wind up the administration of the trust and distribute the trust property to the persons entitled to it.

Notes and Questions

1. Traditionally, courts have been reluctant to imply powers for trustees, but somewhat more willing to imply powers for personal representatives. To what extent, and why, do you think that powers implied for personal representatives should differ from powers implied for trustees?

2. Testator left the residue of his estate, which included company stock, to his three children in equal shares. One of the brothers was the executor who, acting pursuant to statute allowing distribution in kind or cash, proposed to distribute less stock to one brother who otherwise would obtain voting control of the company and cash to compensate for the smaller number of shares. He and his other brother would receive significantly more shares. Should the executor be required to distribute equal shares? *See Harp v. Pryor*, 578 S.E.2d 424 (Ga. 2003).

3. Testators and settlors can alter virtually all of the rules legislatures and courts set. For the overwhelming percentage of estates and trusts, clauses describing fiduciary power or liability never reach litigation. Rather, fiduciaries simply rely upon such clauses in the day-to-day course of business. This reality makes drafting particularly important.

Depending upon the nature of a fiduciary's situation, well-drafted documents grant a wide range of powers. A "simple" will covering modest assets should provide basic authority to act, usually without the need for court approval. If a business is involved, more detailed provisions will be appropriate. Because of the ongoing nature of a trust, trustee powers provisions often are very long and detailed. Documents can also alter duties, by adding more or waiving those the law otherwise imposes.

Problem

Assume your jurisdiction has adopted Uniform Trust Code § 816. In drafting your client's will to create a contingent testamentary trust for his minor children, what powers in section 816 would you seek to exclude or modify, and why?

Selected References

John H. Langbein, *Mandatory Rules in the Law of Trusts*, 98 Nw. U. L. Rev. 1105 (2004).

Arthur B. Laby, *Resolving Conflicts of Duty in Fiduciary Relationships*, 54 Am. U. L. Rev. 75 (2004).

Melanie B. Leslie, *Trusting Trustees: Fiduciary Duties and the Limits of Default Rules*, 94 Geo. L.J. 67 (2005).

Robert J. Rose Pink, *Punctilio of an Honor—A Trustee's Duties*, 28 ACTEC J. 101 (2001).

Robert H. Sitkoff, *An Agency Costs Theory of Trust Law*, 89 Cornell L. Rev. 621 (2004).

2. Fiduciary Access to Digital Assets

a. Background

Fiduciaries, including the personal representatives of *decedents'* estates, trustees, agents under powers of attorney, and conservators (guardians), are responsible for managing assets. To effectively discharge their managerial responsibilities, fiduciaries must *necessarily* have access to financial information and other personal records. Obtaining such information has become complicated over the past several decades, however, due to our society's increasing reliance on digital forms of communication, such as e-mail and social media. Similarly, there has been a steady shift in preference toward online banking, e-commerce, and even digital currency, such as Bitcoin.

Despite the obvious importance of fiduciary access to digital assets, significant difficulties exist. First, state and federal computer privacy laws often pose barriers to administration of digital assets by preventing third parties from accessing a user's personal account information.[5] Additionally, Internet service providers (ISPs) use terms of service agreements (TOSAs), along with password and encryption protection, which prevent fiduciaries from easily accessing the digital assets.

Although a few states had enacted some type of legislation on access by fiduciaries to digital assets, the Uniform Fiduciary Access to Digital Assets Act (UFADAA), which was approved in July 2014 by the Uniform Law Commission, comprehensively provided for access by fiduciaries to digital assets by personal representatives, trustees, agents under powers of attorney, and conservators (guardians). Although well intended, the UFADAA was vigorously opposed by many service providers, including Yahoo, Google, and Facebook, which promoted alternative and much more restrictive legislation: the Privacy Expectations Afterlife Choices Act (PEAC Act). *See* Karin Prangley, *War and Peace in Digital Assets: The Providers' PEAC Act Wages War with UFADAA*, 29 Prob. & Prop. J. 40 (July/August 2015).

---

5. *See* Stored Communications Act, 18 U.S.C. §§ 2701–11, enacted in 1986; Computer Fraud and Abuse Act of 1984, 18 U.S.C. § 1030. For a more in-depth analysis regarding federal digital privacy laws, see James D. Lamm, Christina L. Kunz, Damien A. Riehl & Peter John Rademacher, *The Digital Death Conundrum: How Federal and State Laws Prevent Fiduciaries from Managing Digital Property*, 68 U. Miami L. Rev. 385 (2014). Similar laws exist at the state level. *See* Conn. Gen. Stat. Ann. § 53a-251 (West 1984) ("A person is guilty of the computer crime of unauthorized access to a computer system when, knowing that he is not authorized to do so, he accesses or causes to be accessed any computer system without authorization."); *see also* N.Y. Penal Code § 156.00 (McKinney 2006) ("A person is guilty of unauthorized use of a computer when he or she knowingly uses, causes to be used, or accesses a computer, computer service, or computer network without authorization.").

b. Revised Fiduciary Access to Digital Assets Act

i. In General

In response to opposition by the service providers to UFADAA, the Uniform Law Commission in 2015 approved a revised UFADAA (RUFADAA).[6] *See generally* Suzanne Brown Walsh and Catherine Anne Seal, *The Revised Uniform Fiduciary Access to Digital Assets Act: Striking a Balance between Privacy Expectations and the Need for Fiduciary Access to Digital Assets,* 12 NAELA J. 101 (2016).

RUFADAA has met with the approval of some service providers, including Google and Facebook, as well as approval from privacy organizations. Widespread enactment of RUFADAA has begun.[7]

The RUFADAA provides a comprehensive set of rules governing the power of fiduciaries to access a user's digital assets. *See generally* Suzanne Brown Walsh and Catherine Anne Seal, *The Revised Uniform Fiduciary Access to Digital Assets Act: Striking a Balance between Privacy Expectations and the Need for Fiduciary Access to Digital Assets,* 12 NAELA J. 101 (2016). "Digital assets" are defined under the RUFADAA as "an electronic record in which an individual has a right or interest," and "expressly excludes underlying assets such as funds in an online banking account."[8] Common examples of digital assets include frequent flyer, hotel, and credit card awards and points, computer files, e-mail accounts, social networking accounts, online photographs and videos, financial information accounts and online sales accounts.

The Uniform Law Commission has provided the following summary of RUFADAA:

> Revised UFADAA gives Internet users the power to plan for the management and disposition of their digital assets in a similar way as they can make plans for their tangible property. In case of conflicting instructions, the act provides a three-tiered system of priorities:
>
> 1. If the custodian[9] provides an online tool, separate from the general terms of service, that allows the user[10] to name another person to have access to the user's digital assets or to direct the custodian to delete the

---

6. Revised Uniform Fiduciary Access to Digital Access Act, Unif. Law Comm'n (2015), http://www.uniformlaws.org/shared/docs/Fiduciary%20Access%20to%20Digital%20Assets/2015_RUFADAA_Final%20Act_2016mar8.pdf [hereinafter RUFADAA].

7. Several states have enacted RUFADAA including: Arizona, Colorado, Connecticut, Florida, Hawaii, Idaho, Illinois, Indiana, Iowa, Maryland, Michigan, Minnesota, Nebraska, New York North Carolina, Oregon, South Carolina, Tennessee, Utah, Vermont, Virginia, Washington, Wisconsin, and Wyoming. RUFADAA will likely be enacted by almost all states.

8. RUFADAA § 2(10) *and comment thereto.*

9. Custodian is defined by RUFADAA § 1(8) as follows: "Custodian" means a person that carries, maintains, processes, receives, or stores a digital asset of a user.

10. User is defined by RUFADAA § 1(26) as follows: "User" means a person that has an account with a custodian.

user's digital assets, Revised UFADAA makes the user's online instructions legally enforceable.[11]

2. If the custodian does not provide an online planning option, or if the user declines to use the online tool provided, the user may give legally enforceable directions for the disposition of digital assets in a will, trust, power of attorney, or other written record.[12]

3. If the user has not provided any direction, either online or in a traditional estate plan, the terms of service for the user's account will determine whether a fiduciary may access the user's digital assets. If the terms of service do not address fiduciary access, the default rules of Revised UFADAA will apply.

Revised UFADAA's default rules attempt to balance the user's privacy interest with the fiduciary's need for access by making a distinction between the "content of electronic communications," the "catalogue of electronic communications", and other types of digital assets.

The content of electronic communications includes the subject line and body of a user's email messages, text messages, and other messages between private parties. A fiduciary may never access the content of electronic communications without the user's consent. When necessary, a fiduciary may have a right to access a catalogue of the user's electronic communications—essentially a list of communications showing the addresses of the sender and recipient, and the date and time the message was sent.

For example, the executor of a decedent's estate may need to access a catalogue of the decedent's communications in order to compile an inventory of estate assets. If the executor finds that the decedent received a monthly email message from a particular bank or credit card company, the executor can contact that company directly and request a statement of the decedent's account.

Other types of digital assets are not communications, but intangible personal property. For example, an agent under a power of attorney who has authority to access the principal's business files will have access under Revised UFADAA to any files stored in "the cloud" as well as those stored in file cabinets. Similarly, an executor that is distributing funds from the decedent's bank account will also have access to the decedent's virtual currency account (e.g. bitcoin).[13]

ii. Access to Digital Assets by Specific Fiduciaries

The RUFADAA allows access to a user's digital assets by the following fiduciaries: personal representatives, agents under powers of attorney, trustees and conservators

11. Most custodians do not have online tools. Exceptions include Facebook, which only allows limited access when a user dies and Google, which allows limited access at death but also during lifetime inactivity by the user.

12. Users may also bar access to some or all of the user's digital assets.

13. See http://www.uniformlaws.org/Act.aspx?title=Fiduciary%20Access%20to%20Digital%20Assets%20Act,%20Revised%20(2015)

(guardians). Different rules apply for access to the content of electronic communications, such as emails, which are subject to federal law restrictions, for which user consent will be necessary, and to all other digital assets, including the catalogue of electronic communications (because access thereto is not restricted by law) for which user consent may not be required. Although fiduciaries by default can generally access digital assets other than the contents of electronic communications, the provisions in a TOSA may override these default access rules. *See* RUFADAA §§4(c), 5(c) and 15(b). A provision in a TOSA may not, however, override a user's consent for fiduciary access to the content of electronic communications. *See* RUFADAA §4(b). Nor can a provision in a TOSA override a user's actual consent for fiduciaries to access other digital assets. *See* RUFADAA §4(b). Although some procedural rules for access may vary among different fiduciaries, all fiduciaries are subject to fiduciary duties while managing digital asserts. *See* RUFADAA §15(a). RUFADAA §6 provides custodians with options for providing fiduciaries with access to digital assets.

Access to digital access by personal representatives

RUFADAA §§7 and 8 provide rules for personal representatives to access a deceased user's digital assets. RUFADAA §7 allows access to the contents of electronic communications, but only if the user consented or a court so directs. RUFADAA §8 will allow a personal representative access to the catalogue of electronic communications and to all other digital access of the deceased user unless otherwise prohibited by the user or a court.

Access to digital access by agents under powers of attorney

RUFADAA §§9 and 10 provide rules for agents under powers of attorney to access the digital assets of their principals. RUFADAA §9 provides in part as follows:

> To the extent a power of attorney expressly grants an agent authority over the content of electronic communications sent or received by the principal and unless directed otherwise by the principal or the court, a custodian shall disclose to the agent the content if the agent provides to the custodian [certain documentation and information.]

RUFADAA §10 provides in part as follows:

> Unless otherwise ordered by the court, directed by the principal, or provided by a power of attorney, a custodian shall disclose to an agent with specific authority over digital assets or general authority to act on behalf of a principal a catalogue of electronic communications sent or received by the principal and digital assets, other than the content of electronic communications, of the principal if the agent gives the custodian [certain documentation and information].

Access to digital access by trustees

RUFADAA §§11-13 provide rules for trustees to access a user's digital assets held in trust. If the original user is also the trustee, RUFADAA §11 allows the trustee to access all digital assets held in trust. RUFADAA §12 allows a trustee who is not the original user to access the content of electronic communications sent or received by an original or successor user and carried, maintained, processed, received, or stored by the custodian in the account of the trust if the trustee gives the custodian [certain documentation and information]. The comments to RUFADAA § 12 explain why express consent by the user is not necessary:

> There should be no question that the trustee with legal title to the digital asset was authorized by the settlor to access the digital assets so transferred, including both the catalogue and content of an electronic communication, and this provides "lawful consent" to allow disclosure of the content of an electronic communication from an electronic-communication service or a remote-computing service pursuant to applicable law.[14]

RUFADAA § 13 allows a trustee who is not the original user to access a catalogue of electronic communications sent or received by an original or successor user and stored, carried, or maintained by the custodian in an account of the trust and any digital assets, other than the content of electronic communications, in which the trust has a right or interest if the trustee gives the custodian [certain documentation and information].

Access to digital access by conservators (guardians)

RUFADAA § 14 allows conservators (guardians) to access a ward's digital assets other than the content of electronic communications if so authorized by a court. The comments to RUFADAA § 14 effectively explain why the content of electronic communications will not be accessible by conservators (guardians): When a conservator is appointed to represent a protected person's interests, the protected person may still retain some right to privacy in their personal communications.

Selected References

Elizabeth Sy, *The Revised Uniform Fiduciary Access to Digital Assets Act: Has the Law Caught Up With Technology*, 32 Tuoro L. Rev. 647, 657–62 (2016).

Jared Walker, *Return of the UFADAA: How Texas and Other States' Adoption of the RUFADAA Can Change the Internet,* 8 Est. Plan. & Community Prop. L.J. 577 (2016).

Suzanne Brown Walsh and, Catherine Anne Seal, *The Revised Uniform Fiduciary Access to Digital Assets Act: Striking a Balance between Privacy Expectations and the Need for Fiduciary Access to Digital Assets,* 12 NAELA J. 101 (2016).

Suzanne Brown Walsh, et al., *You Can't Always Get What You Want: Understanding the Revised Uniform Fiduciary Access to Digital Assets Act,* Trusts & Estates, Nov. 2015, at 25.

14. Express consent in the trust instrument should eliminate any issue about user authorization under federal law.

B. Investments

For most beneficiaries, the true measure of a fiduciary's performance is the extent to which investments prosper under the fiduciary's management. Courts hold personal representatives and trustees to a standard of "prudence." Primarily because of estate administration's shorter time horizon, courts have tended to view a personal representative's duty as more of a holding action to keep things together. While preservation of assets also has been a central tenet of trust administration, trustees must be especially sensitive to the changing needs of beneficiaries over time.

Moreover, like many other topics in this course, the standards for fiduciary investments are shifting. In 1830, *Harvard College v. Amory* gave us the "Prudent Man" rule: "[a trustee should] observe how men of prudence, discretion and intelligence manage their own affairs, not in regard to speculation, but in regard to the permanent disposition of their funds, considering the probable income, as well as the probable safety of the capital to be invested." 26 Mass. (9 Pick) 446, 461 (1830). Here was a flexible statement which could adapt to different circumstances, but such flexibility fell into disfavor.

The boom and bust economic cycles of the nineteenth century led many legislatures to provide "legal lists" of appropriate trust investments. Some lists were mandatory, meaning that a trustee could not go beyond them. Others were permissive, allowing a trustee to buy something not on the list, but effectively placing the burden on the trustee to show that such a move was prudent. The lists tended to favor "safe" investments like government bonds and first mortgages on realty. Common stocks usually were omitted, as too risky.

In the aftermath of the Great Depression of the 1930s, stocks recovered their value much better than bonds or mortgages. By the 1940s, the move was on to broaden the scope of appropriate trust investments. With a push from Professor Scott and the Restatement of Trusts, for which he served as reporter, most states shifted from legal lists back to a more flexible "prudent man"[15] approach.

As fleshed-out by Professor Scott in various sections of his treatise, this prudent man was more conservative than his earlier counterpart. In an influential article, Professor Gordon notes three ways that Scott narrowed the Harvard College approach. Jeffrey N. Gordon, *The Puzzling Persistence of the Constrained Prudent Man Rule*, 62 N.Y.U. L. Rev. 52, 59–61 (1987). First, Scott emphasized "preservation" instead of "permanent disposition" of the estate. In an inflationary economy, nominal preservation of capital can hurt those who hold for long periods. Second, when referring to investments, Scott shifted the prudent man standard from one based on how people would manage their own property to a standard based on those concerned about safeguarding the property of others. Third, Scott drew a hard line between "prudence," which

15. To eliminate the sexism of the old phrase, many statutes and commentators refer to this as a "prudent investor" rule. Because the Second Restatement retained the old term, but the Third Restatement has adopted the modern one, this book hopes to avoid confusion by limiting the "prudent investor" usage to descriptions of the new rule, discussed below.

was mandated, and "speculation," which was prohibited. Thus, new companies, companies which do not pay dividends, and new financial devices were out of bounds. The cumulative impact of these changes was to give the hypothetical prudent man less flexibility when choosing investments.

More recently, economists and others have developed new views about how financial markets work. Collectively known as "modern portfolio theory," these ideas emphasize the risk and return of an entire portfolio, rather than an individual investment in isolation. For an accessible introduction to the theory, see Burton G. Malkiel, A Random Walk Down Wall Street, ch. 9 (5th ed. 1990). Modern portfolio theory is now changing the law of trust investments. In 1992, the American Law Institute issued a new Restatement (Third) of Trusts devoted to articulating a "prudent investor" rule shaped by modern portfolio theory, and in 1994 a similarly-conceived Uniform Prudent Investor Act appeared.

We first examine the traditional prudent-man approach and then turn to the proposed reforms. You should understand, however, that a testator or settlor can override a statutory or judicial standard for investments by either making the standard more or less restrictive than the default state law on investments.

1. The Traditional "Prudent Man"

The following case should send shudders through personal administrators who view themselves as caretakers instead of investors.

In re Estate of Janes

681 N.E.2d 332 (N.Y. 1997)

LEVINE, J.

[Rodney B. Janes died on May 26, 1973, survived by his wife, Cynthia. They had no children. Rodney's will created three trusts; two of them gave Cynthia income for life, with remainder to charities and the third was a direct charitable trust. Rodney's stock portfolio included shares of Eastman Kodak (EK) stock, with a date of death value of almost $1.8 million or approximately $ 135 per share; the EK shares represented slightly more than 71% of the portfolio's total value.

Apart from selling 800 EK shares to settle estate obligations, Lincoln First Bank, the executor, still held the remaining EK shares when it filed its initial accounting for 1973–1980 to which Cynthia and the New York Attorney General (as representative of the charities) objected. At the time of the accounting, the price per share of EK stock was about $ 47 a share.

Cynthia died in 1986. Her executor and the New York Attorney General further objected to the bank's accounts as Rodney's executor for the period 1981–1994.]....

Following a trial on the objections, the Surrogate found [and the Appellate Division agreed] that petitioner, under the circumstances, had acted imprudently and should have divested the estate of the high concentration of Kodak stock by August 9, 1973....

....

I. Petitioner's Liability

Petitioner argues that New York law does not permit a fiduciary to be surcharged for imprudent management of a trust for failure to diversify in the absence of additional elements of hazard, and that it relied upon, and complied with, this rule in administering the estate. Relying on Matter of Balfe (152 Misc 739, 749, mod 245 App Div 22), petitioner claims that elements of hazard can be capsulized into deficiencies in the following investment quality factors: "(i) the capital structure of the company; (ii) the competency of its management; (iii) whether the company is a seasoned issuer of stock with a history of profitability; (iv) whether the company has a history of paying dividends; (v) whether the company is an industry leader; (vi) the expected future direction of the company's business; and (vii) the opinion of investment bankers and analysts who follow the company's stock." Evaluated under these criteria, petitioner asserts, the concentration of Kodak stock at issue in this case, that is, of an acknowledged "blue chip" security popular with investment advisors and many mutual funds, cannot be found an imprudent investment on August 9, 1973 as a matter of law. In our view, a fiduciary's duty of investment prudence in holding a concentration of one security may not be so rigidly limited.

New York followed the prudent person rule of investment during the period of petitioner's administration of the instant estate. This rule provides that "[a] fiduciary holding funds for investment may invest the same in such securities as would be acquired by prudent [persons] of discretion and intelligence in such matters who are seeking a reasonable income and the preservation of their capital" (EPTL 11-2.2 [a] [1]).[16]

Codified in 1970 (see L 1970, ch 321), the prudent person rule's New York common-law antecedents can be traced to King v. Talbot (40 NY 76), wherein this Court stated:

> "[T]he trustee is bound to employ such diligence and such prudence in the care and management [of the trust], as in general, prudent men of discretion and intelligence in such matters, employ in their own like affairs.
>
> "[T]his necessarily excludes all speculation, all investments for an uncertain and doubtful rise in the market, and, of course, *everything that does not take into view the nature and object of the trust, and the consequences of a mistake in the selection of the investment to be made....*
>
> "[T]he *preservation of the fund, and the procurement of a just income therefrom, are primary objects* of the creation of the trust itself, and are to be primarily regarded" *id.*, at 85-86 [emphasis supplied]).

---

16. The recently enacted Prudent Investor Act requires a trustee "to diversify assets unless the trustee reasonably determines that it is in the interests of the beneficiaries not to diversify, taking into account the purposes and terms and provisions of the governing instrument" (EPTL 11-2.3[b][3][C]). The act applies to investments "made or held" by a trustee on or after January 1, 1995 and, thus, does not apply to the matter before us (EPTL 11-2.3[a]).]

No precise formula exists for determining whether the prudent person standard has been violated in a particular situation; rather, the determination depends on an examination of the facts and circumstances of each case (see *Purdy v. Lynch*, 145 NY 462, 475; see also, *Matter of Hahn*, 62 NY2d 821, 824). In undertaking this inquiry, the court should engage in "'a balanced and perceptive analysis of [the fiduciary's] consideration and action in light of the history of each individual investment, viewed at the time of its action or its omission to act'" *Matter of Donner*, 82 NY2d 574, 585 [*quoting Matter of Bank of N.Y.*, 35 NY2d 512, 519]). And, while a court should not view each act or omission aided or enlightened by hindsight (*see Matter of Bank of N.Y., supra*, at 519; *see also, Matter of Clark*, 257 NY 132, 136; *Purdy v. Lynch, supra*, at 475–476), a court may, nevertheless, examine the fiduciary's conduct over the entire course of the investment in determining whether it has acted prudently (*see Matter of Donner, supra*, at 585–586). Generally, whether a fiduciary has acted prudently is a factual determination to be made by the trial court (*see id.; see also, Matter of Rothko*, 43 NY2d 305, 318; *Matter of Hubbell*, 302 NY 246).

As the foregoing demonstrates, the very nature of the prudent person standard dictates against any absolute rule that a fiduciary's failure to diversify, in and of itself, constitutes imprudence, as well as against a rule invariably immunizing a fiduciary from its failure to diversify in the absence of some selective list of elements of hazard, such as those identified by petitioner. Indeed, in various cases, courts have determined that a fiduciary's retention of a high concentration of one asset in a trust or estate was imprudent without reference to those elements of hazard (see *Matter of Donner*, supra, at 585–586; *see also, Matter of Curtiss*, 261 App Div 964, *affd without opn* 286 NY 716; *Cobb v. Gramatan Natl. Bank & Trust Co.*, 261 App Div 1086). The inquiry is simply whether, under all the facts and circumstances of the particular case, the fiduciary violated the prudent person standard in maintaining a concentration of a particular stock in the estate's portfolio of investments.

Moreover, no court has stated that the limited elements of hazard outlined by petitioner are the only factors that may be considered in determining whether a fiduciary has acted prudently in maintaining a concentrated portfolio. Again, as commentators have noted, one of the primary virtues of the prudent person rule "*lies in its lack of specificity*, as this permits the propriety of the trustee's investment decisions to be measured in light of the business and economic circumstances existing at the time they were made" (Laurino, *Investment Responsibility of Professional Trustees*, 51 St. John's L Rev 717, 723 [1977] [emphasis supplied]).

Petitioner's restrictive list of hazards omits such additional factors to be considered under the prudent person rule by a trustee in weighing the propriety of any investment decision, as: "the amount of the trust estate, the situation of the beneficiaries, the trend of prices and of the cost of living, the prospect of inflation and of deflation" (Restatement [Second] of Trusts § 227, comment e). Other pertinent factors are the marketability of the investment and possible tax consequences (id., comment o). The trustee must weigh all of these investment factors as they affect the principal objects of the testator's or settlor's bounty, as between income beneficiaries and remainder persons, including decisions regarding "whether to apportion the investments between high-yield or high-growth securities". . . .

Moreover, and especially relevant to the instant case, the various factors affecting the prudence of any particular investment must be considered in the light of the "circumstances of the trust itself rather than [merely] the integrity of the particular investment" (9C Rohan, NY Civ Prac-EPTL P 11-2.2 [5], at 11-513, n 106 [1996]). As stated in a leading treatise:

> "[t]he trustee should take into consideration the circumstances of the particular trust that he is administering, both as to the size of the trust estate and the requirements of the beneficiaries. He should consider each investment *not as an isolated transaction but in its relation to the whole of the trust estate*" (3 Scott, Trusts § 227.12, at 477 [4th ed]).

Our case law is entirely consistent with the foregoing authorities. Thus, in *Matter of Bank of N. Y.* (35 NY2d 512, supra), although we held that a trustee remains responsible for imprudence as to each individual investment in a trust portfolio, we stated:

> "The *record of any individual investment is not to be viewed exclusively, of course, as though it were in its own water-tight compartment*, since to some extent individual investment decisions may properly be affected by considerations of the performance of the fund as an entity, as in the instance, for example, of individual security decisions based in part on considerations of diversification of the fund or of capital transactions to achieve sound tax planning for the fund as a whole. The focus of inquiry, however, is nonetheless on the individual security as such and factors relating to the entire portfolio are to be weighed only along with others in reviewing the prudence of the particular investment decisions" (35 NY2d, at 517, *supra* [emphasis supplied]).

Thus, the elements of hazard petitioner relies upon as demonstrating that, as a matter of law, it had no duty to diversify, suffer from two major deficiencies under the prudent person rule. First, petitioner's risk elements too narrowly and strictly define the scope of a fiduciary's responsibility in making any individual investment decision, and the factors a fiduciary must consider in determining the propriety of a given investment.

A second deficiency in petitioner's elements of hazard list is that all of the factors relied upon by petitioner go to the propriety of an individual investment "exclusively . . . as though it were in its own water-tight compartment" *Matter of Bank of N. Y., supra*, at 517), which would encourage a fiduciary to treat each investment as an isolated transaction rather than "in its relation to the whole of the trust estate" (3 Scott, *op. cit.*, at 477). Thus, petitioner's criteria for elements of hazard would apply irrespective of the concentration of the investment security under consideration in the portfolio. That is, the existence of any of the elements of risk specified by petitioner in a given corporate security would militate against the investment even in a diversified portfolio, obviating any need to consider concentration as a reason to divest or refrain from investing. This ignores the market reality that, with respect to some investment vehicles, concentration itself may create or add to risk, and essentially takes lack of diversification out of the prudent person equation altogether.

Likewise, contrary to petitioner's alternative attack on the decisions below, neither the Surrogate nor the Appellate Division based their respective rulings holding petitioner liable on any absolute duty of a fiduciary to diversify. Rather, those courts determined that a surcharge was appropriate because maintaining a concentration in Kodak stock, under the circumstances presented, violated certain critical obligations of a fiduciary in making investment decisions under the prudent person rule. First, petitioner failed to consider the investment in Kodak stock in relation to the entire portfolio of the estate (*see Matter of Bank of N. Y., supra*, at 517; 3 Scott, op. cit., at 477), i.e., whether the Kodak concentration itself created or added to investment risk. The objectants' experts testified that even high quality growth stocks, such as Kodak, possess some degree of volatility because their market value is tied so closely to earnings projections (cf., Turano and Radigan, *op. cit.*, at 409). They further opined that the investment risk arising from that volatility is significantly exacerbated when a portfolio is heavily concentrated in one such growth stock.

Second, the evidence revealed that, in maintaining an investment portfolio in which Kodak represented 71% of the estate's stock holdings, and the balance was largely in other growth stocks, petitioner paid insufficient attention to the needs and interests of the testator's 72-year-old widow, the life beneficiary of three quarters of his estate, for whose comfort, support and anticipated increased medical expenses the testamentary trusts were evidently created. Testimony by petitioner's investment manager, and by the objectants' experts, disclosed that the annual yield on Kodak stock in 1973 was approximately 1.06%, and that the aggregate annual income from all estate stockholdings was $ 43,961, a scant 1.7% of the $ 2.5 million estate securities portfolio. Thus, retention of a high concentration of Kodak jeopardized the interests of the primary income [*54] beneficiary of the estate and led to the eventual need to substantially invade the principal of the marital testamentary trust.

Lastly, there was evidence in the record to support the findings below that, in managing the estate's investments, petitioner failed to exercise due care and the skill it held itself out as possessing as a corporate fiduciary (see *Matter of Donner*, 82 NY2d, at 578, *supra*; Restatement [Second] of Trusts § 227, Comment on Clause [a]). Notably, there was proof that petitioner (1) failed initially to undertake a formal analysis of the estate and establish an investment plan consistent with the testator's primary objectives; (2) failed to follow petitioner's own internal trustee review protocol during the administration of the estate, which advised special caution and attention in cases of portfolio concentration of as little as 20%; and (3) failed to conduct more than routine reviews of the Kodak holdings in this estate, without considering alternative investment choices, over a seven-year period of steady decline in the value of the stock.

Since, thus, there was evidence in the record to support the foregoing affirmed findings of imprudence on the part of petitioner, the determination of liability must be affirmed *Matter of Donner*, 82 NY2d, at 584, *supra*).

II. Date of Divestiture

As we have noted, in determining whether a fiduciary has acted prudently, a court may examine a fiduciary's conduct throughout the entire period during which the investment at issue was held (see *Matter of Donner*, 82 NY2d, at 585–586, *supra*). The court may then determine, within that period, the "reasonable time" within which divesture of the imprudently held investment should have occurred (see *Matter of Weston*, 91 NY 502, 510–511). What constitutes a reasonable time will vary from case to case and is not fixed or arbitrary (see *id.*, at 510–511). The test remains "the diligence and prudence of prudent and intelligent [persons] in the management of their own affairs" *id.*, at 511 [citations omitted]). Thus, in Donner, we upheld both the Surrogate's examination of the fiduciary's conduct throughout the entire period during which the investment at issue was retained in finding liability, and the Surrogate's selection of the date of the testator's death as the time when the trustee should have divested the estate of its substantial holdings in high-risk securities (82 NY2d, at 585-586, *supra*).

Again, there is evidentiary support in the record for the trial court's finding, affirmed by the Appellate Division, that a prudent fiduciary would have divested the estate's stock portfolio of its high concentration of Kodak stock by August 9, 1973, thereby exhausting our review powers on this issue. Petitioner's own internal documents and correspondence, as well as the testimony of Patterson, Young, and objectants' experts, establish that by that date, petitioner had all the information a prudent investor would have needed to conclude that the percentage of Kodak stock in the estate's stock portfolio was excessive and should have been reduced significantly, particularly in light of the estate's over-all investment portfolio and the financial requirements of Mrs. Janes and the charitable beneficiaries.

III. Damages

[The Court of Appeals agreed with the Appellate Division's measure of damages.

. . . .

Accordingly, the order of the Appellate Division should be affirmed, without costs.

Chief Judge Kaye and Judges Titone, Bellacosa, Smith, Ciparick and Wesley concur.

Order affirmed, without costs.

Notes

1. Although the *Janes* court did not hold that a fiduciary subject to the prudent man standard has the duty to diversify, the majority position and the position taken under the Restatement (Second) of Trusts § 228 is that there is the duty to diversify unless under the circumstances diversification would be imprudent. As will be seen, a trustee has the general duty to diversify under the prudent investor standard.

2. Compare the more forgiving approach by courts when a statute or instrument authorizes a fiduciary to retain initial assets. *See, e.g., In re Williams*, 631 N.W.2d 398 (Minn. Ct. App. 2001) (no surcharge for failing to diversify initial trust holdings because Minnesota prudent man statute authorizes retention of original assets); *In re Chase Manhattan Bank*, 26 A.D.3d 824 (N.Y. 2006) (no surcharge for retaining stock where testator provided that stock should not be disposed of for purposes of diversification). However, liability may attach if the fiduciary fails to exercise prudence in managing the initial investments. *See Will of Dumont*, 791 N.Y.S.2d 868 (Sur. Ct. 2004) (imprudence in retaining stock justified $20 million surcharge against corporate trustee), *rev'd, In re Chase Manhattan Bank*, 26 A.D.3d 824 (N.Y. 2006) (imprudence could not be found based on hindsight analysis).

3. Sometimes diversification can be risky and imprudent under the circumstances. A trustee's decision to diversify a trust funded solely with one stock caused significant capital gains when the stock was sold and the proceeds invested in the bank's common trust fund. In part because of the conflict of the bank investing in its own fund, the court in *Malachowski v. Bank One, Indianapolis*, 590 N.E.2d 559 (Ind. 1992), said the beneficiaries stated a claim for breach of fiduciary duty. *See also In re Scheidmantel*, 868 A.2d 464 (Pa. Super. Ct. 2005) (decision to diversify and method of diversification not only imprudent but grossly negligent).

4. Diversification may not be required, indeed non-diversification may be warranted, based on special circumstances. *See, e.g., In re Trust Created by Inman*, 693 N.W.2d 514 (Neb. 2005) (sale of family farm not allowed based on special importance to beneficiaries).

5. Under the prudent person standard, a trustee can properly invest in fixed income even if the investment erodes the value of the principal since the duty is to preserve the principal. *See, e.g., In re Trust Created by Martin*, 664 N.W.2d 923 (Neb. 2003).

6. Beneficiaries may challenge a trustee's investment strategy because it is not impartial. *See In re Dwight's Trust*, 128 N.Y.S.2d 23 (Sup. Ct. 1952) (trustee surcharged for selling U.S. Savings Bonds at a loss in order to purchase tax-exempt securities for a high-tax-bracket life tenant); *Dennis v. Rhode Island Hosp. Trust Nat'l Bank*, 744 F.2d 893 (1st Cir. 1984) (trustee surcharged in part for maximizing income at the expense of failing to maintain rental property). *But cf. Law v. Law*, 753 A.2d 443 (Del. 2000) (taking into account all facts and circumstances, no breach of duty of impartiality to remainder beneficiaries when trustees invested solely in tax exempt securities).

7. Trustee investment decisions might also involve conflicts of interest between the trustee and the beneficiaries. *See In re Hubbell*, 97 N.E.2d 888 (N.Y. 1951). Sophie left close corporation stock to her husband, Henry, who was both a trustee and president-director-shareholder of the company. Henry as trustee sold stock to the company. With fewer shares outstanding, Henry increased his personal share of the company's stock. The remainderman who would have lost control of the company sought, and got, a surcharge. *See also In re Estate of Swiecicki*, 460 N.E.2d 91 (Ill. App.

Ct. 1984) (bank serving as guardian surcharged for holding a ward's funds in savings accounts or certificates of deposit at the bank); *but see Cleveland Trust Co. v. Eaton*, 256 N.E.2d 198 (Ohio 1970) (a corporate fiduciary which owns its own shares may vote those shares in elections to the corporate board of directors).

SEC Rule 10b-5 poses problems for trustees because it makes insiders liable for trading on the basis of material "inside information." The commercial department of a corporate trustee may learn inside information about a client's new product or impending loss. If the trust department learned the facts and traded the client's stock, it could violate 10b-5. If it knew and did not react, it could violate its duty to make prudent investments. Banks typically respond to this dilemma by barring the flow of insider information from the commercial to the trust department. *See generally* Daniel M. Schuyler, *From Sulphur to Surcharge? Corporate Trustee Exposure under SEC Rule 10b-5*, 67 Nw. U. L. Rev. 42 (1972).

8. Are investments for foreign companies appropriate for domestic trustees?

Selected References

Jeffrey N. Gordon, *The Puzzling Persistence of the Constrained Prudent Man Rule*, 62 N.Y.U. L. Rev. 52 (1987).

Stephen P. Johnson, *Trustee Investment: The Prudent Person Rule or Modern Portfolio Theory, You Make the Choice*, 44 Syracuse L. Rev. 1175 (1993).

2. The Prudent Investor

One response to the development of modern portfolio theory was the American Law Institute's decision to revise the Restatement of Trusts and articulate a new "Prudent Investor Rule." Professor Halbach served as reporter for the project.

Restatement (Third) of Trusts

§ 90. General Standard of Prudent Investment

The trustee is under a duty to the beneficiaries to invest and manage the funds of the trust as a prudent investor would, in light of the purposes, terms, distribution requirements, and other circumstances of the trust.

(a) This standard requires the exercise of reasonable care, skill, and caution, and is to be applied to investments not in isolation but in the context of the trust portfolio and as a part of an overall investment strategy, which should incorporate risk and return objectives reasonably suitable to the trust.

(b) In making and implementing investment decisions, the trustee has a duty to diversify the investments of the trust unless, under the circumstances, it is prudent not to do so.

(c) In addition, the trustee must:

(1) conform to fundamental fiduciary duties of loyalty (§ 78) and impartiality (§ 79);

(2) act with prudence in deciding whether and how to delegate authority and in the selection and supervision of agents (§ 80); and

(3) incur only costs that are reasonable in amount and appropriate to the investment responsibilities of the trusteeship (§ 88).

(d) The trustee's duties under this Section are subject to the rule of § 91, dealing primarily with contrary investment provisions of a trust or statute.

Edward C. Halbach, Jr., *Trust Investment Law in the Third Restatement*

77 Iowa L. Rev. 1151, 1154–55, 1167–70 (1992)

The prudent investor project was undertaken with a clear recognition that trust investment law should reflect and accommodate current knowledge and concepts in the financial community. While seeking to incorporate the lessons of modern experience and research, a scrupulous effort was made to avoid either endorsing or excluding particular theories of economics or investment. In addition, an important objective in drafting the prudent investor rule was to preserve the flexibility necessary for the incorporation of future learning and developments. Therefore, Restatement doctrine should be carefully limited to draw only on consistent themes of legitimate financial theories and to express only those principles upon which general agreement exists.

In short, an effort was made to provide but not to exceed what was required to articulate standards by which the conduct of trustees can be guided and judged, while also protecting settlor objectives and the interests of trust beneficiaries. The rules are designed to be general and flexible enough to adapt to the changes that may occur over time in the financial world. They are also designed to be flexible enough to allow prudent use of any investments and techniques that are suitable to the different abilities of different trustees and to the varied purposes and circumstances of the diverse array of trusts to which the prudent investor rule will inevitably apply.

Accordingly, the prudent investor rule is intended to liberate expert trustees to pursue challenging, rewarding, non-traditional strategies when appropriate to a particular trust. It is also designed to provide unsophisticated trustees with reasonably clear guidance to practical courses of investment that are readily identifiable, expectedly rewarding and broadly adaptable.

The terms of the prudent investor rule in the new Restatement begin by returning, with modest reformulation, to the essence of the Harvard College dictum in an effort to restore that opinion's originally intended generality and flexibility. The terms of the rule then continue in an effort to modernize trust investment law and to make its underlying principles and the relevant financial considerations more readily understandable. This was intended to discourage a repetition of earlier difficulties and temptations in application and elaboration.

The language of the rule and the accompanying commentary were thus designed to preserve the law's adaptability. The mandates of the prudent investor rule were confined to those that seemed essential to: (i) a meaningful duty of prudence, based on its traditional elements of care, skill and caution; (ii) the protection and implementation of fiduciary goals; and (iii) supplying useful guidance to trustees, their counsel and courts, taking account of the varied needs and objectives of individual trusts and trustees. . . .

A. Duty with Respect to Portfolio Risk Level

Risk, in a comprehensive sense, is unavoidable in trust investing, and the type of risk that is rewarded by a realistic prospect of increased return is not inherently bad. Because of the direct relationship between this "market risk" and portfolio return expectations, reasonable decisions about the degree of risk become an integral part of a trustee's ongoing investment strategy. It is thus implicit in the fiduciary duties of care and caution that trustees should make conscious judgments from time to time concerning a suitable overall level of risk and return to be pursued for each portfolio they administer. Each judgment should be based on an assessment of the particular trust's distribution requirements and risk tolerance, together with a consideration of its specific terms, general purposes and pertinent circumstances.

Case law and prior Restatements have tended to condemn "speculation" and excessive risk without definition, as if an objectionable degree of risk can be recognized without regard to a trust's circumstances and objectives. Individual trusts have such different purposes and obligations that anything approaching a universal standard of risk for trust portfolios is unwarranted.

Furthermore, beneficiaries can be disserviced by excessive conservatism as well as by excessive risk taking. Opportunities for gain and a trust's overall return requirements must be balanced against its and the beneficiaries' capacity to withstand the inevitable, but not unalterable, hazards of an adverse outcome over any given period of time. Outcomes are particularly uncertain over relatively short periods, justifying the prudent investor rule's emphasis on investment time horizons and other aspects of a trust's tolerance for volatility. Because of the different degrees of risk implicit in permitting significant variations in trust risk-return objectives, the new Restatement emphasizes that prudence is tested by the reasonableness of the trustee's conduct and not by the performance of the trust's investments.

The prudent investor rule does not, however, abandon the trust law's traditional preference for investment conservatism. It simply attempts to recognize and take account of the great diversity of the situations trust investment law will inevitably govern. Accordingly, even though a general requirement of conservatism continues normally to be inferred from the duty to use caution, the degree of conservatism required and thus the overall degree of risk permitted for a particular trust is ultimately a matter for interpretation and reasonable judgment on a trust-by-trust basis.

B. Duty to Diversify

Sound diversification is fundamental to the management of uncompensated risk. It is, therefore, ordinarily required of trustees, not simply as a means of moderating the dangers inherent in investing but as a means of minimizing uncompensated risk. The importance of diversification is consistently stressed in investment literature ranging from popular advice columns to the most scholarly, and is regularly emphasized in case law, although not always in terms of a legal requirement. . . .

. . . The commentary [to § 90] explains that the ordinary duty [to diversify] applies unless the obligations of both prudent risk management and impartiality can be satisfied without diversifying or unless special considerations make it undesirable to diversify in a particular trust situation. These special considerations might be adverse tax consequences, an inability to realize by sale the full value the trust property has within the particular trust and family setting, or the property's special relation to settlor objectives or properly relevant interests of the beneficiaries.

Asset allocation decisions are a central feature of investment strategy and a starting point in formulating a plan of diversification. They deal with the categories of investments to be included in a trust portfolio and the proportions of a trust estate to be allocated to each. . . .

Basic asset classifications might begin with cash equivalents, debenture and asset-backed debt securities, real estate, and corporate stocks. Both debt and equity categories might further be divided by their general risk-reward or income-versus-growth characteristics, by their tax status, by the domestic, foreign or other characteristics of the issuers, and the like. There is no defined set of asset categories to be considered by fiduciary investors, nor does a trustee's general duty to diversify investments assume that all basic categories are to be represented in a trust's portfolio. In fact, given the wide variety of defensible investment strategies and the wide variations in trust purposes, terms, obligations and other circumstances, the diversification concerns of new section 90 do not necessarily preclude an asset allocation plan that emphasizes a particular category of investments, provided the requirements of caution and impartiality can be accommodated in a manner suitable to the objectives of the trust.

. . . [E]vents affecting the economy do not affect the value of all investments in the same way, so that effective diversification depends not only on the number of assets in a trust portfolio but also on the extent to which their responses to economic events tend to cancel one another. Thus, an otherwise dubious, volatile investment can make a significant contribution to risk management if the shifts in its returns tend not to correlate with the movements of other investments in the portfolio. This is a major reason why diversification is to be valued by trustees, and why the prudence of a particular investment is to be judged by its role in the trust portfolio, rather than in isolation. With pooled investing currently available for nearly all categories of assets, thorough diversification is practical for virtually all trustees, thereby facilitating efforts to create a portfolio that carries only the rewarded or "market" element of risk.

Notes and Questions

1. Modern Portfolio Theory also prompted the Uniform Prudent Investor Act (1994). 7B Unif. Law. Ann. § 281 (2000). Section 2(c) provides the following list of "circumstances that the trustee shall consider in investing and managing trust assets":

(1) general economic conditions;

(2) the possible effect of inflation or deflation;

(3) the expected tax consequences of investment decisions or strategies;

(4) the role that each investment or course of action plays within the overall trust portfolio, which may include financial assets, interests in closely held enterprises, tangible and intangible personal property, and real property;

(5) the expected total return from income and the appreciation of capital;

(6) other resources of the beneficiaries;

(7) needs for liquidity, regularity of income, and preservation or appreciation of capital; and

(8) an asset's special relationship or special value, if any, to the purposes of the trust or to one or more of the beneficiaries.

2. All jurisdictions have now enacted the Uniform Prudent Investor Act or some variant thereof. Significantly, the Act applies, as a default rule, to both newly created trusts and, for periods after the date of enactment, to trusts that were in existence before the enactment of the Uniform Prudent Investor Act. Section 1(b) of the Act allows a settlor to eliminate, or otherwise override, duties under the prudent investor act. *See e.g. Carter v. Carter*, 985 N.E.2d 1146 (Il. App. 2012) (duty to diversify eliminated so investment in only tax-free municipals permitted).

3. The Uniform Prudent Management of Institutional Funds Act (UPMIFA), which was approved in 2006, generally adopts the UPIA as the standard for institutions managing charitable trusts and charitable corporations.

4. Sometimes preserving purchasing power over time is particularly important. For example, because charitable trusts often are designed to run forever, their trustees must balance the generation of current income with the need to maintain the principal so it can provide support indefinitely. *See Woodward School for Girls v. City of Quincy*, 13 N.E.3d 579 (Mass. 2014) (trustee of charitable trust breached duty of prudence by failing to take inflation into account to preserve principal and thereby assure benefits for income beneficiary). Should that principle also apply to individuals? For example, would it be wise to recommend that your clients consider including trust language directing the trustee to preserve the purchasing power of both the principal and the income beneficiaries?

5. The Prudent Investor Act has begun to come under attack primarily because it encourages trustees to engage in risk taking which can seriously harm trust beneficiaries who have no remedies as long as the trustees acted prudently. *See generally*

Stewart E. Sterk, *Rethinking Trust Law Reform: How Prudent Is Modern Prudent Investor Doctrine?*, 95 Cornell L. Rev. 851 (2010).

Problems Involving the Prudent Investor Rule

1. Ron is a longtime client who enjoys speculation, partly for the fun of the bet. He uses part of his portfolio to "play the market" and would like his trustee to have the flexibility to do the same. Draft language which will satisfy Ron's desire to encourage speculation and the trustee's need for protection against liability.

2. You live and practice law in Hopewell, a community of 10,000, the county seat of a rural county. Thirty miles away is a major metropolitan area, and many Hopewell residents commute there to work. You represent Richard, the income beneficiary of a trust for which Hopewell Bank serves as trustee. Over the last several years, the trust has produced an income yield significantly below the average income yield of trusts managed by major banks in the metropolitan area. Hopewell Bank's trust officer, in spite of Richard's repeated urgings, refuses to invest more than a small percentage of the trust funds in other than government bonds and first mortgages. He also refuses to resign to permit appointment of another trustee. Should Richard sue to force broader investments, or to remove the trustee? What evidence would you develop to support such a suit?

3. Jane's Uncle Henry named her as trustee of a relatively modest fund to help pay college expenses of his grandchildren. Jane divided the assets among a checking account, a savings account, and certificates of deposit. Eight years later, Mary, the first grandchild to go to college, complains to you that the fund has hardly grown since Henry died.

(a) What advice do you offer Mary?

(b) How would you have advised Jane?

4. Gilbert, a longtime client, is the trustee of his mother's testamentary trust, which pays income to Gilbert and his siblings for their lives and then distributes the principal to their children. Advise him about whether to make the following investments:

(a) Solartel. This is a new company formed to produce and market solar powered telephones. According to the local financial page, the stock is predicted to be a hot seller because of expected heavy demand for the product. Solartel's president is the device's inventor.

(b) Suburban farm land. The city is growing northwest, and Gilbert spotted a "for sale" sign on a farm just beyond the closest suburb.

(c) A downtown office building. After weathering some defections to the suburbs over the last few years, downtown has stabilized. The building has a few open spaces, but several established tenants.

Selected References

Robert J. Aalberts & Percy S. Poon, *Derivatives and the Modern Prudent Investor Rule: Too Risky or Too Necessary?*, 67 Ohio St. L.J. 525 (2006).

Fredric J. Bendremer, *Modern Portfolio Theory and International Investments under the Uniform Prudent Investor Act*, 35 Real Prop. Prob. & Tr. J. 791 (2001).

Alyssa A. DiRusso & Kathleen M. Sablone, *Statutory Techniques for Balancing the Financial Interests of Trust Beneficiaries*, 39 U.S.F. L. Rev. 261 (2005).

Joel C. Dobris, *Speculations on the Idea of "Speculation" in Trust Investing: An Essa* y, 39 Real Prop. Prob. & Tr. J. 439 (2004).

Joel C. Dobris, *SRI—Shibboleth or Canard (Socially Responsible Investing, That Is)*, 42 Real Prop. Tr. & Est. L.J. 755 (2008)

Trent S. Kiziah et al., *The Persistent Preference for Inception Assets*, 40 ACTEC L.J. 151 (2014).

Beavis Longstreet, Modern Investment Strategy and the Prudent Man Rule (1986).

Stacy K. Mullaney, *Complex Securities Laws and the Eligibility of Trusts to Make Alternative Investments*, 24 Prob. & Prop. 38 (Nov./Dec. 2010).

John Jeffrey Pankauski & Robert E. Conner, *Looking for there Exists: A Fiduciary's Sell Strategy Under the Prudent Investor Act*, 20 Prob. & Prop. 6, 40 (Nov./Dec. 2006).

William Sanders, *Resolving the Conflict Between Fiduciary Duties and Socially Responsible Investing*, 35 Pace L. Rev. 535 (2015).

Max M. Schanzenbach & Robert H. Sitkoff, *Did Reform of Prudent Trust Investment Laws Change Trust Portfolio Allocation?*, 50 J.L. & Econ. 681 (2007).

Stewart E. Sterk, *Rethinking Trust Law Reform: How Prudent Is Modern Prudent Investor Doctrine?*, 95 Cornell L. Rev. 851 (2010).

3. Delegation and Direction

Trust management has become increasingly complex. Indeed, in many trusts one or even more than one trustee cannot be expected to handle all of the trustee functions. As a result, multi-participant trusts are becoming more common. Delegation of certain duties provides one solution but the trustee or trustees are still required to monitor the performance of the delegee and can be liable for properly doing so. Alternatives to slicing and dicing trustee functions include the use of directed trusts and trust protectors.

a. Delegation

Reversing the earlier prohibition on delegation to agents other than for ministerial acts or when the trustee had no reasonable alternative, Restatement (Third) of Trusts § 80 permits delegation to an agent by a trustee if "a prudent person of comparable skill might delegate those responsibilities to others." *Accord* UTC § 807. This change was precipitated by the delegation developments in the prudent investor area as explained below.

John H. Langbein, *Reversing the Nondelegation Rule of Trust-Investment Law*

59 Mo. L. Rev. 105, 110 (1994)

The nondelegation rule has been a familiar feature of the doctrinal landscape of the Anglo-American law of trusts. In the formulation of the Restatement of Trusts (Second) of 1959, the rule places the trustee "under a duty to the beneficiary not to delegate to others the doing of acts which the trustee can reasonably be required personally to perform." The nondelegation rule was thought to apply with particular force to the trustee's investment responsibilities. The Restatement (Second) says flatly: "A trustee cannot properly delegate to another power to select investments."

The new Restatement of Trusts (Third): Prudent Investor Rule, completed in 1992, rejects the nondelegation rule of the 1959 Restatement.... Not only does the Restatement (Third) approve delegation, it imposes upon the trustee a positive duty to act prudently in considering "whether and how to delegate" investment functions....

The case for permitting trustees to delegate various aspects of trust administration, especially investment functions, is straightforward. The circumstances of modern life that have resulted in ever greater specialization and expertise elsewhere in economic and administrative life affect trust administration as well. The trust originated as a relatively passive or inactive stakeholder's device, primarily used for conveying real property within the family. Over the last century or so, awesome changes have occurred in the patterns of private wealth-holding. When ancestral land was the characteristic trust asset, trust administration required of the trustee relatively little expertise or authority. Trustees were mostly stakeholders, and the family lived on the estate and managed its affairs. Today, by contrast, financial instruments have become the typical assets of the trust, and these assets require active fiduciary administration. Managing a portfolio of marketable securities is as demanding a specialty as stomach surgery or nuclear engineering. There is no more reason to expect the ordinary individual serving as a trustee to possess the requisite investment expertise than to expect ordinary citizens to possess expertise in gastroenterology or atomic science.

It is inevitable, therefore, that well-intentioned trustees will seek out and rely upon outside advisors in the conduct of the investment function. When the law forbids the trustee from delegating the investment function, the trustee engages expert advice but purports to make an independent decision about whether to follow that advice. If the investment is subsequently challenged, the legal dispute then concerns the delegation question—that is, "Did the trustee exercise a judgment independent of the advisor?" By contrast, when trust law permits the trustee to delegate investment responsibilities to outside professionals, the delegation doctrine directs attention to a more useful question, which is whether the trustee used due care in selecting, instructing, and monitoring the agent. The traditional rule forbidding delegation disserved trust beneficiaries by preventing open discussion of the standards and safeguards appropriate to delegation.

Uniform Prudent Investor Act

Section 9. Delegation of Investment and Management Functions.

(a) A trustee may delegate investment and management functions that a prudent trustee of comparable skills could properly delegate under the circumstances. The trustee shall exercise reasonable care, skill, and caution in:

(1) selecting an agent;

(2) establishing the scope and terms of the delegation, consistent with the purposes and terms of the trust; and

(3) periodically reviewing the agent's actions in order to monitor the agent's performance and compliance with the terms of the delegation.

(b) In performing a delegated function, an agent owes a duty to the trust to exercise reasonable care to comply with the terms of the delegation.

(c) A trustee who complies with the requirements of subsection (a) is not liable to the beneficiaries or to the trust for the decisions or actions of the agent to whom the function was delegated.

(d) By accepting the delegation of a trust function from the trustee of a trust that is subject to the law of this State, an agent submits to the jurisdiction of the courts of this State.

Comment

This section of the Act reverses the much-criticized rule that forbad trustees to delegate investment and management functions.

Professor Sterk seriously questions the wisdom of allowing trustees to delegate their investment responsibilities.

Stewart E. Sterk, *Rethinking Trust Law Reform: How Prudent Is Modern Prudent Investor Doctrine?*

95 Cornell L. Rev. 851, 899–900, 903 (2010)

Neither the Restatement (Third), . . . [Section 9 of] UPIA, nor the commentary that accompanied reform of the "no delegation" rule clearly stated the issue at stake: if a trustee delegates investment duties, who—the trustee or the trust beneficiaries—should bear the loss that results from the delegate's wrongdoing if the delegate proves insolvent or unavailable? . . . .

If the principal risk at issue is the risk of delegate insolvency, the natural question to start with is which party—the trustee or the trust beneficiaries—was in a better position to assess and avoid that risk? The issue is an easy one: the trustee selected the delegate and had the opportunity to investigate the delegate's background and financial condition, whereas the beneficiaries had no role in selecting or evaluating the delegate. Basic economic principles suggest placing the risk on the trustee—the party in the best position to avoid or to spread the risk. . . .

Are there countervailing reasons to place the risk of loss on the trust beneficiaries rather than on the trustee? The limited commentary on the liability issue emphasizes two incentives the new rule would generate. First, persons without investment expertise would be more willing to accept appointment as trustees. Second, trustees would become more willing to delegate investment responsibility to those with greater expertise. . . .

Although the justifications advanced for the rule authorizing delegation of investment responsibilities were all focused on the family member-trustee, the rule itself was broader in scope, applying equally to professional trustees and individual trustees. No persuasive reasons have been advanced for permitting professional trustees to avoid liability to trust beneficiaries by the device of delegating investment responsibility to investment advisors. Yet the Restatement (Third) and the UPIA sanction that result.

In a stable or rising market, most beneficiaries are unlikely to be hurt substantially by the Restatement (Third) rule. Actions for imprudent investing tend to be less frequent. Fewer investment advisors become insolvent—especially those prudently selected by the trustee. As a result, the Restatement (Third) rule does little harm. By contrast, in a falling market, in which investors are losing money and investment firms that cut corners to generate high returns now find themselves in serious financial straits, the Restatement (Third) rule does threaten to harm innocent beneficiaries without generating any obvious social benefits. The time has come to abandon that rule and replace it with one that entitles a trustee to seek and to pay for investment advice but leaves the trustee as a guarantor for any breaches committed by the investment advisor.

---

b. Direction

In contrast with delegation, direction involves the settlor empowering a person to direct that a trustee follow that person's directions with respect to investments and possibly other trustee functions, including other administrative duties and where applicable, discretionary distribution decisions. For example, the settlor might wish to have a family member serve as trustee but have a third person, a trust investment advisor, direct the trustee on making investments. Or, the settlor might want to have a corporate trustee but provide that a family member can direct the trustee on discretionary trust distributions.

There are two important issues in the directed trust area, which typically arise under directed-trustee statutes.[17] The first, which ultimately involves the liability of a directed trustee for actions or inactions of a trust advisor, is whether the directed trustee has some duty to ensure that the trust advisor's directions are appropriate or whether the directed trustee has the absolute duty to follow the trust advisor's directions. The default rule of UTC § 808(b) is that a directed trustee must follow the advisor's direction "unless the attempted exercise is manifestly contrary to the terms of the trust or the trustee knows the attempted exercise would constitute a serious breach of a fiduciary duty that the person holding the power owes to the beneficiaries of the trust." However, the comments to UPC § 808 provide that the settlor may require that the directed trustee "must accept the decision of the power holder without question," thereby overriding any duties on the part of the directed trustee. *But cf.* 3d Rest. Trusts § 75 (providing limited duties that cannot be overridden).

A few states have specific directed-trustee statutes. *See, e.g.*, Fla. Stat. § 736.0703 (duty not to follow direction if directed trustee has actual knowledge that advisor engaged in willful misconduct). In at least South Dakota and Wyoming, the directed trustee effectively has an absolute duty to follow the advisor's direction. *See* S.D. Codified Laws § 55-1B-2 and Wyo. Stat. § 4-10-808. In other words, the directed trustee will not be liable for following the trust advisor's directions.

The second important issue in directed trusteeships is whether the trust advisor is a fiduciary.[18] If the trust advisor is a fiduciary, then the trust beneficiaries or trustees should be able to obtain redress if the advisor breaches a fiduciary duty within the scope of the advisor's powers. *See, e.g., Matter of Beatrice B. Davis Family Heritage Trust*, 388 P.3d 964 (Nev. 2017) (by accepting role as trust advisor over Nevada trust, nonresident advisor can be sued in Nevada). Although a trust advisor is presumptively a fiduciary under UPC § 808(d), the comments to UPC § 808 allow a settlor to provide that the standards of a fiduciary do not apply

---

17. Section 75 of the Restatement (Third) of Trusts recognizes that a settlor may require a trustee to follow directions from a third party even if a jurisdiction does not have a directed-trustee statute, which is true in many states.

18. If the advisor has a power to direct for his or her sole benefit, the advisor does not hold the power in a fiduciary capacity. *See* 3d Rest. Trusts § 75, cmt. d.

to the advisor. Other states also allow a settlor to override the trust advisor's status as a fiduciary. *See, e.g.*, S.D. Codified Laws § 55-1B-4. On the other hand, other states mandatorily impose a fiduciary standard on a trust advisor. *See, e.g.*, N.H. Rev. Stat. Ann. § 564-B:12-1201(a) and Wyo. Stat. § 4-10-808(d). *Accord* 3d Rest. Trusts § 75, cmt. e.

Notes and Question

1. A liberal delegation rule could generate more business for investment companies. By 2040, $10 trillion may pass from one generation to the next, much of it in trust. If more individuals become trustees, investment companies will be offering to sell their own expertise. *See* Lynn Asinof, *Revised Standards May Make It Easier to Choose a Trustee for Your Estate*, Wall St. J., Jan. 16, 1995, at C1, col. 3.

2. Trustees act at their peril if they delegate jobs that they should do themselves. *See, e.g., Jacob v. Davis*, 738 A.2d 904 (Md. Ct. Spec. App. 1999) (trustee breached the duty not to delegate by allowing another trustee to make all the discretionary distribution decisions); *In re Acker*, 513 N.Y.S.2d 786 (App. Div. 1987) (trustee who held himself out as gift and estate tax expert liable for hiring accountant to prepare fiduciary income tax return).

3. Another recent development involves the use of trust protectors, who can be given a wide range of discretionary powers, including termination and modification powers. A few states have specific statutes dealing with trust protectors. *See, e.g.*, Alaska Stat. § 13.36.370 and S.D. Codified Laws § 55-1B-6. UTC § 808 provides the same rules for trust protectors as are provided for directed trusteeships. For example, unless the settlor provides otherwise, a trustee must follow the direction of a trust protector absent unusual circumstances; in addition, the trust protector is presumptively a fiduciary. *Cf.* 3d Rest. Trusts § 75. A recent case holds that a trust protector is a fiduciary. *See Robert T. McLean Irrevocable Trust v. Davis*, 283 S.W.3d 786 (Mo. Ct. App. 2009) (as a fiduciary, trust protector liable for failing to prevent trust losses incurred by a former trustee); *Robert T. McLean Irrevocable Trust*, 418 S.W.3d 482 (Mo. App. 2014) (after remand, directed verdict in favor of trust protector upheld because no damages resulted from any breach).

4. The settlor in *Minassian v. Rachins*, 152 So. 3d 719 (Fla. Dist. Ct. App. 2014), had included a provision granting the trust protector "sole and absolute discretion" to modify the trust terms to either benefit the beneficiaries *or* to further the settlor's intent. To resolve issues being litigated, the trust protector amended an ambiguous provision in a way that had the effect of disadvantaging some beneficiaries. Because the settlor had intended to avoid litigation, the court upheld the trust protector's approach.

5. Should a trustee's compensation be affected if a trust provides for a trust advisor or trust protector?

Uniform Directed Trust Act

The Uniform Law Commission will likely approve a Uniform Directed Trust Act, which will replace UTC § 808's treatment of directed trusts. Under the Uniform Act, trust directors, including advisors and protectors, will be treated as fiduciaries. A directed trustee will not be liable for following directions absent willful misconduct. The Act will also apply to trustees who are directed by other trustees.

Problem

Laurel's will established a trust for her daughter, Mary Jane, and her two grandchildren, Charles and Robert. Mary Jane was the trustee, but had no investment expertise. Charles, a stockbroker, offered to help. He made the investment decisions and also embezzled over $300,000 from the trust. Should Mary Jane be liable for the loss?

Selected References

Richard C. Ausness, *The Role of Trust Protectors in American Trust Law*, 45 Real Prop. Tr. & Est. L.J. 319 (2010).

Dennis I. Belcher, *Not My Fault-The Devil Made Me Do It! Responsibilities and Duties of a Delegating or Directed Trustee*, 41 Heckerling Inst. on Est. Plan. ch. 13 (2007).

John P.C. Duncan & Anita M. Sarafa, *Achieve the Promise-and Limit the Risk-of Multi-Participant Trusts*, 36 ACTEC L.J. 769 (2011).

Lawrence A. Frolik, *The Next Big Thing*, 50 Real Prop. Tr. & Est. L.J.267 (2015).

Al W. King III & Pierce H. McDowell III, *Delegated vs. Directed Trusts*, 145 Tr. & Est. 26 (July 2006).

Philip J. Ruce, *The Trustee and the Trust Protector: A Question of Fiduciary Power. Should a Trust Protector Be Held to a Fiduciary Standard?*, 59 Drake L. Rev. 67 (2010).

Stewart E. Sterk, *Rethinking Trust Law Reform: How Prudent Is Modern Prudent Investor Doctrine?*, 95 Cornell L. Rev. 851 (2010).

Stewart E. Sterk, *Trust Protectors, Agency Costs, and Fiduciary Duty*, 27 Cardozo L. Rev. 2761 (2006).

4. Settlor's Directions

One of the most important issues in trust law is to what extent may a settlor override a particular trustee duty. The Uniform Trust Code allows a settlor great freedom in overriding trustee duties but some duties cannot be overridden, in effect, trustees are mandatorily required to carry out certain duties. *See* UTC § 105 (default and mandatory rules). A most significant mandatory duty is contained in UTC § 105(b)(3) which bars a settlor from altering "the requirement that a trust and its terms be for the benefit of its beneficiaries, and that the trust have a purpose that is lawful, not contrary to public policy, and possible to achieve." As illustrated by the next case, the first question is whether the settlor effectively overrode a specific trustee duty. Thereafter, we will focus on the current debate whether the benefit-the-beneficiaries rule of UTC § 105(b)(3) applies to bar a settlor from changing the duty to diversify investments under the Prudent Investor Rule.[19]

Americans for the Arts v. Ruth Lilly Charitable Remainder Annuity Trust

855 N.E.2d 592 (Ind. Ct. App. 2006)

BAKER, JUDGE

The primary question presented by this appeal is whether National City Bank of Indiana (National City), as trustee of two charitable trusts created by Ruth Lilly's (Ruth) estate plan, was required to diversify the trust assets. Although as a general rule, trustees have a duty to diversify, the trust instrument may modify that duty by permitting the trustee to retain certain—or all—trust assets. Concluding that the relevant documents at issue herein sufficiently relieved National City of the duty to diversify the trust assets, we affirm the judgment of the trial court.

FACTS

[The case involves] two charitable remainder annuity trusts (CRATs) [that were created by National City, Ruth's conservators, with court approval][20] CRAT # 1 provides Ruth with a lifetime annuity and CRAT # 2 gives money to six of her nieces and nephews for five years. Both CRATs name the same three charities as remainder beneficiaries—appellant-respondent The Poetry Foundation (Poetry), which is to receive 35% of the remaining assets of the CRATs, appellant-respondent Lilly Endowment, Inc. (Lilly Endowment), which will also receive 35% of the remaining assets, and appellant-respondent Americans for the Arts (AFTA), which will receive 30% of the remaining assets. National City is the trustee of, and has sole investment discretion for, both trusts.

The language of the trust documents that is at issue in this case is contained in paragraph 10 of the CRATs and is the same in both documents. In pertinent part, paragraph 10(b) provides that, in its capacity as trustee of the CRATs, National City:

19. Section 27(2) of the Restatement (Third) of Trusts similarly advances the benefit-the-beneficiary rule. *See also* 3d Rest. Trusts § 90–92 (providing prudent investor rule).

20. A CRAT is a charitable trust that typically provides a minimum annuity to a non-charitable beneficiary with remainder to a qualified charitable organization. A CRAT is designed to obtain tax benefits.

shall have the following powers and rights and all others granted by law

> (b) *To retain indefinitely any property received by the trustee* and invest and reinvest the trust property in stocks, bonds, mortgages, notes, shares of stock of regulated investment companies or other property of any kind, real or personal, including interests in partnerships, limited liability companies, joint ventures, land trusts or other title-holding trusts, investment trusts or other business organizations as a limited or general partner, shareholder, creditor or otherwise, and *any investment made or retained by the trustee in good faith shall be proper despite any resulting risk or lack of diversification or marketability and although not of a kind considered by law suitable for trust investments.*

On January 18, 2002, the CRATs were funded as planned—entirely with Lilly stock—3,155,404 shares in CRAT # 1 and 657,376 shares in CRAT # 2. On that date, Lilly stock was selling at approximately $ 75 per share, giving the CRATs a combined initial value of approximately $ 286 million. By March 2002, National City had formulated a draft Investment Policy Statement for the CRATs, the purpose of which was "to identify and present the investment objectives, investment guidelines and performance measurement standards" for the CRATs' assets. Appellants' App. p. 2507–14. National City sold significant portions of the Lilly stock held by the CRATs by July 2002, and by October 2002, most of the Lilly stock—the value of which had declined significantly since January 2002—had been sold and the CRATs were fully diversified.

In November 2002, National City petitioned the probate court to approve of "its formulation and implementation of the diversification of the investment in Eli Lilly and Company stock held by the [CRATs]." Id. p. 183. Poetry and AFTA objected and counterclaimed, alleging that the bank's delay in diversifying was negligent, a breach of fiduciary duty, and a violation of the Indiana Uniform Prudent Investor Act (PIA),[21] and seeking to surcharge the bank for the alleged resulting loss to the CRATs.

III. Retention Clause

The appellants contend that the clause in the trust documents providing general authorization for National City to retain investments (the Retention Clause) does not override or nullify the statutory provision of the prudent investor rule requiring the trustee to diversify the trust assets. The Retention Clause, which is found at the beginning of paragraph 10(b) in the CRATs, provides that National City is empowered to "retain indefinitely any property received by the trustee . . . ."

The PIA provides generally that a trustee "shall invest and manage trust assets as a prudent investor would . . . ." Ind. Code § 30-4-3.5-2(a). The Act goes on to mandate that a trustee "shall diversify the investments of the trust unless the trustee reasonably determines that, because of special circumstances, the purposes of the trust are better served without diversifying." Id. § -3 (emphasis added). The PIA, however,

21. Ind. Code § 30-4-3.5-1 et seq.

also provides that the prudent investor rule "may be expanded, restricted, eliminated, or otherwise altered by the provisions of a trust. A trustee is not liable to a beneficiary to the extent that the trustee acted in reasonable reliance on the provision of the trust." Id. § -1(b).

The appellants concede that the prudent investor rule, including the duty to diversify, may be altered by the trust document. They insist, however, that in this case, the general power contained within the Retention Clause is insufficient to override the duty to diversify. They look first to the Restatement (Third) of Trusts, which provides as follows:

> A general authorization in an applicable statute or in the terms of the trust to retain investments received as part of a trust estate does not ordinarily abrogate the trustee's duty with respect to diversification or the trustee's general duty to act with prudence in investment matters.

Restatement (Third) of Trusts § 229 cmt. d. First, we observe that the Restatement is "not a statute whose precise wording is entitled to deference as an act of an equal branch of government." *PSI Energy, Inc. v. Roberts*, 829 N.E.2d 943, 958 (Ind. 2005). Furthermore, we observe that comment (d) goes on to provide that the terms of a trust "may permit the trustee to retain all of the investments made by the settlor, or a larger proportion of them than would otherwise be permitted." Thus, the Restatement (Third) of Trusts leaves open a comfortable window enabling the settlor to lessen the trustee's duty to diversify by including a clause to that effect in the trust instrument.

Turning next to case law, we observe that the issue presented here is one of first impression. But the appellants direct our attention to a number of cases that they claim provide a generally applicable rationale in support of the argument. In all of these cases, the court concluded that a general retention clause was insufficient to exempt the trustee from the duty to diversify and essentially required that the retention clause explicitly name the specific stock to be retained. After reviewing the cases, however, we conclude that they are nearly all inapposite to the situation presented here because they either involve stock that was in some way directly related to the trustee or an allegation that the trustee acted in bad faith. See *Robertson v. Central Jersey Bank & Trust Co.*, 47 F.3d 1268, 1271 (3rd Cir. 1995) (95% of trust assets were trustee's own corporate stock); *Rutanen v. Ballard*, 424 Mass. 723, 678 N.E.2d 133, 137-38 (Mass. 1997) (allegation that trustee acted in bad faith); *First Alabama Bank of Huntsville, N.A. v. Spragins*, 515 So.2d 962, 963-64 (Ala. 1987) (70% of trust assets were trustee's own corporate stock). Here, on the other hand, National City is in no way connected to Lilly nor have the appellants alleged that the bank acted in bad faith. Thus, the extra layer of protection and specificity that may be required in such cases is not needed here.

Recently, in *Wood v. U.S. Bank, N.A.*, the Ohio Court of Appeals considered a trust document that granted the trustee the power "[t]o retain any securities in the same form as when received, including shares of a corporate Trustee . . . , even though all of such securities are not of the class of investments a trustee may be permitted by law to make and to hold cash uninvested as they deem advisable and proper." 160 Ohio App. 3d 831, 2005 Ohio 2341, 828 N.E.2d 1072, 1074-75 (Ohio Ct. App. 2005). Notwithstanding the fact that the trust referenced the specific stock in question, the court held that "even if the trust document allows the trustee to 'retain' assets that would normally be suitable, the trustee's duty to diversify remains, unless there are special circumstances." *Id.* at 1074.

We observe, however, that the Wood court held that the trust instrument could have eliminated the duty to diversify if it had included the requisite authorizing language:

> Had [the settlor] wanted to eliminate [the trustee's] duty to diversify, he could simply have said so. He could have mentioned that duty in the retention clause. Or he could have included another clause specifically lessening the duty to diversify. But he did not. We hold that the language of a trust does not alter a trustee's duty to diversify unless the instrument creating the trust clearly indicates an intention to do so.

Id. at 1077-78 (emphasis added). Here, on the other hand, the CRATs explicitly eliminate the duty to diversify and exonerate the trustee for its failure to do so. Specifically, the documents authorize National City to "retain indefinitely" the trust assets and then proceed to provide explicitly that "any investment made or retained by the trustee in good faith shall be proper despite any resulting risk or lack of diversification . . . ." *Id.* p. 863–64 (emphasis added). Thus, the CRATs contain precisely the type of language suggested by the Wood court, inasmuch as they include a clause explicitly lessening the duty to diversify.

The record herein reveals no relationship between National City and the Lilly stock that was retained as an asset of the CRATs for a period of time. Furthermore, there is no allegation that National City acted in bad faith and no evidence supporting a conclusion that it engaged in self-dealing. Under these circumstances, we conclude that the general Retention Clause in the CRATs combined with the clause explicitly lessening the trustee's duty to diversify is sufficient to except National City from the default duty to diversify trust assets.

III. Exculpatory Clause

[The court also rejected the argument that the exculpatory clause applied since the clause could only apply to exculpate the trustee from breaching a duty to diversify, which had been overridden in the trust. The court further found the trustee acted in good faith in failing to diversify.]

The judgment of the trial court is affirmed.

SULLIVAN, J., and MAY, J., concur.

Notes

1. Compare the Hershey Trust litigation in Chapter 8 where the trustees were enjoined from selling securities for diversification purposes despite the settlor's grant of authority to sell the securities.

2. A trustee has the general duty to obtain court approval to deviate from any mandated administrative provision if a change in circumstances warrants. *See* 3d Rest. Trust § 66 and UTC § 412. Thus, even if a trustee is required by the trust instrument to retain specific assets, a trustee may have the duty to obtain court approval to deviate from the trust mandate if circumstances have changed significantly.

The Cooper-Langbein Debate

The court in *Americans for the Arts* assumed if the trusts in issue effectively overrode the duty to diversify trust assets then that directive should control based on UPIA § 1(b):

> (b) The prudent investor rule, a default rule, may be expanded, restricted, eliminated, or otherwise altered by the provisions of a trust. A trustee is not liable to a beneficiary to the extent that the trustee acted in reasonable reliance on the provisions of the trust.

Notwithstanding the express language of UPIA § 1(b),[22] Professor John Langbein (Yale) in his article, *Mandatory Rules in the Law of Trusts*, 98 Nw. U. L. Rev. 1105 (2004), took the position that UTC § 105(b)(3), bars a settlor from overriding the duty to diversify absent the special circumstances exception found in UPIA § 3:

> **Diversification.** A trustee shall diversify the investments of the trust unless the trustee reasonably determines that, because of special circumstances, the purposes of the trust are better served without diversifying.

Langbein's position is that, absent special circumstances, the settlor's attempt to override the duty to diversify trust investments should be ignored because then the trust will not be mandatorily administered in the interests of the beneficiaries as required by UTC § 105(3) ("the requirement that a trust and its terms be for the benefit of its beneficiaries, and that the trust have a purpose that is lawful, not contrary to public policy, and possible to achieve"). The mandatory rule of UTC § 105(3) is referred to as "the benefit-the-beneficiaries" rule and in Langbein's view, the rule provides the rationale for denying effect to the age-old rule that capricious trust purposes would not be recognized. For Langbein, the settlor's wishes for non-diversification are capricious and

22. Relying on North Dakota's adoption of UPIA § 1(b), the court in *Nelson v. First National Bank & Trust Co. of Williston*, 543 F.3d 432 (8th Cir, 2008), held that the trustee had no duty to diversify when the trust explicitly overrode the duty of diversification.

would therefore violate the inviolate "benefit-the-beneficiaries" rule of UTC § 105(3).

John H. Langbein, *Mandatory Rules in the Law of Trusts,* 98 Nw. U. L. Rev. 1105, 1112, 1115 (2004)

[E]ven though most rules of trust law (such as the duties to diversify and to invest prudently) are default rules rather than mandatory rules, it does not follow that the settlor is free to authorize any conceivable departure from the default rules. A default rule is one that the settlor can abridge, but only to the extent that the settlor's term is "for the benefit of [the] beneficiaries." The requirement that there be benefit to the beneficiaries sets outer limits on the settlor's power to abridge the default law. Trust law's deference to the settlor's direction always presupposes that the direction is beneficiary-regarding.

When, . . . trust assets are held for investment, and are easily diversifiable at no cost or at acceptable cost, I believe that the courts will come to view the advantages of diversification as so overwhelming that the settlor's interference with effective diversification will be treated as inconsistent with the requirement that the trust terms must be for the benefit of the beneficiaries. Settlor-directed underdiversification is an avoidable harm, akin to the harm that the courts have prevented by intervening against settlors' directions to waste or destroy trust property.

Professor Jeffery Cooper (Quinnipiac) in his article, *Empty Promises: Settlor's Intent, The Uniform Trust Code, and the Future of Trust Investment Law,* 88 B.U. L. Rev. 1165 (2008), took exception to Langbein's view. Cooper believes that a settlor should be able to override the duty to diversify even if special circumstances do not exist because that is what UPIA § 1(b) expressly provides. In fact, UPIA was published 6 years before the UTC. Cooper also suggests some of the problems in not respecting a settlor's wishes and that in any event, enterprising states will make clear that a settlor's nondiversification wishes will be respected.[23]

Professor Langbein took umbrage with Cooper's attack including his "extreme textualist interpretation of the default character of the duty to

23. Cooper pointed to Ohio, which adopted the UTC but departed from the benefit-the-beneficiaries rule. See Jeffrey A. Cooper, *Empty Promises: Settlor's Intent, The Uniform Trust Code, and the Future of Trust Investment Law,* 88 B.U. L. Rev. 1165, 1205, n.191 (2008). A couple other states, including Georgia and New Hampshire, have made it statutorily clear that the duty to diversify can be effectively overridden beyond special circumstances). See, e.g., N.H. § 564-B:9-901 ("A trustee is not liable to a beneficiary to the extent that the trustee . . . determined not to diversify the investments of a trust in good faith in reliance on the express terms of the trust . . .")

diversify."[24] Langbein also responded to Cooper's hypothetical which Cooper posited as "foolish.": a settlor who wanted the trustee to retain IBM stock because the settlor felt that under-diversification would maximize the benefit for the beneficiaries. To Langbein, the "foolish" prohibition on selling IBM was capricious because it would seriously impair objective value for the beneficiaries; as a result, the prohibition should be unenforceable.[25]

Cooper responded that Langbein's textual reading did exactly the same thing by ignoring the default nature of UPIA's diversification rule. Cooper also attempted to expose Langbein's "black or white" position on diversification.

Jeffrey A. Cooper, *Shades of Gray: Applying the Benefit-the-Beneficiaries Rule to Trust Investment Directives*, 90 B.U. L. Rev. 2383, 2398 (2010)

Rather than simply rooting out cases of obvious caprice that "offend outer limits of rationality," Professor Langbein seems to apply the rule to set aside any investment restriction that defies modern portfolio theory and the six Nobel laureates who helped develop it. In marked contrast to traditional notions of capricious trust terms and public policy considerations, there is no suggestion that Professor Langbein sees the enforceability of trust investment restrictions as involving questions of degree. Rather, he gives the impression that prudence and caprice are as easy to distinguish as black and white. Either an investment directive objectively maximizes the trust's profit potential under principles of modern portfolio theory or it is capricious. There seems to be no middle ground....

To illustrate how expansive this rule could become, I offer one final hypothetical. Suppose a trust settlor has just spent his entire fortune on a single holding he considers seriously undervalued in the current marketplace and establishes a trust to hold this solitary investment. His trustees are authorized to loan out the investment as needed to generate income, but he wants the underlying asset kept for the foreseeable future to capitalize on its appreciation potential. The investment is nothing as mundane as stock in IBM or Enron. It is an old oil painting imported from Amsterdam. The settlor's investment imperative: "Keep the Rembrandt."

What would modern portfolio theory say to this final example? I contend that the answer is clear. From the standpoint of modern portfolio theory, there is no justification for limiting an investment portfolio to a single holding—one painting—in a single asset class—artwork. If courts adopt that as the

---

24. See Langbein, *Burn the Rembrandt? Trust Law's Limits on the Settlor's Power to Direct Investments*, 90 B. U. L. Rev. 375, 391 (2008).

25. *Id.* at 388.

relevant test under the benefit-the-beneficiaries rule, they would find this provision capricious and set it aside. The trustee holding our hypothetical artwork thus would have no choice. She must sell the Rembrandt.

With this final example, we have slid to the bottom of a very slippery slope. Evaluating trust investment directives should involve questions of degree—subtle shades of gray rather than stark contrasts between black and white. Trust investment law should be flexible enough to respond to these gradations.

Notes

1. Compare the Hershey Trust litigation on Pages 380–381, where the trustees were enjoined from selling securities for diversification purposes despite the settlor's grant of authority to sell the securities.

2. A trustee has the general duty to obtain court approval to deviate from any mandated administrative provision if a change in circumstances warrants. *See* 3d Rest. Trust § 66 and UTC § 412. Thus, even if a trustee is required by the trust instrument to retain specific assets, a trustee may have the duty to obtain court approval to deviate from the trust mandate if circumstances have changed significantly.

Selected References

Jeffrey A. Cooper, *Empty Promises: Settlor's Intent, the Uniform Trust Code, and the Future of Trust Investment Law*, 88 B.U. L. Rev. 1165 (2008), *Speak Clearly and Listen Well: Negating the Duty to Diversify Trust Investments*, 33 Ohio N.U. L. Rev. 903 (2007), and *Shades of Gray: Applying the Benefit-the-Beneficiaries Rule to Trust Investment Directives*, 90 B.U. L. Rev. 2383 (2010).

Trent S. Kiziah, *The Trustee's Duty to Diversify: An Examination of the Developing Case Law*, 36 ACTEC L.J. 357 (2010).

John H. Langbein, *Burn the Rembrandt? Trust Law's Limits on the Settlor's Power to Direct Investments*, 90 B.U. L. Rev. 375 (2010) and *Mandatory Rules in the Law of Trusts*, 98 Nw. U. L. Rev. 1105 (2004).

C. Principal and Income Issues

Fiduciaries regularly receive and disburse money and other assets. At different stages of administration, a fiduciary typically must decide how to credit (or charge) particular receipts and disbursements among various beneficiaries. Suppose David's will gave Andy some IBM stock. David's executor may need to interpret the will to see whether Andy should also get IBM dividends which came in after the will's execution. Similarly, a fiduciary must allocate each receipt or expense which arises during the estate or trust administration. Finally, when the trust or estate terminates the fiduciary must divide assets between the income and principal beneficiaries.

We open our discussion with the traditional principal and income allocation rules that evolved to guide fiduciaries and still apply in a variety of situations. Then we turn to two newer approaches. We discuss how trustees can use their power of adjustment to harmonize principal and income allocation rules with the prudent investor standard in situations where distinctions between principal and income are unimportant. Finally, we consider the unitrust paradigm and the conversion of existing trusts to unitrusts as another way to facilitate the modern portfolio theory of investing.

1. Principal and Income Allocation Rules

Uniform principal and income acts have provided fiduciaries with guidance since 1931 when the National Conference of Commissioners on Uniform State Laws promulgated the first Uniform Principal and Income Act. *See* 7B Unif. Law. Ann. 183. Only Vermont still uses that version. The Conference revised the Act in 1962, and about six states follow the revised version. *See* 7B Unif. Law. Ann. 145. In 1997, a new principal and income act was adopted which has been already enacted in some form in all other states.

As explained in the prefatory note to the Uniform Principal and Income Act of 1997 (1997 UPIA):

> Revision is needed to support the now widespread use of the revocable living trust as a will substitute, to change the rules in those Acts that experience has shown need to be changed, and to establish new rules to cover situations not provided for in the old Acts, including rules that apply to financial instruments invented since 1962.

As further explained, the 1997 UPIA revises the rights of beneficiaries in four question areas:

- How is income earned during the probate of an estate to be distributed to trusts and to persons who receive outright bequests of specific property, pecuniary gifts, and the residue?
- When an income interest in a trust begins (i.e., when a person who creates the trust dies or when she transfers property to a trust during life), what property is principal that will eventually go to the remainder beneficiaries and what is income?
- When an income interest ends, who gets the income that has been received but not distributed, or that is due but not yet collected, or that has accrued but is not yet due?
- After an income interest begins and before it ends, how should its receipts and disbursements be allocated to or between principal and income?

The 1997 UPIA makes three types of changes in the traditional sections: it clarifies existing rules in the 1962 Act, changes existing rules under the prior acts, and provides new rules to reflect new situations that had arisen since adoption of the 1962 Act. The excerpt which follows offers a sampling of traditional sections in the 1997 Uniform Principal and Income Act.

Uniform Principal and Income Act (1997)

Section 102. Definitions.

In this [Act]:

(4) "Income" means money or property that a fiduciary receives as current return from a principal asset. The term includes a portion of receipts from a sale, exchange, or liquidation of a principal asset, to the extent provided in [Article] 4.

(8) "Net income" means the total receipts allocated to income during an accounting period minus the disbursements made from income during the period, plus or minus transfers under this [Act] to or from income during the period.

(10) "Principal" means property held in trust for distribution to a remainder beneficiary when the trust terminates.

Section 103. Fiduciary Duties; General Principles.

(a) In allocating receipts and disbursements to or between principal and income, and with respect to any matter within the scope of [Articles] 2 and 3, a fiduciary:

(1) shall administer a trust or estate in accordance with the terms of the trust or the will, even if there is a different provision in this [Act];

(2) may administer a trust or estate by the exercise of a discretionary power of administration given to the fiduciary by the terms of the trust or the will, even if the exercise of the power produces a result different from a result required or permitted by this [Act];

(3) shall administer a trust or estate in accordance with this [Act] if the terms of the trust or the will do not contain a different provision or do not give the fiduciary a discretionary power of administration; and

(4) shall add a receipt or charge a disbursement to principal to the extent that the terms of the trust and this [Act] do not provide a rule for allocating the receipt or disbursement to or between principal and income.

(b) In exercising the power to adjust under Section 104(a) or a discretionary power of administration regarding a matter within the scope of this [Act], whether granted by the terms of a trust, a will, or this [Act], a fiduciary shall administer a trust or estate impartially, based on what is fair and reasonable to all of the beneficiaries, except to the extent that the terms of the trust or the will clearly manifest an intention that the fiduciary shall or may favor one or more of the beneficiaries. A determination in accordance with this [Act] is presumed to be fair and reasonable to all of the beneficiaries.

Section 301. When Right to Income Begins and Ends.

(a) An income beneficiary is entitled to net income from the date on which the income interest begins. An income interest begins on the date specified in the terms of the trust or, if no date is specified, on the date an asset becomes subject to a trust or successive income interest.

(b) An asset becomes subject to a trust:

(1) on the date it is transferred to the trust in the case of an asset that is transferred to a trust during the transferor's life;

(2) on the date of a testator's death in the case of an asset that becomes subject to a trust by reason of a will, even if there is an intervening period of administration of the testator's estate; or

(3) on the date of an individual's death in the case of an asset that is transferred to a fiduciary by a third party because of the individual's death.

(c) An asset becomes subject to a successive income interest on the day after the preceding income interest ends, as determined under subsection (d), even if there is an intervening period of administration to wind up the preceding income interest.

(d) An income interest ends on the day before an income beneficiary dies or another terminating event occurs, or on the last day of a period during which there is no beneficiary to whom a trustee may distribute income.

Section 302. Apportionment of Receipts and Disbursements When Decedent Dies or Income Interest Begins.

(a) A trustee shall allocate an income receipt or disbursement other than one to which Section 201(1) applies to principal if its due date occurs before a decedent dies in the case of an estate or before an income interest begins in the case of a trust or successive income interest.

(b) A trustee shall allocate an income receipt or disbursement to income if its due date occurs on or after the date on which a decedent dies or an income interest begins and it is a periodic due date. An income receipt or disbursement must be treated as accruing from day to day if its due date is not periodic or it has no due date. The portion of the receipt or disbursement accruing before the date on which a decedent dies or an income interest begins must be allocated to principal and the balance must be allocated to income.

(c) An item of income or an obligation is due on the date the payer is required to make a payment. If a payment date is not stated, there is no due date for the purposes of this [Act]. Distributions to shareholders or other owners from an entity to which Section 401 applies are deemed to be due on the date fixed by the entity for determining who is entitled to receive the distribution or, if no date is fixed, on the declaration date for the distribution. A due date is periodic for receipts or disbursements that must be paid at regular intervals under a lease or an obligation to pay interest or if an entity customarily makes distributions at regular intervals.

Section 401. Character of Receipts.

(a) In this section, "entity" means a corporation, partnership, limited liability company, regulated investment company, real estate investment trust, common trust fund, or any other organization in which a trustee has an interest other than a trust or estate to which Section 402 applies, a business or activity to which Section 403 applies, or an asset-backed security to which Section 415 applies.

(b) Except as otherwise provided in this section, a trustee shall allocate to income money received from an entity.

(c) A trustee shall allocate the following receipts from an entity to principal:

(1) property other than money;

(2) money received in one distribution or a series of related distributions in exchange for part or all of a trust's interest in the entity;

(3) money received in total or partial liquidation of the entity; and

(4) money received from an entity that is a regulated investment company or a real estate investment trust if the money distributed is a capital gain dividend for federal income tax purposes.

(f) A trustee may rely upon a statement made by an entity about the source or character of a distribution if the statement is made at or near the time of distribution by the entity's board of directors or other person or group of persons authorized to exercise powers to pay money or transfer property comparable to those of a corporation's board of directors.

Section 404. Principal Receipts.

A trustee shall allocate to principal:

(1) to the extent not allocated to income under this [Act], assets received from a transferor during the transferor's lifetime, a decedent's estate, a trust with a terminating income interest, or a payer under a contract naming the trust or its trustee as beneficiary;

(2) money or other property received from the sale, exchange, liquidation, or change in form of a principal asset, including realized profit, subject to this [article];

(3) amounts recovered from third parties to reimburse the trust because of disbursements described in Section 502(a)(7) or for other reasons to the extent not based on the loss of income;

(4) proceeds of property taken by eminent domain, but a separate award made for the loss of income with respect to an accounting period during which a current income beneficiary had a mandatory income interest is income;

(5) net income received in an accounting period during which there is no beneficiary to whom a trustee may or must distribute income; and

(6) other receipts as provided in [Part 3].

Section 501. Disbursements from Income.

A trustee shall make the following disbursements from income . . . :

(1) one-half of the regular compensation of the trustee and of any person providing investment advisory or custodial services to the trustee;

(2) one-half of all expenses for accountings, judicial proceedings, or other matters that involve both the income and remainder interests;

(3) all of the other ordinary expenses incurred in connection with the administration, management, or preservation of trust property and the distribution of income, including interest, ordinary repairs, regularly recurring taxes assessed against principal, and expenses of a proceeding or other matter that concerns primarily the income interest; and

(4) recurring premiums on insurance covering the loss of a principal asset or the loss of income from or use of the asset.

Section 502. Disbursements from Principal.

(a) A trustee shall make the following disbursements from principal:

(1) the remaining one-half of the disbursements described in Section 501(1) and (2);

(2) all of the trustee's compensation calculated on principal as a fee for acceptance, distribution, or termination, and disbursements made to prepare property for sale;

(3) payments on the principal of a trust debt;

(4) expenses of a proceeding that concerns primarily principal, including a proceeding to construe the trust or to protect the trust or its property;

(5) premiums paid on a policy of insurance not described in Section 501 (4) of which the trust is the owner and beneficiary;

(6) estate, inheritance, and other transfer taxes, including penalties, apportioned to the trust; and

(7) disbursements related to environmental matters . . . .

(b) If a principal asset is encumbered with an obligation that requires income from that asset to be paid directly to the creditor, the trustee shall transfer from principal to income an amount equal to the income paid to the creditor in reduction of the principal balance of the obligation.

Notes

1. Among the more well-known principal and income rules is the "Massachusetts rule" for allocating cash and stock dividends. Now widely-accepted by statute and case law, the rule allocates cash dividends and dividends payable in the form of stock of another corporation to income, but dividends payable in the stock of the issuing corporation to principal. *See* George T. Bogert, Trusts §§ 115, 116 (6th ed. 1987). In contrast, 1997 UPIA § 401(c) allocates all stock dividends to principal.

2. 1977 UPIA clarifies and changes earlier rules for allocating a portion of a receipt to income and a portion to principal.[26] For example, § 409(c) apportions receipts from IRA accounts as follows: 90 percent to principal and 10 percent to income. The same 90-10 sharing arrangement applies to most liquidation assets, defined as assets "whose value will diminish or terminate because the asset is expected to produce receipts for a period of limited duration." 1977 UPIA § 410. Examples of liquidating assets include patents and copyrights.

3. 1977 UPIA § 413 changes the rule that required a portion of the proceeds from the sale of unproductive property be allocated to income. Under 1997 UPIA § 413(b), the receipt is allocated entirely to principal.

4. 1977 UPIA § 503(b) changes the rules for depreciation by generally authorizing a trustee to "transfer to principal a reasonable amount of net cash receipts from a principal asset that is subject to deprecation." Under the 1962 UPIA, a trustee was required to change income for a reasonable depreciation allowance.

5. The Uniform Law Commission has begun a study to revise the 1997 Uniform Principal and Income Act to take into account new investment assets and other recent developments.

6. For a sampling of the sorts of disputes that can arise over allocation, consider the following:

(a) Corporate distribution allocable to income under 1997 UPIA § 401(b) because not partial liquidation under UPIA § 401(d)(2) based on amount received by trust. *In re Estate of Thomas*, 21 Cal. Rptr. 3d 741 (Ct. App. 2004).

(b) Income earned before a life tenant's death, but not paid until later, goes to the life tenant's estate. *Appeal of New Britain Bank & Tr. Co.*, 472 A.2d 1305 (Conn. 1983). *Accord* 1997 UPIA § 303.

(c) Income earned on proceeds of property sold to meet probate administration expenses was allocated to principal. *Proctor v. American Security & Tr. Co.*, 98 F.2d 599 (D.C. Cir. 1938). 1997 UPIA § 103(a)(4) provides that receipts shall be added to principal and disbursements charged against principal unless otherwise provided in the Act.

26. As with other rules under 1997 UPIA, these rules for apportionment are default rules that the decedent or settlor can change.

(d) Payment of attorney fees under the 1962 UPIA are chargeable against principal. *See In re Bame*, 263 B.R. 594 (D. Minn. 2001) (attorneys' fees to defend trust principal cannot be paid from bankrupt's estate where bankrupt was has income beneficiary of a trust). *Accord* 1977 UPIA § 502(a)(4).

Selected References

Joel C. Dobris, *Why Trustee Investors Often Prefer Dividends to Capital Gain and Debt Investments to Equity—A Daunting Principal and Income Problem*, 32 Real Prop. Prob. & Tr. J. 255 (1997).

Mark R. Gillett & Katheleen R. Guzman, *Managing Assets: The Oklahoma Uniform Principal and Income Act*, 56 Okla. L. Rev. 1 (2003).

Ronald R. Volkmer, *Nebraska's Updated Principal and Income Act: Apportioning, Allocating, and Adjusting in the New Trust World*, 35 Creighton L. Rev. 295 (2002).

2. *Trustee's Adjustment Power*

As the following excerpt indicates, traditional rules for allocating principal and income no longer fit well with modern theories of trust investment.

Jeffrey N. Gordon, *The Puzzling Persistence of the Constrained Prudent Man Rule*

62 N.Y.U. L. Rev. 52, 99–101 (1987).

The most important aspect of trust law cast into doubt by the acceptance of an unconstrained rule on portfolio theory grounds is the traditional allocation of investment returns. No principle in the law of trusts seems more settled than the rule that income beneficiaries receive ordinary cash dividends from common stock ownership and remaindermen receive capital gains if the stock is sold. The only skirmishing is on the edges of the rule, regarding, for example, the allocation of extraordinary cash dividends or stock dividends. Acceptance of port-folio theory, however, would undermine the traditional rule. The economic models on which portfolio theory relies all calculate investment returns based on the total return during a specific period—cash payouts (dividends and interest) plus gain or loss. The analysis of covariance or co-movement among securities returns, which provides the basis for determining the amount of risk a particular security adds to a portfolio, depends upon this total return definition.

A division of a firm's return between income and capital gain is highly artificial from the perspective of financial economics. Imagine two firms, A and B. For every hundred dollars of shareholders' equity, each earns ten dollars. A, thinking its primary business has reached a no-growth steady state, pays out all earnings as dividends. B, thinking its business provides additional investment opportunities, reinvests all earnings, which leads to an increase in the price of its shares. Each firm is providing comparable economic return to its share-holders; only the form is different. But a trustee holding A must pay out all dividends to income beneficiaries, even if, because of inflation, the purchasing power of the remainder interest, the A stock in the portfolio, is meanwhile depreciating. A trustee holding B can pay out nothing to income beneficiaries, even if the remainder interest is increasing in value because of B's decision to reinvest earnings that would otherwise be available to an income beneficiary.

To assure fairness between income beneficiaries and remaindermen, the trustee may have to adopt an investment policy that mixes A and B stock. Alternatively, present law apparently allows the trustee to refuse to hold B. The result in either case will be a portfolio that is not optimally diversified; it has not been assembled with the objective of producing the greatest expected returns for the risk. It is easy to see why systematic exclusion of companies with low dividends but high reinvestment rates will upset a diversification scheme. But there is no assurance that a portfolio that emphasizes balance between high and low dividend-paying securities will be well-diversified in other respects. The allocation of total returns between income and principal compelled by settled trust law is profoundly inconsistent with the portfolio theory paradigm.

Many endowment funds have adopted a solution that could be adapted to private trusts. It would be possible to tally portfolio results on a total return basis but set standards for allocation of returns between income and remainder interest based on assumptions regarding normalized annual returns. While theoretically correct, such a solution presents practical problems in trust administration because of the inevitable conflicts among income beneficiaries and remaindermen over the appropriate assumptions. Thus, the revision of the Uniform Principal and Income Act to work out the practical details of a total return allocation scheme would be particularly helpful in making a portfolio theory approach readily available to private trusts.

In response to calls for reform, the Uniform and Principal Act of 1997 grants the trustee the power to make adjustments between principal and income. The following excerpts from the Act's Prefatory Note explain the need for a more flexible approach:

> [One of the purposes for the Act] is to provide a means for implementing the transition to an investment regime based on principles embodied in the Uniform Prudent Investor Act, especially the principle of investing for total return rather than a certain level of "income" as traditionally perceived in terms of interest, dividends, and rents.
>
> ....
>
> Coordination with the Uniform Prudent Investor Act
>
> The law of trust investment has been modernized. See Uniform Prudent Investor Act (1994); Restatement (Third) of Trusts: Prudent Investor Rule (1992) (hereinafter

Restatement of Trusts 3d: Prudent Investor Rule). Now it is time to update the principal and income allocation rules so the two bodies of doctrine can work well together. This revision deals conservatively with the tension between modern investment theory and traditional income allocation. The starting point is to use the traditional system. If prudent investing of all the assets in a trust viewed as a portfolio and traditional allocation effectuate the intent of the settlor, then nothing need be done. The Act, however, helps the trustee who has made a prudent, modern portfolio-based investment decision that has the initial effect of skewing return from all the assets under management, viewed as a portfolio, as between income and principal beneficiaries. The Act gives that trustee a power to reallocate the portfolio return suitably. To leave a trustee constrained by the traditional system would inhibit the trustee's ability to fully implement modern portfolio theory.

Uniform Principal and Income Act (1997)

Section 104. Trustee's Power to Adjust.

(a) A trustee may adjust between principal and income to the extent the trustee considers necessary if the trustee invests and manages trust assets as a prudent investor, the terms of the trust describe the amount that may or must be distributed to a beneficiary by referring to the trust's income, and the trustee determines, after applying the rules in Section 103(a), that the trustee is unable to comply with Section 103(b).

(b) In deciding whether and to what extent to exercise the power conferred by subsection (a), a trustee shall consider all factors relevant to the trust and its beneficiaries, including the following factors to the extent they are relevant:

(1) the nature, purpose, and expected duration of the trust;

(2) the intent of the settlor;

(3) the identity and circumstances of the beneficiaries;

(4) the needs for liquidity, regularity of income, and preservation and appreciation of capital;

(5) the assets held in the trust; the extent to which they consist of financial assets, interests in closely held enterprises, tangible and intangible personal property, or real property; the extent to which an asset is used by a beneficiary; and whether an asset was purchased by the trustee or received from the settlor;

(6) the net amount allocated to income under the other sections of this [Act] and the increase or decrease in the value of the principal assets, which the trustee may estimate as to assets for which market values are not readily available;

(7) whether and to what extent the terms of the trust give the trustee the power to invade principal or accumulate income or prohibit the trustee from invading principal or accumulating income, and the extent to

which the trustee has exercised a power from time to time to invade principal or accumulate income;

(8) the actual and anticipated effect of economic conditions on principal and income and effects of inflation and deflation; and

(9) the anticipated tax consequences of an adjustment.

(c) A trustee may not make an adjustment:

(1) that diminishes the income interest in a trust that requires all of the income to be paid at least annually to a spouse and for which an estate tax or gift tax marital deduction would be allowed, in whole or in part, if the trustee did not have the power to make the adjustment;

(2) that reduces the actuarial value of the income interest in a trust to which a person transfers property with the intent to qualify for a gift tax exclusion;

(3) that changes the amount payable to a beneficiary as a fixed annuity or a fixed fraction of the value of the trust assets;

(4) from any amount that is permanently set aside for charitable purposes under a will or the terms of a trust unless both income and principal are so set aside;

(5) if possessing or exercising the power to make an adjustment causes an individual to be treated as the owner of all or part of the trust for income tax purposes, and the individual would not be treated as the owner if the trustee did not possess the power to make an adjustment;

(6) if possessing or exercising the power to make an adjustment causes all or part of the trust assets to be included for estate tax purposes in the estate of an individual who has the power to remove a trustee or appoint a trustee, or both, and the assets would not be included in the estate of the individual if the trustee did not possess the power to make an adjustment;

(7) if the trustee is a beneficiary of the trust; or

(8) if the trustee is not a beneficiary, but the adjustment would benefit the trustee directly or indirectly.

(d) If subsection (c)(5), (6), (7), or (8) applies to a trustee and there is more than one trustee, a cotrustee to whom the provision does not apply may make the adjustment unless the exercise of the power by the remaining trustee or trustees is not permitted by the terms of the trust.

(e) A trustee may release the entire power conferred by subsection (a) or may release only the power to adjust from income to principal or the power to adjust from principal to income if the trustee is uncertain about whether possessing or exercising the power will cause a result described in subsection (c)(1) through (6) or (c)(8) or if the trustee determines that possessing or exercising the power will or may deprive the trust of a tax benefit or impose a tax burden not described in subsection (c). The release may be permanent or for a specified period, including a period measured by the life of an individual.

(f) Terms of a trust that limit the power of a trustee to make an adjustment between principal and income do not affect the application of this section unless it is clear from the terms of the trust that the terms are intended to deny the trustee the power of adjustment conferred by subsection (a).

Note and Question

1. 1997 UPIA was amended to add UPIA § 105 pursuant to which a court is barred from changing a fiduciary's decision to exercise or not exercise a discretionary power, including decisions under § 104, unless an abuse of fiduciary discretion occurred.

2. Because § 104 of the 1997 UPIA bars a trustee who is a beneficiary from exercising the adjustment power, its application will be limited since many settlors want a trust beneficiary to be the sole trustee. Do you foresee any other problems under the 1997 Act's adjustment power?

Problem

Laura's will established a trust giving her children, Greg and Julia, life estates, with the remainder to Laura's grandchildren. She named Greg and Julia as co-trustees. In that role, they recently sold stock for a substantial gain and allocated the gain to their own accounts. The trust agreement says, "The Trustees have absolute discretion to allocate receipts and disbursements between principal and income. Their decisions shall be final and not subject to question by any court or any beneficiary hereof." Greg's son, Andy, believes the capital gain should have gone into principal and asks your advice about what to do. What do you recommend?

Selected Reference

S. Alan Medlin, *Limitations on the Trustee's Power to Adjust*, 42 Real Prop. Prob. & Tr. J. 717 (2008).

3. The Noncharitable Unitrust Alternative

A different way of conceptualizing trusts has emerged to make traditional distinctions between "principal" and "income" irrelevant. A "unitrust" views trust assets as a whole. Unitrusts are also called Total Return Trusts.

The unitrust concept is well-known in the world of charitable trusts. Since 1969, tax benefits from trusts that included non-charitable and charitable beneficiaries may be obtained only for prescribed trust forms: the charitable unitrust is one of the two principal forms sanctioned.

In its most basic formulation, a charitable unitrust (referred to as a "CRUT") requires that a beneficiary annually receive a fixed percentage of the fair market value of the trust's assets, valued annually. Under the standard charitable remainder unitrust, where a charity is the remainder beneficiary, a noncharitable beneficiary must receive an annual payout of at least five percent. I.R.C. §664(d)(2). The annual payout will vary each year because it will be based on the value of the trust's assets as revalued each year.

In re Heller

849 N.E.2d 262 (N.Y. 2006)

ROSENBLATT, J.:

In September 2001, New York enacted legislation that transformed the definition and treatment of trust accounting income. The Uniform Principal and Income Act (Estates, Powers and Trusts Law [EPTL] article 11-A) and related statutes (L 2001, ch 243), including the optional unitrust provision (EPTL 11-2.4), are designed to facilitate investment for total return on a portfolio. The appeal before us centers on the optional unitrust provision, which permits trustees to elect a regime in which income is calculated according to a fixed formula and based on the net fair market value of the trust assets. We hold that a trustee's status as a remainder beneficiary does not in itself invalidate a unitrust election made by that trustee, and that a trustee may elect unitrust status retroactively to January 1, 2002, the effective date of EPTL 11-2.4.

I.

In his will, after making certain other gifts of personal property and money, Jacob Heller created a trust to benefit his wife Bertha Heller, should she survive him, and his children. Heller provided that his entire residuary estate be held in trust during Bertha's life. He appointed his brother Frank Heller as trustee and designated his sons Herbert and Alan Heller as trustees on Frank's death. Every year Bertha was to receive the greater of $40,000 or the total income of the trust. Heller named his daughters (Suzanne Heller and Faith Willinger, each with a 30% share) and his sons and prospective trustees (Herbert and Alan Heller, each with a 20% share) as remainder beneficiaries.

Jacob Heller died in 1986, and his wife Bertha survives him. When Heller's brother Frank died in 1997, Herbert and Alan Heller became trustees. From that year until 2001, Bertha Heller received an average annual income from the trust of approximately $190,000. In March 2003, the trustees elected to have the unitrust provision apply, pursuant to EPTL 11-2.4 (e) (1) (B) (I). As required by EPTL 11-2.4 (e) (1) (B) (III), they notified trust beneficiaries Bertha Heller, Suzanne Heller and Faith Willinger. The trustees sought to have unitrust treatment applied retroactively to January 1, 2002, the effective date of EPTL 11-2.4. As a result of that election, Bertha Heller's annual income was reduced to approximately $70,000.

Appellant Sandra Davis commenced this proceeding, as attorney-in-fact for her mother Bertha Heller, and on August 1, 2003 moved for summary judgment, seeking, among other things, an order annulling the unitrust election and revoking the Letters of Trusteeship issued to Herbert and Alan Heller. She also sought a determination that the election could not be made retroactive to January 1, 2002. Surrogate's Court granted the branch of Sandra Davis's summary judgment motion that sought to void the trustees' retroactive application of the unitrust election, but denied the branches of her motion seeking annulment of the unitrust election itself and other relief.

Davis appealed Surrogate's Court's order, and Herbert and Alan Heller crossappealed. The Appellate Division affirmed the order to the extent that it denied Davis's summary judgment motion and reversed so much of the order as annulled the retroactive application of the unitrust election. It also granted leave to appeal and certified the following question to us: "Was the opinion and order of [the Appellate Division] dated August 15, 2005, properly made?" We conclude that it was and now affirm.

II.

The 2001 legislation that forms the subject of this appeal was designed to make it easier for trustees to comply with the demands of the Prudent Investor Act of 1994.[27] In addition to enacting EPTL article 11-A (Uniform Principal and Income Act), the Legislature both added EPTL 11-2.3 (b) (5) to the Prudent Investor Act and included the optional unitrust provision, EPTL 11-2.4.

Under the former Principal and Income Act (EPTL 11-2.1),[28] a trustee was required to balance the interests of the income beneficiary against those of the remainder beneficiary (see EPTL 11-2.1 [a] [1]), and was constrained in making investments by the Act's narrow definitions of income and principal (see EPTL 11-2.1 [b]). A trustee who invested in non-appreciating assets would ensure reasonable income for any income beneficiary, but would sacrifice growth opportunities for the trust funds, as inflation eroded their value; if the trustee invested for growth, remainder beneficiaries would enjoy an increase in the value of the trust at the expense of income beneficiaries.[29] Moreover, the need to invest so as to produce what the former Principal and Income Act defined as income led to investment returns that failed to represent the benefits envisaged as appropriate by settlors.[30]

---

27. *See e.g.* Legislative Memorandum in support of the Fifth Report of the EPTL-SCPA Legislative Advisory Committee, 14 Warren's Heaton, Surrogates' Courts, Appendix 5.03 at App. 5-171 (6th ed rev).

28. The former Principal and Income Act (EPTL 11-2.1) was superseded by the Uniform Principal and Income Act (EPTL article 11-A) enacted in 2001. The former act does not apply to receipts and expenses received or incurred after January 1, 2002 (EPTL 11-2.1 [m]).

29. *See* Turano, Practice Commentaries, McKinney's Cons Laws of NY, Book 17B, EPTL Article 11-A, 2006 Pocket Part, at 82-83; *see also* Fifth Report of the EPTL-SCPA Legislative Advisory Committee, 14 Warren's Heaton, Surrogates' Courts, Appendix 5.01 at App. 5-4 to 5-13 (6th ed rev).

30. *See* 14 Warren's Heaton, Surrogates' Courts at App. 5-4 to 5-5.

The Prudent Investor Act encourages investing for total return on a portfolio. Unless the governing instrument expressly provides otherwise, the Act requires that trustees "pursue an overall investment strategy to enable the trust to make appropriate present and future distribution to or for the benefit of the beneficiaries under the governing instrument, in accordance with risk and return objectives reasonably suited to the entire portfolio" (EPTL 11-2.3 [b] [3] [A]) (emphasis added). The 2001 legislation allows trustees to pursue this strategy uninhibited by a constrained concept of trust accounting income. First, the Prudent Investor Act now authorizes trustees "to adjust between principal and income to the extent the trustee considers advisable to enable the trustee to make appropriate present and future distributions in accordance with clause (b) (3) (A) if the trustee determines, after applying the rules in article 11-A, that such an adjustment would be fair and reasonable to all of the beneficiaries, so that current beneficiaries may be given such use of the trust property as is consistent with preservation of its value" (EPTL 11-2.3 [b] [5] [A]).

A trustee investing for a portfolio's total return under the Prudent Investor Act may now adjust principal and income to compensate for the effects of the investment decisions on distribution to income beneficiaries (*see* 14 Warren's Heaton, Surrogates' Courts at App. 5-25 to 5-27). Alternatively, the optional unitrust provision lets trustees elect unitrust status for a trust (EPTL 11-2.4), by which income is calculated according to a fixed formula.

In a unitrust pursuant to EPTL 11-2.4, an income beneficiary receives an annual income distribution of "four percent of the net fair market values of the assets held in the trust on the first business day of the current valuation year" (EPTL 11-2.4 [b] [1]), for the first three years of unitrust treatment. This is true regardless of the actual income earned by the trust. Starting in the fourth year, the value of the trust assets is determined by calculating the average of three figures: the net fair market value on the first business day of the current valuation year and the net fair market values on the first business days of the prior two valuation years (see EPTL 11-2.4 [b] [2]). Income generated in excess of this amount is applied to principal.

Under the 2001 legislation, then, a trustee may invest in assets, such as equities, that outperform other forms of investment in the long term but produce relatively low dividend yields for an income beneficiary, and still achieve impartial treatment of income and remainder beneficiaries. The trustee may accomplish this either by adjusting as between principal and income (*see* 14 Warren's Heaton, Surrogates' Courts at App. 5-25 to 5-27) or by electing unitrust status with the result that the income increases in proportion to the value of the principal (*id.* at App. 5-14). If a trust's assets are primarily interests in non-appreciating investments producing high yields for income beneficiaries, a unitrust election may initially result in a substantial decrease in the distribution to any income beneficiary, at least until the portfolio is diversified. This case presents such a scenario.

III.

Davis argues that the trustees are barred as a matter of law from electing unitrust status because they are themselves remainder beneficiaries, and that, in any case, they may not elect unitrust status retroactively to January 1, 2002. The Appellate Division held that the legislation does not impede unitrust election by an interested trustee, that such an election is not inconsistent, per se, with common-law limitations on the conduct of fiduciaries and that the statute permits trustees to select retroactive application. We agree.

EPTL 11-2.3 (b) (5), the 2001 statute that gives trustees the power to adjust between principal and income, expressly prohibits a trustee from exercising this power if "the trustee is a current beneficiary or a presumptive remainder-man of the trust" (EPTL 11-2.3 [b] [5] [C] [vii]) or if "the adjustment would benefit the trustee directly or indirectly" (EPTL 11-2.3 [b] [5] [C] [viii]). Tellingly, the Legislature included no such prohibition in the simultaneously enacted optional unitrust provision, EPTL 11-2.4. Moreover, in giving a list of factors to be considered by the courts in determining whether unitrust treatment should apply to a trust, the Legislature mentioned no absolute prohibitions (see EPTL 11-2.4 [e] [5] [A]), and created a presumption in favor of unitrust application (EPTL 11-2.4 [e] [5] [B]). We conclude that the Legislature did not mean to prohibit trustees who have a beneficial interest from electing unitrust treatment.

It is certainly true that the common law in New York contains an absolute prohibition against self-dealing, in that "a fiduciary owes a duty of undivided and undiluted loyalty to those whose interests the fiduciary is to protect" (*Birnbaum v. Birnbaum*, 73 N.Y.2d 461, 466, 541 N.Y.S.2d 746, 539 N.E.2d 574 [1989]. "The trustee is under a duty to administer the trust solely in the interest of the beneficiaries" (Restatement [Second] of Trusts § 170 [1]). In this case, however, the trustees owe fiduciary obligations not only to the trust's income beneficiary, Bertha Heller, but also to the other remainder beneficiaries, Suzanne Heller and Faith Willinger. That these beneficiaries' interests happen to align with the trustees' does not relieve the trustees of their duties to them. Here, we cannot conclude that the trustees are prohibited from electing unitrust treatment as a matter of common law principle.

That the trustees are remainder beneficiaries does not, by itself, invalidate a unitrust election. Nevertheless, a unitrust election from which a trustee benefits will be scrutinized by the courts with special care. In determining whether application of the optional unitrust provision is appropriate, it remains for Surrogate's Court to review the process and assure the fairness of the trustees' election, by applying relevant factors including those enumerated in EPTL 11-2.4 (e) (5) (A). Application of these factors here presents questions of fact precluding summary judgment.

IV.

Davis seeks to reinstate Surrogate's Court's determination that the unitrust election could not be made retroactive to January 1, 2002. In our view, however, the

Legislature structured EPTL 11-2.4 so that it could be applied retroactively. EPTL 11-2.4 (d) (1) provides that a trustee who elects unitrust status may specify the date on which the interest of a beneficiary begins. Thus, the statute vests trustees with authority to determine the effective date of unitrust elections.

Moreover, EPTL 11-2.4 (b) (6) instructs a trustee who elects unitrust treatment to "determine the unitrust amount properly payable for any preceding and current valuation year of the trust" (emphasis added), unless the election is "expressly made effective prospectively as permitted under clause (e) (4) (a)." The trustee is then required to pay to, or recover from, the current beneficiary the difference between the unitrust amount and any amount actually paid for any completed valuation year. (EPTL 11-2.4 [b] [6].) This provision envisages retroactive application of a unitrust regime. The required recomputation of preceding years' beneficial interests would serve no purpose if retroactive application were barred.

EPTL 11-2.4 (e) (4) (A), on which Surrogate's Court relied, is not to the contrary. This section provides that the optional unitrust provision "shall apply to a trust ... as of the first year of the trust in which assets first became subject to the trust, unless the governing instrument or the court in its decision provides otherwise, or unless the election in accordance with clause (e)(1)(B) is expressly made effective as of the first day of the first year of the trust commencing after the election is made." On the most plausible interpretation of this less than lucid provision, EPTL 11-2.4 (e) (4) (A) actually contemplates retroactivity, insofar as it provides the initial funding of the trust as a default starting point for unitrust treatment of a trust created on or after January 1, 2002. Certainly, EPTL 11-2.4 (e) (4) (A) should not be read as taking away from trustees the authority given them by EPTL 11-2.4 (d) (1) to specify the effective date of a unitrust election.

We therefore hold that a trustee may elect unitrust status for a trust retroactively to January 1, 2002, the effective date of EPTL 11-2.4. Appellant's remaining contentions lack merit.

Accordingly, the order of the Appellate Division should be affirmed, with costs, and the certified question answered in the affirmative.

Order affirmed, with costs, and certified question answered in the affirmative.

In 2001, Delaware, New Jersey, New York, and Missouri enacted legislation that gives a trustee discretion to convert an existing trust, which uses the traditional definition of income, to a unitrust. As of this writing, over 30 states have unitrust conversion statutes. Also, in many unitrust conversion states, statutory authority exists for a settlor to create an initial unitrust.[31] The required unitrust percentage for

31. States may also allow a unitrust to be converted to an income only trust. *See, e.g.*, Ariz. Rev. Stat. § 14-11014(2).

conversion and creation vary; for example, New York requires a four percent unitrust while in Missouri the unitrust percentage may be between three percent and percent.

Other details on conversion vary among the states. For example, in Delaware conversion is subject to numerous safeguards, such as notice of proposed conversion to trust beneficiaries who are given the opportunity to object. Judicial approval for conversion may be required if a beneficiary objects or if not all beneficiaries are competent. On the other hand, in New York unitrust conversion for certain trusts can be made by the trustee even if the trust beneficiaries object, and as the Heller case holds, even if the trustee making the conversion is also a beneficiary.

The mechanism for converting an existing income trust to a unitrust is by redefining income or net income under the existing trust in unitrust terms. Consider how New York's definition of "net income" under its percent unitrust regime makes the distinctions between principal and income irrelevant (N.Y. Est. Powers & Trusts Law § 11-2.4(a)):

> (A) Unless the terms of the trust provide otherwise, the net income of any trust to which this section applies shall mean the unitrust amount as determined hereunder.
>
> (B) Unitrust Amount.
>
> (1) For the first three years of the trust, the "unitrust amount" for a current valuation year of the trust shall mean an amount equal to four percent of the net fair market values of the assets held in the trust on the first business day of the current valuation year.
>
> (2) commencing with the fourth year of a trust, the "unitrust amount" for a current valuation year of the trust shall mean an amount equal to four percent multiplies by a fraction, the numerator of which shall be the sum of (A) the net fair market values of the assets held in the trust on the first business day of the current valuation year and (B) the net fair market values of the assets held in the trust on the first business day of each prior valuation year, and the denominator of which shall be three.

By averaging yearly values after three years, the statute effectively creates a smoothing rule to compensate for fluctuating values.

Question

An alternative to a unitrust would be to use the traditional trust model—income to A for life, remainder to B—with the discretionary power of invasion in the trustee for the benefit of A. Do you see any disadvantages to such traditional trusts? Do you see any disadvantages to unitrusts?

Selected References

Patrick J. Collins & Josh Stampfli, *Promises and Pitfalls of Total Return Trusts*, 27 ACTEC J. 205 (2001).

Joel C. Dobris, *Why Five? The Strange, Magnetic, and Mesmerizing Affect of the Five Percent Unitrust and Spending Rate on Settlors, Their Advisers, and Retirees*, 40 Real Prop. Prob. & Tr. J. 39 (2005).

Alvin J. Golden, *Total Return Unitrusts: Is This a Solution in Search of a Problem?*, 28 ACTEC J. 121 (2002).

Robert B. Wolf, *Total Return Trusts-A Decade of Progress, But Are We There Yet?*, 32 ACTEC J. 5, 101 (2006).

D. Other Fiduciary Duties

A wide variety of specific duties add detail to the general standard of prudence, including: keeping accounts, enforcing claims, and furnishing information.[32] *See generally* 3d Rest. Trusts §§ 76–84. The cases that follow give texture to such black-letter lists.

Estate of Baldwin

442 A.2d 529 (Me. 1982)

McKusick, C.J.

This probate proceeding centers on the Port Clyde General Store, the principal asset of the estate of the late Stephen L. Baldwin. The guardian of the decedent's minor children, displeased with the executor's handling of that asset, brought a petition in the Knox County Probate Court asking, among other things, that the executor, The Connecticut National Bank, be surcharged as appropriate. The probate judge found that the Bank as executor had met its fiduciary obligations under Maine law, and the children's representative brings this appeal. The probate judge's finding was clearly erroneous; we therefore reverse and remand the case to the Probate Court for determination of the appropriate surcharge to be levied against the executor.

I.

On May 30, 1979, Stephen L. Baldwin, a Maine domiciliary, died in a Downeast Airlines plane crash, leaving a widow, Tracy C. Baldwin, and three minor children by a former marriage. The children, aged 13 and younger, lived in Westport, Connecticut, with their mother, now Mrs. McKane. In his will the decedent divided his

32. Duties with respect to co-fiduciaries are considered in connection with *Estate of Rothko* on Page 694.

estate into two equal shares, one share to go to the widow and the other, to his three children.

After his 1976 divorce from his former wife, Stephen Baldwin, then a Connecticut resident, had remarried; and in late 1978 he and his second wife Tracy moved to Port Clyde, Maine, where he had bought all the assets and operating business of the Port Clyde General Store. At the hearing in this proceeding, the general store was described as a "mom and pop" operation. The Baldwins lived in an apartment over the store. The property included a wharf that served the Monhegan Island mail boat and also had a small lunchroom operated during the summer. Its gross revenues, warranted by its prior owners to be about $260,000 per year, were heavily dependent upon the seasonal tourist business on Monhegan and on the mainland in the vicinity of Port Clyde village. At the time of Baldwin's death on May 30, 1979, less than eight months after his purchase of the Port Clyde properties, he held title to all of the real estate, and the store business was operated by Stephen L. Baldwin, Inc., of which he owned 90% of the stock and his wife Tracy, 10%. After Baldwin's death his widow continued to live in the upstairs apartment and operated the general store by herself.

In his will, made in 1977 when he lived in Connecticut, Baldwin nominated as executor The Connecticut National Bank, located in Bridgeport, Connecticut. After Stephen Baldwin's death, the Bank at first filed declination of the appointment, but later withdrew it at the urging—as the Bank's trust officer, Mr. Bedworth, later testified—of Baldwin's family in Connecticut who "had been customers of ours for many years." The Bank was appointed executor by the Knox County Probate Court on October 26, 1979. In the course of the following year, the children's mother and other representatives became concerned that the widow was not running the store well and repeatedly urged the Bank to supervise the store and to obtain from the widow sufficient information to evaluate the store's performance. The Bank resisted those importunities, maintaining "a neutral posture" for fear its action "could be interpreted as intimidation" by the widow. No one at the Bank ever inspected the store or audited its operation. No one at the Bank ever had any meaningful discussion with the widow about her business experience or her management of the store. The Bank never received, or ever requested, periodic financial reports from the widow. . . . By early summer 1980 the Bank knew—its trust officer later testified—that the store was "not doing well."

On October 1, 1980, the children's guardian initiated the present proceeding by filing in the Probate Court a petition asking that the necessary persons be compelled to give account of the operations of the Port Clyde General Store; that the Bank be surcharged if it were found not to have met its fiduciary obligations; and that the Bank, if necessary, be ordered to take over the store. Two weeks after the children's petition was filed, the Bank sent the widow a letter asking her for the first time to account for her operation of the store. On October 17 the Bank petitioned the Probate Court for a license to sell real estate, representing that the estate's liquid assets were insufficient to meet its obligations. . . .

II.

Under the case law and the statute applicable to the administration of this estate prior to January 1, 1981, the effective date of the Probate Code, the fiduciary obligations of an executor are defined in very general terms. Under the prior statute, 18 M.R.S.A. § 4054 (1965), the executor must "exercise the judgment and care under the circumstances then prevailing, which men of prudence, discretion and intelligence exercise in the management of their own affairs."[33] The executor is required to use good faith and prudence consistent with his duty. . . . But good faith and prudence are not alone enough; the executor must take care to enlighten his judgment. . . . The executor must preserve from depletion the total fund in which all of the beneficiaries will share. . . . The executor must be impartial among beneficiaries. . . . An executor representing that he has more skill than an ordinary person is under a duty to use that skill. See Restatement (Second) of Trusts § 174 (1959). The executor is under a general duty not to delegate to others the responsibilities of administering and distributing the estate. *See id.*, § 171. . . .

III.

Upon its appointment as executor of the Baldwin estate on October 26, 1979, the Bank was immediately faced with a situation crying out for its speedy attention. . . .

For the five months since Stephen Baldwin died, his widow had been operating the store and occupying the second floor apartment in the store building. As equal beneficiaries under the Baldwin will, the second wife and the three minor children, under the custody and guardianship of Mrs. McKane, had by law become vested with title to the real estate as tenants in common. Continued operation of the store business held a great risk of operating losses; but, at the same time, its operation in a satisfactory fashion for a limited period might help to maintain the resale value of the real estate and the store business as an operating unit. Since the second Mrs. Baldwin rather than the children would in the natural course of events desire to take the Port Clyde General Store in distribution of her half of the net estate, it might be seen by some, as later claimed by the children's representatives, that it was in her personal interest in the short run to operate the store in a way to depress the property's value for purposes of distribution. The potential for suspicion and animosity between the widow and the first wife who served as guardian of the children was obvious from the outset, and that potential quickly turned into reality when the Bank within a couple of months started to receive demands for information about the store from the children's representatives.

It also should have been clear to the Bank at an early date—at the latest on expiration of the six-month period for filing claims against the estate—that funds would have to be raised from the Port Clyde properties in order to pay debts and expenses

33. Under the Probate Code, the standard has been changed to that of "a prudent person dealing with the property of another." 18-A M.R.S.A. § 7-302(a) (1981), made applicable to personal representatives by id. § 3-703(a).

of administration. . . . The Bank had a duty to take into account the wishes of the widow who enjoyed the lifestyle she and her deceased husband acquired with the purchase of the Port Clyde General Store; at the same time, it had to administer and distribute the estate with impartiality.

IV.

With the 20-20 vision of hindsight, we can now see what optimally an executor of the Baldwin estate should have exercised himself to do promptly upon his appointment. The executor should at once have informed himself of the nature of the Port Clyde properties and the quality of the store management by the widow, by an on-site inspection in person, aided by a knowledgeable appraiser and a competent accountant. Recognizing that an executor cannot countenance continuation of a losing business—except as it might be briefly justified to maintain the sale value of the real estate or of the going concern—the executor should have promptly determined the profit-and-loss prospects of the store. If the widow's bookkeeping methods were inadequate to permit meaningful financial reporting on a frequent periodic basis, and she was to be left in control and management of the store, the executor should have seen that she had help in setting up at least a minimally adequate system for that purpose. Simultaneously, the executor should have determined as quickly as possible the debts and probable expenses of administration and the taxes, if any, in order to know whether liquid or liquifiable assets of the estate were adequate to discharge those obligations so that sale of the Port Clyde real estate would not be required. Through such investigation, the executor would have immediately found that the store was operating at a loss and also that at least part of the Port Clyde properties would have to be sold to pay the estate's debts and expenses. Armed with those findings, the executor would have been compelled to proceed promptly to a decision on how to distribute or sell the Port Clyde business and real estate. That decision was his alone to make and he was duty-bound to make it with diligence. . . . He could and should have given the widow an opportunity to take the Port Clyde General Store as her distributive share upon her making an appropriate compensating payment to the estate; but the executor's negotiations with her to that end should not have been permitted to delay an early offer of the properties for sale to others.

V.

No executor, any more than any other human being or human institution, can be expected to be endowed with foresight that is always equal to hindsight. Nor is it true that a single judgment call will always be the one and only judgment call that will satisfy the standard of prudence imposed upon executors. Nonetheless, even allowing for the limitations on human foresight and even giving a reasonable range for the prudent exercise of judgment, this court sees from a recitation of "what might have been" in the administration of Stephen Baldwin's estate at least two legally critical shortcomings in the Bank's performance as executor of the Port Clyde properties during the period between October 26, 1979, and October 17, 1980.

First, the Bank, at no time during that year and least of all within the limited time required for expeditious settlement of the estate, did anything to investigate adequately the nature, value, existing management, and profit-and-loss circumstances of the store.

Second, during that year the Bank exercised no judgment, informed or otherwise, on the disposition of the Port Clyde General Store, whether by sale or distribution or a mixture, and took no action whatever to resolve that issue. Rather, as to the Port Clyde General Store, it abdicated its affirmative obligation to settle and distribute the estate expeditiously. It passively stood by in a hope that the warring beneficiaries would come to an agreement for the disposition of the major asset of the estate.

By way of confession and avoidance, the Bank puts forth a variety of defenses, none of which we find excuse its fiduciary lapses. First, the Bank complains that it initially declined the nomination as executor and agreed to withdraw its declination only at the urging of relatives of the decedent who had long been its customers. The reasons for the Bank's accepting the Probate Court's appointment as executor are entirely irrelevant. . . . Regardless who persuaded the Bank to change its corporate mind, its appointment imposed the same responsibilities upon it as are imposed upon any executor.

As a second justification for its inaction, the Bank on appeal asserts that the impartiality mandated of an executor . . . prevented the Bank from taking any initiative in resolving the issue of the disposition of the Port Clyde General Store. Mr. Bedworth testified that exceptionally acute differences and animosities among the beneficiaries made him fearful that affirmative action on the Bank's part would give offense and involve the Bank as a disputant. The Bank's error was fundamental. . . . The inherent conflicts between the beneficiaries, which should have been apparent to the Bank from the start and which soon broke out into open conflict, would to a prudent executor have been clear warning signals that this estate required particularly aggressive attention and that the Bank would rely at its peril on the parties' reaching a negotiated settlement to take the place of what it was appointed to decide and do. . . .

As a third justification, the Bank's trust officer at trial urged that the Bank necessarily relied upon the widow's management of the store because the Bank lacked expertise to run the store itself, the estate could not afford to hire an outside manager, and the Bank knew no one in Maine to examine and report on the store's functioning. . . . Obviously, the inappropriateness of appointing the Bank as executor of such property does not excuse the Bank for its failure to carry out the trust it nonetheless accepted. The Bank plainly failed to demonstrate the skills that the law expects of the professional fiduciary it holds itself out to be. See Restatement (Second) of Trusts § 174. The fact that the Baldwin estate did not consist of a neat portfolio of listed securities provides no excuse for the Bank's abdication of its responsibilities.

In sum, the Bank's after-the-fact justifications reveal an unduly relaxed conception of its duty as executor of an estate whose principal asset consists of a small, closely held business. We conclude that the Bank did not live up to its fiduciary obligations and that the children's prayer for a surcharge against the Bank should have been granted. On this record the Probate Court's finding to the contrary was clearly erroneous.

Notes and Questions

1. What should the bank have done differently?

2. Personal representatives have the authority to continue a business for the purpose of liquidating it, but quick liquidation may not be the best way to preserve the concern's value. Without authorization in the will or from a court order, however, executors usually will lack the power to continue the decedent's business. *See In re Estate of Kurkowski*, 409 A.2d 357 (Pa. 1979) (surcharging widow for continuing, without authorization, to run decedent's business for 20 months).

3. A related problem is how to keep the cash flow going. Absent authorization, executors cannot borrow money for the business, nor can they use general estate assets. *Compare In re Estate of Muller*, 248 N.E.2d 164 (N.Y. 1969) (without specific authorization, general assets are not available to continue the business), *with Willis v. Sharp*, 21 N.E. 705 (N.Y. 1889) (language authorizing the executor to "sell or make such other disposition of my real and personal estate as the safe conduct of such business shall seem to require" was enough to allow executor to buy business goods on credit, with the general estate assets liable for the debt).

In deciding whether a testator intended to allow the executor to use the general assets of the estate to help maintain a business, should a court consider whether the decedent held the business as a corporation, a partnership, or a sole proprietorship?

4. The UPC gives personal representatives a wide range of powers they can exercise without specific court authorization. The list reads like those which appear in many wills and can serve as a model for drafting. The powers can only be exercised "reasonably for the benefit of the interested persons." UPC § 3-715.

Problem

Don has come to you for a will. He owns educational testing service, and his best friend, Kurt, is his manager. Don wants to give his parents half of his estate and Kurt the other half. He also wants to name Kurt as his executor. What provisions regarding Don's executor would you recommend?

Johnson v. Johnson

967 A.2d 274 (Md. Ct. App. 2009)

Opinion by Matricciani, J.

This case arises from a dispute between a trust beneficiary and its trustee. Appellant, Catherine A. Moreland Johnson (Catherine), is trustee and stepmother to appellee and trust beneficiary, James Michael Johnson (James). Unsuccessful in his efforts to obtain an accounting of the trust from Catherine, James filed a Petition for Court Assumption of Jurisdiction of Trust Estate and Related Relief in the Circuit Court for Calvert County. Catherine opposed the petition, asserting that James lacked a cognizable interest in the trust. After a hearing on the matter, the circuit court ordered Catherine to provide an accounting of the trust at issue, the Johnson Family Trust (the "Trust"), to James by April 25, 2008. In response, Catherine noted this timely appeal.

QUESTIONS PRESENTED

Appellant presented one question for our review, which we have reworded and divided into two questions.

> I. Did the trial court err in finding that James had an interest in the Johnson Family Trust and that as a result of that interest he was entitled to an accounting?
>
> II. Did the trial court err in finding that the language in the Trust purporting to eliminate the Trustee's duty to provide an accounting was ineffective and that James was still entitled to an accounting of the trust?

Finding no error, we shall affirm the trial court's judgment.

. . . .

DISCUSSION . . . .

II. The Trust

The Johnson Family Trust was created on August 25, 2004, by Edward R. Johnson and Catherine A. Moreland Johnson, his wife. They were named as "Trustors" and "Co-Trustees" and they established the Trust, according to its express language, with the intent that, while they were both living, they would each equitably own an undivided one-half interest in all property subject to the Trust. This was to be accomplished by the use of the federal gift tax exemption for transfers between husband and wife. Trust property, which was listed in an attached "Schedule A," constituted the "Trust Estate" and, due to its gifting provisions, the beneficial interest of the first Trustor to die was to be exactly equal to that of the surviving Trustor. Trust, Article I.

On February 14, 2006, Edward was the first to die. Pursuant to the Trust instrument, the Trust Estate was then to be divided into two shares. Trust A was to be created to take advantage of the federal estate tax exclusion and other tax provisions. The remaining portion of the decedent's interest was to be distributed to an irrevocable Trust B.

The surviving Trustor (Catherine) is entitled to the income and potentially all of the principal of Trust A during her lifetime, if needed her health, maintenance, reasonable comfort and support. She has a power of appointment to dispose of the undistributed income and principal of Trust A by her Last Will and Testament. If the power is not exercised, upon her death, the Trust A corpus is to be added to Trust B and distributed according to its terms.

Catherine has the same lifetime entitlement to the income and to principal of Trust B if needed for her health, maintenance, or support. She has a limited power of appointment over the Trust B estate which authorizes her to leave it to one or more of any children and/or other descendants of both Trustors in such shares as she may deem appropriate. Trust, Article IV. If Catherine does not exercise this limited power, distribution of the Trust B corpus is governed by the Trust's Article VI, which expressly names Edward's son, James, as a beneficiary, if he survives Catherine.

III. James's Interest in the Trust

[The court first determined that James, as taker in default of Catherine's exercise of her powers of appointment, had a future interest in Trust A and Trust B.]

IV. The Right to an Accounting

Having determined that James possesses a future interest in the [entire] Trust, we must consider the trial court's decision that his interest gives rise to a right to an accounting.

According to the Restatement of Trusts,[34] a trust is defined as a "fiduciary relationship with respect to property, arising from a manifestation of intention to create that relationship and subjecting the person who holds title to the property to duties to deal with it for the benefit of charity or for one or more persons[.]" 1 Restatement (Third) of Trusts § 2 at 17 (2003) ("Restatement"). Thus, a fiduciary relationship exists between the trustee and the beneficiary. Beneficiaries are the people, "upon whom the settlor manifested an intention to confer beneficial interests (vested or contingent) under the trust[.]" 2 Restatement, § 48 cmt. a at 236. Beneficiaries can hold a variety of interests:

> The interests of a beneficiary may be a present or future interest; and an interest may or may not be subject to conditions with respect to the recipients or the extent of the interest. Furthermore, an interest may be subject to the discretionary decisions of a trustee or another, or subject to a power of appointment or a power of revocation or amendment. In fact, there is practically no limit to the variety of interests a settlor may create.

2 Restatement, § 49 cmt. b at 243-44 (internal references omitted).

Because James has a future interest in the Trust, despite the uncertainty of his actually benefitting from that future interest, we hold that he is entitled to an accounting from the Trustee. Maryland Code (1974, 2001 Repl. Vol.), § 14-405(j)(1) of the Estates and Trust Article ("ET") lists several categories of people who are permitted to request an accounting of trust property and transactions. The relevant parties included in the list are "The beneficiary or the beneficiary's legal representative." ET § 14-405(j)(1)(ii). In response, "(2)The trustee shall provide a written accounting of all trust property and trust transactions for the previous year, or for a longer period

34. We can find no case law indicating that Maryland has expressly adopted the Restatement of Trusts, but we recognize it as a leading authority with respect to the issue before us.

if needed for tax purposes, upon request by and at reasonable times to a person authorized in paragraph (1) of this subsection." ET § 14-405 (j)(2). In *In re Clarke's Will*, 198 Md. 266, 81 A.2d 640 (1951), the Court of Appeals expounded on who was permitted to request an accounting. The Court stated that, "[i]f the petitioner has any interest at all he is entitled to invoke the court's protection." *Id.* at 273 (citations omitted). The Court continued by explaining that "[t]he mere fact that future interests are involved will not defeat the power to declare rights ...." *Id.*

When last confronted with this issue, we relied on *In re Clarke's Will*, 198 Md. 266, 81 A.2d 640, Austin W. Scott and William Fratcher's The Law of Trusts, and George Bogert's Treatise on the Law of Trusts and Trustees and we held that "[t]he fact that a beneficiary has only a future interest ... does not preclude him from compelling the trustee to account." *Jacob v. Davis*, 128 Md. App. 433, 448, 738 A.2d 904 (1999).[35]

Other jurisdictions however, have limited the requests for accounting from beneficiaries with conditional or contingent interests to instances where "waste, mismanagement or dissipation of assets appear or can be shown." *Barnhart v. Barnhart*, 415 Ill. 303, 114 N.E.2d 378, 388 (Ill. 1953). A number of those decisions are cited in the case of *Kenny v. Citizens Nat. Trust & Sav. Bank of Los Angeles*, 269 P.2d 641 (Cal. App. 1954), which stated: "So substantial is the equitable interest of the contingent remainderman of a trust, that many jurisdictions allow the maintenance of various types of actions and proceedings by a contingent beneficiary against a trustee, for good cause shown, in order to have his possible eventual interest properly secured and protected." *Id.* at 649. At least one federal court in Maryland has acknowledged the entitlement of a beneficiary with a future interest alone to request an accounting to prevent dissipation of assets, but only in exceptional circumstances. *Davidson v. Blaustein*, 247 F. Supp. 225, 227 (D. Md. 1965) (citing *In re Clarke's Will, supra*).[36] Our view of the Maryland authorities does not disclose such a burden on the beneficiary to make such a showing. Thus, James is entitled to make a reasonable request for an accounting[37] based upon his status as a Trust beneficiary who possesses a future interest in the Trust estate.

---

35. At argument, appellant's counsel attempted to distinguish our decision in *Jacob v. Davis*, 128 Md. App. 433, 738 A.2d 904, by contrasting its context of testamentary trusts to the present case, where the Johnsons established an inter vivos trust, one which he characterized as a private trust pursuant to which Catherine managed her own monies. Thus, he contended that Jacobs should not control here and the trustee should not have to account for transactions involving merely her own funds. For the reasons stated herein, we disagree.

36. In *Jacob v. Davis, supra*, we expressed our view that the Davidson decision "represents and unduly restrictive view of a beneficiary's right to an accounting." 128 Md. App. At 449 n. 6.

37. ET § 14-405(j)(2) imposes time constraints and requires that requests for accountings be made by and at reasonable times. Maryland case law also suggests that the requests must be reasonable. In Jacob v. Davis, this Court explained that the beneficiary is entitled to an accounting if the requests are made at "a reasonable time and place." *Jacob*, 128 Md. App. At 448. Additionally, the Court of Appeals has noted that while in the ordinary case, beneficiaries are entitled to an accounting, the right is not absolute. *Shipley v. Crouse*, 279 Md. 613, 625, 370 A.2d 97 (1977).

Appellant also argues that the Trust instrument grants her, as surviving trustor, discretion to distribute the remainder of the Trust at her death. But, as we have held, *supra*, this contingency is insufficient to deny James's interest or to avoid her obligation to provide him an accounting.

Alternatively, Catherine contends that if James is entitled to an accounting, it should be limited to Trust B. We disagree and conclude that James can request an accounting of the entire Trust. While his interest in Trust B is more defined, he has an interest in Trust A and how Catherine manages it. While Catherine is living, she has access to both trusts and the management of Trust A potentially affects the proceeds available for Trust B. In short, the trusts are inextricably linked and limiting James's right to an accounting of Trust B will not satisfy the Trustee's legal responsibility to him.

V. The Limitations in the Trust

Catherine contends that the circuit court's order to provide an accounting contravenes the explicit terms of the Trust, making it contrary to Maryland case law that states that the settlor's intent is controlling. James asserts that Maryland law requires a trustee to provide an accounting upon a beneficiary's request.

Catherine argues that three express provisions of the Trust show the settlor's specific intent that no trustee have an obligation to provide an accounting: first, the section that states: "The TRUSTEE shall not be required at any time to file any account in any court, nor shall the TRUSTEE be required to have any account judicially settled." Trust, Article X(C); second, the language that states the Trustors' express intent to create a private trust; and, third, the Trust language that states: "TRUSTORS direct that only the information concerning the benefits held for or distributable to any particular beneficiary be revealed to such beneficiary and that no person shall be entitled to information concerning benefits held for or distributable to any other person." Trust, Article XVI(P). These three provisions, Catherine contends, override James's legal right to request an accounting. She argues that Trustors have the ability to modify their legal obligation to provide an accounting by explicitly eliminating it in the Trust's provisions.

This Court encountered a similar issue in *Jacob v. Davis*, 128 Md. App. at 450-51. In that case, appellees argued that a section of the contested will relieved the trustee of accounting to the beneficiaries. *Id.* at 446. The provision in *Jacob* read:

> My Trustee shall be excused from filing any account with any court; however, my Trustee shall render an annual (or more frequent) account and may, at any other time, including at the time of the death, resignation, or removal of any Trustee, render an intermediate account of my Trustee's administration to such of the then current income beneficiaries who are of sound mind and not minors at the time of such accounting.

Id. We stated that, "[t]o our knowledge, no Maryland appellate decision ha[d] addressed the extent to which a decedent or testator [could] limit the common law duty of a trustee to account in a court of equity." *Id.* at 450.[38] We further stated that there were not statutes or rules addressing this issue. *Id.* at 450. Thus, we turned to a recognized authority on Trusts, Bogert's, The Law of Trusts and Trustees. The *Jacob* Court quoted, but did not expressly adopt, Bogert's explanation of the role of a trustee and the reasons why a Trustor should not be permitted to avoid his duty to account. *Id.* at 450-51. Bogert's statement reads as follows:

> A [testator] who attempts to create a trust without any accountability in the trustee is contradicting himself. A trust necessarily grants rights to the beneficiary that are enforceable in equity. If the trustee cannot be called to account, the beneficiary cannot force the trustee to any particular line of conduct with regard to the trust property or sue for breach of trust. The trustee may do as he likes with the property, and the beneficiary is without remedy. If the court finds that the settlor really intended a trust, it would seem that accountability in chancery or other court must inevitably follow as an incident. Without an account the beneficiary must be in the dark as to whether there has been a breach of trust and so is prevented as a practical matter from holding the trustee liable for a breach.

The Law of Trusts and Trustees, § 973 at 467.

> The Restatement of Trusts also outlines the fiduciary duties of a trustee, explaining:
>
> [F]iduciary principles include (i) the general duty to act, reasonably informed, with impartiality among the various beneficiaries and interests and (ii) the duty to provide the beneficiaries with information concerning the trust and its administration. This combination of duties entitles the beneficiaries (and also the court) not only to accounting information but also to relevant, general information concerning the bases upon which the trustee's discretionary judgments have been or will be made.

Restatement, § 50 cmt. b at 260 (2003) (internal references omitted). It continues: "It is contrary to sound policy, and a contradiction in terms, to permit the settlor to relieve a "trustee" of all accountability." Id. at cmt. c at 262. We now adopt this reasoning and conclude that a trustor cannot, by including limitations in the Trust instrument, circumscribe the trustee's duty to account to beneficiaries.

This conclusion is in line with recognized Maryland law regarding trusts and accountings. In *In re Clarke's Will*, 198 Md. 266, 81 A.2d 640, the Court of Appeals

---

38. Our research uncovered no additional authority in Maryland or elsewhere since we last addressed this issue in *Jacob* in 1999. However, cf. *Stix v. Comm'r*, 152 F.2d 562 (2d Cir. 1945) (stating, "No language, however strong, will entirely remove any power held in trust from the reach of a court in equity."); *In re Clark*, 174 Iowa 449, 154 N.W. 759, (1915) (stating, "It cannot be that the creator of a trust by will can absolutely exclude the courts from controlling any and all expenditures from the trust fund[.]"); *Carrier v. Carrier*, 226 N.Y. 114, 123 N.E. 135 (1919) (stating, "His discretion, however broad, did not relieve him from obedience to the great principles of equity which are the life of every trust.").

liberally interpreted the class of beneficiaries who would be permitted to request an accounting. By broadly construing who was entitled to an accounting, the Court of Appeals recognized the importance of accountings for maintaining the integrity of trusts. *See also Ehlen v. Ehlen*, 63 Md. 267 (1885) (responding to interested party's petition, court affirmed the order for trustee to bring into court the securities and money held in trust after it was shown that property was in danger).

Permitting a trustor to eliminate the duty to account to beneficiaries would be contrary to the Court of Appeals' decisions regarding who is entitled to an accounting. We conclude that, despite the language in the Trust attempting to eliminate Catherine's duty to account, James is entitled to request an accounting and Catherine is required to provide it.

JUDGMENT AFFIRMED. COSTS TO BE PAID BY APPELLANT.

Uniform Trust Code

Section 813. Duty to Inform and Report.

(a) A trustee shall keep the qualified beneficiaries of the trust reasonably informed about the administration of the trust and of the material facts necessary for them to protect their interests. Unless unreasonable under the circumstances, a trustee shall promptly respond to a beneficiary's request for information related to the administration of the trust.

(b) A trustee:

(1) upon request of a beneficiary, shall promptly furnish to the beneficiary a copy of the trust instrument;

(2) within 60 days after accepting a trusteeship, shall notify the qualified beneficiaries of the acceptance and of the trustee's name, address, and telephone number;

(3) within 60 days after the date the trustee acquires knowledge of the creation of an irrevocable trust, or the date the trustee acquires knowledge that a formerly revocable trust has become irrevocable, whether by the death of the settlor or otherwise, shall notify the qualified beneficiaries of the trust's existence, of the identity of the settlor or settlors, of the right to request a copy of the trust instrument, and of the right to a trustee's report as provided in subsection (c); and

(4) shall notify the qualified beneficiaries in advance of any change in the method or rate of the trustee's compensation.

(c) A trustee shall send to the distributees or permissible distributees of trust income or principal, and to other qualified or nonqualified beneficiaries who request it, at least annually and at the termination of the trust, a report of the trust property, liabilities, receipts, and disbursements, including the source and amount of the trustee's compensation, a listing of the trust assets and, if feasible, their respective market values. Upon a vacancy in a trusteeship, unless a cotrustee remains in office, a report must be sent to the qualified beneficiaries by the former trustee. A personal representative, [conservator], or [guardian] may send the qualified beneficiaries a report on behalf of a deceased or incapacitated trustee.

Comment

The Uniform Trust Code employs the term "report" instead of "accounting" in order to negate any inference that the report must be prepared in any particular format or with a high degree of formality. The reporting requirement might even be satisfied by providing the beneficiaries with copies of the trust's income tax returns and monthly brokerage account statements if the information on those returns and statements is complete and sufficiently clear. The key factor is not the format chosen but whether the report provides the beneficiaries with the information necessary to protect their interests.

Notes

1. UTC § 813 imposes a duty on trustees to inform and report to qualified beneficiaries. UTC § 103(13) defines a qualified beneficiary as:

> a beneficiary who, on the date the beneficiary's qualification is determined:
>
> (A) is a distributee or permissible distributee of trust income or principal;
>
> (B) would be a distributee or permissible distributee of trust income or principal if the interests of the distributees described in subparagraph (A) terminated on that date; or
>
> (C) would be a distributee or permissible distributee of trust income or principal if the trust terminated on that date.

2. *Johnson v. Johnson* raises two important issues: (1) Are all future interest beneficiaries entitled to information from the trustee?[39] (2) May a settlor dispense with the trustee's duty to account? The UTC, which Maryland has now enacted, addresses both issues.

Since only qualified beneficiaries are generally entitled to information under the UTC, certain remote and contingent beneficiaries may not be entitled to information. Moreover, under the Code's virtual representation doctrine, contingent beneficiaries who are qualified beneficiaries may not need to actually receive information. *See* § UTC 304. Also, a court may appoint a representative for a qualified beneficiary even if not for purposes of litigation. *See* § UTC 305.

---

39. *See Marshall & Ilsley Trust Co., N.A. v. Woodward*, 848 N.E.2d 1175 (Ind. Ct. App.2006) (named contingent beneficiary entitled to an accounting).

The trustee's duty to provide certain information, including the duty to notify qualified beneficiaries of the existence of an irrevocable trust, was made mandatory under the original UTC (*see* UTC § 105(b)(8)), as was the duty to respond to requests for reports and other information. *See* UTC § 105(b)(9). However, the Code recognizes the desire of some settlors to keep knowledge from younger beneficiaries. For qualified beneficiaries under age 25, UTC § 105(b)(8) permits the settlor to waive notice of the existence of the trust, the trustee, and the right to request an annual report.

Restatement (Third) Trusts § 82 also imposes the duty to furnish information to beneficiaries. Rather than the UTC's age approach, it employs the concept of fairly representative beneficiaries thereby

> "balancing considerations of practicality for trustees and the importance in most trusts of reflecting the diversity of the beneficial interests and beneficiary concerns. Thus, the trustee's duty under this requirement is to make a good-faith effort to select and inform a limited number of beneficiaries whose interests and concerns are fairly representative of—*i.e.*, likely to coincide with—those of the trust's beneficiaries generally."

3d Rest. Trusts § 82, cmt. (a)(1).

Non-UTC states vary in their approaches to the trustee's duty to furnish information to beneficiaries. For example, Georgia makes the trustee's duty mandatory, whereas Alaska, Delaware, and South Dakota allow settlors to keep trusts secret.

3. As matters have developed, the UTC notification and reporting provisions have proved the Code's most controversial, primarily because some settlors desire to prevent beneficiaries from even knowing of the trust's existence. As a result, the question of whether to make some of § 813's provisions mandatory and non-waivable was left to the enacting states. The UTC indicates optional provisions by placing them in brackets, and the UTC's mandatory, non-waivable terms are identified in § 105. To make the controversial notification and reporting provisions optional, therefore, UTC §§ 105(b)(8) and 105(b)(9) were bracketed. As explained in the 2004 Comments to UTC § 105:

> The placing of these provisions in brackets does not mean that the Drafting Committee recommends that an enacting jurisdiction delete Sections 105(b)(8) and 105(b)(9). The Committee continues to believe that Sections 105(b)(8) and (b)(9), enacted as is, represent the best balance of competing policy considerations. Rather, the provisions were placed in brackets out of a recognition that there is a lack of consensus on the extent to which a settlor ought to be able to waive reporting to beneficiaries, and that there is little chance that the states will enact Sections 105(b)(8) and (b)(9) with any uniformity.

By 2011, the lack of consensus on providing information and reports to beneficiaries in UTC states had become clearly evident. *See generally* Lauren Z. Curry, *Agents in Secrecy: The Use of Information Surrogates in Trust Administration*, 64 Vand. L. Rev.

925 (2011) (detailing how UTC states approach notification and reporting requirements). In fact, over 10 UTC states, including Arkansas, Kansas, and Virginia, now allow the settlor to affirmatively waive the trustee's duty to inform and report to any beneficiary by removing the duty as a mandatory trust rule.[40] Following the lead of the District of Columbia, at least four UTC states (Maine, Missouri, Ohio, and Oregon) now allow a surrogate to receive information and reports in lieu of a beneficiary.[41]

Since 2011, several states have enacted the UTC with differing approaches to the secret trust issue. Minnesota, Mississippi, and Wisconsin permit secret trusts; Kentucky employs the surrogate approach (as does Florida) while Maryland has enacted the mandatory provisions of UTC § 105(b)(8) and (9).[42]

Restatement (Third) Trusts § 82, General Comment, makes clear that the settlor may limit access to information but the duty to provide information "may not be dispensed with entirely or to a degree or for a time that would unduly interfere with the underlying purposes effectiveness of the information requirements."

4. Even if an enacting state imposes a mandatory duty on trustees to furnish beneficiaries information on request, UTC § 105(b)(9) would allow a state to permit only qualified beneficiaries to receive requested information. Restatement (Third) Trusts § 82 requires all requesting beneficiaries to receive information subject to reasonable restrictions if imposed by the settlor.

5. UTC § 603(a) and Restatement (Third) Trusts § 74(1)(b), as explained by Comment to Restatement (Third) Trusts § 82, effectively make the settlor, while competent, the exclusive person entitled to notices and reports on the theory that the settlor has the equivalent of ownership of the trust property. By a 2004 amendment, UTC § 603(a) would leave it to the enacting state to decide that beneficiaries have no rights even if the settlor is incapacitated. *JP Morgan Chase Bank, N.A. v. Longmeyer*, 275 S.W.3d 697 (Ky. 2009), reflects the opposite end of the spectrum regarding required notice requirements. (Under Kentucky law, which is patterned under UPC § 7-303, a trustee is required to give notice to beneficiaries of a revocable trust that they had been removed as beneficiaries by the settlor). *See generally* Turney P. Berry, David M. English & Dana G. Fitzsimons, Jr., *Longmeyer Exposes (or Creates) Uncertainty About the Duty to Inform Remainder Beneficiaries of a Revocable Trust*, 35 ACTEC J. 125 (2009).

---

40. *See, e.g.*, Ark. Code Ann. § 28-73-105. *See* Lauren Z. Curry, *Agents in Secrecy: The Use of Information Surrogates in Trust Administration*, 64. Vand. L. Rev. 925, 937 (2011) (listing states that do not mandatorily require a trustee to inform and report).

41. *See, e.g.*, Ohio. Rev. Code Ann. § 5801.04(C). *See generally* Curry, *supra* note 30, *at 939*.

42. Nebraska has not only enacted the mandatory duty of UTC § 105(b)(9) to respond to requests but also makes mandatory the trustee's duty to keep qualified beneficiaries reasonably informed about the trust and material facts necessary to protect their interests. *See Rafert v. Meyer*, 859 N.W.2d 332 (Neb. 2015) (holding ineffective a trust provision waiving trustee's duty to notify beneficiaries about material facts).

6. Trustees also have the duty to "earmark" trust funds and not to commingle them. *See* UTC § 810 and 3d Rest. Trusts § 84. Earmarking means labeling assets as trust assets to avoid confusion about whether they are the personal assets of the trustee. Commingling involves mixing assets of different trusts with each other, or with the trustee's own assets. Often documents or statutes authorize commingling so trustees can pool smaller trust funds and achieve efficiencies of scale.

7. Trustees also have important distribution duties upon trust termination. Under UTC § 817(b), the trustee must expeditiously distribute trust property to the beneficiaries but can withhold sufficient amounts to pay winding up expenses, debts, and taxes. *See generally* 3d Rest. Trusts § 89.

Problems

1. You are the trust officer in charge of the Garcia Trust, whose main asset is a small office building in your downtown area. The roof leaks and should be replaced, but the trust lacks the necessary funds. What should you do?

2. State Bank & Trust Co. has come to you for advice. They serve as trustee for several trusts which limit or end beneficiaries' interests in specific situations. For example, some terminate income interests "upon the remarriage" of the surviving spouse. Others authorize payment of education expenses "while the beneficiary is pursuing the education diligently." How should the bank protect itself against liability for distributing funds inappropriately?

Selected References

Frances H. Foster, *Privacy and the Elusive Quest for Uniformity in the Law of Trusts*, 38 Ariz. St. L.J. 713 (2006).

Thomas P. Gallanis, *The Trustee's Duty to Inform*, 85 N.C. L. Rev. 1595 (2007).

Joseph Kartiganer & Raymond H. Young, *The UTC: Help for Beneficiaries and Their Attorneys*, Prob. & Prop. 18 (Mar./Apr. 2003).

Donald Kozusko, *In Defense of Quiet Trusts*, 143 Tr. & Est. 20 (Mar. 2004).

Kevin D. Millard, *The Trustee's Duty to Inform and Report Under the Uniform Trust Code*, 40 Real Prop. Prob. & Tr. J. 373 (2005).

Robert Whitman, *Full Disclosure Is Best*, 143 Tr. & Est. 59 (July 2004).

E. Liability to Third Parties

Under traditional rules, fiduciaries may be personally liable for contracts even if the contract is within the fiduciary's authority, and they may be personally liable for torts even when they have personally done no wrong. *See* Thomas E. Atkinson, Law of Wills §§ 118, 119 (2d ed. 1953); George T. Bogert, Trusts §§ 125, 129 (6th ed. 1987). When fiduciaries have acted properly, they usually will have a right of indemnification against the estate or trust. If that entity has plenty of assets, the liability should pose no problem; if the claim exceeds the assets, however, the fiduciary will bear the loss. Of course, if the contract were beyond the scope of the trustee's power or if the tort resulted from the trustee's own negligence, then personal liability would attach without a right of indemnification.

Fiduciaries can avoid contract liability only if the contract explicitly excludes personal liability. Even signing in a representative capacity, like "Warren Magnuson, Executor of the Estate of Andrew Magnuson," is not enough to avoid liability under the traditional rule. Among the most common defendants are those who arrange for burial, and then find the estate assets are too small to cover the cost. *See, e.g., Smolka v. Chandler*, 20 A.2d 131 (Del. 1941).

In response to the harshness of these traditional rules, many states have reversed them. In this context, the UPC treats estates and trusts as "quasi-corporations," with personal representatives and trustees liable as an agent would be. Thus, unless the contract provides otherwise, "a personal representative is not individually liable on a contract properly entered into in his fiduciary capacity in the course of administration of the estate unless he fails to reveal his representative capacity and identify the estate in the contract." UPC § 3-808(a). Under UTC § 1010(a), absent a contract provision to the contrary, a trustee can avoid personal liability on a contract properly entered into if the trustee merely discloses that the contract was entered into in a fiduciary capacity. *Accord* 3d Rest. Trusts § 106(1). Similarly, under the UPC a fiduciary is personally liable for torts only if personally at fault. UPC § 3-808(b) (personal representative). *Accord* UTC § 1010(b) and 3d Rest. Trusts § 106(2) (trustee).

Fiduciary liability for environmental damage has changed in recent years. Prior to 1996 amendment of the Comprehensive Environmental Response, Compensation, and Liability Act of 1980 (CERCLA), a fiduciary could be held personally liable for environmental damage caused by the release or threatened release of certain hazardous substances from property that was owned by an estate or trust. *See City of Phoenix v. Garbage Servs. Co.*, 827 F. Supp. 600 (D. Ariz. 1993) (imposing personal liability on fiduciaries for contaminated landfill site under CERCLA). In 1996, the relevant CERCLA provision, 42 U.S.C. § 9607, was amended to limit fiduciary liability to the assets held in a fiduciary capacity, absent negligence on the fiduciary's part. *See* 42 U.S.C. § 9607(n). The negligence exception is discussed in *Canadyne-Georgia Corp. v. NationsBank*, 183 F.3d 1269 (11th Cir. 1999). UTC § 1010(b) specifically exculpates a trustee who is not personally at fault from liability for environmental law violations.

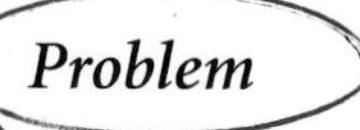

Several years ago you prepared a revocable living trust for Carol and Loren Barton as they prepared for semi-retirement. They moved to a vacation community and bought a small resort with several cabins, a store, and a gas station. They put all of the property in the trust and named Carol as Trustee, Loren as her successor, and you as the alternative successor. After the deaths of Carol and Loren, the trust was to serve as a source of funds for their grandchildren's college educations and terminate when the youngest grandchild alive at Loren's death reached age 30.

Loren died two years ago, and Carol died last week. They have three grandchildren, ages 8, 12, and 15. What are your initial concerns as you prepare to take over as successor trustee?

§ 10.04 Remedies for Breach of Fiduciary Duties

Beneficiaries who have suffered from breaches of duty have available a wide range of remedies against their fiduciaries, which are generally considered equitable in character.[43] *See* 3d Rest. Trusts § 95. Removal is perhaps the ultimate remedy. *See, e.g., Conte v. Ditta*, 312 S.W.3d 951 (Tex. App. 2011) (removal of individual trustee); *In re Estate of Jones*, 93 P.3d 147 (Wash. 2004) (removal of estate's personal representative); *McNeil v. McNeil*, 798 A.2d 503 (Del. 2002) (removal of corporate trustee). However, these remedies may be barred under certain circumstances.

One developing and interesting issue is whether trust (or will) beneficiaries are precluded from seeking judicial resolution because the instrument requires that issues be resolved by arbitration or some other non-judicial method of resolution. Some courts have held that mandatory arbitration clauses are not enforceable because trusts and wills are not subject to state laws enforcing arbitration agreements in contracts. *See, e.g., McArthur v. McArthur*, 168 Cal. Rptr. 3d 785 (Cal. App. 2014) and *Schoneberger v. Oelze*, 96 P.3d 1078 (Ariz. Ct. App. 2004) (*superseded by* Ariz. Rev. Stat. Ann. § 14-10205. *But see Rachel v. Reitz*, 403 S.W.3d 840 (Tex. 2013) (provision binding). *See generally* Gary E. Spitko, *The Will as an Implied Unilateral Arbitration Contract*, 68 Fla. L. Rev. 49 (2016); Erin Katzen, *Arbitration Clauses in Wills and Trusts: Defining the Parameters for Mandatory Arbitration of Wills and Trusts*, 24 Quinnipiac Prob. L.J. 118 (2011); Bridget A. Logstrom, Bruce M. Stone & Robert W. Goldman, *Resolving Disputes with Ease and Grace*, 31 ACTEC J. 235 (2005). *See also* Jonathan G. Blattmachr, *Reducing Estate and Trust Litigation Through Disclosure, In Terrorem Clauses, Mediation and Arbitration*, 36 ACTEC L.J. 547 (2010).

---

43. The traditional rule has been that a settlor as such lacks standing to sue a trustee for breach of a private trust or to enforce the terms of a trust. See 3d Rest. Trusts § 94, cmt d(2). A settlor of a charitable trust may have standing; indeed UTC § 405(c) confers standing on the settlors of a charitable trust. *Accord* 3d Rest. Trusts § 94.

A. Remedies in General

Uniform Trust Code

Section 1001. Remedies for Breach of Trust.

(a) A violation by a trustee of a duty the trustee owes to a beneficiary is a breach of trust.

(b) To remedy a breach of trust that has occurred or may occur, the court may:

(1) compel the trustee to perform the trustee's duties;

(2) enjoin the trustee from committing a breach of trust;

(3) compel the trustee to redress a breach of trust by paying money, restoring property, or other means;

(4) order a trustee to account;

(5) appoint a special fiduciary to take possession of the trust property and administer the trust;

(6) suspend the trustee;

(7) remove the trustee as provided in Section 706;

(8) reduce or deny compensation to the trustee;

(9) subject to Section 1012, void an act of the trustee, impose a lien or a constructive trust on trust property, or trace trust property wrongfully disposed of and recover the property or its proceeds; or

(10) order any other appropriate relief.

Comment

Traditionally, remedies for breach of trust at law were limited to suits to enforce unconditional obligations to pay money or deliver chattels. See Restatement (Second) of Trusts §§ 198 (1959). Otherwise, remedies for breach of trust were exclusively equitable, and as such, punitive damages were not available and findings of fact were made by the judge and not a jury. See Restatement (Second) of Trusts §§ 197 (1959). The Uniform Trust Code does not preclude the possibility that a particular enacting jurisdiction might not follow these norms.

Section 1002. Damages for Breach of Trust.

(a) A trustee who commits a breach of trust is liable to the beneficiaries affected for the greater of:

(1) the amount required to restore the value of the trust property and trust distributions to what they would have been had the breach not occurred; or

(2) the profit the trustee made by reason of the breach.

(b) Except as otherwise provided in this subsection, if more than one trustee is liable to the beneficiaries for a breach of trust, a trustee is entitled to contribution from the other trustee or trustees. A trustee is not entitled to contribution if the trustee was substantially more at fault than another trustee or if the trustee committed the breach of trust in bad faith or with reckless indifference to the purposes of the trust or the interests of the beneficiaries. A trustee who received a benefit from the breach of trust is not entitled to contribution from another trustee to the extent of the benefit received.

In re Estate of Rothko

372 N.E.2d 291 (N.Y. 1977)

Cooke, J.

Mark Rothko, an abstract expressionist painter whose works through the years gained for him an international reputation of greatness, died testate on February 25, 1970. The principal asset of his estate consisted of 798 paintings of tremendous value, and the dispute underlying this appeal involves the conduct of his three executors in their disposition of these works of art. In sum, that conduct as portrayed in the record and sketched in the opinions was manifestly wrongful and indeed shocking.

Rothko's will was admitted to probate on April 27, 1970 and letters testamentary were issued to Bernard J. Reis, Theodoros Stamos and Morton Levine. Hastily and within a period of only about three weeks and by virtue of two contracts each dated May 21, 1970, the executors dealt with all 798 paintings.

By a contract of sale, the estate executors agreed to sell to Marlborough A.G., a Liechtenstein corporation (hereinafter MAG), 100 Rothko paintings as listed for $1,800,000, $200,000 to be paid on execution of the agreement and the balance of $1,600,000 in 12 equal interest-free installments over a 12-year period. Under the second agreement, the executors consigned to Marlborough Gallery, Inc., a domestic corporation (hereinafter MNY), "approximately 700 paintings listed on a Schedule to be prepared", the consignee to be responsible for costs covering items such as insurance, storage restoration and promotion. By its provisos, MNY could sell up to 35 paintings a year from each of two groups, pre-1947 and post-1947, for 12 years at the best price obtainable but not less than the appraised estate value, and it would receive a 50% commission on each painting sold, except for a commission of 40% on those sold to or through other dealers.

Petitioner Kate Rothko, decedent's daughter and a person entitled to share in his estate by virtue of an election under EPTL 5-3.3,[44] instituted this proceeding to remove the executors, to enjoin MNY and MAG from disposing of the paintings, to rescind the aforesaid agreements between the executors and said corporations, for a return of the paintings still in possession of those corporations, and for damages....

---

44. Rothko's children had been disinherited by the will, which left the residuary estate to a charitable foundation. EPTL section 5-3.3 allowed the bequest to be set aside to the extent it exceeded one-half of the estate, and since has been repealed. [Eds.]

Following a nonjury trial covering 89 days and in a thorough opinion, the Surrogate found: that Reis was a director, secretary and treasurer of MNY, the consignee art gallery, in addition to being a coexecutor of the estate; that the testator had a 1969 inter vivos contract with MNY to sell Rothko's work at a commission of only 10% and whether that agreement survived testator's death was a problem that a fiduciary in a dual position could not have impartially faced; that Reis was in a position of serious conflict of interest with respect to the contracts of May 21, 1970 and that his dual role and planned purpose benefited the Marlborough interests to the detriment of the estate; that it was to the advantage of coexecutor Stamos as a "not-too-successful artist, financially", to curry favor with Marlborough and that the contract made by him with MNY within months after signing the estate contracts placed him in a position where his personal interests conflicted with those of the estate, especially leading to lax contract enforcement efforts by Stamos; that Stamos acted negligently and improvidently in view of his own knowledge of the conflict of interest of Reis; that the third coexecutor, Levine, while not acting in self-interest or with bad faith, nonetheless failed to exercise ordinary prudence in the performance of his assumed fiduciary obligations since he was aware of Reis' divided loyalty, believed that Stamos was also seeking personal advantage, possessed personal opinions as to the value of the paintings and yet followed the leadership of his coexecutors without investigation of essential facts or consultation with competent and disinterested appraisers, and that the business transactions of the two Marlborough corporations were admittedly controlled and directed by Francis K. Lloyd. It was concluded that the acts and failures of the three executors were clearly improper to such a substantial extent as to mandate their removal under SCPA 711 as estate fiduciaries. The Surrogate also found . . . that the contracts for sale and consignment of paintings between the executors and MNY and MAG provided inadequate value to the estate, amounting to a lack of mutuality and fairness resulting from conflicts on the part of Reis and Stamos and improvidence on the part of all executors; that said contracts were voidable and were set aside by reason of violation of the duty of loyalty and improvidence of the executors, knowingly participated in and induced by MNY and MAG; . . . The Surrogate held that the present value at the time of trial of the paintings sold is the proper measure of damages as to MNY, MAG, Lloyd, Reis and Stamos. . . . It was held that Levine was liable for $6,464,880 in damages, as he was not in a dual position acting for his own interest and was thus liable only for the actual value of paintings sold MNY and MAG as of the dates of sale, and that Reis, Stamos, MNY and MAG, apart from being jointly and severally liable for the same damages as Levine for negligence, were liable for the greater sum of $9,252,000 "as appreciation damages less amounts previously paid to the estate with regard to sales of paintings." . . .

The Appellate Division . . . affirmed on the opinion of Surrogate Midonick, with additional comments. . . .

. . . [T]he assertions that there were no conflicts of interest on the part of Reis or Stamos indulge in sheer fantasy. Besides being a director and officer of MNY, for which there was financial remuneration, however slight, Reis, as noted by the

Surrogate, had different inducements to favor the Marlborough interests, including his own aggrandizement of status and financial advantage through sales of almost one million dollars for items from his own and his family's extensive private art collection by the Marlborough interests.... Similarly, Stamos benefited as an artist under contract with Marlborough and, interestingly, Marlborough purchased a Stamos painting from a third party for $4,000 during the week in May, 1970 when the estate contract negotiations were pending.... The conflicts are manifest....

The measure of damages was the issue that divided the Appellate Division (*see* 56 A.D.2d, at p. 500, 392 N.Y.S.2d at p. 872). The contention of Reis, Stamos, MNY and MAG, that the award of appreciation damages was legally erroneous and impermissible, is based on a principle that an executor authorized to sell is not liable for an increase in value if the breach consists only in selling for a figure less than that for which the executor should have sold. For example, Scott states:

> "The beneficiaries are not entitled to the value of the property at the time of the decree if it was not the duty of the trustee to retain the property in the trust and the breach of trust consisted merely in selling the property for too low a price" (3 Scott, Trusts [3d ed.], § 208.3, p. 1687 [emphasis added]).
>
> "If the trustee is guilty of a breach of trust in selling trust property for an inadequate price, he is liable for the difference between the amount he should have received and the amount which he did receive. He is not liable, however, for any subsequent rise in value of the property sold". (Id., § 208.6, pp. 1689–1690.)

A recitation of similar import appears in Comment d under Restatement, Trusts 2d (§ 205): "d. Sale for less than value. If the trustee is authorized to sell trust property, but in breach of trust he sells it for less than he should receive, he is liable for the value of the property at the time of the sale less the amount which he received. If the breach of trust consists only in selling it for too little, he is not chargeable with the amount of any subsequent increase in value of the property under the rule stated in Clause (c), as he would be if he were not authorized to sell the property. See § 208." (Emphasis added.) However, employment of "merely" and "only" as limiting words suggests that where the breach consists of some misfeasance, other than solely for selling "for too low a price" or "for too little", appreciation damages may be appropriate. Under Scott (§ 208.3, pp. 1686–1687) and the Restatement (§ 208), the trustee may be held liable for appreciation damages if it was his or her duty to retain the property, the theory being that the beneficiaries are entitled to be placed in the same position they would have been in had the breach not consisted of a sale of property that should have been retained. The same rule should apply where the breach of trust consists of a serious conflict of interest—which is more than merely selling for too little.

The reason for allowing appreciation damages, where there is a duty to retain, and only date of sale damages, where there is authorization to sell, is policy oriented. If a trustee authorized to sell were subjected to a greater measure of damages he might be reluctant to sell (in which event he might run a risk if depreciation ensued). On the other hand, if there is a duty to retain and the trustee sells there is no policy reason to protect the trustee; he has not simply acted imprudently, he has violated an integral condition of the trust.

"If a trustee in breach of trust transfers trust property to a person who takes with notice of the breach of trust, and the transferee has disposed of the property . . . [i]t seems proper to charge him with the value at the time of the decree, since if it had not been for the breach of trust the property would still have been a part of the trust estate" (4 Scott, Trusts [3d ed.], § 291.2; . . . This rule of law which applies to the transferees MNY and MAG also supports the imposition of appreciation damages against Reis and Stamos, since if the Marlborough corporations are liable for such damages either as purchaser or consignees with notice, from one in breach of trust, it is only logical to hold that said executors, as sellers and consignors, are liable also pro tanto. . . .

Restatement (Third) of Trusts

§ 81 Duty with Respect to Co-Trustees

(1) If a trust has more than one trustee, except as otherwise provided by the terms of the trust, each trustee has a duty and the right to participate in the administration of the trust.

(2) Each trustee also has a duty to use reasonable care to prevent a co-trustee from committing a breach of trust and, if a breach of trust occurs, to obtain redress.

§ 102. Liability of Multiple Trustees: Contribution

(1) Except as otherwise provided in this Section, if two or more trustees are liable for a breach of trust, they are jointly and severally liable, with contribution rights and obligations between or among them reflecting their respective degrees of fault.

(2) A trustee who committed a breach in bad faith is not entitled to contribution unless the trustee or trustees from whom contribution is sought also acted in bad faith.

(3) A trustee who benefited personally from the breach is not entitled to contribution to the extent of that benefit.

Notes and Questions

1. What did Levine do wrong? When you consider whether to serve as a co-fiduciary or whether to advise someone else to do so, remember Levine's fate. *See Dardovitch v. Haltzman*, 190 F.3d 125 (3d Cir. 1999) (co-trustee's good faith did not excuse liability for breach of trust by another co-trustee).

2. Courts do not typically award punitive damages, but in egregious cases, punitive damages may be permissible. *See* 3d Rest. Trusts § 100, cmt. d. Were the "appreciation damages" levied against the defendants other than Levine really just punitive damages for what the court saw as outrageous behavior? *See* Richard V. Wellman, *Punitive Surcharges Against Disloyal Fiduciaries-Is Rothko Right?*, 77 Mich. L. Rev. 95 (1978).

Artists' works often appreciate substantially after their deaths. For example, it was reported in the London Sunday Times that in May 2007, Rothko's "White Center (Yellow, Pink, Lavender on Rose)" sold for almost $73 million! *See* http://www.timesonline.co.uk/tol/news/world/us_and_americas/article1797653.ece.

3. When calculating damages caused by the trustee's improper discretionary distributions to an income beneficiary, the trustee may be liable to remainder beneficiaries for the total amount of improper distributions with interest accruing from the date of the life income beneficiary's death. *See Reliance Trust Co. v. Candler*, 751 S.E.2d 47 (Ga. 2013) (reversing a jury award that calculated prejudgment interest running from the date of each encroachment, reasoning that any interest accruing on trust corpus would have been distributed to the income beneficiary).

4. Where a trustee causes loss to the trust by breaching the duty of care and simultaneously breaches the duty of loyalty by engaging in self-dealing, the trustee may be liable for both restoration damages and for disgorgement of profits that were the result of the wrongdoing. A beneficiary's recovery will not be limited to restoration damages if restoration damages will not ensure that both remedial goals are fulfilled. *See Miller v. Bank of Am., N.A.*, 352 P.3d 1162 (N.M. 2015) (remanding the case back to the trial court on the issue of damages where the record was unclear as to whether both restoration and disgorgement were accomplished).

5. Setting damages for imprudent investments poses different problems. Consistent with § 100 of the Restatement (Third) of Trusts, UTC § 1002(a)(1) adopts a lost profits approach. It asks what the trust property would have been worth had the trust property been prudently invested and, where applicable, uses benchmark portfolios (market indicies) to determine value. *See* Estate of Wilde, 708 A.2d 273 (Me. 1998) (measure of damages based on S&P 500 Index). *In re Janes*, which involved the imprudent retention of Kodak stock, the court of appeals applied the traditional measure of damages (681 N.E.2d at 339–340):

> Where, as here, a fiduciary's imprudence consists solely of negligent retention of assets it should have sold, the measure of damages is the value of the lost capital . . . Thus, the Surrogate's reliance on Matter of Rothko in imposing a "lost profit" measure of damages is inapposite, since in that case the fiduciary's misconduct consisted of deliberate self-dealing and faithless transfers of trust property . . . .
>
> In imposing liability upon a fiduciary on the basis of the capital lost, the court should determine the value of the stock on the date it should have been sold, and subtract from that figure the proceeds from the sale of the stock or, if the stock is still retained by the estate, the value of the stock at the time of the accounting . . . .
>
> Whether interest is awarded, and at what rate, is a matter within the discretion of the trial court. . . . Dividends and other income attributable to the retained assets should offset any interest awarded. . . .

6. If some investments in a portfolio do well, but others do poorly, a trustee may face the "anti-netting" rule, which can apply in a variety of situations. It says that a trustee who breaches trust duties may not offset gains against losses if the breaches were separate and distinct. 3d Rest. Trusts § 213.

At first blush, the anti-netting rule would seem to cause problems for those endorsing modern portfolio theory, which focuses on total gains or losses. The two rules are not at odds, however, because modern portfolio theory applies to determine whether there is a breach. The anti-netting rule applies only if there has been a breach. *See* 3d Rest. Trusts § 101, cmt. a. Moreover, the anti-netting rule may not apply at all, because the investment decisions may well have been interrelated, rather than separate and distinct. *See id.*, cmt. f.

7. Rather than damages, a beneficiary may seek to retrieve particular property. If the trustee has already sold the property to a bona fide purchaser, however, this remedy will not be available. *See* 3d Rest. Trusts § 109. There are four major limitations to the bona fide purchaser rule: (a) the purchase must be for value, (b) the transaction must be legal, (c) the right of the purchaser must be legal, rather than equitable, and (d) the purchaser must have no notice of the breach. *See* 3d Rest. Trusts § 110.

8. Can a third person be liable for dealing with a trustee who exceeds his, her or its authority? At common law third persons were strictly liable, which effectively imposed on them a duty to inquire whether the trustee was acting properly. Section 7 of the Uniform Trustees' Powers Act reversed the rule; third persons would only be liable if they had actual knowledge that the transaction constituted a breach of trust. UTC § 1012(b) takes an intermediate position by eliminating the duty to inquire whether the trustee was acting properly if the third person acted in good faith.

9. The duties of trustees and their consequent liability for breaches involving actions or inactions by trust advisors and trust protectors is largely undeveloped. *See generally* John P.C. Duncan & Anita M. Sarafa, Achieve the Promise-and Limit the Risk-of Multi-Participant Trusts, 36 ACTEC L.J. 769 (2011).

10. Under the American rule, litigants are generally not entitled to recover attorney fees even if successful. *But see* UTC § 1004 (allowing court to award attorney fees "as justice and equity may require"), which was applied in *Shelton v. Tamposi,* 62 A.3d 741(N.H. 2013) (award justified by trustee's bad faith). *Cf. In re Trust No. T-1 of Trimble,* 826 N.W.2d 474 (Iowa 2013) (no compelling reasons to require trustee to pay attorney's fees). However, fiduciaries may have their attorney fees paid from estate or trust property even if surcharged for fiduciary breaches. *See McNeil v. McNeil,* 798 A.2d 503 (Del. 2002); *Regions Bank v. Lowrey,* 154 So. 3d 101 (Ala. 2014) (allowing attorney fees payable from trust assets when trustee successfully defended against a $13 million claim for breach of fiduciary duty brought by beneficiaries).

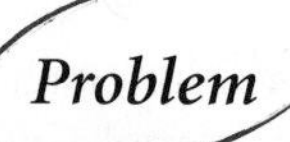

Problem

Tom held some farmland as trustee for some clients who sought to avoid probate. Because his daughter, Ina, needed a new house, Tom gave her that land. Without knowing of the breach of trust upon which her title rested, Ina built a house on the property. When the beneficiaries learn of the breach, should a court order the property's return to them? If so, should Ina be entitled to any credit for her improvements?

Selected References

Dominic J. Campisi, *The Perils of Prosperity: What Goes Up Will Likely Result in Surcharge*, 35 Heckerling Inst. on Est. Plan., ch. 12 (2001).

Charles F. Gibbs & Maureen S. Bateman, *Feuding Fiduciaries*, 144 Tr. & Est. 44 (July 2005).

John P.C. Duncan & Anita M. Sarafa, *Achieve the Promise-and Limit the Risk-of Multi-Participant Trusts*, 36 ACTEC L.J. 769 (2011).

Ray D. Madoff, *Mediating Probate Disputes: A Study of Court Sponsored Programs*, 38 Real Prop. Prob. & Tr. J. 697 (2004).

John Pankauski, Laurence A. Steckman & Robert E. Conner, *Punitive Damages Against Fiduciaries, Probate Cases, and Equitable Relief*, 25 Prob. & Prop. 43 (May/June 2011).

Stewart E. Sterk, *Trust Protectors, Agency Costs, and Fiduciary Duty*, 27 Cardozo L. Rev. 2761 (2006).

Peter T. Wendel, *The Evolution of the Law of Trustee's Powers and Third Party Liability for Participating in a Breach of Trust: An Economic Analysis*, 35 Seton Hall L. Rev. 971 (2005).

Robert Whitman, *Resolution Procedures to Resolve Trust Beneficiary Complaints*, 39 Real Prop. Prob. & Tr. J. 829 (2005).

B. Bars to Relief

In re Williams

591 N.W.2d 743 (Minn. Ct. App. 1999)

Huspeni, J.

In this consolidated appeal, appellants Robert H. Williams and Robert K. Williams challenge the dismissal of their surcharge action against respondent-trustee Norwest Bank Minnesota, National Association (Norwest), contending the district court erred in concluding that (1) a corporate trustee may rely upon an exculpatory clause in a trust instrument; and (2) the language of the particular exculpatory clause at issue here protects Norwest. . . .

FACTS

In his last will and testament, dated August 22, 1949, and codicil thereto, dated August 29, 1950, James T. Williams created a trust. . . . From 1979 until 1997, the trustees were appellant Robert H. Williams, Margaret Linstroth, and respondent Norwest.

James T. Williams, the trust's creator, was the founder of the Creamette Company, and Creamette stock originally accounted for 98% of the trust's value. In 1979, Creamette was acquired by Borden, Inc. As part of the Borden acquisition, the trust's Creamette stock was exchanged for Borden common stock. As of January 1, 1980, nearly 100% of the total market value of the trust was in Borden stock. The trust owned 630,948 shares of Borden stock at that time.

Beginning in 1980, the trustees began selling shares of Borden stock because of a perceived need to diversify trust assets. As of December 31, 1989, the last date through which trusteeship accounts have been settled and allowed by the district court, the trust owned 600,000 shares of Borden common stock at a value of $ 36.375 per share, and that stock accounted for 39.3% of the total market value of the trust.

From 1990 through 1994, the trustees generally voted to defer further divestment of Borden stock. The Williams trust's board of trustees makes decisions by majority vote, so although Robert Williams moved to sell Borden stock, Norwest and Linstroth were able to defeat the motions. Norwest and Linstroth apparently felt that it would be prudent to hold Borden stock until the price of the stock rose in value. Borden stock ultimately lost value. The trustees disposed of most of the trust's Borden stock by exchanging it for RJR Nabisco stock. For purposes of this stock exchange, Borden common stock was valued at $ 14.25 per share. Because Borden stock was previously valued at $ 36.375 per share, this exchange represented a significant loss in the value of the trust.

By petition dated June 6, 1996, trustees Linstroth and Norwest sought approval of the trustees' annual accounts for the trusteeship from 1990 to 1995. Appellant Robert H. Williams filed objections to the petition, claiming that Norwest, as corporate trustee, was responsible for the trust's loss in value from 1990 to 1995 and should be surcharged for the trust's losses.

Norwest eventually asserted that article VIII, section 12 of the trust instrument protects it from liability. That clause states:

> No Trustee shall be liable for the default or doing of any other Trustee, whether the act be one of misfeasance or nonfeasance, nor shall he be held liable for any loss by reason of any mistake or errors of judgment made by him in good faith in the execution of the trust.

The district court dismissed the action against Norwest on the basis of this clause because the court found that Norwest did not act with malfeasance and therefore was not liable.

ISSUES

I. May Norwest, as corporate trustee, use the exculpatory clause in the trust instrument as a shield to liability for breach of trust without violating public policy?

II. Does the exculpatory clause at issue shield Norwest from liability? [Other issues omitted]

ANALYSIS

I. Public policy

Appellant contends that allowing corporate trustees to use exculpatory clauses as a shield to liability for breach of trust violates public policy. We disagree. In *Schlobohm v. Spa Petite, Inc.*, 326 N.W.2d 920 (Minn. 1982), and *Walton v. Fujita Tourist Enterprises Co.*, 380 N.W.2d 198 (Minn. App. 1986), *review denied* (Minn. March 21, 1986), Minnesota courts examined exculpatory clauses generally and held that such clauses are valid so long as two conditions are met. Before enforcing an exculpatory clause, Minnesota courts look to see

> (1) whether there was a disparity of bargaining power between the parties (in terms of a compulsion to sign a contract containing an unacceptable provision and the lack of ability to negotiate elimination of the unacceptable provision) and
>
> (2) the types of services being offered or provided (taking into consideration whether it is a public or essential service).
>
> *Schlobohm*, 826 N.W.2d at 923 (citations omitted).

Here, there is no evidence suggesting either that there was a disparity of bargaining power between Norwest and the trust's creator, James T. Williams, or that Norwest somehow compelled Williams to add the exculpatory clause. Moreover, numerous organizations are able to act as corporate trustees, and this particular trust was designed to benefit only private individuals. Thus, service as a corporate trustee for the Williams trust does not appear to be the type of public or essential service discussed in Schlobohm. We conclude that Norwest may raise the exculpatory clause in this case without violating Minnesota's public policy.

II. Application of the exculpatory clause to Norwest

A. The first portion of the clause

. . . Generally, exculpatory clauses are not favored by the law and are strictly construed against the benefitted party. Schlobohm, 326 N.W.2d at 923. If an exculpatory clause is either ambiguous in scope or attempts to release the benefitted party from liability for intentional, willful, or wanton acts, the clause will not be enforced. Id.

Here, the district court found that under the Williams trust instrument, "trustees cannot be held liable for any act of misfeasance or nonfeasance but only for acts of malfeasance." However, the "misfeasance or nonfeasance" portion of the clause states that "no trustee shall be liable for the default or doing of any other trustee," thereby preventing a trustee from incurring liability only for the acts of other trustees. The clause does not protect a trustee from his or her own act of misfeasance or nonfeasance; the clause only relieves a trustee of liability for his or her own acts when loss is suffered "by reason of any mistake or error of judgment made by [the trustee] in good faith in the execution of his trust." Thus, while there may be situations in which the exculpatory clause will eliminate a trustee's liability, the "misfeasance or nonfeasance" portion of the clause does not define those situations.

B. The second portion of the clause

Norwest contends that even if the district court incorrectly interpreted the clause, that portion relieving a trustee of liability for mistakes or errors of judgment made in good faith applies to Norwest's benefit. (citation omitted). Appellant argues that this language cannot aid Norwest because Norwest was negligent in failing to vote to divest the trust of Borden stock, and the language of the exculpatory clause does not exculpate a trustee for negligence.

We note initially that courts have long distinguished between negligence-type claims and mistakes or "mere errors of judgment." See *Sjobeck v. Leach*, 213 Minn. 360, 365, 6 N.W.2d 819, 821–22 (1942) ("Mere error of judgment * * * does not create liability."); *In re Will of McCann*, 212 Minn. 233, 238, 240, 3 N.W.2d 226, 229, 230 (1942) (indicating that exculpatory clause stating "my said trustees shall not be liable for any mistake of judgment" did not protect the trustees from negligence); *Fortune v. First Trust Co.*, 200 Minn. 367, 379, 274 N.W. 524, 530 (1937) ("The distinction between negligence and mere errors of judgment must be borne in mind.' Trustees acting honestly, with ordinary prudence and within the limits of their trust, are not liable for mere errors of judgment.' '') (citation omitted). Moreover, this distinction has existed since before the trust instrument at issue here was created. Thus, we can reasonably assume that the trust creator was aware of these distinctions and could have exculpated a trustee for negligent acts had he wished to do so.

Because our task is to find the intent of the trust's creator, and trust instruments are to be strictly construed, we conclude that while the exculpatory clause protects a trustee from liability for "mistakes or errors of judgment," it does not do so for negligent acts.

Norwest concedes that it is a professional trustee and has greater skills in the area of trusts than does a person of ordinary prudence. Therefore, Norwest was under a duty to use those skills under Minn. Stat. §§ 501B.10, subd. 1(a) (1994). Further, failure of a professional to meet a minimum standard of care is not a mere error in judgment. *Wartnick v. Moss & Barnett*, 490 N.W.2d 108, 116 (Minn. 1992).

Generally, expert testimony is required to establish the standard of care and breach of that standard, unless the conduct can be evaluated by a jury in the absence of expert testimony. *Id.* A review of the record convinces us that a material fact issue exists as to whether Norwest met the minimum standard of care for a professional trustee. Appellant's expert investment executive concluded in his affidavit that my professional experience indicates that even under special circumstances, the Borden holding should have represented no more than 10% of trust assets after a maximum of five years.

Moreover, the district court itself observed that "[appellant] raised substantial and serious questions as to whether Norwest breached its fiduciary obligations." We must remand for trial on the issue of possible negligence of Norwest. . . .

Uniform Trust Code

Section 1008. Exculpation of Trustee.

(a) A term of a trust relieving a trustee of liability for breach of trust is unenforceable to the extent that it:

(1) relieves the trustee of liability for breach of trust committed in bad faith or with reckless indifference to the purposes of the trust or the interests of the beneficiaries; or

(2) was inserted as the result of an abuse by the trustee of a fiduciary or confidential relationship to the settlor.

(b) An exculpatory term drafted or caused to be drafted by the trustee is invalid as an abuse of a fiduciary or confidential relationship unless the trustee proves that the exculpatory term is fair under the circumstances and that its existence and contents were adequately communicated to the settlor.

Comment

Even if the terms of the trust attempt to completely exculpate a trustee for the trustee's acts, the trustee must always comply with a certain minimum standard. As provided in subsection (a), a trustee must always act in good faith with regard to the purposes of the trust and the interests of the beneficiaries.

Notes and Questions

1. Section 96 of the Restatement of Trusts is similar to UTC § 1008. However, a trustee cannot be exculpated from making profit under the Restatement position but can be exculpated under UTC § 1008. Interestingly, New York does not allow a testamentary trustee to be exonerated from liability for acting other than reasonably, diligently, and prudently. *See* N.Y. Estates, Powers and Trusts Law § 11-1.7.

2. In *Americans for the Arts v. Ruth Lilly Charitable Annuity Trust* on Page 650, the trustee, who inserted an exculpatory clause in the trust instrument, was found not to have abused its fiduciary or confidential relationship in inserting the clause. *But see Rafert v. Meyer*, 859 N.W.2d 332 (Neb. 2015) (based on UTC § 1008(b), court refused to recognize exculpatory clause because exculpatory term, which was drafted by trustee, was neither fair nor was its existence communicated to the settlor).

3. Should an exculpatory clause exonerate a trustee from the duty to furnish information to beneficiaries? *See McNeil v. McNeil*, 798 A.2d 503 (Del. 2002) (no).

Trustee exoneration for acts not constituting gross negligence may raise the issue whether a trustee's acts will constitute gross negligence. *See In re Scheidmantel*, 868 A.2d 464 (Pa. Super. Ct. 2005) (trustee's decision to diversify without regard to trust purposes amounted to reckless disregard, which constituted gross negligence). *But see Newcomer v. Nat'l City Bank*, 19 N.E.3d 492 (Ohio Ct. App. 2014) (rejecting beneficiaries' argument that in determining whether trustee acted with reckless indifference to purpose of trust the court should consider the cumulative effects of each individual act of negligence or poor judgment).

Should an exculpatory clause be effective if inserted in a trust that was created by an agent under a power of attorney if the agent names himself as trustee? *See In re Dentler Family Trust*, 873 A.2d 738 (Pa. Super. Ct. 2005) (no).

4. How would the definition of a trust be affected if courts allowed exculpatory provisions to be absolute bars to actions for a trustee's intentional wrongdoing? Should an exoneration clause relieve a trustee from liability for breaching the duty of loyalty?

5. In addition to exoneration (exculpatory) clauses, a fiduciary may escape liability because of actions by the beneficiaries. UTC § 1009 provides the situations: consent, release, or ratification, provided the beneficiaries had knowledge of the material facts and the trustee did not act improperly to obtain the consent, release, or ratification from the beneficiaries. *See also* 3d Rest. Trusts § 97. States vary whether a trustee may condition payment on trust beneficiaries releasing a trustee from liability. *Compare* Cal. Prob. Code § 16004.5 (a) (prohibiting) *with Hastings v. PNC Bank, NA*, 54 A.3d 714 (Md. 2012) (allowing).

6. A beneficiary may also be barred from obtaining relief against a fiduciary by the statute of limitations. *See, e.g., Cundall v. U.S. Bank*, 909 N.E.2d 1244 (Ohio 2009) (statute starts to run when beneficiaries learned of breach). *But cf. Ditta v. Conte*, 298 S.W.3d 187 (Tex. 2009) (action to remove trustee not barred by statute of limitations). UTC § 1005(a) provides that an action must be commenced within one year after the trustee sent a report to the beneficiary "that adequately disclosed the existence of a potential claim for breach of trust and informed the beneficiary of the time allowed for commencing a proceeding." Otherwise the period is five years after the first to occur of: "(1) the removal, resignation, or death of the trustee; (2) the termination of the beneficiary's interest in the trust; or (3) the termination of the trust." UTC § 1005(c). *See In re Theresa Houlahan Trust*, 101 A.3d 599 (N.H. 2014) (when trustee allegedly wrongfully transferred the sole asset of trust property, the beneficiary's claim for breach of fiduciary duty became property of the trust; thus, the trust was not terminated and the statute of limitations did not start running until the trustee's death).

7. Even if the statute of limitations has not run a beneficiary's remedies may be barred by the laches or estoppel doctrines. *See* 3d Rest. Trusts § 98. *But cf. Quick v.*

Pearson, 112 Cal. Rptr. 3d 62 (Ct. App. 2010) (trustee stopped from raising laches defense because of unclean hands).

Problems

1. You represent Local Bank. Draft an exculpatory clause to eliminate or reduce the bank's liability for the breach of fiduciary duties as a testamentary trustee.

2. Lucinda wants you to draft a testamentary trust for her children and her minor grandchildren. Should you recommend a clause dispensing with judicial approval of accounts, and permitting (a) the trustee to account informally to adult beneficiaries, (b) a guardian ad litem to approve accounts for the minors, or (c) the minor's parent or guardian to approve the accounts?

3. Mary Thomas has come to your law office for advice. She has many years' experience as a vice-president and comptroller for MM Industries. She has been approached by Susan Miller, who would like her to serve as Successor Trustee of a trust created by Miller's father, Morris, who died late last month. Mary has also been named as executor under Morris's will of March 6, 2001 (see below).

Morris Miller had been a successful businessman. In the 1990's Morris did a lot of reading about estate planning and on May 8, 2000, he executed a Declaration of Trust he drafted himself with the help of some form books.

The document is typical in most respects. Morris declares himself to hold the trust property (see below) in trust with income to himself for life. He also reserved the power to revoke the trust and to invade the corpus to meet his own needs. After his death, the trust property is to be held, administered, and distributed as follows:

> "(1) $17,000 to my good friend Sam Saif for our poker pals.
>
> "(2) $10,000 to my son Ron.
>
> "(3) $12,000 to be kept in trust with income to Mickey Lehman for life, and at his death, his share shall go to his then living children.
>
> "(4) The remainder of the trust to be held for my daughter Susan, with income to her for her life, and at her death the trust shall end and the trustee shall distribute the property equally among Susan's then-surviving children."

The trust contains a standard spendthrift clause, as well as typical powers of a trustee over management of the trust estate. The trust allows the trustee to invade the corpus on behalf of any income beneficiary "to be sure they can live comfortably."

At the time Morris declared the trust, he had some 1,000 shares of MM Industries reissued from his name to that of Morris Miller, Trustee of the Miller Trust. By the time of his death, the trust held the 1,000 shares, plus about $50,000 in cash and CD's. The MM stock has an estimated value of $700,000.

Mary has also located several other documents:

1. Morris's March 15, 1965 will, properly executed, revoking all other wills and giving everything to his wife Jane.

2. An envelope containing pieces of Morris's torn up will, properly executed, dated June 12, 1966, revoking all prior wills and giving everything to Jane and if she hadn't survived, to Susan. The envelope contains a notation in Morris's hand: "Revoked, August 12, 1972. 1965 will still good. M.M."

3. Morris's May 8, 2000 will, properly executed, revoking all prior wills and giving "all of my property to the successor trustee of my Declaration of Trust dated May 8, 2000, to be held, administered, and distributed under the terms of that document."

4. A March 6, 2001 will identified as "The Last Will and Testament of Morris Miller," signed by Jane Miller and two witnesses. The will revokes all prior wills and contains two dispositive clauses. One gives $20,000 to Ron. The other clause parallels the one in the 2000 will, pouring "all the rest of my property" into the trust.

5. A March 6, 2001 will identified as "The Last Will and Testament of Jane Miller," signed by Morris and two witnesses. The will revokes all prior wills and gives the entire estate to Morris, and if he doesn't survive Jane, to Susan and Ron, equally.

Mary also relates the following facts:

1. At his death Morris owned a house ($125,000), a recreation cabin ($75,000) in joint tenancy with Jane, tangible personal property ($75,000), and cash in his checking account ($8,000).

2. In this state, children have the legal duty to support their parents. Mickey Lehman's mother has a judgment against him for support for the year 2001. She has approached Susan about getting access to the trust fund Morris had told her he had set up for Mickey.

3. Sam Saif is a long-time friend who played weekly poker games with Morris, George Benney, and J.C. Carson.

4. Morris's widow, Jane, is the mother of Susan (born in January 1966) and Ron (born in September 1968). Ron died in December 2001, leaving a wife, Marjorie, and a daughter, Laila. Ron left a will giving everything to Marjorie. Jane suffered a stroke at Morris's funeral and is now in a nursing home, unable to communicate with others.

5. Jane owns the recreation cabin and is income beneficiary of a trust ($400,000) over which she has the power to revoke. Ron is named to take the remainder at her death.

Draft a memo to your senior partner, describing the problems Mary Thomas would face as successor trustee, and as executor, and the approaches she might take should she decide to accept either office.

Selected References

Charles Bryan Baron, *Self-Dealing Trustees and the Exoneration Clause: Can Trustees Ever Profit from Transactions Involving Trust Property?*, 72 St. John's L. Rev. 43 (1998).

Louise Lark Hill, *Fiduciary Duties and Exculpatory Clauses: Clash of the Titans or Cozy Bedfellows?*, 45 U. Mich J.L. Reform 855 (2012)

Melanie B. Leslie, *Trusting Trustees: Fiduciary Duties and the Limits of Default Rules*, 94 Geo. L.J. 67 (2005).

Alan Newman, *You Don't Know What You've Got Till It's Gone: Time-Barred Claims under the Uniform Trust Code*, 48 Real Prop. Tr. & Est. L.J. 459 (2014).

Holland A. Sullivan, Jr., *The Grizzle Bear: Lingering Exculpatory Clause Problems Posed by Texas Commerce Bank*, N.A. v. Grizzle, 56 Baylor L. Rev. 253 (2004).

Finally, as you strive to balance the needs of your private and professional lives, consider some advice from Charles Schultz. Linus wonders, "If you work real hard, and you get everything you've always wanted, is it worth it?" Snoopy responds, "Not if your dog doesn't like you."

Appendix

Sample Documents

A. A "Simple" Will

The following form contemplates a single person with children. An example of a married person's will appears in Chapter 1 on Pages 6.

WILL of ________________

I, ________________, a resident of ________________, ________________, declare this to be my Will and revoke all my former Wills and Codicils.

I. IDENTIFICATIONS AND DEFINITIONS

A. *Identifications*

I am not presently married, and I have three living children: ________________, ________________, and ________________.

B. *Definitions*

For purposes of this document, the following definitions shall apply:

1. CHILD, CHILDREN, DESCENDANT include any person born to or adopted by me or any of my descendants, so long as the person resided while a minor in the household of their parent related to me, regardless of the marital status of the child's parent.

2. SURVIVE means the beneficiary shall be deemed to have survived only if alive on the 91st day following the date of my death.

3. TANGIBLE PERSONAL PROPERTY includes all of my personal and household effects such as jewelry, clothing, automobiles, furniture, furnishings, silverware, books, pictures, and collections. It does not include property such as money, precious metals held for investment, bank accounts, stocks, or securities.

4. PER CAPITA WITH REPRESENTATION divides property into as many equal shares as there are (1) surviving descendants in the nearest generation to the decedent containing one or more then surviving descendants and (2) deceased persons in the same generation who left then surviving descendants. One share shall be given to each surviving descendant in the nearest generation, and the share of each deceased person in the same generation

shall be divided among his or her then surviving descendants in the same manner.

II. TANGIBLE PERSONAL PROPERTY

A. *Specific Gifts*

I give the following items if owned by me at my death to those among the following beneficiaries who survive me:

1. To my son, _________________, the ledger sets from RD Company during the early 1900s kept by my grandfather, _________________, and currently located in my library desk.

2. To my granddaughter, _________________, my copy of *Good Night Moon* signed by the author, Margaret Wise Brown, and currently located on my guest room bookshelf.

B. *Remaining Tangible Personal Property*

1. GIFTS TO MY CHILDREN

I give my children who survive me whatever other tangible personal property I own at my death that they choose, subject to the following:

a. The children shall draw numbers to determine the order of choosing items.

b. Starting with the child who drew the lowest number, each child shall choose one item, in turn. For the purposes of this process, items consisting of more than one piece shall be considered a single item. By way of illustration, my 20-piece set of silverware shall be considered a single item, as shall my 5-volume biography of Thomas Jefferson.

c. The children shall repeat this process until they have chosen all of my tangible personal property that they wish to have, or until there are no more items to choose.

2. REMAINING PROPERTY

My executor shall sell all of my tangible personal property not previously distributed and add the proceeds to the residuary.

III. RESIDUARY ESTATE

A. *Gift to My Descendants*

I give the balance of my estate (except for property over which I have a power of appointment) to my descendants, per capita with representation.

B. *Gift to Charity*

If none of my descendants survive me, I give the balance of my estate (except any property over which I have a power of appointment) to ________________.

IV. ADMINISTRATION

A. *Appointment of Executor*

I appoint ________________ to serve as my executor. If ________________ fails to become or ceases to act as executor, I appoint ________________.

B. *Guardians*

If it becomes necessary to appoint a guardian for one of my children, I nominate ________________of ________________ as guardian of the person and of the estate of that child.

C. *Bond*

I request that bond or other security not be required of any executor or guardian named by this will.

D. *Taxes*

My executor shall pay all taxes payable by reason of my death, without apportionment against any beneficiary of this Will.

E. *Executor Powers*

My executor shall have all the following powers together with any additional but not inconsistent powers granted by law, to be exercised without court order.

1. Pay all my legally enforceable debts out of my estate;
2. Retain any property regardless of diversification, risk, or non-productivity;
3. Sell, lease, mortgage, improve, or repair any real or personal property with the terms my executor decides are in the best interest of my estate;
4. Invest any estate property in securities, or real or personal property;
5. Exercise ownership rights of securities, including the right to vote;
6. Exercise options to purchase securities;
7. Borrow money;
8. Employ agents and delegate powers to them as desirable;
9. Make distributions in cash or in kind;
10. Litigate or settle claims for or against my estate on whatever terms my Executor decides are best; and

11. Perform all other acts necessary for the proper administration and distribution of my estate.

V. MISCELLANEOUS PROVISIONS

A. *Notice*

Any notice under this document shall be deemed given if sent by regular mail to the last known address of the beneficiary or his representative. The guardian of the estate of a beneficiary or the parents or surviving parent or guardian of the person of a minor beneficiary for whose estate no guardian has been appointed, may, in carrying out the provisions of this will, act and receive notice for the beneficiary and sign any instrument of appointment or appearance required of the beneficiary.

B. *No Contest Clause*

Any distribution made in this Will to a person, organization, or combination thereof that contests this Will shall be void.

C. *Applicable Law.* The law of ________________ shall determine the validity and effect of this will.

I have signed this, my Will, on this ________________ day of ________________, ________________.

____

Testator

On this ________________ day of ________________, ________________, we saw ________________, in our presence, sign this instrument. She then declared it to be her Will and requested us to act as witnesses to it. We believe she is of sound mind and memory and not under duress or constraint of any kind. We then, in her presence and in the presence of each other, signed our names as attesting witnesses.

________________ residing at ________________

________________ residing at ________________

Self-Proving Affidavit[1]

State of ________________)

)ss.

County of ________________)

1. [The self-proving affidavit, here based on UPC §2-504(b), is not required. In UPC states, it sets up a conclusive presumption that the signature requirements have been followed. In this mobile society, including the affidavit is good practice in any state, in case the testator dies domiciled in a UPC state. Eds.]

We, ________________, ________________, and ________________, the testator and the witnesses, respectively, whose names are signed to the attached or foregoing instrument, being first duly sworn, do hereby declare to the undersigned authority that the testator signed and executed the instrument as the testator 's will, and that [he] [she] had signed willingly (or willingly directed another to sign for [him][her]), and that [he][she] executed as [his][her] free and voluntary act for the purposes therein expressed, and that each of the witnesses, in the presence and hearing of the testator, signed the will as witness and that to the best of [his][her] knowledge the testator was at that time 18 years of age or older, of sound mind, and under no constraint or undue influence.

________________**Testator**

________________**Witness**

________________**Witness**

Subscribed, sworn to, and acknowledged before me by ________________, the testator, and subscribed and sworn to before me by ________________, and ________________, the witnesses, this ________________ day of ________________, ________________.

____

Notary Public

B. A "Pour-over" Will

A pour-over will likely resemble a simple will. The principal difference is that the pour-over makes a gift—usually through the residuary clause—to a preexisting trust. The testator often has created a revocable trust as part of an integrated estate plan, just prior to executing the will. However, a will can pour over to any trust. *See* UPC § 2-511, reproduced on page 219. "Fail-safe" clauses, giving alternative dispositions, protect against the possibility that there is a problem with the trust.

Although some adjustment of the executor's powers may be appropriate, the simple will above could be converted to a pour-over by changing the residuary clause to read as follows:

III. RESIDUARY ESTATE

A. *Gift to Trust*

I give the balance of my estate (except for property over which I have a power of appointment) to the Trustee of the ________________ Trust dated ________________, ________________, to be added to the trust property and administered under the terms of that trust.

B. *Alternative Gift to Descendants or Charity*

If that trust does not exist or is not valid at my death, I give the balance of my estate (except for property over which I have a power of appointment) to my descendants, per capita with representation; if none of my descendants survive me, I give such property to ________________.

C. A Lifetime Trust

Lifetime trusts generally take one of two approaches. The most common is a "Trust Agreement" between the settlor (or "donor" or "grantor") and the trustee(s). Sometimes settlors, in their individual capacities, agree with themselves, as trustees. Sometimes they agree with third parties, e.g., a bank or a trusted friend. The other option is a "Declaration of Trust," naming oneself as trustee of specifically-identified property.

Trusts can be either revocable or irrevocable. Here is an example of a revocable trust with a third-party trustee.[2]

REVOCABLE TRUST AGREEMENT

This agreement between ________________, as Settlor, and ________________, as Trustee, is entered into in consideration of the mutual covenants of the parties in order to create an amendable and revocable trust of the property described in the attached Schedule A and delivered to the trustee, in addition to such other properties as may from time to time be added hereto. This trust shall be known as "The ________________ Revocable Trust."

ARTICLE 1: DEFINITION OF TERMS

The following definitions shall apply to this document:

1. CHILD, GRANDCHILD, DESCENDANT includes any person born to or adopted by me or any of my descendants, regardless of the marital status of the person's parent at the time of the birth.
2. PER CAPITA WITH REPRESENTATION divides property into as many equal shares as there are (1) surviving descendants in the nearest generation to the decedent containing one or more then surviving descendants and (2) deceased persons in the same generation who left then surviving descendants. One share shall be given to each surviving descendant in the nearest generation, and the share of each deceased person in the same generation shall be divided among his or her then surviving descendants in the same manner.

---

2. In form—but not legal effect—a testamentary trust often looks like a lifetime trust, but because a testamentary trust is part of a will, the trust does not include lifetime support for the trust's creator. Frequently, the will's residuary article establishes the trust, and the trust details follow as sub-parts of that article. We leave it to your imagination to create such a form after reviewing this one.

3. SECURITIES includes stocks, bonds, notes, commercial paper, and certificates of deposit, regardless of class, priorities, or secured position.

4. SURVIVE means that a person must survive by 120 hours the person or event referred to.

ARTICLE 2: ADMINISTRATION DURING SETTLOR'S LIFE

A. *While the Settlor is Able to Manage Her Own Affairs*

1. While the Settlor is able to manage her own affairs, the Trustee shall hold, invest and reinvest the trust assets, collect the trust income, and shall pay all of the net income to the Settlor quarterly or as the Settlor otherwise directs in writing and the Trustee shall pay any part of the trust principal (even to the point of completely exhausting the same) as the Settlor directs in writing.

2. In the absence of such directions, the Trustee shall pay to, or apply for the benefit of, one or more or all of the members of a class consisting of the Settlor and her then living descendants such amounts of the net income and principal (even to the point of completely exhausting the same) as the Trustee, in its sole and absolute discretion, deems advisable to provide adequately for the health, support, and maintenance of any one or more or all of the members of that class, provided that the Settlor's needs shall be given primary consideration.

3. The Trustee shall accumulate any undistributed income and annually add it to principal.

B. *While the Settlor is Unable to Manage Her Own Affairs*

1 During any period during which (in the sole judgment of the Trustee after consulting with the Settlor's physicians and family) the Settlor is unable to manage her own affairs, the Trustee shall pay to, or apply for the benefit of, one or more or all of the members of a class consisting of the Settlor and her then living descendants such amounts of the net income and principal (even to the point of completely exhausting the same) as the Trustee, in its sole and absolute discretion, deems advisable to provide adequately for the health, support, and maintenance of any one or more or all of the members of that class, provided that the Settlor's needs shall be given primary consideration.

2. The Trustee shall accumulate any undistributed income and annually add it to principal.

ARTICLE 3: ADMINISTRATION AFTER SETTLOR'S DEATH

A. *Payments to Estate*

The Trustee shall pay to the Executor or Administrator of the Settlor's estate such amounts as the Executor or Administrator certifies to the Trustee as necessary to pay the debts, funeral expenses, and estate administration expenses of the Settlor. The Trustee may withhold distribution of an amount sufficient in its judgment to cover any liability that may be imposed for estate or other taxes, including penalties and interest, until such liability is finally determined, and may pay such taxes unless such liability is otherwise discharged.

B. *Trust for __________________'s Life*

The Trustee shall hold and administer the remaining trust property for the benefit of __________________ during her life. The Trustee in its discretion may pay to __________________ or use for her benefit, as much of the trust income and principal as the Trustee determines to provide adequately for her health, support, and maintenance. The Trustee may make these distributions directly to __________________ or to third parties on her behalf in such proportions, amounts, and intervals as the Trustee determines to be appropriate.

C. *After __________________'s Death*

1. Upon the death of __________________, the Trustee shall distribute the remainder of the trust property according to the directions of __________________ under the special power of appointment granted to her in Article 4 of this Trust.

2. To the extent that __________________ does not expressly exercise this power of appointment effectively, the Trustee shall distribute the remainder of the trust property to the Settlor's then-surviving descendants according to a per capita with representation division. If the Settlor leaves no then-surviving descendants, the Trustee shall distribute the remainder of the trust property to __________________ [charity].

D. *Transfers to Minors*

If trust assets are distributable to a person under the age of 21 years (a "minor"), the Trustee may, in its absolute discretion:

1. distribute the minor's property to any of the following as custodian under the applicable Uniform Transfers to Minors Act:
   a. his or her parent,
   b. his or her guardian, or
   c. a qualified person (including the Trustee); or
2. continue to hold the property as follows:
   a. Until the minor reaches the age of 21 years, the Trustee may pay to, or apply for the benefit of, the minor such amounts of trust property as the Trustee in its absolute discretion deems advisable to provide adequately for the minor's health, support, maintenance, and

education, accumulating any income not so paid or applied and annually adding the same to principal.

b. If the minor does not reach the age of 21 years, the Trustee shall distribute the minor's trust property to the Executor or Administrator of the estate of the minor.

c. When the minor reaches the age of 21 years, the Trustee shall distribute to that beneficiary the balance of the beneficiary's trust property.

d. The trustee acting under this section D (2) shall have all the duties and powers conferred upon the Trustee by Article 6 of this Agreement.

ARTICLE 4: ________________'S SPECIAL POWER OF APPOINTMENT

Upon ________________'s death, the trustee shall pay all remaining principal and undistributed income, or hold it, according to the directions ____ ________________ makes under the special power of appointment created by this section. ________________ may make such appointment by a written instrument she has signed and delivered to the trustee during her lifetime but after the Settlor's death or by a provision in a will executed after the Settlor's death and specifically referring to the power created by this trust agreement. ________________ may appoint to, or for the benefit of, any one or more of her lineal descendants, in whatever shares she deems appropriate. She may not appoint to herself, her estate, her creditors, or the creditors of her estate. She may appoint the property outright or in trust according to whatever terms she chooses as if the property were her own, subject to the limitations imposed by this section with regard to the persons who may benefit from this trust. In particular, but not by way of further limiting her discretion, she may create new powers of appointment and new present or future interests in any appointee; create new powers of appointment in any other person living at the Settlor's death (including a trustee, except that such new power may not be exercised in favor of persons other than the objects of this power); and impose spendthrift or other lawful restrictions.

ARTICLE 5: SUCCESSOR TRUSTEES

A. *Resignation*

The Trustee may resign at any time by providing written notice to the current income beneficiaries, specifying the effective date of such resignation, which shall not be earlier than 30 days from the notice unless a Successor Trustee is readily available.

B. *Removal*

Any Beneficiary or his/her Guardian may remove a Trustee upon a determination of cause, such as willful misconduct, by a neutral arbiter selected by mutual agreement.

C. *Successor Trustee Appointment*

If a vacancy exists as Trustee, all current income beneficiaries shall have one vote to elect the Successor Trustee, which must be a financial institution authorized to administer trusts.

D. *Successor Trustee Powers*

A Successor Trustee shall succeed to all of the powers, duties, and discretion of the original Trustee unless otherwise provided.

ARTICLE 6: ADMINISTRATIVE, INVESTMENT AND TRUSTEE PROVISIONS

A. *Administrative Provisions*

1. ACCOUNTING AND REPORTS: The Trustee shall keep accurate records and accounts of the administration of the trust property. During the Settlor's lifetime, the Trustee shall provide the Settlor an annual accounting of all receipts and disbursements of the trust account, including an inventory of the trust assets. After the Settlor's death, the Trustee shall annually provide the same to all current income beneficiaries. The written approval of such accounting by the persons entitled to receive accountings shall bind all who are then or may thereafter become entitled to any part of the assets, as to all matters and transactions shown in the account.

2. ALLOCATION AND DIVISION OF ASSETS: In allocation of assets between the beneficiaries of this trust, the Trustee is not required to physically divide the assets into shares to which each beneficiary would be entitled, but may do so through appropriate book entries.

3. PAYMENTS OF EXPENSES:

a. *Legally enforceable claims*: The Trustee shall pay all legally enforceable claims incurred against the trust.

b. *Trustee Compensation*: The Trustee shall be entitled to receive reasonable compensation for services as Trustee.

4. SEVERABILITY: If a court determines that a provision of this instrument is legally unenforceable, the remaining provisions shall continue to be fully effective.

5. COSTS OF UNSUCCESSFUL CHALLENGES: Any beneficiary who commences legal action to contest the validity of this Trust Agreement and does not prevail, shall have the reasonable attorney fees and costs incurred by the Trustee in successfully defending the contest deducted from any amount such beneficiary is entitled to receive.

B. *Powers and Duties of Trustee*

The Trustee shall have the following powers together with any additional but not inconsistent powers granted by law:

1. MANAGEMENT OF TRUST PROPERTY

a. To receive or reject any property given to the trust.

b. To retain, buy, sell, lease, mortgage, improve, or repair any real or personal property at the time and price, and on the terms the Trustee determines to be appropriate.

c. To carry insurance in the kind and amount that the Trustee deems advisable.

d. To enforce any mortgage or lease held by the trust.

e. To deposit funds in a bank and rent a safe deposit box for the protection of trust assets.

2. INVESTMENT POWERS

a. To retain, buy, or sell any security (including its own securities) at the time and price, and on the terms the Trustee determines to be appropriate.

b. To register and carry any property in the Trustee's own name or in the name of its nominee or to hold it unregistered.

c. To exercise ownership rights over securities, including the right to vote.

d. To exercise options to purchase securities.

3. OTHER POWERS

a. To litigate or settle claims for or against this trust on whatever terms the Trustee in its sole discretion determines are in the best interests of the trust.

b. To borrow money from any person or corporation for any trust purpose on whatever terms the Trustee deems proper, to obligate the trust to repay the borrowed money, and to pledge property as security.

c. To make loans to the current income beneficiaries, in amounts, for periods and on such terms as the Trustee in its sole discretion determines are in the best interests of the trust.

d. To employ agents and delegate powers to them as desirable.

e. To make distributions in cash or in kind.

C. *Rule Against Perpetuities*

1. If the Rule Against Perpetuities is deemed to apply to any part of this document, then the following shall apply:

a. *Trust Existence*: The Trustee shall terminate any trust still in existence on the day before 21 years after the death of the last of my lineal descendants living at the time this instrument becomes irrevocable.

b. *Termination*: Upon termination of any trust, the Trustee shall distribute the Trust property on a per capita with representation basis among my descendants.

2. CLASS GIFTS: Whenever necessary to avoid invalidation of a gift because of the Rule Against Perpetuities, any gift to a class of beneficiaries shall be construed to include only those members of the class who survived me.

3. POWER OF APPOINTMENT: Any power of appointment herein granted may not be exercised in a manner that violates the Rule Against Perpetuities, and any attempt to do so shall be entirely without effect. In such event, the Trustee shall distribute the property as if the power of appointment had not been exercised.

D. *Charitable Gifts*

The Trustee shall give the share of any named charity no longer in existence to a similar charity chosen by the Trustee.

E. *Restriction Against Alienation*

No beneficiary shall have any right or power to anticipate, pledge, assign, sell, transfer, alienate, or encumber in any way his or her interest in the income of the trust or his or her interest in the principal of the trust receivable in the future.

F. *Applicable Law*

The law of ________________ shall determine the validity and effect of this trust.

ARTICLE 7: REVOCATION AND AMENDMENT

The Settlor reserves the power, by signed instrument delivered to the trustee during the Settlor's life, to revoke this agreement in whole or in part and to amend it from time to time in any respect, except that the duties and compensation of the Trustee shall not be materially changed without the Trustee's written approval.

IN TESTIMONY WHEREOF, ________________, as Settlor, and ________________, as Trustee, have signed this Trust Agreement on this ________________ day of ________________, ________________.

____

Settlor

____

Trustee

State of ________________)

)ss.

County of ________________)

The above named ________________ and ________________ appeared before me, a Notary Public in and for this County and State, on the ________________ day of _______________, _______________ and acknowledged their signatures on this Trust Agreement.

____

Notary Public

SCHEDULE "A"

I confirm that I have transferred the following described property to the Trustee of The _______________ Trust, subject to the terms and conditions of the foregoing Trust Agreement:

REAL ESTATE:

PERSONAL PROPERTY:

1. Investments
2. Life Insurance

____

Settlor

D. Power of Attorney for Property Management

Many jurisdictions authorize the use of statutory forms that, in turn, rely upon definitions found in the local statute, but not in the form itself. Statutory forms have the advantage of simplicity, so the client/principal is not overwhelmed by language, but the disadvantage that the form itself does not detail the powers actually given the agent. For an example of a statutory form, see Pages 363–368.

Other forms are available from a variety of sources. The example below creates a presently-exercisable power. Some clients may prefer a "springing" power which becomes effective upon their incapacity.[3]

DURABLE GENERAL POWER OF ATTORNEY

I, _______________, revoke any power of attorney I have previously made and appoint _______________ as my attorney and, if my attorney is unable or unwilling to serve, appoint _______________ as my successor attorney with the same powers and duties, to act in my place and for my benefit.

I. Effectiveness and Duration

This power is effective immediately and shall not be affected by my disability or by lapse of time.

3. A springing power should include a means for determining incapacity.

II. Powers

My attorney shall have the authority:

A. *Financial Accounts*: To deal with my accounts at financial institutions (including, without limitation, banks, savings & loan institutions, credit unions, mutual funds managers, and securities dealers); to open and close accounts; to make deposits, withdrawals (by check or otherwise), and transfers.

B. *Tangible Personal Property*: To take possession of my tangible personal property; to buy, sell, license, and encumber such property upon such terms as my attorney thinks appropriate; to execute and deliver appropriate contracts, notes, and other instruments necessary to accomplish these acts.

C. *Real Estate*: To enter, manage, repair, improve, encumber, and insure any of my real property; to buy, sell, or release any interest in real property upon such terms as my attorney thinks appropriate; to execute and deliver appropriate contracts, deeds, mortgages, notes, and other instruments necessary to accomplish these acts. To lease real property upon such terms as my attorney thinks appropriate and to enforce the terms of those leases against any occupiers.

D. *Securities*: To buy, sell, and encumber all stocks, bonds (including United States Treasury Bonds), mutual funds, and any other securities of any kind.

E. *Safe Deposit Box*: To enter any safe deposit box to which I have access.

F. *Property Due Me*: To collect and receive all funds, debts, accounts, and other property due me.

G. *Claims Against Me*: To pay, settle, or otherwise discharge debts or claims against me.

H. *Litigation*: To participate in my name in any legal action in connection with the authority granted in this instrument.

I. *Transfers to Trust*: To transfer any of my assets to the trustee of the ________________ Trust, dated ________________.

J. *Gifts*: To make gifts to my spouse, other relatives, my friends, or charities I have supported.

K. *Disclaimers*: To disclaim any interest in accordance with state and federal law in any property to which I would otherwise succeed.

L. *Taxes*: To execute, acknowledge, and file all federal, state, and local tax returns; to pay amounts due, and contest and appeal any assessments.

M. *Agents*: To employ and dismiss any agents or advisors.

III. Termination

This power of attorney may be terminated either by me or by my attorney by giving written notice to the other. An executed duplicate of this power of attorney, or a photostatic copy thereof, will be conclusive against me and my attorney as to such third party that my attorney's power of attorney has not been terminated and will continue in effect until such third party is advised by written notice from me or my attorney of such termination.

VI. Applicable Law

The law of ________________ shall apply to this instrument.

V. Reserved Powers

In addition to the right to terminate this power, I reserve all rights to do personally any act that my attorney is authorized to perform, and to grant similar powers of attorney to others.

I executed this Durable General Power of Attorney on ________________, ________________.

____

Principal

State of ________________)

)ss.

County of ________________)

The above named ________________ appeared before me, a Notary Public in and for this County and State, on the ________________ day of ________________, ________________ and acknowledged his signature on this instrument.

____

Notary Public

E. Health Care Advance Directives

The form that follows is adapted from the Uniform Health Care Decisions Act. It combines in one form a power of attorney for health care (also known as a "health care proxy"), particular health care directions (commonly known as a "living will"), and authorization for organ donations. With minor edits, any of the parts can stand alone.

Some forms combine authority over property with authority over health care. That approach works where the same person is best for both roles, but has the disadvantage of filling financial files with medical issues and medical files with financial issues.

ADVANCE HEALTH-CARE DIRECTIVE

PART 1

POWER OF ATTORNEY FOR HEALTH CARE

(1) DESIGNATION OF AGENT:

(a) I designate the following individual as my agent to make health-care decisions for me:

____

(name of individual you choose as agent)

____

____

(address) (city) (state) (zip code)

____

(home phone) (work phone)

(b) If I revoke my agent's authority or if my agent is not willing, able, or reasonably available to make a health-care decision for me, I designate as my first alternate agent:

____

(name of individual you choose as first alternate agent)

____

____

(address) (city) (state) (zip code)

____

(home phone) (work phone)

(2) AGENT'S AUTHORITY:

(a) My agent is authorized to make all health-care decisions for me, including decisions to provide, withhold, or withdraw artificial nutrition and hydration and all other forms of health care to keep me alive, except as I state here:

____

____

____

[Add additional sheets if needed.]

(b) I intend that my health-care agent be my personal representative within the meaning of, and have all of the same rights as I would have under, the Health Insurance Portability and Accountability Act of 1996 ("HIPAA"), 42 U.S.C § 1320d and 45 C.F.R §§ 160–164.[4]

(3) WHEN AGENT'S AUTHORITY BECOMES EFFECTIVE: My agent's authority becomes effective when my primary physician determines that I am unable to make my own health-care decisions.

(4) AGENT'S OBLIGATION: My agent shall make health-care decisions for me in accordance with this power of attorney for health care, any instructions I give in Part

4. [To cover the possibility that HIPAA authorization may be appropriate before this power becomes effective, a separate HIPAA form may be advisable. For an example, see the form that follows. Eds.]

2 of this form, and my other wishes to the extent known to my agent. To the extent my wishes are unknown, my agent shall make health-care decisions for me in accordance with what my agent determines to be in my best interest. In determining my best interest, my agent shall consider my personal values to the extent known to my agent.

(5) NOMINATION OF GUARDIAN: If a guardian of my person needs to be appointed for me by a court, I nominate the agent designated in this form.

If that agent is not willing, able, or reasonably available to act as guardian, I nominate the alternate agents whom I have named, in the order designated.

PART 2

INSTRUCTIONS FOR HEALTH CARE

[If you are satisfied to allow your agent to determine what is best for you in making end-of-life decisions, you need not fill out this part of the form. If you do fill out this part of the form, you may strike any wording you do not want.]

(6) END-OF-LIFE DECISIONS: I direct that my health-care providers and others involved in my care provide, withhold, or withdraw treatment in accordance with the choice I have marked below:

[ ] (a) Choice Not to Prolong Life

I do not want my life to be prolonged if (i) I have an incurable and irreversible condition that will result in my death within a relatively short time, (ii) I become unconscious and, to a reasonable degree of medical certainty, I will not regain consciousness, or (iii) the likely risks and burdens of treatment would outweigh the expected benefits, OR

[ ] (b) Choice to Prolong Life

I want my life to be prolonged as long as possible within the limits of generally accepted health-care standards.

(7) ARTIFICIAL NUTRITION AND HYDRATION: Artificial nutrition and hydration must be provided, withheld, or withdrawn in accordance with the choice I have made in paragraph (6) unless I mark the following box. If I mark this box [ ], artificial nutrition and hydration must be provided regardless of my condition and regardless of the choice I have made in paragraph (6).

(8) RELIEF FROM PAIN: Except as I state in the following space, I direct that treatment for alleviation of pain or discomfort be provided at all times, even if it hastens my death:

____

____

(9) OTHER WISHES: [If you do not agree with any of the optional choices above and wish to write your own, or if you wish to add to the instructions you have given above, you may do so here.] I direct that:

____

____

[Add additional sheets if needed.]

PART 3

DONATION OF ORGANS AT DEATH

(10) Upon my death [Mark applicable box]

[ ] (a) I give any needed organs, tissues, or parts, OR

[ ] (b) I give the following organs, tissues, or parts only

____

(c) My gift is for the following purposes [Strike any of the following you do not want.]

(i) Transplant

(ii) Therapy

(iii) Research

(iv) Education

(11) EFFECT OF COPY: A copy of this form has the same effect as the original.

(12) SIGNATURES:

__________________(date) __________________(sign your name)

__________________(address) __________________(print your name)

__________________(city) (state)

SIGNATURES OF WITNESSES:

First witness	Second witness
__________________(print name)	__________________(print name)
__________________(address)	__________________(address)
__________________(city) (state)	__________________(city) (state)
__________________(signature of witness)	__________________(signature of witness)
__________________(date)	__________________(date)

F. HIPAA Authorization

In many states, as in the form above, a health-care power of attorney is effective only in limited circumstances. For example, under New York's Public Health Law § 2981[4], the agent's authority does not commence until the principal's attending physician determines that the principal lacks the capacity to make health-care decisions about himself or herself. This requirement can create problems because the Health Insurance Portability and Accountability Act of 1996 ("HIPAA"), 42 U.S.C § 1320d, prohibits health-care providers from disclosing protected health information (PHI) without a release, and the power of attorney is not effective as a release until after a determination of incapacity.

There are, however, other situations where it could be helpful for someone other than the patient to have access to medical information. What if the principal is in failing health with limited capacity? What if the primary physician, out of deference to a long-time patient, delays making a capacity judgment?[5] What if the primary physician is unavailable? What if the primary physician determines that the patient does have capacity, but the agent thinks the physician is wrong? How can the agent obtain enough information to challenge the decision?

A form like the one below addresses these problems. Note that part (a) applies to a general durable power of attorney, including one of the "springing" variety which becomes effective upon the principal's incapacity. That power could define incapacity without relying on the primary physician. Part (b) refers to a health-care power similar to the one above.

HIPAA Authorization for Release of PHI Relating to Capacity

I, ________________, authorize all health-care providers, including physicians, nurses, dentists, and all other persons (including entities) who may have provided, or be providing me with any type of health care, to disclose protected health information that related directly or indirectly to my capacity to conduct my affairs in a competent manner, including my ability to understand and appreciate the nature and consequences of health-care decisions, including the benefits and risks of and alternatives to any proposed health care, and to reach an informed conclusion thereon to

(a) an agent designated as my attorney-in-fact in a durable power of attorney signed by me when asked to do so by my designated attorney-in-fact for the purpose of determining my capacity as defined in the power of attorney or by governing law; or

(b) an agent designed in a health-care proxy signed by me when asked by my designated agent for the purpose of determining my capacity to make health-care decisions.

This authorization is intended to provide my health-care providers with the authorization necessary to allow each of them to disclose protected health-care information regarding me to the persons described above for the purpose of allowing each of them to make specified determinations regarding my capacity

The information disclosed pursuant to this authorization may be redisclosed and may no longer be protected by the privacy rules of 45 CFR Section 164.

This authorization may be revoked by me in writing at any except to the extent that any health care provider, including an entity, has disclosed protected health information in reliance on this authorization.

5. In New York, the physician must make a capacity determination if requested by a named agent. N.Y. Pub. Health Law § 2983[2].

Unless otherwise validly revoked, this authorization shall expire one year after my death.

____________________ ____________________

Signed Dated

[If signed by a Personal Representative, the authorization must include a description of the Personal Representative's authority to act.]

Index